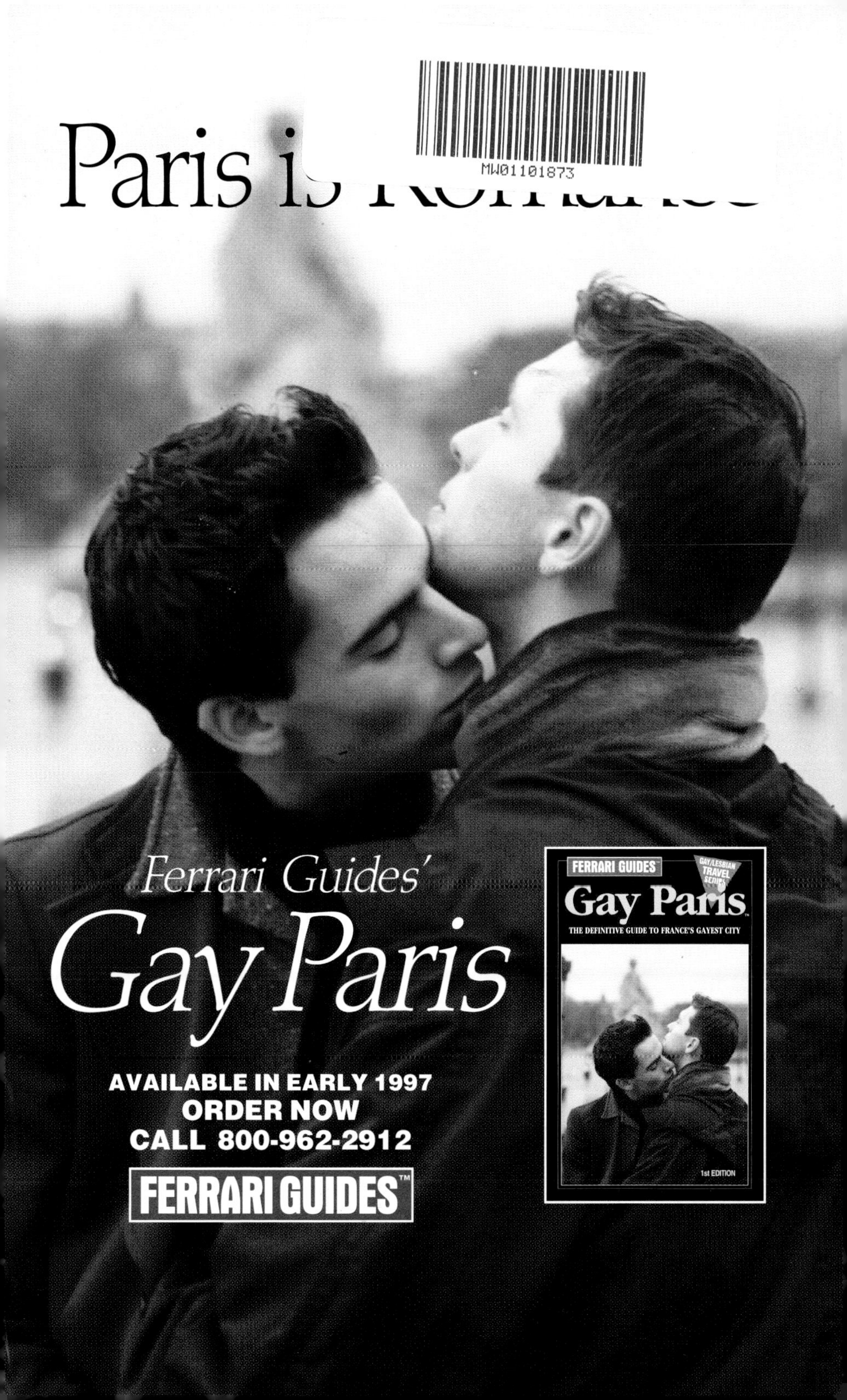

# Paris i

*Ferrari Guides'*

# *Gay Paris*

**AVAILABLE IN EARLY 1997**
**ORDER NOW**
**CALL 800-962-2912**

**FERRARI GUIDES™**

# Inn Places® 1997

**10th Edition**

**Published by**
**Ferrari International Publishing, Inc.**
PO Box 37887
Phoenix, AZ 85069 USA
Tel: (602) 863-2408
Fax: (602) 439-3952
E-mail: ferrari@q-net.com

**Published**
December 1996

Inn Places is a registered trademark of Ferrari International Publishing, Inc.

Ferrari, Marianne
Inn Places 1997

Includes index
ISBN 0-942586-57-3



Listing of a group, organization or business in Inn Places® does not indicate that the sexual orientation of owners or operators is homosexual, nor that the sexual orientation of any given member of that group or client of that business is homosexual, nor that the organization or business specifically encourages membership or patronage of homosexuals as a group. This book is sold without warranties or guarantees of any kind, express or implied, and the authors and publisher disclaim any liability for loss, damage or injury in connection with it.

**Special Sales**
Purchases of 10+ copies of any Ferrari Guides can be made at special discounts by businesses and organizations.

Printed in the United States of America

### On the Cover

## Applewood Inn and Restaurant Russian River, California

Applewood Inn and Restaurant in Guerneville, California, is the first inn to be honored by appearing on the front cover of Inn Places more than once. This year's cover features an Applewood bedroom whose color scheme, decor and lighting effects are ample demonstration of the good taste and attention-to-detail behind every aspect of Applewood's hospitality. See pages 15 and 274 for more information about Applewood.

# CONTENTS

## INTRODUCTION

Contents ..... 5
How to Use This Guide ..... 6

## COLOR SECTION

Index to Color Section ..... 9
Special Color Section ..... 10

## WORLDWIDE LISTINGS

### AFRICA

South Africa ..... 34

### ASIA

Thailand ..... 37

### EUROPE

Belgium ..... 40
Czech Republic ..... 43
Denmark ..... 44
France ..... 46
Germany ..... 55
Greece ..... 63
Iceland ..... 64
Ireland ..... 64
Italy ..... 69
Netherlands ..... 73
Portugal ..... 87
Spain ..... 89
Switzerland ..... 94
UK-England ..... 96
UK-Scotland ..... 125
UK-Wales ..... 129

### PACIFIC REGION

Australia ..... 132
New Zealand ..... 160
French Polynesia/Tahiti ..... 166

### CANADA

Alberta ..... 168
British Columbia ..... 170
Ontario ..... 182
Québec ..... 187
Saskatchewan ..... 194

### CARIBBEAN

British West Indies ..... 196
Dominican Republic ..... 198
Dutch West Indies ..... 199
French West Indies ..... 200
Puerto Rico ..... 201
Virgin Islands-BVI ..... 205
Virgin Islands-US ..... 207

### LATIN AMERICA

Costa Rica ..... 210
Mexico ..... 214

### UNITED STATES

Alaska ..... 224
Arizona ..... 228
Arkansas ..... 240
California ..... 244
Colorado ..... 307
Connecticut ..... 312
Delaware ..... 313
District of Columbia ..... 317
Florida ..... 322
Georgia ..... 358
Hawaii ..... 364
Illinois ..... 387
Iowa ..... 392
Louisiana ..... 393
Maine ..... 403
Maryland ..... 414
Massachusetts ..... 416
Michigan ..... 457
Minnesota ..... 460
Missouri ..... 462
Nevada ..... 465
New Hampshire ..... 466
New Jersey ..... 473
New Mexico ..... 474
New York ..... 487
North Carolina ..... 502
Ohio ..... 510
Oklahoma ..... 511
Oregon ..... 512
Pennsylvania ..... 518
Rhode Island ..... 526
South Carolina ..... 529
South Dakota ..... 531
Tennessee ..... 532
Texas ..... 534
Utah ..... 542
Vermont ..... 546
Virginia ..... 555
Washington ..... 558
West Virginia ..... 574
Wisconsin ..... 576
Wyoming ..... 578

## FORMS

Reader Comment Form ..... 585
The Ferrari Guides™ Order Form ..... 586

## INDICES

RV & Camping Index ..... 581
Women's Index ..... 582
Index to Accommodations ..... 587

# HOW TO USE THIS GUIDE

## How it Is Organized

This book is organized into the following geographical areas: Africa, Asia, Europe, Pacific Region, Canada, Caribbean, Latin America and United States. Each area is organized alphabetically by country and, within each country, alphabetically by state (or province) and city, or just by city.

**SAMPLE LISTING**

TAORMINA • ITALY

**TAORMINA**

**Hotel Villa Schuler**

Gay-Friendly ♀♂

***History & Tradition, Comfort & Romance***

Family-owned *Hotel Villa Schuler* was converted from a Sicilian villa to a hotel in 1905. In recent years the hotel has been extensively refurbished, emphasizing its original elegance, charm and atmosphere. Superbly situated above the Ionian Sea, its unique location offers stupendous views of snow-capped Mount Etna and the Bay of Naxos. Its central position, next to the delightful Botanical Gardens and tennis courts, is just 2 minutes from Taormina's famous traffic-free Corso Umberto. The ancient Greco-Roman theater and the cable-car to the beaches are just a 10-minute walk away.

The hotel is surrounded by its own extensive, shady, terraced gardens, where the fragrance of jasmine and bougainvillaea blossoms blend soothingly, enhancing the comfortable, romantic surroundings. Rooms are spacious, each with private bath/shower, WC, orthopaedic beds and mattresses, direct-dial telephone and electronic safe. Most have balcony/terrace or loggia and seaview. Other amenities include a roof terrace solarium, the palm terrace pavilion, dining and TV rooms (color satellite), small library, piano, 24-hour bar and room service, laundry, parking, garages and central heating.

**Address: Via Roma 17, I-98039**
**Taormina/Sicily Italy.**
**Tel: (39) 942 23481, Fax: (39) 942 23522.**

**Type:** Bed & breakfast hotel & bar.
**Clientele:** Mainly hetero clientele with a gay & lesbian following.
**Transportation:** Airport bus to Taormina, or pick up from airport by arrangement LIT 90.000, taxi from train LIT 20.000.
**To Gay Bars:** 5-minute walk.
**Rooms:** 26 rooms, 1 suite & 4 apartments with single or double beds.
**Bathrooms:** Private: 8 bath/toilets, 15 shower/toilets, 3 sinks. 1 shared bath.
**Meals:** Expanded continental breakfast.
**Vegetarian:** Restaurants nearby.
**Dates Open:** March to December.
**High Season:** Easter, August.
**Rates:** LIT 49.000-LIT 65.000 per person for B&B.
**Credit Cards:** MC, VISA, Amex & Eurocard.
**Rsv'tns:** Recommended, by FAX if possible.
**Reserve Through:** Travel agent or call direct.
**Parking:** Adequate, free on-street parking, garage LIT 12.000 per day.
**In-Room:** Maid & room service, telephone, safe, laundry service.
**On-Premises:** TV lounge, meeting rooms, laundry facilities, solarium, exotic garden, furnished terraces.
**Exercise/Health:** Nearby gym, weights, sauna & massage.
**Swimming:** At nearby ocean beach, shuttle service available.
**Sunbathing:** On the roof or at nearby beach.
**Smoking:** Permitted without restrictions.
**Pets:** Not permitted.
**Handicap Access:** No.
**Children:** Welcomed.
**Languages:** Italian, English, German, French, Spanish & Belgian.

INN PLACES® 1997 77

## Type of Accommodations

Until hospitality professionals agree on standardized definitions of the terms "B&B," "inn" and "guesthouse," ***Inn Places***® continues to honor the terminology chosen by each innkeeper.

## Gay Orientation & Gender

At the top right corner of each listing is the answer to the perennial first question, "How gay is it and is it for men or women?" The range of possible answers is given below. In describing clientele, these answers employ both words and the symbols for male ♂ and female ♀.

| | |
|---|---|
| Men ♂ | Gay male clientele |
| Women ♀ | Female clientele |
| Gay/Lesbian ♂ | Mostly gay men |
| Gay/Lesbian ♀ | Mostly gay women |
| Gay/Lesbian ♀♂ | Gay men and women about 50/50 |
| Gay-Friendly ♀♂<br>Gay-Owned ♀♂ | Mostly straight (non-gay) clientele with a gay and lesbian following, or a place that welcomes gay and lesbian customers |
| Gay-Friendly ♀<br>Gay-Owned ♀ | Mostly straight (non-gay) clientele with a gay female following |
| Gay-Friendly ♂<br>Gay-Owned ♂ | Mostly straight (non-gay) clientele with a gay male following |
| Gay-Friendly 50/50<br>Gay-Owned 50/50 | Half gay and half straight (Symbols indicate gay male ♂ or lesbian ♀ predominance) |

## Q-NET Logo

Placement of the "q-net" logo next to an entry signifies that a detailed entry with color photography appears on the Ferrari Internet sites. **Q-net** is a gay-lesbian site containing comprehensive accommodations and tours listings.

## Member AGLTA & IGTA

AGLTA is the Australian Gay & Lesbian Travel Association. IGTA is the International Gay Travel Association.

## Description

A description of the inn's architecture, ambiance, decor, amenities and services helps you to decide which inn to choose. Information is frequently also given on local activities.

## Addresses

Some businesses do not list their addresses. Others list mailing addresses only. Some have deleted their zip codes to indicate they do not wish to receive advertising solicitations from other publications using this book as a lead list.

## Telephones

Inside the US, area codes appear within parentheses. Outside the US, both country and city codes are used. For example, "Country: Netherlands, City: Amsterdam" is expressed by "(31-20)" followed by the phone number. When calling between two cities which are both within a country's boundaries (not US), always drop the country code and add a zero in front of the city code. Some countries are now dropping the city code and increasing phone numbers to 9 digits.

## Telephones Are Changing

Watch the space just under city headings for notices of changes taking place during 1997.

## All the Facts

Up to 32 facts may be included in a given listing. Variations in the length of listings are determined by the amount of information supplied to us by each establishment.

■ **Type** - Defines the kind of establishment (bed & breakfast, hotel, resort, etc.), and indicates whether restaurants, bars or shops are on the premises.

■ **Clientele** - A more specific and detailed description than provided in the gay orientation & gender line.

■ **Transportation** - Tells you if airport/bus pickup is provided and, if not, the best mode of transport is indicated.

■ **To Gay Bars** - The distance from your lodgings to the nearest gay or lesbian bar(s).

■ **Rooms** - The number and kind of accommodations provided. A cottage or cabin is an accommodation in a freestanding building. A bunkroom is a large room in which beds can be rented singly at a reduced rate. Bed sizes are also indicated.

■ **Bathrooms** - The number and type of private bathrooms and shared bathrooms.

■ **Campsites** - The number and kind of sites provided. Full RV hookups have both electric and sewer unless otherwise noted.

■ **Meals** - Describes meals included with room rate and those available at extra charge. Full breakfast includes meat, eggs and breads with coffee, tea, etc. Continental breakfast consists of breads and jams with coffee, tea, etc.

■ **Vegetarian Food** - Availability indicated.

■ **Complimentary** - Any complimentary foods, beverages or amenities.

■ **Dates Open** - Actual dates, if not open all year.

■ **High Season** - Annual season of high occupancy rate.

■ **Rates** - The range of rates, from lowest to highest, is given. Note: Rates are subject to change at any time and travelers should always request current rates when making reservations.

■ **Discounts** - Amounts and conditions.

■ **Credit Cards** - Lists cards accepted (MC=MasterCard, Amex=American Express). Access is MC in Europe. Bancard is British and Australian.

■ **Reservations** - Tells if required and how far in advance.

■ **Reserve Through** - How to make reservations.

■ **Minimum Stay** - If required, indicates how long.

■ **Parking** - Availability and type.

■ **In-Room** - Facilities provided INSIDE your room (TV, phone, AC, etc).

■ **On-Premises** - Facilities not provided inside your room, but available on the premises.

■ **Exercise/Health** - Availability of facilities such as hot tub, gym, sauna, steam, massage, weights.

■ **Swimming** - Availability, type, location.

■ **Sunbathing** - Areas described.

■ **Nudity** - Indicates if permitted and where.

■ **Smoking** - Restrictions, if any, are noted and availability of non - smokers' rooms is indicated.

■ **Pets** - Indicates if permitted, and restrictions are described.

■ **Handicap Access** - Indicates if accessible, and limitations are described.

■ **Children** - Preferences described.

■ **Languages** - All languages spoken by staff.

■ **Your host** - Name(s) of innkeeper(s).

**Travel Safety** - Constantly changing political and social situations in every nation can increase or decrease the risks of visiting any given destination without warning. This book does not include specific information about health and safety risks that readers may encounter in the places described herein. Travelers should always be mindful of their health and safety when traveling or staying in unfamiliar places.

■ **Advertisements** - The author, editor, and publisher of this book are not responsible for the contents of advertisements that appear in this book and make no endorsements or guarantees about their accuracy.

■ **We Welcome Reader Comments** - Specific information described in the listings, articles and other materials in this book may change without the knowledge of the author, editor and publisher, and the author, editor, and publisher cannot be responsible for the accuracy and completeness of such information or advice. We welcome all information sent to us by readers. We will consider your comments and suggestions in updating the next issue. Information on new areas, not yet covered, are especially valued.

# INDEX

## Inns Featured in the Color Section


**Pacific Region (Australia)**

■ Queensland, Cairns
Fifty-Four Cinderella Street ................ 10

**Canada**

■ Montreal, Quebec
La Conciergerie Guest House ............ 10

**Caribbean**

■ Netherlands Antilles, Saba
Captain's Quarters ................................ 11

**United States**

■ Arizona, Tucson
Tortuga Roja Bed & Breakfast ........... 12
■ California, Laguna Beach
Casa Laguna B&B Inn ........................ 12
■ California, Lake Tahoe Area
Lakeside B 'n B .................................. 13
■ California, Palm Springs
Inn Exile .............................................. 13
Santiago Resort .................................. 14
■ California, Russian River
Applewood Inn and Restaurant .......... 15
Fern Falls ............................................ 14
Highland Dell Inn Bed & Breakfast .... 16
■ California, San Francisco
Inn On Castro ..................................... 17
Lombard Central,
A Super 8 Hotel, The ....................... 17
Renoir Hotel ........................................ 18
San Francisco Cottage ....................... 18
Villa, The ............................................. 19
■ California, Sonoma
Gaige House Inn ................................. 16
■ Delaware, Rehoboth Beach
Silver Lake .......................................... 20
■ Florida, Key West
Rainbow House ................................... 21
■ Hawaii, Kauai
Mahina Kai .......................................... 22
■ Louisiana, New Orleans
Nine Twelve Pauline Street ................ 22
■ Massachusetts, Provincetown
Admiral's Landing Guest House ......... 23
Beaconlite Guest House ..................... 23
Boatslip Beach Club ........................... 24
Commons, The .................................... 24
Eighteen-O-Seven (1807) House ....... 25
■ New Mexico, Taos
Ruby Slipper, The ............................... 25
Inn of the Turquoise Bear ................... 26
■ New York, New Paltz
Golden Bear Farm, The ...................... 27
■ Tennessee, Newport
Christopher Place ............................... 28
■ Texas, Dallas
Courtyard on the Trail ......................... 28
■ Vermont, Andover
Inn at Highview, The ........................... 29
■ Washington, Port Townsend
Ravenscroft Inn ................................... 29
■ Washington, Lopez Island
Inn At Swifts Bay ................................ 30
■ Washington, Seattle
Gaslight Inn ......................................... 31

## Fifty-Four Cinderella Street

Q-NET Women ♀

***Superb Accommodation...Creative Cuisine... Absolute Beachfront...for Women!***

Be pampered in the tropics at a fairy tale hideaway – ***54 Cinderella Street*** – just 10 minutes from Cairns and the airport on Reddens Island at the mouth of the Barron River, in quiet and unspoiled Machans Beach. Spend idyllic days in the large garden with a rock swimming pool complete with creek bed and waterfall, or use the private access to the beach. The coastline, magnificent rainforests, and some of the best reef diving in the world, not to mention excellent tourist shopping and casinos, make Cairns one of the most sought-after tourist destinations in the world.

**Address: 54 Cinderella St, Cairns, QLD 4878 Australia.**
**Tel: (61-70) 550 289, Fax: (61-70) 559 383. E-mail: dsdelmont@c131.aone.net.au.**

**Type:** Bed & breakfast guesthouse with restaurant.
**Clientele:** Mostly gay women
**Transportation:** Car is best. Free pick up from airport, train, bus or ferry dock.
**To Gay Bars:** 4 miles, a 10-minute drive.
**Rooms:** 4 suites with single or queen beds.
**Bathrooms:** Private: 2 bath/shower/toilets, 2 shower/toilets.
**Meals:** Full breakfast.
**Vegetarian:** Inquire, all tastes catered for.

*More facts on page 147*



## La Conciergerie Guest House

Q-NET Gay/Lesbian ♂

***Your Resort in the City!***

***La Conciergerie*** is Montréal's premier guest house. Since our opening in 1985, we have gained an ever-growing popularity among travelers from Canada, the United States, Europe and Australia, winning the 1995 Out & About Editor's Choice Award. The beautiful Victorian home, built in 1885, offers 17 air-conditioned rooms with queen-sized beds and duvet comforters. A complimentary European breakfast is served either in the breakfast room or on an outdoor terrace. The house is within walking distance of most major points of interest, including downtown shopping, Old Montréal, rue St.-Denis, rue Ste.-Catherine, and the East Village, with its many gay shops, restaurants and bars. We're two blocks from the Metro (subway) and there is plenty of on-street parking for those who drive.

**Address: 1019 rue St.-Hubert, Montréal, QC H2L 3Y3 Canada. Tel: (514) 289-9297, Fax: (514) 289-0845, http://www.gaibec.com.**

**Type:** Bed & breakfast.
**Clientele:** Mostly men with women welcome
**Transportation:** Airport bus to Voyageur Bus Station, then walk, or taxi directly for CDN $25. Take a cab if arr. by train.
**To Gay Bars:** 2 blocks to men's & women's bars.
**Rms:** 17 rms w/ queen beds.
**Bathrooms:** 9 private. Shared: 1 bathtub, 3 showers, 3 toilets, 1 full bath.
**Meals:** Expanded continental breakfast.
**Vegetarian:** Bring your own. Vegetarian rest. nearby.
**Dates Open:** All year.
**High Season:** April-Dec.
**Rates:** High season CDN $72-$135, low season CDN $52-$110.

*More facts on page 190*

# Captain's Quarters

Q-NET Gay-Friendly ♀♂

## *The Unspoiled Queen of the Caribbean*

Orchids, tree frogs, crested hummingbirds, sea turtles, hot springs, snorkeling... Enjoy all of this when you stay at ***Captain's Quarters.*** This 16-room Victorian guesthouse (which has hosted royalty, celebrities, and adventurous travelers for more than 30 years) is set in a tropical paradise, a short 10-minute flight from St. Maarten. Rooms feature antique and four-poster beds, many with elegant canopies. From the balconies and patios are stunning views of the Caribbean and mountain scenery. Enjoy the garden dining pavilion, cliffside pool/bar, and some of the friendliest people in the Caribbean.

Saba is a storybook setting of Dutch gingerbread villages that date from the 1850s. Originally settled by pirates and sea captains as a safe haven for their families, "The Rock" was accessible only by footpaths and thousands of steps until "the Road that Couldn't be Built" was handcrafted in the 1950s. Saba will remind you of Switzerland with palm trees! World-class scuba diving, well-marked hiking trails, a pristine rainforest, and spectacular views at every turn make Saba unforgettable.

**Note:** Saba has no beaches. All swimming is from rocks, boats, tidal pools, and hotel swimming pools. However, since you have to fly through St. Maarten anyway, spend a few days there and enjoy some of the best beaches in the world. Then visit us – just minutes away – for a few days.

**Address: Windwardside, Saba Netherlands Antilles.**
**Tel: (5994) 62201, Fax: (5994) 62377, In USA: (212) 289-6031, Fax: 289-1931.**
**E-mail: Rich_Holm@msn.com. http://saba-online.com.**

**Type:** Hotel with restaurant & bar.
**Clientele:** Mostly straight clientele with a gay & lesbian following
**Transportation:** 10-minute flight from St. Maarten, on Wiriair (Wm). Airport transfer included in rates.
**To Gay Bars:** None. All bars on island are friendly.
**Rooms:** 16 rooms with double or queen beds.
**Bathrooms:** All private shower/toilets.
**Meals:** Full American breakfast.
**Vegetarian:** Available upon request.
**Complimentary:** Welcome drink.
**Dates Open:** All year.
**High Season:** Feb, Mar, Apr.
**Rates:** Summer $95-$150, extra person $35. Winter $115-$170, extra person $45, includes tax & service fee.
**Discounts:** For stays of 3 or more nights, group packages. Off-season discounts for groups.
**Credit Cards:** Visa, MC, Amex & Discover.
**Rsv'tns:** Required. Walk-ins based on availability.
**Reserve Through:** Travel agent or call direct.
**Parking:** Ample free off-street parking.
**In-Room:** Balcony & maid service. Some rooms with AC, color cable TV, ceiling fans, refrigerator.
**On-Premises:** Meeting rooms & TV lounge
**Exercise/Health:** Nearby gym.
**Swimming:** Pool on premises. Nearby ocean.
**Sunbathing:** At poolside.
**Smoking:** Permitted.
**Pets:** Permitted with advance approval.
**Handicap Access:** No.
**Children:** Welcome.
**Languages:** English, Dutch, Papiamento & Spanish.

## Tortuga Roja Bed & Breakfast Q-NET Gay/Lesbian ♀♂

### *Come, Share Our Mountain Views*

***Tortuga Roja Bed & Breakfast*** is a 4-acre cozy retreat at the base of the Santa Catalinas, whose windows look out on an open landscape of natural high-desert vegetation. A bicycle and running path along the Rillito River right behind our house can be followed for four miles on either side. Our location is close to upscale shopping and dining and numerous hiking trails. It's an easy drive to the university, local bars and most tourist attractions. Some of our accommodations have fireplaces and kitchens.

**Address: 2800 E River Rd, Tucson, AZ 85718**
**Tel: (520) 577-6822, (800) 467-6822.**

**Type:** Bed & breakfast.
**Clientele:** Good mix of gays & lesbians
**Transportation:** Car is best.
**To Gay Bars:** 10-min. drive.
**Rooms:** 2 rooms & 1 cottage with queen beds.
**Bathrooms:** All private.
**Meals:** Exp. continental break.
**Dates Open:** All year.
**High Season:** Sep.-May.
**Rates:** Please call for rates.
**Discounts:** For weekly & monthly stays.
**Credit Cards:** Disc., MC, VISA.
**Rsv'tns:** Often essential.
**Reserve Through:** Travel agent or call direct.
**Minimum Stay:** 2 nights on holiday weekends.
**Parking:** Ample free off-street parking.
**In-Room:** Color TV, VCR, AC, ceiling fan, radio & telephone. Cottage has kitchen.
**On-Premises:** Laundry facilities & kitchen privileges.

*More facts on page 239*



## Casa Laguna Bed & Breakfast Inn Gay-Friendly ♀♂

### *Sun, Sand & Sea*

***Casa Laguna*** is a unique, 20-room country inn on a terraced hillside, overlooking the Pacific Ocean. Its towering palms hover over meandering paths and flower-splashed patios, swimming pool, aviary and fountains, making this intimate, mission-style inn a visual delight. Many rooms and suites have sweeping views. A cottage, set on its own, has private garden, sun decks and ocean views. The mission house, itself, has two bedrooms and two fireplaces. Laguna Beach combines art, seaside casualness and colorful landscapes for an ideal retreat.

**Address: 2510 South Coast Hwy, Laguna Beach, CA 92651**
**Tel: (714) 494-2996, (800) 233-0449, Fax: (714) 494-5009.**

**Type:** Bed & breakfast inn.
**Clientele:** Mostly straight clientele with a gay & lesbian following
**Transportation:** Car is best. Jitney service from Orange County Airport, about $20.
**To Gay Bars:** One mile to nearest one. There are others in Laguna Beach.
**Rooms:** 15 rooms, 4 suites & 2 cottages. Sgl, dbl or king beds.
**Bathrooms:** All private shower/toilets.
**Meals:** Exp. continental break.
**Vegetarian:** Fruit, cereals & breads available at breakfast.
**Complimentary:** Wine, cheese, snacks, tea & coffee are served each afternoon in the library.
**Dates Open:** All year.
**High Season:** Jul- Labor Day.
**Rates:** Winter $79-$175, summer $90-$225.
**Discounts:** Winter & mid-week discounts.

*More facts on page 250*

# Lakeside B 'n B Tahoe

Gay/Lesbian ♀♂

## *Romantic, Inexpensive, Right on the Water!*

***Lakeside B 'n B Tahoe,*** a private home smack-dab on the water, has antiques, plants and magnificent views of Lake Tahoe and mountains from all three guest rooms. There is a steam room, Jacuzzi, grand piano, fireplace, library, lakeside deck and parklike grounds. Fresh-baked bread and gargantuan gourmet breakfasts are served from a printed, personalized menu with many choices. Fabulous skiing in winter, swimming, boating and nude sunbathing in summer, and 24-hour Nevada gaming action are minutes away. On the quiet Nevada side of North Lake Tahoe, the B&B is 4 hours from San Fran. and 45 minutes from Reno.

**Address: Box 1756, Crystal Bay, NV 89402**
**Tel: (702) 831-8281, Fax: (702) 831-7FAX (7329), E-mail: tahoeBnB@aol.com.**

**Type:** Bed & breakfast.
**Clientele:** Gay & lesbian, good mix of men & women
**Transportation:** Car is best. Carry chains in winter.
**To Gay Bars:** About 1/2 hr drive to Faces in South Lake Tahoe or 45 min to Reno bars.
**Rooms:** 3 rooms with single or queen beds.
**Bathrooms:** 1 private & 1 shared.
**Meals:** Full breakfast from printed menu with many choices, daily gourmet special & fresh-baked bread.
**Vegetarian:** Available whenever a guest wants it.
**Complimentary:** Wine, coffee, other goodies, breakfast in bed if desired.

*More facts on page 254*



# Inn Exile

Men ♂

## *Where Being Gay Is a Way of Life*

Close your eyes and fantasize about a place where the open air calls you to the sparkling pool in the desert sun. Breathe in the dramatic view of towering mountains, while being refreshed by our outdoor mist cooling system. At ***Inn Exile,*** clothing is always optional. There's no need to miss your workout...our gymnasium is here for you. Call or write for brochure.

**Address: 545 Warm Sands Drive, Palm Springs, CA 92264. Tel: (619) 327-6413, (800) 962-0186, Fax: (619) 320-5745. http://www.innexile.com.**

**Type:** Resort.
**Clientele:** Men only
**Transportation:** Car is best.
**To Gay Bars:** Three minutes by car, a 10 minute-walk.
**Rooms:** 26 rooms with king beds.
**Bathrooms:** All private full baths.
**Dates Open:** All year.
**Rates:** $83-$114.
**Discounts:** For 7 nights or more.
**Credit Cards:** MC, VISA, Amex, Discover, Diners, Carte Blanche.
**Rsv'tns:** Required.
**Reserve Through:** Travel agent or call direct.
**Minimum Stay:** Required at times. Please inquire.
**Parking:** Adequate, free off-street and on-street parking.
**In-Room:** Color TV, VCR, video tape library, AC, houseman service, telephone & refrigerator.
**On-Premises:** TV lounge.
**Exercise/Health:** Gym, weights, Jacuzzi, steam room.
**Swimming:** Pools on premises.
**Sunbathing:** At poolside.
**Nudity:** Permitted without restriction.
**Smoking:** Permitted without restriction.

*More facts on page 269*

# Santiago Resort

Men ♂

## *Palm Springs' Most Spectacular Private Men's Resort*

Exotically landscaped and secluded grounds provide a peaceful enclave for the discriminating traveller. Enjoy the most magnificent mountain views that Palm Springs can offer from our terrace level. An oversized diving pool, a 12-man spa and an outdoor cooling mist system complete the setting. Select from 23 poolside, courtyard or terrace suites and studios, all professionally designed and appointed. King-sized beds with feather duvet covers, superior quality towels and linens, shower massages, refrigerators and microwaves set the standard of excellence and luxury that you can expect at the ***Santiago.*** Expanded continental breakfast, courtyard luncheon, film library and Gold's Gym passes are all complimentary. And clothing is forever optional...

**Address: 650 San Lorenzo Rd, Palm Springs, CA 92264-8108. Tel: (619) 322-1300, (800) 710-7729, Fax: (619) 416-0347. Area code changes to (760) Oct, 1997.**

**Type:** Hotel resort.
**Clientele:** Men only
**Transportation:** Car is best. Free pick up from airport or bus.
**To Gay Bars:** A 10-minute walk or a 3-minute drive.
**Rooms:** 10 rooms, 13 suites with king beds.
**Bathrooms:** Private: 19 shower/toilets, 4 bath/toilet/showers.

*More facts on page 271*



# Fern Falls

Gay/Lesbian ♀♂

## *Romance Amidst the Redwoods*

***Fern Falls*** is a hillside habitat in a captivating canyon of Cazadero, whose cascading creeks merge with the languid waters of the Russian River. The custom-designed curved deck of the main house looks over the creek and ravine, and an ozonator spa sits above the waterfall on a hill nestled below a giant boulder. Nearby you can try wine tasting at the Korbel Winery, horseback riding, a soothing enzyme bath and massage at Osmosis, canoeing on the Russian River, or hiking in the redwood forests.

**Address: 5701 Austin Creek Rd, PO Box 228, Cazadero, CA 95421**
**Tel: (707) 632-6108, Fax: (707) 632-6216.**

**Type:** Guesthouse & cottages.
**Clientele:** Gay & lesbian. Good mix of men & women.
**Transportation:** Car is best.
**To Gay Bars:** 12 miles to bars in Guerneville.
**Rooms:** 1 suite & 2 cottages with double or queen beds.
**Bathrooms:** Private.
**Dates Open:** All year.
**High Season:** May-October.
**Rates:** $65-$135.
**Discounts:** Weekly rates.
**Rsv'tns:** Required.
**Reserve Through:** Travel agent or call direct.
**Minimum Stay:** 2 nights on weekends in season.
**Parking:** Adequate free parking.
**In-Room:** Color cable TV, VCR, coffee/tea-making facilities, kitchen, refrigerator. Cabins have fireplaces.

*More facts on page 275*

# Applewood Inn and Restaurant Q-NET Gay-Friendly ♀♂

***Russian River's Preeminent B&B***

It's easy to see why *San Francisco Focus Magazine* called ***Applewood*** "the region's premier bed and breakfast" in July 1995. The beauty of the redwoods, apple trees and vineyards...the relaxing pool and Jacuzzi...the stylish rooms with European down comforters...the marvelous food in a firelit dining room...your willing hosts and two tail-wagging dogs...all await your arrival at this contemporary Eden. Once a mission-style retreat in the redwoods, ***Applewood*** has been transformed into an elegant country inn and restaurant that has become the darling of food critics and editors steering their readers to romantic getaways. Rave reviews have appeared in regional and national magazines and newspapers.

"The inn features richly appointed rooms and a secluded swimming pool. A swim in the pool is more private than anywhere on the river, a couple I met assured me. They live in nearby Napa Valley and stay frequently at the inn because the weather, scenery and stylish accommodations are 'so inviting.'" -- *Los Angeles Times, September 1995.*

Jeff Cox of the *Santa Rosa Press Democrat* says, "I've found a spot...where peace and quiet hang motionless under the boughs of the redwoods and where the relaxed sensibility of a former time seems captured in the graceful lines of a building's architecture. And, while you're enjoying all this, you're also being served marvelous food."

Let ***Applewood*** be your great place to unwind and relax. Drive down country lanes, picnic or taste wine at boutique wineries, raft or canoe the Russian River, take a short drive to the coast to kick up a little sand on the beach, or lounge in bed with a mimosa and someone special.

**Address: 13555 Hwy 116, Guerneville, CA 95446. Tel: (707) 869-9093, (800) 555-8509, E-mail: stay@applewoodinn.com. http://applewoodinn.com.**

**Type:** Inn with restaurant serving 4-course dinners.
**Clientele:** Mostly straight clientele with a gay & lesbian following.
**Transportation:** Car is best. Free pick up from Santa Rosa airport.
**To Gay Bars:** 5-minute drive to men's/women's bars.
**Rooms:** 10 rooms & 6 suites with queen beds.
**Bathrooms:** All private.
**Meals:** Full breakfast included, dinner offered to guests & public Tuesdays thru Saturdays.
**Vegetarian:** Upon request with 1-day notice.
**Complimentary:** Chocolates on pillows, coffee and tea all day.
**Dates Open:** All year.
**High Season:** April-November.
**Rates:** Doubles $125-$250. Off-season (Dec-Mar) $90-$190.
**Credit Cards:** MC, Visa, Amex, Discover.
**Rsv'tns:** Recommended. Essential for dinner.
**Reserve Through:** Travel agent or call direct.
**Minimum Stay:** 1 night mid week, 2 nights on weekends, 3 nights on holiday weekends.
**Parking:** Ample, free off-street parking.
**In-Room:** Color TV, phone & maid service. Suites also have showers for two or Jacuzzi baths, fireplaces & private patios or verandas.
**On-Premises:** Meeting rooms, private dining rooms, public telephone, laundry facilities & fax.
**Exercise/Health:** Jacuzzi, massage. Jacuzzi baths in suites.
**Swimming:** Heated pool on premises, river nearby. 10 minutes to ocean.
**Sunbathing:** At poolside & on private verandas with suites.
**Smoking:** Not permitted.
**Pets:** Not permitted.
**Handicap Access:** Yes, ramps, wide doors, grab bars.
**Children:** Not permitted.
**Languages:** English.
**Your Host:** Darryl & Jim

CALIFORNIA • RUSSIAN RIVER

# Highland Dell Inn Bed & Breakfast

Gay-Friendly 50/50 ♀♂

## *Exceptional Service in a Spectacular Setting*

The landmark ***Highland Dell Inn Bed & Breakfast,*** with its vista of the Russian River, captures the serenity of a more gentle era. Rich, stained glass windows, a gigantic lobby fireplace, heirloom antiques and a collection of historical photos set the tone for arriving guests. The large pool is under the redwoods. The area offers canoeing, swimming, fishing, backpacking, nature trails, horseback riding, cross-country cycling, enzyme baths, and even hot-air ballooning. One of our guests comments, *"The warmth of your hospitality, the charm of this beautiful B&B, delicious food, the view...a perfect getaway. Lady (dog) certainly lives up to her name."*

**Address: 21050 River Blvd, Box 370, Monte Rio, CA 95462-0370**
**Tel: (707) 865-1759, (800) 767-1759, E-mail: highland@netdex.com.**

**Type:** Bed & breakfast inn.
**Clientele:** 50% gay & lesbian & 50% straight clientele. Sometimes more gay than straight
**Transportation:** Car is best.
**To Gay Bars:** 5-minute drive to most gay venues.
**Rooms:** 5 rooms & 3 suites with queen or king beds.
**Bathrooms:** 2 private shower/toilets, 6 private bath/toilet/showers.
**Meals:** Full breakfast.
**Vegetarian:** Available upon request.
**Complimentary:** Tea & coffee. Candies throughout.
**Dates Open:** Open all year

*More facts on page 278*

CALIFORNIA • SONOMA

# Gaige House Inn

Gay-Friendly ♀♂

## *A Star in the Valley of the Moon*

The ***Gaige House Inn,*** a Sonoma designated landmark, is bordered by lazy Calabezas Creek and the wooded hills of the California Coast range. *Fodors* called the location "one of the best sites of any wine country inn" and *Northern California's Best Places* described our guest rooms as "spectacular." Oversized towels, fluffy robes and English toiletries await you, along with direct-dial phones and reading lights with rheostats. Two-course breakfasts, prepared by a professional chef, include fresh-squeezed orange juice and coffee from Peet's, a Bay Area institution. Seven miles from Sonoma, the wooded hamlet of Glen Ellen is a superb base for touring wine country. A dozen notable wineries are several miles away. Relaxing days can be spent combining wine tastings with picnics. Outdoor activities in the area include horseback riding, golfing, hiking and ballooning.

**Address: 13540 Arnold Dr, Glen Ellen, CA**
**Tel: (707) 935-0237, (800) 935-0237, Fax: (707) 935-6411. www.gaige.com.**

**Type:** Inn.
**Clientele:** Mostly straight with a gay & lesbian following
**Transportation:** Car is best.
**To Gay Bars:** 45 mins to Russian River & 25 mins to Santa Rosa gay bars.
**Rooms:** 9 rooms, 1 suite with king or queen beds.
**Bathrooms:** 10 private bath/toilet/shower.

*More facts on page 304*

# Inn On Castro

Gay/Lesbian ♀♂

The innkeepers invite you into a colorful and comfortable environment filled with modern art and exotic plants. All rooms vary in size and have private baths. Meet fellow travelers from all over the world for a memorable breakfast. The ***Inn On Castro's*** location is unique, just 100 yards north of the intersection of Market and Castro, where you are in a quiet neighborhood, yet only a stone's throw away from the Castro Theater, plus dozens of bars, restaurants and shops. With the ***Underground*** almost virtually adjacent to the ***Inn,*** big-name store shopping and cable car, etc. are just a few minutes away. There is literally something for everyone.

**Address: 321 Castro St, San Francisco, CA 94114 Tel: (415) 861-0321.**

**Type:** Bed & breakfast.
**Clientele:** Good mix of gay men & women
**Transportation:** Supershuttle from airport approx $11 per person.
**To Gay Bars:** Less than 1-minute walk to men's/women's bars.
**Rooms:** 6 rooms & 2 suites with double, queen or king beds, self-catering apartment.
**Bathrooms:** All private.
**Meals:** Full breakfast.
**Vegetarian:** Available with advance notice.
**Complimentary:** Afternoon wine, brandy night cap, tea, coffee, juices.
**Dates Open:** All year.
**High Season:** May-October.
**Rates:** Rooms $80-$150.
**Credit Cards:** MC, Visa, Amex.
**Rsv'tns:** Recommended 1 month in advance.
**Reserve Through:** Call direct.
**Minimum Stay:** 2 days on weekends, 3 on holidays, 4 days Folsom Fair, Castro Fair & Gay Lib days.
**Parking:** Adequate on-street parking.
**In-Room:** Color TV on request, telephone, maid service, refrigerator.
**On-Premises:** Lounge & dining room.

*More facts on page 297*

CALIFORNIA • SAN FRANCISCO

# The Lombard Central, A Super 8 Hotel

## *Old-World Charm and Today's Hospitality*

Gay-Friendly ♀♂

***The Lombard Central,*** reminiscent of old San Francisco with an intimate lobby featuring marble floors, etched glass, mahogany columns, and a grand piano, offers guests old-world charm and Super 8 hospitality. At the 100-room hotel, you'll find the attention to detail and personal service exceptional. From making reservations at the hotel's famous Faces Cafe Restaurant to arranging special tours of the city and beyond, the staff is eager to make your stay perfect. We are conveniently located in the heart of downtown San Francisco's performing arts and civic center district, and are only five blocks from the famous cable cars.

**Address: 1015 Geary Blvd, San Francisco, CA 94109. Tel: (415) 673-5232, (800) 777-3210, Fax: (415) 885-2802.**

**Type:** Hotel with breakfast cafe.
**Clientele:** Mostly straight clientele with a gay/lesbian following.
**Transportation:** From airport, car or airport shuttle is best.
**To Gay Bars:** 2 blocks, a 5-minute walk.
**Rooms:** 100 rooms with sgl., double, queen or king beds.
**Bathrooms:** All private bath/shower/toilets.
**Vegetarian:** Available at breakfast & at nearby restaurants.
**Complimentary:** 24-hr coffee & tea, complimentary wine hour weekdays 5:30-6:30 pm.

*More facts on page 298*

## Renoir Hotel

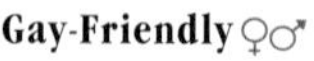

Gay-Friendly ♀♂

### *San Francisco's Newest First Class Downtown Hotel*

The ***Renoir Hotel*** is a newly-renovated historical landmark building, just three blocks from Folsom Street, Polk Street, and three subway stations from the Castro. It is the best bargain in downtown San Francisco, providing charming European ambiance with classical music throughout. The ornate interior includes an original Renard in the reception area and Renoir prints placed tastefully throughout the hotel. The Royal Delight Restaurant serves breakfast, lunch and dinner. Also available are the lounge and lobby cafe and room service. *Inn Places* discount to $69 available most dates (or pick up coupon at Visitors Center).

**Address: 45 McAllister St, San Francisco, CA 94102**
**Tel: (415) 626-5200 or (800) 576-3388.**

**Type:** Hotel with restaurant, bar, espresso bar & gift shop.
**Clientele:** Mostly straight with a gay & lesbian following
**Transportation:** BART subway from Oakland airport to Civic Center Station. Shuttle van from SF Airport to hotel.
**To Gay Bars:** 2 blks. About 10 gay bars within 5 blks.
**Rooms:** 123 rooms & 3 suites with twin, double, queen & king beds.
**Bathrooms:** All private.
**Vegetarian:** Vegetarian items on restaurant & cafe menus.
**Dates Open:** All year.
**High Season:** May 15-Nov 15.

*More facts on page 299*

---

CALIFORNIA • SAN FRANCISCO

## San Francisco Cottage

Gay/Lesbian ♀♂

### *The Perfect San Francisco Experience*

***San Francisco Cottage*** offers a lovely cottage and an elegant studio apartment in the rear garden of a San Francisco Edwardian home. We're on a quiet, residential street, just a five-minute stroll to Castro Street venues. Public transportation is nearby. The studio apartment has contemporary decor, a complete kitchen, living room area opening onto a garden, dining area, queen-sized bed, and a bathroom with shower and claw tub. The loft-like cottage, decorated in Santa Fe-style, has a living room, queen-sized bed, modern kitchen and dining area. French doors open onto a redwood deck and terraced garden.

**Address: 224 Douglass St, San Francisco, CA 94114**
**Tel: (415) 861-3220, Fax: (415) 626-2633.**

**Type:** Self-catering cottage & studio apartment.
**Clientele:** Gay & lesbian
**Transportation:** Shuttle buses or taxi from airport. Best way downtown is metro.
**To Gay Bars:** 3 short blocks to gay bars.
**Rooms:** 1 cottage & 1 apartment with queen beds.
**Bathrooms:** Both private.
**Complimentary:** Tea & coffee set-up in rooms.
**Dates Open:** All year.
**High Season:** Mar-Oct.
**Rates:** $95-$105 per night, $600-$660 per week.
**Discounts:** Weekly & monthly rates.

*More facts on page 300*

# The Villa

Gay/Lesbian ♀♂

## *Spectacular Views of San Francisco*

***The Villa*** is the flagship guesthouse of San Francisco Views rental services. Located atop one of the Castro's legendary hills, this exclusive villa offers a magnificent view of the San Francisco skyline by day and the glitter of city lights by night from our double rooms and suites. Guests have the use of our fireplace lounge, complete kitchen and dining area overlooking our decks and swimming pool. Our fabulous rooms and suites are equipped with television, VCR and telephone with answering machine. We are close to all of the attractions San Francisco is famous for -- just minutes from the financial and shopping districts of downtown San Francisco, and three blocks from the heart of the Castro. We are open all year and short- or long-term rentals are available.

**Address: 379 Collingwood, San Francisco, CA 94114**
**Tel: (415) 282-1367, (800) 358-0123, Fax: (415) 821-3995.**
**E-mail: SFViews@aol.com.**

**Type:** Guesthouse.
**Clientele:** Good mix of gays & lesbians
**Transportation:** Easily accessible by car, or shuttle from airport.
**To Gay Bars:** 3 blocks or a 5-minute walk.
**Rooms:** 4 rooms, 3 suites & 4 apartments with single, double, queen or king beds.
**Bathrooms:** Rooms: private & shared. Apartments have private baths.
**Meals:** Continental breakfast.
**Vegetarian:** Restaurants nearby.
**Dates Open:** All year.
**High Season:** Summer & Fall.
**Rates:** Daily from $80, weekly $500, monthly rates available.
**Discounts:** Please inquire.
**Credit Cards:** MC, Visa, Amex.
**Rsv'tns:** Recommended.
**Reserve Through:** Call direct.
**Minimum Stay:** 2 days.
**Parking:** Free off-street & on-street parking.
**In-Room:** Color cable TV, VCR, telephone, kitchen, refrigerator & maid service.
**On-Premises:** TV lounge, laundry facilities & shared kitchen on each floor.
**Swimming:** Pool on premises, ocean nearby.
**Sunbathing:** At poolside & on common sun decks.
**Smoking:** Permitted inside the rooms. Non-smoking rooms available upon request.
**Pets:** Not permitted.
**Handicap Access:** No.
**Children:** Permitted, but not especially welcome.
**Languages:** English & Spanish.

IGTA

# Silver Lake

Q-NET Gay/Lesbian ♀♂

*"Gem of the Delaware Shore"*

***Silver Lake Guest House*** is "the best of the bunch" (Fodor's Gay Guide), "the best option" (Out & About), and "the gem of the Delaware shore" (The Washington Post). Located in a tranquil waterfront setting in the midst of a waterfowl preserve on Rehoboth Beach's most scenic drive, this beautiful home offers its guests much more than a conventional bed and breakfast. It is also the resort's closest guesthouse to gay Poodle Beach.

The spectacular lake and ocean view from the main house's sprawling columned veranda along with a beautifully landscaped garden provide an inviting introduction to ***Silver Lake.*** Inside, all of the bedrooms have private baths, cable TV and central air conditioning. Some of the rooms have panoramas of the lake and ocean beyond, while others look out on the numerous varieties of pine and evergreen surrounding the property.

Guests may enjoy breakfast quietly in their rooms, on the veranda or patio, or in the second floor sunroom. Here, too, the lake and dunes are on full display. Breakfast includes muffins baked daily, an assortment of fresh fruit, juice, tea, coffee, along with daily newspapers. Behind the main house is the Carriage House with its very private, large two-bedroom apartments. Each has a private entrance, living room, dining area and complete kitchen.

***Silver Lake*** is about quality of life. Whether for a weekend or extended vacation, guests enjoy an ambience of comfort and relaxation in the midst of nature at its best.

**Address: 133 Silver Lake Dr, Rehoboth Beach, DE 19971**
**Tel: (302) 226-2115, (800) 842-2115.**

**Type:** Bed & breakfast guesthouse.
**Clientele:** Gay & lesbian. Good mix of men & women
**Transportation:** Car is best.
**To Gay Bars:** Walking distance.
**Rooms:** 11 rooms & 2 two-bedroom apartments with queen or king beds.
**Bathrooms:** All private.
**Meals:** Expanded continental breakfast.
**Complimentary:** Tea, coffee, juices & fruit.
**Dates Open:** All year.
**High Season:** Summer.
**Rates:** In season $80-$165, off season from $60.
**Discounts:** For longer stays.
**Credit Cards:** MC, Visa, Amex, Discover
**Rsv'tns:** Required.
**Reserve Through:** Call direct.
**Minimum Stay:** 2-3 nights on summer weekends.
**Parking:** Ample, free off-street parking.
**In-Room:** Color cable TV, AC, maid service, kitchens in apartments.
**On-Premises:** Meeting rooms, kitchenette, sun room, lounge, BBQ grills, beach chairs & towels, ice, sodas, outdoor showers, lake front lawn & gardens.
**Exercise/Health:** On jogging & biking course. Gym nearby.
**Swimming:** 5-minute walk to gay ocean beach.
**Sunbathing:** On the beach.
**Smoking:** Permitted.
**Pets:** Permitted in apartments only, by prior arrangement.
**Handicap Access:** Yes, call for details.
**Children:** Not permitted except by prior arrangement.
**Languages:** English.
**Your Host:** Joe & Mark

# Rainbow House

**Q-NET** Women ♀

*Welcome to Paradise!*

At the ***Rainbow House,*** we have everything from a standard room to a deluxe suite. All of our rooms have queen-sized beds, color TV, telephones, air conditioning, as well as Bahama fans and, of course, private bath. We serve an expanded continental breakfast poolside every morning. Enjoy it in our air conditioned pavilion or poolside. It's complimentary to our guests and a wonderful social setting. After breakfast, lounge on one of the sunbathing decks, or sit in the shade while you read a book with the gentle island breezes rustling the palm trees above.

As relaxing and comfortable as the guesthouse is, you may want to venture out to have fun. We can take care of that, too. We have a full-time concierge to help with snorkeling, scuba, kayaking, parasailing, bike trails, beaches, and, of course, Key West's many restaurants. Just turn the corner of our street, and start your shopping exodus. Duval Street has everything you can imagine, from art galleries to T-shirts, from jewelers to sushi bars. Of course, while you're in Key West, you'll have to experience one of our fabulous sunsets. They light up the sky and they're always memorable. And why not watch the sunset from Mallory Square, where you'll see jugglers, sword swallowers, tightrope walkers and characters that'll make you say "Only in Key West!"

There's plenty of nightlife, from rock-and-roll to disco, from piano bars to jazz, all within walking distance. Most of our guests park their cars and leisurely stroll the streets of Old Town Key West. Whatever your vacation needs are...peace and quiet, the laid-back life, sun and fun, romantic or rejuvenating...pamper yourself with the special atmosphere we've created for you at the ***Rainbow House.***

**Address: 525 United St, Key West, FL 33040**
**Tel: (305) 292-1450, (800) 74-WOMYN (800 749-6696).**

**Type:** Bed & breakfast guesthouse.
**Clientele:** Women only
**To Gay Bars:** 5-minute walk to gay/lesbian bars.
**Rooms:** 15 rooms & 9 suites.
**Bathrooms:** All private.
**Meals:** Expanded continental breakfast.
**Dates Open:** All year.
**High Season:** January through April.
**Rates:** $69-$189.
**Credit Cards:** MC, VISA, Discover, Preferred, Amex.
**Rsv'tns:** Strongly recommended.
**Reserve Through:** Call direct or travel agent.
**Minimum Stay:** During holidays.
**Parking:** On-street parking.
**In-Room:** Maid service, color TV, phones, AC. Kitchens available.
**Exercise/Health:** Jacuzzi.
**Swimming:** In pool or 1 block to ocean.
**Sunbathing:** At poolside, on private sun decks or on ocean beach.
**Nudity:** Permitted at poolside.
**Pets:** Not permitted.
**Handicap Access:** One unit available.
**Children:** Not permitted.
**Languages:** English.
**Your Host:** Marion.

# Mahina Kai

Q-NET Gay/Lesbian ♀♂

***Relax and Renew Your Spirit at...***

Kauai's preeminent gay accommodation, ***Mahina Kai.*** This artist's home, a blue-tiled Asian-Pacific villa on two acres of secluded estate grounds on Anahola Bay, overlooks the ocean. The exotic and dramatic design provides a separate guest wing with several tropical decor bedrooms, lanais, a living room and a guest kitchenette. A tropical breakfast is served in the garden courtyard. Enjoy the lagoon pool and hot tub enclosed in a Japanese garden or join other guests in bicycling, snorkeling, hiking along the Na Pali coast trail or taking a helicopter tour or Zodiac boat trip. The B&B is available for retreats of 12-24 people, with a special tea house for group activities.

**Address: PO Box 699, Anahola, Kauai, HI 96703**
**Tel: (808) 822-9451 or (800) 337-1134.**

**Type:** Bed & breakfast.
**Clientele:** Mostly gay & lesbian with some straight clientele
**Transportation:** Car is best. Car rental at airport (no public transportation).
**Rooms:** 3 rooms & 1 2-bedroom apt. with double beds.
**Bathrooms:** 3 private bath/toilet/showers, 1 shared bath/toilet/shower.
**Meals:** Continental breakfast.
**Vegetarian:** Excellent vegetarian food nearby in Kapaa.
**Complimentary:** Tea, coffee & popcorn.
**Dates Open:** All year.
**High Season:** All year.
**Rates:** \$95-\$115.
**Rsv'tns:** Required.

*More facts on page 375*



# Nine Twelve Pauline Street

Gay/Lesbian ♀♂

***New Orleans – A City Spiced with Unusual Charm***

Located in the residential neighborhood of Bywater, a National Historic District, ***912 Pauline Street*** is a raised and renovated Mediterranean-style home with a distinctive Spanish tile roof. About one mile from the French Quarter and four blocks from the Mississippi River, this spacious and bright first-floor, 2-bedroom apartment has a private, lighted entrance, cable TV, stereo and electronic security. The kitchen is stocked with self-catering breakfast foods and beverages. The charm, warmth and affordability of ***912 Pauline Street*** is ideal for visitors wanting to do business in "The Big Easy," or those wanting to reinforce its reputation as "The Big Sleazy."

**Address: 912 Pauline St, New Orleans, LA**
**Tel: (504) 948-6827, E-mail: bareskin@ix.netcom.com.**

**Type:** Bed & breakfast.
**Clientele:** Mostly gay & lesbian with some straight clientele
**Transportation:** Cab from airport, or car.
**To Gay Bars:** 12 blocks, a 10 minute walk, a 2 minute drive.
**Rooms:** 1 apartment with double or queen beds.
**Bathrooms:** Private bath & toilet.
**Meals:** Continental breakfast.
**Vegetarian:** No meat served. 1 vegetarian rest. 2 mi. away.

*More facts on page 400*

## Admiral's Landing Guest House

Gay/Lesbian ♀♂

### *You've Been Waiting a Long Time to Get Away*

***Admiral's Landing Guest House...*** One block from the bay beach, shops and restaurants, offering spacious rooms with private baths, parking and a friendly, social atmosphere. Provincetown has miles of sandy beaches and dunes, wonderful shops and restaurants. Dance the night away or sit and gaze at the moon over Cape Cod Bay. Call or write for photo brochure, or visit our web site.

**Address: 158 Bradford St, Provincetown, MA 02657 Tel: (508) 487-9665, Fax: (508) 487-4437, E-mail: adm158@capecod.net. http://www.ptown.com/ptown/admiralslanding/**

**Type:** Guesthouse & efficiency studios.
**Clientele:** Gay men & women
**Transportation:** Courtesy transportation from airport with prior arrangement.
**To Gay Bars:** 3 blks to men's, 5-mins.' walk to women's.
**Rooms:** 6 doubles & 2 efficiencies.
**Bathrooms:** 4 private & 2 shared. Studio efficiencies have private baths.
**Meals:** Continental breakfast, afternoon snacks.
**Dates Open:** All year. Studios Apr 15-Nov 15 only.
**High Season:** May-Sep.
**Rates:** Summer & holidays: $74-$109; winter: $34-$64; spring/fall $44-$79.
**Discounts:** Group rates.

*More facts on page 425*

---

MASSACHUSETTS • PROVINCETOWN

## Beaconlite Guest House

Gay/Lesbian ♀♂

### *A Provincetown Tradition Like No Other*

Awaken to the aroma of freshly-brewed coffee and home-baked cakes and breads. Relax in the English country house charm of our elegant bedrooms and spacious drawing rooms, complete with open fire, grand piano, and antique furnishings. Multi-level sun decks provide panoramic views of Provincetown. ***Beaconlite's*** exceptional reputation for pampered comfort and caring service has grown by the word of mouth of our many returning guests. We truly become your home away from home! Editor's Choice Award '96 & '97 – Out & About.

**Address: 12 & 16 Winthrop St, Provincetown, MA 02657**
**Tel: (508) 487-9603 (Tel/Fax), (800) 696-9603.**
**Call #16 Winthrop St. at (508) 487-4605 (Tel/Fax), (800) 422-4605.**

**Type:** Guesthouse.
**Clientele:** Mostly men in high season. Good mix of men & women at other times
**Transportation:** Car, ferry or air from Boston. Free airport/ferry pick up provided if arranged.
**To Gay Bars:** 2 minutes' walk to gay bars, 1/2 block to tea dance.
**Rooms:** 12 rooms, 3 suites & 1 apartment with double, queen or king beds.
**Bathrooms:** 5 private bath/toilets & 11 private shower/toilets.
**Meals:** Gourmet continental breakfast.
**Vegetarian:** Available in local restaurants.
**Complimentary:** Coffee & tea.

*More facts on page 427*

## Boatslip Beach Club

Gay/Lesbian ♀♂

***Simply the Best for Over 25 Years!***

The ***Boatslip Beach Club***, beginning its 30th season, is a 45-room contemporary resort on Provincetown Harbor. Thirty-three rooms have glass doors opening onto private balconies overlooking our fabulous deck, pool, private beach and the bay. All rooms have either one queen or two double beds, private baths, direct-dial phones and color cable TV. Off-street parking, morning coffee, admission to Tea Dance and sun cots are all complimentary. We offer a full-service restaurant, poolside grille and raw bar and evening entertainment. Call or write your hosts: ***Peter Simpson and Jim Carlino*** for further information....***YOU OWE IT TO YOURSELF!!!***.

**Address: 161 Commercial St Box 393, Provincetown, MA 02657**
**Tel: (800) 451-SLIP (7547), (508) 487-1669, Fax: (508) 487-6021.**

**Type:** Hotel with restaurant, bar, disco, card & gift shop, & sportswear boutique.
**Clientele:** Gay & lesbian. Good mix of men & women
**Transportation:** Car is best. Walk from ferry.
**To Gay Bars:** Bar on premises, good mix of men & women. Women's bar 2 blks.
**Rooms:** 30 rooms with double beds & 15 rms with qn. beds.
**Bathrooms:** All private bath/toilets.
**Vegetarian:** Available.
**Complimentary:** Morning coffee, sun cots, admission to Tea Dance.
**Dates Open:** Apr-Oct.

*More facts on page 429*

MASSACHUSETTS • PROVINCETOWN

## The Commons

Q-NET Gay/Lesbian ♀♂

***Provincetown Historical Commission's 1995 Best Restoration Award***

Awake to the call of seagulls gliding over Cape Cod Bay at ***The Commons,*** a charming seaside resort nestled in a garden just off lively Commercial Street and across from Cape Cod Bay. In 1995, this mid-19th-century house underwent extensive restoration. All rooms now have new private baths and are furnished with oversized comfortable beds and a blend of modern and antique furnishings. Among the attractions of ***The Commons*** is the bistro-style restaurant, located on Commercial Street. The Bistro serves fresh seafood, wood-oven pizzas, and innovative cuisine with a French accent. Outdoor dining at the streetside cafe and the Upper Deck with harbor views makes it one of Provincetown's liveliest eateries. Cape Cod Bay Beach is steps away, right across Commercial Street. Provincetown's Gallery District begins just down the block; terrific shopping and the outrageous downtown scene are a 10-minute walk at the center of town.

**Address: 386 Commercial St, PO Box 1037, Provincetown, MA 02657**
**Tel: (508) 487-7800, (800) 487-0784.**

**Type:** Guesthouse with restaurant & bar.
**Clientele:** Mostly gay & lesbian with some straight clientele
**Transportation:** Taxi from Provincetown airport.
**To Gay Bars:** Bar on premises. Other bars & disco 8 blocks, a 10-minute walk.
**Rooms:** 12 rooms & 2 suites with single, queen or king beds.
**Bathrooms:** Private: 11 shower/toilets, 3 bath/shower/toilets.

*More facts on page 435*

# 1807 House

Gay/Lesbian ♀♂

## *Comfort and Privacy 50 Yards from the Beach*

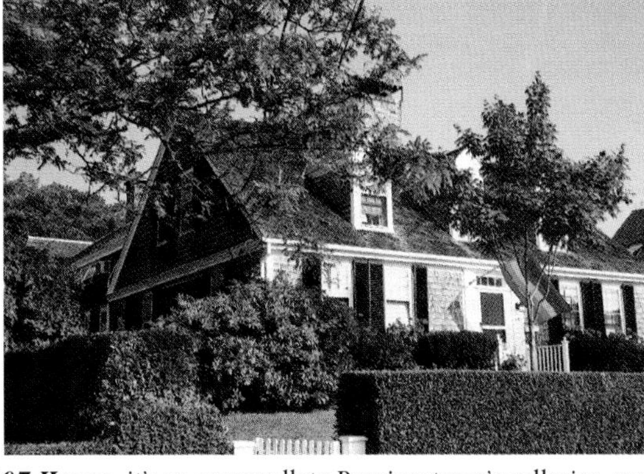

This sought-after spot for discerning gay travelers since 1977 stands just 50 yards from the beach. ***1807 House,*** located in Provincetown's famous West End, is an origianl 1807 cedar-shingled main house facing the beach and bay. The addition joining it to the remodeled carriage house and the separate secluded garden cottage each contain additional studios and apartments with kitchens. Miles of unspoiled sand dunes, beaches, hiking, bicycling, and horse trails are close by. From ***1807 House,*** it's an easy walk to Provincetown's galleries, restaurants, gay bars, and discos.

**Address: 54 Commercial St, Provincetown, MA 02657**
**Tel: (508) 487-2173, E-mail: ptown1807@aol.com.**

**Type:** Bed & breakfast & guesthouse.
**Clientele:** Mostly gay & lesbian with some straight clientele
**Transportation:** Car, plane, ferry, bus. Free pick up from airport or ferry dock.
**To Gay Bars:** 1/2 mile or a 10-minute walk.
**Rooms:** 3 rooms & 5 apartments with single, double or king beds.
**Bathrooms:** 5 private & 3 shared bath/toilet/showers.
**Meals:** Continental breakfast (for rooms).
**Vegetarian:** Excellent restaurants nearby.
**Complimentary:** Setup service.
**Dates Open:** All year.

*More facts on page 437*



# The Ruby Slipper

Q-NET Gay/Lesbian ♀♂

## *A Perfect Balance of Privacy & Personal Attention*

At ***The Ruby Slipper,*** our guest rooms, individually decorated with handmade furniture, have private baths and fireplace or woodstove. Breakfast specialties include scrumptious breakfast burritos, omelettes and banana pancakes. Our lovely grounds are complete with an outdoor hot tub. A vacation in Taos might include hiking, horseback riding, world-class skiing, gallery viewing, shopping or visiting Taos Pueblo. ***The Ruby Slipper*** is Northern New Mexico's most popular and relaxing gay-friendly bed and breakfast. Come see what everybody's talking about!

**Address: PO Box 2069, Taos, NM 87571. Tel: (505) 758-0613.**

**Type:** Bed & breakfast.
**Clientele:** Mostly gay/lesbian with some straight clientele.
**Transportation:** Car is best. 2-1/2 hours from Albuquerque by car. Taxi from bus stop to Ruby Slipper, $5.
**To Gay Bars:** 1-1/4 hours to Santa Fe gay & lesbian bars.
**Rooms:** 7 rooms with double, queen or king beds.
**Bathrooms:** All private.
**Meals:** Full breakfast.
**Vegetarian:** Available.
**Complimentary:** In-room coffee-maker with fresh ground coffee & assorted teas.
**Dates Open:** All year.
**High Season:** Summer, holidays and ski season.
**Rates:** $79-$104 /night for two, $94-$119 for Xmas holidays.
**Discounts:** On weekly stays, if booked directly.
**Credit Cards:** MC, Visa, Amex, Discover.
**Rsv'tns:** Recommended.
**Reserve Through:** Travel agent or call direct.
**Minimum Stay:** 2-3 days on holidays.

*More facts on page 486*

# Inn of the Turquoise Bear

Q-NET Gay/Lesbian ♀♂

***Where the Action Is... Stay Gay in Santa Fe!***

The ***Inn of the Turquoise Bear*** occupies the home of Witter Bynner (1881-1968), a prominent gay citizen of Santa Fe, active in cultural and political affairs. A noted poet, essayist and translator, Bynner was a staunch advocate of human rights and a vocal opponent of censorship.

Bynner's rambling adobe villa, built in Spanish-Pueblo Revival style, is one of Santa Fe's most important historic estates. With its signature portico, tall pines, magnificent rock terraces, meandering paths, and flower gardens, the inn offers guests a romantic retreat close to the center of Santa Fe. As the largest gay-oriented bed & breakfast in Santa Fe, the ***Turquoise Bear*** is the perfect choice for both couples and individuals traveling alone.

Bynner and Robert Hunt, his lover of more than 30 years, were famous for the riotous parties they hosted in this house, referred to by Ansel Adams, a frequent visitor, as "Bynner's Bashes." Their home was the gathering place for the creative and fun-loving elite of Santa Fe and guests from around the world. Their celebrity guests included D.H. & Frieda Lawrence, Igor Stravinsky, Willa Cather, Errol Flynn, Martha Graham, Christopher Isherwood, Georgia O'Keeffe, Rita Hayworth, Thornton Wilder, Robert Frost – and many others.

Ralph and Robert, the new owners of the Witter Bynner Estate, reside on the property. Their goals are to rekindle the spirit of excitement, creativity, freedom and hospitality for which this remarkable home was renowned; to protect, restore and extend the legacy of its famous gay creator; and to provide their guests with the experience of a unique setting that captures the essence of traditional Santa Fe. Whether you are coming to New Mexico for the opera, the art scene, the museums, skiing, hiking, exploring Native American and Hispanic cultures, or just to relax away from it all, the ***Inn of the Turquoise Bear*** is the place to stay in Santa Fe.

**Address: 342 E Buena Vista Street, Santa Fe, NM 87501. Tel: (505) 983-0798, (800) 396-4104, Fax: (505) 988-4225, E-mail: bluebear@roadrunner.com.**

**Type:** Bed & breakfast inn.
**Clientele:** 70% gay & lesbian and 30% straight clientele
**Transportation:** Car is best, shuttle bus from Albuquerque airport.
**To Gay Bars:** 8 blocks, 1 mile, a 20 min walk, a 2 min drive.
**Rooms:** 9 rooms, 2 suites with double, queen or king beds.
**Bathrooms:** Private: 1 bath/toilet, 4 shower/toilets, 4 bath/shower/toilets. Shared: 1 shower only.
**Meals:** Expanded continental breakfast.
**Vegetarian:** Available nearby.
**Complimentary:** Tea, coffee & fruit all day. Wine & cheese in afternoon. Sherry & brandy in common room. Chocolates on pillows.
**Dates Open:** All year.
**High Season:** April-October & December.
**Rates:** Per room, double occupancy: high season $90-$210, low season $80-$180.
**Discounts:** 10% for AAA, AARP. Weekly rate: 10% discount.
**Credit Cards:** MC, Visa, Amex.
**Rsv'tns:** Required, but we accept late inquiries.
**Reserve Through:** Travel agent or call direct.
**Minimum Stay:** Required during certain holidays.
**Parking:** Ample free, walled & gated off-street parking.
**In-Room:** Color cable TV, VCR, fans, telephone, maid service. Some rooms have refrigerators.
**On-Premises:** Meeting rooms, video tape & book libraries, fax (sending & receiving).
**Exercise/Health:** Jacuzzi to be installed late 1996. Nearby gym, weights, Jacuzzi, sauna, steam, massage.
**Swimming:** Pool nearby.
**Sunbathing:** On patios.
**Nudity:** Permitted in various patio areas.
**Smoking:** Permitted on patios, not in rooms or public rooms.
**Pets:** Small pets OK in some rooms.
**Handicap Access:** One guest room accessible, but no access to rest of the building.
**Children:** Over 12 years OK, but children discouraged.
**Languages:** English, Spanish, French, Norwegian, German.
**Your Host:** Ralph & Robert.

# The Golden Bear Farm

Q-NET Gay/Lesbian ♀♂

*A 1784 Country Inn Less Than Two Hours from New York City*

Nestled in a 12-acre country setting, less than two hours from New York City is our historic 1784 stone house, ***Golden Bear Farm.*** The romantic guest rooms are appointed with feather beds and antique furnishings. Weather permitting, breakfasts are served on the outdoor patio overlooking the pool and meadows. The many wonderfully delicious and tempting breakfast offerings include savory Belgian waffles with fresh fruit and strawberry cream, a variety of omelettes, homemade popovers and quiche of the day. There is always a tasty array of fresh juices and a supply of tasty muffins such as maple-pecan, Swiss cheese and zucchini, and German apple.

Each evening, an elegant dinner is served on Wedgewood china and crystal in the candlelit dining room. The meals are prepared by the owner/chefs of the inn who were trained at the renowned Culinary Institute of America. Featured among the choices of entrees are chateaubriand for two, rack of lamb, poached salmon with lemon beurre blanc, and a seafood medly of scallops, shrimp and lobster in a creamy white sauce. Each dish is accompanied with locally grown vegetables. Vegetarian meals and low-fat dishes are always available upon request.

***Golden Bear Farm*** is in close proximity to the Mohonk Mt. House and Minnewaska State Park. Other historic and cultural attractions include FDR's home, the Vanderbilt mansion, old stone houses in New Paltz and Hurley, local college theater and concerts, local wineries, ski areas, Woodstock and West Point. **TO OPEN SPRING, 1997.**

**Address: 1 Forest Glen Rd, New Paltz, NY 12561. Tel: (914) 255-1515.**

**Type:** Country inn.
**Clientele:** Mostly gay & lesbian with some straight clientele
**Transportation:** Car is best. Non-stop bus from NYC. Shuttle to Stewart Airport in Newburg, NY. Free pick up from train in Poughkeepsie or bus in New Paltz.
**To Gay Bars:** 12 mile, a 20 min drive to gay bars.
**Rooms:** 5-7 rooms, 1 suite with double or queen beds.
**Bathrooms:** 5 private bath/toilets, 2 shared bath/shower/toilets.
**Meals:** Continental breakfast Mon-Thurs. Expanded continental breakfast Fri-Sun. Dinner nightly.
**Vegetarian:** Always available with notice at time of reserv.
**Complimentary:** Set-up serv., tea & coffee, mints on pillow.
**Dates Open:** All year.
**High Season:** April-October.
**Rates:** Inquire.
**Discounts:** Inquire.
**Credit Cards:** MC, Visa, Amex.
**Rsv'tns:** Required.
**Reserve Through:** Travel agent or call direct.
**Minimum Stay:** Required on certain holiday weekends.
**Parking:** Ample free off-street parking.
**In-Room:** Ceiling fans, coffee & tea-making facilities, VCR, maid & laundry service. Color TV in some rooms.
**On-Premises:** TV lounge, video tape lib., fax, computer.
**Exercise/Health:** Massage. Spa to be completed in 1998.
**Swimming:** Pool on premises. Minnewaska State Park lake nearby.
**Sunbathing:** Poolside & on patio.
**Nudity:** Permitted poolside.
**Smoking:** Permitted in common rooms.
**Handicap Access:** No.
**Children:** No.
**Languages:** English.
**Your Host:** Robert & Jim.

## Christopher Place

Q-NET Gay-Owned 50/50 ♀♂

***We're Easy to Find, but Hard to Forget***

Surrounded by expansive mountain views, this premiere bed & breakfast includes over 200 acres to explore, a pool, tennis court and sauna. Relax by the marble fireplace in the library, retreat to the game room, or enjoy a hearty mountain meal in our restaurant. Romantic rooms are available with a hot tub or fireplace. Off I-40 at exit 435, ***Christopher Place*** is just 32 scenic miles from Gatlinburg and Pigeon Forge. Perfect for special occasions and gatherings. Rated 4 diamonds by AAA. Gay-owned & -operated.

**Address: 1500 Pinnacles Way, Newport, TN 37821**
**Tel: (423) 623-6555 (Tel/Fax), (800) 595-9441 (for brochure).**

**Type:** Gay-owned & -operated inn with restaurant.
**Clientele:** 50% gay & lesbian clientele
**Transportation:** Car is best. $25 for pick up from airport.
**To Gay Bars:** 40 miles or an hour drive.
**Rooms:** 9 rooms & 1 suite with double, queen or king beds.
**Bathrooms:** Private: 2 bath/toilets, 4 shower/toilets & 4 bath/shower/toilets.
**Meals:** Full breakfast.
**Vegetarian:** Available with 24-hour notice.
**Complimentary:** Afternoon tea & lemonade.
**Dates Open:** All year.
**High Season:** Jul-Oct.
**Rates:** $99-$199.
**Discounts:** Special gift to *Inn Places* readers.
**Credit Cards:** MC & Visa.
**Rsv'tns:** Recommended.
**Reserve Through:** Travel agent or call direct.
**Minimum Stay:** Some holidays or special weekends.
**Parking:** Ample free off-street parking.

*More facts on page 533*



## Courtyard on the Trail

Gay/Lesbian ♀♂

***Maximum Comfort, Privacy and Convenience***

Enter through arched gates into a relaxing and memorable experience at ***Courtyard on the Trail.*** While close to downtown and North Dallas, we are far enough removed to afford guests a country setting in which to kick back and relax. The B&B is decorated with elegant antique and modern furnishings, fine linens and art. Your bedroom has direct access to the pool and courtyard through French doors, affording you maximum comfort, privacy and convenience. Luxuriate in your marble bathroom's extra-large bathtub while contemplating the beautiful clouds painted on a blue sky overhead. Whether you are in town for business or celebrating a special occasion, your host will ensure a personalized, first-class stay.

**Address: 8045 Forest Trail, Dallas, TX 75238. Tel: (214) 553-9700 (Tel/Fax), (800) 484-6260 pin #0465. E-mail: akrubs4u@aol.com.**

**Type:** Bed & breakfast.
**Clientele:** Mostly gay & lesbian with some straight clientele
**Transportation:** Car. Pick up service if prearranged.
**To Gay Bars:** 6 miles, a 15 minute drive.
**Rooms:** 3 rooms with king or queen beds.
**Bathrooms:** 3 private bath/toilet/showers.
**Meals:** Full breakfast. Dinner if prearranged.

*More facts on page 536*

# The Inn at HighView

Q-NET Gay-Friendly ♀♂



***Vermont the Way You Always Dreamed It Would Be...***

...but the way you've never found it, until now. Everyone who arrives at ***The Inn at HighView*** has the same breathless reaction to the serenity of the surrounding hills. The inn's hilltop location offers incredible peace, tranquility and seclusion, yet is convenient to all the activities that bring you to Vermont, such as skiing, golf, tennis and antiquing. Ski cross-country or hike our 72 acres. Swim in our unique rock garden pool. Enjoy our gourmet dinner, relax by a blazing fire, snuggle under a down comforter in a canopy bed, or gaze 50 miles over pristine mountains.

**Address: RR 1, Box 201A, East Hill Road, Andover, VT 05143**
**Tel: (802) 875-2724, Fax: (802) 875-4021.**

**Type:** Inn with restaurant for Inn guests only.
**Clientele:** Mostly straight with a gay & lesbian following
**Transportation:** Car is best. Amtrak to Bellows Falls, VT (19 mi), Albany, NY (83 mi). Taxi from Bellows Falls $20. Limo from Albany $90.
**To Gay Bars:** 1.5 hours by car. Proximity to a bar is NOT the reason to come here!
**Rooms:** 6 rms & 2 suites with sgl., dbl., queen or king beds.
**Bathrooms:** 6 private bath/toilet/showers & 3 private shower/toilets.
**Meals:** Full breakfast with dinner available on most weekend nights at a prix fixe rate.
**Vegetarian:** We specialize in Italian cuisine and have many pasta dishes without meat.
**Complimentary:** Sherry in room & turn-down service. Tea & coffee always. Conferences receive coffee & snacks.

*More facts on page 546*

# Ravenscroft Inn

Gay-Friendly ♀♂



***Take a Short Trip to Far Away...***

One of the most romantic hideaways in the Pacific Northwest is located high on a bluff overlooking historic Port Townsend, the Olympic Peninsula's Victorian seaport. The ***Ravenscroft Inn*** is noted for its colonial style. The Inn offers a unique combination of colonial hospitality, mixed with a casual air that spells comfort to its guests. The hosts take great pleasure in looking after their guests' special requests, whether it's dinner, theatre, concert reservations, or arranging for flowers or champagne, all are carried out with ease and alacrity. Port Townsend and its environs meets all your vacation requirements offering scenic beauty, theatre, unparalleled dining, boating, biking, fishing, kayaking and hiking.

**Address: 533 Quincy St, Port Townsend, WA 98368**
**Tel: (360) 385-2784, (800) 782-2691, Fax: (360) 385-6724.**

**Type:** Bed & breakfast.
**Clientele:** Mainly straight with a gay & lesbian following
**Transportation:** Car is best. Free pick up from Port Townsend Airport (from Seattle via Port Townsend Airways).
**To Gay Bars:** 2 hrs by car.
**Rooms:** 8 rooms & 2 suites with single, queen or king beds.
**Bathrooms:** 4 private bath/shower/toilets & 5 private shower/toilets.

*More facts on page 564*

# Inn At Swifts Bay

Gay-Friendly ♀♂

## *A Small Inn with a National Reputation*

Since 1988, ***The Inn At Swifts Bay*** has gained national recognition as one of the finest accommodations in the beautiful San Juan Islands of Washington State. This elegant country home sits on three wooded acres with a private beach nearby. The inn has five quiet and romantic guest rooms, three with private baths and fireplaces. Two common areas also have fireplaces. The hot tub is at the edge of the woods – we provide robes and slippers. Here's what others say about the inn.

"The most memorable part of the trip...a stay at Inn At Swifts Bay...the setting is beautiful and serene, the accommodations excellent, and the food of gourmet quality!" – *San Francisco Sunday Chronicle-Examiner*

"Stateroom elegant." – *Vogue*

"Entrust yourself to the warm hospitality of the Inn At Swifts Bay. In the morning, one of the greatest pleasures of your stay awaits, a breakfast that is famous island-wide!" – *Brides Magazine*

"Those who appreciate luxury and superb cuisine will find the Inn At Swifts Bay to their liking. The Tudor-style inn is classy, stylish and oh, so comfortable...a breakfast that is nothing short of sensational!" – *West Coast Bed & Breakfast Guide*

**Inn Places Reader Commment:** "The inn is impeccably and tastefully decorated. Everything is done with warmth and quality. All of your needs and desires are met before you know what you want. The inn has a sense of class I have dreamed about, but have never found."

**Address: Lopez Island,, WA 98261**
**Tel: (360) 468-3636, Fax: (360) 468-3637,**
**E-mail: SWIFTINN@aol.com. http://www.pgsi.com/swiftsbay.**

**Type:** Bed & breakfast inn & cottage.
**Clientele:** Mostly straight clientele with a gay/lesbian following
**Transportation:** By car ferry from Anacortes or daily plane from Seattle, Anacortes. Pick up from airport, ferry dock, or marina.
**To Gay Bars:** Drive 1 hr to Bellingham or Everett. 1-1/2 hrs to Seattle bars.
**Rooms:** 2 rooms, 3 suites & 1 cottage with queen beds.
**Bathrooms:** 4 private shower/toilets & 1 shared bath/shower/toilet.
**Meals:** Full breakfast.
**Vegetarian:** Dietary restrictions considered with advance notice at time of reservation.
**Complimentary:** Sherry in living room. Fridge with mineral waters, microwave popcorn & tea.
**Dates Open:** All year.
**High Season:** May-October.
**Rates:** $85-$225.
**Discounts:** For extended stays in off season.
**Credit Cards:** MC, Visa, Discover & Amex.
**Rsv'tns:** Required.
**Reserve Thru:** Call direct.
**Minimum Stay:** Only on holiday weekends.
**Parking:** Ample free off-street parking.
**In-Room:** Maid service.
**On-Premises:** Telephone in library, VCR with film library, refrigerator with ice & mineral water.
**Exercise/Health:** Hot tub & massage (by appointment only), exercise studio & sauna
**Swimming:** Ocean or lake (very cold!).
**Sunbathing:** On beach, patio or lawn.
**Nudity:** Permitted in the hot tub.
**Smoking:** Not permitted inside.
**Pets:** Not permitted.
**Handicap Access:** No.
**Children:** Not permitted.
**Languages:** English, limited German & Portuguese.
**Your Host:** Robert & Christopher.

IGTA

# Gaslight Inn

Q-NET Gay/Lesbian ♀♂

Welcome to ***Gaslight Inn,*** a Seattle four-square house built in 1906. In restoring the inn, we have brought out the home's original turn-of-the-century ambiance and warmth, while keeping in mind the additional conveniences and contemporary style needed by travelers in the nineties. The interior is appointed in exacting detail, with strikingly rich, dark colors, oak paneling, and an enormous entryway and staircase.

***Gaslight Inn's*** comfortable and unique rooms and suites are furnished with quality double or queen-sized beds, refrigerator and television. Additional features for your special needs, such as private bath and phone service, are available in some rooms. Some rooms also have decks with fabulous views or fireplaces. The living room, with its large oak fireplace, is always an inviting room, as is the library. Through the late spring and summer, we encourage you to relax and unwind at poolside with a glass of wine after a long, busy day. This private, in-ground, heated pool with several decks and interesting plant arrangements, is found at the back of the inn.

***Gaslight Inn*** is convenient to central Seattle's every attraction: Volunteer Park, City Center, and to a plethora of gay and lesbian bars, restaurants and retail stores in the Broadway district. All of us at ***Gaslight Inn*** send you a warm advance welcome to Seattle.

**Address: 1727 15th Ave, Seattle, WA 98122. Tel: (206) 325-3654, Fax: (206) 328-4803.**

**Type:** Guesthouse.
**Clientele:** Mostly gay/lesbian with some straight clientele
**Transportation:** Shuttle Express from airport $15. (206) 286-4800 to reserve ride.
**To Gay Bars:** 2 blocks to men's bars, 3 blocks to women's bars.
**Rooms:** 9 doubles, 5 suites.
**Bathrooms:** 11 private, others share.
**Meals:** Expanded continental breakfast.
**Complimentary:** Coffee, tea & juices, fresh fruit, pastries.
**Dates Open:** All year.
**High Season:** Summer.
**Rates:** $68-$148.
**Discounts:** 5% for cash payment.
**Credit Cards:** MC, Visa & Amex.
**Rsv'tns:** Recommended at least 2 weeks in advance.
**Reserve Through:** Call direct.
**Minimum Stay:** 2 days on weekends, 3 days on holidays.
**Parking:** Ample on-street & off-street parking.
**In-Room:** Color TV, maid service & refrigerator.
**On-Premises:** Meeting rooms, living room, library, public telephone.
**Swimming:** Seasonal heated pool.
**Sunbathing:** On private or common sun decks or at poolside.
**Smoking:** Permitted on decks & porches only.
**Pets:** Not permitted.
**Handicap Access:** No.
**Children:** Not permitted.
**Languages:** English.
**Your Host:** Trevor, Stephen & John.

IGTA

WASHINGTON • SEATTLE

AFRICA

# SOUTH AFRICA

## JOHANNESBURG

### The Cottages

Gay-Friendly 50/50 ♀♂

*Come Share Our Paradise*

Treat yourself to the most "Out of Africa" experience in individually decorated stone & thatch cottages, some with their own catering facilities and glorious views. ***The Cottages*** (AD 1905) are set on the Observatory Ridge, a 10-minute drive east of the city and business centres and close to the airport, bars, restaurants and nightlife. Other wonderful facilities include a hiking trail, rock pool, a verdant English garden and unlimited tranquility (at no extra charge!) We look forward to welcoming you to a Johannesburg you never knew existed!

**Address: 30 Gill St, Observatory, Johannesburg 2198 South Africa. Tel: (27-11) 487 2829, Fax: (27-11) 487 2404.**

**Type:** Guesthouse.
**Clientele:** 50% gay & lesbian & 50% hetero clientele
**Transportation:** Car is best. Pick up from airport or train R100.
**To Gay Bars:** 6 blocks, a 10-15 minute walk.
**Rooms:** 4 suites, 9 cottages with single or double beds.
**Bathrooms:** Private.
**Meals:** Full breakfast. Dinners on request.
**Vegetarian:** Available on request.
**Complimentary:** Tea- & coffee-making facilities with tea, coffee & sugar provided.
**Dates Open:** All year.
**High Season:** All year, quiet Christmas period.
**Rates:** Single R220-R250, double R300-R350.
**Discounts:** 7 or more days, less 5%. Monthly, less 10%.
**Credit Cards:** MC, Visa, Amex, Diners.
**Rsv'tns:** Advisable.
**Reserve Through:** Travel agent or call direct.
**Parking:** Ample free parking.
**In-Room:** Coffee/tea-making facilities, color TV, phone, laundry & maid service. Kitchen in 4 units, refrigerator in 5 units, color cable TV in 4 units.
**On-Premises:** Fax.
**Exercise/Health:** Trampoline, hiking trail adjacent.
**Swimming:** Pool on premises.
**Sunbathing:** Poolside & on patio.
**Smoking:** Not permitted in dining room.
**Pets:** Not permitted.
**Handicap Access:** Very hilly terrain, difficult access for the handicapped.
**Children:** Welcome.
**Languages:** English, Afrikaans, Italian, German.
**Your Host:** John & Sonja.

### Joel House

Gay-Owned ♀♂

*A Special Retreat in the Heart of the City*

***Joel House*** (AD 1912) is a delightful original Johannesburg home, restored to offer luxury accommodation in tranquil surroundings, right on the doorstep of all that matters in Johannesburg. Five individually decorated en suite rooms (some with fireplaces) are served by an elegant drawing room, dining room, library, and a delightful English country garden. Fine dining is offered in our Colonial Rajah Room. Personal service is of the highest degree. Tours of Johannesburg are also available on request. Welcome to a special retreat in the heart of the city!

**Address: 61 Joel Rd nr Lily Rd, Berea, Johannesburg 2198 South Africa. Tel: (27-11) 642 4426, mobile: (27-83) 654 5665, Fax: (27-11) 642 5221.**

**Type:** Full-service guesthouse w/ formal Rajah Room restaurant.
**Clientele:** Mostly straight clientele with a gay & lesbian following
**Transportation:** Airport bus or taxi. Free pick up from train station, R60 for airport pick up.
**To Gay Bars:** Gotham City 5 blks, Connections 7 blks.

Champions, Gershwin's Cafe.
**Rooms:** 5 rms with twin, dbl, queen or king beds.
**Bathrooms:** All private.
**Meals:** Full breakfast with other meals optional.
**Vegetarian:** Available upon request.
**Complimentary:** Tea, coffee, juice, soda on arrival. Coffee, tea in library. Turn down sweets, chocolates.
**Dates Open:** All year.
**High Season:** Sept-Mar.
**Rates:** R 200-240 per night singles, R 300-360 per night doubles, breakfast included.
**Discounts:** Group rate for entire house 15% disc.
**Credit Cards:** MC, Visa, Diners, Amex.
**Rsv'tns:** Required.
**Reserve Through:** Travel agent or call direct.
**Parking:** Free off-street secure parking.
**In-Room:** Ceiling fans, telephone, maid, room & laundry service. Oil radiators in winter.
**On-Premises:** TV lounge & meeting rooms. Glorious garden with fountain & pond for outdoor dining.
**Exercise/Health:** Walk our 3 dogs. Private tennis courts nearby.
**Swimming:** 5 minutes to public swimming pool.
**Sunbathing:** In the garden.
**Smoking:** Permitted.
**Pets:** 2 cats & 3 dogs in residence, not necessary to bring your own.
**Children:** Permitted over 14 years of age. Accommodation free if sharing with parents.
**Languages:** English, Afrikaans, some German, American.
**Your Host:** Mark.

# PIKETBERG

## Noupoort Guest Farm

**Gay-Owned ♀♂**

***Noupoort Guest Farm*** is only 1-1/2 hours' drive from Cape Town on the western slopes of the Piketberg mountains, a little-known paradise set amongst spectacular rock formations. If you can appreciate crisp mountain air, scenic walks in unspoilt splendor, wholesome country fare, outdoor activity, star-filled skies, and an open hearth in the evenings, make ***Noupoort Guest Farm*** your country getaway. It is ideal for that relaxing break you deserve, whether you choose to be indulged and catered for, or simply prefer to self-cater in the privacy of your own country cottage. Gay theatre weekends with cabaret take place here four times a year.

**Address: PO Box 101, Piketberg 7320 South Africa.**
**Tel: (27-0261) 5754, Fax: (27-0261) 5834,**
**E-mail: noupoort@mickey.iaccess.za.**

**Type:** Mountain retreat on a guest farm.
**Clientele:** Mostly hetero clientele with 25% gay & lesbian clientele in-season
**Transportation:** Car is best. Daily bus service from Cape Town to Piketberg. Nominal charge for pick up at Piketberg.
**Rooms:** 14 rooms in 10 cottages with single, 3/4 or queen beds.
**Bathrooms:** All private.
**Vegetarian:** Available with prior notice.
**Dates Open:** All year.
**Rates:** R90-R245. Choose self-catering or dinner, bed & breakfast.
**Discounts:** Group bookings encouraged.
**Credit Cards:** MC, Visa, Amex, Diners.
**Rsv'tns:** Required.
**Reserve Through:** Call direct.
**Parking:** Ample free off-street parking.
**In-Room:** Dining room, fireplace, kitchen, refrigerator, coffee/tea-making facilities & private braai.
**On-Premises:** Conference room with flipcharts, projector, VCR & monitor, TV lounge. BBQ & sun deck.
**Exercise/Health:** Sauna & basic work-out gym, Jacuzzi & weights.
**Swimming:** Pool on premises.
**Sunbathing:** At poolside, on patio & common sun decks.
**Nudity:** Permitted on special weekends.
**Pets:** Not permitted.
**Children:** No children under 12 years of age.
**Languages:** English, Afrikaans, Xhosa.
**Your Host:** Brent.

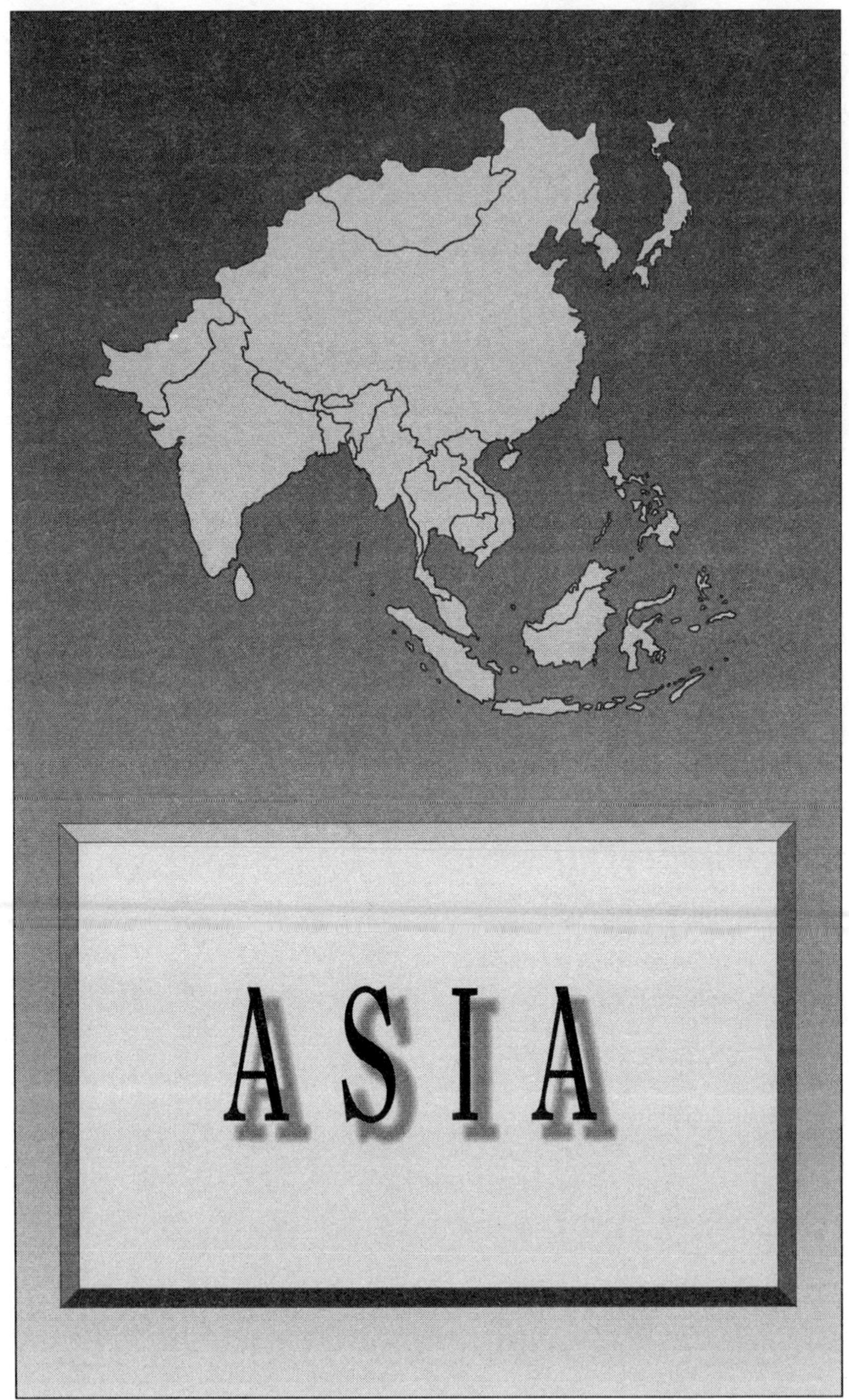
ASIA

# THAILAND

## CHIANG MAI

### Coffee Boy Cottages

**Men ♂**

The ***Coffee Boy,*** widely regarded as Thailand's leading gay bar, also provides luxury cottages individually designed in Lanna style and set in lush, tropical surroundings. The cottages are situated 1 km from the centre of the ancient city of Chiang Mai. The staff are able to recommend reputable, local tour operators and guides, travel agents, retail outlets and car, motorbike or bicycle rentals. The adjacent ***Coffee Boy Bar,*** a 70-year-old, traditional solid teak building set in lush, tropical gardens, where the new cottages have been built, is open daily from 8:30pm-1:00am, with a nightly Go-Go Boy Show and a spectacular cabaret show on Fri., Sat. and Sun. The ambiance of the bar is typically Thai, with quiet background music in a traditional setting. Over 50 charming young men ensure that the guests' needs are fully cared for.

Chiang Mai, which means New City, was founded in 1926. The old city is surrounded by moats, and parts of the old wall still exist. Over 300 temples dominate the skyline. The city is accessible from all parts of Thailand by bus, train or air and has all the cultural advantages of Bangkok, but is small enough to explore on foot and has no traffic jams or air pollution. It is noted for its temperate climate, low humidity and cool nights. Numerous attractions, such as Hill Tribe villages, dot the surrounding area, and the Golden Triangle is a short distance away. Trekking in the hills is popular. Elephants are still widely used in the jungle. A highlight of your trip may be a visit to the Elephant Training Camp or an elephant safari. Thailand's highest peak is also nearby. The flora and fauna, spectacular waterfalls, hot geysers, ancient temples and archaeological sites will give an everlasting impression of Thailand's beauty.

Great restaurants offer a range of cuisines, including Thai, Chinese, Burmese, vegetarian and Western. After dinner, many visitors head for the Night Bazaar, where you can hone your bargaining skills. Chiang Mai has six gay men's bars, including our famous Coffee Boy Bar, so there is a remarkable choice of delightful, young men to entertain the visitor. There is also a large number of discos, at which gay people are very welcome.

**Address: 248 Toong Hotel Rd, Chiang Mai 50000 Thailand.**
**Tel: (66-53) 247 021 (Tel/Fax), bar tel: (66-53) 244 458.**

**Type:** Luxury cottages.
**Clientele:** Men
**Transportation:** Free pick up from airport or train.
**To Gay Bars:** Coffee Boy gay bar is adjacent, 5 other gay bars nearby.
**Rooms:** 9 rooms & 4 luxury cottages.
**Bathrooms:** All private baths with showers, basins, western-style toilets.
**Meals:** Full American breakfast.
**Complimentary:** Cold drinks, light snacks all day.
**Dates Open:** All year.
**High Season:** Oct-Feb.
**Rates:** 500, 700 or 900 Baht per night.
**Discounts:** 15% during off season.
**Credit Cards:** MC & VISA.
**Rsv'tns:** Preferred, with 30 day advance deposit.
**Reserve Through:** Travel agent or call direct.
**Parking:** Ample free off-street parking.
**In-Room:** AC, sitting room, refrigerator, teak furniture & fittings reflecting North Thailand's architectural heritage in luxury cottages. AC, ceiling fans, refrigerator, maid & laundry service.
**On-Premises:** Tropical gardens, water-lily pond, private entrance to Coffee Boy Bar.
**Sunbathing:** On the patio.
**Smoking:** No restrictions.
**Languages:** Thai, English.
**Your Host:** Narong.

# Lotus Hotel

Gay/Lesbian ♂

## *The Center of Gay Chiang Mai*

Nightly, the street in front of the ***Lotus Hotel*** becomes the lively center of gay Chiang Mai. Across from the hotel is the largest and most popular gay club in town – The Adams Apple Club. Four floors of gay entertainment include a restaurant serving Western and Thai dishes, a snooker and reading lounge, a gift shop, private rooms with traditional Thai massage, a showplace with 40 go-go dancers swaying to the latest pop music, and a karaoke facility.

The gay ***Lotus Hotel*** in Chaing Mai is perfectly located in the busiest district with easy access to local Thai markets, shopping centers, movie theaters, banks, and post offices. A popular feature of the hotel is a tropical garden with its very busy Bamboo Bar that sells inexpensive drinks. Deep in the garden there is a Thai Sala where customers can relax amidst lush vegetation, have a soothing Thai massage, or just relax and watch Thai boys pump up their muscles.

All the rooms have en suite bathrooms and are equipped with air conditioning, mini bar, stereo, TV, and VCR. Amenities are of top quality: therapeutic mattresses, soft pillows, and cotton linens. The hotel also: serves meals at any time to your room or the terrace, has laundry service, rents cars, offers guided tours around Chiang Mai, confirms tickets and reservations, has a video and book library, and has a very friendly staff.

**Address: 2/25 Soi Viangbua, Tambol Chang-Phuk, Amphur Muang, Chiang Mai 50300 Thailand.**
**Tel: (66-53) 215 376, 215 462, Fax: (66-53) 221 340.**

**Type:** Gay-owned hotel with bar, restaurant, kiosk shops, drag & boys show, karaoke, massage.
**Clientele:** Mostly men with women welcome & some hetero clientele
**Transportation:** Free pick up from airport, bus, train station. Taxi 100 baht.
**To Gay Bars:** Opposite hotel.
**Rooms:** 6 rooms with king & queen beds & 3 suites.
**Bathrooms:** All private.
**Vegetarian:** Available on restaurant menu.
**Complimentary:** Fruit for regular customers.
**Dates Open:** All year.
**High Season:** Nov-Apr 15 & Aug.
**Rates:** High season 650-1650 Baht.
**Discounts:** 20% in low season or for stays over one month.
**Credit Cards:** MC & VISA.
**Rsv'tns:** Required.
**Reserve Through:** Travel agent or call direct.
**Parking:** Limited free parking.
**In-Room:** Color TV, video tape library, AC, phone, refrigerator, maid, room & laundry service. VCR in suite, ceiling fans extra.
**On-Premises:** Bar, terrace & garden.
**Sunbathing:** Private sun decks in the garden.
**Smoking:** Permitted without restrictions.
**Pets:** Not permitted.
**Handicap Access:** No.
**Children:** Not permitted.
**Languages:** Thai, English, French & Arabic.

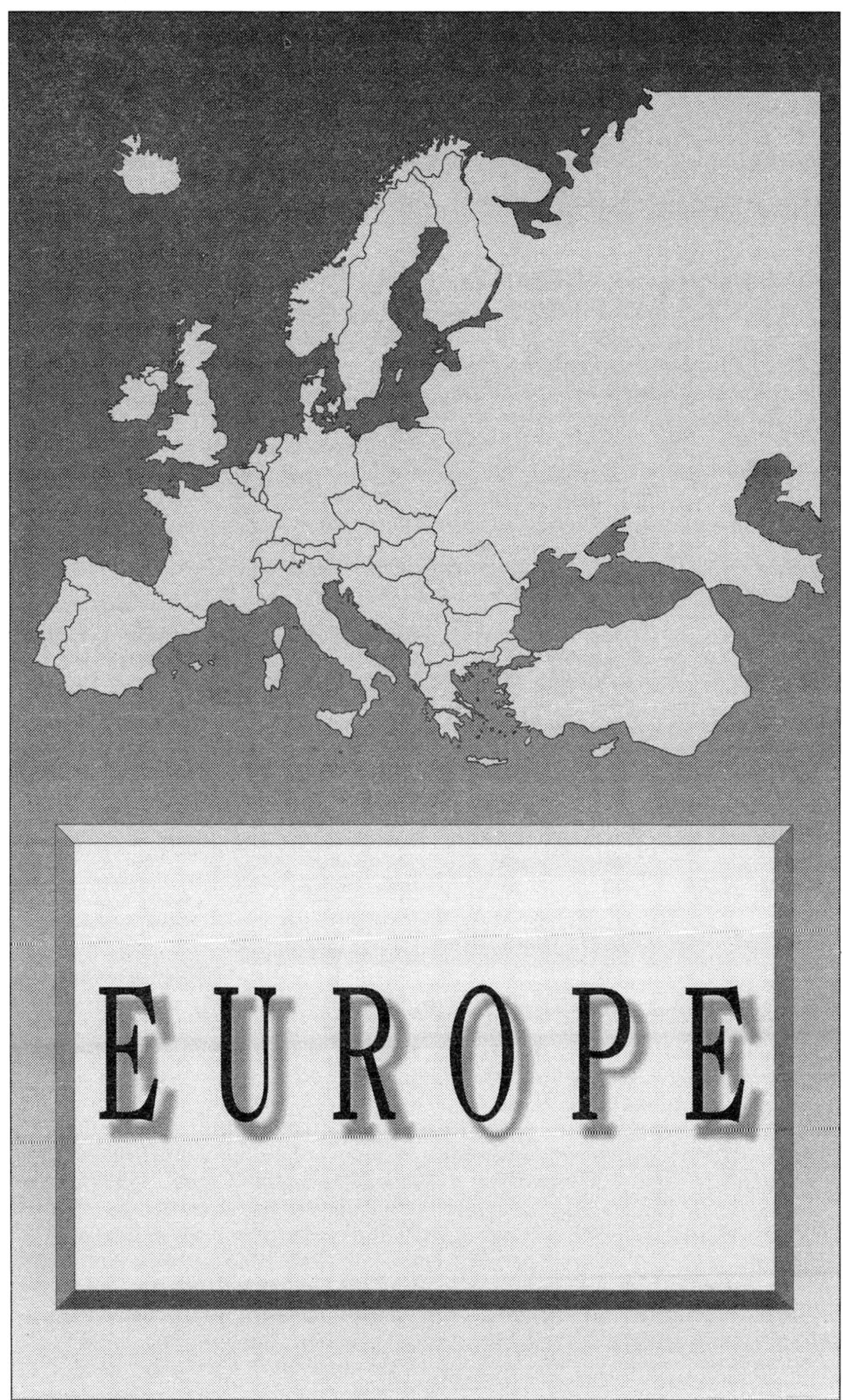
EUROPE

# BELGIUM

## BRUGGE

### Hostellerie Ten Lande

Gay/Friendly 50/50 ♀♂

*A Splendid Gay-Owned Hotel in Beernem*

Surrounded by woods just a stone's throw from the E40 Highway is ***Hostellerie Ten Lande.*** The hotel's eight double rooms, with comfortable, contemporary furnishings, have private baths, phones with direct outside lines, and fully stocked mini-bars for guests' pleasure. While at ***Hostellerie Ten Lande,*** enjoy the gastronomic cuisine that serves everything from the aperitif to the after-dinner coffee. The restaurant also has several larger rooms ideal for banquets and meetings. We are near Brugge, the coast, an 18-hole golf course, and a Motor Yacht marina on the Gent-Brugge Canal. There is also plenty of private parking. For guests' convenience, the hotel staff are willing to cater for individual requirements.

**Address: Reigerlostraat 25, Beernem 8730 Belgium. Tel: (32-50) 79 10 00, Fax: (32-50) 79 12 84.**

**Type:** Hotel with restaurant & bar.
**Clientele:** 50% gay & lesbian, 50% hetero clientele
**Transportation:** Car is best. Pick up from airport, train or ferry dock 8 Bfr per km.
**To Gay Bars:** 10-minute drive to Ravel (Brugge).
**Rooms:** 8 double rooms.
**Bathrooms:** Private.
**Meals:** Full breakfast.
**Vegetarian:** Available.
**Complimentary:** Mints on pillow.
**Dates Open:** All year.
**High Season:** Jul-Aug.
**Rates:** 2000 Bfr-2500 Bfr.
**Credit Cards:** Eurocard, VISA, Bancard.
**Rsv'tns:** Required.
**Reserve Through:** Call direct.
**Parking:** Large private car park.
**In-Room:** Color cable TV, telephone, mini-bar, refrigerator, room & laundry service.
**On-Premises:** Meeting rooms, laundry facilities, business services.
**Exercise/Health:** Nearby gym with weights, Jacuzzi, sauna, massage.
**Swimming:** Nearby pool, ocean, river.
**Sunbathing:** On beach & in garden.
**Smoking:** Permitted. Non-smoking rooms available.
**Handicap Access:** No.
**Children:** No.
**Languages:** Dutch, French, German, English.

### Hotel Kerlinga

Q-NET Gay-Friendly ♀♂

*Vriendelijke Bediening – Friendly Service*

A short 10-minute train ride from Brugge, the seaside city of Blankenberge is an ideal holiday getaway destination. Blankenberge offers sea and sandy beaches, a traffic-free shopping centre, good restaurants, a scenic pier and yacht harbour, and the entertainment of a casino. ***Hotel Kerlinga*** is situated within walking distance of the town and is easy travelling distance to many points, including Brugge, Gent and Ostend. It is only 120 kilometres to Brussels, Belgium's capital, 35 kilometres to Holland, and Paris is approximately a four-hour drive from us. Brugge is a historic city offering many interesting activities and places to visit. From boat trips on the canals, horse-drawn carriage rides, and famous museums and churches to the lace centre, windmills, breweries and parks, there is plenty to take in.

We serve a substantial breakfast daily, and all meals are prepared by the proprietors, using only the finest-quality foods. Vegetarian and other special diets can be catered for. The on-premises bar and TV lounge are available for our guests' enjoyment. All 16 rooms have private bath, safe, telephone and radio, and television and minibar are available upon request. The friendly staff at ***Hotel Kerlinga*** are happy to help you in any way. We love children. Groups are also welcome and our rates are very reasonable. **The hotel is currently being remodeled and will be ready by Easter, 1997.**

**Address: Kerkstraat 146, Blankenberge 8370 Belgium. Tel: (32-50) 41 17 91, Fax: (32-50) 42 99 26.**

**Type:** Hotel with restaurant & bar.
**Clientele:** Mostly hetero with a gay/lesbian following
**Transportation:** Car is best. Free pick up from train.
**To Gay Bars:** A 20-minute drive to gay bars.
**Rooms:** 16 rooms with twin or double beds.
**Bathrooms:** All private bathrooms.
**Meals:** Full breakfast.
**Vegetarian:** Can be provided on request.
**Complimentary:** Beverages at breakfast.
**Dates Open:** April-Oct. After Easter 1997, hotel will be open all year.
**High Season:** Jun-Aug.
**Rates:** Please inquire.
**Discounts:** For groups of at least 20 persons & for child. und. 12 years of age.
**Credit Cards:** MC, Diners, Eurocard, Visa.
**Rsv'tns:** Recommended.
**Reserve Through:** Travel agent or call direct.
**Parking:** On-street pay parking.
**In-Room:** Maid service, safe, telephone, radio. TV & minibar on request.
**On-Premises:** TV lounge.
**Swimming:** Nearby pool & ocean.
**Sunbathing:** At beach.
**Smoking:** Permitted.
**Pets:** Permitted, except in dining room.
**Handicap Access:** Yes, lift (elevator) is accessible.
**Children:** Welcomed.
**Languages:** Flemish, French, English, German.
**Your Host:** Josephine.

# GHENT AREA

## Bungalow 't Staaksken

Gay/Lesbian ♀♂

### *A Flemish Bungalow/Cottage in the Heart of the Meetjesland Lake Area, Where Time Stands Still...*

The willow-lined canals, lush green pastures and extensive soft, sandy dunes of Flanders need no introduction; their beauty has been captured for centuries by some of the world's greatest artists. The Meetjesland, however, is known only to a discerning few, yet it has much to offer anyone seeking peace and quiet. It is one of those rare corners of Western Europe where time has virtually stood still and man has barely changed the face of nature. Today, it is a land of creeks and polders, tall fields of maize, "sleeping" dikes and old smugglers routes in the north and woodlands in the south which contain beautiful castles and castle farms. The terrain is ideal for cycling, walking, relaxing and fishing.

***Bungalow 't Staaksken,*** our country bungalow, is situated atop an old dike, 2 kilometres from the gastronomic village of Assenede. With a population of 7,000, Assenede is one of the oldest villages in Flanders and enjoys the distinction of having many restaurants of international repute. In particular, we can recommend the restaurant Den Hoek with its creative dinners, beautiful art interior and green surroundings with creeks and dikes. We offer you a free appetizer when you

*continued next page*

dine at Edward's place. After dinner, you are welcome to spend the rest of the evening at his brother Marius' artcafe, Cafe Passe, where we offer you, free, one of the good Belgian beers.

Assenede is on the Belgium/Netherlands border, only 20-45 minutes from the towns of Ghent to the south, Brugges (the Venice of the North) to the west, and Antwerp (Belgium's premier gay city) to the east. Also easily accessible are the cities of Brussels and Middelburg (Netherlands). The resort town of Knokke, on the Nordsee coast, is a 30-minute drive. There are also very good connections by car or train (Eurostar/TGV) to Paris, London, Amsterdam and Cologne.

***Bungalow 't Staaksken*** has furniture in the Flemish style and sleeps up to five guests in one single and two double rooms. From the sitting room/terrace a panoramic view encompasses the garden, lake and surrounding fields and pasture land. Flanders is also known for its year-round art and music fesitvals. Activities in the Assenede area include tennis, bowling, golf, sailing, surfing, horse riding, cable gliding. Also available are free guided walks with your host, Jan. ***Bungalow 't Staaksken*** is rated 4 Shamrocks. Colour brochure on request.

**Address: Staakstraat 136/138A, Assenede 9960 Belgium.**
**Tel: (32-9) 344 0954 (Tel/Fax).**

**Type:** Bed & breakfast & self-catering, 4-shamrock-rated bungalow.
**Clientele:** Mostly gay & lesbian with hetero clientele welcome
**Transportation:** Car is best. Free pick up from train & bus. Pick up from Zeebrugge & Breskens (Holland) ferry dock, 400 BF.
**To Gay Bars:** 2 miles. A 20-min drive to Ghent, 35-min drive to Antwerp.
**Rooms:** 3 rooms & self-catering bungalow. Single & double beds.
**Bathrooms:** 1 bath/shower/toilet & 1 shared toilet.
**Meals:** Full Belgian breakfast in B&B. Bungalow self-catering. Dinner on request (Belgian & Mauritian specialties).
**Vegetarian:** Available 1 mile away.
**Complimentary:** Tea & coffee on arrival with Belgian chocolates & cakes, flowers.
**Dates Open:** All year.
**High Season:** July-August, Christmas & New Year.
**Rates:** Bungalow: Low: 10,200 BF/wk, 4,500 BF (2n)/wknd, 7,200 BF (4n) midweek; High: 15,200 BF/wk. B&B: 1,200 BF (1 person), 1,800 BF (2 people). Extra person 750 BF.
**Discounts:** Bungalow: 5% off on 2 weeks or more low season. 10% to ECMC members.
**Rsv'tns:** Required.
**Reserve Through:** Call, fax or mail direct.
**Minimum Stay:** 2 nights.
**Parking:** Adequate free covered parking.
**In-Room:** Bungalow: color cable TV, radio, well-appointed kitchen, VCR on request, laundry service.
**On-Premises:** Meeting & dining rooms, TV lounge, BBQ, large garden, fax.
**Exercise/Health:** Nearby gym, weights, Jacuzzi, sauna, steam & massage.
**Swimming:** Lake & pond on premises. Nearby tropical in- & outdoor pool. 30km to Nordsee coast.
**Sunbathing:** On private sun decks or in the garden.
**Nudity:** Permitted on sun terrace, in garden w/discretion & at nude beaches (Paulinapolder 10km, Nordsee 30km).
**Smoking:** Permitted outside only, not in house.
**Pets:** No.
**Handicap Access:** Yes.
**Children:** No. Permitted only on special request when there are no other guests.
**Languages:** Dutch, English, French, German, Creole, some Danish.
**Your Host:** Jan & Margaret.

# CZECH REPUBLIC

## PRAGUE

### Penzion David Hotel

Gay/Lesbian ♀♂

***Penzion David*** is a 1920's bourgeois house built on a slope next to a green hill area. The last owner was a pop singer. The house has been beautifully renovated with many modern features, including a terrace, a garden, a sauna and a restaurant and bar. The staff is friendly. All rooms have private baths, telephone, satellite TV and clock radio. The main tourist attractions of Prague can be easily reached by tram or metro (yellow line "B", metro station Radlicka) which is a five-minute walk from the hotel.

**Address: Holubova 5, Praha 5 150 000 Czech Republic.**
**Tel: (42-2) 900 11 293 or 294, Fax: (42-2) 549 820.**

**Type:** Hotel with restaurant, sauna & bar.
**Clientele:** Mostly gay & lesbian with some hetero clientele
**Transportation:** Tram #14 to Laurová terminal, then 2-min walk. Or yellow metro line B, Radlicka station, then a 5 min walk.
**To Gay Bars:** On the premises.
**Rooms:** 6 suites with double beds, additional single beds available.
**Bathrooms:** All en suite shower/toilets.
**Meals:** Expanded continental breakfast.
**Vegetarian:** Available upon request.
**Dates Open:** All year.
**Rates:** DM 80-DM 120 (CZK 1360-2040) per person per night.
**Rsv'tns:** Recommended.
**Reserve Through:** Call or fax direct.
**Parking:** Ample on-street parking.
**In-Room:** Maid service, colour cable TV & telephone.
**On-Premises:** Restaurant, bar, terrace & garden.
**Exercise/Health:** Sauna.
**Swimming:** 10-minute walk to municipal swimming pool.
**Sunbathing:** In the garden.
**Smoking:** Permitted.
**Pets:** Not permitted.
**Handicap Access:** No.
**Children:** Not permitted.
**Languages:** Czech, German & English.

## Prague Home Stay

**Gay/Lesbian ♀♂**

***Prague Home Stay*** offers inexpensive rooms, not only at the above address, but even in a number of other rooms in the homes of our friends, members of Lambda Prague. Our own rooms provide quiet rest in a residential area, within easy 24-hour reach by tram of all parts of the city. The city, itself, is miraculous, with impressive architecture and historical monuments, hidden beauties and even ghosts. Your hosts will take the time to talk with guests and help them get to know this fascinating city.

**Address: Pod Kotlárkou 14, Prague 5 150 000 Czech Republic.**
**Tel: (42-2) 527 388. Phone may be altered in 1997, for information, call (42-2) 5721 0862.**

**Type:** Lodging & kitchen privileges in a private home.
**Clientele:** Mostly gay & lesbian with some hetero clientele
**Transportation:** Metro B (Yellow Line) to station Andel, then 5 stops by trams No 4,7,9, stop Kotlárka.
**To Gay Bars:** 10-20 minutes by municipal transport or car.
**Rooms:** 1 single, 2 doubles with single beds & 1 suite with double bed.
**Bathrooms:** 2 rooms share 1 bath.
**Complimentary:** Tea & coffee.
**Dates Open:** All year.
**Rates:** USD $20-$34 per person, per night (CZK 560-900).
**Rsv'tns:** Required by telephone.
**Reserve Through:** Call direct.
**Minimum Stay:** 2 nights.
**Parking:** Ample on-street parking. Room for 1 car on premises.
**In-Room:** Telephone upon request.
**On-Premises:** Kitchen privileges for 2 rooms.
**Sunbathing:** At the swimming pool.
**Smoking:** Permitted.
**Pets:** Not permitted.
**Handicap Access:** No.
**Children:** Not permitted.
**Languages:** Czech, Slovak, English, German, Russian & Polish.

# DENMARK

## KØBENHAVN (COPENHAGEN)

## Hotel Windsor

**Q-NET Gay/Lesbian ♀♂**

### *Reasonable Accommodations Near the Central Station*

***Hotel Windsor*** offers centrally located and immaculately clean accommodations at prices reasonable for Denmark! You can walk to the gay bars and you can bring back friends, even to breakfast. Certain floors are designated for men only and have a somewhat bath house atmosphere. The hotel is accessed by a stairway, so be prepared to climb steps. We have cable TV in all rooms, and both telephone and fax service are in reception. Our staff is ready to help you with information about sightseeing, of which Tivoli Garden is the most spectacular example, with many restaurants, free shows, and an amusement park.

**Address: Frederiksborggade 30, Kobenhavn 1360 Denmark.**
**Tel: (45) 33 11 08 30, telefax: (45) 33 11 63 87.**

**Type:** Hotel with restaurant open for breakfast only.
**Clientele:** Exclusively gay
**Transportation:** Airport bus to central station, then bus or taxi.
**To Gay Bars:** 5-minute walk to men's bar, 10-minute walk to women's.
**Rooms:** 10 singles, 10 doubles, 1 triple, 1 quad, 1 apartment.
**Bathrooms:** 4 private, 1 shared bath per floor, sinks in room.

**Meals:** Continental breakfast.
**Vegetarian:** We can recommend vegetarian restaurant.
**Dates Open:** All year.
**High Season:** Mid May-early October.
**Rates:** Single Dkr 325.00-450.00, double Dkr 450-600.
**Credit Cards:** MC, Visa, Access, Eurocard.
**Rsv'tns:** Required, especially in high season.
**Reserve Through:** Call direct.
**Parking:** Ample off-street pay parking, some free on-street after 6 PM.
**In-Room:** Maid service, laundry service, cable color TV & refrigerator.
**On-Premises:** TV lounge, public telephones.
**Swimming:** Public pool nearby, nude beach accessible by train.
**Sunbathing:** 2-minute walk to sunbathing area.
**Nudity:** Permitted on men-only floor.
**Smoking:** Permitted without restrictions.
**Pets:** Not permitted.
**Handicap Access:** No! Many stairs!
**Children:** Permitted.
**Languages:** Danish, English, Norwegian, Swedish, German, French, Italian.
**Your Host:** John.

# SKAGEN

## Finns Pension

**Gay/Lesbian ♀♂**

***Finns Pension*** is a beautiful old wood house decorated in the old style. It's a great place to stay for a holiday in this very special corner of Denmark, the most famous holiday place in the country. Enjoy the sun drenched beaches, lovely scenery, and outstanding local museums. The owner is gay and promotes a relaxed atmosphere for gay people.

**Address: Ostre Strandvej 63, Skagen 9990 Denmark.**
**Tel: (45) 98 45 01 55.**

**Type:** Hotel with restaurant for guests.
**Clientele:** Mostly gay & lesbian with some hetero clientele
**Transportation:** Car or train is best. Free pick up from train.
**Rooms:** 6 rooms with single or double beds.
**Bathrooms:** Sinks in rooms. Shared: 2 full baths, 1 shower & 1 WC.
**Meals:** Expanded continental breakfast. Optional lunch & dinner.
**Vegetarian:** Available if ordered before arrival.
**Dates Open:** All year.
**High Season:** May 1-Aug 31.
**Rates:** High season: single Dkr 325-475, double Dkr 575-675. Low season: single Dkr 300-425, double Dkr 525-625.
**Discounts:** 10% for stays of 3+ days, 15% for stays of 7+ days.
**Credit Cards:** MC, VISA, Eurocard, JGB.
**Rsv'tns:** Required.
**Reserve Through:** Call direct.
**Parking:** Limited free off-street parking.
**In-Room:** Radio & room service.
**On-Premises:** Garden, library, lounge, telephone, & laundry facilities.
**Exercise/Health:** Small weights.
**Swimming:** Public pool 1 km. Ocean beach nearby.
**Sunbathing:** At the beach or in the garden.
**Nudity:** Permitted at the beach.
**Smoking:** Permitted. No non-smoking rooms available.
**Pets:** Permitted.
**Handicap Access:** No. Stairs to rooms.
**Children:** Permitted, but maximum of 2.
**Languages:** Danish, English, German, & Swedish.

# FRANCE

## BRITTANY

### Chez Jacqueline

**Women ♀**

***Jaqueline Boudillet*** offers her quiet, rural home as a bed and breakfast for women only. Here you can enjoy the peaceful countryside, visit many nearby touristic areas or simply stay at home. The home has a women's library, a lovely garden and musical instruments which guests are free to play. Guests are encouraged to take advantage of activities including swimming, riding, walking through forests, by the lakes or the sea-side.

**Address: c/o Jacqueline Boudillet, La Croix Cadio, St Donant, Brittany 22800 France.**
**Tel: June through Sept: (33) 96 73 81 22, Oct-May: Paris (33-1) 47 39 94 54.**

**Type:** Bed & breakfast in a big country house in Brittany.
**Clientele:** Women only
**Transportation:** Car is best.
**Rooms:** 3 doubles.
**Bathrooms:** 2 shared.
**Meals:** FF 20 for continental breakfast.
**Dates Open:** Jun-Sep, sometimes May. Use mail address above. Rest of year, use Paris addr.
**Rates:** Room FF 200.00.
**Rsv'tns:** Required. Call ahead. Oct-May in Paris: 6, rue du Port, 92110 Clichy, (1) 47 39 94 54.
**Reserve Through:** Call direct.
**Parking:** Ample free off-street parking.
**On-Premises:** TV room.
**Swimming:** Ocean beach 20 minutes by car.
**Sunbathing:** In the garden.
**Smoking:** Permitted.
**Pets:** Only dogs who love cats are permitted.
**Handicap Access:** 1 bedroom is on ground floor.
**Children:** Not permitted.
**Languages:** French, English & some German.

## BURGUNDY REGION

### La Salamandre

**Gay-Owned ♀♂**

#### *18th-Century Home in the Wine Country of Burgundy*

Passing through the hilly region of Burgundy, you'll find ***La Salamandre***, our beautifully decorated 18th-century home surrounded by a large park-like area populated with old trees. Without sacrificing the charm of the past, we have completely renovated the house to the standards of modern comfort. The atmosphere of the surrounding vineyards and hills turns a simple country walk or bike ride into a memorable visual experience, especially for city folk whose eyes crave distances and panoramas. The Chateau de Cormatin (17th century), only a dozen kilometers away, is a striking example of the architecture of the time. And the area abounds with equestrian centers and scenic places to ride.

At the end of an active day, guests enjoy gathering for a good meal in a warm convivial atmosphere. Wine to accompany your meal can be purchased from our wine list, which is small, but includes a variety of good wines. After dinner, guests can repare to the salon whose corner library and fireplace set the tone for relaxation.

**Address: Au Bourg, Salornay sur Guye 71250 France.**
**Tel: (33) 385 59 91 56, Fax: (33) 385 59 91 67.**

**Type:** Guesthouse. Town of Salornay is close to the cities of Mâcon, Dijon & Lyon & is a short drive NE of the town of Cluny.
**Clientele:** Mostly hetero clientele with a gay & lesbian following
**Transportation:** Car is best. Train (TGV) from Paris to Mâcon Loché station, then bus or taxi. Free pick up from train upon request.
**To Gay Bars:** 18 miles (30 min drive) to gay disco. 1-1/2 hrs to Lyon gay bars & activities.
**Rooms:** 4 rooms, 1 suite with single or double beds.
**Bathrooms:** Private: 2 bath/toilets, 3 shower/toilets.
**Meals:** Expanded continental breakfast included in rate. Three-course dinner for guests FF 120.
**Vegetarian:** Available if requested in advance.
**Complimentary:** Chocolates on pillow.
**Dates Open:** All year.
**High Season:** July-September.
**Rates:** Single FF 270, double FF 390, suite FF 490 (for 2-3 persons).
**Discounts:** From 4 nights, 10% discount on above rates.
**Credit Cards:** MC, Visa, Eurocard.
**Rsv'tns:** Recommended in high season & on weekends.
**Reserve Through:** Call direct.
**Parking:** Ample free off-street parking.
**In-Room:** Telephone, maid service.
**On-Premises:** TV lounge, meeting rooms.
**Exercise/Health:** Bicycle on premises. Nearby golf, horse riding, fishing.
**Swimming:** At nearby river & lake.
**Smoking:** Permitted in lounge. All rooms are non-smoking.
**Pets:** Not permitted.
**Handicap Access:** No.
**Children:** Welcome.
**Languages:** French, English, German, Italian.
**Your Host:** Guy & Jean-Pierre.

# DOMME

## La Dordogne Camping de Femmes

Women ♀

For those who have never seen the countryside of France, staying at ***La Dordogne Camping de Femmes*** is a special experience. In addition to the camaraderie with other women from many countries, you can bicycle or hike through the rolling, green countryside, or explore the fascinating caves and ancient castles nearby. Most accommodations consist of tent sites. There are also three caravans, which can be rented, and a bungalow tent, which is furnished, has a kitchen, etc., and accommodates two people. There are two bars on the premises, one for smokers and one for non-smokers. Wild womyn don't get the blues. They go to a women's campground for Dutch hospitality with a French accent.

**Address: St.-Aubin de Nabirat, Domme 24250 France.**
**Tel: (33) 553 28 50 28.**

**Type:** Campground.
**Clientele:** Women only
**Transportation:** 8 km from railway station, taxis available.
**To Gay Bars:** 2 hrs by car to Toulouse.
**Campsites:** 20 tent sites, 4 electric, 3 caravans (campers), 2 toilets, 2 hot & 1 cold shower, laundry facilities, 2 bars, library.
**Vegetarian:** Always.
**Complimentary:** Snack bar on the campground.
**Dates Open:** May-Sept.
**High Season:** Jul-Aug.
**Rates:** FF 45.00 per day per woman for tent sites. Caravan with electric, FF 1200 per week for 2 persons.
**Rsv'tns:** Required.
**Reserve Through:** Call direct.
**Parking:** Off-street private parking.
**On-Premises:** Meeting rooms, TV lounge, laundry facilities for guests.
**Exercise/Health:** Tennis, volleyball, pingpong hall, jeu de boule on the premises, nearby canoeing, riding, walking & bicycle trips.
**Swimming:** At pool on premises.
**Sunbathing:** At poolside & tent sites.
**Nudity:** Topless only.
**Smoking:** Permitted outdoors & in one of the bars.
**Pets:** Permitted.
**Children:** Only girls over 14 years old.
**Languages:** Dutch, German, French, English.

# PARIS

## Hotel Central Marais

Gay/Lesbian ♂

### *In the Middle of Everything*

***Hotel Central Marais*** is a small, exclusively gay hotel in the Marais, the old, aristocratic, historic quarter of central Paris. Surrounded by the principal gay bars and restaurants, it is a 5-minute walk from Notre Dame, La Bastille and Les Halles. The 17th-century hotel has been carefully restored to enhance the charm of its old-world character, while providing modern conveniences.

Accommodations consist of two double-bedded rooms per floor, with a bathroom off the short lobby between. A small, communal salon is available to guests on the first floor. Guests are substantially on their own, with limited guest services. On the ground floor is the famous Belle Epoque bar, *Le Central,* a popular gay rendezvous. Available in the building opposite is a 2-room apartment with kitchenette, bath and small balcony. We speak English and French. A bientôt – Maurice

*NOTE: Hotel entry with intercom at 2, rue Ste. Croix de la Bretonnerie (corner building).*

**Address: 33, rue Vieille-du-Temple (Enter: 2, rue Ste, Croix de la Brctonnerie), Paris 75004 France.**
**Tel: (33-1) 48 87 56 08, Fax: (33-1) 42 77 06 27.**

**Type:** Hotel above a popular men's bar & 2-room apartment across street.
**Clientele:** Mostly men with women welcome
**Transportation:** From: CDG airport Bus Train (RER); Orly airport ORLY VAL (RER) to Chatelet Les Halles Sta, exit Centre Georges Pompidou.
**To Gay Bars:** On the premises or 12 gay bars within 10 minutes walk.
**Rooms:** 7 rooms with double beds.
**Bathrooms:** One shared bath per floor, private bath 5th floor (no lift).
**Meals:** Continental breakfast 35 FF per day, available 8:30-13:00.
**Dates Open:** All year.
**High Season:** All year.
**Rates:** Hotel: FF 400 single, FF 485 double. Apt: FF 595 (1-2 people), FF 720 (3-4 people).
**Credit Cards:** MC, Visa & Eurocard.
**Rsv'tns:** Required.
**Reserve Through:** Call direct.
**Minimum Stay:** Apartment. 3 days.
**Parking:** Parking is difficult. Parking garage under Hotel de Ville.
**In-Room:** Maid service & telephone.
**On-Premises:** TV lounge, meeting room & gay bar.
**Exercise/Health:** Gym, weights, Jacuzzi, sauna, steam & massage all available nearby.
**Swimming:** At nearby pool.
**Sunbathing:** By the river.
**Smoking:** Permitted.
**Pets:** Not permitted.
**Handicap Access:** No.
**Children:** Not permitted.
**Languages:** French & English.

IGTA

## Hotel des Nations

Gay-Friendly ♀♂

### *In the Heart of Paris' Quartier Latin, Near the Gay Nightlife of the Marais*

Dance all night, walk along the Seine, get up early or stay up late to see the sun rise over Notre Dame. You're in the Latin Quarter, smack in the center of Paris, yet in a neighborhood of overarching trees, cafe society, the Pantheon and the Sorbonne. It's a neighborhood that is very close to the gay nightlife of the Marais, yet free of the frenetic pace of the center city. At ***Hotel des Nations,*** we endeavor to set a peaceful mood of soft lights, warmth and friendliness that will put you right at ease. In your room, you will find all the convenience of modern decor and amenities, such as direct-dial phone, radio, TV and individual safes. You'll find the bar a congenial meeting place for business encounters and the lounge, with its pleasant hearthside, a cozy nook for evenings of relaxation.

**Address: 54 rue Monge, Paris 75005 France. Tel: (33-1) 43 26 45 24, Fax: (33-1) 46 34 00 13, http://www.hotel.co.uk/helan.**

**Type:** Hotel with bar.
**Clientele:** Mostly hetero clientele with a gay/lesbian following
**Transportation:** Metro Place Monge & Cardinal Lemoine.
**To Gay Bars:** 1 mile, 10-minutes by metro.
**Rooms:** 38 rooms with single & double beds.
**Bathrooms:** Private: 20 bath/toilets, 18 shower/toilets.
**Vegetarian:** Vegetarian restaurant nearby.
**Dates Open:** All year.
**High Season:** May-June, September-October.
**Rates:** Double 560 FF-630 FF.
**Discounts:** 15% for seniors.
**Credit Cards:** MC, Visa, Amex, Diners, Eurocard, JCB.
**Rsv'tns:** Required.
**Reserve Through:** Travel agent or call direct. Sabre CN 29594, Galileo CN 70816, Amadeus CN PARDES, Worldspan CN DESNA.
**Parking:** On-street public pay parking.
**In-Room:** Color cable TV, VCR, maid service.
**Smoking:** Permitted. Non-smoking rooms available.
**Pets:** Permitted.
**Handicap Access:** No.
**Children:** Welcome.
**Languages:** French, English, Brazilian Portuguese, Spanish, Italian.
**Your Host:** Bernard.

IGTA

## Hotel Louxor

Gay-Friendly 50/50 ♀♂

### *We are a 2-Star Hotel*

In a peaceful street, close to the northern and eastern railway stations and a few minutes from the main boulevards, department stores and entertainment centres of Paris, you will find the ***Hotel Louxor,*** a charming building, constructed at the turn of the century. You'll enjoy your intimate, individualized room and the quiet lounge where breakfast is served. You'll also appreciate the restful surroundings in the reading lounge. Here is a hotel which has not lost the human touch and where you will feel at home.

*continued next page*

**Address: 4 rue Taylor, Paris 75010 France.**
**Tel: (33-1) 42 08 23 91, Fax: (33-1) 42 08 03 30.**

**Type:** Hotel.
**Clientele:** 50% gay & lesbian & 50% hetero clientele
**To Gay Bars:** 6 blocks to gay bars or a 10-minute walk.
**Rooms:** 30 rooms with single or double beds.
**Bathrooms:** All private shower/toilets.
**Meals:** Breakfast FF25.
**Dates Open:** All year except Feb.
**Rates:** Single FF 225-255, double FF 290, double with 2 beds FF 330.
**Credit Cards:** MC, Visa & Eurocard.
**Rsv'tns:** Required by fax with credit card number as guarantee.
**Reserve Through:** Travel agent or call direct.
**Parking:** Off-street parking.
**In-Room:** Color TV, direct-dial telephone, quiet lounge & reading lounge.
**Smoking:** Permitted without restrictions in the room. No public smoking sections.
**Pets:** Permitted.
**Handicap Access:** No.
**Children:** Permitted.
**Languages:** French & English.

## Private Paris Accommodations

Gay ♂

### *Your Home in Paris*

Next time you're in Paris, why not rent a charming studio apartment in an 18th-century building on the pedestrian Rue Bourbon le Chateau (behind the church of St. Germain) in the heart of the Left Bank St. Germain des Pres? Its convenient location makes it easy to walk to just about anywhere in Central Paris. To help you get accustomed to the area, the trilingual owner is happy to show you around the neighborhood. You are just a few blocks from Café de Flor and Les Deux Magots. Around the corner is the Place Furstemberg, and a six-day-a-week open-air market is down the street, convenient for food and flower shopping.

The photo shown is a view from one of our apartments. We also have another accommodation with views of the Eiffel Tower and Paris.The studio apartment has been entirely rebuilt with a modern bath and kitchen and has parquet floors and high-beamed ceilings. It is furnished with a mixture of contemporary and antique furniture with a king-sized bed and double pullout sofa. Guests will also find a TV (with English cable) and a telephone. Two tall windows face the street on the second floor. We also offer accommodations in San Francisco, California. Call to make reservations.

**Address: Contact: NY B&B Reservation Center, in New York, USA,**
**Tel: (212) 977-3512.**

**Type:** Private apartment in St. Germain des Pres on Left Bank.
**Clientele:** Gay
**Transportation:** Metro or taxi.
**To Gay Bars:** Walking distance to many.
**Rooms:** 1 studio apt.
**Bathrooms:** Private shower/toilet.
**Rates:** Available on request.
**Credit Cards:** Amex.
**Rsv'tns:** Required.
**Reserve Through:** Travel agent or call direct.
**Minimum Stay:** 4 days.
**Parking:** On-street parking or parking in paid public garage.
**In-Room:** Color cable TV, telephone, kitchenette, refrigerator & weekly maid service.
**Swimming:** 10-minute walk to floating pool on the Seine.
**Smoking:** Permitted.
**Pets:** Inquire.
**Handicap Access:** No.
**Children:** Welcome.
**Languages:** French, English, Spanish & Italian.

# SOUTHWEST FRANCE - RURAL

## Hilltop Cantegrive Farmhouses

Gay-Friendly ♀

### *A Tranquil Hideaway in Foie Gras, Chateaux and Wine Country*

Perched on a hilltop in 50 private acres, ***Cantegrive*** is a 17th-century Perigordian country estate, 75 miles east of Bordeaux and 18 miles east of Bergerac on the Dordogne River. Our thick stone walls of local yellow sandstone have stood for centuries, supporting massive oak beams and a dizzyingly steep gabled roof of handcrafted tiles – admire their golden beauty as you relax with a glass of Bergerac wine.

The Dordogne/Perigord region is French countryside at its best. This is Eleanor of Aquitane country where troubadours sang in fairy tale castles. Later, this peaceful area became the site of centuries of bitter warfare between French and English kings. Medieval castles and fortified bastide villages still bear testimony to those fierce times. Even earlier, prehistoric man settled here wich is evidenced by many caves with their fascinating wall paintings and sculpture.

Amid all these traces of earlier times, today's visitor can also enjoy canoeing, biking, horseback riding, tennis – a cornucopia of outdoor activity! And, do not forget that France, food and wine go together. Village markets abound with fresh local produce, cheeses, foie gras and wines. Cozy restaurants dot the countryside, offering local fare at prices kind to your wallet. For quieter moments, stroll or jog on our forest trails. Or, relax and enjoy your spacious house, nicely furnished in antique and wicker. On warm evenings, admire the magnificent sunsets from your own terrace, or take the chill off cool seasons in front of your natural stone fireplace.

**Address: Bidot Haut, St. Avit Sénieur (Bergerac) 24 440 France.**
**Tel: (33) 553 22 01 94, Fax (33) 553 27 87 85.**

**Type:** 2 self-catering houses.
**Clientele:** Mostly hetero clientele with a gay female following
**Transportation:** Car essential. Airports at Bordeaux & Bergerac. Free pick up from train in Bergerac.
**To Gay Bars:** 45 miles (1 hr) north to Perigueux or 2 hrs to Bordeaux.
**Rooms:** 2- & 3-bedroom houses with single, double or queen beds.
**Bathrooms:** Private, tiled with tub & shower.
**Meals:** Self-catering cottages.
**Vegetarian:** Ample supply of fresh local seasonal produce. Available upon request at local restaurants.
**Complimentary:** Welcome wine on arrival. Figs & plums in season from own trees. Firewood in season from own forests.
**Dates Open:** All year.
**High Season:** July-August.
**Rates:** Houses per week: 2-bedroom US $450-US $700, 3-bedroom US $900-US $1200.
**Discounts:** For long-term & off-season, on request.
**Rsv'tns:** Necessary with deposit.
**Reserve Through:** Directly.
**Minimum Stay:** 1 week, Saturday-Saturday.
**Parking:** Plenty of space on-site for parking.

*continued next page*

**In-Room:** Each house has Satellite TV, fireplace, dishwasher, microwave, refrigerator/freezer, oven, linen & towels.
**On-Premises:** Laundry facilities, Weber grill for each house. Central oil heat, fax.
**Exercise/Health:** Petanque, badminton.
**Swimming:** 20 x 50 ft. pool.
**Sunbathing:** At pool, or as you like on property.
**Smoking:** Preferably outdoors.
**Pets:** No.
**Handicap Access:** No.
**Children:** Permitted if well-behaved.
**Languages:** French, English, German, Finnish, Swedish.
**Your Host:** Joan & Aune.

## Mondès

**Women ♀**

### *A Women's Inn in France's Armagnac Region*

Combine beautiful countryside with the charm of French culture, the warm atmosphere of home, the camaraderie of summer camp and the feeling of land inhabited only by women and then you have ***Mondès.*** Owners Dorothee and Monika immediately welcome you, making you feel at home and comfortable with their friendly hospitality. Women staying at ***Mondès*** have breakfast and dinner together outside in the warm sunshine while enjoying the view of a medieval chateau in the distance. During the conversation around the table, you can meet women from all parts of Europe, and the world, and hear German, English and French spoken. There is always much laughter and friendliness and sometimes guitar playing and singing.

**Address: Courrensan, Gondrin 32330 France.**
**Tel: (33) 562 06 59 05. In France dial: 0562 06 59 05.**

**Type:** Inn & campground.
**Clientele:** Women only
**Transportation:** Car is best, train to Agen + bus to Gondrin.
**To Gay Bars:** 150 km to Toulouse.
**Rooms:** 5 doubles. Also a small house with 1 double bdrm, kitchen, toilet/shower, living room, patio.
**Bathrooms:** 1 bathroom with 2 showers shared.
**Campsites:** 20 tent sites with two toilets & 3 showers.
**Meals.** Full breakfast buffet & gourmet vegetarian dinners.
**Vegetarian:** Mostly organic vegetarian. Organic lamb from own farm occasionally.
**Dates Open:** All year.
**High Season:** Jul-Aug.
**Rates:** Per person per day: FF 180 breakfast & dinner, FF 40 camping, FF 145 camping, breakfast & dinner. Small house: FF 300 per day.
**Discounts:** Inquire
**Rsv'tns:** Required.
**Reserve Through:** Call direct.
**Minimum Stay:** 3 days.
**Parking:** Adequate parking on own land.
**On-Premises:** Meeting rooms, laundry facilities, & living room with fireplace.
**Exercise/Health:** Bicycles, volleyball & swimming. Horseriding & tennis nearby.
**Swimming:** In lake on private ground.
**Sunbathing:** Everywhere.
**Nudity:** Permitted around the lake.
**Smoking:** Permitted everywhere except in rooms.
**Pets:** Not permitted.
**Handicap Access:** Yes.
**Children:** Permitted. Males up to 8 years old.
**Languages:** French, German & English.
**Your Host:** Dorothee & Monika.

## Roussa

Women ♀

### *Come and Fall in Love*

***Roussa*** is a 200-year-old renovated farmhouse with a beautiful, big garden, German-run, but international in atmosphere and clientele. You will find all holiday activities nearby, but no mass tourism. Come, and fall in love with the vineyards and the fields of sunflowers and corn which surround us. You'll enjoy discovering charming small towns and marketplaces and exploring musketeer castles, medieval fortifications and Roman ruins. Terribly tempting dining specialties await you in Gascony, including famous wines. You can get in touch with a lesbian network through ***Roussa,*** making interesting contacts along the way. By the way, at ***Roussa,*** you can rent a beautiful conference room and organize, or participate in, group activities of all sorts. Ask about our program. Gabriele, Monika and Chantal, with their pets (cats, hens, sheep), wish you a warm welcome.

**Address: Courrensan, Gondrin 32330 France.**
**Tel: (33) 62 06 58 96, Fax: (33) 62 64 45 34.**

**Type:** Guesthouse & camping.
**Clientele:** Women only
**Transportation:** Car recommended. Pick up service from bus or train station.
**Rooms:** 7 rooms with single & double beds.
**Bathrooms:** 2 shared bath/shower/toilets & 3 shared WCs.
**Campsites:** 10 tent sites.
**Meals:** Generous breakfast & vegetarian dinner.
**Vegetarian:** Always.
**Complimentary:** Cocktails, wine, tea, coffee, juices & snacks.
**Dates Open:** All year except Nov.
**High Season:** Jul-Sept.
**Rates:** Per person: FF 150 high season, FF 130 off season.
**Discounts:** Call for details.
**Rsv'tns:** Call for reservations.
**Reserve Through:** Call direct.
**Minimum Stay:** 2 nights.
**Parking:** Adequate free off-street parking.
**On-Premises:** TV lounge, meeting rooms, laundry service.
**Exercise/Health:** Bicycles to rent on premises. Horseback riding & tennis nearby.
**Swimming:** Nearby pool & lake.
**Sunbathing:** In the garden.
**Smoking:** Permitted.
**Pets:** Dogs permitted, if they don't eat our cats.
**Handicap Access:** No.
**Children:** Welcome, boys only to age 10.
**Languages:** German, French & English.
**Your Host:** Gabriele, Monika & Chantal.

## Saouis

Women ♀

Surrounded by vineyards, fields and woods, ***Saouis*** is situated 80 km from the Pyrenees and 120 km from the Atlantic Coast. For 7 years, women from many different countries have spent their holidays here in this beautiful, tranquil spot, spoiling themselves with the sun, fresh air and fine cuisine. The house has 5 double rooms and plenty of space outdoors for tent camping. For women interested in outdoor activities, we have a 6x14-meter swimming pool on premises, and a paved tennis court 1-1/2 km, from the house. Horseback riding is one km. away. For women who have come without cars, transportation is available, for a fee, to the Pyrenees or the Atlantic Coast. It is also possible, without leaving the farm, to find quiet corners for peaceful solitude, sunbathing, reading and relaxing. If you appreciate good, healthy food, you will not be disappointed with the dishes we prepare! Reservations are required in advance.

**Address: Cravencères, Nogaro 32110 France.**
**Tel: (33) 62 08 56 06.**

**Type:** Guesthouse.
**Clientele:** Women only
**Transportation:** Car is best. Pick up from bus in Manciet (near Mont-de-Marsan).
**To Gay Bars:** 150 km Toulouse Bagdam Cafe, & Bordeaux.
**Rooms:** 5 doubles.
**Bathrooms:** 2 shared hot

*continued next page*

showers & 2 WCs.
**Campsites:** 10 tent sites, 2 hot showers, 1 cold shower, & 2 WCs.
**Meals:** Expanded continental breakfast and dinner.
**Vegetarian:** Mainly vegetarian meals, but also seafood & meat dishes.
**Complimentary:** Cocktails, "floc" (a regional specialty), & pousse rapier.
**Dates Open:** Mar-Oct.
**High Season:** July-Aug.
**Rates:** Rooms FF 170, camping FF 130-FF 150, with breakfast & dinner.
**Rsv'tns:** Recommended in July & Aug.
**Reserve Through:** Call direct.
**Minimum Stay:** 3-day minimum for rooms.
**Parking:** Adequate, free parking.
**Swimming:** At lake 5 km away. 6x14-meter swimming pool on premises.
**Sunbathing:** In the garden.
**Nudity:** Permitted.
**Smoking:** Permitted.
**Pets:** Permitted.
**Handicap Access:** No.
**Children:** Permitted, but boys to age 10 only.
**Languages:** French, German, & English.
**Your Host:** Dagmar.

# TOURS

## Prieuré des Granges

**Gay-Friendly ♀♂**

### *Stay in a French Country Castle 1 Hour From Paris*

The Loire Valley, where the French kings built their castles, is the best place to experience the history of France. ***Prieuré des Granges*** is an old mansion dating from the 17th and 19th centuries and surrounded by a garden full of aged trees and a swimming pool. All the large, southern-facing guest rooms overlook the garden, each one with its own bath (or shower) and private WC and each furnished with antiques. We have taken great pleasure in arranging for our guests a most interesting stay in this region. We are only 15 minutes by car from the town of Tours, the true capital of the Loire Valley. In Savonnieres and Tours, you will find a variety of restaurants to choose from. Tennis, horseback riding, an 18-hole golf course, antique galleries, as well as tourist attractions, such as the museums of Tours and many castles, are all within easy reach.

**Address: 37510 Savonnieres, Touraine France.**
**Tel: (33) 02 47 50 09 67, Fax: (33) 02 47 50 06 43.**

**Type:** Bed & breakfast with antique shop.
**Clientele:** Mostly hetero with a gay & lesbian following
**Transportation:** Car is best. Train to Tours, then taxi. TGV fast train, 55 minutes from Paris.
**To Gay Bars:** 6 miles or 15 minutes by car.
**Rooms:** 6 rooms, 1 with twin beds, 1 suite.
**Bathrooms:** Private: 3 bath/toilets, 3 shower/toilets, 1 bath/shower/toilet.
**Meals:** Continental breakfast.
**Vegetarian:** Vegetarian restaurant in Tours.
**Dates Open:** Mar 15-Dec 31.
**High Season:** July-Sept.
**Rates:** 550 FF-650 FF for 2 people, breakfast included. Suite (4 beds) 900 FF.
**Discounts:** 10% for 4 nights.
**Credit Cards:** Required for guarantee only.
**Rsv'tns:** Required.
**Reserve Through:** Travel agent or call direct.
**Parking:** Free private parking on the property.
**In-Room:** Telephone.
**On-Premises:** Meeting rooms & TV lounge.
**Exercise/Health:** Tennis & horseback riding. Golf nearby.
**Swimming:** Pool on premises.
**Sunbathing:** At poolside.
**Smoking:** Permitted without restrictions.
**Pets:** Permitted in the downstairs rooms.
**Handicap Access:** No.
**Children:** Welcomed if well-behaved.
**Languages:** French & English.
**Your Host:** Philippe, Serge & Xavier.

IGTA

# GERMANY

## BERLIN

### ARCO Hotel — Norddeutscher Hof

Gay-Friendly 50/50 ♀♂

#### *The New ARCO Hotel*

In January, 1996, the ***ARCO*** reopened on a quiet sidestreet two blocks from the central Wittenbergplatz. The pleasant, safe neighbourhood, right in the gay area, offers a wide range of restaurants, bars, shops and cafés. The 21 renovated rooms (most on the ground and first floors) all have telephones, safes, TV, radio, alarm clock and most have a private bath or shower. The helpful ***ARCO*** staff is especially proud of the terrace and the quiet, shady garden and is looking forward to welcoming you in its new environment.

**Address: Geisbergstr. 30, Berlin 10777 Germany.**
**Tel: (49-30) 218 21 28, Fax: (49-30) 211 33 87.**

**Type:** Hotel/pension.
**Clientele:** 50% gay & lesbian & 50% hetero clientele
**Transportation:** 5-minute walk from Wittenbergplatz U-bahn station. 3 U-bahn lines & several bus stops nearby.
**To Gay Bars:** 2-8 minute walk.
**Rooms:** 14 double rooms, 7 single rooms, 1 apartment.
**Bathrooms:** 14 private, 7 shared.
**Meals:** Breakfast buffet.
**Dates Open:** All year.
**Rates:** Singles DM 70-DM 135, doubles DM 110-DM 175.
**Credit Cards:** MC, Visa, Amex, Diners.
**Rsv'tns:** Preferred.
**Reserve Through:** Call direct.
**Parking:** On the street or in nearby garage.
**In-Room:** Maid service, phone, safe, TV, radio, alarm clock.
**On-Premises:** Small lounge, terrace, garden.
**Exercise/Health:** Gym nearby.
**Swimming:** Lake nearby.
**Sunbathing:** At the lake or in the park.
**Nudity:** Permitted in park or at the lake.
**Smoking:** Permitted.
**Pets:** Permitted.
**Handicap Access:** Yes. Please inquire.
**Children:** Permitted.
**Languages:** German, English, French, Spanish, Portuguese.
**Your Host:** Jacques & Rolf.

### Artemisia, Women Only Hotel

Women ♀

***Artemisia,*** the hotel for women only, is located just minutes from the Kurfürstendamm, Berlin's most exciting avenue. Newly renovated and redecorated in soothing pastels, our hotel offers rooms with modern furniture, telephones and spacious, private bathrooms. ***Artemisia's*** special features also include a sun deck with an impressive view of Berlin.

At ***Artemisia,*** travelling women find complete comfort and convenience. If you come to Berlin, for business or pleasure, ***Artemisia's*** personal, woman-identified atmosphere will make your stay a memorable experience.

**Address: Brandenburgischestrasse 18, Berlin 10707 Germany.**
**Tel: (49-30) 873 89 05, or 873 63 73, Fax: (49-30) 861 86 53.**

**Type:** Hotel with bar.
**Clientele:** Women only
**Transportation:** Taxi or U-bahn: Konstanzerstrasse, airport bus to Adenauerplatz.
**To Gay Bars:** 10-minute drive to women's bars.
**Rooms:** 7 rooms & 1 suite with single or double beds.
**Bathrooms:** 1 private bath/toilet & 7 private shower/toilets.
**Meals:** Lavish buffet-style breakfast with eggs, cereal, fruits, vegetables, yogurt, cheeses & meats, jams, etc.
**Vegetarian:** Buffet breakfast has a variety of items to please everyone.
**Complimentary:** Bar with room service.
**Dates Open:** All year.
**Rates:** Single 99.00-200.00 DM, double 169.00-220.00 DM.
**Discounts:** On stays exceeding 1 week (7 nights).
**Credit Cards:** MC, VISA, Amex, Eurocard & Diners.
**Rsv'tns:** Recommended!
**Reserve Through:** Call direct.

*continued next page*

**Parking:** Adequate free on-street parking.
**In-Room:** Maid & laundry service, telephone, heat. In suite only: color cable TV.
**On-Premises:** Meeting rooms, TV lounge, cocktail lounge, women's art displays.
**Sunbathing:** On common sun deck.
**Smoking:** Permitted without restriction except during breakfast (no smoking).
**Pets:** Not permitted.
**Handicap Access:** No.
**Children:** Permitted, but males only up to 14 yrs.
**Languages:** German, English, Italian & French.

## Pension Niebuhr

**Gay-Friendly 50/50 ♂**

### *Willkommen, Bienvenue, Welcome*

***Pension Niebuhr*** follows an old Berlin tradition: You are accommodated in a house built in the beginning of this century, with converted former apartments, so you'll get a feeling of privacy. Rooms are typically spacious, with high ceilings. All have been newly furnished during the last two years and don't look like most hotel rooms. The interior is modern and decorated with paintings by young Berlin artists. Seven of the 12 rooms have private bathrooms, cable TV, telephone and clock/radio. The other five have sinks with hot water and a shared shower and toilet on the same floor. As a special free service, an extended breakfast is served in the room any time after 7 a.m.

In the well-known district of Berlin-Charlottenburg, ***Pension Niebuhr*** is centrally located, yet in a quiet neighborhood. Kurfürstendamm, the popular main street for shopping and strolling, is within a three-minute walk. The S-Bahn-station Savignyplatz is about 200 meters from us. From there it's just one station to Zoologischer Garten, the former main station of West Berlin. The surrounding area offers a wide choice of international restaurants with their typical cuisine, several little galleries, bars and antique shops. A VERY IMPORTANT NOTE: THIS IS A SAFE AREA.

Willi, the friendly host, is always glad to take the time to chat and share information about this great city.

**Address: Niebuhrstr 74, Berlin 10629 Germany.**
**Tel: (49-30) 324 95 95 or 324 95 96, Fax: (49-30) 324 80 21.**

**Type:** Pension.
**Clientele:** 50% hetero with a gay male following
**Transportation:** Bus (NR 109) from airport to Bleibtreustr, then 3-minute walk. From Zoo station, S-Bahn to Savignyplatz.
**To Gay Bars:** About 10 minutes by bus to gay bar area or 5-min walk to nearest bar.
**Rooms:** 12 rooms.
**Bathrooms:** 7 private showers/toilets, 5 rooms share.
**Meals:** Expanded continental breakfast.
**Vegetarian:** Vegetarian breakfast by request. Restaurants also offer vegetarian food.
**Complimentary:** Coffee, tea, juices, sparkling wine, coke & mineral water.
**Dates Open:** All year.
**Rates:** Single DM 95,00-DM 140,00. Double DM 125,00-DM 170,00.
**Discounts:** On stays exceeding 7 nights. Winter rates from Nov-Feb.
**Credit Cards:** MC, VISA, Amex & Eurocard.
**Rsv'tns:** Required.
**Reserve Through:** Call direct.
**Parking:** Limited on-street parking, DM 5 per day. Empty spaces hard to find.
**In-Room:** Color cable TV, telephone, maid & room service.
**On-Premises:** Fax machine.
**Exercise/Health:** Nearby gym, sauna & massage.
**Swimming:** Pool & lake 1 km away.
**Sunbathing:** At the park or lake.
**Nudity:** Permitted at the lake or partly common pool.
**Smoking:** Permitted without restrictions.
**Pets:** Permitted.
**Handicap Access:** No.
**Children:** Not especially welcome.
**Languages:** German & English.
**Your Host:** Willi.

## Tom's House Berlin

**Men** 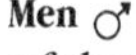

HOUSE BERLIN

You will appreciate the old-world charm of the spacious, individually furnished rooms in this grand turn-of-the-century Berlin apartment house. You will relax in our homelike atmosphere, and you will not believe the buffet breakfast we serve from 10:00 a.m. till 1:00 p.m. You have your choice of yogurt, cereal, cheese, meat, smoked salmon, fruit salad, freshly baked German rolls, bread, eggs, marmalade, honey, jam, and sometimes even champagne! ***Tom's House Berlin*** is located in the gayest part of town. You can walk to a number of gay night spots, saving the expense of taxis or rental cars. Convenience is important, and our guests return year after year, because at ***Tom's House Berlin*** they always feel comfortable and at ease.

**Address: Eisenacher Str. 10, Berlin 10777 Germany.**
**Tel: (49-30) 218 55 44, Fax: (49-30) 213 44 64.**

**Type:** Bed & breakfast guesthouse predominantly for leather men.
**Clientele:** Men only
**Transportation:** Taxi 20 minutes from Tegel, 10 minutes from Tempelhof, 30 minutes from Schönefeld airports.
**To Gay Bars:** Next door to men's bars.
**Rooms:** 8 rooms with single or double beds.
**Bathrooms:** All rooms have sinks. 3 toilets & showers are shared by all.
**Meals:** Buffet breakfast: Eggs, cereal, yogurt, smoked salmon, meat, cheese, bread, rolls, orange juice, milk, jam, honey etc.
**Complimentary:** Free city map & boot jack in each room.
**Dates Open:** All year.
**Rates:** DM 130.00-DM 180.00.
**Rsv'tns:** Required, as early as possible.
**Reserve Through:** Call direct.
**Parking:** Adequate easy on-street parking & garage for off-street pay parking.
**In-Room:** Maid service. Some rooms have refrigerator.
**On-Premises:** TV lounge.
**Exercise/Health:** Nearby gym & sauna.
**Swimming:** In lake far away.
**Sunbathing:** In nearby public park.
**Nudity:** Permitted in public park.
**Smoking:** Permitted without restrictions.
**Pets:** Dogs only.
**Handicap Access:** No.
**Children:** Not permitted.
**Languages:** German, English & Danish.

IGTA

# BRUNKEN/ WESTERWALD

## Lichtquelle, Frauenbildungsstätte

**Women ♀**

***Lichtquelle,*** a women's seminar center, is a place for healing, meditation and therapy. Here women can find support on their journey of self-formation and self-discovery. When there are no seminars being held, women can come for an individual retreat. English, French and German speakers will feel comfortable at our seminars, which can involve dancing, music, therapy and many other subjects. They are usually held from Friday to Sunday, but some are longer.

**Address: Hochstr. 11, Brunken 57539 Germany.**
**Tel: (49-2742) 71587.**

**Type:** Healing retreat.
**Clientele:** Women only
**Transportation:** Car is best, pick up provided from train.
**To Gay Bars:** 15 miles (20 km).
**Rooms:** 2 doubles, 2 quads.
**Bathrooms:** 1 big shared bathroom.
**Meals:** Full board.
**Vegetarian:** Serve vegetarian food only (mainly macrobiotic).
**Complimentary:** Juices, mineral water.
**Dates Open:** All year.
**Rates:** DM 55 per person.
**Rsv'tns:** Required.
**Reserve Through:** Please write for reservations.
**Parking:** Adequate, free off-street parking.
**On-Premises:** Meeting rooms.
**Smoking:** Not permitted.
**Pets:** Not permitted.
**Handicap Access:** No.
**Children:** Not permitted.
**Languages:** German, English, French.

# CHARLOTTENBERG

## Frauenlandhaus

**Women ♀**

The ***Frauenlandhaus*** at Charlottenberg is a bed & breakfast guesthouse for women only. There is a large garden and many single rooms are now available in a new building. Workshops are offered here, involving topics such as massage, nutrition, self-defense, Tantra, voice awareness and expression, magic, spirituality, and writing.

**Address: Holzappeler Str 3, Charlottenberg 56379 Germany.**
**Tel. (49-6439) 7531.**

**Type:** Bed & breakfast guesthouse with workshops.
**Clientele:** Women only
**Transportation:** Car or train. Pick up from train.
**To Gay Bars:** 50 miles to Frankfurt, 60 miles to Cologne.
**Rooms:** Large number of rooms available.
**Bathrooms:** All shared.
**Meals:** Buffet breakfast, lunch, dinner.
**Vegetarian:** Always. Only vegetarian food.
**Complimentary:** Coffee & tea any time. No alcohol.
**Dates Open:** All year.
**Rates:** Dormitory DM 17, double DM 22, single DM 27. Each meal DM 14.
**Discounts:** Group rates, children's rates.
**Rsv'tns:** Required.
**Reserve Through:** Call direct.
**Parking:** Free parking.
**In-Room:** Coffee/tea-making facilities, kitchen, video tape library.
**On-Premises:** Meeting rooms, telephone, piano.
**Exercise/Health:** Sauna, massage, yoga, meditation room, bicycles.
**Swimming:** Nearby lake.
**Sunbathing:** On private sun decks or in the garden.
**Nudity:** Permitted in the garden.
**Smoking:** Permitted only in smoking room & in the garden.
**Pets:** Not permitted.
**Handicap Access:** No.
**Children:** Permitted, boys to the age of 12.
**Languages:** German, English & Italian.

# DÜSSELDORF

## Hotel Alt Graz

Gay-Friendly 50/50 ♀♂

### *Our Gay Staff Will Make You Feel at Home*

***Hotel Alt Graz,*** located in the centre of town, is just a short walk to Central Station, several international restaurants, and plenty of shopping. A ten-minute walk from the hotel is the Altstadt, which is known as the longest bar in the world, with its hundreds of bars, discos, and restaurants. Düsseldorf offers sightseers many attractions. Visit sea lions, piranhas, penguins and crocodiles at the Aqua Zoo, spend a day at the Kunsthalle art museum or the Goethe museum, or cheer on the ice hockey team, which has won five of the last six playoffs. For your convenience, we have installed a new lift and each of our rooms has a direct-dial telephone and cable TV. Our complimentary English breakfast will get you off to a good start each morning. Please keep in mind that we are usually booked during every exhibition, so it is imperative that you make your reservations early.

**Address: Klosterstrasse 132, Düsseldorf 40211 Germany.
Tel: (49-211) 36 40 28, Fax: (49-211) 36 95 77.**

**Type:** Bed & breakfast hotel.
**Clientele:** 50% hetero & 50% gay & lesbian clientele
**To Gay Bars:** 5-minute walk to gay/lesbian bars.
**Rooms:** 11 singles, 11 doubles & 2 triples with single & matrimonial beds.
**Bathrooms:** 10 private, others share.
**Meals:** Expanded continental breakfast.
**Dates Open:** All year.
**Rates:** Single DM 75-DM 145, double/twin DM 120-DM 245, 3-beds DM 155-DM 275.
**Credit Cards:** MC, VISA, Amex, Diners, Eurocard.
**Rsv'tns:** Required.
**Reserve Through:** Travel agent or call direct.
**Parking:** On-street parking.
**In-Room:** Telephone, color TV, maid service.
**Smoking:** Permitted without restrictions.
**Pets:** Not permitted.
**Languages:** German, English.

# HAMBURG

## Künstler-Pension Sarah Petersen

Gay/Lesbian ♀♂

### *The Artist Pension*

Located directly in the center of the beautiful seaport city of Hamburg, ***Künstler-Pension Sarah Petersen*** is keeping with the tradition of the famous European artist pensions of the twenties and thirties. Writers, actors, musicians, fashion designers and all people who like the special atmosphere of a small familiar hotel are part of the good spirit our little guesthouse has to offer. Another reason to stay here is the rare early 19th century architecture and the creative furnishings. Our concept: A minimum of hotel and a maximum of private house interior. The ***Künstler-Pension Sarah Petersen*** is

*continued next page*

surrounded by museums, coffee houses, small stores, restaurants and gay bars. A five-minute walk and you are at the big city lake Alster, with parks and open-air cafes. In December, 1996 we will move to Lange Reihe 88, on the same sunny side of the street just 200 metres from our current location.

**Address: Lange Reihe 50, (moving December '96 to Lange Reihe 88), Hamburg 20099 Germany.**
**Tel: (49-40) 24 98 26 (Tel/Fax).**

**Type:** Guesthouse with small picturesque hotel bar.
**Clientele:** Good mix of gay men & women with 30% straight clientele
**Transportation:** Airport bus to Hauptbahnhof.
**To Gay Bars:** 1/2 block or 4 minutes by foot.
**Rooms:** 6 rooms.
**Bathrooms:** 6 private sinks & 2 shared baths. In-room shower boxes may be installed for 1997.
**Meals:** Expanded (meatless) continental breakfast.
**Vegetarian:** Breakfast. Several restaurants & coffeehouses nearby serve vegetarian food.
**Complimentary:** Tea, coffee, juices, beer, wine & champagne.
**Dates Open:** All year.
**High Season:** July-Sept.
**Rates:** Single DM 79.00, double DM 98.00, triple DM 140.00, apartment DM 180.00.
**Credit Cards:** Eurocard.
**Rsv'tns:** Required with deposit.
**Reserve Through:** Call direct or write.
**Parking:** Free on-street parking, parking house around the corner.
**In-Room:** B&W & color TV, room service.
**On-Premises:** House bar for guests & friends.
**Swimming:** 10-minute walk to indoor public pool.
**Sunbathing:** 5 minutes to Lake Alster.
**Smoking:** Permitted without restrictions.
**Pets:** Cats only.
**Handicap Access:** No.
**Children:** Permitted.
**Languages:** German & English.

# OSTFRIESLAND

## Frauenferienhof Ostfriesland

Women ♀

### *Ride Horses on the Moors... Indulge in a Massage... Dream by the Fireplace...*

On the windswept plains not far from the North Sea, we have established a place for women, for us and for our animals, and a place for you to enjoy an unusual vacation amongst other women from many places. ***Frauenferienhof Ostfriesland*** means "A place for women to vacation in Ostfriesland." You can have as active or as meditative a vacation as you like. You can bicycle or ride Icelandic horses over the lowlands and through the moors, meadows and woods. Or you can relax under the broad skies of Ostfriesland and repose in our garden, relax in the sauna or just dream by the fireplace. When you feel like it, you can join other women in lively conversation, games or dancing, or indulge yourself in a Reflexology treatment or massage. We also offer courses and programs, whose subjects change from year to year. We provide food which is mainly organically grown. As a rule, guests do their own cooking.

**Address: Zum Lengener Meer 2, Friedeburg-Bentstreek 26446 Germany.**
**Tel: (49-4956) 4956 (Tel/Fax).**

**Type:** Women's retreat with courses & program.
**Clientele:** Women only
**Transportation:** Pick up from bus, train.
**Rooms:** 3 doubles, 2 triples, 1 single.
**Bathrooms:** 2 shared.
**Meals:** Meals included.
**Vegetarian:** Only vegetarian.
**Dates Open:** All year.
**Rates:** DM 50 per day (meals included), not including course.
**Rsv'tns:** Required.
**On-Premises:** Meeting rooms.
**Exercise/Health:** Sauna.
**Swimming:** At nearby lake.
**Nudity:** Permitted in the garden.
**Smoking:** Permitted in the designated living room only.
**Pets:** Not permitted.
**Handicap Access:** Yes.
**Children:** Permitted, boys under 10 years old only.
**Languages:** German, English.

# SIMMELSDORF

## Hotel Sonnenhof

Men ♂

### *Fantastic Days and Hot Nights for Gay Men*

***Hotel Sonnenhof*** is the largest exclusively gay vacation and weekend getaway in Germany. Here, within our house and grounds, like-minded gay men relax in an atmosphere both uninhibited and discreet. Nudism? No problem! In this clothing-optional environment, each person can enjoy the sun – dressed or undressed – as he pleases.

You'll find us north of Munich, about midway between Nürnberg and Bayreuth. The 3-story main house has common rooms where guests dine and socialize, a late-night disco bar, as well as a TV lounge with video and games. Guest rooms are well-furnished, some with private bath and balconies. Our round swimming pool (8-meter in diameter) has an area of 650 square meters and is unequaled in the German gay scene. In winter, cross-country and downhill skiing are popular. Nearby castles and limestone caves make for interesting side trips at all times of the year. Canoeing, riding and tennis are also available.

Gay events held at ***Hotel Sonnenhof*** throughout the year include showtime with Miss Mara, a drag extravaganza, the election of Mr. Sonnenhof, and various drag and strip show events.

**Address: Ittling 36, Simmelsdorf 91245 Germany.**
**Tel: (49-9155) 823, Fax: (49-9155) 7278.**
**E-mail: SONNENHOF.HOTEL@t-online.de.**
**http://ourworld.compuserve.com/homepages/GAY_HOTEL/.**

**Type:** Hotel with disco/bar.
**Clientele:** Men only
**Transportation:** Car is best. Pick up from train station. (Simmelsdorf free, Lanf/Peg DM 30,00.)
**To Gay Bars:** 45 miles or a 40-minute drive.
**Rooms:** 20 rooms & 1 apartment with single or double beds.
**Bathrooms:** Private: 3 shower/toilet, 17 sink only.
**Meals:** Buffet breakfast, dinner.
**Complimentary:** Tea, coffee, cake, ice, cocktails & snacks.
**Dates Open:** Closed in January. Call for details.
**High Season:** May-September, December.
**Rates:** Single DM 65,00 to DM 70,00. Double DM 130,00 to DM 170,00.
**Discounts:** Varies per season. Please inquire.
**Rsv'tns:** Required.
**Reserve Through:** Call direct.
**Minimum Stay:** Single day is DM 10,00 more per person.
**Parking:** Free off-street parking.
**On-Premises:** TV lounge & reading room.
**Exercise/Health:** Sauna. Skiing nearby.
**Swimming:** Pool on premises.
**Sunbathing:** At poolside.
**Nudity:** Permitted poolside.
**Smoking:** Not permitted.
**Pets:** Permitted.
**Handicap Access:** No.
**Children:** Not especially welcome.
**Languages:** German, English.

# TIEFENBACH

## Frauenferienhaus Tiefenbach/Silbersee

**Women ♀**

***Frauenferienhaus Tiefenbach/Silbersee*** combines a rural vacation retreat and conference center for women in the beautiful countryside of Germany near the border of the Czech Republic. The geography of the area makes it ideal for a variety of outdoor activities, from hiking and swimming in summer to skiing in the winter. We welcome lesbian and straight women who travel by themselves, in couples or in groups. Feminist psychodrama groups are possible.

**Address: Hammer 22, Tiefenbach 93464 Germany. Tel: (49-9673) 499.**

**Type:** Retreat with classes available.
**Clientele:** Women only
**Transportation:** Car, train or bus.
**Rooms:** 1 single, 4 doubles & 1 triple with single or double beds.
**Bathrooms:** 1 en suite, 3 shared.
**Vegetarian:** Available at extra cost.
**Dates Open:** All year.
**High Season:** December, January, July & August.
**Rates:** DM 25.00 per woman per night. DM 65.00 per woman per night includes vegetarian meals.
**Rsv'tns:** Required.
**Reserve Through:** Call direct.
**Parking:** Ample on-street parking.
**On-Premises:** Meeting rooms & garden.
**Exercise/Health:** Bicycles, horseback riding, nearby sauna & bath hall.
**Swimming:** Lake on premises.
**Sunbathing:** On lake beach & on the lawn.
**Smoking:** Not permitted.
**Pets:** Not permitted.
**Handicap Access:** Partially.
**Children:** Not especially welcome.
**Languages:** German, English.

# ZÜLPICH-LÖVENICH

## Frauenbildungshaus Zülpich-Lövenich

**Women ♀**

The ***Frauenbildungshaus Zülpich-Lövenich*** is a very beautiful, rebuilt old farmhouse of wooden construction, with a large, quiet garden. This is a place for women to meet and to take various classes. The women stay for a week or weekend to learn together, live together, or do whatever together. Our classes include dancing, voice awareness, and introduction to healing methods such as Shiatsu, as well as computer courses. If there is room after course visitors have signed up, we take women who wish to stay for just a holiday, just to be lazy, go swimming in the nearby lake, take a bicycle ride, or visit the prehistoric places nearby and follow the traces of our ancestresses.

**Address: Prälat-Franken-Str. 13, Zülpich-Lövenich 53909 Germany. Tel: (49-2252) 6577.**

**Type:** Retreat with classes available.
**Clientele:** Women only
**Transportation:** Car is best.
**To Gay Bars:** 60 km or 30 minutes by car.
**Rooms:** 1 apartment with single & double beds.
**Bathrooms:** 1 private shower/toilet, 6 shared shower/toilets.
**Meals:** We supply groceries, guests do cooking.
**Vegetarian:** Always.
**Dates Open:** All year.
**Rates:** DM 50.00-DM 65.00 per woman per night, food included.
**Discounts:** Social discounts for the classes. (3 for each class possible.)
**Rsv'tns:** Required.
**Reserve Through:** Call direct.
**Parking:** Adequate free on-street parking.
**On-Premises:** Meeting rooms.
**Exercise/Health:** Bicycles.
**Swimming:** At nearby lake.
**Sunbathing:** In the garden.
**Nudity:** In the garden.
**Smoking:** Not permitted in the house.
**Pets:** Not permitted.
**Handicap Access:** Yes.
**Children:** Permitted. Boys allowed only to age 10.
**Languages:** German & English.

# GREECE

## MYKONOS

### Hotel Elysium

Q-NET Gay/Lesbian ♀♂

*The Most IN Island in the Mediterranean*

You are captivated at first glance by the ever-changing patterns of blue and white on the walls, the narrow streets and the wonderful, sandy beaches, with waters in all shades of blue. Such intensive contrasts in colour, and such harmonious shapes, can be found on no other island. Mykonos is a place where sun, sea and entertainment come together in a superb, natural setting, to create the perfect atmosphere for your holiday. And, you'll find ***Hotel Elysium*** the perfect environment in which to enjoy it.

The hotel was built in a traditional Mykonian architectural style in 1989 and offers panoramic views of Mykonos Old Town and the ocean. Each of the hotel's 42 rooms and three suites have ceiling fans, hairdryers, direct-dial phones, stereo music, refrigerator, safe box and color satellite TV. For relaxation and fitness there is a swimming pool, Jacuzzi, and a fully-equipped fitness center with sauna. The breakfast is American Buffet. Other features of ***Hotel Elysium*** include a snack-bar, living room, TV lounge, pool bar, private parking, guest laundry facilities and beach towels. All facilities into ***Hotel Elysium*** are free of charge.

**Address: School of Fine Arts, Mykonos Town, Mykonos 84600 Greece.**
**Tel: (30-289) 23952, 24210, 24684, Fax: (30-289) 23747.**

**Type:** Hotel with restaurant & bar.
**Clientele:** Mostly gay with some straight clientele
**Transportation:** Car is best, free hotel bus pick up from airport or port.
**To Gay Bars:** 2 minute walk.
**Rooms:** 43 rooms & 3 apartments with single, double or king beds.
**Bathrooms:** All private.
**Meals:** American buffet breakfast.
**Complimentary:** Juices.
**Dates Open:** April to November.
**High Season:** July 1 through September 15.
**Rates:** Doubles 26,000-34,000 drachmas, suites 43,000-48,000 drachmas, depending on season.
**Discounts:** 5% for stays of a week or more.
**Credit Cards:** VISA, Amex, Diners & Eurocard.
**Rsv'tns:** Required.
**Reserve Through:** Travel agent or call direct.
**Parking:** Free off-street parking.
**In-Room:** Color TV, telephone, hair dryer, refrigerator, maid & laundry service.
**On-Premises:** TV lounge, meeting rooms.
**Exercise/Health:** Jacuzzi, sauna, gym, weights.
**Swimming:** Pool on premises, nearby ocean beach.
**Sunbathing:** At poolside.
**Nudity:** Permitted poolside.
**Smoking:** Permitted.
**Pets:** Permitted.
**Children:** Not permitted.
**Languages:** Greek, English, French, Italian & Spanish.

# ICELAND

## REYKJAVIK

### Room With a View

Gay/Lesbian ♀♂

## *Panoramic Rooftop Apartments in Iceland*

Haven't you always wanted to visit Iceland and stay for a few days – or perhaps a few weeks? If so, make your stay a memorable one and rent an apartment in downtown Reykjavík. Ideal for long stays, ***Room With a View's*** luxurious, fully furnished apartments have separate bedroom, TV, stereo equipment, laundry facilities, kitchen, and Jacuzzi. Inspiring panoramic views of the city, sea, mountains and midnight sun can be seen from each apartment's large balcony. Downstairs we have added a coffee shop which is open daily 9am-10pm.

**Address: Laugavegur 18, 6th floor, Reykjavik 101 Iceland.**
**Tel: (354) 552 7262 (Tel/Fax), E-mail (mark all e-mail with name Arni Einarsson): mm@centrum.is.**

**Type:** Rental apartments with bookshop & coffee shop on premises.
**Clientele:** Mostly gay & lesbian with some hetero clientele
**Transportation:** Bus from airport to town terminal, then bus, taxi or walking.
**To Gay Bars:** Next door to apartments.
**Rooms:** Two 1-bedroom apartments with queen beds, sleep 1-4 persons.
**Bathrooms:** Private bath/shower/toilets.
**Dates Open:** All year.
**High Season:** May-August.
**Rates:** US $63.
**Discounts:** Please inquire.
**Credit Cards:** MC, VISA, Amex, Eurocard.
**Rsv'tns:** Recommended.
**Reserve Through:** Travel agent or call direct.
**Minimum Stay:** 3 days.
**Parking:** Ample on-street parking.
**In-Room:** Fully furnished, color TV, kitchen, coffee/tea-making facilities, refrigerator, laundry facilities.
**On-Premises:** Laundry facilities, video tape library.
**Exercise/Health:** Jacuzzi, steam.
**Swimming:** Nearby pool.
**Sunbathing:** On roof.
**Nudity:** Permitted on roof.
**Smoking:** Permitted on balcony.
**Pets:** Not permitted.
**Handicap Access:** There is an elevator.
**Children:** Welcome.
**Languages:** Icelandic, English, Danish.
**Your Host:** Arni.

# IRELAND

## CORK

### Amazonia

Women ♀

## *The Welcome of Amazonia and Ireland Make an Unforgettable Vacation*

From the hilltop windows of ***Amazonia*** you can look upon the beautiful, rolling, green hills of Ireland and the Atlantic Ocean. The beach is at the bottom of the hill and is very safe for swimming and sports. The walks to the nearby pubs afford marvelous views of the ocean rolling in along the rocky coastline. We have bikes, canoes, body boards, tennis racquets and golf clubs free for the guests' use and we can arrange horseback riding for you. Breakfast, which is either vegetarian or a full Irish fry, is served from 9:00 until 12:00 and you can eat as much or as little as you like! There is free tea and coffee all day. We prepare excellent vegetarian evening meals (optional) with lots of homemade wine and beer. We want you to feel at home and enjoy our Irish hospitality.

**Address: Coast Road, Fountainstown, Myrtleville, Cork Ireland. Tel: (353-21) 831 115.**

**Type:** Bed & breakfast guesthouse with campsites.
**Clientele:** Women only
**Transportation:** Car or bus from Cork city. Pick up from arrival point in Cork city (airport, ferry dock) £5.00.
**To Gay Bars:** 10 miles or 30 minutes by car.
**Rooms:** 2 log cabins, 3 rooms with single, twin or queen beds & a house tent with double bed.
**Bathrooms:** Private & shared.
**Campsites:** 3 tent sites with complete use of facilities & breakfast in the main house.
**Meals:** Full breakfast served until 12:00. Optional vegetarian evening meal, including home-made wine & beer, for £12 extra.
**Vegetarian:** As breakfast option or excellent evening meal.
**Complimentary:** Tea or coffee all day.
**Dates Open:** All year except Christmas.
**High Season:** May-Sep.
**Rates:** Cabins & rooms £14-£18 per woman, house tent £10/woman. Camping £4 per tent + £6 per woman (includes breakfast & use of house).
**Discounts:** 50% off for children under 10 years.
**Rsv'tns:** Required during high season.
**Reserve Through:** Call direct.
**Parking:** Ample off-street free parking.
**In-Room:** B&W TV, coffee/tea-making facilities & room service.
**On-Premises:** TV lounge, library & laundry service.
**Exercise/Health:** Kayaks, bicycles, wind surfers, snorkeling equipment. Nearby tennis club, horse riding arranged.
**Swimming:** In nearby ocean or river.
**Sunbathing:** On the patio or in the garden.
**Nudity:** Permitted in the garden.
**Smoking:** Limited to garden.
**Pets:** Permitted. We have dogs & cats.
**Handicap Access:** Yes. Bungalow allows reasonable wheelchair access.
**Children:** Welcomed.
**Languages:** English, German, French & Italian.
**Your Host:** Penny & Aine.

# DUBLIN

## Dunsany Bed & Breakfast

Gay-Friendly 50/50 ♀♂

### *A Friendly Welcome is Assured – Visit Once and You'll Want to Return*

***Dunsany Bed & Breakfast*** assures you of a warm Irish welcome. This delightful Victorian house with its period features has been lovingly maintained by its owners. A haven in a bustling city, the house is situated in a quiet cul-de-sac with a bowling green to the front and fields behind, truly a country-like setting. We offer you a full Irish breakfast (or a vegetarian version, if you prefer) to sustain you on your travels, and tea and coffee are available all day. Dublin city has many attractions for the visitor, including cultural, historical and, of course, social! The city and its sights are easily accessible by bus, car, taxi, or on foot. Dublin is also renowned for easy access to sea, mountains and countryside – well worth a visit!

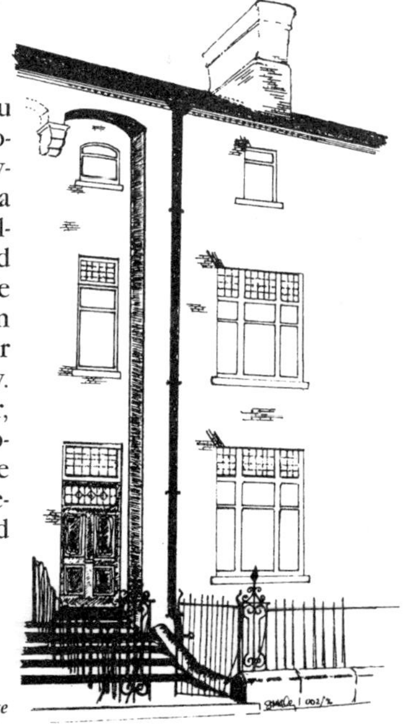

**Address: 7 Gracepark Gardens, Drumcondra, Dublin 9 Ireland. Tel: (353-1) 857 1362, Mobile: (353-88) 695 051.**

*continued next page*

**Type:** Bed & breakfast.
**Clientele:** 50% gay & lesbian & 50% hetero clientele
**Transportation:** Airport bus 41 to Drumcondra, or taxi from airport (about £8), excellent bus service from city centre.
**To Gay Bars:** 2 miles, a 25 min. walk, a 10 minute drive.
**Rooms:** 3 rooms with single or double beds.
**Bathrooms:** Private: 1 shower/toilet, Shared: 1 shower only, 1 WC only.
**Meals:** Full Irish breakfast.
**Vegetarian:** Vegetarian breakfast available. Vegetarians catered for nearby (5 min walk) or in city centre (2 miles).
**Complimentary:** Tea & coffee.
**Dates Open:** All year. Closed Dec 24-26.
**High Season:** June-August.
**Rates:** £20-£25 per person, no single supplement.
**Discounts:** For stays of 3 nights or more.
**Rsv'tns:** Required.
**Reserve Through:** Call direct.
**Parking:** Ample free on-street parking.
**On-Premises:** TV lounge.
**Smoking:** Permitted in TV lounge only.
**Pets:** Permitted.
**Handicap Access:** No.
**Children:** Permitted.
**Languages:** English, French.
**Your Host:** Anne & Maureen.

## Fairfield Lodge

**Gay/Lesbian ♀♂**

Our luxury double studio apartment, ***Fairfield Lodge,*** is set in a glorious award-winning garden and is designed to provide all of the peace and tranquility that you would expect in Ireland. It is within easy reach of our bustling city, only 15 minutes by car from Dublin's city centre. For your convenience, there is also a bus stop outside the gate which takes you into Dublin every seven minutes. The studio is newly decorated and furnished to the highest standards. It is totally self-contained with secured parking.

**Address: Monkstown Ave, Monkstown County, Dublin Ireland.**
**Tel: (353-1) 280 3912 (Tel/Fax). E-mail: JSB@Indigo.ie**

**Type:** Studio apartment for 2 with own entrance.
**Clientele:** Gay & lesbian
**Transportation:** Bus stop outside the gate, but car is handy. Pick up from airport & train £10.
**To Gay Bars:** 20 min drive into city center.
**Rooms:** 1 studio apartment with double bed.
**Bathrooms:** Private.
**Meals:** Breakfast food items supplied in studio's kitchen.
**Complimentary:** Tea & coffee.
**Dates Open:** All year.
**High Season:** May-Sept.
**Rates:** £40 per night, but vary depending on no. of nights. Single supplement on request.
**Discounts:** Inquire during off season (Oct-end of April).
**Rsv'tns:** Required.
**Reserve Through:** Travel agent or call direct.
**Parking:** Adequate free off-street parking, locked up at night.
**In-Room:** Color TV, VCR on request, telephone, refrigerator, kitchen, maid service, coffee & tea-making facilities.
**Sunbathing:** In garden, weather permitting.
**Smoking:** Permitted.
**Pets:** Not permitted.
**Handicap Access:** No.
**Children:** No.
**Languages:** English, French, German, Italian.
**Your Host:** John.

# Frankies Guesthouse

Q-NET Gay/Lesbian ♂

## *Céad Mile Fáilte – A Million Thanks*

Established in 1989 in a mews-style building over 100 years old, ***Frankies*** offers year-round accommodations exclusively for gays. Dublin has an expanding gay scene, which offers a variety of venues for those looking for adventure, and ***Frankies*** is located close to the bars, clubs and saunas. Our beautiful south-facing roof terrace & sun deck is surrounded with tropical potted plants and is a good place to relax after a day of sightseeing. We have recently added a sauna and a bar on premises for our guests to enjoy. Dublin is a capital city of many charms and delights. From magnificent Dublin Castle and the supreme architecture of the city's cathedrals, to Phoenix Park (the largest enclosed park in Europe), the choice is endless.

Travellers wishing to tour outside Dublin will find breathtaking scenery along the coast road which leads to sandy beaches and sand dunes, well worth the trip for those who enjoy the smell of the sea and a sense of freedom. You'll be glad you visited Ireland, a country renowned for its hospitality and friendliness.

In early 1997 we will be opening a place in Athens, Greece. Please contact us here in Dublin for more details.

**Address: 8 Camden Place, Dublin 2 Ireland.**
**Tel: Reservations: (353-1) 478 3087 (Tel/Fax) or (353-1) 475 2182.**

**Type:** Guesthouse with bar.
**Clientele:** Mostly men with women welcome
**Transportation:** Airport bus to city bus sta., taxi from bus sta. approx £3. Taxi from airport approx £10.
**To Gay Bars:** 8 minutes walking.
**Rooms:** 12 rooms with single or double beds & an apartment in town.
**Bathrooms:** 5 en suite. Shared: 2 bath/shower/toilets, 1 WC. All have hand wash basin.
**Meals:** Full Irish breakfast.
**Vegetarian:** Available on request.
**Complimentary:** Tea & coffee.
**Dates Open:** All year.
**High Season:** July, August, & September.
**Rates:** Singles from £18.00-£27.50. Doubles from £44.00-£55.00.
**Discounts:** On extended stays.
**Credit Cards:** MC, Visa, Amex & Eurocard.
**Rsv'tns:** Required.
**Reserve Through:** Call direct.
**Parking:** Ample, free on-street parking.
**In-Room:** Color TV & maid service.
**On-Premises:** TV lounge.
**Exercise/Health:** Sauna.
**Sunbathing:** On the roof terrace.
**Smoking:** Permitted without restrictions.
**Pets:** Not permitted. We have our own dogs.
**Handicap Access:** Yes, some ground floor rooms.
**Children:** Not permitted.
**Languages:** English, Chinese & Malay.
**Your Host:** Joe & Frankie.

# TINAHELY

## Stoneybroke House

**Gay/Lesbian ♀♂**

### *Experience the Garden of Ireland in an Irish Country Home*

***Stoneybroke House*** is an Irish Country House in County Wicklow, the Garden of Ireland, situated 1-1/2 miles from the historic town of Tinahely, and approximately 60 miles south of Dublin. The original house is more than 200 years old and has recently been extended and refurbished. It enjoys spectacular views across the local river and on across the valley and surrounding hills.

Emphasis is on your comfort and relaxation coupled with high-quality food, lovingly prepared in our own kitchen. Our menu features eight entrees, including Wicklow leg of lamb butterfly-style and marinated in olive oil, garlic, rosemary and lemon juice; Wicklow sirloin steak served with a mushroom and red wine sauce; Chicken breast a la Stoneybroke with a whole grain mustard, white wine & cream sauce, garnished and stuffed with olives; Salmon steak with a traditional Hollandaise sauce; and for vegetarians, a special vegetable Kiev.

We look forward to your visit. You are assured a warm welcome and, upon your departure, we hope that you leave us as new-found friends.

**Address: Ballinamanogue, Tinahely, Co. Wicklow Ireland.**
**Tel: (353-402) 38236.**

**Type:** Inn with restaurant & wine bar.
**Clientele:** Gay & lesbian. Good mix of men & women
**Transportation:** Car is best.
**To Gay Bars:** Dublin airport limousine. Limousine hire service available. Pick up £70 one way.
**Rooms:** 4 rooms with single or double beds.
**Bathrooms:** 2 private with bath or shower, others share.
**Meals:** Full breakfast, dinner.
**Vegetarian:** Available at time of booking, if requested.
**Complimentary:** Tea & coffee on arrival. Biscuits in room.
**Dates Open:** All year.
**High Season:** June-September.
**Rates:** £35-£50.
**Discounts:** 1 night free in 7. Weekend & mid-week discount packages.
**Credit Cards:** MC, Visa, Amex, Eurocard.
**Rsv'tns:** Required.
**Reserve Through:** Call direct.
**Minimum Stay:** 2 nights.
**Parking:** Ample free off-street parking.
**In-Room:** Colour TV, coffee & tea-making facilities, hair dryer, clock radio, bathrobes, room, maid & laundry service.
**On-Premises:** TV lounge, restaurant & wine bar.
**Sunbathing:** On private & common sun decks, on patio, in gardens.
**Nudity:** Permitted in house.
**Smoking:** No restrictions. Non-smoking rooms available.
**Pets:** Not permitted.
**Handicap Access:** No
**Children:** No.
**Languages:** English.
**Your Host:** Richard & Liam.

# ITALY

## ACQUI TERME

### La Filanda Guesthouse

Q-NET Women ♀

## *A Woman's Cultural Center and Guesthouse*

This romantic Italian villa, surrounded by a huge wild garden, imposing old trees, and the lovely hills of the Piemonte region, was created by female artists. The ancient city of Acqui Terme, famous for its thermal baths and traffic-free center, is within walking distance, while Genova, Milan and the Mediterranean Sea are 40 miles away (a one-hour drive). Piemonte is well-known for its superb cuisine and high-class wines, such as Barolo and Barbaresco – a gourmet's delight! At ***La Filanda*** we organize a yearly workshop program along diverse cultural lines. We hope to see you soon.

**Address: Reg. Montagnola No. 4, Acqui Terme 15011 Italy.**
**Tel: (39-144) 32 39 56 (Tel/Fax).**

**Type:** Guesthouse & cultural center with music room & workshops.
**Clientele:** Women only
**Transportation:** Train from Genova to Acqui Terme (1 hour), then taxi. Pick up from train 10,000 lire.
**To Gay Bars:** 40 miles, 1-hour drive to Genova, Milan or Turin gay bars.
**Rooms:** 7 rooms with single or double beds.
**Bathrooms:** Shared: 2 bath/shower/toilets, 2 showers only, 2 WCs only.
**Vegetarian:** Restaurants in town have vegetarian dishes.
**Dates Open:** March-October. Open in winter during special periods, on request.
**High Season:** June-Sep.
**Rates:** Double 45,000 LI, single 60,000 LI (35 Sfr-55 Sfr).
**Discounts:** Special group rates.
**Rsv'tns:** Required.
**Reserve Through:** Call direct.
**Parking:** Free parking.
**On-Premises:** 2 fully equipped kitchens, living rooms, video library, books, music/cassettes.
**Exercise/Health:** Health center nearby with sauna & massage.
**Swimming:** Pool & river nearby.
**Sunbathing:** In garden & on terrace.
**Nudity:** Permitted in garden.
**Smoking:** Permitted everywhere.
**Pets:** Permitted if well-behaved.
**Handicap Access:** No.
**Children:** Welcome. Boy children welcome up to 10 years of age.
**Languages:** Italian, German, English, French.
**Your Host:** Regula, Sibylla.

# FIRENZE (FLORENCE)

## Morandi alla Crocetta

Gay-Friendly ♀♂

### *The Special Feeling of a Genteel Tuscan Home*

In the quiet, distinguished atmosphere of a former convent, ***Morandi alla Crocetta*** follows an ancient tradition of hospitality. Its location is close to every point of artistic and cultural interest, such as the Statue of David, the Archaeological Museum and the Academy of Fine Arts. This is a hotel for those seeking a small and comfortable place filled with character and charm, in the city centre and yet away from the typical tourist establishments.

**Address: Via Laura 50, Firenze 50121 Italy.**
**Tel: (39-55) 2344747, Fax: (39-55) 2480954,**
**E-mail: Hotel.Morandi@dada.it. www.dada.it/Hotel.Morandi.**

**Type:** Guesthouse.
**Clientele:** Mostly straight clientele with a gay & lesbian following
**Transportation:** Taxi from airport US $15. From train station $7.00.
**To Gay Bars:** 2 blocks to gay/lesbian bars.
**Rooms:** 10 rooms.
**Bathrooms:** All private.
**Meals:** Continental breakfast 18.000 Lire per person.
**Dates Open:** All year.
**High Season:** Easter, Apr-May, Sept-Oct.
**Rates:** 110.000-200.000 Lire.
**Credit Cards:** MC, VISA, Amex, Diners, Access, Eurocard.
**Rsv'tns:** Recommended. Fax or phone O.K.
**Reserve Through:** Call direct.
**Parking:** Limited on-street parking.
**In-Room:** Maid & room service, color satellite TV, telephone, AC, mini-bar refrigerator & laundry service.
**Exercise/Health:** Nearby gym & weights.
**Smoking:** Permitted without restrictions.
**Pets:** Permitted if small and well-behaved.
**Handicap Access:** No.
**Children:** Permitted.
**Languages:** Italian, English, & limited French & German.

# ISOLA D'ELBA

## Casa Scala

Q-NET Women ♀

### *An Italian Home on a Picturesque Island*

Picture Elba Island, covered with lush vegetation such as wild rosemary, anise, blackberries, grapes (small, family-owned vineyards), cactus, and trees as varied as apricot, lemon, almond, pine, fir, eucalyptus, cypress, and palm. Amidst this splendor is ***Casa Scala.*** This small, Italian house with four apartments and two sun terraces is surrounded by a garden with trees and flowers and has a view of some of the many tree-covered hills. The nearby hills are a brilliant red, due to iron-rich land. Abandoned mine sites are cluttered with stones and rocks waiting to be scooped up by hand. ***Casa Scala*** is just a few minutes by bike (available for the duration of your stay for a small fee) from one of the sandy beaches. Boating excursions to some of the caverns (accessible only by sea) are also available.

**Address: Loc. Filetto No 9, Marina di Campo, Isola d'Elba 57034 Italy.**
**Tel: (39-565) 977 777, Fax: (39-565) 977 770.**

**Type:** Cottage with workshops available.
**Clientele:** Women only
**Transportation:** Car is best or train from Florence to Elba, pick up from bus station Marina di Campo.
**Rooms:** 4 apartments with single beds.
**Bathrooms:** Each apartment has its own bath.
**Meals:** Continental breakfast with workshop.
**Dates Open:** March-October.
**High Season:** July-August.
**Rates:** DM 1,000 for two-week workshop (includes accommodations & breakfast), or DM 35-DM 40 per

night (35,000-40,000 Lire).
**Credit Cards:** Eurocheck.
**Rsv'tns:** Required.
**Reserve Through:** Call direct.
**Minimum Stay:** One week in general. Single days for women from overseas.
**Parking:** Adequate free off-street parking.
**In-Room:** VCR, video tape library, kitchen, refrigerator, coffee & tea-making facilities.
**On-Premises:** Meeting rooms, garden.
**Swimming:** Nearby ocean beach.
**Sunbathing:** In the garden, on the beach.
**Nudity:** Permitted in the garden.
**Smoking:** Permitted.
**Pets:** Not permitted.
**Handicap Access:** No.
**Children:** Boys not permitted after 10 years of age.
**Languages:** German, Italian, English.
**Your Host:** Marianne & Elvira.

# ROMA (ROME)

## Hotel Scalinata di Spagna

Gay-Friendly ♀♂

***Hotel Scalinata di Spagna*** has one of the best possible locations, right in the center of Rome and at the top of the famous Spanish Steps. At the foot of the steps is American Express's central office and in the surrounding streets, some of the most famous stores and finest restaurants in the world. Each room has private bath, air conditioning, telephone, security box, and a TV. Breakfast is served on the terrace overlooking all of Rome. Parking is nearby.

**Address: Piazza Trinità dei Monti 17, Roma 00187 Italy.**
**Tel: Bookings: (39-6) 679 3006 or 699 40896, Fax: (39-6) 699 40598.**

**Type:** Bed & breakfast with roof garden.
**Clientele:** Mostly straight clientele with a 20%-30% gay/lesbian following
**Transportation:** Taxi or Metro to Piazza di Spagna.
**To Gay Bars:** 5-minute walk to gay bar.
**Rooms:** 2 singles, 12 doubles, 3 triples.
**Bathrooms:** All private.
**Meals:** Expanded continental breakfast.
**Complimentary:** Tea, coffee, juices, candy on pillow.
**Dates Open:** All year.
**High Season:** June-October, except August.
**Rates:** Single Ll 250,000-Ll 350,000, double Ll 300,000-Ll 380,000.
**Credit Cards:** MC, Visa, Amex.
**Rsv'tns:** Required, two months in advance or at last moment.
**Reserve Through:** Call direct.
**Parking:** 35,000 Ll/day or on street, a 5-minute walk.
**In-Room:** Mini bar, radio, AC, TV, telephone, safe deposit box, and maid, room & laundry service.
**On-Premises:** TV lounge, public telephone.
**Exercise/Health:** Convenient to Borghese Garden for jogging. Steam, sauna, Jacuzzi, gym, 5 min away at Villa Borghese.
**Swimming:** Ocean beaches 20 miles by train.
**Sunbathing:** On beach or roof deck.
**Smoking:** Permitted without restrictions.
**Pets:** Permitted.
**Handicap Access:** Yes.
**Children:** Permitted.
**Languages:** Italian, English, Spanish, French, German.

# TAORMINA

## Hotel Villa Schuler

Gay-Friendly ♀♂

### *History & Tradition, Comfort & Romance*

Family-owned ***Hotel Villa Schuler*** was converted from a Sicilian villa to a hotel in 1905. In recent years the hotel has been extensively refurbished, emphasizing its original elegance, charm and atmosphere. Superbly situated above the Ionian Sea, its unique location offers stupendous views of snow-capped Mount Etna and the Bay of Naxos. Its central position, next to the delightful Botanical Gardens and tennis courts, is just 2 minutes from Taormina's famous traffic-free Corso Umberto. The ancient Greco-Roman theater and the cable-car to the beaches are just a 10-minute walk away.

The hotel is surrounded by its own extensive, shady, terraced gardens, where the fragrance of jasmine and bougainvillaea blossoms blend soothingly, enhancing the comfortable, romantic surroundings. Rooms are spacious, each with private bath/shower, WC, orthopaedic beds and mattresses, direct-dial telephone and electronic safe. Most have balcony/terrace or loggia and seaview. Other amenities include a roof terrace solarium, the palm terrace pavilion, dining and TV rooms (color satellite), small library, piano, 24-hour bar and room service, laundry, parking, garages and central heating. You have the choice of having breakfast served in your room, in the dining room or on the panoramic palm terrace overlooking the entire coastline. Tennis courts nearby. Regular shuttle-service to the beaches (May-Oct). Multilingual staff.

**Address: Via Roma 17, Taormina/Sicily 98039 Italy. Tel: (39) 942 23481, Fax: (39) 942 23522. E-mail: schuler@cys.it. http://www.cys.it/schuler.**

**Type:** Bed & breakfast hotel & bar.
**Clientele:** Mainly hetero clientele with a gay & lesbian following
**Transportation:** Airport bus to Taormina, or pick up from airport by arrangement LIT 95.000, taxi from train LIT 20.000.
**To Gay Bars:** 5-minute walk.
**Rooms:** 26 rooms, 1 suite & 4 apartments with single or double beds.
**Bathrooms:** Private: 8 bath/toilets, 15 shower/toilets, 3 sinks. 1 shared bath.
**Meals:** Expanded continental breakfast.
**Vegetarian:** Restaurants nearby.
**Dates Open:** February 1-November 16, 1997.
**High Season:** Easter, August.
**Rates:** LIT 51.000-LIT 68.500 per person for B&B.
**Credit Cards:** MC, VISA, Amex, Eurocard, Diners.
**Rsv'tns:** Recommended, by FAX if possible, with credit card guarantee.
**Reserve Through:** Travel agent or call direct.
**Parking:** Adequate, free on-street parking, garage LIT 12.000 per day.
**In-Room:** Maid & room service, telephone, safe, laundry service.
**On-Premises:** TV lounge with satellite TV, meeting rooms, laundry facilities, solarium, exotic garden, furnished terraces.
**Exercise/Health:** Nearby gym, weights, sauna & massage.
**Swimming:** At nearby ocean beach, shuttle service available.
**Sunbathing:** On the roof terrace or at nearby beach.
**Smoking:** Permitted without restrictions.
**Pets:** Not permitted.
**Handicap Access:** No.
**Children:** Welcomed.
**Languages:** Italian, English, German, French, Spanish & Belgian.

# NETHERLANDS

## AMSTERDAM

### Amsterdam House BV

Q-NET Gay-Friendly ♀♂

## *A Luxurious Apartment or Houseboat for the Price of a Hotel Room*

If you need excellent business or tourist accommodations in Amsterdam, call ***Amsterdam House,*** in the heart of the gay center, available for long- and short-term rentals. Close to the main railway station and other major transport intersections, all of the apartments and houseboats are spacious, with luxuriously furnished rooms, fully equipped kitchens and bathrooms, direct telephone, hi-fi set and TV. A fax, answering machine, and photocopier are available on request, as is secretarial service. Of course, all apartments and houseboats are provided with bed linen and towels, and maid service is included. Some apartments have a sauna and a grand piano and most of the apartments overlook the picturesque Amsterdam canals. All houseboats are comfortably heated. Your stay will be unforgettable and something special when you stay in the "Venice of the North."

For easy access to the Amsterdam International Airport, the business and commercial sections of town, and the other downtown amenities offered by one of Europe's greatest capitals, stay in one of the apartments or houseboats offered by ***Amsterdam House.***

Amsterdam House

Address: Amstel 176a, Amsterdam 1017 AE Netherlands.
Tel: (31-20) 62 62 577, Fax: (31-20) 62 62 987,
USA: (904) 677-5370, (800) 618-1008, Fax: (904) 672-6659.

**Type:** Apartment hotel.
**Clientele:** Mostly hetero with a gay & lesbian following
**To Gay Bars:** Some apartments are steps away & most are only 1 minute away.
**Rooms:** 35 apartments & 10 houseboats.
**Bathrooms:** All private.
**Dates Open:** All year.
**High Season:** June-Sep.
**Rates:** Hfl 125-Hfl 425.
**Discounts:** Long stays.
**Credit Cards:** MC, VISA, Amex & Diners.
**Rsv'tns:** Preferred.
**Reserve Through:** Travel agent or call direct.
**Parking:** Adequate on-street parking, depending on traffic.
**In-Room:** Color TV, telephone, kitchen, refrigerator, maid & laundry service.
**On-Premises:** Meeting rooms & laundry facilities. Some houseboats have terraces.
**Exercise/Health:** Many exercise facilities in the neighborhood.
**Sunbathing:** At the beach.
**Smoking:** Permitted. Non-smoking rooms available.
**Pets:** Permitted.
**Handicap Access:** Some accommodations are accessible.
**Children:** Permitted.
**Languages:** Dutch, German, Spanish, English, French.
**Your Host:** Willemina & Cyril.

# Amsterdam Toff's

Gay-Friendly 50/50 ♀♂

## *Your Holiday Home in Amsterdam*

***Amsterdam Toff's*** are self-contained, self-catering, serviced apartments in an area known as "De Pijp," overlooking the Boerenwetering canal and situated close to museums and art galleries. This is the real Amsterdam, the Amsterdam that the tourist does not normally see, yet it is only 15 minutes' walk from the Leidseplein. These 100-year-old buildings were rebuilt in 1990, and their interiors have been completely renovated with modern comforts in mind.

Each apartment is outfitted with color TV, a fully-equipped kitchen with an oven (not often found in Amsterdam) and bathroom. ***Amsterdam Toff's*** are listed and recommended by both the Amsterdam Tourist Board and the Netherlands Reservations Centre. Amsterdam guide service is available to our guests. Our guests frequently make comments, such as, "What luck to get this place." "Fantastic–a very nice apartment." "Much better than a hotel stay." Next time you're in Amsterdam, try staying in ***Amsterdam Toff's***, where you can relax and be truly comfortable and on your own.

**Address: Ruysdaelkade 167, Amsterdam 1072 AS Netherlands. Tel: (31-20) 67 38 529, Fax: (31-20) 66 49 479.**

**Type:** Self-catering serviced apartments.
**Clientele:** 50% gay & lesbian & 50% straight clientele
**Transportation:** Train from airport to central station, then Tram 24 or taxi.
**To Gay Bars:** 10 minutes by taxi to main gay/lesbian areas.
**Rooms:** 4 apartments with single or double beds & 1 bed/settee.
**Bathrooms:** All private bath/shower/WCs.
**Dates Open:** All year.
**High Season:** April through August.
**Rates:** Hfl 175/night, Hfl 950/week, Hfl 2,800/month (prices include city tourist tax). Special off season rates available.
**Discounts:** 5% discount for cash.
**Credit Cards:** MC, Visa, Amex & Eurocard. 5% surcharge for credit cards.
**Rsv'tns:** Deposit or credit card number for all reservations.
**Reserve Through:** Travel agent, but prefer to deal direct.
**Minimum Stay:** 3 days.
**Parking:** Limited on-street parking. Pay parking.
**In-Room:** Color cable TV, telephone, kitchen, refrigerator, coffee & tea-making facilities. VCR on request.
**On-Premises:** Pay phone.
**Swimming:** Short train ride to ocean beach. Municipal pool nearby.
**Nudity:** Nudist beaches 30 minutes out of town at Zandvoort.
**Smoking:** Permitted without restrictions.
**Pets:** Not permitted.
**Handicap Access:** No, because of steep stairway.
**Children:** Welcome.
**Languages:** Dutch, English, German, & basic French.
**Your Host:** Russell & Trevor.

## Anco Hotel-Bar

Q-NET Men ♂

### *Welcoming Leathermen from all over the World*

The *ANCO* is a gay-owned and -operated hotel-bar that welcomes leathermen from all over the world. It is located in a historic canal building which dates from 1640, and is situated between the leather district (Warmoesstraat) and Amsterdam's famous red light district. The Central Railway Station is just a short walk from the hotel.

**Address: Oudezijds Voorburgwal 55, Amsterdam 1012 EJ Netherlands.**
**Tel: (31-20) 624 11 26, Fax: (31-20) 620 52 75.**

**Type:** Hotel & bar for leathermen.
**Clientele:** Men only
**Transportation:** Train from airport to central station, then taxi or 5-minute walk.
**To Gay Bars:** On premises & nearby.
**Rooms:** 11 rooms, 2 dormitories & 1 suite with private bath.
**Bathrooms:** Private: 14 sinks. Shared bath/shower/toilet on each floor.
**Meals:** Expanded continental breakfast.
**Dates Open:** All year.
**High Season:** June 1-October 31.
**Rates:** HFL 60.00-130.00. With private bath & TV HFL 185.00.
**Credit Cards:** All major cards accepted.
**Rsv'tns:** Required at least 4 weeks in advance in high season.
**Reserve Through:** Call or fax direct.
**Minimum Stay:** 2 nights during high season.
**In-Room:** Maid service, color cable TV, 24hr gay video.
**On-Premises:** Meeting room, gay bar.
**Swimming:** 20 miles to nude beach & lakeside Amsterdam.
**Sunbathing:** At the beach.
**Nudity:** Permitted. 30-minute train ride to nude beach.
**Smoking:** Permitted without restrictions.
**Pets:** Not permitted.
**Handicap Access:** No.
**Children:** Not permitted.
**Languages:** Dutch, English, German, Italian & French.
**Your Host:** Kees.

# C&G Bed & Breakfast House

Gay/Lesbian ♂

## *Finest Hospitality in the Heart of Amsterdam*

Our two modern houses form a private enclave in the beautiful Iordaan residential quarter of Amsterdam. We offer you great rates in this unique accommodation in the world's gayest city. The gay owners proudly offer to share with you the comfort of these well-furnished houses. Our deluxe rooms, some with antique decor, each have their own distinctive style and the shared bath/toilets are modern and immaculately clean. Each house has a cozy living room and dinning room area with cable TV. Complimentary continental breakfast is served here each morning and coffee and tea facilities are available all day. Here, also, is the telephone, where you can receive calls from anywhere and place local calls as necessary.

The ***C&G Bed & Breakfast House*** accommodations are so centrally located that you can walk to the museums, the Royal Palace, the major department stores and, of course, Amsterdam's famous gay bars. Intimate restaurants and cafes and shops of all kinds abound in the streets of the surrounding neighborhood. In summertime, guests can use the roof garden at the top of each house for sunning and socializing with other guests.

Your hosts are longtime residents of Amsterdam who can advise you on getting around the city and tell you what to expect of various gay venues. For any further information, please contact us. We will be very pleased to inform you about our very nice houses! Please remember, we must know your arrival time in advance.

**Address: PO Box 15889, Amsterdam 1001 NJ Netherlands.**
**Tel: (31-20) 422 7996.**

**Type:** Private housing.
**Clientele:** Mostly men with women welcome
**To Gay Bars:** A 5 to 8 minute walk to gay bars.
**Rooms:** 6 rooms with single or double beds.
**Bathrooms:** 2 shared bath/shower toilets, 4 shared WC only.
**Meals:** Continental breakfast.
**Dates Open:** All year.
**Rates:** Single or double: Hfl 100 .
**Credit Cards:** Accepted only for using pre-reservation.
**Rsv'tns:** Required.
**Reserve Through:** Call direct.
**Minimum Stay:** 2 days & nights.
**Parking:** On-street parking.
**In-Room:** Telephone, color cable TV, kitchen, refrigerator, coffee & tea-making facilities, maid service.
**On-Premises:** Roof garden.
**Swimming:** Pool & ocean nearby.
**Sunbathing:** On roof.
**Smoking:** Permitted throughout house.
**Pets:** Not permitted.
**Handicap Access:** No.
**Children:** No.
**Languages:** Dutch, English, Spanish, French, Italian, Portuguese, German.

## Centre Apartments Amsterdam

Gay/Lesbian ♀♂

### *Apartments and Studios Smack Dab in the Middle of Amsterdam*

For a weekend or holiday, the comfort, convenience and affordability of ***Centre Apartments Amsterdam*** is unsurpassed. You will find complete quiet and privacy while being located immediately adjacent to Centraal Station, the city's transportation hub; Damrak; Dam Square; some of the city's busiest shopping streets; and the Warmoesstraat, Amsterdam's most famous gay district.

Fourteen apartments and studios are new, some within restored old houses. They are spotlessly clean, fully furnished, and provide a home-away-from-home atmosphere. Guests can choose between one- or three-room apartments accommodating a maximum of four persons or studios for three. The apartments are furnished with one large double bed and a single bed, and the studios have double beds. Both include cable TV, stereo tower with tape deck or CD player. A VCR is available for rent in some of the accommodations. The modern kitchens are fully equipped and the bathrooms are spacious, modern, and immaculate. Double-glazed windows ensure quiet. Pets are not allowed, and the units are not suitable for children. All apartments and studios include linen and towels.

Nearby you can find the Albert Heijn supermarket; neighborhood shops for baked goods, coffee and tea, and flowers; restaurants; bars; coffee shops; the Dam; the Royal Palace; and Madame Tussaud's. Next door is the unique Amstelkring, a 17th-century canal house famous for its clandestine Roman Catholic church and authentic period rooms. At one end of the street is the famous red-light district, while at the other end are the city's legendary leather bars.

The proprietors speak English, Spanish, Italian, German, Portuguese, and French and accept all credit cards, but prefer cash. Our rates are as follows: Apartment: per day Hfl 165-Hfl 185; per week Hfl 1100-Hfl 1200. Studio: per day Hfl 135-Hfl 145; per week Hfl 950-Hfl 1050. We must know your arrival time in advance.

**Address: Heintje Hoekssteeg 27, PO Box 15889, Amsterdam 1001 NJ Netherlands.**
**Tel: (31-20) 627 25 03, Fax: (31-20) 625 11 08.**

## Hotel "The Village"

**Gay-Friendly 50/50 ♀♂**

### *You Don't Need an Expensive Taxi*

Situated on the Kerkstraat, Amsterdam's gayest street, ***Hotel "The Village"*** places you right in the middle of what's happening. This is where you want to be: in the center of town within easy reach of nightlife, restaurants, museums and other attractions. The hotel has 2-, 3- and 4-person rooms with shower and bathroom and there is a café on the premises. You get your own key to the front door.

**Address: 25 Kerkstraat, Amsterdam 1017 GA Netherlands.**
**Tel: (31-20) 626 9746, Fax: (31-20) 625 4081.**

**Type:** Hotel with bar for residents, café downstairs.
**Clientele:** 50% gay & lesbian & 50% straight clientele
**Transportation:** Tram 1, 2 & 5 from central station.
**To Gay Bars:** Close to all gay/lesbian bars.
**Rooms:** 10 rooms for 1-5 people. Guests receive their own front door key.
**Bathrooms:** All private.
**Meals:** Dutch breakfast.
**Dates Open:** All year.
**Rates:** Summer Hfl 125, winter Hfl 120.
**Reserve Through:** Call direct.
**In-Room:** The larger rooms have sofas, tables & easy chairs. All rooms have refrigerators & colour TVs.
**Nudity:** Short train ride to nude beach.
**Smoking:** Permitted without restrictions.
**Pets:** Not permitted.
**Languages:** Dutch & English.

## Hotel Aero

**Gay/Lesbian ♂**

***Hotel Aero*** is conveniently located in the heart of Amsterdam. All rooms have been converted to satisfy modern tastes and are provided with every comfort and convenience. Most rooms have telephones and TV with VCR. Our Tavern de Pul, with its inviting Dutch atmosphere, is a place where everyone drops in and feels in his element.

**Address: Kerkstraat 49, Amsterdam-C 1017 GB Netherlands.**
**Tel: (31-20) 622 77 28, Fax: (31-20) 638 8531.**

**Type:** Hotel with bar & gay-sex shop downstairs.
**Clientele:** Mostly men with women welcome
**Transportation:** Taxi or trams or walking.
**To Gay Bars:** All within walking distance & many on the same street.
**Rooms:** 4 singles, 12 doubles.
**Bathrooms:** 11 private, others shared.
**Meals:** Full breakfast
**Dates Open:** All year.
**Rates:** Hfl 120-Hfl 145.
**Credit Cards:** MC, Visa, Amex, Eurocard.
**Rsv'tns:** Required two weeks in advance.
**Reserve Through:** Call direct.
**Parking:** Off- & on-street parking available.
**In-Room:** Color TV, telephone & VCR in most rooms.
**Swimming:** Ocean & lake beaches nearby.
**Nudity:** 30-minute train ride to nude beach.
**Smoking:** Permitted without restrictions.
**Pets:** All permitted.
**Handicap Access:** No.
**Children:** Not permitted.
**Languages:** Dutch, English, Spanish, French, German.
**Your Host:** Pedro.

# Hotel Sander

**Gay/Lesbian ♀♂**

This attractive 4-star hotel is situated only a block away from the Van Gogh Museum and the Concertgebouw (Concert Hall) and is just a ten-minute walk from the Kerkstraat gay area, a gay fitness centre and both the day and night saunas. ***Hotel Sander*** is also only a fifteen-minute walk from the most famous women's cafe in Amsterdam.

This 5-storey hotel has an elevator, so less athletic guests needn't worry about climbing the famous steep stairs of Amsterdam. The reception staff speaks English, German, French, Spanish, Italian and Portuguese and operates 24 hours a day, as does our fully licensed bar, *The Portal*. Guests can order snacks and refreshments at any time of the day or night. Room service is available from approximately 8:00-22:00, and a same-day laundry and dry-cleaning service operates Monday through Friday.

All room rates include Dutch continental breakfast served in the spacious breakfast room adjacent to the bar area and ground floor reception. A large variety of side orders can be ordered from our breakfast staff. In warm weather, patio doors open onto a flower-filled terrace and garden where guests can relax in an oasis of calm in the middle of a bustling city.

All guest rooms include colour cable TV, direct-dial telephone, radio, individual safe and en suite WC and shower. Some rooms also have bathtubs. ***Hotel Sander*** is easy to reach from Schiphol Airport via the train to Station Zuid/WTC. From there, take either Bus 63 to Jacob Obrechtstraat (10 minutes), Tram 5 to the Concert Hall (10 minutes) or a taxi (approximately 15 guilders). From the Central Railway Station, take Tram 16 to Jacob Obrechtstraat (15 minutes).

**Address: Jacob Obrechtstraat 69, Amsterdam 1071 KJ Netherlands.**
**Tel: (31-20) 6627574, Fax: (31-20) 6796067.**

**Type:** Hotel with bar.
**Clientele:** Mostly gay & lesbian with some hetero clientele
**Transportation:** To Jacob Obrechtstraat: From Schiphol Airport, train to station Zuid then Bus 63; From Central Station, Tram 16.
**To Gay Bars:** 1 mile. A 10-minute walk or 5-minute drive.
**Rooms:** 20 rooms with single or double beds.
**Bathrooms:** All private.
**Meals:** Expanded continental breakfast.
**Vegetarian:** Our bar serves some vegetarian snacks 24 hours a day. 5-minute walk to vegetarian restaurant.
**Dates Open:** All year.
**High Season:** 1 April-1 November, X-mas-New Year.
**Rates:** Hi: single HFL 125-165, dble HFL 145-195, twin HFL 155-210. Low: single HFL 100-125, dble HFL 125-165, twin HFL 145-185.
**Credit Cards:** MC, VISA, Amex, Diners, Eurocard.
**Rsv'tns:** Required.
**Reserve Through:** Call direct.
**Parking:** Adequate free on-street space. Pay parking covered garage HFL 17.50 (24hr).
**In-Room:** Color cable TV, telephone, coffee/tea-making facilities, room & laundry service.
**On-Premises:** 24-hour bar & snack service.
**Exercise/Health:** Nearby gym, weights, Jacuzzi, sauna, steam & massage.
**Swimming:** Nearby pool, lake & ocean.
**Sunbathing:** At the beach.
**Smoking:** Permitted in bar, lounge & most rooms. Some non-smoking bedrooms available.
**Pets:** Not permitted.
**Handicap Access:** Yes. Elevator.
**Children:** Not especially welcome.
**Languages:** Dutch, English, German, French, Spanish, Italian & Portuguese.

IGTA

## Hotel Seven Bridges

Gay-Owned ♂

***Hotel Seven Bridges*** is located overlooking one of the picturesque canals of Amsterdam. You'll never need your car, as you can walk to all the sights of this city and there is no better way to capture the flavor of the place and its people. For comfort and convenience, there is no better location than the Seven Bridges.

**Address: Reguliresgracht 31, Amsterdam 1017 LK Netherlands. Tel: (31-20) 623-1329.**

**Type:** Hotel.
**Clientele:** Mainly hetero clientele with 30% gay & lesbian clientele
**To Gay Bars:** 3 min walk.
**Rooms:** 1 single, 10 dbls.
**Bathrooms:** 6 private, others share.
**Meals:** Dutch breakfast served in your room.
**Dates Open:** All year.
**Rates:** Double room including breakfast Hfl 135.00-Hfl 230.00.
**Discounts:** MC, Amex, Visa.
**Rsv'tns:** Required.
**Reserve Through:** Call direct.
**Minimum Stay:** Generally 3 nights.
**Parking:** Limited on-street parking, 7-minute walk to 2 garages.
**In-Room:** Color TV, maid service, telephones in some rooms.
**Smoking:** Permitted without restrictions.
**Pets:** Not permitted.
**Handicap Access:** Difficult accessibility.
**Children:** Not encouraged.
**Languages:** Dutch, English, German, French, Spanish.

## Hotel Wilhelmina

Gay-Friendly ♀♂

***Hotel Wilhelmina*** is centrally located in the heart of Amsterdam's shopping and cultural centre, convenient to museums, the concert hall, Vondel Park, the World Trade Centre and the Central Station. Schiphol Amsterdam Airport is a 10-minute drive away. The hotel is recommended in the Michelin Hotel Guide, the Amsterdam Tourist Office, most European automobile clubs and airlines. The efficient management, inspired by great hospitality, will do all to enhance the pleasure and comfort of your stay. Breakfast is served in the hotel, and an enormous variety of restaurants can be found in the vicinity.

**Address: Koninginne Weg 167-169, Amsterdam 1075 CN Netherlands. Tel: (31-20) 662 5467, Fax: (31-20) 679 2296, Telex: WILHL NL.**

**Type:** Hotel.
**Clientele:** Mostly straight clientele with a gay & lesbian following
**Transportation:** Trams 2 & 16 to Valeriusplein.
**To Gay Bars:** 1 km to Kerkstraat gay bars.
**Rooms:** 19 rooms with single or double beds.
**Bathrooms:** En suite: 14 shower/toilets, 5 sinks. Shared: 3 showers, 3 WCs.
**Meals:** Full Dutch breakfast.
**Vegetarian:** Vegetarian breakfast. Vegetarian restaurants nearby.
**Dates Open:** All year.
**High Season:** March-November.
**Rates:** Hfl 75-Hfl 175.

**Discounts:** Please inquire.
**Credit Cards:** Most major credit cards.
**Rsv'tns:** Required.
**Reserve Through:** Call direct.
**Parking:** Adequate free on-street parking.
**In-Room:** Maid, room & laundry service, color cable TV, direct-dial telephone.
**On-Premises:** Private dining rooms, TV lounge & bicycle storage.
**Sunbathing:** On the patio.
**Smoking:** Not permitted in dining room, lounge, toilets, or passageways.
**Pets:** Not permitted.
**Handicap Access:** No.
**Children:** Permitted.
**Languages:** Dutch, German & English.

## Liliane's Home; Guesthouse for Women Only

Women ♀

### *Small, Comfortable & Personal*

***Liliane's Home*** is located in a renovated manor in the stately Plantagebuurt and provides short- or extended-stay women-only lodging in the heart of Amsterdam. Public transportation access is excellent. Your room will be on one of two floors located directly above the owner's own home. This intimate arrangement ensures personal attention in a warm and comfortable environment. Common rooms include living room, kitchen and bath facilities.

This combination of central location and comfortable, intimate, personal service, provides all the necessary ingredients for a pleasant and successful visit to Amsterdam.

Public transportation access is excellent. The bus, tram and metro all stop at the door, and transportation to and from Schiphol Airport is optimal. Downtown cultural centers, movies, galleries and a variety of nightlife are all within walking distance.

**Address: Sarphatistraat 119, Amsterdam 1018 GB Netherlands. Tel: (31-20) 627 4006 (Tel/Fax).**

**Type:** Guesthouse.
**Clientele:** Women only
**Transportation:** From Schiphol Airport, train to Central Station, then subway to Weesperplein or tram 6, 7, 10. Pick up, Hfl 45.
**To Gay Bars:** 2 blocks or a 10-minute walk.
**Rooms:** 5 rooms & 2 apartments with single or double beds.
**Bathrooms:** 4 private sinks only. Shared: 2 bathtub, 4 shower & 4 WC only. Apartments have private bath.
**Meals:** Breakfast included.
**Vegetarian:** Vegetarian restaurants nearby.
**Complimentary:** Tea & coffee. Soft drinks & beer, Hfl 1,5.
**Dates Open:** All year.
**Rates:** Per room: Hfl 65 1 person, Hfl 110 2 people, Hfl 150 3 people. Apts: Hfl 160 2 people, Hfl 185 3 people, Hfl 240 4 people.
**Discounts:** 5% for longer than 7 days.
**Rsv'tns:** Required.
**Reserve Thru:** Call direct.
**Minimum Stay:** 2 days.
**Parking:** Limited on-street pay parking. Covered private parking, 1 car Hfl 25/day.
**In-Room:** Color cable TV, coffee/tea-making facilities, maid & laundry service. Apartments have kitchen & balcony.
**On-Premises:** Meeting rooms, garage, big living room & kitchen.
**Exercise/Health:** Massage. Nearby gym, weights, sauna, steam & massage.
**Sunbathing:** On the patio & balcony.
**Smoking:** Permitted in living room. Sleeping rooms are non-smoking!
**Pets:** Not permitted.
**Handicap Access:** 1 garden room.
**Children:** Not especially welcome.
**Languages:** Dutch, English & German.
**Your Host:** Liliane.

## Maes B&B

**Gay/Lesbian ♀♂**

***Maes B&B's*** recently renovated turn-of-the-century home has quaint, comfortable guest rooms decorated in the style of that period, with the accent on cozy homelike ambiance. Awaken to fresh croissants, just part of the extended continental breakfast served. Our quiet street in the Concertgebouw area is near trams, the Concertgebouw, the Rijksmuseum, and the Van Gogh and the Stedelijk museums. Numerous restaurants and nightspots are within walking distance, as is the Albert Cuyp street market and the trendy shopping street, PC Hooftstraat.

**Address: Nicolaas Maesstraat 94A, Amsterdam 1071 RE Netherlands.**
**Tel: (31-20) 679 4496,**
**Mobile: (31-6) 54 721 002,**
**Fax: (31-20) 679 5595,**
**E-mail: Maesbb94@XS4ALL.NL. http://www.XS4ALL.NL/~MaesBB94.**

**Type:** Bed & breakfast.
**Clientele:** Mostly gay & lesbian with some hetero clientele
**Transportation:** Airport: train to Sta. Zuid/WTC, then tram #5 to Concertgebouw. Central Sta: tram #5 or #16 to Concertgebouw. Or taxi.
**To Gay Bars:** 10-20 minutes by foot.
**Rooms:** 3 rooms with single, twin or king beds.
**Bathrooms:** 3 private sinks. Shared: 1 bath, 1 shower & 2 WCs.
**Meals:** Expanded continental breakfast.
**Complimentary:** Tea & coffee available from guest pantry all day.
**Dates Open:** All year.
**High Season:** April-October.
**Rates:** Hfl 65.00-Hfl 120.00.
**Discounts:** On stays of 7 or more nights.
**Credit Cards:** MC, Diners, Amex, Eurocard.
**Rsv'tns:** Required.
**Reserve Through:** Call or E-mail direct.
**Minimum Stay:** 2 nights on weekends.
**Parking:** Paid parking (parking meters).
**On-Premises:** Laundry facilities & guest pantry with refrigerator & coffee/tea-making facilities. Telephone & fax services.
**Exercise/Health:** Nearby gym, weights, Jacuzzi, sauna, steam & massage.
**Swimming:** In nearby North Sea & city swimming pools.
**Sunbathing:** On the beach or in the parks.
**Nudity:** Permitted at the beach & in some parks.
**Smoking:** Not permitted.
**Pets:** Not permitted.
**Handicap Access:** No.
**Children:** Welcome.
**Languages:** Dutch, English, some French & German.
**Your Host:** Ken & Hugo.

## Riverside Apartments

Gay-Friendly 50/50 ♀♂

### *A Wide Variety of Accommodations in Central Amsterdam and Beyond*

***Riverside Apartments*** offers both short-term and long-term rentals, with most short-term accommodations within walking distance of most gay bars and discos. For those staying for six months or longer, apartments and houses are available along the canals, in the suburbs and in surrounding towns. Rates vary from Fl. 1,000 to Fl. 1,750 per week for single or double occupancy during low season, and from Fl. 1,500 to Fl. 2,000 during high season. Daily rates are available on request and require a minimum stay of four days. The rates for a stay of six months or more depend on the type of accommodation required, as well as its location. Monthly rates vary from Fl. 1,500 to Fl. 5,000 and, in most cases, a deposit of one or two month's rent is required.

Singles, doubles and larger parties can also be accommodated in hotels, apartments and houses. All accommodations have private facilities, cable TV, refrigerator and coffee- and tea-making facilities. Some have fax, answering machines and minibars, and most have private kitchens, telephones and VCRs. In some cases breakfast is included in the rate. As a rule, all major credit cards are accepted. Parking is difficult in the center of the city and is expensive. Maid service is available and varies with the accommodation. It is sometimes included on a daily basis, sometimes two or three times a week, and some accommodations are serviced only before checking in and after checking out.

In most cases, pets are not allowed and smoking is permitted. Although most places are not handicap-accessible, there are some which are accessible and which do allow pets. Children are not especially welcomed in most short-term rentals. The owner, Jerry, speaks Dutch, English, German and French. Please call direct.

**Address: Weteringschans 187 E, Amsterdam 1017 XE Netherlands.
Tel: (31-20) 627 9797, Fax: (31-20) 627 9858.
E-mail: geuje@worldonline.nl.**

# Singel Suite — The Bed & Breakfast Suites

Gay-Friendly ♀♂

## *Overlooking One of the Prettiest Canals in the Heart of Amsterdam*

The ***Singel Suites*** are on the first and second floors of a classic Amsterdam *grachtenpand* house. Both overlook one of the prettiest canals in the heart of Amsterdam. It is in this area where, gay or straight, Amsterdam's rich and famous live. The apartments have a separate living room and bedroom. The first-floor apartment has a Jacuzzi-bath bathroom next to the private patio, and both apartments overlook the canal and Amsterdam bridges.

Although the ***Singel Suite*** has preserved its original 17th-century style, it has luxury, modern comfort, and more. Surrounded by culture, canals, and antique shops, the famous Spui, Rembrandtsplein, Leidseplein, cinemas, museums and the flowermarket are close by. We are also near the city's most well-known clubs & restaurants, among them the gay bars and discos of Reguliersdwarsstraat. Guests at ***Singel Suite*** will find something better than the average hotel. They will find luxury, comfort and privacy.

**Address: Singel 420, Amsterdam 1016 AK Netherlands.**
**Tel: (31-20) 625 8673, Fax: (31-20) 625 8097.**

**Type:** Bed & breakfast apartment suite.
**Clientele:** We don't question our guests' orientation
**Transportation:** Train from airport to Central Station, then trams 1, 2, or 5 (a 10-minute ride) to Koningsplein, or taxi direct.
**To Gay Bars:** 1 block or a 2-minute walk.
**Rooms:** 2 apartments with king & extra bed.
**Bathrooms:** Private full baths.
**Meals:** Expanded continental breakfast in Suite.
**Vegetarian:** Available nearby.
**Complimentary:** Cheese, sausages & a variety of appetizers in the minibar.
**Dates Open:** All year.
**Rates:** Hfl 245 for two persons.
**Discounts:** Weekly rates, 3 day weekend.
**Credit Cards:** MC, Visa, Amex, Diners & Eurocard.
**Rsv'tns:** Preferred.
**Reserve Through:** Fax or call direct.
**Minimum Stay:** Depends on time of arrival. If in the morning, 2 days.
**Parking:** Limited on-street pay parking. Best to park in parking garage.
**In-Room:** Color cable TV, VCR, video tape & international libraries, direct-dial phone, refrigerator, bathrobes, bathing salts, free coffee/tea-making & limited kitchen facilities & maid service.
**On-Premises:** Fax. Car rental service available from Singel Suite.
**Exercise/Health:** Jacuzzi on premises. Nearby gym, weights, Jacuzzi, sauna steam & massage. 45 minutes to lakes & rental boats.
**Swimming:** Nearby pool. 30 minutes to ocean, 20 minutes to lake.
**Sunbathing:** At nearby pool, 30 mins to beach or lakes, 10 mins to Vondelpark.
**Nudity:** 15-20 minutes to nude area.
**Smoking:** Permitted.
**Pets:** Small pets permitted with deposit.
**Handicap Access:** No.
**Children:** Welcome.
**Languages:** Dutch, French, English & German.
**Your Host:** Anthony & Jacqueline.

## Sunhead of 1617

Q-NET Gay/Lesbian ♀♂

### *The GENEROUS Dutch Treat!*

Located in one of the oldest listed canal houses of rustic Amsterdam, this small and friendly bed-and-delicious-breakfast offers the best value for your money. ***Sunhead's*** very central, yet quiet, location is a five-minute walk from Central Station and virtually all the city's historical, cultural and gay amenities such as the Anne Frank House, the Homo monument, the Royal Palace, several historical churches and synagogues, the "Begijn" courtyard, the Theater museum and the Warmoesstraat and Reguliersdwarsstraat gay district. Our area is famous for its boutiques, good restaurants and cafés.

The third-floor rooms overlook Amsterdam's loveliest canal and gabled roofs. Each room has vaulted ceilings, Japanese-inspired decor, skylighting, a modern toilet and shower, cable TV, a VCR, a fridge, coffee/tea-making facilities, daily maid service and fresh flowers and plants galore! This 17th-century house has no elevator, so expect to use the stairs.

Full breakfast is served in the privacy of your own room or in the dining room from 8:30 a.m. till late, and optional dinner is served upon request. Other amenities include in-house pay phone, fax and IBM PC. Guests also have access to the city center's best equipped gym with licensed trainer (US $10 per visit).

**Address: Herengracht 152, Amsterdam 1016 BN Netherlands.**
**Tel: (31-20) 626 1809, Fax: (31-20) 626 1823. E-mail: sunhead@xs4all.nl.**

**Type:** Bed & breakfast.
**Clientele:** Mostly gay & lesbian with some hetero clientele
**Transportation:** Pick up from airport Hfl 35.00. Pick up from train Hfl 10.00.
**To Gay Bars:** 4 blocks or a 5-minute walk.
**Rooms:** 2 rooms & 1 apartment with single or double beds.
**Bathrooms:** All private.
**Meals:** Full breakfast.
**Vegetarian:** Available upon request. Many vegetarian restaurants & cafes nearby.
**Complimentary:** Welcome fruit basket & bottle of house wine. Tea & coffee.
**Dates Open:** All year.
**High Season:** July, August & December.
**Rates:** Hfl 145-135 per room for 2. Hfl 105 per room for single. Self-catering apartment for 2: Hfl 185 (Hfl 40 per extra person, maximum 5 people).
**Discounts:** 5% for cash.
**Credit Cards:** MC, Visa, Amex, Diners, JCB, Eurocard.
**Rsv'tns:** Advisable.
**Reserve Through:** Travel agent or call direct.
**Minimum Stay:** 2 days on weekends.
**Parking:** Adequate on-street pay parking. Free evenings & Sundays.
**In-Room:** Color cable TV, VCR, telephone, fans, refrigerator, coffee/tea-making facilities, maid & laundry service.
**On-Premises:** Fax machine.
**Exercise/Health:** Nearby gym, weights, Jacuzzi, sauna, steam & massage.
**Swimming:** Nearby pool, ocean & lake.
**Sunbathing:** In the park.
**Smoking:** Permitted in some rooms.
**Pets:** Not permitted.
**Handicap Access:** No.
**Children:** Welcome.
**Languages:** Dutch, English, Tagalog, Cebuano, French & German.
**Your Host:** Carlos & Roelf-Jan.

## Westend Hotel & Cosmo Bar

Gay/Lesbian ♂

Located on Kerkstraat, site of one of the heaviest concentrations of gay nightlife in Amsterdam, the ***Westend*** offers you comfortable rooms with shared showers, very centrally located to all gay bars and tourist attractions. Right downstairs from your room is an assortment of gay nightlife, interesting cafes, a gay video shop, and even a night sauna.

**Address: Kerkstraat 42, Amsterdam 1017 GM Netherlands.**
**Tel: (31-20) 624 80 74, Fax: (31-20) 622 99 97.**

**Type:** Bed & breakfast with bar.
**Clientele:** Mostly men with women welcome
**Transportation:** Train to Central Station, then taxi or tram line 1, 2 or 5.
**To Gay Bars:** Men's bars & sauna on the same & next block.
**Rooms:** 5 doubles also available for single use.
**Bathrooms:** 2 shared toilets & 2 shared showers.
**Dates Open:** All year.
**High Season:** July, August, September.
**Rates:** Single Hfl 85.00. Room with double bed Hfl 120.00. Twin bedded room Hfl 140.00. Triple Hfl 180.00.
**Credit Cards:** MC, Visa, Amex, Diners & Eurocard.
**Rsv'tns:** Required 2 weeks in advance.
**Reserve Through:** Call direct.
**Parking:** Limited on-street parking with meters. 15-min walk to guarded parking.
**In-Room:** Color cable TV with CNN, maid service, telephone, refrigerator & coffee & tea-making facilities.
**Sunbathing:** On beach 1/2 hour away.
**Nudity:** 30-minute train ride to nude beach.
**Smoking:** Permitted without restrictions.
**Pets:** Small pets permitted.
**Handicap Access:** No.
**Children:** Not permitted.
**Languages:** Dutch, English, French & German.
**Your Host:** Herman.

# DONKERBROEK

## 't Zijpad

Women ♀

***'t Zijpad,*** meaning the "she" or "side path," is a small-scale holiday resort for those seeking the peace of the countryside and contact with nature. We're in a charming and pastoral region of natural beauty on the edge of the Ontwijk estate woodlands, an area with many birds, protected plant species, deer and other wildlife perfect for camping, bicycling and woodland walks. You need to be a Sherlock Holmes to find other tourists! The region affords opportunities for cultural sightseeing, as well. Quiet villages and historical towns, which preserve the old Frisian atmosphere, dot the countryside.

Accommodations are simple, practical and comfortable. The Garden House is a large room overlooking garden and woods and features a private shower. The cottage (women-only during July & August) is a detached summer house with sitting room, kitchen, colour TV and a sleeping loft. Bed & breakfast accommodations are in a small sitting room with bedroom upstairs. The camping area occupies 70 acres of woodland and walking paths and is always exclusively for women, with room for eight tents, each emplacement screened by wildflowers and bushes to ensure a degree of privacy. A table in a central area is for use by everyone. Those not traveling with camping equipment can rent tents, mattresses, storm lanterns and other necessities for a reasonable fee. Macrobiotic produce from our garden is also available. The locale offers a wide selection of restaurants to choose from.

**Address: Balkweg 8, Donkerbroek 8435 VP Netherlands.**
**Tel: (31-516) 491752.**

**Type:** Bed & breakfast guesthouse, campground.
**Clientele:** Mostly women with some men welcome
**Transportation:** Charge for pick up from bus, train.
**Rooms:** 1 room, 1 apartment, 1 cottage & 1 cabin with single beds.
**Bathrooms:** All shared.
**Campsites:** 8 tent sites with cooling containers &

cooking tiles. 2 covered dishwashing basins. Campers use guesthouse facilities.
**Meals:** Expanded continental breakfast for B & B only.
**Complimentary:** Tea, coffee, juices, homemade preserves.
**Dates Open:** All year.
**High Season:** April 1-October 15, Christmas, New Years, Easter, 1 week in February.
**Rates:** Cottage Hfl 250 per week. B&B in house add'tl Hfl 30 per person per day. Camping Hfl 8 per night. Cabin & Garden Room Hfl 195 per week. Plus tax.
**Rsv'tns:** Required.
**Reserve Thru:** Call direct.
**Minimum Stay:** Apt & cottage, 1 week, B&B, campground, 1 night.
**Parking:** Adequate, free off-street parking.
**In-Room:** Color TV, kitchen, refrigerator.
**Swimming:** Public pools in villages, river 50 m, lake 10 km.
**Sunbathing:** At campgrounds, terraces, in large garden & in woods.
**Smoking:** Permitted, but not in bedrooms.
**Pets:** Permitted by prior arrangement, female dogs only.
**Children:** Permitted, but no facilities, campground no males over 12.
**Languages:** Dutch, German, English, French & Frisian.

# PORTUGAL

## ALGARVE

### Casa Amigos

Men ♂

## *An Intimate Guesthouse in the Algarve*

In two acres of gardens surrounded by orange and lemon groves with mountain views, you can't help but relax. ***Casa Amigos,*** an exclusive gay guesthouse, is situated just 12 miles inland from the main resort of Albufeira, 35 minutes from Faro International Airport, three hours from Lisbon, and two hours from the Spanish city of Seville. Local Portuguese restaurants are nearby and the guesthouse is only 15 minutes from the nearest gay beach and clubs of Albufeira. All rooms lead directly onto the pool terrace.

**Address: Larga Vista, Foral, S.B. Messiness, Algarve 8357 Portugal. Tel: (351-82) 56597 (Tel/Fax), or London tel: (44-181) 743 7417.**

**Type:** Bed & breakfast guesthouse with bar.
**Clientele:** Men only
**Transportation:** Pick up arranged.
**To Gay Bars:** 15-minute drive to bar.
**Rooms:** 3 rooms & 1 suite with single & double beds.
**Bathrooms:** All en suite.
**Meals:** Expanded continental breakfast. Evening meals & BBQ by arrangement.
**Vegetarian:** Available upon request.
**Complimentary:** Welcoming cocktail, tea & coffee in rooms.
**Dates Open:** April-October.
**High Season:** May-October.
**Rates:** From 5000-6600 escudos per person, per night.
**Discounts:** Large booking of 6-8.
**Rsv'tns:** Required.
**Reserve Through:** Travel agent or call direct.
**Parking:** Ample free, own car park.
**In-Room:** Color TV & maid service.
**On-Premises:** Meeting rooms, TV lounge, poolside bar & food services.
**Exercise/Health:** Weights on premises. Nearby gym, weights, Jacuzzi, sauna & steam.
**Swimming:** Pool on premises. 15-minute drive to ocean.
**Sunbathing:** At poolside, on patio, roof & at the beach.
**Nudity:** Permitted at poolside & at gay beach (20-minute drive).
**Smoking:** Permitted.
**Pets:** Not permitted.
**Handicap Access:** 2 ground floor rooms.
**Children:** Not permitted under 18 years.
**Languages:** English, Portuguese & a little German.
**Your Host:** Roy.

IGTA

## Casa Marhaba

Gay/Lesbian ♂

### "Marhaba" Means "Welcome" - We Mean to Make You Just That

***Casa Marhaba*** is set on one acre in a pleasant rural area, 1 km from the nearest beach, 5 km from Carvoeiro and Lagoa, and 50 km west of Faro International Airport. All five of our double rooms have en suite bathrooms with showers. We serve a substantial continental breakfast on the poolside terrace and picnic lunches and pub-style snacks are available to order. Barbecue by the pool or enjoy the TV lounge with satellite TV and video facilities.The Algarve region provides a perfect mix of contrasts: unspoiled countryside with miles of beaches, quaint and historical villages with lively towns and resorts, deep sea fishing and coastal boat trips, and great restaurants offering a wide range of cuisine. We will be delighted to recommend restaurants, beaches, and bars or help you with any other aspect of your holiday.

**Address: Rua de Benagil, Alfanzina, Lagoa 8400 Portugal.**
**Tel: (351-82) 358720 (Tel/Fax).**

**Type:** Bed & breakfast guesthouse with bar.
**Clientele:** Mostly men with women welcome
**Transportation:** Faro Airport, then rental car. Pick up can be arranged for a fee.
**To Gay Bars:** 10 miles or a 15-minute drive.
**Rooms:** 5 rooms with single or double beds.
**Bathrooms:** 5 private shower/toilets.
**Meals:** Expanded continental breakfast.
**Vegetarian:** Available upon advanced request. Vegetarian food nearby.
**Complimentary:** Welcome cocktail.
**Dates Open:** April thru October.
**High Season:** April thru October.
**Rates:** Single: £192/week, £34 per night. Double: £235/week, £40 per night.
**Rsv'tns:** Required.
**Reserve Through:** Call direct.
**Parking:** Ample free off-street parking.
**In-Room:** Maid & laundry service.
**On-Premises:** TV lounge with satellite TV & video facilities.
**Swimming:** Pool on premises, ocean nearby.
**Sunbathing:** At poolside, on patio & private sun decks.
**Nudity:** Permitted on special sun deck poolside.
**Smoking:** Permitted throughout.
**Pets:** Not permitted.
**Handicap Access:** No.
**Children:** Not especially welcome.
**Languages:** English & French.
**Your Host:** Tony & Sam.

## Casa Pequena

Gay/Lesbian ♂

### All the Comforts of Home...

Situated in 1100 square metres of gardens on a hillside overlooking the village and beach of Praia da Luz, ***Casa Pequena*** is, first and foremost, our home. As such, you will find it comfortable and well-furnished with the usual amenities, including TV, video, audio equipment and a good library of books, all available to our guests. We have two guest rooms, each with adjacent bath/shower and we provide all linens, towels and beach towels. We also have a swimming pool, extensive terraces and sun-beds. If you want to explore, we can advise you where to visit and explain the eccentricities of gay nightlife in Portugal. You will have your own key so you can come and go as you please.

**Address: Apartado 133, Praia da Luz, Lagos, Algarve 8600 Portugal.**
**Tel: (351-82) 789068 (24-hr tel/fax).**

**Type:** Guesthouse with honour bar.
**Clientele:** Mostly gay men with women welcome
**Transportation:** Car is best. Pick up from airport, train, bus. 3,250 escudos from Faro airport. Free from Lagos.
**To Gay Bars:** 5 km or 10 minutes by car.
**Rooms:** 2 rooms with

single or double bed.
**Bathrooms:** Private adjacent to room: 1 shower/toilet, 1 bath/shower/toilet.
**Meals:** Expanded continental breakfast. Other meals can be provided at reasonable cost.
**Vegetarian:** Available upon request. Most restaurants have non-meat dishes.
**Complimentary:** Tea & coffee.
**Dates Open:** All year.
**High Season:** April/May-end of October.
**Rates:** 5000 escudos per night single. 8,500 escudos per night double.
**Discounts:** 10% if both rooms booked by same party (4 persons).
**Rsv'tns:** Required.
**Reserve Through:** Call direct.
**Minimum Stay:** 3 nights minimum charge though you can stay for fewer nights.
**Parking:** Ample free off-street parking.
**On-Premises:** TV lounge. Entire house is available for guests.
**Exercise/Health:** Nearby hotel/sports centre with gym, weights, Jacuzzi, sauna, steam & massage.
**Swimming:** Pool on premises, ocean nearby.
**Sunbathing:** At poolside, on common sun decks & at nearby beaches (some nude & gay).
**Nudity:** Permitted wherever guests feel comfortable.
**Smoking:** Permitted everywhere except in bedrooms.
**Pets:** Not permitted. 3 resident cats.
**Handicap Access:** No.
**Children:** Not especially welcome.
**Languages:** Portuguese, English, French.
**Your Host:** Jim & Geoff.

# SPAIN

## ASTURIAS

### Casa Lorenzo

Gay-Friendly 50/50 ♀♂

*On Spain's Spectacular Northwest Coast...*

A true Spanish country villa nestled on a lush, gently sloping hillside is ideally situated on Spain's northwest coast along the area known as Costa Verde in the Province of Asturias. Peaceful and relaxing, this region of Spain remains relatively undiscovered by many tourists. This historic area is filled with attractions such as the charming fishing villages of Cudillero and Luarca, and the spectacular rocky coastline, containing narrow estuaries and small beaches. It takes all day to explore this verdant span termed by locals as a "natural paradise."

Lodgings at ***Casa Lorenzo*** are comprised of two spacious bright and sunny guest rooms upstairs, pleasant and comfortably furnished, and both with views overlooking the quaint village and views of the beach. The cozy guest room across the hall sleeps two and has a view of hillside forest and afternoon sun. A massive shared bath, as well as a downstairs half bath are decorated in the Andalusian style. A large living room for guests is furnished with antiques and has panoramic views. Your gateway to Asturias will be Oviedo, an approximately 45-minute flight from Madrid. Day excursions can be arranged for guests.

**Address: c/o David Braddy, Palo Alto Travel, 535 Ramona #7, Palo Alto, CA 94301. Tel: (415) 323-2626, (800) 359-3922, Fax: (415) 323-2684.**

**Type:** Gay-owned inn in town of S. Pedro de la Ribera, 30 min from Oviedo.
**Clientele:** 50% gay & lesbian & 50% straight clientele
**Transportation:** 30-minute drive from Oviedo, a 5-hour drive from Madrid to Oviedo. Pick up from Oviedo airport US$20 each way.
**Rooms:** 1 room, 2 suites with single or double beds.
**Bathrooms:** 1 shared bath/shower/toilet, 1 shared WC only.
**Meals:** Expanded continental breakfast. Dining by reservation, chef on premises.
**Vegetarian:** Prepared on request & available at local restaurants.
**Complimentary:** Evening wine service or juices, bottled mineral water.
**Dates Open:** All year.
**High Season:** June-Aug.
**Rates:** US $69-US $99.
**Discounts:** 10% on stays over 3 days, 10% for renting both suites.
**Credit Cards:** MC, VISA, Amex. Credit cards accepted in advance only with 3% surcharge.
**Rsv'tns:** Required. Payment in full 30 days prior to arrival, 25% cancellation fee.
**Reserve Through:** Travel agent or call direct.
**Parking:** Limited free parking.
**In-Room:** Maid, room & laundry service.

*continued next page*

**On-Premises:** Large living room for guests, breakfast room.
**Swimming:** Nearby ocean, river.
**Sunbathing:** At beach, on patio.
**Nudity:** Permitted at nearby nude beach.
**Smoking:** Permitted on outside patio & in garden.
**Pets:** Not permitted.
**Handicap Access:** No.
**Children:** Not especially welcome.
**Languages:** Spanish, English.
**Your Host:** Lorenzo.

# BALEARIC ISLANDS - IBIZA - JESUS

## Casa Alexio

Men ♂

On top of a rise above the bay of Talamanca is placed the very private guesthouse called *Casa Alexio,* far away from any road noise, but only 3 minutes by car to town. From the breakfast terrace, one has a wonderful view over Ibiza Town, the harbor and the sea reaching to the neighboring island of Formentera. A pool with bar, terraces and a comfortable living room with cable TV add to your comfort. The beach is a five-minute walk.

**Address: Barrio Ses Torres 16, Jesús, Ibiza 07819 Spain.**
**Tel: (34-71) 31 42 49, Fax: (34-71) 31 26 19.**

**Type:** Guesthouse with 24 hr self-service poolside bar.
**Clientele:** Men only
**Transportation:** Free pick up service or taxi from airport.
**To Gay Bars:** 1.7 miles or 3 minutes by car.
**Rooms:** 15 rooms with king beds.
**Bathrooms:** All private bathrooms.
**Meals:** Breakfast included.
**Dates Open:** All year.
**High Season:** April through October.
**Rates:** Single 6,000 Pts-10,000 Pts, double 12,000 Pts-16,000 Pts.
**Discounts:** Special off-season rates.
**Credit Cards:** Visa, MC, Amex, Eurocard.
**Rsv'tns:** Required.
**Reserve Through:** Travel agent or call direct.
**Parking:** Free off-street parking.
**In-Room:** Satellite TV, AC, maid and laundry service.
**On-Premises:** TV lounge, meeting rooms, laundry facilities.
**Exercise/Health:** Whirl pool. Workout possibilities in pool area.
**Swimming:** Pool, ocean beach next door.
**Sunbathing:** At poolside or on beach.
**Nudity:** Permitted at the pool. Nude beach nearby.
**Smoking:** Permitted without restrictions.
**Pets:** Not permitted.
**Children:** Not permitted.
**Languages:** Spanish, English, German, French, Italian, Dutch, Portuguese.

# BALEARIC ISLANDS - MALLORCA - PALMA

## Hotel Rosamar

Gay-Friendly ♀♂

### *Relax and Just Do Nothing*

The ***Hotel Rosamar,*** privately owned and recently refurbished, offers comfortable accommodation together with a friendly bar and a large, attractive garden terrace. All rooms have private bathrooms and terraces. It has a very easy, relaxed atmosphere. The hotel is situated in the midst of Palma's night life area with all the gay bars and discos situated on the same street and within walking distance of the hotel. There is also a small, interesting beach a ten-minute walk away.

Mallorca is the largest of the Balearic Islands off the eastern coast of Spain. It is extremely beautiful with many changes of landscape and one of the most stunning beaches in Europe. Chopin, George Sand, Robert Graves, and now Michael Douglas are some of the people who have made their homes here.

**Address: Avenida Joan Miro 74, Palma de Mallorca 07015 Spain.**
**Tel: (34-71) 732723, Fax: (34-71) 283828.**

**Type:** Hotel with bar.
**Clientele:** Mostly hetero with a gay & lesbian following
**Transportation:** Taxi or airport bus to Plaza España, then taxi. Or taxi or direct from airport. Hire car best for sightseeing.
**To Gay Bars:** All the present gay bars are located on the same street as the hotel.
**Rooms:** 40 rooms with single or double beds.
**Bathrooms:** All en suite.
**Meals:** Continental breakfast.
**Vegetarian:** 2 or 3 restaurants in Palma city 10 minutes away.
**Dates Open:** March 20th to January 8th.
**High Season:** July, August, September.
**Rates:** Per night per room: Double Pta 4,600-Pta 5,100, single Pta 3,800-Pta 4,300.
**Credit Cards:** MC, VISA & Eurocard.
**Rsv'tns:** Required.
**Reserve Through:** Travel agent or call direct.
**Parking:** Ample free off-street parking.
**In-Room:** Telephone, towels changed daily, most rooms with balconies.
**On-Premises:** Terrace, sun deck, meeting rooms & TV lounge.
**Exercise/Health:** Sauna 50 metres away.
**Swimming:** In the ocean.
**Sunbathing:** On common sun deck.
**Nudity:** Permitted on the sun deck at the discretion of other guests.
**Smoking:** Permitted.
**Pets:** Not permitted.
**Handicap Access:** No.
**Children:** Permitted only if WELL-controlled, otherwise NO!!!
**Languages:** Spanish, English, German, Italian, French.
**Your Host:** Bill & Basilio.

IGTA

# MADRID

## Hostal Hispano

Gay/Lesbian ♀♂

### *Come to Madrid!*

You will find ***Hostal Hispano*** right in the center of Madrid quite close to the Gran Vía. There is good access to both public and private transportation, and gay bars are only one block away. The recently restored hotel has 20 rooms, all of them with private bathrooms. Each room has color TV, telephone, and music channels.

**Address: Hortaleza 38, Madrid 28004 Spain.**
**Tel: (34-1) 531 4871, Fax: (34-1) 521 8780.**

**Type:** Hotel.
**Clientele:** Mostly gay & lesbian with some hetero clientele
**Transportation:** Bus & taxi.
**To Gay Bars:** 1 block.
**Rooms:** 20 rooms with single or double beds.
**Bathrooms:** 20 private & 2 shared bath/toilet/showers.
**Dates Open:** All year.
**Rates:** Single Pta 4,200, double Pta 5,500.
**Credit Cards:** Visa, MC.
**Rsv'tns:** Required.
**In-Room:** Color TV, telephone, maid & laundry service.
**On-Premises:** TV lounge, meeting rooms, laundry facilities.
**Exercise/Health:** Nearby gym, sauna, steam, massage.
**Swimming:** Nearby pool.
**Smoking:** Permitted throughout hotel. No non-smoking rooms available.
**Pets:** Not permitted.
**Handicap Access:** Yes.
**Children:** Welcome.
**Languages:** Spanish, English, French.

# SITGES

## Hotel Romàntic i La Renaixença

Gay/Lesbian ♀♂

### *Two Lovely Hotels in the Center of Sitges*

***Hotel Romàntic & Hotel Renaixença*** are in the center of Sitges, a resort town with a long tradition as a vacation spot and center for culture. ***Hotel Romàntic's*** spacious garden is open daily, with snack and drink service. Occupying three adjacent townhouses, its rooms have baths, period furniture and many have terraces overlooking the garden. ***Hotel Renaixença's*** 16 nicely decorated rooms have private bath and WC. There is easy access, by foot, to the beach, shopping and nightlife. Nearby transportation services places as diverse as the local waterpark and the city of Barcelona.

**Address: Carrer de Sant Isidrc 33, Sitges 08870 Spain.
Tel: (34-3) 894 8375, Fax: (34-3) 894 8167.**

**Type:** Bed & breakfast hotel with bar & solarium.
**Clientele:** Mostly gay & lesbian with some hetero clientele
**Transportation:** From Barcelona aiport, train to El Prat de Llobregat then train to Sitges. Taxi.
**To Gay Bars:** Centrally-located to all gay bars.
**Rooms:** 85 rooms with single or double beds.
**Bathrooms:** All private.
**Meals:** Continental breakfast, buffet breakfast.
**Dates Open:** La Renaixença all year. Hotel Romàntic Mar 15-Oct 19, '97.
**Rates:** 6,300 Pts-11,600 Pts plus VAT.
**Credit Cards:** VISA, Amex, Diners & Eurocard.
**Rsv'tns:** Required, but call-ins welcome.
**Reserve Thru:** Call direct.
**Minimum Stay:** 1 day.
**Parking:** Off-street public pay parking.
**In-Room:** Telephone & maid service. Top rooms have ceiling fans.
**On-Premises:** Meeting rooms, TV lounge & solarium.
**Swimming:** Ocean beach and swimming pool nearby.
**Sunbathing:** On roof, private & common sun decks.
**Nudity:** 1/2 hr walk to nudist beach.
**Smoking:** Permitted without restrictions.
**Pets:** Permitted.
**Children:** Welcome.
**Languages:** Catalan, Spanish, English, French & Italian
**Your Host:** Gonçal.

# TARRAGONA

## MontyMar

Q-NET Women ♀

### *Get Close to Nature without Giving up Comfort*

Miami Playa is a small settlement on the Mediterranean Sea coast. In this garden city, between the nearby mountains and the sea, and only 600 meters from the beach, you will find the Spanish-Moorish-style *MontyMar*. All rooms are on the ground floor with a little terrace facing our beautiful, quiet and peaceful patio with water-basin, fountain, plants and flowers. Here you can sunbathe, enjoy your drinks, or eat your meals. In addition to our dinners, you can find many nearby restaurants with Spanish, French, and German specialities. We have about 4 km of sandy beach divided in 2 open beaches and about 8 small bays. You will also find our marvelous large nude beach 6 km to the south. None of our beaches is overcrowded, even in high season. For more mobility you can rent cars, bicycles, or motor-scooters, or take the train to the villages or towns (Barcelona, Tarragona, Tortosa) along the coast. Motor- and sailing-boat trips can be arranged for small groups. If you like nature but don't want to give up comfort, you will enjoy your vacation in our cherished surroundings at *MontyMar*.

**Address: Av Principe de España, Apdo (Box) 113, Miami Playa, Tarragona 43892 Spain.**
**Tel: (34-77) 81 05 30.**

**Type:** Guesthouse.
**Clientele:** Mostly women with men welcome
**Transportation:** Car is best. (Car rental at Barcelona airport.)
**To Gay Bars:** 17 km to Salou (25 min by car).
**Rooms:** 8 rooms.
**Bathrooms:** All private.
**Meals:** Full breakfast of eggs, yoghurt, cereals, meat, cheese, milk, orange juice, etc. Snacks & dinner at extra charge.
**Vegetarian:** Available upon request.
**Complimentary:** Welcome drink.
**Dates Open:** Apr 1 to Oct 15 (in May women only), Dec 15 to Jan 15 for women only.
**High Season:** July-August.
**Rates:** DM 80-103 (approx $60-$75 USD), double occupancy including breakfast, taxes. Pay in dollars, DM or pesetas.
**Discounts:** For groups of 10 or more people, upon request. 10% for individuals for stays of 11 or more days.
**Rsv'tns:** Accepted with prepayment for 3 nights.
**Reserve Through:** Call direct.
**Parking:** Adequate free off-street parking.
**In-Room:** Maid, room & laundry service.
**On-Premises:** Meeting rooms.
**Swimming:** 600 meters to ocean beach.
**Sunbathing:** On the patio, beach, private or common terraces.
**Nudity:** Nude beach 6 km away.
**Smoking:** Permitted without restrictions.
**Pets:** Permitted upon request with extra charge, US $2 daily.
**Children:** Welcome. May & Christmas when women only, permitted upon request.
**Languages:** Spanish, German, English, Hebrew.
**Your Host:** Ulla & Christel.

# SWITZERLAND

## BASEL

### White Horse Hotel

Gay-Friendly ♀♂

*The White Horse* is a small hotel in the center of Basel. The hotel's modern atmosphere is reflected in each room, as well as in the especially welcoming breakfast room. Its huge two-storey glass panel window admits ample sunlight, brightening up this always pleasant morning space. Our continental breakfast, much more than the usual, spoils our guests with a buffet area brimming with a variety of fresh bread, yoghurts, fresh fruit, etc.

WHITE HORSE

All our rooms have a shower, WC, television and telephone. Our rates include service, taxes and a Swiss breakfast buffet. The bar is open to everybody, especially our guests, and in the summer, the courtyard is used for relaxing and enjoying drinks until late at night. You can take nice long walks along the river Rhine, only one block away. We look forward to welcoming you the next time you visit Switzerland.

**Address: Webergasse 23, Basel 4005 Switzerland. Tel: (41-61) 691 57 57, Fax: (41-61) 691 57 25.**

**Type:** Hotel with a bar for residents.
**Clientele:** Mostly straight clientele with a gay & lesbian following (20%-50%)
**Transportation:** Airport bus to central station, then taxi, or direct streetcar #8 to "Rheingasse."
**To Gay Bars:** 5-minute walk to gay/lesbian bar.
**Rooms:** 5 singles, 5 doubles, 6 with queen beds.
**Bathrooms:** All private showers & toilets.
**Meals:** Expanded continental breakfast.
**Dates Open:** All year.
**High Season:** Spring & autumn.
**Rates:** Single SF 95.00-125.00, double & queen SF 125.00-185.00.
**Discounts:** 10% to guests with a copy of Inn Places.
**Credit Cards:** Visa, Eurocard, Diners.
**Rsv'tns:** Required 2 wks in advance.
**Reserve Through:** Call direct.
**Parking:** Limited on-street parking.
**In-Room:** TV, telephone, alarm clock, color TV.
**On-Premises:** Public telephone, shoeshine & cigarette machines.
**Smoking:** Permitted without restrictions.
**Pets:** Limited (1 dog or cat).
**Handicap Access:** No.
**Children:** Permitted.
**Languages:** German, French, English, Spanish, Italian.

# ZÜRICH

## Hotel Goldenes Schwert

Gay/Lesbian ♀♂

### *Switzerland's Only Truly Gay Hotel*

The relaxed and informal atmoshpere of ***Hotel Goldenes Schwert*** radiates from the front desk to each of the guestrooms. Located in the heart of the Old Town, near the financial district and just two minutes from the famous Bahnhofstrasse shops, the hotel offers the charm and warmth of a quality hotel. There are 25 large rooms and three suites, and single rooms have French beds. All rooms have private bath, hair dryer & cosmetic box, color TV, VCR, direct-dial phone. Some rooms have attractive balconies. The popular one-and-only T&M gay disco is on premises, and other gay venues are a short walk away.

**Address: Marktgasse 14, Zürich 8001 Switzerland. Tel: (41-1) 266 1818, Fax: (41-1) 266 1888. E-mail: hotel@gaybar.ch. http://www.gaybar.ch.**

**Type:** Hotel with bar & disco.
**Clientele:** Mostly gay & lesbian with some hetero clientele
**Transportation:** Airport hotel bus on request, or taxi. 12 km from airport.
**To Gay Bars:** T&M disco on premises, others a 2 min walk.
**Rooms:** 22 rooms, 3 suites, 5 theme rooms with single or double beds.
**Bathrooms:** All private bath/toilets.
**Meals:** Continental breakfast Sfr 9.50.
**Dates Open:** All year.
**High Season:** May-Sept.
**Rates:** Single Sfr 99; Double Sfr 130-150; Suites Sfr 290-320.
**Discounts:** 20% after 4 days.
**Credit Cards:** MC, Visa, Amex, Diners, Eurocard.
**Rsv'tns:** Required.
**Reserve Through:** Travel agent or call direct.
**Parking:** Adequate on-street pay parking.
**In-Room:** Maid & laundry service, telephone, color cable TV, VCR.
**Exercise/Health:** Nearby gym, Jacuzzi, sauna, steam, massage.
**Swimming:** Lake.
**Sunbathing:** At beach.
**Smoking:** Permitted everywhere. No non-smoking rooms available.
**Pets:** Permitted.
**Handicap Access:** No.
**Children:** No.
**Languages:** German, English, French.
**Your Host:** Thomas.

# UK - ENGLAND

## AVON

### The Lodge

Men ♂

## *An Englishman's Home is His Castle*

It is said that an "Englishman's home is his castle," but this Englishman's Castle is his Home! The buildings, Banwell Castle and ***The Lodge,*** are set in 21 acres of grounds and gardens, with fine views to The Mendips and The Welsh Hills. Completed in 1847, Banwell Castle is of historical and architectural interest.

***The Lodge*** is a charming Victorian Gate House Lodge, full of Olde World charm and atmosphere. It is peaceful, romantic and intimate, for those very special occasions, either weekend or mid-week breaks. Also of interest is Banwell Village, a pleasant rural Somerset Village, with 4 pubs and a selection of shops. Visitors will take pleasure in strolling through the older parts of the village which have buildings dating back to the 17th century.

**Address: Banwell Castle, Banwell, Avon BS24 6NX England.**
**Tel: (44-1934) 823 122, Fax: (44-1934) 823 946.**

**Type:** Bed & breakfast.
**Clientele:** Mostly men with women welcome
**Transportation:** Car is best, free pick up from bus or train.
**To Gay Bars:** 20 minutes by car.
**Rooms:** 4 doubles/singles.
**Bathrooms:** 2 shared.
**Meals:** Full English break.
**Vegetarian:** Always available.
**Complimentary:** Fresh fruit, tea, coffee.
**Dates Open:** All year.
**High Season:** July, August, September.
**Rates:** £25.00 per person per night.
**Discounts:** 10% for 2 or more nights.
**Rsv'tns:** Required.
**Reserve Thru:** Call direct.
**Parking:** Ample off-street parking.
**In-Room:** Color TV, laundry service, maid & room service.
**On-Premises:** TV lounge.
**Swimming:** Five miles to pool or ocean beach.
**Sunbathing:** On roof.
**Smoking:** Permitted in TV lounge.
**Pets:** Permitted by prior arrangement.
**Handicap Access:** No.
**Children:** Not permitted.
**Languages:** English.
**Your Host:** Chris.

# BATH

## The Kennard Hotel

Gay-Friendly ♀♂

### *A Georgian Town House of Charm and Character*

Staying at ***The Kennard Hotel*** gives you a chance to discover and enjoy a true Georgian Town House. Now restored to a charming small hotel with its own special character, it was originally built in 1794 during Bath's grand era of elegance and prosperity. Each of its 13 bedrooms are thoughtfully and individually furnished for your comfort. The original Georgian kitchen, now a delightful garden-style bistro, is the setting for a full choice of English or continental breakfasts. Quietly situated in Henrietta Street, its city centre location is ideal – just over Pulteney Bridge, only minutes from the Abbey and Roman Baths and with easy access from London or the Station.

**Address: 11 Henrietta Street, Bath, Avon BA2 6LL England.**
**Tel: (44-1225) 310472, Fax: (44-1225) 460054,**
**E-mail: kennard@dircon.co.uk.**

**Type:** Bed & breakfast hotel.
**Clientele:** Mostly hetero with a gay & lesbian following
**To Gay Bars:** 5-minute walk.
**Rooms:** 10 doubles & 2 singles.
**Bathrooms:** 10 private, others share.
**Meals:** Full English break.
**Vegetarian:** Available upon request.
**Complimentary:** Coffee & tea-making facilities in room.
**Dates Open:** All year.
**Rates:** £58-£75.
**Credit Cards:** MC, VISA, Amex & Diners.
**Rsv'tns:** Required.
**Reserve Thru:** Call direct.
**Parking:** On-street parking.
**In-Room:** Colour TV, direct-dial phone, hair dryers, tea & coffee.
**Children:** Not permitted.
**Languages:** English.

# BIRMINGHAM

## The Fountain Inn

Gay/Lesbian ♂

Built as a traditional Victorian public house, ***The Fountain Inn*** retains much of its original character. With guest accommodations refurbished to the highest standards, ***The Fountain Inn*** offers its guests a warm and welcoming stay. All rooms are en suite or have separate, private toilet and tea- and coffee-making facilities, telephone, central heating and colour TV with satellite movie channel and in-house video channel. Guest keys give 24-hour access.

***The Fountain Inn's*** very popular, ground-floor gay bar is only a 5- to 10-minute walk from the other gay bars and clubs, the main railway station and Birmingham's shopping and entertainment areas. Birmingham is known as the "Second City" (London being the first!), and is at the heart of the motorway network, with London approximately 1-1/2-hour's drive away and "Shakespeare

*continued next page*

country" only a half-hour's drive. Birmingham now boasts one of the largest conference centers, exhibition centers and international airports in Europe.

**Address: 102 Wrentham St, Birmingham, West Midlands B5 6QL England. Tel: (44-121) 622 1452, Fax: (44-121) 622 5387. In USA call (407) 994-3558, Fax: (407) 994-3634.**

**Type:** Guesthouse inn. Our bar has pub food & is open evenings & Sat & Sun days.
**Clientele:** Mostly men with women welcome
**Transportation:** Car, 5-min taxi ride from railway station (£2), taxi from Birmingham International Airport approx £12.
**To Gay Bars:** Five min walk to nearest bars & discos.
**Rooms:** 5 rooms with single or double beds.
**Bathrooms:** Private: 1 bath/toilet, 3 shower/toilet, 1 shower/wash basin & toilet.
**Meals:** Full breakfast. Continental breakfast served in bedroom.
**Vegetarian:** Available on request before arrival.
**Complimentary:** Tea/coffee making facilities & biscuits.
**Dates Open:** All year.
**Rates:** £25.00-£45.00 per night.
**Discounts:** 10% for 3 nights & over, if booked direct.
**Credit Cards:** MC, Visa.
**Rsv'tns:** Required.
**Reserve Through:** Travel agent or call direct.
**Parking:** Free off-street parking for 5 cars, on-street pay parking, free weekends.
**In-Room:** Color TV with in-house, non-porn video channel, movie channel via satellite, telephone, coffee/tea-making facilities & maid service.
**On-Premises:** Meeting rooms.
**Smoking:** Permitted.
**Pets:** Not permitted.
**Handicap Access:** No.
**Children:** Not permitted.
**Languages:** English.
**Your Host:** Erick.

# BLACKPOOL

## Ashbeian Hotel

**Gay-Friendly 50/50 ♀♂**

### *Your Happiness is Our Concern*

***The Ashbeian*** is a small, intimate guesthouse best suited to those who like superb home cooking, comfort and personal service in quiet surroundings. Well situated, it is yards from the beach with its lights, the tower, shops, restaurants and most theatres. For those liking a drink, we have a very pleasant bar with popular entertainment in our sister hotel over the road, which you may use while enjoying the more peaceful atmosphere here. ***The Ashbeian*** has been awarded "Three Crowns Recommended" by the English Tourist Board for 1996.

**Address: 49 High St, Blackpool FY1 2BH England. Tel: (44-1253) 26301 (Tel/Fax). In September 1997: (44-1253) 626 301 (Tel/Fax).**

**Type:** Guesthouse.
**Clientele:** 50% gay & lesbian & 50% hetero clientele
**Transportation:** Car or train.
**To Gay Bars:** A 2-minute walk to gay bars.
**Rooms:** 5 rooms with single or double beds.
**Bathrooms:** 5 private shower/toilets.
**Meals:** Full breakfast. Evening meals at £7.
**Vegetarian:** Always available.
**Complimentary:** Teas & coffee in bedrooms.
**Dates Open:** All year.
**High Season:** During Illuminations — Sept-Oct.
**Rates:** £10-£22 B&B. Evening meals at £7.
**Credit Cards:** MC, Visa.
**Rsv'tns:** Required.
**Reserve Through:** Travel agent or call direct.
**Parking:** Ample on-street pay parking.
**In-Room:** Color TV with remote, coffee & tea-making facilities, maid & laundry service.
**Exercise/Health:** Nearby gym, weights, Jacuzzi, sauna, massage.
**Swimming:** Nearby pool, ocean.
**Sunbathing:** At beach.
**Your Host:** Graham.

## Tremadoc Guest House

**Gay/Lesbian** ♀♂

***Tremadoc*** is a large, comfortable licensed guesthouse overlooking the sea and located only minutes from the town centre, North Station, North Pier, Gynn Square and the Promenade and five minutes from pubs and clubs. Rooms have hot and cold water, shaver points and colour TV. Front door and bedroom keys are supplied on arrival. There is a bar for guests, and a colour TV lounge for guests' use. Guests receive a concessionary pass to the Flamingo, a popular gay club. Breakfast is included, with evening meal optional. Singles are always welcome. There are nightly Illuminations – 6-1/2 miles of lights – from the first week of September until early November.

**Address: 127-129 Dickson Rd, North Shore, Blackpool FY1 2EU England. Tel: (44-1253) 24 001.**

**Type:** Guesthouse.
**Clientele:** Good mix of gay men & women
**Transportation:** Bus or train from London or Manchester to Blackpool, then taxi.
**To Gay Bars:** 5 minutes to gay bars.
**Rooms:** 9 rooms with single, double & bunk beds.
**Bathrooms:** 2 shower rooms & 3 toilets.
**Meals:** Full English breakfast. Optional evening meal £4.00.
**Vegetarian:** Available upon request.
**Complimentary:** Free pass to Flamingo.
**Dates Open:** All year.
**High Season:** Sep. through beginning of Nov.
**Rates:** High season £15.00. Low season £11.00.
**Discounts:** Winter specials available on request.
**Rsv'tns:** Required for Illumination weekends.
**Reserve Thru:** Call direct. 24 hour answering service.
**Parking:** Ample free on-street parking.
**In-Room:** Tea-making facilities.
**On-Premises:** Colour TV lounge.
**Exercise/Health:** All available in nearby big hotel.
**Swimming:** Ocean beach across the road.
**Sunbathing:** On beach.
**Smoking:** Permitted without restrictions.
**Pets:** Not permitted.
**Handicap Access:** No.
**Languages:** English.

# BOURNEMOUTH

## The Creffield

**Gay/Lesbian** ♂

### *Exclusively Gay Hotel With the Air of a Country Home*

A well-appointed red-brick, late Edwardian house, ***The Creffield*** was originally built as a rich man's family summer home. It stands on its own grounds with a car park to the fore and a large private garden to the rear. All of the bedrooms are en-suite and the single rooms aren't single rooms at all, but small doubles. Our two largest bedrooms have four-poster beds. Breakfast is served either in the conservatory or outside on the patio. It is an easy walk from ***The Creffield*** to all of Bournemouth's main venues. If, like the hotel's owner, you have a car, like a drink, but don't much relish the thought of walking your

*continued next page*

feet off, then this is the place for you. Park your car in the free car park and five licensed venues are a hop, skip and a jump away (no taxis necessary).

**Address: 7 Cambridge Road, Bournemouth BH2 6AE England. Tel: (44-1202) 317 900.**

**Type:** Bed & breakfast guesthouse with bar on premises.
**Clientele:** Mostly men with women welcome
**Transportation:** Car, train from London, taxi.
**To Gay Bars:** A 2 minute walk to gay bars.
**Rooms:** 9 rooms with singles or doubles. 2 rooms have 4-poster beds.
**Bathrooms:** All private shower/toilets.
**Meals:** Full breakfast.
**Vegetarian:** Always available.
**Complimentary:** Tea & coffee. Courtesy trays in each room.
**Dates Open:** All year.
**High Season:** June-September.
**Rates:** Single £24-£30; Double £42-£48; 4-poster £48-£54.
**Discounts:** 10% on stays of 7 or more nights.
**Reserve Through:** Call direct.
**Minimum Stay:** Two nights during high season.
**Parking:** Adequate free, well-lit off-street parking.
**In-Room:** Color TV, coffee & tea-making facilities, maid service.
**On-Premises:** Meeting room, TV lounge, full central heating, large private garden.
**Exercise/Health:** Nearby gym, sauna, steam.
**Swimming:** Pool & ocean nearby.
**Sunbathing:** On patio.
**Smoking:** Permitted in rooms, bar & smoking room. There is a non-smoking "dry" lounge.
**Pets:** Permitted. Must be kept on a lead.
**Handicap Access:** No.
**Children:** Absolutely not.
**Languages:** English.
**Your Host:** Roger.

## Ravensbourne Hotel

**Gay-Owned 50/50 ♀♂**

You'll get a warm and friendly welcome at ***Ravensbourne Hotel*** when you visit this Edwardian town noted for its many trees. Our house has a family atmosphere where guests can feel at home. The seaside is not far away, but if you're not in the mood to wander, our private English country garden is perfect for sunning, weather permitting. Your host will orient you with details of local amenities and other information.

**Address: 17 Westby Rd, Boscombe, Bournemouth BH5 1HA England. Tel: (44-1202) 309 770.**

**Type:** Guesthouse with bar, disco & shops.
**Clientele:** 50% gay & lesbian & 50% hetero clientele
**To Gay Bars:** 3 min walk to gay bar.
**Rooms:** 10 doubles.
**Bathrooms:** 1 shared, 1 WC each floor.
**Meals:** Full English breakfast, evening meal optional 7 British pounds.
**Vegetarian:** Available upon request.
**Complimentary:** Tea.
**Dates Open:** All year.
**Rates:** Summer £17.00, winter £12.00.
**Rsv'tns:** Preferred in summer.
**Reserve Thru:** Call direct.
**Parking:** 3 off-street spaces, 1 on-street.
**In-Room:** Color cable TV, maid & laundry service.
**Swimming:** At nearby nude ocean beach, gay frequented.
**Sunbathing:** At beach, on patio.
**Smoking:** Permitted except in dining room, shower, landings
**Pets:** Small dogs OK.
**Handicap Access:** No.
**Children:** Permitted.
**Languages:** English.

# BRIGHTON

## Alpha Lodge Private Hotel

**Gay/Lesbian ♂**

### *THE Gay Hotel for Single People*

As Brighton's longest established exclusively gay hotel (since 1980), ***Alpha Lodge*** welcomes gay men and women year round. We are situated in a pleasant Regency square, overlooking the Victorian Palace Pier, a few yards from the beach and most gay clubs. Local gay saunas and nude bathing beaches are nearby. Our well-appointed, intimate hotel, originally built in the early 1800's, is run by Derrick and Charles, both of whom are actively gay. It is run as a continuous house party.

Five rooms have double beds, each with its own private shower. The remainder, with single beds, are both with and without private showers. All rooms have colour TV, radio/alarm clocks, intercom and hot drink facilities, and, of course, self-controlled central heating. There are adequate public showers, toilets, a bathroom and a cosy lounge with an open fire and colour TV. Our full English breakfast is renowned. The Steine Room Suite, consists of Turkish Bath, rest area with an open fire and colour TV, shower area, hair dryer, toilet and lockers. Towels and wraps are provided, and the facility is free to residents Wednesday, Friday and Saturday for 1-1/2 hours in early evening.

All guests have front door keys, and there are no petty restrictions. Friends may be brought in at all times. There is a safe for valuables (free). Everything is geared to make one's stay comfortable and relaxing. A full fire certificate has been issued. A map of Gay Brighton, a privilege card for entry to the gay clubs, and a welcoming drink upon arrival are all provided as part of the basic charge for the room. We are not licensed, but alcoholic drinks may be brought into the hotel, where ice and mixers are available 24 hours a day. We look forward to your joining us.

**Address: 19 New Steine, Brighton, E Sussex BN2 1PD England.**
**Tel: (44-1273) 609 632, Fax: (44-1273) 690 264.**

**Type:** Guesthouse with a steam-room suite.
**Clientele:** Mostly men with women welcome. Exclusively gay
**Transportation:** Take taxi or No. 7 minibus from the station.
**To Gay Bars:** 2-minute walk to gay & lesbian bars.
**Rooms:** 10 rooms with single & double beds.
**Bathrooms:** 1 shared bath, 7 showers (2 shared) & 5 shared toilets.
**Meals:** Full English breakfast. Cold soft drinks at low cost 24 hours.
**Vegetarian:** Available with overnight notice.
**Complimentary:** Coffee, tea, soft drink on arrival. Unlimited hot drinks in the rooms.
**Dates Open:** All year. Closed in December for vacation.
**High Season:** July, Aug & Bank Holidays, mid-season May/June & Sept/Oct.
**Rates:** Low season: £21-£42 per room; mid-season: £22-£44; high season: £23-£46.
**Discounts:** 7th night free to all & 10% to members of gay groups.
**Credit Cards:** MC, VISA, Amex & Eurocard.
**Rsv'tns:** Recommended in summer 10 days in advance.
**Reserve Through:** Travel agent or call direct.
**Minimum Stay:** One night. Longer stays on bank holidays.
**Parking:** Free & pay parking on the street at or near the hotel.
**In-Room:** Color TV, beverage-making facilities, radio/alarm clock & intercom in all rooms. Room service for continental breakfast.
**On-Premises:** TV lounge, public telephone, meeting rooms & refrigerator for cold sodas.
**Exercise/Health:** Steam room (free on Wed., Fri. and Sat. evenings).
**Swimming:** Pool, ocean beach nearby.
**Sunbathing:** On the beach.
**Nudity:** 10-minute walk to public nudist beach.
**Smoking:** Permitted without restrictions.
**Pets:** Not permitted.
**Handicap Access:** No.
**Children:** Not permitted.
**Languages:** English.
**Your Host:** Derrick & Charles.

## Barrington's Private Hotel

**Gay-Friendly 50/50 ♀♂**

Luxury rooms and a full English breakfast enhance your stay at ***Barrington's Private Hotel.*** We are located opposite the Royal Pavilion and two minutes from *Revenge* nightclub and ocean beach.

**Address: 76 Grand Parade, Brighton BN2 2JA England.**
**Tel: (44-1273) 604 182.**

**Type:** Hotel with licensed lounge bar.
**Clientele:** 50% gay & lesbian & 50% hetero clientele
**Rooms:** Luxury rooms with double & twin beds.
**Bathrooms:** Private showers, shared baths.
**Meals:** Full English breakfast.
**High Season:** June-September.
**Rates:** £16-£20 per person.
**Reserve Thru:** Call direct.
**Parking:** Free parking behind hotel
**In-Room:** Remote control colour TV, radios & intercom.
**Swimming:** 2-minute walk to ocean.
**Smoking:** Permitted.
**Pets:** Small pets permitted.
**Handicap Access:** No.
**Children:** Permitted over 5 years of age.
**Languages:** English.
**Your Host:** Barry.

## Brighton Court Craven Hotel

**Gay/Lesbian ♀♂**

The ***Brighton Court Craven Hotel*** is open year-round, and in 1993 was voted "Hotel of the Year" in the United Kingdom.

**Address: 2 Atlingworth St, Brighton BN2 1PL England.**
**Tel: (44-1273) 607710.**

**Type:** B&B hotel with bar.
**Clientele:** Gay & lesbian. A good mix of men & women
**Transportation:** Train or bus from Gatwick airport (30 minutes).
**To Gay Bars:** A 3-min. walk.
**Rooms:** Rooms have single or double beds.
**Bathrooms:** 10 private bath/shower/toilets, 3 shared WCs only.
**Meals:** Full breakfast.
**Vegetarian:** Available any morning.
**Complimentary:** Tea, coffee & chocolate facilities in rooms.
**Dates Open:** All year.
**High Season:** April-Sept.
**Rates:** Midweek £33 & £17, weekends £36 & £19.
**Discounts:** On stays of 1 week, midweek rates.
**Rsv'tns:** Required.
**Reserve Thru:** Call direct.
**Parking:** Ample on-street parking. Parking is quite safe.
**In-Room:** Coffee/tea-making facilities, colour TV, laundry service.
**On-Premises:** Meeting rooms, TV lounge.
**Swimming:** Nearby ocean & pool.
**Sunbathing:** On beach.
**Smoking:** Permitted anywhere.
**Pets:** Permitted.
**Handicap Access:** Yes, one ground-floor room.
**Children:** Please inquire.
**Languages:** English, Arabic, Hebrew.
**Your Host:** Bryan & Nagib.

## Catnaps Private Guest House

**Gay/Lesbian ♂**

***Catnaps*** is situated close to the sea, about 8 minutes' walk from the Royal Pavilion, unique to Brighton and actually the historical reason for the growth of the town in the 18th-19th centuries. We aim for a family atmosphere and we like guests to feel welcome. All rooms have hot and cold water and are centrally heated. Showers and toilets are in a separate area of the house and are easily reached from the bedrooms. Guests have their own keys to the house.

**Address: 21 Atlingworth St, Brighton, E Sussex BN2 1PL England.**
**Tel: (44-1273) 685 193, Fax: (44-1273) 622 026.**

**Type:** Guesthouse.
**Clientele:** Mostly men with women welcome
**Transportation:** Taxi or bus from station.
**To Gay Bars:** 5-minute walk to gay & lesbian bars.
**Rooms:** 7 rooms.
**Bathrooms:** Shared baths & toilets. 2 rooms have private showers, all have sinks.
**Meals:** Full English breakfast.
**Complimentary:** Tea & coffee upon arrival.
**Dates Open:** All year.
**High Season:** June-Aug.
**Rates:** Single £18 for 1 night. £35 twin. Double £36 for a night with shower, £34 without shower.
**Discounts:** On longer stays.
**Rsv'tns:** Preferred.
**Reserve Thru:** Call direct.
**Parking:** Adequate free on-street parking.
**In-Room:** Tea or coffee delivered to room.
**On-Premises:** TV lounge & public telephone.
**Swimming:** Pool & ocean beach are nearby.
**Sunbathing:** On the beach.
**Nudity:** 5-minute walk to nude beach.
**Smoking:** Permitted without restrictions.
**Pets:** Permitted with prior arrangement. Owner responsible for pets.
**Handicap Access:** No.
**Children:** Not normally, but open to requests.
**Languages:** English, limited French.
**Your Host:** Malcolm & Charlie.

## Coward's Guest House

**Men ♂**

***Coward's Guest House*** is a Regency-style guesthouse in the heart of Brighton's gay area, five minutes' walk from gay bars and clubs. Brighton is a very gay town with a lively gay nightlife. The town is known for its Regency architecture and for The Pavilion, a winter palace which was built by the Prince Regent. The train from London takes only 50 minutes, making Brighton an easy commute to London's tourist attractions.

**Address: 12 Upper Rock Gardens, Brighton BN2 1QE England.**
**Tel: (44-1273) 692677.**

**Type:** Guesthouse.
**Clientele:** Men only
**Transportation:** Brighton Station, then taxi.
**To Gay Bars:** Many gay pubs & clubs within 5 min walk.
**Rooms:** 2 singles, 4 doubles & 2 triples with single & double beds.
**Bathrooms:** 4 en suite. All rooms have showers.
**Meals:** Full English or vegetarian breakfast.
**Vegetarian:** Anytime.
**Complimentary:** Tea & coffee in all rooms.
**Dates Open:** All year.
**High Season:** April - Oct.
**Rates:** Summer: double £42-£55, single £24-£26. Winter: double £38-£50, single £21-£23.
**Credit Cards:** Visa, Access.
**Rsv'tns:** Required.
**Reserve Thru:** Call direct.
**Parking:** Free on-street parking.
**In-Room:** Color TV.
**Swimming:** At nearby sea.
**Sunbathing:** On the beach.
**Smoking:** Permitted.
**Pets:** Not permitted.
**Handicap Access:** No.
**Children:** Not permitted.
**Languages:** English.
**Your Host:** Gerry & Cyril.

## George IV Hotel

Gay-Friendly 50/50 ♀♂

### *Our Welcome is Warm Throughout the Year*

Only 100 yards from the sea, Brighton's ***George IV Hotel*** offers comfortable accommodation in a beautiful five-floor Regency building. Our small, gay-run motel is situated in the city centre, a five-minute walk to the gay bars and nightclubs. In addition, we have a licenced bar on premises for residents and their friends. We also maintain a connection with the gay-friendly Sussex Arts Club, which has a licenced restaurant and further accommodation.

All of our rooms have single or queen-sized beds, full ensuite baths, colour television and telephone, as well as tea- & coffee-making facilities. Our rates range from £25 for a single room to £70 for a double room with a sea view. From Gatwick Airport it is a short 20-minute train ride to Brighton. Genuine guest comments about our room with a sea view include "A handsome house in which to lodge a friend." "The seafront at the garden's end." "Perfect views of an historic pier." "The welcome is warm throughout the year."

**Address: 34 Regency Square, Brighton BN1 2FJ England.**
**Tel: (44-1273) 321 196.**

**Type:** Hotel with licenced bar for residents & their friends.
**Clientele:** 50% gay & lesbian & 50% hetero clientele
**Transportation:** 20 min from Gatwick Airport on train.
**To Gay Bars:** A 5 min walk to gay bars.
**Rooms:** 8 rooms with single or double beds.
**Bathrooms:** All private.
**Meals:** Continental breakfast included. Full English breakfast £3.95.
**Complimentary:** Tea & coffee tray in room.
**Dates Open:** All year.
**High Season:** April-November.
**Rates:** £25 single, £70 double with sea view.
**Discounts:** 10% on stays of 7 nights or more.
**Credit Cards:** MC, Visa, Diners, Eurocard, Electron.
**Rsv'tns:** Better to book ahead.
**Reserve Through:** Call direct.
**Parking:** Ample on-street pay parking. Underground car park next to hotel.
**In-Room:** Color TV, telephone, coffee & tea-making facilities.
**On-Premises:** Lounge.
**Exercise/Health:** Nearby gym.
**Swimming:** 100 yards to the sea.
**Smoking:** Permitted.
**Pets:** Not permitted.
**Handicap Access:** No.
**Children:** Welcome.
**Languages:** English.
**Your Host:** Brian.

## Hudsons Guest House

Gay/Lesbian ♀♂

***Hudsons*** is an early 19th century gentleman's residence, which has been skillfully converted to an exclusively gay guest house. Concealed behind louvered doors in each room, are shower and washbasin, wardrobes and tea- and coffee-making facilities. All rooms also have colour TV, and some have sofas. Also of high standard is the decor, which was coordinated by Next Interiors. Devonshire Place is a quiet road in the middle of Brighton's gay village, so clubs and bars are only a five-minute walk from our door. Also nearby are the Royal Pavilion, the sea, beaches, the pier and the town centre.

***Hudsons*** is the only gay hotel inspected by, and whose standards are approved by, the Tourist Authority. The quality and warmth of ***Hudsons*** has established it in the fine tradition of English hospitality. We promise to do our best to make sure you go away wishing the next visit were tomorrow.

**Address: 22 Devonshire Place, Brighton, E Sussex BN2 1QA England. Tel: (44-1273) 683 642, Fax: (44-1273) 696 088.**

**Type:** Guesthouse.
**Clientele:** Good mix of gay men & women
**Transportation:** Train to Brighton Station then taxi or No. 7 bus.
**To Gay Bars:** Within easy walking distance (2 mins) of all gay bars.
**Rooms:** 9 rooms with single, queen or king beds.
**Bathrooms:** All have private showers, 1 has shower/toilet en suite.
**Meals:** Proper English breakfast in dining room with homemade preserves.
**Vegetarian:** Just ask, one of us is vegetarian! Superb vegetarian restaurants nearby.
**Complimentary:** Tea, coffee, sherry, juice, biscuits & free Brighton map at check-in, concessions to clubs.
**Dates Open:** All year.
**Rates:** Single £20.00-£28.00, double £34.00-£46.00 (includes breakfast for two).
**Discounts:** Mid-week, extended stay.
**Credit Cards:** MC, VISA & Amex.
**Rsv'tns:** A good idea, but not always necessary.
**Reserve Through:** Travel agent or call direct.
**Minimum Stay:** Bank holidays or weekends.
**Parking:** On-street parking nearby.
**In-Room:** Washbasins, private shower, tea-making facilities, colour TV, central heating, telephone, laundry service, maid service.
**On-Premises:** Guests lounge.
**Exercise/Health:** Nearby gym, weights, Jacuzzi, sauna, steam, massage.
**Swimming:** At nearby ocean beach & pool.
**Sunbathing:** Patio and nearby beach.
**Nudity:** Permitted at nearby beach (10 mins).
**Smoking:** Not permitted in dining room.
**Pets:** Not permitted.
**Handicap Access:** No.
**Children:** Not permitted.
**Languages:** English, some French, German.
**Your Host:** Frank & Graham.

IGTA

## Shalimar Hotel

Gay/Lesbian ♂

### *Undisputedly: Brighton's Most Centrally Located Hotel for Clubs and Bars*

***Shalimar*** has been under the personal supervision of your internationally known hosts, Kevin and Lawrence, since 1983. All rooms are tastefully decorated and have color TV, vanity units and shaving points. Front rooms have sea views. Deluxe rooms have full bath, fridge and a private balcony overlooking the sea and pier. Not to be missed is our Victoria Suite, complete with four-poster bed. An excellently cooked breakfast is included. A free map gives you the locations of gay bars and clubs, and a privilege pass for entry to clubs is also provided. We now have a full residents' bar, the Backroom Bar, which is proving very popular and is a fun place to meet other guests. Send for our brochure. You will not be disappointed. Special discount on presentation of Inn Places.

**Address: 23 Broad St, Marine Parade, Brighton, Sussex BN2 1TJ England. Tel: (44-1273) 605 316.**

**Type:** Hotel with backroom resident's bar.
**Clientele:** Mostly men with women welcome
**Transportation:** Car, taxi or bus. Nearest airport London Gatwick, then 1/2 hour by train to Brighton.
**To Gay Bars:** 2 min. by foot.
**Rooms:** 10 rooms with single, double or queen beds.
**Bathrooms:** 5 private & 3 private showers only. Shared: 1 full bath, 1 WC.
**Meals:** Full breakfast.
**Vegetarian:** Available upon request.
**Complimentary:** Tea, coffee in rooms.
**Dates Open:** All year.
**High Season:** April through October.
**Rates:** £35-£50/two per.
**Discounts:** 10% on stays of 1 week or longer.
**Credit Cards:** MC, VISA, Amex, Diners, Eurocard, JCB.
**Rsv'tns:** Preferred.
**Reserve Through:** Travel agent or call direct.
**Minimum Stay:** 3 days during bank holidays only.
**Parking:** Adequate on-street parking.
**In-Room:** Colour TV, telephone, coffee & tea-making facilities & room service. Deluxe rooms with refrigerators.
**On-Premises:** Backroom bar, fun bar.
**Exercise/Health:** Nearby gym, weights, Jacuzzi, sauna, steam, massage.
**Swimming:** Nearby pool. 2 minutes to the beach.
**Sunbathing:** On beach.
**Nudity:** 10 minutes to nude beach.
**Smoking:** Permitted except in dining room, non-smokers' rooms available.
**Pets:** Not permitted.
**Handicap Access:** No.
**Children:** Not permitted.
**Languages:** English.
**Your Host:** Kevin & Lawrence.

## Sinclairs Guest House

Gay/Lesbian ♂

### *Exclusively Gay*

***Sinclairs*** is a historically listed building located within minutes of the major Brighton gay area, the famous Regency Pavilion and the sea. All bedrooms have color TV, alarm clock radios, free tea- and coffee-making facilities and central heating. Some have refrigerators and en-suite facilities. A full English breakfast is served till late in the morning, and a continental one till midday. ***Sinclairs*** is exclusively gay and provides a detailed, up-to-date map of the gay area. The garden is available in summer for relaxing in the sun. All guests have room and front door keys, and friends of guests are welcome.

**Address: 23 Upper Rock Gardens, Brighton BN2 1QE England.**
**Tel: (44-1273) 600 006 and (44-1831) 248 361.**

**Type:** Bed & breakfast guest house.
**Clientele:** Mostly men with women welcome
**Transportation:** Train to Brighton station, then taxi.
**To Gay Bars:** 5-minute walk to nearest gay bar or club.
**Rooms:** 5 rooms & 1 suite with single or double beds.
**Bathrooms:** 3 en suite, 3 sinks only, 1 shared WC, & 2 shared bath/shower/toilet.
**Meals:** Full breakfast.
**Vegetarian:** Upon request with no extra charge.
**Complimentary:** Tea & coffee in room.
**Dates Open:** All year.
**High Season:** July-September.
**Rates:** £16.00-£21.50 per person.
**Credit Cards:** MC, VISA & Eurocard.
**Rsv'tns:** Preferred.
**Reserve Thru:** Call direct.
**Parking:** Adequate on-street parking.
**In-Room:** Color TV, fridge, hair dryer, clock radios, coffee/tea-making facilities.
**On-Premises:** Lounge.
**Swimming:** Ocean beach.
**Sunbathing:** On beach & in garden.
**Nudity:** Permitted on the public beach.
**Smoking:** Permitted without restrictions.
**Pets:** Not permitted.
**Handicap Access:** No.
**Children:** Not permitted.
**Languages:** English, Spanish, French, German, Italian, Portuguese.

# CORNWALL

## Penryn House

**Gay/Lesbian ♀♂**

### *A Picturesque Cornish Seaside Getaway*

Polperro is probably the most photographed and painted Cornish fishing village with its whitewashed fishermen's cottages and colourful fishing fleet bobbing in the harbour. It is conveniently located for British Rail and is easily accessible by car, just 30 minutes from the city of Plymouth. ***Penryn House*** is set in its own grounds a short seven-minute walk to the picturesque harbour. Ensuite rooms are comfortably furnished, centrally heated, and the candlelit restaurant offers excellent cuisine using the best of local seafood and produce. Parking is available on the grounds. Ask about our Gay Murder Mystery Weekends and women-only holidays.

**Address: The Coombs, Polperro, Cornwall PL13 2RG England. Tel: (44-1503) 272 157.**

**Type:** Hotel with restaurant & bar.
**Clientele:** Gay & lesbian with some hetero clientele
**Transportation:** Train to nearby town of Looe.
**To Gay Bars:** 40 minutes to gay bars.
**Rooms:** 10 doubles, 2 twins.
**Bathrooms:** 12 ensuite.
**Meals:** Full English breakfast & dinner.
**Vegetarian:** Always available.
**Complimentary:** Tea & coffee in rooms.
**Dates Open:** All year.
**High Season:** July & August.
**Rates:** £26 per person, per night (£52 per room) high season.
**Discounts:** Low & mid-season discounts available.
**Credit Cards:** Visa, MC, Amex.
**Rsv'tns:** Recommended during high season.
**Reserve Through:** Phone or fax direct.
**Parking:** Parking on grounds.
**In-Room:** Television, telephone, alarm clock, courtesy tray, hair dryers, radio.
**On-Premises:** Bar, restaurant, log fires in cooler months.
**Swimming:** Nearby pool & beach.
**Sunbathing:** At nearby beach.
**Smoking:** Permitted in bar.
**Pets:** Welcome.
**Handicap Access:** No.
**Your Host:** Christine & Isa.

## Rosehill in the Fern

**Gay/Lesbian ♀♂**

Cornwall is a beautiful, rural part of England, with fabulous beaches, cliffs and a warm climate (by British standards!). ***Rosehill in the Fern*** is about 8 miles from Truro, the small city which is the main town in Cornwall, with its magnificent cathedral built out of Cornish granite. We are also about 8 miles from the village of Portreath, where there is a thriving gay club. The spectacular north Cornish coast, with its golden beach and breathtaking cliffs, is only five minutes by car. Our house is a very attractive eighteenth-century country house set in two acres of garden and woodland. The property is secluded but conveniently located for all that Cornwall has to offer, and is ideal for either a quiet "get away from it all" break, or a more energetic touring holiday.

The interior of the house is quietly and tastefully decorated and furnished, the emphasis being on country-house-style comfort, where guests are able to enjoy privacy or each other's company by choice. We have a large drawing room and dining room. Each bedroom is spacious and comfortably furnished with double or twin beds. Our two principal rooms have access through French windows to their own private patio with room to sit outside. The en suite bathrooms are appointed to a very high standard with bath, shower, wash basin and WC. Guests are given a front door key and are encouraged to come and go as they wish. We aim to provide a high standard of comfort and good home cooking in order to ensure that our guests feel welcome and at home.

**Address: Roseworthy, Camborne, Cornwall TR14 0DU England. Tel: (44-1209) 712 573.**

**Type:** Guesthouse (private hotel).
**Clientele:** Mainly gay & lesbian with some hetero clientele
**Transportation:** Car is best. Pick up airport, train, bus or ferry dock.
**To Gay Bars:** 10 miles to Perranporth.
**Rooms:** 3 rooms with single or double beds.
**Bathrooms:** All private.
**Meals:** Full English break.
**Vegetarian:** We cater to special dietary needs with advance notice.
**Dates Open:** All year.
**High Season:** April-Sept.
**Rates:** £25.00 per person per night in high season, £20.00 during off season.
**Discounts:** Weekly and fortnightly rates.
**Credit Cards:** MC, Visa & Eurocard.
**Rsv'tns:** Greatly appreciated.
**Reserve Thru:** Call direct.
**Parking:** Ample free off-street parking.
**In-Room:** Color TV, coffee & tea-making facilities.
**On-Premises:** TV lounge & meeting rooms.
**Exercise/Health:** Nearby gymnasium and leisure centre.
**Swimming:** At nearby full-sized heated pool or ocean.
**Sunbathing:** On the patio, lawn & at the beach.
**Smoking:** Permitted in public rooms, discouraged in sleeping rooms.
**Pets:** Dogs welcome by arrangement.
**Handicap Access:** Not equipped for severe disabilities.
**Children:** Not permitted.
**Languages:** English.
**Your Host:** Barry.

## Ryn Anneth

Gay/Lesbian ♀♂

### *Join Us for Exclusively Gay Lodgings & Tea in an English Garden*

***Ryn Anneth*** is a small, exclusively gay, very friendly guesthouse in a quiet cul-de-sac close to beaches and the town centre. We have a reputation for cleanliness, cozy comfort and a sociable atmosphere. St. Ives is arguably the most beautiful town in Cornwall, and Cornwall one of the most beautiful counties in England. Nearby attractions range from prehistoric sites to modern theme parks and the new St. Ives Tate modern art gallery which opened in 1993.

**Address: Southfield Place, St Ives, Cornwall TR26 1RE England. Tel: (44-1736) 793 247.**

**Type:** Bed & breakfast.
**Clientele:** Exclusively gay & lesbian
**Transportation:** Taxi or short walk from railway station.
**To Gay Bars:** Occasional gay/lesbian venues at various locations.
**Rooms:** 1 single, 3 doubles, & space for an extra person.

*continued next page*

**Bathrooms:** 2 ensuite, 2 shared.
**Meals:** Full breakfast.
**Vegetarian:** An hour's notice or pot luck. Vegetarian cafes in town.
**Complimentary:** Tea, coffee, soft drinks. A glass or two of homemade wine for all brave & sociable guests.
**Dates Open:** All year.
**High Season:** Jun - Sept.
**Rates:** £18-£22.
**Rsv'tns:** Preferable during high season.
**Reserve Thru:** Call direct.
**Parking:** Ample, free on-street parking & nearby cheap carpark.
**In-Room:** Color TV, laundry service for long stay guests & just shout for tea/coffee.
**On-Premises:** Large lounge meeting room. TV if necessary, but considered a waste of time with so much beautiful Cornwall around you.
**Exercise/Health:** Available nearby.
**Swimming:** At ocean beach nearby & other hotel pools open to the public.
**Sunbathing:** On the patio, in the garden or on nearby beaches.
**Smoking:** Not permitted in dining room before meals.
**Pets:** Permitted if in strict control. No elephants please.
**Handicap Access:** No, St. Ives is very hilly.
**Children:** No.
**Languages:** English.

# COTSWOLDS

## Crestow House

Gay-Friendly ♀♂

### *English Victorian Stone Country House in a Picturesque Cotswold Village*

***Crestow House*** was built in 1870 out of Cotswold sandstone by a local wool merchant. The generously-sized rooms and 12 foot ceilings speak of the affluence this region once knew. Stow is on the Fosse Way, the old wool route built at the time of the Roman occupation. The concluding battles of the English Civil War took place in the fields outside Stow. The town still preserves its Mediaeval stocks and has one of the oldest pubs in Britain. The wool trade has since given way to the antiques business, with Stow having about 20 antique dealers. There is also a twice-yearly horse trading fair (mid May and October) where gypsies from England and Ireland trade their ponies. The area is filled with castles and stately homes with formal, world-renowned gardens and is also known for its high quality food. We would be glad to recommend some of our fine local restaurants or cook for you if you let us know in the morning that you would like to eat with us that evening. Stow is about a 2-hour drive from London (1-1/4-hour train ride from Paddington Station), 20 minutes north of Oxford and 15 minutes south of Stratford-on-Avon, home of the Royal Shakespeare Company.

***Crestow House*** is three-storied with a large conservatory, living room, dining room, large country breakfast room and back veranda, with some of the best views and sunsets in Britain. The house has a large walled back garden with heated swimming pool. The middle floor consists of four double bedrooms with en suite bathroom/toilets, antique furnishings, English country decor and modern double beds. The floor-to-ceiling windows make the best of the beautiful countryside that surrounds the house. The owners live on the upper floor.

**Address: Stow-on-the-Wold, Gloucestershire GL54 1JY England.**
**Tel: (44-1451) 830 969, Fax: (44-1451) 832 129,**
**E-mail: 100620.773@compuserve.com.**

**Type:** Bed & breakfast country manor house.
**Clientele:** Mostly straight with a gay & lesbian following
**Transportation:** Car is best. Train service available from London's Paddington Station to Moreton-In-Marsh.
**To Gay Bars:** 15 miles or 35 minutes by car.
**Rooms:** 4 rooms with double or king (2 twin) beds.
**Bathrooms:** All en suite.
**Meals:** Expanded continental breakfast.
**Vegetarian:** Available upon prior request. 5-minute walk to restaurant.
**Complimentary:** Tea or coffee on arrival, pre-dinner sherry.
**Dates Open:** All year except Jan.
**High Season:** June-Sept.
**Rates:** £25-£34/person.
**Discounts:** For 2 nights or longer.
**Credit Cards:** MC, Visa.
**Rsv'tns:** Preferred.
**Reserve Thru:** Call direct.
**Parking:** Free off-street parking.
**In-Room:** Color TV, laundry service.
**On-Premises:** Laundry facilities. Can send/receive fax.
**Exercise/Health:** Sauna & fitness equipment on premises.
**Swimming:** Pool on premises.
**Sunbathing:** At poolside.
**Smoking:** Not permitted.
**Pets:** Not permitted.
**Handicap Access:** No.
**Children:** Not especially welcome.
**Languages:** English, Spanish, Italian & German.
**Your Host:** Frank & Jorge.

# DERBYSHIRE

## Hodgkinson's Hotel & Restaurant

**Gay-Friendly 50/50 ♀♂**

***Hodgkinson's Hotel and Restaurant,*** built over 200 years ago, was purchased in run-down condition by Malcolm and Nigel and has been undergoing renovations ever since. Current restoration projects include the 1/4-acre of terraced gardens, affording fine views of the valley. The main project, however, is the opening of the caves which have been used as cellars until recent times. They form part of the labyrinth which runs through the hillside, supposedly dating back to Roman times. Malcolm's hairdressing salon, Redken-appointed, is now well-established, used by the local community & hotel guests.

**Address: South Parade, Matlock Bath, Derbyshire DE4 3NR England. Tel: (44-1629) 582 170, Fax: (44-1629) 584 891.**

**Type:** Hotel and hairdressing salon.
**Clientele:** 50% gay & lesbian & 50% hetero clientele
**Transportation:** Car is best, free pick up from train.
**To Gay Bars:** 3/4 hour to Derby, Nottingham, Sheffield.
**Rooms:** 6 doubles.
**Bathrooms:** All private shower & toilet en suite.
**Meals:** Full breakfast.
**Vegetarian:** Available to order.
**Complimentary:** Tea & coffee in rooms.
**Dates Open:** All year.
**Rates:** £45.00-£80.00 double, £30.00 single.
**Discounts:** For special breaks & 2-night weekends.
**Credit Cards:** MC, Visa, Amex, Access.
**Rsv'tns:** Recommended.
**Reserve Through:** Call direct.
**Parking:** Adequate off-street parking.
**In-Room:** Color TV, telephone, room & laundry service.
**On-Premises:** Meeting rooms.
**Exercise/Health:** Sauna.
**Swimming:** 2 miles to pool.
**Smoking:** Permitted without restrictions.
**Pets:** Permitted, but not in dining room.
**Handicap Access:** No.
**Children:** Permitted.
**Languages:** English.
**Your Host:** Malcolm & Nigel.

# DEVON

## White House Hotel

Gay-Friendly ♀♂

### *A Small Hotel of Unusual Charm*

The ***White House Hotel*** is a lovely Grade II listed building with great aesthetic and architectural appeal. Set in an acre of lawned and terraced gardens on the edge of a South Devon village, the house has a unique atmosphere reminiscent of an altogether quieter and less hurried age.

Now think of South Devon: imagine a land of thatched cottages, cream teas, green fields, secret byways, where the climate is kind and where, for centuries, travellers have sought peace and quiet. Our special part of this beautiful and historic corner of England is called the South Hams, a name derived from the old English word "Hamme," meaning an enclosed or sheltered place.

To the west of us are Kingsbridge and the Salcombe Estuary, famous for its sailing. To the north are Totnes and the wild expanses of Dartmoor. To the east is picturesque Dartmouth, and sweeping 'round us to the south is the spectacular South Hams coastline with its rugged cliffs, sandy beaches and quiet coves, most of it protected by the National Trust.

Returning from a day spent out and about, guests can relax over a drink in the Normandy Bar Lounge, a cosy room in the oldest part of the house. Doctor Smalley's Drawing Room, from which French doors open onto the terrace and garden, offers elegant and comfortable surroundings in which to chat over the day's happenings.

The newly built Garden Room Restaurant makes a delightful setting for sampling our delicious food cooked on the kitchen range. We take advantage of the best fresh local produce and are always happy to cater for individual tastes.All our bedrooms are en suite and each is individual in its furnishings and character. Books and pictures abound, the garden beckons and cocktails await you on the terrace.

**Address: Chillington, Kingsbridge, South Devon TQ7 2JX England.**
**Tel: (44-1548) 580580, Fax: (44-1548) 581124.**

**Type:** Hotel with restaurant.
**Clientele:** Mainly hetero clientele with a gay/lesbian following
**Transportation:** Car is best. Pick up from train approx £17.
**To Gay Bars:** 25 mi to Plymouth & 18 mi via ferry to Torquay.
**Rooms:** 8 rooms with single or double beds.
**Bathrooms:** 5 priv. bath/toilets, 3 priv. shower/toilets.
**Meals:** Full breakfast. 4-course dinner available.
**Vegetarian:** Avail. anytime.
**Complimentary:** Tea, coffee on arrival, beverage trays in all bedrooms.
**Dates Open:** Apr-Dec.
**High Season:** Jun-Sep.
**Rates:** Low season: £33.00-£52.00 per person. High season: £36.00-£56.00 per person.
**Discounts:** 10% for 2 or more nights on Dinner Room & Breakfast inclusive terms.
**Credit Cards:** MC, Visa, Amex.
**Rsv'tns:** Required.
**Reserve Thru:** Call direct.
**Minimum Stay:** 2 nights on weekends.
**Parking:** Ample free private parking on grounds.
**In-Room:** Color TV, telephone, video tape library, coffee/tea-making facilities, room & maid service.
**On-Premises:** TV lounge & laundry facilities.
**Swimming:** Ocean beach 2 miles away.
**Sunbathing:** At beach or in garden.
**Nudity:** Permitted at nudist beach 6 miles away.
**Smoking:** Permitted in bar lounge & bedrooms.
**Pets:** Dogs permitted by prior arrangement. Not allowed in public rooms.
**Children:** Permitted over 5 years of age.
**Languages:** English, French, & German.
**Your Host:** David & Michael.

# ISLE OF WIGHT

## The Edgecliffe Hotel

Gay-Friendly ♀♂

### *Always a Warm Welcome*

Minutes from the famous cliff top walk, the ***Edgecliffe*** is a charming and comfortable, well-run hotel with an enviable reputation for its first-class food and relaxed, friendly atmosphere. From the moment you enter, you know you are in a hotel that cares about its guests and as a result, a non-smoking regime has been adopted. The hotel is fully centrally heated and guests have their own bedroom and front door keys to allow complete freedom. Our tastefully decorated bedrooms are light, spacious and airy. Most are en-suite and each offers a full array of comforts including shaver socket, hair dryer, colour TV – and beautiful views.

Enjoy a hearty breakfast to start the day or savour our expertly cooked five-course evening dinner. We offer a choice of menus to suite every palatte, including vegetarian. Sunny Shanklin is an ideal holiday destination with its picturesque old village, history, entertainment and easy access to wonderful walking country. We have maps and guidebooks, as well as walking itineraries for you. Our aim is to ensure that the ***Edgecliffe Hotel*** offers all that you seek to make your stay a memorable one.

Address: 7 Clarence Gardens, Shanklin, Isle of Wight PO3 6HA England. Tel: (44-1983) 866 199 (Tel/Fax).

**Type:** Hotel with bar & small fitness room.
**Clientele:** Mostly hetero with a gay & lesbian following
**Transportation:** Ferries cross to the island from Portsmouth & Southampton, then train or bus to Shanklin.
**To Gay Bars:** No gay bars here.
**Rooms:** 10 rooms with single, queen or bunk beds.
**Bathrooms:** Private: 4 shower/toilets, 2 bath/toilet/shower, 6 sinks only. Shared: 1 bath/shower/toilet, 2 WCs only.
**Meals:** Full breakfast, dinner.
**Vegetarian:** We offer a full vegetarian choice at breakfast & dinner.
**Complimentary:** Full range of beverages in rooms, with biscuits.
**Dates Open:** All year.
**High Season:** July-August.
**Rates:** Low £15.00-£19.00, mid £16.00-£22.00, high £18.50-£26.50.
**Discounts:** Group bookings 5%-10%.
**Credit Cards:** MC, Visa, Amex, Diners, Eurocard.
**Rsv'tns:** Required.
**Reserve Through:** Travel agent or call direct.
**Parking:** Adequate on-street parking.
**In-Room:** Colour TV, coffee & tea making facilities, maid service.
**On-Premises:** Video tape library, TV lounge.
**Exercise/Health:** Gym, weights. Nearby gym, weights, Jacuzzi, sauna, steam, massage.
**Swimming:** Nearby pool & ocean.
**Sunbathing:** On patio.
**Smoking:** We are a non-smoking establishment.
**Pets:** Not permitted.
**Handicap Access:** No.
**Children:** Welcome.
**Languages:** English, some French & German.
**Your Host:** Gary & John.

# LONDON

## Bromptons Guesthouse

Q-NET Gay-Owned & -Operated ♂

### *Accommodations in the Centre of Gay London*

Experience the ever-growing, lively, fun gay scene from ***Bromptons Guesthouse,*** in the heart of Earls Court gay village, London. Guests are within 250 yards walking distance of all Earls Court nightlife, restaurants, shopping, and close enough to experience London's history, theatre, and many galleries. London's airports are within easy reach.

***Bromptons*** is personally run by Peter and Jeremy who are pleased to offer expert advice on how to get the best out of your London vacation. The guesthouse's spacious, clean, well-decorated rooms all have a double bed (including singles), colour TV, direct-dial phones, coffee- and tea-making facilities, and iron/ironing boards. We provide up-to-date magazines and maps in each room for your personal use, which give all the latest information about what's happening on London's vibrant gay scene.

Our proximity to Earls Court underground station makes travelling within London extremely easy, and we are on a direct line with Heathrow Airport. For longer stays we offer a discount of one night per week, and we'll be pleased to quote for very long visits. Come to London at any time of the year – there is always plenty to do and see. We are busy throughout the year, and an early reservation is recommended.

**Address: PO Box 629, London SW5 9XF England.**
**Tel: (44-171) 373 6559, Fax: (44-171) 370 3923.**

**Type:** Guesthouse.
**Clientele:** Exclusively gay. Mostly men
**Transportation:** From Heathrow: tube to Earls Court. From Gatwick: Express train to Victoria, then tube to Earls Court.
**To Gay Bars:** 250 yards.
**Rooms:** 10 (for single or double occupancy).
**Bathrooms:** 5 private, others share.
**Dates Open:** All year.
**Rates:** Guesthoues: £45-£75.
**Discounts:** 10% for cash payment. Guesthouse: weekly rate, pay for 6 nights.
**Credit Cards:** MC, VISA, Amex.
**Rsv'tns:** Required.
**Reserve Through:** Call direct.
**Parking:** Off-street parking (but not recommended in Central London).
**In-Room:** Daily maid service, TV, phones, coffee & tea-making facilities, irons & hairdryers.
**Exercise/Health:** Nearby gym.
**Sunbathing:** At Hyde Park
**Smoking:** Permitted without restrictions.
**Pets:** Not permitted.
**Handicap Access:** No.
**Children:** Not permitted.
**Languages:** English & Hebrew.
**Your Host:** Peter & Jeremy.

## Clone Zone Luxury Apartments

Q-NET **Gay/Lesbian ♂**

Modern ***Clone Zone Luxury Aparments*** are fitted out to the highest specification and one, a quasi-penthouse, sleeps four comfortably and is fully equipped with a comprehensive kitchen, lounge and bathroom with bath and shower. The apartments are situated above the Clone Zone shop, centrally located in the heart of the London gay scene and near Heaven and G.A.Y., two of the biggest gay discos in Europe.

Soho is central to the capital's principle tourist attractions – Buckingham Palace, the National Portrait Gallery, Piccadilly Theatreland, shopping and wonderful restaurants. History, culture and fun are at your the doorstep. Come at the end of May for the Soho Pink Weekend. The first week of July sees the week of Pride events culminating on July 5th of the carnival with 20,000 visitors. In August, see the Summer Rites carnival. In fact, at any given time of year London has so much to offer.

Clone Zone is one of the world's largest chains of lesbian and gay stores and is located throughout the U.K. The stores stock an original and extensive range of leatherwear, rubberwear, underwear and fashionwear, as well as books, magazines, toys, videos and a wide selection of greeting cards and postcards.

**Address: 64 Old Compton St, Soho, London W1 England.**
**Tel: Reservations: (44-171) 287 3530, Fax: (44-171) 287 3531.**

**Type:** Self-contained apartment.
**Clientele:** Mostly men with women welcome
**Transportation:** Heathrow Airport tube to Piccadilly tube.
**To Gay Bars:** Short walk to all gay venues.
**Rooms:** 1 apartment with king bed & double sofa bed. Sleeps up to 4 & 3 dbl rms.
**Bathrooms:** Private bath/toilet/shower.
**Vegetarian:** Avail. nearby.
**Dates Open:** All year.
**High Season:** June-Sept.
**Rates:** From £50 to £100 per night.
**Discounts:** 10% for E.C.M.C., M.S.C & Bears Club.
**Credit Cards:** MC, Visa, Amex, Diners & Eurocard.
**Rsv'tns:** Required.
**Reserve Thru:** Call direct.
**Parking:** Ample pay parking.
**In-Room:** Color TV, AC, telephone, coffee & tea-making facilities.
**On-Premises:** Shop.
**Exercise/Health:** Nearby gym, weights, Jacuzzi, sauna, steam & massage.
**Pets:** Not permitted.
**Handicap Access:** No.
**Children:** Not especially welcome.
**Languages:** English.

# Number Seven Guesthouse

Gay/Lesbian ♀♂

## *Best UK Gay Hotel, 1994 & 1995*

***Number Seven Guesthouse,*** an exclusively lesbian and gay accommodation in an elegant Victorian townhouse, was voted Hotel/Guesthouse of the Year in 1994 & 1995 by readers of the UK gay national newspaper *The Pink Paper.*

The guesthouse, situated in a quiet, tree-lined avenue in Brixton (a lively cosmopolitan area of the London borough of Lambeth – one of the six inner London boroughs) is ideally situated for sightseeing, shopping, and the gay scene. It is also extremely well served by public transportation throughout the day and night, with good connections to the rail, tube (underground zone 2), bus, and night bus. The international terminal for EuroStar trains direct to Paris and Brussels is a short taxi ride; Heathrow and Gatwick airports are just 35-55 minutes. The guesthouse is only five minutes' walk from The Fridge, voted the best London gay club, and Sub-Station South, one of London's newest gay clubs.

Since 1992, ***Number Seven*** has striven to improve the facilities offered to its international clientele. The guesthouse, tastefully decorated in striking colours, has all modern facilities yet maintains many original features. All bedrooms have private bathrooms, direct-dial phones, ceiling fans, colour cable TVs, tea and coffee, hair dryers, pine furnishings, and central heating. The Honeymoon Suite with its own corner bath and bidet is popular. Laundry service, iron and ironing board, fax, and photocopier are available on request.

A complimentary full English breakfast is available every morning in the conservatory overlooking the beautiful walled garden. Try over-easy eggs with British bacon, sausage, tomatoes/beans, mushrooms, and ***Number Seven's*** world-famous hash browns. If you like a Caribbean flavour, add some plantain or, for the taste of real England, try some black pudding. If you can't manage all that, try the continental or vegetarian menu. There's fresh fruit, yogurt, and, of course, as much tea, coffee, and orange juice as you can drink. Your gay hosts, John and Paul, will be happy to provide you with up-to-date information on London's gay scene to ensure you have a great time.

Address: 7 Josephine Ave, London SW2 2JU England.
Tel: (44-181) 674 1880, Fax: (44-181) 671 6032,
E-mail: johnpaul@noseven.demon.co.uk/.
http://www.noseven.demon.co.uk/.

**Type:** Bed & breakfast guesthouse.
**Clientele:** Gay & lesbian. Good mix of men & women
**Transportation:** Main line train, tube, bus, car, or taxi from London airports, intercity train stns; pick ups cost petrol plus time.
**To Gay Bars:** 4 min walk or 4 min by tube to a variety of gay & lesbian bars & clubs.
**Rooms:** 8 rooms with single, twin, double, triple or queen beds.
**Bathrooms:** 4 en suite bath/shower/toilets & 4 en suite shower/toilets.
**Meals:** Full, buffet, continental or expanded continental breakfasts included in room rate.
**Vegetarian:** Vegetarian breakfast always available. Good local vegetarian restaurants.
**Complimentary:** Tea & coffee on arrival & in rooms.
**Dates Open:** All year.
**Rates:** £49-£99.
**Credit Cards:** MC, VISA.
**Rsv'tns:** Required. Preferred credit card booking.
**Reserve Thru:** Call direct.
**Minimum Stay:** 2 nights weekends & other holidays.
**Parking:** Ample easy off-street free parking in front of guesthouse.
**In-Room:** Clock/radio, remote CTV w/video & satellite link, direct-dial telephone, ceiling fans, tea/coffee-making facilities, Bahama fans, hair dryer, maid & laundry service. Iron & ironing board upon request.
**On-Premises:** Pay phone, dining room with maps & guides, conservatory, private walled garden, photo copier, fax machine, message service.
**Exercise/Health:** Weights, rowing machine, situp bench available upon request. Recreation centre & park nearby.
**Swimming:** 2 pools 1/2 mile away.
**Sunbathing:** In front & back gardens.
**Smoking:** Permitted without restrictions in bedrooms.
**Pets:** Not permitted.
**Handicap Access:** No. 3 steps to front door, no wide doorways.
**Children:** Not permitted.
**Languages:** English, British Sign Language.
**Your Host:** Paul & John.

IGTA

## One-Sixty (160) Regents Park Road

Gay/Lesbian ♀♂

### *The Best Bed and Breakfast in London*

Chris welcomes you to his comfortable and elegant Victorian home. ***160 Regents Park Road,*** with just two bedrooms, is a friendly alternative to London's larger gay hotels: Offering a relaxed base for your sightseeing, trips to the theatre and ventures into the city's varied gay night life. The townhouse is on three floors (many stairs, no lift!) leading finally to an impressive roof garden.

The style throughout is an eclectic mix of antiques, prints and drawings, with many ultra-modern fittings. The larger bedroom, with book-lined walls, wooden floor and Oriental carpet, is reminiscent of a gentleman's library. A stunningly modern shower room adjoins and includes a toilet, washbasin and a really powerful shower. The smaller room is airy and light, with its own washbasin and use of the sumptuous bathroom on the floor below. Both rooms have remote-controlled color TV, bathrobes, hairdryer and telephones with itemised billing. Your breakfast choice is so "full," it may leave you feeling that way! Only the best ingredients are used, such as quality jams, breads and pastries, free-range eggs and bacon.

Our area is one of the most charming and celebrated corners of London, with a "village" atmosphere that has attracted millionaires and the famous. The range of shopping and eating could hardly be bettered, including stores of every necessity and a choice of over a dozen restaurants. From Primrose Hill, itself, there are won-

*continued next page*

derful views over London and close by are the open spaces of Hampstead Heath and Regents Park. From our Underground station, Chalk Farm, Piccadilly Circus is just 15 minutes away. In fact, ***160 Regents Park Road*** is the ideal compromise, close to the city centre, but without its noise and hassle. With all my experience and knowledge of what London has to offer, I hope you will share your time with me.

**Address: Primrose Hill, London NW1 8XN England.**
**Tel: (44-171) 586 5266 (Tel/Fax).**

**Type:** Bed & breakfast.
**Clientele:** Mostly gay & lesbian with occasional hetero clientele
**Transportation:** Subway, car or taxi. From airports subway is Chalk Farm station.
**To Gay Bars:** 10 min. to gay pubs and cafés in Camden Town & Hampstead.
**Rooms:** 2 rooms with double or queen bed.
**Bathrooms:** 1 en suite shower/toilet, 1 shared bath/shower/toilet.
**Meals:** Extensive English breakfast menu.
**Vegetarian:** Available with minimum notice. Vegetarian restaurant in neighborhood.
**Complimentary:** Tea, coffee, juices, & chilled water.
**Dates Open:** All year except Dec 15-Jan 1.
**Rates:** Small double, £45.00 for 1, £60.00 for 2 or large double, £75.00 for 2.
**Discounts:** For periods longer than 7 nights.
**Credit Cards:** MC, VISA & Eurocard.
**Rsv'tns:** Required.
**Reserve Through:** Travel agent or call direct.
**Minimum Stay:** 2 nights.
**Parking:** Adequate on-street parking.
**In-Room:** Color TV, maid service & telephone.
**On-Premises:** Dining room for daytime tea, coffee; roof terrace in summer; glazed dome for winter sitting; laundry facilities.
**Swimming:** At nearby covered public pools.
**Sunbathing:** On the roof.
**Smoking:** Permitted, but not encouraged.
**Pets:** Not permitted.
**Handicap Access:** No.
**Children:** Inquire.
**Languages:** English, French & Italian.
**Your Host:** Chris.

# MANCHESTER

## Clone Zone Manchester Holiday Apartment

**Gay/Lesbian ♀♂**

### *Your Gay Manchester Holiday Apartment*

The most appealing aspect of the ***Clone Zone Manchester Holiday Apartment*** is its central location in the heart of Manchester's gay and lesbian village. The apartment is close to principal tourist attractions: guided tours of the sets of "Coronation Street" and other well-known shows, the G-Mex Concert and Exhibition Center, museums, art galleries, theatres, stately homes, and the Liverpool and Blackpool seasides. The apartment is also within walking distance of the metro and bus and rail stations. In August there's a famous village charity carnival weekend, attracting thousands of visitors to the gay village. The apartment, two floors above the world-famous Clone Zone gay and lesbian retail chain store, is equipped with colour TVs, a bathroom with shower, telephone, and tea- and coffee-making facilities. One room has a bed settee that will accommodate an extra two persons.

**Address: 39 Bloom St, Manchester M1 3LY England.**
**Tel: (44-161) 236 1398, Fax: (44-161) 236 5178.**

**Type:** Apartment.
**Clientele:** Gay & lesbian. Good mix of men & women
**To Gay Bars:** 1 block.
**Rooms:** 1 apartment.
**Bathrooms:** Private bath.
**Dates Open:** All year.
**Rates:** Single £25.00, double £30.00, 3-4 persons £40.00.
**Rsv'tns:** Required.
**In-Room:** Color TV, telephone, coffee/tea-making facilities, kitchen.
**Smoking:** Permitted.
**Pets:** Not permitted.
**Languages:** English.

# NEWCASTLE-UPON-TYNE

## Cheviot View Guest House

Gay/Lesbian ♀♂

### *Anywhere Else is a Compromise*

One of England's most highly recommended gay guesthouses, ***Cheviot View Guest House*** offers exceptional standards of service and comfort. Indulge yourself in luxury! Linden, of *APN Magazine* called it "...the best gay guest house I've ever stayed in..." *Northern Scene* called it "One of the best gay hotels in England." Here, you can enjoy Newcastle's sparkling and exciting nightlife, explore the coast and the magnificence of Northumbria. Our brochure gives details of champagne weekends, mini-breaks and day trips in our chauffeur-driven Daimler Sovereign. Member of the British Hospitality Association.

**Address: 194 Station Rd, Wallsend, Newcastle NE28 8RD England. Tel: (44-191) 262 0125, mobile: (0378) 863 469, Fax: (44-191) 262 2626.**

**Type:** Guesthouse with cocktail bar.
**Clientele:** Gay men & women, about 50/50
**Transportation:** Metro from city centre (10 min.) is best.
**To Gay Bars:** 10 minutes by car or metro.
**Rooms:** 5 rooms with single, double or king beds.
**Bathrooms:** Private: 1 bath/toilet, 1 shower/toilet. Shared: 1 bath/shower/toilet.
**Meals:** Full English breakfast.
**Vegetarian:** Available at breakfast.
**Complimentary:** Tea, coffee, biscuits & orange juice in rooms, mnts on pillows. Free entry to all gay clubs.
**Dates Open:** All year.
**Rates:** £18.00-£50.00.
**Discounts:** For stays of 5 nights or more.
**Credit Cards:** All major credit & debit cards & Amex.
**Rsv'tns:** Recommended.
**Reserve Thru:** Call direct.
**Parking:** Ample free off-street parking.
**In-Room:** Exceptional standards of service & comfort. Color TV, telephone, hair dryer, razor points, radio/alarm clock, coffee/tea-making facilities, room service.
**On-Premises:** Drawing room & Empire Lounge, laundry facilities.
**Swimming:** Nearby pool & ocean beach.
**Sunbathing:** At the beach.
**Smoking:** Permitted in cocktail bar. Drawing room & all bedrooms are non-smoking.
**Pets:** Small dogs permitted.
**Handicap Access:** Yes. Please check for full details.
**Children:** Permitted.
**Languages:** English/ French.
**Your Host:** Colin & Scott.

## Stratford Lodge

Gay/Lesbian ♀♂

### *Quality Accommodation & Friendly Atmosphere, Exclusively for Gay & Lesbian Guests*

Situated in a tree-lined crescent, ***Stratford Lodge*** is a mid-Victorian property only minutes from the amenities of the city centre. Throughout its refurbishment, every effort has been made to retain its original features and character and to present them in a tasteful and comfortable light. We provide quality accommodations, contemporary and antique furnishings, easy parking and a friendly atmosphere exclusively for gay and lesbian guests. Our double and king rooms are of comfortable proportions. All rooms have colour satellite TV, and a tea and coffee tray. Continental breakfast is served in your room. New to our B&B is a French-style room with canopy, a master bedroom with a king-sized four-poster bed and a Victorian-style room with brass bed, open fireplace and Victorian antique furnishings. Our 300-ft gardens running down to Jesmond Vale are a combination of terraced patios, meadow with pond and woodland.

**Address: 8 Stratford Grove Terrace, Heaton, Newcastle upon Tyne NE6 5BA England. Tel: (44-191) 265 6395, mobile: (44-831) 879182.**

**Type:** Bed & breakfast.
**Clientele:** Gay & lesbian. Good mix of men & women
**Transportation:** Metro from airport, then taxi, or taxi from British Rail Station.
**To Gay Bars:** 1 mile or a 20-minute walk or 5-minute drive.
**Rooms:** 5 rooms with single, double or king bed.

*continued next page*

**Bathrooms:** 1 bathroom per floor.
**Meals:** Expanded continental breakfast.
**Vegetarian:** Vegetarian continental breakfast available. Vegetarian restaurants in city.
**Complimentary:** Tea & coffee tray in each room. Free entry into local gay clubs.
**Dates Open:** All year.
**Rates:** £19.00-£48.00.
**Discounts:** Special business rates available & student discounts.
**Rsv'tns:** Required.
**Reserve Through:** Call direct.
**Parking:** Ample on-street parking.
**In-Room:** Color satellite TV, tea/coffee making facilities & laundry service.
**On-Premises:** TV lounge with satellite TV.
**Exercise/Health:** Traditional Swedish massage, aromatherapy massage, solarium & sauna. Nearby gym, weights, Jacuzzi & steam.
**Swimming:** Nearby pool & ocean.
**Sunbathing:** On patio & beach.
**Nudity:** Permitted in sauna.
**Smoking:** Permitted except for sauna area.
**Pets:** Not permitted.
**Children:** Not especially welcome.
**Languages:** English.
**Your Host:** David.

# NORFOLK

## Warham Old Post Office Cottage

Gay-Friendly ♀♂

### *Bed & Breakfast Tranquility in North Norfolk*

***Warham Old Post Office Cottage*** offers a perfect setting for a quiet break in the country. It has many exposed beams and other period features, as well as home comforts. All rooms have wash basins, wardrobes, and tea/coffee making facilities. The common lounge has an inglenook fireplace, comfortable seating, and a colour TV. The village pub, Three Horseshoes, is adjacent to the cottage. Home cooking is the speciality for lunches and evening meals. Beaches and many attractions are nearby.

**Address: c/o Three Horseshoes Free House, In Warham near Wells-next-the-Sea NR23 1NL England.**
**Tel: (44-1328) 710 547.**

**Type:** Bed & breakfast inn with restaurant & bar.
**Clientele:** Mainly straight with 20% gay & lesbian clientele
**Transportation:** Car is best.
**To Gay Bars:** In Norwich, 1 hr by car.
**Rooms:** 2 singles, 3 doubles.
**Bathrooms:** Private: 1 bath, 2 WCs. Others share.
**Meals:** Full breakfast.
**Vegetarian:** Available at all times.
**Complimentary:** Tea & coffee in rooms.
**Dates Open:** All year.
**High Season:** Easter-Sept
**Rates:** Low season £17.00-£19.00 per person, high season £19.00-£22.00.
**Discounts:** Inquire.
**Rsv'tns:** Not always required.
**Reserve Thru:** Call direct.
**Parking:** Ample free off-street parking.
**In-Room:** Laundry service.
**On-Premises:** TV lounge, meeting rooms.
**Swimming:** At nearby ocean beach.
**Sunbathing:** At nearby ocean beach.
**Smoking:** Permitted in public rooms only, all bedrooms are non-smoking.
**Pets:** Permitted by prior arrangement.
**Handicap Access:** 1 downstairs suite, not wheelchair suitable.
**Children:** Not permitted.
**Languages:** English.
**Your Host:** Ian & Mac.

# NOTTINGHAMSHIRE

## Bathley Guest House

Gay/Lesbian ♂

***Bathley Guest House*** is an exclusively gay bed & breakfast two minutes from the city's gay life. Conveniences include late keys and no restrictions, tea making facilities in all rooms, weekly rates on request. Concessions for admission to gay bars and sauna are available to our guests. Special midweek breaks are also available and women are welcome. Just 10 minutes' walk from our house is the Nottingham Castle, where the sheriff of Nottingham lived. Sherwood Forest is only 20 minutes by car. There, you can view the Major Oak, Robin Hood's hiding place. In Nottingham is Britain's oldest inn, Trip to Jerusalem, built in 1650.

**Address: 101 Bathley St, Trent Bridge, Nottingham NG2 2EE England. Tel: (44-115) 9862 463.**

**Type:** B & B guesthouse with bar for residents.
**Clientele:** Mostly men with women welcome
**To Gay Bars:** 2 minutes from gay bars.
**Rooms:** 8 rooms with single & double beds.
**Bathrooms:** 2 shared.
**Meals:** Full English breakfast.
**Complimentary:** Concessions to local gay clubs & gay & lesbian sauna.
**Dates Open:** All year.
**Rates:** Sgl. £18.00, dbl. £30.00, twin rooms £30.00.
**Discounts:** Special mid-week rates.
**Reserve Through:** Travel agent or call direct.
**Parking:** Ample free on-street parking.
**In-Room:** Tea/coffee making facilities.
**On-Premises:** TV lounge.
**Smoking:** Permitted in lounge.
**Pets:** Welcome.
**Handicap Access:** No.
**Children:** Gay parents with children welcome.
**Languages:** English.
**Your Host:** Keith & Jeff.

# SHROPSHIRE

## Cockford Hall

Gay-Friendly ♀♂

### *Your Country Retreat*

Experience the tranquil comfort of this idyllic rural area in the midst of "houseman's country." ***Cockford Hall,*** a restored Georgian house, is set in 20 acres on a wooded hillside above the historic town of Clun, surrounded by an inspirational landscape of gentle rolling hills, patchwork fields and hidden valleys. The charm of ***Cockford Hall,*** with its many features of architectural and historical interest has been carefully preserved. You will receive a warm welcome and a high standard of accommodation with fine antiques, elegant furnishings, fresh flowers and well-appointed rooms. Relax to the crackle of log fires, the rhythmic ticking of old clocks, and relish hearty breakfasts and candlelit dinners with real English food. In July, 1996, we received the top-quality grade "Deluxe" from the English Tourist Board.

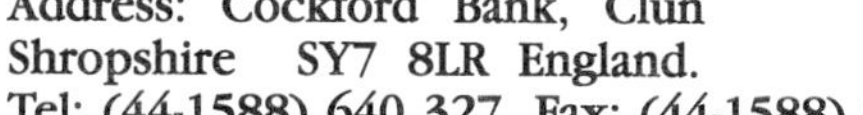

**Address: Cockford Bank, Clun Shropshire SY7 8LR England. Tel: (44-1588) 640 327, Fax: (44-1588) 640 881.**

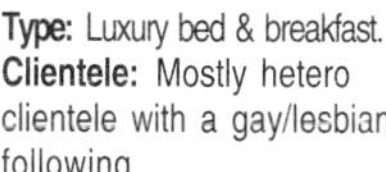

**Type:** Luxury bed & breakfast.
**Clientele:** Mostly hetero clientele with a gay/lesbian following
**Transportation:** Car is best. Free pick up from train.
**Rooms:** 1 room, 1 suite, 1 apartment with single or queen beds.
**Bathrooms:** All private bath/toilets.
**Meals:** Full breakfast. 3-course dinner available by prior arrangement, from £15.
**Vegetarian:** Available by prior arrangement. Vegetarian food also available nearby.
**Complimentary:** Sherry, tea & coffee in room, welcome fruit tray, etc.
**Dates Open:** All year.
**Rates:** £25-£35/person.
**Discounts:** For longer stays of 3 days or more.
**Credit Cards:** MC, Visa.
**Rsv'tns:** Required.
**Reserve Through:** Travel agent or call direct.
**Parking:** Ample free covered off-street parking.
**In-Room:** Colour TV, VCR, telephone, coffee & tea-making facilities, maid service.
**On-Premises:** Video tape library, laundry facilities.
**Swimming:** Nearby pool, ocean, river, lake.
**Sunbathing:** On patio, private sun decks, in garden, in woods.
**Smoking:** Not permitted in bedrooms or dining room. Inquire about smoking areas.
**Pets:** Permitted by prior arrangement.
**Handicap Access:** No, steps.
**Children:** Premises not suitable for young children.
**Languages:** English, German.
**Your Host:** Roger & Burkhard.

# SOMERSET

## Bales Mead

Gay-Friendly 50/50 ♀♂

### *The Ritz in Miniature*

***Bales Mead*** is a small, elegant Edwardian country house, offering superb, luxurious accommodation in an outstanding setting. The peaceful location has magnificent panoramic views of both the sea and the rolling countryside of Exmoor. All three double bedrooms are exquisitely furnished, offering every modern comfort and facility. Breakfast is served in the elegant dining room or *al fresco* in the summer, weather permitting. ***Bales Mead*** provides an excellent base for walking or touring Exmoor and the North Devon Coast.

**Address: West Porlock, Somerset TA24 8NX England.**
**Tel: (44-1643) 862565.**

**Type:** Country house bed & breakfast.
**Clientele:** 50% gay & lesbian & 50% hetero clientele
**Transportation:** Car is best, train from London to Taunton then bus to Porlock is possible.
**To Gay Bars:** 1-1/2 hours.
**Rooms:** 3 doubles.
**Bathrooms:** 2 private baths, others share.
**Meals:** Expanded continental or full breakfast.
**Vegetarian:** Always available.
**Complimentary:** Tea, coffee & hot chocolate making facilities, mineral water, mints & toffees.
**Dates Open:** All year except Xmas & New Years.
**High Season:** May-October.
**Rates:** From £25.00.
**Rsv'tns:** Recommended.
**Reserve Through:** Call direct.
**Parking:** Parking available for 6 cars in private drive in front of house.
**In-Room:** Color TV, radio alarm clocks, hairdryers, & tea & coffee makers.
**On-Premises:** Central heating & log fire in winter. Lounge & dining room for breakfast. Private gardens available for sitting & relaxing.
**Swimming:** Nearby pool & ocean beach.
**Sunbathing:** At the beach.
**Smoking:** Not permitted.
**Pets:** Not permitted.
**Handicap Access:** No.
**Children:** Not permitted.
**Languages:** English, French, Spanish, & German.
**Your Host:** Stephen & Peter.

# TORQUAY

## Cliff House Hotel at the Beach

Gay/Lesbian ♀♂

### *England's First and Foremost Gay Hotel*

Originally a millionaire's home, ***Cliff House,*** celebrating its 23rd year, is an exclusive, luxury hotel with a secluded garden at sea's edge. Here one can view the sea from the terrace that fronts the comfortable bar lounge. This gracious house has the elegance of a bygone age with the advantages of modern amenities. All bedrooms have a bathroom en suite. Full central heating warms us in cooler months, which are so delightful in this beautiful part of the country. There are ample parking facilities. Old friends meet, and newfound friends are made, and no one ever wants to leave. A visit to England is not the same unless you visit ***Cliff House.***

**Address: St. Marks Rd, Meadfoot Beach, Torquay TQ1 2EH England.**
**Tel: (44-1803) 294 656, Fax: (44-1803) 211 983.**

**Type:** Hotel with restaurant & bar.
**Clientele:** Good mix of gay men & women
**Transportation:** Train or bus from London. Pick up from train.
**To Gay Bars:** A 5-minute walk or 2-minute drive.
**Rooms:** 16 rooms with single or double beds.
**Bathrooms:** All private bath/toilets.
**Meals:** Full English breakfast.
**Vegetarian:** With prior arrangement.
**Complimentary:** Tea & coffee in room.
**Dates Open:** All year.
**High Season:** Easter, June-October and Christmas.
**Rates:** £21-£26. Accounts

subject to V.A.T.
**Discounts:** Party discounts.
**Credit Cards:** MC, VISA, Access & Switch.
**Rsv'tns:** Required during high season.
**Reserve Through:** Call direct.
**Parking:** Ample on- and off-street parking.
**In-Room:** Color TV, coffee & tea-making facilities & room service.
**On-Premises:** TV lounge, bar & public telephone.
**Exercise/Health:** Steam room, Jacuzzi, massage and gym.
**Swimming:** Ocean beach.
**Sunbathing:** On the beach, sun deck or in the secluded garden.
**Nudity:** Permitted in the secluded garden.
**Smoking:** Permitted without restrictions.
**Pets:** Dogs are permitted, but not in public rooms.
**Handicap Access:** Yes, 2 rooms.
**Children:** Not permitted.
**Languages:** English.
**Your Host:** Alan & Robbie.

## Ravenswood Hotel

**Gay-Owned** ♀♂

***Ravenswood*** is a friendly hotel overlooking Torwood Gardens. Bedrooms are attractive, well-appointed and equipped with hot and cold water, shaver points, colour TV and tea-making facilities. Some have private bathroom or shower. Rates include breakfast, and the licensed restaurant is available for lunch and dinner. Free parking is nearby. We're 350 yards from the harbour, main shopping centre and entertainment. A pleasant walk takes you to popular beaches.

**Address: 535 Babbacombe Rd, Torquay, South Devon TQ1 1HQ England.
Tel: (44-1803) 292 900 (Tel/Fax).**

**Type:** Hotel with residents' bar & public restaurant.
**Clientele:** Mostly hetero clientele with a 20% gay/lesbian following
**To Gay Bars:** 4-min. walk to gay/lesbian bars.
**Rooms:** 12 doubles.
**Bathrooms:** 9 private & others share.
**Meals:** Full English breakfast. Dinner optional.
**Vegetarian:** Available upon request that morning.
**Complimentary:** Tea & coffee in rooms.
**Dates Open:** All year.
**High Season:** Summer.
**Rates:** £14.00-£20.00 per person.
**Credit Cards:** MC, VISA, Access, & Eurocard.
**Rsv'tns:** Required.
**Reserve Through:** Call direct.
**Parking:** Free car park.
**In-Room:** Maid service, colour cable TV, telephone, wash basin, tea & coffee makers, & late-night keys.
**On-Premises:** TV lounge with video & tape library.
**Swimming:** 5-minute walk to ocean beach. 20-minute walk to nude beach.
**Sunbathing:** On beach.
**Smoking:** Permitted without restrictions.
**Pets:** Permitted if well supervised.
**Handicap Access:** No.
**Children:** Permitted.
**Languages:** English, Deaf Sign Language.

## Red Squirrel Lodge

**Gay-Owned** ♀♂

### *The English Tourist Board Rated Us Three Crowns!*

A superb Victorian villa, ***Red Squirrel Lodge*** is in a quiet, peaceful area surrounded by spacious gardens. We are located near shops, buses and railway station, yet are only 200 yards from Torquay's finest beach. It is most beautifully furnished and has been established as a distinctive hotel for many years. You will be welcomed by resident proprietors John and David. A courtesy car from the bus and railway station is available.

**Address: Chelston Rd, Torquay, TQ2 6PUEngland.
Tel: (44-1803) 605 496, Fax: (44-1803) 690 170.
E-mail: squirrel@mail.zynet.com.co.uk.**

**Type:** Hotel with bar.
**Clientele:** Mainly hetero clientele with a 20% gay & lesbian following
**Transportation:** Car is best, or train from London Paddington Stn. Free pick up from bus or train.
**To Gay Bars:** 5 min. by car.
**Rooms:** 14 rooms with single, dbl & queen beds.
**Bathrooms:** All private.
**Meals:** Full English breakfast. Optional dinner extra charge.
**Vegetarian:** Available with 24 hour notice.
**Complimentary:** Tea & coffee-making facilities in rooms. Tea, coffee, & soft drink upon arrival.
**Dates Open:** All year.
**Rates:** £20.00 per person low season, £30.00 per person high season.
**Discounts:** For 2 or more nights in low season.
**Credit Cards:** MC, Visa, Amex.
**Rsv'tns:** Required with deposit.

*continued next page*

**Reserve Through:** UK travel agent or call direct.
**Minimum Stay:** 3 nights high season (July-Aug).
**Parking:** Adequate, free off-street parking.
**In-Room:** Color TV & maid service.
**On-Premises:** TV lounge, pay phone, & separate bar for residents & friends.
**Exercise/Health:** Sport & leisure center 1/2 mile with gym, sauna, & Jacuzzi.
**Swimming:** At pool 1/2 mile away or ocean 250 yards.
**Sunbathing:** In extensive gardens.
**Nudity:** Permitted on nude beach 3 miles away.
**Smoking:** Permitted except in dining room.
**Pets:** Permitted except in dining room, bar & lounge.
**Handicap Access:** Yes. 3 ground floor rooms.
**Children:** Not permitted.
**Languages:** English.
**Your Host:** John & David.

# WARWICKSHIRE

## Ellesmere House

Gay/Lesbian ♂

### *A Friendly Welcome to the Heart of England*

***Ellesmere House*** is an elegant, early Victorian town residence with spacious rooms furnished in antiques. It has been modernized to a high standard of comfortable accommodation and is situated in a quiet, tree-lined avenue within walking distance of all the facilities of this attractive regency town. Shakespeare's Stratford, The Castles at Warwick and Kenilworth are all within easy reach.

**Address: 36 Binswood Ave, Royal Leamington Spa, Warwickshire CV32 5SQ England. Tel: (44-1926) 424 618.**

**Type:** Bed & breakfast homestay.
**Clientele:** Mostly men with women welcome
**Transportation:** Own vehicle is best, but train, bus OK.
**To Gay Bars:** Warwick gay bar 3 miles.
**Rooms:** 3 rooms with single or double beds.
**Bathrooms:** 2 private bath/toilets & 1 private shower/toilet.
**Meals:** Full English breakfast.
**Dates Open:** All year.
**Rates:** £28.00-£40.00.
**Rsv'tns:** Required.
**Reserve Thru:** Call direct.
**Parking:** Adequate, free on-street parking.
**In-Room:** Color TV.
**Sunbathing:** In garden.
**Smoking:** Not encouraged.
**Pets:** Not permitted.
**Children:** Not permitted.
**Languages:** English, Spanish, limited French, Italian.
**Your Host:** Francisco & Colin.

# YORKSHIRE

## Bull Lodge

Gay-Friendly ♀♂

### *"The History of York is the History of England"*

***Bull Lodge*** is a modern, detached residence on a quiet side street, 3/4 mile from the city centre and close to the University and Barbican Leisure Centre. We're on a bus route and have private, enclosed parking. Single, twin, or double bedrooms are available. Twins and doubles can be with or without private shower and toilet. All rooms have tea & coffee facilities, colour TV, clock-radio, and direct-dial telephones. A full-choice English breakfast is served, evening meals can be ordered, and snacks and drinks are available.

York can be busy all year, so booking ahead is always a good idea. In the winter, weekends are usually busy, and June through October is busy almost every day. Allow at least two days to enjoy this beautiful city and its many sights and attractions. York is also an excellent base to explore the surrounding countryside, the moors and the dales, to visit Castle Howard of "Brideshead Revisited" fame, or nearby Bronte country. If you're touring the U.K., relax for a few days here, between the busy cities of Edinburgh and London.

**Address: 37 Bull Lane, Lawrence St, York YO1 3EN England. Tel: (44-1904) 415522 (Tel/Fax).**

**Type:** Guesthouse.
**Clientele:** Mostly straight clientele with a gay/lesbian following
**Transportation:** Convenient direct bus from train/bus stations. Pick up by prior arrangement if minimum 2 night advance booking.
**To Gay Bars:** 1 mile.
**Rooms:** 1 single, 6 doubles, 1 twin.
**Bathrooms:** 3 private, 2 shared. Ground floor with private suitable for disabled.
**Meals:** Full English breakfast. Evening meal additional charge (low season only).
**Complimentary:** Tea & coffee.
**Dates Open:** End January to mid-December.
**High Season:** June thru October.
**Rates:** 1997: summer £16-£20; winter £14.50-£17.
**Discounts:** £1 per person per night for more than 4 nights. Off-season breaks.
**Rsv'tns:** Recommended for weekends & summer period.
**Reserve Through:** Travel agent or call direct.
**Parking:** Private enclosed parking. Garage for motorbikes & bicycles.
**In-Room:** Color TV, tea/coffee makers, radio alarm clocks, hot & cold water, maid service, telephone.
**On-Premises:** Non-smoking TV lounge with books & games.
**Swimming:** 10-minute walk to Barbican pool & leisure centre.
**Smoking:** Permitted except in lounge & dining room.
**Pets:** Permitted.
**Handicap Access:** Yes, ground floor en suite double room.
**Children:** Permitted, minimum age 3 years.
**Languages:** English.
**Your Host:** Roy & Dennis.

## Interludes

**Gay-Friendly 50/50 ♀♂**

### *Little "Scene," But Great Scenery*

***Interludes*** is an elegant Georgian townhouse with sea views, peacefully situated in a conservation area, yet close to beach, town centre, theatres, castle, etc. The hotel is licensed, and, because of our connections with the Stephen Joseph Theatre (artistic director Alan Ayckbourn), has a theatrical theme. The bedrooms are well equipped. ***Interludes*** is informal, friendly and most relaxing. Scarborough is an attractive resort, and is an ideal centre for exploring the nearby North Yorkshire Moors National Park and the historical towns of York and Whitby.

**Address: 32 Princess St, Old Town, Scarborough, North Yorkshire YO11 1QR England.**
**Tel: (44-1723) 360 513, Fax: (44-1723) 368 597.**

**Type:** Hotel.
**Clientele:** 50% gay & lesbian & 50% hetero clientele
**Transportation:** Car, bus or train (rail link to Manchester Airport).
**Rooms:** 5 rooms with twin, king, canopy & four poster beds.
**Bathrooms:** 4 en suite, 1 with sink & adjacent shower & toilet.
**Meals:** Full breakfast with 4 course dinner available at additional cost.
**Vegetarian:** Available with prior notification.
**Complimentary:** Tea, coffee, chocolate, juice, etc.
**Dates Open:** All year.
**High Season:** July-September.
**Rates:** £45 standard, £50 superior per double room.
**Discounts:** Single occupancy, 5%-15% groups of 7 or more, special pckg with Stephen Joseph Theatre. 12-1/2% for 7 or more days, 5% 4-6 days.
**Credit Cards:** MC, VISA.
**Rsv'tns:** Wise to confirm availability.
**Reserve Through:** Call direct.
**Minimum Stay:** Required public holiday weekends.
**Parking:** Adequate free on-street parking, limited during high season.
**In-Room:** Color TV, coffee & tea-making facilities & maid service.
**On-Premises:** Laundry facilities.
**Swimming:** Nearby pool & ocean beach.
**Sunbathing:** On the patio, at the beach.
**Nudity:** 20 miles to unofficial public nude beach.
**Smoking:** Permitted in lounge & outside. All bedrooms are non-smoking.
**Pets:** Not permitted.
**Handicap Access:** No.
**Children:** Not permitted.
**Languages:** English.
**Your Host:** Bob & Ian.

## Pauleda House Hotel

**Gay-Friendly ♂**

***Pauleda House Hotel*** is a small, comfortable family-run hotel, situated less than one mile from York's beautiful Minister and city centre. York is a comparatively small place and other than the abundance of stately homes, abbeys, etc. on the outskirts, the historical attractions are all within walking distance of each other. Our building itself is a fine example of the Victorian style. We are very close to the picturesque village green which gives a feeling of rural tranquillity while being only a 10-minute walk to the city centre. The River Ouse is close by, this being an alternative pleasant walk into the city.

GUEST COMMENTS: "The best B&B we have ever stayed in! All the little extra touches and the decor make it a great break;" and "1st-class hotel, all staff very helpful, superb food, room kept very clean...Thanks for making our stay so enjoyable."

**Address: 123 Clifton, York YO3-6BL England.**
**Tel: (44-1904) 634745, Fax (44-1904) 621327.**

**Type:** Hotel with restaurant.
**Clientele:** Mainly hetero clientele with a gay male following
**Transportation:** By car, taxi from railway or bus station approx £2.50
**To Gay Bars:** Less than one mile from York Arms & White Horse.
**Rooms:** 12 rooms with single, double or queen beds (5 of which are 4-poster beds)
**Bathrooms:** All private shower/toilets.
**Meals:** Continental, expanded continental, or full breakfast. Optional evening meals.
**Vegetarian:** Available upon prior request.
**Complimentary:** Tea & coffee.
**Dates Open:** All year.
**High Season:** April to October.
**Rates:** Rooms £18.00-£30.00 per person per night.
**Credit Cards:** MC, VISA, Access, Connect, Switch, Diners, Eurocard & Delta.
**Rsv'tns:** Required but walk-ins welcome.
**Reserve Through:** Call direct.
**Parking:** Ample free on-street & off-street parking. Private lot.
**In-Room:** Satellite color TV, telephone, maid service, radio/alarm, hairdryer, shoe cleaning, sewing kits, tissues.
**On-Premises:** Meeting rooms, ironing facilities, lounge, bar, dining room.
**Swimming:** At local swimming pools or river yards away.
**Smoking:** Permitted except in dining room.
**Pets:** Not permitted.
**Handicap Access:** No.
**Children:** Not permitted.
**Languages:** English.
**Your Host:** Paul.

# UK - SCOTLAND

## AVIEMORE

### Auchendean Lodge Hotel

**Gay-Friendly ♀♂**

We are more a home than a hotel. So, come and relax in the Scottish Highlands in our Edwardian hunting lodge. ***Auchendean Lodge Hotel*** is an elegant, comfortable country hotel furnished with antiques and fine paintings. When you stay here, plan on enjoying interesting, award-winning food, good wines and malt whiskies, spectacular views of Spey and the Cairngorm Mountains, walking, fishing, golfing and skiing. Our hotel is set in a magnificent garden on the edge of 200 acres of mature forest. Call Ian or Eric for a brochure. Although our clientele is not exclusively gay, you will be warmly welcomed.

**Reader's Comment:** "The Scottish dinners were superb. The hosts were very friendly and welcomed us warmly. The other guests, while not gay, were friendly and very nice. I would recommend this hotel without reservation, but plan on TWO nights. One night will make you want another." *–Richard H., St. Louis, MO*

**Address: Dulnain Bridge near Grantown-on-Spey, Inverness-Shire PH26 3LU Scotland.**
**Tel: (44-1479) 851 347 (Tel/Fax).**

**Type:** Inn with restaurant.
**Clientele:** Mostly hetero with a gay & lesbian following
**Transportation:** Car is best.
**To Gay Bars:** 2 hrs by car.
**Rooms:** 8 rooms with single, double or queen beds.
**Bathrooms:** Private: 5 bath/- or shower/toilets, 3 sinks. Shared: 1 shower & 2 WC.
**Meals:** Full breakfast with dinner optional at £23.50.
**Vegetarian:** Available with advance notice.
**Complimentary:** Tea, coffee, biscuits.
**Dates Open:** All year.
**High Season:** Easter thru early October, Xmas & New Year.
**Rates:** B&B, summer £21.00-£46.00, winter £16.50-£33.00; B&B + dinner, summer add £23.50.
**Discounts:** 10% for 3 days or more on dinner, bed & breakfast rates.
**Credit Cards:** MC, VISA, Amex, Diners. Commission charged.
**Rsv'tns:** Recommended.
**Reserve Through:** Call direct.
**Parking:** Ample free off-street parking.
**In-Room:** Color TV, coffee & tea-making facilities, room & laundry service.
**Exercise/Health:** Walking, fishing, golfing, skiing.
**Swimming:** Nearby pool, river, lake.
**Sunbathing:** In adjacent woods.
**Smoking:** Permitted in bedrooms & 1 lounge.
**Pets:** Permitted. Large gardens & woods attached to premises.
**Handicap Access:** Yes, restaurant. Flight of steps to bedrooms.
**Children:** Permitted.
**Languages:** English, French.

## AYR

### Roseland Guest House

**Gay-Friendly ♀♂**

Ayr, a seaside resort on Scotland's west coast, is situated 3 miles from Alloway, the birthplace of Scotland's national poet, Robert Burns. Long miles of golden sand, superb sports and recreational facilities and family entertainments have helped make Ayr one of Britain's premier coastal resorts. The area is renowned for its golf courses, where you can follow in the footsteps of the golfing greats. Royal Troon, 10 miles north, is the venue for the 1997 British Open. Ayr Racecourse annually

*continued next page*

hosts the Scottish Grand National (April) and the Scottish Gold Cup (Sept). The town annually hosts Scotland's premier Flower Show in August. History abounds in the area, where the coastline is dotted with dramatic castles perched on clifftops, including Culzean Castle, the area's top tourist attraction, which houses the flat given by the British to President Eisenhower for his lifetime use.

***Roseland Guest House,*** which offers a quiet, peaceful haven, is virtually in the town centre, which has a large variety of shops and entertainment. There are several restaurants in town, which offer local fare, and numerous others offering international cuisine. It's a great location for a quiet, restful holiday within easy travelling distance of Glasgow (45 mins), your direct point of entry to the country, and Scotland's capital, Edinburgh (1hr 45 mins). Your host, Ron, looks forward to welcoming you to ***Roseland.***

**Address: 15 Charlotte Street, Ayr KA7 1DZ Scotland.**
**Tel: (44-1292) 283435 (Tel/Fax).**

**Type:** Bed & breakfast.
**Clientele:** Mostly hetero with gay & lesbian following
**Transportation:** Car or train from Glasgow Airport to Ayr then taxi.
**To Gay Bars:** One hour by car or train to Glasgow.
**Rooms:** 4 rooms with single & double beds.
**Bathrooms:** 4 private sinks, 1 shared shower & 1 shared toilet.
**Meals:** Full breakfast.
**Complimentary:** Tea, coffee & biscuits in room.
**Dates Open:** All year.
**High Season:** July-August.
**Rates:** £16.00-£28.00 per person B&B.
**Discounts:** 10% for 7 or more nights.
**Rsv'tns:** Preferred.
**Reserve Through:** Call direct.
**Parking:** Ample on-street pay parking.
**In-Room:** Color TV, coffee & tea-making facilities, maid service.
**On-Premises:** Communal lounge.
**Swimming:** Five min walk to pool, 2 min walk to beach.
**Sunbathing:** At nearby beach.
**Smoking:** Permitted everywhere.
**Pets:** Not permitted.
**Handicap Access:** No.
**Children:** Not especially welcome.
**Languages:** English.
**Your Host:** Ron.

# EDINBURGH

## The Amaryllis Guest House

**Gay/Lesbian ♀♂**

Lesbian-owned and -run, ***The Amaryllis Guest House*** is a newly refurbished Georgian Town House, centrally located and within walking distance of the city centre. Late breakfast is available for those who enjoy Edinburgh's great gay nightlife.

**Address: 21 Upper Gilmore Place, Edinburgh EH3 9NL Scotland.**
**Tel: (44-131) 229 3293.**

**Type:** Guesthouse.
**Clientele:** Mainly gay & lesbian with some hetero clientele
**To Gay Bars:** 10 minutes by taxi or bus.
**Rooms:** 1 double, 1 twin, 3 family, 2 en-suite.
**Bathrooms:** 2 shared baths.
**Meals:** Full breakfast. Early or late trays are always available.
**Vegetarian:** Available on request.
**Complimentary:** Tea & coffee.
**Dates Open:** All year.
**High Season:** June-October.
**Rates:** £15-£28 per person.
**Credit Cards:** Visa, Access, MC.
**Reserve Through:** Call direct.
**Parking:** Adequate on-steet parking at night. Limited on-street parking by day. Some private parking.
**In-Room:** TV, coffee & tea-making facilities.
**Smoking:** Permitted in all rooms.
**Pets:** Not permitted.
**Children:** Permitted.
**Languages:** English.

## Aries Guest House

Gay/Lesbian ♀♂

### *Capital Accommodation, Superb Value*

A friendly Scottish welcome is assured to all guests who stay at the ***Aries Guest House.*** Lesbian-run and -owned, the guesthouse is centrally located in Edinburgh, within minutes of Princes Street, the castle, Old Town, theatres, shops, cinemas, clubs and gay nightlife.

**Address: 5 Upper Gilmore Place, Edinburgh EH3 9NW Scotland. Tel: (44-131) 229 4669.**

**Type:** Bed & breakfast guesthouse.
**Clientele:** Mostly gay & lesbian with some hetero clientele
**Transportation:** Taxi, bus or car.
**To Gay Bars:** 15-minute walk, 5-minute drive.
**Rooms:** 5 rooms with single, double or king beds.
**Bathrooms:** Private & shared.
**Meals:** Full Scottish breakfast, early/late trays available on request.
**Vegetarian:** Available on request.
**Complimentary:** Tea & coffee.
**Dates Open:** All year.
**High Season:** June-Oct.
**Rates:** £13-£22.
**Discounts:** Child discounts 30%.
**Rsv'tns:** Required.
**Reserve Through:** Call direct.
**Parking:** Adequate on-street parking at night. Limited pay parking during day.
**In-Room:** Color TV, coffee/tea-making facilities, maid service.
**On-Premises:** TV lounge.
**Exercise/Health:** Nearby gym, weights, Jacuzzi, sauna, massage.
**Swimming:** Pool nearby.
**Sunbathing:** In city parks.
**Smoking:** Permitted in all rooms.
**Pets:** Permitted.
**Handicap Access:** Ground-floor rooms accessible.
**Children:** Welcome.
**Languages:** English.
**Your Host:** Stella.

## The Armadillo Guest House

Gay/Lesbian ♀♂

***The Armadillo Guest House,*** highly commended by the Tourist Board of Scotland, is newly refurbished throughout to an excellent standard and provides a friendly, warm atmosphere. We have maps and full information on gay and happy life here in Scotland. Come and join in the fun of "Tartan Kilt" country, only at ***The Armadillo.***

**Address: 12 Gilmore Place, Edinburgh EH3 9NQ Scotland. Tel: (44-131) 229 6457.**

**Type:** Guesthouse.
**Clientele:** Mostly gay & lesbian with some hetero clientele
**Transportation:** Bus, taxi.
**To Gay Bars:** A 20-minute walk or 5-minute drive.
**Rooms:** 6 rooms with single or double beds.
**Bathrooms:** Shared: 3 bath/shower/toilets, 3 WCs, 3 showers & 1 bathtub.
**Meals:** Full breakfast. Late breakfast also available.
**Vegetarian:** Always available to guests.
**Complimentary:** Tea, coffee & set-up service.
**Dates Open:** All year.
**High Season:** July through October.
**Rates:** Double/twin £15 £20. Single £16-£26.
**Discounts:** For longer stays.
**Rsv'tns:** Required.
**Reserve Through:** Call direct.
**Parking:** Limited off-street & on-street parking.
**In-Room:** Color TV, telephone, coffee/tea-making facilities, room, maid & laundry service.
**On-Premises:** Laundry facilities.
**Pets:** Permitted.
**Handicap Access:** No.
**Languages:** English.

## Mansfield House

**Gay/Lesbian ♀♂**

***Mansfield House*** is elegantly furnished with many antiques and is considered to be THE place to stay in Edinburgh. It is centrally located and is near the local gay clubs, bars, discos, restaurants and shops.

**Address: 57 Dublin St, Edinburgh EH3 6NL Scotland.**
**Tel: (44-131) 556 7980 (Tel/Fax).**

**Type:** Guesthouse.
**Clientele:** Good mix of gays & lesbians
**Rooms:** 5 rooms with double beds.
**Bathrooms:** 1 en suite with shower, bidet. Four rooms share 1 toilet & shower.
**Meals:** Continental breakfast available at breakfast bar.
**Complimentary:** Tea, coffee in room.
**Dates Open:** All year.
**High Season:** June-Sept.
**Rates:** £30-£50. En suite: £40-£55.
**Credit Cards:** Inquire.
**Rsv'tns:** Required.
**Reserve Through:** Travel agent or call direct.
**Parking:** Limited off-street parking.
**In-Room:** Color TV, maid service, & ceiling fans in most rooms, private refrigerator in some rooms.
**On-Premises:** Public pay phone.
**Smoking:** Permitted.
**Pets:** Not permitted.
**Handicap Access:** No.
**Children:** Not permitted.
**Languages:** English.

## Regis House

**Gay-Friendly 50/50 ♀♂**

***Regis House*** is situated on a residential street near the city centre, five minutes from Princess Street. We provide comfortable guest lodgings and guests have their own keys.

**Address: 57 Gilmore Place, Edinburgh EH3 9NT Scotland.**
**Tel: (44-131) 229 4057.**

**Type:** Guesthouse.
**Clientele:** 50% gay & lesbian & 50% hetero clientele
**To Gay Bars:** 5 minutes to French Connection, Blue Oyster.
**Rooms:** 6 doubles.
**Bathrooms:** 1 en suite, others share.
**Meals:** Continental breakfast.
**Complimentary:** Tea, coffee.
**Dates Open:** All year.
**High Season:** August/September.
**Rates:** £15-£20.
**Credit Cards:** MC, Visa, Amex, Access.
**Rsv'tns:** Required.
**Reserve Through:** Call direct.
**Parking:** Adequate on-street parking.
**In-Room:** Color TV, maid service.
**Smoking:** Permitted.
**Pets:** Not permitted.
**Handicap Access:** No.
**Children:** Permitted.
**Languages:** English, German.

# ISLE OF BUTE

## Ardmory House Hotel

**Gay-Friendly ♂**

### *Fall in Love With This Restful Scottish Hotel*

Golf, fishing, birdwatching, and walking are restful and relaxing pastimes for guests on the Isle of Bute, approximately 60 minutes from Glasgow and 30 minutes on the ferry from Wemyss Bay. ***Ardmory House Hotel*** sits in its own grounds on a hill overlooking Rothesay Bay, commanding an outstanding view over the Bay, Firth of Clyde, and Loch Striven. Although the hotel's clientele is not exclusively gay, gays are warmly welcomed. Contact Donald or Bill for a brochure.

**Address: Ardmory Road, Ardbeg, Isle of Bute PA20 0PG Scotland.**
**Tel: (44-1700) 502346 (Tel/Fax).**

**Type:** Hotel with restaurant & bar.
**Clientele:** Mostly hetero with a gay male following
**Transportation:** Car is best, or rail from Glasgow, ferry, taxi.
**To Gay Bars:** 1-1/2 hours to gay bars.
**Rooms:** 5 rooms with single or double beds.
**Bathrooms:** Private: 3 shower/toilets, 2 bath/shower/toilets.
**Meals:** Full breakfast. Dinner available.
**Vegetarian:** Available at breakfast, dinner or bar meal.
**Complimentary:** Tea, coffee, fruit basket & quarter bottle of wine in all rooms.
**Dates Open:** All year.
**High Season:** July-August.
**Rates:** B&B: single £30, double £55. Dinner B&B: single £42.50, double £85.
**Discounts:** Dinner B&B: 10% on stays of 3 or more days.
**Credit Cards:** MC, VISA, Amex, Diners.
**Rsv'tns:** Required.
**Reserve Through:** Travel agent or call direct.
**Parking:** Ample free off-street parking.
**In-Room:** Colour TV, telephone, coffee/tea-making facilities, maid & room service, limited laundry serv.
**On-Premises:** Laundry facilities.
**Swimming:** Nearby pool & ocean.
**Sunbathing:** In garden.
**Smoking:** Not permitted in bedrooms or restaurant.
**Pets:** Permitted.
**Handicap Access:** Please inquire.
**Children:** No.
**Languages:** English.
**Your Host:** Donald & Bill.

# UK - WALES

## AMMANFORD - DYFED

### Apple Cottage

Women ♀

*Apple Cottage,* situated in an area of outstanding natural beauty, is a semi-detached, self-contained, stone cottage that is more than 200 years old. The living area of this clean and cozy 1-bedroom accommodation, has an exposed painted stone wall with an open fire range, color television and fitted wool carpet and rugs. The fully-equipped kitchen includes an electric cooker and small fridge. Patio doors lead to a small, furnished patio area which overlooks a large, enclosed garden. The upstairs bedroom is furnished with antiques and has a velux window for extra light. From the front of the cottage are views of a wide grazing common with the Black Mountain as a backdrop. It is 2 miles to the Brecon Beacons National Park, about 10 miles to the Vale of Neath, known for magnificent and abundant waterfalls and 13 miles to Swansea City.

**Address: 35 New Rd, Gwaun-Cae-Gurwen, Ammanford, Dyfed SA18 1UN Wales. Tel: (44-1269) 824072.**

**Type:** Self-contained stone cottage.
**Clientele:** Mostly women with men welcome
**Transportation:** Bus, taxi.
**To Gay Bars:** 30-min drive to Swansea gay bars.
**Rooms:** 1 bedroom with 1 double & 1 single bed.
**Bathrooms:** Private shower/toilet with pine wash stand.
**Meals:** Upon request.
**Vegetarian:** Available.
**Dates Open:** All year.
**High Season:** Jun 11-Sep 24, Easter, Christmas & New Year.
**Rates:** High season: £135-£150 per week. Off-season £120 per week. £25 per night.
**Rsv'tns:** Required, with deposit. Balance paid immediately on arrival.
**Reserve Through:** Call direct.
**Minimum Stay:** 2 nights.
**Parking:** Off-street parking.
**In-Room:** Fully-equipped kitchen, color TV, open fire range, oil central heat, hot water, linens, thermostatically-controlled shower.
**On-Premises:** Large enclosed garden.
**Exercise/Health:** Horseback riding, water sports, climbing, walking & swimming.
**Swimming:** On coast, in rivers.
**Sunbathing:** In garden.
**Smoking:** Permitted.
**Pets:** Permitted.
**Handicap Access:** Yes.
**Children:** Yes.
**Languages:** English.

# BRECON BEACONS

## Tybesta Tolfrue

Gay/Lesbian ♀♂

### *In the Heart of Brecon Beacons National Park*

Hosts Richard and Steve warmly welcome travellers to their listed 18th-century townhouse. Ideally situated in the town of Brecon, 45 miles north of Cardiff, ***Tybesta Tolfrue's*** location offers ample opportunity for guests to go walking, pony trekking, cycling, sailing, or to simply relax. The attractive bedrooms are standard to full en suite, and offer amenities such as a full breakfast, in-room tea- and coffee-making facilities and colour TV.

**Address: Brecon, Wales. Tel: (44-1874) 611 115.**

**Type:** Bed & breakfast.
**Clientele:** Gay & lesbian. Good mix of men & women
**Transportation:** Car is best. Nat'l Express Coach Network or rail to Merthyr Tydfil, then local bus service.
**To Gay Bars:** 45 miles to Cardiff, a 45-60 minute drive.
**Rooms:** 4 rooms with single or double beds.
**Bathrooms:** Private: 1 bath/toilet, 1 shower/toilet. 1 shared bath/shower/toilet.
**Meals:** Full breakfast.
**Vegetarian:** Vegetarian breakfast on request. Available locally for lunch & dinner.
**Complimentary:** Tea, coffee in rooms.
**Dates Open:** All year.
**High Season:** July & August.
**Rates:** £17.50-£19.50 per person per night.
**Rsv'tns:** Required when possible. Deposit required.
**Reserve Through:** Call direct.
**Minimum Stay:** Required over bank holiday periods.
**Parking:** Ample free off- & on-street parking.
**In-Room:** Colour TV, coffee/tea-making facilities, maid service.
**On-Premises:** TV lounge.
**Exercise/Health:** Nearby gym with weights, Jacuzzi, sauna & steam.
**Swimming:** Pool nearby.
**Sunbathing:** On patio.
**Smoking:** Permitted in rooms.
**Pets:** Permitted by prior arrangement.
**Handicap Access:** No.
**Children:** No.
**Languages:** English.
**Your Host:** Richard & Steve.

# CARDIFF

## Courtfield Hotel

Gay-Friendly ♀♂

The ***Courtfield Hotel*** is a tastefully-decorated hotel close to Cardiff Castle and the city centre. Our setting is a wide and tree-lined avenue with stately homes and buildings. Our hotel, restaurant and bar have a mixed clientele. Gay bars are just 10 minutes away. Guests have their own keys.

**Address: 101 Cathedral Rd, Cardiff CF1 9PH Wales. Tel: (44-1222) 227 701 (Tel/Fax).**

**Type:** Hotel with restaurant & bar.
**Clientele:** Mostly straight clientele with a gay & lesbian following
**Transportation:** Cardiff (Wales) airport, then taxi to city.
**To Gay Bars:** 10 minutes to gay bars.
**Rooms:** 16 rooms with single & double beds.
**Bathrooms:** 4 private shower/toilets. Shared: 2 bath/shower/toilets, 1 WC.
**Meals:** Full Welsh breakfast.
**Vegetarian:** Vegetarians catered for.
**Complimentary:** Tea & coffee facilities in rooms.
**Dates Open:** All year.
**Rates:** Single £20-£30, double £35-£45.
**Discounts:** 10% on long-term stays.
**Credit Cards:** MC, Visa, Amex, Access, Diners, Eurocard.
**Rsv'tns:** Required 1 week in advance.
**Reserve Through:** Travel agent or call direct.
**Parking:** On-street parking.
**In-Room:** Maid & room service, color TV, telephone, tea making facilities & clock radio.
**On-Premises:** Meeting rooms.
**Swimming:** Pool nearby.
**Smoking:** Permitted without restrictions.
**Pets:** Permitted by prior arrangement.
**Handicap Access:** No.
**Children:** Permitted.
**Languages:** English, Dutch, German & French.

# SNOWDONIA NATIONAL PARK

## Dewis Cyfarfod

Women ♀

### *Women's Guesthouse with Art Courses*

***Dewis Cyfarfod*** is a small, friendly, licensed women's guesthouse offering a warm welcome and a high standard of service. The house is set in an elevated position on five acres of woodland overlooking the River Dee in the Snowdonia National Park three miles from Bala and the largest natural lake in Wales. There are excellent facilities locally for many outdoor sports with equipment for hire and tuition available. Art tuition and residential courses in drawing, painting and sculpture are available at ***Dewis Cyfarfod.***

**Address: Llandderfel, near Bala, Gwynedd LL23 7DR Wales.**
**Tel: (44-1678) 530 243.**

**Type:** Licensed guesthouse with art courses.
**Clientele:** Women only
**Transportation:** Car is best.
**To Gay Bars:** 40 miles.
**Rooms:** 2 rooms with single or double beds.
**Bathrooms:** 2 ensuite shower/toilet.
**Meals:** Full or continental breakfast.
**Vegetarian:** With prior notice.
**Complimentary:** Tea & coffee.
**Dates Open:** All year.
**Rates:** £16-£18.
**Rsv'tns:** Required.
**Reserve Thru:** Call direct.
**Parking:** Ample free off-street parking.
**In-Room:** TV, tea & coffee-making facilities.
**On-Premises:** Sm. bar lounge.
**Exercise/Health:** Nearby weights, sauna & massage.
**Swimming:** 3 miles to swimming pool & lake.
**Sunbathing:** Anywhere on our 5 acres.
**Nudity:** Anywhere.
**Smoking:** Permitted anywhere. One non-smoking sleeping room.
**Pets:** Not permitted.
**Handicap Access:** Partially. Ground-floor rooms.
**Children:** Not especially welcome.
**Languages:** English, French, Spanish, German.

## Pennant Hall

Gay/Lesbian ♂

### *Where the Spectacular Welsh Mountains Meet the Sea*

***Pennant Hall*** is a period building set in its own floodlit grounds overlooking the sea. The village nestles between two headlands at the foot of the Snowdonia National Park with Mount Snowdon as its centrepiece. A warm and friendly welcome awaits our guests, all of whom are gay and are predominantly men. This ten-bedroom hotel is elegantly appointed with a bar, restaurant and large sauna suite. These are open to non-residents, thus ensuring a convivial atmosphere. When in the U.K., a visit to North Wales is a must. With its own language, culture, historic castles, mountains and spectacular scenery, you will be captivated by its mystery and sense of adventure. At the heart of all this, ***Pennant Hall*** awaits.

**Address: Beach Road, Penmaenmawr Conwy LL34 6AY North Wales.**
**Tel: (44-1492) 622 878.**

**Type:** Hotel with restaurant & bar.
**Clientele:** Mostly men with women welcome
**Transportation:** Car is best. Train, then taxi (a 2-min walk). Free pick up from train.
**To Gay Bars:** 6 miles, a 10-minute drive.
**Rooms:** 10 rooms with single or double beds.
**Bathrooms:** 10 private shower/toilets.
**Meals:** Expanded continental breakfast.
**Vegetarian:** Vegetarian menu available.
**Complimentary:** Tea & coffee in rooms.
**Dates Open:** All year.
**High Season:** June-Sept.
**Rates:** £25 all year.
**Credit Cards:** MC, Visa.
**Rsv'tns:** Required.
**Reserve Through:** Travel agent or call direct.
**Parking:** Ample free off-street parking.
**In-Room:** Colour TV, coffee & tea-making facilities.
**On-Premises:** TV lounge.
**Exercise/Health:** Jacuzzi, sauna, steam, sun room.
**Swimming:** Ocean nearby.
**Sunbathing:** On private sun decks, patio & at beach.
**Nudity:** Permitted in sun terrace & sauna area.
**Smoking:** Permitted in bar. Inquire about non-smoking area.
**Pets:** Small dogs permitted.
**Children:** No.
**Languages:** English, Welsh.
**Your Host:** Terry.

PACIFIC REGION
AUSTRALIA

# NEW SOUTH WALES

## BERRY

### Tara Country Retreat

Gay/Lesbian ♀♂

***Australia's Most Popular Country Gay Guesthouse***

At ***Tara Country Retreat*** we especially welcome overseas guests, and are happy to take them on a tour of the surrounding tourist spots and koala and kangaroo parks. ***Tara*** is a convenient stop-off for travel between Sydney, Canberra and Melbourne. Facilities include swimming pool, spa, game room, TV and video. We can arrange for tennis, canoeing and guided bushwalks. ***Tara*** is only 9 km from historic Berry, famous for fine restaurants and antique shops. It's 15 minutes from Seven Mile Beach and adjoins the nature reserve and rainforests of the Kangaroo Valley.

**Address: 219 Wattamolla Rd, Berry, NSW 2535 Australia.**
**Tel: (61-44) 641 472, Fax: (61-44) 642 265. E-mail: rods@kpk.com.au.**
**http://www.ozemail.com.au/~rods.**

**Type:** Guesthouse & campground with restaurant, bar & a variety of village shops.
**Clientele:** Good mix of gay men & women
**Transportation:** Car is best. Free pick up from train or bus, AUD $75 for pick up from airport.
**To Gay Bars:** Nearest bars are in Sydney, Canberra, or Wollongong. 50 miles or 1 hour.
**Rooms:** 6 rooms with single or queen beds.
**Bathrooms:** 2 shared showers & 2 shared WCs.
**Campsites:** 10 tent sites with use of guesthouse facilities. 2 RV parking sites.
**Meals:** Full country breakfast, other meals at extra charge.
**Vegetarian:** Available upon request.
**Complimentary:** Tea & coffee, wine with meals.
**Dates Open:** All year.
**High Season:** Dec & Jan.
**Rates:** AUD $50-AUD $120, campsites AUD $10.
**Discounts:** For midweek stays.
**Credit Cards:** MC, Visa, Amex, Bancard, Diners.
**Rsv'tns:** Recommended.
**Reserve Through:** Travel agent or call direct.
**Parking:** Ample free off-street parking.
**In-Room:** Coffee & tea-making facilities.
**On-Premises:** TV lounge, meeting rooms & laundry facilities.
**Exercise/Health:** Jacuzzi, weights, massage, gym.
**Swimming:** Pool on premises, nearby swimming holes & river. 15-min drive to ocean.
**Sunbathing:** At pool or riverside, on ocean beach.
**Nudity:** Permitted in pool area & Jacuzzi at discretion of other guests.
**Smoking:** Permitted without restrictions.
**Pets:** Dogs & cats permitted.
**Handicap Access:** Yes.
**Children:** No.
**Languages:** English.

IGTA agta

# BLUE MOUNTAINS

## Bygone Beautys Cottages

Q-NET Gay-Friendly ♀♂

### *From Pure Relaxation to Total Indulgence*

From modest mountain cottages to executive residences, from romantic settings for two to cottages designed for 10 people or more, ***Bygone Beautys Cottages*** has a range of fully self-contained accommodations set in beautiful gardens in the heart of the Blue Mountains. The cottages are conveniently located to the sights of the Blue Mountains and to many recreational activities available in the area.

On arrival, guests will find chocolates and fresh flowers greeting them in each of the fully self-equipped cottages. The kitchens are stocked with ingredients for a traditional Aussie breakfast of bacon, eggs, tomatoes, bread, cereals, oranges for juice, and fresh fruit. The bathrooms, some with spas, have a generous supply of fluffy towels and bath toiletries. Most of the cottages have central heating and, for that extra mountain atmosphere, a burning log fire in the living room. The ***Bygone Beautys*** tearooms serve delicious complimentary Devonshire tea to guests at any time during their stay.

**Address: 20-22 Grose St, Leura, NSW 2780 Australia.**
**Tel: (61-47) 84 3117, (61-47) 84 3108, Fax: (61-47) 58 7257.**

**Type:** Bed & breakfast cottages with restaurant & bric-a-brac & craft shop.
**Clientele:** Mostly hetero clientele with a gay & lesbian following
**Transportation:** Car or train, then taxi.
**To Gay Bars:** 55 km, an hour by car.
**Rooms:** 14 cottages with double, queen or king beds.
**Bathrooms:** All private.
**Meals:** Full breakfast.
**Vegetarian:** Available upon request.
**Complimentary:** Devonshire tea, chocolates, coffee, tea, milk.
**Dates Open:** All year.
**High Season:** June-September.
**Rates:** Per person per night from AUD $60-AUD $115.
**Discounts:** For groups, extended periods of stay, children.
**Credit Cards:** Amex, VISA, MC.
**Rsv'tns:** Required.
**Reserve Through:** Call direct.
**Minimum Stay:** Required.
**Parking:** Ample free off-street parking.
**In-Room:** Color TV, VCR, kitchen, refrigerator, coffee/tea-making facilities & laundry service.
**Exercise/Health:** Tennis court & Jacuzzi on one property, bushwalking, abseiling, rock climbing.
**Sunbathing:** In the garden.
**Smoking:** Permitted in all areas.
**Pets:** Not permitted.
**Handicap Access:** Yes.
**Children:** Welcome.
**Languages:** English.

iglta

# COFFS HARBOUR

## Santa Fe Luxury Bed & Breakfast

Gay-Owned ♀♂

***Santa Fe*** is not only the romance of Santa Fe, but the irresistible appeal of its lifestyle...a casual elegance.Tucked away in a secluded valley just 10 minutes north of Coffs Harbour and only 2 minutes from beautiful Sapphire Beach, discover this unique peaceful retreat set in 5 acres of subtropical gardens, waterfalls and natural bushland. Take a stroll through the gardens, feed the Koi fish or relax around the large salt water pool that is set in terraced lawns and gardens. Enjoy a log fire, the adobe BBQ area and healthy breakfasts served on the deck.

**Address: The Mountain Way, Coffs Harbour, NSW 2450 Australia.**
**Tel: (61-66) 537 700, Fax: (61-66) 537 050.**

**Type:** Bed & breakfast.
**Clientele:** 10% gay & lesbian clientele
**Transportation:** Free pick up from airport & train.
**Rooms:** 3 rooms with single, queen or king beds.
**Bathrooms:** 3 private shower/toilets.
**Meals:** Full breakfast.
**Vegetarian:** Available upon request.
**Complimentary:** Tea & coffee.
**Dates Open:** All year.
**High Season:** Nov-Feb.
**Rates:** Winter (May-Sept) AUD $125. Summer (Oct-Apr) AUD $145.
**Credit Cards:** MC, VISA & Bancard.
**Rsv'tns:** Required.
**Reserve Thru:** Call direct.
**Parking:** Ample free off-street parking.
**In-Room:** Color TV, VCR, video tape library, ceiling fans, coffee/tea-making facilities & room service.
**On-Premises:** TV lounge & laundry facilities.
**Swimming:** Pool & spa jet on premises. Nearby ocean, 5 minutes to gay beach.
**Sunbathing:** At poolside, on common & private sun decks & at the beach.
**Smoking:** Permitted outside only.
**Pets:** Not permitted.
**Children:** Not especially welcome.
**Languages:** English.
**Your Host:** Sharon, Ben & Alan.

# NORTHERN NEW SOUTH WALES

## A Slice of Heaven Rural Retreat for Women

Women ♀

### *Staying at A Slice of Heaven Doesn't Cost You the Earth*

***A Slice of Heaven Rural Retreat for Women*** is a 12 acre permaculture paradise, peaceful, secluded and strategically situated on the Pacific Highway near Murwillumbah in Northern NSW, one half hour from Byron Bay and the Coolangatta. We offer bed and breakfast either in-house or in separate private accommodation. There are two guest rooms in the main house and a self-contained studio in the newly appointed barn, just past the tropical orchard and tennis court. There is another separate studio adjacent to the games room, beside the saltwater pool and summer house. Gourmet dinners and lunches are available upon request. Facilities include a saltwater billabong-style pool and spa, tennis court, pool table, mini gym, large bath and bush walks. Join us for Women's Fair Day and in February for Women's Sports Day. Tariffs are $80 per double and $60 per single. If you want to be pampered then our place is for you. For reservations call Carly on (066) 779276.

**Address: Lot 3 Pacific Highway,, Stokers Siding, NSW 2484 Australia.**
**Tel: (61-66) 779 276, mobile: (61-15) 590 299.**
**E-mail: spower@medeserv.com.au.**
**http://www.powerup.com.au/~qldq/soh.html.**

**Type:** Rural retreat B&B.
**Clientele:** Women only
**Transportation:** Car is best. Free pick up for railway (Murwillumbah, NSW) or air (Coolangatta Airport/ Gold Coast QLD).
**To Gay Bars:** 30 minutes by car.
**Rooms:** 2 rooms, 1 suite & 1 cottage with single or double beds.
**Bathrooms:** 2 private bath/toilets & 2 private shower/toilets.

*continued next page*

**Meals:** Expanded continental breakfast.
**Vegetarian:** Readily available upon request.
**Complimentary:** Tea, coffee, pre dinner drinks & liqueur coffee with other meals.
**Dates Open:** All year.
**Rates:** AUD $60 per single, AUD $80 per double.
**Discounts:** Stay 7 nights, pay for 6.
**Rsv'tns:** Required.
**Reserve Through:** Call direct.
**Parking:** Ample free off-street parking.
**In-Room:** Color TV, ceiling fans, refrigerator, coffee & tea-making facilities.
**On-Premises:** TV lounge, meeting rooms & games room with VCR & video tape library. BBQ area at private lake.
**Exercise/Health:** Gym, Jacuzzi, massage, tennis court, pool table & bush walks.
**Swimming:** Pool on premises & private lake.
**Sunbathing:** At poolside, on patio & common sun decks.
**Smoking:** Permitted on verandahs & outside.
**Pets:** Not permitted.
**Handicap Access:** Yes.
**Children:** Not especially welcome.
**Languages:** English.
**Your Host:** Carly & Fae.

agta

# SYDNEY

## The Barracks

Men ♂

### *Sydney's Only Male-Only Accommodation*

If you want to stay only five minutes' walk from the gay bars of Oxford St., ***The Barracks*** is for you. Our renovated Victorian has six stylishly furnished guest bedrooms, and a large TV lounge with current reading material. Four rooms have either balconies or direct access to the courtyard. One of these has stunning city views, another has a private bathroom. Breakfast is served from 7:00 a.m. till noon, for the convenience of late risers. We run a clean, uncluttered guesthouse, which you will find a pleasant and comfortable base from which to discover Sydney.

**Address: 164 B Bourke St, Darlinghurst, Sydney, NSW 2010 Australia.**
**Tel: (61-2) 9360 5823,**
**Fax: (61-2) 9361 4584.**

**Type:** Bed & breakfast guesthouse.
**Clientele:** Men only
**Transportation:** Taxi to & from airport AUD $15-AUD $20.
**To Gay Bars:** Three blocks or a 5-minute walk.
**Rooms:** 6 rooms with queen beds, 1-bedroom apartment sleeping up to 3.
**Bathrooms:** 1 private shower/toilet, 5 sinks. Shared: 3 showers, 1 bath, 1 toilet.
**Meals:** Continental breakfast.
**Complimentary:** Coffee, tea, fruit juice.
**Dates Open:** All year.
**Rates:** AUD $70-AUD $110.
**Discounts:** Seventh night free except Mardi Gras weekend.
**Credit Cards:** MC, Visa, Amex, Bancard.
**Rsv'tns:** Suggested.
**Reserve Through:** Travel agent or call direct.
**Parking:** Adequate off-street parking.
**In-Room:** Ceiling fans & maid service.
**On-Premises:** TV lounge, laundry facilities, BBQ & private courtyard.
**Exercise/Health:** Nearby gym, sauna, weights, steam & massage.
**Swimming:** 5-minute walk to pool. Ocean beach 8 kms, harbor beach 3 kms.
**Sunbathing:** At the beach, on patio & private sun decks.
**Nudity:** Permitted in the courtyard.
**Smoking:** Permitted in most of the house. Non-smoking rooms available.
**Pets:** Not permitted.
**Handicap Access:** Not wheelchair accessible.
**Children:** Not permitted.
**Languages:** English.
**Your Host:** Bryce & Don.

## Brickfield Hill Bed & Breakfast Inn

Gay/Lesbian ♀♂

### *Quality Service, Understated Elegance*

Restored to reflect its original domestic plan, this four-storey Victorian terrace house accommodates up to eight guests. It is located in Surry Hills, close to Oxford Street and the city. There are numerous excellent restaurants in the neighbourhood which is fast becoming one of Sydney's most sought after inner-city residential addresses. The city, Sydney Harbour and the opera house are only minutes away by taxi or underground, or you can hop on a bus for a day at one of Sydney's South Pacific beaches.

Service at ***Brickfield Hill Bed and Breakfast Inn*** is personal, yet unobtrusive. Rooms with or without private bathrooms are available. Three rooms on the upper two levels have balconies with pleasant views, and breakfast is served in the dining room and on its adjoining verandah.

**Address: 403 Riley St, Surrey Hills, Sydney, NSW 2010 Australia.**
**Tel: (61-2) 9211 4886 (Tel/Fax).**

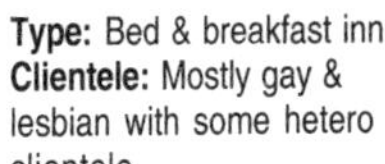

**Type:** Bed & breakfast inn.
**Clientele:** Mostly gay & lesbian with some hetero clientele
**Transportation:** Taxi or city shuttle direct from Sydney Airport, or airport bus to Central Station, then taxi or walk.
**To Gay Bars:** 3 blocks to Oxford St (The Golden Mile), an 8 minute walk, a 1 minute drive.
**Rooms:** 4 rooms with double or queen beds.
**Bathrooms:** Private: 1 bath/toilet, Shared: 1 bath/shower/toilet.
**Meals:** Expanded continental breakfast.
**Vegetarian:** Vegetarians are catered for. Good neighbourhood restaurants also have vegetarian food.
**Complimentary:** Tea & coffee.
**Dates Open:** All year.
**High Season:** February-March.
**Rates:** AUD $95-AUD $145.
**Credit Cards:** MC, Visa.
**Rsv'tns:** Required.
**Reserve Through:** Call direct.
**Parking:** Limited on- & off-street parking. If parking is needed, please reserve a parking space when booking your room.
**In-Room:** Colour TV, coffee & tea-making facilities, maid service.
**On-Premises:** Meeting rooms, phone, fax & limited word processing service.
**Exercise/Health:** Nearby gym, weights, Jacuzzi, sauna, steam, massage.
**Swimming:** Pool, ocean & harbour nearby.
**Sunbathing:** Some rooms have private verandahs.
**Smoking:** The inn is completely non-smoking.
**Pets:** Not permitted.
**Handicap Access:** No.
**Children:** No.
**Languages:** English, Japanese, French, German, Italian.
**Your Host:** Ivano & David.

IGTA

## Furama Hotel Central

Gay-Friendly ♀♂

Featuring 182 luxurious rooms, this modern Australian-owned and -built hotel offers complete privacy and convenience in a comfortable and relaxing environment. ***Furama Hotel Central's*** spacious and well-appointed rooms feature many amenities, including colour TV, reverse cycle air-conditioning, direct-dial ISD/STD telephones, executive desks and mini bars. An international a la carte restaurant is on premises and offers extensive food and wine selections. We are minutes from the airport, a step away from Central Railway Station, and a short stroll to Darling Harbour, Chinatown, city centre, theatres and major sporting facilities.

**Address: 28 Albion St, Surrey Hills, Sydney, NSW 2010 Australia. Tel: (61-2) 9281 0333, Fax: (61-2) 9281 0222.**

**Type:** Hotel with restaurant & bar.
**Clientele:** Mostly hetero with a gay & lesbian following
**Transportation:** Airport bus to hotel or taxi.
**To Gay Bars:** 4 blocks, 1/2 mile, a 15 min walk, a 3 min drive.
**Rooms:** 182 rooms with single or queen beds.
**Bathrooms:** All private bath/toilet/showers.
**Vegetarian:** Vegetarian options on menu at restaurants.
**Complimentary:** Tea & coffee facilities in rooms.
**Dates Open:** All year.
**Rates:** AUD $165.
**Credit Cards:** Visa, Diners, Amex, Bancard.
**Rsv'tns:** Required.
**Reserve Through:** Travel agent or call direct.
**Parking:** Ample off-street pay, covered parking.
**In-Room:** Color TV, telephone, AC, coffee & tea-making facilities, refrigerator, maid, room & laundry service.
**On-Premises:** Meeting rooms, business services.
**Exercise/Health:** Gym, weights, Jacuzzi, sauna.
**Swimming:** Pool on premises.
**Sunbathing:** Poolside & on common sun decks.
**Smoking:** Permitted in rooms only. Non-smoking rooms available.
**Handicap Access:** Yes.
**Children:** Welcome.
**Languages:** English.
**Your Host:** Bruce.

## Furama Hotel Darling Harbour

Gay-Friendly ♀♂

### *Affordable Luxury!*

***Furama Hotel Darling Harbour*** is ideally situated opposite the Sydney Entertainment Centre, next to Chinatown and is at the gateway to Sydney's famous Darling Harbour Convention and shopping complexes. It is just a short walk from the hotel to the monorail, major theatre's, cinemas, main department stores, the business district and other major tourist attractions. This international-standard hotel is partly located in a historic Woolstore. Its Executive Suites and Deluxe and Superior Rooms offer a wide range of amenities from complimentary toiletries to express check out. Experience the atmosphere of a turn-of-the-century coffee and spices mill at Shipley's restaurant. It offers fresh, modern cuisine and features a great range of Hunter Valley wines.

**Address: 68 Harbour Street, Darling Harbour, Sydney, NSW 2000 Australia. Tel: (61-2) 9281 0400, Fax: (61-2) 9281 1212.**

**Type:** Hotel with restaurant.
**Clientele:** Mostly hetero with a gay & lesbian following
**Transportation:** Airport bus to Furama, or taxi or car.
**To Gay Bars:** 4 blocks, 1/2 mile, a 15 min walk, a 3 min drive.
**Rooms:** 236 rooms, 14 suites with single or queen beds.
**Bathrooms:** All private bath/toilet/showers.
**Vegetarian:** Vegeterian menu options in hotel restaurants.
**Complimentary:** Tea & coffee facilities.
**Dates Open:** All year.
**Rates:** AUD $165.
**Credit Cards:** Visa, Diners, Amex, Bancard.
**Rsv'tns:** Required.
**Reserve Through:** Travel agent or call direct.
**Parking:** Ample off-street pay, covered parking.
**In-Room:** Color TV, telephone, AC, coffee & tea-making facilities, refrigerator, maid, room & laundry service.
**On-Premises:** Meeting rooms, business services.
**Exercise/Health:** Nearby gym.
**Smoking:** Permitted in rooms. No non-smoking rooms available.
**Pets:** Not permitted.
**Handicap Access:** Yes.
**Children:** Welcome.
**Languages:** English.
**Your Host:** Bruce.

## Governors on Fitzroy B&B

**Gay/Lesbian ♀♂**

### *An Australian B&B in the Heart of Sydney*

Whether traveling for pleasure or business, ***Governors on Fitzroy B&B Guesthouse*** will be your home in Sydney. Our quiet location is a sanctuary from the busy city of Sydney, yet conveniently just half a mile from the city centre. The B&B was established in 1987, with refurbishment of an 1863 terrace-style house. Six guest rooms provide comfortable, private accommodation and a full American-style breakfast is served each morning. Our private garden, lounge and TV rooms are available for guest use. Your hosts live on the property and are available for travel information and tips on making your stay in Sydney the best!

**Address: 64 Fitzroy St, Surry Hills, NSW 2010 Australia.**
**Tel: (61-2) 9331 4652,**
**Fax: (61-2) 9361-5094,**
**E-mail: governor@zip.com.au.**

**Type:** Bed & breakfast.
**Clientele:** Good mix of gays & lesbians
**Transportation:** Taxi from airport approximately AUD $15.
**To Gay Bars:** 2 blocks to men's/women's bars.
**Rooms:** 6 rooms with double & queen beds.
**Bathrooms:** 5 private sinks, 2 shared bath/shower/toilets & 2 shared toilets.
**Meals:** Full American-style breakfast.
**Vegetarian:** Upon request.
**Complimentary:** Coffee, tea available 24 hours.
**Dates Open:** All year.
**High Season:** February-March, during Gay & Lesbian Mardi Gras.
**Rates:** Single AUD $75, double AUD $95.
**Discounts:** Weekly rate for 6-night stay.
**Credit Cards:** MC, VISA, Amex.
**Rsv'tns:** Recommended.
**Reserve Through:** Call direct.
**Minimum Stay:** 5 nights during Mardi Gras.
**Parking:** Limited on-street parking.
**In-Room:** Maid service.
**On-Premises:** Meeting rooms, telephone, fax, piano, library, TV lounge, private garden.
**Exercise/Health:** Spa on premises. Nearby gym, sauna & massage.
**Swimming:** 20-min drive to ocean.
**Sunbathing:** On common sun decks or ocean beach.
**Nudity:** Permitted in spa area.
**Smoking:** Permitted, but not in bedrooms.
**Pets:** Not permitted.
**Handicap Access:** No.
**Children:** Not permitted.
**Languages:** English.

## Manor House Boutique Hotel

Gay/Lesbian ♂

### *The Ultimate in Gay Boutique Hotels*

***The Manor House,*** built circa 1850, was the original residence of the first Lord Mayor of Sydney. Now totally refurbished and renovated to its former glory, it is one of Sydney's finest boutique hotels. This two-story terrace mansion features ornate ceilings, cornices and chandeliers, along with extensive balconies, lead light windows and a polished timber staircase. There are 18 boutique accommodation rooms, a fully licensed restaurant and bar, a heated outdoor spa pool and cabana.

***The Manor House*** is situated in one of Sydney's premier entertainment districts, only 300 metres from Oxford Street which is internationally renowned for its abundance of restaurants, bars and night clubs.

**Address: 86 Flinders St, Darlinghurst, Sydney, NSW 2010 Australia.**
**Tel: (61-2) 9380 6633, Fax: (61-2) 9380 5016.**

**Type:** Hotel with restaurant & bar.
**Clientele:** Mostly men with women welcome
**Transportation:** Taxi or car.
**To Gay Bars:** 1 block, a 2 min walk.
**Rooms:** 18 rooms with single, queen or king beds.
**Bathrooms:** Private: 6 shower/toilets, 12 bath/toilet/showers.
**Meals:** Buffet breakfast.
**Vegetarian:** Available on request. An abundance of restaurants for vegetarians only 2 mins away.
**Complimentary:** Tea & coffee.
**Dates Open:** All year.
**High Season:** Feb & Oct.
**Rates:** Low season $100-$200, high season $150-$250.
**Credit Cards:** MC, Visa, Amex, Diners, Bancard.
**Rsv'tns:** Required.
**Reserve Through:** Travel agent or call direct.
**Minimum Stay:** 1 week minimum required during high season.
**Parking:** Limited off-street parking.
**In-Room:** Color TV, VCR, telephone, coffee & tea-making facilities, refrigerator.
**On-Premises:** Video tape library.
**Exercise/Health:** Jacuzzi. Nearby gym, weights, Jacuzzi, sauna, steam, massage.
**Swimming:** Pool, ocean on premises & nearby.
**Sunbathing:** Poolside & at beach.
**Smoking:** Permitted. Non-smoking rooms available.
**Handicap Access:** Yes.
**Children:** No.
**Languages:** English.

IGTA agta

## The Observatory Hotel

Gay-Friendly ♀♂

### *Five-Star Luxury Tailored to the Individual*

Part of the distinctive collection of Orient-Express Hotels, ***The Observatory*** is Sydney's most personal hotel, providing every conceivable luxury in the style of a period Australian home. Its 100 luxurious guest rooms feature CD's, video and marble bathrooms. The private Drawing Room, Globe Bar, restaurants and Health and Leisure Club offer a relaxed atmosphere ideal for both business and pleasure. Located just minutes from the CBD, ***The Observatory*** has also established a fine reputation as a conference venue.

**Address: 89-113 Kent St, Sydney, NSW 2000 Australia.**
**Tel: (61-2) 9256 2222, Fax: (61-2) 9256 2233.**

**Type:** Hotel with restaurant, bar, gift shop & health & leisure club.
**Clientele:** Mostly straight clientele with a gay & lesbian following
**Transportation:** Bus, taxi or train. Pick up from airport in limousine, one way AUD $55 (domestic)-AUD $65 (international).
**To Gay Bars:** 30-minute walk or 10-minute drive.
**Rooms:** 75 rooms, 21 suites & 4 handicap-accessible rooms with single, double, queen or king beds.
**Bathrooms:** All private full baths.
**Vegetarian:** Available upon request. 10 minutes to vegetarian restaurants.
**Complimentary:** Mineral water upon turndown.
**Dates Open:** All year.
**High Season:** Feb-Mar, Oct-Nov.
**Rates:** From AUD $330.
**Discounts:** Corporate & contract rates negotiable with Director of Sales.
**Credit Cards:** MC, Visa, Amex, Diners, Bancard & JCB.
**Rsv'tns:** Required.
**Reserve Through:** Travel agent or call direct.
**Parking:** Limited covered parking, AUD $15 per day per car.
**In-Room:** Color cable TV, VCR, video tape library (concierge), AC, telephone, refrigerator, room, maid & laundry service. Coffee/tea-making facilities in suites.
**On-Premises:** Meeting rooms & secretarial services.
**Exercise/Health:** Gym, weights, Jacuzzi, sauna, steam, massage & flotation tank on premises. Nearby health club.
**Swimming:** Pool on premises. Pool & ocean nearby.
**Sunbathing:** On private sun decks & at the beach.
**Smoking:** Permitted except in 1 restaurant & on non-smoking floor.
**Pets:** Not permitted.
**Handicap Access:** Yes.
**Children:** Welcome.
**Languages:** English, French, basic Japanese & Italian.
**Your Host:** Patrick.

## Park Lodge Hotel

Gay-Owned 50/50 ♀♂

### *The Olympic City's Best Value and Friendliest People*

Old-world charm describes ***Park Lodge Hotel,*** a Victorian-style boutique hotel built in 1880, situated opposite Sydney's spacious Moore Park and Royal Agriculture Society Showground. The hotel is only 10 minutes from both of Sydney's airports and is in the heart of Sydney's gay area, only a short bus ride from the city centre, the beautiful harbour, and renowned ocean beaches. The hotel has 20 rooms, most with en suite facilities, and a delightful courtyard oasis in the bustling city environment. Enjoy continental breakfast in the quaint breakfast room or sunny courtyard. Of course, the numerous nearby Oxford Street restaurants are renowned for offering inexpensive, top-quality cuisine.

**Address: 747 South Dowling St, Moore Park, Sydney, NSW 2016 Australia. Tel: (61-2) 9318 2393, Fax: (61-2) 9318 2513.**
**E-mail: pklodge@geko.net.au. http://www.geko.net.au/~pklodge/.**

**Type:** Hotel.
**Clientele:** 50% gay & lesbian & 50% hetero clientele
**Transportation:** Taxi (about AUD $15).
**To Gay Bars:** 3 blocks, a 7-minute walk, a 2-minute drive.
**Rooms:** 20 rooms with single, double, queen, king or bunk beds.
**Bathrooms:** 18 private bath/toilets, 2 shared bath/toilets.
**Meals:** Continental breakfast.
**Vegetarian:** Non-meat selections at breakfast.
**Complimentary:** In-room tea/coffee, mints on pillow.
**Dates Open:** All year.
**High Season:** Sydney Gay & Lesbian Mardi Gras (Feb-March).
**Rates:** Low season (winter) AUD $60-AUD $95, high season (summer) AUD $80-AUD $120.
**Discounts:** On longer stays & referrals.
**Credit Cards:** MC, Visa, Amex, Diners, Bancard, EFTPOS.
**Rsv'tns:** Required during high season.
**Reserve Through:** Travel agent or call direct.
**Parking:** Limited on-street parking.
**In-Room:** Color TV, VCR rental, ironing facilities, telephone, refrigerator, pay laundromat, coffee/tea-making facilities, maid service.
**On-Premises:** Courtyard, laundry facilities, video tape library.
**Exercise/Health:** Massage by appointment. Nearby gym, weights, Jacuzzi, sauna, steam, massage.
**Swimming:** Nearby pool, ocean.
**Sunbathing:** At beach & in courtyard.
**Smoking:** Permitted in room & outside areas.
**Pets:** Considered on request.
**Handicap Access:** Ground-floor room.
**Children:** Welcome, but no extra provisions other than beds, cots & interconnecting rooms.
**Languages:** English.

## Simpsons of Potts Point

Gay-Friendly ♀♂

### *Sydney's Finest Heritage Inn*

Erected in 1892 as the stylish residence of a local politician, ***Simpsons of Potts Point*** was meticulously restored in 1988 to form a unique 14-room boutique hotel. Experience the ambiance of large, spacious rooms, grand halls, and original stained-glass widows of this national trust listed building. Fabrics of William Morris designs recreate the original arts and crafts decoration of the period. ***Simpsons*** is located in Sydney's best restaurant area, within walking distance to the CBD and Oxford Street's gay venues.

**Address: 8 Challis Ave, Potts Point, NSW 2011 Australia. Tel: (61-2) 356 2199, Fax: (61-2) 356 4476.**

**Type:** Inn.
**Clientele:** Mostly hetero with 10% gay & lesbian clientele
**Transportation:** Taxi is best, or airporter bus. Inn is near good bus & train services.
**To Gay Bars:** 5 blocks, a 15 min walk, a 5 min drive.
**Rooms:** 13 rooms & 1 suite with single or queen beds.
**Bathrooms:** Private: 4 bath/toilets, 10 shower/toilets.
**Vegetarian:** Excellent vegetarian restaurants nearby.
**Complimentary:** Tea, coffee & cookies served in glass conservatory.
**Dates Open:** All year.
**High Season:** Summer (December-February).
**Rates:** AUD $145-AUD $245.
**Credit Cards:** MC, Visa, Amex, Diners, Bancard.
**Rsv'tns:** Required.
**Reserve Through:** Travel agent or call direct.
**Parking:** Limited free off-street parking.
**In-Room:** Colour TV, AC, telephone, ceiling fans, refrigerator, maid, room & laundry service.
**On-Premises:** Meeting rooms, TV lounge.
**Exercise/Health:** Nearby gym, weights, Jacuzzi, sauna, steam, massage.
**Swimming:** Pool nearby.
**Smoking:** Permitted. Non-smoking rooms available.
**Pets:** Not permitted.
**Handicap Access:** No.
**Children:** No.
**Languages:** English, German.
**Your Host:** Peter.

## Sydney Star Accommodation

Q-NET Gay/Lesbian ♀♂

### *You'll Always Feel Welcome*

When staying away from home for business or pleasure it is refreshing to find a friendly, cozy atmosphere to relax and feel welcome in. The ***Sydney Star Accommodation*** combines all the style and elegance of a European pensione with the service and security of a modern hotel.

It's a new, fresh approach to affordable accommodation in colourful downtown Darlinghurst, the heart of Sydney's gay and lesbian community. This stylish private hotel is conveniently located in a quiet oasis on Darlinghurst Road, just minutes from Oxford Street and Kings Cross. Darlinghurst, known for its history and vitality, is a short stroll from the inner city, and is alive with restaurants, cafes, galleries, and boutiques. The 10 comfortable rooms of the guesthouse apartments are private and fully serviced, with single, twin, and double suites available, each with kitchen and colour TV. You'll find surprisingly inexpensive city living – special weekly rates are available.

This charming, quaint, boutique-style hotel is popular with the creative and fashion industries, presenting a delightful alternative to a high tariff and impersonal atmosphere. You'll always feel welcome at the ***Sydney Star Accommodation*** where you'll find old-fashioned courtesy in the heart of Sydney.

**Address: 275 Darlinghurst Rd, Darlinghurst, NSW 2010 Australia.**
**Tel: (61-414) 677 778 (24-hour mobile phone), Fax: (61-2) 9331 1000.**

**Type:** Guesthouse apartments.
**Clientele:** Mostly gay & lesbian with some hetero clientele
**Transportation:** 15-minutes by taxi or bus from airport, very close to train & ferry.
**To Gay Bars:** 2 blocks, a 10-minute walk, a 3-minute drive.
**Rooms:** 10 suites, 20 apartments with single, double, queen or bunk beds.
**Bathrooms:** Private: 15 shower/toilets, 1 bath/shower/toilet, 30 sinks. Shared: 15 bath/shower/toilets.
**Meals:** Expanded continental breakfast.
**Complimentary:** Each room has kitchen, fridge, microwave, sink, a selection of teas, fresh-ground coffee & cereal.
**Dates Open:** All year.
**High Season:** Oct-April.
**Rates:** Double AUD $90, twin AUD $80, single AUD $60.
**Discounts:** Weekly & monthly packages.
**Credit Cards:** MC, Visa, Amex, Diners, Bancard, Discover.
**Rsv'tns:** Advisable.
**Reserve Through:** Travel agent or call direct. 1 week minimum booking.
**Minimum Stay:** Inquire.
**Parking:** Ample on- & off-street parking.
**In-Room:** Color TV, telephone, refrigerator, kitchen, coffee/tea-making facilities.
**Exercise/Health:** Nearby gym, weights, Jacuzzi, sauna, steam, massage.
**Swimming:** Nearby pool, ocean, beautiful beaches.
**Sunbathing:** At beach.
**Smoking:** Permitted on balcony & in courtyard, not encouraged in rooms.
**Pets:** Not permitted.
**Handicap Access:** No.
**Children:** No.
**Languages:** Australian English, Dutch, French, German.
**Your Host:** Robert.

## Victoria Court Sydney

Q-NET Gay-Friendly ♀♂

### *Victorian Charm in the Heart of Sydney*

The focal point of ***Victoria Court*** is the verdant courtyard conservatory where, to the accompaniment of twittering free-flying birds, guests can enjoy their breakfast. ***Victoria Court*** is comprised of two elegant Victorian terrace houses, built in 1881, that were restored and modernised. Here in an informal atmosphere, amidst Victorian charm, guests are offered friendly and personalised service.

Not unexpectedly, no two rooms are alike: most have marble fireplaces, some have balconies that offer views over National Trust classified Victoria Street, and others feature patios. For romantics there are even some rooms with four-poster beds. Guests can relax and read the daily papers or browse through books in the fireplaced lounge. All rooms have en suite bathrooms, hairdryers, coffee- and tea-making facilities, colour televisions, AM/FM radios, and direct dial telephones for local and international calls.

The historic boutique hotel is centrally located on a quiet, leafy street in lively Potts Point, the heart of Sydney's bohemian scene. The hotel is an ideal base from which to explore Sydney. It is within minutes of the Opera House, Oxford Street, the Central Business District with its superb shopping, the Harbour, Chinatown, and beaches. In the immediate vicinity are some of Sydney's most renowned restaurants and clubs, as well as innumerable others with menus priced to suit all pockets. The wide variety of cuisines includes Australian, Italian, French, Thai, Chinese, Japanese, and Indian, to name but a few. Public transport, car rental, travel agencies, and banks are within easy reach. An airport shuttle bus operates to and from the hotel, while, for those with their own transport, security parking is available. E-mail: vicsyd@ozemail.com.au(fe)

**Address: 122 Victoria Street, Sydney-Potts Point, NSW 2011 Australia.**
**Tel: (61-2) 9357 3200, Fax: (61-2) 9357 7606.**
**Toll-free in Australia: (1800) 63 05 05.**

**Type:** Bed & breakfast hotel.
**Clientele:** Mostly hetero clientele with a gay/lesbian following
**Transportation:** Taxi, airport bus, train or bus.
**To Gay Bars:** 1 block, a 5-minute walk.
**Rooms:** 23 rooms with single, queen or king beds.
**Bathrooms:** All private.
**Meals:** Buffet breakfast.
**Vegetarian:** Vegetarian restaurants nearby.
**Complimentary:** Coffee, tea.
**Dates Open:** All year.
**High Season:** December-March.
**Rates:** AUD $75-AUD $210.
**Discounts:** Long-term & corporate rates.
**Credit Cards:** MC, VISA, Amex, Diners, Bancard, Eurocard.
**Rsv'tns:** Recommended.
**Reserve Through:** Travel agent or call direct.
**Parking:** Limited covered parking.
**In-Room:** AC, telephone, colour TV, refrigerator, coffee/tea-making facilities, ceiling fans, laundry & maid service.
**Exercise/Health:** Nearby gym with weights, Jacuzzi, sauna, steam, massage.
**Swimming:** Nearby pool, ocean, river.
**Sunbathing:** At beach.
**Smoking:** Permitted in rooms & public areas. Non-smoking rooms available.
**Pets:** Not permitted.
**Handicap Access:** Yes.
**Children:** No.
**Languages:** English, German, French, Spanish.

# QUEENSLAND

## BRISBANE

### Allender Apartments

Gay-Friendly ♀♂

*Allender* is a beautifully appointed apartment block in a safe area close to the downtown centre, venues, clubs, pubs, restaurants, shops, and taxis. Each spacious and clean apartment is tastefully furnished with ultra-modern decor, fully-equipped separate kitchens, self-controlled heat and air, huge full-length mirrored wardrobes, direct dial phones, television, and security door intercom. Washing and drying facilities are also available. As a small, owner-operated establishment, we provide individual attention to your needs, as well as current tourist information.

**Address: 3 Moreton St, New Farm, Brisbane, QLD 4005 Australia.**
**Tel: (61-7) 3358 5832, Fax: (61-7) 3254 0799.**

**Type:** 8 apartments, 3 studios, 4 1-br & 1 2-br.
**Clientele:** Mostly hetero with a gay & lesbian following
**Transportation:** Airport shuttle to downtown transit centre, then taxi, or taxi direct from airport (14km).
**To Gay Bars:** 1 mile, a 15-minute walk or 3-minute drive.
**Rooms:** 8 self-contained apartments with single, double or queen beds. Shortly adding 3 more studios.
**Bathrooms:** All private.
**Complimentary:** Tea & coffee.
**Dates Open:** All year.
**High Season:** Jan, Apr, Sep.
**Rates:** AUD $50-$55 single or double occupancy. 1- & 2-br AUD $75.
**Credit Cards:** MC, Visa, Bancard.
**Rsv'tns:** Preferred.
**Reserve Through:** Travel agent or call direct.
**Minimum Stay:** 3 day advance minimum or 1 or 2 days subject to availability.
**Parking:** Ample on-street parking.
**In-Room:** Color TV, AC, telephone, security door intercom, kitchen, refrigerator, coffee/tea-making facilities & maid service.
**On-Premises:** Laundry facilities.
**Swimming:** Nearby pool.
**Sunbathing:** At poolside.
**Smoking:** Permitted in rooms.
**Pets:** Not permitted.
**Handicap Access:** No.
**Children:** Children stay occasionally.
**Languages:** English.
**Your Host:** Peter.

### Edward Lodge

Gay/Lesbian ♂

## *Brisbane's Finest Gay Accommodation*

***Edward Lodge*** was built in the 1920s in a tudor style. The rooms are all large, comfortably furnished and serviced each day. The lounge/breakfast room opens onto the courtyard where a generous complimentary continental breakfast is served until midday. Amenities also include 24-hour tea/coffee-making facilities and a spa. ***Edward Lodge,*** located in the cosmopolitan Brisbane suburb of New Farm, is close to gay venues, cafes and restaurants, and a range of shopping, transportation and entertainment facilities. A stay at ***Edward Lodge*** is a relaxing and friendly experience.

**Address: 75 Sydney St, New Farm, Brisbane, QLD 4005 Australia.**
**Tel: (61-7) 3254 1078, Fax: (61-7) 3254 1062.**

**Type:** Bed & breakfast guesthouse.
**Clientele:** Mostly men with women welcome
**Transportation:** Bus, ferry or taxi.
**To Gay Bars:** 2 km.
**Rooms:** 8 rooms with twin or queen beds.
**Bathrooms:** 8 private shower/toilets.
**Meals:** Expanded continental breakfast.
**Complimentary:** Tea, coffee.

*continued next page*

**Dates Open:** All year.
**High Season:** Mid year.
**Rates:** Single AUD $60, double AUD $70.
**Credit Cards:** MC, VISA, Bancard, Diners, Amex.
**Rsv'tns:** Recommended.
**Reserve Through:** Travel agent or call direct.
**Parking:** Ample on-street parking.
**In-Room:** Telephone, ceiling fans, color TV, VCR, refrigerator, laundry service.
**On-Premises:** TV lounge, video tape library.
**Exercise/Health:** Jacuzzi. Nearby gym.
**Swimming:** Nearby pool.
**Nudity:** Permitted in Jacuzzi.
**Smoking:** Permitted outside only.
**Pets:** Not permitted.
**Handicap Access:** No.
**Children:** Not permitted.
**Languages:** English.
**Your Host:** Gary & Grant.

aglta

# BUNDABERG

## Field of Dreams

**Gay/Lesbian ♀♂**

### *Dreaming Down Under*

Escape from the big city to ***Field of Dreams,*** a tranquil hideaway with cool, relaxing verandahs, well-appointed bedrooms, BBQ, swimming pool and spa. Night skies reveal more stars than can be imagined, and while watching the passage of meteors across the sky, one could be forgiven for forgetting that the rest of the world still actually exists. Our large ranch-style home is about 40 minutes inland from Bundaberg (north of Brisbane) and the coast, yet within easy reach of local attractions including whale watching, turtle rookeries and the Great Barrier Reef.

**Address: Lot 24, Woodswallow Dr, MS 882, Gin Gin, QLD 4671 Australia. Tel: (61-71) 573 024, Fax: (61-71) 573 025, E-mail: fod@ozemail.com.au.**

**Type:** Bed & breakfast guesthouse.
**Clientele:** Mostly gay & lesbian with some hetero clientele
**Transportation:** Car is best. Free pick up from Bundaberg airport, bus, train.
**To Gay Bars:** 3 hours by car.
**Rooms:** 4 rooms with queen beds.
**Bathrooms:** Shared.
**Meals:** Continental breakast.
**Vegetarian:** Available by request.
**Complimentary:** Tea & coffee 24 hrs.
**Dates Open:** All year.
**Rates:** Single AUD $60-AUD $70, double AUD $110-AUD $135.
**Discounts:** For tertiary students, artists, retirees, etc.
**Credit Cards:** MC, Visa.
**Rsv'tns:** Required.
**Reserve Thru:** Call direct.
**Parking:** Ample free off-street parking.
**In-Room:** Colour TV.
**On-Premises:** TV lounge, video tape library, laundry facilities.
**Swimming:** Pool on premises. Ocean nearby.
**Sunbathing:** Poolside, on patio, at beach.
**Smoking:** Permitted outside.
**Pets:** Permitted.
**Handicap Access:** No.
**Children:** Not especially welcomed.
**Languages:** English, Mandarin Chinese, Hokkien, Bahasa Malaysia.
**Your Host:** Kim & Kay Hock.

IGTA

# CAIRNS

## Fifty-Four Cinderella Street

Q-NET Women ♀

### *Superb Accommodation... Creative Cuisine...Absolute Beachfront...for Women!*

Be pampered in the tropics at a fairy tale hideaway – ***54 Cinderella Street*** – just 10 minutes from Cairns and the airport on Reddens Island at the mouth of the Barron River, in quiet and unspoiled Machans Beach. Spend idyllic days in the large garden with a rock swimming pool complete with creek bed and waterfall, or use the private access to the beach. The coastline, magnificent rainforests, and some of the best reef diving in the world, not to mention excellent tourist shopping and casinos, make Cairns one of the most sought-after tourist destinations in the world.

**Address: 54 Cinderella St, Cairns, QLD 4878 Australia.**
**Tel: (61-70) 550 289, Fax: (61-70) 559 383.**
**E-mail: dsdelmont@c131.aone.net.au.**

**Type:** B&B guesthouse with restaurant.
**Clientele:** Mostly gay women
**Transportation:** Car is best. Free pick up from airport, train, bus or ferry dock.
**To Gay Bars:** 4 miles, a 10-minute drive.
**Rooms:** 4 suites with single or queen beds.
**Bathrooms:** All private
**Meals:** Full breakfast.
**Vegetarian:** Inquire, all tastes catered for.
**Dates Open:** All year.
**Rates:** Single AUD $80, double AUD $110.
**Credit Cards:** Visa, Bancard.
**Rsv'tns:** Required, if possible.
**Reserve Through:** Travel agent (61-2) 9380 6244, fax (61-2) 9361 3729, or call direct.
**Parking:** Ample free off-street parking.
**In-Room:** Color satellite TV, VCR, ceiling fans, coffee/tea-making facilities, room & laundry service.
**On-Premises:** Meeting rooms, video library, fax, internet, E-mail.
**Exercise/Health:** Surf skiing & fishing. Nearby gym, weights, massage.
**Swimming:** Pool & ocean on premises.
**Nudity:** Permitted on property & at beach.
**Smoking:** Permitted anywhere.
**Children:** No.
**Your Host:** David & Lynda.

## Turtle Cove Resort Cairns

Q-NET Gay/Lesbian ♀♂

### *Turtle Cove is Gay Heaven*

Once you get to ***Turtle Cove*** you'll soon know why it's one of the world's most popular gay resorts. Just 30 minutes from Cairns International Airport by one of our courtesy coaches, your choice of accommodation is a garden cabin, one of our new elevated ocenview terraces, or a beachfront room with only lawn, sand and the odd palm tree between you and the Coral Sea. All rooms feature queen and single beds, en suite bathrooms, airconditioning, ceiling fans, television with in-house video, radio, phones, refrigerator and tea- and coffee-making facilities. The resort features a fully stocked cocktail bar open from early to late, and a licensed restaurant serving great tropical food. Complimentary breakfasts are served on the terrace, and lunch and dinner are available by the pool and under the stars.

Without a doubt, the highlight of ***Turtle Cove*** is our exclusively gay and totally private beach. With the backdrop of tropical rainforest, it has one of the best locations in the world, gay or straight. It's ideal for sunning, relaxing under an umbrella, swimming, or cruising. You'll share it with fellow guests, visiting locals and, if you are lucky, one of the large turtles which nest there each year.

Other facilities include a large pool above the beach, two Jacuzzis, extensive tropical gardens and lawns, rental cars, a resort shop, tour desk, mini gym and all-gay trips to the world heritage rainforests, as well as the Great Barrier Reef. The Reef is a wonder of the world and we visit it twice a week, in all-gay company, on a luxury boat for snorkeling and diving. Our location is private, but many restaurants, bars and clubs are within 30 minutes of the resort. When considering Australia, we invite you to include ***Turtle Cove.*** We look forward to making it the highlight of your vacation downunder.

**Address: Captain Cook Hwy, PO Box 158, Smithfield, Cairns, Far North QLD 4878 Australia. Tel: (61-70) 591 800, Fax: (61-70) 591 969, E-mail: turtlecove@iig.com.au. http://www.iig.com.au/turtle_cove/.**

**Type:** Beachfront resort with full-service restaurant, bar & resort shop.
**Clientele:** Good mix of men & women
**Transportation:** Bus from airport passes by our front door. Free pick up from airport, RR or bus station, city hotel.
**To Gay Bars:** 35 minutes to Cairns gay bar. Bus from resort Sat nights.
**Rooms:** 27 rooms with single, double or queen beds.
**Bathrooms:** All rooms have private showers & toilets.
**Meals:** Tropical & continental buffet breakfast.
**Vegetarian:** Available in our restaurant.
**Complimentary:** Tea & coffee in rooms, airport transfers, welcome drink on arrival.
**Dates Open:** All year.
**Rates:** AUD $94-AUD $144. AUD $18 per night for 2nd person.
**Discounts:** For most of year: stay 7, pay for 6.
**Credit Cards:** MC, Visa, Amex, Diners, Bankcard.

**Rsv'tns:** Suggested.
**Reserve Through:** Travel agent or call direct.
**Parking:** Ample free off-street covered parking.
**In-Room:** Colour TV, AC, refrigerator, telephone, ceiling fans, coffee/tea-making facilities, room & maid service. Rooms serviced daily. In-house video, video tape library.
**On-Premises:** Meeting rooms, private dining rooms & laundry facilities.
**Exercise/Health:** Jacuzzi, massage, beach equipment, volleyball, gym & weights.
**Swimming:** Pool, beachfront & river swimming hole on premises.
**Sunbathing:** At poolside, on our patio, common sun decks & on the beach.
**Nudity:** Permitted poolside & on the beach.
**Smoking:** Permitted without restrictions.
**Pets:** Not permitted.
**Handicap Access:** Yes. Mostly single story with minimal steps.
**Children:** Not permitted.
**Languages:** English, Dutch, German & French.
**Your Host:** Bert & Michael.

IGTA agta

## Witchencroft

Women ♀

Welcome to ***Witchencroft,*** two very private and comfortable self-contained units for women only. Relax and enjoy a nature-based holiday in five acres of gardens on the Atherton Tablelands. We specialise in 4WD and bushwalking tours to suit your individual interests. This is an ideal base from which to escape the tourism of Cairns and explore a great diversity in sightseeing options, including the World Heritage tropical rainforest. There is all-year-round fine weather within an hour of ***Witchencroft!*** Your host is a fourth generation north Queenslander, and a great source of local information.

**Address: Write: Jenny Maclean, PO Box 685, Atherton, QLD 4883 Australia. Tel: (61-70) 912 683, E-mail: jj@bushnet.qld.edu.au.**

**Type:** Guesthouse on a 5-acre organic farm.
**Clientele:** Women only
**Transportation:** Free pickup from Atherton, bus from Cairns daily.
**To Gay Bars:** 90 kms to Cairns.
**Rooms:** 2 apartments with double beds.
**Bathrooms:** All private shower/toilets.
**Campsites:** Tent sites, powered sites.
**Meals:** Self-cater or enjoy our vegetarian cuisine.
**Vegetarian:** Strictly vegetarian.
**Complimentary:** Tea, coffee & milk.
**Dates Open:** All year.
**High Season:** July, August.
**Rates:** Single US $60, double US $80.
**Discounts:** Garden work exchange.
**Rsv'tns:** Required.
**Reserve Thru:** Call direct.
**Minimum Stay:** Two nights.
**Parking:** Ample parking.
**In-Room:** Color TV, ceiling fans, kitchen, refrigerator, coffee & tea-making facilities.
**Exercise/Health:** Bushwalks.
**Swimming:** 10 minutes to rivers & lakes.
**Sunbathing:** In the garden.
**Nudity:** Permitted.
**Smoking:** Permitted outdoors.
**Pets:** Permitted with restrictions because of resident livestock.
**Handicap Access:** Yes.
**Children:** Permitted.
**Languages:** English, some French & German.

# NOOSA

## Guys Bed & Breakfast Noosa Heads

Men ♂

David welcomes you to ***Guys Bed & Breakfast,*** a small, comfortable guesthouse. Good food and cleanliness matter most to me and my guests. ***Guys*** is tastefully furnished with many antiques. A complimentary full English breakfast is served on the patio and evening meals are available for an additional fee. ***Guys*** offers a warm, friendly, homey atmosphere. David, your host, is dedicated to making each visit a memorable occasion for every guest. As if you were staying with a friend, beautiful Noosa welcomes you.

**Address: PO Box 964, Noosa Heads, QLD 4567 Australia. Tel: (61-74) 749 322.**

**Type:** Bed & breakfast.
**Clientele:** Men only
**Transportation:** Pick up from airport or bus.
**To Gay Bars:** 5 min by car to Aqua Bar Cafe & Restaurant.
**Rooms:** 1 single, 3 doubles.
**Bathrooms:** 1 shower, 1 separate toilet, others share.

*continued next page*

**Meals:** Full breakfast (2-course dinner available AUD $12).
**Vegetarian:** Available upon request with 1 day's notice.
**Complimentary:** Tea & coffee, mints on pillow.
**Dates Open:** All year.
**Rates:** Low season, single AUD $48, double AUD $75.
**Discounts:** AUD $5 per night on stays of 7 or more days.
**Rsv'tns:** Required.
**Reserve Through:** Call direct.
**Parking:** Limited covered parking.
**In-Room:** Ceiling fans, maid service.
**On-Premises:** TV lounge, laundry facilities for guests.
**Swimming:** At nearby ocean beach.
**Sunbathing:** On common sun decks.
**Nudity:** Nudist-friendly.
**Smoking:** Permitted.
**Pets:** Not permitted.
**Handicap Access:** No.
**Children:** Not permitted.
**Languages:** English.
**Your Host:** David.

## Noosa Cove

**Gay/Lesbian ♂**

### *The Gay Beach Resort Capital of Australia*

You'll be met at the airport or terminal by our Mercedes Benz, then whisked to ***Noosa Cove,*** a resort set in the most sought-after location in Noosa near Australia's best beach. Our location overlooking Noosa's fabulous national park, provides access to many natural coves and beaches, including the famous gay naturist beach, Alexandria Bay. Guests can indulge in physical activities, such as bushwalking, surfing, windsurfing, waterskiing, boating, fishing, sailing and swimming, or just enjoy sun-baking by the private pool. Apartments in a sub-tropical garden and pool setting have two bedrooms, sunny balcony, kitchen and colour TV with remote in the main bedroom. The gay nightclub and restaurant are situated 2 minutes' walk from your apartment.

**Address: 82 Upper Hastings St, Noosa, QLD 4567 Australia.**
**Tel: (61-7) 544 926 68 (Tel/Fax), mobile (018) 061911.**

**Type:** Holiday apartments & guesthouse.
**Clientele:** Mostly men with women welcome
**Transportation:** Pick up from airport & bus.
**To Gay Bars:** 1 block or 400 yards. 3 minutes by foot or 1 minute by car.
**Rooms:** 3 spacious, fully self-contained apartments & 1-bedroom studio unit with queen beds.
**Bathrooms:** All private.
**Vegetarian:** At 43 beachside restaurants within a 3-minute walk.
**Complimentary:** Tea & coffee.
**Dates Open:** All year.
**High Season:** 1st 2 weeks of January & school & public holidays.
**Rates:** High season, AUD $100-AUD $140 per night. Low season AUD $75-AUD $95 per night. Guesthouse AUD $50 per night.
**Credit Cards:** VISA, Amex & Bancard.
**Rsv'tns:** Recommended.
**Reserve Through:** Travel agent or call direct.
**Parking:** Ample free off-street covered parking.
**In-Room:** Color TV, VCR, telephone, ceiling fans, coffee & tea-making facilities, kitchen, refrigerator & laundry service.
**Exercise/Health:** Gym & weights on premises. Nearby gym, weights, Jacuzzi/spa, sauna & massage.
**Swimming:** Pool in apartment complex. Nearby ocean & river.
**Sunbathing:** At poolside, on private sun decks, or at the beach.
**Nudity:** Permitted at poolside or at the beach.
**Smoking:** Permitted.
**Handicap Access:** 1 apartment on ground level.
**Children:** Not permitted.
**Languages:** English.
**Your Host:** Alan.

# SOUTH AUSTRALIA

## ADELAIDE

## Greenways Apartments

**Gay-Friendly ♀♂**

Adelaide, our state capital, features traditional stone architecture and wide encircling parklands. This elegant city is situated near one of the world's most famous winegrowing districts, and its residents are relaxed and friendly. These features, combined with the picturesque backdrop of the Adelaide Hills, give Adelaide an atmosphere found nowhere else in Australia. South Australia was the first Australian state to legalize homosexuality. ***Greenways*** provides excellent, comparatively cheap accommodations in fully furnished, self-contained private apartments. It is situated near city center and gay venues. Hosts are gay-friendly and are willing to assist with local information and they especially welcome international travelers.

**Address: 45 King William Rd, North Adelaide, SA 5006 Australia. Tel: (61-8) 8267 5903, Fax: (61-8) 8267 1790.**

**Type:** Holiday apartments.
**Clientele:** Mostly straight clientele with a gay & lesbian following
**Transportation:** Taxi best from airport, bus or train station.
**To Gay Bars:** 1 mile to gay/lesbian bars.
**Rooms:** 25 apartments with single or double beds.
**Bathrooms:** All private.
**Dates Open:** All year.
**Rates:** 1-bdrm AUD $67, 2-bdrm AUD $95 & up, 3-bdrm AUD $135 & up.
**Discounts:** AUD $5/night on stays of 7 days or longer (private bookings only).
**Credit Cards:** MC, VISA, Bancard, Diners, Amex.
**Rsv'tns:** Required 1 month in advance.
**Reserve Through:** Travel agent or call direct.
**Minimum Stay:** 3 days.
**Parking:** Ample free off-street parking.
**In-Room:** Telephone, kitchenette, refrigerator, weekly maid service, AC/heat, color TV.
**On-Premises:** Coin-operated laundry facilities.
**Exercise/Health:** Public gym, spa & sauna 3/4 mi.
**Swimming:** Public pool 3/4 mile, ocean 15 miles.
**Sunbathing:** At public pool, on ocean beach (nude beach 1 hour).
**Smoking:** Permitted without restrictions.
**Pets:** Not permitted.
**Handicap Access:** No.
**Children:** Permitted.
**Languages:** English.

## Rochdale

Gay/Lesbian ♀♂

### *One of Adelaide's Special Secrets!*

Adelaide's only accommodation provider for gay men and women, ***Rochdale*** is a private, traditional bed and breakfast. The residence is a typical late '20's Adelaide residence, with spacious, well-appointed rooms and an air of understated elegance. Wood panelling is used extensively throughout the formal living areas and open fires warm the study, lounge and one of the guest rooms. The gardens provide areas suited to quiet, secluded relaxing, reading and alfresco dining. We are within strolling distance of shopping and restaurants, conveniently located for easy access to the city and Adelaide Hills and serviced with public transport.

**Address: 349 Glen Osmond Rd, Glen Osmond, SA 5064 Australia. Tel: (61-8) 8379 7498, Fax: (61-8) 8379 2483.**

**Type:** Bed & breakfast.
**Clientele:** Gay & lesbian preferred accommodation
**Transportation:** Car or public transport from city centre. Free pick up (by arrangement only) from airport, bus or train.
**To Gay Bars:** 7 min. by car.
**Rooms:** 3 rooms with queen or double beds.
**Bathrooms:** 2 private shower/toilets, 1 shared bath/shower/toilet.
**Meals:** Full cooked breakfast. 3-course gourmet dinner & luncheon picnic hamper available at additional cost with prior arrangement.
**Vegetarian:** Available with prior arrangement.
**Complimentary:** Morning or afternoon tea upon arrival, tea & coffee, Port in rooms.
**Dates Open:** All year.
**Rates:** AUD $70 single, AUD $90 double, dinner B&B AUD $180 minimum 2 persons.
**Credit Cards:** MC, Visa, Amex, Diners & Australian Bankcard.
**Rsv'tns:** Required.
**Reserve Through:** Travel agent or call direct.
**Parking:** Limited free off-street parking.
**On-Premises:** TV lounge, meeting rooms.
**Exercise/Health:** Nearby gym, weights, Jacuzzi, sauna, steam & massage.
**Swimming:** Nearby pool & ocean.
**Sunbathing:** On the patio, in garden.
**Nudity:** Permitted in private garden. 1 hour to nude beach.
**Smoking:** Permitted outside only.
**Pets:** Not permitted.
**Handicap Access:** One bathroom is accessible.
**Children:** Adult-oriented accommodation.
**Languages:** English.
**Your Host:** Peter & Brian.

# TASMANIA

## HOBART

### Corinda's Cottages

Gay Hosts ♀♂

#### *Awaken to the Sound of Birdsong!*

Overlooking a cobbled courtyard are the converted coach-house and servant's quarters of ***Corinda,*** an award-winning National Trust Classified property in the heart of Hobart. Its historic outbuildings are now delightful gay-owned, self-contained cottages. ***Corinda's*** gardens are a real delight. Lime trees and hedges of box and yew create formal enclosed areas, each with its own colour scheme. Though only a five-minute stroll from Sullivans Cove, the property has a real "country" feel as it adjoins the Queens Domain, a large park teaming with birdlife.

**Address: 17 Glebe St, Glebe, Hobart, TAS Australia.**
**Tel: (61-03) 62 34 1590, Fax: (61-03) 62 34 2744.**

**Type:** Self-contained cottages.
**Clientele:** 50% gay & lesbian & 50% straight clientele
**Transportation:** Car is best.
**To Gay Bars:** 1 mile, a 15-min walk, a 5-min drive.
**Rooms:** 2 cottages with single, dbl. or queen beds.
**Bathrooms:** Private: 1 shower/toilet, 1 bath/shower/toilet.
**Meals:** Expanded continental breakfast.
**Vegetarian:** Vegetarian restaurants nearby.
**Complimentary:** Tea, coffee, decaf, fruit juice, range of condiments, fudge.
**Dates Open:** All year.
**High Season:** Jan-Feb.
**Rates:** AUS $150 per cottage (2 per.), all year round.
**Discounts:** 20% to readers of Ferrari Guides if booked directly through us.
**Credit Cards:** Visa, Bancard.
**Rsv'tns:** Required.
**Reserve Through:** Travel agent or call direct.
**Parking:** Ample, free, on- & off-street parking.
**In-Room:** Color TV, refrigerator, kitchen, coffee & tea-making facilities, maid & laundry service.
**On-Premises:** Laundry facilities & use of phone/fax.
**Exercise/Health:** Nearby gym, weights, Jacuzzi, sauna, steam, massage.
**Swimming:** Nearby pool, ocean & river.
**Sunbathing:** At beach & in garden.
**Smoking:** Permitted anywhere. Non-smoking rooms available.
**Pets:** Not permitted.
**Handicap Access:** No.
**Children:** No children under 12.
**Languages:** English, Dutch.
**Your Host:** Wilmar & Matthew.

## LAUNCESTON

### Brickfields Terrace

Gay-Friendly ♀♂

#### *Part of Tasmania's Heritage*

Spoil yourself with the elegance and comfort of 4-1/2 star Victorian townhouses (circa 1889) that overlook century-old elm trees and park land in the heart of Launceston. Two terraces offer spacious warm rooms filled with freshly picked flowers and potpourri. Beautiful decorative touches and charming antique furniture lend an air of sophistication. Share a crackling log fire during the crisp winter evenings, browse through a wonderful array of magazines, and feast on delicious handmade fudge. Your exclusive occupancy ensures complete privacy. Whether you are looking for a romantic retreat or simply a chance to relax with friends, ***Brickfields Terrace*** is the perfect choice.

**Address: 64 & 68 Margaret St, Launceston, TAS 7250 Australia.**
**Tel: (61-03) 6330 1753, Fax: (61-03) 6330 2334.**

**Type:** Historic terraces.
**Clientele:** Mostly hetero with a gay/lesbian following
**Transportation:** Car, airport bus to front door, taxi.
**To Gay Bars:** A 15-minute walk, a 5-minute drive (limited venues).
**Rooms:** 2 cottages with single or queen beds.
**Bathrooms:** All private.
**Meals:** Expanded continental breakfast.
**Vegetarian:** Available in nearby restaurant on request.
**Complimentary:** Tea, coffee, handmade Tasmanian fudge, champagne for special occasions.
**Dates Open:** All year.
**High Season:** January-April.
**Rates:** AUD $140-AUD $208.
**Discounts:** Seasonal discounts available on application.
**Credit Cards:** MC, Visa, Bankcard.
**Rsv'tns:** Required.
**Reserve Through:** Travel agent or call direct.
**Parking:** Ample free on- & off-street parking.
**In-Room:** Colour TV, telephone, refrigerator, fully equipped kitchen, open fire, games, magazines, books, radio, lunch & dinner room service, coffee/tea-making facilities from neighbouring restaurant.
**On-Premises:** Laundry facilities.
**Exercise/Health:** Nearby gym with weights, sauna, steam, massage.
**Swimming:** Nearby pool & river.
**Smoking:** Permitted outside only. Terraces are smoke-free.
**Pets:** Not permitted.
**Handicap Access:** No.
**Children:** Welcome.
**Languages:** English.
**Your Host:** Sarah.

# VICTORIA

## DAYLESFORD

### The Balconies

Gay/Lesbian ♀♂

***Relax on the Balconies and Enjoy the View of Beautiful Lake Daylesford***

Your hosts, Geof and Theo invite you to experience their hospitality midst the picturesque surroundings of Daylesford, Australia's largest gay-populated country town, and Hepburn Springs. Here, in the heart of the mineral springs and central goldfields, gays and lesbians have been building a base of gay businesses and properties since 1992. Established in that same year, and one of the first gay properties here, ***The Balconies*** is set in three acres with views of Lake Daylesford. Guests enjoy a heated indoor pool and spa or a stroll around beautiful Lake Daylesford after breakfast. Some prefer to sit on the balcony and watch the ducks. Remember to bring bottles to take home some mineral water, and bread to feed the ducks.

**Address: 35 Perrins St, Daylesford, VIC 3460 Australia.
Tel: (61-3) 53 48 1322.**

**Type:** Bed & breakfast with in-house dinner.
**Clientele:** Good mix of gays & lesbians
**Transportation:** Car, train & bus. Free pick up from train & bus.
**To Gay Bars:** 3 blocks or a 10-minute walk to Friday-night only gay bar.
**Rooms:** 5 rooms with single or queen beds.
**Bathrooms:** 2 private shower/toilets. Others share.
**Meals:** Expanded continental breakfast.
**Vegetarian:** Can be arranged.

*continued next page*

**Complimentary:** Tea, coffee & cake.
**Dates Open:** All year.
**Rates:** AUD $75-$135.
**Discounts:** Mid-week Sun to Thur. Full price 1st night & half price for each following night.
**Credit Cards:** MC, Visa & Bancard.
**Rsv'tns:** Required.
**Reserve Through:** Travel agent or call direct.
**Parking:** Free off-street parking.
**In-Room:** Coffee & tea-making facilities.
**On-Premises:** TV lounge, video library & laundry facilities.
**Exercise/Health:** Jacuzzi on premises, nearby massage.
**Swimming:** Heated indoor pool on premises. Nearby pool, river & lake.
**Sunbathing:** On the patio.
**Nudity:** Permitted in indoor pool room.
**Smoking:** Permitted in games room or on balconies. All bedrooms are non-smoking.
**Pets:** Not permitted.
**Handicap Access:** Yes.
**Children:** Not especially welcome.
**Languages:** English, Greek, Italian & French.
**Your Host:** Geof & Theo.

# MELBOURNE

## California Motor Inn

**Gay-Friendly 50/50 ♀♂**

### *Stylish...and Affordable*

The ***California Motor Inn*** is close to Melbourne's "must see" attractions, yet is located in an elegant suburb amidst Victorian grandeur. Newly renovated suites are inviting and spacious with TVs, direct dial phones, refrigerators, and tea- and coffee-making facilities. At the end of the day when it's time to relax, stop for a drink in the bar before dining in the licensed restaurant with its friendly atmosphere, fresh cuisine, and fine wines. A cosy dinner and breakfast can be served in your room or you can help yourself at the breakfast buffet.

**Address: 138 Barkers Rd, Hawthorn, VIC 3122 Australia.**
**Tel: (61-3) 9818 0281, Fax: (61-3) 9819 6845. Toll free in Australia: (1800) 331166. Ask for Jay. E-mail: llylew@mpx.com.au.**

**Type:** Motel with restaurant & bar.
**Clientele:** 50% gay & lesbian & 50% hetero clientele
**Transportation:** Airport bus to city, then tram or taxi.
**To Gay Bars:** 1-1/2 miles, a 10-minute drive.
**Rooms:** 80 rooms with single, double or queen beds.
**Bathrooms:** All private, 2 rooms have spas.
**Dates Open:** All year.
**Rates:** AUD $84-$205.
**Credit Cards:** MC, Visa, Amex, Diners, Bancard.
**Rsv'tns:** Required.
**Reserve Through:** Travel agent or call direct.
**Parking:** Ample free off-street parking.
**In-Room:** Color TV, phone, refrigerator, AC, coffee- & tea-making facilities, room & laundry service.
**On-Premises:** Meeting rooms, laundry facilities, fax, photocopier, secretarial services.
**Exercise/Health:** Nearby gym with weights & massage.
**Swimming:** Pool on premises.
**Sunbathing:** At poolside.
**Smoking:** Permitted. Non-smoking rooms available.
**Pets:** Not permitted.
**Handicap Access:** No.
**Children:** Welcome.
**Languages:** English.
**Your Host:** Jay.

IGLTA

## The Gatehouse

**Men ♂**

### *A Guesthouse Catering to the Male S&M Scene*

Each of the four double rooms at ***The Gatehouse*** has a mezzanine above its own private playroom. Equipped with dual-purpose sling beds and eye hooks for bondage scenes, the playrooms all have lights fitted with dimmer switches, as well as in-house, volume controllable music piped into each room. The rooms are centrally-heated for winter and equipped with air conditioning for summer. A help-yourself breakfast is inclusive, and the kitchen area, restocked daily, includes microwave, electric kettle, and a toaster.

**Address: 10 Peel St, Collingwood, VIC 3066 Australia.**
**Tel: (61-3) 9417 2182, Fax: (61-3) 9416 0474.**

**Type:** S&M guesthouse with playrooms.
**Clientele:** Men only
**Transportation:** Taxi from airport.
**To Gay Bars:** 1 block, a 3-minute walk.
**Rooms:** 4 rooms with double beds.
**Bathrooms:** Shared: 1 bath/shower/toilet, 1 WC only.
**Meals:** Continental breakfast.
**Vegetarian:** Vegetarian cafes & restaurants nearby.
**Complimentary:** Tea, coffee, juice.
**Dates Open:** All year.
**Rates:** AUD $70 (rate includes complementary entry to Club 80 private men's club).
**Discounts:** Weekly rate AUD $420 (for 7-night consecutive stay).
**Credit Cards:** MC, VISA, Amex, Diners.
**Rsv'tns:** Required.
**Reserve Through:** Travel agent or call direct.
**Parking:** Adequate free on- & off-street parking.
**In-Room:** AC, maid service, playroom, mezzanine bed.
**On-Premises:** TV lounge, public phone.
**Exercise/Health:** Nearby gym with sauna.
**Swimming:** Nearby pool & bay.
**Nudity:** Permitted.
**Smoking:** Permitted without restrictions.
**Pets:** Not permitted.
**Handicap Access:** No.
**Children:** No.
**Languages:** English.

## Laird O'Cockpen Hotel

**Men ♂**

### *Enjoy the Ambience*

Stay at the ***Laird*** and enjoy top class accommodation in house or at our annex, Norwood. Built in 1888, just 3km from the C.B.D. (city centre), the hotel reflects the charm of Melbourne. All our rooms are serviced daily and our friendly staff are here to make you feel at home. ***The Laird*** music/video bar is the most popular gay mens' bar, perfect for socializing. Sunday nights we host "Bootscoot" and BBQ. Nuggets bar is home to the leather scene, with two clubs meeting weekly. Included in our low tariff is free entry to Club 80, Australia's most famous gay mens' club, and Peel dance bar is just a short walk away. You have all the facilities of a great city at your doorstep.

**Address: 149 Gipps St, Collingwood 3067, Melbourne, VIC Australia. Tel: (61-3) 9417 2832, Fax: (61-3) 9417 2109.**

**Type:** Hotel with bar & beer garden.
**Clientele:** Men only
**Transportation:** Taxi from the airport.
**To Gay Bars:** Men's bar on premises. Others one block away.
**Rooms:** 9 rooms with double or queen beds.
**Bathrooms:** Shared: 2 bath/showers, 1 shower & 3 toilets.
**Meals:** Continental breakfast.
**Vegetarian:** Vegetarian cafés & restaurants nearby.
**Complimentary:** Tea, coffee & juice.
**Dates Open:** All year.
**Rates:** AUD $55 per room.
**Discounts:** Weekly rate AUD $330, for 7-night consecutive stay.
**Credit Cards:** MC, VISA, Amex, Diners Club, Bankcard.
**Rsv'tns:** Required.
**Reserve Through:** Call direct.
**Parking:** Adequate on-street parking.
**On-Premises:** TV lounge, laundry facilities, public telephone, 2 bars with pool table, pinball, video games, beer garden.
**Smoking:** Permitted without restrictions.
**Pets:** Not permitted.
**Handicap Access:** No.
**Children:** Not permitted.
**Languages:** English.

## The Melbourne Guesthouse

**Men ♂**

### *Melbourne's Most Stylish and Comfortable Gay Men's Accomodation*

***The Melbourne Guesthouse*** is 10 minutes via tram from the city, an ideal location for tourists or businessmen seeking stylish gay accommodation. Enjoy superbly appointed, centrally-heated rooms, a large living and dining area overlooking a landscaped garden, a fully appointed kitchen, luxurious bathrooms, full laundry facilities, telephone, off-street parking and BBQ facilities. Other amenities

*continued next page*

include TV, video and stereo. Continental breakfast, fresh fruit, tea and coffee are available 24 hours. We are close to gay venues in Prahran and St. Kilda and to Chapel Street shopping, cafes and restaurants.

**Address: 26 Crimea St, St Kilda, VIC 3182 Australia.**
**Tel: (61-3) 9510 4707.**

**Type:** Guesthouse.
**Clientele:** Men
**Transportation:** Taxi from airport or airport bus to Spencer St Station, then taxi.
**To Gay Bars:** 1.5 km. A 20-minute walk or 5-min. drive.
**Rooms:** 6 rooms with double or queen beds.
**Bathrooms:** 1 private, others share.
**Meals:** Continental breakfast.
**Complimentary:** Tea, coffee, fruit juice & biscuits. Cup-a-soups in winter.
**Dates Open:** All year.
**High Season:** Dec-Mar.
**Rates:** AUD $65-$85.
**Credit Cards:** MC, Visa & Bancard.
**Rsv'tns:** Required.
**Reserve Thru:** Call direct.
**Parking:** Adequate free off-street parking (3 vehicle spaces).
**In-Room:** Refrigerator & maid service.
**On-Premises:** TV lounge, telephone & laundry facilities.
**Swimming:** Nearby pool & Port Phillip Bay.
**Sunbathing:** On garden lawn or at the beach.
**Smoking:** Permitted outside only.
**Pets:** Not permitted.
**Handicap Access:** No.
**Children:** No.
**Languages:** English.

## One Sixty-Three Drummond Street

Gay/Lesbian ♀♂

### *You Will be Pleasantly Surprised*

***163 Drummond Street*** comprises two magnificent Victorian mansions, authentically renovated, retaining all their original features including marble fireplaces, tiled entrance halls with Persian runners and winding cedar staircases. A 19th-century elegance together with 20th-century comforts and amenities distinguishes this guesthouse. The atmosphere is warm; one where friends, newcomers and their guests can relax in the communal living and dining areas furnished with antiques and artwork. We are committed to informality and generosity with 24-hour access to all facilities. ***163 & 169*** are located two minutes away from Melbourne's famous Italian restaurant Mecca, Lygon Street, the theaters, Chinatown and the central business center. We overlook the majestic gardens and The Exhibition Building.

**Address: 163 Drummond Street, Carlton, Melbourne, VIC 3053 Australia.**
**Tel: (61-3) 9663 3081.**

**Type:** Bed & breakfast guesthouse.
**Clientele:** Good mix of gays & lesbians
**Transportation:** Taxi from airport (approx. AUD $22). Shuttle pick up from "163."
**To Gay Bars:** A 20-minute walk or 5-minute drive.
**Rooms:** 11 rooms with single, double, queen or king beds.
**Bathrooms:** 4 ensuite bathrooms, 4 private sinks only. 2 shared bath/shower/toilets, 1 shared WC only.
**Meals:** Expanded continental breakfast, tea or coffee is 24 hours, self-service.
**Vegetarian:** 5-minute walk to a vegetarian restaurant.
**Complimentary:** Beverages, self-service 24 hours in dining room. Confectionery, biscuits & fruit.
**Dates Open:** All year.
**High Season:** Summer & autumn.
**Rates:** AUD $45-$105.
**Discounts:** Weekly rates.
**Credit Cards:** MC, Visa & Bancard.
**Rsv'tns:** Required.
**Reserve Through:** Travel agent or call direct.
**Parking:** Adequate off-street parking, covered car park.
**In-Room:** Color TV, ceiling fans, AC.
**On-Premises:** TV lounge & laundry facilities.
**Exercise/Health:** Nearby gym, weights, Jacuzzi, sauna, steam & massage.
**Swimming:** Nearby pool.
**Sunbathing:** On the patio.
**Smoking:** Permitted in courtyard gardens & balconies.
**Pets:** Not permitted.
**Handicap Access:** No.
**Children:** Not especially welcome.
**Languages:** English.
**Your Host:** Ian.

aglta

# WARRNAMBOOL

## King's Head

Gay/Lesbian ♀♂

### *Come and Try Our Royal Hospitality*

Only seven kilometres from the city centre, opposite a whale nursery, lies ***King's Head.*** This luxury accommodation has magnificent river and rural views with its own private fishing jetty. Each room has a queen-sized bed and private facilities. Personalised friendly service ensures your stay will be one to remember. The B&B has no children's facilities. A two-bedroom fully self-contained unit is also available for long- or short-term rental in Warrnambool.

**Address: PO Box 658, Warrnambool, VIC 3280 Australia. Tel: (61-3) 5561 4569, Fax: (61-3) 5562 4085. E-mail: kinghead@ansonic.com.au. http://www.ansonic.com.au/kingshead.**

**Type:** Bed & breakfast, self-contained town house.
**Clientele:** Good mix of gays & lesbians
**Transportation:** By arrangement.
**Rooms:** 3 rooms with double & queen beds.
**Bathrooms:** 2 private.
**Campsites:** By arrangement.
**Meals:** By arrangement.
**Vegetarian:** By arrangement.
**Dates Open:** All year.
**High Season:** Jan., Easter.
**Rates:** From AUD $95.
**Discounts:** For AGLTA members.
**Credit Cards:** VISA, MC, Amex.
**Rsv'tns:** Required.
**Reserve Thru:** Call direct.
**Parking:** Available.
**In-Room:** TV, video & fridge.
**On-Premises:** BBQs & fishing jetty.
**Exercise/Health:** Spa.
**Swimming:** Opposite beach & river.
**Sunbathing:** At beach.
**Nudity:** Inquire.
**Smoking:** Permitted outside.
**Pets:** Not permitted.
**Handicap Access:** No.
**Children:** No.
**Languages:** English, limited German.
**Your Host:** Kevin & Max.

agta

# WESTERN AUSTRALIA

# PERTH

## Abaca Palms

Men ♂

### *A Gay Men's Oasis in the City*

As Perth's only exclusively gay guesthouse, ***Abaca Palms*** is where gay guys stay. This large 1930's Art Deco-character house features ornate ceilings and offers the best at affordable prices. ***Abaca Palms*** is a refuge for guys who like to mingle with their own kind and who like their privacy. Relax and enjoy yourselves in the private, friendly and spacious subtropical surroundings. Near all transportation, public transport is adjacent, minutes from the city and its venues. Our motto is "You arrive as strangers, and leave as friends." **Guest Comments:** "A fantastic welcome and super hospitality. It is impossible not to feel at home here." – Martyn P., Berlin, Ger-

*continued next page*

many. "Very convenient location, first-rate hospitality...I highly recommend the inn." – Mark D., Los Gatos, CA.

**Address: 34 Whatley Crescent, Mount Lawley, Perth, WA 6050 Australia. Tel: (61-9) 271 2117, mobile (041) 996 0571. Toll-free in Australia: (1800) 24 2117. Tel. as of March '97: (61-89) 271 2117.**

**Type:** Bed & breakfast guesthouse with dining room.
**Clientele:** Men only
**Transportation:** Train or bus. Free airport transfers.
**To Gay Bars:** 1/2 km.
**Rooms:** 8 rooms, 3 ensuite.
**Bathrooms:** 3 showers, 2 toilets.
**Meals:** Full breakfast. Optional 4-5 course sumptuous dinner AUD $25.
**Complimentary:** Tea, coffee, afternoon scones, bottle of champagne, fresh fuit basket.
**Dates Open:** All year.
**High Season:** Nov to Apr.
**Rates:** Summer AUD $50 (s)-AUD $85 (d). Specials available.
**Discounts:** 7 nights for the price of 6.
**Credit Cards:** MC, Bancard, Visa.
**Rsv'tns:** Required.
**Reserve Through:** Travel agent or call direct.
**Parking:** Adequate free off-street parking.
**In-Room:** Room service.
**On-Premises:** TV lounge, extensive video library, meeting room, private dining room, conservatory, laundry facilities.
**Exercise/Health:** Weights & Jacuzzi. Free use of squash, tennis racquets & golf clubs at nearby facility.
**Swimming:** 10 km to gay beach.
**Sunbathing:** In garden, Jacuzzi & on patio.
**Nudity:** Permitted.
**Smoking:** Permitted outside in conservatory. Non-smoking sleeping room available.
**Children:** Not especially welcome.
**Languages:** English.
**Your Host:** Lloyd.

## The Lawley on Guildford

Gay/Lesbian ♀♂

### *The Ultimate Address When in Perth*

Australian hospitality surrounds ***The Lawley on Guildford,*** a 1920's two-storey residence, located in one of Perth's older established city areas. The B&B has three large bedrooms, a cozy guest lounge with log fire, high ceilings, leadlight windows, a large dining room, wood paneling, an enclosed conservatory, and private garden spaces with grass tennis court. Guests are only minutes (by train or taxi) to the heart of the city and all Northbridge venues. ***The Lawley*** is the place to stay for warm, friendly hospitality when in Perth.

**Address: 72 Guildford Rd, Mount Lawley, WA 6050 Australia. Tel: (61-9) 272 5501 (Tel/Fax), mobile (015) 995 178.**

**Type:** Bed & breakfast.
**Clientele:** Mostly gay & lesbian with some hetero clientele
**Transportation:** Taxi from airport. Free pickup from airport.
**To Gay Bars:** 2-1/2 miles, a 7-minute drive.
**Rooms:** 3 rooms with double or queen beds.
**Bathrooms:** 1 private bath/shower/toilet, 2 private shower/WC only.
**Meals:** Expanded continental breakfast.
**Vegetarian:** Available at cafes & restaurants, a 20-minute walk.
**Complimentary:** Chocolates, water jug set up, tea & coffee.
**Dates Open:** All year.
**High Season:** Sept.-Mar.
**Rates:** AUD $55-AUD $80.
**Discounts:** Weekly rates.
**Credit Cards:** MC, VISA.
**Rsv'tns:** Required.
**Reserve Through:** Travel agent or call direct.
**Parking:** Adequate off-street parking.
**In-Room:** Colour TV, AC, maid service.
**On-Premises:** Meeting rooms, TV lounge, public phone, laundry facilities, guest refrigerator, all-day coffee/tea-making facilities.
**Exercise/Health:** Weights, Jacuzzi, grass tennis court, bicycles for hire on premises. Nearby sauna, steam & massage.
**Swimming:** River nearby.
**Sunbathing:** On patio & in private gardens on premises.
**Smoking:** Permitted in enclosed conservatory smoking area. All rooms non-smoking.
**Pets:** Not permitted.
**Handicap Access:** No.
**Children:** No.
**Languages:** English.
**Your Host:** Ian.

## Swanbourne Guest House

Gay/Lesbian ♂

### *Your Tranquil Retreat Between City and Surf*

This four-star RAC-rated private residence, ten minutes outside central Perth, is set in lush gardens overlooking trees and Australian flora. A rear patio offers privacy for nude sunbathing. Golf, tennis and swimming pool are within walking distance. On our complimentary bikes, you can make the gay beach in 10 minutes. Claremont's yuppie, cosmopolitan atmosphere, restaurants, bars and shops, all top class, are also close by. The ***Swanbourne's*** cool, Mediterranean interior and large, exquisitely appointed rooms make it a perfect haven from stressful, hectic city living, whilst offering all the amenities and activities a cosmopolitan city has to offer.

Perth, on the edge of the Indian Ocean, has superb beaches and the coastline offers breathtaking views and beautiful swimming locations. The comfortable dry heat and gusty cooling afternoon breezes make Perth a watersports-lover's paradise. Scub diving, sailing, water skiing and windsurfing are favourites among the locals and are readily available for all to try.

Perth also offers a wide variety of restaurants – seafood, Italian, French, Greek, Chinese and Japanese – a variety of boutiques and great food halls. Ten kilometres to the south of ***Swanbourne*** stands Freemantle, an old sailing port which has been converted into bustling outdoor markets and promenades. Ten kilometres to the north, adjacent to the city centre, is Northbridge, an exciting night spot which caters to every taste – family restaurants, bars, nightclubs and cabarets. For those wishing to venture further afield, the possibilities are endless. Visit Margaret River with its world-renowned wineries, the Karri forests and spectacular coastlines, or feed the world-famous Monkey Mia dolphins in their natural environment. Drive inland and witness Australia's barren, arresting outback, or make a trip to Rottnest, an exotic island located 26 kilometres off the mainland.

**Address: 5 Myera St, Swanbourne, Perth, WA 6010 Australia.**
**Tel: (61-9) 383 1981, mobile (018) 902 107, Fax: (61-9) 385 4595.**

**Type:** Bed & breakfast guesthouse.
**Clientele:** Mostly gay men with gay women welcome
**Transportation:** Airport bus to Perth, then taxi. Free pick up from train or bus.
**To Gay Bars:** 4 miles or 10 minutes by car.
**Rooms:** 4 rooms, 1 suite, & 1 apartment with single, double, queen beds or king.
**Bathrooms:** 3 private. Shared: 2 bathtubs, 2 showers & 1 full bath.
**Meals:** Continental breakfast with eggs & fresh fruit when in season.
**Vegetarian:** Vegetarian food nearby.
**Complimentary:** Tea, coffee, mints on pillows & fresh flowers daily.
**Dates Open:** All year.
**High Season:** Nov-Apr.
**Rates:** AUD $55-AUD $85.
**Discounts:** One day free for weekly stays.
**Credit Cards:** MC, Visa, Bancard.
**Rsv'tns:** Required.
**Reserve Thru:** Call direct.
**Minimum Stay:** 2 nights.
**Parking:** Ample free off-street covered parking.
**In-Room:** Color TV, VCR, video tape library, telephone, ceiling fans, kitchen, refrigerator, coffee & tea-making facilities, room & laundry service.
**On-Premises:** Meeting rooms, TV lounge, laundry facilities, courtyard with BBQ. Cars for hire.
**Exercise/Health:** Gym, weights on premises. Nearby Jacuzzi, sauna, steam & massage.
**Swimming:** Nearby pool, ocean, river, lake & beach.
**Sunbathing:** On private & common sun decks, patio, lawn or at the beach. Gay nude beach 2 km.
**Nudity:** Permitted on back patio.
**Smoking:** Permitted outside.
**Children:** Not especially welcome.
**Languages:** English.

agta

PACIFIC REGION
NEW
ZEALAND

# NORTH ISLAND

## AUCKLAND

### Aspen Lodge

Gay-Friendly ♀♂

#### *Pink on the Outside, Warm & Inviting on the Inside*

***Aspen Lodge*** is a budget bed & breakfast hotel, offering you comfortable, quiet accommodation in a friendly, homey atmosphere. The central downtown location puts you within a 5-minute walk of City Centre, restaurants, bus depots, railway station, ferry terminal, and airport bus service. In addition to providing guests with a good, healthy breakfast, beverage-making facilities, laundry facilities, and a TV lounge, we can arrange rental cars, campervans, and sightseeing tours. We do NOT provide frills, but we DO provide clean and comfortable budget accommodations in a central downtown location.

**Address: 62 Emily Place, Auckland, North Island, New Zealand. Tel: (64-9) 379 6698, Fax: (64-9) 377 7625.**

**Type:** Bed & breakfast.
**Clientele:** Mostly hetero with 20% gay & lesbian clientele
**Transportation:** Supershuttle from airport to door NZ $10 per person.
**To Gay Bars:** 5-minute walk to gay bar & sauna.
**Rooms:** 14 singles, 6 doubles (1 dbl bed) & 6 twins (2 single beds).
**Bathrooms:** 5 shared showers & 6 shared toilets.
**Meals:** Continental breakfast.
**Vegetarian:** 5-minute walk.
**Complimentary:** Tea & coffee.
**Dates Open:** All year.
**High Season:** November-May.
**Rates:** Single NZ $49, twin NZ $69.
**Discounts:** Winter, May 1-Sept 30. Yearly winter specials available.
**Credit Cards:** MC, Visa, Amex, Diners & JBC.
**Rsv'tns:** Required, especially in high season.
**Reserve Through:** Travel agent or call direct.
**Parking:** Limited on-street pay parking. 1st come, first served.
**In-Room:** Maid service.
**On-Premises:** TV lounge, laundry facilities, public telephones.
**Exercise/Health:** 5 min to nearby gym, weights, sauna, steam, massage.
**Swimming:** 5 min to nearby pool.
**Sunbathing:** On the patio.
**Smoking:** Permitted in designated areas only, rooms are non-smoking.
**Pets:** Not permitted.
**Handicap Access:** No.
**Children:** Permitted.
**Languages:** English, Dutch, German, French.
**Your Host:** Sarah & Phillip.

## BAY OF ISLANDS

### Orongo Bay Homestead

Gay-Friendly 50/50 ♀♂

#### *Reserve a Piece of Paradise*

***Orongo Bay Homestead*** offers historic charm and fine cuisine on the coast in the Bay of Islands. This historic First American Consulate (c. 1863) is now an exclusive, lovingly restored retreat with natural spring water. Sequestered in 17 private acres of bush, lake and lawns, there are sweeping views over a tranquil bush-framed bay towards New Zealand's birthplace. Just a 50-minute flight from Auckland, the ***Homestead*** is central to yachting, gentle walks, sea-kayaking, vintage aircraft flightseeing, unspoiled beaches and world-record game fishing. The many amenities and features found here include attentive service, wood-panelled ceilings, private bathrooms, natural wool bedding, fluffy bathrobes, complimen-

*continued next page*

tary natural skin-care creams and a dry Finnish sauna. Maori co-hosts Chris Swannell and *Foodwriters'* award-winner chef Michael Hooper, feature health-conscious, luxurious cuisine from ocean, farm, organic gardens and exotic orchard, plus a fabulous "champagne brunch." Oysters are served live, harvested from the bay just before dinner.

**Address: Aucks Road, RD1, Russell, Bay of Islands New Zealand. Tel: (64-9) 403 7527, Fax: (64-9) 403 7675.**

**Type:** Guesthouse with dining room & historic wine cellar.
**Clientele:** 50% gay & lesbian & 50% hetero clientele
**Transportation:** Car or 50-min flight from Auckland. Inquire about fee for pick up from airport, ferry dock & Rolls Royce limo service from airport (35 mins).
**Rooms:** 2 rooms & 2 suites with sgl., queen or king beds.
**Bathrooms:** All private.
**Meals:** Full breakfast with champagne. Property is organic & pesticide-free, free-range hens.
**Vegetarian:** By arrangement vegetarian & all dietary requirements are welcome (low-fat, low-cholesterol, etc).
**Complimentary:** Chocolate chunk cookies, fresh tea & coffee, fresh herbal tisanes, homemade cognac truffles, spring water.
**Dates Open:** All year.
**High Season:** 25 Dec-31 Apr.
**Rates:** Per person: winter NZ $135-185 per person, summer NZ $135-$225, includes champagne brunch.
**Discounts:** 10% "family" discount during low season, advance payment.
**Credit Cards:** MC, Diners, Visa, Amex.
**Rsv'tns:** Essential.
**Reserve Through:** Travel agent or call direct.
**Parking:** Ample free off-street parking.
**In-Room:** Maid & laundry service. Suites have coffee & tea-making facilities & refrigerator.
**On-Premises:** TV lounge, meeting rooms.
**Exercise/Health:** Sauna, massage. Nearby bush walks, tennis, golf, sailing, game fishing.
**Swimming:** Ocean, diving nearby.
**Sunbathing:** On hills & fields of estate, on patio, private & common sun decks, at beach.
**Smoking:** Permitted on covered verandahs. House is smoke-free.
**Pets:** Not permitted.
**Handicap Access:** Yes.
**Children:** No. Inquire if booking all 4 rooms.
**Languages:** English, some Danish, Maori & French.
**Your Host:** Michael & Chris.

# ROTORUA

## Troutbeck

Gay/Lesbian ♂

### *Gay Homestay with Trout Fishing from the Garden's Edge*

***Troutbeck*** lies five kilometres from Rotorua on a half-acre of landscaped garden on the banks of the Waiteti Stream by its outlet into Lake Rotorua. Right from the banks of the stream at the foot of our garden, guests can fly fish for Rainbow or Brown trout from December to May. And you can troll the lake all year, using our dinghy and private landing ramp. ***Troutbeck*** is the first Lockwood house built in New Zealand in 1953 of Californian redwood, a prototype of many in the country, all renowned for their quality wooden construction and open-plan design. We're close to the thermal areas and Maori culture. Golf courses are nearby.

**Address: 16 Egmont Rd, PO Box 242, Ngongotaha, Rotorua New Zealand. Tel: (64-7) 357 4795.**

**Type:** Homestay.
**Clientele:** Mostly men with women welcome
**Transportation:** Car is best. Will pick up from airport, train or bus.
**Rooms:** 3 rooms with king or queen beds.
**Bathrooms:** 2 shared baths.
**Meals:** Full breakfast. Opt. lunch & dinner with wine.
**Vegetarian:** Available on request.
**Complimentary:** Tea & coffee.
**Dates Open:** All year.
**High Season:** Dec-April.
**Rates:** Single NZ $40, double NZ $60.
**Credit Cards:** MC, Visa, Amex, Bancard.
**Rsv'tns:** Preferred.
**Reserve Through:** Travel agent or call direct.
**Parking:** Adequate free off-street parking.
**In-Room:** Refrigerator, maid, room & laundry service.
**On-Premises:** TV lounge with VCR, laundry facilities.
**Exercise/Health:** Nearby gym.
**Swimming:** At nearby lake.
**Sunbathing:** On private 1/2 acre of land.
**Nudity:** Permitted while sunning in private garden.
**Smoking:** We prefer no smoking.
**Pets:** We prefer no pets.
**Handicap Access:** No, there are steps.
**Languages:** English, Tongan.
**Your Host:** Ken & Tali.

# WELLINGTON

## The Mermaid

Q-NET Women ♀

***The Mermaid,*** a turn-of-the-century character building, is situated in Wellington's inner city Aro Valley, an historic area with picturesque Victorian Villas. The four individually decorated rooms all have views, either of the tree-lined garden or of the surrounding hillsides. One room has private facilities, while the others share a bathroom with tub. All have luxurious robes, towels and fragrant soaps for your extra comfort. We're a 10-minute walk from downtown cafes, shops, theatres, the nearest gay bar (which holds regular women's events) and Wellington's waterfront. Owner, Francesca, will be happy to share her knowledge of local dining, theater, activities and events to make your stay completely personalised and memorable.

**Address: 1 Epuni St, Brooklyn, Wellington New Zealand.**
**Tel: (64-4) 384 4511 (Tel/Fax), E-mail: mermaid@sans.vuw.ac.nz.**

**Type:** Guesthouse.
**Clientele:** Women only
**Transportation:** Airport shuttle, bus from railway station to Aro Valley. Pickup from airport, NZ$10 per person.
**To Gay Bars:** 5 blocks, a 15 minute walk, a 5 minute drive.
**Rooms:** 4 rooms with single, double or queen beds.
**Bathrooms:** 1 private shower/toilet, 1 shared bath/shower toilet.
**Meals:** Buffet breakfast.
**Vegetarian:** Restaurant nearby.
**Complimentary:** Tea, coffee, wine on arrival, fresh fruit.
**Dates Open:** All year.
**High Season:** Dec-Jan.
**Rates:** NZ$65-NZ$110.
**Discounts:** 10% on stays of over 1 week.
**Credit Cards:** MC, Visa, Amex.
**Rsv'tns:** Required.
**Reserve Thru:** Call direct.
**Parking:** Adequate off-street parking.
**In-Room:** Television, VCR, coffee/tea-making facilities.
**On-Premises:** Pool table, library, telephone.
**Exercise/Health:** Massage by appointment. Nearby gym, Jacuzzi, massage.
**Swimming:** Nearby pool & ocean.
**Sunbathing:** On common sun decks, on patio.
**Smoking:** Permitted outside.
**Pets:** Not permitted.
**Handicap Access:** No.
**Children:** Welcome.
**Languages:** English, Greek.
**Your Host:** Francesca.

# SOUTH ISLAND

# CHRISTCHURCH

## Frauenreisehaus (The Homestead)

Women ♀

***Frauenreisehaus (The Homestead)*** is the only women's backpackers hostel in New Zealand. A very spacious, 2-story, 100-year-old house built of double brick and concrete exterior, it is warm in the winter and cool in the summer (late January through early May). There is accommodation for 36 people in 4 double bed/single rooms, 2 twin bed rooms and 5 bunk rooms. There is plenty of common room in our TV lounge/library, with books and magazines in English, Japanese and German, a video and HBO (Sky TV, as we call it here), as well as a large games room with a pool table and board games.

Two large, airy, sunny kitchens are fully-equipped and stocked with crockery, glasses, cutlery, cooking utensils and free herbs and spices. The crockery is fine German china and the glasses crystal, a welcome change from the plastic and tin utensils most backpackers use. The beautiful dining room has French doors opening

*continued next page*

onto a small garden with fish pond and waterfall. The bedrooms are spacious and clean. Linen, duvets, pillows, local telephone calls, washing facilities and bicycles are provided free. There are four shower and toilet areas and plenty of hot water. We do not limit the number of showers as many hostels do. Guests can expect a very warm welcome. We greet each person, show her around the house and introduce her to other guests to make her feel at home. Our rates are almost the cheapest in the country, even though we provide the highest standard of accommodation that we can.

Only minutes from the city centre and information centre, we also provide information about our local area and the South Island of New Zealand. Christchurch is a beautiful garden city, with much to interest the traveller. For excitement, bungee jump, parachute dive or paraglide. For culture, enjoy free plays and concerts. There is stunning scenery, winter skiing, and an hour away are hot pools and whale watching.

**Address: 272 Barbadoes St, Christchurch New Zealand.**
**Tel: (64-3) 366 2585.**

**Type:** Backpackers hostel.
**Clientele:** Women only. Mostly hetero with a gay female following
**Transportation:** Courtesy transport from train, bus or within the city. Within 6-minutes walk of the "Square" central city.
**To Gay Bars:** 5 blocks or a 10-minute walk.
**Rooms:** 4 double bed/ single rooms, 2 twin bed rooms & 5 bunk rooms (4 with 4 beds, 1 with 6 beds).
**Bathrooms:** 4 shared bath/shower/toilets.
**Campsites:** 3 tent sites.
**Vegetarian:** Good vegetarian food can be bought only 3 blocks away.
**Complimentary:** Tea, coffee & hot chocolate.
**Dates Open:** All year.
**High Season:** November until May.
**Rates:** Bunk rooms NZ $12, twin rooms NZ $15, single rooms NZ $18.
**Discounts:** NZ $1 upon presentation of VIP card.
**Rsv'tns:** Required.
**Reserve Through:** Call direct.
**Parking:** Adequate free off-street parking.
**On-Premises:** TV lounge, game room, dining room, outdoor dining area & laundry facilities.
**Swimming:** Nearby pool, ocean & river.
**Sunbathing:** At the beach.
**Smoking:** Smoking permitted outside.
**Pets:** Not permitted.
**Handicap Access:** No.
**Children:** Not especially welcome.
**Languages:** English.
**Your Host:** Sandra.

## Rainbow House

**Gay/Lesbian ♂**

### *Where Comfort is Affordable & Diversity is Appreciated*

Located high on the side of St. Martins Valley, only 10 minutes from downtown Christchurch, ***Rainbow House*** offers a lovely view of the city. Mt. Vernon Park, hiking tracks and beaches are nearby, while skiing is one hour away. The sleeping quarters in our modern pole house are breezy and spacious with a private sun deck. In addition, a generous and delicious breakfast is prepared for you each morning. We are always able to give up-to-date referrals to places and events that you may wish to explore during your visit to Christchurch and New Zealand.

**Address: 9 The Crescent, Christchurch 8002 New Zealand.**
**Tel: (64-3) 337 1438, E-mail: m.fraser@student.canterbury.ac.nz.**

**Type:** Bed & breakfast guesthouse inn.
**Clientele:** Mostly men with women welcome
**Transportation:** Car. Pick up from airport (NZ$ 12), bus, train. Free ride to city & return 10:30am-11pm.
**To Gay Bars:** 3 miles, an 8 min drive, a 30 min walk.
**Rooms:** 4 rooms with single or queen beds.
**Bathrooms:** Shared: 1 bath/shower/toilet, 1 bathtub only, 1 shower only.
**Meals:** Full breakfast.
**Vegetarian:** Request when booking. Vegetarian restaurants nearby.
**Complimentary:** Tea, coffee, soda.
**Dates Open:** All year.
**High Season:** Nov-Mar.
**Rates:** NZ$ 38-NZ$ 58.
**Rsv'tns:** Required.
**Reserve Through:** Travel agent or call direct.
**Parking:** Adequate free off-street parking.
**In-Room:** Maid & laundry ser.
**On-Premises:** TV lounge, video tape library, meeting rms, laundry facilities, E-mail.
**Exercise/Health:** Nearby gym, weights, Jacuzzi, sauna, steam, massage.
**Swimming:** Nearby pool, ocean.
**Sunbathing:** On common sun decks.
**Nudity:** Permitted on sun decks.
**Smoking:** No smoking inside.
**Children:** No.
**Languages:** English.
**Your Host:** Martin & Robbie.

PACIFIC REGION
PACIFIC
ISLANDS

# FR. POLYNESIA/TAHITI

## MOORE A ISLAND

### Residence Linareva

Gay-Friendly 50/50 ♀♂

## *Just What you Need!*

Here, at the foot of lush, green hills, on the shores of a lagoon, we have created an environment of tropical ease for gay, lesbian and other visitors from far away. Each of the typical Tahitian grass bungalows at ***Residence Linareva*** has its own character. Special care has been taken in decorating them with traditional crafts. Also enjoy the most exquisite French cuisine in the unique surroundings of our floating pub-restaurant and over-water terrasse. Charmingly converted from a former inter-island trading boat, this small, but delightful, floating restaurant specializes in fresh local seafood with a definite European flair and provides a romantic setting for cocktails at sunset.

**Address: PO Box 1, Haapiti, Moorea French Polynesia.**
**Tel: (689) 56 15 35 (Tel/Fax).**

**Type:** Residence with floating bar-restaurant.
**Clientele:** 50% gay & lesbian & 50% hetero clientele
**Transportation:** From Moorea airport, taxi or rental car. From dock, bus or rental car. Rental cars & scooters available.
**To Gay Bars:** A 5-minute drive.
**Rooms:** 3 rooms, 1 suite & 1 bungalow with king beds.
**Bathrooms:** All private shower & toilet.
**Dates Open:** All year.
**Rates:** 7,200-15,600 Pacific Francs.
**Discounts:** 25% for stays of at least 7 nights.
**Credit Cards:** MC, Visa.
**Rsv'tns:** Required.
**Reserve Through:** Travel agent or call direct.
**Parking:** Free parking.
**In-Room:** Color TV, ceiling fans, kitchen, refrigerator, coffee/tea-making facilities & maid service.
**Exercise/Health:** Bicycles, outrigger canoes, masks, snorkels.
**Swimming:** At deep water spot at end of pier or at nearby sand beaches.
**Sunbathing:** On private sun decks & beach.
**Nudity:** Permitted in garden & on raft.
**Pets:** Not permitted.
**Handicap Access:** No.
**Children:** Not especially welcome.
**Languages:** French, English & Italian.

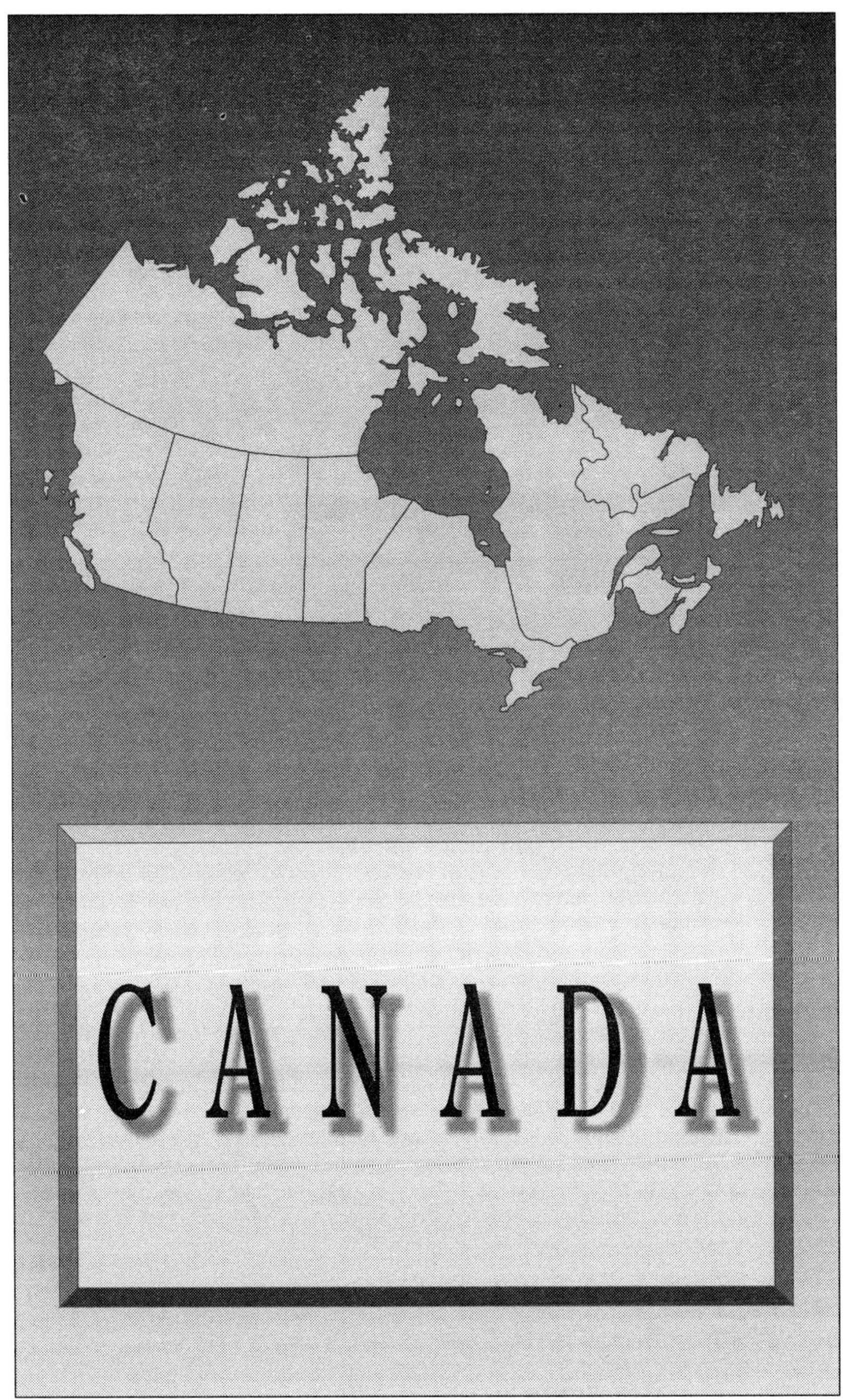
CANADA

# ALBERTA

## CALGARY

### The Foxwood Bed & Breakfast

Gay/Lesbian ♀♂

***Western Hospitality in the Heart of Calgary***

***The Foxwood,*** a charming character home in the heart of Calgary, was originally built in 1910. The home offers four different sleeping rooms, The Winston, The Chelsea, The Rockport and The Dora-Rose, each with its own style and antique decor. To enhance the character of the Edwardian period, we have accented the home with antiques and collectibles. Many of the items are unique and we encourage you to wander through our home to enjoy them all.

We chose the name ***Foxwood*** for very obvious reasons. Our two four-legged family members, Winston and Chelsea, are brother and sister wire-haired Fox Terriers, and anyone who loves high-energy, intelligent companions will love these dogs. Even though our dogs are part of our family, they are not allowed in guest rooms, nor are they allowed to have any "people food." They are well-trained and are not allowed out the front door.

We invite you to share and experience our home and our beautiful city, both of which are known for their Western hospitality. ***The Foxwood*** is conveniently located just off 17th Avenue SW, also known as "Uptown 17." This historic area hosts a variety of unique shops and great restaurants. We are also close to local clubs for dancing, or just getting together with friends. Calgary has long been known for hosting the world's largest rodeo, The Calgary Stampede; every July over one million people attend, and the growing "Gay Rodeo," although smaller, is becoming a Western Canadian tradition! If winter travel is in your plans, take advantage of some of the Canadian Rockies' best skiing, with the '88 Winter Olympic ski hills only one hour from ***The Foxwood.*** All year round, we take pride in everything Calgary has to offer. Whether fitness, entertainment, or simple relaxation is in your plans, ***The Foxwood*** will provide the comfortable place to start!

**Address: 1725-12 St SW, Calgary, AB T2T 3N1 Canada.**
**Tel: (403) 244-6693.**

**Type:** Bed & breakfast.
**Clientele:** Mostly gay & lesbian with some straight clientele
**Transportation:** Car, airport pick up, taxi. Pick up from airport CDN $15, from bus CDN $6.
**To Gay Bars:** 10 blocks, a 10 minute walk, a 2-5 minute drive.

**Rooms:** 4 rooms with single, double or queen beds.
**Bathrooms:** Private: 4 sinks only. Shared: 2 bath/shower/toilets, 1 WC only.
**Meals:** Full breakfast.
**Vegetarian:** Available with advance notice, when making reservation.
**Complimentary:** Coffee, tea, snacks, ice, before-bed mints or chocolates.
**Dates Open:** All year.
**High Season:** May-Oct.
**Rates:** Low season (Nov-Apr): CDN $50-CDN $70; high season (May-Oct) CDN $60-CDN $75.
**Discounts:** 10% off on stays of over 4 consecutive nights. Group discount (full house) 10%.
**Credit Cards:** MC, Visa.
**Rsv'tns:** Required.
**Reserve Thru:** Call direct.
**Minimum Stay:** 2 nights on holiday weekends.
**Parking:** Adequate free on-street parking. Winter plug-ins available.
**In-Room:** Color cable TV, robes, blow dryers, maid service. 2 rooms have VCR.
**On-Premises:** TV lounge, video tape library, laundry facilities.
**Exercise/Health:** Weights. Nearby gym, Jacuzzi, massage & tanning.
**Swimming:** Nearby pool & river.
**Sunbathing:** On patio.
**Smoking:** Permitted on outside patio & porches only.
**Pets:** Not permitted.
**Handicap Access:** No.
**Children:** Welcome over 12 years of age.
**Languages:** English.
**Your Host:** Brent & Devon.

## Westways Guest House

Gay/Lesbian ♂

### *Calgary's Only Guesthouse for the Community*

***Westways*** is a 1914 Heritage home, offering four tastefully-appointed bedrooms with private baths. After an active day, guests can relax in a hot tub or on the secluded deck. Each morning offers a choice of a traditional English, Canadian or health-conscious breakfast prepared by an award-winning chef and served in an Edwardian dining room. While bus and tram stops are nearby, we're just a ten-minute walk to bars and restaurants, and twenty minutes' walking to downtown. **GUEST COMMENT:** *"Very helpful host, quiet location, excellent breakfast, comfortable."* E.S., Milan, Italy.

**Address: 216 25th Ave SW, Calgary, AB T2S 0L1 Canada.**
**Tel: (403) 229-1758 (Tel/Fax), E-mail: westways@canuck.com.**
**http://www.xcite.com/westways.**

**Type:** Bed & breakfast.
**Clientele:** Mostly men with women welcome
**Transportation:** Near rapid transport & bus. Pick up from airport CDN $12.
**To Gay Bars:** 10-minute walk.
**Rooms:** 4 rooms with double or queen beds.
**Bathrooms:** All private.
**Meals:** Full cooked breakfast.
**Vegetarian:** Available.
**Complimentary:** Tea & coffee in kitchen. Fresh fruit.
**Dates Open:** All year.
**High Season:** July.
**Rates:** CDN $60-$90 double, CDN $40-$60 single.
**Discounts:** Weekly rates.
**Credit Cards:** MC, VISA, Amex.
**Rsv'tns:** Required.
**Reserve Through:** Travel agent or call direct.
**Parking:** Ample free off-street & on-street parking.
**In-Room:** Ceiling fans, telephone, maid & laundry service.
**On-Premises:** TV lounge & laundry facilities.
**Exercise/Health:** Jacuzzi.
**Swimming:** Pool in nearby sports arena.
**Smoking:** Permitted in kitchen, on porch & by hot tub.
**Pets:** Permitted.
**Handicap Access:** No.
**Children:** Not especially welcome.
**Languages:** English.
**Your Host:** Jonathon.

# BRITISH COLUMBIA

## SALT SPRING ISLAND

### Blue Ewe

**Gay/Lesbian ♀♂**

## *A Memorable Escape*

The ***Blue Ewe*** is a private retreat on over 5 acres of secluded quiet with ponds, forested paths and ocean and mountain views. Wildlife shares the place with farm and domestic animals and friendly people. Canada's Super Natural Gulf Islands, and adjacent US San Juan Islands, offer peace, quiet and close-to-nature activities. Car ferry service from Washington State, Vancouver and Victoria is fast and frequent. Walkers and cyclists are guaranteed priority service and we pick up at the dock. Lots of artists and artisans offer unique things in not-too-close-by shops.

**Address: 1207 Beddis Rd, Salt Spring Island, BC V8K 2C8 Canada. Tel: (250) 537-9344.**

**Type:** Bed & breakfast.
**Clientele:** Mostly gay & lesbian, plus their families & friends
**Transportation:** Car is best. Pick up from ferry docks & sea plane dock.
**To Gay Bars:** 30 miles or a 90-minute drive.
**Rooms:** 4 rooms & 1 cottage with single, queen or king beds.
**Bathrooms:** 2 private shower/toilets, 2 shared bath/shower/toilets.
**Meals:** Full breakfast.
**Vegetarian:** Always available on the premises & at nearby establishments.
**Complimentary:** Fridge space available.
**Dates Open:** All year.
**High Season:** Easter to Thanksgiving.
**Rates:** CDN $74-$150.
**Discounts:** 1 day free on 7-day stay. CDN $15 off all rates for single occupancy.
**Credit Cards:** MC & VISA.
**Rsv'tns:** Recommended
**Reserve Through:** Travel agent or call direct.
**Parking:** Adequate free off-street parking.
**On-Premises:** Meeting rooms.
**Exercise/Health:** Jacuzzi, sauna, massage & trails. Nearby gym, weights, massage & track.
**Swimming:** Nearby pool, ocean & lake.
**Sunbathing:** On private & common sun decks & in forest glens.
**Nudity:** Permitted in hot tub, sauna, on decks & in private wooded glens.
**Smoking:** Permitted on covered veranda, decks.
**Pets:** Permitted by prior arrangement.
**Handicap Access:** No.
**Children:** OK if accompanied by parent (under 1, over 5 to 12). Others prior arrangement.
**Languages:** English.

### Green Rose

**Gay-Friendly 50/50 ♀♂**

***Green Rose Farm & Guest House*** is a wonderfully restored 1916 Salt Spring Island farmhouse, set amidst 17 acres of field, orchards and forest. Guest rooms evoke the mood of old summer homes somewhere near the sea. Guests enjoy crisp, uncluttered spaces and, in the morning, a memorable breakfast inspired by the season. ***Green Rose*** is approximately 1-1/2 miles north of Ganges, the largest village on Salt Spring. The nearest ferry terminal is four miles away at Long Harbour. Fulford and Vesuvius terminals are also easily accessible. Nearby, are boat, kayak and bicycle rentals.

**Address: 346 Robinson Rd, Salt Spring Island, BC V8K 1P7 Canada. Tel: (250) 537-9927.**

**Type:** Bed & breakfast guesthouse.
**Clientele:** 50% gay & lesbian & 50% straight clientele
**Transportation:** Ferry from Vancouver or Victoria.
**Rooms:** 3 rooms with queen beds.
**Bathrooms:** 1 private bath/toilet & 2 private shower/toilet.

**Meals:** Full breakfast.
**Vegetarian:** Available by arrangement.
**Complimentary:** Sherry in room.
**Dates Open:** All year.
**High Season:** June-September.
**Rates:** CDN $110.
**Credit Cards:** MC & VISA.
**Rsv'tns:** Recommended, although not always necessary.
**Reserve Through:** Call direct.
**Minimum Stay:** 2 nights on holiday weekends (Canadian).
**Parking:** Ample off-street parking.
**On-Premises:** Living room with fireplace for guests' use.
**Swimming:** Nearby lake.
**Smoking:** Permitted outside only.
**Pets:** Not permitted.
**Handicap Access:** No.
**Children:** Not especially welcome.
**Languages:** English.

## Summerhill Guest House

Gay-Friendly 50/50 ♀♂

### *The Romance of Island Living*

At water's edge, ***Summerhill*** evokes peace and serenity. Tasteful and understated, the guest rooms overlook either magnificent Sansum Narrows or pastoral meadows. All have private baths, cozy duvets and excellent bedside reading lamps. Relax by the fire in the spacious oceanside sitting room or escape to sun-drenched decks and watch the eagles glide by. Tantalizing breakfasts are served overlooking the sea. While on Salt Spring, explore nature or browse the numerous shops and galleries in the village. Connections from Vancouver and Seattle.

**Address: 209 Chu-An Drive, Salt Spring Island, BC V8K 1H9 Canada. Tel: (250) 537-2727, Fax: (250) 537-4301.**

**Type:** Bed & breakfast.
**Clientele:** 50% gay & lesbian & 50% straight clientele
**Transportation:** Ferry (walk-on or with car) or float plane. Free pick up from ferry dock or float plane dock.
**Rooms:** 3 rooms with single or queen beds.
**Bathrooms:** 1 private shower/toilet & 2 private bath/toilet/showers.
**Meals:** Full breakfast.
**Vegetarian:** Available upon request. Vegetarian food & restaurant nearby.
**Complimentary:** Welcoming wine, beer, coffee, tea, juice. Room snacks.
**Dates Open:** All year.
**High Season:** May-Sep.
**Rates:** CDN $90-$120.
**Credit Cards:** MC & VISA.
**Rsv'tns:** Recommended.
**Reserve Thru:** Call direct.
**Parking:** Ample free off-street parking.
**On-Premises:** Sitting & dining rooms, fireplace & guest refrigerator.
**Exercise/Health:** Nearby gym, weights & massage.
**Swimming:** Nearby ocean & lake access.
**Sunbathing:** On the roof, common sun decks & at the beach.
**Smoking:** Permitted outside.
**Pets:** Not permitted.
**Handicap Access:** No.
**Children:** Adults only.
**Languages:** English.
**Your Host:** Michael & Paul.

# TOFINO

## The West Wind Guest House

Q-NET Gay/Lesbian ♀♂

### *A Fine West Coast Experience in Any Season*

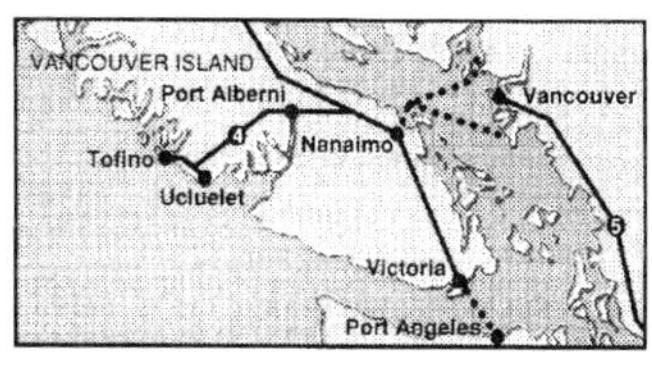


In this area of pounding surf and windswept shores is ***The West Wind Guest House,*** situated on two acres of wooded privacy. Tofino is a year-round haven for beachcombers and storm watchers alike. You can go whale watching, kayaking, and hiking and enjoy the beauty of endless beaches and ancient rainforest. The West Coast ambiance of the guesthouse includes feather beds, goose down duvets, antique furnishings, and tranquil gardens. Fine restaurants, grocery stores, pubs, and galleries are nearby.

*continued next page*

**Address: 1321 Pacific Rim Hwy, Tofino, BC V0R 2Z0 Canada.**
**Tel: (250) 725-2224, Fax: (250) 725-2212.**

**Type:** Private cottages.
**Clientele:** Good mix of gays & lesbians
**Transportation:** Car is best. Complimentary aiport or bus pick up/drop off.
**To Gay Bars:** 4-1/2 hours to Victoria.
**Rooms:** 2 cottages.
**Bathrooms:** Private baths.
**Complimentary:** Coffee, teas, fruit basket.
**Dates Open:** All year.
**High Season:** May-Sep.
**Rates:** Winter CDN $75-$110 double, summer CDN $110-$185 dbl (addt'l person CDN $20).
**Discounts:** On extended stays in low season.
**Credit Cards:** MC, Visa & Amex.
**Rsv'tns:** Required.
**Reserve Through:** Travel agent or call direct.
**Minimum Stay:** 2 nights.
**Parking:** Private covered parking.
**In-Room:** VCR, video tape library, kitchen, refrigerator, coffee/tea-making facilities, ceiling fans.
**On-Premises:** Video library, laundry facilities, phone.
**Exercise/Health:** Hot tub, gym, mountain bikes for loan, hiking, beachcombing, kayaking, canoeing, golfing, surfing.
**Swimming:** 5 minute-walk to ocean & beaches.
**Sunbathing:** On private sun decks, private garden & at the beach.
**Nudity:** Clothing optional with discretion. Nude sunbathing in private garden & decks.
**Smoking:** Permitted on outdoor deck areas only.
**Pets:** Sorry, not permitted.
**Handicap Access:** No.
**Children:** Permitted.
**Languages:** English.

## Wind Rider, A Guest House for Women

Women ♀

### *A Guesthouse for Women on Canada's Rugged West Coast*

The ***Wind Rider,*** a guesthouse for women is on the rugged West Coast of Vancouver Island where the wild open ocean meets some of the last remaining virgin temperate rainforest in the world. Enjoy spectacular sunset views from our spacious open deck overlooking Meares Island and Clayoquot Sound. Located in the heart of Tofino, around the corner from shops and restaurants, the ***Wind Rider*** is minutes away from the West Coast's renowned beaches. Also on-site is our Women's Training Centre and wilderness programs. We are a non-profit society run by and for women.

**Address: Box 548, 231 Main St, Tofino, BC V0R 2Z0 Canada.**
**Tel: (250) 725-3240, Fax: (250) 725-3280. E-mail: whole@island.net.**

**Type:** Women's guesthouse, training & education centre & wilderness programs.
**Clientele:** Women only
**Transportation:** Car or bus.
**Rooms:** 3 rooms with single, double or queen beds.
**Bathrooms:** Shared: 1 bath/shower/toilet, 1 WC only.
**Vegetarian:** Vegetarian cafes around the corner.
**Dates Open:** All year.
**High Season:** May-September.
**Rates:** CDN $18-$75.
**Discounts:** 15% for workshop participants.
**Rsv'tns:** Always preferred, but required during off-season.
**Reserve Through:** Call direct.
**Parking:** Adequate free on- & off-street parking.
**In-Room:** Telephone, maid service.
**On-Premises:** Lounge with VCR only, video tape library, equipped kitchen, meeting rooms.
**Exercise/Health:** Jacuzzi. Massage nearby.
**Swimming:** Ocean nearby.
**Sunbathing:** On common sun decks.
**Nudity:** Inquire.
**Smoking:** Permitted outside only. House is non-smoking
**Pets:** Not permitted.
**Handicap Access:** Not at this time, we are working on it.
**Children:** Welcome.
**Languages:** English, some French-speakers on staff.

# VANCOUVER

## The Albion Guest House

Q-NET Gay/Lesbian ♀♂

### *A Country Retreat in the City*

Imagine yourself in a beautiful sitting room with freshly-cut flowers, relaxing in front of a fireplace, sipping your complimentary aperitif. This is a typical scene at ***The Albion Guest House,*** a turn-of-the-century character home on a quiet, tree-lined residential street in the city. The inn's peaceful ambiance, immediately apparent from the playful statuettes which greet you as you arrive, fosters a warm feeling for all who visit. *Twist,* a Seattle gay newspaper, has commented that the innkeepers are "soft-spoken, generous and accommodating," and that their "personal flair for service and detail is seen in their individual decorations of the guest rooms." The inn's restful rooms are bright, spacious and individually decorated, all with comfortable iron beds covered with thick feather mattresses, fine cotton linens and down-filled duvets. Guests experience a sumptuous breakfast in the formal dining room, which has been whimsically handpainted by a local artist, or in the sunny courtyard. Breakfast can include home-baked breads, pastries, omelettes, "Eggs on a Cloud," old fashioned oatmeal or an array of fresh fruits, juices and other healthful goodies.

Later, you may want to take advantage of the free bicycle rentals to explore Vancouver on your own. Chinatown and Gastown are just a few minutes away, as well as the expo "Skytrain." It's just three minutes' walk to popular restaurants, Starbuck's coffee shop, delicatessens, parks, art galleries, theatre and shopping. Vancouver's gambling casinos, Queen Elizabeth Theatre, Ford Centre for the Performing Arts and Van Dusen Gardens are also nearby. Area attractions include boating, parasailing, windsurfing and nude sunbathing at Wreck Beach. A health club is nearby. It's a 30-minute drive to the famous Capilano Suspension Bridge or Grouse Mountain, a major ski area with a panoramic view of Vancouver. The airport is just 15 minutes away. After a long day you can soak in the 6-person hot tub! ***The Albion Guest House*** has been selected for inclusion in *Best Places to Stay in the Pacific Northwest* and is AAA approved.

**Address: 592 West Nineteenth Ave, Vancouver, BC V5Z 1W6 Canada.**
**Tel: (604) 873-2287, Fax: (604) 879-5682, E-mail: hle@bull.com.**

**Type:** Bed & breakfast guesthouse.
**Clientele:** Gay & lesbian, good mix of men & women
**Transportation:** Car, taxi, shuttle or bus. 1 block to public transportation.
**To Gay Bars:** 8 minutes by car.
**Rooms:** 4 rooms with queen beds.
**Bathrooms:** 2 private with toilet, sink, shower & bathtub; 2 shared with toilet, sink & shower.
**Meals:** Full breakfast. Lunch if prearranged.
**Vegetarian:** If prearranged. Vegetarian restaurant 1 block away.
**Complimentary:** Sherry, wine, coffee, beverages on request & chocolates on pillows. Local calls.
**Dates Open:** All year.
**High Season:** May-September.
**Rates:** CDN $60-CDN $155.
**Discounts:** Negotiable for extended stays.

*continued next page*

**Credit Cards:** MC, VISA & Amex.
**Rsv'tns:** Recommended.
**Reserve Through:** Call direct.
**Parking:** Ample free covered parking. On-street parking is easy to find also.
**On-Premises:** Complimentary bicycle/luggage storage, fireplace, refrigerator & fresh spring water.
**Exercise/Health:** Nearby fitness facility.
**Swimming:** Nearby indoor & outdoor pools & ocean beach.
**Sunbathing:** On common sun decks & patio.
**Smoking:** Permitted outdoors only. Non-smoking establishment.
**Pets:** Not permitted.
**Handicap Access:** No.
**Children:** Permitted.
**Languages:** English & French.
**Your Host:** Howard & Carole.

IGTA

## Colibri Bed & Breakfast

**Gay/Lesbian ♀♂**

### *Calm in the City Centre*

In the heart of the gay West End of beautiful Vancouver is ***Colibri.*** With unpretentious calm and a warm welcome, you'll find your home here while you discover the city, or yourself. Shop till you drop or take time for your inner self. ***Colibri*** is just blocks to scenic beaches, hectares of forest, and kilometres of oceanside promenade. Come, be yourself with us. A European-style bed and breakfast for those who value a sense of home while on the road.

**Address: 1101 Thurlow St, Vancouver, BC V6E 1W9 Canada.**
**Tel: (604) 689-5100, Fax: (604) 682-3925.**

**Type:** Bed & breakfast.
**Clientele:** Mostly gay & lesbian with some hetero clientele
**Transportation:** Airport bus to Century Plaza, then walk 1 block west.
**To Gay Bars:** 2 blocks.
**Rooms:** 5 rooms with single, double, queen or king beds.
**Bathrooms:** 2 shared bath/shower/toilets.
**Meals:** High season: full breakfast. Low season: continental breakfast.
**Vegetarian:** By arrangement on arrival. Restaurants nearby (1-1/2 blocks).
**Complimentary:** Beverage on arrival. In summer fresh Belgian chocolates on pillows at turn-down.
**Dates Open:** All year.
**High Season:** May-October.
**Rates:** May-Oct CDN $95-$140. Nov-May CDN $55-$85.
**Discounts:** By arrangement on long stays in low season.
**Credit Cards:** MC, VISA & Amex.
**Rsv'tns:** Highly recommended.
**Reserve Through:** Call/fax direct.
**Minimum Stay:** 2 days in high season.
**Parking:** Available.
**In-Room:** Maid & laundry service.
**Exercise/Health:** Nearby gym, weights, Jacuzzi, sauna, steam & massage.
**Swimming:** At Olympic-sized heated indoor pool 4 blocks away or nearby ocean.
**Sunbathing:** On common sun decks & at the beach.
**Nudity:** Nude beach 20 minutes by bus.
**Smoking:** Permitted on front & back decks & on room balconies.
**Pets:** Not permitted. Resident cat.
**Handicap Access:** Regrettably not.
**Children:** By arrangement.
**Languages:** English, French & Spanish.

## Columbia Cottage Guest House

**Gay-Friendly ♀♂**

### *A Tranquil Oasis in the City with Fabulous Gourmet Breakfasts*

On a tree-lined street, featuring an English country garden with a fountain flowing into the fish pond covered with waterlilies, ***Columbia Cottage*** offers peace and tranquility. Our breakfasts are fabulous – perhaps a baked apple, basted eggs with mango salsa, English scones, fresh orange juice, or those wonderful BC berries with crême-Anglaise. We're a five-minute drive to gay clubs downtown or to Q.E. Park for a romatic evening stroll to watch the sunset. Vancouver offers many attractions, so plan to stay a few days for complete satisfaction.

**Address: 205 West 14th Ave, Vancouver, BC Canada.**
**Tel: (604) 874-5327, Fax: (604) 879-4547.**
**http://www.novamart.com/columbia.**

**Type:** Bed & breakfast.
**Clientele:** 20% gay & lesbian & 80% hetero clientele
**Transportation:** Car or cab. 15 minutes from international airport.
**To Gay Bars:** 5-minute drive to Vancouver's gay clubs.
**Rooms:** 4 double rooms & 1 garden suite with single, double, queen or king beds.
**Bathrooms:** All private.
**Meals:** Full gourmet breakfast.
**Vegetarian:** Available, as well as other special diets, if requested at time of booking.
**Complimentary:** Robes, slippers, coffee, tea, sherry & local calls.
**Dates Open:** All year.
**High Season:** May-October.
**Rates:** Summer single CDN $100-$135, double CDN $125-$160. Winter single CDN $80, double CDN $95.
**Discounts:** For extended stays, business traveler.
**Credit Cards:** MC, Visa.
**Rsv'tns:** Recommended.
**Reserve Through:** Call direct.
**Parking:** Ample free parking.
**In-Room:** Maid & laundry service, telephone, refrigerator, kitchen, coffee/tea-making facilities.
**On-Premises:** Private dining room, enclosed garden.
**Exercise/Health:** Nearby gym, massage.
**Swimming:** 10 minutes from most beaches. Walk to nearby pool.
**Sunbathing:** On the patio, at the beach.
**Nudity:** 15-minute drive to nude beaches.
**Smoking:** Permitted outside only.
**Pets:** Not permitted.
**Handicap Access:** No.
**Children:** Permitted over 8 years old.
**Languages:** English, German.
**Your Host:** Alisdair & Susanne.

## Hawks Avenue Bed & Breakfast

Women ♀

### *A Quiet and Comfortable Women's Bed & Breakfast*

A bright and spacious room awaits you at ***Hawks Avenue Bed & Breakfast.*** Our heritage three-level townhouse is in Vancouver's Strathcona neighbourhood, a section of town rich in character and colour. We're ten minutes from downtown restaurants, shopping, theatres, clubs and galleries, as well as historic Gastown, Chinatown and Commercial Drive – renowned for its coffee bars and alternative atmosphere. Your room opens onto two decks, one of which overlooks a small park, and has a queen-sized bed, colour TV, telephone and a private half bathroom. We serve an expanded continental breakfast. There is ample street parking and non-smokers are preferred.

**Address: 734 Hawks Avenue, Vancouver, BC V6A 3J3 Canada.**
**Tel: (604) 253-0989.**

**Type:** Bed & breakfast.
**Clientele:** Women only
**Transportation:** Car, taxi from airport, or airport bus to downtown, then taxi.
**To Gay Bars:** 10 blocks, 1 mile, a 20 minute walk, a 5 minute drive.
**Rooms:** 1 room with queen bed.
**Bathrooms:** Private sink & toilet. Shared bath/shower/toilet.
**Meals:** Expanded continental breakfast.
**Vegetarian:** Available. Vegetarian restaurant & organic grocery are nearby.
**Dates Open:** All year.
**High Season:** May-September.
**Rates:** Summer: single CDN $75, double CDN $85. Winter: single CDN $65, double CDN $75.
**Discounts:** 10% on stays of over 2 nights.
**Rsv'tns:** Required.
**Reserve Through:** Call direct.
**Parking:** Ample free on-street parking.
**In-Room:** Color cable TV, telephone.
**Exercise/Health:** Nearby gym, weights, Jacuzzi, sauna, steam, massage.
**Swimming:** Nearby pool, ocean.
**Sunbathing:** On private sun decks, at beach.
**Smoking:** Permitted outside. Entire house is non-smoking.
**Pets:** Not permitted.
**Handicap Access:** No.
**Children:** No.
**Languages:** English.
**Your Host:** Louise.

# Nelson House

Q-NET Gay/Lesbian ♀♂

## *No Boring Old B&B!*

***Nelson House*** is a large, 1907 Edwardian on a quiet, residential street, only minutes' walk from the business district, shopping, entertainment, Stanley Park and the beaches. Glowing fireplaces and the wagging tail of a Springer Spaniel ensure a warm welcome. Every spacious corner guestroom suggests a different travel itinerary. Will it be Sailor's, Vienna, Klondyke or Hollywood? The third-floor studio suite, with Far Eastern ambiance, a fireplace, deck, kitchen and Jacuzzi ensuite, is especially appealing. We are often complimented on our breakfast food, fun and conversation. Visit awhile. After all, Vancouver is right at your doorstep.

**Address: 977 Broughton St, Vancouver, BC V6G 2A4 Canada.**
**Tel: (604) 684-9793, Fax: (604) 684-4141.**

**Type:** Bed & breakfast.
**Clientele:** Mostly gay & lesbian with some hetero clientele
**Transportation:** By car or airport bus to Landmark Hotel, walk or taxi remaining 2 blocks.
**To Gay Bars:** Four blocks.
**Rooms:** 4 rooms & 1 suite with double or queen beds.
**Bathrooms:** 3 private (1 with Jacuzzi), 1 shared. Guestrooms have wash basins.
**Meals:** Full breakfast.
**Vegetarian:** Available upon request, prior notice appreciated. Plenty of veggies nearby.
**Complimentary:** 2 kitchenettes stocked with tea & coffee.
**Dates Open:** All year, except Christmas thru New Year.
**High Season:** May through mid-October.
**Rates:** Low season CDN $58-$108, high season CDN $78-$155.
**Discounts:** Available by week in low season.
**Credit Cards:** MC & VISA.
**Rsv'tns:** Required.
**Reserve Through:** Travel agent or call direct.
**Minimum Stay:** 2 nights on holiday weekends only.
**Parking:** Ample free off-street parking.
**In-Room:** Maid service, some rooms with kitchens, some refrigerators. Studio has cable colour TV.
**On-Premises:** TV lounge, VCR, stereo, house telephone, complimentary storage of bicycles & bags
**Exercise/Health:** Massage. Nearby gym, weights, Jacuzzi, sauna, steam & massage.
**Swimming:** Five- to ten-minute walk to ocean beach.
**Sunbathing:** On beach or private sun decks.
**Nudity:** Directions available to excellent clothing-optional beaches.
**Smoking:** Permitted on front porch or in garden.
**Pets:** Not permitted.
**Handicap Access:** No.
**Children:** Permitted by prior arrangement, 12 or older only.
**Languages:** English & French.
**Your Host:** David & O'Neal.

IGTA

## "O Canada" House

Gay-Friendly ♀♂

### *The Home of Canada's National Anthem*

*"O Canada" House* offers the ultimate in old-world charm and hospitality in a beautifully restored 1897 Victorian home, located in a quiet downtown neighbourhood near fine shopping, dining and entertainment. The home is large enough to ensure maximum privacy and comfort. Its spacious main floor contains a large entry with open staircase, front and rear parlors, and a dining room with a serving pantry stocked with goodies. Our wrap-around porch looks out into an English garden. Five large bed/sitting rooms have private baths and are decorated in a late Victorian style with designer linens. We serve gourmet breakfasts and early-evening sherry in the front parlor.

**Address: 1114 Barclay St, Vancouver, BC V6E 1H1 Canada.**
**Tel: (604) 688-0555. http://www.bbcanada.com/919.html.**

**Type:** Bed & breakfast.
**Clientele:** Mostly straight with a gay & lesbian following
**Transportation:** Car is best, taxi, airport shuttle bus.
**To Gay Bars:** 3 blocks, a 5 minute walk, a 3 minute drive.
**Rooms:** 5 rooms with king or queen beds.
**Bathrooms:** Private: 4 shower/toilets, 1 bath/toilet/shower.
**Meals:** Full breakfast.
**Vegetarian:** Available nearby.
**Complimentary:** Sherry in front parlor in late afternoon. Mints on pillows, cookies in room. Available 24 hrs: snacks, fruit juices, pop, coffee, tea.
**Dates Open:** All year.
**High Season:** May-October.
**Rates:** High season: CDN $150-CDN $195. Low season CDN $125-CDN $160.
**Discounts:** For extended stays, singles, AAA members.
**Credit Cards:** MC, Visa.
**Rsv'tns:** Required.
**Reserve Through:** Travel agent or call direct.
**Minimum Stay:** 2 days on weekends.
**Parking:** Adequate free off-street parking.
**In-Room:** Color cable TV, VCR, telephone, refrigerator, maid service.
**On-Premises:** Meeting rooms, TV lounge, video tape library, fax. Front & rear parlors have fireplaces.
**Exercise/Health:** Nearby gym, weights, Jacuzzi, sauna, steam, massage.
**Swimming:** Nearby pool, ocean, short walk to beaches.
**Sunbathing:** At beach.
**Smoking:** Permitted on front porch.
**Pets:** Not permitted.
**Handicap Access:** No.
**Children:** Children ages 12 & over welcome.
**Languages:** English.
**Your Host:** Mike & Jim.

## Rural Roots Bed and Breakfast

Gay/Lesbian ♀♂

### *Luxurious, Affordable, Country Setting at Vancouver's Doorstep*

Less than one hour from Vancouver, Canada, and two hours from Seattle, ***Rural Roots*** is a luxury, country B&B on ten parklike acres with gardens, an orchard, rolling pastures, grazing cows and a small forest. Relax in the hot tub, breakfast in a Victorian conservatory and lounge on the sun decks. Let us be your "getaway" from the city or, when touring, make us your base for Vancouver and the many recreational opportunities of the Pacific Northwest. After a busy day, return to the relaxed pace of ***Rural Roots*** to enjoy the best of both worlds, rural and urban.

**Address: 4939 Ross Road, Mt. Lehman, BC V4X 1Z3 Canada. Tel: (604) 856-2380, Fax: (604) 857-2380, E-mail: rroots@uniserve.com.**

**Type:** Bed & breakfast.
**Clientele:** Gay & lesbian. Good mix of men & women
**Transportation:** Car is best.
**To Gay Bars:** 33 miles or an hour drive to Vancouver gay bars.
**Rooms:** 4 rooms with twin, double, queen or king beds.
**Bathrooms:** 3 private bath/toilets, 1 shared shower/toilet.
**Meals:** Full breakfast.
**Vegetarian:** Available upon request. Vegetarian restaurants nearby.
**Complimentary:** Tea, coffee & soft drinks.
**Dates Open:** All year.
**Rates:** CDN $55-$95.
**Discounts:** 10% off third and subsequent nights.
**Rsv'tns:** Required.
**Reserve Thru:** Call direct.
**Parking:** Ample free parking.
**In-Room:** Color TV.
**On-Premises:** TV lounge, guest kitchen, laundry facilities.
**Exercise/Health:** Jacuzzi. Recreation centre 20 minutes away, exercise equipment.
**Swimming:** Pool at recreation centre, 60 minutes to ocean.
**Sunbathing:** On common sun decks.
**Nudity:** Permitted in hot tub area.
**Smoking:** Permitted outdoors only.
**Pets:** Permitted. Kennelled at night.
**Handicap Access:** No.
**Children:** Not especially welcome.
**Languages:** English, French & Spanish.
**Your Host:** Jim & Len.

# VICTORIA

## Claddagh House Bed & Breakfast

Gay/Lesbian ♀♂

A warm welcome awaits you in our 1913 heritage home. At ***Claddagh House B&B,*** you can step back from the pressures of everyday life and give yourself up to the relaxation and charm of an authentic Irish B&B experience. Expect cheerful hospitality and attention to your comfort. Enjoy a quiet time or conversation with new friends on the front porch or balcony, or perhaps an evening in front of a fire. For significant occasions, enhance your experience with our *Celebrations Package.* Two-night *Island Escape Packages* include your choice of relaxation treatments.

**Address: 1761 Lee Ave, Victoria, BC V8R 4W7 Canada. Tel: (250) 370-2816, Fax: (250) 592-0228.**

**Type:** Bed & breakfast.
**Clientele:** Mostly gay & lesbian with some hetero clientele
**Transportation:** Easy access to city by car, bus, bicycle, taxi, tour companies.
**To Gay Bars:** 8 min by car to gay & lesbian bars.
**Rooms:** 4 rooms with double, queen or king beds.
**Bathrooms:** 3 private bath/toilet & 1 shared bath/shower/toilet.
**Meals:** Hearty breakfast from homemade & home-grown foods.
**Vegetarian:** Lacto-ovo vegetarian always available.
**Complimentary:** Tea, coffee, cookies & Irish Milsèan confectionery.
**Dates Open:** All year.
**High Season:** May through September.
**Rates:** CDN $65-$125 for two, CDN $50-$100 for one.
**Discounts:** 7th consecutive night free. Frequent-sleeper discounts for return guests.
**Credit Cards:** MC & VISA.
**Rsv'tns:** Recommended & preferred.
**Reserve Through:** Travel agent or call direct.
**Minimum Stay:** 2 nights on holiday weekends.
**Parking:** Ample free on-street parking.
**In-Room:** Coffee & tea-making facilities.
**On-Premises:** TV lounge, laundry facilities, front porch, garden & fireplace.
**Exercise/Health:** Health & recreation centre & bicycle rental 1 block. Massage, reflexology & aromatherapy with advance notice.
**Swimming:** Pool 1 block, ocean beach 5-min drive.
**Sunbathing:** At ocean beach or in garden.
**Smoking:** Permitted outdoors.
**Pets:** Pets by arrangement. Resident cat, Polly, has private quarters.
**Handicap Access:** No.
**Children:** Welcome.
**Languages:** English.
**Your Host:** Maggie.

# Oak Bay Guest House

Gay-Friendly ♀♂

At this classic inn, established since 1922, we have your comfort and pleasure at heart. Guests at ***Oak Bay Guest House*** enjoy the peaceful location, scenic walks a block from the ocean, and the beautiful gardens that surround. All eleven rooms have private bathrooms. There are two sitting rooms decorated with antiques, a library and gas fireplace. We are frequently complimented on our home-cooked breakfast. Golf, village shopping, fine dining and a city bus tour are accessible from our location, just minutes from downtown. Come, and enjoy.

**Address: 1052 Newport Ave, Victoria, BC V8S 5E3 Canada.**
**Tel: (250) 598-3812, (800) 575-3812,**
**E-mail: OakBay@beds-breakfasts.com.**
**http://beds-breakfasts.com/OakBay.**

**Type:** Inn.
**Clientele:** Mostly straight clientele with a gay & lesbian following
**Transportation:** Car is best. Bus stop right outside.
**To Gay Bars:** 2 miles or 10 mins by car.
**Rooms:** 11 rooms with single or queen beds.
**Bathrooms:** All private bath/toilets.
**Meals:** Full breakfast.
**Vegetarian:** Available upon request.
**Complimentary:** Tea & coffee.
**Dates Open:** All year.
**High Season:** Jun-Sept.
**Rates:** CDN $65-$120 winter, CDN $120-$160 summer.
**Credit Cards:** MC, Visa, Amex.
**Rsv'tns:** Required.
**Reserve Through:** Call direct.
**Parking:** Ample free off-street & on-street parking.
**In-Room:** Coffee & tea-making facilities.
**On-Premises:** TV lounge.
**Swimming:** Nearby pool, lake & ocean beach.
**Sunbathing:** On the beach.
**Smoking:** Non-smoking guesthouse.
**Pets:** Not permitted.
**Handicap Access:** No.
**Children:** Not permitted.
**Languages:** English.

## Ocean Wilderness

**Gay-Friendly ♀♂**

### *An Elegant Jewel in a Wilderness Setting*

***Ocean Wilderness*** has 9 guest rooms on five forested acres of oceanfront with breathtaking view of forests, the Straits of Juan de Fuca and the Olympic Mts.

Large, and beautifully decorated rooms with private baths and bed canopies. A silver service of coffee is delivered to your door as a gentle wake-up call. Home baking makes breakfast a special treat. A fun seafood dinner on the beach is available Thursday and Sunday. The hot tub, in a Japanese gazebo, is popular with weary vacationers. Book your time for a private soak. Several rooms have private soak tubs for two, overlooking the ocean.

**Address: 109 West Coast Rd RR#2, Sooke, BC V0S 1N0 Canada.**
**Tel: (250) 646-2116, (800) 323-2116, Fax: (250) 646-2317.**

**Type:** Bed & breakfast inn with gift shop.
**Clientele:** Mostly straight with gay/lesbian following
**Transportation:** Car is best.
**To Gay Bars:** 30 miles.
**Rooms:** 9 rooms with single, queen or king beds.
**Bathrooms:** All private.
**Meals:** Full breakfast. Seafood dinner on the beach Thurs & Sun available at extra charge.
**Vegetarian:** Available with prior notification or upon arrival.
**Complimentary:** Wake up coffee to your door on silver service, 24-hr beverage station.
**Dates Open:** All year.
**High Season:** May-October.
**Rates:** Summer (June 1-Sept 30) CDN $85-$175, winter (Oct 1-May 30) CDN $65-$140.
**Discounts:** Winter rates + 3 nights for the price of 2
**Credit Cards:** MC, VISA.
**Rsv'tns:** Req'd in season.
**Reserve Through:** Travel agent or call direct.
**Parking:** Off-street parking.
**In-Room:** Room service, telephone, bar refrigerator, maid service.
**On-Premises:** Beach, wilderness, wildlife, landscaped gardens, hot tub in gazebo overlooking ocean.
**Exercise/Health:** Hot tub, massage by appointment.
**Swimming:** Ocean beach & river.
**Sunbathing:** On beach, patio, private sun decks.
**Nudity:** Permitted on private sun decks.
**Smoking:** Permitted outdoors only, all rooms non-smoking.
**Pets:** Permitted by prior arrangement.
**Handicap Access:** Yes, 1 room.
**Children:** Permitted occasionally, please inquire. Must be adult oriented.
**Languages:** English.

## The Weekender Bed & Breakfast

**Gay/Lesbian ♀♂**

### *A Seaside Bed & Breakfast*

***Weekender Bed & Breakfast*** is located just steps from the ocean, along Victoria's scenic drive. Our location is but a short distance from Beacon Hill Park, Cook Street Village, Fairfield Shopping Plaza, local restaurants, nightlife and most tourist attractions. The inn's spacious, bright rooms all have private baths. The deluxe suite has ocean views and a private sun deck.

**Address: 10 Eberts St, Victoria, BC V8S 5L6 Canada.**
**Tel: (250) 389-1688.**

**Type:** Bed & Breakfast.
**Clientele:** Mostly gay & lesbian with some hetero clientele
**Transportation:** Car is best. Taxi from city centre, about $9.00. Free pick up from bus & Clipper Catama-

ran foot passenger term.
**To Gay Bars:** 2 miles or 30 minutes by foot, 5 minutes by car.
**Rooms:** 3 rooms with queen beds.
**Bathrooms:** 3 private bath/toilets.
**Meals:** Expanded continental breakfast.
**Vegetarian:** Always available.
**Complimentary:** Complimentary beverage on check-in. Fresh fruit always available.
**Dates Open:** Weekends November-April, full-time May-October.
**High Season:** Mid-May to mid-October.
**Rates:** High season CDN $84-99. Low season CDN $69-$82.
**Credit Cards:** MC & VISA.
**Rsv'tns:** Recommended & preferred.
**Reserve Through:** Call direct.
**Minimum Stay:** 2 nights on holiday weekends & special events days.
**Parking:** Ample on-street parking.
**In-Room:** Maid service.
**Exercise/Health:** Massage. Nearby YMCA & YWCA.
**Sunbathing:** On private sun decks.
**Smoking:** Permitted outdoors only.
**Pets:** Not permitted.
**Handicap Access:** No.
**Children:** Not especially welcomed.
**Languages:** English.
**Your Host:** Michael.

# WHISTLER MOUNTAIN

## The Whistler Retreat

Q-NET Gay/Lesbian ♀♂

### *Whistler's Favorite Gay & Lesbian B&B*

Discovering ***The Whistler Retreat,*** brings downhill and cross-country skiing, snowshoeing, snowmobiling, hiking, mountain biking, swimming, sunbathing, golf, tennis, canoeing, and horseback riding to your doorstep. This spacious alpine home, located just five minutes north of Whistler Village, has spectacular mountain views, three fireplaces, queen-sized beds, an outdoor Jacuzzi, a sauna, and a pool table. Whistler, a world-renowned mountain resort, has been rated one of the best places in the world to ski by *Snow Country Magazine* and *SKI Magazine.*

**Address: 8561 Drifter Way, Whistler, BC V0N 1B8 Canada.**
**Tel: (604) 938-9245 (Tel/Fax).**

**Type:** Bed & breakfast.
**Clientele:** Gay & lesbian. Good mix of men & women
**Transportation:** Car is best.
**To Gay Bars:** 70 miles to Vancouver bars.
**Rooms:** 3 rooms with queen beds.
**Bathrooms:** 2 shared bath/shower/toilets.
**Meals:** Full breakfast.
**Vegetarian:** Available on request.
**Dates Open:** All year.
**High Season:** December-March.
**Rates:** Low season: single CDN $65, double CDN $79. High season: single CDN $85, double CDN $99.
**Discounts:** 10% on stays of 3 or more nights.
**Credit Cards:** MC, Visa.
**Rsv'tns:** Recommended.
**Reserve Through:** Travel agent or call direct.
**Parking:** Ample free off-steet parking.
**In-Room:** Maid service.
**On-Premises:** TV lounge, video tape library, pool table, laundry facilities.
**Exercise/Health:** Jacuzzi, sauna. Nearby gym, weights, Jacuzzi, sauna, steam, massage, squash & tennis courts, ice skating.
**Swimming:** Nearby pool, lake.
**Sunbathing:** On common sun decks, at beach.
**Nudity:** Permitted in sauna & Jacuzzi. Nude sunbathing at nearby beach.
**Smoking:** Permitted except in bedrooms.
**Pets:** Not permitted.
**Handicap Access:** No.
**Children:** No.
**Languages:** English.

IGTA

# ONTARIO

## HAMILTON

### Cedars Tent & Trailer Park

Gay/Lesbian ♀♂

***Cedars Tent & Trailer Park*** is the only mixed campground in Ontario. We've been in business for ten years, building and improving each year. Come visit us on our 130 green Ontario acres.

**Address: PO Box 195, Millgrove, ON L0R 1V0 Canada.**
**Tel: (905) 659-7342 or 659-3655.**

**Type:** Campground with rental trailers, clubhouse, restaurant & bar.
**Clientele:** Good mix of gay men & women
**Transportation:** Car is best.
**To Gay Bars:** 5 miles to gay bars.
**Bathrooms:** Shower & toilet building plus outhouses throughout.
**Campsites:** 600 campsites with shared shower facilities.
**Meals:** Full-service restaurant on premises.
**Dates Open:** April 1st through October 15th.
**Rates:** CDN $13.50 per person per day.
**Reserve Through:** Call direct.
**Parking:** Ample free parking.
**On-Premises:** Clubhouse, bar, dance floor & game rooms.
**Exercise/Health:** Recreational area.
**Swimming:** Pool.
**Sunbathing:** At poolside.
**Smoking:** Permitted without restrictions.
**Pets:** Permitted. Must be on a leash.
**Handicap Access:** Yes.
**Children:** Welcome. Children under 12 free, parent responsible.
**Languages:** English & French.

## OTTAWA/HULL

### Le jardin des Trembles

Women ♀

***For Every Season There is a Good Reason to Visit...***

***Le jardin des Trembles,*** a women's B&B bordering on the beautiful Gatineau Hills, minutes from downtown Ottawa. We have two attractive bedrooms and our continental breakfast includes fresh croissants and breads, homemade jams, teas, coffees and juices. The house is non-smoking, but smoking is permitted on the sun deck. Our house is bright and cheerful. Goudou, our small dog, and Danielle and Francine, your hosts, welcome you to Québec, "La belle province" for an incredible adventure in the art of total relaxation and to experience excellent cuisine in a completely French ambiance.

**Address: 29 rue des Chardonnerets, Hull, QC Canada.**
**Tel: (819) 595-8761, Fax: (819) 595-0515,**
**E-mail: cw002@freenet.carleton.ca.**

**Type:** Bed & breakfast.
**Clientele:** Women only
**Transportation:** Car is best, pick up from airport, train or bus CDN $15.
**To Gay Bars:** 5 miles, a 15-minute drive.
**Rooms:** 2 rooms with double or queen beds.
**Bathrooms:** Shared bath/shower/toilet.
**Meals:** Continental breakfast.
**Vegetarian:** Always available, vegetarian food stores nearby.
**Complimentary:** Tea, coffee, juice, chocolate on pillows.
**Dates Open:** All year.
**High Season:** June 15-Sept 15.
**Rates:** CDN $45-CDN $55.
**Discounts:** 15% on stays of 5 days or longer. Special rates for long weekends.
**Rsv'tns:** Required.
**Reserve Through:** Call direct.
**Minimum Stay:** 1 night.

**Parking:** Adequate on-street parking.
**In-Room:** Ceiling fans, maid service.
**On-Premises:** TV lounge, video tape library, laundry facilities, fax, computer, e-mail, Internet.
**Exercise/Health:** Nearby tennis courts, cross-country & downhill skiing, bike & hiking trails.
**Swimming:** Nearby pool, river, lake.
**Sunbathing:** On private sun decks.
**Smoking:** Permitted on sun deck, outside.
**Pets:** Small dogs only.
**Handicap Access:** No.
**Children:** No.
**Languages:** English, French.
**Your Host:** Danielle & Francine.

## Rideau View Inn

Gay-Owned 50/50 ♀♂

### *Victorian Elegance in the Heart of Ottawa*

***Rideau View Inn*** is a large Edwardian home built in 1907 with seven elegant guest rooms. It is located in the center of the city on a residential street just steps from fine restaurants, shopping, Parliament Hill and public transport. We offer a gourmet breakfast in our gracious dining room from 7:30-9:00am. Our guests are encouraged to relax in front of the fireplace in the living room, enjoy a leisurely stroll beside the Rideau Canal or a game of tennis in nearby public courts.

**Address: 177 Frank St, Ottawa, ON K2P 0X4 Canada.**
**Tel: (613) 236-9309, (800) 658-3564, Fax: (613) 237-6842,**
**E-mail: rideau@istar.ca. http://home.istar.ca/~rideau/.**

**Type:** Bed & breakfast.
**Clientele:** 50% gay & lesbian & 50% hetero clientele
**Transportation:** Taxi.
**To Gay Bars:** 10-minute walk to gay/lesbian bars.
**Rooms:** 7 rooms with single, double or queen beds.
**Bathrooms:** 2 private bath/toilets & 4 shared bath/shower/toilets.
**Meals:** Full breakfast.
**Vegetarian:** Available with 1 days notice.
**Complimentary:** Tea & coffee.
**Dates Open:** All year.
**Rates:** CDN $58-$85.
**Discounts:** 15% discount on bookings of 7 days or more.
**Credit Cards:** MC, Visa, Amex & Enroute.
**Rsv'tns:** Required 1 week in advance.
**Reserve Through:** Travel agent or call direct.
**Minimum Stay:** On holiday weekends only.
**Parking:** Adequate free on- & off-street parking.
**In-Room:** AC & telephone.
**On-Premises:** TV lounge.
**Sunbathing:** On common sun decks.
**Smoking:** Smoke-free home.
**Pets:** Not permitted.
**Handicap Access:** No.
**Children:** Permitted.
**Languages:** English, French.
**Your Host:** George.

# STRATFORD

## Burnside

Gay-Friendly 50/50 ♀♂

***Burnside*** is an ancestral, turn-of-the-century home featuring many family heirlooms and antiques, redecorated in light, airy colors. Our host is a horticultural instructor and an authority on local and Canadian geneology. Relax amid flowers and herbs in the gardens overlooking Lake Victoria. We are a mere 12 minutes' walk from the Stratford, Avon and Tom Patterson theatres and a short walk from interesting shops and good restaurants. Nearby is the Avon Trail, part of a network of trails enabling one to walk from London, Ontario to Niagara Falls. We will pick up guests at the train or bus stations.

**Address: 139 William St, Stratford, ON N5A 4X9 Canada.**
**Tel: (519) 271-7076, Fax: (519) 271-0265**

**Type:** Bed & breakfast.
**Clientele:** 50% gay & lesbian & 50% hetero clientele
**Transportation:** Car is best. Free pick up from train & bus station. Use Stratford Airporter from airport to our front door.
**To Gay Bars:** 5-minute walk to gay/lesbian bar (Down the Street Bar & Cafe).
**Rooms:** 4 rooms with single/twin, double or king beds.
**Bathrooms:** Shared: 1 full bath, 2 bathtubs, 2 showers & 1 toilet room.

*continued next page*

**Meals:** Full or expanded continental breakfast.
**Vegetarian:** Cater to special diets.
**Complimentary:** Ice provided.
**Dates Open:** All year.
**High Season:** July & August.
**Rates:** Student CDN $25, single CDN $45, twin & double CDN $65, king CDN $70.
**Discounts:** For stays of over 2 nights.
**Rsv'tns:** Preferred.
**Reserve Through:** Call direct.
**Minimum Stay:** 2 nights on July & August weekends.
**Parking:** Adequate free off-street parking.
**In-Room:** Central AC/heat, refrigerator.
**On-Premises:** Private dining room, TV lounge with color cable TV, VCR & limited video tape library, & spacious gardens.
**Exercise/Health:** Whirlpool tub & massage.
**Swimming:** Lions Club pool 1/2 block, YMCA pool 3 blocks.
**Sunbathing:** At Grand Bend Beach & Shakespeare Conservation Park.
**Nudity:** Permitted on lower level.
**Smoking:** Permitted outside.
**Pets:** Not permitted.
**Handicap Access:** No.
**Children:** Permitted but not encouraged during festival season (May-Oct).
**Languages:** English, limited French.
**Your Host:** Les & Don.

# TORONTO

## Catnaps 1892 Downtown Guesthouse

Q-NET Gay/Lesbian ♀♂

### *Toronto's Purrfect Place to Be*

Stay at ***Catnaps*** and enjoy personal, friendly attention. Our newly-renovated century home right downtown is the oldest Toronto gay and lesbian guesthouse. Each room has a different personality, and all are cozy and comfortable. We're close to 24-hour public transportation, and guests have use of kitchen and laundry facilities. Relax in a casual, informal atmosphere just steps from all Toronto has to offer...theatre, nightlife, shopping, world-famous tourist attractions. Next time you're passing through, stay with us and help us celebrate 17 years.

**Address: 246 Sherbourne St, Toronto, ON M5A 2S1 Canada.**
**Tel: (416) 968-2323, Reservations: (800) 205-3694, Fax: (416) 413-0485,**
**E-mail: catnaps@onramp.ca.**

**Type:** Bed & breakfast guesthouse.
**Clientele:** Good mix of gay men & women
**To Gay Bars:** 2 blocks or 1/4 mile. 5 minutes by foot.
**Rooms:** 9 rooms.
**Bathrooms:** 1 private toilet only, 2 shared bath/shower/toilets.
**Meals:** Expanded continental breakfast with fresh-baked goods.
**Vegetarian:** Readily available.
**Complimentary:** Coffee & tea all day.
**Dates Open:** All year.
**High Season:** May through September (Victoria Day through Labour Day).
**Rates:** Rooms CDN $39-$65.
**Discounts:** Coupons sent to our mailing list. Off-season weekly & monthly rates.
**Credit Cards:** MC & VISA.
**Rsv'tns:** Recommended.
**Reserve Through:** Call direct.
**Minimum Stay:** 2 nights on holiday weekends.
**Parking:** Adequate off-street parking, CDN $5 per night.
**In-Room:** Color cable TV, AC, clock radios, ceiling fans & maid service.
**On-Premises:** Laundry facilities, kitchen, tourist information, courtesy phone.
**Exercise/Health:** Gym, weights, sauna, steam, massage & Jacuzzi nearby.
**Swimming:** Lake Ontario (Toronto Islands), YMCA & other clubs nearby.
**Sunbathing:** On beach at Toronto Islands and on house sun decks (private & common).
**Smoking:** Permitted in some guest rooms, kitchen, garden & decks.
**Pets:** Small pets permitted by prior arrangement.
**Handicap Access:** No.
**Children:** Welcomed, some restrictions. Reservations required.
**Languages:** English, French & German.

## Divine Lake Nature's Sport & Spa Resort

**Gay-Friendly ♀♂**

Gay-friendly ***Divine Lake*** is in Muskoka amid 86 acres of lovely nature 2 hours north of Toronto. Cottages and chalets with fireplaces and kitchenettes are available. There are two lounges, a bar, a restaurant, heated pool, hot tub, Finnish sauna, tennis court, table-tennis, pool table, TV-video room, and conference rooms. Outdoor activities include boating, windsurfing, fishing, hiking on breath-taking trails, cross-country skiing, and motorboat tours. Stay with us at ***Divine Lake Nature's Sport & Spa Resort,*** in Canada.

**Tel: (705) 385-1212, Fax: (705) 385-1283. Information & reservations (Canada & USA): (800) 263-6600.**

**Type:** Resort with restaurant, bar, shops.
**Clientele:** Gay & straight clientele
**Transportation:** Free pick up from Port Sydney bus station & Huntsville train station.
**To Gay Bars:** In Toronto, a 2-hour drive.
**Rooms:** 10 cottages, 9 chalets.
**Bathrooms:** All private.
**Meals:** Full breakfast, dinner.
**Vegetarian:** Available on request when booking.
**Complimentary:** Tea & coffee.
**Dates Open:** All year.
**High Season:** June- Oct.
**Rates:** CDN $91-$122 per person per night. Cottage for 2, from CDN $600 per week, without meals.
**Discounts:** Special packages available.
**Credit Cards:** MC, Visa & Amex.
**Rsv'tns:** Required.
**Reserve Through:** Travel agent or call direct.
**Parking:** Ample free parking.
**In-Room:** Fireplace, color TV, VCR, kitchen, refrigerator, maid service.
**On-Premises:** Meeting rooms, TV lounge, laundry facilities for guests.
**Exercise/Health:** Health spa with steam/herb sauna, massage, mudpacks, gym, tennis court. Spa packages available.
**Swimming:** Heated pool on premises, lake.
**Sunbathing:** Poolside, on sun deck, at the beach.
**Smoking:** In designated dining rm. area, lounge; non-smoking rms. available.
**Handicap Access:** Yes, bathroom.
**Languages:** French, English & German.

IGTA

## The Dundonald House

**Gay/Lesbian ♀♂**

### *An Oasis of Calm in Busy Downtown Toronto*

From the moment you walk through our marvelous stained-glass front door you are a guest in our home, ***The Dundonald House.*** Built in 1907, the bed and breakfast's grandeur and comfort places it among the stately homes of Toronto. Guestrooms are uncluttered and comfortable, and breakfast is served in our contemporary glass and chrome dining room. Our location on a small street between Church and Yonge streets, truly makes us an oasis in this exciting area of downtown Toronto. The Church/Wellesley corner is the center of Toronto's large gay community, and shops, cafes, restaurants and Yonge St. are within walking distance.

**Address: 35 Dundonald Street, Toronto, ON M4Y 1K3 Canada.**
**Tel: (416) 961-9888, (800) 260-7227, Fax: (416) 961-2120.**
**E-mail: dundonal@idirect.com. http://www2.cglbrd.com/dundonald.**

**Type:** Bed & breakfast.
**Clientele:** Gay & lesbian. Good mix of men & women
**Transportation:** Taxi. Pick up from airport, train or bus, charge negotiable.
**To Gay Bars:** 1 block, a 2 min drive.
**Rooms:** 7 rooms with single, double or queen beds.
**Bathrooms:** Shared: 2 bathtubs only, 3 showers only, 2 bath/shower/toilets.
**Meals:** Full breakfast.
**Vegetarian:** Special requests available. Vegetarian restaurant on Dundonald St.
**Comp.:** Mints on pillows.
**Dates Open:** All year.
**High Season:** May-Sep.
**Rates:** CDN $60-$125.
**Credit Cards:** MC, Visa, Amex.
**Rsv'tns:** Required.
**Reserve Through:** Travel agent or call direct.
**Parking:** Ample pay parking.
**In-Room:** AC, laundry service.
**On-Premises:** TV lounge, video tape library.
**Exercise/Health:** Jacuzzi, sauna, massage. Nearby gym, weights, Jacuzzi, sauna, steam, massage.
**Swimming:** Nearby pool & lake.
**Sunbathing:** On patio & private sun decks.
**Smoking:** Permitted in designated areas. Non-smoking rooms available.
**Pets:** Not permitted.
**Languages:** English, Italian, Portuguese, Spanish.
**Your Host:** Warren & Dave.

# Ten Cawthra Square B&B & Guesthouse

Q-NET Gay/Lesbian ♀♂

## *Living in Style*

Take your ease in our elegantly appointed Edwardian home, a beautiful retreat in the heart of Toronto's vibrant gay village. The salon, with its fireplace and grand piano, looks out onto a quiet, tree-shaded street. ***Ten Cawthra Square B&B's*** spacious guest rooms provide private terraces and a continental breakfast is served in a bright country kitchen.

The entire city and all of its attractions are quickly and easily accessible via the nearby subway. A few steps across the adjacent park you will find the most inviting array of shops, restaurants, cafes & nightclubs that Toronto has to offer. The city's best theatres, museums and galleries are also all at your doorstep. No matter what you do, you are certain to enjoy yourself in this enchanting atmosphere with all the comforts of home.

**Address: 10 Cawthra Square, Toronto, ON M4Y 1K8 Canada.**
**Tel: (416) 966-3074, (800) 259-5474, Fax: (416) 966-4494,**
**E-mail: host@cawthra.com.**

**Type:** Bed & breakfast guesthouse.
**Clientele:** Mostly gay & lesbian with some straight clientele
**Transportation:** Airport bus to subway. Readily accessible by all means of transportation. Fee for pick up.
**To Gay Bars:** 2 blocks, a 5-minute walk.
**Rooms:** 3+ rooms with double or queen beds.
**Bathrooms:** Shared: 2 bath/shower/toilets & 1 WC.
**Meals:** Expanded continental breakfast.
**Vegetarian:** Generally. Excellent vegetarian restaurants & supplies within a few blocks.
**Complimentary:** Sherry in room, tea & coffee, mints on pillow.
**Dates Open:** All year.
**High Season:** All year.
**Rates:** CDN $79-CDN $125 (introductory rates still in effect).
**Discounts:** Please inquire.
**Credit Cards:** MC, Visa.
**Rsv'tns:** Required.
**Reserve Through:** Travel agent or call direct.
**Parking:** Ample covered off-street parking.
**In-Room:** Color TV, VCR, ceiling fans, AC, laundry service.
**On-Premises:** Meeting rooms, business service (complete home office: access to Internet, fax, PC, copier, etc.), laundry facilities.
**Exercise/Health:** Jacuzzi, massage. Nearby gym, weights, Jacuzzi, sauna, steam, massage, cycling & running trails, tennis.
**Swimming:** Nearby pool & lake.
**Sunbathing:** On private & common sun decks, patio.
**Smoking:** Permitted outdoors only. Strictly non-smoking inside.
**Pets:** Permitted if socialized & restricted. There are 2 house dogs on premises.
**Handicap Access:** No.
**Children:** No.
**Languages:** English, ASL.
**Your Host:** Ric & Frank.

IGTA

# QUEBEC

## MONTRÉAL

### Alacoque Bed & Breakfast

Gay-Friendly 50/50 ♀♂

*"My Pleasure to Welcome You"*

An authentic town house from the early 1900s, ***Alacoque Bed & Breakfast*** features authentic pinewood floors, antique furnishings and fireplaces. Accommodations include two beautiful suites with two bedrooms, fireplaces, kitchen and private baths. Our location is excellent for accessing Montreal's many cultural activities which take place throughout the year. We are a one-minute walk from the Place des Arts and a 10-minute walk from the gay village and McGill University. Your host and owner is from Lyon, France and he will be happy to help you discover the "French" flavour of his establishment. Member: Montreal Tourist Office.

**Address: 2091 St-Urbain, Montreal, PQ H2X 2N1 Canada. Tel: (514) 842-0938, Fax: (514) 842-7585.**

**Type:** Bed & breakfast.
**Clientele:** 50% gay & lesbian & 50% hetero clientele
**Transportation:** Taxi or bus.
**To Gay Bars:** 15 blocks, 1 mile to gay bars, a 10 minute walk, a 5 minute drive.
**Rooms:** 8 rooms, 2 suites with single, double or queen beds.
**Bathrooms:** 2 private bath/shower/toilets, 4 shared bath/shower/toilets.
**Meals:** Full breakfast with fresh croissants.
**Vegetarian:** Available within a 5 minute walk.
**Dates Open:** All year.
**High Season:** May-October.
**Rates:** Singles: CDN 35-CDN $50. Twins, doubles & triples: CDN $45-CDN $85.
**Discounts:** On long stays.
**Credit Cards:** Visa.
**Rsv'tns:** Required, if possible.
**Reserve Through:** Call direct.
**Parking:** Adequate free covered on- & off-street parking.
**In-Room:** AC, color TV, ceiling fans, laundry & room service.
**On-Premises:** TV lounge, laundry facilities
**Exercise/Health:** Nearby gym, weights, Jacuzzi, sauna, steam, massage.
**Swimming:** Pool nearby.
**Sunbathing:** On patio.
**Smoking:** Please ask for smoking room.
**Pets:** Ask when making reservation.
**Handicap Access:** No.
**Children:** Welcome.
**Languages:** French, English.
**Your Host:** Christian.

# Au Bon Vivant Guest House

**Gay/Lesbian ♂**

## *A Fine Home for the Discerning Traveller*

Welcome to the ***Au Bon Vivant Guest House.*** Ideally located in the gay village, we are steps from the Metro, Latin Quarter, clubs, restaurants, and Lafontaine Park. We are also adjacent to gay-friendly Plateau Mount-Royal and within easy access to tourist attractions. Our three guest rooms share a bath and common living room. The colour scheme, Persian carpets and antiques were specifically chosen to create a calming, warm and inviting atmosphere. Our motto, "A fine home for the discerning traveller," hopefully describes the ambience we have created. We sincerely hope your stay with us is enjoyable and that you visit us again.

**Address: 1648 Amherst, Montréal, QC H2L 3L5 Canada.**
**Tel: (514) 525-7744, Fax (514) 525-2874.**

**Type:** Bed & breakfast guesthouse
**Clientele:** Mostly men with women welcome
**Transportation:** Airport bus to Berri terminal.
**To Gay Bars:** 1 block.
**Rooms:** 4 rooms with single, double or queen beds.
**Bathrooms:** 2 shared bath/shower/toilet.
**Meals:** Buffet breakfast.
**Vegetarian:** Available upon request.
**Complimentary:** Tea, coffee & juice.
**Dates Open:** All year.
**High Season:** May-Oct.
**Rates:** High CDN $59-$89. Low CDN $40-$75.
**Discounts:** 10%-15% for stays of 7 or more days during low season.
**Credit Cards:** MC, VISA & Amex.
**Rsv'tns:** Required.
**Reserve Through:** Travel agent or call direct.
**Parking:** Adequate off-street parking.
**In-Room:** Ceiling fans, AC.
**On-Premises:** TV lounge & laundry facilities.
**Exercise/Health:** Nearby gym, weights, Jacuzzi, sauna, steam & massage.
**Swimming:** Nearby pool.
**Sunbathing:** On common sun decks.
**Smoking:** Not permitted.
**Pets:** Not permitted.
**Handicap Access:** No.
**Children:** No.
**Languages:** French, English & some Spanish.
**Your Host:** Marcel & Derek.

# Aux Berges

Men ♂

## *Canada's Finest All Male Hotel*

From the time *Aux Berges* was founded in 1967, it has acquired an atmosphere which is relatively unique among establishments having a constant flow of guests. The fact that they are from various countries and backgrounds certainly helps to make their stay with us a most pleasant and memorable experience. We regard ourselves as a large family, and would gladly welcome you to join us. Our staff are always ready to help you with any problems you might have during your stay in Montréal.

**Address: 1070 rue Mackay, Montréal, QC H3G 2H1 Canada.**
**Tel: (514) 938-9393, (800) 668-6253, Fax: (514) 938-1616.**

**Type:** Hotel.
**Clientele:** Men only
**Transportation:** Airport bus to Sheraton Center Hotel, then 5-minute walk, or taxi directly from airport CDN $25.
**To Gay Bars:** 1 block to gay bar.
**Rooms:** 42 rooms with double beds.
**Bathrooms:** 29 private, 13 shared.
**Meals:** Continental breakfast.
**Dates Open:** All year.
**High Season:** May-October.
**Rates:** CDN $65-CDN $100.
**Discounts:** On 7-day stay, 2 days free (good Nov-Mar.).
**Credit Cards:** MC, Visa, Amex, Diners Club, En Route & Discover.
**Rsv'tns:** Recommended.
**Reserve Through:** Travel agent or call direct.
**Parking:** Adequate on- & off-street parking.
**In-Room:** Color TV with video, in-house movies, AC, telephone, laundry & maid service.
**On-Premises:** Kitchen facilities, TV lounge, snack bar.
**Exercise/Health:** Jacuzzi, dry & steam saunas.
**Swimming:** Pool & lake nearby.
**Sunbathing:** On private sun deck & terrace.
**Nudity:** Permitted on the sun deck, terrace & sauna area.
**Smoking:** Permitted without restrictions.
**Pets:** Small pets permitted.
**Handicap Access:** No.
**Children:** Not permitted.
**Languages:** French, English, German & Spanish.
**Your Host:** Serge & Christian.

## Château Cherrier B&B

Gay/Lesbian ♀♂

*Château Cherrier* is a magnificent Tudor building decorated throughout with authentic period furniture. Large original oils of the same period adorn the sitting room and entry. Our strategic location near the gay village, restaurants, boutiques and nightlife, is further enhanced by a private parking lot, a rarity in the area. Leo and Jacques invite you to experience Montréal.

**Address: 550 rue Cherrier, Montréal, QC H2L 1H3 Canada. Tel: (514) 844-0055, (800) 816-0055, Fax: (514) 844-8438.**

**Type:** Bed & breakfast in a private home.
**Clientele:** Mainly gay/lesbian with some hetero clientele
**Transportation:** Taxi from airport 20 minutes. Limousine service (flat rate charge).
**To Gay Bars:** 4 blks to rue Ste-Catherine gay bars.
**Rooms:** 8 rooms with double & twin beds & a fourfold.
**Bathrooms:** 1 private bath/toilet/shower, 2 shared showers, & 4 shared toilets.
**Meals:** Full breakfast prepared by Chef Leo.
**Complimentary:** Ice cubes.
**Dates Open:** April 1-November 30.
**Rates:** CDN $50-$75+.
**Credit Cards:** MC, VISA, Amex.
**Rsv'tns:** Required.
**Reserve Through:** Travel agent or call direct. TAC 15%.
**Minimum Stay:** 3 nights long weekends or grand event.
**Parking:** Free private valet parking.
**In-Room:** AC, fan, color cable TV and maid service.
**On-Premises:** 2 living rooms, laundry service on long stays, shared refrigerator, safety box.
**Smoking:** Permitted in lounge only, not in rooms.
**Languages:** French, English, Spanish.

## La Conciergerie Guest House

Q-NET Gay/Lesbian ♂

### *Your Resort in the City!*

*La Conciergerie* is Montréal's premier guest house. Since our opening in 1985, we have gained an ever-growing popularity among travelers from Canada, the United States, Europe and Australia, winning the 1995 Out & About Editor's Choice Award. The beautiful Victorian home, built in 1885, offers 17 air-conditioned rooms with queen-sized beds and duvet comforters. A complimentary European breakfast is served either in the breakfast room or on an outdoor terrace.The house is within walking distance of most major points of interest, including downtown shopping, Old Montréal, rue St.-Denis, rue Ste.-Catherine, and the East Village, with its many gay shops, restaurants and bars. We're two blocks from the Metro (subway) and there is plenty of on-street parking for those who drive.

**Address: 1019 rue St.-Hubert, Montréal, QC H2L 3Y3 Canada. Tel: (514) 289-9297, Fax: (514) 289-0845, http://www.gaibec.com.**

**Type:** Bed & breakfast.
**Clientele:** Mostly men with women welcome
**Transportation:** Airport bus to Voyageur Bus Station, then walk, or taxi directly for CDN $25. Take a cab if arriving by train.
**To Gay Bars:** 2 blocks to men's & women's bars.
**Rooms:** 17 rooms with queen beds.
**Bathrooms:** 9 private. Shared: 1 bathtub, 3 showers, 3 toilets, 1 full bath.
**Meals:** Expanded continental breakfast.
**Vegetarian:** Bring your own. Vegetarian restaurants nearby.
**Dates Open:** All year.
**High Season:** April-December.
**Rates:** High season CDN $72-$135, low season CDN $52-$110.
**Discounts:** On 7-day stays in off-season.
**Credit Cards:** MC, Visa, Amex & Diners.
**Rsv'tns:** Recommended.
**Reserve Through:** Call direct.
**Minimum Stay:** 3 nights on long weekends.
**Parking:** Ample free on-street parking.
**In-Room:** Maid service & AC.
**On-Premises:** Meeting rooms, TV lounge, public telephone, central AC/heat, laundry facilities, private terrace, gardens, & kitchen privileges.
**Exercise/Health:** Jacuzzi & small gym on premises. Massage by appointment only.
**Swimming:** At nearby pool.
**Sunbathing:** On common sun deck & roof.
**Nudity:** Permitted on roof & Jacuzzi.
**Smoking:** Permitted, except in bedrooms.
**Pets:** Permitted with prior notice.
**Handicap Access:** No.
**Children:** Not permitted.
**Languages:** French & English.
**Your Host:** Luc & Michael.

IGTA

## La Douillette

**Women ♀**

### *Love to Travel, but Hate to Leave Home & Cat? Borrow Mine!*

***La Douillette*** is a private home with small garden, purring cat and wonderful cuisine. The house, furnished with antiques, conveys a feeling of tranquility. Each room is supplied with local maps and information about current events, to help you enjoy this great city of Montréal to the fullest. I will also be pleased to advise you in any way that will help you enjoy your stay. In summer, relax and enjoy a home-cooked breakfast in our flower garden. Bienvenue à toutes! *Micheline*

**Address: 7235 de Lorimier St, Montréal, QC H2E 2N9 Canada. Tel: (514) 376-2183.**

**Type:** Bed & breakfast.
**Clientele:** Women only
**Transportation:** Pickup from airport when possible, CDN $15.00. Bus from airport to Bonaventure Subway Stn, then to Fabre Stn.
**To Gay Bars:** 15 minutes by car or metro.
**Rooms:** 3 rooms with double or queen beds.
**Bathrooms:** 1 shared bath/shower/toilet.
**Meals:** Full breakfast.
**Vegetarian:** Available at all times.
**Complimentary:** Juices, tea, coffee & chocolates.
**Dates Open:** All year.
**High Season:** Spring, summer & autumn.
**Rates:** CDN $40-$60.
**Rsv'tns:** Recommended.
**Reserve Through:** Call direct.
**Parking:** Ample on-street parking.
**In-Room:** Ceiling fans.
**On-Premises:** TV/stereo lounge.
**Swimming:** At free nearby pool or river.
**Smoking:** Permitted with some restrictions.
**Pets:** Not permitted.
**Handicap Access:** No.
**Children:** Permitted with restrictions.
**Languages:** French, English, Spanish & German.
**Your Host:** Micheline.

## Le St. Christophe Bed & Breakfast

Men ♂

### *An Unexpected Canadian Treat*

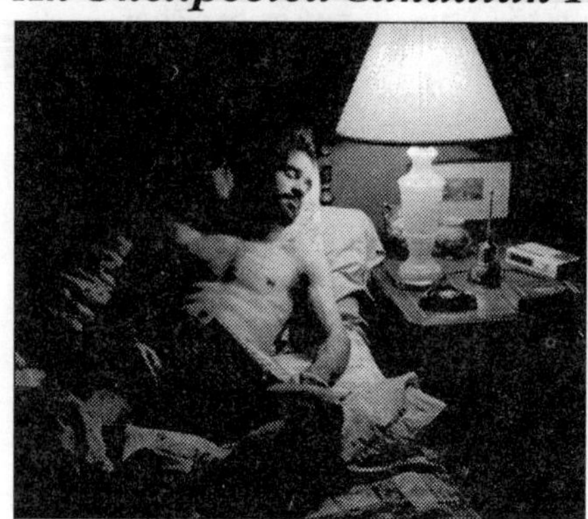

A Montreal-style townhouse built in 1875, ***Le St-Christophe*** is now fully restored to offer guests all the modern luxuries while maintaining the charm of the past. For more than nine years we have collected and filled our inn with antiques and memorabilia to enchant and delight you. There is always something new to discover at ***Le St-Christophe.***

We offer five spacious guest rooms: The Library, The French Canadian, The Sunrise, The Gallery and The China Room, each decorated in a different theme. Some have their own private baths, others share bathrooms, and all have color TVs and VCRs. There are two common rooms for your enjoyment. The first one is a great place for relaxing, reading or just socializing. It houses our collection of sailing ships reminiscent of the type Captain Jacques St-Pierre, the original owner of the house, once sailed. The second common room, also a nice place in which to spend some time, has a working fireplace, a small library of gay reading materials and a four-man Jacuzzi.

As one of your day's highlights, a full breakfast is served each morning from 9:00 am to 11:00 am either in our dining room or on the breakfast deck. Seated at your own table, you can expect eggs Benedict, omelets, or Stephen's famous French toast. We also offer our guests the use of our very private rooftop sun deck, where you will find sun all day and a million stars at night. Clothing is optional, of course. ***Le St-Christophe*** is located in the East end of Montreal in the area known as the gay village. It is one block from Ste-Catharine St., where all of the gay bars and restaurants are situated, and is within walking distance of places like Old Montreal, rue St-Denis and China Town.

**Address: 1597 St.-Christophe, Montréal, QC H2L 3W7 Canada.**
**Tel: (514) 527-7836.**

**Type:** Bed & breakfast guesthouse with full breakfast.
**Clientele:** Men only
**Transportation:** Airport bus to Voyageur bus station. Walk one block. Take metro to Berri if arriving by train.
**To Gay Bars:** 1 block.
**Rooms:** 5 rooms with double beds.
**Bathrooms:** 2 private shower/toilets, 1 private sink. 2 shared full baths.
**Meals:** Full breakfast.
**Vegetarian:** Available by pre-arrangement.
**Complimentary:** Fruits, coffee & tea.
**Dates Open:** All year.
**High Season:** Easter through Thanksgiving.
**Rates:** CDN $50-$69. High season CDN $60-$79.
**Discounts:** On 7-day stays in off season.
**Credit Cards:** MC & VISA.
**Rsv'tns:** Required.
**Reserve Through:** Call direct.
**Minimum Stay:** 3 nights on long weekends.
**Parking:** Ample, free on-street parking.
**In-Room:** Color TV & VCR with video tapes, ceiling fans, maid service.
**On-Premises:** 2 lounges, private dining room, laundry service, working fireplace, breakfast deck.
**Exercise/Health:** Jacuzzi.
**Swimming:** Nearby pool.
**Sunbathing:** On private sun decks.
**Nudity:** Permitted.
**Smoking:** Permitted without restrictions.
**Pets:** Permitted with prior notice.
**Handicap Access:** No.
**Children:** Not permitted.
**Languages:** French & English.
**Your Host:** Stephen.

## Pension Vallières

Women ♀

### *We Welcome You to Montréal!*

We extend a warm welcome to guests at ***Pension Vallières,*** our cozy, quiet home in Montréal. The house is decorated in an "Art Deco" style and we offer two choices of accommodation. We have a bedroom with queen-sized bed, as well as a fully-equipped studio with a private entrance. Amenities in the studio include kitchenette, private bath, pool table, color cable TV and a stereo. You may choose from a variety of hearty breakfasts, which, if you like, we will serve in your room. To help make the most of your stay in Montréal, your hostess, Lucille, is available to take you on a sightseeing tour of this beautiful city.

**Address: 6562, Delorimier St, Montréal, QC H2G 2P6 Canada. Tel: (514) 729-9552.**

**Type:** Bed & breakfast.
**Clientele:** 95% women, men welcome
**Transportation:** Pick up from airport, train (CDN $25-$35), bus. #18 bus from airport to Bonaventure Subway Sta, then to Beaubien Station
**To Gay Bars:** 10 minutes by Métro.
**Rooms:** 1 room & 1 bachelor studio (private bath) with double or queen bed.
**Bathrooms:** 1 private bath/shower/toilet & 1 shared bath/shower/toilet.
**Meals:** Full breakfast.
**Vegetarian:** 5-minute walk to vegetarian food store.
**Complimentary:** Tea, herbal tea, coffee & juice.
**Dates Open:** All year.
**High Season:** Spring, summer, autumn.
**Rates:** 1 person CDN $50, 2 people CDN $60, each addt'l person CDN $15.
**Discounts:** 10% for stays of over 8 nights.
**Rsv'tns:** Required.
**Reserve ThrU:** Call direct.
**Parking:** Ample on-street parking.
**In-Room:** Ceiling fan, coffee/tea-making facilities, room & maid service. Studio has color cable TV, kitchen.
**On-Premises:** Pool table, stereo & laundry facilities.
**Sunbathing:** Beach on Notre Dame islands.
**Smoking:** Permitted without restriction.
**Pets:** Not permitted.
**Children:** Permitted.
**Languages:** French & English.
**Your Host:** Lucille.

# QUÉBEC

## Le Coureur des Bois

Gay/Lesbian ♀♂

***Le Coureur des Bois*** is located in a historic stone house typical of the early French Canadian period. Well-maintained, the interior of the house is modern. Seven guest rooms, each with its own character, are simply furnished with emphasis on cleanliness and comfort. None of our rooms have private bath, but with 3 full baths to 7 rooms, we've yet to have anyone complain. Fresh fruit, croissants, rolls, muffins, cheeses, cereals and coffee make up the continental breakfast. What distinguishes us from the competition is our unique location within the walled city and the famous ***Coureur des Bois*** hospitality.

**Address: 15 rue Ste.-Ursule, Québec, QC G1R 4C7 Canada. Tel: (418) 692-1117, (800) 269-6414.**

**Type:** Guesthouse.
**Clientele:** Good mix of gay men & women
**Transportation:** Taxi from airport or train.
**To Gay Bars:** 6-minute walk to gay/lesbian bars.
**Rooms:** 7 rooms with double or queen beds.
**Bathrooms:** 3 shared.
**Meals:** Our continental breakfast is a hearty combination of croissants, muffins, sweet breads, fruit dishes, cereals & assorted beverages.
**Vegetarian:** Available with advance notice.
**Dates Open:** All year.
**High Season:** Apr-Nov.
**Rates:** CDN $42-$92.
**Credit Cards:** MC, VISA, Amex & Diners.
**Rsv'tns:** Recommended.
**Reserve Through:** Travel agent or call direct.
**Parking:** 4-minute walk to underground parking for CDN $6 per day.
**In-Room:** Maid service.
**On-Premises:** TV lounge, outdoor terrace, & fridge in lounge.
**Swimming:** River & lake 15 minutes by car.
**Sunbathing:** On the terrace.
**Smoking:** Permitted, but not in bedrooms.
**Pets:** Permitted by prior arrangement.
**Children:** Not permitted.
**Languages:** French & English.
**Your Host:** Jean Paul & Mark.

# SASKATCHEWAN

## RAVENSCRAG

### Spring Valley Guest Ranch

**Gay-Owned 50/50 ♀♂**

Enjoy bed and breakfast at ***Spring Valley Guest Ranch*** in a cozy 3-story, 1913-era home where the home-cooked meals are prepared in "The Country" Tearoom. The tearoom specializes in croissants and serves three meals daily. For a different experience, you can stay in a log cabin. Wood, water and outdoor washrooms are furnished. Activities include horseback riding, lawn games and hiking. The area is excellent for naturalists, photographers, historians, hikers or anyone who can appreciate silence and solitude.

**Address: Box 10, Ravenscrag, SK S0N 0T0 Canada.**
**Tel: (306) 295-4124.**

**Type:** Bed & breakfast & campground with restaurant.
**Clientele:** 50% gay & lesbian & 50% straight clientele
**Transportation:** Private auto best.
**To Gay Bars:** No gay bars in area.
**Rooms:** 4 doubles in house. 2 doubles in log cabin.
**Bathrooms:** 1 shared in house. Outdoor facilities for cabin.
**Campsites:** Unlimited space for tents, trailers, RV's but no water or electrical hook-ups.
**Meals:** Full breakfast for B&B guests.
**Vegetarian:** Fresh vegetables available, no special dishes cooked.
**Dates Open:** All year.
**High Season:** July-August.
**Rates:** Log cabin & house: single CDN $35, double CDN $55.
**Discounts:** Group discounts for wilderness camp.
**Credit Cards:** MC, Visa.
**Rsv'tns:** Required one week in advance.
**Reserve Through:** Call direct.
**Parking:** Ample free parking.
**In-Room:** Maid service, room service.
**On-Premises:** Laundry facilities, public telephone, TV lounge, refrigerator.
**Exercise/Health:** Horseback riding on the ranch.
**Sunbathing:** On lawn.
**Smoking:** Permitted in TV lounge and restaurant.
**Pets:** Permitted, except in restaurant & kitchen.
**Handicap Access:** No.
**Children:** Permitted but no cribs or facilities for infants.
**Languages:** English.
**Your Host:** Jim.

CARIBBEAN

# BRITISH WEST INDIES

## JAMAICA

### Hotel Mocking Bird Hill

Q-NET Gay-Friendly ♀♂

***Where Your Heart Will Sing & Your Soul Will Fly***

The breathtaking mountain views and ocean vistas at ***Hotel Mocking Bird Hill*** will refresh your spirit. This elegant, charming retreat nestled in 6.5, lush, tropical acres has spacious, airy rooms with original art, while the hotel's gallery offers insight into Jamaican art and culture. The clientele is international and the cuisine is creative, using only fresh local produce, some from the hotel's own gardens. This intimate hotel with warm hospitality and personal touches from the innkeepers is also environmentally friendly. Nearby are rainforests, mountains, and numerous waterfalls, romantic coves, and beautiful beaches.

**Address: PO Box 254, Port Antonio Jamaica.**
**Tel: (809) 993-7267, (809) 993-7134, Fax: (809) 993-7133.**
**E-mail: mockbrd@toj.com.**

**Type:** Private, intimate hotel with restaurant, bar, gallery.
**Clientele:** Straight clientele with a gay & lesbian following
**Transportation:** From Kingston: car rental or taxi. From Montego Bay: Inland flight to Port Antonio airport with free transfer to hotel.
**Rooms:** 10 rooms with single, queen or king beds.
**Bathrooms:** 7 en suite shower/toilets, 3 en suite bath/toilet/showers.
**Meals:** Additional charge for meals.
**Vegetarian:** Meals included in menu.
**Complimentary:** Welcome cocktail. Fresh fruit & flowers in room, small gift.
**Dates Open:** All year.
**High Season:** Dec 15-Apr 30.
**Rates:** For double room: Summer '97 US $95-$110. Winter '96/97 US $130-$150.
**Discounts:** Group rates (10 or more people), long stays, repeat guests. Call/fax for off-season specials. Jan 6-Feb 28 & May 1-June 30.
**Credit Cards:** MC, Visa, Eurocard, Amex.
**Rsv'tns:** Recommeded. Walk-ins welcome.
**Reserve Through:** Travel agent or call/fax direct.
**Parking:** Ample free off-street parking.
**In-Room:** Ceiling fans, safe, laundry service, balcony with ocean view.
**On-Premises:** TV lounge, telephone, babysitters, special tours & hikes arranged.
**Exercise/Health:** Walking/jogging trail, horseback riding, hiking. Massage with prior appointment.
**Swimming:** Pool, ocean, rivers, waterfalls.
**Sunbathing:** At poolside, beach or in the garden.
**Smoking:** Permitted. Non-smoking rooms available.
**Pets:** Not permitted. Dogs & cats on premises
**Handicap Access:** Yes. Limited, with no special facilities.
**Children:** Welcome, but not encouraged.
**Languages:** English, German & French.
**Your Host:** Barbara & Shireen.

# Muscle & Art B&B

Q-NET Gay/Lesbian ♂

## *It's Summer All Year in Kingston*

Gay-owned and -operated, ***Muscle & Art B&B*** is a certified member of the Jamaican Tourist Board Bed & Breakfast Programme. Its household setting offers an opportunity for social and cultural exchange in a comfortable suburban area 20 minutes from Kingston's business centre and a public beach. Divine fusion cuisine, reggae music and making new friends will enhance your stay at ***Muscle & Art B&B.***

**Address: 1 Denham Ave, Meadowbrook Estates, Kingston 19 Jamaica.**
**Tel: (809) 933-1372 (Tel/Fax).**

**Type:** Bed & breakfast.
**Clientele:** Mostly men with women welcome
**Transportation:** Car is best.
**To Gay Bars:** 15-20 minutes from 2 gay bars/ private parties.
**Rooms:** 2 doubles, 1 single.
**Bathrooms:** Private & shared.
**Meals:** Complimentary breakfast (fusion cuisine), dinner served at extra cost.
**Vegetarian:** On menu & upon request.
**Complimentary:** Fresh fruit juice. Alcohol served at extra cost.
**Dates Open:** All year.
**High Season:** Nov-Apr.
**Rates:** US $45.
**Discounts:** Group rates for 3 or more persons; on stays of 10 days or more.
**Rsv'tns:** Required, please inquire.
**Reserve Through:** Travel agent or call or fax direct.
**Minimum Stay:** 2 nights.
**Parking:** On premises & free on-street parking.
**In-Room:** Maid service, fan.
**On-Premises:** Art gallery, cable TV, phone, fax, video, library, laundry & refrigerator. Info on gay-friendly areas, dress codes, etc. Tour guide can arrange excursions.
**Exercise/Health:** Jogging.
**Swimming:** 35 minutes to swimming.
**Nudity:** Permitted in house.
**Smoking:** Permitted outside.
**Pets:** Not permitted.
**Handicap Access:** No.
**Children:** No.
**Languages:** English.
**Your Host:** Lawrence.

## Tingalaya's Bed & Breakfast

Gay-Friendly ♀♂

### *A Country-Style Respite in Negril, Jamaica*

The caress of the sun... the splash of the sea... the fragrance of jasmine, and the sweet birdsong in the air are all yours in a natural seaside setting at ***Tingalaya's Bed & Breakfast.*** We are an intimate friendly retreat with a genuine Jamaican flavour. Guests sleep in beautiful terra-cotta thatched roof casitas, artistically decorated in tropical colors, the walls radiating the hue of the setting sun. ***Tingalaya's*** is great for singles, couples and groups of up to 12. Complimentary bicycles are available. We're on West End Road in Negril, Jamaica.

**Address: Write: 440 Ontario St, Toronto, ON M5A 2W1 Canada. Tel: Reservation number in Canada: (416) 924-4269. Tel. in Negril: (809) 957-0126. http://www.patriciamarsh.com/Tingalayas/main.html.**

**Type:** 2 separate terra-cotta units in southwest styles.
**Clientele:** Mostly straight clientele with a gay & lesbian following
**Transportation:** We can arrange paid transportation from Montego Bay.
**Rooms:** Each unit has 2 adjoining rooms with double beds. 2 rooms have addt'l loft, sleeping 2.
**Bathrooms:** Private bath ensuite.
**Campsites:** Yes.
**Meals:** Breakfast. Other meals upon request or use of kitchen.
**Vegetarian:** Yes.
**Complimentary:** Refreshments on arrival.
**Dates Open:** Year round.
**High Season:** Dec 1-Apr 30.
**Rates:** US $75-US $100 per room.
**Discounts:** May-Nov 25% discount.
**Rsv'tns:** Required.
**Minimum Stay:** 1 week.
**Parking:** Available.
**In-Room:** Maid service, porches with garden views, ceiling fan.
**On-Premises:** Outside kitchen & dining area.
**Swimming:** Small, rugged area on property with deep water & no beach. Only good swimmers unless it is calm.
**Sunbathing:** Beach, sand areas for private nude sunbathing.
**Nudity:** Permitted in private nude sunbathing area.
**Smoking:** We prefer that guests smoke outdoors.
**Handicap Access:** No.
**Children:** Must be supervised.
**Languages:** English.

# DOMINICAN REPUBLIC

## CABARETE

## Purple Paradise

Women ♀

### *Magic at the Rainbow's End*

Enjoy tranquility on an endless sandy beach. Chill out in the Jacuzzi and slide into the pool nestled in a lush garden. Savor scrumptious meals. Engage in quiet conversation in spacious, comfortable common areas, or simply admire the magnificent sea view. Visit our mountains and magical caves. Venture to nearby Cabarete for handmade gifts by local artisans. Do everything...or do nothing. At ***Purple Paradise,*** the choice is yours.

**Address: Mail: Hell Von Gogh, EPS D#184, PO Box 02-5548, Miami, FL 33102 USA. Tel: (809) 571-0637, Fax: (809) 571-0691.**

**Type:** Guesthouse with bar & art shop.
**Clientele:** Women only
**Transportation:** Taxi from airport direct to guesthouse.
**Rooms:** 5 rooms with single or double beds.
**Bathrooms:** All private shower/toilets.
**Vegetarian:** Served daily & vegetarian food nearby.
**Complimentary:** Welcome drink.
**Dates Open:** Nov-May, July-Sept.
**High Season:** December-March.
**Rates:** Winter $65 per night, summer $55 per night.
**Rsv'tns:** Required.
**Reserve Through:** Call direct.
**Parking:** Adequate free off-street parking.
**In-Room:** Maid service.
**On-Premises:** Indoor & outdoor lounge areas.
**Exercise/Health:** Jacuzzi on premises. Nearby gym, weights, massage, tennis, golf, windsurfing, scuba, snorkeling, mountain bikes, riding.
**Swimming:** Pool & ocean on premises. Nearby ocean & river.
**Sunbathing:** At poolside, on roof, patio, common & private sun decks & at the beach.
**Nudity:** Permitted in the pool.
**Smoking:** As the villa is "open air," smoking is permitted.
**Pets:** Not permitted.
**Handicap Access:** No.
**Children:** Not especially welcome.
**Languages:** Spanish, English, Dutch, German, French & Italian.

# DUTCH WEST INDIES

## SABA

### Captain's Quarters

Q-NET Gay-Friendly ♀♂

#### *The Unspoiled Queen of the Caribbean*

Orchids, tree frogs, crested hummingbirds, sea turtles, hot springs, snorkeling... Enjoy all of this when you stay at ***Captain's Quarters.*** This 16-room Victorian guesthouse (which has hosted royalty, celebrities, and adventurous travelers for more than 30 years) is set in a tropical paradise, a short 10-minute flight from St. Maarten. Rooms feature antique and four-poster beds, many with elegant canopies. From the balconies and patios are stunning views of the Caribbean and mountain scenery. Enjoy the garden dining pavilion, cliffside pool/bar, and some of the friendliest people in the Caribbean.

Saba is a storybook setting of Dutch gingerbread villages that date from the 1850s. Originally settled by pirates and sea captains as a safe haven for their families, "The Rock" was accessible only by footpaths and thousands of steps until "the Road that Couldn't be Built" was handcrafted in the 1950s. Saba will remind you of Switzerland with palm trees! World-class scuba diving, well-marked hiking trails, a pristine rainforest, and spectacular views at every turn make Saba unforgettable.

*continued next page*

**Note:** Saba has no beaches. All swimming is from rocks, boats, tidal pools, and hotel swimming pools. However, since you have to fly through St. Maarten anyway, spend a few days there and enjoy some of the best beaches in the world. Then visit us – just minutes away – for a few days.

**Address: Windwardside, Saba Netherlands Antilles.**
**Tel: (5994) 62201, Fax: (5994) 62377, In USA: (212) 289-6031, Fax: 289-1931. E-mail: Rich_Holm@msn.com. http://saba-online.com.**

**Type:** Hotel with restaurant & bar.
**Clientele:** Mostly straight clientele with a gay & lesbian following
**Transportation:** 10-minute flight from St. Maarten, on Wiriair (Wm). Airport transfer included in rates.
**To Gay Bars:** None. All bars on island are friendly.
**Rooms:** 16 rooms with double or queen beds.
**Bathrooms:** All private shower/toilets.
**Meals:** Full American breakfast.
**Vegetarian:** Available upon request.
**Complimentary:** Welcome drink.
**Dates Open:** All year.
**High Season:** Feb-Apr.
**Rates:** Summer $95-$150, extra person $35. Winter $115-$170, extra person $45, includes tax & service fee.
**Discounts:** For stays of 3 or more nights, group packages. Off-season discounts for groups.
**Credit Cards:** Visa, MC, Amex & Discover.
**Rsv'tns:** Required. Walk-ins based on availability.
**Reserve Through:** Travel agent or call direct.
**Parking:** Ample free off-street parking.
**In-Room:** Balcony & maid service. Some rooms with AC, color cable TV, ceiling fans, refrigerator.
**On-Premises:** Meeting rooms & TV lounge.
**Exercise/Health:** Nearby gym.
**Swimming:** Pool on premises. Nearby ocean.
**Sunbathing:** At poolside.
**Smoking:** Permitted.
**Pets:** Permitted with advance approval.
**Handicap Access:** No.
**Children:** Welcome.
**Languages:** English, Dutch, Papiamento & Spanish.

IGTA

# FRENCH WEST INDIES

## ST BARTHELEMY

### Hostellerie des Trois Forces

**Gay-Friendly ♀♂**

Authentic peacefulness is the soul of ***Hostellerie des Trois Forces,*** established by a French chef. Eight private cottages, some with private baths, have handmade wooden furnishings designed to complement the different zodiac signs. The hand-hewn, mountaintop restaurant serves French and Creole and vegetarian specialities and has a wood fire grill and a rolling flambé dessert cart. One guest said: "Don't miss Hubert's cooking, especially his salade des Trois Forces and filet mignon a la dijon." The restaurant has been reviewed by publications such as *GQ, Vogue, NY Times, Los Angeles Times, Conde Nast,* and *Caribbean Travel and Life.* Hubert received the 1995 gold medal award from the Academie de la Marnite d'Or for French cuisine. This academy has been in existence since 1657.

**Address: Vitet 97133, St. Barthelemy French West Indies.**
**Tel: Direct: (590) 276-125, Fax: (590) 278-138.**

**Type:** Inn with French & Creole & vegetarian restaurant & bar.
**Clientele:** Mostly straight clientele with a gay & lesbian following
**Transportation:** Taxi or rental car (we can reserve your car).
**To Gay Bars:** No gay bars on the island.
**Rooms:** 7 cottages, with four under construction.
**Bathrooms:** All private.
**Meals:** Continental breakfast, full breakfast available by special order.
**Vegetarian:** Food is love. We make French Creole vegetarian.
**Dates Open:** All year.
**High Season:** December through March.
**Rates:** US $75-$170.
**Credit Cards:** MC, VISA, Amex.
**Rsv'tns:** Required in high season, penalty for no-shows, cancellations.
**Reserve Through:** Travel agent or call or fax direct.
**Parking:** Adequate, free, off-street parking.
**In-Room:** Maid, room & laundry service, AC and every room has petit frigidaire.

**Exercise/Health:** Massage with polarity, yoga, astrological readings available.
**Swimming:** Pool on premises, ocean beach nearby.
**Sunbathing:** At poolside, on beach.
**Nudity:** Women can go topless by the pool. St. Barth has a nude beach.
**Smoking:** Permitted without restrictions.
**Pets:** Not permitted.
**Handicap Access:** No.
**Children:** Permitted.
**Languages:** English, French, German, some Spanish.

# PUERTO RICO

## PONCE

### Michael and Sebastian's

Gay/Lesbian ♀♂

*"The Pearl of the South"*

Welcome to ***Michael and Sebastian's!*** We take pride in helping you enjoy our friendly, casual and comfortable atmosphere while you discover Ponce, "The Pearl of the South." This southern part of the island is known for its warm, dry weather and true sense of hospitality. We are conveniently located in the center of Ponce, the second-largest city in Puerto Rico, and are a short walk to the Museum of Art and the restored Historical – Colonial downtown area. Shopping, movies, restaurants and several local colleges are also close at hand. The Hacienda "Buena Vista" coffee plantation, "Tibes" Indian Ceremonial Park, beaches, mountains and other local attractions are all within short driving distance.

Address: PO Box 221, Ponce, PR. Tel: (787) 284-0631 (Tel/Fax).

**Type:** Bed & breakfast.
**Clientele:** Mostly gay & lesbian with some straight clientele
**Transportation:** Car is best. Taxi service available in the area.
**To Gay Bars:** 2 miles, a 10 minute drive.
**Rooms:** 3 rooms with double or queen beds.
**Bathrooms:** 2 shared bath/shower/toilets.
**Meals:** Full breakfast.
**Vegetarian:** Available upon request. Vegetarian food nearby.
**Complimentary:** Coffee & tea.
**Dates Open:** All year.
**High Season:** November-March.
**Rates:** $40-$55.
**Discounts:** 10% on weekly stays.
**Credit Cards:** MC, Visa.
**Rsv'tns:** Required.
**Reserve Through:** Call direct.
**Minimum Stay:** 2 nights on weekends.
**Parking:** Adequate off-street parking.
**In-Room:** AC, maid service.
**Exercise/Health:** Nearby gym, weights, sauna, steam.
**Swimming:** Nearby pool, ocean.
**Sunbathing:** On patio, at beach.
**Smoking:** Permitted on terrace or patio.
**Pets:** Not permitted.
**Handicap Access:** No.
**Children:** No.
**Languages:** Spanish, English, French.

## SAN JUAN

### Embassy Guest House - Condado

Gay/Lesbian ♀♂

Welcome to the ***Embassy Guest House-Condado*** in the center of Condado, only steps to the beach in San Juan. Awaken to aqua-colored waters off Condado Beach. Relax under a coco palm. Dine at Panaché, our beachfront restaurant and bar. Or, enjoy nearby water and jet skiing, scuba diving, fishing, tennis, golf etc. The San Juan night, with casinos, discos, and shows, is nearby, as is shopping in Old San Juan. The ***Embassy*** staff helps you enjoy your stay, so come see why Puerto Rico is called the "Shining Star of the Caribbean."

*continued next page*

**Address: 1126 Calle Seaview-Condado, San Juan, PR 00907**
**Tel: (787) 725-8284 or (787) 724-7440, Fax: (787) 725-2400.**

**Type:** Guesthouse with restaurant & bar on the beach.
**Clientele:** Mainly gay/lesbian with some straight clientele
**Transportation:** Taxi or limo from airport, approx $15. 15-min drive.
**To Gay Bars:** On premises, others 4 blocks away.
**Rooms:** 1 suite, 7 doubles, 7 quads.
**Bathrooms:** All private.
**Vegetarian:** Upon request in Panache Restaurant.
**Complimentary:** Coffee, tea.
**Dates Open:** All year.
**High Season:** December 1st through May 1st.
**Rates:** $65-$145 Dec 15 to Apr 30, $45-$85 May 1 to Dec 14.
**Discounts:** 10% on weekly stays during off-season.
**Credit Cards:** MC, Visa, Amex.
**Rsv'tns:** Recommended.
**Reserve Through:** Travel agent or call direct.
**Minimum Stay:** 2 days on holidays & in season.
**Parking:** Ample, free on-street parking.
**In-Room:** Maid & room service, color TV, AC, ceiling fans, refrigerators & coffeemakers.
**On-Premises:** Restaurant, bar, TV lounge & public telephones.
**Swimming:** Ocean beach.
**Sunbathing:** On beach or sun decks.
**Smoking:** Permitted without restrictions.
**Pets:** Not permitted.
**Handicap Access:** Yes.
**Children:** Permitted, no infants, please.
**Languages:** Spanish, English, French.

IGTA

## Numero Uno Guest House

Q-NET Gay-Friendly 50/50 ♀♂

### *We Get Rave Reviews!*

Among the many accolades our Caribbean guesthouse has received over the years are: "***Numero Uno***...our home away from home..." – *The Washington Post,* October 1995; "***Numero Uno:*** With a name like that there's little doubt which of Ocean Park's flower-fringed guesthouses is the most stylish." – *Diversion,* July 1996; "...wonderfully relaxing..." – *The Washington Post,* January 1996.

In its Sunday, February 27, 1994 article the *San Francisco Examiner* quoted our guests' comments as follows: "On our recent trip to Puerto Rico, we were fortunate enough to have stayed at the ***Numero Uno.*** This charming guest house is located between Isla Verde and Condado and is ideally situated between the San Juan airport (15 minutes) and Old San Juan (10 minutes). Before we had even checked into our rooms, our hosts, Esther and Chris, served us a cold drink from the complete bar by the pool.

Chris was trained as a chef in New York and offers his culinary skills each night for those wanting to have dinner there. We took advantage of this our first night: fresh seafood kebabs (swordfish, scallops and shrimp), rice pilaf, tossed salad, fresh baby asparagus, homemade chocolate cheesecake and coffee. Even if you can't get a room here, it's worth it just to eat here. Dinner is served by the pool, and reservations are required. ***Numero Uno Guest House*** has been renovated over the past two years, and all of the rooms are spacious, with either double or king-sized beds and private baths, and include a continental breakfast. Rooms fronting the ocean are booked far in advance." – Sue I. and John T., Foster City

**Address: Calle Santa Ana #1, Ocean Park, San Juan, PR 00911**
**Tel: (787) 726-5010, (787) 727-5482.**

**Type:** Guesthouse with restaurant & bar.
**Clientele:** 50% gay & lesbian & 50% straight clientele
**Transportation:** Taxi, 10 min. from airport, fixed $12.
**To Gay Bars:** 4-6 blks.
**Rooms:** 12 rooms & 6 apartments with double, queen or king beds.
**Bathrooms:** All rooms have private bath/toilets or shower/toilets.
**Meals:** Expanded continental breakfast.
**Vegetarian:** We have several vegetarian options on our menu. Several health food stores/rests. nearby.
**Dates Open:** All year.
**High Season:** We book up in advance for December thru April.
**Rates:** Low sea. (May-Nov): $70-$105; high sea. (Dec-Apr): $85-$135.
**Discounts:** Inquire.
**Credit Cards:** MC, Visa, Amex.
**Rsv'tns:** Required.
**Reserve Through:** Travel agent or call direct.
**Minimum Stay:** 3 days during high season.
**Parking:** Adequate on-street parking.
**In-Room:** AC, ceiling fans, maid service.
**Exercise/Health:** Massage. Nearby gym, weights, Jacuzzi, sauna, steam, massage.
**Swimming:** Pool & ocean on premises.
**Sunbathing:** Poolside, on patio, at beach.
**Smoking:** Permitted, no non-smoking rooms available.
**Pets:** Permitted with some restrictions. Please call for details.
**Handicap Access:** Yes.
**Children:** Welcome.
**Languages:** Span., English.

IGTA

# Ocean Walk Guest House

Gay/Lesbian ♀♂

## *Where Europe Meets the Caribbean*

Formerly a series of Spanish-style homes located directly on the best part of San Juan's beach, ***Ocean Walk*** is now a very casual resort complex with 40 comfortable rooms in a beautiful courtyard setting, with pool, bar and grill. On the large, elevated sun deck, you can enjoy a piña colada, while the sun sets, in a spectacular display of colors, on the horizon. After midnight, all is quiet, and you will hear only the gentle pounding of the surf. Yet, the fast-paced nightlife and the casinos are within walking distance.

**Address: Calle Atlantic No 1, Ocean Park, San Juan, PR 00911**
**Tel: (787) 728-0855 or (800) 468-0615, Fax: (787) 728-6434.**

**Type:** Guesthouse with restaurant & bar.
**Clientele:** Gay & lesbian w/ some hetero clientele
**Transportation:** Taxi or rental car from San Juan Int'l Airport approx $12.
**To Gay Bars:** 10 min walk or short taxi ride.
**Rooms:** 40 rooms & 5 apartments with single, double & king beds.
**Bathrooms:** 34 private shower/toilets. 6 rooms share bath/shower/toilet.
**Meals:** Breakfast & lunch.
**Vegetarian:** Available upon request.
**Complimentary:** Coffee, tea, muffins, fruit on the patio (mornings until 11:00).
**Dates Open:** All year.
**High Season:** Dec 15-Apr 15.
**Rates:** US $40-$85 in sum. US $55-$130 in win.
**Discounts:** 10% airline discounts, weekly rates for minimum 2 weeks.
**Credit Cards:** MC, VISA, Amex, Discover & Eurocard.
**Rsv'tns:** Recommended.
**Reserve Through:** Travel agent or call direct.
**Minimum Stay:** 4 nights, Dec 16-March 1, if Sat or Sun is involved.
**Parking:** Adequate on-street parking.
**In-Room:** Color cable TV, ceiling fans & maid service. Some rooms have AC.
**On-Premises:** Telephones.
**Swimming:** At pool on premises or ocean beach.
**Sunbathing:** At poolside, beach & com. sun decks.
**Smoking:** Permitted.
**Pets:** Special permission required.
**Handicap Access:** Yes. Limited & with assistance.
**Children:** Welcomed.
**Languages:** English, Spanish, French & German.

IGTA

# VIEQUES ISLAND

## New Dawn Caribbean Retreat & Guest House

Gay/Lesbian ♀

### *Best of All Worlds...*

Enjoy both mountain rest AND beach life on this unspoiled Caribbean island of Vieques. Its location on 5 acres of Pilon hillside, dotted with hibiscus, bougainvillaeas & grazing horses makes ***New Dawn Caribbean Retreat & Guest House*** a complete environment of natural beauty. The main house is flower-covered and built for outdoor living with spacious decks. There are also a women's bunkhouse and tent sites. ***New Dawn*** was designed for people who like to go barefoot & who don't need all the comforts of home, but seek a truly relaxed, peaceful atmosphere.

**Address: PO Box 1512, Bo Pilon, Rt 995, Vieques, PR 00765**
**Tel: (787) 741-0495.**

**Type:** Guesthouse & campground retreat with restaurant & bar.
**Clientele:** Mostly women with men welcome, some straight clientele
**Transportation:** Rent a car or call on arrival for $5 pick up from airport or ferry dock.
**To Gay Bars:** San Juan gay/lesbian bars 2 hrs away on main island of Puerto Rico.
**Rooms:** 6 rooms & bunkhouse which sleeps six. Single, bunk & queen beds.
**Bathrooms:** Share 1 toilet indoors, 6 showers & 2 toilets outdoors.
**Campsites:** 4 wooden platform tent sites (tents not included), outside showers, bath house w 2 toilets, volleyball, horseshoes, snorkeling gear, horses, bicycles.
**Meals:** Restaurant & bar open in season. Communal kitchen May-Nov.
**Vegetarian:** Available upon request.
**Dates Open:** All year.
**High Season:** Dec-Apr.
**Rates:** Rooms $40-$50, camping $10/person, bunkhouse $18 plus tax/person, May-Dec weekly, 6 bdrm guesthouse $1100 per week
**Discounts:** May 16-Dec 14 reduced private weekly rental for entire retreat.
**Rsv'tns:** Deposit required.
**Reserve Through:** Travel agent or call direct (leave message!).
**Parking:** Ample free off-street parking.
**In-Room:** Guesthouse only: telephone, laundry service, kitchen, refrigerator, ceiling fans, TV & VCR.
**On-Premises:** Meeting rooms, laundry facilities, bike rentals, boogie boards, snorkeling gear.
**Exercise/Health:** Bikes, windsurfing, volleyball, horseshoes, croquet, & horseback riding. Massage available.
**Swimming:** Ocean beach.
**Sunbathing:** On beach, private & common sun decks, patio or roof, tent sites.
**Nudity:** Permitted in campsites at discretion of campers.
**Smoking:** Permitted outside, not in dorm or sleeping areas.
**Pets:** No, we have our own animals to care for.
**Handicap Access:** Yes, special WC. Limited to 1st fl of guest house, bunkhouse, camping.
**Children:** Permitted. Children under 2 years free.
**Languages:** Spanish & English.
**Your Host:** Gail.

# VIRGIN ISLANDS - BVI

## COOPER ISLAND

### Cooper Island Beach Club

Gay-Friendly ♀♂

*A Casual Caribbean Beachfront Resort*

***Cooper Island Beach Club*** is on a 1 1/2-mile by 1/2-mile island, where there are no roads, nightclubs, malls or fast food outlets. Your principal activities will be sunning, swimming, snorkeling, reading, writing and enjoying relaxing meals. Our beachfront restaurant and bar offers dramatic sunset views. Sheltered from the sun, you can enjoy a cool drink with the Caribbean Sea lapping the sand only a few feet away. Our rooms, too, are on the beach, with open-plan living room, kitchen, balcony, bathroom and a shower that is almost outdoors!

**Address: Cooper Island, British VI.**
**USA office: PO Box 512, Turners Falls, MA 01376.**
**Tel: (413) 863-3162, (800) 542-4624 (USA office),**
**Fax: (413) 863-3662. E-mail: info@cooper-island.com.**

**Type:** Beach resort with restaurant, bar, & scuba dive shop.
**Clientele:** Mainly straight with gay & lesbian following
**Transportation:** Pick up from ferry dock, no charge on scheduled trips.
**Rooms:** 12 rooms with queen beds.
**Bathrooms:** All private shower/toilets.
**Vegetarian:** Available for lunch & dinner with prior notice.
**Dates Open:** All year.
**High Season:** December 15th to April 15th.
**Rates:** Per night for 2: US $75 (Jun 1-Oct 30); US $145 (Dec 15-Apr 15); US $95 (Apr 15-May 31 & Nov 1-Dec 14). Meal and/or dive packages available.
**Discounts:** Weekly discounts available.
**Credit Cards:** MC, VISA, with 5% handling charge.
**Rsv'tns:** Required.
**Reserve Through:** Travel agent or call direct.
**Parking:** Boat moorings available.
**In-Room:** Ceiling fans, kitchen, refrigerator & maid service.
**Exercise/Health:** Full scuba facilities & watersports.
**Swimming:** In the ocean.
**Sunbathing:** On the beach.
**Pets:** Not permitted.
**Handicap Access:** No.
**Children:** Permitted, preferably over 10 yrs old.
**Languages:** English.

# TORTOLA

## Villas of Fort Recovery Estate

Gay-Friendly ♀♂

### *"A Bit of Britain in the Sun"*

A great place for a romantic getaway, the ***Villas of Fort Recovery Estate*** boasts its own private beach, fresh-water swimming pool and 17th-century Dutch fort. The luxury three- to four-bedroom house on the beach and the one- and two-bedroom seaside and penthouse villas afford spectacular views of six islands. All accommodations include daily continental breakfast, air-conditioning, cable TV, kitchen and housekeeping service. Each stay of seven nights inludes one dinner, served by butler service in the privacy of your villa, and a snorkel excursion, per guest. Expert yoga classes and massages are available for deep rest and relaxation.

**Address: Box 239, Road Town, Tortola BVI.**
**Tel: (809) 495-4354, (800) 367-8455, Fax: (809) 495-4036,**
**E-mail: FTRHOTEL@caribsurf.com.**

**Type:** Bed & breakfast hotel & villa resort with restaurant.
**Clientele:** Mostly straight clientele with a gay/lesbian following.
**Transportation:** Taxi.
**Rooms:** 17 villas with king beds.
**Bathrooms:** All private shower/toilets.
**Meals:** Continental breakfast.
**Vegetarian:** Menu has vegetarian choices. There are lots of vegetarian foods on the island.
**Complimentary:** One welcome dinner per guest for each 7-night stay.
**Dates Open:** All year.
**High Season:** November-June.
**Rates:** Summer: 1br \$125-\$135, 2br \$210, 3-4 br \$378-\$429. Winter: 1br \$185-\$195, 2br \$295, 3-4 br \$535-\$629.
**Credit Cards:** MC, Visa, Amex.
**Rsv'tns:** Required.
**Reserve Through:** Travel agent or call direct.
**Parking:** Adequate free parking.
**In-Room:** AC, ceiling fans, color cable TV, kitchen, refrigerator, maid & room service.
**On-Premises:** Meeting rooms, E-mail, fax, phone, typing.
**Exercise/Health:** Massage & yoga classes. Nearby gym, weights.
**Swimming:** Pool & the Caribbean.
**Sunbathing:** Poolside, at beach, on private patio.
**Nudity:** Please inquire.
**Pets:** Not permitted.
**Handicap Access:** No.
**Children:** Welcome.
**Languages:** English, Spanish.

IGTA

# VIRGIN ISLANDS - US

## ST CROIX

### On The Beach Resort

Q-NET Gay/Lesbian ♀♂

***The Virgin Island's Only Gay-Owned Beachfront Resort – Our 18th Year!***

"In my travels throughout the world, there are but a few most highly recommended places and ***On the Beach Resort*** is one of these," said Bobby Stevens, *The Guide,* Jan. 1995. "For warmth, comfort, and tranquility, it is unsurpassed."

The resort provides attractive and immaculate accommodations, two beachfront patios, two fresh water pools, a wonderful gourmet restaurant and a beachfront bar. Explore unspoiled and secluded beaches, swim, snorkel, sail, bask in the Caribbean sun or spend romantic evenings viewing breathtaking sunsets. ***"On the Beach Resort*** on the tiny island of St. Croix is magical. It was the best vacation I've ever taken." – *Frances Stevens, Curve Magazine, Feb. 1995.*

**Guest Comment:** "My 12th visit ...I can't imagine staying anywhere else. [The host's] personal attention to every detail is obvious. The Gourmet restaurant is the finest on the island. I shall return!" – Curt K., Virginia Beach, VA

**Address: PO Box 1908, Frederiksted, St. Croix, USVI 00841-1908**
**Tel: (809) 772-1205 or (800) 524-2018 (Toll-free reservations).**

**Type:** Beachfront resort with restaurant & bar.
**Clientele:** Gay & lesbian, good mix of men & women
**Transportation:** Taxi from airport $10 for 2.
**To Gay Bars:** Gay bar on premises. "Last Hurrah" gay bar & disco in Frederiksted.
**Rooms:** 10 rooms, 4 suites & 6 apartments with queen & king beds.
**Bathrooms:** All have private shower & toilet.
**Meals:** All rates include continental breakfast. Gourmet restaurant on premises.
**Vegetarian:** Available in restaurant.
**Complimentary:** Welcome cocktail.
**Dates Open:** All year.
**High Season:** December 15th thru April 15th.
**Rates:** Low-season $50-$110, high-season $105-$180.
**Discounts:** Special summer package rates, discounts for returning guests.
**Credit Cards:** MC, Visa, Amex.
**Rsv'tns:** Required.
**Reserve Through:** Travel agent or call direct.
**Minimum Stay:** Low-season 3 nights, high season 1 week.
**Parking:** Ample free off-street parking.
**In-Room:** AC, ceiling fans, coffee/tea-making facilities, kitchen, refrigerator & maid service.
**On-Premises:** TV lounge, gourmet restaurant & beachfront bar.
**Exercise/Health:** Massage.
**Swimming:** 2 pools on premises or ocean beach.
**Sunbathing:** At poolside & on ocean beach or common sun decks.
**Nudity:** Permitted on nearby isolated beaches.
**Smoking:** Permitted without restrictions.
**Pets:** Permitted with prior approval.
**Handicap Access:** No.
**Children:** Permitted with prior approval.
**Languages:** English, Spanish.
**Your Host:** Bill.

IGTA

# ST THOMAS

## Blackbeard's Castle

Gay-Friendly 50/50 ♀♂

The tower at ***Blackbeard's Castle,*** built in 1697 to scan the Caribbean for pirates and enemy ships, is a national historic site. It provides a spectacular backdrop for the oversized fresh water pool and terrace. The views are exceptional! Spacious and quiet guest rooms provide all the expected amenities. It is an intimate inn whose owner-manager team offers all the personal touches that make a vacation memorable. Accolades include: *VOGUE:* "...remarkable view...an excellent restaurant." *AMEX:* "A first-class hotel and restaurant." *PRACTICAL GOURMET:* "...best restaurant on St. Thomas."

**Address: PO Box 6041, St Thomas, USVI 00804**
**Tel: (809) 776-1234, (800) 344-5771, Fax: (809) 776-4321.**

**Type:** Hotel with restaurant, bar, & piano lounge with live jazz 8pm-midnight.
**Clientele:** 50% gay & lesbian & 50% straight clientele
**Transportation:** Taxi is best from airport.
**To Gay Bars:** 5-minute drive to gay/lesbian bars.
**Rooms:** 12 doubles, 4 junior suites, & 4 apartment suites.
**Bathrooms:** All private.
**Meals:** Continental breakfast.
**Vegetarian:** Available upon request.
**Complimentary:** Welcome cocktail.
**Dates Open:** All year.
**High Season:** December 15th-April 30th.
**Rates:** Summer $75-$145. Winter $110-$190.
**Credit Cards:** MC, Visa, Amex, Discover & Diners.
**Rsv'tns:** Required.
**Reserve Through:** Travel agent or call direct.
**Minimum Stay:** 3 days during high season.
**Parking:** Free adequate off-street parking.
**In-Room:** Cable color TV, AC, direct dial telephones, safes, daily maid service & kitchens in apartment suites.
**On-Premises:** Gardens.
**Exercise/Health:** Massage by appointment.
**Swimming:** In 2 swimming pools.
**Sunbathing:** At poolside.
**Smoking:** Permitted without restrictions.
**Pets:** Not permitted.
**Handicap Access:** No.
**Children:** Permitted, over 16.
**Languages:** English, Portuguese, Spanish, German & French.

IGTA

LATIN
AMERICA

# COSTA RICA

## QUEPOS-MANUEL ANTONIO

### Hotel Casa Blanca de Manuel Antonio S.A.

Q-NET Gay/Lesbian ♀♂

***Admittedly, our Hotel is Definitely NOT the Main Attraction Here...***

...because we are within 15 minute's walking distance to Playita, the one and only gay beach in the whole country. ***Hotel Casa Blanca*** guesthouse is on a hillside overlooking the beaches. A steady ocean wind makes your stay comfortable and our private atmosphere makes you feel at home. Relax in our tropical garden, 2 pools, or on the sun deck. If you like action, we can arrange beach or mountain horseback riding, boat trips into the mangroves, guided tours to Manuel Antonio National Park, multiday excursions to untouched tropical islands, and any number of water adventures. Nearby Quepos provides ample nightlife with discos and casinos.

HOTEL CASA BLANCA DE ML. ANT. S.A.

**Address:** Apdo 194, Quepos-Manuel Antonio 6350 Costa Rica.
**Tel:** (506) 777-0253 (Tel/Fax), **E-mail:** cblanca@sol.racsa.co.cr.
http://bertha.pomona.edu/cblanca/.

**Type:** Hotel guesthouse.
**Clientele:** Exclusively for gay & lesbian guests, their relatives & friends
**Transportation:** Pick up provided by Sansa (400 Colones per person), TravelAir ($4 dollars per person) & Directo (free).
**To Gay Bars:** 175 km to San Jose (4-hr drive). Local bars mixed, especially in high season.
**Rooms:** 4 rooms, 2 suites & 4 apartments with single, double or king beds.
**Bathrooms:** All private.
**Meals:** Breakfast at additional charge of $5 plus tax.
**Vegetarian:** Available upon request on premises & at nearby restaurants.
**Complimentary:** Tea & coffee.
**Dates Open:** All year.
**High Season:** November-April.
**Rates:** USD, tax not included. Double: Low $40-high $70. Apt: Low-$50-high $90. Suites: Low $90-high $140, $10 per extra bed.
**Discounts:** 15% for airlines.
**Credit Cards:** VISA, MC, Amex & Eurocard.
**Rsv'tns:** Required.
**Reserve Through:** Travel agent or call direct.
**Parking:** Adequate free off-street parking. Guarded private parking lot.
**In-Room:** All with ceiling fans & laundry service. Suites with kitchenette. Apartments with kitchenette, refrigerator & panoramic views.
**On-Premises:** Refrigerators & freezers outside of rooms. Laundry facilities, phone, tropical garden, flight & hotel reservation services.
**Exercise/Health:** Massage upon request. Gym, weights & massage in downtown Quepos.
**Swimming:** Pool on premises, gay beach within walking distance. Nearby pool & river.
**Sunbathing:** At poolside, in the garden, on common sun decks & at the beach.
**Nudity:** Permitted poolside, in the pool, in the garden & on the sun deck.
**Smoking:** Permitted without restrictions.
**Pets:** Permitted. Must have entered country legally & have all the paperwork.
**Handicap Access:** Yes. No stairs for suites, 4 rooms, garden & poolside.
**Children:** Not especially welcome.
**Languages:** Management: Spanish, English & German. Cleaning staff: Spanish, little English.
**Your Host:** Harald & Rainer.

IGTA

# SAN JOSE

## Hotel Colours, The Guest Residence San Jose

Gay/Lesbian ♀♂

### *Experience Not Just a Place, But a State of Mind*

***Colours,*** the premier guesthouse of Costa Rica, is of Spanish-style architecture and located in San Jose, the capital city. Our location is conveniently set in an exclusive residential district a few minutes from the new Plaza Mayor mall, the US Embassy and several neighborhood parks. From here, it's just a 10-minute ride to central San José and only a block to pharmacies, grocery store, liquor store, bars, restaurants and a weekly farmers' market. If you are a first-time visitor, you may wish to be met and escorted directly to the ***Residence*** (a complimentary service with reservations of seven nights or more). Upon arrival and settling in, an orientation is offered, covering currency exchange, what's where in the neighborhood, massage, city access for shopping, sightseeing, restaurants and nightlife. Our multilingual staff members advise guests of guided day excursions to attractions outside San José, such as volcanos, biological reserves, rainforests, island/beach boat cruises, whitewater river rafting, bungee jumping and others.

From the main balcony of the poolside house, you look out over the enclosed garden and pool area, with a view in the distance of the mountain ranges surrounding the city. Take some time for sunning beside the solar-heated pool and have your complimentary tropical breakfast there or in the dining room. Join us at poolside again at cocktail hour, as we gather to meet and mingle with other guests and their friends. Our facility features various types of guest rooms to suit your taste and personal budget. All ten rooms are furnished with varied bed sizes, Bahamian paddle fans, clock radios and security safes. Telephones are soon to be installed. Also on the property are three large social rooms, one of which features English-speaking cable television. Whether your goal is to relax and unwind, adventure out and explore this tropical country, or both, ***Colours*** is a carefree place for it ALL to happen.

Speak to our friendly reservations staff about our other distinctive lodgings – ***Colours, The Guest Mansion*** in romantic Key West, and ***Colours, The Mantell Guest Inn*** in exciting South Miami Beach.

**Address: c/o Colours Destinations,
255 W 24th St, Miami Beach, FL 33140 USA.
Tel: (800) ARRIVAL (277-4825) or (305) 532-9341.
Local San Jose (506) 232-3504.**

**Type:** Hotel guesthouse.
**Clientele:** Gay & lesbian. Good mix of men & women
**Transportation:** Taxi from airport or inquire about airport transfers.
**To Gay Bars:** 10 minutes to gay bars.
**Rooms:** 10 rooms with single, double, queen or king beds.
**Bathrooms:** Priv. & shared.
**Meals:** Expanded continental breakfast or full breakfast. Other meals may be arranged.
**Complimentary:** Evening happy hour & turndown mints.

*continued next page*

**Dates Open:** All year.
**High Season:** Dec-May.
**Rates:** US $59-$109.
**Discounts:** On extended stays, prepayments, for single occupancy, inquire for others.
**Credit Cards:** All major credit cards.
**Rsv'tns:** Suggested.
**Reserve Through:** Travel agent or call direct.
**Minimum Stay:** On some holidays.
**Parking:** Ample, free, on-street parking.
**In-Room:** Maid & laundry service, ceiling fans & security safes.
**On-Premises:** TV lounge, meeting rooms & guest refrigerator.
**Exercise/Health:** Full health club facilities & massage nearby.
**Swimming:** Pool on premises.
**Sunbathing:** At poolside.
**Nudity:** Permitted poolside.
**Smoking:** Permitted, except in TV lounge.
**Pets:** Not permitted.
**Handicap Access:** No.
**Children:** Not permitted.
**Languages:** Spanish, English, limited French, German & Italian.

IGTA

## Hotel Kekoldi

Q-NET **Gay-Friendly** ♀♂

### *Unique in Costa Rica – Young and Informal*

The staff of ***Hotel Kekoldi*** is young and easygoing like you are. The historic building is uniquely styled, reflecting the colorful atmosphere of the sunny Caribbean islands, and is decorated with sensational paintings by famous English artist Helen Eltis. The hotel is located in the historic Barrio Amón, only minutes by foot to the center and all touristic points of interest as well as to restaurants, bars, discos, and cinemas. There are 14 large rooms with king-sized beds, private bathrooms with hot water, telephones, and breakfast, bar, and laundry services.

**Address: Avenida 9, Calle 3 Bis, across from INVU, San José Costa Rica.**
**Tel: (506) 223-3244, Fax: (506) 257-5476,**
**E-mail: kekoldi@sol.racsa.co.cr.**
**www.costaricainfo.com/kekoldi.html**

**Type:** Hotel with bar & breakfast restaurant.
**Clientele:** Mostly hetero clientele with a gay/lesbian following
**Transportation:** Bus or taxi from airport, approximately $10.
**To Gay Bars:** 2 blocks, an 8-minute walk.
**Rooms:** 14 rooms with single or king beds.
**Bathrooms:** 14 private shower/toilets.
**Vegetarian:** Available nearby.
**Dates Open:** All year.
**High Season:** Dec-April.
**Rates:** Single $24-$32, double $34-$45.
**Discounts:** On extended stays.
**Credit Cards:** MC, VISA.
**Rsv'tns:** Suggested.
**Reserve Through:** Travel agent or call direct.
**Parking:** Adequate on-street pay parking.
**In-Room:** Tele., ceiling fans, maid & laundry serv.
**On-Premises:** TV lounge, video tape library.
**Sunbathing:** At beach, accessible by bus.
**Smoking:** Permitted.
**Pets:** Permitted, inquire in advance.
**Handicap Access:** No.
**Children:** Welcome.
**Languages:** Spanish, English, German.
**Your Host:** Edgar.

## Joluva Guesthouse & Villa La Roca Beach House

Gay/Lesbian ♂

### *Stay at the Right Place...At the Right Price!*

The friendliness of our all-gay, bilingual (Spanish and English) crew at ***Joluva Guesthouse*** creates a relaxing and welcoming atmosphere. Our rates are friendly, too, and include a continental breakfast with tropical fruits. Our rooms are clean and spacious and have beds with luxury orthopedic mattresses. We're always ready to assist you with vacation plans, arranging tours or trips, or local information. All gay activities and cultural attractions are within walking distance. Each room at ***Villa La Roca,*** our new beach house in Manuel Antonio, has an ocean view and bathroom with hot shower. We serve breakfast each morning.

**Address: Calle 3B, AVS 9 y 11 #936, San Jose & Manuel Antonio Beach Costa Rica.**
**Tel: (506) 223 7961, Fax: (506) 257 7668. Villa La Roca direct (506) 777-1349. USA reservations & info (800) 298-2418.**
**E-mail: joluva@sol.racsa.co.cr.**

**Type:** Bed & breakfast.
**Clientele:** Mostly men with women welcome
**Transportation:** Bus or taxi from airport or pick up for extra fee of approx $15.
**To Gay Bars:** 2 blocks or 10 minutes by foot.
**Rooms:** Guesthouse: 8 rooms with single or double beds. Villa: 6 rooms.
**Bathrooms:** Guesthouse: 6 private, 2 shared. Villa: 6 private.
**Meals:** Continental breakfast with tropical fruits.
**Vegetarian:** We can direct you to vegetarian establishments.
**Complimentary:** Coffee all day.
**Dates Open:** All year.
**High Season:** December-May.
**Rates:** USD $15-$70 (add $5 per extra person).
**Discounts:** 10% for 7 nights stay, 15% for 14 nights or more.
**Credit Cards:** MC, Visa, Amex.
**Rsv'tns:** Required.
**Reserve Through:** Travel agent or call direct.
**Parking:** San Jose: limited on-street parking or guarded pay lots which we strongly recommend. Villa: free parking.
**In-Room:** Color cable TV.
**On-Premises:** VCR available at $3.00 for 24 hours. Includes all selections from our video library.
**Swimming:** At the beach.
**Sunbathing:** At the beach.
**Nudity:** Gay nude beach at La Playita Manuel Antonio.
**Smoking:** Permitted but strongly discouraged.
**Pets:** Not permitted.
**Handicap Access:** No special provisions. Please inquire.
**Children:** Not especially welcomed.
**Languages:** English, Spanish & Polish.
**Your Host:** Alejandro & Peter.

IGTA

# MEXICO

## ACAPULCO

### Acapulco Las Palmas

Q-NET Men ♂

*Paradise Complete*

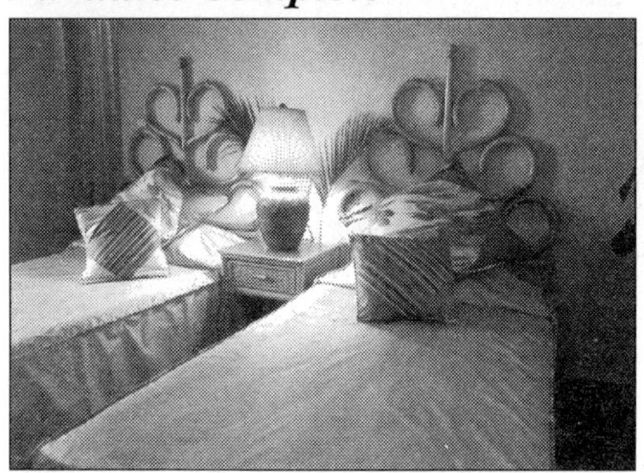

Enjoy five-star luxury and comfort at Acapulco's extraordinary new gay guesthouse, ***Acapulco Las Palmas.*** This gem of colonial Mexican architecture is located on the slopes of Paradise Mountain, within the Golden Zone of the Costera. A relaxed, open-air feeling characterizes the entire villa, which is uniquely set on four terrace levels overlooking Acapulco. Behind high walls, lush and exotic tropical vegetation flanks an elegant courtyard with cascading waterfalls and a dark-blue swimming pool overlooked by our colorful cocktail lounge, El Bar. Our fifteen carefully-appointed rooms and suites, each with a different theme, have air conditioning, ceiling fans, TV/VCR, telephone, fresh flowers and mints on pillows.

A short walk from the villa, you can explore a craft market, shops and boutiques filled with silver. Gay clubs and many restaurants dot the Costera, where cruising continues till the wee hours. After a day at the beach, guests ascend the curving staircase to the elegant sun terrace (clothing optional), where, against the backdrop of a magnificent view of Acapulco, they can enjoy cocktails and complimentary hors d'oeuvres at the palapa-covered giant Jacuzzi bar. The open-air restaurant on the second level offers complimentary continental breakfast and a full a la carte menu at reasonable prices. The lunch menu offers a variety of salads, sandwiches and the chef's offering of the day. For those who prefer it, room service is available at almost any hour of the day.

**Address: 155 Avenida Las Conchas, Fracto. Farallon, Acapulco, GRO 39690 Mexico.**
**Tel: (52-74) 87 08 43, Fax: (52-74) 87 12 82.**
**E-mail: condesa@mpsnet.com.mx.**

**Type:** Guesthouse villas with restaurant & bar.
**Clientele:** Men only
**Transportation:** Plane. Free limo pick up at airport.
**To Gay Bars:** A 10 min walk, a 2 min drive.
**Rooms:** 15 rooms, 2 suites with single or double beds.
**Bathrooms:** Private: 15 shower/toilets, 2 bath/shower/toilets. Suite has Jacuzzi.
**Meals:** Continental breakfast.
**Vegetarian:** Available upon request.
**Complimentary:** Drink on arrival. Bar snacks at evening cocktail time. Fresh flowers & plants in each room or suite, mints on pillow, bottled water in rooms.
**Dates Open:** All year.
**High Season:** November-April.
**Rates:** High season: US $100-$225, low season: US $90-$200. Inclusive of tax, etc.
**Credit Cards:** MC, Visa, Diners.
**Rsv'tns:** Required.
**Reserve Through:** Travel agent or call direct.
**Minimum Stay:** 3 days.
**Parking:** Ample free on-street parking.
**In-Room:** AC, ceiling fans, phones, color cable TV, VCR, maid, room & laundry service.
**On-Premises:** Video tape library, fashion & model photography, motion picture location by prior arrangement.
**Exercise/Health:** Jacuzzi, massage.
**Swimming:** Pool. Nearby ocean.
**Sunbathing:** Poolside, on patio, roof & common sun decks.
**Nudity:** Permitted poolside & on top sun terrace.
**Smoking:** Permitted in rooms, on open terrace & in bar.
**Pets:** Inquire.
**Handicap Access:** No. Due to the number of levels, our staff's assistance is necessary. It is their pleasure to help guests requiring assistance.
**Children:** No.
**Languages:** Spanish, English.
**Your Host:** Bobby & David.

IGTA

## Casa Le Mar

Gay/Lesbian ♂

### *Gay Paradise*

***Casa Le Mar*** is a beautiful Mexican-style, luxury villa in the Condesa area of the city. It has four spacious bedrooms with a variety of beds, private baths, AC, and ceiling fans. It also has a lounge, dining room, kitchen, and a patio with pool, wet bar and sun deck. Your host will often find time to take guests (new friends) by jeep to Pie de la Cuesta (Sunset Beach) for an afternoon at the sea and lagoon to enjoy a Red Snapper fish dinner and one of the most beautiful sunsets in the world. "I try to make traveling affordable for the single traveler."

**Address: Lomas del Mar 32-B, Acapulco 39690 Mexico.**
**Tel: (52-74) 84 10 22 or (52-74) 84 68 54. Fax: (52-74) 84 68 54.**

**Type:** Bed & breakfast in a private, open-air villa with self-serve bar.
**Clientele:** Mostly men with women genuinely welcome
**Transportation:** Free pick up from airport & bus.
**To Gay Bars:** 1/2 block.
**Rooms:** 1 double w/garden bath, 2 king size w/ balcony, 1 king size suite; all overlooking waterfall & pool.
**Bathrooms:** All Private.
**Meals:** Full breakfast.
**Vegetarian:** Available upon request with 1 day's notice.
**Complimentary:** Set-up service, tea, coffee, sodas, mints on pillows, sometimes fruit or flowers in room.
**Dates Open:** All year.
**Rates:** Bed & breakfast $60-$80 (inclusive, tax, etc).
**Rsv'tns:** Recommended. Necessary for pick up at airport.
**Reserve Through:** Travel agent or call direct.
**Parking:** Ample free parking.
**In-Room:** B/W TV, AC, ceiling fans, maid & laundry service.
**On-Premises:** Meeting rooms, TV lounge, two floors of common area, pool with cascade, patio, wet bar, reading room, dining room (mi casa, su casa).
**Exercise/Health:** 2-min walk to gay-friendly gym.
**Swimming:** Pool on premises, 1-min walk to ocean beach, 1/2 hr to lagoon.
**Sunbathing:** At poolside, beach, on patio, private & common sun decks.
**Smoking:** Non-smoking room reserved, open-air house.
**Pets:** Not permitted.
**Handicap Access:** Sorry, not accessible.
**Languages:** English, Spanish.

# BAJA CALIFORNIA SUR

## La Concha Beach Resort

Gay-Friendly ♀♂

### *A Hidden Jewel in the Sea of Cortez*

Long white sandy beaches, calm blue-green waters, breathtaking sunsets, an abundance of water sports... Where is this haven? ***La Concha Beach Resort*** in La Paz. It's the perfect destination for vacationers and business travelers. This modern city offers so much: whale watching, world-class scuba diving, sea kayaking, snorkeling with sea lions, sport fishing, exploring deserted islands, great shopping, and fine dining. Just two miles from downtown La Paz in a secluded setting, this resort has 107 air-conditioned rooms and suites, a full-service restaurant, two bars, and an outdoor pool overlooking the sea.

**Address: Kilómetro 5 Carretera a Pichilingue, CP 23010, La Paz, BCS Mexico.**
**Tel: In USA: (619) 260-0991, Fax: (619) 294-7366 or (800) 999-BAJA (2252).**

**Type:** Hotel with restaurant & gift shop.
**Clientele:** Mostly hetero clientele
**Transportation:** Airport to La Paz, then airport shuttle. Airport pick up US $16 roundtrip per person (outside service).
**To Gay Bars:** 3 miles, a 5-minute drive.
**Rooms:** 103 rooms, 2 suites, 11 concominlums with single or king beds.
**Bathrooms:** All private shower/toilets.
**Vegetarian:** Available at hotel restaurant.
**Dates Open:** All year.
**High Season:** July-August.
**Rates:** US $65-US $85 for standard rooms.
**Discounts:** AAA.
**Credit Cards:** MC, Visa, Amex.
**Reserve Through:** Travel agent or call direct.
**Parking:** Ample free off-street parking.
**In-Room:** Color cable TV, telephone, refrigerator, AC, maid, room & laundry service. Condos have kitchen.
**On-Premises:** Meeting rooms, video tape library.
**Swimming:** Pool & ocean on premises.
**Sunbathing:** At poolside & at beach.
**Smoking:** Permitted. Non-smoking rooms available.
**Pets:** Not permitted.
**Handicap Access:** No.
**Children:** Welcome.
**Languages:** Spanish, English.

# CUERNAVACA

## Casa Aurora

Gay/Lesbian ♀♂

### *Study Spanish in the Eternal Spring City*

Cuernavaca, the city of the Eternal Spring, is a one hour's drive from Mexico City, on the road to Acapulco. The city's many attractions include the Palace of Cortes, a 16th-century cathedral, the Borda Gardens (once the summer home of Emperor Maximillian and Charlotte), the Brady Museum, the San Anton waterfall,

Siqueiros Workshop (named for the famed muralist) and its Spanish-language schools. One of them, the gay-friendly CETLALIC language center, offered a three-week lesbian program in 1996 and, hopefully, will have a gay one next year. One of our guest's comments: "*Casa Aurora* is a restored Colonial home, downtown near everything. Once inside, you find an oasis where you can relax, take a siesta in one of the hammocks or listen to fascinating stories of Mexico's history told by your host..."

**Address: Arista No. 12, Centro, Cuernavaca, Mor. 62000 Mexico. Tel: (52 73) 18 63 94.**

**Type:** Bed & breakfast or guesthouse.
**Clientele:** Mostly gay & lesbian with some hetero clientele
**Transportation:** Plane or bus from Mexico City. Taxi from bus station to house.
**To Gay Bars:** 10 blocks to Shadee disco/bar. A 15 min walk, a 5 min drive.
**Rooms:** 3 rooms with single, double or king bed.
**Bathrooms:** 1 private bath/toilet/shower, 1 shared bath/toilet/shower.
**Meals:** Continental breakfast or 3 meals.
**Vegetarian:** Owner only cooks vegetarian.
**Dates Open:** All year.
**High Season:** Summer (May-August).
**Rates:** B&B: US $18. Three meals: US $24.
**Discounts:** For 2 guests in same room: B&B US $32; Three meals: US $42.
**Rsv'tns:** Preferred.
**Reserve Thru:** Call direct.
**Minimum Stay:** No, but prefer longer stays and students of Spanish.
**Parking:** Adequate pay parking, parking lot around the corner.
**In-Room:** Each room has a terrace with a hammock.
**On-Premises:** Small garden, laundry facilities.
**Swimming:** Nearby pool. 1 hour to Las Estacas resort.
**Sunbathing:** In garden.
**Smoking:** Owner doesn't smoke, smoking permitted in terraces, garden & in rms.
**Handicap Access:** Yes. Rooms are all in one floor or on ground floor.
**Languages:** Spanish, English, French.
**Your Host:** Antonio.

# PUERTO VALLARTA

## Casa Fantasía

Q-NET Gay/Lesbian ♂

### *Where Your Dreams Become Reality*

A jewel in the heart of Puerto Vallarta's gay district awaits. Situated behind tall brick walls to ensure guest privacy, *Casa Fantasía* consists of three separate houses – traditional Old-World-style Mexican haciendas totaling 10,000 square feet of luxury accommodations. The elegant yet informal common areas include sunken living rooms, covered terraces and intimate conversation areas. Eight large bedrooms each contain a private full bath, and guests may choose from twin or king-sized beds. The houses are filled with antique furnishings, limited edition prints and original oil paintings, as well as hundreds of curios and objets d'art which can hold one's attention for hours. All rooms, both common and guest, have plants and/or fresh flowers daily. Outside, the terrace provides a relaxing, regenerating environment with a staffed bar for guests and their friends adjacent to the swimming pool, along with chaise lounges, lounge chairs and tables.

Located in Colonia Emiliano Zapata, Puerto Vallarta's gay district, *Casa*

*continued next page*

***Fantasía*** is just a block from the beach and a short five-to-ten-minute beach walk to the famous "blue chairs." Vallarta's premier disco, Club Paco Paco, is but two blocks away and the other popular bars, Los Balcones and Zótano, are a leisurely five-minute stroll over the new bridge into downtown. Within a ten-minute walk one can find world-class restaurants, more modest dining, craft and curio shops, museums, clothing stores, a gym and much, much more. The staff at ***Casa Fantasía*** can also arrange tickets for Vallarta's many paid diversions – day-long excursions to Yelapa, evening dinner cruises, jungle tours, horseback riding, deep-sea fishing, snorkeling, parasailing and the like.

So come, let your new friends at ***Casa Fantasía*** pamper you in a style to which you will quickly become accustomed. Call or write for our brochure. ***Casa Fantasía:*** a new standard in Puerto Vallarta!

**Address: Apartado Postal #387 Centro, Puerto Vallarta, Jalisco CP 48300 Mexico.**
**Tel: (52-322) 2 19 04, Fax: (52-322) 2 19 23 (effective 12-96). Toll-free in USA: (888) 636-2539. E-mail: nenalex@aol.com.**

**Type:** Bed & breakfast guesthouse. On-premises restaurant & bar opening spring, 1997.
**Clientele:** Mostly men with women welcome. Some straight clientele
**Transportation:** Airport taxi to B&B.
**To Gay Bars:** 2 blocks, 1/4 mile, a 5 minute walk, a 2 minute drive.
**Rooms:** 6 rooms with single or king beds.
**Bathrooms:** 6 private bath/toilet/showers.
**Meals:** Full or buffet breakfast. Selection alternates, there is no menu.
**Vegetarian:** By request and available nearby.
**Complimentary:** Afternoon beverages (wine, sherry, etc), welcome fruit basket, always something on pillow.
**Dates Open:** All year.
**High Season:** Mid-November to mid-April.
**Rates:** Low season: USD $30-USD $75; High season: USD $52-USD $95.
**Rsv'tns:** Required.
**Reserve Through:** Travel agent or call direct.
**Minimum Stay:** 3 days.
**Parking:** Ample on-street parking.
**In-Room:** Ceiling fans, laundry & maid service.
**On-Premises:** TV lounge, video tape library, fax, phone, computer, Internet. Bar & rest. to open spg, '97.
**Exercise/Health:** Massage. Nearby gym, weights, massage.
**Swimming:** Pool on premises. Nearby ocean & river.
**Sunbathing:** Poolside, on patio, at beach.
**Smoking:** Permitted in all areas & in all rooms.
**Languages:** Spanish, English.
**Your Host:** Daniel & Luis.

IGTA

## Casa Panoramica

Q-NET **Gay/Lesbian** ♀♂

Dramatically-situated on a hillside, ***Casa Panoramica*** is a 11,000-square-foot villa on 5 levels with spectacular and breathtaking views of the Bahia de Banderas and the town below. While remaining convenient to both beach and downtown, the villa's lofty vantage point catches the cool cross breezes from the mountains. Four separate dining areas, two large terraces for swimming and dining and a small terrace with BBQ provide a variety of relaxing environments. The villa accommodates 12 people comfortably, with complete housekeeping services provided.

**Address: Apdo. Postal 114, Puerto Vallarta, Jalisco 48300 Mexico.**
**Tel: (800) 745-7805, Fax: (808) 324-1302 in CA, USA. Or call direct (52-322) 23656. E-mail: CasaPano@pvnet.com.**

**Type:** Bed & breakfast in a private 7 bedroom villa.
**Clientele:** 75% men & 25% women
**Transportation:** Airport combi vans.
**To Gay Bars:** 1-12 blocks to gay bars.
**Rooms:** 7 rooms with double, queen & king beds.
**Bathrooms:** All private.
**Meals:** Full breakfast.
**Vegetarian:** Upon request.
**Complimentary:** Coffee, tea.
**Dates Open:** Closed in Aug.
**High Season:** Nov-May.
**Rates:** $85-$95 Nov-May, $65-$75 June-Oct.
**Discounts:** On stays over two weeks.
**Credit Cards:** MC, Visa, Amex.
**Rsv'tns:** Recommended 30 days in advance.
**Reserve Through:** Travel agent or call direct.
**Minimum Stay:** During Christmas.
**Parking:** Adequate, free, off-street parking.
**In-Room:** Maid & laundry service, ceiling fans.
**On-Premises:** Laundry facilities.
**Exercise/Health:** 7 blocks to new fully-equipped gym.
**Swimming:** Pool on premises, ocean beach 3 blks.
**Sunbathing:** At poolside, on patio, common sun decks or beach.
**Smoking:** Permitted without restrictions.
**Pets:** Not permitted.
**Handicap Access:** Not accessible.
**Children:** Ages 6 and up permitted.
**Languages:** Spanish, English.

IGTA

## Doin' It Right — in Puerto Vallarta

Gay/Lesbian ♀♂

### *Vallarta is Tropical, Affordable, Gay-Friendly and CLOSE!*

Discover a wonderful tropical rainforest paradise in Puerto Vallarta. Party all night, shop and dine till you drop. Vallarta has something for everyone – cobblestone streets, spectacular lightening shows above the bay... This warm destination is in the same latitude as Hawaii, but much closer and a quarter of the cost. There are restaurants that rival San Francisco's and New York's, friendly locals, tourist police, one of the best water systems in Mexico, wonderful shopping and water sports. Gay life is visible both on the gay beach and in the city's growing number of gay nightspots. You also have a choice of gay excursions. How about a day of snorkeling or a sunset cruise or jungle and horseback riding tours, all organized by a gay company?

At ***Doin' It Right,*** we specialize in Puerto Vallarta, with over 150 properties available to make sure you have the amenities you are looking for. We are the US and Canada reservation line for Hotel Paco Paco Descanso del Sol and Vallarta Cora gay hotels. And we can connect you with any of the gay tours

*continued next page*

and excursions available in the area. Upcoming Doin' It Right tours include: Investment, Mother/Son & Mother/Daughter Mother's Day, Pampering/Chill, Taking Care of the Caretakers, AIDS Grief Processing, Travel Agent/Writer Familiarization, Shopping Tours, New Years White Party and more. Get a group of your friends, family, club or coworkers together and rent your own private villa (starting at only US $145/night) with your own houseman serving you margaritas by your own private pool, while your cook prepares the delectable dishes of her culture (amenities vary by property).

Beachfront to jungle... touristy to remote... party to tranquil... rustic and basic apartments to the most luxurious and elegant villas... independent to the utmost in pampering... we have it all – gay, mainstream, corporate, family reunions, tours to transfers – from one to 400 people. Let the specialists at Doin' It Right take care of ALL your Puerto Vallarta arrangements.

**Address: 150 Franklin #208, San Francisco, CA 94102**
**Tel: (415) 621-3584, USA & Canada: (800) 936-3646, Fax: (415) 621-3576.**

## Mission San Francisco

**Q-NET Gay-Friendly ♀♂**

### *Your Private Casa Overlooking the Bay*

Allow yourself to experience the extraordinary ***Mission San Francisco*** and its panoramic bay view. From your private luxurious home, you'll view the bay, tropical hillsides, margarita sunsets, nighttime city lights and palm studded village. Relax under the dome of the master bedroom suite or sun yourself on the very private rooftop terrace. ***Mission San Francisco*** is in the heart of the village, within walking distance of the gay beach, Mexican bazaar, supermarket, bars and restaurants. Included are 3 bedrooms and 2 baths, with additional rooms available. Weekly and monthly rates. NOTE: Also available in Mexico City, in the very heart of the Zona Rosa, is our one-bedroom rooftop apartment "Casita del Cielo," renting at only $800 per month.

**Tel: (916) 933-0370 (Tel/Fax), E-mail: mpizza@quiknet.com.**

**Type:** Two rental homes.
**Clientele:** Mostly hetero with a gay & lesbian following
**Transportation:** Airport taxi to home approximately $5.
**To Gay Bars:** 6 blocks or a 10-minute walk.
**Rooms:** 1 3-bedroom, 2 bath home & 1 5-bedroom, 4 bath home with single, double & king beds.
**Bathrooms:** Private bath/ toilets.
**Complimentary:** Refrigerator stocked with beer & soft drinks upon arrival.
**Dates Open:** All year.
**Rates:** $295-$495 per week, per home (not per person).
**Discounts:** 4th week free.
**Rsv'tns:** Required.
**Reserve Through:** Call direct.
**Minimum Stay:** Rates are by the week.
**Parking:** Ample on-street parking.
**In-Room:** Completely furnished homes with ceiling fans, color cable TV & full kitchens.
**Exercise/Health:** Nearby gym.
**Swimming:** 6 block walk to gay beach.
**Sunbathing:** On private sun decks or nearby beach.
**Smoking:** Permitted.
**Pets:** Not permitted.
**Handicap Access:** No.
**Children:** Welcome.
**Languages:** Spanish, English.
**Your Host:** Mike.

## Palapas in Yelapa

**Gay-Friendly 50/50 ♀♂**

Our ***Palapas in Yelapa*** are comfortable, simple cabin accommodations in tropical surroundings with spectacular ocean views. All or our palapas (cabins) have gas stoves, cooking utensils, silverware, bathrooms with showers, kerosene lamps, mosquito nets, hammocks, tables, chairs and beds with linens. In town, there are restaurants, shops and a doctor.

Yelapa is hidden in a crescent cove where blue-green waters roll on white sands. Thatched roofs spot the shore and disappear into the dense jungle hillside. A rolling river flows down the palm-covered mountains and gently fills the peaceful bay. The tropical secluded village has many exotic birds, lagoons, waterfalls and colorful flowering trees. Combined with balmy breezes and spectacular reddish-orange sunsets, Yelapa is a paradise hideaway.

**Address: c/o Antonio & Lucinda Saldaña, Apartado Postal 2-43, Puerto Vallarta, Jalisco Mexico.**
**Tel: (52-322) 491 97.**

**Type:** Palapas (cabins).
**Clientele:** 50% gay & lesbian & 50% straight clientele
**Transportation:** Plane to Puerto Vallarta, then boat ride to Yelapa.
**Rooms:** 5 cabins accommodating 2-6 people.
**Bathrooms:** All private showers & toilets.
**Dates Open:** All year.
**High Season:** Nov-Apr.
**Rates:** USD $10-$35 per night, per cabin.
**Discounts:** Stays over 1 month, group rates.
**Rsv'tns:** Required, plus 50% deposit.
**Reserve Through:** Call direct.
**Minimum Stay:** 1 week usually required with 50% deposit (flexible).
**In-Room:** Gas stoves, cooking utensils, silverware, beds/linens, kerosene lamps, mosquito nets, tables, chairs & hammocks.
**Swimming:** Ocean & river a 5-minute walk.
**Sunbathing:** On ocean beach.
**Nudity:** On private decks.
**Smoking:** Permitted.
**Pets:** Permitted.
**Handicap Access:** No.
**Children:** Welcome.
**Languages:** Spanish & English.
**Your Host:** Antonio & Lucinda.

# Vallarta Cora

**Gay/Lesbian ♂**

## *Very Active, Very Lively!*

***Vallarta Cora*** is a hotel/apartment with 14 units on four floors. All units have one bedroom (with one double and one twin bed), 1-1/2 bath (with huge oval-shaped Mexican tile bathtubs big enough for two), daily maid service, kitchenettes, AC, fans, balcony and bottled water. A dusk-till-dawn clothing-optional swimming pool sits between twin towers facing each other. Your own key allows you to come and go as you please, as well as have your own guests. On premises are a beauty shop and fax and e-mail service. ***Vallarta Cora*** is also home to Amadeus Tours.

**Address: Calle Pilitas #174, Colonia Emiliano Zapatas, Puerto Vallarta, Jalisco 48380 Mexico.**
**Tel: (52-322) 32815 (Tel/Fax), E-mail: coragay@pvnet.com.mex.**
**Reservations: (800) 936-3646 (in USA & Canada) or Tel/Fax: (415) 621-3576.**

**Type:** Apartments.
**Clientele:** Mostly gay male & some lesbian clientele
**Transportation:** Taxis.
**To Gay Bars:** 4 blocks.
**Rooms:** 14 apartments with single or double beds.
**Bathrooms:** All private.
**Meals:** 2 blocks to restaurants. Catered meals available.
**Vegetarian:** Available nearby.
**Dates Open:** All year.
**High Season:** Oct 15-April 30.
**Rates:** Summer US $40-$50, winter: US $50-$75.
**Discounts:** 7th night free on weekly stays. Monthly discounts available.
**Reserve Through:** Call direct, 800 reservation line, or travel agent.
**Minimum Stay:** High season: 3 nights. Holidays: 7 nights.
**Parking:** Limited free off-street parking.
**In-Room:** AC, ceiling fans, refrigerator, kitchen, maid service.
**On-Premises:** Fax, phone, e-mail/internet access.
**Exercise/Health:** Gym nearby with 30% discount for our guests.
**Swimming:** Pool on premises. 2 blocks to gay beach, 1/2 block to mainstream beach.
**Sunbathing:** At poolside & beach.
**Nudity:** Pemitted poolside from dusk to dawn, if guests are quiet.
**Smoking:** Permitted without restriction.
**Pets:** Upon approval.
**Handicap Access:** 5 steps to lower apartment.
**Children:** Upon approval.
**Languages:** Spanish, English, French.
**Your Host:** Mario & Mario.

UNITED
STATES

# ALASKA

## ANCHORAGE

### Arctic Feather B&B

Q-NET Gay/Lesbian ♀♂

## *Share the Warm Alaskan Energy*

You'll be warmed by the charm of the *Arctic Feather B&B,* located in an older, quiet neighborhood within easy walking distance of downtown. Many restaurants, shops, the Anchorage Museum of History and Art, a gay bar, and three parks are close by. The B&B is located several blocks from the train station, where you can catch a train north to Denali Park and the tallest mountain in North America at 20,320 feet or take the train south to Seward to enjoy a panoramic view of mountains and the Turnagain Arm. Adjacent to the train station is Ship Creek where you can watch 40-pound king salmon swim upstream to spawn.

The *Arctic Feather B&B* has one guest bedroom with a private bath and two guest bedrooms which share a bath; all rooms have comfortable queen-sized beds. A large cedar deck surrounded by mature birch trees overlooks the Cook Inlet. Anchorage is located on the edge of the inlet with the Chugach mountains in the background and is home to half of the total Alaskan population of 500,000. A pleasant pastime is exploring the more than 125 miles of scenic biking/walking trails.

While visiting Alaska, you should definitely plan on traveling outside Anchorage. Unspoiled wilderness is close by; take an hour trip south to Portage Glacier or travel an equal distance north to Eklutna Indian cemetery. Your host highly recommends a day trip to Prince William Sound out of Whittier or Seward and can steer you to the only licensed lesbian ship captain in the state. Having been a resident of Anchorage for the past 20 years, the host will be glad to assist with suggestions on how to make your visit to the beautiful state a memorable one. Alaska is a very young state. Come share the vibrant energy!

**Address: 211 W Cook, Anchorage, AK 99501. Tel: (907) 277-3862.**

**Type:** Bed & breakfast.
**Clientele:** Mostly gay & lesbian with some straight clientele.
**Transportation:** Taxi or rental car.
**To Gay Bars:** 15-min walk or 3-min drive to the Raven, 10-min drive to The Wave.
**Rooms:** 3 rooms with queen beds.
**Bathrooms:** 1 private bath/toilet, 2 shared bath/shower/toilets.
**Meals:** Cont. breakfast.
**Vegetarian:** Available.
**Complimentary:** Tea & coffee.
**Dates Open:** All year.
**High Season:** Summer (June-September).
**Rates:** Summer $75-$95, winter $45-$65.
**Rsv'tns:** Required.
**Reserve Through:** Travel agent or call direct.
**Parking:** Ample free off-street parking.
**In-Room:** Telephone.
**On-Premises:** Laundry facilities.
**Exercise/Health:** Bikes.
**Swimming:** Pool nearby.
**Smoking:** Permitted outside only. All rooms non-smoking.
**Pets:** Not permitted.
**Handicap Access:** No.
**Children:** Permitted.
**Languages:** English.

## Aurora Winds, An Exceptional B&B Resort

Q-NET Gay/Lesbian ♀♂

### *Only One Thing Is Missing – YOU!*

Far exceeding the standards expected by today's most discriminating traveler, the 5,200-square foot ***Aurora Winds*** has five sumptuous guest suites, each with its own private bathroom on two secluded acres overlooking Anchorage. The professionally decorated and furnished B&B has an atmosphere of quiet elegance and a contemporary style with an Alaskan home ambiance. Each of the nonsmoking guest rooms is furnished with queen-sized beds, televisions, VCRs, phones, and private sitting areas. Mornings, you have your choice of breakfast selections. Either a full complement of culinary delights or an expanded continental breakfast is available in the dining room or, if you prefer, in bed.

You will be pleasantly surprised by the many amenities the ***Aurora Winds*** has to offer, including a 10-person Jacuzzi where you can visit with other guests and enjoy a glass of wine following your workout in the exercise room. You might wish to relax in the sauna, play a game of billiards, watch a video on the 52-inch surround sound TV, or just curl up with your best friend in front of one of the four fireplaces.

As your hosts, we strive to provide you with all the services you may need. The ***Aurora Winds*** is less than 20 minutes from many local attractions. In addition to the unlimited natural wonders that you will find in Anchorage, there are also three gay bars, five bookstores, and a thriving gay community. We look forward to providing you with the special type of hospitality that only Alaskans can offer.

**Address: 7501 Upper O'Malley, Anchorage, AK 99516**
**Tel: (907) 346-2533, E-mail: awbnb@alaska.net.**

**Type:** Bed & breakfast.
**Clientele:** Good mix of gay men & women with some straight clientele
**Transportation:** Car is best & advised. Pick up available with prior arrangement
**To Gay Bars:** Approximately 15 minutes.
**Rooms:** 5 suites with queen beds.
**Bathrooms:** All private.
**Meals:** Expanded continental breakfast or full breakfast available.
**Vegetarian:** Available with advance notice.
**Complimentary:** Coffee, tea, sodas, mineral waters, & evening nightcap.
**Dates Open:** All year.
**High Season:** May 15-September 15.
**Rates:** Winter $65-$105 & summer $85-$125.
**Discounts:** For longer stays. Inquire for others.
**Credit Cards:** MC, VISA & Amex.
**Rsv'tns:** Recommended, especially during high season.
**Reserve Through:** Travel agent or call direct.
**Parking:** Ample free off-street parking.
**In-Room:** Telephone & color TV.
**On-Premises:** Meeting rooms, billiards room, TV lounge, theatre room, laundry facilities, & kitchen privileges.
**Exercise/Health:** Exercise room, free weights & 10-person Jacuzzi.
**Swimming:** 3 minutes to year-round Olympic indoor pool.
**Sunbathing:** On the common sun deck.
**Nudity:** Permitted in the hot tub.
**Smoking:** In designated areas only. All sleeping & common areas are non-smoking.
**Pets:** Permitted, on approval.
**Handicap Access:** Partial.
**Children:** Permitted on approval only.
**Languages:** English. Emergency translator available.
**Your Host:** Bill & James

## Cheney Lake Bed & Breakfast

**Gay-Friendly ♀♂**

***Cheney Lake Bed & Breakfast*** is located on Cheney Lake in a quiet residential neighborhood. We have a great view of the mountains from the living and dining rooms, while the lake can be viewed from each bedroom and the deck. Curl up beside the fireplace, watch videos, soak in the hot tub, or chat with your hosts who are long-time Alaskans and can offer numerous suggestions on how to enjoy the beauty and adventure of Anchorage and Alaska.

**Address: 6333 Colgate Dr, Anchorage, AK 99504**
**Tel: (907) 337-4391, Fax: (907) 338-1023,**
**E-mail: cheneybb@alaska.net.**

**Type:** Bed & breakfast.
**Clientele:** Mostly straight with a gay/lesbian following.
**Transportation:** Car is best.
**To Gay Bars:** 10-15 minute drive to 3 bars.
**Rooms:** 3 rooms with king beds.
**Bathrooms:** Private: 2 bath/toilet/showers, 1 shower/toilet.
**Meals:** Continental breakfast.
**Vegetarian:** Available upon request.
**Complimentary:** Coffee, tea, sodas, beer, wine, juice. Candy & nuts in room.
**Dates Open:** All year.
**Rates:** Summer $85, winter $65.
**Credit Cards:** MC, VISA.
**Rsv'tns:** Preferred.
**Reserve Through:** Travel agent or call direct.
**Parking:** Ample free on- & off-street parking.
**In-Room:** Color TV, VCR, phone, ceiling fans, maid service.
**On-Premises:** Laundry facilities, TV lounge, video tape library, fax, copier, computer.
**Exercise/Health:** Nearby gym with weights.
**Smoking:** Permitted on outside deck. Non-smoking home.
**Pets:** Not permitted.
**Handicap Access:** No.
**Children:** No.
**Languages:** English.
**Your Host:** Mary & Janetta.

# FAIRBANKS

## Alta's Bed and Breakfast

**Q-NET Gay/Lesbian ♀♂**

This log home with modern amenities in a wilderness setting, only twenty miles from downtown Fairbanks, makes ***Alta's Bed & Breakfast*** a piece of Alaska's interior to be experienced. In summer, you can fish, hike, soak in the hot tub and enjoy the midnight sun. In winter you can rent snowmobiles, ski or watch the Northern Lights from the solarium. Plan your stay for the Alaska Women's Festival, Solstice Party or even the Winter Carnival in March.

**Address: PO Box 82290, Fairbanks, AK 99708 Tel: (907) 389-2582.**

**Type:** Bed & breakfast.
**Clientele:** Mostly gay & lesbian with some straight clientele
**Transportation:** Free pick up from airport, train & bus can be arranged.
**To Gay Bars:** Fairbanks, Fri & Sat late evenings at the Palace Saloon.
**Rooms:** 1 single & 1 king.
**Bathrooms:** 1 private shower/toilet & 1 shared bath/shower/toilet.
**Campsites:** 2 RV parking only.
**Meals:** Full breakfast.
**Vegetarian:** Available upon request.
**Complimentary:** Soda, coffee, tea & juices.
**Dates Open:** All year.
**Rates:** $50-$75.
**Credit Cards:** MC & VISA through Triangle Tours, Anchorage.
**Rsv'tns:** Preferred.
**Reserve Through:** Travel agent or call direct.
**Parking:** Ample free parking. Heated garage for rental cars in winter.
**In-Room:** Maid service upon request.
**On-Premises:** TV lounge, laundry facilities & solarium dining room.
**Exercise/Health:** Hiking, cross-country skiing & snowmobiling.
**Sunbathing:** On common sun decks.
**Nudity:** Clothing optional on deck.
**Smoking:** Permitted outside only. All rooms are non-smoking.
**Pets:** Not permitted.
**Handicap Access:** No.
**Children:** Permitted.
**Languages:** English, Spanish, Russian.
**Your Host:** Pete.

# HOMER

## Island Watch B&B

Gay-friendly ♀♂

### *"A Room With a View"*

Situated in a quiet location, five minutes from Homer, ***Island Watch B&B*** provides a rural feeling within the city limits. Our spacious, cozy accommodations feature views of Kachemak Bay and the Kenai Mountain Range. We offer four units, two of which are ideal for guests who want a very private space. One of our units is made for the physically-challenged. Breakfasts are served family-style in the main house. Nearby walking trails and picnic areas are at your disposal and there are bikes for rent.

**Address: PO Box 1394, Homer, AK 99603**
**Tel: (907) 235-2265.**

**Type:** Bed & breakfast.
**Clientele:** Mostly straight clientele with a 30% gay & lesbian following
**Rooms:** 2 rooms, 1 suite & 1 cabin.
**Meals:** Full breakfast with fresh eggs, fruit & grains.
**Vegetarian:** No meat served.
**Dates Open:** Year round.
**Rates:** $75-$100 per couple, $50 single.
**Discounts:** 10% for over 3 days.
**Credit Cards:** Discover, MC, Visa.
**Parking:** On premises.
**Exercise/Health:** Bikes for rent, hiking trails.
**Smoking:** Permitted outside.
**Pets:** No.
**Handicap Access:** Yes. 1 room.
**Children:** Welcome.
**Languages:** English.

# ARIZONA

## FLAGSTAFF

### Chalet in the Pines

Gay/Lesbian ♂

*A Chalet in the Pines, 15 Miles from Flagstaff, Arizona*

Nestled in the mountains of northern Arizona, at Pinewood Country Club in Munds Park, Arizona, is cozy ***Chalet in the Pines.*** The chalet is surrounded by national forest with over 200 miles of logging trails to hike, cross-country ski or just explore. The chalet has a large fireplace, vaulted ceilings, entertainment center and large redwood deck, as well as formal dining and catering available for those special occasions. Country club facilities are available, including golf, tennis, pool and dining. Whether you are by yourself or with a special friend, you'll find the atmosphere here relaxing, quiet and enjoyable.

A 2-1/2 hour drive to the Flagstaff area from Phoenix takes you through a variety of landscapes which change as the elevation gets higher. When you arrive in Flagstaff, you are definitely in the pines. The city is presided over by the rather stately presence of the San Francisco Peaks, two ancient volcanic mountains which stay snow-covered till very late each spring. Flagstaff's Snow Bowl has downhill skiing, and there are lots of crosscountry skiing trails in the area. Another two hours north lies the Grand Canyon. It's an easy day trip to the Petrified Forest, where you can see and touch giant trees that were turned to stone eons ago and see a movie depicting the wetter, warmer environs that once characterized the area. Even closer to Flagstaff is the Meteor Crater. Its huge size will amaze you even more when you tour its museum and find out how small was the meteor which created it. Another nice day trip takes you winding down the mountains along Oak Creek to Sedona. The scenery is incredible, and dining choices abound.

**Address: PO Box 25640, Munds Park, AZ 86017. Tel: (520) 286-2417.**

**Type:** Bed & breakfast at a country club.
**Clientele:** Mostly men with women welcome
**Transportation:** Car is best (15 mi from Flagstaff, 110 mi from Phoenix).
**To Gay Bars:** 15 miles to gay bars in Flagstaff.
**Rooms:** 3 rooms, 1 suite with single, dbl or king beds.
**Bathrooms:** 1 private full bath, 2 shared full baths.
**Meals:** Expanded continental & full breakfast. Dinner available.
**Complimentary:** Tea, coffee, cocktails, set up service.
**Dates Open:** All year.
**High Season:** July-August.
**Rates:** Single \$75, double \$110-\$125.
**Discounts:** Weekly 10%.
**Rsv'tns:** Preferred.
**Reserve Thru:** Call direct.
**Parking:** Ample off-street parking.
**In-Room:** Color cable TV, VCR, tele., maid service.
**On-Premises:** Laundry facilities, video tape library, fireplace.
**Exercise/Health:** Jacuzzi. Nearby sauna & country club.
**Swimming:** Nearby country club pool.
**Sunbathing:** On common sun decks at chalet & poolside at country club.
**Smoking:** Permitted on the deck.
**Pets:** Permitted with owner's approval.
**Handicap Access:** No.
**Children:** No.
**Languages:** English.
**Your Host:** Mike & Steve.

## The Inn at 410 Bed & Breakfast

Gay-Friendly ♀♂

### *The Place with the Personal Touch*

"***The Inn at 410 B&B*** skips over excellence and moves toward perfection," said one guest. From this charming 1907 Craftsman home, you can explore the Grand Canyon, Indian country, Sedona, and Oak Creek Canyon. Nine spacious guest rooms, some with fireplaces or whirlpools, are uniquely decorated. Afternoon cookies fresh from the oven and scrumptious gourmet breakfasts are available. Walk to shops, galleries, and restaurants in historic downtown Flagstaff and enjoy hiking, mountain biking, and skiing in the San Francisco peaks.

**Address:** 410 North Leroux St, Flagstaff, AZ 86001
**Tel:** (520) 774-0088, (800) 774-2008.

**Type:** Bed & breakfast.
**Clientele:** Mostly straight clientele with a gay/lesbian following.
**Rooms:** 5 rooms, 4 suites with single, queen or king beds.
**Bathrooms:** Private: 1 shower/toilets, 8 bath/toilet/showers.
**Meals:** Full breakfast.
**Vegetarian:** Breakfasts are vegetarian. Vegans, please inform innkeepers.
**Complimentary:** Coffee, tea, hot chocolate. In dining room: cookies, iced tea in summer, hot cider in winter.
**Dates Open:** All year.
**High Season:** April/May-October.
**Rates:** $110-$165.
**Credit Cards:** MC, VISA.
**Rsv'tns:** Advisable on weekends, holidays, high season.
**Reserve Through:** Travel agent or call direct.
**Minimum Stay:** 2 nights on weekends Apr-Oct, 3 nights some holidays.
**Parking:** Ample free off-street parking.
**In-Room:** AC, coffee/tea-making facilities, refrigerator, ceiling fans, maid service.
**On-Premises:** Games, books, fireplace, garden gazebo.
**Exercise/Health:** Massage on premises. Nearby gym with weights, Jacuzzi, sauna, steam, massage.
**Swimming:** Pool nearby.
**Smoking:** Not permitted anywhere on property.
**Pets:** Not permitted, kennel nearby.
**Handicap Access:** Yes. Dining room & 1 guest room wheelchair accessible.
**Children:** Welcome if well-behaved & -supervised. No cribs or highchairs on premises.
**Languages:** English.
**Your Host:** Howard & Sally.

# PHOENIX

## Arizona Royal Villa

Men ♂

Enjoy Palm Springs-style accommodations in downtown Phoenix. Accommodations are available for long or short stays, ranging from one day to several months. The walled complex is totally private, with keyed entry. Rooms range from small hotel rooms to furnished one-bedroom apartments. The pool and Jacuzzi are open year-round. ***The Arizona Royal Villa*** is popular, because of the amenities, competitive rates and strategic location to all the bars. Book early to avoid disappointment! Day passes available for $10.

**Address:** 1110 E Turney Ave, Phoenix, AZ 85014
**Tel:** (602) 266-6883 (Tel/Fax). **Email:** azroyalvil@aol.com.

**Type:** Bed & breakfast motel.
**Clientele:** Men only
**Transportation:** Car is best. $10 for pick up from airport.
**To Gay Bars:** Walking distance to 1 local gay bar & rest., others 1 mile away.
**Rooms:** 3 rooms, 3 suites & 3 apartments with queen beds.
**Bathrooms:** All private.
**Meals:** Continental breakfast.
**Dates Open:** All year.
**High Season:** Oct-May.
**Rates:** High season (Oct-May) from $55.95. Low season (Jun-Sep) from $45.95.
**Credit Cards:** MC, VISA, Amex.
**Rsv'tns:** Recommended.
**Reserve Through:** Travel agent or call direct.
**Minimum Stay:** Two nights on holiday weekends.
**Parking:** Adequate free parking.
**In-Room:** Color cable TV, AC, coffee & tea-making facilities, kitchen, refrigerator.
**On-Premises:** Laundry facilities.

*continued next page*

**Exercise/Health:** Jacuzzi, weights.
**Swimming:** Heated pool on premises (in season only).
**Sunbathing:** At poolside.
**Nudity:** Permitted.
**Smoking:** Permitted.
**Pets:** Not permitted.
**Handicap Access:** No.
**Children:** Not permitted.
**Languages:** English, some French, Italian, Spanish.

## Arizona Sunburst Inn

Men ♂

### *"A Man's Resort" in the Heart of Phoenix*

The ***Arizona Sunburst Inn*** provides a unique setting in the Valley of the Sun that is totally private, yet in the heart of the city. Only blocks away from the gay bars and the only all-male, clothing-optional resort in Phoenix, we offer spacious rooms with queen-sized beds, cable TV, some private baths and some shared baths. A tropical-garden-like yard is complete with patios, a large heated pool and a hot tub.

**Address: 6245 N 12th Place, Phoenix, AZ 85014**
**Tel: (602) 274-1474, (800) 974-1474.**

**Type:** Bed & breakfast resort.
**Clientele:** Men only.
**To Gay Bars:** 6 blocks.
**Rooms:** Seven rooms with queen beds.
**Bathrooms:** Private & shared.
**Meals:** Expanded continental breakfast.
**Dates Open:** All year.
**High Season:** Oct to May.
**Rates:** $59-$99.
**Credit Cards:** MC, VISA, Amex.
**Rsv'tns:** Required.
**Reserve Through:** Call direct.
**Parking:** Ample off-street & on-street parking.
**In-Room:** Color cable TV, AC, coffee/tea-making facilities & maid service.
**On-Premises:** Kitchen.
**Exercise/Health:** Hot tub & massage on premises. Nearby gym, weights, sauna & steam.
**Swimming:** Pool on premises.
**Sunbathing:** On the patio area around the pool.
**Nudity:** Clothing optional.
**Smoking:** Permitted on patio. No smoking in rooms.
**Pets:** Not permitted.
**Handicap Access:** No.
**Children:** No.
**Languages:** English.
**Your Host:** Bill & Wayne.

## Larry's B & B

Gay/Lesbian ♂

### *A Gay Place to Stay*

At ***Larry's B & B,*** our large private home offers three guest rooms, with shared bath or private bath, living and family rooms, all at economical rates. Guests enjoy the beauty of Phoenix's weather in the privacy of our pool area, surrounded by walls and tropical vegetation. We are near both golf and tennis facilities. Full breakfast is included, lunch and dinner are available by arrangement. Pickup at Sky Harbor Airport is $10.00.

**Address: 502 W Claremont Ave, Phoenix, AZ 85013-2974**
**Tel: (602) 249-2974.**

**Type:** A true bed & breakfast in our home.
**Clientele:** Mostly gay men with women welcome. Some straight clientele such as relatives or friends
**Transportation:** Pick up from bus, airport or train for $10.
**To Gay Bars:** 5 minutes to gay/lesbian bars.
**Rooms:** 3 rooms with queen or king beds.
**Bathrooms:** 1 private bath/toilet, 1 shared full bath.
**Meals:** Full breakfast, lunch & dinner by arrangement.
**Vegetarian:** Upon request.
**Complimentary:** Tea, coffee & soft drinks. Wine or hard drinks with meals.
**Dates Open:** All year.
**High Season:** January through April.
**Rates:** Singles $45-$50 daily, $250-$300 weekly. Doubles $50-$65 daily, $300-$400 weekly.
**Discounts:** $5 off 2nd to 6th day per room on daily rate.
**Rsv'tns:** Preferred.
**Reserve Through:** Call direct.
**Parking:** Ample free off-street parking.
**In-Room:** Telephone, color TV & ceiling fans, AC.
**On-Premises:** Central AC/heat, TV lounge, laundry facilities & use of refrigerators.
**Exercise/Health:** Jacuzzi.
**Swimming:** Pool, not heated in winter.
**Sunbathing:** At poolside, on patio & common sun decks.
**Nudity:** Permitted in backyard, please inquire.
**Smoking:** Permitted without restrictions.
**Pets:** Permitted.
**Handicap Access:** Yes.
**Children:** Permitted.
**Languages:** English, limited Japanese, Spanish.

## Stewart's B&B

**Gay/Lesbian ♂**

### *A Welcoming B&B*

Conveniently located in North Central Phoenix, this frontier-style home offers a friendly home feeling that says "Welcome." At ***Stewart's B&B,*** enjoy the patio setting, sunbathe next to the moss-covered fountain, feed the goldfish, or hold hands with someone special in front of the patio's beehive fireplace on a cool winter evening. Guests can hike in the nearby Phoenix Mountain Preserve, follow the canals through the city on foot or on bicycles, and dine at some of the nearby world-renowned restaurants.

**Address: 1319 E. Hayward, Phoenix, AZ**
**Tel: (602) 861-2500, Fax: (602) 861-0242, E-mail: stewphx@aol.com.**

**Type:** Bed & breakfast.
**Clientele:** Mostly men with women welcome. Especially leather-friendly
**Transportation:** $10 pick up from airport by arrangement.
**To Gay Bars:** 6 miles, a 5-minute drive.
**Rooms:** 3 rooms with double or queen beds.
**Bathrooms:** Shared bath/shower/toilet.
**Meals:** Expanded continental breakfast.
**Vegetarian:** Available on special request, if possible to accommodate.
**Complimentary:** Coffee, tea, pop.
**Dates Open:** All year.
**Rates:** Double $55, Queen $75, $10 extra per person per room.
**Discounts:** 20% discount after 4th night.
**Credit Cards:** MC, VISA.
**Rsv'tns:** Required.
**Reserve Through:** Call direct.
**Parking:** Ample free off-street parking. Trailer parking possible.
**In-Room:** AC/air cooler, telephone.
**On-Premises:** TV lounge, video tape library, laundry facilities, fax, e-mail, computer, copy machine.
**Exercise/Health:** Weights/workout machine.
**Sunbathing:** On patio.
**Nudity:** Permitted throughout house & on patio.
**Smoking:** Permitted outside only. House non-smoking.
**Pets:** Permitted if small, well-trained & friendly.
**Handicap Access:** No.
**Children:** No.
**Languages:** English, some German & Spanish.
**Your Host:** Stewart.

## Windsor Cottage

**Gay/Lesbian ♂**

### *Where Everyone Is Treated Like Royalty*

Feel like a king or queen when you stay at ***Windsor Cottage,*** two English Tudor-style cottages with full baths, living areas, sleeping areas and fresh flowers. French doors open to the pool surrounded by beautiful gardens where breakfast is served. Located in the heart of Phoenix, ***Windsor Cottage*** is central to the very best that Phoenix has to offer. Only minutes away from museums, theaters, symphonies, sports, restaurants, shops, parks, and the bars, it is nestled in the Willow Historic District of Central Phoenix. Massage is available onsite by appointment and bikes are available for explorers.

**Address: 62 West Windsor, Phoenix, AZ 85003. Tel: (602) 264-6309.**

**Type:** Bed & breakfast guesthouse cottages
**Clientele:** Mostly men with women welcome.
**Transportation:** Car, airport Super Shuttle ($7), pick up from airport or train by arrangement, $10.
**To Gay Bars:** 2 miles.
**Rooms:** 2 cottages with queen beds.
**Bathrooms:** Private shower/toilet.
**Meals:** Expanded continental breakfast.
**Vegetarian:** Please inquire.
**Complimentary:** Soda, bottled water.
**Dates Open:** All year.
**High Season:** October-May.
**Rates:** $55-$125.
**Credit Cards:** MC, Visa, Amex.
**Rsv'tns:** Required.
**Reserve Through:** Travel agent or call direct.
**Minimum Stay:** Required.
**Parking:** Ample free off-street parking.
**In-Room:** Color cable TV, phone, ceiling fans, AC, coffee/tea-making facilities, refrigerator, microwave, laundry service.
**On-Premises:** Laundry facilities.
**Exercise/Health:** Massage, bikes on premises.
**Swimming:** Pool on premises.
**Sunbathing:** At poolside.
**Nudity:** Permitted at poolside.
**Smoking:** Permitted outdoors & at poolside only.
**Pets:** Not permitted.
**Handicap Access:** Yes.
**Children:** No.
**Languages:** English.
**Your Host:** Greg & John.

# SEDONA

## Cozy Cactus

**Gay-Friendly ♀♂**

Overlooking the valley between Sedona's red rock cliffs and one of John Wayne's favorite movie locations, Wild Horse Mesa, we invite you to share the sunsets from our patio, as they play across the nearby red cliffs. ***Cozy Cactus*** is a ranch-style home, comfortably furnished with family heirlooms and theatrical memorabilia from our professional careers. Each guest room has large windows and private bath. Each pair of bedrooms share a sitting room with fireplace and small kitchen, perfect for two couples traveling together.

**Address: 80 Canyon Circle Dr, Sedona, AZ 86351**
**Tel: (520) 284-0082, (800) 788-2082. Fax: (520) 284-4210.**

**Type:** Bed & breakfast.
**Clientele:** Mostly straight clientele with a gay & lesbian following.
**Transportation:** Car is best.
**To Gay Bars:** 120 miles to Phoenix.
**Rooms:** 5 rooms with single, queen or king beds.
**Bathrooms:** All private bath/toilets.
**Meals:** Full breakfast.
**Vegetarian:** Available.
**Complimentary:** Refreshments available in the afternoon.
**Dates Open:** All year.
**High Season:** March-May, September-November.
**Rates:** $95-$115 for 2 people.
**Discounts:** Special weekly rates. AAA & Senior discount 10%.
**Credit Cards:** MC, VISA, Amex & Discover.
**Rsv'tns:** Recommended.
**Reserve Through:** Travel agent or call direct.
**Parking:** Ample free off-street parking.
**In-Room:** AC, refrigerator, & maid service. Fireplace in sitting area.
**On-Premises:** TV lounge & laundry facilities.
**Exercise/Health:** 3 major golf courses in town.
**Swimming:** 10 minutes to community pool. 15 minutes to swimming hole at Slide Rock.
**Sunbathing:** On the patio.
**Smoking:** Permitted on patios only.
**Pets:** Not permitted.
**Handicap Access:** Yes.
**Children:** Welcome.
**Languages:** English, Italian & ASL.

## The Huff 'n Puff Straw Bale Inn

**Gay/Lesbian ♀♂**

Do the following things tickle your fancy? Canoeing the Verde River while being followed by great blue heron... Wading in Wet Beaver Creek and then sunbathing on huge red boulders... Spotting roadrunners and quail on your return to the inn... Scouting Indian ruins and seeing petroglyphs... If so, then make your reservation now at ***The Huff 'n Puff Straw Bale Inn,*** just 19 miles from Sedona. Please note that this is a non-toxic home, no perfumes or hair spray, please.

**Address: PO Box 406, Rimrock, AZ 86335. Tel: (520) 567-9066.**

**Type:** Inn.
**Clientele:** Mostly gay & lesbian with some straight clientele
**Transportation:** Car is best or airport shuttle to Camp Verde. Pickup from Camp Verde (airport shuttle) $10.
**To Gay Bars:** 47 miles, a 55 min drive.
**Rooms:** 2 rooms with queen beds.
**Bathrooms:** Private: 1 shower & toilet, 1 bath/shower/toilet.
**Campsites:** RV parking only. 1 indoor bath with tub & shower.
**Meals:** Continental breakfast.
**Vegetarian:** Available (cooked) for lunch & dinner, $10 per person per meal.
**Complimentary:** Tea & coffee.
**Dates Open:** All year.
**Rates:** $50-$60.
**Discounts:** Up to 1/2 of fee is work exchangeable.
**Reserve Through:** Travel agent or call direct.
**Minimum Stay:** Not required, but $5 extra for stays of only 1 night.
**Parking:** Ample free off-street parking.
**In-Room:** Swamp cooler, color cable TV (satellite).
**On-Premises:** Tours of Indian ruins can be arranged.
**Exercise/Health:** Massage.
**Swimming:** In nearby creek.
**Sunbathing:** In yard.
**Smoking:** Both rooms non-smoking. No smoking allowed.
**Pets:** Permitted, except for Jan-Feb & must be on leash.
**Handicap Access:** Yes. Wheelchair ramp, handicap shower, non-toxic home (no perfumes or hair spray, please).
**Children:** Welcome.
**Languages:** English.
**Your Host:** Susan.

## Marti's Guest Ranch

Q-NET Gay/Lesbian ♀♂

### *A Paradise For Bird Watching and Nature Walks*

Come relax and enjoy yourself in a private, rustic guest cottage on a historical 65-acre ranch beside Oak Creek. You'll experience memorable sunsets as ducks, geese and heron settle for the night on the banks of the creek. Cool, splashing creek waters, coyotes, hawks and cows call to you. ***Marti's Guest Ranch*** includes two bedrooms, private bath, a living room, sun room, cable TV with VCR and movies. The fully equipped kitchen is stocked with coffee, tea and condiments. We're 20 minutes from a gaming casino, 30 minutes from Sedona or Old Town Cottonwood and 45 minutes from Jerome Ghost Town.

**Address: Mail: Cornville Ranch, PO Box 605, Cornville, AZ 86325**
**Tel: (520) 634-4842, E-mail: MartiMac@Sedona.net.**

**Type:** Cottage.
**Clientele:** Gay & lesbian. Good mix of men & women
**Transportation:** Car is best.
**Rooms:** 1 cottage with single or double beds.
**Bathrooms:** 1 private bath/toilet/shower.
**Meals:** Continental breakfast.
**Vegetarian:** Available upon request.
**Complimentary:** Tea, coffee, Artesian well water, sparkling apple cider, condiments, cookies, soda, milk & bagels, muffins or rolls & juice, popcorn, soups, flowers.
**Dates Open:** All year.
**Rates:** $50-$170.
**Rsv'tns:** Required.
**Reserve Through:** Call direct.
**Parking:** Ample free covered off-street parking. No RV or motor home parking.
**In-Room:** Color cable TV, VCR, window AC, ceiling fans, coffee & tea-making facilities, kitchen, refrigerator. Telephone for local calls.
**On-Premises:** Video tape, book & game libraries.
**Swimming:** At river on premises.
**Sunbathing:** On river banks.
**Smoking:** Permitted on outside porch. Non-smoking rooms available.
**Pets:** Not permitted.
**Handicap Access:** No.
**Children:** No.
**Languages:** English.

## Paradise by the Creek B&B

Women ♀

### *Serenity Awaits You at Our Red Rock Hideaway*

Nestled in a green valley amidst red rock canyons, our cozy ranch home sits on a quiet lane surrounded by willows and cottonwoods. You can swim in the creek or laze on its banks and watch the sun set orange on spectacular Cathedral Rock. ***Paradise by the Creek's*** two guest rooms with shared bath are perfect for two couples travelling together, but if it's just a getaway for the two of you, then the whole suite is yours. Wait till you see the stars in the Sedona sky!

**Address: 215 Disney Lane, Sedona, AZ**
**Tel: (520) 282-7107, E-mail: drdeb@sedona.net.**

**Type:** Bed & breakfast.
**Clientele:** Mostly women with men welcome
**Transportation:** Car is best. We're 2 hours north of Phoenix.
**To Gay Bars:** 120 miles. None in Sedona.
**Rooms:** 2 rooms with double or queen beds.
**Bathrooms:** 1 private bath/toilet/shower, 1 shared bath/shower/toilet.
**Campsites:** RV parking only, electric hook up only.
**Meals:** Cont. breakfast.
**Vegetarian:** Vegetarian restaurants in Sedona township, 3 miles away.
**Complimentary:** Plenty of fresh fruit & orange juices.
**Dates Open:** All year.
**Rates:** $75 for 1-2 people, $100 for 3-4 people.
**Discounts:** For stays of 5 days or more.
**Rsv'tns:** Required.
**Reserve Thru:** Call direct.
**Parking:** Ample free off-street parking.
**In-Room:** AC, telephone, ceiling fans, refrigerator, coffee & tea-making facilities.
**Exercise/Health:** Nearby massage, floats, healings, psychic readings.
**Swimming:** Creek nearby.
**Sunbathing:** In priv. garden.
**Smoking:** Permitted outside, rooms are non-smoking.
**Handicap Access:** No, but willing to accommodate special needs on individual basis.
**Children:** Welcome. There are pets, farm animals, creek & trees for them to explore.
**Languages:** English.
**Your Host:** Cheryl & Debbie.

## Paradise Ranch

**Women ♀**

If you are looking for a quiet place to relax from your daily routine or are interested in bringing someone special to a beautiful retreat, ***Paradise Ranch*** offers a guesthouse for women who want to experience the beauty of Sedona in a safe environment. Fill your lungs with our perfect clean air and bubble your cares away in the privacy of our hot tub, surrounded by beautiful trees and clear blue sky. Get in touch with your soul in our sweat lodge. Let yourself be pampered at ***Paradise Ranch,*** the area that the Yavapi Indians called the home of the Great Mother.

**Address: 135 Kachina Dr, Sedona, AZ 86336. Tel: (520) 282-9769.**

**Type:** Guesthouse.
**Clientele:** Women only.
**Transportation:** Car is best.
**Rooms:** 1 cottage with double bed.
**Bathrooms:** 1 private.
**Complimentary:** Tea & coffee.
**Dates Open:** All year.
**Rates:** $85 to $125 per night.
**Rsv'tns:** Required.
**Reserve Through:** Call direct.
**Parking:** Ample free parking.
**In-Room:** Color TV, evap cooler, kitchen, refrigerator, laundry service.
**On-Premises:** Meeting rooms.
**Exercise/Health:** Jacuzzi, massage, sweat lodge, life readings, life force transfusions, crystal healings.
**Swimming:** Creek.
**Nudity:** Permitted in Jacuzzi & while sunbathing.
**Smoking:** Not permitted.
**Pets:** Not permitted.
**Handicap Access:** No.
**Children:** Not permitted.
**Languages:** English, some German, some Spanish.

# TUCSON

## Adobe Rose Inn Bed & Breakfast

**Gay-Friendly ♀♂**

### *"What is More Agreeable Than One's Home?" – Cicero*

Casual comfort best describes the atmoshpere of ***The Adobe Rose Inn,*** a beautifully restored 1933 adobe home located in the historic Sam Hughes neighborhood, just two blocks from the university. There are three charming lodgepole-furnished rooms in the main house, two of which have cozy, beehive fireplaces and stained-glass windows. There are also two private cottages that are ideally suited for longer stays. All rooms have cable television and private baths, as well as access to the very private bougainvillea-draped swimming pool and hot tub. The property is gated and surrounded by six-foot adobe walls, providing privacy and enhancing the quiet of this prestigious neighborhood.

**Address: 940 N Olsen Ave, Tucson, AZ 85719**
**Tel: (520) 318-4644, (800) 328-4122, Fax: (520) 325-0055.**

**Type:** Bed & breakfast.
**Clientele:** Mostly straight clientele with a gay/lesbian following
**Transportation:** Rental car, taxi or shuttle.
**To Gay Bars:** 2 miles, a 5-minute drive.
**Rooms:** 3 rooms, 2 cottages with single, queen or king beds.
**Bathrooms:** Private: 3

shower/toilets, 2 bath/toilet/showers.
**Meals:** Full breakfast.
**Vegetarian:** Always available (meat always served on the side), special diet meals with advance notice.
**Complimentary:** Cookies, lemonade.
**Dates Open:** All year.
**High Season:** Jan.-Apr.
**Rates:** Summer $45-$55, Sept-Dec $70-$85, Jan-May $95-$105.
**Discounts:** Senior (60+) discounts.
**Credit Cards:** MC, Visa, Eurocard, Discover.
**Rsv'tns:** Reservations suggested, walk-ins welcome.
**Reserve Through:** Travel agent or call direct.
**Minimum Stay:** Required at certain times of the year.
**Parking:** Ample on- & off-street parking.
**In-Room:** Maid service, kitchen, refrigerator, ceiling fans, phone, AC, color cable TV, VCR, coffee/tea-making facilities.
**Exercise/Health:** Hot tub on premises. Nearby gym, weights, Jacuzzi, sauna, steam, massage.
**Swimming:** Pool on premises.
**Sunbathing:** Poolside, on common sundecks, on patio.
**Smoking:** Permitted outside only, all rooms are non-smoking.
**Pets:** Not permitted.
**Handicap Access:** No.
**Children:** No.
**Languages:** English.

## Casa Alegre Bed & Breakfast Inn

Gay-Friendly ♀♂

### *Warmth & Happiness of a Bygone Era*

Our distinguished, 1915 craftsman-style bungalow is just minutes from the University of Arizona and downtown Tucson. At *Casa Alegre,* each guest room has private bath and its decor reflects an aspect of Tucson's history, such as the mining industry or the Indian Nation. The Arizona sitting room opens onto the inn's serene patio and pool area, and is equipped with TV/VCR. A scrumptious full breakfast is served in the sun room, formal dining room or outside on the patio. Shopping, dining and entertainment are all within walking distance.

**Address: 316 East Speedway Blvd, Tucson, AZ 85705**
**Tel: (520) 628-1800, (800) 628-5654, Fax: (520) 792-1880.**

**Type:** Bed & breakfast.
**Clientele:** Mostly straight with a gay & lesbian following.
**Transportation:** Car is best. Shuttle service from airport $15 maximum.
**To Gay Bars:** 3 blocks.
**Rooms:** 5 rooms with queen or king beds.
**Bathrooms:** All private bath/toilets.
**Meals:** Full breakfast.
**Vegetarian:** Available upon request.
**Complimentary:** Cool soft drinks & snacks by pool in summer, tea & goodies in front of fireplace in winter.
**Dates Open:** All year.
**High Season:** September 1 through May 31.
**Rates:** Summer $55-$70, rest of year $75-$95.
**Discounts:** 10% senior, corporate, week or longer stays.
**Credit Cards:** MC, VISA, Discover.
**Rsv'tns:** Preferred.
**Reserve Through:** Travel agent or call direct.
**Parking:** Ample free on-street & off-street covered parking.
**In-Room:** AC, ceiling fans, maid service.
**On-Premises:** Meeting rooms, TV lounge & guests' refrigerator on covered patio.
**Exercise/Health:** Spa on premises. Nearby gym, weights, sauna, steam & massage.
**Swimming:** Pool on premises.
**Sunbathing:** At poolside or on patio.
**Nudity:** Permitted in pool & patio area with discretion.
**Smoking:** Permitted outside only.
**Pets:** No facilities available for pets.
**Handicap Access:** No.
**Children:** Permitted under close supervision of parents because of antiques & pool.
**Languages:** English.

## Casa Tierra Adobe Bed & Breakfast Inn

Gay-Friendly ♀♂

### *The Quintessential Desert Experience*

*Casa Tierra* is located on five acres of beautiful Sonoran desert, fifteen miles west of Tucson and minutes from The Desert Museum and Saguaro National Park. This area is famous for its unique Saguaro cacti, spectacular mountain views and brilliant sunsets. Our rustic adobe home with vaulted brick ceilings, interior arched courtyard and Mexican furnishings, recalls haciendas found in old Mexico. Each guest room has a private bath, queen-sized bed, microwave oven, small refrigerator, private entrance and a patio overlooking the desert landscape. After a day of sightseeing, hiking or birding, enjoy the Jacuzzi or just relax with us in the quiet of the desert.

**Address: 11155 West Calle Pima, Tucson, AZ 85743**
**Tel: (520) 578-3058 (Tel/Fax).**

**Type:** Bed & breakfast inn.
**Clientele:** Mostly straight with a gay & lesbian following.
**Transportation:** Car is necessary.
**To Gay Bars:** 15 miles or 25 minutes.
**Rooms:** 3 rooms with queen beds.
**Bathrooms:** 2 private bath/shower/toilets & 1 private shower/toilet.
**Meals:** Full breakfast.
**Vegetarian:** Always.
**Complimentary:** Tea & coffee self-serve bar, fruit in room.
**Dates Open:** Sept 1-May 31.
**High Season:** Feb, Mar, Apr & holidays.
**Rates:** $85-$95. $10 extra for single night stay, $10 for a third person.
**Discounts:** 10% for 7 or more days.
**Rsv'tns:** Suggested.
**Reserve Through:** Call direct.
**Minimum Stay:** Two nights or $10 extra.
**Parking:** Ample free off-street parking.
**In-Room:** Telephone, ceiling fans, evaporative coolers, microwave & refrigerator.
**Exercise/Health:** Jacuzzi. Massage by appointment.
**Sunbathing:** On the patio.
**Nudity:** Permitted in the Jacuzzi with discretion.
**Smoking:** Permitted on outside private patios only.
**Pets:** Not permitted.
**Handicap Access:** No.
**Children:** Welcomed, age 3 and older.
**Languages:** English & small amounts of Spanish.
**Your Host:** Karen & Lyle.

## Catalina Park Inn

Gay Owned ♀♂

### *Comfort, Style and Elegance*

Overlooking Catalina Park, this historic residence offers you a comfortable environment of understated elegance. Our guest rooms are handsomely furnished with antiques and are equipped with most of the comforts of home. Enjoy a hearty breakfast in the dining room or in our lush perennial garden. We are superbly located in Tucson's

West University Historic District, within walking distance of the University of Arizona and Fourth Avenue's eclectic shops, restaurants, and nightlife. ***Catalina Park Inn*** offers a high level of comfort, privacy, and friendly service.

**Address: 309 East 1st St, Tucson, AZ 85705**
**Tel: (520) 792-4541, Fax: (520) 792-0838, Reservations: (800) 792-4885.**

**Type:** Gay-owned bed & breakfast inn.
**Clientele:** Friendly gay, lesbian & straight clientele.
**Transportation:** Car is best. Shuttle services from airport $15 maximum.
**To Gay Bars:** 3 blocks.
**Rooms:** 2 rooms, 1 suite & 1 cottage with queen beds.
**Bathrooms:** All private.
**Meals:** Full breakfast.
**Vegetarian:** Available on request. Restaurant & organic market a short walk from the inn.
**Complimentary:** Coffee & tea at all times from the Butler's Pantry.
**Dates Open:** All year.
**High Season:** Sept 1-May 31.
**Rates:** Low season (summer) $65-$85. Rest of year $90-$115.
**Discounts:** 10% for stays of a week or longer.
**Credit Cards:** VISA, MC.
**Rsv'tns:** Preferred.
**Reserve Through:** Call direct or travel agent.
**Parking:** Ample free on-street parking.
**In-Room:** Color remote cable TV, telephone, robes, alarm clock radio, hairdryer, iron & ironing board, fresh flowers, full-length mirror, maid service. Two rooms have private porches.
**On-Premises:** Large living room with fireplace, space for a small meeting or reception.
**Exercise/Health:** Facilities close by.
**Swimming:** Public pools & YMCA nearby.
**Smoking:** Limited to outside areas: garden, porches.
**Pets:** Not permitted.
**Handicap Access:** No.
**Children:** Over 10 years welcomed.
**Languages:** English, a bit of French.
**Your Host:** Paul & Mark.

## Dillinger House Bed & Breakfast

Q-NET Gay/Lesbian ♀♂

### *Dillinger Slept Here...*

The ***Dillinger House Bed & Breakfast*** is a delightful, historic house with two guest cottages in the West University District of Tucson. The house is two blocks from the main campus of the University of Arizona, as well as a very short walk to 4th Avenue which has become the cultural and arts center of Tucson. Every other Saturday night there is an event called Downtown Saturday Night, where the entire 4th Avenue and Downtown stores and galleries are open with live music and outside vendors.

The ***Dillinger House*** was occupied by the infamous John Dillinger and his gang of outlaws and was also the site of Dillinger's capture, as featured in the PBS documentary *Dillinger, Public Enemy #1*. The house is also the only registered national historic residence in Tucson. We have preserved the historic flavor of the property and welcome your stay.

We provide a continental breakfast each morning, including fresh organic juices, coffee, tea and an array of tasty specialties. A hot breakfast is available upon request. The cottages are fully self-contained with coffeemakers, bath and shower and cable TV. We have also fully landscaped our property to provide privacy and comfort for relaxing in the Jacuzzi, sunbathing or just taking advantage of Tucson's wonderful winter climate.

*continued next page*

We are just three blocks from IBT's, Tucson's hottest gay club, and are within a 3-mile radius of The Venture "N", Ain't Nobody's Biz and The Plug. We are also within walking distance of Tucson's Lesbian and Gay Center, WINGSPAN, as well as many other gay-owned businesses, coffee shops, a natural food store and vegetarian restaurants. Our central location provides easy access to Interstate 10, museums, hiking, restaurants, theater, movies and much more!!

**Address: 927 N. 2nd Ave, Tucson, AZ 85705**
**Tel: (520) 622-4306 (Tel/Fax). E-mail: muchmor@azstarnet.com.**

**Type:** Bed & breakfast.
**Clientele:** Mostly gay & lesbian with some straight clientele
**Transportation:** Car is best.
**To Gay Bars:** 3 blocks, a 10 min walk.
**Rooms:** 2 cottages with double beds.
**Bathrooms:** Private: 1 bath/toilet, 1 shower/toilet.
**Meals:** Expanded continental breakfast.
**Vegetarian:** Available on request. 3 blocks to vegetarian restaurant.
**Complimentary:** Coffee & tea in room.
**Dates Open:** Sept 1-July 1 (after July 1, please call).
**High Season:** Nov 1-May 10.
**Rates:** Winter $85-$115, summer $60-$90.
**Discounts:** One free night with five paid.
**Rsv'tns:** Required.
**Reserve Through:** Travel agent or call direct.
**Minimum Stay:** 2 nights on holiday weekends & during gem show.
**Parking:** Ample free parking. Covered parking in 1-br house.
**In-Room:** AC, ceiling fans, color cable TV, telephone, coffee & tea-making facilities, refrigerator, maid service. One cottage has kitchen.
**On-Premises:** TV lounge, laundry facilities.
**Exercise/Health:** Jacuzzi. Nearby gym, weights, Jacuzzi, sauna, steam, massage.
**Swimming:** Nearby river & lake.
**Sunbathing:** On patio.
**Nudity:** Permitted in Jacuzzi only.
**Smoking:** Permitted outside only.
**Pets:** Not permitted.
**Handicap Access:** No.
**Children:** No.
**Languages:** English.
**Your Host:** Sam & Mark.

## Montecito House

Women ♀

### *Mom, I'm Home!*

Experience the friendly, relaxed atmosphere of ***Montecito House,*** my home, not a business. My B & B is a hobby, a way to meet people from around the world. Discussions at breakfast over fresh grapefruit juice from the tree in my yard are usual. Many guests meet here once and establish friendships that grow each year. Returning guests often mention the feeling of coming home again.

**Address: PO Box 42352, Tucson, AZ 85733. Tel: (520) 795-7592.**

**Type:** Bed & breakfast.
**Clientele:** Mostly lesbian with men welcome. Some straight clientele.
**Transportation:** Car is best, pick up from airport, bus $10.
**To Gay Bars:** 2 miles.
**Rooms:** 2 rooms with double beds.
**Bathrooms:** 1 private bath/toilet & 1 shared bath/shower/toilet.
**Campsites:** RV parking with electric only, share inside bathroom.
**Meals:** Continental breakfast.
**Vegetarian:** Available upon prior arrangement.
**Complimentary:** Tea, soda, coffee, juices, fresh fruit, nuts, crackers.
**Dates Open:** All year.
**High Season:** February.
**Rates:** Summer $30-$35, winter $35-$40.
**Discounts:** On weekly rates with reservation.
**Rsv'tns:** Recommended.
**Reserve Through:** Call direct.
**Minimum Stay:** $10 surcharge for 1-night stay
**Parking:** Ample, free off-street & on-street parking.
**In-Room:** Color TV, AC, telephone, maid service.
**On-Premises:** TV lounge, pinball, laundry facilities, use of kitchen if pre-arranged.
**Exercise/Health:** Nearby Jacuzzi/spa, massage, golf, tennis.
**Swimming:** In nearby pool.
**Sunbathing:** At poolside or on patio.
**Nudity:** Permitted in the house with consent of other guests.
**Smoking:** Permitted on outside front porch only.
**Pets:** Not permitted, cat & dog in residence.
**Handicap Access:** Baths not accessible.
**Children:** Not encouraged, but call to discuss.
**Languages:** English.
**Your Host:** Fran.

# Tortuga Roja Bed & Breakfast

Q-NET Gay/Lesbian ♀♂

## *Come, Share Our Mountain Views*

***Tortuga Roja Bed & Breakfast*** is a 4-acre cozy retreat at the base of the Santa Catalinas, whose windows look out on an open landscape of natural high-desert vegetation. A bicycle and running path along the Rillito River right behind our house can be followed for four miles on either side. Our location is close to upscale shopping and dining and numerous hiking trails. It's an easy drive to the university, local bars and most tourist attractions. Some of our accommodations have fireplaces and kitchens.

**Address: 2800 E River Rd, Tucson, AZ 85718**
**Tel: (520) 577-6822, (800) 467-6822.**

**Type:** Bed & breakfast.
**Clientele:** Good mix of gays & lesbians
**Transportation:** Car is best.
**To Gay Bars:** 10-min. drive.
**Rooms:** 2 rooms & 1 cottage with queen beds.
**Bathrooms:** All private.
**Meals:** Expanded continental breakfast.
**Dates Open:** All year.
**High Season:** Scp-May.
**Rates:** Please call for rates.
**Discounts:** For weekly & monthly stays.
**Credit Cards:** Discover, MC, VISA.
**Rsv'tns:** Often essential.
**Reserve Through:** Travel agent or call direct.
**Minimum Stay:** 2 nights on holiday weekends.
**Parking:** Ample free off-street parking.
**In-Room:** Color TV, VCR, AC, ceiling fan, radio & telephone. Cottage has kitchen.
**On-Premises:** Laundry facilities & kitchen privileges.
**Swimming:** Pool & hot tub on premises.
**Sunbathing:** At poolside & on the patio.
**Nudity:** Permitted poolside & in hot tub.
**Smoking:** Permitted outdoors only.
**Pets:** Not permitted.
**Handicap Access:** Limited. Not wheelchair accessible.
**Children:** Permitted in guest cottage only.
**Languages:** English.

IGTA

# ARKANSAS

## EUREKA SPRINGS

### Arbour Glen B&B Victorian Inn & Guesthouse

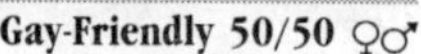

Gay-Friendly 50/50 ♀♂

***Kindle Your Romance in Old-World Elegance!***

***The Arbour Glen,*** circa 1896, sits on a hillside overlooking the Eureka Springs historical district. Our tree-covered hollow is the perfect picturesque setting for relaxation and enjoyment and is home to hummingbirds, deer, and rare birds. ***The Arbour Glen*** has been completely restored with comfort in mind. Each guest room is decorated with antiques, handmade quilts, brass and iron bedsteads, and fresh flowers. We serve a full gourmet breakfast, with china, silver and fanciful linen, on the veranda overlooking the hollow. Our guests enjoy sipping coffee, while watching the deer and the birds. Though only steps away from downtown shops and restaurants, our location provides a secluded setting, very private and relaxing and comfortable. Spacious, shady verandas with swings overlook the rock and flower garden, complete with fish pond and fountain. There is a nearby nature trail for walking. Accommodations have hardwood floors with hand-hooked area rugs; clawfoot tub.

Adding to the luxury are country club privileges that are available at nearby Holiday Island for you to swim, golf, or enjoy a game of tennis. Eureka Springs is a real Victorian village, nestled in the Ozark Mountains of Arkansas. The narrow, winding streets, hand-cut limestone walls and hillside parks and homes take advantage of the natural Ozark Mountain setting. One can discover shops and galleries filled with unique items not found anywhere else, many of which are lovingly and patiently handcrafted. Your stay here will definitely be an unforgettable experience.

**Address: 7 Lema, Eureka Springs, AR 72632**
**Tel: (501) 253-9010, (800) 515-GLEN(4536).**

**Type:** Bed & breakfast.
**Clientele:** 50% gay & lesbian & 50% straight clientele.
**Transportation:** Car is best. Pick up from airport.
**To Gay Bars:** 5 blocks. An 8-min walk or 3-min drive.
**Rooms:** 5 suites with double or queen beds.
**Bathrooms:** All private.
**Meals:** Full gourmet breakfast.
**Vegetarian:** Available with prior notification.
**Complimentary:** Mints, tea, coffee, soft drinks & afternoon desserts upon request.
**Dates Open:** All year.
**High Season:** April-Oct & holidays.
**Rates:** Low season \$65-\$115, high season \$75-\$125.
**Discounts:** On reservations for more than 3 nights. Honeymoon packages available.
**Credit Cards:** MC, Discover, Visa, Amex.
**Rsv'tns:** Required.
**Reserve Through:** Travel agent or call direct.
**Minimum Stay:** 2 nights on weekends, 3 nights on holiday & festival weekends.
**Parking:** Ample free off-street parking.
**In-Room:** Color cable TV, VCR, AC, ceiling fans, refrigerator, coffee & tea-making facilities, fireplaces, Jacuzzis for two & maid service.
**On-Premises:** Nature trail.
**Exercise/Health:** Jacuzzi & nature trail.
**Swimming:** In nearby river, lake & country club.
**Sunbathing:** On the premises or at nearby lakes.
**Smoking:** Permitted outside on verandas only.
**Pets:** Not permitted.
**Handicap Access:** No.
**Children:** Not especially welcome.
**Languages:** English.
**Your Host:** Jeffrey.

## Dairy Hollow House

Gay-Friendly ♀♂

### *The Sweetness of the Good Life*

A friendly innkeeper to welcome you... the smell of hot apple cider with cinnamon on a cool day... a quilt-covered bed... a jug of tulips... herb and flower gardens... everywhere, delight. Relax into the sweetness of the good life at ***Dairy Hollow House.*** Accommodations are in two homes on either side of a peaceful, wooded green valley, just a mile from historic downtown Eureka and easily accessible to its many attractions. Choose either the Farmhouse or the Main House: each has its own magic. Peace, quiet and a definite out-in-the-country feeling reign in the old-fashioned rooms of our lovingly restored 1880's Farmhouse. A hidden-away, off-road setting and rocker-laden porch help make this Ozark home the perfect spot to while away an afternoon. A bubbling hot tub, immaculately maintained, is hidden among the dogwoods above the flower-filled garden (Main House guests enjoy the use of the hot tub, too).

On historic Spring Street, our inviting late-40's bungalow-style Main House suites afford spaciousness, luxury and a place a little closer to "where the action is." The suites are generously-sized and beautifully appointed, with a feeling of unpretentious luxury. Each suite has its own living/sitting room, two are large enough to sleep four guests, and one suite boasts its own balcony. You'll love the fanciful tile work throughout the house, too. Special-event dinners at our small, elegant restaurant feature old-fashioned service and up-to-the-minute cuisine, served in a pretty garden-like room. Everything's from scratch and ingredients are seasonal and regional.

Accolades include *Uncommon Lodgings,* Editor's Choice: "... innkeepers (who) are very, very nice people, who like what they're doing and know how to do it very well indeed." *Arkansas Gazette:* "Nothing has been overlooked in an all-out effort to provide comfort and pleasure for guests." *Christian Science Monitor:* "A delightful country inn (with) marvelous, delectable fare." Named "Best Inn of the Year" and *New York Times* "Correspondent's Choice," the inn has also been singled out for praise in *USA TODAY, Chocolatier, Out & About, Gourmet, Conde Nast Traveler* and *Glamour Magazine.* We try to live up to that praise daily.

**Address: 515 Spring Street, Eureka Springs, AR 72632-3032**
**Tel: (501) 253-7444, (800) 562-8650, Fax: (501) 253-7223.**
**E-mail: 74762.1652@compuserve.com. http://www.dairyhollow.com.**

**Type:** Inn with restaurant & shop with cookbooks & children's books by co-innkeeper, Crescent.
**Clientele:** Mostly straight with a gay & lesbian following
**Transportation:** Car is best.
**To Gay Bars:** 1-1/2 miles, a 5 min drive, a 15 min walk. Gay-owned venues nearby.
**Rooms:** 3 rooms, 3 suites with dbl, queen or king beds.
**Bathrooms:** Private 4 bath/toilets, 2 shower/toilets.
**Meals:** Full breakfast.
**Vegetarian:** Just let us know, preferably when making reservation (owners are vegetarian). Good vegetarian dining nearby.
**Complimentary:** Inn-made cookies each day, hot or cold beverage in room each day, spring water in each mini-fridge. Rooms have coffee-makers & are stocked with coffees, teas, cocoa.

*continued next page*

**Dates Open:** Rooms: Feb-Dec (closed Jan). Restaurant: 6 special event dinners per year.
**High Season:** Oct is busiest, then Je-Aug.
**Rates:** Regular: $135-$185. October, holidays: $155-$205.
**Discounts:** On longer stays. Eleventh-hour Escape rates if call day of reservation.
**Credit Cards:** MC, Visa, Amex, Diners, Discover.
**Rsv'tns:** Not required, but safest for weekends.
**Reserve Through:** Travel agent or call direct.
**Minimum Stay:** 2 nights on weekends, 3 nights some holidays.
**Parking:** Ample free on- & off-street parking.
**In-Room:** AC, refrigerator, coffee- & tea-making facilities, maid service. Kitchen in 2 suites. Telephone optional.
**On-Premises:** Fax & copy machine available.
**Exercise/Health:** Jacuzzi. Nearby steam & massage.
**Swimming:** Lake nearby.
**Sunbathing:** At beach.
**Smoking:** Not permitted.
**Pets:** Not permitted.
**Handicap Access:** Restaurant is accessible, rooms are not.
**Children:** 1 suite set up for families.
**Languages:** English, some French.
**Your Host:** Ned & Crescent.

## Greenwood Hollow Ridge

**Gay/Lesbian ♀♂**

### *It's Gay in the Ozarks!*

***Greenwood Hollow Ridge*** is a country home located on 5 heavily-wooded acres in Eureka Springs, the little Switzerland of the Ozarks. We are the only EXCLUSIVE lodging in the area, a live-and-let-live community that charms every visitor. The entire downtown shopping district is listed on the National Register of Historic Places. Popular attractions include the Passion Play, arts & crafts fairs, music festivals, the Vintage Train Ride and watersports. Our guests have country club privileges for golf and tennis. Come and be gentled in the privacy of our quiet, country setting in the woods.

**Address: Rte 4, Box 155, Eureka Springs, AR 72632. Tel: (501) 253-5283.**

**Type:** Bed & breakfast.
**Clientele:** Exclusively gay! Good mix of gay men & women
**Transportation:** Car is a must! Free pickup from airport.
**To Gay Bars:** 2 miles to gay/lesbian bar.
**Rooms:** 3 rooms & 1 apartment with single, double & king beds.
**Bathrooms:** 1 private bath/toilet, 1 private shower/toilet, shared full bath.
**Campsites:** RV parking only.
**Meals:** Full breakfast.
**Vegetarian:** Available on request.
**Complimentary:** Welcome wine.
**Dates Open:** Closed Feb.
**High Season:** May -Oct.
**Rates:** Summer $45-$65, winter $35-$45.
**Rsv'tns:** Encouraged.
**Reserve Through:** Travel agent or call direct.
**Parking:** 5 acres of parking.
**In-Room:** Color TV, ceiling fans, AC & kitchen.
**On-Premises:** Meeting rms.
**Exercise/Health:** Jacuzzi & exercycle.
**Swimming:** 15-minute drive to lake.
**Sunbathing:** On patio or private sun deck.
**Nudity:** Permitted at spa.
**Pets:** Small pets OK.
**Handicap Access:** Yes, ramps.
**Children:** Not welcomed.
**Languages:** English & Spanish.

## Pond Mountain Lodge & Resort

**Gay-Friendly 50/50 ♀♂**

### *Get the Peak Experience...*

Mountain breezes, panoramic views, and thoughtful hospitality await at historic Eureka Springs' ***Pond Mountain Lodge & Resort.*** Both a bed & breakfast and resort, casually elegant ***Pond Mountain*** is located just two miles south of Eureka Springs at the county's highest elevation. Guests enjoy fishing ponds, swimming pool, horseback riding, Jacuzzi suites, TV/VCRs, billiards room, refrigerators, microwaves, gourmet coffee service, complimentary champagne and hearty breakfasts each morning. Warm and unintrusive hosting, and the serenity and beauty of 150 acres of mountain wonder make this the ideal respite. Catch our web page.

**Address: Rt 1 Box 50, Eureka Springs, AR 72632**
**Tel: (501) 253-5877. Reservations only: (800) 583-8043.**

**Type:** B&B resort with riding stables. Cabin with spa room.
**Clientele:** 50% gay & lesbian & 50% straight clientele
**Transportation:** Car is best.
**Rooms:** 2 rooms & 4 suites with single, double, queen or king beds. 2-bedroom cabin.
**Bathrooms:** All private.
**Meals:** Full buffet breakfast (except cabin).
**Vegetarian:** Breakfast on request. Several excellent restaurants nearby.
**Complimentary:** Champagne, non-alcoholic sparkling cider, popcorn. Gourmet coffee, candy in room. Winter: sherry.
**Dates Open:** All year.
**High Season:** Apr 15-Nov 5.
**Rates:** High season $75-$140. Winter $60-$140. Rates for 2, $7.50 per additional person. Cabin $140 year-round.
**Discounts:** 10% on stays of more than 3 days, rental of more than 3 units, or "family" AARP. 5% AARP.
**Credit Cards:** MC, VISA, Discover.
**Rsv'tns:** Recommended for weekends for Jacuzzi suites.
**Reserve Through:** Travel agent or call direct.
**Minimum Stay:** 2 nights for special events (6 weekends per year).
**Parking:** Ample free off-street parking.
**In-Room:** Color TV, VCR, video tape library, AC, coffee/tea-making facilities, refrigerator, kichen. Some ceiling fans. Telephone in guest house.
**On-Premises:** Meeting room.
**Exercise/Health:** Jacuzzi in suites, massage by appointment. Hiking on 150 acres, fishing in private ponds. Horseback riding add'l fee.
**Swimming:** Pool on premises. Nearby river & lake.
**Sunbathing:** At poolside & on common sun decks.
**Smoking:** Permitted on outside covered verandah only. All rooms non-smoking.
**Pets:** Not permitted.
**Handicap Access:** Yes, cabin.
**Children:** Welcome. Separate building has family units which accommodate children.
**Languages:** English.
**Your Host:** Judy.

## Rock Cottage Gardens

Gay-Friendly 50/50 ♀♂

### *The Pride of the Hills*

From the luxurious linens on our queen-sized beds to the whirlpool tubs for two, every detail of ***Rock Cottage Gardens'*** five private guest cottages has been conceived with your comfort in mind. Experience the magical quality of Eureka Springs for yourself! See why we, and so many other "family" members, have kept coming back to Eureka Springs. We hope you will give us the pleasure of sharing our home, and our home town, with you.

**Address: 10 Eugenia St, Eureka Springs, AR 72632**
**Tel: (501) 253-8659 or (800) 624-6646.**

**Type:** Bed & breakfast cottages.
**Clientele:** 50% gay & lesbian & 50% straight clientele
**Transportation:** Car is best. Air to Fayetteville, AR, Tulsa, OK, or Springfield, MO results in 1-3 hr drive to Eureka Springs.
**Rooms:** 5 cottages with queen beds. Each will accommodate 2 adults.
**Bathrooms:** All private bath/toilets.
**Meals:** Full breakfast.
**Vegetarian:** Available upon request.
**Complimentary:** Refrigerators stocked with drinks. Hot chocolate, herbal tea & ground coffee in cottage.
**Dates Open:** All year.
**High Season:** April thru October.
**Rates:** $95-$110.
**Discounts:** Weekdays during off season.
**Credit Cards:** MC, Visa, Discover.
**Rsv'tns:** Recommended.
**Reserve Through:** Call direct.
**Minimum Stay:** 2 days on weekends.
**Parking:** Ample free off-street parking.
**In-Room:** Color cable TV, AC, refrigerator, coffee-maker, electric tea kettle, ceiling fans, maid service.
**Exercise/Health:** Massage services available in town.
**Swimming:** 10 minutes to Table Rock Lake & Beaver Lake.
**Sunbathing:** On the beach.
**Smoking:** Permitted outdoors only. All cottages are non-smoking.
**Pets:** Not permitted.
**Handicap Access:** No.
**Children:** Not permitted.
**Languages:** English.

# CALIFORNIA

## ANAHEIM - ORANGE COUNTY

### Country Comfort Bed & Breakfast

Gay/Lesbian ♀♂

## *Country Comfort, City Sights!*

Gay and lesbian travelers to the Orange County area will find themselves right at home here! We are only 7 miles from Disneyland and the Anaheim Convention Center, 5 miles from the *new* Anaheim Pond and the Anaheim Stadium, all of them on the same street leading to our B&B! Beaches are within 20 miles and you'll enjoy our solar-heated pool and Jacuzzi, too. Other nearby attractions include Knott's Berry Farm, the Orange County Performing Arts Center, the Los Angeles Theater District, Universal Studios, Magic Mountain, the Queen Mary, Catalina, Sea World, San Diego Zoo and the Wild Animal Park. In case you are looking for a few "wild animals" of a different sort, dance or dine at 11 local gay and lesbian clubs and bars!

We offer guests country-style hospitality in a quiet residential neighborhood in Orange. Our home is noted for its unique glass architecture looking out onto the Orange Hills. Private rooms are decorated for your comfort and pleasure, including bathrobes, cable TV, telephone, rocking chair, antiques and ceiling fan. The *Blue Room* has a private atrium entrance, perfect for relaxing by yourself or with a friend. Everyone is welcome to relax in the family room with super-screen TV, VCR and laser-disks. For the person with special needs, the home is handicap-accessible with adaptive equipment available on prior notice. Exercise equipment for the fitness buff is also available.

Breakfast is bountiful, tailored to satisfy your individual needs. Our stuffed French toast has a reputation all its own, served country style. Early birds can enjoy their juice and cappuccino by the pool.

It's *your* holiday! We invite you to spend your time with us...in ***Country Comfort.***

**Address: 5104 E Valencia Drive, Orange, CA 92669 -1217**
**Tel: (714) 532-2802, Fax: 997-1921, E-mail: gerilopker@aol.com.**

**Type:** Bed & breakfast.
**Clientele:** Gay & lesbian, good mix of men & women.
**Transportation:** Car is best. Pick up from Disneyland Hotel, airport shuttle stop or Anaheim Amtrack station (small charge may apply).
**To Gay Bars:** 10 mi. by car.
**Rooms:** 2 rooms with trundle, queen or king bed.
**Bathrooms:** 1 private bath/toilets & 1 private shower/toilet.
**Meals:** Full breakfast.
**Vegetarian:** Upon request, many local restaurants.
**Complimentary:** Tea, coffee, soft drinks, wine, beer.
**Dates Open:** All year.
**Rates:** $65.
**Discounts:** For extended stays (over 5 days).
**Credit Cards:** None.
**Rsv'tns:** Recommended 1-2 weeks in advance. Occasional last-minute rooms available. Call first.
**Reserve Through:** Travel agent or call direct.
**Minimum Stay:** Prefer 2 nights.
**Parking:** Ample free on-street parking.
**In-Room:** Cable color TV,

telephone, ceiling fans, maid service, refrigerator.
**On-Premises:** TV lounge, laundry facilities, copier, fax, computer rental.
**Exercise/Health:** Jacuzzi, treadmill, exercise bike, mini-trampoline. Nearby gym, massage.
**Swimming:** Pool on premises, 15 miles to ocean. Hydrotherapy spa.
**Sunbathing:** At poolside, on common sun decks, patio or nearby beach.
**Smoking:** Permitted outdoors on patio, atrium & sun deck.
**Handicap Access:** Yes, 1 story no barriers. Bath equip. available with prior arrangement.
**Children:** Permitted when the stay is private (no other booked guests).
**Languages:** English, Signing.
**Your Host:** Joanne & Geri.

# BERKELEY

## Elmwood House B&B

**Gay-Friendly ♀♂**

Our home was built in 1902, as the residence for University of California Latin Professor Wm. Augustus Merrill and his family. ***Elmwood House*** is a brown-shingled, redwood-trimmed epitome of the Berkeley Bay Tradition of turn-of-the-century architecture. We're conveniently located between the fashionable Elmwood shopping district and the U. of C., Berkeley campus. Dining, shopping and entertainment areas of this college town are nearby. Excellent public transit to San Francisco and adjoining Bay Area sights are at your doorstep. Enjoy your visit in the style of Old Berkeley!

**Address: 2609 College Avenue, Berkeley, CA 94704-3406**
**Tel: (510) 540-5123 (Tel/Fax), (800) 540-3050,**
**E-mail: elmwoodhse@aol.com.**

**Type:** Bed & breakfast.
**Clientele:** Mainly straight with gay/lesbian following
**Transportation:** Shuttle bus, public transit or car.
**To Gay Bars:** About 1 mile.
**Rooms:** 4 rooms with double & queen beds.
**Bathrooms:** 2 private & 1 shared.
**Vegetarian:** Available at nearby restaurants.
**Dates Open:** All year.
**High Season:** Last two weeks of May.
**Rates:** $50-$95 plus tax.
**Discounts:** 10% for stays of 7 or more days.
**Credit Cards:** MC, Visa, Amex.
**Rsv'tns:** Required.
**Reserve Thru:** Call direct.
**Minimum Stay:** One-night service charge.
**Parking:** Adequate free on-street & off-street parking.
**In-Room:** Maid service, telephone.
**On-Premises:** TV lounge, meeting rooms.
**Exercise/Health:** Gym nearby.
**Swimming:** 15 min walk to pool, 20 min drive to lake, 1 hr drive to beach.
**Smoking:** 100% non-smoking.
**Pets:** Not permitted. We have 2 resident cats.
**Handicap Access:** No.
**Children:** Not encouraged.
**Languages:** English, some French & a little German.

# BIG BEAR LAKE AREA

## Beary Merry Mansion

**Women ♀**

***Your Private Hideaway That's Not Too Far Away!***

Just under two hours from LA and Orange Counties, awaits your *private* home in Big Bear Lake, ***Beary Merry Mansion.*** Your stress level will melt like spring snow when you settle in to this cozy country charmer! Great for parties of four, PERFECT for parties of two! Winter and spring offer fabulous snow skiing at any of the three major resorts nearby. Summer and fall feature fishing and lake sports. Specialty shops are open year-round. Enjoy a refreshing change from hotel and B&B vacations. Come "up the hill" to your *private* home in the mountains.

**Big Bear Lake, CA**
**Tel: (407) 872-1286, (800) 288-6805 (answers Scott-Powell),**
**Fax: (407) 872-3202.**

**Type:** Private cabin.
**Clientele:** Mostly women with men welcome
**Transportation:** Car is best. However, there is a small craft airport with taxi service.
**To Gay Bars:** 1 hour down the mountain to San Bernardino.
**Rooms:** 2-bedroom cabin with full kitchen, living room & bath. Master has 1 queen bed. Other room has 2 twin beds.
**Bathrooms:** Private bath.
**Dates Open:** All year.
**High Season:** Winter ski season.
**Rates:** Winter $100-$165 per night. Summer/spring $85-$95 per night.
**Discounts:** Monday thru Thursday (excluding holidays), 15% discount on daily rates.
**Rsv'tns:** Required without exceptions.
**Reserve Thru:** Call direct.
**Minimum Stay:** 2 nights. 3 nights on holidays.
**Parking:** Adequate free off-street parking.
**In-Room:** Color TV, VCR, microwave oven, kitchen & refrigerator.
**Swimming:** At nearby Big Bear Lake.
**Sunbathing:** On private sun deck.
**Smoking:** Not permitted.
**Pets:** Not permitted.
**Handicap Access:** No.
**Children:** Not permitted.
**Languages:** English.

## Smoketree Resort

**Q-NET Gay-Friendly ♀♂**

***Smoketree Resort*** was originally built in the late 40's and early 50's and was frequented by movie stars over the years. All of our rooms have been recently upgraded. Our location in the San Bernardino Mountains is on three acres close to Big Bear Lake and a national forest. The main lodge house has five suites with bath and fireplace. There are also 25 cabins for two or for up to eight people. We are close to the village. You can walk to shopping and restaurants. Skiing, mountain biking, hiking and boating are only a few minutes away.

**Address: 40210 Big Bear Blvd, PO Box 2801, Big Bear Lake, CA 92315**
**Tel: (909) 866-2415 or (800) 352-8581.**

**Type:** Bed & breakfast & cabins in Big Bear ski resort area.
**Clientele:** Mostly straight with 10% gay & lesbian following
**Transportation:** Car is best. Free pick up from Big Bear Airport.
**To Gay Bars:** San Bernardino, 1 hour & 30 minutes.
**Rooms:** 5 suites & 25 cabins.

**Bathrooms:** All private.
**Meals:** Continental breakfast in the B&B.
**Complimentary:** Coffee, tea & hot chocolate in room.
**Dates Open:** All year.
**Rates:** Low season \$39-\$185, High season \$59-\$220.
**Credit Cards:** MC, Visa, Amex & Discover.
**Rsv'tns:** Suggested.
**Reserve Through:** Travel agent or call direct.
**Minimum Stay:** Required in high season.
**Parking:** Ample free off-street parking.
**In-Room:** Color TV, telephone, maid service. Cabins have kitchens.
**Exercise/Health:** 2 Jacuzzis & massage.
**Swimming:** 2 heated pools on premises, 5 minutes to lake.
**Sunbathing:** At poolside.
**Smoking:** No smoking in office & B&B.
**Pets:** Small pets, \$10 per night. May not be left unattended.
**Handicap Access:** No.
**Children:** Permitted.
**Languages:** English.
**Your Host:** Joseph & Russell.

# CLEARLAKE AREA

## Sea Breeze Resort

Gay-Friendly ♀♂

### *Glistening Water, Tree-Covered Mountains, Clear Blue Skies*

***Sea Breeze*** is a lakefront resort on California's largest natural lake. Enjoy swimming, boating and fishing just steps away from your tastefully-decorated, impeccably-clean cottage with fully-equipped kitchen. Relax and enjoy our beautifully-landscaped grounds, and picturesque lake and mountain views. Exclusively for our guests are a covered lighted pier, boat slips/mooring, launching ramp, beach, swim float, picnic tables, chaise lounges and Weber barbecues. For those seeking more arduous activities, boat and jet ski rentals, parasailing, glider rides and top name entertainment are a short distance away.

**Address: 9595 Harbor Dr, (Mail: PO Box 653), Glenhaven, CA 95443
Tel: (707) 998-3327.**

**Type:** Resort with cottages.
**Clientele:** Mostly straight clientele with a gay & lesbian following.
**Transportation:** Car is best.
**Rooms:** 6 cottages with full kitchens, 1 room with refrigerator. Single, double, queen or king beds.
**Bathrooms:** All private bath/toilet/showers.
**Campsites:** 3 RV parking only sites, 3 with electric, sewer & water. No separate shower/toilet facilities.
**Vegetarian:** Available at nearby restaurants.
**Complimentary:** Coffee, tea, hot cocoa & ice.
**Dates Open:** Apr 1st through Oct 31st.
**High Season:** June through September.
**Rates:** \$55-\$85.
**Credit Cards:** MC, VISA.
**Reserve Through:** Call direct.
**Minimum Stay:** 3-night minimum on holidays.
**Parking:** Ample free off-street parking. Ample parking for boat trailers on-site
**In-Room:** Color cable TV, AC, ceiling fans, coffee/tea-making facilities, kitchen & refrigerator.
**Swimming:** Lake on premises.
**Sunbathing:** At the beach & on the lawns.
**Smoking:** Permitted without restrictions.
**Pets:** Not permitted.
**Handicap Access:** No.
**Children:** Well-disciplined children welcome.
**Languages:** English.
**Your Host:** Phil & Steve.

# GOLD COUNTRY - SIERRA FOOTHILLS

## Rancho Cicada

Gay/Lesbian ♂

### *Get Back to Nature in the Heart of the Gold Country*

***Rancho Cicada*** retreat is located on a beautiful, isolated and private stretch of the Cosumnes River, in the Gold Country of the Sierra foothills, about 50 miles east of Sacramento. Peacocks stroll through rock gardens and lawns in our natural riverside setting. Private groups often rent the entire facility and enjoy activities such as swimming, sunbathing, hot tubbing, croquet, volleyball or floating on air mattresses. There is also good fishing, and nature hikes are led by the owner/naturalist. The retreat is not listed in any telephone directory, and is only discreetly advertised. **Guest comment:** *"Rancho Cicada is a terrific alternative to the B&B circuit." –Ernie, SF CA*

**Address: PO Box 225, Plymouth, CA 95669. Tel: (209) 245-4841.**

**Type:** Camping retreat with platform tents & cabins.
**Clientele:** Mostly men with women welcome
**Transportation:** Car is best.
**To Gay Bars:** 1 hour by car.
**Rooms:** 2 cabins with queen beds.
**Bathrooms:** 2 private in cabins, shared at campsites.
**Campsites:** 22 tents on platforms. Tents equipped with queen, double or single mattress. Hot showers, wash basins & flush toilets in separate men/women facilities.
**Meals:** Provided on weekends.
**Vegetarian:** When private group rents entire facility, caterer will prepare vegetarian dishes.
**Complimentary:** Coffee available in cabins.
**Dates Open:** Cabins, all year. Tents, May 1-Oct 1.
**High Season:** June, July & August.
**Rates:** Tents $60-$100 per person for entire weekend. Cabins $200 for entire weekend, $350 per week.
**Rsv'tns:** Required.
**Reserve Through:** Call direct.
**Minimum Stay:** On weekends.
**Parking:** Ample free parking.
**In-Room:** Color TV, VCR, ceiling fans, refrigerator & coffee/tea-making facilities in cabins only.
**On-Premises:** Fully furnished kitchen with refrigerator & large adjustable BBQ. 900 sq. ft. deck for meetings & dancing.
**Exercise/Health:** 2 Jacuzzis
**Swimming:** River with several swimming holes within walking distance.
**Sunbathing:** On private cabin sun decks, on common sun decks & large lawn.
**Nudity:** This is a clothing-optional retreat.
**Smoking:** Permitted in designated areas. Non-smoking rooms available.
**Pets:** Not permitted.
**Handicap Access:** No.
**Children:** Not permitted.
**Languages:** English.
**Your Host:** David & Mark.

# IDYLLWILD

## The Pine Cove Inn

Gay-Friendly ♀♂

Picture yourself in one of the nine A-frame chalets at ***The Pine Cove Inn,*** surrounded by natural landscaping and enjoying the clear, crisp mountain air. You're up at 6,300 feet, and the views are nothing less than incredible. Your individually-decorated room has private bath, fridge and microwave oven. Six rooms have fireplaces and six have private decks or porches with magnificent mountain views. In winter, our toboggan run will carry you down a mountain of fun.

**Address: PO Box 2181, Idyllwild, CA 92549**
**Tel: (909) 659-5033, Fax: (909) 659-5034.**

**Type:** Bed & breakfast & conference center.
**Clientele:** 25% gay & lesbian & 75% straight clientele.
**Transportation:** Car is best.
**To Gay Bars:** 1 hour to Palm Springs' gay/lesbian bars.
**Rooms:** 9 doubles.
**Bathrooms:** All private.
**Meals:** Full breakfast.

**Vegetarian:** Just let us know when you make your reservation.
**Complimentary:** Tea & coffee in room.
**Dates Open:** All year.
**Rates:** $70-$90 plus 10% tax.
**Discounts:** On mid-week stays (Sun-Thurs).
**Credit Cards:** MC, Visa, Amex.
**Rsv'tns:** Recommended.
**Reserve Through:** Travel agent or call direct.
**Minimum Stay:** 2 nights on weekends, 3 nights on holiday weekends.
**Parking:** Ample, free, off-street parking.
**In-Room:** Fridge, microwave oven.
**On-Premises:** TV lounge, meeting rooms, lodge with fireplace, books, games, puzzles.
**Sunbathing:** On private sun decks.
**Smoking:** Some rooms non-smoking. Smoking permitted outdoors, in TV lounge & lodge.
**Pets:** Not permitted.
**Handicap Access:** Limited accessibility.
**Children:** Permitted, $10 extra 12 years and older.
**Languages:** English.
**Your Host:** Bob & Michelle.

# JULIAN

## Leelin Wikiup B&B

Gay-Friendly ♀♂

### *A Casual Retreat in a Rural Mountain Setting*

Sit outside and enjoy the breeze and shade trees by day or the star-filled skies at night. Three large romantic suites (two with firplaces, one with a two-person tub) make up ***Leelin Wikiup B&B.*** The B&B is located one mile from Julian on three heavily wooded acres. Birds and small animals abound and resident, friendly dogs, cats, and llamas love attention from guests. Breakfasts are a special treat: the large, gourmet family-style meals rival any in town.

**Address: 1645 Whispering Pines, PO Box 2363, Julian, CA 92036**
**Tel: (619) 765-1890, (800) 6WIKIUP (694-5487), (800) LAMAPAK (526-2725), Fax: (619) 765-1512.**

**Type:** Bed & breakfast.
**Clientele:** Mostly straight clientele with a gay/lesbian following
**Transportation:** Car from San Diego is best, bus available.
**To Gay Bars:** 60 miles to San Diego gay bars.
**Rooms:** 1 room, 2 suites with queen or king beds.
**Bathrooms:** 3 private bath/shower/toilets.
**Meals:** Expanded continental breakfast. Weekends: Full breakfast.
**Vegetarian:** Available with advance notice. Restaurants locally.
**Complimentary:** Coffee, other hot & cold drinks in rooms. Pastries in-room on arrival, evening snacks.
**Dates Open:** All year.
**High Season:** Sept-Dec & Apr-May.
**Rates:** $105-$140.
**Discounts:** Please inquire.
**Credit Cards:** MC, Visa.
**Rsv'tns:** Required.
**Reserve Through:** Travel agent or call direct.
**Minimum Stay:** 2 days on weekends, 3 days some holiday weekends.
**Parking:** Ample off-street parking.
**In-Room:** Kitchenette, coffee/tea-making facilities, refrigerator, ceiling fans, fireplaces.
**On-Premises:** TV lounge, video tape library, outdoor lounging areas.
**Exercise/Health:** Massage on premises. Nearby boating, llama trekking, horseback riding. Jetted hot tub under stars.
**Swimming:** Pool & lake nearby.
**Sunbathing:** On common sun decks.
**Smoking:** Permitted in limited smoking areas outside.
**Pets:** Dogs permitted if small, social, housetrained & quiet.
**Handicap Access:** No.
**Children:** Older, well-mannered, quiet, schoolaged children welcome.
**Languages:** English, Spanish available.
**Your Host:** Lee & Linda.

# LAGUNA BEACH

## Casa Laguna Bed & Breakfast Inn

Gay-Friendly ♀♂

### *Sun, Sand & Sea*

*Casa Laguna* is a unique, 20-room country inn on a terraced hillside, overlooking the Pacific Ocean. Its towering palms hover over meandering paths and flower-splashed patios, swimming pool, aviary and fountains, making this intimate, mission-style inn a visual delight. Many rooms and suites have sweeping views. A cottage, set on its own, has private garden, sun decks and ocean views. The mission house, itself, has two bedrooms and two fireplaces. Laguna Beach combines art, seaside casualness and colorful landscapes for an ideal retreat.

**Address: 2510 South Coast Hwy, Laguna Beach, CA 92651**
**Tel: (714) 494-2996, (800) 233-0449, Fax: (714) 494-5009.**

**Type:** Bed & breakfast inn.
**Clientele:** Mostly straight clientele with a gay & lesbian following
**Transportation:** Car is best. Jitney service from Orange County Airport, about $20.
**To Gay Bars:** One mile to nearest one. There are others in Laguna Beach.
**Rooms:** 15 rooms, 4 suites & 2 cottages. Single, double or king beds.
**Bathrooms:** All private shower/toilets.
**Meals:** Expanded continental breakfast.
**Vegetarian:** Fruit, cereals & breads available at breakfast.
**Complimentary:** Wine, cheese, snacks, tea & coffee are served each afternoon in the library.
**Dates Open:** All year.
**High Season:** July until Labor Day.
**Rates:** Winter $79-$175, summer $90-$225.
**Discounts:** Winter & midweek discounts.
**Credit Cards:** MC, Visa, Amex, Diners, Bancard, Eurocard & Discover.
**Rsv'tns:** Required, but walk-ins accepted.
**Reserve Through:** Travel agent or call direct.
**Minimum Stay:** Only on national holidays.
**Parking:** Ample free off-street parking.
**In-Room:** Color cable TV, telephone, ceiling fans & maid service. Some rooms with refrigerators. Kitchens in the 4 suites & 2 private homes.
**On-Premises:** Meeting rooms & TV lounge/library.
**Swimming:** Pool.
**Sunbathing:** At poolside, on the patio & common sun decks.
**Smoking:** Permitted. Non-smoking rooms available.
**Pets:** Small pets permitted with prior arrangements.
**Handicap Access:** No.
**Children:** Permitted, but must be attended by an adult at all times.
**Languages:** English, Spanish.

## Coast Inn

Gay/Lesbian ♂

The *Coast Inn* is the oldest and most popular gay resort in America, providing year-round fun right on the Pacific Ocean, with the world's most beautiful beaches. All rooms have color TV, phones, private baths, and a sun deck or balcony overlooking the private bathing beach. We are also home to the world famous "Boom Boom Room," with dancing to the hottest and latest music til 2 am. We are 2 minutes from the West Street gay beach and 15 minutes from San Onofre nude beach. Dana Point Harbor is only five miles away and provides some of the finest surfing, windsurfing, sailing, fishing, snorkling, and scuba diving in Southern California. Disneyland is 30 miles away. Laguna Beach itself has a lot of fine shopping and dining and is home of The Pageant of the Masters.

**Address: 1401 S Coast Hwy, Laguna Beach, CA 92651**
**Tel: (714) 494-7588, (800) 653-2697, Fax: (714) 494-1735.**

**Type:** Resort hotel with restaurant & "Boom Boom Room" bar & disco.
**Clientele:** Mostly men with women welcome.
**Transportation:** Rental car from LAX or San Diego Airport or John Wayne Airport, 12 mi north.
**To Gay Bars:** World famous "Boom Boom Room" on the premises. 3 other bars in walking distance.
**Rooms:** 23 rooms
**Bathrooms:** Each room has a private bath & sun deck or balcony.
**Vegetarian:** We have a full menu in the restaurant with some vegetarian food available.
**Dates Open:** All year.
**High Season:** Apr-Oct.
**Rates:** $60-$160.
**Discounts:** Stay 6 nights & get the 7th night free.
**Credit Cards:** MC, VISA, Amex, Diners, Discover.
**Rsv'tns:** Strongly suggested.
**Reserve Through:** Travel agent or call direct.
**Minimum Stay:** 2-nights on weekends.
**Parking:** Limited free off-street parking.
**In-Room:** Color cable TV, telephone, maid service, & room service.
**Swimming:** In the ocean.
**Sunbathing:** On the beach & on private common sun decks.
**Nudity:** Permitted on sun decks.
**Smoking:** Permitted everywhere.
**Pets:** Not permitted.
**Handicap Access:** No.
**Children:** Not permitted.
**Languages:** English.

# LAKE TAHOE AREA

## The Bavarian House

Gay/Lesbian ♀♂

The Bavarian House

### *Breathe the Pine-Scented Mountain Air Year-Round*

Amidst the pristine beauty of the Sierra Nevada is ***The Bavarian House,*** a spacious bed and breakfast nestled on a mountainside on the south shore of Lake Tahoe.

In summer, enjoy hiking, biking, swimming, horseback riding, or exploring the exquisite granite peaks, lakes, and forestland. Return home and take in the cool pine-scented mountain air and breathtaking views from one of the large decks. Winter is the time for skiing (Heavenly Valley, Tahoe's largest ski resort is just four blocks away), snowmobiling, horse-drawn

*continued next page*

sleigh rides, roaring fires, hot cider, and watching the snow quietly fall. Casinos and restaurants are close by for year-round entertainment.

***The Bavarian House*** has three generous guest rooms (for a maximum of six guests), each with a private bath, king-sized bed, and TV/VCR and rustic mountain decor. Rates include daily maid service, a hearty breakfast and access to a large video library. The greatroom, with its large river rock fireplace and vaulted, beamed ceilings, is a comfortable place to talk with friends, sample some wine and cheese, or just relax in front of a cozy fire. The loft, overlooking the greatroom, has game tables, a reading lounge, and a piano. A separate, three-bedroom chalet is also available – perfect for couples or groups. Join your hosts, Jerry and Kevin, and you'll understand why guests return again and again.

**Address: PO Box 624507, Lake Tahoe, CA 96154**
**Tel: (800) 431-4411, (916) 544-4411.**

**Type:** Bed & breakfast guesthouse.
**Clientele:** Good mix of gays & lesbians
**Transportation:** Shuttle or rental car from Reno airport (1 hr), or taxi from South Lake Tahoe Airport (15-min drive).
**To Gay Bars:** 10 minutes by car.
**Rooms:** 3 rooms with king beds.
**Bathrooms:** All private bath/toilets.
**Meals:** Full breakfast.
**Vegetarian:** Available with advance notice.
**Complimentary:** Wine & cheese upon arrival. Set-ups, coffee, tea & juices.
**Dates Open:** All year.
**Rates:** $95-$125.
**Rsv'tns:** Required.
**Reserve Through:** Call direct.
**Minimum Stay:** $15 premium for 1-night stay.
**Parking:** Adequate free off-street parking.
**In-Room:** Color cable TV, VCR, video tape library & maid service.
**Swimming:** At nearby lake.
**Sunbathing:** On common sun decks or nearby beach.
**Nudity:** 30-minute drive to nude beach.
**Smoking:** Permitted outside.
**Pets:** Not permitted.
**Handicap Access:** Not wheelchair accessible.
**Children:** Not permitted.
**Languages:** English.

## Holly's

Q-NET **Women ♀**

### *A Special Vacation Place for Women*

What do you call a place where you can get away from it all, smell the fresh pine air, be with friends or alone, where you can cook your own meals or go out on the town? It's called ***Holly's*** at beautiful Lake Tahoe! Our place is 2 blocks from the beach, close to all shopping, 2 miles from the casinos, and close to all hiking and bicycling trails. In the winter, the skiing is great! We're only 2 miles from Heavenly Valley and close to many other downhill ski areas. Snowmobiling, snowboarding and x-country trails are also in the vicinity. So, whether you are looking for relaxation, entertainment, fun in the snow or the summer sun, there is something for everyone in every season.

Our main desire is to provide a place where women can be themselves in an environment that is safe, supportive, relaxed, and most of all, fun! Our grounds are situated in a woodsy 2 acres close to downtown. For privacy, we've surrounded the property with 110 cords of split firewood stacked 7 feet high. Many guests have called ***Holly's*** "a wonderful oasis in the middle of South Lake Tahoe, two blocks from the lake."

We want women to feel at home. Our cozy, clean cabins and rooms are decorated in rustic elegance. Our accommodations allow for privacy as well as group interaction. So if this is something you're looking for, we think you'll enjoy our place. This is a special place for all open and accepting women to vacation or celebrate special occassions. We also welcome well-behaved boys and girls and well-behaved, non-aggressive, loving dogs. They will love it here as much as their moms. Almost everyone comes back time and time again, so we invite you to come to ***Holly's*** and find out for yourself. Member: Gay Innkeepers of Tahoe.

**Address: PO Box 13197, South Lake Tahoe, CA 96151**
**Tel: (916) 544-7040, (800) 745-7041, E-mail: hollys@oakweb.com.**

**Type:** Vacation place for women with cabins & guest rooms.
**Clientele:** Women only
**Transportation:** Car is best.
**To Gay Bars:** 2-1/2 miles or an 8-minute drive.
**Rooms:** 3 rooms & 9 cabins with queen beds.
**Bathrooms:** Mostly private baths.
**Meals:** Continental breakfast.
**Complimentary:** Tea, coffee & muffins in cabins.
**Dates Open:** All year.
**High Season:** Major holidays, Dec thru March, June thru September.
**Rates:** $85-$185.
**Discounts:** Cabins only: off-season 20% off midweek, 7th night free. In season, 8th night free.
**Rsv'tns:** Required.
**Reserve Through:** Call direct.
**Minimum Stay:** Yes.
**Parking:** Ample off-street parking.
**In-Room:** Color cable TV, VCR, stereos, ceiling fans, fully equipped kitchen, coffee/tea-making facilities & fireplaces.
**On-Premises:** Laundry, bikes, video library, ping pong, volleyball, badminton, recreation & conference room.
**Exercise/Health:** Hot tub. Nearby gym, weights, sauna, steam, massage, hiking, golf, mountain bike trails, water sports.
**Swimming:** 2 blocks from lake, pool nearby.
**Sunbathing:** Decks, lawn and nearby lakeside beach.
**Nudity:** Permitted in hot tub only.
**Smoking:** Permitted outside only. All cabins & rooms are non-smoking.
**Pets:** Well-behaved dogs with prior approval only.
**Handicap Access:** No.
**Children:** Well-behaved boys & girls.
**Languages:** English.

IGTA

## Inn Essence

**Gay/Lesbian ♀♂**

### *A Special Place for You!*

Nestled in the mountains at Lake Tahoe, amidst the world famous ski resorts and casinos, is ***Inn Essence.*** Gourmet chef for the stars and interior designer, Patrick Finn opens his home to you. The beautifully appointed rooms are just waiting to pamper you. Enjoy an aromatherapy spa, or massage after a day of hiking, skiing, snowmobiling, swimming, sunbathing and more. Then snuggle in by the fire or enjoy an exciting show at the casinos. ***Inn Essence*** will truly be "a special place for you"! (Other homes available for groups.)

**Address: 865 Lake Tahoe Blvd, South Lake Tahoe, CA 96150**
**Tel: (916) 577-0339, Fax: (916) 577-0118, (800) 57 TAHOE.**
**Vacation rentals: (800) 344-9364.**

**Type:** Bed & breakfast guesthouse.
**Clientele:** Gay & lesbian clientele.
**Transportation:** Car or plane.
**To Gay Bars:** 9 miles.
**Rooms:** 2 rooms with king or queen beds.
**Bathrooms:** 1 shared bath/shower toilet with spa tub & essential oils.
**Meals:** Full gourmet breakfast. Lunch, dinner & catering available.
**Vegetarian:** Always available.
**Complimentary:** Tea, coffee, morning newspapers, gourmet treats, mints on pillow & turndown service.
**Dates Open:** All year.
**Rates:** $79-$99. Rates slightly higher on holidays.
**Discounts:** Available for extended stays & for groups.
**Rsv'tns:** Required.
**Reserve Through:** Call direct.
**Minimum Stay:** Holidays, weekends.
**Parking:** Ample free off-street & on-street parking.
**In-Room:** Color cable TV,

*continued next page*

VCR, video library, telephone, maid, room & laundry service, private entrances.
**On-Premises:** TV lounge, laundry facilities.
**Exercise/Health:** Jacuzzi, massage.
**Swimming:** Pool in summer season. River & lake nearby.
**Sunbathing:** On common sun decks, poolside or at the beach.
**Nudity:** Permitted at gay nude beach.
**Smoking:** Permitted in smoking areas outside. Non-smoking rooms.
**Pets:** Not permitted.
**Handicap Access:** No.
**Languages:** English.
**Your Host:** Patrick.

## Lakeside B 'n B Tahoe

Gay/Lesbian ♀♂

### *Romantic, Inexpensive, Right on the Water!*

***Lakeside B 'n B Tahoe,*** a private home smack-dab on the water, has antiques, plants and magnificent views of Lake Tahoe and mountains from all three guest rooms. There is a steam room, Jacuzzi, grand piano, fireplace, library, lakeside deck and parklike grounds. Fresh-baked bread and gargantuan gourmet breakfasts are served from a printed, personalized menu with many choices. Fabulous skiing in winter, swimming, boating and nude sunbathing in summer, and 24-hour Nevada gaming action are minutes away. On the quiet Nevada side of North Lake Tahoe, the B&B is 4 hours from San Francisco and 45 minutes from Reno.

**Address: Box 1756, Crystal Bay, NV 89402**
**Tel: (702) 831-8281, Fax: (702) 831-7FAX (7329),**
**E-mail: tahoeBnB@aol.com.**

**Type:** Bed & Breakfast.
**Clientele:** Gay & lesbian, good mix of men & women
**Transportation:** Car is best. Carry chains in winter.
**To Gay Bars:** About 1/2 hr drive to Faces in South Lake Tahoe or 45 min to Reno bars.
**Rooms:** 3 rooms with single or queen beds.
**Bathrooms:** 1 private & 1 shared.
**Meals:** Full breakfast from printed menu with many choices, daily gourmet special & fresh-baked bread.
**Vegetarian:** Available whenever a guest wants it.
**Complimentary:** Wine, coffee, other goodies, breakfast in bed if desired.
**Dates Open:** All year.
**High Season:** Dec-Apr (skiing season) & Jun-Oct.
**Rates:** $59-$135.
**Rsv'tns:** Required.
**Reserve Thru:** Call direct.
**Minimum Stay:** $15 premium for one-night stays.
**Parking:** Ample free off-street parking.
**In-Room:** Color cable TV, VCR & huge video tape library.
**On-Premises:** Library, giant screen TV, fireplace, bearskin rug, grand piano, many musical instruments, laundry facilities & lakeside decks with dramatic views of Lake Tahoe.
**Exercise/Health:** Jacuzzi & steam room in suite, not always available to all. Swim, boat, ski, horseback ride, hike, nearby health club.
**Sunbathing:** At lakeside, on private & common sun decks. Nude beach nearby.
**Nudity:** Permitted if OK with other guests.
**Smoking:** Outside only.
**Pets:** Permitted, but have to get along with my pets.
**Handicap Access:** No. Steep steps & steep access to lake.
**Children:** Welcomed.
**Languages:** English, some French & Spanish.
**Your Host:** Steven.

## SierraWood Guest House

Gay/Lesbian ♀♂

### *The Privacy Is a Luxury in Itself*

***SierraWood*** is a romantic, cozy chalet in the woods, where you've dreamed of taking a special friend for an exciting vacation together or getting away by yourself for relaxation and renewal. Here, beside a rippling stream, we're surrounded by U.S. Forest preserve. For those who want to balance the peace and privacy of the wooded chalet, the glittering allure of Lake Tahoe's gaming casinos, superstar entertainers, clubs, restaurants and nightlife is only a few miles away. In summer, you can charter ***SierraWood's*** own 25-foot *Lancer* for an exciting day on the waters of Lake Tahoe. Your hosts will serve cocktails and lunch, while you soak in the sun and the sights. On another day, try hiking through flowering meadows to the pristine alpine lakes nearby. The winter delight is downhill and cross-country skiing at one of three major ski resorts.

The chalet is an inviting, 6-bedroom, 4-bath home whose unique architecture incorporates open-beam cathedral ceilings, pine paneling and both a rock fireplace and an antique potbelly stove. There are bay windows, floor-to-ceiling windows, and skylights, plus an outdoor redwood hot tub with a view of the river, white fir and aspen woods. Our convivial cocktail hour begins with a soak in the hot tub. Then we join in the warm glow of a sumptuous dining table, sparkling with candlelight, Waterford crystal and the laughter and good conversation of happy company. A healthy breakfast is also included in the daily fare.

**Address: PO Box 11194, Tahoe Paradise, CA 96155-0194**
**Tel: (916) 577-6073, (800) 700-3802.**

**Type:** Bed & breakfast guesthouse with dinner included.
**Clientele:** Good mix of gay men & women
**Transportation:** Car is best. Free pick up from airport & bus.
**To Gay Bars:** 12 miles to gay/lesbian bar & the casinos.
**Rooms:** 4 rooms with double, queen or king beds.
**Bathrooms:** 1 private bath, 2 private sinks, 2 shared bath/shower/toilets.
**Meals:** Full breakfast & dinner.
**Vegetarian:** Available with 3 days' notice.
**Complimentary:** BYOB, setups provided, tea & coffee, beverages, mints on pillow, wine with dinner.
**Dates Open:** All year.
**Rates:** Single $80, double $110-$125. Holidays $90-$150.
**Rsv'tns:** Preferred 2 days in advance.
**Reserve Through:** Travel agent or call direct.
**Minimum Stay:** 2 days on holidays.
**Parking:** Ample free parking.
**In-Room:** Telephone, VCR, maid, room & laundry service.
**On-Premises:** Fireplace, lounge with color TV, laundry facilities.
**Exercise/Health:** Weights & hot tub with Jacuzzi.
**Swimming:** River on premises, lake nearby, nude beach 45 min.
**Sunbathing:** On beach or common sun decks.
**Nudity:** On decks & in hot tub.
**Smoking:** Permitted without restrictions.
**Pets:** Small pets permitted, if housebroken.
**Handicap Access:** No.
**Children:** Not permitted.
**Languages:** English.
**Your Host:** David & LeRoy.

# LOS ANGELES

## The Grove Guest House

**Gay/Lesbian ♀♂**

### *Luxury and Privacy – Moments from West Hollywood*

You can't beat ***The Grove Guest House*** for privacy and relaxation. Enjoy your own spacious, luxurious villa with separate bedroom. Located in a quiet and historic neighborhood, it features a glamorous black-bottom pool and spa amidst lush tropical landscaping. Leather furniture, artwork, a VCR, a private phone, romantic bedroom lighting, and a refrigerator stocked with goodies are just some of the amenities. When you're ready for adventure, the heart of West Hollywood is just minutes away, with gay fun, clubs, and shops. Enjoy the comfort, quality, and privacy this villa has to offer – you may never want to leave!

**Address: 1325 N Orange Grove Ave, Los Angeles -West Hollywood, CA 90046. Tel: (213) 876-7778, Fax: (213) 876-3170.**

**Type:** Guesthouse.
**Clientele:** Gay & lesbian
**Transportation:** Car is best, taxi or LAX super shutle.
**To Gay Bars:** 1 block. A 5-minute walk or 2-minute drive.
**Rooms:** 1 large villa with separate bedroom.
**Bathrooms:** Private shower/toilet.
**Meals:** Continental breakfast & snacks.
**Vegetarian:** Lots of vegetarian food nearby.
**Complimentary:** Kitchen is well stocked with a range of food & goodies.
**Dates Open:** All year.
**Rates:** $125 per day for 2 people. Additional people & selected dates slightly higher.
**Discounts:** On extended stays.
**Rsv'tns:** Required.
**Reserve Through:** Travel agent or call direct.
**Parking:** Ample free parking.
**In-Room:** Eat-in kitchen, color cable TV, VCR, video tape & book library, AC, ceiling fans, phone, refrigerator, microwave, coffee & tea-making facilities.
**Exercise/Health:** Jacuzzi on premises. Nearby gyms offer discounts to our guests.
**Swimming:** Pool on premises. Nearby pool & ocean.
**Sunbathing:** At poolside.
**Nudity:** Permitted by pool & spa.
**Smoking:** Permitted, but not in bedroom, please.
**Pets:** Not permitted.
**Handicap Access:** No.
**Children:** Not especially welcome.
**Languages:** English, French.
**Your Host:** Oliver.

## Holloway Motel

**Gay/Lesbian ♀♂**

***The Holloway*** is a 22-unit motel centrally located in West Hollywood. This Southern California-style wooden stucco structure has traditional furnishings, very reasonable rates, and a warm, friendly feeling. Each room has color cable TV, air conditioning, phone, shower, toilet, and maid service. ***The Holloway*** is adjacent to restaurants and close to several gay and lesbian bars. We are also near Hollywood, Beverly Hills, and Sunset Strip, and under 30 minutes from most major Southern California attractions.

**Address: 8465 Santa Monica Blvd, West Hollywood, CA 90069 Tel: (213) 654-2454.**

**Type:** Motel.
**Clientele:** Mostly gay & lesbian with some straight clientele.
**Transportation:** Car, taxi or LAX super shuttle.
**To Gay Bars:** 4 blocks.
**Rooms:** 20 rooms & 2 suites with single or queen beds.
**Bathrooms:** Each room has its own shower & toilet.
**Vegetarian:** Available nearby.
**Dates Open:** All year.
**Rates:** $55 per night including tax, Sun-Thurs; $65, Fri-Sat. For studios add $10-$15 per night. Higher on holidays.
**Discounts:** Available for advance payment & extended stay.
**Credit Cards:** MC & VISA.
**Rsv'tns:** Recommended.
**Reserve Thru:** Call direct.
**Parking:** Free off-street parking.
**In-Room:** Color cable TV, AC, telephone, maid service.
**Exercise/Health:** Several gyms down the street.
**Smoking:** Permitted. Non-smoking rooms available.
**Pets:** Not permitted.
**Handicap Access:** No.
**Children:** Permitted.
**Languages:** English & Spanish.
**Your Host:** Rudy & Dave.

## Le Montrose Suite Hotel De Gran Luxe

Q-NET Gay-Friendly ♂

### *Indulge Yourself...Stay With Us at Le Montrose*

Nestled in a quiet, residential area two blocks from the world-famous Sunset Strip, ***Le Montrose*** is a most pleasant alternative, offering 128 charming suites, friendly, personalized service, and attention to details with the special grace of a European-style hotel. Each suite includes sunken living room, cozy fireplace, refrigerator, color TV with VCR and twice-daily maid service. If you need to be in constant touch with your office, you'll value the state-of-the-art, multiline telephone with dataport, fax machines, and voice mail services in each suite. Most suites at ***Le Montrose*** include a kitchenette, and many offer private balconies with a breathtaking city view.

You can enjoy suite service dining in your suite or on the rooftop terrace, with a panoramic view of the west side. Superb dining indoors is available at the intimate Library Restaurant. Relax in the heated pool and spa, or catch a game of tennis on the lighted court. Both are located on the rooftop. Complimentary bicycles are available for exploring the surrounding West Hollywood area. Among the many attractions within a 7-mile radius of the hotel are Universal Studios, Mann's Chinese Theater, Pacific Design Center, Rodeo Drive, Cedars Sinai Medical Center and the Beverly Center. Ask about the Salon Room, which has 1,300 square feet of function space for small meetings or receptions. Other hotel services include valet laundry service, on-property laundry facilities, underground valet parking, in suite movies with Nintendo, currency exchange, full concierge and business services and a new, state-of-the-art fitness center with on-call private trainer and masseuse.

**Address: 900 Hammond St, West Hollywood, CA 90069**
**Tel: (310) 855-1115, (800) 776-0666, Fax: (310) 657-9192.**

**Type:** Hotel with restaurant.
**Clientele:** Mostly straight clientele with a gay male following
**Transportation:** Car is best.
**To Gay Bars:** 2 blocks or a 10-minute walk.
**Rooms:** 128 suites. 13 1-bedroom & 60 executive suites with kitchens. 36 junior suites with refrigerator (no kitchen). Double, queen or king beds.
**Bathrooms:** All private.
**Vegetarian:** Available upon request of guest.
**Complimentary:** Welcome fresh fruit. Departure, cookies & milk.
**Dates Open:** All year.
**Rates:** $190-$475.
**Discounts:** 35% discount if you ask for Ferrari Rate.
**Credit Cards:** MC, VISA, Amex, Diners & others.
**Rsv'tns:** Required. Call (800) 776-0666.
**Reserve Through:** Travel agent or call direct.
**Parking:** Ample covered pay parking.
**In-Room:** Color cable TV, VCR, premier movies & Nintendo, fax machines, AC, telephones (3 per suite), fireplaces, kitchen, refrigerator, coffee/tea-makers, room & laundry service, and maid service twice daily.
**On-Premises:** Meeting rooms & laundry facilities.
**Exercise/Health:** Full service fitness center. Free tennis & free bicycles for guest use. Rooftop terrace with Jacuzzi.
**Swimming:** Heated pool on premises. 10 miles to beaches.
**Sunbathing:** At poolside or on the roof.
**Smoking:** Permitted. Non-smoking rooms are available.
**Pets:** Permitted with deposit.
**Handicap Access:** Yes.
**Children:** Permitted.
**Languages:** English, Spanish, French, German, Japanese, Chinese & Romanian.

IGTA

## Le Parc Hotel

Gay-Friendly ♀♂

### *West Hollywood's Great Little Hotel*

For those who prefer their luxury hotel to be more of a refuge from LA's fast lane than a tribute to it, we suggest ***Le Parc Hotel.*** Gracefully set in one of West Hollywood's most peaceful residential neighborhoods, you'll feel like you are miles away from the action, when in reality you are conveniently right in the middle of it. ***Le Parc Hotel*** offers elegant seclusion within walking distance of the bars, restaurants, sports clubs and businesses that make West Hollywood a world-renowned gay destination. Whether traveling for business (Pacific Design Center, The Beverly Center, Melrose's art galleries or antique shops) or pleasure (Revolver, Mickys, Rage, Trunks, The Palms) your destination is just a short walk away.

Our 154 luxury suites provide a living room with fireplace, balcony, kitchenette, video cassette player, Nintendo, multiline phones, walk-in closets and complimentary cable TV. As a truly full-service hotel, we offer morning and evening maid service, room service, free morning newspaper, and Cafe Le Parc, a private restaurant exclusively for guests of the hotel.

Casual and comfortable, with the feeling of an exclusive country club, ***Le Parc*** is a haven when your hectic day is over. While West Hollywood's best health clubs, World Gym and Bally's Sports Connection are just around the corner, the hotel has its own facilities exclusively for guests' use, including a well-equipped gym and sauna, as well as a rooftop pool, jacuzzi and tennis and basketball courts. ***Le Parc Hotel*** not only requests, but respects your business and community, and is committed to giving back to the gay and lesbian community via philanthropic endeavors. From the private guests-only restaurant, to the hotel's meeting and banquet rooms to the friendly service and amenities, ***Le Parc Hotel*** specializes in the fine art of casual elegance.

**Address: 733 N. West Knoll Dr, West Hollywood, CA 90069**
**Tel: (310) 855-8888 , Reservations USA only: (800) 578-4837,**
**Fax: (310) 659-7812.**

**Type:** Hotel with restaurant and bar.
**Clientele:** Mostly straight clientele with a gay and lesbian following.
**Transportation:** Car is best.
**To Gay Bars:** 1-3 blocks.
**Rooms:** 154 suites with single, double & king beds.
**Bathrooms:** All private.
**Vegetarian:** Two restaurants & health food store nearby

**Complimentary:** Welcome fresh fruit basket, limousine service.
**Dates Open:** All year.
**Rates:** Deluxe suite $225; One-bedroom suite $275; Premier Suite $250.
**Discounts:** 30% discount if you mention Inn Places.
**Credit Cards:** MC, VISA, Amex, Diners, JCB.
**Rsv'tns:** Required.
**Reserve Through:** Travel agent or call direct.

**Parking:** Adequate covered off-street pay parking (either valet or self-park).
**In-Room:** Color cable TV, Nintendo, AC, telephone, kitchen, refrigerator, microwave, coffee & tea-making facilities, maid, room, & laundry service.
**On-Premises:** Meeting rooms, coin laundry facilities.
**Exercise/Health:** Gym, weights, Jacuzzi, sauna, massage.

**Swimming:** Heated pool on premises.
**Sunbathing:** On rooftop.
**Smoking:** Permitted, non-smoking rooms available.
**Pets:** Permitted in deluxe suites only with $50 fee.
**Handicap Access:** Yes.
**Children:** Permitted, under 17 stay free with parent.
**Languages:** English, Spanish, Arabic, French.
**Your Host:** Dona & Josh.

# Le Rêve Hotel

Gay-Friendly ♀♂

## *Le Rêve...The Dream*

The hotel of your dreams, conveniently located in the foothills of West Hollywood, offers all the comfort and charm of old European tradition. ***Le Rêve Hotel*** offers personalized service at its best so you can fully enjoy the quiet elegance of West Hollywood. For a touch of romance, visit the rooftop garden pool and soothe yourself in the mineral spa. Savor your favorite dish while taking in the breathtaking view of Hollywood Hills, or call our 24-hour suite service if you prefer to dine quietly and cozily by firelight in your suite. Pamper yourself with a massage by a licensed masseur or masseuse in the privacy of your suite. For movie buffs, a VCR and an array of videos is provided for your pleasure.

Each of the hotel's 80 luxurious suites comes individually appointed with fireplaces, spacious baths, hair dryers, mini bars, refrigerators, multiline telephones, cable color TVs, kitchenettes, and private balconies (in most suites). Other amenities include same-day laundry and dry cleaning, coin-operated laundry machines, and 24-hour fax service for business travelers. For small meetings, the hotel can accommodate up to 20 people.

***Le Rêve Hotel*** is just minutes away from some of Los Angeles' most exciting attractions: the Hollywood Walk of Fame, Grauman's Chinese Theater, Universal Studios, Rodeo Drive, the Hollywood Bowl, the La Brea Tar Pits, Museum Row, the Beverly Center, and Saks Fifth Avenue. If you're hungry, dine in any of West Hollywood's famous restaurants: Spago's, Planet Hollywood, and the House of Blues or sample the trendy clubs on Sunset Strip, or the coffee houses on Melrose. The hotel's unequaled guest service, charm, beauty, and unsurpassed value are secrets worth sharing with those who expect only the best. Guests say "It is unbelievable" and "It's simply marvelous." We say "It's a dream come true!"

**Address: 8822 Cynthia Street, West Hollywood, CA 90069**
**Tel: (310) 854-1114, (800) 835-7997, Fax: (310) 657-2623.**

**Type:** All-suite de luxe boutique hotel.
**Clientele:** Mostly straight clientele with a gay & lesbian following
**Transportation:** Car is best. Taxi from LAX approximately $30.
**To Gay Bars:** One block.
**Rooms:** 72 singles & 5 doubles.
**Bathrooms:** All private.
**Vegetarian:** Some available on room service menu.
**Complimentary:** Fruit basket and non-alcoholic beverage upon arrival.
**Dates Open:** All year.
**Rates:** $135-$225, plus tax. Check for promotional rates.
**Discounts:** Monthly stays & groups of 10 or more rooms.
**Credit Cards:** MC, Visa, Amex, Diners, Discover.
**Reserve Through:** UTELL, travel agent or call direct.
**Parking:** Self parking in underground garage ($6 per day).
**In-Room:** AC, color TV, telephone, refrigerator, kitchen, room service, maid service & laundry service.
**On-Premises:** Laundry facilities.
**Exercise/Health:** Jacuzzi
**Swimming:** Pool on premises.
**Sunbathing:** By the pool & on the roof.
**Smoking:** One floor is non-smoking.
**Pets:** Not permitted.
**Handicap Access:** No.
**Children:** Permitted.
**Languages:** English, Spanish, French, Arabic, Polish.

## Ramada Hotel West Hollywood

Q-NET Gay-Friendly 50/50 ♀♂

### *Affordable Luxury in the Heart of Gay Los Angeles*

Located between Beverly Hills and Hollywood, the ***Ramada West Hollywood*** is within walking distance to all of the area's popular cafes, restaurants, bars and nightclubs. Universal Studios and most tourist attractions are located within 10 minutes. Built in 1989 and renovated in 1995, the hotel has 175 rooms and suites, an outdoor pool, discount healthclub memberships and Enterprise car rental. There is also a clothing boutique and a food court which includes Starbucks Coffee, Pizzeria Uno's, Baja Buds Mexican Restuarant, Wok Deli – Chinese, Bagel Bakery and Juice Shop.

**Address: 8585 Santa Monica Blvd, West Hollywood, CA 90069**
**Tel: (310) 652-6400, (800) 845-8585, Fax: (310) 652-2135.**

**Type:** Hotel with restaurant, food court, clothing store & car rental agency.
**Clientele:** 50% gay & lesbian & 50% straight clientele
**Transportation:** From LAX airport: shuttle $12 per person each way, taxi $25 each way.
**To Gay Bars:** 4 blocks, 1/2 mile, a 10-minute walk, a 5-minute drive.
**Rooms:** 135 rooms, 40 suites with double, queen or king beds.
**Bathrooms:** All private bath/toilet/showers.
**Vegetarian:** Available at hotel restaurant, 2 vegetarian restaurants nearby.
**Complimentary:** Daily newspaper, afternoon & evening coffee.
**Dates Open:** All year.
**High Season:** April 30-September 30.
**Rates:** Summer $99-$259, winter $89-$209.
**Discounts:** AAA, AARP, government, entertainment card. 15% off when mentioning the Ferrari Guides. All accepted upon availability.
**Credit Cards:** MC, Visa, Amex, Diners, Discover.
**Rsv'tns:** Reservations suggested, walk-ins welcome.
**Reserve Through:** Travel agent or call direct.
**Minimum Stay:** Required during special events.
**Parking:** Ample on-street & covered pay parking ($8 per day).
**In-Room:** Color cable TV, AC, telephone, coffee/tea-making facilities, maid, room & laundry service.
**On-Premises:** Laundry facilities.
**Exercise/Health:** Nearby gym, weights, Jacuzzi, sauna, steam.
**Swimming:** Pool on premises.
**Sunbathing:** At poolside.
**Smoking:** Permitted by the pool area & in smoking rooms.
**Pets:** Not permitted.
**Handicap Access:** Yes.
**Children:** Welcome.
**Languages:** English, Spanish, French.
**Your Host:** David.

IGTA

## Saharan Motor Hotel

Gay-Friendly ♂

The ***Saharan Motor Hotel*** is conveniently located in the heart of Hollywood. We're surrounded by famous restaurants, night clubs, theaters and shopping centers, not to mention many of the most popular gay night spots. Minutes from downtown LA, Universal Studios, Dodger Stadium, the Hollywood Bowl, the Chinese Theater and the Farmers' Market, the ***Saharan*** is equally convenient for both the business and the vacation traveler.

**Address: 7212 Sunset Blvd, Los Angeles, CA 90046**
**Tel: (213) 874-6700, Fax: (213) 874-5163.**

**Type:** Motel.
**Clientele:** Mostly straight clientele with a 20%-30% gay male following.
**Transportation:** Super shuttle from LAX.
**To Gay Bars:** 4 blocks to men's bars.
**Rooms:** 54 rooms & 8 suites with double, queen or king beds.
**Bathrooms:** All private.
**Complimentary:** Coffee all day.
**Dates Open:** All year.
**High Season:** May-September.
**Rates:** Summer $40-$75, rest of year $36-$70.
**Credit Cards:** MC, VISA, Amex & Diners.
**Rsv'tns:** Recommended.
**Reserve Through:** Travel agent or call direct.
**Parking:** Adequate free parking.
**In-Room:** Maid service, satellite color TV, telephones & AC.
**Swimming:** Pool on premises or 20 minutes to ocean beach.
**Sunbathing:** At poolside or on beach.
**Smoking:** Permitted without restrictions.
**Pets:** Not permitted.
**Handicap Access:** No.
**Children:** Permitted.
**Languages:** English, Spanish, Japanese & Chinese.

## San Vicente Inn & Resort

Gay/Lesbian ♂

West Hollywood's ***San Vicente Inn*** recently re-opened with new owners, a new pool and expanded decks and spa. Still West Hollywood's only gay B&B, the ***San Vicente*** offers Key West-style accommodations just a few steps from the action on Santa Monica Blvd, a short walk from the Pacific Design Center and minutes from Beverly Hills, Hollywood, Silverlake and Century City. Rooms have AC, TV, phone and answering machine. The pool is solar heated and surrounded by gardens and clothing-optional sun decks.

**Address: 845 San Vicente Blvd, West Hollywood, CA 90069**
**Tel: (310) 854-6915, Fax: (310) 289-5929.**

**Type:** Bed & breakfast guesthouse.
**Clientele:** Mostly men with women welcome
**Transportation:** Shuttle service from the airport or rental car.
**To Gay Bars:** 2 blocks.
**Rooms:** 8 rooms & 8 cabanas with double or queen beds.
**Bathrooms:** 12 private bath/shower/toilets, 8 shared bath/shower/toilets.
**Meals:** Expanded continental breakfast.
**Vegetarian:** 5-minute walk.
**Complimentary:** Tea, coffee, juice.
**Dates Open:** All year.
**Rates:** $59-$139 plus tax.
**Discounts:** Stay 6 nights, get 7th night free.
**Credit Cards:** MC, Visa, Amex, Diners, Discover.
**Rsv'tns:** Required, but walk-ins OK.
**Reserve Through:** Travel agent or call direct.
**Parking:** Ample free off-street & on-street parking.
**In-Room:** Color TV, AC, telephones, kitchen, refrigerator, coffee/tea-making facilities & maid service.
**Exercise/Health:** Jacuzzi.
**Swimming:** Pool on premises.
**Sunbathing:** At poolside or on common sun decks.
**Nudity:** Permitted poolside.
**Smoking:** Permitted outside.
**Pets:** Not permitted.
**Handicap Access:** No.
**Children:** Not especially welcome.
**Languages:** English & Spanish.
**Your Host:** Terry & Rocky.

# MARINA DEL REY

## The Mansion Inn

Gay-Friendly ♀♂

***The Mansion Inn*** is a charming, European-style inn with a bed and breakfast ambiance. Completely remodeled, it's very clean and well maintained and has a relaxing environment with a friendly, unpretentious staff. The great location is within walking distance of Venice Beach and close to many attractions. Enjoy the beach during the day, local gay bars in the evening, or motor 20 minutes to West Hollywood nightspots. Many restaurants are also within walking distance. If you like small, intimate places to stay, come visit ***The Mansion Inn.*** We would love to see you.

**Address: 327 Washington Blvd, Marina del Rey, CA 90291**
**Tel: (310) 821-2557, (800) 828-0688, Fax: (310) 827-0289.**

**Type:** European inn with courtyard cafe.
**Clientele:** Mostly straight clientele with a 30% gay & lesbian following.
**Transportation:** Shuttle from LAX $8 per person, taxi from LAX $16.
**To Gay Bars:** 20-min walk or 5-10-min drive. 25-min drive to West Hollywood.

*continued next page*

**Rooms:** 26 with 1 queen bed, 6 with 2 queen beds, 6 with 2 twin beds, 5 loft suites with queen bed upstairs, queen sleeper sofa downstairs.
**Bathrooms:** All private.
**Meals:** Expanded continental breakfast with bagels, English muffins, sweet rolls, hot & cold cereals, fruit, juices, coffee, teas.
**Dates Open:** All year.
**High Season:** June 1 through September 30.
**Rates:** $69-$125 USD.
**Discounts:** AAA, seniors, midweek specials, Quests Memberships, some other discount memberships & corporate rates.
**Credit Cards:** MC, VISA, Amex, Diners, Discover, En Route.
**Rsv'tns:** Required.
**Reserve Through:** Travel agent or call direct.
**Parking:** Adequate free off-street covered parking.
**In-Room:** Color TV, AC, telephone, refrigerator, maid service, laundry service.
**On-Premises:** Courtyard patio & cafe.
**Exercise/Health:** 5-min drive to Golds Gym & World Gym.
**Swimming:** 1 block to ocean beach.
**Sunbathing:** On the beach.
**Smoking:** Permitted. Some non-smoking rms available.
**Pets:** Not permitted.
**Handicap Access:** Yes. Elevator, wide hallways, many equipped baths.
**Children:** Permitted. Under 12 stay free with existing bedding.
**Languages:** English, Spanish, Norwegian, French.

# MENDOCINO COUNTY

## Annie's Jughandle Beach B&B Inn

Gay-Friendly ♀♂

### *Century-old Swedish Farmhouse Heritage*

Not only does our lovingly cared for 1880's Victorian farmhouse provide whale watching and ocean views, its front door opens to the Jughandle State Reserve. Come celebrate nature as you wander across ocean meadows and explore Mendocino's fabulous coast. Four miles north of Mendocino village and three miles south of Ft. Bragg's Noyo Harbor, you'll relax in a comfortable country setting. Gourmet breakfasts at ***Annie's*** are served in the company of visitors from around the world. We welcome you without imposing ourselves on you, whether you've come to explore or relax.

**Address: 32980 Gibney Ln, Ft. Bragg, CA**
**Tel: (707) 964-1415, Fax: (707) 961-1473.**

**Type:** Bed & breakfast cottage.
**Clientele:** Mainly straight with a gay & lesbian following.
**Transportation:** Car is best.
**Rooms:** 4 rooms & 1 suite with queen beds.
**Bathrooms:** All private: 1 bath/toilet, 1 bath/shower/toilet, 3 shower/toilets.
**Meals:** Full breakfast.
**Vegetarian:** Available upon request.
**Dates Open:** All year.
**High Season:** June-Nov.
**Rates:** Winter $85-$140, summer $99-$159.
**Credit Cards:** MC, Visa.
**Rsv'tns:** Advised during season.
**Reserve Through:** Travel agent or call direct.
**Minimum Stay:** For over Saturday night we require a second day.
**Parking:** Ample free off-street parking.
**In-Room:** Ceiling fans, maid service.
**On-Premises:** Meeting rooms.
**Swimming:** At nearby ocean, river, lake.
**Sunbathing:** At beach.
**Smoking:** Inn is non-smoking. Permitted outside only.
**Children:** Well-behaved children are welcome, but we screen.
**Languages:** English, Cajun French.
**Your Host:** Jean & Shannon.

## Sallie & Eileen's Place

Q-NET Women ♀

***Sallie & Eileen's Place*** offers a safe and comfortable place for women near Mendocino, state parks, beaches, hiking, biking, horseback riding, river canoeing and a large women's community. The A-frame is a studio with fireplace and rockers, double bed and a large private bathroom with sunken tub. The cabin has lots of windows, and is wonderful in the rain. It also has a private yard and deck, a woodburning stove, and a loft bedroom with queen bed.

**Address: Box 409, Mendocino, CA 95460. Tel: (707) 937-2028**

**Type:** Studio cottage and a guesthouse.
**Clientele:** Women only
**Transportation:** Car.
**To Gay Bars:** 3 1/2 hours by car.
**Rooms:** 2 cottages with double or queen beds.
**Bathrooms:** All private bath/toilets.
**Complimentary:** Mints, special blend of coffee, regular & decaf.
**Dates Open:** All year.
**High Season:** Spring break, summer & Christmas.

**Rates:** A-frame $65, cabin $80 for 1-2, $15 each add'l woman, plus county tax.
**Discounts:** Weekly rates, mid-week specials during fall & winter.
**Rsv'tns:** Required.
**Reserve Thru:** Call direct.
**Minimum Stay:** 2 nights, 3-4 on holiday weekends.
**Parking:** Ample free off-street parking.
**In-Room:** Kitchen, refrigerator & coffee/tea-makers. Fireplace in A-frame. Ceiling fans in cabin.
**Exercise/Health:** Hot tub $5 a day per person.
**Swimming:** 3 miles to ocean and river beaches.
**Sunbathing:** A-frame has private sun deck. Cabin has sun deck and its own yard.
**Nudity:** Permitted anywhere on the land.
**Smoking:** Not permitted in A-frame, permitted in cabin.
**Pets:** Dogs in cabin only, $5 per day per dog.
**Handicap Access:** No.
**Children:** Permitted in cabin only. $10 to age 12. No boy children over 10.
**Languages:** English, Spanish & French.
**Your Host:** Sallie & Eileen.

# NAPA VALLEY

## Willow Retreat

Gay-Friendly ♀♂

Secluded on forty acres in the hills behind Napa and Sonoma Valleys, ***Willow*** is the perfect retreat for those seeking escape from hectic city life. Swim and sun by the pool, play tennis on a hillside court surrounded by vineyards, bike, jog or walk on forest trails and country roads, stroll our grounds and treat yourself to just-picked blackberries, apples, walnuts, figs and plums. Tour the area's wineries, take a mud and mineral bath in Calistoga, try an early-morning hot air balloon ride or a glider plane ride, or picnic and ride horseback nearby.

**Address: 6517 Dry Creek Rd, Napa Valley, CA 94558. Tel: (707) 944-8173.**

**Type:** Retreat facility for group events or individuals.
**Clientele:** Everyone welcome. Sexual preference is unimportant.
**Transportation:** Car is best. Pick up from bus can be arranged. Airport limo to Napa or Sonoma from SF or Oakland airports.
**To Gay Bars:** 1 1/2 hr to San Francisco bars. 1 hr to Russian River bars.
**Rooms:** 12 rooms with single, queen or king beds.
**Bathrooms:** 10 private baths/toilets & 2 shared.
**Meals:** Cont. breakfast.
**Vegetarian:** Always available.
**Dates Open:** All year.
**High Season:** May-Oct.
**Rates:** Single $55-$75. Double $80-$110. Triple $115-$140. Quad $135-$165.
**Discounts:** 10% on 4 days or more. Group rates.
**Credit Cards:** MC & VISA.
**Rsv'tns:** Required.
**Reserve Thru:** Call direct.
**Minimum Stay:** Two nights on weekends Apr-Oct.
**Parking:** Ample free off-street parking.
**In-Room:** Self-controlled electric heat.
**On-Premises:** Living/dining room, community kitchen, & public phone.
**Exercise/Health:** Sauna, massage & hot tub.
**Swimming:** Pool on premises.
**Sunbathing:** At poolside.
**Nudity:** Permitted in pool & hot tub areas only.
**Smoking:** Permitted in designated outside areas.
**Handicap Access:** Yes.
**Children:** Permitted.
**Languages:** English.

# PALM SPRINGS - CATHEDRAL CITY

## Alexander Resort

Men ♂

### *Chill Out in Beautiful Palm Springs*

Epitomizing the serenity of the casual Palm Springs lifestyle is ***Alexander Resort.*** Its spacious, mist-cooled grounds have fountain, pool, spa and a fabulous mountain view. Guests enjoy hospitality that is both gracious and friendly. Rooms are furnished in desert hues, with direct-dial phones, refrigerators and remote color TV with adult videos. Use our bikes to explore many bike paths or enjoy Village Fest every Thursday evening nearby. Complimentary breakfast and light lunch are served at poolside daily, with parties on major holidays.

**Address: 598 Grenfall Rd, Palm Springs, CA 92264**
**Tel: (619) 327-6911 or (800) 448-6197.**

*continued next page*

**Type:** Garden court guesthouse.
**Clientele:** Men only.
**Transportation:** Car is best but bus & cabs are available. Free pick up from airport or bus.
**To Gay Bars:** 2-minute drive to gay bars. 15 minutes to clubs.
**Rooms:** 3 rooms, 3 studios with kitchens & 2 deluxe studios with kitchens & private patios. Twin or king beds.
**Bathrooms:** 6 private bath/toilets & 2 private shower/toilets.
**Meals:** Expanded continental breakfast & light lunch.
**Vegetarian:** Available on request.
**Complimentary:** Fruit & in-room coffee & tea. Iced tea poolside.
**Dates Open:** All year.
**High Season:** Dec-Jun.
**Rates:** $79-$99 in season. Specials off season.
**Discounts:** 10% for 7 days, 15% for 14 days & 20% for 30 days. More for longer stays and off season.
**Credit Cards:** MC, VISA, Discover & Amex.
**Rsv'tns:** Strongly recommended!
**Reserve Through:** Travel agent or call direct.
**Minimum Stay:** 2 nights on weekends in season. Longer for holiday periods.
**Parking:** Ample free off-street parking.
**In-Room:** Maid service, color TV, male video channel, VCR, telephone, AC/heat, kitchen, refrigerator, shower massage & coffee/tea service.
**On-Premises:** Laundry facilities, gas BBQ, & video library.
**Exercise/Health:** Jacuzzi, bicycles. Masseurs available at extra charge. Large gym nearby (passes available).
**Swimming:** In the pool.
**Sunbathing:** At poolside or on the patio.
**Nudity:** Permitted in all outside areas.
**Smoking:** Permitted without restrictions.
**Handicap Access:** All facilities are at ground level.
**Children:** Not permitted.
**Languages:** English.
**Your Host:** Bud & Chuck.

## Atrium/Vista Grande/Mirage

Q-NET Men ♂

### *If You Don't Stay at the Mirage, You'll Wish You Had!*

Palm Springs's unique new exotic male playground, ***Atrium/Vista Grande/Mirage,*** is set in a multi-level tropical environment. Some of the giant, contoured boulders, on which you can sunbathe nude or watch the night stars, weigh over 20,000 pounds. Individual flagstone paths lead to rooms overlooking the waterfall grotto with its ring of fire. Both pools, the Jacuzzi and the atrium have outdoor mist systems. Our gym, fire pit, bar, large natural stone BBQ, botanical gardens, open-beam ceilings and private patios are worth the trip.

**Address: 574 Warm Sands Dr, Palm Springs, CA 92264**
**Tel: (619) 322-2404 or (800) 669-1069. Fax: (619) 320-1667,**
**E-mail: mirage4men@aol.com.**

**Type:** Private male resort.
**Clientele:** Men only
**Transportation:** Free pick up from the airport & bus.
**To Gay Bars:** Close to gay bars & restaurants.
**Bathrooms:** All private.
**Complimentary:** Coffee maker, fresh coffee, tea, cream, & sugar.
**Dates Open:** All year.
**High Season:** All year.
**Rates:** $79-$165.
**Discounts:** Airline personnel.
**Credit Cards:** All credit cards.
**Rsv'tns:** Recommended.
**Reserve Through:** Travel agent or call direct.
**Minimum Stay:** 2 days on weekends.
**Parking:** Adequate, free, off-street parking.
**In-Room:** Color TV, VCR, laundry & maid service, AC, telephone, & kitchen.
**On-Premises:** Laundry facilities (free).
**Exercise/Health:** 2 Jacuzzis & micro-cool outdoor mist.
**Swimming:** 2 pools on premises.
**Sunbathing:** At poolside or on the sun decks.
**Nudity:** Permitted everywhere.
**Smoking:** Permitted without restrictions.
**Handicap Access:** No.
**Children:** Not permitted.
**Languages:** English, German, Dutch, limited French.
**Your Host:** Bob & Alvin.

IGTA

## Bee Charmer Inn

Q-NET Women ♀

### *A Sweet Retreat for Women in Palm Springs*

Created for today's pleasure-seeking women, the ***Bee Charmer Inn*** is unmatched in comfort and luxury with 13 beautiful rooms meticulously furnished in soft southwestern pastels. This luxury hotel is located in the heart of Palm Springs, minutes from all clubs, restaurants, recreational venues, and attractions of the fabulous gay desert. The French doors open onto a sparkling pool, inviting you to relax and enjoy the glittering sunshine and breathtaking scenery. An occasional holiday BBQ or cocktail hors d'oeuvres create a chance to make new friends from all over the world.

**Address: 1600 E Palm Canyon Dr, Palm Springs, CA 92264**
**Tel: (619) 778-5883.**

**Type:** Resort.
**Clientele:** Women only
**Transportation:** Rental car from airport (approx 1 mile), taxi.
**To Gay Bars:** 1 mile.
**Rooms:** 14 rooms with queen & king beds, sleeper sofas.
**Bathrooms:** All private.
**Meals:** Continental breakfast.
**Dates Open:** All year.
**High Season:** Sept 1-July 5.
**Rates:** $77-$97 high season, $57-$77 low season.
**Credit Cards:** All credit cards accepted.
**Rsv'tns:** Recommended.
**Reserve Through:** Call direct or travel agent.
**Minimum Stay:** During holidays & special events.
**Parking:** Free on-site parking.
**In-Room:** Color TV, AC, refrigerator & micowave.
**Swimming:** Pool on premises.
**Sunbathing:** Poolside.
**Nudity:** Tops optional.
**Smoking:** Permitted outside only.
**Languages:** English.

## Canyon Club Hotel

Men ♂

### *Size DOES Matter!*

***Canyon Club*** is large enough to be exciting, but private enough to be clothing optional. With 32 rooms, there are enough people around to make for lively camaraderie day and night.

Recently renovated, the rooms are clean, comfortable, and uncluttered. With air conditioning (not evaporative coolers); remote-controlled, color, cable TV; telephone; and refrigerator, the one- and two-bed rooms are highly appealing. There are also several 24-hour, in-house, all-male video channels. Some rooms are available with full kitchens and some have private patios. Ample common areas, including a large lobby with a cozy fireplace for cool fall and winter evenings, await those times that you'd prefer to spend in the company of your fellow guests.

The 50-foot pool is surrounded by a private, spacious, sunny courtyard, where you can relax the day away, meet the other guests, read, relax, and enjoy the views. You can work on the perfect tan – with or without tan lines; the entire facility (except the lobby) is clothing optional. Both the sauna and steam room are especially invigorating on cool fall and winter evenings or after a hard day around the pool. The 16-man capacity spa is among the largest of any gay hotel in Palm Springs.

*continued next page*

In the evening, take a short walk to the center of downtown Palm Springs where you're sure to find restaurants or shops to your liking. ***Canyon Club*** is within five to 15 minutes drive of all the gay restaurants and nightspots of Palm Springs and adjacent cities, and is about a one-hour drive from Ontario International Airport and a two-hour drive from Los Angeles or San Diego. http://www.tenpct.com/canyonclub

**Address: 960 N Palm Canyon Dr, Palm Springs, CA 92262**
**Tel: (619) 322-4367 or (800) 295-2582, Fax: (619) 322-4024,**
**E-mail: CanyonClub@tenpct.com.**

**Type:** Hotel.
**Clientele:** Men only.
**Transportation:** Car is best, one mile from airport.
**To Gay Bars:** 1 block or 10-minute drive.
**Rooms:** 32 rooms with dbl, queen or king beds.
**Bathrooms:** 30 private bath/toilet/showers, 2 private shower/toilets.
**Meals:** Cont. breakfast.
**Dates Open:** All year.
**High Season:** Spring & fall.
**Rates:** $59-$89.
**Discounts:** On stay of 5 nights.
**Credit Cards:** MC, VISA, Amex & Discover.
**Rsv'tns:** Recommended.
**Reserve Thru:** Call direct.
**Minimum Stay:** Most weekends & holidays.
**Parking:** Ample free off-street parking.
**In-Room:** Color cable TV, AC, telephone, refrigerators & maid service. Some full kitchens & private patios. Two in-house video channels.
**On-Premises:** Lobby with fireplace.
**Exer./Health:** Full gym, Jacuzzi, dry sauna & steam rm.
**Swimming:** Large pool on premises.
**Sunbathing:** At poolside & on the patio.
**Nudity:** Clothing optional everywhere except lobby.
**Smoking:** Permitted. No non-smoking rooms.
**Children:** Not welcome.
**Languages:** English.

## Columns Resort

**Men ♂**

### *A Man's Private Paradise*

The ***Columns*** provides a relaxing, comfortable setting to enjoy in solitude or with new friends. Our newly-decorated rooms surround a large, heated pool and spa, in a tropical courtyard. Clothing is optional at all times, and our Cool Mist and air conditioning ensure your total comfort while you enjoy our mountain views. Each spacious room includes a kitchen and dining area, coffee maker, private bath, phone, color cable TV, VCR and firm, queen-sized bed. Our large tape collection is available at your leisure. We pride ourselves on our tranquil, sharing environment and cleanliness. Come, relax with us.

**Address: 537 Grenfall Rd, Palm Springs, CA 92264**
**Tel: (619) 325-0655, (800) 798-0655, Fax: (619) 322-1436,**
**E-mail: rescolumns@aol.com.**

**Type:** Private resort hotel.
**Clientele:** Men only
**Transportation:** Car is best. Free pick up from airport, train or bus with prior arrangement.
**To Gay Bars:** 3-4 blocks to men's bars.
**Rooms:** 7 studios with queen beds & kitchens.
**Bathrooms:** All private shower/toilets.
**Meals:** Expanded continental breakfast provided daily.
**Complimentary:** Coffee/cream/sugar in rooms. Soft drinks, iced tea, lemonade & snacks available. Icebreakers 1/2x wk
**Dates Open:** All year.
**High Season:** Jan-Jun.
**Rates:** $59-$95.
**Discounts:** 10% on 6 days & to repeat guests. 1 day free for 7 or more nights.
**Credit Cards:** MC, VISA, Amex, Discover.
**Rsv'tns:** Highly recommended!
**Reserve Through:** Travel agent or call direct.
**Minimum Stay:** 2 nights on weekends, longer on some holidays.
**Parking:** Ample, free, off-

street parking.
**In-Room:** Maid service, AC, remote color cable TV & VCR, kitchen, refrigerator, coffee/tea-making facilities, telephone, ceiling fans, video tape library.
**On-Premises:** Barbeque, bicycles, fax/copier, modem, lap counter at pool.
**Exercise/Health:** Jacuzzi, bicycles, micro-cool outdoor mist, add'l charge for massage. Gym passes available.
**Swimming:** Pool on premises.
**Sunbathing:** At poolside.
**Nudity:** Permitted inside compound.
**Smoking:** Permitted without restrictions.
**Pets:** Not permitted.
**Handicap Access:** No.
**Children:** Not permitted.
**Languages:** English.
**Your Host:** Jack & Blaine.

## Desert Paradise Hotel

Q-NET Men ♂

### *An Ambiance of Style & Sophistication*

Lush garden settings and majestic mountain views create the mood at ***Desert Paradise Hotel.*** Our attention to detail and dedication to service afford each guest a truly memorable experience. Stylish accommodations include private bath, telephone, color TV, VCR, air conditioning and kitchens. Exotic grounds, a poolside mix of music and laughter, and proximity to the excitement of Palm Springs combine to meet your every expectation. This is a gentleman's resort of the highest caliber, representing the best the desert has to offer!

**Address: 615 Warm Sands Dr, Palm Springs, CA 92264**
**Tel: (619) 320-5650, (800) 342-7635, Fax: (619) 320-0273.**

**Type:** Hotel.
**Clientele:** Men only
**Transportation:** Car or taxi. 5 minute taxi ride to hotel.
**To Gay Bars:** 5 minutes by car to bars.
**Rooms:** 10 rooms & 2 suites with queen or king beds.
**Bathrooms:** All private shower/toilets.
**Meals:** Fresh fruit expanded continental breakfast.
**Vegetarian:** Available upon request.
**Complimentary:** Snacks, beverages. Beverages available with breakfast.
**Dates Open:** All year.
**High Season:** Oct-Jun.
**Rates:** $75-$135, subject to change.
**Discounts:** Weekly rates, please inquire.
**Credit Cards:** All major cards including MC, VISA, Amex, Diners & Discover.
**Rsv'tns:** Preferable to assure availability.
**Reserve Through:** Travel agent or call direct.
**Minimum Stay:** 2 nights on weekends, longer on some holidays.
**Parking:** Ample free off-street parking.
**In-Room:** Color cable TV, VCR, film library, AC, maid service, telephone, kitchen, microwave, refrigerator.
**On-Premises:** Fax, laundry facility for guests, large poolside patio area, lush garden settings.
**Exercise/Health:** Spa, nearby gym.
**Swimming:** Pool on premises.
**Sunbathing:** At poolside.
**Nudity:** Permitted everywhere.
**Smoking:** Permitted except in lobby.
**Pets:** Small pets permitted with restrictions. Inquire first.
**Handicap Access:** No.
**Children:** No children.
**Languages:** English.
**Your Host:** Basil & Larry.

## El Mirasol Villas

Gay/Lesbian ♀♂

### *Experience Our Style, Discover Our Magic....*

***El Mirasol Villas,*** in 1995 celebrated 20 years as Palm Springs' leading gay resort, occupies villas built by Howard Hughes for one of his mistresses, their guests, and himself. Gay men, lesbians, and bisexuals from around the world are now welcomed within this extravagantly landscaped relaxing property. The uniformed staff is dedicated to providing the level of service which keeps our guests returning again and again. That over a third of our guests are by enthusiastic referral, speaks for itself.

**Address: 525 Warm Sands Dr,, Palm Springs, CA 92264**
**Tel: (619) 327-5913, (800) 327-2985, Fax: (619) 325-8931.**

**Type:** Resort hotel.
**Clientele:** Gay men, lesbians & bisexuals.
**Transportation:** Drive. Fly to Palm Springs Regional Airport (free pick up) or Ontario (rent car or use limo, 1 hr).
**To Gay Bars:** A few blocks to neighborhood bars, 10-minutes to dance bars.
**Rooms:** 6 suites & 9 cottages.
**Bathrooms:** All private.
**Meals:** Continental breakfast & lunch.
**Vegetarian:** Available by arrangement at time of reservation.
**Complimentary:** Lemonade, iced tea, bottled water all day.
**Dates Open:** All year.
**Rates:** $95-$260.
**Discounts:** On extended stays.
**Credit Cards:** All major credit cards.
**Rsv'tns:** Recommended.
**Reserve Through:** Travel agent or call direct.
**Minimum Stay:** Required at times. Please inquire.
**Parking:** Ample, free off-street parking.
**In-Room:** Color cable TV & VCRs in living- & bedrooms. AC, telephone, some kitchens, refrigerator & maid service.
**On-Premises:** Laundry facilities, video library, fax & copier.
**Exercise/Health:** Jacuzzi, bicycles, nearby gyms. Massage by appointment.
**Swimming:** Two pools on premises.
**Sunbathing:** At poolside, on private sun decks or on patio.
**Nudity:** Permitted around 1 of the pools.
**Smoking:** Permitted.
**Pets:** Permitted by prior arrangment, fee.
**Children:** Not permitted.
**Languages:** English, French, Spanish.
**Your Host:** John.

IGTA

## INNdulge Palm Springs

Men ♂

### *Warm Sands' Newest Playground for Men*

Pamper, pleasure, and gratify yourself at Warm Sands' newest resort for gay travelers. ***INNdulge,*** located in Palm Springs' premier gay area of 15 gay resorts, has 20 large rooms surrounding a secluded, private courtyard with an expansive 24-hour heated pool and a large whirlpool spa. Of course, clothing is forever optional! Spoil yourself with a complimentary Euro-breakfast of croissants, juice, breads, and coffee and daily afternoon "vins et fromages" by the pool. Inquire about the weekday specials – and summer rates, which can be up to 50% off.

**Address: 601 Grenfall Rd, Palm Springs, CA 92264**
**Tel: (619) 327-1408, (800) 833-5675, Fax: (619) 327-7273.**

**Type:** Inn.
**Clientele:** Men only.
**Transportation:** Car is best. Free pick up from airport (5 blocks away).
**To Gay Bars:** 5 blocks, a 10-minute walk, a 3-minute drive.
**Rooms:** 18 rooms & 2 suites with king beds.
**Bathrooms:** 20 private shower/toilets.
**Meals:** Continental breakfast.
**Vegetarian:** None available.
**Complimentary:** Afternoon poolside wine & cheese service 5:00pm-6:00pm.
**Dates Open:** All year.
**High Season:** January-May.
**Rates:** Winter $75-$125, summer $59-$99.
**Discounts:** Summer discounts up to 50%.
**Credit Cards:** MC, Visa, Amex, Discover.
**Reserve Through:** Travel agent or call direct.
**Parking:** Ample free off-street parking.
**In-Room:** Color cable TV, VCR, AC, coffee/tea-making facilities, telephone, refrigerator, maid & laundry service. Some rooms with kitchen.
**On-Premises:** Video tape library, laundry facilities.

**Exercise/Health:** Nearby gym, weights.
**Swimming:** Pool on premises.
**Sunbathing:** At poolside.
**Nudity:** Permitted throughout pool area & courtyard.
**Smoking:** Permitted.
**Pets:** Small, well-trained pets permitted.
**Handicap Access:** No.
**Children:** No.
**Languages:** English, French.
**Your Host:** John & Jean-Guy.

IGTA

## Inn Exile

Men ♂

### *Where Being Gay Is a Way of Life*

Close your eyes and fantasize about a place where the open air calls you to the sparkling pool in the desert sun. Breathe in the dramatic view of towering mountains, while being refreshed by our outdoor mist cooling system. At *Inn Exile,* clothing is always optional. There's no need to miss your workout...our gymnasium is here for you. Call or write for brochure.

**Address: 545 Warm Sands Drive, Palm Springs, CA 92264**
**Tel: (619) 327-6413, (800) 962-0186, Fax: (619) 320-5745.**
**http://www.innexile.com.**

**Type:** Resort.
**Clientele:** Men only
**Transportation:** Car is best.
**To Gay Bars:** Three minutes by car, a 10 minute-walk.
**Rooms:** 26 rooms with king beds.
**Bathrooms:** All private full baths.
**Dates Open:** All year.
**Rates:** $83-$114.
**Discounts:** For 7 nights or more.
**Credit Cards:** MC, VISA, Amex, Discover, Diners, Carte Blanche.
**Rsv'tns:** Required.
**Reserve Through:** Travel agent or call direct.
**Minimum Stay:** Required at times. Please inquire.
**Parking:** Adequate, free off-street and on-street parking.
**In-Room:** Color TV, VCR, video tape library, AC, houseman service, telephone & refrigerator.
**On-Premises:** TV lounge.
**Exercise/Health:** Gym, weights, Jacuzzi, steam room.
**Swimming:** Pools on premises.
**Sunbathing:** At poolside.
**Nudity:** Permitted without restriction.
**Smoking:** Permitted without restriction.
**Pets:** Not permitted.
**Handicap Access:** Yes.
**Children:** Not permitted.
**Languages:** English.
**Your Host:** John & Carter.

IGTA

## InnTrigue

Men ♂

### *The Two Worlds of InnTrigue Await You*

You'll be intrigued by these two deluxe adjoining properties in the heart of Palm Springs. They have spacious, colorfully landscaped courtyards and magnificent mountain vistas. Relax around the totally private, CLOTHING OPTIONAL sparkling pools and secluded spas of ***InnTrigue.*** The poolside one- and two-bedroom suites have private patios, fully equipped kitchens, king-sized beds, remote cable TV with VCR, and an extensive video library. Complimentary Gold's Gym passes are available. Out & About Editor's Choice Award.

**Address: 526 Warm Sands Dr, Palm Springs, CA 92264**
**Tel: (619) 323-7505, (800) 798-8781, Fax: (619) 323-1055.**

**Type:** Private male resort.
**Clientele:** Men only.
**Transportation:** Car is best. Free pick up from the airport or bus station.
**To Gay Bars:** Within walking distance of gay bars & restaurants.
**Rooms:** 28 rooms.
**Bathrooms:** All private.
**Meals:** Cont. breakfast & evening social gathering.
**Complimentary:** Coffee & tea. Occasional cookouts, large cocktail parties & holiday dinners.
**Dates Open:** All year.
**Rates:** $75-$135.
**Discounts:** For extended stays. Please inquire.
**Credit Cards:** All major credit cards.
**Rsv'tns:** Recommended.
**Reserve Through:** Travel agent or call direct.
**Minimum Stay:** 2 nights on weekends
**Parking:** Adequate free off-street parking.
**In-Room:** Color cable TV, VCR, male video tape library, AC, phone, kitchen, refrigerator, coffee/tea-makers, houseman service.
**On-Premises:** Laundry facilities, cool-mist system, security access gate.
**Exercise/Health:** 2 Jacuzzis, pool table. Complimentary Gold's Gym day passes, massage by appt., bicycles.
**Swimming:** 2 pools on premises.
**Sunbathing:** At poolside & on patios.
**Nudity:** Permitted everywhere.
**Smoking:** Permitted without restrictions.
**Pets:** Inquire.
**Handicap Access:** Yes.
**Children:** Not permitted.
**Languages:** English.
**Your Host:** Michael, Terry & Don.

IGTA

## Inntimate

Gay/Lesbian ♂

### *For the Discerning Palm Springs Visitor*

A private guesthouse catering to the needs of the discerning Palm Springs visitor, ***Inntimate*** is a wonderful hideaway for a romantic weekend, an escape from the world, or just peace and quiet with all the amenities. Our four totally refurbished luxury suites surround the beautiful secluded fountain and pool area with its panoramic view of the mountains. Each suite has a kitchen, living area, king-sized bed, cable color TV, VCR, stereo and telephone.

**Address: 556 Warm Sands Dr, Palm Springs, CA 92264**
**Tel: (619) 778-8334, (800) 695-3846, Fax: (619) 778-9937.**

**Type:** Private guesthouse.
**Clientele:** Mostly men with women welcome
**Transportation:** Car is best. Free pick up from airport or bus.
**To Gay Bars:** 5 blocks, a 10 minute walk a 3 minute drive.
**Rooms:** 4 suites with king beds.
**Bathrooms:** Private: 1 bath/toilet, 3 shower/toilets.
**Meals:** Pre-stocked kitchen with beverages & breakfast & snack items.
**Vegetarian:** 10 minute walk to excellent vegetarian restaurant.
**Complimentary:** Bottle of wine. Pre-stocked kitchens with breakfast & snack items & non-alcoholic beverages.
**Dates Open:** All year.
**High Season:** October-June.
**Rates:** $135-$200.
**Discounts:** On weekly & monthly stays.
**Credit Cards:** Mc, Visa, Amex, Diners, Discover.
**Rsv'tns:** Required.
**Reserve Through:** Travel agent or call direct.
**Minimum Stay:** 2 nights on weekends, 3 nights on holiday weekends.
**Parking:** Adequate free off-street parking.
**In-Room:** Color cable TV, VCR, AC, evaporative coolers, ceiling fans, telephone, stereo systems, kitchen, refrigerator, coffee & tea-maker & maid service.
**On-Premises:** Fax.
**Exercise/Health:** Massage by appointment. Nearby gym, passes available.
**Swimming:** Pool on premises.
**Sunbathing:** Poolside & on patio.
**Smoking:** Permitted in pool area & in 3 suites. 1 suite is non-smoking.
**Pets:** Not permitted.
**Handicap Access:** No.
**Children:** No.
**Languages:** English.
**Your Host:** Ken.

## Santiago Resort

**Men ♂**

### *Palm Springs' Most Spectacular Private Men's Resort*

Exotically landscaped and secluded grounds provide a peaceful enclave for the discriminating traveller. Enjoy the most magnificent mountain views that Palm Springs can offer from our terrace level. An oversized diving pool, a 12-man spa and an outdoor cooling mist system complete the setting. Select from 23 poolside, courtyard or terrace suites and studios, all professionally designed and appointed. King-sized beds with feather duvet covers, superior quality towels and linens, shower massages, refrigerators and microwaves set the standard of excellence and luxury that you can expect at the ***Santiago.*** Expanded continental breakfast, courtyard luncheon, film library and Gold's Gym passes are all complimentary. And clothing is forever optional...

**Address: 650 San Lorenzo Rd, Palm Springs, CA 92264-8108**
**Tel: (619) 322-1300, (800) 710-7729, Fax: (619) 416-0347.**
**Area code changes to (760) Oct, 1997.**

**Type:** Hotel resort.
**Clientele:** Men only
**Transportation:** Car is best. Free pick up from airport or bus.
**To Gay Bars:** A 10-minute walk or a 3-minute drive.
**Rooms:** 10 rooms, 13 suites with king beds.
**Bathrooms:** Private: 19 shower/toilets, 4 bath/toilet/showers.
**Meals:** Expanded continental breakfast, lunch.
**Vegetarian:** Available.
**Complimentary:** Gold's gym passes.
**Dates Open:** All year.
**High Season:** February-March.
**Rates:** $99-$129.
**Discounts:** On extended stays.
**Credit Cards:** MC, Visa, Amex, Discover.
**Rsv'tns:** Recommended.
**Reserve Through:** Travel

*continued next page*

agent or call direct.
**Minimum Stay:** Required at times, please inquire.
**Parking:** Ample free off-street parking.
**In-Room:** Color cable TV, VCR, AC, telephone, refrigerator, microwave, houseman service.
**On-Premises:** Outdoor pavilion with fireplace, video tape library, fax, photocopier, laundry facilities.
**Exercise/Health:** Jacuzzi, nearby gym.
**Swimming:** Diving pool on premises.
**Sunbathing:** At poolside.
**Nudity:** Permitted without restriction.
**Smoking:** Permitted without restriction.
**Pets:** Not permitted.
**Handicap Access:** Yes.
**Languages:** English, French.

IGTA

## Triangle Inn

Men ♂

### *Everything... Except Ordinary!*

Finally... a secluded resort geared to the gay male traveler that will exceed your expectations. As you pass through the gate to our sun-drenched tropical gardens, you will be allured by the refreshing, sparkling pool and soothing Jacuzzi.

You can select from our studios, junior, one- and two-bedroom suites. For your added pleasure, our rooms include all the modern conveniences of today: remote color TV & VCR, stereo with CD & tape players, private telephones, large private baths, complete with oversized fluffy towels and blow dryers. All rooms also have central air conditioning, offering refrigerated air, evaporative cooling and heat systems. The junior, one- and two-bedroom suites come with fully-equipped kitchens and the studios offer a kitchenette. All just steps from our sparkling, heated pool and soothing Jacuzzi... where swimsuits are optional. Enjoy our own daily "Palm Springs" breakfast buffet served poolside. Call for a free color brochure.

The ***Triangle Inn*** is an experience well worth repeating again and again. It is a delightful feast for the eyes and a soothing embrace for the troubled spirit, a place where one can make new friends or surrender to peace and solitude. Either way, there is always something here to remind us that life is worth living. Visitors return home with recharged batteries, ready once more to face the challenges of every-day life. The ***Triangle Inn*** is an experience that will linger on long after the end of the vacation.

**Address: 555 San Lorenzo, Palm Springs, CA 92264**
**Tel: (619) 322-7993, (800) 732-7555.**

**Type:** Inn.
**Clientele:** Men only.
**Transportation:** Free pick up from Palm Springs airport.
**To Gay Bars:** 5- to 10-minute drive to all gay bars.
**Rooms:** 3 rooms & 6 suites with queen or king beds.
**Bathrooms:** All private bath/toilets.
**Meals:** Expanded continental breakfast.
**Dates Open:** All year.
**High Seas:** Oct 1-June 21.
**Rates:** $69-$189. Inquire for summer value rates.
**Discounts:** Inquire.
**Credit Cards:** MC, VISA & Amex.
**Rsv'tns:** Required.
**Reserve Through:** Travel agent or call direct.
**Minimum Stay:** Inquire for specific minimums.
**Parking:** Ample free off-street parking.
**In-Room:** AC, maid service, telephone, stereo, CD, color TV, VCR, kitchen & refrigerator.
**On-Premises:** Video tape library.
**Exercise/Health:** Jacuzzi, massage by appointment & bicycles.
**Swimming:** Pool on premises.
**Sunbathing:** At poolside with microcool outdoor cooling system.
**Nudity:** Permitted poolside.
**Smoking:** Permitted without restrictions.
**Handicap Access:** Inquire.
**Children:** Not permitted.
**Languages:** English.
**Your Host:** Kevin & Matthew.

IGTA

## The Villa

**Gay/Lesbian ♂**

Palm Springs is fast becoming the number one gay destination in the U.S., and ***The Villa*** is its largest, finest gay resort. Though a popular gathering spot, ***The Villa*** offers uncrowded luxury on 2-1/2 acres of lushly-planted grounds. You can dine on the patio, lounge in the Poolside Bar, enjoy an espresso or wander off to a quiet corner beneath the over 70 palms on the property. Our 45 rooms, originally built by Elizabeth Arden, have been lovingly restored.

**Address: 67-670 Carey Rd, Cathedral City, CA 92234**
**Tel: (619) 328-7211. Reservations (800) VILLA OK, Fax: (619) 321-1463.**

**Type:** Resort with pool bar & restaurant.
**Clientele:** Mostly men with women welcome
**Transportation:** Car or cab.
**To Gay Bars:** 1/2 mile by car to men's bars.
**Rooms:** 45 rooms with double or queen beds.
**Bathrooms:** All private.
**Meals:** Cont. breakfast.
**Dates Open:** All year.
**High Season:** Jan-July 4.
**Rates:** Off season $44.95-$84.95, in season $49.95-$102.95, holidays $89.95-$117.95.
**Discounts:** Off season: 1 night free on 2-night stay. In season: Tue, Wed, Thurs free with 2 prior nights stay.
**Credit Cards:** MC, VISA & Amex.
**Rsv'tns:** Recommended.
**Reserve Through:** Travel agent or call direct.
**Minimum Stay:** 2-4 days on holidays.
**Parking:** Ample off-street parking.
**In-Room:** Separate entrances, remote control color TV/radio, direct-dial phone, maid services, refrigerators, microwaves, AC.
**On-Premises:** Meeting room, fireplace dining room, public telephone.
**Exercise/Health:** Sauna, Jacuzzi, massage.
**Swimming:** Pool on premises.
**Sunbathing:** At poolside or on lawn.
**Smoking:** Permitted. Non-smoking rooms available.
**Handicap Access:** Please inquire.
**Languages:** English, limited Spanish.

# RUSSIAN RIVER

## Applewood Inn and Restaurant

Q-NET Gay-Friendly ♀♂

### *Russian River's Preeminent B&B*

Once a mission-style retreat in the redwoods, ***Applewood*** has been transformed into an elegant country inn and restaurant that has become the darling of food critics and editors steering their readers to romantic getaways. It's easy to see why *San Francisco Focus Magazine* called ***Applewood*** "the region's preeminent bed and breakfast" in July 1995. The beauty of the redwoods, apple trees and vineyards...the relaxing pool and Jacuzzi...the stylish rooms with European down comforters...the pleasure of sitting by the fire or reading in the library...the marvelous food in a firelit dining room...your willing hosts and two tail-wagging dogs...all await your arrival at this contemporary Eden.

**Address: 13555 Hwy 116, Guerneville, CA 95446**
**Tel: (707) 869-9093, (800) 555-8509,**
**E-mail: stay@applewoodinn.com. http://applewoodinn.com.**

**Type:** Inn with restaurant serving 4-course dinners.
**Clientele:** Mostly straight clientele with a gay & lesbian following.
**Transportation:** Car is best. Free pick up from Santa Rosa airport.
**To Gay Bars:** 5-minute drive to men's/women's bars.
**Rooms:** 10 rooms & 6 suites with queen beds.
**Bathrooms:** All private.
**Meals:** Full breakfast included, dinner offered to guests & public Tuesdays thru Saturdays.
**Vegetarian:** Upon request with 1-day notice.
**Complimentary:** Chocolates on pillows, coffee and tea all day.
**Dates Open:** All year.
**High Season:** April-November.
**Rates:** Doubles $125-$250. Off-season (Dec-Mar) $90-$190.
**Credit Cards:** MC, Visa, Amex, Discover.
**Rsv'tns:** Recommended. Essential for dinner.
**Reserve Through:** Travel agent or call direct.
**Minimum Stay:** 1 night midweek, 2 nights on weekends, 3 nights on holiday weekends.
**Parking:** Ample, free off-street parking.
**In-Room:** Color TV, phone & maid service. Suites also have showers for two or Jacuzzi baths, fireplaces & private patios or verandas.
**On-Premises:** Meeting rooms, private dining rooms, public telephone, laundry facilities & fax.
**Exercise/Health:** Jacuzzi, massage. Jacuzzi baths in suites.
**Swimming:** Heated pool on premises, river nearby. 10 minutes to ocean.
**Sunbathing:** At poolside & on private verandas with suites.
**Smoking:** Not permitted.
**Pets:** Not permitted.
**Handicap Access:** Yes, ramps, wide doors, grab bars.
**Children:** Not permitted.
**Languages:** English.
**Your Host:** Darryl & Jim.

## Fern Falls

Gay/Lesbian ♀♂

### *Romance Amidst the Redwoods*

***Fern Falls*** is a hillside habitat in a captivating canyon of Cazadero, whose cascading creeks merge with the languid waters of the Russian River. The custom-designed curved deck of the main house looks over the creek and ravine, and an ozonator spa sits above the waterfall on a hill nestled below a giant boulder. Nearby you can try wine tasting at the Korbel Winery, horseback riding, a soothing enzyme bath and massage at Osmosis, canoeing on the Russian River, or hiking in the redwood forests.

**Address:** 5701 Austin Creek Rd, PO Box 228, Cazadero, CA 95421 **Tel:** (707) 632-6108, **Fax:** (707) 632-6216.

**Type:** Guesthouse & cottages.
**Clientele:** Gay & lesbian. Good mix of men & women.
**Transportation:** Car is best.
**To Gay Bars:** 12 miles to bars in Guerneville.
**Rooms:** 1 suite & 2 cottages with double or queen beds.
**Bathrooms:** Private.
**Dates Open:** All year.
**High Season:** May-Oct.

**Rates:** $65-$135.
**Discounts:** Weekly rates.
**Rsv'tns:** Required.
**Reserve Through:** Travel agent or call direct.
**Minimum Stay:** 2 nights on weekends in season.
**Parking:** Adequate free parking.
**In-Room:** Color cable TV, VCR, coffee/tea-making facilities, kitchen, refrigerator. Cabins have fireplaces.

**On-Premises:** Video tape library, fax, phone, laundry facilities.
**Exercise/Health:** Jacuzzi. Nearby gym, massage.
**Swimming:** Creek on premises. Nearby ocean, river & waterfall.
**Sunbathing:** On private & common sun decks.
**Nudity:** Permitted on decks, in garden & at creek.

**Smoking:** Permitted outside on decks.
**Pets:** Permitted in cottages if well-behaved.
**Handicap Access:** No. Terrain is hilly & steep.
**Children:** Permitted, must be supervised & well-behaved.
**Languages:** English.
**Your Host:** Darrel & Peter.

# Fern Grove Inn

Q-NET Gay-Friendly 50/50 ♀♂

## *Sonoma Wine Country, Majestic Redwoods & the Scenic Russian River*

For a leisurely weekend or an extended getaway, ***Fern Grove Inn,*** surrounded by the Sonoma Wine Country, is a heavenly relaxing retreat. Individually decorated cottages with freshly cut flowers, romantic fireplaces, and private entrances ensure your comfort. Cottages range from spacious one-bedroom suites with fireplaces to intimate guest rooms with sitting areas. Two villas offer the ultimate in privacy. Original pine paneling and an eclectic blend of antique and contemporary furniture complete the setting.

Start your day with freshly brewed gourmet coffee and a leisurely buffet breakfast featuring renowned homemade muffins and pastries served in the relaxed atmosphere of the common room. The morning newspapers, soft classical music, a warming fire, and good conversation will stimulate your spirits.

Later in the day you can practice the fine art of relaxation or explore the back roads of the neighborhood. For wine connoisseurs, Sonoma County boasts more than 70 award-winning wineries. Golf, tennis, bicycling, horseback riding, hiking, and nature walks are just around the corner – or enjoy a lazy canoe ride down the Russian River. For a daring adventure, try soaring above the vineyards in a hot air balloon, followed by a gourmet champagne brunch.

For the beachcomber in search of solitude, the rugged Sonoma Coast is just minutes away. Peer out to sea to view playful seals and watch for migrating whales. Bodega Bay, a quaint fishing village where the Hitchcock classic "The Birds" was filmed, is a great place to explore. At the end of the day, dine at local restaurants – from simple country French bistros to the bastions of California cuisine. Nightclub dancing, jazz combos, a symphony orchestra, and a repertory theater are also nearby.

**Address: 16650 River Rd, Guernewood Park, CA 95446**
**Tel: (707) 869-9083, (800) 347-9083, Fax: (707) 869-2948.**

**Type:** Bed & breakfast with cottages.
**Clientele:** 50% gay & lesbian & 50% straight clientele
**Transportation:** Car is best or SFO Airport Express Bus to Santa Rosa & local bus to Guerneville.
**To Gay Bars:** 1 blk to men's/women's bars, dancing.
**Rooms:** 2 villas, 9 suites & 6 studio cottages with queen beds.
**Bathrooms:** All private.
**Meals:** Expanded continental breakfast.
**Vegetarian:** Nearby rests.
**Complimentary:** Coffee & tea all day. Juice or sherry in the afternoon.
**Dates Open:** All year.
**High Season:** Apr-Oct.
**Rates:** $89-$199.
**Discounts:** Inquire about mid-week or off-season.
**Credit Cards:** MC, Visa, Amex, Discover.
**Rsv'tns:** Recommended.
**Reserve Through:** Travel agent or call direct.
**Minimum Stay:** 2 nights most weekends. 3 nights holiday weekends.
**Parking:** Ample off-street parking.
**In-Room:** Color TV, VCR, refrigerator, & maid service.
**On-Premises:** Common room, guest telephone, book & video library.
**Exercise/Health:** Golf, tennis, horseback riding, jogging, hiking, canoeing, enzyme baths, & health club all nearby.
**Swimming:** Pool on premises. 12 miles to ocean beach. River across hwy.
**Sunbathing:** At poolside or on river or ocean beaches.
**Smoking:** Not permitted in cottages.
**Children:** Permitted, but not encouraged.
**Languages:** English & some Spanish.

# Golden Apple Ranch

Q-NET Gay-Friendly 50/50 ♀♂

## *Gateway to the Sonoma Coast & Wine Country*

***Golden Apple Ranch,*** gateway to the Russian River wine country, is a secluded retreat built among the towering redwoods and overlooking Bodega Bay. The lodge gallery and great room invite guests to read, relax, paint or dream the day away...while the private suites offer total seclusion. From the ranch, one can arrange to be chauffered through the wine country in our Classic Silver Cloud Rolls Royce or our luxury Continental convertible. Your host, John Stillion, is known for his gracious hospitality in seeing to guest's individual needs. We hope you can join us this season. We cater many gay weddings.

**Address: 17575 Fitzpatrick Lane, Occidental, CA 95465**
**Tel: (707) 874-3756, Fax: (707) 874-1670.**

**Type:** Art gallery lodge overlooking magnificent redwood groves.
**Clientele:** 50% gay & lesbian & 50% straight clientele
**Transportation:** By car. Deluxe ground transportation available upon request.
**To Gay Bars:** 12 miles or 20 minutes.
**Rooms:** 5 suites & private 3-bedroom gatehouse cottage.
**Bathrooms:** All private.
**Meals:** Continental breakfast 8-11 am included. Lunch & dinner available at extra charge.
**Vegetarian:** Full vegetarian lunch & dinner available upon request.
**Complimentary:** Champagne, wine, or tea on arrival. Sherry or hot tea in the evening.
**Dates Open:** All year.
**High Season:** April-December.
**Rates:** $95-$165. Gatehouse $285 per night.
**Discounts:** Guests staying 3 or more nights will receive a 20% discount on lodging.
**Rsv'tns:** Required.
**Reserve Through:** Travel agent or call direct.
**Parking:** Ample parking in motor court & grounds.
**In-Room:** Maid service. Satellite color TV available in most suites.
**On-Premises:** Meeting rooms, TV lounge, weddings & celebrations.
**Exercise/Health:** Personalized massage available upon request. Internationally renowned osmosis baths in nearby Freestone.
**Swimming:** Public beaches 5 miles.
**Sunbathing:** On the roof or in the grassy meadow below the lodge.
**Nudity:** Permitted on the roof, grassy meadow, and public nude beach 10 miles away.
**Smoking:** Permitted on private decks, terraces & motor court.
**Pets:** Most welcome with prior arrangement.
**Handicap Access:** Yes.
**Children:** Most welcome with prior arrangement.
**Languages:** English & Spanish.
**Your Host:** John Stillion.

## Highland Dell Inn Bed & Breakfast

Gay-Friendly 50/50 ♀♂

### *Exceptional Service in a Spectacular Setting*

The landmark ***Highland Dell Inn Bed & Breakfast,*** with its vista of the Russian River, captures the serenity of a more gentle era. Rich, stained glass windows, a gigantic lobby fireplace, heirloom antiques and a collection of historical photos set the tone for arriving guests. The large pool is under the redwoods. The area offers canoeing, swimming, fishing, backpacking, nature trails, horseback riding, cross-country cycling, enzyme baths, and even hot-air ballooning. One of our guests comments, *"The warmth of your hospitality, the charm of this beautiful B&B, delicious food, the view...a perfect getaway. Lady (dog) certainly lives up to her name."*

**Address: 21050 River Blvd, Box 370, Monte Rio, CA 95462-0370**
**Tel: (707) 865-1759, (800) 767-1759, E-mail: highland@netdex.com.**

**Type:** Bed & breakfast inn.
**Clientele:** 50% gay & lesbian & 50% straight clientele. Sometimes more gay than straight
**Transportation:** Car is best.
**To Gay Bars:** 5-minute drive to most gay venues.
**Rooms:** 5 rooms & 3 suites with queen or king beds.
**Bathrooms:** 2 private shower/toilets, 6 private bath/toilet/showers.
**Meals:** Full breakfast.
**Vegetarian:** Available upon request.
**Complimentary:** Tea & coffee. Candies throughout.
**Dates Open:** Open all year except for Jan 2-Feb 1.
**High Season:** May-Oct.
**Rates:** Summer $75-$200 & winter $60-$200.
**Discounts:** Inquire.
**Credit Cards:** MC, Visa, Amex, Discover, Eurocard.
**Rsv'tns:** Required.
**Reserve Through:** Travel agent or call direct.
**Minimum Stay:** 2 nights on weekends. 3 nights some holidays.
**Parking:** Ample, free off-street parking.
**In-Room:** Maid service, color cable TV, tele. Suites have VCR, coffee/tea-making facilities & refrigerator.
**On-Premises:** Meeting rooms, video tape library, fax & copy service.
**Exercise/Health:** Massage. Nearby gym, massage, weights.
**Swimming:** Seasonal pool on premises. 6 miles to ocean beach & river nearby.
**Sunbathing:** At poolside or on the beach.
**Smoking:** Permitted on sun porch only. All rooms are non-smoking.
**Pets:** Pets up to 40 pounds with pet deposit in 1st floor rooms only + $15.
**Handicap Access:** Yes, with assistance to building.
**Languages:** English.
**Your Host:** Glenn & Anthony.

## Highlands Resort

Gay/Lesbian ♀♂

***Highlands Resort*** is a country retreat on 4 wooded acres. You can plan your day while soaking in the outdoor hot tub, swim and sun at the pool or barbecue a meal with friends. Challenge another group to Trivial Pursuit, read a book or curl up in front of the fireplace. This is a place for relaxing. The resort feels like a mountaintop, yet is only a short walk to fine restaurants, shops, nightclubs.

**Address: PO Box 346, 14000 Woodland Dr, Guerneville, CA 95446**
**Tel: (707) 869-0333, Fax: (707) 869-0370.**

**Type:** Inn and campground.
**Clientele:** Good mix of gay men & women.
**Transportation:** Car is best.
**To Gay Bars:** 2 blocks to men's/women's bars. A 5-minute walk or 2-min drive.
**Rooms:** 10 rooms, 1 suite

& 6 cottages with double, queen or king beds.
**Bathrooms:** 10 private, others share.
**Campsites:** 20 tent sites with 3 showers & 2 restrooms.
**Meals:** Continental breakfast on weekends.
**Dates Open:** All year.
**High Season:** Apr-Oct.
**Rates:** Summer $40-$105, winter $40-$80.
**Credit Cards:** MC, VISA, Amex & Discover.
**Rsv'tns:** Recommended.
**Reserve Through:** Travel agent or call direct.
**Minimum Stay:** 2 nights over weekends.
**Parking:** Ample free parking.
**In-Room:** Maid service, 2 kitchens.
**On-Premises:** TV lounge.
**Exercise/Health:** Hot tub.
**Swimming:** Pool on premises.
**Sunbathing:** At poolside or on the patio.
**Nudity:** Permitted around pool & hot tub.
**Smoking:** Permitted in designated areas.
**Pets:** Permitted by special arrangement.
**Handicap Access:** No.
**Children:** Not especially welcome.
**Languages:** English.
**Your Host:** Lynette & Kenneth.

## House of a Thousand Flowers

Gay-Friendly 50/50 ♀♂

Designed so that each room has its own spectacular view of the forest and the valley below, ***The House of a Thousand Flowers*** sits high on a bluff overlooking the Russian River. It is surrounded by sunny decks, intimate gardens, and walkways. There are two comfortably furnished guest rooms with private entrances, a shared bath, and an enclosed spa on the deck. There is a fireplace in the living room and an extensive book, music, and movie library for the guests. There are many activities, sunny beaches, quaint inns, and fine restaurants nearby.

**Address: 11 Mosswood Circle, Cazadero, CA 95421**
**Tel: (707) 632-5571, Fax: (707) 632-6215.**

**Type:** Bed & breakfast.
**Clientele:** 50% gay & lesbian & 50% straight clientele.
**Transportation:** Pick up from airport in Santa Rosa, pick up from bus $10.
**To Gay Bars:** 9 miles or 10 minutes by car.
**Rooms:** 2 rooms with queen beds.
**Bathrooms:** 1 shared bath/shower/toilet.
**Meals:** Full breakfast.
**Vegetarian:** Always available.
**Complimentary:** Afternoon wine, after dinner liqueur.
**Dates Open:** All year.
**High Season:** July-Sept.
**Rates:** One rate, $85-$90 per couple, $60 single.
**Credit Cards:** MC, VISA.
**Rsv'tns:** Required.
**Reserve Thru:** Call direct.
**Parking:** Free parking.
**On-Premises:** TV lounge, meeting rooms, laundry facilities.
**Exercise/Health:** Jacuzzi.
**Swimming:** At nearby river & ocean beach.
**Sunbathing:** At beach & common sun decks.
**Nudity:** Permitted on common sun deck by appointment only.
**Smoking:** Permitted in designated areas, non-smoking rooms available.
**Pets:** Not permitted.
**Handicap Access:** No.
**Children:** Not permitted.
**Languages:** English.
**Your Host:** Dave & Bob.

## Huckleberry Springs

Gay-Friendly 50/50 ♀♂

Located on 56 wooded acres, ***Huckleberry Springs*** offers private cottage accommodations in an intimate and peaceful setting. Four modern cottages offer guests all amenities, including VCR, queen beds, skylights and wood-burning stoves. The lodge boasts dramatic views from its mountaintop location and is a cozy spot to sit, read or relax. Guests sunbathe on the pool decks or on the large deck. Breakfast and dinner are served in the lodge. Massage is available on premises and canoeing, hiking, bicycling, golf, tennis, wineries and the ocean are nearby.

**Address: PO Box 400, Monte Rio, CA 95462**

*continued next page*

**Tel: (707) 865-2683, (800) 822-2683, E-mail: thelmaliv@aol.com.**

**Type:** Cottages & B&B on 56 acres one mile from the river.
**Clientele:** 50% gay & lesbian & 50% straight clientele
**Transportation:** Rental car is best.
**To Gay Bars:** 6 miles.
**Rooms:** 4 cottages with queen beds.
**Bathrooms:** All private.
**Meals:** Full breakfast. Dinner by reservation.
**Vegetarian:** With advance notice upon reservation.
**Complimentary:** Tea, coffee & spring water.
**Dates Open:** March 2-December 14.
**High Season:** May through September.
**Rates:** $145 double occupancy. Full breakfast included in rate.
**Credit Cards:** MC, VISA & Amex.
**Rsv'tns:** Required.
**Reserve Through:** Travel agent or call direct.
**Minimum Stay:** 2 days.
**Parking:** Ample free parking.
**In-Room:** Ceiling fans, hairdryers, woodstoves, refrigerator, VCR, stereos, coffee & tea-making facilities.
**On-Premises:** Catering, kitchen with advance request, meeting rooms & TV lounge.
**Exercise/Health:** Jacuzzi, massage cottage, by appointment.
**Swimming:** Pool on premises, river nearby.
**Sunbathing:** Poolside, private & common sun decks, at nearby ocean, riverside beaches.
**Nudity:** Permitted in the hot tub.
**Smoking:** No smoking on property.
**Pets:** Not permitted.
**Handicap Access:** Only the lodge.
**Children:** Not permitted.
**Languages:** English & Spanish.

IGTA

## Jacques' Cottage

Gay/Lesbian ♂

### *The Ultimate in Privacy*

Amidst oaks, redwoods, and fruit trees, ***Jacques' Cottage*** is located in the heart of California wine country, only minutes from the wineries and fine restaurants that made Sonoma County famous. Many gay clubs and restaurants are 10 minutes away. Fishing, canoeing, or swimming at the gay beach (five minutes from the cottage) are possible in the tranquil Russian River. At ***Jacques' Cottage,*** enjoy a hot tub under the stars, lounge by the pool, or have a glass of wine on your private deck overlooking the vineyards.

**Address: 6471 Old Trenton Road, Forestville, CA 95436**
**Tel: (707) 575-1033, (800) 246-1033, Fax: (707) 573-8911.**
**E-mail: jacques@wco.com. www.wco.com/~jacques/.**

**Type:** Large, private guest cottage.
**Clientele:** Mostly men with women welcome
**Transportation:** Car is best.
**To Gay Bars:** 8 miles to all the bars.
**Rooms:** 1 cottage with 2 queen beds.
**Bathrooms:** Private bath/toilet/shower.
**Complimentary:** Coffee & coffee-maker in cottage.
**Dates Open:** All year.
**High Season:** May-end of Oct.
**Rates:** $100-$125.
**Discounts:** Weekly rates available.
**Rsv'tns:** Required.
**Reserve Through:** Travel agent or call direct.
**Minimum Stay:** 2 nights.
**Parking:** Ample, free off-street parking.
**In-Room:** Color TV, VCR, video tape library, laundry service, private phone line, bathrobes, kitchen, refrigerator, coffee & tea making facilities, CD.
**On-Premises:** Sun deck.
**Exercise/Health:** Free weights poolside, Jacuzzi on premises. Nearby gym, massage.
**Swimming:** Pool on premises. River with gay beach 2 miles, or lake 35 miles away.
**Sunbathing:** At poolside or on private sun deck.
**Nudity:** Permitted.
**Smoking:** Permitted.
**Pets:** Permitted.
**Handicap Access:** No.
**Children:** Permitted.
**Languages:** English.
**Your Host:** Jacques.

## Mountain Lodge Resort

Gay-Friendly 50/50 ♀♂

Discover ***Mountain Lodge Resort,*** one of the Russian River's best-kept secrets. Explore the possibilities! Peaceful gardens and secluded decks nestle into the artfully landscaped grounds. The pool and hot tubs overlook the Russian River. Gay bars of the area are a short distance away.

**Address: PO Box 169, 16350 1st St, Guerneville, CA 95446**
**Tel: (707) 869-3722, Fax: (707) 869-0556.**

**Type:** Condo-style ground level units.
**Clientele:** 50% gay & lesbian & 50% straight clientele
**Transportation:** Car is best from San Francisco.
**To Gay Bars:** 2-minute walk to gay & lesbian bars.
**Rooms:** 3 apartments with queen beds.
**Bathrooms:** All private baths.
**Dates Open:** All year.
Weekly/monthly rentals based on availability.
**High Season:** May through September.
**Rates:** Summer $49-$125. Winter $40-$95. Based on double occupancy.
**Discounts:** For stays of three nights or more Sunday-Thursday or for a week or more.
**Credit Cards:** MC, Visa, Amex, Discover.
**Reserve Through:** Travel agent or call direct.
**Minimum Stay:** On holiday weekends.
**Parking:** Ample off-street parking. Gated security, key access only.
**In-Room:** Color cable TV, kitchen, refrigerator, coffee & tea-making facilities & maid service.
**On-Premises:** Laundry facilities.
**Exercise/Health:** Jacuzzi. Steam in one resort room.
**Swimming:** Pool & river on premises.
**Sunbathing:** At poolside, on the beach, or on private & common sun decks.
**Nudity:** Permitted in spas after dark with discretion.
**Smoking:** Permitted without restrictions.
**Pets:** Not permitted.
**Children:** Permitted. Small children at pool between 3 & 6 pm only.
**Languages:** English.

## Paradise Cove

Gay/Lesbian ♀♂

### *A Unique Place to Stay on the Russian River*

***Paradise Cove*** is a luxurious, unique, adult resort where service and comfort are top priorities. All cabins have private baths, sundecks and fireplaces. The grounds were carefully planned to highlight seasonal changes in this northern California forest and wine country setting. From the spectacular burst of color in our rhododendron dell to cascading vines of Burmese honeysuckle, passion flower, palms and lilies of the Nile, there is even a hint of the tropics.

**Address: 14711 Armstrong Woods Rd, Guerneville, CA 95446**
**Tel: (707) 869-2706 or (800) 880-2706.**

**Type:** Resort.
**Clientele:** Good mix of gay men & women
**Transportation:** Car.
**To Gay Bars:** 1 mile to men's/women's bars.
**Rooms:** 15 rooms with queen beds, fireplaces & sun decks.
**Bathrooms:** All private shower/toilets.
**Meals:** Coffee, tea, breakfast cakes on weekends, holidays.
**Dates Open:** All year.
**High Season:** May-September.
**Rates:** Off-season $50-$105, in-season $65-$135.
**Discounts:** Weekly rates & off-season packages may apply.
**Credit Cards:** MC, VISA, Amex & Discover.
**Rsv'tns:** Recommended.
**Reserve Through:** Call direct.
**Minimum Stay:** On holiday & special-event weekends.
**Parking:** Adequate free off-street parking.
**In-Room:** Wet bars, some have color cable TV.
**On-Premises:** Public telephones.
**Exercise/Health:** Hydrotherapy spa.
**Swimming:** In heated pool, nearby river 1 mi, ocean 15 mi.
**Sunbathing:** At poolside, on private sun decks.
**Nudity:** Permitted on private sun decks.
**Smoking:** Permitted without restrictions.
**Pets:** Not permitted.
**Handicap Access:** No.
**Children:** Discouraged.
**Languages:** English.

## Rio Villa Beach Resort

Gay-Friendly 50/50 ♀♂

***Rio Villa*** is a cluster of resort cabins, units and suites surrounded by spacious decks, abundant gardens and lush lawns, sheltered by the redwoods. Decor reflects the warmth of old-world charm. Newly-remodeled rooms have kitchens, private baths, sofas, king and queen beds, color TV, outdoor BBQs and private sun decks. A stroll through the old-fashioned herb and flower gardens along the river leaves one refreshed and grateful. Weekends, a buffet breakfast of homemade coffee cakes, muffins, fresh fruit, juices and coffee is served on the redwood patio.

**Address: 20292 Hwy 116, Monte Rio, CA 95462**
**Tel: (707) 865-1143, Fax: (707) 865-0115. E-mail: riovilla@wclynx.com.**

**Type:** Beach resort.
**Clientele:** 50% gay & lesbian & 50% straight clientele
**Transportation:** Car is best.
**To Gay Bars:** 10 minutes to men's/women's bars.
**Rooms:** 10 rooms, 2 suites & 2 cottages with double, queen & king beds.
**Bathrooms:** Private: 12 shower/toilets, 1 full bath & 1 sink. 1 shared shower.
**Meals:** Continental breakfast on weekends.
**Complimentary:** Tea & coffee in all kitchen units.
**Dates Open:** All year.
**High Season:** May-September.
**Rates:** High season $65-$150. Low season $57.50-$150.
**Discounts:** Multiple-day packages available. Off-season bargains.
**Credit Cards:** MC, Visa, Amex & Discover.
**Rsv'tns:** Preferred.
**Reserve Through:** Call direct.
**Minimum Stay:** High season weekends & holidays.
**Parking:** Ample, free, off-street parking.
**In-Room:** Color cable TV, kitchen, refrigerator & maid service.
**Exercise/Health:** Nearby Jacuzzi & massage.
**Swimming:** River on the premises, ocean beach nearby.
**Sunbathing:** On beach, private & common sun decks & patio.
**Smoking:** Permitted.
**Pets:** Not permitted.
**Children:** Permitted but not encouraged.
**Languages:** English.

## The Willows

Q-NET Gay/Lesbian ♀♂

### *Where Tourists Are Treated Just Like Home Folk!*

***The Willows*** guesthouse offers a country home vacation on five spectacular acres overlooking the Russian River. In the main lodge, there are thirteen private, cozy bedrooms, some with fireplaces and color TVs, all with direct-dial telephones. Nine bedrooms have private baths. In the spacious living room, you will enjoy a large stone fireplace, extensive library and grand piano. A sun deck with hot tub and sauna extends the length of the lodge. On the rambling, well-tended property, ideal for tent camping, you'll find quiet, wooded seclusion and sunny, landscaped lawns, which slope down to the private dock on the river. Use of the canoes is provided at no additional charge. Guests at ***The Willows*** are served a complimentary breakfast of fresh fruit, pastries, juice and coffee, and are welcome to make use of the community kitchen and outdoor barbecues. Many excellent

restaurants are a short walk away. At ***The Willows,*** you'll find a relaxed, intimate, and friendly atmosphere, where you can get away from it all, yet be in the heart of the maddening fun on the Russian River.

**Address: PO Box 465, 15905 River Rd, Guerneville, CA 95446**
**Tel: (707) 869-2824, (800) 953-2828.**

**Type:** Riverfront guesthouse inn with tent camping.
**Clientele:** Good mix of gay men & women
**Transportation:** Car is best.
**To Gay Bars:** 2 blocks (1/4 mi). 10-minute walk or 1-minute drive.
**Rooms:** 13 rooms with queen beds.
**Bathrooms:** 9 private, 4 shared.
**Campsites:** Can accommodate 120 tent campers. RV access, no hook-ups. Full toilet & shower facilities, 4 showers for men, 2 showers for women, 2 toilets for each.
**Meals:** Expanded continental breakfast.
**Vegetarian:** At nearby restaurants.
**Complimentary:** Tea & coffee served all day.
**Dates Open:** All year.
**High Season:** May thru September.
**Rates:** Rooms $59-$119, special weekday rates.
**Credit Cards:** MC, VISA, Amex & Discover.
**Rsv'tns:** Required.
**Reserve Through:** Travel agent or call direct.
**Minimum Stay:** 2 nights on weekends (rooms only during peak season).
**Parking:** Ample free on- & off-street parking.
**In-Room:** Color cable TV, some VCRs, video tape library, telephone, ceiling fans, maid service.
**On-Premises:** Large community kitchen. Private dock with canoes & paddleboat on river.
**Exercise/Health:** Hot tub, sauna & massage. Gym in town.
**Swimming:** In the river.
**Sunbathing:** On the beach or common sun deck, 5 acres of park-like grounds.
**Nudity:** Permitted in designated areas.
**Smoking:** Permitted outside the lodge. All rooms non-smoking.
**Pets:** Not permitted.
**Handicap Access:** No.
**Children:** Not permitted.
**Languages:** English.

# SACRAMENTO

## Hartley House Inn

Q-NET Gay-Friendly 50/50 ♀♂

### *A New Standard of Excellence*

***Hartley House,*** a stunning turn-of-the century mansion, combines modern comforts with the warmth and charm of a bygone era. The home's stately character is preserved in original inlaid hardwood floors, stained woodwork, leaded and stained glass windows, and original brass light fixtures. Authentic antique furnishings, period artworks, and collectibles decorate the parlor, dining room, and guest rooms. Mornings, savor generous breakfasts of freshly baked muffins, fresh fruit, coffees, teas, and a variety of home made specialties. The elegant decor, relaxed atmosphere and convenient location are all qualities that bring guests back time and time again.

**Address: 700 Twenty-Second St, Sacramento, CA 95816-4012**
**Tel: (916) 447-7829, (800) 831-5806, Fax: (916) 447-1820,**
**E-mail: randy@hartleyhouse.com. http://www.hartleyhouse.com.**

**Type:** Bed & breakfast.
**Clientele:** 50% gay & lesbian & 50% straight clientele
**Transportation:** Car is best, airporter to door approx $10.
**To Gay Bars:** 5 blocks to gay/lesbian bars.
**Rooms:** 5 rooms with dbl, queen or king beds.
**Bathrooms:** All private.
**Meals:** Full breakfast.
**Vegetarian:** Always available. Special menu items with advance notice.

*continued next page*

**Complimentary:** Cookies, beverages, turndown service with mints on pillow.
**Dates Open:** All year.
**High Season:** Spring-fall.
**Rates:** $89-$150.
**Discounts:** Corp. & government discounts avail.
**Credit Cards:** MC, Visa, Amex, Discover, Carte Blanche, Diners, JCB, ATM cards.
**Rsv'tns:** Recommended.
**Reserve Through:** Travel agent or call direct.
**Minimum Stay:** On holiday weekends only.
**Parking:** Ample, free on- & off-street parking.
**In-Room:** Maid, room & laundry service, color cable TV, stereo/cassette clock radios, AC, ceiling fans, fine robes, soaps & shampoos, phones with modem ports (no charge for local calls or long distance access).
**On-Premises:** Meeting room, dining room, library, fax & copy facilities.
**Exercise/Health:** Massage on premises with appointment. Discount at nearby local health club.
**Swimming:** In lake, river or nearby pool.
**Sunbathing:** On beach/patio.
**Smoking:** Permitted outdoors.
**Children:** Permitted if older and by prior arrangement.
**Languages:** English & Spanish.
**Your Host:** Randy.

# SAN DIEGO

## Balboa Park Inn

Q-NET Gay/Lesbian ♀♂

### *More Than You'll Pay For...*

***Balboa Park Inn*** is a collection of 26 distinctive, immaculate and beautifully-appointed suites, located in the heart of San Diego's gay community. We're just footsteps (1-1/2 blocks) from Balboa Park and the world famous San Diego Zoo. Nearby are the numerous cafes, shops, restaurants and nightclubs of Hillcrest, the city's gayest area of town. A short drive will find you at the Pacific's doorstep, including Black's Beach, a favorite spot for nude sunbathing. Rent a car to see the sights, or use our comprehensive public transportation system. We're just minutes from the airport, train station and bus terminal downtown, and only 20 miles from Tijuana, Mexico, the world's most visited city.

The ***Balboa Park Inn*** is your affordable, "family"-oriented destination in San Diego. Stay with us. We promise that you'll always get more than you paid for!

**Address: 3402 Park Blvd, San Diego, CA 92103**
**Tel: (619) 298-0823, (800) 938-8181, Fax: (619) 294-8070.**

**Type:** Bed & breakfast inn.
**Clientele:** Good mix of gay men & women, with some straight clientele
**Transportation:** Car is best or taxi from airport.
**To Gay Bars:** 6 blocks to men's, 3 blocks to women's bar. A 15-minute walk or 5-minute drive.
**Rooms:** 19 suites & 7 rooms with single, queen or king beds.
**Bathrooms:** All private.
**Meals:** Expanded continental breakfast.
**Complimentary:** Coffee, tea or hot chocolate in suite.
**Dates Open:** All year.
**High Season:** Summer.
**Rates:** $80-$190 plus tax.
**Discounts:** For established business accounts.
**Credit Cards:** MC, Visa, Amex, Diner's, Carte Blanche, Discover.
**Rsv'tns:** Required 3-4 wks. ahead in summer.
**Reserve Through:** Travel agent or call direct.
**Minimum Stay:** 3 days on holiday weekends.
**Parking:** Ample, free, on-street parking.
**In-Room:** Color cable TV, VCR, telephone, AC, kitchen, refrigerator, coffee/tea-making facilities, ceiling fans, room, laundry & maid service.
**On-Premises:** Maids do laundry.
**Swimming:** Pool nearby, 10-15-min drive to ocean beach, 30-min drive to Black's Beach.
**Sunbathing:** On private and common sun decks.
**Smoking:** Permitted without restrictions.
**Handicap Access:** Yes, one room.
**Children:** Permitted.
**Languages:** English, Spanish.

IGTA

## The Beach Place

**Gay/Lesbian ♂**

Minutes from downtown, Hillcrest and most tourist attractions, the Ocean Beach section of San Diego retains the charm of a small town. No high-rise hotels block the view or prevent access to the beach. At ***The Beach Place,*** you enjoy the privacy of your own apartment with deck, small garden, full kitchen with microwave, bedroom with queen bed and living room with color TV and adult films. The central courtyard has a gazebo with a huge hot tub, as well as a patio for sunbathing.

**Address: 2158 Sunset Cliffs Blvd, San Diego, CA 92107**
**Tel: (619) 225-0746.**

**Type:** Guesthouse.
**Clientele:** Mostly men with women welcome
**Transportation:** Car is best.
**To Gay Bars:** 10-minute drive to numerous bars in Hillcrest, Pacific Beach & Point Loma.
**Rooms:** 4 suites with queen beds.
**Bathrooms:** All private.
**Complimentary:** Tea, coffee, sugar, salt, pepper & utensils.
**Dates Open:** All year.
**Rates:** $60 per night or $350 per week for 2 people. $15 per night per additional guest.
**Rsv'tns:** Required.
**Reserve Through:** Travel agent or call direct.
**Minimum Stay:** 2 days.
**Parking:** Adequate off-street covered parking.
**In-Room:** Kitchen with microwave & refrigerator, color cable TV, ceiling fans & maid service.
**On-Premises:** Gas barbeque available in the courtyard.
**Exercise/Health:** Jacuzzi.
**Swimming:** 4 blocks to ocean beach.
**Sunbathing:** On the patio & private sun decks.
**Nudity:** Permitted on sun decks.
**Pets:** Sometimes with prior arrangement.
**Children:** Permitted at times with prior arrangement.
**Languages:** English

IGTA

## Dmitri's Guesthouse

**Gay/Lesbian ♂**

Overlooking downtown in one of San Diego's historic turn-of-the-century neighborhoods, ***Dmitri's*** is minutes from the convention center, Gaslamp entertainment area, Horton Plaza shopping, Balboa Park, our famous zoo, the Old Globe Theatre, the Aerospace Museum, Old Town, the bays and beaches, and just blocks from the stops for bright red trolleys that go to Tijuana, Mexico. A variety of accommodations with private baths include continental breakfast served at poolside.

**Address: 931 21st St, San Diego, CA 92102. Tel: (619) 238-5547.**

**Type:** Guest house.
**Clientele:** Mostly men with women welcome
**Transportation:** Pickup from airport, bus or train, $6.
**To Gay Bars:** 6 blocks to gay/lesbian bars.
**Rooms:** 5 doubles with queen beds, or 1-2 double beds.
**Bathrooms:** 3 private, 2 shared.
**Meals:** Continental breakfast.
**Complimentary:** Tea & coffee.
**Dates Open:** All year.
**High Season:** July-September.
**Rates:** 2 people $55-$85, $15 per extra person.
**Discounts:** Weekly rates available.
**Credit Cards:** MC, Visa.
**Rsv'tns:** Required.
**Reserve Through:** Travel agent or call direct.
**Minimum Stay:** 2 nights on weekends.
**Parking:** Adequate free on-street parking.
**In-Room:** Maid service, color TV, kitchen.
**On-Premises:** Telephone, TV lounge.
**Exercise/Health:** Hot tub.
**Swimming:** Pool.
**Sunbathing:** At poolside or on common sundecks.
**Nudity:** Yes.
**Smoking:** Permitted outdoors.
**Pets:** Not permitted.
**Handicap Access:** No.
**Children:** Not permitted.
**Languages:** English, limited Spanish.

## Kasa Korbett

Gay/Lesbian ♀♂

### *Where a Guest is at Home*

Each room in ***Kasa Korbett,*** a comfortable 70-year-old craftsman-design house, is appointed in its own theme. Enjoyable breakfasts are served each morning in your room, the dining room, or on the patio deck (dinner plans are available). Relax in the living room with a video, unwind in the patio spa, or nap in the backyard hammock year-round. A new pedestrian bridge connects our quiet residential neighborhood with the Hillcrest/Uptown area. Here you will find bars for every taste, various bookstores and coffeehouses, and gay-owned and gay-friendly restaurants and shops.

**Address: 1526 Van Buren Ave, San Diego, CA 92103**
**Tel: (619) 291-3962, (800) 757-KASA (5272), Fax: (619) 298-9150.**

**Type:** Bed & breakfast home.
**Clientele:** Gay & lesbian. Good mix of men & women
**Transportation:** Car is best. Taxi is inexpensive. Free pick up from airport, train, bus.
**To Gay Bars:** 4 blocks, an 8 min walk, a 4 min drive.
**Rooms:** 2 rooms, 1 suite with queen beds.
**Bathrooms:** 1 private bath/toilet/shower, 1 shared bath/shower/toilet.
**Meals:** Expanded continental breakfast.
**Vegetarian:** By guest request. Many restaurants, health food stores nearby.
**Complimentary:** Tea, coffee, juice, soda. Sherry in room.
**Dates Open:** All year.
**High Season:** April-October.
**Rates:** $59-$89.
**Discounts:** Stay 5 nights, 6th night free. Long-term stay: up to 40% discount.
**Rsv'tns:** Required.
**Reserve Through:** Travel agent or call direct.
**Parking:** Ample on- & off-street parking.
**In-Room:** Telephone, color TV, maid & room service.
**On-Premises:** TV lounge, video tape library, laundry facilities.
**Exercise/Health:** Jacuzzi, massage. Nearby gym, weights, sauna, steam.
**Swimming:** Pool & ocean nearby.
**Sunbathing:** On common sun decks.
**Smoking:** No smoking except in patio area.
**Pets:** Not permitted.
**Handicap Access:** Yes. Wheelchair accessibility to all rooms.
**Children:** No.
**Languages:** English.
**Your Host:** Bob.

## Keating House

Gay-Friendly 50/50 ♀♂

### *This Is No Addam's Family Victorian!*

***Keating House*** is a bright, sunny bed and breakfast overflowing with light, color and flowering plants. Over 100 years old, it has retained the charm and glamour of the turn-of-the-century. But this is no museum! We're a take-your-shoes-off relax-and-stay-awhile kind of place. Touring "America's finest city" can be exhausting, but not when you start and end your day with us. Have the time of your life, then, we'll return you to your world refreshed, relaxed and rejuvenated.

**Address: 2331 Second Ave, San Diego, CA 92101-1505**
**Tel: (619) 239-8585, (800) 995-8644, Fax: (619) 239-5774.**

**Type:** Bed & breakfast inn.
**Clientele:** 50% gay & lesbian & 50% straight clientele
**Trans:** Bus, taxi, or car.
**To Gay Bars:** Short drive or cab ride to men's & women's clubs.
**Rooms:** 8 rooms with

double or queen beds.
**Bathrooms:** 2 private bath/toilets & 3 shared bath/showers.
**Meals:** Full, sumptuous breakfast served every morning.
**Complimentary:** Beverages.
**Dates Open:** All year.
**Rates:** Rooms $60-$85 per night. Third person $25.
**Discounts:** 10% for 5 days or more.
**Credit Cards:** MC, VISA, Amex & Discover.
**Rsv'tns:** Required.
**Reserve Through:** Travel agent or call direct.
**Minimum Stay:** 2 nights on holidays & Valentine's weekend.
**Parking:** Unlimited, free on-street parking.
**On-Premises:** Large front porch. 2 lush sun & shade gardens.
**Swimming:** 10 minutes to ocean beaches. 15 minutes to Coronado Island.
**Sunbathing:** In the sun garden.
**Smoking:** Permitted outside only.
**Pets:** Not permitted.
**Handicap Access:** No.
**Children:** Permitted.
**Languages:** English, French, limited Spanish.

IGTA

## Park Manor Suites Hotel

Gay-Friendly 50/50 ♀♂

### *"San Francisco Charm" in Gay Hillcrest*

At ***Park Manor Suites Hotel*** we pride ourselves on our friendly staff and hospitality. Eighty elegantly appointed suites boast full kitchens, dining areas and baths, as well as cable and color TV. Enjoy incredible views while lunching at the Top of the Park Penthouse. Its Monday-Friday lunch menu consists of daily specials to please every palate at reasonable prices. Evening dining at Inn at the Park restaurant features dishes prepared by our chef who is specially trained in European-style cuisine. Located adjacent to Balboa Park at Sixth Avenue and Spruce Street, we are within walking distance to all gay restaurants and bars.

**Address: 525 Spruce St, San Diego, CA 92103**
**Tel: (619) 291-0999, (800) 874-2649, Fax: (619) 291-8844.**

**Type:** Hotel with restaurant & bar.
**Clientele:** 50% gay & lesbian & 50% straight clientele
**Transportation:** Car or taxi.
**To Gay Bars:** 1 block walking distance.
**Rooms:** 80 single, double & triple suites.
**Bathrooms:** All private.
**Meals:** Continental breakfast.
**Dates Open:** All year.
**Rates:** $79-$169.
**Discounts:** Senior citizens 10%.
**Credit Cards:** MC, Visa, Amex, Discover.
**Reserve Through:** Travel agent or call direct.
**Parking:** Free parking.
**In-Room:** Color TV, ceiling fans, telephone, kitchen, refrigerator & maid service.
**On-Premises:** Meeting rooms, laundry facilities, catering.
**Sunbathing:** Across street at Balboa Park.
**Smoking:** Non-smoking suites available.
**Pets:** Permitted with $50 deposit.
**Handicap Access:** Yes.
**Children:** Permitted with no restrictions.
**Languages:** English, Spanish, French & German.

IGTA

# SAN FRANCISCO

## Alamo Square Bed & Breakfast Inn

Gay-Friendly ♀♂

### *Fine Service...Gracious Surroundings*

A complex of two Victorian mansions, an 1895 Queen Anne and an 1896 Tudor Revival, is today the ***Alamo Square Inn,*** a unique and gracious bed and breakfast in San Francisco's largest historical district. A variety of accommodations are available, from cozy guest rooms to the luxurious Oriental-influenced suites overlooking the sweeping San Francisco skyline. Take breakfast in the filtered sunlight of our morning room, in the solarium or in the atrium.

**Address: 719 Scott St, San Francisco, CA 94117**
**Tel: (415) 922-2055, (800) 345-9888,**
**Fax: (415) 931-1304.**
**http://www.alamoinn.com.**

**Type:** Inn.
**Clientele:** Mostly straight clientele with a gay & lesbian following
**Transportation:** Airport shuttle $11 per person or taxi $25.
**To Gay Bars:** 10-minute walk to Castro St. gay & lesbian bars.
**Rooms:** 9 rooms, 3 suites & 1 apartment with single, queen or king beds.
**Bathrooms:** 13 private bath/toilets.
**Meals:** Full breakfast.
**Vegetarian:** Upon request.
**Complimentary:** Cocktail set-ups, coffee, tea, sherry & wine.
**Dates Open:** All year.
**High Season:** July-September.
**Rates:** $85-$275.
**Discounts:** 10% off for 7 or more days.
**Credit Cards:** MC, Visa, Amex.
**Rsv'tns:** Required.
**Reserve Through:** Travel agent or call direct.
**Minimum Stay:** 2 nights on weekend bookings.
**Parking:** Free off-street parking for up to 14 cars.
**In-Room:** Maid, room & laundry service & telephone. Some have refrigerators & TV.
**On-Premises:** Laundry facilities & meeting rooms.
**Exercise/Health:** Private Jacuzzi in one suite. Massage by appointment. Tennis courts in the park across the street.
**Sunbathing:** On common sun decks.
**Smoking:** Permitted outside.
**Pets:** Not permitted.
**Handicap Access:** No.
**Children:** Permitted.
**Languages:** English, French, German, Italian.

## Andora Inn

Gay/Lesbian ♀♂

### *Affordable Elegance*

San Francisco's newest and most elegant B&B, ***The Andora Inn,*** is located in Mission Dolores, one of the city's oldest and most colorful districts. A fully restored 1875 Italianate Victorian Manor, guest rooms and spacious suites feature high ceilings, queen-sized beds and color TVs with remote and built-in VCRs. The inn is in the center of San Francisco's most progressive hot spots, and museums, galleries and The Castro are nearby. Hot dance clubs and notorious leather bars are in the South of Market Area, a short 10-15 minute walk from us. Guests will leave here with many "tales of the city," and a longing to return.

**Address: 2434 Mission St, San Francisco, CA 94110**
**Tel: (415) 282-0337, (800) 967-9219, Fax: (415) 282-2608.**

**Type:** Bed & breakfast with restaurant & bar.
**Clientele:** Mostly gay & lesbian with some straight clientele
**Transportation:** Airport shuttle, taxi, BART, limo.
**To Gay Bars:** 6 blocks, a 15-minute walk, a 5-minute drive.
**Rooms:** 11 rooms, 2 suites, 1 apartment wit double or queen beds.
**Bathrooms:** Private & shared.
**Meals:** Expanded continental breakfast. Restaurant & bar on premises featuring Latino & California cuisine.
**Vegetarian:** Always available.
**Complimentary:** Tea & coffee in afternoons.
**Dates Open:** All year.
**High Season:** June-November.
**Rates:** $69-$199.
**Credit Cards:** MC, VISA, Amex.
**Rsv'tns:** Required.
**Reserve Through:** Travel agent or call direct.
**Parking:** Ample covered pay parking.
**In-Room:** Color cable TV, VCR, telephone, housekeeping daily.
**On-Premises:** Meeting rooms, library with fireplace, video tape library.
**Exercise/Health:** Nearby gym, weights, tennis courts.
**Sunbathing:** On patio.
**Smoking:** Permitted on outside patio only.
**Pets:** Not permitted.
**Handicap Access:** No.
**Children:** No.
**Languages:** English, Spanish.
**Your Host:** Jose, Brian.

IGTA

# Anna's Three Bears

**Gay-Friendly 50/50 ♀♂**

## *Your Escape in San Francisco*

World travelers of the Edwardian Golden Age maintained a "pied-a-terre" in their favorite city. In today's hustle and bustle, ***Anna's Three Bears*** could be yours. A magnificently restored 100-year-old Edwardian, the ***Bears*** is an adventure in days gone by when elegance, graciousness and thoughtfulness were a way of life.

More than just a place to stay, the proprietors of ***Anna's Three Bears*** have created the ultimate retreat. Entirely furnished with antiques gathered from around the world, each suite has a stunning view of downtown San Francisco and the Bay, spacious living and dining rooms, fully-stocked kitchens, fireplaces, lavish linens, and handmade quilts. Each and every bed is a marvelous example of old-world craftsmanship.

Located on a quiet residential street in historic Buena Vista Gardens, we are just a few steps from world renowned restaurants and bars, as well as the excitement of the Castro. The house invokes an atmosphere that is perfect for that magical romantic getaway for two or a magical adventure with friends. Imagine hosting a candlelit dinner surrounded by historical elegance, then retiring to an evening together in front of a roaring fire as you marvel at the spectacular night view which lies before you.

***Anna's Three Bears*** is one of the most charming and unusual inns you'll ever find. Come and experience San Francisco in grand style and indulge yourself in a way you could never imagine.

**Address: 114 Divisadero St, San Francisco, CA 94117**
**Tel: (800) 428-8559, (415) 255-3167, Fax: (415) 552-2959.**

**Type:** Bed & breakfast luxury suites.
**Clientele:** 50% gay & lesbian & 50% straight clientele
**Transportation:** Car. Public transport is 1 & 2 blocks away.
**To Gay Bars:** 4 blocks or an 8-minute walk to The Castro.
**Rooms:** 3 suites with single, double, queen or king beds.
**Bathrooms:** All private.
**Meals:** Continental breakfast.
**Vegetarian:** Several very good vegetarian restaurants nearby.
**Complimentary:** Kitchen stocked with tea, coffee, fruit, muffins, bread, milk, juices, etc.
**Dates Open:** All year.
**High Season:** August, September & December.
**Rates:** $225-$295 double daily, $25 per additional person. $1250-$1650 double weekly, $100 per additional person.
**Credit Cards:** MC, Visa, Amex.
**Rsv'tns:** Recommended.
**Reserve Through:** Travel agent or call direct.
**Minimum Stay:** 2 nights minimum, 14-day cancellation notice required.
**Parking:** Adequate on-street parking. Short term permit available.
**In-Room:** Color cable TV, telephone, refrigerator, stocked kitchen, coffee & tea-making facilities & maid service.
**On-Premises:** Private liv-

ing & dining rooms.
**Smoking:** Smoking permitted on back decks only.
**Pets:** Not permitted.
**Handicap Access:** Yes, ground floor apartment. Not handicap-equipped.
**Children:** Not especially welcome.
**Languages:** English.
**Your Host:** Michael.

IGTA

## Atherton Hotel

Gay-Friendly ♀♂

### *European Charm in the Heart of San Francisco*

Constructed in 1927, the ***Atherton Hotel*** was renovated this past year to enhance its "Old San Francisco" feel. The lobby's original marble floor, molded ceiling and etched glass project the ambiance of an intimate European inn. The Atherton Grill, serving continental cuisine, breakfast and Sunday champagne brunch, also offers dinner mid-May through October. Our English-style pub, The Abbey room, decorated with antique abbey altar panels, offers a full bar from 5 pm. The hotel is walking distance to the Cable Cars, Union Square and theaters. With intimate charm and friendly service, we have proudly served our community for over 15 years.

**Address: 685 Ellis St, San Francisco, CA 94109**
**Tel: (415) 474-5720, (800) 474-5720, Fax: (415) 474-8256.**

**Type:** Hotel with restaurant and bar.
**Clientele:** Mostly straight clientele with a gay & lesbian following
**Transportation:** Shuttle from airport about $10, taxi maximum $30. All major public transportation lines nearby.
**To Gay Bars:** 1 block to men's bars on Polk Street, 10 minutes' drive to Castro (3 metro stops).
**Rooms:** 75 rooms with twin, queen or king beds.
**Bathrooms:** All private baths.
**Complimentary:** Coffee from 7:30am-2pm, weekday am limo service to downtown destinations.
**Dates Open:** All year.
**High Season:** June-October.
**Rates:** US $69-$119.
**Discounts:** AAA, senior.
**Credit Cards:** MC, Visa, Amex, Diners, Discover.
**Rsv'tns:** Required.
**Reserve Through:** Travel agent or call direct.
**Minimum Stay:** 2 nights during Gay Pride & Folsom St. Fair.
**Parking:** Adequate on-street pay parking.
**In-Room:** Color TV, telephone & maid service.
**On-Premises:** Private dining rooms.
**Exercise/Health:** Nearby gym.
**Swimming:** In nearby ocean.
**Smoking:** Not permitted in lobby. Non-smoking rooms available.
**Pets:** Not permitted.
**Handicap Access:** No.
**Children:** Children under 12 with accompanying parents stay free.
**Languages:** English, German, Spanish, Italian, French, Tagalog.
**Your Host:** Naomi & Garey.

## Beck's Motor Lodge

**Gay-Friendly 50/50 ♀♂**

If you've searched for a hotel with moderately-priced, comfortable accommodations in a picturesque neighborhood setting, discover ***Beck's Motor Lodge*** on world-famous Market St. In the midst of the Castro area and convenient to everything, it is surrounded by tree-lined streets, quaint shops and Victorian homes. It's easy to relax with special touches like in-room fresh coffee service, refrigerators, parking, color cable TV and our private sun deck with lovely views of the city. Our staff is friendly and accommodating.

**Address: 2222 Market St, San Francisco, CA 94114**
**Tel: (415) 621-8212, (800) 227-4360, Fax: (415) 241-0435.**

**Type:** Motel.
**Clientele:** 50% gay & lesbian & 50% straight clientele.
**Transportation:** Airport shuttles.
**To Gay Bars:** 1 block.
**Rooms:** 57 rooms with queen or king beds.
**Bathrooms:** All private.
**Vegetarian:** Amazing Grace is 1 block away.
**Complimentary:** Coffee in room.
**Dates Open:** All year.
**High Season:** May through October.
**Rates:** $70-$105.
**Discounts:** Senior citizen & AAA 10%.
**Credit Cards:** Visa, MC, Amex, Diners & Discover.
**Rsv'tns:** Required.
**Reserve Through:** Travel agent or call direct.
**Parking:** Adequate free off-street parking.
**In-Room:** Color cable TV, telephone, refrigerator, maid service & coffee & tea-making facilities. 10 rooms have AC.
**On-Premises:** Laundry facilities for guests.
**Exercise/Health:** Gym & weights nearby.
**Swimming:** 3-1/2 miles to ocean beach.
**Sunbathing:** On common sun decks.
**Smoking:** Permitted in all rooms.
**Pets:** Not permitted.
**Handicap Access:** No ramps, but doors are wide.
**Children:** Welcomed.
**Languages:** English, Spanish, French & Tagalog.
**Your Host:** Irene.

## Black Stallion Inn

**Gay/Lesbian ♂**

Located in the heart of the Castro, the ***Black Stallion Inn*** provides a quiet and relaxing atmosphere for those visiting San Francisco. This renovated Victorian flat is on the itinerary of many tours of the area. Guests can make themselves at home in front of the wood-burning stove in the common room or on the spacious sun deck. There is a modern, shared kitchen for lunches and evening meals. The inn is located a block-and-a-half from gay bars and has its own private social club, which guests may attend.

**Address: 635 Castro St, San Francisco, CA 94114**
**Tel: (415) 863-0131, Fax: (415) 863-0165.**

**Type:** Bed & breakfast.
**Clientele:** Mostly men
**Transportation:** Door-to-door airport shuttle to B&B, approximately $8-$12 each. Taxi $35 including tip.
**To Gay Bars:** 1-1/2 blocks to countless gay bars.
**Rooms:** 4 rooms.
**Bathrooms:** Shared: 2 baths & 1 half bath.
**Meals:** Expanded continental breakfast.
**Vegetarian:** Health & vegetarian store opposite B&B.
**Complimentary:** Coffee, tea, & juice avail. all day.
**Dates Open:** All year.
**High Season:** Jun-Oct.
**Rates:** Single $80-$95, double $95-$110.
**Discounts:** Off-season & weekday specials. *Inn Places* discount.
**Credit Cards:** MC, Visa, Amex, Discover, Novus.
**Rsv'tns:** Highly recommended.
**Reserve Through:** Travel agent or call direct.
**Minimum Stay:** On weekends, holidays & special events.
**Parking:** On-street pay & free. 1 garage space or 1 secured space $10 night.
**In-Room:** Maid service. Guests share telephone & answering service.
**On-Premises:** Kitchen with fireplace, large sun deck, laundry facilities, private social club, cable TV in communal lounge.
**Exercise/Health:** Within 3 blocks of 3 full service gay gyms.
**Swimming:** Nearby pool & ocean.
**Sunbathing:** On common sun decks & at the beach. 2-3 miles to gay beach, nudist beach.
**Nudity:** Permitted anywhere inside the inn.
**Smoking:** Permitted if smokers are considerate.
**Pets:** Permitted, $100 damage deposit, +$15/night.
**Children:** Not especially welcome.
**Languages:** English, German.
**Your Host:** Mark.

## Bock's Bed & Breakfast

Gay/Lesbian ♀♂

### *In Operation Since 1980*

***Bock's*** is a lovely 1906 Edwardian residence in the Parnassus Heights area of San Francisco with beautiful views of the city. Golden Gate Park is two blocks away and public transportation is nearby. Host, Laura Bock, has restored the original virgin redwood walls of the dining and entry rooms as well as the mahogany inlaid oak floors of the latter. The latest renovation project was completed with the addition of a new bathroom & the restoration of two original pocket doors on the main floor. Laura's enthusiasm and touring tips about her native city are enjoyed by an international clientele.

Address: 1448 Willard St, San Francisco, CA 94117
Tel: (415) 664-6842, Fax: (415) 664-1109.

**Type:** Bed & breakfast.
**Clientele:** Mostly gay & lesbian/some straight clientele
**Transportation:** From airport take one of the van shuttles outside the 2nd level.
**To Gay Bars:** 1 mile to gay/lesbian bars.
**Rooms:** 3 rooms with single, dbl or queen beds.
**Bathrooms:** 1 private, 1 private sink, others share full bath.
**Meals:** Expanded continental breakfast.
**Vegetarian:** I can accommodate special needs & there is vegetarian food nearby.
**Complimentary:** Coffee, tea, hot chocolate service in rooms. Small, shared guest refrigerator.
**Dates Open:** All year.
**High Season:** May through October.
**Rates:** $40-$75 +tax. $10 each add'l person, +tax.
**Discounts:** 10% discount for stays of a week or more.
**Credit Cards:** None.
**Rsv'tns:** Recommended.
**Reserve Thru:** Call direct.
**Minimum Stay:** 2 nights.
**Parking:** On-street parking. Inexpensive lot 2 blocks.
**In-Room:** Color TV, tele., electric hot pot, radios, coffee/tea-making facilities.
**On-Premises:** Laundry facilities, guest refrigerator.
**Swimming:** Pool nearby, ocean beach 3 miles.
**Sunbathing:** On private or common sun decks.
**Smoking:** Non-smokers only.
**Pets:** Not permitted.
**Children:** Permitted.
**Languages:** English, smattering of French.
**Your Host:** Laura

## Carl Street Unicorn House

Women ♀

***Carl Street Unicorn House*** is a small Victorian house located near San Francisco's Golden Gate Park within walking distance of great restaurants and cafes, the aquarium, museums, and a variety of interesting shops. There is a collection of over 200 ethnic dolls, many pieces of artwork and antiques befitting a Victorian home. Your host resides on the top floor, while guests occupy the ground floor.

Address: 156 Carl St, San Francisco, CA 94117
Tel: (415) 753-5194.

**Type:** Bed & breakfast.
**Clientele:** Mostly women with men welcome, some straight clientele.
**Transportation:** Airport shuttle van to door.
**To Gay Bars:** 5-10 minutes' drive to gay/lesbian bars.
**Rooms:** 2 rooms with double beds.
**Bathrooms:** 1 shared bath/shower/toilet.
**Meals:** Expanded continental breakfast.
**Complimentary:** Tea & coffee.
**Dates Open:** All year.
**High Season:** Summer.
**Rates:** $40-$50, $5 extra for 1 night stay.
**Discounts:** 10% on stays of 7 days or more.
**Rsv'tns:** Required.
**Reserve Through:** Call direct.
**Minimum Stay:** Required on weekends.
**Parking:** On-street parking.
**On-Premises:** TV lounge.
**Swimming:** 5 min drive to pool.
**Sunbathing:** On the patio.
**Smoking:** Not permitted.
**Handicap Access:** No.
**Children:** Permitted if over 6 years.
**Languages:** English.

## The Cartwright Hotel

Gay-Friendly ♀♂

### *Union Square is the Place to Be*

***The Cartwright Hotel*** on Union Square proudly combines old-world charm with modern amenities. The deluxe accommodations include antique-filled guest rooms, lobby, and library. All rooms have private baths, honor bars, cable TV, and Nintendo. Complimentary continental breakfast, afternoon tea service, wine hour, and work-out facilities are among the extra amenities that guests enjoy at this B&B-style hotel. The friendly and well-trained staff is sensitive to every traveler's needs. ***The Cartwright Hotel*** is convenient to both the Polk and Castro Street districts.

**Address: 524 Sutter St, San Francisco, CA 94102**
**Tel: (415) 421-2865, (800) 227-3844, Fax: (415) 983-6244.**

**Type:** Hotel.
**Clientele:** Mostly straight clientele with a gay/lesbian following
**Transportation:** Car or shuttle from SFO airport. Pick up from airport $10 one way.
**To Gay Bars:** 3 blocks, a 10-minute walk, a 5-minute drive.
**Rooms:** 109 rooms, 5 suites with single or queen beds.
**Bathrooms:** All private.
**Meals:** Expanded continental breakfast, afternoon tea, evening wine hour.
**Vegetarian:** Many restaurants nearby.
**Complimentary:** Afternoon tea, evening wine hour.
**Dates Open:** All year.
**High Season:** June-October.
**Rates:** $109-$149.
**Credit Cards:** MC, VISA, Amex, Diners, Bancard, Eurocard, Discover.
**Rsv'tns:** Required.
**Reserve Through:** Travel agent or call direct.
**Parking:** Ample covered pay parking.
**In-Room:** Color cable TV, AC, telephone, coffee/tea-making facilities, maid, room & laundry service.
**On-Premises:** Meeting rooms, TV lounge.
**Exercise/Health:** Nearby gym, weights, Jacuzzi, sauna, steam, massage.
**Swimming:** Nearby pool.
**Smoking:** Non-smoking rooms available.
**Pets:** Not permitted.
**Handicap Access:** Yes.
**Children:** Welcome.
**Languages:** English, Spanish, German, French, Chinese, Japanese.
**Your Host:** Peter & Lisa.

IGTA

## Castillo Inn

Gay/Lesbian ♂

### *Your Home Away from Home*

The ***Castillo Inn*** is a short five-minute walk to Market and Castro Streets and one block to major public transportation. The inn has four rooms that are very clean and share a bath. Three of the rooms have queen-sized beds and one room has a double bed. A deluxe continental breakfast is included, and a voice mail answering service, a telephone and fax are available for guests. The ***Castillo Inn*** is a non-smoking establishment and our rates range from $55 to $75. Ask us about our two-bedroom suite.

**Address: 48 Henry St, San Francisco, CA 94114**
**Tel: (415) 864-5111, (800) 865-5112, Fax: (415) 641-1321.**

**Type:** Bed & breakfast.
**Clientele:** Mostly men with women welcome
**Transportation:** Shuttle or taxi.
**To Gay Bars:** 2 blocks, a 2-5 min walk.
**Rooms:** 4 rooms, 1apartment with double or queen beds.
**Bathrooms:** Suite or apartment has private bath/toilet/shower. 1 shared bath/shower/toilet.
**Meals:** Expanded continental breakfast.
**Vegetarian:** Available nearby.
**Dates Open:** All year.
**High Season:** July-October.
**Rates:** $55-$75.
**Discounts:** Please inquire.
**Credit Cards:** MC, Visa, Amex.
**Rsv'tns:** Required.
**Reserve Through:** By travel agent January-March. Call direct other times.
**Minimum Stay:** Sometimes required.
**Smoking:** Permitted outside, non-smoking rooms available.
**Pets:** Not permitted.
**Handicap Access:** No.
**Languages:** English, Spanish.

## Chateau Tivoli

**Gay-Friendly 50/50 ♀♂**

### *The Greatest Painted Lady In the World*

***Chateau Tivoli*** is an authentic period restoration of a Victorian mansion built in 1892. The book *Painted Ladies Revisited* calls it "...the greatest Painted Lady in the world." Fully licensed as a hotel Bed & Breakfast, the residence features eight guest bedrooms. The building exterior has become a San Francisco landmark, painted in twenty-two different colors and shades, and highlighted with brilliant gold leafing. The roof is multi-colored slate tile, mounted in a special diamond pattern and surrounded by fabulous iron grill work. The interior is resplendent with hardwood floors, stately columns and numerous stained glass windows. There are four woodburning fireplaces. The walls and ceilings in bedrooms and hallways are covered in Bradbury & Bradbury wallpaper and accented by gold leaf and various faux treatments.

The mansion has been so faithfully restored that guests experience the sensation of a timetravel journey back to San Francisco's romantic golden age of opulence. Here, they are surrounded by genuine antiques and art from the estates of Cornelius Vanderbilt, Charles de Gaulle, J. Paul Getty, the Countess of Richelieu and the famous San Francisco madame, Sally Stanford. Spacious and grand, the rooms and suites feature elegant canopy beds and marble baths, balconies and views, fireplaces and stained glass, towers and turrets, each facet contributing to the atmosphere that makes ***Chateau Tivoli*** a truly unforgettable experience.

**Address: 1057 Steiner St, San Francisco, CA 94115**
**Tel: (415) 776-5462, (800) 228-1647, Fax: (415) 776-0505.**

*continued next page*

**Type:** Bed & breakfast.
**Clientele:** 50% gay & lesbian & 50% straight clientele.
**Transportation:** Airport bus to downtown, then taxi.
**To Gay Bars:** Ten minutes to gay & lesbian bars.
**Rooms:** 5 doubles, 3 suites (one with 2 bedrooms).
**Bathrooms:** 4 private, others share with only one other room.
**Meals:** Expanded continental breakfast Mon-Fri, full champagne breakfast Sat & Sun.
**Complimentary:** Wine, coffee, tea, herb tea, juice, etc.
**Dates Open:** All year.
**High Season:** March-October.
**Rates:** $80-$200.
**Discounts:** For 4 or more days.
**Credit Cards:** MC, VISA & Amex.
**Rsv'tns:** Required.
**Reserve Through:** Travel agent or call direct.
**Minimum Stay:** None.
**Parking:** Ample, on-street parking in residential neighborhood.
**In-Room:** Maid service, telephone.
**On-Premises:** Meeting rooms.
**Sunbathing:** On patio.
**Smoking:** Limited to porches, balconies and patio.
**Pets:** Not permitted.
**Children:** Valuable antiques in all areas. Parents must take full responsibility.
**Languages:** English.
**Your Host:** Chris, Sonny, Laurie.

## The Essex Hotel

Q-NET Gay-Friendly ♀♂

***The Essex Hotel,*** totally renovated in recent years, is centrally located and within walking distance of all major points, including Cable Car line, Union Square, Chinatown, theaters and many fine restaurants. Polk Street is only a block away and gay men's bars are two blocks away. The Airporter shuttle to our front door is only $9. The hotel has a European atmosphere, pleasant, comfortable double rooms with high-quality furnishings, color TV, maid service, and direct dial phones. Most rooms have private baths.

**Address: 684 Ellis St, San Francisco, CA 94109**
**Tel: (415) 474-4664, (800) 453-7739, Fax: (415) 441-1800. In CA (800) 443-7739.**

**Type:** Hotel.
**Clientele:** Mostly straight clientele with a gay & lesbian following
**Transportation:** Airporter shuttle $9.00.
**To Gay Bars:** 2 blocks to men's bars.
**Rooms:** 100 rooms with single or queen beds.
**Bathrooms:** 50 private bath/toilets, others share. 100 private sinks.
**Complimentary:** Coffee.
**Dates Open:** All year.
**Rates:** Single $59, double $69.
**Discounts:** 10% to holders of Inn Places, subject to room availability.
**Credit Cards:** MC, VISA & Amex.
**Rsv'tns:** Suggested.
**Reserve Through:** Travel agent or call direct.
**Parking:** Adequate on-street pay parking.
**In-Room:** Color TV, direct dial phone, maid service.
**On-Premises:** Public tele phone, central AC/heat.
**Smoking:** Permitted without restrictions.
**Pets:** Not permitted.
**Handicap Access:** No.
**Children:** Permitted.
**Languages:** English, French, German.

## Inn On Castro

Gay/Lesbian ♀♂

The innkeepers invite you into a colorful and comfortable environment filled with modern art and exotic plants. All rooms vary in size and have private baths. Meet fellow travelers from all over the world for a memorable breakfast. The ***Inn On Castro's*** location is unique, just 100 yards north of the intersection of Market and Castro, where you are in a quiet neighborhood, yet only a stone's throw away from the Castro Theater, plus dozens of bars, restaurants and shops. With the ***Underground*** almost virtually adjacent to the ***Inn,*** big-name store shopping and cable car, etc. are just a few minutes away. There is literally something for everyone.

**Address: 321 Castro St, San Francisco, CA 94114. Tel: (415) 861-0321.**

**Type:** Bed & breakfast.
**Clientele:** Good mix of gay men & women
**Transportation:** Supershuttle from airport approx $11 per person.
**To Gay Bars:** Less than 1-minute walk to men's/women's bars.
**Rooms:** 6 rms & 2 suites with double, queen or king beds, self-catering apartment.
**Bathrooms:** All private.
**Meals:** Full breakfast.
**Vegetarian:** Available with advance notice.
**Complimentary:** Afternoon wine, brandy night cap, tea, coffee, juices.
**Dates Open:** All year.
**High Season:** May-Oct.
**Rates:** Rooms $80-$150.
**Credit Cards:** MC, Visa, Amex.
**Rsv'tns:** Recommended 1 month in advance.
**Reserve Thru:** Call direct.
**Minimum Stay:** 2 days on weekends, 3 on holidays, 4 days Folsom Fair, Castro Fair & Gay Lib days.
**Parking:** Adequate on-street parking.
**In-Room:** Color TV on request, telephone, maid service, refrigerator.
**On-Premises:** Lounge & dining room.
**Exercise/Health:** Gym, weights, jacuzzi, sauna, steam & massage across the street.
**Swimming:** Nearby pool.
**Sunbathing:** On private sun decks.
**Smoking:** Permitted on patio, front porch, rear deck.
**Handicap Access:** Patio suite is handicap-accessible.
**Children:** Permitted but not encouraged.
**Languages:** English, French, German & Dutch.

## The Inn San Francisco

Q-NET Gay-Friendly ♀♂

### *Distinctly San Franciscan Warmth & Hospitality*

Feel the years slip away, as you step through the massive, wooden doors of the ***Inn San Francisco.*** Each of the guest rooms is individually decorated with antique furnishings, fresh flowers, marble sinks, polished brass fixtures and exquisite finishing touches. All are extraordinarily beautiful and the feeling of classic, old-world elegance and grandeur is carried throughout. In the garden, under the shade of an old fig tree, an enchanting gazebo shelters the inviting hot tub.

**Address: 943 S Van Ness Ave, San Francisco, CA 94110**
**Tel: (415) 641-0188, (800) 359-0913, Fax: (415) 641-1701.**

**Type:** Bed & breakfast inn.
**Clientele:** Mixed, straight clientele with very strong gay/lesbian following
**Transportation:** Airport Shuttle $10 per person.
**To Gay Bars:** 8 blocks to men's & women's bars.
**Rooms:** 16 rooms, 5 suites & 1 apartment with single, double or queen beds.

*continued next page*

**Bathrooms:** 17 private bath/shower/toilets, 5 share.
**Meals:** Full buffet break.
**Vegetarian:** Our breakfast includes a huge array of fresh fruits, granola, homemade breads or muffins & a cheese plate.
**Complimentary:** Coffee, tea, sherry complimentary in parlor, truffles in room.
**Dates Open:** All year.
**Rates:** Rooms $85-$225.
**Discounts:** Stays of 1 week or longer.
**Credit Cards:** Visa, MC, Amex, Diners, Carte Blanche, Discover.
**Rsv'tns:** Required.
**Reserve Thru:** Call direct.
**Minimum Stay:** Weekends, particularly on holidays, require a 2 night stay, but we are flexible. Call.
**Parking:** Several covered garages w/electric door openers, parking $10/night.
**In-Room:** Maid & laundry service, color TV, telephone, refrigerator.
**On-Premises:** Laundry facilities.
**Exercise/Health:** Redwood hot tub in tropical gazebo.
**Sunbathing:** On private & common sun decks, patios & on rooftop.
**Smoking:** Not permitted in parlor.
**Children:** Permitted.
**Languages:** English, Spanish, Chinese, limited French.

IGTA

## The Lombard Central, A Super 8 Hotel

**Gay-Friendly** ♀♂

### *Old-World Charm and Today's Hospitality*

***The Lombard Central,*** reminiscent of old San Francisco with an intimate lobby featuring marble floors, etched glass, mahogany columns, and a grand piano, offers guests old-world charm and Super 8 hospitality. At the 100-room hotel, you'll find the attention to detail and personal service exceptional. From making reservations at the hotel's famous Faces Cafe Restaurant to arranging special tours of the city and beyond, the staff is eager to make your stay perfect. We are conveniently located in the heart of downtown San Francisco's performing arts and civic center district, and are only five blocks from the famous cable cars.

**Address: 1015 Geary Blvd, San Francisco, CA 94109**
**Tel: (415) 673-5232, (800) 777-3210, Fax: (415) 885-2802.**

**Type:** Hotel with breakfast cafe.
**Clientele:** Mostly straight clientele with a gay/lesbian following.
**Transportation:** From airport, car or airport shuttle is best.
**To Gay Bars:** 2 blocks, a 5-minute walk.
**Rooms:** 100 rooms with single, double, queen or king beds.
**Bathrooms:** All private bath/shower/toilets.
**Vegetarian:** Available at breakfast & at nearby restaurants.
**Complimentary:** 24-hr coffee & tea, complimentary wine hour weekdays 5:30 pm-6:30 pm.
**Dates Open:** All year.
**High Season:** July-August.
**Rates:** $74-$99.88.
**Discounts:** Weekend & midweek specials, senior rates. All special rates subject to availability.
**Credit Cards:** VISA, Amex, Discover, MC, Diners.
**Rsv'tns:** Recommended in high season.
**Reserve Through:** Travel agent or call direct.
**Parking:** Adequate pay parking.
**In-Room:** Color TV, telephone, ceiling fans, maid & laundry service.
**On-Premises:** Meeting rooms, fax available.
**Exercise/Health:** Nearby gym.
**Smoking:** Permitted in smoking rooms. Non-smoking rooms available.
**Pets:** Not permitted.
**Handicap Access:** No.
**Children:** Welcome.
**Languages:** English, Spanish, German.

## The Metro Hotel

**Gay-Friendly 50/50 ♀♂**

### *A Great Discovery*

A small, affordable hotel with 24 rooms on two floors, ***The Metro Hotel*** is situated in a historic district of San Francisco, walking distance to The Castro, The Haight and Golden Gate Park. We have new interiors with private baths, as well as the convenience of delicious food at The Metro Cafe. Let us make your stay in San Francisco a memorable event with our friendly atmosphere, secluded English garden, and cafe. Our convenient location is only 10 minutes by bus from downtown San Francisco, and 8 blocks from the Castro District.

**Address: 319 Divisadero St, San Francisco, CA 94117**
**Tel: (415) 861-5364, Fax: (415) 863-1970.**

**Type:** Hotel.
**Clientele:** 50% gay & lesbian & 50% straight clientele.
**Transportation:** Car or airport shuttle.
**To Gay Bars:** 8 blocks to men's bars.
**Rooms:** 24 rooms with suites, double or queen beds.
**Bathrooms:** All private.
**Vegetarian:** Available at The Metro Cafe on premises.
**Dates Open:** All year.
**High Season:** Summer.
**Rates:** $50-$94.
**Discounts:** Call to see what is available at the time.
**Credit Cards:** MC, VISA, Amex, Discover.
**Rsv'tns:** Required. 24-hour cancellation notice also required.
**Reserve Through:** Travel agent or call direct.
**Parking:** Free parking 6pm-9am.
**In-Room:** Cable color TV, telephone, maid service.
**Sunbathing:** On patio.
**Smoking:** Permitted.
**Pets:** Not permitted.
**Handicap Access:** No.
**Children:** Permitted.
**Languages:** English, Spanish, Chinese.
**Your Host:** Dean.

## Renoir Hotel

**Gay-Friendly ♀♂**

### *San Francisco's Newest First Class Downtown Hotel*

The ***Renoir Hotel*** is a newly-renovated historical landmark building, just three blocks from Folsom Street, Polk Street, and three subway stations from the Castro. It is the best bargain in downtown San Francisco, providing charming European ambiance with classical music throughout. The ornate interior includes an original Renard in the reception area and Renoir prints placed tastefully throughout the hotel. The Royal Delight Restaurant serves breakfast, lunch and dinner. Also available are the lounge and lobby cafe and room service. *Inn Places* discount to $69 available most dates (or pick up coupon at Visitors Center).

**Address: 45 McAllister St, San Francisco, CA 94102**
**Tel: (415) 626-5200 or (800) 576-3388.**

*continued next page*

**Type:** Hotel with restaurant, bar, espresso bar & gift shop.
**Clientele:** Mostly straight with a gay & lesbian following
**Transportation:** BART subway from Oakland airport to Civic Center Station. Shuttle van from SF Airport to hotel.
**To Gay Bars:** 2 blocks. About 10 gay bars within 5 blocks.
**Rooms:** 123 rooms & 3 suites with twin, double, queen & king beds.
**Bathrooms:** All private.
**Vegetarian:** Vegetarian items on restaurant & cafe menus.
**Dates Open:** All year.
**High Season:** May 15-Nov 15.
**Rates:** High season $99-$150, low season $69-$150.
**Discounts:** Inn Places rate: $69.
**Credit Cards:** All major credit cards.
**Rsv'tns:** Required.
**Reserve Through:** Travel agent or call direct.
**Minimum Stay:** Gay Day Parade weekends & some sold-out periods, for last minute reservations.
**Parking:** Ample off-street pay parking & valet parking. Lot $10 day, valet $12 day.
**In-Room:** Color TV, telephone, maid, room & laundry service.
**On-Premises:** Meeting rooms. Executive level offers modem hookups for computers.
**Exercise/Health:** YMCA 1 block from hotel with 7 floors of facilities. Non-member admission $13 per day.
**Swimming:** At nearby YMCA pool.
**Nudity:** 7 miles to nude beaches.
**Smoking:** Permitted in half the rooms & the bar. Non-smoking rooms available.
**Pets:** Not permitted.
**Handicap Access:** Yes. 3 handicap rooms. Ramp provided upon request.
**Children:** Welcome.
**Languages:** English, German, French, Russian, Spanish/Portuguese, Cantonese/Mandarin/Tagalog
**Your Host:** Steve.

## San Francisco Cottage

**Gay/Lesbian ♀♂**

### *The Perfect San Francisco Experience*

***San Francisco Cottage*** offers a lovely cottage and an elegant studio apartment in the rear garden of a San Francisco Edwardian home. We're on a quiet, residential street, just a five-minute stroll to Castro Street venues. Public transportation is nearby. The studio apartment has contemporary decor, a complete kitchen, living room area opening onto a garden, dining area, queen-sized bed, and a bathroom with shower and claw tub. The loft-like cottage, decorated in Santa Fe-style, has a living room, queen-sized bed, modern kitchen and dining area. French doors open onto a redwood deck and terraced garden.

**Address: 224 Douglass St, San Francisco, CA 94114 Tel: (415) 861-3220, Fax: (415) 626-2633.**

**Type:** Self-catering cottage & studio apartment.
**Clientele:** Gay & lesbian
**Transportation:** Shuttle buses or taxi from airport. Best way downtown is metro.
**To Gay Bars:** 3 short blocks to gay bars.
**Rooms:** 1 cottage & 1 apartment with queen beds.
**Bathrooms:** Both private.
**Complimentary:** Tea & coffee set-up in rooms.
**Dates Open:** All year.
**High Season:** March through October.
**Rates:** $95-$105 per night, $600-$660 per week.
**Discounts:** Weekly & monthly rates.
**Credit Cards:** MC & VISA.
**Rsv'tns:** Required.
**Reserve Through:** Travel agent or call direct.
**Minimum Stay:** 2 nights.
**Parking:** Ample on-street parking.
**In-Room:** Color cable TV, VCR, stereo, telephone, kitchen & refrigerator.
**On-Premises:** Laundry facilities.
**Exercise/Health:** 5-minute walk to gay gym.
**Sunbathing:** On private sun deck & patio.
**Pets:** Not permitted.
**Handicap Access:** No.
**Languages:** English.

IGTA

## Twenty-Four Henry Guesthouse

**Gay/Lesbian ♀♂**

***24 Henry Guesthouse*** is a serene, non-smoking environment in San Francisco's gay Castro district. Within a block or two of the house are scores of cafes, shops, bars, and public transportation. Each beautifully appointed guest room has a private phone with answering machine. Our Victorian parlour/lounge is the setting for an extended continental buffet every morning where you may meet travelers from other parts of the globe. Also, consider our fully equipped multiroom Castro Suites for a romantic or business getaway.

**Address: 24 Henry St, San Francisco, CA 94114. Tel: (800) 900-5686, (415) 864-5686, Fax: (415) 864-0406, E-mail: WalteRian@aol.com.**

**Type:** Guesthouse.
**Clientele:** Everyone is welcome.
**Transportation:** Shuttle from airport to our door.
**To Gay Bars:** 2 blocks.
**Rooms:** 1 single, 9 doubles with queen beds.
**Bathrooms:** 6 private, 4 shared.
**Meals:** Ext. cont. buffet.
**Vegetarian:** Available upon request.
**Complimentary:** Hosts will help with travel planning.
**Dates Open:** All year.
**Rates:** Rooms $55-$95.
**Credit Cards:** MC, VISA, Amex.
**Rsv'tns:** Advised, preferably 2-3 weeks in advance.
**Reserve Through:** Travel agent or call direct.
**Minimum Stay:** 2 days.
**Parking:** Adequate on-street parking.
**In-Room:** Individual phone lines with answering machines, no charge for local calls.
**On-Premises:** TV lounge, library.
**Smoking:** Non-smoking.
**Children:** Permitted.
**Languages:** English, Spanish.
**Your Host:** Rian & Walter.

IGTA

## The Villa

**Gay/Lesbian ♀♂**

### *Spectacular Views of San Francisco*

***The Villa*** is the flagship guesthouse of San Francisco Views rental services. Located atop one of the Castro's legendary hills, we offer magnificent views of the city from our double rooms and suites. Guests have the use of our fireplace lounge, complete kitchen and dining area overlooking our decks and swimming pool. Suites are equipped with TV, VCR and telephone with answering machine. We are minutes from the financial and shopping districts of downtown San Francisco, three blocks from the heart of the Castro and are open all year. Short- or long-term rentals available.

**Address: 379 Collingwood, San Francisco, CA 94114 Tel: (415) 282-1367, (800) 358-0123, Fax: (415) 821-3995. E-mail: SFViews@aol.com.**

*continued next page*

**Type:** Guesthouse.
**Clientele:** Good mix of gays & lesbians
**Transportation:** Easily accessible by car, or shuttle from airport.
**To Gay Bars:** 3 blocks or a 5-minute walk.
**Rooms:** 4 rooms, 3 suites & 4 apartments with single, double, queen or king beds.
**Bathrooms:** Rooms: private & shared. Apartments have private baths.
**Meals:** Continental breakfast.
**Vegetarian:** Restaurants nearby.
**Dates Open:** All year.
**High Season:** Summer & Fall.
**Rates:** Daily from $80, weekly $500, monthly rates available.
**Discounts:** Please inquire.
**Credit Cards:** MC, Visa, Amex.
**Rsv'tns:** Recommended.
**Reserve Through:** Call direct.
**Minimum Stay:** 2 days.
**Parking:** Free off-street & on-street parking.
**In-Room:** Color cable TV, VCR, telephone, kitchen, refrigerator & maid service.
**On-Premises:** TV lounge, laundry facilities & shared kitchen on each floor.
**Swimming:** Pool on premises, ocean nearby.
**Sunbathing:** At poolside & on common sun decks.
**Smoking:** Permitted inside the rooms. Non-smoking rooms available upon request.
**Pets:** Not permitted.
**Handicap Access:** No.
**Children:** Permitted, but not especially welcome.
**Languages:** English & Spanish.

IGTA

## The Willows

Q-NET **Gay/Lesbian** ♀♂

### *Your Haven Within The Castro*

Housed in a 1904 Edwardian, ***The Willows*** derives its name from the handcrafted bentwood willow furnishings which grace each room. Complementing these unique pieces are antique dressers and armoires, plantation shutters, cozy comforters and fine English wallpaper borders. Each of our eleven guest bedrooms also has the country freshness of flowers, potted plants and dried floral arrangements. As an added comfort to each room, we provide direct dial telephones, alarm clock radios, kimono bathrobes, and fine Crabtree & Evelyn soaps.

***The Willows*** is noted for its homey atmosphere and personal, friendly service. In the morning, wake up to a newspaper at your door followed by the pampered touch of breakfast served in bed. To help you plan your day's activities, our innkeepers are always available with helpful suggestions and directions. The sitting room welcomes guests to gather in the evening for cheese and conversation. Upon returning to the Inn at night, guests will appreciate the touch of a turned-down bed softly illuminated by the warmth of a glowing table lamp and a port nightcap, our classic finish to another day at ***The Willows***. At the crossroads to the city's efficient transportation system, each of San Francisco's unique neighborhoods, attractions and convention sites are easily accessible. Dotting our neighborhood are a wide range of fine restaurants, specialty and second hand shops, gyms, bars and a vintage '30s movie palace.

**Address: 710 14th St, San Francisco, CA 94114**
**Tel: (415) 431-4770, Fax: (415) 431-5295.**

**Type:** Bed & breakfast inn.
**Clientele:** Gay & lesbian. Good mix of men and women.
**Transportation:** Airport shuttle to the inn $10.
**To Gay Bars:** 1/2 block to men's bar, 3 to women's.
**Rooms:** 10 rooms & 1 suite with single or queen beds.
**Bathrooms:** 4 shared water closets, 4 shared showers, sinks in all rooms.
**Meals:** Expanded continental breakfast.
**Vegetarian:** Vegetarian-only restaurant (Amazing Grace) 1/2 block away.
**Complimentary:** Sherry nightcap with chocolate truffle.
**Dates Open:** All year.
**High Season:** June 15th-

November 15th.
**Rates:** $64-$125.
**Discounts:** Midweek off season.
**Credit Cards:** MC, VISA, Discover, Amex.
**Rsv'tns:** Recommended 2 weeks in advance.
**Reserve Through:** Call direct.
**Minimum Stay:** 2 nights on weekends.
**Parking:** Adequate on-street, limited off-street pay parking.
**In-Room:** TV on request, direct dial telephone, alarm clock radios, maid & room service, refrigerator in some rooms.
**On-Premises:** TV lounge area, refrigerator in pantry.
**Exercise/Health:** Co-ed & women's gyms 1 block.
**Swimming:** Nearby pool & ocean.
**Smoking:** Permitted without restrictions.
**Pets:** Not permitted.
**Handicap Access:** No.
**Children:** Not permitted.
**Languages:** English, German.

# SANTA BARBARA

## Glenborough Inn

Gay-Friendly ♀♂

### *Have Breakfast in Bed in a Romantic B&B*

You step into the past, where life was quieter and the pace relaxed. Your room is fresh, immaculate, old-fashioned, with plants, fresh flowers and antiques. You might meet others around the fireplace, or in the gardens for hors d'oeuvres, or indulge yourself in the enclosed garden hot tub for private use. Pamper yourself with a gourmet breakfast delivered to your room. Leave your car, and take the shuttle to the beach or around town. The ***Glenborough Inn*** is Santa Barbara's most romantic gay-owned, gay-friendly B&B.

**Address: 1327 Bath St, Santa Barbara, CA 93101**
**Tel: (805) 966-0589, (800) 962-0589, Fax: (805) 564-8610.**

**Type:** Bed & breakfast inn.
**Clientele:** Mostly straight clientele with a gay/lesbian following.
**Transportation:** Taxi from airport or train station.
**To Gay Bars:** 5 minutes by car to gay bars.
**Rooms:** 7 rooms & 4 suites with king, queen & full beds.
**Bathrooms:** 11 private bath/shower/toilets.
**Meals:** Full gourmet breakfast brought to room.
**Vegetarian:** No meat is served at the inn. Special diets accommodated with continental breakfast.
**Complimentary:** Evening refreshments & hors d'oeuvres, hot drinks & cookies nightly.
**Dates Open:** All year.
**High Season:** June-Oct.
**Rates:** $100-$225.
**Discounts:** Midweek corporate rates for guests on business.
**Credit Cards:** MC, VISA, Amex, Diners & Discover.
**Rsv'tns:** Recommended (not usually needed midweek).
**Reserve Through:** Travel agent for Mon-Thurs stays or call direct.
**Minimum Stay:** 2 nights on weekends & 3 nights for 3-day holidays.
**Parking:** Ample free off- and on-street parking.
**In-Room:** Telephones & maid service.
**On-Premises:** Parlour, gardens, guest refrigerator & fax.
**Exercise/Health:** Outdoor enclosed (garden) Jacuzzi on sign-up basis.
**Swimming:** At nearby ocean beach.
**Sunbathing:** In gardens & at nearby beach.
**Nudity:** Nude beach nearby.
**Smoking:** ALL rooms are non-smoking; smoking permitted in gardens & patios.
**Pets:** Not permitted.
**Handicap Access:** No.
**Children:** Not especially welcomed.
**Languages:** English, Spanish & sign language.
**Your Host:** Michael, Steve, Cathi.

## Ivanhoe Inn

Gay-Friendly ♀♂

This lovely Victorian house, surrounded by a white picket fence entwined with colorful flowers, is now the ***Ivanhoe Inn.*** Accommodations, including comfortable suites and a separate cottage, are individually decorated. Each morning, a picnic basket will appear outside your door with a continental breakfast in it. Each suite has a kitchen, so you may make your own coffee, then eat in the privacy of your room, or on the sunny patio or garden. The Santa Barbara area is renowned for its wineries and fine restaurants. The beach is just a few blocks from our door.

**Address: 1406 Castillo St, Santa Barbara, CA 93101**
**Tel: (805) 963-8832, (800) 428-1787, Fax: (805) 966-5523.**

**Type:** Bed & breakfast & separate cottage.
**Clientele:** Mostly straight clientele with a gay/lesbian following
**Transportation:** Taxi or airport limo. Pick up from train.
**To Gay Bars:** Close to gay/lesbian bars.
**Rooms:** 1 room, 3 suites & 1 2-bdrm cottage with queen or king beds.
**Bathrooms:** Private: 1 shower/toilet, 2 bath/toilet/showers. 2 shared full baths.
**Meals:** Expanded continental breakfast.
**Complimentary:** Wine & cheese on arrival. Crackers, coffee, tea, hot chocolate, wine & condiments in room.
**Dates Open:** All year.
**High Season:** Apr.-Sep.
**Rates:** $57-$195, $20 per extra person.
**Discounts:** On extended stays. 40% off Sun thru Thur except holidays and special days.
**Credit Cards:** MC, VISA, Amex & Diners.
**Rsv'tns:** Preferred.
**Reserve Through:** Travel agent or call direct.
**Minimum Stay:** 2 nights on weekends.
**Parking:** Ample off-street & on-street parking.
**In-Room:** Color cable TV, ceiling fans, kitchen, refrigerator, coffee/tea-making facilities, maid service.
**On-Premises:** Laundry facilities.
**Exercise/Health:** Complimentary bikes.
**Swimming:** 14 blocks to ocean beach.
**Sunbathing:** On beach.
**Nudity:** Nude beach nearby.
**Smoking:** Not permitted except on patios.
**Pets:** Permitted in cottage & downstairs rooms.
**Children:** Permitted.
**Languages:** English, limited Spanish.
**Your Host:** Mary.

# SONOMA

## Gaige House Inn

Gay-Friendly ♀♂

### *A Star in the Valley of the Moon*

The ***Gaige House Inn,*** a Sonoma designated landmark, is bordered by lazy Calabezas Creek and the wooded hills of the California Coast range. *Fodors* called the location "one of the best sites of any wine country inn" and *Northern California's Best Places* described our guest rooms as "spectacular." Oversized towels, fluffy robes and English toiletries await you, along with direct-dial phones and reading lights with rheostats. Two-course breakfasts, prepared by a professional chef, include fresh-squeezed orange juice and coffee from Peet's, a Bay Area institution. Seven miles from Sonoma, the wooded hamlet of Glen Ellen is a superb base for touring wine country. A dozen notable wineries are

several miles away. Relaxing days can be spent combining wine tastings with picnics. Outdoor activities in the area include horseback riding, golfing, hiking and ballooning.

**Address: 13540 Arnold Dr, Glen Ellen, CA**
**Tel: (707) 935-0237, (800) 935-0237, Fax: (707) 935-6411.**
**www.gaige.com.**

**Type:** Inn.
**Clientele:** Mostly straight with a gay & lesbian following
**Transportation:** Car is best.
**To Gay Bars:** 45 mins to Russian River & 25 mins to Santa Rosa gay bars.
**Rooms:** 9 rooms, 1 suite with king or queen beds.
**Bathrooms:** 10 private bath/toilet/shower.
**Meals:** Full breakfast.
**Vegetarian:** Available upon request. Limited restaurant offerings.
**Complimentary:** Complimentary wine hour 4:30pm-6:00pm. Free soda, juice, bottled water & cookies 24 hours.
**Dates Open:** All year.
**High Season:** July-Oct.
**Rates:** $135-$255.
**Credit Cards:** MC, Visa, Amex, Discover.
**Rsv'tns:** Required.
**Reserve Through:** Travel agent or call direct.
**Minimum Stay:** 2 days on weekends.
**Parking:** Ample free off-street parking.
**In-Room:** Color cable TV, AC, ceiling fans, telephone, reading lights with rheostats, maid service. Some rooms have fireplaces.
**On-Premises:** Meeting rooms, TV lounge, corp. conferences, faxes, shaded hammock, picnic deck.
**Exercise/Health:** Nearby gym, massage.
**Swimming:** 20'x40' pool on premises.
**Sunbathing:** At poolside, on common sun decks.
**Smoking:** Permitted outside only.
**Languages:** English, French, Spanish.
**Your Host:** Ken & Greg.

## Sonoma Chalet B&B

**Gay-Friendly ♀♂**

### *A Wine Country Getaway*

One of the first bed and breakfast inns established in Sonoma, our Swiss-style farmhouse and country cottages are situated on three acres, blocks from Sonoma's historic square. Relax in ***Sonoma Chalet's*** uniquely decorated rooms with fireplace or wood-burning stove, antiques, quilts and collectibles. Cross a wooden bridge to the popular fairy-tale-like Honeymoon Cottage. Complimentary bicycles are available for the more ambitious, or simply relax in the outdoor Jacuzzi. Enjoy a delightful continental breakfast served in your cottage or on the deck overlooking a 200-acre ranch.

**Address: 18935 Fifth St West, Sonoma, CA 95476**
**Tel: (707) 938-3129, (800) 938-3129.**

**Type:** Bed & breakfast.
**Clientele:** Mostly straight clientele with gays & lesbians welcome
**Transportation:** Car is best.
**To Gay Bars:** 1-hour drive to San Francisco & Russian River resorts.
**Rooms:** 2 rooms, 1 suite & 3 cottages with double or queen beds.
**Bathrooms:** 4 private. & 1 shared.
**Meals:** Expanded continental breakfast.
**Complimentary:** Tea & coffee. Sherry in room.
**Dates Open:** All year.
**High Season:** April-Oct.
**Rates:** $75-$150.
**Credit Cards:** MC, VISA & Amex.
**Rsv'tns:** Required.
**Reserve Through:** Travel agent or call direct.
**Minimum Stay:** 2 nights on weekends & holidays during high season.
**Parking:** Ample free parking.
**In-Room:** Ceiling fans, refrigerator, coffee & tea-making facilities.
**Exercise/Health:** Free use of bicycles, Jacuzzi on premises. Nearby gym, weights & massage.
**Smoking:** Permitted outside only.
**Pets:** Not permitted.
**Handicap Access:** No.
**Children:** By prior arrangement.
**Languages:** English.
**Your Host:** Joe.

# SONOMA COUNTY

## Asti Ranch

**Women ♀**

***Asti Ranch*** is a charming one-bedroom cottage, with full kitchen, in a rural wine growing region 1-1/2 hours north of San Francisco. The ranch has eight sheep, two llamas, as well as ducks and geese on the pond. It is close to the premium wineries of Sonoma and Napa counties and only 1/2 hour from a major lesbian/gay resort. Fish, swim or canoe in the Russian river. Excellent restaurants and shopping are close by and it is only 45 minutes to the Pacific Ocean.

**Address: 25750 River Rd, Cloverdale, CA 95425**
**Tel: (707) 894-5960, Fax: (707) 894-5658.**

**Type:** Cottage.
**Clientele:** Women only.
**Transportation:** San Francisco Airport, then 2 hours north. Airport shuttle available to Santa Rosa.
**To Gay Bars:** 1/2 hour drive.
**Rooms:** 1 cottage with queen bed & double futon.
**Bathrooms:** Private bath/shower/toilet.
**Complimentary:** Tea, coffee & 1 bottle of wine en suite.
**Rates:** Week $500-$750, weekend $200-$250.
**Rsv'tns:** Required.
**Reserve Through:** Call direct.
**Minimum Stay:** 2 nights.
**Parking:** Ample free off-street parking.
**In-Room:** Ceiling fans, kitchen, refrigerator, coffee & tea-making facilities.
**Exercise/Health:** Nearby gym, Jacuzzi & massage.
**Swimming:** Nearby river & lake.
**Sunbathing:** On the patio or by the pond.
**Smoking:** Not permitted.
**Pets:** Not permitted.
**Handicap Access:** Yes.
**Children:** Not especially welcome.
**Languages:** English.

## Whispering Pines B&B

**Gay-Friendly 50/50 ♀♂**

A ranch-style home in a peaceful wooded area, ***Whispering Pines B&B*** is located in the middle of the Sonoma/Napa wine country. What a perfect place in which to relax away from city life, enjoy the sounds of nature and gaze at myriad stars while soaking in the hot tub at night! Full breakfast is served in the dining room or on the deck. We are close to wineries, balloon and glider rides, mud baths and massage, restaurants and more. Your congenial hostesses have many ideas of enjoyable things to do.

**Address: 5950 Erland Rd, Santa Rosa, CA 95404**
**Tel: (707) 539-0198 (Tel/Fax).**

**Type:** Bed & breakfast.
**Clientele:** 50% gay & lesbian & 50% straight clientele.
**Transportation:** Car is best.
**To Gay Bars:** 10 miles, a 15 min drive.
**Rooms:** 2 rooms with double or queen beds.
**Bathrooms:** 2 private bath/toilets, 2 private shower/toilets.
**Meals:** Full breakfast.
**Vegetarian:** Available nearby & on request.
**Complimentary:** Wine & fruit in room.
**Dates Open:** All year.
**Rates:** $85-$115 year round.
**Credit Cards:** MC, Visa.
**Rsv'tns:** Required.
**Reserve Through:** Call direct.
**Parking:** Ample off-street parking.
**In-Room:** AC, ceiling fans, VCR.
**On-Premises:** Video tape library, garden seating.
**Exercise/Health:** Exercycle, Jacuzzi.
**Swimming:** Pool. River nearby.
**Sunbathing:** Poolside.
**Smoking:** Permitted outside. No non-smoking rooms available.
**Pets:** Permitted in outside kennel.
**Handicap Access:** No.
**Children:** No.
**Languages:** English.
**Your Host:** Sharon & Jeannie.

# COLORADO

## ASPEN

### Hotel Aspen

Q-NET Gay-Friendly ♀♂

**_Best Way to Stay in Aspen_**

This striking, contemporary 45-room hotel on Main Street has large, beautifully-appointed rooms with king or queen beds, wet bars, cable TV, air conditioning, in-room safes, refrigerators, and private baths. Most rooms open onto terraces or balconies and some have private Jacuzzis. Guests relax year-round under beautiful mountain skies on our patio courtyard with its heated swimming pool and two Jacuzzis. In the lounge, take in incredible panoramic views while enjoying a complimentary mountain breakfast or afternoon wine and cheese in the lounge.

***Hotel Aspen*** is the perfect home base from which to enjoy what the spirited town of Aspen has to offer. In winter, there is world-class skiing. Summer sports include golf, tennis, swimming, hiking, biking, river rafting and trout fishing. For the culturally-minded, there are daily concerts, dance and theater. And whatever the season, there are numerous shops, galleries and restaurants.

From the moment you arrive, our professional staff caters to your needs, ensuring a vacation that goes beyond expectation. ***Hotel Aspen*** is centrally located, just a short stroll from everything, and is convenient to free public transportation. The airport is only three miles from town and the city of Denver is a scenic 3-1/2 hour drive from Aspen.

**Address: 110 W Main St, Aspen, CO 81611**
**Tel: (970) 925-3441, (800) 527-7369, Fax: (970) 920-1379.**

**Type:** Hotel with breakfast & meeting room.
**Clientele:** Mainly straight with a gay & lesbian following
**Transportation:** Car. City provides shuttle transport from airport. Amtrak from Denver to Glenwood Sprgs.
**To Gay Bars:** About 3 blks.
**Rooms:** 40 rooms & 5 suites with double, queen or king beds.
**Bathrooms:** All private.
**Meals:** Expanded continental buffet breakfast.
**Vegetarian:** At almost all restaurants. Best in Aspen, Explore Booksellers & Coffeehouse, is only 2 blocks.
**Complimentary:** Apres-ski receptions in season.
**Dates Open:** All year.
**High Season:** Ski season: Xmas thru New Year, 2nd wk of Feb thru 3rd wk of Mar, July 4th.
**Rates:** Summer, $59-$160/night; winter $69-$295/night.
**Discounts:** Inquire. Mention *Inn Places* for 10% disc.
**Credit Cards:** MC, Visa, Amex, Diners & Discover.
**Rsv'tns:** Strongly suggested.
**Reserve Through:** Travel agent or call direct.
**Minimum Stay:** At certain times. Inquire.
**Parking:** Ample free off-street & on-street parking.
**In-Room:** Cable color TV, AC, telephone, refrigerator, coffee/tea-maker & maid service. 4 rooms with Jacuzzi.
**On-Premises:** Meeting rooms, valet service.
**Exercise/Health:** Gym & outside Jacuzzi. Day passes available at the Aspen Athletic Club.
**Swimming:** On premises large outdoor heated pool. 25 miles to Reudi Reservoir.
**Sunbathing:** At poolside or on private sun decks.
**Smoking:** Permitted in rms, not in common areas.
**Pets:** Dogs permitted in some rooms.
**Handicap Access:** Yes. All 1st-floor rooms.
**Children:** Permitted.
**Languages:** English, Spanish, German, French & Australian.

# ASPEN AREA

## Rising Star Ranch

Q-NET Gay/Lesbian ♀♂

### *A Gay Guest Ranch in the Rockies*

***Rising Star Ranch,*** located 46 miles west of Aspen, Colorado, is a year-round guest ranch/resort for gay women and men. Whether your ideal vacation includes lots of activity in a beautiful mountain setting, pampering in an upscale resort environment, or some combination of the two, ***Rising Star Ranch*** will exceed your expectations. Packaged weekly rates include lodging, meals, all shuttles (to airport, rafting, skiing, shopping, etc.) and all ranch activities, including horseback riding, water skiing and jet skiing, overnight camp-outs, fly-fishing, hiking, cross-country skiing, snow-mobiling, nightly dances and the courteous attention of our staff. Whitewater rafting and downhill skiing at Aspen, Vail and Snowmass are close by and are priced separately.

The ranch is surrounded on three sides by thousands of acres of national forest land with trails to secluded lakes, old mine sites and breathtaking views. The Frying Pan River, a gold-medal trout stream, forms the ranch's fourth boundary. Nestled in a lush meadow surrounded by towering pines and aspen, ***Rising Star Ranch*** provides accommodations for 58 guests. Choose from luxury suites with a private fireplace, Jacuzzi and sitting room...bedrooms with private baths...and bedrooms with shared baths. After a full day's activity, you'll be glad to climb into a lodgepole-pine bed, complete with soft, cotton sheets and down comforter. Oversized towels, bathrobes, and high-quality toiletries extend the overall feeling of being pampered. Massages and facials will help ease the remnants of city stress.

Our chef will tantalize your palate with a variety of delicious meals, ranging from elegant entrees to fiesta dinners and outdoor barbecues. Fresh-baked cookies will await you each afternoon, and we'll even cook to order the trout you caught in the nearby Frying Pan River. Not only will we accommodate your dietary requirements, we'll even ask you ahead of time to tell us your favorite beverage and other food preferences, and we'll do our best to have them on hand for your arrival. Our goals are: 1) For you to declare this your best vacation ever, and 2) For you to visit us again!

**Address: Meredith, CO. Tel: (888) GAY-RNCH (429-7624).**

**Type:** Resort guest ranch with 40% men and women & 60% women-only weeks.
**Clientele:** Gay & lesbian. Good mix of men & women
**Transportation:** Fly into Aspen or Eagle. The ranch provides for pick up from airport, train, etc.
**To Gay Bars:** Bar on premises.
**Rooms:** Rooms & suites with king or queen beds. Accommodates 58 guests.
**Bathrooms:** Private: 8 private bath/toilet/showers, 12 Jacuzzi/toilet/showers. Shared: 9 bath/shower/toilets.
**Meals:** Full breakfast, lunch, dinner, all snacks.
**Vegetarian:** We accommodate vegetarian requirements with ad-

vance notice.
**Complimentary:** Afternoon & late-night snacks; beer & wine with dinner; softdrinks, coffee & tea. Our kitchen is open to guests.
**Dates Open:** Depends on weather, approximately June 1-Oct 15 & Nov 15-April 15.
**High Season:** June-Aug, Thanksgiving, Christmas, New Year.
**Rates:** Summer $1200-$1500 per week; Ski season $1000-$1350 per week.
**Discounts:** Negotiable, depends on size of group & time of year.
**Rsv'tns:** Required.
**Reserve Through:** Travel agent or call direct.
**Parking:** Ample free off street parking. Ranch provides comprehensive free shuttle service, cars not necessary.
**In-Room:** Suites have private fireplaces, Jacuzzi, sitting room. All rooms have color TV, VCR, down comforters, coffee/tea-making facilities, maid service. Limited laundry service.
**On-Premises:** Meeting rooms, TV lounge, laundry facilities, video tape library, reading library.
**Exercise/Health:** Gym, weights, Jacuzzi, sauna, massage, facials. Motorboat, jet ski, snow shoes, tennis & basketball court, softball field, bicycles, canoes, horses.
**Swimming:** Pool on premises, nearby lake.
**Sunbathing:** Poolside.
**Smoking:** Permitted outside only. All rooms non-smoking.
**Pets:** Not permitted.
**Handicap Access:** Yes.
**Children:** We are adults only.
**Languages:** English.
**Your Host:** Carol & Susan.

IGTA

# COLORADO SPRINGS

## Pikes Peak Paradise B&B

Q-NET Gay-Friendly 50/50 ♀♂

### *We're So Happy, You Might Even Say We're...Gay!*

Take: a Southern mansion and hospitality and an unexcelled view of Pikes Peak. Mix with: romantic atmosphere and privacy, a fireplace, queen- and king-sized beds with fresh sheets, and a gourmet breakfast. Add: friendly hosts eager to make you feel at home and a pinch of good conversation. Fold in: a basketful of dreams yet-to-be, a plentiful supply of "glad-to-be-gay." Shake and bake with: enjoyment. It will yield: a large bundle of unforgettable moments and memories at ***Pikes Peak Paradise.***

**Address:** PO Box 5760, Woodland Park, CO 80866
**Tel:** (719) 687-7112, (800) 354-0989, **Fax:** (719) 687-9008,
**E-mail:** woodlandco@aol.com.

**Type:** Bed & breakfast.
**Clientele:** 50% gay & lesbian & 50% straight clientele
**Transportation:** Car.
**To Gay Bars:** 25 minutes to Colorado Springs gay/lesbian bars.
**Rooms:** 5 rooms with queen & king beds.
**Bathrooms:** 3 private bath/toilets & 2 private shower/toilets.
**Meals:** Full gourmet breakfast. Breakfast in bed available.
**Vegetarian:** Available upon request.
**Complimentary:** Tea, coffee, peanuts, soft drinks, mints on pillows.
**Dates Open:** All year.
**High Season:** May-October.
**Rates:** $95-$175.
**Discounts:** $15 off per night for gays/lesbians (specify when reserving). Oct 15-May 15, Sun-Thurs: 2 nights for price of 1.
**Credit Cards:** MC, Visa, Amex, Discover.
**Rsv'tns:** Requested.
**Reserve Through:** Travel agent or call direct.
**Parking:** Ample free off-street parking.
**In-Room:** Ceiling fans, refrigerator, fireplace, hot tub.
**On-Premises:** Public telephones & living room.
**Exercise/Health:** Massage $50/hour. Jacuzzi.
**Swimming:** 10 miles to public pool.
**Sunbathing:** On patio. 3 rooms have private deck.
**Nudity:** Permitted on private deck & in hot tub.
**Smoking:** Permitted outdoors.
**Pets:** Toy breed dogs & declawed cats by prior arrangement.
**Handicap Access:** Yes, 1 deluxe room with Jacuzzi tub.
**Children:** Permitted if over 12 yrs.
**Languages:** English.
**Your Host:** Tim, Martin & Priscilla.

# DENVER

## Mile Hi Bed/Breakfast

Gay/Lesbian ♂

### *Home Away from Home*

***Mile Hi Bed/Breakfast*** offers contemporary lodging at reasonable rates, with king-sized bed, private bath, color TV, VCR, mini-bar, air-conditioning, phone, breakfast, a library, video selections, laundry facilities, massage, and discount coupons. ***Mile Hi*** is in a lovely, centrally located, Spanish-style condo complex in the heart of the gay area, near Cheesman Park. It is only one block to buses. Clubs, bars, and eateries are nearby. Your host will be glad to assist you with information about places to go and things to do. Please kick off your shoes, relax, and enjoy my home, while you're away from yours! NOTE: Owner may be moving, please call B&B for updated information.

**Address:** Denver, CO. **Tel:** (303) 831-8266 or (800) 513-7827.

**Type:** In home stay.
**Clientele:** Mostly men with women welcome
**To Gay Bars:** 4 blocks.
**Rooms:** 1 rooms with king bed.
**Bathrooms:** 1 private tub/shower/toilet.
**Meals:** Expanded continental breakfast. Dinners available with advance notice, nominal charge.
**Vegetarian:** Available with advance notice.
**Complimentary:** Set-up service, tea, coffee, pop.
**Dates Open:** All year.
**Rates:** $40-$60, subject to change.
**Discounts:** Special weekly rate available.
**Rsv'tns:** Preferred.
**Reserve Through:** Travel agent or call direct.
**Parking:** Ample off-street parking.
**In-Room:** Color TV, VCR, video tape library, telephone & refrigerator.
**On-Premises:** Laundry facilities.
**Exercise/Health:** Massage on premises. Year-round sauna & Jacuzzi.
**Swimming:** Pool in summer.
**Sunbathing:** On the patio.
**Nudity:** Please inquire.
**Smoking:** Permitted outside only.
**Pets:** Not permitted.
**Handicap Access:** No.
**Children:** Not permitted.
**Languages:** English.
**Your Host:** Bob.

## P.T. Barnum Estate

Gay/Lesbian ♀♂

Built in 1878, the ***P.T. Barnum Estate*** consists of a main house with 14 rooms and several outbuildings. We're located seven minutes from downtown Denver's business area, Mile Hi Stadium, hotels, restaurants and drinking establishments. The estate's grounds abound with flowers, and the house has antiques and other items of interest, making this a truly different and unusual bed and breakfast experience. Enjoy the ambiance and nostalgia of yesteryear by staying with Bart and Herb at the ***P.T. Barnum Estate.*** Our guests comments: Great! Wonderful! Fantastic! We'll be back! Terrific location!

**Address:** Denver, Colorado. **Tel:** (303) 698-0045.

**Type:** Bed & breakfast.
**Clientele:** Mostly gay, lesbian & bisexual
**Transportation:** Car is best. Taxi, one block to city bus line.
**To Gay Bars:** 12 blocks to gay/lesbian bars.
**Rooms:** 2 doubles.
**Bathrooms:** 1 private & 1 shared.
**Meals:** Expanded continental breakfast.
**Complimentary:** Tea, coffee & juice.
**Dates Open:** All year.

**Rates:** $50-$80 per night. **Discounts:** Weekly. **Rsv'tns:** Recommended. **Reserve Through:** Travel agent or call direct. **Parking:** Adequate on-street parking in a safe neighborhood. **On-Premises:** Color TV, telephones with free local calls. **Smoking:** Permitted on balconies. **Pets:** Not permitted. **Handicap Access:** No. **Children:** Not permitted. **Languages:** English, German, Japanese. **Your Host:** Bart & Herb.

## Victoria Oaks Inn

Q-NET Gay/Lesbian ♀♂

The warmth and hospitality of ***Victoria Oaks Inn*** is apparent the moment you enter this historical, restored 1896 mansion. Elegant, original oak woodwork, tile fireplaces and dramatic hanging staircase replete with ornate brass chandelier, set the mood for a delightful visit. The nine guest rooms are finished with stylish, restored antiques from the turn-of-the-century and have panoramic views through leaded glass windows and soft colors throughout. The individual character and appointments of ***Victoria Oaks Inn*** are designed for your personal comforts in your home-away-from-home. Whether your visit is for business or pleasure, ***Victoria Oaks*** is conveniently located near Denver's bustling business and financial district, numerous shopping areas and varied tourist attractions.

The mansion is quietly nestled blocks from many of Denver's finest restaurants and close to major traffic arteries, providing quick access for any excursion. The historic Capitol Hill district offers special attractions, including the Unsinkable Molly Brown House, Botanic Gardens and the domed State Capitol Building. Within walking distance are the city park, the zoo, the Museum of Natural History and Imax Theatre. As a home you'd love to come home to, whether for a night or for the week, ***Victoria Oaks*** stands proudly apart. As a small inn, we offer personalized services not often available at larger hotels. Begin each morning with an inspiring continental breakfast, including freshly-squeezed orange juice, blended coffee and teas and a choice of fresh pastries, croissants, bagels and fresh fruits with the morning paper. Start your evening with a complimentary glass of wine from our wine cellar.

**Address: 1575 Race St, Denver, CO 80206**
**Tel: (303) 355-1818, (800) 662-OAKS (6257), Fax: (303) 331-1095.**

**Type:** Bed & breakfast. **Clientele:** Mostly gay & lesbian with some straight clientele **Transportation:** Taxi. **To Gay Bars:** 4 blks to gay/lesbian bars. **Rooms:** 9 doubles. **Bathrooms:** 7 private, 2 share. **Meals:** Expanded continental breakfast. **Complimentary:** Tea, coffee, juices, beer, wine & sodas. **Dates Open:** All year. **High Season:** June-August. **Rates:** $50-$85. **Discounts:** Weekly and group rates. **Credit Cards:** MC, Visa, Amex, Diners & Discover. **Rsv'tns:** Recommended 2 weeks in advance. **Reserve Through:** Travel agent or call direct. **Parking:** Adequate free off-street parking. **In-Room:** Maid & laundry service & telephone. **On-Premises:** Meeting rooms, private dining rooms, TV lounge & laundry facilities. **Sunbathing:** In the backyard. **Smoking:** Permitted without restrictions. **Pets:** Not permitted. **Handicap Access:** No. **Children:** Permitted if well-behaved. **Languages:** English. **Your Host:** Clyde.

# CONNECTICUT

## MYSTIC

### The Adams House

Gay-Friendly ♀♂

***"Quaint & Cozy...Friendly...Beautiful...& Relaxing"***

***Adams House*** is a 1790's-era house on a full acre of lush greenery and flower gardens, offering a homey colonial atmosphere featuring old fashioned fireplaces in the dining room and two bedrooms. Guests can choose between the main house and the ***Garden Cottage,*** a self-contained building just far enough away to ensure total privacy. Breakfast is a delicious medley of fresh fruit, homemade muffins and hot entrées with fabulous coffee. Guests' comments: "Quaint, cozy, fun, relaxing." "A perfect getaway." "Friendly, beautiful." "A blessing."

**Address: 382 Cow Hill Rd, Mystic, CT 06355**
**Tel: (860) 572-9551.**

**Type:** Bed & Breakfast.
**Clientele:** Mostly straight clientele with gays & lesbians welcome.
**Transportation:** Plane to Groton, taxi, train or ferry to New London, then taxi. Free pick up (usually) from Mystic train station.
**To Gay Bars:** 9 miles to New London.
**Rooms:** 6 rooms with queen beds & 1 room with double & queen beds.
**Bathrooms:** 7 private.
**Meals:** Full breakfast.
**Vegetarian:** Always available.
**Complimentary:** Hot or iced tea on arrival or request.
**Dates Open:** All year.
**High Season:** Memorial Day to Labor Day.
**Rates:** $95-$175. Off-season rates available.
**Discounts:** Sun-Thur nights, 3rd night half price. November through April negotiable.
**Credit Cards:** MC, VISA, Amex & Discover.
**Rsv'tns:** Recommended for weekends & Jun-Sep.
**Reserve Through:** Call direct.
**Minimum Stay:** 2 nights on weekends & holidays.
**Parking:** Ample free off-street parking.
**In-Room:** AC & maid service. Garden Cottage has color cable TV, refrigerator.
**On-Premises:** TV lounge.
**Exercise/Health:** Sauna in Garden Cottage.
**Swimming:** 20-30 minutes by car to several beaches, 1 nude.
**Sunbathing:** On the lawn or at the beaches.
**Nudity:** At nude beach.
**Smoking:** Permitted in yard only.
**Pets:** Not permitted.
**Handicap Access:** Garden Cottage accessible, 2 steps.
**Children:** Welcome in Garden Cottage.
**Languages:** English.
**Your Host:** Mary Lou & Greg.

# DELAWARE

## MILTON

### Honeysuckle

Women ♀

*A Haven for Women Near the Sea*

Come to ***Honeysuckle*** and enjoy the easy-going atmosphere at our popular Victorian inn and adjoining houses, Wisteria and Larkspur, near the Delaware beaches. Women feel at home in the comfortable spaces that our houses provide. Our sauna and outdoor hot tubs are year-round favorites. In summer, stroll our porches, decks and gardens to the large in-ground pool with privacy fencing. Snuggle by the fireside in winter. VCRs, stereos, games, a canoe and our library of women's books and music will keep you busy between trips to the beaches, restaurants and outlet malls.

**Address: 330 Union St, Milton, DE 19968**
**Tel: (302) 684-3284.**

**Type:** Inn & 2 adjoining houses.
**Clientele:** Women only
**Transportation:** Car is best.
**To Gay Bars:** 12 miles to Rehoboth gay/lesbian bars.
**Rooms:** 4 rooms & 2 private rental houses with double or queen beds. Each private house accommodates up to 6 people.
**Bathrooms:** 2 private bath/whirlpool tubs. Others shared. Outdoor shower by pool.
**Meals:** Full breakfast at inn only.
**Vegetarian:** Upon request.
**Complimentary:** Coffee and teas.
**Dates Open:** All year.
**High Season:** Summer (June through September).
**Rates:** $80-$150.
**Discounts:** 10% for 7 days or more.
**Credit Cards:** MC, Visa.
**Rsv'tns:** Required.
**Reserve Through:** Travel agent or call direct.
**Minimum Stay:** On holiday weekends only.
**Parking:** Ample free off-street parking.
**In-Room:** Inn: self-controlled AC/heat & one room with whirlpool in bath. Houses: AC/heat, private hot tub, whirlpool/massage room.
**On-Premises:** TV lounge & kitchens.
**Exercise/Health:** Sauna, outdoor hot tub & whirlpool in private baths. Massage available.
**Swimming:** Pool on premises.
**Sunbathing:** At poolside or on the beaches.
**Nudity:** Permitted poolside.
**Smoking:** Permitted outdoors.
**Pets:** Not permitted, excellent kennel nearby.
**Handicap Access:** 1 house available with 1st-floor bedroom/bath.
**Children:** Not permitted.
**Languages:** English.
**Your Host:** Mary Ann & Julie.

IGTA

# REHOBOTH BEACH

## The Mallard Guest Houses

Gay/Lesbian ♀♂

### *Rehoboth's Newest Quaze!*

***The Mallard Guest Houses*** provide comfortable accommodations in this quaint Atlantic seashore community nestled just south of Delaware Bay. Our in-town location is very convenient to bars, fine restaurants and shopping. The inn is decorated in fine furnishings. Enjoy a warm afternoon at the beach or visit our town's many attractions. Enjoy the best of Rehoboth, while staying at the best in Rehoboth.

**Address: 67 Lake Ave, Rehoboth Beach, DE 19971**
**Tel: (302) 226-3448.**

**Type:** Guesthouses. Three locations in Rehoboth.
**Clientele:** Gay & lesbian. Good mix of men & women
**Transportation:** Car is best.
**To Gay Bars:** 1/2 block.
**Rooms:** 20 rooms.
**Bathrooms:** 9 private & others share.
**Meals:** Cont. breakfast.
**Comp.:** Coffee & tea.
**Dates Open:** All year.
**High Season:** Memorial Day-Labor Day.
**Rates:** $65-$150.
**Credit Cards:** MC, Visa.
**Rsv'tns:** Required.
**Reserve Through:** Travel agent or call direct.
**Parking:** Adequate off-street parking.
**On-Premises:** TV lounge.
**Swimming:** 2 blocks to ocean beach.
**Sunbathing:** On private sun decks & at the beach.
**Smoking:** Permitted in designated areas. All rooms are non-smoking.
**Pets:** Sometimes in off season.
**Handicap Access:** Not fully accessible.
**Children:** Inquire.
**Languages:** English.

## The Rams Head

Q-NET Men ♂

### *European Hospitality in a Masculine Environment*

Not far from the madding crowd lies a private haven, protected from intruding eyes by its surrounding walls and lush gardens. We call this place ***The Rams Head.*** Unique in the Rehoboth Beach area, it is bordered by fields and forests, yet is only minutes from the beach, bars, restaurants, tax-free outlet malls, and shops. According to the *Washington Post,* "The Rams Head is an upscale retreat for gay men in an area that seems to have more gay or gay-friendly establishments than Munich has beer halls."

***The Rams Head*** is proud to be the only exclusively all-male bed and breakfast resort in the Rehoboth Beach area. Discover relaxed and comfortable European hospitality in a distinctly East Coast seashore setting. We are a totally enclosed compound, complete with heated pool, gymnasium with universal equipment, free weights & ten-man sauna, enclosed private hot tub/spa, and an outdoor poolside cabana – where we host full breakfast in the morning and complimentary open bar in the afternoon. Comfortably-appointed accommodations are bright, spacious and individually decorated in traditional style. Each bedroom has a queen-sized bed, private bath, color TV, VCR, hair dryers, central air, and refrigerator. Pamper yourself in a man-to-man environment.

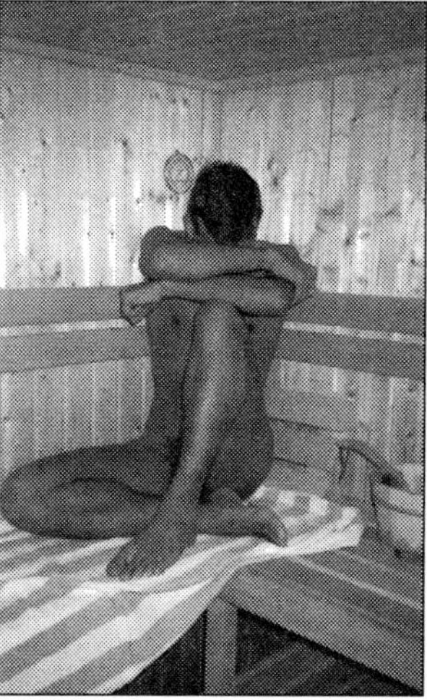

**Address: RD 2 Box 509, Rehoboth Beach, DE 19971-9702**
**Tel: (302) 226-9171.**

**Type:** Bed & breakfast.
**Clientele:** Men only
**Transportation:** Car is best.
**To Gay Bars:** 1 mile to dance bar, 2 miles to cruise bars.
**Rooms:** 2 economy rooms, 5 deluxe rooms & 2 suites, all with queen beds.
**Bathrooms:** All private.
**Meals:** Full breakfast.
**Complimentary:** Non-alcoholic & alcoholic beverages served poolside during day.
**Dates Open:** May 1-October 1.
**High Season:** May 1-October 1.
**Rates:** $100-$140.
**Credit Cards:** MC, Visa, Discover, Amex.
**Rsv'tns:** Required.
**Reserve Through:** Call direct.
**Minimum Stay:** 2 days in season, 3 days on holidays.
**Parking:** Ample, free off-street parking.
**In-Room:** Housekeeping service, color cable TV, VCR, refrigerator, hair dryer.
**On-Premises:** Library, sitting lounge, cabana with open bar.
**Exercise/Health:** Full gym with free weights, universal & 10-man sauna, gazebo with hot tub.
**Swimming:** Heated pool on premises, ocean beach 2 miles.
**Sunbathing:** At poolside & on the beach.
**Nudity:** Permitted poolside & in spa & sauna area.
**Smoking:** Permitted without restriction.
**Pets:** Not permitted.
**Handicap Access:** No.
**Children:** Not permitted.
**Languages:** English.
**Your Host:** Jim & Carl.

## Rehoboth Guest House

**Gay/Lesbian ♀♂**

### *Rehoboth's Oldest Continually Running Gay Guesthouse*

***Rehoboth Guest House,*** is a charming Victorian beach house 1-1/2 blocks from the beach on a residential street close to gay shopping & dining. Feel at home in 12 airy, white-washed rooms with large windows and painted floors. Relax over continental breakfast in the sun room or rock on the flower-lined front porch. Enjoy sun decks, gay beaches, outdoor cedar showers, Saturday evening wine and cheese, or nearby shops, restaurants and bars. Whether you are taking a long vacation or grabbing a weekend, you will always feel relaxed and welcome. Newly renovated.

**Address: 40 Maryland Ave, Rehoboth, DE 19971**
**Tel: (302) 227-4117, (800) 564-0493.**

**Type:** Bed & breakfast guesthouse.
**Clientele:** Mostly gay & lesbian with some hetero clientele
**Transportation:** Car is best.
**To Gay Bars:** 1 block.
**Rooms:** 12 rooms & 1 apartment sleeping 4. Dbl, queen & king beds.
**Bathrooms:** Private & shared baths.
**Meals:** Cont. breakfast.
**Complimentary:** Wine & cheese in backyard or living room on Sat afternoon.
**Dates Open:** May-Oct.
**High Season:** May-Oct.
**Rates:** Sept 16-May 15, $45-$55; May 16-Sept 15, $55-$110; Apartment $125-$150.
**Discounts:** Special rates for Sun thru Thur stays.
**Credit Cards:** MC, VISA.
**Rsv'tns:** Required.
**Reserve Through:** Travel agent or call direct.
**Minimum Stay:** 2 nights weekends, holiday weekends 3 nights.
**Parking:** Most rooms with free off-street parking, limited free on-street parking.
**In-Room:** All rooms have AC & ceiling fans.
**On-Premises:** 2 sun decks, front porch with rockers, 2 picnic tables in backyard, 2 outdoor, en-

*continued next page*

closed showers/dressing rooms with hot water.
**Exercise/Health:** Gym a few blocks away on boardwalk.
**Swimming:** 1-1/2 blocks to beach, short walk to gay beaches.
**Sunbathing:** On common sun decks or at the beach.
**Smoking:** Permitted on porch or decks.
**Languages:** English.

## Silver Lake

Q-NET Gay/Lesbian ♀♂

### *"Gem of the Delaware Shore"*

***Silver Lake Guest House*** is "the best of the bunch" (Fodor's Gay Guide), "the best option" (Out & About), and "the gem of the Delaware shore" (The Washington Post). Located in a tranquil waterfront setting in the midst of a waterfowl preserve on Rehoboth Beach's most scenic drive, this beautiful home offers its guests much more than a conventional bed and breakfast. It is also the resort's closest guesthouse to gay Poodle Beach.

The spectacular lake and ocean view from the main house's sprawling columned veranda along with a beautifully landscaped garden provide an inviting introduction to ***Silver Lake.*** Inside, all of the bedrooms have private baths, cable TV and central air conditioning. Some of the rooms have panoramas of the lake and ocean beyond, while others look out on the numerous varieties of pine and evergreen surrounding the property.

Guests may enjoy breakfast quietly in their rooms, on the veranda or patio, or in the second floor sunroom. Here, too, the lake and dunes are on full display. Breakfast includes muffins baked daily, an assortment of fresh fruit, juice, tea, coffee, along with daily newspapers.

Behind the main house is the Carriage House with its very private, large two-bedroom apartments. Each has a private entrance, living room, dining area and complete kitchen. ***Silver Lake*** is about quality of life. Whether for a weekend or extended vacation, guests enjoy an ambience of comfort and relaxation in the midst of nature at its best.

**Address: 133 Silver Lake Dr, Rehoboth Beach, DE 19971**
**Tel: (302) 226-2115, (800) 842-2115.**

**Type:** Bed & breakfast guesthouse.
**Clientele:** Gay & lesbian. Good mix of men & women
**Transportation:** Car is best.
**To Gay Bars:** Walking distance.
**Rooms:** 11 rooms & 2 two-bedroom apartments with queen or king beds.
**Bathrooms:** All private.
**Meals:** Expanded continental breakfast.
**Complimentary:** Tea, coffee, juices & fruit.
**Dates Open:** All year.
**High Season:** Summer.
**Rates:** In season $80-$165, off season from $60.
**Discounts:** For longer stays.
**Credit Cards:** MC, Visa, Amex, Discover
**Rsv'tns:** Required.
**Reserve Thru:** Call direct.
**Minimum Stay:** 2-3 nights on summer weekends.
**Parking:** Ample, free off-street parking.
**In-Room:** Color cable TV, AC, maid service, kitchens in apartments.
**On-Premises:** Meeting rooms, kitchenette, sun room, lounge, BBQ grills, beach chairs & towels, ice, sodas, outdoor showers, lake front lawn & gardens.
**Exercise/Health:** On jogging/biking course. Gym nearby.
**Swimming:** 5-minute walk to gay ocean beach.
**Sunbathing:** On the beach.
**Smoking:** Permitted.
**Pets:** Permitted in apartments only, by prior arrang.
**Handicap Access:** Yes.
**Children:** Not permitted except by prior arrangement.
**Languages:** English.
**Your Host:** Joe & Mark

## The Summer Place

Gay/Lesbian ♀♂

### *In the Heart of Gay Rehoboth*

Rehoboth's largest gay-owned hotel, ***Summer Place Hotel*** is located on the ocean block with a sun deck overlooking the Atlantic Ocean. Known for 100 years as "Yellow House," this property was recently remodeled from the foundation up. Each room has a private bath, television, air conditioning, heat and telephone. The one-bedroom condos have a kitchen that includes a dishwasher, microwave, stove and refrigerator. Comfortable, clean and quiet, we're in an excellent location in the heart of gay Rehoboth, just a walk to all bars and restaurants. Open year round.

**Address: 30 Olive Ave, Rehoboth Beach, DE 19971**
**Tel: (302) 226-0766, (800) 815-3925, Fax: (302) 226-3350.**

**Type:** Hotel.
**Clientele:** Mostly gay & lesbian with some straight clientele
**Transportation:** Car is best.
**To Gay Bars:** A 1-minute walk.
**Rooms:** 23 rooms, 5 apartments.
**Bathrooms:** All private.
**Dates Open:** All year.
**High Season:** June-August.
**Rates:** Rooms: $40-$145 per day. Apartments: $60-$175 per day.
**Credit Cards:** Visa, MC, Discover, Amex, Nexus.
**Minimum Stay:** 1-3 nights.
**Parking:** Parking pass available.
**In-Room:** AC, telephone, color cable TV. Apartments also have dishwasher, stove, microwave, refrigerator.
**On-Premises:** Sun deck overlooking ocean.
**Swimming:** 1 minute to beach.
**Smoking:** Smoking & non-smoking rooms available.
**Pets:** No.
**Handicap Access:** 1st floor accommodations easy to enter.
**Your Host:** Dan.

# DISTRICT OF COLUMBIA

## WASHINGTON

**For weekend getaways outside of Washington, or a lovely rural stopover 2 to 4 hours outside the city, see Huttonsville and Lost River, West Virginia.**

## The Brenton

Gay/Lesbian ♂

Dating from 1891, ***The Brenton*** is located in the Dupont Circle neighborhood, 12 blocks north of the White House. Rooms are spacious and well-appointed, with antiques, art and Oriental carpets on handsome wood floors. The rooms are air conditioned, have direct-dial phones with answering machines and most have ceiling fans. In the European tradition, the baths are shared, and our beds are ultra-firm. The cozy front parlor welcomes you to relax with new friends and the staff encourages questions about local sights, activities and dining. Make yourself at home, and enjoy Washington as the locals do.

**Address: 1708 16th St NW, Washington, DC 20009**
**Tel: (202) 332-5550, (800) 673-9042, Fax: (202) 462-5872.**

**Type:** Guesthouse.
**Clientele:** Mostly men with women welcome.
**Transportation:** Metro to Dupont Circle, then short walk.
**To Gay Bars:** 2 blocks to gay bar.
**Rooms:** 8 rooms with single, double, queen or king beds.
**Bathrooms:** 3 shared bath/shower/toilets, 1 shared toilet.
**Meals:** Expanded continental breakfast.
**Complimentary:** Cocktail hour in evening, coffee, tea, always.
**Dates Open:** All year.
**High Season:** March through October.
**Rates:** $69-$99.
**Credit Cards:** MC, VISA, Amex & Discover.
**Rsv'tns:** Recommended.

*continued next page*

**Reserve Through:** Travel agent or call direct.
**Parking:** Limited on-street pay parking.
**In-Room:** Maid service, telephone, AC, ceiling fans.
**On-Premises:** Dining rooms, TV lounge.
**Exercise/Health:** Nearby gym.
**Smoking:** Permitted without restrictions.
**Pets:** Not permitted.
**Handicap Access:** No.
**Children:** Not permitted.
**Languages:** English.
**Your Host:** Bob.

# Capitol Hill Guest House

**Gay-Friendly 50/50 ♀♂**

***Capitol Hill Guest House*** is a Victorian row house with original woodwork and appointments, ideally located in the historic Capitol Hill district. Formerly home to congressional pages, the house has ten moderately-priced rooms. We're a short walk from the Capitol and the mall, close to the Eastern Market, fine restaurants and the Smithsonian Museums. Whether for business or pleasure, the convenience and charm of our house will make your stay comfortable and fun.

**Address: 101 Fifth St NE, Washington, DC 20002. Tel: (202) 547-1050.**

**Type:** Bed & breakfast guest house.
**Clientele:** 50% gay & lesbian & 50% straight clientele. Gay owned & operated.
**Transportation:** Taxi from airport, metro from Union Station.
**To Gay Bars:** 6-7 blocks to men's or women's bars.
**Rooms:** 10 rms with single, dbl or queen beds.
**Bathrooms:** Private & shared.
**Meals:** Cont. breakfast.
**Vegetarian:** Available at nearby restaurants.
**Complimentary:** Sherry in living room.
**Dates Open:** All year.
**High Season:** Spring & fall.
**Rates:** $45-$110.
**Discounts:** For senior citizens.
**Credit Cards:** VISA, MC, Amex (with surcharge), Discover.
**Rsv'tns:** Recommended.
**Reserve Through:** Travel agent or call direct.
**Parking:** Adequate, free, on-street parking, permits provided.
**In-Room:** B&W TV for fee.
**On-Premises:** Refrigerator in the hall.
**Swimming:** 6 blocks to indoor public pool.
**Smoking:** Permitted on porch or in backyard.
**Pets:** Not permitted.
**Handicap Access:** No.
**Children:** Permitted, if over 8 years.
**Languages:** English, Spanish, Portuguese, American Sign Language.
**Your Host:** Antonio.

# Eighteen Thirty-Six California St

**Gay/Lesbian ♀♂**

## *Victorian Romance...Today's Comfort*

***1836 California St,*** our small, elegant bed and breakfast inn, offers a luxurious haven on a quiet street midway between the international restaurants and antique shops of Adams Morgan and the galleries and vibrant nightlife of Dupont Circle. This centrally located 1900 Victorian townhouse has been beautifully restored and decorated with period pieces and contemporary art. Fireplaces grace public rooms and some bedrooms, and an extensive library is scattered throughout. Accommodations consist of four comfortably appointed bedrooms that share two baths and two suites with private baths.

**Address: 1836 California St NW, Washington, DC 20009**
**Tel: (202) 462-6502, Fax: (202) 265-0342.**

**Type:** Bed & breakfast.
**Clientele:** Mostly gay & lesbian with some straight clientele
**Transportation:** 6 minutes from Dupont metro stop.
**To Gay Bars:** 4 blocks.
**Rooms:** 4 rooms & 2 suites with queen beds. 2 rooms also have twin beds.
**Bathrooms:** Private: 2 bath/toilets. Shared: 2 bath/shower/toilets, 1 toilet.
**Meals:** Continental breakfast.
**Vegetarian:** Breakfast is vegetarian. Many nearby restaurants offer vegetarian food.
**Dates Open:** All year.
**Rates:** $60-$95.
**Credit Cards:** MC, Visa & Amex.
**Rsv'tns:** Required.
**Reserve Through:** Call direct.
**Parking:** Limited on-street, covered, pay parking.
**In-Room:** Color cable TV, AC, ceiling fans & telephone.
**On-Premises:** Meeting rooms & dining room.
**Exercise/Health:** Nearby gym, weights, Jacuzzi, sauna, steam & massage.
**Sunbathing:** On patio & common sun deck.
**Smoking:** Permitted on sun deck & patio only.
**Pets:** Not permitted.
**Handicap Access:** No.
**Children:** Not especially welcome.
**Languages:** English, Turkish & Portuguese.

## Embassy Inn

Gay-Friendly ♀♂

***The Embassy Inn*** is a charming, gay-friendly B&B on historical 16th St. We offer a relaxing, friendly atmosphere and convenience to metro stops, restaurants, grocery store and nightlife. You'll enjoy personalized service, continental breakfast, and evening sherry, as you relax in the warm lobby with a great selection of books and magazines. Our staff is always happy to help with dining suggestions, tourist information or directions. The inn is a great value and is easily accessible to all of Washington's sights. The neighborhood is quaint and offers something for everyone.

**Address: 1627 16th St, Washington, DC**
**Tel: (202) 234-7800 or (800) 423-9111, Fax: (202) 234-3309.**

**Type:** Hotel inn.
**Clientele:** Mostly straight clientele with a gay & lesbian following
**Transportation:** Taxi from airport. Metro Red line from Union Station to Dupont Circle, then 4-1/2 blocks to inn.
**To Gay Bars:** 2 blocks to men's bar, 5 blocks to Dupont Circle gay & lesbian bars.
**Rooms:** 38 rooms with single & double beds.
**Bathrooms:** All private shower/toilets.
**Meals:** Expanded continental breakfast.
**Complimentary:** Evening sherry year-round, coffee/tea 24 hours.
**Dates Open:** All year.
**High Season:** April-May & September-October.
**Rates:** High season $69-$99, low season $69-$89.
**Discounts:** On extended stays, weekend rates, government (business) travel, based on availability.
**Credit Cards:** MC, Visa, Amex, Carte Blanche & Diner's.
**Rsv'tns:** Preferred. Must be guaranteed with credit card.
**Reserve Through:** Travel agent or call direct.
**Parking:** Limited on-street parking, 24-hr pay garage 8 blocks away.
**In-Room:** Telephone, color cable TV, free HBO, AC, maid service.
**On-Premises:** Dry cleaning service.
**Smoking:** Not permitted in main lobby. Non-smoking rooms available. Limited smoking rooms.
**Pets:** Not permitted.
**Handicap Access:** No.
**Children:** Permitted.
**Languages:** English, German & Spanish.

## The Kalorama Guest House at Kalorama Park

Q-NET Gay-Friendly ♀♂

### *Your Home in Washington, DC*

***The Kalorama Guest House*** is the place to call home when you are in D.C. We are located on a quiet, tree-lined street, only a short walk from two of Washington's most trendy neighborhoods, Dupont Circle and Adams Morgan. You'll be near a potpourri of bars, ethnic restaurants, nightspots, antique shops and the underground metro. After staying in a bedroom decorated tastefully with Victorian antiques and enjoying a continental breakfast, an evening aperitif and our nationally-known hospitality, we're sure you'll make our house your home whenever you visit Washington. If you prefer a smaller, more intimate guesthouse, please inquire about our other property, ***The Kalorama Guest House at Woodley Park.***

**Address: 1854 Mintwood Pl NW, Washington, DC 20009**
**Tel: (202) 667-6369, Fax: (202) 319-1262.**

*continued next page*

**Type:** Bed & breakfast.
**Clientele:** Gay-friendly establishment. Mostly straight clientele with a gay & lesbian following
**Transportation:** Taxi or subway are best.
**To Gay Bars:** 4 blocks to men's bars at Dupont Circle.
**Rooms:** 29 rooms & 2 suites with double or queen beds.
**Bathrooms:** 12 private, 19 rooms share (2-3 rooms per bath).
**Meals:** Continental breakfast.
**Complimentary:** Sherry in parlor (afternoon aperitif), lemonade in summer.
**Dates Open:** All year.
**High Season:** Mar-Jun & Sep-Oct.
**Rates:** Rooms $50-$95, suites $80-$115.
**Discounts:** AAA.
**Credit Cards:** MC, VISA, Amex, Diners.
**Reserve Through:** Travel agent or call direct.
**Minimum Stay:** 2 nights required occasionally.
**Parking:** Pay parking off-street and free on-street parking.
**In-Room:** AC, maid & laundry service. Some rooms with ceiling fans.
**On-Premises:** Meeting rooms, TV lounge, guest fridge, laundry facilities.
**Exercise/Health:** Gym with weights nearby.
**Swimming:** In nearby pool.
**Sunbathing:** On landscaped backyard.
**Smoking:** Discouraged in breakfast room. Non-smoking rooms available.
**Children:** Prefer those over 10 years old.
**Languages:** English.
**Your Host:** Tammi & Rick.

IGTA

## The William Lewis House

Q-NET Gay/Lesbian ♂

### *Washington's Finest Bed & Breakfast*

You are always welcome at ***The William Lewis House,*** Washington's finest bed & breakfast. We are conveniently located near Logan Circle, in the heart of the gay community. We are very close to 17th Street, Dupont Circle, Adams Morgan and The Mall. Three different subway lines are within walking distance of the house, the closest of which is the U Street Station on the Green Line. Many of Washington's best restaurants are within a short walk of the house.

Built just after the turn of the century in 1904, this classically inspired house has been painstakingly and faithfully restored to its original grandeur through an intensive and meticulous eleven-year process. It is appointed with antiques, authentic reproduction wall papers and working gas lights. ***The William Lewis House*** is a warm and charming reflection of the quality of a bygone era. Relax in the gilded parlor or richly paneled dining room in front of one of four working fireplaces. The spacious rooms are appointed with family heirlooms and antique carpets. Each bed has cotton linens, feather mattresses and pillows to add to your comfort. Handmade chocolates are delivered to your bedside each evening by request. A full breakfast is served Saturday, Sunday and Monday. An expanded continental breakfast is served Tuesday through Friday.

In addition to the antique luxuries of a completely restored house, ***The William Lewis House*** also offers many modern conveniences such as direct-dial telephones with answering machines and ceiling fans in each guest room. A hot tub is located in the garden to help relax you after a long day of touring. Your hosts Theron, Dave and their lovable pup, Winston, will welcome you and try to make you feel as though you are staying with friends. We will provide you with pertinent information about the things that have brought you to Washington, as well helpful suggestions about activities in the community.

**Address: 1309 R St NW, Washington, DC**
**Tel: (202) 462-7574, (800) 465-7574, Fax: (202) 462-1608.**

**Type:** Bed & breakfast.
**Clientele:** Mostly gay men, all welcome
**Transportation:** Metro to U St or Dupont Circle, then a short walk.
**To Gay Bars:** 4 blocks. A 5-minute walk.
**Rooms:** 4 rooms with double beds.
**Bathrooms:** 2 shared bath/shower/toilets. 1 shared WC/toilet.
**Meals:** Expanded continental or full breakfast.
**Vegetarian:** Many vegetarian restaurants nearby.
**Complimentary:** Coffee, tea & snacks always. Homemade chocolates at your bedside.
**Dates Open:** All year.
**Rates:** $65-$75.
**Discounts:** On extended stays.
**Credit Cards:** Visa, MC, Discover, Amex.
**Rsv'tns:** Required.
**Reserve Through:** Travel agent or call direct.
**Parking:** Adequate on-street parking.
**In-Room:** Ceiling fans, direct-dial phone with answering machine, maid service.
**On-Premises:** Laundry facilities.
**Exercise/Health:** Hot tub in garden (bring your swimsuit). Nearby gym.
**Swimming:** Nearby pool.
**Sunbathing:** In nearby parks.
**Smoking:** Permitted in garden only.
**Pets:** Not permitted.
**Handicap Access:** No.
**Languages:** English.
**Your Host:** Theron & Dave.

## Windsor Inn

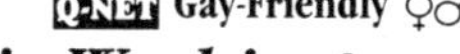

### *A Relaxing Oasis in Washington*

A relaxed atmosphere and personalized service typify the ***Windsor Inn,*** a charming art deco-style bed and breakfast on historical 16th Street, convenient to the metro and a variety of restaurants. We're happy to help with dining suggestions, tourist information, etc. Rooms are comfortable and pleasantly decorated. Our nine suites have beautiful ceiling borders and a basket of special soaps and shampoo, extra-thick towels and small refrigerators. The ***Windsor*** is also close to nightlife and sights. We are a friendly alternative to the larger convention hotels.

**Address: 1842 16th St NW, Washington, DC 20009**
**Tel: (202) 667-0300, (800) 423-9111,**
**Fax: (202) 667-4503.**

**Type:** Hotel inn.
**Clientele:** Mostly straight clientele with a gay & lesbian following
**Transportation:** Taxi from airport. From Union Station take metro red line to Dupont Circle, then walk 5-1/2 blocks.
**To Gay Bars:** 3 blocks to men's bars & 5 blocks to gay & lesbian bars.
**Rooms:** 44 rooms & 2 suites with single, double or queen beds.
**Bathrooms:** All private.
**Meals:** Expanded continental breakfast & evening sherry.
**Complimentary:** Sherry in lobby all year, coffee & tea 24 hours.
**Dates Open:** All year.
**High Season:** April, May & September.
**Rates:** High season $69-$150, low season $59-$99.
**Discounts:** On extended stays, govt. ID, weekend rates (space-available).
**Credit Cards:** MC, Visa, Amex, Diners, Carte Blanche.
**Rsv'tns:** Preferred with a credit card guarantee.
**Reserve Through:** Travel agent or call direct.
**Parking:** On-street parking, some limitations.
**In-Room:** Maid service, telephone, color cable TV, free HBO, AC, refrigerator in 2 suites & 7 rooms.
**On-Premises:** Small conference room, same-day laundry service, dry cleaning.
**Smoking:** Lobby non-smoking. Most rooms are non-smoking.
**Pets:** Not permitted.
**Handicap Access:** No.
**Children:** Permitted.
**Languages:** English, limited Spanish & French.

# FLORIDA

## AMELIA ISLAND

### Amelia Island Williams House

Gay-Friendly ♀♂

***A Historic Bed & Breakfast with a Heritage of Elegance***

"The most exquisite B&B in Florida and one of the most exquisite B&Bs in the South...the uncontested gem of Amelia Island." "Top Inn of the Year 1995" – *Country Inns magazine* This 1856 ante-bellum mansion is the town's oldest and most historic home, featuring outstanding architectural details and antiques and art dating from the 1500s. Eight guest suites include a regal anniversary suite with original Napoleonic antiques. Breakfast is served in the opulent red and gold dining room. From ***The Amelia Island Williams House*** enjoy 13 miles of unspoiled beaches, horseback riding, golf, tennis, fishing, and shopping in restored historic downtown.

**Address: 103 S 9th St, Amelia Island, FL 32034**
**Tel: (904) 277-2328, (800) 414-9257.**

**Type:** Bed & Breakfast.
**Clientele:** Mainly straight clientele with a gay & lesbian following.
**Transportation:** Car. 30 minutes from Jacksonville International Airport.
**To Gay Bars:** 45-min drive.
**Rooms:** 8 rooms with king or queen beds.
**Bathrooms:** All private.
**Meals:** Full breakfast.
**Vegetarian:** Vegetarian food available upon request. Will cook for dairy allergies.
**Complimentary:** Wine & cheese in afternoon.
**Dates Open:** All year.
**High Season:** Summer.
**Rates:** $135-$165/night.
**Credit Cards:** MC & VISA.
**Rsv'tns:** Required.
**Reserve Through:** Travel agent or call direct.
**Minimum Stay:** Req'd during spec. events weekends.
**Parking:** Ample off-street & on-street parking.
**In-Room:** Color cable TV, video tape library, VCR, AC, ceiling fans & maid service.
**On-Premises:** Formal English walking garden.
**Exercise/Health:** 2 rooms have private Jacuzzis. Massage on call.
**Swimming:** Nearby ocean.
**Sunbathing:** At the beach.
**Smoking:** Not permitted in house. Permitted on porch & in courtyard only.
**Pets:** Not permitted. Pet boarding service available at vet's or in private home.
**Handicap Access:** Yes.
**Children:** Not especially welcome. 12 years & up OK.
**Languages:** English.

# DAYTONA BEACH

## The Villa

Q-NET Gay/Lesbian ♀♂

### *Live Like Royalty*

Live like royalty in our national-register historical Spanish mansion, constructed in 1929 by the finest craftsmen. ***The Villa*** grandly overlooks two-plus acres of landscaped grounds in the heart of Daytona Beach. The interior, particularly the public areas, continues the Spanish theme of the exterior. The present proprietor has beautifully and authentically furnished the mansion in keeping with the architecture of the period with massive sideboards, carved chairs and art objects from the owner's collection filling the building. The mansion with its impressive moldings and stencilled ceilings, the work of the famous Mizner Studios, is one of the finest examples of Spanish Colonial Revival architecture, rivaling mansions in Palm Beach and Miami.

Guests appreciate the secluded tropical garden, swimming pool and spa, private sun deck and public areas. Stay in guest rooms named for nobility: the King Juan Carlos, Queen Isabella, Marco Polo and Christopher Columbus rooms are decorated with the finest period pieces. ***The Villa*** is located within walking distance of Daytona's world-famous beach, fine dining, shopping and nightlife. Saint Agustine, America's oldest city, is only 45 minutes away. Orlando, home of Disney World and other theme parks, is just an hour's drive. Cape Canaveral, site of shuttle launches, is less than an hours' drive.

The staff is more than happy to advise guests on a variety of activities, car rentals and special events. Groups may rent the entire villa on a weekly basis and arrangements can be made for cooking, maid service and car and driver. A stay at ***The Villa*** will take you back to a period of grand living. It is without a doubt one of the finest accommodations catering to the travelling community.

**Address: 801 N Peninsula Dr, Daytona Beach, FL 32118**
**Tel: (904) 248-2020 (Tel/Fax).**

**Type:** Bed & breakfast.
**Clientele:** Mainly gay & lesbian with some straight clientele
**Transportation:** Car or taxi. Pick up from airport or train can be arranged.
**To Gay Bars:** 12 blocks.
**Rooms:** 4 rooms with queen or king beds.
**Bathrooms:** All private.
**Meals:** Expanded continental breakfast.
**Complimentary:** Tea, coffee & soft drinks.
**Dates Open:** All year.
**Rates:** $65-$185.
**Credit Cards:** MC, Visa, Amex.
**Rsv'tns:** Req'd in most cases.
**Reserve Through:** Travel agent or call direct.
**Minimum Stay:** Required during peak season & special events.
**Parking:** Ample free off-street parking.
**In-Room:** Maid service, color TV, AC.
**On-Premises:** TV lounge, use of refrigerator.
**Exercise/Health:** Hot spring spa. Nearby gym, weights & tanning salons.
**Swimming:** Pool on premises, 4 blocks to ocean beach.
**Sunbathing:** At poolside.
**Nudity:** Permitted on pool deck only.
**Smoking:** Permitted outside only.
**Children:** Not permitted.
**Languages:** English.

IGTA

# FT LAUDERDALE

## Admiral's Court

Gay-Friendly 50/50 ♀♂

### *A Superior Waterfront Resort*

***Admiral's Court*** is located on a scenic waterway in one of central Ft. Lauderdale's most desirable locations. Walk to the beach or to fashionable Las Olas Boulevard's shopping, dining and nightlife. Our well-kept, clean and affordable resort accommodations range from large efficiencies to rooms and suites. All rooms offer cable TV, AC and overhead fans. Our goal is to provide our guests with a relaxing, enjoyable, friendly and quiet ambiance. We look forward to your visit and to your enjoying the diversity that Ft. Lauderdale offers its guests every day of the year.

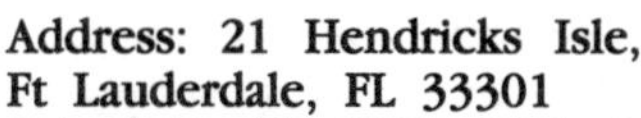

**Address: 21 Hendricks Isle, Ft Lauderdale, FL 33301**
**Tel: (954) 462-5072, (800) 248-6669, Fax: (954) 763-8863.**

**Type:** Motel.
**Clientele:** 50% gay & lesbian & 50% straight clientele.
**Transportation:** Car is best. Water taxi & bus service available.
**To Gay Bars:** 1 mile.
**Rooms:** 20 rooms & 12 apartments with king or queen beds.
**Bathrooms:** All priv. baths.
**Dates Open:** All year.
**High Season:** Feb-Apr.
**Rates:** Winter $75-$145, summer $50-$100.
**Discounts:** Weekly rates, plus summer special: every 4th week free.
**Credit Cards:** MC, VISA, Amex.
**Rsv'tns:** Required.
**Reserve Through:** Travel agent or call direct.
**Parking:** Ample off-street parking.
**In-Room:** Color cable TV, AC, ceiling fans, telephone, maid service.
**On-Premises:** Laundry facilities, BBQ.
**Swimming:** 2 pools.
**Sunbathing:** On private sun decks, at poolside.
**Nudity:** Permitted.
**Smoking:** Permitted. Non-smoking rooms available.
**Handicap Access:** We have ground-level rooms.
**Children:** No.
**Languages:** English, Spanish.
**Your Host:** Vic & Jann.

IGTA

## The Bahama Hotel

Gay-Friendly ♀♂

### *In the Center of Fort Lauderdale Beach*

Comfortable furnished rooms, overlooking the center of Fort Lauderdale Beach and the Atlantic Ocean, will put you in a vacation frame of mind. At ***Bahama Hotel***, let yourself relax in a large, heated, fresh-water pool. Stretch out for tanning on our patio which gets sun all day. Refreshments are always close by in our tropical patio bar. Enjoy fine cuisine morning, noon, and evening in our Deck Restaurant overlooking the bright blue waters of the Atlantic.

**Address: 401 N Atlantic Blvd (A1A), Fort Lauderdale, FL 33304**
**Tel: (954) 467-7315, (800) 622-9995, Fax: (954) 467-7319.**

**Type:** Hotel with restaurant & bar.
**Clientele:** Mostly straight clientele with a small gay following
**Transportation:** Car or taxi from airport.
**To Gay Bars:** 5 miles or 10-minute drive.
**Rooms:** 43 rooms, 1 suite, 23 efficiency cottages with double or king beds.
**Bathrooms:** Private baths.
**Meals:** Full breakfast.
**Vegetarian:** Available upon request.
**Complimentary:** Coffee in lobby.
**Dates Open:** All year.
**High Season:** Dec-April.
**Rates:** Low season $69-$159, high season $95-$275.
**Credit Cards:** MC, VISA,

Amex, Diners, Discover.
**Rsv'tns:** Required.
**Reserve Through:** Travel agent or call direct.
**Minimum Stay:** Required during holidays & special events.
**Parking:** Adequate free off-street parking.
**In-Room:** Color cable TV, AC, tele., kitchen, refrigerator, maid & room service.
**On-Premises:** Laundry facilities.
**Exercise/Health:** Weights & massage on premises.
Gym nearby.
**Swimming:** Pool on premises. Ocean nearby.
**Sunbathing:** At poolside, on common sun decks, on ocean beach.
**Smoking:** Permitted. Non-smoking rooms available.
**Pets:** Permitted. Dogs under 20 lbs.
**Handicap Access:** Yes.
**Children:** Welcome.
**Languages:** English, French, Spanish, Portuguese.

IGTA

## Big Ruby's Guesthouse

**Men ♂**

### *Lounge Poolside at this Tropical Resort*

Lounge by the large swimming pool with cascading waterfall at ***Big Ruby's*** tropical Key West-style guesthouse. The clothing-optional pool area is surrounded by a tropical lush garden. All rooms at the guesthouse have been recently repainted and upgraded. Amenities in the rooms include cable TV, refrigerators, ceiling fans, AC, and microwaves.

**Address: 908 NE 15th Ave, Ft Lauderdale, FL 33304**
**Tel: (954) 523-RUBY (7829), Fax: (954) 523-7051.**
**Toll-free (888) BIG RUBY (523-7829).**

**Type:** Guesthouse.
**Clientele:** Men only.
**Transportation:** Airport 15 minutes.
**Rooms:** 5 doubles, 3 singles, 2 suites.
**Bathrooms:** All private.
**Meals:** Continental breakfast in season.
**Complimentary:** Weekly BBQ in season.
**Dates Open:** All year.
**High Season:** Dec-Apr.
**Rates:** In-season $45-$115, off-season $25-$55. Weekly rates on request.
**Discounts:** To local residents off season.
**Credit Cards:** MC, VISA, & Amex.
**Rsv'tns:** Recommended in high season.
**Reserve Through:** Travel agent or call direct.
**Parking:** Ample free off-street parking.
**In-Room:** Maid, room & laundry service, color TV, AC & refrigerator.
**Exercise/Health:** Weights, workout area.
**Swimming:** Pool on premises. Ocean beach 1 mile.
**Sunbathing:** At poolside, on beach, or common sun deck.
**Nudity:** Permitted by the pool & around house.
**Smoking:** Permitted.
**Pets:** Small pets permitted.
**Children:** Not permitted.
**Languages:** English, Spanish.
**Your Host:** Derek & Scott.

## King Henry Arms

**Gay/Lesbian ♂**

### *The Best Is Yet to Come: YOU!*

***King Henry Arms,*** with its friendly, home-like atmosphere and squeaky-clean accommodations, is just the place for that romantic getaway. Spend your days relaxing amidst the tropical foliage by our pool, or at the ocean beach, just 300 feet away. Enjoy your evenings at the many restaurants and clubs, before returning to the quiet comfort of your accommodations. Truly a jewel by the sea.

**Address: 543 Breakers Ave, Ft. Lauderdale, FL 33304-4129**
**Tel: (954) 561-0039 or (800) 205-KING (5464).**

**Type:** Motel.
**Clientele:** Mostly men with women welcome.
**Transportation:** Car or taxi from Ft. Lauderdale airport.
**To Gay Bars:** 2 miles to gay/lesbian bars.
**Rooms:** 4 rooms, 6 suites & 2 apartments with single, double or king beds.
**Bathrooms:** All private bath/toilet/showers.
**Meals:** Cont. breakfast.
**Vegetarian:** Restaurants & stores nearby.
**Dates Open:** All year.
**High Season:** Winter mths.
**Rates:** Spring thru fall $45-$60, winter $77-$99.
**Discounts:** 10% on 8-30 nights, 15% on 31-60 nights and 20% on 61 nights or more, plus summer specials.
**Credit Cards:** MC, VISA, Amex, Discover, Novus.
**Rsv'tns:** Prefer 1 month in advance, earlier in season.
**Reserve Through:** Travel agent or call direct.
**Minimum Stay:** 7 nights in high season.
**Parking:** Adequate free off-street parking.
**In-Room:** Maid service, color cable TV, telephone, AC, safe & refrigerator. Apartments & suites have kitchens.
**On-Premises:** Laundry facilities.

*continued next page*

**Exercise/Health:** Gym nearby.
**Swimming:** Pool on premises, ocean beach nearby.
**Sunbathing:** At poolside, on beach or patio.
**Smoking:** Permitted without restrictions.
**Pets:** Not permitted.
**Children:** Not especially welcomed.
**Languages:** English.
**Your Host:** Don & Roy.

IGTA

## Orton Terrace

Gay/Lesbian ♀♂

### *The INN Place for the IN Men*

***Orton Terrace*** is located in the Central Beach area only steps from the beach. We offer a quiet, relaxing and friendly atmosphere with the largest apartment accommodations found in the area. The one- and two-bedroom apartments have full-sized kitchens and 27" TVs. All rooms feature phones, cable TVs, safes, refrigerators and microwaves. Videos and VCRs are also available. Our grounds feature pool, BBQ and a quiet tropical courtyard setting.

**Address: 606 Orton Ave, Ft. Lauderdale, FL 33304**
**Tel: (954) 566-5068, Fax: (954) 564-8646.**
**Toll-free in USA, Canada & Caribbean: (800) 323-1142.**

**Type:** Motel.
**Clientele:** Mostly gay & lesbian with some straight clientele
**Transportation:** Taxi.
**To Gay Bars:** 3 miles, a 6-min drive, a 45-min walk.
**Rooms:** 7 2-bedroom apartments with single, double or queen beds.
**Bathrooms:** All private.
**Meals:** Cont. breakfast.
**Dates Open:** All year.
**High Season:** Dec-Feb & Apr.
**Rates:** Dec 1-May 1: $75, $99, $170. May 1-Dec 1: $42, $52, $90.
**Credit Cards:** MC, Visa, Amex, Discover.
**Rsv'tns:** Required.
**Reserve Through:** Travel agent or call direct.
**Minimum Stay:** Please inquire.
**Parking:** Adequate free off-street parking.
**In-Room:** AC, ceiling fan, color cable TV, VCR, video tape library, phone, coffee/tea making facilities, kitchen, refrigerator, maid service.
**On-Premises:** Laundry facilities.
**Swimming:** Pool on premises. Ocean nearby.
**Sunbathing:** Poolside, on patio, at beach.
**Smoking:** Not permitted.
**Children:** Please inquire.
**Languages:** English.

IGTA

## The Palms on Las Olas

Men ♂

### *Fort Lauderdale's Finest Guest Suites*

Affordable luxury in classic fifties style awaits at ***The Palms on Las Olas.*** Spacious accommodations, ranging from simple hotel rooms to grand one bed room suites, include AC, remote control cable TV, telephones and, in season, a full continental breakfast. We're in the heart of "chic" Las Olas Boulevard, one mile from the beach, and close to shops, restaurants and bars. This is the most central, safe location available. Relax by the pool, or take a water taxi from our private dock and explore the canals and waterways of Old Fort Lauderdale.

**Address: 1760 E Las Olas Blvd, Ft. Lauderdale, FL 33301**
**Tel: (954) 462-4178, (800) 550-POLO (7656), Fax: (954) 463-8544.**

**Type:** Guesthouse motel.
**Clientele:** Gay men only
**Transportation:** Car is best.
**To Gay Bars:** 5 blocks or 1/2 mile. An 8-minute walk or 2-minute drive.
**Rooms:** 2 rooms, 5 suites, 1 cottage & 6 efficiencies with single, queen or king beds.
**Bathrooms:** All private.
**Meals:** Expanded continental breakfast, high season only.
**Dates Open:** All year.
**High Season:** Dec-Apr.
**Rates:** Summer $60-$90, winter $80-$145.
**Credit Cards:** MC, Visa, Amex.
**Rsv'tns:** Requested.
**Reserve Through:** Travel agent or call direct.
**Minimum Stay:** 3 days during high season.
**Parking:** Ample free off-street parking.
**In-Room:** Color cable TV, AC, telephones, coffee/tea-making facilities, maid, room & laundry service. Efficiencies & apartments with full kitchens.
**On-Premises:** Laundry facilities & fax.
**Exercise/Health:** Nearby gym.
**Swimming:** Heated pool on premises, ocean nearby.
**Sunbathing:** At poolside & on common sun decks.

**Nudity:** Permitted poolside.
**Smoking:** Permitted.
**Pets:** Not permitted.
**Children:** No.
**Languages:** English.

## The Royal Palms

Men ♂

### *Five-Star Luxury Beneath Towering Palms*

Welcome to the award-winning ***Royal Palms,*** Fort Lauderdale's only five-star accommodation for gay men. Come and experience our tropical paradise for that special vacation, where atmosphere, attention to detail and service are unequaled. At ***The Royal Palms,*** nestled beneath towering palms, all accommodations surround the secluded tropical garden, pool and sun deck, where a complimentary breakfast is served. We are within minutes of shops, bars and restaurants and two blocks from the main Fort Lauderdale beach. ***The Royal Palms*** was chosen as one of the top three gay accommodations in the United States by Out & About Newsletter, January 1996, and received its 1996 Five Palm Award.

**Address: 2901 Terramar St, Ft Lauderdale, FL 33304**
**Tel: (954) 564-6444 or Fax: (954) 564-6443.**

**Type:** Hotel with wine & beer bar.
**Clientele:** Men only.
**Transportation:** Car is best, but taxi service very good.
**To Gay Bars:** 3 miles (10-min drive).
**Rooms:** 8 rooms, 4 suites with king & queen beds.
**Bathrooms:** All private.
**Meals:** Expanded continental breakfast.
**Dates Open:** All year.
**High Season:** Mid-December-May.
**Rates:** Summer $90-$150, winter $135-$195.
**Discounts:** 3-4 in season.
**Credit Cards:** MC, VISA & Amex.
**Rsv'tns:** Strongly recommended.
**Reserve Through:** Travel agent or call direct.
**Minimum Stay:** 3 days in high season.
**Parking:** Ample free off-street parking.
**In-Room:** Color cable TV, VCR, CD players, video tape & CD libraries, AC, ceiling fans, telephone, kitchen, refrigerator, coffee/tea-making facilities & maid service.
**Exercise/Health:** Nearby gym, weights, Jacuzzi & sauna.
**Swimming:** Heated pool on premises, nearby ocean beach.
**Sunbathing:** At poolside, on beach, patio, private sun decks.
**Nudity:** Permitted.
**Smoking:** Permitted.
**Pets:** Not permitted.
**Children:** Not permitted.
**Languages:** English, Spanish & French.
**Your Host:** Richard & Rick.

# KEY WEST

## Alexander's Guesthouse

Gay/Lesbian ♂

### *A Guesthouse for Your Lifestyle*

From the moment you arrive at ***Alexander's,*** you will appreciate our thoughtful service and our attention to detail. Built as a private residence in 1910 in what is now known as Old Town, ***Alexander's*** was established as a guesthouse in 1981. This European guesthouse offers all of the luxuries. Our lovely common living areas set the mood. Handsome quarters await you, each one unique and with amenities chosen to anticipate your needs. Our bright, comfortable rooms all have bahama fans, AC, TV, VCRs, phone and refrigerators.

The secluded grounds, radiant throughout the day, are a haven for sun-worshippers. Guests can soak up the sun all day on our multi-level decks, or stroll through the lush, sunny tropical garden surrounding the heated pool. Sunbathe poolside or revel in your sense of freedom on one of our private sun decks above the gardens. If you're in the mood for a swim, frolic in the pool beneath cascading bougainvillaea. Evenings, gather by the pool with fellow guests for the complimentary evening cocktail hour.

Truly representative of Key West at its finest, Fleming Street is replete with classic Conch houses, antique stores, food markets, a ship chandlery, the public library and more. Key West is legendary for its incomparable weather and liberal attitudes. Favored daytime activities range from watersports to gallery hopping. Only a short walk away is Duval Street, where nights of celebration and revelry await you. Its clubs, restaurants and bars offer fun and entertainment lasting until the early morning.

**Address: 1118 Fleming St, Key West, FL 33040**
**Tel: (305) 294-9919 or (800) 654-9919.**

**Type:** Guesthouse.
**Clientele:** 75% men, 25% women
**Transportation:** Taxi from the airport.
**To Gay Bars:** 6-7 blocks to men's & women's bars.
**Rooms:** 12 doubles, 5 quads
**Bathrooms:** 15 private, 2 shared.
**Meals:** Expanded continental breakfast.
**Complimentary:** Daily happy hour.
**Dates Open:** All year.
**High Season:** December 15-April 15.
**Rates:** Winter $120-$250, summer $80-$180.
**Credit Cards:** MC, Visa, Amex, Discover.
**Rsv'tns:** Recommended.
**Reserve Through:** Travel agent or call direct.
**Minimum Stay:** Minimum for most holidays & special events.
**Parking:** Adequate free on-street parking.
**In-Room:** Self-controlled AC, VCRs, color TV with remote, telephone, maid service, refrigerator & ceiling fans.
**Swimming:** In pool or at nearby ocean beach.
**Sunbathing:** On private & common sun decks, on the beach & at poolside.
**Nudity:** Permitted for sunbathers on 2nd & 3rd floor sun decks.
**Smoking:** Permitted without restrictions.
**Pets:** Not permitted.
**Handicap Access:** No.
**Children:** Not permitted.
**Languages:** English.

IGTA

## Atlantic Shores Resort

**Gay/Lesbian ♀♂**

### *You've Spent the Day Before – Now Spend the Night*

Welcome to a Key West gay landmark: completely rehabbed in 1995, the ***Atlantic Shores Resort*** has been transformed into a whimsically tropical art deco mecca. The Shores is directly on the ocean and half a block off Duval Street in the "gayer" part of town. Amenities include Diner Shores Restaurant, the infamous clothing-optional Pool Bar and Grill, Cinema Shores (an outdoor movie theater), and the world-renowned Tea Dance by the Sea on Sunday evenings. You've spent the day before, now spend the night. Timing is everything. Call now.

**Address: 510 South St, Key West, FL 33040**
**Tel: (305) 296-2491, (800) 526-3559, Fax: (305) 294-2753.**

**Type:** Hotel with restaurant, pool bar & grill.
**Clientele:** Mainly gay & lesbian with some straight clientele
**Transportation:** Airport taxi or car is best.
**To Gay Bars:** Gay bar on premises.
**Rooms:** 59 rooms & 14 suites with double, queen or king beds.
**Bathrooms:** All private.
**Vegetarian:** Available in Diner Shores & Pool Bar on premises.
**Dates Open:** All year.
**Rates:** Summer $69-$99, winter $99-$250.
**Discounts:** Please inquire.
**Credit Cards:** MC, Visa, Amex, Diners, Discover, Carte Blanche, Eurocard, Bancard.
**Rsv'tns:** Highly recommended.
**Reserve Through:** Travel agent or call direct.
**Minimum Stay:** Please inquire.
**Parking:** Adequate free parking.
**In-Room:** Color cable TV, AC, telephone, refrigerator, coffee machine, microwave, maid service.
**On-Premises:** Fax, copy machine.
**Exercise/Health:** Nearby gym, weights & massage.
**Swimming:** Pool on premises, also on ocean front.
**Sunbathing:** At poolside.
**Nudity:** Permitted in Pool Bar & Grill.
**Smoking:** Permitted.
**Pets:** Not permitted.
**Handicap Access:** Limited accessibility. Check availability.
**Children:** No.
**Languages:** English, Spanish, Polish.

IGTA

## Big Ruby's Guesthouse

**Gay/Lesbian ♂**

On our quiet little lane, in peace and privacy, our three guesthouses, each in traditional historic design, stand secluded behind a tall fence. Inside ***Big Ruby's,*** luxury touches are everywhere. Immaculate rooms have sumptuous beds with four king-sized pillows and superthick bath sheets for towels. Awaiting you outside are a beautiful lagoon pool, spacious decks and lounge areas in a completely private tropical garden. Full breakfast is served at poolside. Evenings, we gather by the pool for wine and the easy companionability of good conversation. You'll never feel so welcome, so comfortable, so at home.

**Address: 409 Applerouth Lane, Key West, FL 33040-6534**
**Tel: (305) 296-2323 or (800) 477-7829.**

*continued next page*

**Type:** Guesthouse.
**Clientele:** Mostly men with women welcome
**Transportation:** Fly to Key West, 15 min by cab (less than $12) to guesthouse.
**To Gay Bars:** Less than 1/2 block.
**Rooms:** 17 rooms with queen or king beds.
**Bathrooms:** Private: 12 shower/toilet, 3 full baths. 2 shared full baths.
**Meals:** Full breakfast every morning. Dinners on Christmas, New Year & Thanksgiving.
**Complimentary:** Wine served each evening from 6pm-8pm except Sunday.
**Dates Open:** All year.
**High Season:** December 21-April 30.
**Rates:** Winter $115-$200, summer $78-$128.
**Discounts:** 10% on stays of 7 days or more between 5/1-12/20, excluding holidays.
**Credit Cards:** MC, Visa, Amex, Discover, Diners Club, Carte Blanche.
**Rsv'tns:** Recommended.
**Reserve Through:** Travel agent or call direct.
**Minimum Stay:** On holidays.
**Parking:** Limited off-street parking.
**In-Room:** Maid service, color cable TV, AC, Bahama fan, refrigerator, 4 king-sized pillows, huge, thick towels, laundry service, video library. Some rooms with VCR.
**On-Premises:** TV lounge, public telephone.
**Exercise/Health:** Rainforest (outdoor tropical shower). Nearby gym & massage.
**Swimming:** Pool, nearby ocean beach.
**Sunbathing:** At poolside, on private or common sun decks, ocean beach.
**Nudity:** Permitted poolside & in sunning yard.
**Smoking:** Permitted without restrictions. 2 non-smoking rooms available.
**Pets:** Not permitted.
**Handicap Access:** Yes.
**Children:** Not permitted.
**Languages:** English.
**Your Host:** George & Frank.

IGTA

## Blue Parrot Inn

Gay-Friendly 50/50 ♀♂

### *Hatched in 1884 and Still Flying High*

The ***Blue Parrot,*** in the heart of historic Old Town, is a tropical, secluded, quiet and clean retreat near famous Duval Street. Our pool is heated during the cooler months and is delightfully usable year round. Beaches, clubs, restaurants and shops are only a very short walk away. We are just two blocks from famous Duval Street where fine restaurants coexist with a crazy assortment of bars, ranging from elegant garden affairs to funky rock-and-roll joints with peanut-covered floors. All water activities are nearby, including diving, and snorkeling on America's only living coral reef. The atmosphere is relaxed and friendly; the music is usually classical. Brochure available.

**Address: 916 Elizabeth St, Key West, FL 33040**
**Tel: (305) 296-0033, (800) 231-BIRD (2473), Fax: (305) 296-5697,**
**E-mail: BLUPAROTIN@AOL.COM.**

**Type:** Bed & breakfast.
**Clientele:** 50% gay & lesbian & 50% straight clientele
**Transportation:** Key West International Airport, then taxi.
**To Gay Bars:** 4 blocks, a 5 min walk.
**Rooms:** 10 rms with single, dbl or queen beds.
**Bathrooms:** Private: 7 shower/toilets, 3 bath/toilet/showers.
**Meals:** Expanded continental breakfast.
**Vegetarian:** Vegetarian food 1 block.
**Dates Open:** All year.
**High Season:** January-April.
**Rates:** Summer $70-$160, winter $105-$180.
**Discounts:** AAA, AARP & on stays of 5 nights or longer.
**Credit Cards:** MC, Visa, Amex, Diners, Eurocard.
**Rsv'tns:** Required.
**Reserve Through:** Travel agent or call direct.
**Minimum Stay:** Required only on weekends, some holidays & special events.
**Parking:** Adequate free on-street parking.
**In-Room:** AC, color cable TV, telephone, refrigerator, ceiling fans, maid service.
**On-Premises:** Fax & photocopy service, bicycle rentals.
**Exercise/Health:** Massage. Nearby gym,

weights, massage.
**Swimming:** Pool on premises. Ocean nearby.
**Sunbathing:** Poolside, on private & common sun decks, at beach.
**Nudity:** Permitted on elevated sun deck with separate entrance.
**Smoking:** Permitted anywhere.
**Pets:** Not permitted.
**Handicap Access:** Yes.
**Children:** Adults only.
**Languages:** English.
**Your Host:** Larry & Frank.

IGTA

## The Brass Key Guesthouse

Gay/Lesbian ♂

### *The Only Thing Missing is You!*

Key West's premier gay and lesbian guesthouse offers attentive service and luxury accommodations in a traditional Conch-style setting of wide verandas, louvered plantation shutters and ceiling fans. Expansive sun decks, a sparkling heated pool and a whirlpool spa glisten within ***The Brass Key's*** private, hedged compound featuring flowering hibiscus, bouganvillaea, jasmine and seven varieties of exotic palms.

Located on a quiet street in the heart of Old Town's finest neighborhood, ***The Brass Key*** is surrounded by restored homes, galleries, restaurants and shops and is just minutes from the nightlife of world-famous Duval Street. The harborfront is but two blocks away, offering casual waterside restaurants and salty bars, as well as gay sailing excursions and seaplane adventures.

The sixteen guest rooms and one-bedroom suites at ***The Brass Key*** are light and airy, featuring handcrafted furniture and traditional antiques, tropical fabrics and local artworks. Each offers king/queen bed, air-conditioning, telephone with voicemail, color television with VCR and videocassette library, hair dryer, Caswell-Massey toiletries, refrigerator and nightly turndown.

While the amenities and service of ***The Brass Key*** are first-class, the atmosphere is always friendly and laid-back: guests enjoy morning conversation during the breakfast buffet; later, many spend the day relaxing together in the sun chaises surrounding the pool. For the energetic, ***The Brass Key*** often arranges group charters for an afternoon snorkel cruise or sunset champagne sail. The evening's cocktail hour provides a further chance to share the day's exploits (and the previous night's misdeeds) and to finalize dinner and club plans.

***The Brass Key*** has been featured by *The Advocate, Conde Nast Traveler, Genre,* and was recently awarded *Out & About's* highest rating "Five Stars - Exceptional." Join us soon and let our staff and guests welcome you to the native warmth and exotic verve of the Caribbean.

**Address: 412 Frances St, Key West, FL 33040**
**Tel: (305) 296-4719, (800) 932-9119, Fax: (305) 296-1994.**

**Type:** Bed & breakfast guesthouse.
**Clientele:** Mostly men with women very welcome
**Transportation:** Airport pick up $10.
**To Gay Bars:** 5-7 blocks to gay & lesbian bars.
**Rooms:** 14 rms & 2 suites with queen or king beds.
**Bathrooms:** All private.
**Meals:** Expanded continental breakfast.
**Complimentary:** Afternoon cocktails.
**Dates Open:** All year.
**High Season:** Mid-December - mid-April.
**Rates:** Winter $140-$265.

*continued next page*

Summer $65-$150.
**Credit Cards:** Amex, Discover, MC, Visa.
**Rsv'tns:** Highly recommended.
**Reserve Through:** Travel agent or call direct.
**Minimum Stay:** Required holidays, special events.
**Parking:** Ample free on-street parking.
**In-Room:** AC, ceiling fan, phone w/ voicemail, color cable TV, VCR, videocassette library, hair dryer, refrigerator, bathrobes, laundry, maid & turndown service.
**On-Premises:** Spacious living room with breakfast area.
**Exercise/Health:** Whirlpool spa on premises & gym nearby. Bicycles at guesthouse.
**Swimming:** Heated pool on premises. Ocean beach half mile.
**Sunbathing:** Poolside & on sun decks.
**Nudity:** Permitted on rooftop sun deck.
**Smoking:** Non-smoking rooms available.
**Pets:** Not permitted.
**Handicap Access:** Yes. Wheelchair ramp. 1 guestroom/bath for the physically challenged.
**Children:** Not permitted.
**Languages:** English.

IGTA

## Chelsea House

Q-NET Gay-Friendly 50/50 ♀♂

*Chelsea House* is a uniquely open, restored 19th-century, two-story home with 18 guestrooms and two-bedroom suite. All rooms (except for one) have semi-private or private balconies. The suite has a full kitchen, living room, hardwood floors and two private balconies. Our acre of land, two blocks from Duval Street, has extensive, tropical gardens, pool and clothing-optional sun deck, and on-property parking. We provide a thorough orientation for guests and are always around to lend friendly advice. Experience the unique ambiance of this historic Old Town, adult-only home and the special attention to individual needs from an informed, experienced staff. Gay-owned and -operated.

**Address:** 707 Truman Ave, Key West, FL 33040
**Tel:** (305) 296-2211, USA & Canada: (800) 845-8859, **Fax:** (305) 296-4822.
**E-mail:** chelseahse@aol.com.

**Type:** Guesthouse.
**Clientele:** 50% gay & lesbian & 50% straight clientele
**Transportation:** Fly to Key West International. $16 per person round trip for airport pick up.
**To Gay Bars:** 2 blocks.
**Rooms:** 18 rooms & one 2-bedroom suite with double, queen or king beds.
**Bathrooms:** All private.
**Meals:** Continental breakfast buffet.
**Vegetarian:** Available nearby.
**Complimentary:** Cuban coffee & iced tea all day. Chocolates at nightly turndown.
**Dates Open:** All year.
**High Season:** December 15-April 17.
**Rates:** Summer $79-$115, winter $118-$170, spring $98-$145.
**Discounts:** 10% for 7 or more days in summer.
**Credit Cards:** MC, Visa, Discover, Bancard & Eurocard.
**Rsv'tns:** Preferred.
**Reserve Through:** Travel agent or call direct.
**Minimum Stay:** On holidays & special events.
**Parking:** Adequate free off-street parking.
**In-Room:** Color cable TV, AC, ceiling fans, telephone, safe, hair dryer, refrigerator, coffee/tea-making facilities & maid service.
**Exercise/Health:** Nearby full-service health facility & water sports.
**Swimming:** Pool on premises, Gulf of Mexico nearby.
**Sunbathing:** At poolside or clothing-optional sun deck above pool building.
**Nudity:** Permitted on clothing-optional sun deck.
**Smoking:** Permitted.
**Pets:** Permitted with exception.
**Handicap Access:** Yes.
**Children:** Not permitted.
**Languages:** English, German, French.
**Your Host:** Gary & Jim.

## Coconut Grove

Gay/Lesbian ♂

Enjoy unparalleled views of Old Town and the Gulf of Mexico from our rooftop decks at ***Coconut Grove Guest House.*** The widow's walk provides a private spot to tan, take in the ocean air or experience Key West's sunsets. Friendliest service and largest, best suites in town.

**Address: 817 Fleming St, Key West, FL 33040**
**Tel: (305) 296-5107, (800) 262-6055.**

**Type:** Guesthouse.
**Clientele:** Mostly men with women welcome
**Transportation:** Taxi.
**To Gay Bars:** 3 blocks to men's/women's bars.
**Rooms:** 5 singles, 11 doubles, 2 suites, 4 1-bedroom apartments in annex across the street.
**Bathrooms:** 20 private, 2 shared.
**Meals:** Cont. breakfast.
**Dates Open:** All year.
**High Season:** December 20th-April 15th.
**Rates:** High season, $85-$200. Low season, $55-$100.
**Credit Cards:** MC, Visa.
**Reserve Through:** Travel agent or call direct.
**Minimum Stay:** Required at certain times.
**Parking:** On-street parking.
**In-Room:** Maid serv., color TV, kitchen, ref. & AC.
**On-Premises:** Meeting rooms, telephone.
**Exercise/Health:** Gym, weights.
**Swimming:** Pool.
**Sunbathing:** At poolside & common sun decks, or roof.
**Nudity:** Permitted at the pool & sun decks.
**Smoking:** Permitted without restrictions.
**Children:** Not permitted.
**Languages:** English, German, French, Swedish.

IGTA

## Colours, The Guest Mansion Key West

Gay/Lesbian ♀♂

### *Experience Not Just a Place, But a State of Mind*

This Victorian mansion in the center of Old Town has undergone a contemporary conversion, yet retains its original details, such as chandeliers, 14-foot ceilings and polished wood floors. Accommodations at ***Colours, The Guest Mansion Key West*** vary from simple sitting rooms to suites. Amenities include cable TV, paddle fan, private baths, air conditioning and balconies with hammocks. Stroll half a block to the shops and entertainment of Duval St, and celebrate colourful sunsets at our pool with our complimentary cocktails. Evenings, find your bed turned down, a mint on your pillow and fresh bath linen after returning from Key West's nightlife, a late affair lasting till dawn.

**Address: 410 Fleming St, Key West, FL 33040. Tel: Reservations: (800) ARRIVAL (277-4825) or (305) 532-9341, Fax: (305) 534-0362.**

**Type:** Guesthouse hotel.
**Clientele:** Mostly gay & lesbian with some straight clientele
**Transportation:** Free pick up from airport or bus if staying 7 nights or more (otherwise $15 roundtrip per person).
**To Gay Bars:** 1-2 blocks to bars & discos.
**Rooms:** 7 rooms & 5 suites (2 with kitchens) with single, double, queen or king beds.
**Bathrooms:** 10 private & 2 shared.
**Meals:** Expanded continental breakfast.
**Complimentary:** Sunset cocktails and impromptu parties. Movie library & turndown service with mints on pillows.
**Dates Open:** All year.
**High Season:** Winter
**Rates:** Summer $54-$135 & winter $82-$185, double occupancy.
**Discounts:** For single occupancy, longer stays & prepayment. Inquire for other.
**Credit Cards:** MC, Visa, Amex & Discover.
**Rsv'tns:** Recommended.
**Reserve Through:** Travel agent or call direct.
**Minimum Stay:** On some holidays.
**Parking:** Limited on-street parking.
**In-Room:** Phone, refrigerators, AC, ceiling fans & maid service. Some have color cable TV & full kitchens.

*continued next page*

**On-Premises:** TV lounge with video tape library.
**Exercise/Health:** Massage & full health club facilities nearby.
**Swimming:** Heated pool on premises. Only 4-10 blocks to ocean beaches.
**Sunbathing:** At poolside, on sun deck or ocean beach.
**Nudity:** Permitted at poolside.
**Smoking:** Permitted, but not in TV lounge.
**Pets:** Not permitted.
**Handicap Access:** No.
**Children:** Not permitted.
**Languages:** English, limited Spanish & French.

IGTA

## Coral Tree Inn

**Men ♂**

***Coral Tree Inn*** is a newly renovated resort in the heart of Old Town, across the street from The Oasis, our mother house. Ten suites open onto balconies, with multi-level sun decks cascading from the 3rd level down to the pool, courtyard and whirlpool under the trellis and the coral tree. Tastefully decorated rooms have AC, color cable TV, Bahama fans, refrigerators, hair dryers, coffee-makers, and robes to wear during your visit. Clothes are optional and complete concierge services are available in 4 languages. You will find our hospitality genuine and generous.

**Address: 822 Fleming St, Key West, FL**
**Tel: (305) 296-2131 or (800) 362-7477.**

**Type:** Guesthouse with beer & wine bar.
**Clientele:** Men only
**Transportation:** Taxi from airport.
**To Gay Bars:** 3-1/2 blocks.
**Rooms:** 10 rooms with queen beds.
**Bathrooms:** All private.
**Meals:** Expanded continental breakfast.
**Complimentary:** Wine & hors d'oeuvres at sunset for an hour by the pool.
**Dates Open:** All year.
**High Season:** December 16-May 1.
**Rates:** Summer $110, winter $165.
**Discounts:** Airline flight service.
**Credit Cards:** MC, Visa, Amex.
**Rsv'tns:** Strongly advised.
**Reserve Through:** Travel agent or call direct.
**Minimum Stay:** Required on holidays & special events.
**Parking:** Limited free on-street parking. Car is not really needed.
**In-Room:** Color TV, AC, ceiling fans, refrigerator, maid service.
**Exercise/Health:** Jacuzzi & use of 2 Jacuzzis at The Oasis.
**Swimming:** Pool & nearby ocean beach. Use of 2 pools at The Oasis.
**Sunbathing:** At poolside or on common sun decks.
**Nudity:** Permitted in public areas.
**Smoking:** Permitted.
**Pets:** Not permitted.
**Handicap Access:** No.
**Children:** Not permitted.
**Languages:** English (even British), Russian, German, Spanish & Turkish.

## Curry House

**Men ♂**

### *Key West's Premiere Guest House for Men*

If you find many of your new friends speak with an intriguing accent, it's because the ***Curry House*** is internationally popular. With only nine rooms, getting to know your fellow guests happens naturally while lounging by our black lagoon pool or at our daily happy hour. As your hosts, we're wholeheartedly at your service. Your room will be immaculate, your bed as comfortable as any you've ever slept in. ***Curry House*** is a short 3-block stroll from Duval Street, Key West's lively mainstream.

**Address: 806 Fleming St,**
**Key West, FL 33040**
**Tel: (305) 294-6777, (800) 633-7439,**
**Fax: (305) 294-5322.**

**Type:** B&B guesthouse.
**Clientele:** Men only
**Transportation:** Airport taxi, approx. $6.
**To Gay Bars:** 4 blocks to men's bars.
**Rooms:** 9 rooms with double & queen beds.
**Bathrooms:** 7 private.
**Meals:** Full breakfast.
**Vegetarian:** Available nearby.
**Complimentary:** Free cocktail hour from 4-6 PM.
**Dates Open:** All year.
**High Season:** January through May.
**Rates:** Summer $75-$95, winter $120-$150.
**Credit Cards:** MC, Visa, Amex.
**Rsv'tns:** Recommended during in-season (3-6 months in advance).
**Reserve Through:** Call direct or travel agent.
**Minimum Stay:** 3 nights in high season, 1 night on summer weekends.
**Parking:** Ample free on-street parking.
**In-Room:** Refrigerator, maid service, AC, ceiling fans.
**On-Premises:** Public telephone.
**Exercise/Health:** Jacuzzi.
**Swimming:** Pool or ocean beach.
**Sunbathing:** At poolside or on private or common sun decks.
**Nudity:** Permitted at poolside and on balconies.
**Smoking:** Permitted without restrictions.
**Pets:** Not permitted.
**Handicap Access:** No.
**Children:** Not permitted.
**Languages:** English.

IGTA

## Duval House

**Gay-Friendly 50/50 ♀♂**

### *A Traditional Inn in Paradise*

Outside our front gate lie the galleries, sidewalk cafes and exciting nightlife of Duval Street. Yet, within the ***Duval House*** compound, seven historic Victorian houses are surrounded by magnificent tropical gardens. Relax under our century-old Banyan tree, swim in our romantic pool, enjoy a free buffet breakfast on a sunny deck. We pride ourselves on being friendly and open to all. Rooms feature wicker and antiques, with ceiling fans, Caribbean colors, and restful porches or balconies for you to enjoy the gentle island tradewinds.

**Address: 815 Duval St, Key West, FL 33040**
**Tel: (305) 294-1666 or (800) 22-DUVAL.**

**Type:** Inn.
**Clientele:** 50% gay & lesbian & 50% straight clientele
**Transportation:** Taxi from airport.
**To Gay Bars:** 1/2 block to men's & 3 blocks to women's bars.
**Rooms:** 26 rooms & 3 suites with double or queen beds.
**Bathrooms:** 27 private shower/toilets & 2 shared showers.
**Meals:** Expanded continental breakfast.
**Dates Open:** All year.
**High Season:** December 22nd thru April 15th.
**Rates:** High season $120-$190, low season $85-$140.
**Discounts:** 10% weekly during off-season.
**Credit Cards:** MC, Visa, Amex, Discover & Diners.
**Rsv'tns:** Recommended.
**Reserve Through:** Travel agent or call direct.
**Parking:** Adequate off-street parking.
**In-Room:** AC, maid service, suites have kitchen & ceiling fans.
**On-Premises:** TV lounge.
**Exercise/Health:** Nearby gym, weights, sauna & steam.
**Swimming:** Pool on premises, ocean beach nearby.
**Sunbathing:** At poolside, private sun decks, or on ocean beach.
**Smoking:** Permitted without restrictions.
**Pets:** Not permitted.
**Handicap Access:** No.
**Children:** Under 16 years discouraged.
**Languages:** English, German.

## Equator

Men ♂

### *The New Age of Male Accommodation*

***Equator*** ushers in a new millennium in Key West men's resorts. The deluxe suites, apartments with pocket kitchens and bungalows create a world of whimsy and comfort unlike any other. Our spacious accommodations feature specialty lighting, Italian tile floors, wooden blinds, security access, instant hot water, climate control and pastel interior tones and accessories. Luxuriate in our tropical setting with a black lagoon pool, orchids, sunning decks, waterfall, keystone fountain and monsoon shower. ***Equator***, a place where time stands still... poised on the edge of the 21st century.

**Address: 818 Fleming St, Key West, FL 33040**
**Tel: (305) 294-7775, (800) 278-4552, Fax: (305) 296-5765.**

**Type:** Guesthouse.
**Clientele:** Men only
**Transportation:** Taxi from airport.
**To Gay Bars:** 5 blocks to gay bars.
**Rooms:** 12 rooms, 4 suites, 1 cottage with queen or king beds.
**Bathrooms:** 17 private shower & toilets.
**Meals:** Full breakfast.
**Vegetarian:** Available across the street.
**Complimentary:** Cocktails, turndown service, room snacks.
**Dates Open:** All year.
**High Season:** Mid-December thru May.
**Rates:** High season $115-$175, mid-season $95-$125, summer $60-$105.
**Credit Cards:** MC, Visa, Amex.
**Rsv'tns:** Required.
**Reserve Through:** Travel agent or call direct.
**Minimum Stay:** Required.
**Parking:** Car not necessary, but limited on-street parking available.
**In-Room:** AC, ceiling fans, color cable TV, VCR available, video tape library, phone, refrigerator, maid service, some rooms have kitchen.
**Exercise/Health:** Gym, weights, massage, steam, Jacuzzi.
**Swimming:** Pool on premises, ocean nearby.
**Sunbathing:** Poolside, on private sun decks, on roof, at beach.
**Nudity:** Permitted.
**Smoking:** Permitted outside.
**Pets:** Not permitted.
**Handicap Access:** Yes.
**Children:** No.
**Languages:** English.
**Your Host:** Joe & Bill.

IGTA

## Heron House

Gay-Friendly ♀♂

### *Feel Free...Feel Relaxed...Feel Welcomed*

Amidst orchids, bougainvillaea, jasmine and palms, a secluded tropical garden fantasy awaits you. This warm and friendly place to relax and dream is ***Heron House.*** Spacious sun decks surround a sparkling pool. Our light, airy and spacious rooms are a careful mix of old and new and have a tropical flare with wicker, casual and comfortable furnishings. Luxurious marble bathroom vanities reflect an attention to detail.

**Address: 512 Simonton St, Key West, FL 33040**
**Tel: (305) 294-9227, (800) 294-1644, Fax: (305) 294-5692.**
**E-mail: heronKW@aol.com. http://sla-keys.com/heronhouse.**

**Type:** Guesthouse.
**Clientele:** Mostly straight clientele with a gay & lesbian following
**Transportation:** Car or airport, then taxi.
**To Gay Bars:** 1 block to men's bars.
**Rooms:** 21 rooms with double, queen or king beds.
**Bathrooms:** All private bath/toilets.
**Meals:** Deluxe continental breakfast.
**Vegetarian:** 1 block away.
**Dates Open:** All year.
**High Season:** Dec 20-April 30.
**Rates:** Winter: Dec 20-Apr 30 $149-$249; Shoulder: May 1-30 & Oct 20-Dec 19 $109-$199; Summer: June 1-Oct 19 $99-$179.
**Credit Cards:** MC, Visa, Amex, Diners.
**Rsv'tns:** Recommended.
**Reserve Through:** Travel agent or call direct.
**Minimum Stay:** During holidays and special events.
**Parking:** Ample on-street parking.
**In-Room:** Maid service, ceiling fans, AC, color TV, refrigerators, telephones, private entrances.
**Exercise/Health:** Some rooms have Jacuzzis.
**Swimming:** Pool, ocean beach.
**Sunbathing:** At poolside, on roof or on private or common sun decks.
**Nudity:** Permitted on sun deck.
**Smoking:** Permitted without restrictions.
**Pets:** Not permitted.
**Handicap Access:** Yes. Ramps.
**Children:** Not permitted.
**Languages:** English.

## The Island Key Courts of Key West

Q-NET Gay-Friendly ♀

### *Go Native in Key West! Best Values! Best Rates!*

We are the only Key West accommodation offering a special welcome package for women, and a detailed insider's guide to all Key West activities & attractions of interest to women. We invite you to go native and live like a Key Wester at the ***Island Key Courts.*** For a price similar to that of a standard room-with-bath accommodation, we offer a charming cottage-style Island Residence – a complete, self-contained apartment suite with the convenience and savings of a fully equipped kitchen and the roomy comfort of a Studio Residence, a One-Bedroom Residence or a Two-Bedroom, Two-Bath Residence. (Our residences sleep 1-9 guests!) A real, laid-back hideaway – and all within easy walking distance of downtown bars, boutiques, restaurants and Atlantic beaches!

With our condo format, you will have total peace and privacy: No crowded lobbies, no miles of hallways – most of our 14 units have a private entrance from the garden. There is no intrusive staff, just meticulous daily maid service and friendly concierges ready to direct you to the best of the insider's Key West.

In additon to our best values and reasonable rates, as a guest of the ***Island Key Courts*** you will receive a wonderful, free extra – a complimentary membership to the plush, private beach club at a nearby luxury resort, located just a few blocks from us. You will have unlimited access to a private, sandy beach, a sparkling pool, a complete health club with fully equipped gym and spa, two fabulous restaurants and three tropical bars – plus exciting discounts on food, beverages and gift shop purchases with your Island Key Court Guest Card.

**Address: 910 Simonton St (office) & 817 Catherine St, Key West, FL 33040. Tel: (305) 296-1148, (800) 296-1148, Fax: (305) 292-7924, E-mail: rayebv@aol.com.**

*continued next page*

**Type:** Apartment suites & guestrooms.
**Clientele:** Mostly straight clientele with a strong lesbian following
**Transportation:** Taxi from Key West airport (5-minute drive), car from Miami (3-hour drive).
**To Gay Bars:** 5 blocks, a 7-minute walk, a 3-minute drive.
**Rooms:** 14 apartments with single, queen & king beds, rollaways.
**Bathrooms:** All private: 7 bath/toilets, 7 shower/toilets.
**Vegetarian:** Vegetarian restaurants in town.
**Dates Open:** All year.
**High Season:** Christmas-Easter.
**Rates:** Summer $55-$199, winter $99-$299.
**Discounts:** Various.
**Credit Cards:** MC, Visa, Amex, Diners.
**Rsv'tns:** Required.
**Reserve Through:** Call direct or travel agent.
**Minimum Stay:** Required during holidays & special events.
**Parking:** Adequate free on-street parking.
**In-Room:** Color cable TV, AC, phone, ceiling fans, full kitchen, coffee/tea-making facilities, maid service.
**Exercise/Health:** Complimentary membership at nearby private health club.
**Swimming:** Complimentary membership at same private pool & beach club.
**Sunbathing:** By the pool & at the beach.
**Pets:** Not permitted.
**Handicap Access:** No.
**Children:** Yes.

## La-Te-Da Hotel

**Gay/Lesbian ♀♂**

### *A Place of Fantasy and Fun*

The fabled La Terraza, known affectionately as ***La-Te-Da,*** recently reopened after a total restoration. This European-style hotel is set in a compound, arranged around a glorious private pool framed by tropical palms. The main building houses a gourmet restaurant, a disco and a terrace bar, all with an ambiance of romance and charm. Originally built as a private residence, in 1892 the legendary Cuban patriot, Martí, used the balcony of the main house as a rallying place for raising funds for the liberation of Cuba. ***La-Te-Da*** is within walking distance of all Old Town attractions, as well as beaches, shopping and watersports.

**Address: 1125 Duval St, Key West, FL 33040**
**Tel: (305) 296-6706, (800) 528-3320, Fax: (305) 296-0438.**

**Type:** Hotel with restaurant, show bar.
**Clientele:** Mostly gay & lesbian with some straight clientele
**Transportation:** Car or taxi.
**To Gay Bars:** A 2 minute walk to gay bars.
**Rooms:** 16 rooms with king or queen beds.
**Bathrooms:** All private.
**Vegetarian:** Available on property.
**Complimentary:** One welcome cocktail.
**Dates Open:** All year.
**High Season:** Christmas thru Easter.
**Rates:** Summer $60-$120, winter $120-$240.
**Discounts:** 10% to walk-ins, summer.
**Credit Cards:** MC, Visa, Amex, Discover.
**Reserve Through:** Travel agent or call direct.
**Minimum Stay:** Required during holidays.
**Parking:** Limited on-street parking.
**In-Room:** AC, color cable TV, ceiling fans, telephone, coffee & tea-making facilities, maid & room service.
**On-Premises:** Restaurant, show bar, meeting rooms.
**Exercise/Health:** Nearby gym, weights, Jacuzzi, sauna, massage.
**Swimming:** Pool & ocean on premises.
**Sunbathing:** Poolside, on private & common sun decks, on patio.
**Nudity:** Permitted on clothing-optional sun deck.
**Smoking:** Permitted anywhere. No non-smoking rooms available.
**Pets:** Not permitted.
**Handicap Access:** Yes.
**Children:** No.

## Lightbourn Inn

Q-NET Gay-Friendly ♀♂

### *Your Home Away from Home*

The ***Lightbourn Inn,*** a classic Queen Anne-style mansion, is listed on the national register of historical structures. In 1992, the inn was honored with the Historical Preservation Award and the Key West Chamber of Commerce Business for Beauty Award. The 10 comfortably furnished guest rooms have private bath, television, telephone, air conditioning, and ceiling fan. Our delightful collection of teddy bears is the largest in Key West. Mornings are leisurely outside by the pool area, where a gourmet buffet breakfast is served. Ratings of three-diamonds from AAA and four-palms from Out and About guarantee your comfort.

**Address: 907 Truman Ave, Key West, FL 33040**
**Tel: (305) 296-5152, (800) 352-6011, Fax: (305) 294-9490.**

**Type:** B&B guesthouse.
**Clientele:** 40% gay and lesbian clientele
**Transportation:** Taxi from airport.
**To Gay Bars:** 3 blocks.
**Rooms:** 10 rooms with queen or king beds.
**Bathrooms:** 10 private shower & toilets.
**Meals:** Buffet breakfast.
**Vegetarian:** Available nearby.
**Dates Open:** All year.
**High Season:** Dec 15-May 16.
**Rates:** Summer $88-$188, Winter $128-$188.
**Discounts:** 10% AAA.
**Credit Cards:** MC, VISA, Diners, Discover.
**Rsv'tns:** Required.
**Reserve Through:** Travel agent or call direct.
**Minimum Stay:** Required during hoidays & special events.
**Parking:** Adequate off-street parking.
**In-Room:** AC, telephone, color cable TV, ceiling fans, maid service.
**Exercise/Health:** Nearby gym, weights, Jacuzzi, sauna, steam & massage.
**Swimming:** Pool on premises, ocean nearby.
**Sunbathing:** At poolside & on common sun decks.
**Nudity:** Permitted on upper sun deck.
**Smoking:** Permitted outdoors only.
**Pets:** Not permitted.
**Handicap Access:** Yes.
**Children:** Not especially welcomed.
**Languages:** English.
**Your Host:** Scott & Kelly.

## Lighthouse Court

Men ♂

***Lighthouse Court*** is Key West's largest, most private guest compound. A variety of restored conch houses connected by decking, nestled in lush tropical foliage, it combines the charm of days past with contemporary taste and design. Accommodations include rooms, apartments and suites. Rooms have TV, air conditioning and/or Bahama fans, refrigerators, and many have kitchen facilities. Located one block from historic Duval Street, ***Lighthouse Court*** is a short stroll from shops, galleries, beaches, sailing & snorkeling as well as Key West's famous nite life.

**Address: 902 Whitehead St, Key West, FL 33040. Tel: (305) 294-9588.**

**Type:** Guesthouse with restaurant, bar & health club.
**Clientele:** Men only
**Transportation:** Taxi from airport.
**To Gay Bars:** 1 block to Duval St bars.
**Rooms:** 4 singles, 30 doubles, 4 suites & 4 efficiencies.

*continued next page*

**Bathrooms:** 38 private & 4 shared.
**Vegetarian:** Breakfast & lunch.
**Dates Open:** All year.
**High Season:** Jan 20 thru Easter, Fantasy Fest-late October, New Years' Eve.
**Rates:** $60-$235.
**Credit Cards:** MC, Visa.
**Rsv'tns:** Preferred.
**Reserve Through:** Call direct.
**Minimum Stay:** Required on holidays.
**Parking:** Ample free on-street parking.
**In-Room:** Maid & room service, AC, ceiling fans, fridge, telephone & TV.
**On-Premises:** Meeting rooms, TV lounge, beer-and-wine bar.
**Exercise/Health:** Jacuzzi, health club on premises, gym, weights, massage.
**Swimming:** Pool on premises, ocean beach nearby.
**Sunbathing:** At poolside, on roof, common sun decks, or on beach nearby.
**Nudity:** Permitted.
**Smoking:** Permitted without restrictions.
**Pets:** Not permitted.
**Handicap Access:** Inquire.
**Children:** Not permitted.
**Languages:** English, French.

## Mangrove House

Men ♂

### *Intimate and Friendly in the Key West Tradition*

Located in the centre of historic Old Town Key West, this charming "Eyebrow" house offers spacious and comfortable accommodations exclusively for gay men. Nestled in a lush tropical setting, ***Mangrove House*** is quiet and secluded yet steps away from the heart of Duval Street. All units have private bath, phone, air conditioning and cable TV. Clothing is optional around the beautiful solar-heated pool and hot tub. A copious continental breakfast is served poolside every morning and complimentary refreshments are available throughout the afternoon.

**Address: 623 Southard St, Key West, FL**
**Tel: (800) 294-1866, (305) 294-1866, Fax: (305) 294-8757.**

**Type:** Guesthouse.
**Clientele:** Men only
**Transportation:** Car, taxi from airport, walk from bus depot.
**To Gay Bars:** 2 blocks or a 3-minute walk.
**Rooms:** 2 rooms & 2 apartments with double or queen beds.
**Bathrooms:** 4 private bath/toilets.
**Meals:** Continental breakfast.
**Complimentary:** Refreshments in the afternoon.
**Dates Open:** All year.
**High Season:** December-April.
**Rates:** Low season $70-$110, high season $95-$160, Fantasy Fest $135-$205.
**Discounts:** 10% for stays of 7 or more nights except during Fantasy Fest.
**Credit Cards:** MC, VISA, Amex, Discover.
**Rsv'tns:** Highly recommended.
**Reserve Through:** Travel agent or call direct.
**Minimum Stay:** 3 nights for holidays, 4 nights for Fantasy Fest.
**Parking:** Ample on-street parking on safe residential street.
**In-Room:** Color cable TV, telephone, AC, ceiling fans & maid service. Apartment has kitchen, refrigerator & coffee/tea-making facilities.
**Exercise/Health:** Jacuzzi & weights on premises. Nearby gym, massage.
**Swimming:** Pool on premises. Nearby ocean.
**Sunbathing:** At poolside.
**Nudity:** Permitted in pool area.
**Smoking:** Permitted without restrictions.
**Pets:** Not permitted.
**Handicap Access:** No. 4 steps from street to rooms.
**Children:** Not especially welcome.
**Languages:** English, French, German & Italian.

## Newton Street Station

**Men ♂**

### *Join Us in Our Corner of Paradise*

***Newton Street Station***, formerly the home of the stationmaster of the Florida East Coast Railway, is an intimate guesthouse in a quiet, residential section of Old Town Key West. Rooms are individually-decorated and breakfast is served on the tropical sun deck. Lounge by the pool, nude, if you like, enjoy the tropical gardens, or work out on the exercise deck. Visit shops and galleries, or enjoy some of the finest water sports in the country. ***Newton Street Station*** is one of the friendliest, all-men's guesthouses in Key West, where our goal is to make you feel welcome.

**Address: 1414 Newton St, Key West, FL 33040**
**Tel: (305) 294-4288, (800) 248-2457, Fax: (305) 292-5062.**
**http//www.travelbase.com/destinations/keywest/newton-street-station.**

**Type:** Guesthouse.
**Clientele:** Men only
**Transportation:** Inexpensive taxi ride from airport.
**To Gay Bars:** 5 minutes by car to men's bars.
**Rooms:** 6 rooms & 1 suite with double beds.
**Bathrooms:** 4 private, 2 shared & 1 half-bath.
**Meals:** Cont. breakfast.
**Dates Open:** All year.
**High Season:** Dec 15th-Apr 30th.
**Rates:** Winter $80-$120, summer $60-$80.
**Discounts:** 10% for a week or more, or for members of nudist/naturist groups.
**Credit Cards:** MC, Visa, Amex.
**Rsv'tns:** Highly recommended.
**Reserve Through:** Travel agent or call direct.
**Minimum Stay:** During holidays & special events.
**Parking:** Ample free on-street parking.
**In-Room:** Maid service, color cable TVs, AC, ref, phone, some ceiling fans.
**On-Premises:** TV lounge & free local phone calls.
**Exercise/Health:** Weights & bicycles
**Swimming:** Pool or nearby ocean.
**Sunbathing:** At poolside, on private & common sun decks, or patio.
**Nudity:** Permitted anywhere on premises.
**Smoking:** Permitted without restrictions.
**Languages:** English, limited French & limited German.
**Your Host:** John.

IGTA

## Oasis, A Guest House

**Men ♂**

***Oasis, A Guest House*** is Key West's most elegant guesthouse, a magnificently restored 1895 mansion in the historic district, where you capture the true charm and excitement of this idyllic isle. Multi-level sun decks allow secluded sunbathing, plus breathtaking views of town and gulf. Tastefully-appointed rooms have AC, private bath, color TV, Bahama fans and robes to wear during your visit. We have two of the island's largest private pools (one heated) and Forida's largest Jacuzzi. The sun decks and pools are open 24 hours a day, clothes optional. Share the tranquil beauty of our home and experience our genuine and generous hospitality.

**Address: 823 Fleming Street, Key West, FL 33040**
**Tel: (305) 296-2131 or (800) 362-7477, Fax: (305) 296-5972.**

**Type:** Guesthouse with beer & wine bar.
**Clientele:** Men only
**Transportation:** Taxi from airport.
**To Gay Bars:** 4 blocks to men's/women's bars.
**Rooms:** 19 rooms with queen beds.
**Bathrooms:** 19 private bath/toilets.
**Meals:** Expanded continental breakfast.
**Complimentary:** Wine party every evening with hors d'oeuvres by the main pool.
**Dates Open:** All year.
**High Season:** Jan-April.
**Rates:** Summer $95-$125, winter $145-$179.
**Discounts:** 10% airline travel agents.
**Credit Cards:** MC, Visa, Amex.
**Rsv'tns:** Preferred.
**Reserve Through:** Travel agent or call direct.
**Minimum Stay:** During holidays & special events.
**Parking:** Plenty of on-street parking.
**In-Room:** Maid service, color TV, refrigerator, AC & ceiling fans.
**Exercise/Health:** Jacuzzi.
**Swimming:** 2 large pools on premises.
**Sunbathing:** At poolside or on private sun decks.
**Nudity:** Permitted.
**Smoking:** Permitted without restrictions.
**Languages:** English, Spanish, German & Russian.
**Your Host:** Victor Arguello

IGTA

# Pilot House Guest House & Duval Suites

Gay-Friendly 50/50 ♀♂

## *Home of Southernmost Hospitality*

***Pilot House*** is a grand two-story Victorian mansion built, circa 1900, by Julius Otto as his private home. Today the structure stands proud in the center of the Key West historical district known as Old Town. It boasts verandas and porches with hand-milled spindels and gingerbread trim. After the labored restoration in 1990, receiving the prestigious "Excellence Award for Preservation" by the Florida Keys Preservation Board, we opened the doors to the mansion as a guest residence. ***Pilot House*** is appointed with a careful blend of antiques and decorated with tropical furnishings, accommodating the discriminating tastes of experienced travelers. We offer unique lodging accommodations with six guest rooms to choose from, all with private bath, color cable TV, phone, air conditioning and paddle fans. Newly added to the tropical paradise of the ***Pilot House*** compound are the brand-new poolside cabana suites, which feature in-room Jacuzzis, mini-bars and modern tropical decor. Each has its own outside entrance and selected "smoking-allowed" suites are also available.

A few blocks away, and surrounded by the casual, upscale eateries and galleries of Duval St., are our new ***Duval Suites.*** Each suite has a mini-bar or kitchenette and its own deck overlooking either Duval St. or the tropical garden below. The garden, complete with Jacuzzi, offers shady respite from the world outside. Kayak the Keys with a wildlife expert, take a bicycle tour with a native, discover our tropical reef scuba diving with a pro, see our famous sunset aboard a schooner sailboat. After a full day of fun and sun, come back to our secluded spa and relax in our tropical garden and patio. A casual dinner in a popular eatery and the nightlife of the famous Duval Street is just a half block from our back door. Our staff is on hand to provide you with information to our palm-studded island that only a local can share with you.

**Address: 414 Simonton St & 724 Duval St, Key West, FL 33040**
**Tel: (800) 648-3780, (305) 294-8719, Fax: (305) 294-9298,**
**E-mail: PGuesthous@aol.com.**

**Type:** Guesthouse.
**Clientele:** 50% gay & lesbian & 50% straight clientele
**Transportation:** Taxi.
**To Gay Bars:** 2 blocks.
**Rooms:** PH: 6 rooms, 6 suites w/ dbl or queen beds. DS: 6 rooms w/ queen beds & 1- or 2-br cottages.
**Bathrooms:** All private.
**Dates Open:** All year.
**High Season:** January, February, March.
**Rates:** \$135-\$300 in season, \$85-\$175 off-season.
**Discounts:** 10% weekly.
**Credit Cards:** Visa, Amex, Diners Club, Carte Blanche, Discover, Eurocard.
**Rsv'tns:** Preferred.
**Reserve Through:** Travel agent or call direct.
**Minimum Stay:** 3 nights or more on hol. & spec. events.
**Parking:** Limited public pay parking.
**In-Room:** Color cable TV, private line phone, AC, ceiling fans, queen beds, coffee/tea-making facilities, kitchens, ref., maid service.
**On-Premises:** Botanical garden.
**Exercise/Health:** Jacuzzi, bike rack with nearby rentals.
**Swimming:** Pool at Pilot House, 4 blocks to gulf.
**Sunbathing:** At poolside. On sun deck for penthouse.
**Nudity:** Permitted poolside.
**Smoking:** Permitted on balconies, patios & in cabana rooms.
**Pets:** Not permitted.
**Handicap Access:** Yes.
**Children:** Not especially welcome.
**Languages:** English.

## Pines of Key West

Gay/Lesbian ♂

### *We Host the Nicest People in the World!*

***The Pines,*** Key West's original exclusively gay guesthouse, offers the perfect combination of congenial atmosphere and relaxation. We are located only a few minutes' walk from Key West's finest beaches, bars, shops and restaurants. Join us for continental breakfast on the patio, then sun all day long by our large pool. Our spacious hot tub provides an ideal setting to meet new friends and adapt to Key West's casual island atmosphere. Come to ***The Pines*** and experience the best vacation of your life!

**Address: 521 United St, Key West, FL 33040**
**Tel: (305) 296-7467 or (800) 282-PINE (7463).**

**Type:** Guesthouse.
**Clientele:** Mostly men with women welcome
**Transportation:** Car or taxi from airport.
**To Gay Bars:** All bars within walking distance.
**Rooms:** 14 rooms with double, queen or king beds.
**Bathrooms:** All private.
**Meals:** Continental breakfast.
**Dates Open:** All year.
**High Season:** December 15th-April 30th.
**Rates:** Summer $70-$90, winter $95-$150.
**Discounts:** Weekly rates during summer, approx. $10 off for stays of 7 or more nights.
**Credit Cards:** MC, Visa, Amex, Discover, Diners.
**Rsv'tns:** Recommended.
**Reserve Through:** Call direct or travel agent.
**Minimum Stay:** Fantasy Fest 7 days, summer holidays 3, Xmas/New Years 7.
**Parking:** Adequate, free off-street & on-street parking.
**In-Room:** Color cable TV, telephone, AC, maid service, refrigerator & ceiling fans.
**Exercise/Health:** Jacuzzi.
**Swimming:** Pool on premises, ocean beach 2 blks.
**Sunbathing:** At poolside & 2nd floor sun deck.
**Nudity:** Permitted at poolside or on common sun deck.
**Smoking:** Permitted.
**Pets:** Not permitted.
**Children:** Not permitted.
**Languages:** English.

IGTA

## Rainbow House

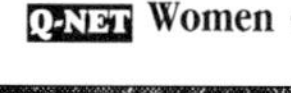

Women ♀

### *Welcome to Paradise!*

At the ***Rainbow House,*** we have everything from a standard room to a deluxe suite. All of our rooms have queen-sized beds, color TV, telephones, air conditioning, as well as Bahama fans and, of course, private bath. We serve an expanded continental breakfast poolside every morning. Enjoy it in our air conditioned pavilion or poolside. It's complimentary to our guests and a wonderful social setting. After breakfast, lounge on one of the sunbathing decks, or sit in the shade while you read a book with the gentle island breezes rustling the palm trees above.

As relaxing and comfortable as the guesthouse is, you may want to venture

*continued next page*

out to have fun. We can take care of that, too. We have a full-time concierge to help with snorkeling, scuba, kayaking, parasailing, bike trails, beaches, and, of course, Key West's many different restaurants. Just turn the corner of our street, and start your shopping exodus. Duval Street has everything you can imagine, from art galleries to T-shirts, from jewelers to sushi bars. Of course, while you're in Key West, you'll have to experience one of our fabulous sunsets. They light up the sky and they're always memorable. And why not watch the sunset from Mallory Square, where you'll see jugglers, sword swallowers, tightrope walkers and characters that'll make you say "Only in Key West!"

There's plenty of nightlife, from rock-and-roll to disco, from piano bars to jazz, all within walking distance. As a matter of fact, most of our guests park their cars and leisurely stroll the streets of Old Town Key West. Whatever your vacation needs are...peace and quiet, the laid-back life, sun and fun, romantic or rejuvenating...pamper yourself with the special atmosphere we've created for you at the ***Rainbow House.***

**Address: 525 United St, Key West, FL 33040**
**Tel: (305) 292-1450, (800) 74-WOMYN (800 749-6696).**

**Type:** Bed & breakfast guesthouse.
**Clientele:** Women only
**To Gay Bars:** 5-minute walk to gay/lesbian bars.
**Rooms:** 15 rms & 9 suites.
**Bathrooms:** All private.
**Meals:** Expanded continental breakfast.
**Dates Open:** All year.
**High Season:** Jan-April.
**Rates:** $69-$189.
**Credit Cards:** MC, VISA, Discover, Preferred, Amex.
**Rsv'tns:** Strongly recommended.
**Reserve Through:** Call direct or travel agent.
**Minimum Stay:** During holidays.
**Parking:** On-street parking.
**In-Room:** Maid service, color TV, phones, AC. Kitchens available.
**Exercise/Health:** Jacuzzi.
**Swimming:** In pool or 1 block to ocean.
**Sunbathing:** At poolside, on private sun decks or on ocean beach.
**Nudity:** Permitted poolside.
**Handicap Access:** One unit available.
**Children:** Not permitted.
**Languages:** English.
**Your Host:** Marion.

IGTA

## Sea Isle Resort

**Men ♂**

### *More than a Guesthouse...Paradise*

***Sea Isle*** is in the very heart of Old Town Key West, close to beaches, water sports of both the Gulf and the Atlantic and a short stroll from shops, restaurants, art galleries and nightspots. You'll be impressed with your guest room. It's comfortable, handsome and immaculate, with private bath, air conditioning and telephone. Stay in good shape using our Nautilus equipment and free weights. Swim in the pool, then stretch out on the poolside deck or the secluded sun decks; all clothing optional.

**Address: 915 Windsor Lane, Key West, FL 33040**
**Tel: (305) 294-5188 or (800) 995-4786, Fax: (305) 296-7143.**

**Type:** Resort/compound.
**Clientele:** Mostly gay men
**To Gay Bars:** 3 blocks.
**Rooms:** 16 doubles, 6 quads & 2 suites.
**Bathrooms:** All private.
**Meals:** Cont. breakfast.
**Complimentary:** Cocktail parties on weekends.
**Dates Open:** All year.
**High Season:** Dec-April.
**Rates:** For 2 people, summer $75-$185, winter $110-$250, extra person $20 per night.
**Credit Cards:** MC, Visa, Amex, Discover.
**Rsv'tns:** Strongly suggested.
**Reserve Thru:** Call direct.
**Minimum Stay:** In winter & on holidays.
**Parking:** Ample off-street parking.
**In-Room:** Color TV, telephone, AC & mini-ref.
**On-Premises:** Lrg priv. courtyard.
**Exercise/Health:** Nautilus, free weights & hot tub.
**Swimming:** Large, climate-controlled pool on premises, ocean beach nearby.
**Sunbathing:** At poolside, on beach, on private sun decks.
**Nudity:** Permitted.
**Smoking:** Permitted without restrictions.
**Pets:** $10.00 add'l charge per day for pets.
**Handicap Access:** With assistance.
**Children:** Not permitted.
**Languages:** English.
**Your Host:** Randy & Jim.

IGTA

# Sheraton Key West All-Suite Resort

Gay-Friendly ♀♂

## *Island Suites in the Key West Tradition*

***Sheraton Key West,*** an all-suite hotel, is located right across from popular Smathers Beach on the Atlantic Ocean side of the island. Our friendly staff will meet your every need and you'll enjoy the familiar Sheraton service and quality that you have come to depend on. All of our accommodations are comfortable suites with lots of room and amenities. There is free shuttle service into Old Town and we offer moped rental services. Rooms include a wet bar, microwave and coffee maker. We also offer a fitness center and pool with cascading waterfall.

**Address: 2001 S Roosevelt Blvd, Key West, FL 33040**
**Tel: (305) 292-9800, Fax: (305) 294-6009.**

**Type:** Resort with restaurant, shops & bar.
**Clientele:** Mostly straight clientele with a gay/lesbian following
**Transportation:** Hotel car or taxi from airport. Pick up from airport.
**To Gay Bars:** 1.5 miles, a 10-minute drive.
**Rooms:** 180 suites with double or king beds.
**Bathrooms:** All private bath/toilets.
**Vegetarian:** In restaurant on property.
**Complimentary:** Coffee & tea in all suites.
**Dates Open:** All year.
**High Season:** Dec 22-Apr 15.
**Rates:** High season $200-$450, low season $140-$300.
**Discounts:** AAA, AARP.
**Credit Cards:** MC, Visa, Amex, Diners, Eurocard, Discover.
**Rsv'tns:** Suggested.
**Reserve Through:** Travel agent or call direct.
**Parking:** Ample free off-street parking.
**In-Room:** AC, telephone, color cable TV, coffee & tea-making facilities, refrigerator, maid & room service.
**On-Premises:** Laundry facilities, meeting rooms.
**Exercise/Health:** Gym, weights, Jacuzzi.
**Swimming:** Pool. Ocean nearby.
**Sunbathing:** Poolside, on private sun decks, at beach.
**Smoking:** Permitted in rooms. Non-smoking rooms available.
**Pets:** Not permitted.
**Handicap Access:** Yes.
**Children:** Welcome. There are poolside activities & toys.
**Languages:** English, German, Spanish, Portuguese.

IGTA

## Simonton Court Historic Inn & Cottages

**Gay-Friendly 50/50 ♀♂**

### *Once You Stay Here, You'll Always Come Back*

***Simonton Court*** is an elegant, yet relaxed retreat for body and soul in the heart of Old Town Key West, America's Caribbean island. A collection of gracefully restored Old Town Key West buildings, the property dates from the 1880s and Key West's cigar-making era. It is an *exceptionally* romantic, quiet resort setting for adults, perfectly situated less than a block from lively Duval Street and just three blocks from Key West's harbor and Mallory Square. All forms of entertainment – unique shops, excellent restaurants, live theater and a bar for everyone's taste – are only a short walk away. America's only living coral reef makes for some of the finest diving, snorkeling, fishing and boating experiences anywhere in the world.

A lovely private garden compound, with hot tub and three separate pools, brick paths, tin roofs, French doors and lush foliage canopies create the ambiance for three levels of accommodation. An old cigar-makers' factory, now the Inn, and a building called the Manor House, offer charming rooms, each unique and each with either kitchenette or refrigerator. Cottages, with wood floors and wicker furniture, are ideal for 2-6 people, with 2-3 separate sleeping areas and private porches and/or decks. The Mansion, built in the Victorian era, is now the property's most elegant accommodation, offering an unsurpassed level of service. Some of the Mansion's suites have outdoor decks, and one has a most private widow's walk for sweeping panoramic views of the city and ocean, with an in-room Jacuzzi – *very* romantic! A few rooms can be combined into suites; two rooms in the Manor House form a private suite with a pool and deck for the exclusive use of the suite when combined.

The staff is friendly and helpful, but low-key, never intrusive. A luscious complimentary continental breakfast is served every morning and can be carried into one of many garden alcoves or porches.

**Address: 320 Simonton St, Key West, FL 33040**
**Tel: (800) 944-2687, (305) 294-6386, Fax: (305) 293-8446.**

**Type:** Cottage inn.
**Clientele:** 50% gay & lesbian & 50% straight clientele
**Transportation:** Taxi or airport shuttle 10 min from airport.
**To Gay Bars:** 4 blocks to gay & lesbian bars.
**Rooms:** 2 rooms, 14 suites & 6 cottages with bunk, double, queen or king beds.
**Bathrooms:** All private shower/toilets.
**Meals:** Expanded continental breakfast.
**Vegetarian:** Vegetarian food available at several restaurants within 4 blocks.
**Dates Open:** All year.
**High Season:** Dec 15-May 1 & all national holidays.
**Rates:** In season $150-$350, mid season $130-$255, low season $110-$200.
**Discounts:** Airline.
**Credit Cards:** MC, VISA, Amex & Discover.
**Rsv'tns:** Recommended.
**Reserve Through:** Travel agent or call direct.
**Minimum Stay:** 2 days weekends, 5 days Christmas, New Year, Fantasy Fest, 4 days high season.
**Parking:** Ample on-street or pay parking.
**In-Room:** Color cable TV, VCR, AC, phone, ceiling fans, fridge., coffee tea-makers, maid service. Some units with kitchens.
**Exercise/Health:** Hot tub.
**Swimming:** 3 heated pools. 3 blocks to beach.
**Sunbathing:** At poolside or on beach.
**Smoking:** Permitted without restrictions.
**Languages:** English.

IGTA

# MIAMI - SOUTH BEACH

## Colours, The Mantell Guest Inn

Gay/Lesbian ♀♂

### *Experience Not Just a Place, But a State of Mind*

Close your eyes and imagine a boardwalk, white sandy beaches, turquoise waters, warm ocean breezes, a refreshing late afternoon swim in a secluded tropical pool under swaying palms and clear blue skies, the culinary delights of South Beach's finest restaurants, and dancing 'til dawn at the hottest clubs. All of this is possible when you stay at ***Colours, The Mantell Guest Inn,*** a historic art deco hotel, completely renovated in 1994. The 25+ uniquely appointed studios have kitchens; some have terraces and ocean views. Speak to our reservations staff about Colours' other distinctive lodgings: ***Colours, The Guest Mansion*** in romantic Key West, and ***Hotel Colours, The Guest Residence*** in San Jose, Costa Rica.

**Address: 255 West 24th St, South Miami Beach, FL 33140**
**Tel: (305) 538-1821 Local. Reservations: (800) ARRIVAL, (305) 532-9341, Fax: (305) 534-0362.**

**Type:** Hotel inn guesthouse.
**Clientele:** Mostly gay & lesbian with some straight clientele
**Transportation:** Super shuttle from Miami Int'l Airport. Pick up from airport $20-$30 roundtrip per person.
**To Gay Bars:** 2 blocks or a 5-minute walk.
**Rooms:** 25+ studios with single, double or queen beds.
**Bathrooms:** All private bath/toilets.
**Meals:** Expanded continental breakfast.
**Dates Open:** All year.
**High Season:** November-May.
**Rates:** Summer (June-Oct) $59-$139, winter $79-$159.
**Discounts:** Single occupancy, length of stay, method of payment & prepayment.
**Credit Cards:** MC, Visa, Amex & Discover.
**Rsv'tns:** Recommended.
**Reserve Through:** Travel agent or call direct.
**Minimum Stay:** Required for certain events, holidays.
**Parking:** Adequate free on-street parking.
**In-Room:** Color TV, AC, telephone, kitchen, refrigerator, coffee/tea-making facilities & maid service.
**On-Premises:** Laundry facilities & fax.
**Exercise/Health:** Gym & weights on premises. Nearby Jacuzzi, sauna, steam & massage.
**Swimming:** Pool on premises, ocean nearby.
**Sunbathing:** At poolside, beach, on patio & common & private sun decks.
**Nudity:** At your own option.
**Smoking:** No smoking in TV lounge. Non-smoking rooms available.
**Pets:** Not permitted.
**Handicap Access:** Not fully.
**Children:** Adult-oriented hotel, children not especially welcomed.
**Languages:** English, Spanish & French.

IGTA

## European Guest House

Q-NET Gay/Lesbian ♀♂

Enjoy old world charm and beautifully-appointed rooms with unexpected modern amenities at ***European Guest House,*** South Beach's only gay bed & breakfast. We're 6 blocks from sandy beaches. The legendary moonlight, balmy ocean breezes and golden, sun-baked days are here for the taking. Air conditioning, refrigerator, private baths and remote control cable TV are in each room, while a hot tub and tropical gardens outside await your pleasure. Our low rates and laid-back atmosphere make your vacation most memorable.

**Address: 721 Michigan Ave, Miami Beach, FL 33139**
**Tel: (305) 673-6665, Fax: (305) 672-7442,**
**E-mail: sobegaybb@aol.com.**

**Type:** Bed & breakfast guesthouse.
**Clientele:** Good mix of gay men & women
**Transportation:** City shuttle from airport, $10.
**To Gay Bars:** 10-min walk from gay/lesbian bars.
**Rooms:** 10 rooms & 2 suites with queen or king beds.
**Bathrooms:** 8 private, 4 shared.
**Meals:** Full buffet breakfast.
**Complimentary:** Coffee all day, pastries in the afternoon.
**Dates Open:** All year.
**High Season:** November-April.
**Rates:** Summer $59-$89, winter $69-$99.
**Discounts:** On weekly or monthly stays. May-Nov '97: 3 nights $119, 1wk $269, single occ., some exceptions may apply.
**Credit Cards:** MC, Visa, Amex, Diners, Discover.
**Rsv'tns:** Recommended, 4 wks in advance.
**Reserve Through:** Travel agent or call direct.
**Minimum Stay:** 3 days on major holidays.
**Parking:** Ample free off-street parking.
**In-Room:** Maid service, AC, telephone, refrigerator, remote control cable TV.
**On-Premises:** Meeting rooms, laundry facilities, private dining room, TV lounge, sun deck and tropical garden.
**Exercise/Health:** Jacuzzi.
**Swimming:** Ocean beach 5 blocks from house.
**Sunbathing:** Near jacuzzi, on beach, private or common sun decks or patio.
**Nudity:** Permitted.
**Smoking:** Not permitted in rooms, but allowed everywhere else.
**Pets:** Permitted.
**Handicap Access:** No.
**Children:** Not permitted.
**Languages:** English, Spanish, French, German.

## The Jefferson House

Gay/Lesbian ♀♂

***THE House on the Beach...***

is ***Jefferson House,*** located in the midst of the historical Art Deco District of South Beach. Famous Miami Beach and exciting Ocean Drive are a few blocks from our door, as are the diverse restaurants and clubs of the area. All of our air conditioned rooms have private baths and queen-sized beds, and are tastefully appointed to add warmth and charm. Enjoy the friendly hospitality of a fine breakfast served on our deck overlooking a lovely tropical garden and pool. Come and experience the camaraderie that ***The Jefferson House*** has to offer.

**Address: 1018 Jefferson Ave, Miami Beach, FL 33139**
**Tel: (305) 534-5247, Fax: (305) 534-5953.**

**Type:** Bed & Breakfast.
**Clientele:** Mostly gay & lesbian with some straight clientele.
**Transportation:** Car, taxi, shuttle or bus.
**To Gay Bars:** 3 blocks. A 5-minute walk or 2-minute drive.
**Rooms:** 6 rooms & 1 suite with queen beds.
**Bathrooms:** All private shower/toilets.
**Meals:** Full breakfast.
**Vegetarian:** Available upon request.
**Complimentary:** Set-up service.
**Dates Open:** All year.
**High Season:** Dec 15-Mar 15 & holidays.
**Rates:** High season $95-$150, mid season $75-$120.
**Discounts:** TAC 10%.
**Credit Cards:** MC, Visa, Amex.
**Rsv'tns:** Required.
**Reserve Through:** Travel agent or call direct.
**Minimum Stay:** Required on weekends.
**Parking:** Limited on-street parking.
**In-Room:** TV, AC, radio, maid service & phones with free local calls.
**On-Premises:** Laundry facilities.
**Exercise/Health:** Nearby gym, weights, tennis, track & basketball. Special rates for guests.
**Swimming:** Pool on premises, ocean nearby.
**Sunbathing:** On the patio or at the beach.
**Smoking:** Permitted anywhere.
**Pets:** Not permitted.
**Handicap Access:** No.
**Children:** Not especially welcome.
**Languages:** English, Spanish & a little German.
**Your Host:** Jonathan & Jeffrey.

IGTA

## Miami River Inn

**Gay-Friendly ♀♂**

### *Enjoy the Charm of the Past Complemented by the Technology of Today*

***Miami River Inn*** is located in the ethnically diverse Miami River Neighborhood of East Little Havana. Centrally located across the Miami River from downtown, the inn is an oasis in the heart of Miami. The "compound" consists of five wooden cottages surrounding a pool and Jacuzzi in a lush tropical setting full of flowers,soaring palms and other native greenery. South Beach, Coconut Grove, Key Biscayne and Coral Gables are all within a 15-minute drive. Downtown & Little Havana are within walking distance.

**Address: 118 SW South River Dr, Miami, FL 33130**
**Tel: (305) 325-0045, (800) HOTEL 89 (468-3589), Fax: (305) 325-9227,**
**E-mail: miami100@ix.netcom.com.**

**Type:** Bed & breakfast with furnished apartments.
**Clientele:** Mostly straight clientele with a gay & lesbian following.
**Transportation:** Car is best. Taxi or SuperShuttle from airport. Pick up for large parties can be arranged for a fee.
**To Gay Bars:** 5 miles or a 10-minute drive.
**Rooms:** 40 rooms & 14 apartments with single, double, queen or king beds.
**Bathrooms:** All private.
**Meals:** Expanded continental breakfast.
**Vegetarian:** Available at nearby restaurants.
**Complimentary:** Glass of wine at check-in.
**Dates Open:** All year.
**High Season:** November-April.
**Rates:** Nov 1-Apr 30 $89-$125, May 1-Oct 31 $69-$125.
**Discounts:** Gov't rate $59, AAA 10%, AARP 10%, Airline & travel 25%.
**Credit Cards:** MC, VISA, Amex, Diners, Discover & Carte Blanche.
**Rsv'tns:** Preferred. Necessary during high season.
**Reserve Through:** Call direct.
**Parking:** Ample free parking in enclosed lot. Locked at night with guest access.
**In-Room:** Color cable TV, AC, ceiling fans, telephone & maid service.
**On-Premises:** Lounge, meeting rooms, fax, copier, conference call & laundry facilities (coin operated).
**Exercise/Health:** Jacuzzi on premises. Nearby gym, Jacuzzi, sauna, steam, massage, walking/running path, tennis & golf.
**Swimming:** Pool on premises.
**Sunbathing:** At poolside.
**Smoking:** Prohibited in rooms & closed public spaces.
**Pets:** Permitted if guests stay in an apartment for a week or more.
**Handicap Access:** Yes. General access & rooms.
**Children:** Welcome.
**Languages:** English, Spanish.
**Your Host:** Sallye, Jane & Adam.

## Normandy South

Q-NET Men ♂

### *If Gauguin Had Stopped Here, He May Never Have Made it to Tahiti!*

Standing on a palm-lined street in a quiet, safe, residential neighborhood close to the convention center, ***Normandy South*** is a Mediterranean revival home among similar architectural gems dating from Art Deco's heyday, the Roaring 20s.

Within easy walking distance of South Beach's ever-expanding choice of gay clubs, trendy restaurants and chic (and funky!) shops, we welcome the sophisticated male traveler who demands a prime location, luxury and elegance without formality and stuffiness.

Guest accommodations are generous, each with a new marble and tile bath en suite, and are poshly furnished with queen- and king-sized beds, exciting, original art and colorful dhurries. In addition to three doubles and three suites (one with its own terrace) in the main house, there are two doubles in the carriage house at the opposite end of the spectacular "Miami Vice" pool.

When not out dancing, shopping or cruising the gay beaches, guests are encouraged to lounge poolside, perfecting a no-tan-line tan, socialize in the Jacuzzi or work off those extra piña coladas in the 44-foot lap lane. For a change of pace, one can slip off to the shaded grotto and luxuriate in the hot tub beneath a thatched chickee, or snooze in the oversized hammock. As might be expected in this tropical hideaway, clothing is optional both inside and outside. Should one choose, a freshly-plucked hibiscus or jasmine tucked behind one's ear is raiment enough. What is not optional is smoking. Guests are strictly limited to non-smokers, no exceptions. Here, one is free to enjoy, without interference, the freshly-scented ocean breezes and fragrant blossoms that abound.

**Address: Miami Beach, FL**
**Tel: (305) 674-1197, Fax: (305) 532-9771.**

**Type:** Guesthouse.
**Clientele:** Men only
**Transportation:** Super Shuttle or taxi direct from airport to guesthouse.
**To Gay Bars:** 10 minutes to Warsaw, Westend, Hombre, Twist, Kremlin, Salvation, Loading Zone & others.
**Rooms:** 5 rooms & 3 suites with queen or king beds.
**Bathrooms:** All private.
**Meals:** Tropical continental breakfast.
**Dates Open:** All year.
**High Season:** November through April.
**Rates:** Winter $100-$150, summer $80-$120.
**Credit Cards:** MC, Visa & Amex.
**Rsv'tns:** Recommended.
**Reserve Through:** Travel agent or call direct.
**Minimum Stay:** Varies with season & holiday.
**Parking:** Ample, free off-street parking.
**In-Room:** Full-range cable TV, central air, maid & complimentary laundry service, refrigerator, VCR w/fun flics, ceiling fans.
**Exercise/Health:** Gym & Jacuzzi with massage by appointment.
**Swimming:** Heated pool w/ lap lane on premises. Five minutes to gay beaches.
**Sunbathing:** At poolside, on private or common sun decks & at public beaches.
**Nudity:** Clothing optional inside, poolside, on sun decks, in grotto, at nude gay beach.
**Smoking:** Accommodations are for non-smokers only.
**Pets:** Permitted with prior arrangement.
**Handicap Access:** No.
**Children:** Not permitted.
**Your Host:** Hank & Bruce.

IGTA

## Richmond Hotel

Gay-Friendly ♂

### *A Truly Distinctive South Beach Experience*

***The Richmond*** represents a return to a gentler era when Miami Beach was the winter capital of North America. Launched prior to the outbreak of World War II, it was the creation of a modern-day Marco Polo whose travels took him from the capitals of Europe to the trade routes of Asia and, finally, to the warm sands of South Florida. ***The Richmond*** was designed by Miami Beach's most famous Art Deco architect, L. Murray Dixon, and was one of the first oceanfront hotels on Collins Avenue. The restoration of this oceanfront Art Deco masterpiece in the heart of South Beach has resulted in the creation of a small luxury hotel offering beautiful accommodation in a fabulous location. Its service is reminiscent of the days when our guests were picked up by our Woody station wagon at Miami's old FEC railway station and were greeted personally by our parents and grandparents.

As part of our effort to create a truly distinctive South Beach experience, the Verandah dining terrace offers fantastic creations combining the savory tastes of the Old South with great American favorites, all served in South Beach's most romantic setting. Guests enjoy a free, deluxe continental breakfast every morning as the sun begins to rise over the sparkling blue waters of the Atlantic. A wonderful place for a gay or lesbian holiday, its perfect location is a short walk to the gay beach, the pulsating night clubs and world-famous Ocean Drive and Lincoln Road. Shopping, dining, dancing until dawn... all just steps away from the most peaceful oasis in South Beach – ***The Richmond.***

**Address: 1757 Collins Ave, Miami Beach, FL 33139**
**Tel: (305) 538-2331, (800) 327-3163, Fax: (305) 531-9021.**

**Type:** Hotel with restaurant.
**Clientele:** Mostly straight with a gay male following
**Transportation:** From airport: taxi $23 or Super Shuttle $10 per person.
**To Gay Bars:** 5 blocks, an 8 min walk, a 2 min drive.
**Rooms:** 99 rooms with queen beds.
**Bathrooms:** 99 private bath/toilets.
**Meals:** Continental breakfast.
**Dates Open:** All year.
**High Season:** Dec-April.
**Rates:** Winter $145-$225, summer $125-$165.
**Discounts:** Corporate rates available.
**Credit Cards:** MC, Visa, Diners, Amex.
**Rsv'tns:** Required.
**Reserve Through:** Travel agent or call direct.
**Minimum Stay:** 3-night minimum required during certain holiday periods.
**Parking:** Adequate off-street pay parking. Valet only: $12 overnight, unlimited in/out.
**In-Room:** AC, color cable TV, telephone, maid, room & laundry service.
**On-Premises:** Meeting rooms, business services.
**Exercise/Health:** Gym & Jacuzzi on premises. Nearby weights, sauna, steam, massage.
**Swimming:** Pool & ocean on premises.
**Sunbathing:** Poolside, on private sun decks, at beach.
**Smoking:** Permitted in hotel common areas & guest rooms. Non-smoking rooms available.
**Handicap Access:** Yes.
**Children:** No.
**Languages:** English, Portuguese, Spanish, French, Creole.
**Your Host:** Pat & Allan.

IGTA

# Your Private Art Deco Apartment in South Beach

Gay ♂

## *Feel the Flavor... Taste the Atmosphere of South Beach and Miami*

Choose between our two apartments situated in a beautifully-landscaped Art Deco structure directly across from Flamingo Park in Miami's South Beach. The building, just five minutes from the beach at Ocean Drive, has two apartments, which together occupy the entire second floor. The identical layouts include two bedrooms, two bathrooms, a living room with a small balcony, a dining room and a fully-equipped kitchen. All rooms are of ample dimensions and have central air conditioning and heat. Both apartments are furnished in the Art Deco style. One of them was even featured in *House and Garden* magazine. Above ***Your Private Art Deco Apartment*** is a large decked roof garden for sunning, entertaining and barbecues.

Flamingo Park has twenty-two tennis courts, all open to the public. Some of the best tennis "pros" in the country are available for training sessions by easily-arranged appointment. But, if you enjoy gay nightlife, you may find it difficult to schedule a morning lesson, for South Beach's gay scene has enough variety to keep you partying every night till the wee hours.

Many of the buildings in the area have been purchased and restored by gay people whose creative renovations have turned South Beach into an architectural showplace. Lots of clever retail ideas have been turned into reality, so be prepared to window shop at least part of the time. The South Beach atmosphere is distinctively its own... relaxed, with a perpetual undercurrent of excitement. On your way across the causeway to Miami, you see brilliant white cruise ships with colorful smoke stacks moving sedately into and out of the harbor. Cross over and feel the faster pulse of Miami, sample the Latin dance bars, or visit one of the many Cuban restuarants for authentic Cuban dishes, like fried plantains, black bean soup, or rice with moros.

**Address: New York Bed & Breakfast Reservation Service, Suite 221, 331 West 57th St, New York, NY 10019**
**Tel: (212) 977-3512, (800) 747-0868.**

**Type:** Private apartments.
**Clientele:** Gay
**Transportation:** Taxi.
**To Gay Bars:** 3 blocks.
**Rooms:** 2 apartments with queen beds.
**Bathrooms:** Private.
**Dates Open:** All year.
**Credit Cards:** Amex.
**Rsv'tns:** Required.
**Reserve Through:** Travel agent or call direct.
**Minimum Stay:** 1 week.
**Parking:** Adequate on- & off-street parking.
**In-Room:** AC, color cable TV, telephone, kitchen, coffee & tea-making facilities.
**Swimming:** Ocean nearby.
**Sunbathing:** On roof.
**Handicap Access:** No.
**Children:** Welcome.
**Languages:** English, French, Spanish.

# ORLANDO

## Things Worth Remembering

Gay/Lesbian ♀♂

### *Movie, Television, Broadway & Sports Memorabilia*

Dustin Hoffman's bust from the movie "Hook," Jane Alexander's dress from "The Great White Hope," and Christina Ricci's pajama's from "Mermaids" are among the items for you to view at ***Things Worth Remembering,*** a B&B decorated with collectibles, memorabilia and autographs. Whether you choose to relax among the collectibles, stroll through our garden with its blooming rose bushes, or simply watch the birds in flight, this will be a vacation you will never forget. Your hosts are business professionals with many interesting inside stories from their years as Disney World employees.

**Address: 7338 Cabor Ct, Orlando, FL 32818**
**Tel: (407) 291-2127 (Tel/Fax, call before faxing), (800) 484-3585 (code 6908).**

**Type:** Bed & breakfast.
**Clientele:** Gay & lesbian. Good mix of men & women
**Transportation:** Car is best. Free pick up from airport, train & bus.
**To Gay Bars:** A 15 min drive to gay bars.
**Rooms:** 1 room with queen bed.
**Bathrooms:** Private bath/toilet.
**Campsites:** Front drive parking with electric hook up for 1 RV.
**Meals:** Continental breakfast.
**Vegetarian:** Full access to kitchen. Special requests OK.
**Complimentary:** Guest fridge with drinks, water, snacks.
**Dates Open:** All year.
**Rates:** $65-$75.
**Discounts:** 10% discount if you mention Inn Places ad. Stay 1 week, 7th day free.
**Rsv'tns:** Required.
**Reserve Through:** Travel agent or call direct.
**Parking:** Adequate free off-street parking.
**In-Room:** AC, ceiling fans, telephone, color cable TV, VCR, kitchen, refrigerator, coffee & tea-making facilities, maid & laundry service.
**On-Premises:** Video tape library.
**Exercise/Health:** Nearby gym, weights, Jacuzzi, sauna, steam, massage.
**Swimming:** Nearby pool, ocean, river, lake & water parks.
**Sunbathing:** On patio.
**Smoking:** Permitted outside only.
**Pets:** Not permitted.
**Handicap Access:** Please inquire.
**Languages:** English.
**Your Host:** James & Lindsey.

# ST PETERSBURG - CLEARWATER

## The Frog Pond Guesthouse

Gay-Friendly 50/50 ♀♂

### *"Build a Pond and They Will Come"*

Named for the croaking amphibians that inhabited the garden pond when it was built, ***The Frog Pond Guesthouse*** offers its guests a relaxing atmosphere in a unique setting. Its features include vintage and wicker furniture, queen-sized beds, hardwood floors, French doors, a spacious patio, and a billiards/game room. Take a sunset stroll along the water or watch the sailboats at the pier. Located in the historical district of St. Petersburg's Old Northeast, the guesthouse is conveniently located to the Gulf beaches, Florida International and Dali Museums, Busch Gardens, and Florida Aquarium in Tampa. It's only 90 minutes to Disney World and other major attractions in Orlando.

**Address: 145 29th Avenue North, St. Petersburg, FL 33704**
**Tel: (813) 823-7407 (Tel/Fax), Fax: (813) 620-1040,**
**E-mail: wenrob@aol.com.**

*continued next page*

**Type:** Guesthouse with garden pond.
**Clientele:** 50% gay & lesbian & 50% straight clientele.
**Transportation:** Car is best, airport shuttle available.
**To Gay Bars:** A 5-minute drive, 30-minute drive to Tampa bars.
**Rooms:** 1-bedroom apartment with queen bed.
**Bathrooms:** 1 private bath/toilet/shower.
**Meals:** Continental breakfast upon arrival.
**Vegetarian:** Vegetarian restaurants 5 minutes away.
**Complimentary:** Tea, coffee in room, mints on pillows, fresh flowers & other amenities.
**Dates Open:** All year.
**High Season:** December 15-May 31.
**Rates:** High season $65/night, low season $55/night.
**Discounts:** Weekly & monthly discounts.
**Credit Cards:** MC, VISA.
**Rsv'tns:** Recommended.
**Reserve Through:** Travel agent or call direct.
**Minimum Stay:** 2 nights on weekends.
**Parking:** Ample free off-street parking.
**In-Room:** Color cable TV, VCR, ceiling fans, AC, kitchen, refrigerator, coffee/tea-making facilities
**On-Premises:** Fax, typing & computer service, video tape library, laundry facilities.
**Exercise/Health:** Nearby gym with weights & massage.
**Swimming:** Nearby pool & ocean.
**Sunbathing:** On beach & patio.
**Smoking:** Permitted outside.
**Pets:** Not permitted.
**Languages:** English.
**Your Host:** Wendy.

## Sea Oats by the Gulf

**Gay-Friendly 50/50 ♀♂**

***Sea Oats,*** on lovely Treasure Island, is minutes from St. Petersburg, directly on the Gulf of Mexico. The hotel, with its traditional Key West charm, is modern with beautifully-appointed apartments, efficiencies and studios overlooking the Gulf. Rooms are individually climate controlled, have color cable TV and fully-equipped kitchenette with microwave. Other amenities include a private yard bordered by palm trees and an eight person Jacuzzi. John's Pass, where you can charter boats, go parasailing, take dinner cruises or enjoy many fine restaurants and shops, is one block away. We are AAA approved.

**Address: 12625 Sunshine Lane, Treasure Island, FL 33706**
**Tel: (813) 367-7568 , Fax: (813) 397-4157.**

**Type:** Motel.
**Clientele:** 50% gay & lesbian & 50% straight clientele.
**Transportation:** Car is best. Limo from Tampa airport available. $10 each way (40 minute ride).
**To Gay Bars:** All within 5-20 minutes.
**Rooms:** 1 room & 10 apartments with double & queen beds.
**Bathrooms:** 7 private shower/toilets & 4 private bath/toilet/showers.
**Dates Open:** All year.
**High Season:** Jan-May.
**Rates:** Low $35-$95, high $50-$110.
**Discounts:** 2 week or longer stay.
**Credit Cards:** MC & VISA.
**Reserve Thru:** Call direct.
**Minimum Stay:** Required weekends only, Fri/Sat.
**Parking:** Adequate free on-street parking.
**In-Room:** Color cable TV, AC, kitchen, refrigerator, coffee/tea-making facilities, maid & laundry service. Some with ceiling fans.
**On-Premises:** Laundry facilities.
**Exercise/Health:** Jacuzzi on premises. Nearby gym.
**Swimming:** Ocean on the premises & nearby.
**Sunbathing:** On the patio, in the backyard or at beach.
**Nudity:** Permitted in Jacuzzi area if you book it.
**Smoking:** Permitted.
**Pets:** Permitted. Extra flat $10 fee. Small dog, no cats.
**Children:** Welcome if well-behaved.
**Languages:** English.
**Your Host:** JoAnn & Christie.

# SARASOTA

## The Dragon's Den

**Gay/Lesbian ♂**

### *A Special Place to Stay in Sarasota*

Sarasota is the cultural center of Florida's Gulf Coast, offering beautiful beaches, museums, art galleries and theater galore! Just minutes away from all of this is ***The Dragon's Den,*** a private guest suite, located in a lovely home in a park-like setting. The suite includes a bedroom, full bath and a sitting room with its own private entrance. After a full day of activity, relax in total privacy in the sparkling pool and adjoining ceramic tile hot tub. Shopping, restaurants and gay bars are nearby. Everyone is welcome here.

**Address: Sarasota, FL. Tel: (941) 923-2646.**

**Type:** B&B guesthouse.
**Clientele:** Mostly men with women welcome
**Transportation:** Car is necessary.
**To Gay Bars:** 3-5 miles, 10-minute drive.
**Rooms:** 1 suite with double bed.
**Bathrooms:** Private bath/toilet/shower.
**Meals:** Continental breakfast.
**Vegetarian:** Available nearby.
**Complimentary:** Wine, beer, cocktail on arrival, setups available.
**Dates Open:** All year.
**High Season:** Dec 15-Apr 15.
**Rates:** Single $30, double $50.
**Discounts:** 7th day free.
**Rsv'tns:** Required with 1st night's deposit.
**Reserve Through:** Call direct.
**Parking:** Ample off-street parking.
**In-Room:** Color cable TV, AC, ceiling fans, reading material, refrigerator, coffee & tea-making facilities, maid & laundry service.
**On-Premises:** Phone, large, screened lanai, grill privileges.
**Exercise/Health:** Jacuzzi, massage. Nearby gym with weights, sauna & steam.
**Swimming:** Pool on premises. Beaches nearby.
**Sunbathing:** At poolside.
**Nudity:** Permitted poolside.
**Smoking:** Permitted poolside only.
**Pets:** Not permitted.
**Handicap Access:** No.
**Children:** No.
**Languages:** English.
**Your Host:** Steven.

# SEBASTIAN

## The Pink Lady Inn

Women ♀

### *A Victorian Lady with Modern Amenities*

Built in 1904, this renovated private home is filled with antiques, family heirlooms, *and* many modern amenities. Each room of ***The Pink Lady Inn*** has its own style from white wicker in the Key West room, to the cast iron and brass bed in the Provincetown room. Each room contains a fridge, microwave, and cable TV. Swim, surf, or walk the beaches. Explore the Indian River Lagoon, a diverse estuary and pelican island, by watercraft, bicycle, or foot. Jet ski, sailboard, canoe, and boat rentals are only a few blocks away. Snorkeling, diving, and fishing are also available.

**Address: 1309 Louisiana Ave, Sebastian, FL 32958**
**Tel: (407) 589-1345.**

**Type:** Inn.
**Clientele:** Mostly lesbian with some hetero clientele
**Transportation:** Car is best.
**To Gay Bars:** 15 miles, a 20-minute drive.
**Rooms:** 2 rooms with double or queen beds.
**Bathrooms:** Private sink , shared bath/shower/toilet.
**Campsites:** RV parking only, electric only. Share bath in inn.
**Meals:** Expanded continental breakfast.
**Vegetarian:** Vegetarian breakfast always available.
**Complimentary:** Coffee, tea, bottled water, popcorn for microwave.
**Dates Open:** All year.
**Rates:** $45-$55.
**Discounts:** Weekly rates available.
**Rsv'tns:** Required.
**Reserve Thru:** Call direct.
**Minimum Stay:** Required during certain periods.
**Parking:** Ample off-street parking. Enough for boat or RV up to 32 feet.
**In-Room:** Color cable TV, central AC, coffee/tea-making facilities, microwave, refrigerator, ceiling fans.
**On-Premises:** TV lounge/parlor, video tape library.
**Exercise/Health:** Bicycle ergometer, stair stepper, treadmill. Gym with massage nearby.
**Swimming:** In-ground pool with therapy jets on premises. Ocean & river nearby.
**Sunbathing:** Poolside, on roof, patio or at beach.
**Smoking:** Permitted outside only. Both rooms non-smoking.
**Pets:** Well-behaved pets welcome with advance notice, shaded kennel area provided.
**Handicap Access:** No.
**Children:** No.
**Languages:** English.
**Your Host:** Carol & Barbara.

# TAMPA

## Birdsong Bed and Breakfast

Women ♀

### *Experience the Natural Beauty of Florida Woodlands*

***Birdsong B&B*** offers a tranquil atmosphere on five wooded acres adjacent to a wildlife preserve and the Alafia River. Created especially for women, the contemporary spacious private room has its own entrance, kitchen and bath. Hawks, owls, towhees and whippoorwills call from the oak and pine woodland, providing inspiration for creative work, relaxation or romance. Horseback riding, canoeing, camping, swimming, hiking and bike trails are only minutes away. Secluded, yet centrally located, ***Birdsong*** is less than an hour to beaches, downtown Tampa, and Orlando attractions.

**Address: Tampa, FL. Tel: (813) 654-8179.**

**Type:** Bed & breakfast.
**Clientele:** Women only.
**Transportation:** Car.
**To Gay Bars:** 35-minute drive to Tampa bars.
**Rooms:** 1 room with queen bed, sofa bed & kitchen.
**Bathrooms:** Private shower/toilet.
**Meals:** Expanded continental breakfast.
**Complimentary:** Fruit juices, coffee, tea, kitchen staples.
**Dates Open:** All year.
**High Season:** December-April.
**Rates:** $60.
**Rsv'tns:** Required.
**Reserve Through:** Call direct.
**Minimum Stay:** 2 nights on weekends.
**Parking:** Ample free off-street parking.
**In-Room:** Color TV, AC, ceiling fans, telephone, kitchen, refrigerator, microwave oven, coffee & tea-making facilities.
**On-Premises:** Massage therapist available.
**Exercise/Health:** Nearby canoe & horse rentals, hiking/biking trails.
**Swimming:** Nearby lake & Gulf of Mexico beaches.
**Sunbathing:** Anywhere.
**Nudity:** Permitted in certain areas.
**Smoking:** Permitted outside.
**Pets:** Permitted on approval.
**Handicap Access:** Limited. Call to inquire.
**Children:** Permitted on approval.
**Languages:** English.

## Gram's Place B&B Guesthouse

Gay/Lesbian ♀♂

### *A Casual Taste of Amsterdam & Key West in the Center of Tampa*

***Gram's Place*** is a relaxing, laid-back eclectic Key West-style B&B, featuring the music of Jazz, Blues, Folk Country, Rock & Roll, etc. The cottages were named in honor of legendary singer/songwriter Gram Parsons (1946-1973). There are three rooms with shared baths (private sinks in the rooms) and three rooms with private baths, queen-sized beds, and hardwood floors. Each house has a kitchen and dining area. The neighborhood is located two miles NW of downtown Tampa and historic Ybor City. You'll find ***Gram's Place*** most comfortable with the feel of a faraway island.

**Address: 3109 N Ola Ave, Tampa, FL 33603**
**Tel: (813) 221-0596 (Tel/Fax), Beeper: 292-1415.**

**Type:** Bed & breakfast cottages.
**Clientele:** 70% gay/lesbian & 30% straight clientele.
**Transportation:** We offer personal shuttle service, for half the price of cab fare, to bars, restaurants, airport, train & bus.
**To Gay Bars:** 1/2 mile & 2 blocks to restaurant, bar & disco.
**Rooms:** 7 rooms with 2 kitchens & 2 dining rooms.
**Bathrooms:** 4 private, others share.
**Meals:** Continental breakfast.
**Complimentary:** Coffee, orange juice, Coca Cola machine on premises.
**Dates Open:** All year. May be closed during July & August. Please inquire.
**High Season:** Dec-Apr.
**Rates:** $45-$100.

**Discounts:** Weekly & monthly rates.
**Credit Cards:** MC, VISA, Amex.
**Reserve Through:** Travel agent or call direct.
**Parking:** Ample on- & off-street free parking in a well-lit area.
**In-Room:** Color HBO & cable TV, AC, ceiling fans, telephone & maid service.
**On-Premises:** TV lounge, laundry facilities, kitchen privileges, BYOB pub. Occasional live music in courtyard.
**Exercise/Health:** Jacuzzi & outside shower/toilet facilities, waterfalls.
**Swimming:** Public pools nearby. 30 minutes to ocean beach.
**Sunbathing:** On the private sun deck by the Jacuzzi.
**Nudity:** Permitted if other guests do not mind.
**Smoking:** Prefer outside smoking, but not mandatory.
**Pets:** Permitted, with restrictions.
**Handicap Access:** No.
**Children:** Permitted over 5.
**Languages:** English.
**Your Host:** Mark.

# WEST PALM BEACH

## Hibiscus House B&B

**Gay-Lesbian ♀♂**

### *Tropical Elegance at Its Best*

Recapture early Florida at the ***Hibiscus House B&B.*** Originally built as the mayor's mansion, the house has seven guest rooms individually decorated with antiques, all with private baths and private terraces. The suite has a terrace, living room, bedroom and bath. The poolside cottage sleeps 6 and has a kitchen. Relax with a complimentary cocktail by the tropical pool or take our bikes and explore Palm Beach in leisurely fashion. Your hosts, Raleigh & Colin, are always accessible. Our clientele come as guests and leave as friends!

**Address: 501 30th St, West Palm Beach, FL 33407**
**Tel: (561) 863-5633, (800) 203-4927.**

**Type:** Bed & breakfast.
**Clientele:** Mainly gay & lesbian with some straight clientele.
**Transportation:** Pick up service available from airport, bus, train, port, rental car advised.
**To Gay Bars:** 10-minute drive.
**Rooms:** 5 rooms, 1 suite & 1 cottage with queen beds.
**Bathrooms:** 2 private bath/toilets & 5 private shower/toilets.
**Meals:** Full breakfast.
**Vegetarian:** Available with advance notice.
**Complimentary:** Cocktails, tea, coffee, soda, chocolates on pillow.
**Dates Open:** All year.
**High Season:** December through April.
**Rates:** Low season $55-$120, high season $75-$150.
**Discounts:** For long-term stays.
**Credit Cards:** MC, VISA, Amex.
**Rsv'tns:** Required.
**Reserve Through:** Travel agent or call direct.
**Parking:** Ample, free off-street parking.
**In-Room:** Maid service, color TV, telephone, AC & ceiling fans.
**On-Premises:** Laundry facilities & kitchen privileges.
**Swimming:** In pool on premises or 15 minutes to ocean.
**Sunbathing:** At poolside or on patios & private sun decks.
**Nudity:** Permitted with discretion.
**Smoking:** Permitted with restrictions.
**Pets:** Small pets permitted.
**Handicap Access:** No.
**Children:** Not permitted.
**Languages:** English.
**Your Host:** Raleigh & Colin.

# GEORGIA

## ATLANTA

### Ansley Inn

Q-NET Gay-Friendly ♀♂

***Experience Atlanta from the INN-SIDE...***

Nestled in the heart of midtown Atlanta, in historic Ansley Park, ***Ansley Inn*** offers exceptional residental living and beautiful conference and reception facilities in a turn-of-the-century English Tudor mansion. Previously home to Atlanta clothier and philanthropist, George Muse, and then an exclusive boarding house for young, single women, the house underwent a monumental 2-1/2 year refurbishing program after being purchased by the present owners in 1987. Massive fireplaces, crystal chandeliers, original impressionistic art, marble floors and period pieces from Chippendale, Queen Anne and Empire all create a magical ambiance you will remember long after your visit.

A stay at ***Ansley Inn*** enables you to have the best of both the old world and the new. Each uniquely decorated room is equipped with cable color TV, phone, wet bar, bath with Jacuzzi, climate control and ample closet space. Some rooms have fireplaces and many have four poster beds. Continental breakfast is served in the dining room and, in the afternoon, appetizers and set ups await you in the living room. We also offer the morning paper, catered lunch and dinner in your room, same day laundry and dry-cleaning, 24-hr concierge serv., and health club privileges.

***Ansley Inn*** is located in the middle of everything that makes Atlanta wonderful. We're just minutes from Downtown's Underground, a few short blocks from the theatre district, and we're surrounded by the greenery of five public parks. Our neighbors include High Museum, Woodruff Arts Center, and Atlanta Botanical Gardens. MARTA, Atlanta's award-winning subway system, is within walking distance.

We consider it our pleasure as well as our responsibility to help you feel comfortable during your visit with us. Our concierge staff will be happy to assist you with dinner reservations, taxis, rental car arrangements, business information and services, or whatever else it takes to make things run smoothly for you.

**Address: 253 15th St NE, Atlanta, GA 30309**
**Tel: (404) 872-9000, (800) 446-5416, Fax: (404) 892-2318.**

**Type:** Inn.
**Clientele:** Mostly straight clientele with a gay & lesbian following.
**Transportation:** MARTA or taxi.
**To Gay Bars:** 6 blocks or 1/4 mile. A ten-minute walk or 5-minute drive.
**Rooms:** 22 rooms, 4 suites & 2 apartments with queen beds.
**Bathrooms:** All private.
**Meals:** Expanded continental breakfast.
**Vegetarian:** Available with

24-hr notice.
**Complimentary:** Tea, coffee & set-up service.
**Dates Open:** All year.
**Rates:** $115-$500.
**Discounts:** 20% corporate.
**Credit Cards:** MC, VISA, Amex, Diners, Discover.
**Reserve Through:** Travel agent or call direct.
**Parking:** Ample, free off-street parking.
**In-Room:** Color cable TV, AC, telephone, ceiling fans, kitchen, refrigerator, maid, laundry & room service.
**On-Premises:** Meeting rooms. Business services available upon request.
**Exercise/Health:** Jacuzzi & massage. Nearby gym & massage.
**Swimming:** Pool on premises. Nearby river & lake.
**Sunbathing:** At poolside.
**Smoking:** Permitted with some restrictions in public space.
**Pets:** Permitted.
**Handicap Access:** Yes.
**Children:** Welcome.
**Languages:** English, limited Spanish.
**Your Host:** Tim.

## The Bonaventure

Gay-Friendly 50/50 ♀♂

### *A Victorian Oasis in Midtown Atlanta*

***The Bonaventure,*** a Victorian oasis in midtown Atlanta, is nestled in a fragrant grove of dogwoods, azaleas and magnolias. Experience the comfort, irresistible charm and funky elegance of this exquisitely restored and appointed Victorian home. Formerly home to the Griffith School of Music, the premier learning center for stringed instruments, the house is soon to be declared an historical property. Antiques fill the house with style ranging from Victorian to Art Nouveau. Four light-filled bedrooms, each with its own fireplace, have comfortable beds with fine cotton linens, and the Master Bedroom with private bath, features a separate sunroom overlooking the garden and pond.

Relax with an aperitif or fresh juice on the veranda or in the parlour. Wander the lovely grounds to discover the wisteria-draped archway which leads to the goldfish pond and turtle spa. Breakfast includes freshly baked croissants and pastries from Alon's bakery, fresh juices, excellent coffee and teas, plus a variety of seasonal fruits. At guests' request wine and cheese may be served in early evening.

Many of Atlanta's better restaurants are just blocks away in the vibrant midtown/Virginia Highland neighborhood: Babettes, Harvest Moon, Cafe Diem, Surin, Terra Cotta and many others. There is also an eclectic mix of blues and jazz clubs, bars, boutiques, art galleries, antique shops and unusual coffee shops within easy walking distance. Check out our homepage on the web for more pictures and info: http://www.mindspring.com/~friedato.

**Address: 650 Bonaventure Ave, Atlanta, GA 30306**
**Tel: (404) 817-7024, Fax: (404) 249-9988,**
**E-mail: friedato@mindspring.com.**

**Type:** Bed & breakfast guesthouse.
**Clientele:** 50% gay & lesbian & 50% straight clientele
**Transportation:** MARTA to North Ave stn, then taxi; MARTA to N. Ave Stn, #2 Ponce de Leon bus to Bonaventure Ave, then 1/2 block to B&B. Free pick up from MARTA when available.
**To Gay Bars:** 2 blocks, 1/4 mile, 3 min walk, 1 min drive.
**Rooms:** 3 rooms, 1 suite, 1 cottage with single or double beds.
**Bathrooms:** Private: 1 bath/toilet, 1 shower/toilet, 1 bath/shower/toilet. Shared: 1 bath/shower/toilet, 1 WC only.

*continued next page*

**Meals:** Expanded continental breakfast.
**Vegetarian:** Vegetarian breakfast always available. Numerous restaurants nearby.
**Complimentary:** Sherry, coffee, tea, cocoa, fresh juices, mineral water. Cheese platter with wine optional at cocktail hour.
**Dates Open:** All year.
**Rates:** $100-$150.
**Discounts:** Inquire.
**Credit Cards:** Visa.
**Rsv'tns:** Required.
**Reserve Through:** Travel agent or call direct.
**Parking:** Ample free secured off-street parking.
**In-Room:** AC, color cable TV, maid & room service. Cordless telephone available.
**On-Premises:** Laundry facilities, TV lounge, video tape library, fax & computer available, music, lovely private gardens with fish pond.
**Exercise/Health:** Nearby gym & weights.
**Sunbathing:** On the roof & by the pond.
**Smoking:** Permitted on veranda & in garden. All rooms are non-smoking.
**Pets:** Not permitted.
**Handicap Access:** No.
**Children:** Not especially welcome. Well-behaved children ages 12 & up are tolerated.
**Languages:** English, French.
**Your Host:** Mary Beth.

## Candler Park Patio Apartment

**Gay/Lesbian ♀♂**

### *Your Private Patio Apartment in the Candler Park Area*

Enter your own private terrace apartment through a stone patio on the grounds of our 1920's Mediterranean-style home. ***Candler Park Patio Apartment*** was designed by noted early century Atlanta architect Leila Ross Wilburn, featured in Atlanta's History Center exhibit. Our Candler Park location is close to the Little Five Points area and within easy reach of downtown Atlanta, Olympic Circle, Carter Center, Emory University, and, of course, the gay nightlife of Atlanta. Since we work out of our home, we're always close by to answer questions and lend assistance. Some guests enjoy viewing the garden-themed printed apparel and gift items we design and manufacture, as well as imported folk art and crafts from various cultures.

**Address: 612 Clifton Rd NE, Atlanta, GA 30307**
**Tel: (404) 373-6072, (800) 392-5999, Fax: (404) 377-7637.**

**Type:** Bed & breakfast patio apartment.
**Clientele:** Gay & lesbian. Good mix of men & women
**Transportation:** Car is best.
**To Gay Bars:** 1 mile, a 5 min drive.
**Rooms:** 1 apartment with single or double beds.
**Bathrooms:** Private.
**Meals:** Continental breakfast.
**Vegetarian:** 5 blocks to vegetarian restaurant.
**Complimentary:** Kitchen stocked with breakfast items.
**Dates Open:** All year.
**Rates:** $72.
**Discounts:** For stays of 1 week or longer.
**Credit Cards:** MC, Visa, Discover.
**Rsv'tns:** Required.
**Reserve Through:** Travel agent or call direct.
**Parking:** 1 space on premises & plenty of on-street parking.
**In-Room:** AC, color cable TV, telephone, kitchen, refrigerator, coffee & tea-making facilities.
**On-Premises:** Laundry facilities, fax.
**Smoking:** Smoking OK.
**Pets:** Not permitted.
**Handicap Access:** No.
**Children:** 1 child can be accommodated.
**Languages:** English, some Spanish.

## Gaslight Inn Bed & Breakfast

Q-NET Gay-Friendly ♀♂

### *Extravagantly Decorated – One of Atlanta's Finest Bed & Breakfast Inns*

Built in 1913 and completely renovated in 1990, ***The Gaslight Inn*** is one of Atlanta's finest bed and breakfast inns. This extravagantly decorated craftsman-style home has been featured in numerous local and national publications which attest to its world-class quality. These include *Better Homes and Gardens, Southern Homes, Atlanta Homes and Lifestyles,* as well as *The Atlanta Journal* and *Constitution Magazine.* ***The Gaslight Inn*** has also been on several tours, including those sponsored by the American Society of Interior Designers, the International Furnishings and Design Association, and the Atlanta Preservation Center. Equally spectacular is the home's walled garden, showcased on both the Gardens for Connoisseurs Tour, sponsored by the Atlanta Botanical Garden, and the Fernbank Natural History Museum Garden Tour.

The original granite step at curbside, used by passengers to disembark from horse-drawn carriages, is the first clue that this is truly a unique and historic inn. Flickering gas lanterns outside, original gas lighting inside, and five working fireplaces continue the ***Gaslight Inn's*** history and tradition. The inn offers a variety of accommodations from affordable, elegant rooms to luxurious suites. Some rooms feature exquisite, 18th-century hand-painted furniture, while others offer private decks with garden overlooks, whirlpools and a separate steam bath. Private, detached carriage house rooms are also available. All rooms have private baths and television, and include an elaborate continental breakfast prepared by the proprietor, an avid chef published in the magazine *Bon Appétit.*

Located in Atlanta's Virginia-Highland neighborhood, we are within blocks of the finest restaurants, shops, theaters and art galleries in Atlanta. The Carter Presidential Library, Fernbank Natural History Museum, the home of "MIss Daisy" from the movie "Driving Miss Daisy," Emory University, Piedmont Perk, and the Callanwolde Fine Arts Center are within walking distance.

**Address: 1001 Saint Charles Avenue, Atlanta, GA 30306**
**Tel: (404) 875-1001, Fax: (404) 876-1001,**
**E-mail: gaslight n@aol.com. http://www.gaslightinn.com.**

**Type:** Bed & breakfast.
**Clientele:** Mostly straight clientele with a gay/lesbian following
**Transportation:** Car, taxi, subway train, then bus.
**To Gay Bars:** 8 blocks, 1 mile, a 10 min walk, a 3 min drive.
**Rooms:** 3 rooms, 3 suites wtih single, queen or king beds.
**Bathrooms:** All private: 1 shower/toilet, 5 bath/toilet/showers.
**Meals:** Expanded continental breakfast.
**Vegetarian:** Total vegetarian, one block.
**Complimentary:** Tea, coffee & wine.
**Dates Open:** All year.
**High Season:** All year.
**Rates:** $85-$195.
**Credit Cards:** MC, Visa, Amex, Discover.
**Rsv'tns:** Required.
**Reserve Through:** Travel agent or call direct.
**Parking:** Ample free on- & off-street parking.

*continued next page*

**In-Room:** AC, ceiling fans, color cable TV, VCR, telephone, refrigerator, coffee & tea-making facilities, maid service. One room has kitchen.
**On-Premises:** TV lounge, 6 working fireplaces.
**Exercise/Health:** Jacuzzi, steam. Nearby gym, weights, massage.
**Sunbathing:** On private sun decks.
**Smoking:** Permitted on porches & decks. All rooms non-smoking.
**Pets:** Not permitted.
**Handicap Access:** Yes, 2 rooms are accessible.
**Children:** No.
**Languages:** English.
**Your Host:** Jim & Shannon.

## Triangle Pointe

Gay/Lesbian ♂

### *For Those Who Want to Get Away from It All...*

Away from the hustle and bustle of city life is ***Triangle Pointe,*** a guest suite in a private home. It is located 70 miles north of Atlanta with a view that elicits exclamations. Sit on the deck or screened porch and watch the sun go down behind the mountains or relax in the hot tub and gaze at the brightest stars you've ever seen. Nearby activities include panning for gold, hiking, horseback riding, golfing, canoeing, rafting, tubing, and shopping in historic Dahlonega.

**Address: Route 4, Box 242, Dahlonega, GA 30533-9238**
**Tel: (706) 867-6029, Fax: (706) 867-6030.**

**Type:** Bed & breakfast.
**Clientele:** Mostly men with women welcome.
**Transportation:** Car is essential.
**To Gay Bars:** 70 miles, an 80-minute drive to Atlanta.
**Rooms:** 1 room with queen bed.
**Bathrooms:** Private shower/toilet.
**Meals:** Full breakfast.
**Vegetarian:** By arrangement with reservation.
**Complimentary:** Tea, coffee, ice.
**Dates Open:** All year.
**High Season:** 2nd-4th weeks of October.
**Rates:** $69.
**Discounts:** 10% for single occupancy.
**Rsv'tns:** Required.
**Reserve Through:** Call direct.
**Minimum Stay:** 2 nights preferred.
**Parking:** Ample off-street parking.
**In-Room:** AC, color satellite cable TV, VCR, phone, ceiling fans.
**On-Premises:** Video tape library.
**Exercise/Health:** Jacuzzi on premises.
**Sunbathing:** On private sun decks.
**Nudity:** Permitted on deck & in hot tub.
**Smoking:** Permitted only outside, on decks & screened porch.
**Pets:** Not permitted.
**Handicap Access:** No.
**Children:** No.
**Languages:** English, some Spanish.
**Your Host:** Howard.

## Upper Echelons

Gay/Lesbian ♀♂

### *Glamour – Glamour*

For business or pleasure, come visit Atlanta, a brave and beautiful city, a city "too busy to hate." Come celebrate at ***Upper Echelons,*** a secure, serene, sophisticated, petite penthouse in the heart of downtown Atlanta. A dramatic and romantic condo with black laquered kitchen, mirrored walls and all the amenities awaits the two of you.

**Address: 215 Piedmont Ave NE, Atlanta, GA**
**Tel: (770) 642-1313.**

**Type:** Luxuriously furnished downtown petite penthouse.
**Clientele:** Men and women
**Transportation:** Car is best.
**To Gay Bars:** 2 miles.
**Rooms:** 1 studio with kitchen.
**Bathrooms:** Private bath.
**Vegetarian:** Restaurants nearby.
**Dates Open:** All year.
**Rates:** $79 per night. 3 or more nights $69 per night.
**Discounts:** Weekly & monthly rates available.
**Rsv'tns:** Required. Please, no calls after 10 pm EST.
**Reserve Through:** Call direct.
**Minimum Stay:** 2 nights.
**Parking:** Secured parking spot at front door.
**Swimming:** Pool on premises.
**Sunbathing:** At poolside.
**Smoking:** Permitted.
**Pets:** Not permitted.
**Languages:** English.

# SAVANNAH

## Nine Twelve Barnard Bed & Breakfast

Gay/Lesbian ♀♂

### *A Victorian B&B in the Hostess City of the South*

Don and Kevin warmly welcome you to ***912 Barnard,*** a restored double house in the heart of Savannah's Victorian district. Our home is within walking distance of shops, restaurants, museums and beautiful Forsyth Park, the crown-jewel of Savannah's historic squares. Antique furnishings and four original fireplaces set the decor. On the first floor is the double parlor living room-dining room, full kitchen and laundry facilities. Upstairs, two graciously appointed guest rooms await. We serve continental breakfast, complimentary beverages and, of course, plenty of assistance for sightseeing, shopping or dining.

**Address: 912 Barnard St, Savannah, GA 31401. Tel: (912) 234-9121.**

**Type:** Bed & breakfast.
**Clientele:** Exclusively gay & lesbian.
**Transportation:** Car, bus or taxi.
**To Gay Bars:** 12 blocks, a 5-minute drive.
**Rooms:** 1 shared bath/shower/toilet & one 1/2 bath.
**Meals:** Expanded continental breakfast.
**Vegetarian:** Available upon prior request & at nearby deli.
**Complimentary:** Coffee & tea. Evening wine or sherry in room.
**Dates Open:** All year.
**High Season:** March-September.
**Rates:** $69 per night.
**Discounts:** $5 for cash payment.
**Rsv'tns:** Required.
**Reserve Thru:** Call direct.
**Parking:** Adequate free on-street parking.
**In-Room:** Color TV, VCR, phone, ceiling fans, fireplaces, AC, maid service.
**On-Premises:** Laundry facilities, video tape library.
**Exercise/Health:** 1 block to tennis courts, walking & running paths.
**Swimming:** 15 minutes to ocean & Tybee Beach, gay beach nearby.
**Sunbathing:** On common sundecks, at beach.
**Nudity:** Inquire.
**Smoking:** Permitted outside only, rooms are non-smoking.
**Pets:** Not permitted.
**Handicap Access:** No.
**Children:** No.
**Languages:** English.
**Your Host:** Kevin & Don.

# SENOIA

## Culpepper House B&B

Gay-friendly ♀

Romance is waiting as you step back 120 years to casual Victorian elegance at the ***Culpepper House B&B.*** Share a special evening in a four-poster, canopy bed next to a fireplace, with sounds of the night coming through the window. Wake to a gourmet breakfast then take a tandum bike ride through the historic town, visit area shops and picturesque countryside, or just sit on the porch and rock. We're less than 1 hour from Atlanta, Warm Springs, Callaway Gardens and the mountains.

**Address: 35 Broad St, Senoia, GA. Tel: (770) 599-8182.**

**Type:** Bed & breakfast.
**Clientele:** Mostly straight clientele with a gay female following.
**Transportation:** Car is best. 30 miles from the Atlanta Airport.
**To Gay Bars:** 30 miles.
**Rooms:** 3 rooms with single, queen or king beds.
**Bathrooms:** 3 private baths.
**Meals:** Full breakfast.
**Vegetarian:** Available upon request.
**Complimentary:** Evening refreshments of wine, soft drinks, nuts, etc. Turn-down service with mint.
**Dates Open:** All year.
**Rates:** $85.
**Discounts:** 10% weekly.
**Credit Cards:** MC, VISA & Amex.
**Reserve Through:** Call direct.
**Parking:** Ample free parking.
**In-Room:** Black & white TV, AC.
**On-Premises:** TV lounge & fax.
**Swimming:** Nearby pool & lake.
**Smoking:** No smoking except on porch.
**Pets:** Permitted with restrictions. Please inquire.
**Handicap Access:** No.
**Children:** Not especially welcome.
**Languages:** English.
**Your Host:** Maggie & Barb.

# HAWAII

## HAWAII - BIG ISLAND

### Hale Aloha Guest Ranch

Q-NET Gay/Lesbian ♀♂

***Find the Real Spirit of Aloha at a Hillside Hideaway***

Discover the "house of welcome and love" with its spacious lanais and spectacular ocean views. ***Hale Aloha*** is nestled at 1,500 feet in the lush South Kona hillside. Guests will enjoy the peace and tranquillity of the five-acre park-like citrus and macadamia nut plantation which borders a state forest preserve. Stroll, get a massage, relax in the Jacuzzi, sunbathe, or be more adventurous and bike and snorkel. The City of Refuge and Kealakekua Bay (famous for its tropical fish, sea turtles and often-present dolphins) are right down below, and Volcano National Park is a scenic 68 miles away.

**Address: 84-4780 Mamalahoa Hwy, Captain Cook, HI 96704**
**Tel: (808) 328-8955 (Tel/Fax), (800) 897-3188,**
**E-mail: halealoha@aol.com.**

**Type:** B&B guest ranch.
**Clientele:** Mostly gay & lesbian with some straight clientele
**Transportation:** Car is best.
**To Gay Bars:** A 25-minute drive to Kona gay bar.
**Rooms:** 3 rooms, 1 suite, 2 studio apartments with king, queen or double beds.
**Bathrooms:** Master suite: private double shower/ Jacuzzi, bath/toilet. Apartments: private shower/ toilet. 3 rooms share bath/ toilet.
**Meals:** Full breakfast.
**Vegetarian:** Available at breakfast & at local stores & restaurants.
**Complimentary:** Refreshments on arrival, Kona coffee, iced tea.
**Dates Open:** All year.
**High Season:** Holidays.
**Rates:** $60-$100.
**Discounts:** 10% on stays of 4 nights.
**Credit Cards:** MC, Visa, Diners, Discover, JCB.
**Rsv'tns:** Required.
**Reserve Through:** Travel agent or call direct.
**Minimum Stay:** 2 nights on weekends & holidays.
**Parking:** Ample free off-street parking.
**In-Room:** Maid service. Apartments & 3 rooms share kitchen.
**On-Premises:** Video tape library, kitchenette, color TV & VCR, coffee & tea-making facilities.
**Exercise/Health:** Jacuzzi, massage, mountain bikes, snorkel gear, boogie boards.
**Swimming:** Nearby ocean.
**Sunbathing:** On common sun decks, on private areas throughout 5-acre property, at beach.
**Nudity:** Permitted while sunbathing, in Jacuzzi & at nude beach near Kona.
**Smoking:** Permitted outside. All rooms are non-smoking.
**Pets:** Not permitted.
**Handicap Access:** Downstairs rooms can be entered through sliding glass door.
**Children:** Please inquire.
**Languages:** English, German.
**Your Host:** Johann & Lennart.

IGTA

## Hale Kipa 'O Pele

Gay/Lesbian ♀♂

### *Romance Flows Where Lava Glows!*

***Hale Kipa 'O Pele*** bed and breakfast is named for the sacred spirit, Madame Pele, goddess of fire, ruler of Hawaii's volcanoes and protector of the forest. It is believed that Pele's spirit guards the property even today! Situated on the volcanic slopes of Mt. Hualalai, above the sunny southern Kona coast, the tropical estate and plantation-style home are distinctly unique. A majestic volcanic dome graces the entrance drive. The house surrounds an open-air atrium with lava rock waterfall, koi pond and a tiled walkway providing a private entrance to each room-suite.

The *Maile* is a corner room with spacious sitting area, private bath and intimate covered patio. The *Ginger* has a large walk-in closet, private bath with sunken tub and sliding glass doors that access the wooden deck and provide a view of the gardens. The expansive *Pele Bungalow* has a cozy bedroom, full bath, living room, mini-kitchen and a large private covered patio overlooking the fruit tree grove.

A covered wooden lanai wraps around the entire front of the home, providing full panoramic views of the lush landscape. Enjoy a buffet-style tropical continental breakfast at YOUR leisure on the lanai or in the dining room. After a day of activities, relax in the garden Jacuzzi or enjoy movies on the Pro-Logic Surround Sound(tm) system.

***Hale Kipa 'O Pele*** is a close 5 miles to the beach and all activities. Guests can enjoy scuba diving, para-sailing, deep sea fishing, helicopter tours, or walk along the scenic shores and quaint village-style shops of old Kona Town.

We cater to both singles and couples seeking the true "ALOHA" spirit and a serene and romantic atmosphere that only a tropical-style bed and breakfast can offer! Our guests will be rejuventated by exotic Hawaii, and the enthusiasm of both hosts who truly cherish this small part of the world known as PARADISE!

**Address: PO Box 5252, Kailua-Kona, HI 96745**
**Tel: (800) LAVAGLO, (808) 329-8676,**
**E-mail: halekipa@aol.com.**

**Type:** Bed & breakfast & bungalow.
**Clientele:** Good mix of gays & lesbians
**Transportation:** Rental car is best. Airport courtesy pick up for travel industry employees.
**To Gay Bars:** 6 miles.
**Rooms:** 2 suites with queen beds, 1 bungalow with 1 queen bed & 2 twin beds.
**Bathrooms:** All private bath/shower/toilets.
**Meals:** Tropical island-style continental breakfast.
**Complimentary:** Refreshments upon arrival, wine & cheese at sunset.
**Dates Open:** All year.
**Rates:** $65-$115 plus room & state taxes.
**Discounts:** 10% for 7 nights & for travel industry/ airline employees.
**Credit Cards:** MC, Visa.
**Rsv'tns:** Required.
**Reserve Through:** Travel agent or call direct.
**Minimum Stay:** Usually 2 nights.
**Parking:** Adequate free off-street parking.
**In-Room:** Ceiling fans & maid service. Bungalow has mini-kit., cable TV & VCR.
**On-Premises:** TV lounge with theatre sound & video tape library. Expansive covered decks.
**Exercise/Health:** Jacuzzi on premises. Gym & racquetball nearby.
**Swimming:** Nearby ocean.
**Sunbathing:** On Jacuzzi sun deck, the lawn or at the beach.
**Nudity:** Permitted in the Jacuzzi & at nude beach.
**Smoking:** Permitted outside & on covered decks.
**Pets:** Not permitted.
**Children:** Not especially welcome.
**Languages:** English.

## Hale Ohia Cottages

Q-NET Gay-Owned 50/50 ♀♂

### *Volcano Magic Unleashed*

There are many special places in Hawaii, but few rival the serenity and magic of ***Hale Ohia,*** the historic Dillingham summer estate located on several acres of exquisitely landscaped grounds. It is across Highway 11 from the village of Volcano and one mile from Hawaii Volcanoes National Park. Built in 1931, ***Hale Ohia*** is comprised of a main residence, a guest cottage, a gardener's cottage and numerous support structures. *Hale Ohia Cottage,* once a gardener's cottage, has three bedrooms, a large living room, fully furnished kitchen, covered lanai and covered parking. *Hale Lehua Cottage,* the oldest of the cottages, was originally built as a private study. This one-bedroom cottage is graced by a lava rock fireplace and has limited cooking facilities and a covered lanai with garden views. The *Iiwi* and *Camellia* suites each have private entrances and private bath with leaded glass windows and comfortable sitting and reading areas. The two-bedroom *Dillingham Suite* in the main residence offers the quiet elegance of a 1930's kamaaina home. Under the sugi trees is *Ihilani Cottage,* our deluxe private cottage under the sugi trees, featuring a private fountained garden, fireplace, kitchenette and antique leaded windows.

Nestled in a botanical garden setting, our complex affords guests a unique view of Hawaii's past. The gardens were developed over thirty years by a resident Japanese gardener who left the natural volcanic terrain untouched while gently grooming it into the most beautiful botanical garden in Volcano. While staying at ***Hale Ohia,*** discover the mystique of Volcano. Walk through lush fern forests, see newly created lands and feel the energy and magic of Kilauea, the most active volcano on earth and home to Pele, the goddess of fire. After a day of hiking, enjoy a book under a wisteria-covered gazebo or relax in the heated Japanese soaking tub under huge sugi pines. We have been featured in *The New York Times "Sophisticated Traveler"* and *National Geographic Traveler Magazine,* December 1994, and *Travel & Leisure,* January 1996.

**Address: PO Box 758, Volcano, HI 96785**
**Tel: (800) 455-3803 or (808) 967-7986, Fax: (808) 967-8610.**

**Type:** Bed & breakfast & cottages.
**Clientele:** 50% gay & lesbian & 50% straight clientele
**Transportation:** Car is best.
**To Gay Bars:** 26 miles.
**Rooms:** 4 suites & 3 cottages with single, double or queen beds.
**Bathrooms:** All private shower/toilets.
**Meals:** Cont. breakfast.
**Vegetarian:** Vegetarian health food store nearby.
**Complimentary:** Tea & coffee.
**Dates Open:** All year.
**High Season:** Nov 15-Jan 15 & June 15-Sep 5.
**Rates:** $75-$95.
**Discounts:** Travel agents, ASU, Kamaaina. 2 or more nights.
**Credit Cards:** MC & Visa.
**Rsv'tns:** Suggested.
**Reserve Through:** Travel agent or call direct.
**Parking:** Ample free off-street covered parking.
**In-Room:** Kitchen, refrigerator, coffee/tea-maker, maid & laundry service.
**On-Premises:** Meeting rms.
**Exercise/Health:** Steam, massage & heated Japanese furo.
**Swimming:** In nby ocean.
**Sunbathing:** In priv. sun area.
**Smoking:** Smoking permitted outside only.
**Pets:** Not permitted.
**Handicap Access:** Yes. One unit is barrier free.
**Children:** Welcomed over 6 years of age.
**Languages:** English.

IGTA

# Kalani Oceanside Eco-Resort

Q-NET Gay/Lesbian ♀♂

## *Kalani Eco-Resort = Heaven on Earth*

***Kalani ("Heaven on Earth") Oceanside Eco-Resort*** is the only coastal lodging facility within Hawaii's largest conservation area. Here, you are treated to Hawaii's real aloha comfort, traditional culture, healthful cuisine and extraordinary adventures: thermal springs, a naturist dolphin beach, snorkel pools, kayaking, waterfalls, crater lake and spectacular Volcanoes National Park. Come for an anytime getaway or for one of several annual week-long events: Gay Spirit, LesBiGay, WildWomen, Pacific Men, Hula Heritage, Adventure Camp, Body Electric, Dance & Music Festivals, and Healing Arts. Our international, native, gay and lesbian staff welcome you!

**Address: Box 4500-IP, Kehena Beach, HI 96778-9724**
**Tel: (800) 800-6886, (808) 965-7828, Fax: (808) 965-9613,**
**E-mail: kh@ILHawaii.net.**
**http://randm.com/kh.html.**

**Type:** Eco-resort with restaurant & native gift shops.
**Clientele:** 70% gay & lesbian & 30% straight clientele. Women very welcome
**Transportation:** Rental car is best. Airport pick up $25.
**To Gay Bars:** 30 miles or a 45-minute drive.
**Rooms:** 35 lodge rooms & 8 cottage units with single, double, queen or king beds.
**Bathrooms:** 23 private & 20 shared.
**Campsites:** 20 tent sites with convenient hot showers & restrooms.
**Meals:** Continental breakfast included with rooms.
**Vegetarian:** Always available.
**Complimentary:** Tea, coffee, juices.
**Dates Open:** All year.
**Rates:** Rooms $45-$75, cottages $85. With meal plan $70-$110. Campsites $15-$40 per person. Week-long adventures & events $550-$1,100.
**Discounts:** 10-20% to senior citizens, island natives, vacation (long-term) rentals.
**Credit Cards:** MC, VISA, Amex & Diners Club.
**Rsv'tns:** Preferred.
**Reserve Through:** Travel agent or call direct.
**Parking:** Ample, free off-street parking.
**In-Room:** Maid service. Some rooms have kitchens.
**On-Premises:** Meeting rooms, private dining rooms, TV lounge, laundry facilities, kitchens.
**Exercise/Health:** Weights, Jacuzzi, sauna & massage.
**Swimming:** Olympic pool on premises. Ocean beach, river, lake & snorkel tidal pools nearby.
**Sunbathing:** At poolside, oceanfront on beach or on common sun decks.
**Nudity:** Permitted anytime oceanfront at ocean beach or after 7pm at pool & spa.
**Smoking:** Permitted outdoors.
**Pets:** Not permitted.
**Handicap Access:** Yes.
**Children:** Permitted. Families housed together to afford privacy for others.
**Languages:** English, Spanish, French, German & Japanese.
**Your Host:** Richard, Delton & Dottie.

## Kealakekua Bay B&B

Gay-Friendly 50/50 ♀♂

### *Kealakekua Bay, the Unspoiled Jewel of Kona, Awaits You*

The spirit of Aloha will envelope you at ***Kealakekua Bay B&B.*** In a landscaped five-acre tropical estate of colorful, fragrant flowers and plants, fruit trees and many varieties of exotic palms, this B&B and guesthouse is a peaceful and secluded sojourn from the tensions of mainland life. The luxurious Mediterranean-style villa overlooks the pristine bay on the sunny and warm south Kona Coast of Hawaii's Big Island, in the heart of Kona coffee country. Although guests are only a short stroll from beautiful Kealakekua Bay, famous for its frolicking spinner dolphins and unparalleled fine swimming, snorkeling, scuba diving, and kayaking, they are less than 30 minutes form the many fine shops, restaurants, and historical attractions of the town of Kailua-Kona.

The villa offers two large tastefully appointed bedrooms and the stunning master suite, all with private entrance, bath, queen or king bed, and breathtaking views of the bay, coastal areas, and the pali (cliffs) of the adjacent conservation land and state historical park. Guests may avail themselves of the spacious library and entertainment room with cable TV, VCR, and stereo. An expanded continental breakfast, featuring many locally grown tropical fruits and Kona coffee, is served each morning on the upper-level dining lanai overlooking the bay.

The separate two-bedroom, two-and-a-half-bath guesthouse provides the option of even more privacy and seclusion. Featuring a fully equipped kitchen, laundry room, additional sleeping areas, and its own lanai with a spectacular view of the bay, this house can comfortably accommodate parties of up to eight.

Your host has explored the Big Island for many years and is eager to share with you its fascinating history, myriad attractions, and off-the-beaten-track wonders. Come experience the peace and the benevolence of this truly special vacation destination.

**Address: PO Box 1412, Kealakekua, HI 96750**
**Tel: (808) 328-8150, (800) 328-8150.**

**Type:** Bed & breakfast & guesthouse.
**Clientele:** 50% gay & lesbian & 50% straight clientele.
**Transportation:** Rental car from Kailua-Kona airport.
**To Gay Bars:** 18 miles to The Mask in Kailua-Kona.
**Rooms:** 3 suites & one 2-bedroom guesthouse with queen or king beds.
**Bathrooms:** B&B: 3 private bath/toilet/showers; Guesthouse: private 2-1/2 baths.
**Meals:** Expanded continental breakfast.
**Vegetarian:** Breakfast is vegetarian, 5-10 miles to restaurants & deli.
**Complimentary:** Daily filtered water supplied.
**Dates Open:** All year.
**High Season:** Thanksgiving-Memorial Day.
**Rates:** $80-$225.
**Discounts:** Guesthouse: 10% weekly discount.
**Rsv'tns:** Required.
**Reserve Through:** Travel agent or call direct.
**Minimum Stay:** 2 nights in B&B, 3 nights in guesthouse.
**Parking:** Ample off-street parking.
**In-Room:** Refrigerators, ceiling fans, maid service. Master suite & guesthouse have telephone.
**On-Premises:** TV lounge, video tape library, exten-

sive book library with large collection of Hawaiiana, laundry facilities.
**Exercise/Health:** Jacuzzi in master suite.
**Swimming:** Nearby ocean.
**Sunbathing:** At beach.
**Nudity:** Permitted in guesthouse.
**Smoking:** Permitted outside only.
**Pets:** Not permitted.
**Handicap Access:** Yes.
**Children:** Welcome in separate guesthouse.
**Languages:** English.

## Our Place Papaikou's B&B

Q-NET Gay-Friendly 50/50 ♀♂

### *A Private, Lush, Tropical Retreat*

Four miles north of Hilo, ***Our Place Papaikou's B&B*** is a cedar home set amid a lush tropical garden overlooking a stream. The Great Room, splendid with its cathedral ceiling, has a library, fireplace, grand piano, and cable TV with VCR for guests to enjoy. Four rooms share a Hawaiian-style lanai that looks out over Kupue stream. Nearby attractions include surfing and snorkeling at beaches and ocean parks, the Hawaii Tropical Botanical Garden, Rainbow Falls, and Hawaii Volcanoes National Park.

**Address: PO Box 469, Papaikou, HI 96781**
**Tel: (808) 964-5250 (Tel/Fax), (800) 245-5250,**
**E-mail: rplace@aloha.net.**

**Type:** B&B with licensed acupuncturist.
**Clientele:** 50% gay & lesbian & 50% straight clientele
**Transportation:** Car is best.
**Rooms:** 4 rooms with king, queen & double beds.
**Bathrooms:** 1 private bath/toilet/shower, 1 shared bath/shower/toilet.
**Meals:** Expanded continental breakfast.
**Vegetarian:** Breakfast is vegetarian.
**Dates Open:** All year.
**High Season:** December-April.
**Rates:** $55-$75.
**Discounts:** 10% senior discount.
**Rsv'tns:** Required.
**Reserve Through:** Travel agent or call direct.
**Minimum Stay:** 2 nights.
**Parking:** Ample free off-street parking.
**In-Room:** Color cable TV, VCR, phone, ceiling fans, refrigerator, maid & laundry service.
**On-Premises:** Refrigerator, TV lounge with cable TV & VCR.
**Exercise/Health:** Nearby gym with weights & Jacuzzi.
**Swimming:** River on premises, ocean nearby.
**Sunbathing:** At nearby beach.
**Smoking:** Permitted on covered lanai.
**Pets:** Not permitted.
**Handicap Access:** No.
**Children:** Welcome over 12 years of age.
**Languages:** English.
**Your Host:** Ouida & Sharon.

## Paauhau Plantation House

Gay-Friendly ♀

### *One of Hawaii's Hidden Gems*

Guests have raved about ***Paauhau Plantation House*** on the **Big Island** of Hawaii, calling it *One of Hawaii's hidden gems* and *Probably the best bed and breakfast on the island.* Listed on the National Register of Historic Places, the Plantation House, built in 1921, was completely restored in 1985. It is situated on 5 acres of richly landscaped grounds, fenced-in for privacy and security. All rooms are elegantly and tastefully decorated and there is an ocean view from the main house. The famous Parker Ranch, the active Kilauea volcano and many other scenic attractions are just a short drive away.

**Address: PO Box 1375, Honokaa, HI**
**Tel: (808) 775-7222, (800) 789-7614, Fax: (808) 775-7223.**

**Type:** Bed & breakfast.
**Clientele:** Mostly straight with gay female following
**Transportation:** Car rental is best. Will pick up if necessary with advance notice, $30.
**Rooms:** 4 doubles, 3 cottages.
**Bathrooms:** All private.
**Meals:** Expanded continental breakfast, other meals optional at additional cost.
**Vegetarian:** Host specializes in vegetarian.
**Complimentary:** Herb & regular teas, fresh ground Kona coffee.

*continued next page*

**Dates Open:** All year.
**Rates:** $75-$140. $400 for main plantation house/day.
**Discounts:** Large groups for extended stays.
**Rsv'tns:** Required, but will take walk-ins if space avail.
**Reserve Thru:** Call direct.
**Parking:** Ample free parking.
**In-Room:** Color TV, ceiling fans, kitchen, refrigerator, limited maid service.
**On-Premises:** Laun. facil.
**Exercise/Health:** Tennis & basketball courts.
**Swimming:** Ocean beach.
**Sunbathing:** On patio & private sun decks.
**Nudity:** Permitted on private sun decks.
**Smoking:** Permitted outside only.
**Children:** Permitted.
**Languages:** English.

## Pamalu

Q-NET Gay/Lesbian ♀♂

### *An Island Within an Island*

"A home away from home. I feel like I've been in a different world," is how one guest described the Hawaiian country house ***Pamalu,*** situated on five private acres in sunny Kapoho. Relax on the screened lanai with vaulted ceiling overlooking colorful landscaping and lawns surrounding a 40-foot pool and pavilion with BBQ where you can listen to doves and trade winds in the palms. It's an easy walk to snorkeling with colorful reef fish among underwater coral gardens. Nearby is a lagoon warmed by volcanic vents, a surfing area, and a black sand, clothing-optional beach. Volcano National Park with many hiking trails is an hour's drive.

**Address: RR 2, Box 4023, Pahoa, HI**
**Tel: (808) 965-0830, Fax: (808) 965-6198.**

**Type:** B&B country retreat, 10 min from Pahoa town.
**Clientele:** Mostly gay & lesbian w/some straight clientele
**Transportation:** Car is best (rental car from Hilo airport, a 10 minute drive).
**Rooms:** 3 rooms & 1 suite, all with queen beds
**Bathrooms:** Private: 1 shower/toilet, 3 bath/toilet/ showers.
**Meals:** Expanded continental breakfast.
**Vegetarian:** Vegetarian store a 10-minute drive.
**Complimentary:** Tea, coffee, juice.
**Dates Open:** All year.
**Rates:** $60-$100.
**Discounts:** 10% for 1 week.
**Rsv'tns:** Required.
**Reserve Through:** Travel agent or call direct.
**Minimum Stay:** 2 nights.
**Parking:** Ample free off-street parking.
**In-Room:** Computer phone jack.
**On-Premises:** TV lounge, video tape library.
**Exercise/Health:** Nearby gym, weights, massage, acupuncture.
**Swimming:** Pool on premises, nearby lagoon, 20-min to black sand beach.
**Sunbathing:** At poolside, on patio, at beach.
**Nudity:** Permitted IN pool & at beach (20-25 min away).
**Smoking:** Permitted outside & at poolside pavillion.
**Handicap Access:** Inquire.
**Children:** Please inquire.
**Languages:** English.

## R.B.R. Farms

Gay/Lesbian ♂

***R.B.R. Farms*** is, to this day, a working macadamia nut and coffee plantation. The old plantation home has been totally renovated and a swimming pool added. The house is secluded, accessed only by an unimproved 3/4-mile-long drive. ***R.B.R. Farms*** is privately-owned and -managed, so it retains the personal touch and attention to detail that sets us apart among outstanding bed and breakfasts in the world. ***R.B.R. Farms...*** a place to come, to stay, to remember, to return.

**Address: PO Box 930, Captain Cook, HI 96704**
**Tel: (800) 328-9212, Tel/Fax: (808) 328-9212.**

**Type:** Bed & breakfast.
**Clientele:** Mostly men with women welcome.
**Transportation:** Rental car is best.
**To Gay Bars:** Kona has a gay bar.
**Rooms:** 4 rooms & 1 cottage with single, queen or king beds.
**Bathrooms:** 1 private bath/toilet, 4 shared bath/shower/toilets.
**Meals:** Full breakfast.
**Vegetarian:** Available upon request.
**Complimentary:** Soft drinks, iced tea daytimes at pool, mints on pillow.
**Dates Open:** All year.
**Rates:** $60-$150.
**Credit Cards:** MC, VISA.
**Rsv'tns:** Required.
**Reserve Through:** Travel agent or call direct.
**Minimum Stay:** Usually two nights.
**Parking:** Ample free parking.
**In-Room:** Color cable TV, VCR, ceiling fans & maid service.
**On-Premises:** Public telephones.
**Exercise/Health:** "21-minute ab" gym, Jacuzzi & massage.
**Swimming:** Pool on premises, ocean beach nearby.
**Sunbathing:** At poolside, on common sun decks & on the beach.
**Nudity:** Permitted at poolside & on private decks.
**Smoking:** Not permitted in rooms. Permitted on grounds & common areas.
**Pets:** Not permitted.
**Handicap Access:** No.
**Children:** Not permitted.
**Languages:** English.
**Your Host:** Bob & Jane.

# The Samurai

**Gay/Lesbian ♀♂**

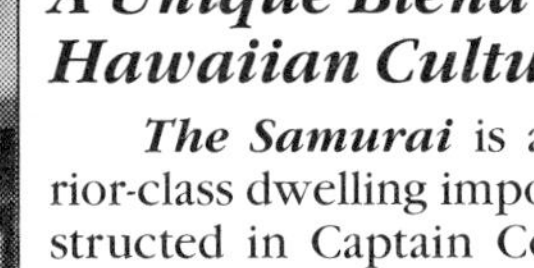

## *A Unique Blend of Japanese and Hawaiian Culture*

***The Samurai*** is an authentic Japanese warrior-class dwelling imported from Japan and reconstructed in Captain Cook, Hawaii. The trickling waterfall and koi ponds nestled in temple grass form an intimate Japanese entry garden recreating a moment in Old Japan. Upon entering the house, exposed cypress beams, shoji screens, fusuma doors, and tatami mats further emphasize the unique Japanese flavor of this old inn. Sitting on a promontory overlooking majestic Kealakekua Bay, and a breathtaking view of the southern Kona Coast, it is not hard to understand why ***The Samurai*** is renowned to Hawaii's gay visitors.

For a Zen experience of simple luxury, honorable guests may choose the Tatami Room, situated in the original historic part of the house and furnished in old Japanese style (with the exception of a "western" king-sized bed). It features an adjoining indoor/outdoor living and dining lanai – where one can sunbathe, watch the incredible sunsets or read in complete privacy. For a more traditional, yet equally beautiful accommodation, one may choose the Shogun Room – a studio apartment, beautifully furnished in a mission oak and Japanese antique blend. Both accommodations have full kitchens and private baths. The more modest Kimono Room offers a private lanai, refrigerator and a private, unattached bath. All rooms have lanai from which to enjoy the dazzling views and access to the hot tub.

Your host, Douglass, who has lived in the area for 10 years, restored and opened the inn in 1989. He holds an M. Ed. in counseling and, in addition to appre-

*continued next page*

ciating the Japanese aesthetic, has a deep reverence for Hawaiian values and culture. He will be delighted to share his knowledge and Aloha with you.

**Address: 82-5929 Mamalahoa Hwy, Captain Cook, HI 96704**
**Tel: (808) 328-9210, Fax: (808) 328-8615.**

**Type:** Bed & breakfast.
**Clientele:** Mostly gay/lesbian with some friendly straights
**Transportation:** Rental cars are necessary on the big island.
**To Gay Bars:** 20 minutes.
**Rooms:** 3 doubles & 1 apartment.
**Bathrooms:** 3 private. 2 of the rooms share 1 bath.
**Meals:** Continental tropical breakfast.
**Complimentary:** Tea, coffee, & juice.
**Dates Open:** All year.
**High Season:** Winter & late summer.
**Rates:** $55-$85 all year.
**Discounts:** On stays longer than a week.
**Credit Cards:** MC, Visa.
**Rsv'tns:** Required.
**Reserve Through:** Travel agent or call direct.
**Parking:** Free off-street parking.
**In-Room:** Color TV, VCR, refrigerator. 2 rooms have kitchen.
**On-Premises:** TV lounge, meeting rooms, & laundry facilities.
**Exercise/Health:** Hot tub.
**Swimming:** 15-minute drive to ocean beach.
**Sunbathing:** On private decks.
**Nudity:** Permitted on private decks. 30-minute drive to gay nude beach.
**Smoking:** Permitted on the lanais.
**Pets:** Not permitted.
**Handicap Access:** Accessibility to one room on the 1st floor.
**Children:** Permitted.
**Languages:** English & American Sign Language.
**Your Host:** Douglass.

## Volcano Ranch: Inn & Bunkhouse

Q-NET Gay ♂

### *Hawaii's Newest Gay Paradise*

For luxury or budget accommodation, *INN*dulge yourself at Hawaii's *NEWEST GAY PLAYGROUND!* ***Volcano Ranch: Inn & Bunkhouse*** is *the ONLY place in Hawaii with natural steam baths and caves* and 25 acres of clothing-optional PRIVACY. Each huge open-beam bedroom opens into a vaulted Great Room, and has an ocean view, full bath, queen beds, and first-rate amenities. The separate "Bunkhouse" facility has gang showers and clean bunks. At night, view the glow of the volcano, the moon and twinkling lights on the ocean or, if you like "action," visit the 24-hour "public" steam cave on premises.

**Address: 13-3775 Kalapana Hwy, Pahoa, HI 96778**
**Tel: (808) 965-8800.**

**Type:** Inn and bunkhouse.
**Clientele:** Mostly men
**Transportation:** Car is best. Pickup from airport $20.
**To Gay Bars:** 3 miles, a 7-min drive to The Godmothers restaurant & bar.
**Rooms:** 4 suites with 8 queen beds, bunkhouse with 12 bunks.
**Bathrooms:** Private: 4 bath/toilet/showers, 2 sink/washbasins. Shared: 6 showers only, 2 WCs only.
**Campsites:** 4 electric, sewer & water hookups.
**Meals:** Continental breakfast. Full kitchen for guests. 10 restaurants in Pahoa town (a 3-mile drive).
**Vegetarian:** Available at 4 restaurants in Pahoa town.
**Complimentary:** Coffee & tea.
**Dates Open:** All year.
**High Season:** National holidays.
**Rates:** Inn: suites $70-$120. Bunkhouse $20.
**Discounts:** 10% if more than 2 per suite; 8th day free for all rooms & bunks.
**Rsv'tns:** Required.
**Reserve Through:** Travel agent or call direct.
**Minimum Stay:** 2 days/nights.
**Parking:** Ample free unlimited off-street parking.
**In-Room:** Color TV, VCR, refrigerator, maid service.
**On-Premises:** TV lounge, meeting rooms, coffee & tea facilities, full kitchen, 7' concert Grand piano.
**Exercise/Health:** Weights, Jacuzzi, sauna, steam rooms w/ showers, steam caves on premises, massage, wholistic treatments, nervetherapy, table tennis, hiking trails.
**Swimming:** Pool on premises. Ocean, thermal pool nearby.
**Sunbathing:** Anywhere on premises, poolside, on private & common sun decks, at beach.
**Nudity:** Permitted anywhere on ranch.
**Smoking:** Permitted outside only.
**Pets:** Not permitted.
**Handicap Access:** Yes.
**Children:** Age 12 or older only, upon approval.
**Languages:** English.

## Wood Valley B&B Inn

Q-NET Women ♀

### *Off the Tourist Track, But Close to Power Spots*

Glimpse old Hawaii at our secluded plantation home on twelve acres of pasture and gardens near Volcano National Park and beaches of green or black sand. From ***Wood Valley Bed & Breakfast*** one can see the ocean, watch the weather change and experience the serene seclusion of one of the Big Island's more mystical and enchanted places. We serve a home-grown breakfast each morning which features fruit from the orchard, eggs from the coop and Kona coffee. Lomi Lomi massage is available, and you can relax in our outdoor hot tub or steam bath. Our clientele is mostly women, with men welcome.

**Address: PO Box 37, Pahala, HI 96777**
**Tel: (808) 928-8212, (800) 854-6754, Fax: (808) 928-9400,**
**E-mail: jessie@aloha.net. http://civic.net/webmarket/hawaii/jessie.**

**Type:** Bed & breakfast with a farm atmosphere.
**Clientele:** Mostly women with men welcome
**Transportation:** Rent a car and arrive in daylight hours. Car is essential.
**To Gay Bars:** 60 miles to Kona gay bars.
**Rooms:** 1 single, 2 doubles.
**Bathrooms:** Unique outdoor bathing & indoor shared toilet.
**Campsites:** Tent sites, toilet & shower.
**Meals:** Full breakfast, food options are limited, please call ahead. Kitchen privileges.
**Vegetarian:** All vegetarian cuisine.
**Complimentary:** Welcome to graze in orchard & garden.
**Dates Open:** All year.
**High Season:** November-March.
**Rates:** Single $35, double $55 with 10% tax.
**Discounts:** 11th day free. Work exchange available, please inquire.
**Credit Cards:** None.
**Rsv'tns:** Recommended, with deposit.
**Reserve Through:** Call direct.
**Parking:** Ample free off-street parking.
**In-Room:** Telephone.
**On-Premises:** Satellite TV, laundry facilities, shared lanai, kitchen, dining room & VCR with tapes of local interest.
**Exercise/Health:** Walking trails, steam bath, massage available.
**Swimming:** Ocean beach is 15 miles away.
**Sunbathing:** On the beach, in the backyard.
**Nudity:** Clothing is optional.
**Smoking:** Permitted outdoors.
**Pets:** Not permitted.
**Handicap Access:** No.
**Children:** Permitted with prior arrangement.
**Languages:** English.

# KAUAI

## Aloha Kauai Bed & Breakfast

Gay/Lesbian ♀♂

### *Seclusion and Hawaiian Hospitality*

Above the lazy Wailua River in ***Aloha Kauai,*** Hawaii speaks in the soft murmur of wind chimes, the sweet smell of tropical flowers, and the shimmery water of the pool. Close to Kapaa town beaches and Donkey Beach, this B&B is a hideaway conveniently located within minutes of restaurants, shops, and scenic attractions. It is close to spectacular Opaekaa Falls, hiking trails in the forests of Sleeping Giant, and freshwater spots at the Wailua Reservoir. Choose from four rooms: the Hibiscus Room, the Bamboo Room, the Orchid Suite, or the Pool House.

**Address: 156 Lihau St, Kapaa, HI 96746**
**Tel: (808) 822-6966, (800) 262-4652.**

**Type:** Bed & breakfast.
**Clientele:** Gay & lesbian. Good mix of men & women.
**Transportation:** Car is best.
**To Gay Bars:** 5 miles or a 5-minute drive.
**Rooms:** 4 rooms with single, queen or king beds.
**Bathrooms:** Private & shared.
**Meals:** Full breakfast.
**Vegetarian:** Available upon request.
**Complimentary:** Sunset refreshments (cocktails, sodas, etc.).

*continued next page*

**Dates Open:** All year.
**Rates:** $60-$85.
**Rsv'tns:** Required.
**Reserve Through:** Travel agent or call direct.
**Parking:** Ample off-street parking.
**In-Room:** Color cable TV, VCR, ceiling fans, maid service.
**On-Premises:** Meeting rooms, TV lounge.
**Exercise/Health:** Nearby gym with weights, Jacuzzi, sauna, steam, massage.
**Swimming:** Pool on premises. Nearby pool, ocean, river.
**Sunbathing:** At poolside, on patio & at beach.
**Smoking:** Permitted on patios & other outside areas.
**Pets:** Not permitted.
**Handicap Access:** Yes.
**Children:** No.
**Languages:** English.
**Your Host:** Dan & Charlie.

IGTA

# Kalihiwai Jungle Home

Gay-Friendly 50/50 ♀♂

## *Be Tarzan or Jane in Our Jungle Home*

Spectacular waterfall, jungle and mountain views await you at ***Kalihiwai,*** a beautiful rental on the Northshore of the Garden Island of Kauai. Beautifully furnished, this ***luxury*** rental is decorated with antique Hawaiian art and has a marble bathroom with Jacuzzi bathtub, marble fireplace, and a hammock for two on the balcony which overlooks the jungle and waterfall. Ideally located, it is the perfect place for a dream vacation. ***Kalihiwai*** is situated on half an acre of tropical splendor, affording spectacular glassed-in panoramic views from each room.

Address: PO Box 717, Kilauea, HI 96754
Tel: (808) 828-1626 (Tel/Fax),
E-mail: thomasw@aloha.net. http://www.hshawaii.com/kvp/jungle/.

**Type:** Vacation rental.
**Clientele:** 50% gay & lesbian & 50% straight clientele.
**Transportation:** Car is best. Airport less than 1 mile from home.
**To Gay Bars:** 15 miles or a 30-minute drive.
**Rooms:** 1 bedroom with queen bed.
**Bathrooms:** Private bath with Jacuzzi bathtub.
**Vegetarian:** Vegetarian health food restaurants nearby.
**Complimentary:** Papayas & bananas on arrival.
**Dates Open:** All year.
**Rates:** $100-$150 per day, depending on length of stay.
**Discounts:** For longer stays of 1-4 weeks & for a single person.
**Rsv'tns:** Required.
**Reserve Through:** Travel agent or call direct.
**Minimum Stay:** Required.
**Parking:** Adequate free parking on premises.
**In-Room:** Telephone, ceiling fans, private full kitchen, coffee/tea-making facilities, laundry service. Maid service extra. Color TV on request.
**On-Premises:** Laundry facilities, fax & private phone.
**Exercise/Health:** Nearby gym, weights, Jacuzzi, sauna, steam, massage, facial.
**Swimming:** Nearby Olympic-sized lap pool, ocean, river & lake.
**Sunbathing:** On the patio & beach.
**Nudity:** Permitted in house & on balcony.
**Smoking:** No smokers permitted.
**Pets:** Not permitted.
**Handicap Access:** No, upstairs unit.
**Children:** Welcome.
**Languages:** English.
**Your Host:** Thomas & Doug.

## Mahina Kai

Q-NET Gay/Lesbian ♀♂

### *Relax and Renew Your Spirit at...*

Kauai's preeminent gay accommodation, ***Mahina Kai.*** This artist's home, a blue-tiled Asian-Pacific villa on two acres of secluded estate grounds on Anahola Bay, overlooks the ocean. The exotic and dramatic design provides a separate guest wing with several tropical decor bedrooms, lanais, a living room and a guest kitchenette. A tropical breakfast is served in the garden courtyard. Enjoy the lagoon pool and hot tub enclosed in a Japanese garden or join other guests in bicycling, snorkeling, hiking along the Na Pali coast trail or taking a helicopter tour or Zodiac boat trip. The B&B is available for retreats of 12-24 people, with a special tea house for group activities.

**Address: PO Box 699, Anahola, Kauai, HI 96703 Tel: (808) 822-9451 or (800) 337-1134.**

**Type:** Bed & breakfast.
**Clientele:** Mostly gay & lesbian with some straight clientele
**Transportation:** Car is best. Car rental at airport (no public transportation).
**Rooms:** 3 rooms & 1 2-bedroom apartment with double beds.
**Bathrooms:** 3 private bath/toilet/showers, 1 shared bath/toilet/shower.
**Meals:** Cont. breakfast.
**Vegetarian:** Excellent vegetarian food nearby in Kapaa.
**Complimentary:** Tea, coffee & popcorn.
**Dates Open:** All year.
**High Season:** All year.
**Rates:** $95-$115.
**Rsv'tns:** Required.
**Reserve Through:** Travel agent or call direct.
**Minimum Stay:** 3 nights.
**Parking:** Ample free off-street parking.
**In-Room:** Color TV, ceiling fans. Apartment has color cable TV, VCR, ceiling fans & refrigerator.
**On-Premises:** Coffee/tea-making facilities, meeting rooms, TV lounge, library & fax machine.
**Exercise/Health:** Spa.
**Swimming:** In our pool or at ocean beach across rd.
**Sunbathing:** At poolside, on beach, on private or common sun decks.
**Nudity:** Permitted on the grounds, 2 miles to nude gay beach.
**Smoking:** Permitted on lanai only. Rooms are non-smoking.
**Pets:** Not permitted.
**Handicap Access:** No.
**Languages:** English, French.

## Mala Lani (Heavenly Garden) Guest House

Gay/Lesbian ♀♂

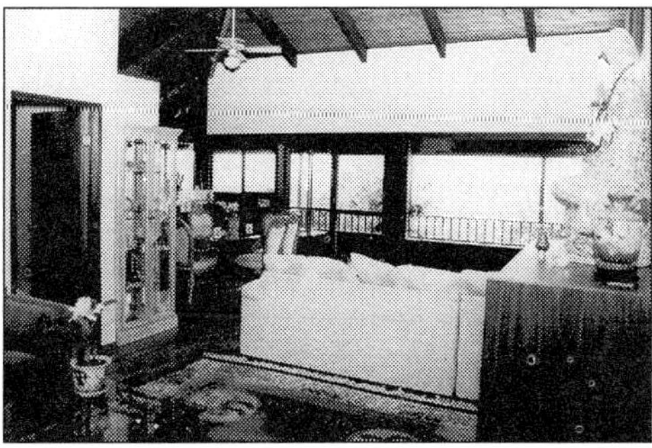

### *A Tropical Retreat that is Private, Relaxing and Friendly*

Write a ticket to your Aloha dreams with a visit to the Garden Isle, steeped in legend, unforgettable beauty and romance. Come experience refined country living on Sleeping Giant Mountain with spectacular mountain and pastoral views. ***Mala Lani,*** set in lush bo-

*continued next page*

tanical gardens, offers all the comforts of home in self-contained, completely private, superbly appointed Pacific Rim decor suites. Close to beaches, shopping and restaurants. Your hosts will welcome you into our home to share the Kauai we have come to know and love. Color brochure on request.

**Address: 5711 Lokelani Rd, Kapaa, Kauai, HI 96746**
**Tel: (808) 823-0422, Fax: (808) 823-0420.**

**Type:** Guesthouse.
**Clientele:** Mostly gay & lesbian with some straight clientele.
**Transportation:** Rental car from airport.
**To Gay Bars:** 10 min by car.
**Rooms:** 1 2-bedroom suite with queen bed & 2 extra-long twin beds. 1 1-bedroom suite with queen bed & queen sofa bed. 1 studio with queen bed.
**Bathrooms:** All private. Outdoor shower w/ hot water.
**Complimentary:** Bananas, papayas & avocados from the garden when in season.
**Dates Open:** All year.
**Rates:** 2-bedroom suite $195, 1 bedroom suite $115, studio $85. Rates for 2 people. $20 per add'l person per night. Tax extra.
**Discounts:** For stays of 7 or more nights.
**Credit Cards:** MC & VISA.
**Rsv'tns:** Required.
**Reserve Through:** Travel agent or call direct.
**Minimum Stay:** 3 nights. $20 surcharge for stays of 1 or 2 nights.
**Parking:** Ample off-street.
**In-Room:** Telephone, cable color TV, VCR, ceiling fans, refrigerator, microwave, coffeemaker. 2-bedroom has gourmet kitchen with dishwasher.
**On-Premises:** BBQ, lawn chaises, individual lanais or patios. XXX video library.
**Exercise/Health:** Soloflex, Jacuzzi. Nearby full gym, massage arranged. State Mt. hiking trail near house.
**Swimming:** 10 minutes to ocean beaches.
**Sunbathing:** Chaise lounges in gardens.
**Nudity:** At Donkey Beach (15 minutes).
**Smoking:** Permitted outdoors only.
**Languages:** English.

# Mohala Ke Ola B&B Retreat

Q-NET **Gay-Friendly** ♀♂

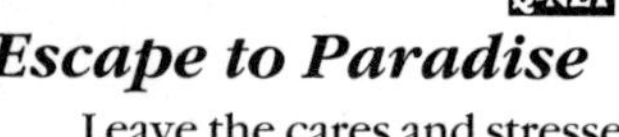

## *Escape to Paradise*

Leave the cares and stresses of civilization behind. Enjoy a Hawaiian lomi-lomi massage or rejuvenate with one of the other body treatments available, including shiatsu, acupuncture and Reiki. ***Mohala Ke Ola B&B Retreat*** is situated high above the lush Wailua River Valley and is surrounded by magical mountain and waterfall views. It provides an ideal location from which to explore the island. We'll gladly share our insights on the best hikes, scenic lookouts, secret beaches, tropical gardens, helicopter and boat tours.

**Address: 5663 Ohelo Rd, Kapaa, Kauai, HI 96746**
**Tel: (808) 823-6398 (Tel/Fax), toll-free (888) GO-KAUAI (465-2824).**
**http://www.hshawaii.com/kvp/mohalakeola/index.html.**

**Type:** Bed & breakfast.
**Clientele:** Mostly straight clientele with a gay & lesbian following.
**Transportation:** Car is best.
**To Gay Bars:** 5 miles or a 10-minute drive to Sideout.
**Rooms:** 3 rms with queen beds. 1 rm with king bed.
**Bathrms:** 3 priv., 1 shared.
**Meals:** Cont. breakfast.
**Vegetarian:** Local Thai & health food store deli.
**Complimentary:** Coffee & tea.
**Dates Open:** All year.
**High Season:** Nov-May.
**Rates:** $65-$95.
**Discounts:** Weekly rate 10%.
**Rsv'tns:** Required.
**Reserve Through:** Travel agent or call direct.
**Minimum Stay:** Prefer 3 nights minimum.
**Parking:** Ample free off-street parking.
**In-Room:** Ceiling fans.
**On-Premises:** TV lounge, meet. rooms & laun. facilities.
**Exercise/Health:** Jacuzzi, massage, acupuncture, lomi lomi, shiatsu, Reiki on premises.
**Swimming:** Pool on premises. Ocean & river nearby.
**Sunbathing:** At poolside or on the beach.
**Nudity:** Permitted in hot tub & pool at discretion of other guests. 15 min to nude beach.
**Smoking:** Permitted outside only.
**Children:** Not especially welcome.
**Languages:** English, Japanese & German.

## Pali Kai

Gay/Lesbian ♀♂

### *"Mountain by the Sea"*

Kauai's spectacular North Shore surrounds you at ***Pali Kai,*** on a hilltop with views of mountains, valley and ocean. All bedrooms in this beautiful home have queen beds with private baths and each has a sweeping ocean view. There is a shared living room with cassette player, books and an island information guide. A hot tub and garden with barbecue overlook the ocean. A luxurious lawn and lush gardens surround the house and a scenic path leads to the Kalihiwai River and beach. Swimming and snorkeling beaches, hiking trails and rivers for kayaking are nearby.

**Address: PO Box 450, Kilauea, Kauai, HI 96754**
**Tel: (808) 828-6691. E-mail: palikai@aloha.net.**
**http://www.tnight.com/web/pali-kai.**

**Type:** Bed & breakfast with panoramic views of mountains, Kalihiwai Valley & the ocean.
**Clientele:** Gay & lesbian. Good mix of men & women
**Transportation:** Car is essential, rent at airport.
**To Gay Bars:** 20 minutes by car.
**Rooms:** 3 rooms with ocean views & private cottage, all queen beds.
**Bathrooms:** All private. 1 with sink/toilet & private outdoor shower.
**Meals:** Self-catering island-style breakfast.
**Dates Open:** All year.
**Rates:** $70 singles, $80 doubles.
**Rsv'tns:** Required.
**Reserve Through:** Travel agent or call direct.
**Minimum Stay:** 3 nights.
**Parking:** Ample off-street parking.
**In-Room:** Telephone, TV, VCR, refrigerator, microwave, ceiling fan, coffee/tea-making facilities & maid service.
**Exercise/Health:** Jogging path to river & beach, hot tub available to all.
**Swimming:** At nearby ocean beaches.
**Sunbathing:** At beach & in front yard.
**Nudity:** In hot tub & at some nearby beaches.
**Smoking:** Permitted outdoors only.
**Languages:** English.

## Royal Drive Cottages

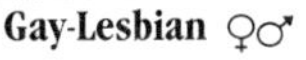

Gay-Lesbian ♀♂

### *A Cozy Tropical Hideaway*

Looking for quiet and privacy? Up in the lush green hills of the Eden-like Wailua district, down a private road, you'll find the beautiful ***Royal Drive*** guest cottages. You look out upon a lush tropical garden, where the temptation to settle under a tree in the garden and never move is strong. Your on-site host is very happy to offer suggestions to help make your stay truly special, guiding you to off-the-beaten-path experiences. From a guest book filled with unsolicited enthusiasm, *Such a wonderful place to rest and heal from life's realities.*

**Address: 147 Royal Drive, Wailua, Kauai, HI 96746**
**Tel: (808) 822-2321 (Tel/Fax).**

**Type:** Cottages.
**Clientele:** Mainly gay/lesbian with some straight clientele.
**Transportation:** Car rental at airport.
**To Gay Bars:** 10 min drive.
**Rooms:** 2 cottages with twin or king beds.
**Bathrooms:** All private.
**Complimentary:** Tropical fruit trees for guests' picking in season.
**Dates Open:** All year.
**Rates:** $80.
**Rsv'tns:** Suggested.
**Reserve Through:** Travel agent or call direct.
**Parking:** Ample free off-street parking.
**In-Room:** Well-equipped kitchenette in each cottage.
**On-Premises:** Laundry facilities.
**Exercise/Health:** Nearby gym. Massage on premises.

*continued next page*

**Swimming:** Ocean beach & river nearby, gay nude beach 15 minutes.
**Sunbathing:** On common sun deck or lawn.
**Nudity:** Permitted on common sun deck.
**Smoking:** Permitted outdoors.
**Pets:** Not permitted.
**Handicap Access:** 3 stairs up to one cottage, 1 step to the other.
**Languages:** English.

# MAUI

## Andrea & Janet's Maui Condos

Q-NET Gay-Friendly 50/50 ♀♂

### *We Provide the Rest!*

***Andrea & Janet's Maui Condos*** offer spacious one- or two-bedroom lesbian-owned deluxe oceanfront Maui condos surrounded by six miles of sand beaches, rolling green lawns, tropical foliage, and swaying palm trees. Enjoy the on-property tennis courts, shuffle board, swimming pool, whirlpool, sauna, and putting green. From December to April, the area becomes the playground for humpback whales and year-round there is excellent diving, snorkeling, surfing, and sailing. Adventure lovers won't be bored with helicopter tours, volcanic crater hikes, Hawaiian luaus, horseback riding, sport fishing, kayaking and surfing.

**Address: Box 424, Puunene, Maui, HI 96784**
**Tel: (808) 879-6702, (800) 289-1522, Fax: (808) 879-6430,**
**E-mail: andrea@maui.net. http://maui.net/~andrea.**

**Type:** Oceanfront condos.
**Clientele:** 50% gay & lesbian & 50% straight clientele
**Transportation:** Car is best.
**To Gay Bars:** 8 miles.
**Rooms:** 1- & 2-bedroom suites on the beach with double, queen & king beds, tropical rattan & wicker decor.
**Bathrooms:** All private.
**Dates Open:** All year.
**Rates:** $90-$135.
**Credit Cards:** MC, Visa, Discover.
**Rsv'tns:** Required.
**Reserve Through:** Travel agent or call direct.
**Minimum Stay:** 5 nights.
**Parking:** Ample free off-street parking.
**In-Room:** Color cable TV, VCR, telephone, ceiling fans, refrigerator, kitchen, coffee/tea-making facilities, laundry service. Maid service optional.
**On-Premises:** BBQ, picnic area.
**Exercise/Health:** Jacuzzi, sauna, tennis, shuffle board, putting green on premises.
**Swimming:** Pool & ocean on premises.
**Sunbathing:** Poolside, on patio & beach.
**Nudity:** Little Beach nude beach 5 miles away, frequented by gays & lesbians.
**Smoking:** Permitted outside only.
**Pets:** Not permitted.
**Handicap Access:** No.
**Children:** Welcome.
**Languages:** English, German.
**Your Host:** Andi, Janet.

IGTA

## Anfora's Dreams

Gay-Friendly 50/50 ♀♂

### *Maui Condos with Your Lifestyle in Mind*

Like a jewel piercing the Pacific Ocean, lush, tropical Maui and her magnificent volcanoes rise out of the sea to warmly caress your soul. ***Anfora's Dreams,*** with both one- and two-bedroom condos, are located in sunny Kihei. Both ocean and park are just across the road. Units are completely furnished in deluxe style, with total comfort in mind. Take a walk along the beach or a refreshing dip in the pool or Jacuzzi. Here, on Maui, you will learn the true meaning of "Maui No Ka Oi." Maui is the best!

**Address: Attn: Dale Jones, PO Box 74030, Los Angeles, CA 90004**
**Tel: (213) 737-0731, Reservations: (800) 788-5046, Fax: (818) 224-4312.**

**Type:** Condo.
**Clientele:** 50% gay & lesbian & 50% straight clientele.
**Transportation:** Car is best.
**To Gay Bars:** 15 miles or 20 minutes by car.
**Rooms:** 2 condos with queen beds.
**Bathrooms:** All private bath/toilets.
**Vegetarian:** Complete kitchens in condos.

**Dates Open:** All year.
**High Season:** November 15 through February 15.
**Rates:** $50-$120.
**Credit Cards:** MC, Visa.
**Rsv'tns:** Required, but can do spot bookings on available basis.
**Reserve Through:** Call direct.
**Parking:** Ample free off-street parking. Assigned space with guest spaces available.
**In-Room:** Color cable TV, telephone, kitchen, refrigerator, ceiling fans, coffee & tea-making facilities. Some with AC.
**On-Premises:** Laundry facilities. 2-bedroom, 2-bath has washer/dryer in unit.
**Exercise/Health:** Jacuzzi, nearby gym.
**Swimming:** Pool on premises, ocean across the road.
**Sunbathing:** At poolside, on patio & nearby beach.
**Nudity:** Nude beach 10 minutes away.
**Pets:** Not permitted on Maui.
**Handicap Access:** Yes. Single only.
**Children:** We welcome all guests with open arms.
**Languages:** English.

## Golden Bamboo Ranch

Gay-Friendly 50/50 ♀♂

### *Tropical Splendor in a Garden Paradise*

This private, seven-acre estate is nestled on the lower slopes of upcountry Maui along the spectacular road to Hana. ***Golden Bamboo Ranch*** is centrally located to all of Maui's bounty—10 minutes from Hookipa windsurfing beach, Twin Falls, with natural swimming pools, or the "cowboy" town of Makawao. We have just renovated a cottage and three plantation house suites, all with unobstructed, panoramic ocean views through horse pastures (we have horses) and forests on one side and a tropical garden and lily pond on the other.

**Address: 422 Kaupakalua Rd, Haiku, Maui, HI 96708**
**Tel: (808) 572-7824 (Tel/Fax), (800) 344-1238,**
**E-mail: golden@maui.net.**

**Type:** Cottage & plantation house suites.
**Clientele:** 50% gay & lesbian & 50% straight clientele.
**Transportation:** Rental car is best.
**To Gay Bars:** 30 minutes to Hamburger Mary's in Wailuku.
**Rooms:** 3 suites & 1 cottage with single, queen or king beds.
**Bathrooms:** 4 private bath/toilet/showers.
**Meals:** Expanded continental breakfast left daily in accommodations.
**Vegetarian:** Available with prior notice. 15-minute drive to 2 vegetarian restaurants & 2 health food stores.
**Dates Open:** All year.
**Rates:** $69-$90.
**Discounts:** For seven or more days.
**Credit Cards:** MC, VISA & Amex.
**Rsv'tns:** Required.
**Reserve Through:** Travel agent or call direct.
**Parking:** Ample free off-street parking.
**In-Room:** Color TV, telephone, ceiling fans, kitchen, refrigerator, coffee/tea-making facilities & maid service.
**On-Premises:** Laundry facilities.
**Exercise/Health:** 5 minutes to Twin Falls hiking path to waterfalls & natural swimming pools.
**Swimming:** Nearby ocean & natural swimming pools.
**Sunbathing:** On the patio & at the beach.
**Nudity:** Permitted on patios & terraces. 30 minutes to super gay nude beach.
**Smoking:** Permitted on patios & terraces. Non-smoking rooms available.
**Pets:** Not permitted.
**Handicap Access:** Yes. Plantation house is ground level.
**Children:** Not especially welcome.
**Languages:** English, French & Spanish.
**Your Host:** Marty & Al.

IGTA

## Hale Makaleka

**Women ♀**

***Hale Makaleka,*** a bed and breakfast for women, is situated on the leeward south shore of the island. We have a large, light and airy room with private bath and private entrance overlooking the garden. Tropical breakfast is served on our upstairs deck from where whales can be seen during winter months. Relax in homey, restful seclusion, chat with us about mainland happenings, stories of Maui, sightseeing, shopping and activities in the lesbian community. Resort activities, dining experiences and white sand beaches are within four miles.

**Address: Kihei, HI 96753. Tel: (808) 879-2971.**

**Type:** Bed & breakfast.
**Clientele:** Women only.
**Transportation:** Rental car.
**To Gay Bars:** 30 minutes to Hamburger Mary's in Wailuku.
**Rooms:** 1 double with private entrance.
**Bathrooms:** Private.
**Meals:** Full trop. breakfast.
**Vegetarian:** Available upon request.
**Dates Open:** All year.
**High Season:** Dec-April.
**Rates:** $60 dbl, $55 sgl.
**Rsv'tns:** Required.
**Reserve Thru:** Call direct.
**Minimum Stay:** 2 days.
**Parking:** Adequate, free off-street parking.
**In-Room:** Color TV, VCR.
**On-Premises:** Laundry facilities, refrigerator & telephone.
**Exercise/Health:** Nearby gyms.
**Swimming:** One mile to ocean beach.
**Sunbathing:** In secluded garden, on nearby beach.
**Nudity:** Permitted in garden & at "Little Beach" 6 miles away.
**Smoking:** Permitted outside.
**Pets:** Not permitted.
**Children:** Not permitted.
**Languages:** English.
**Your Host:** Margaret & Jackie.

## Halfway to Hana House

**Gay-Friendly 50/50 ♀♂**

### *Relax and Rejuvenate...Awaken Your Senses*

A 20-minute drive from Paia town on the Hana road, this cozy private studio is nestled in lush seclusion. Sparkling clean and airy, with a double bed, mini-kitchen, private bath and entrance, ***Halfway to Hana House*** features a breakfast patio overlooking a tropical valley with ocean views. There are banana and bamboo groves, citrus and papaya orchards, a pineapple field, tropical flowers, herb gardens and a lily pond. Your host, a long-time Maui resident and avid outdoor enthusiast gives restuarant and adventure tips, and may even invite you to go snorkeling or kayaking on a Sunday morning.

**Address: PO Box 675, Haiku, Maui, HI 96708**
**Tel: (808) 572-1176, Fax: (808) 572-3609.**

**Type:** Bed & breakfast with champagne, wine, beer available for purchase.
**Clientele:** 50% gay & lesbian & 50% straight clientele (1 studio ensures complete privacy)
**Transportation:** Car is best. No public transportation available.
**To Gay Bars:** 20 miles by car to Wailuku.
**Rooms:** 1 private studio suite with double bed.
**Bathrooms:** 1 private shower/toilet.
**Meals:** Expanded continental breakfast.
**Vegetarian:** All breakfasts.
**Complimentary:** Chocolate-covered macadamia nuts, herb teas.
**Dates Open:** All year.
**High Season:** December through April.
**Rates:** Single $55-$60, double $60-$70.
**Discounts:** 10% for 7 or more days.
**Rsv'tns:** Recommended. Walk-ins welcome if space is available.
**Reserve Through:** Travel agent or call direct.
**Minimum Stay:** 2 nights.
**Parking:** Ample off-street parking area shaded by trees.
**In-Room:** Coffee/tea-making & light cooking facilities, beach mats, shampoo, razors, toothpaste, color TV, radio, tape player.
**On-Premises:** Telephone, refrigerator, laundry facilities, covered patio with table & chairs, lounge chair.
**Exercise/Health:** Nordic track, trampoline, massage.
**Swimming:** Nearby fresh water pools, ocean beach 15 min away, lap pool 20 mi away.
**Sunbathing:** At the beach, on private patio & private grounds.
**Nudity:** Permitted on private patio & in secluded areas on private ground.
**Smoking:** This is a non-smoking environment.
**Pets:** Permitted if specific arrangements are made.
**Handicap Access:** No, pathways are gravel.
**Children:** Permitted over age of 10.
**Languages:** English, limited French & Japanese.

## Huelo Point Flower Farm B&B

Gay-Friendly 50/50 ♀♂

### *"One of the Most Spectacular – and Romantic – B&Bs in Hawaii"*

There is a place of unforgettable beauty, breathtaking views and lush tropical gardens offering the finest in accommodation on Maui's gorgeous North Shore... ***The Huelo Point Flower Farm*** is a private, secluded 2-acre estate perched at the edge of a 300-foot sea cliff, overlooking Waipio Bay. Choose either the glass-walled "Gazebo" cottage at cliff's edge, the spacious Carriage House, or the stunning Main House. All offer exquisite views of the ocean and Mt. Haleakala. Guests really enjoy our 50-foot swimming pool and hot tubs, as well as sampling fresh organic fruits and vegetables from the estate's gardens.

**Address: PO Box 1195, Paia, Maui, HI 96779**
**Tel: (808) 572-1850,**
**E-mail: huelopt@maui.net. http://maui.net/~huelopt.**

**Type:** Bed & breakfast & rental homes.
**Clientele:** 50% gay & lesbian & 50% straight clientele
**Transportation:** Rental car, 1/2 hour from airport.
**To Gay Bars:** 35 minute drive.
**Rooms:** Main house for six w/ double, queen & king beds, cottage w/ queen bed, carriage house w/ 2 queen beds.
**Bathrooms:** All private.
**Meals:** Continental breakfast (cottage only).
**Vegetarian:** Almost always available.
**Complimentary:** Tea & coffee.
**Dates Open:** All year.
**Rates:** Cottage $110/night, carriage house $125/night. Main house $1800/week, plus tax.
**Discounts:** Cottage or carriage house weekly discount of 10%.
**Rsv'tns:** Required. Walk-ins welcome if space is available.
**Reserve Through:** Call direct.
**Minimum Stay:** 2 days.
**Parking:** Ample off-street parking on gated estate.
**In-Room:** Color TV, CD player, telephone, kitchen, & refrigerator.
**On-Premises:** Laundry facilities.
**Exercise/Health:** Jacuzzis, massage.
**Swimming:** Pool on premises. 15 min drive to ocean beach. 10 min drive to waterfalls & natural pools.
**Sunbathing:** At poolside & on the patio.
**Nudity:** Permitted.
**Smoking:** Permitted.
**Pets:** Permitted by request.
**Handicap Access:** Yes.
**Children:** Small children could be a problem because of 300 foot cliff.
**Languages:** English, French, & Russian.
**Your Host:** Guy & Doug.

## Jack & Tom's Maui Condos

Q-NET Gay-Friendly ♀♂

### *Tropical Sun, Sandy Beaches, Gentle Trade Winds...Maui No Ka Oi (is the best)*

Explore the island, play a little tennis, relax by the pools or enjoy the sand and surf of the finest beaches on Maui, including the nude beach at Makena (only minutes away). At the end of your day, return to your private one- or two-bedroom condominium to freshen up for a night out. Or, if you prefer, prepare dinner in your own fully-equipped kitchen and enjoy a quiet evening at home. All units at ***Jack & Tom's Maui Condos*** have either ocean or garden views, are clean, comfortable and are equipped to make you want to stay a lifetime.

**Address:** Write: Margaret Norrie Realty, PO Box 365, Kihei, HI 96753
**Tel:** (800) 800-8608, (808) 874-1048, **Fax:** (808) 879-6932.

**Type:** Priv. condominiums within larger complexes.
**Clientele:** Mostly straight clientele with a gay & lesbian following.
**Transportation:** Car is a must on Maui. We can arrange car rental.
**To Gay Bars:** 12 miles or a 25-minute drive.
**Rooms:** 36 condos with queen or king beds.
**Bathrooms:** All private.
**Dates Open:** All year.
**High Season:** December 15 to April 15.
**Rates:** Summer $35-$90, winter $45-$125.
**Rsv'tns:** Required.
**Reserve Through:** Travel agent or call direct.
**Minimum Stay:** 5 days.
**Parking:** Ample off-street.
**In-Room:** Color cable TV, AC, ceiling fans, telephone, kitchen & laundry facilities. Some units have VCRs, stereos.
**Exercise/Health:** Nearby gym.
**Swimming:** Pool on premises. Ocean beach across the street.
**Sunbathing:** At poolside or on the beach.
**Smoking:** Permitted. Non-smoking units available.
**Handicap Access:** Yes.
**Languages:** English.
**Your Host:** Jack & Tom.

## Kailua Maui Gardens

Gay-Friendly 50/50 ♀♂

### *Stay With Us for a True Tropical Island Experience*

Located in the picturesque village of Kailua, ***Kailua Maui Gardens*** is an undiscovered hideaway on the edge of Maui's vast rainforest. Enchanting pathways and bridges lead you through two acres of fabulous gardens, which surround our well-appointed accommodations, most with ocean views. The house has its own pool, spa and barbecue lanai area. Cottage guests can relax in the garden spa, where they will be surrounded by the lush gardens. Enjoy nearby waterfalls and natural swimming pools. It's an ideal setting for large groups, individuals and couples.

**Address: SR Box 9 (Hana Hwy), Haiku, Maui, HI 96708**
**Tel: (800) 258-8588, (808) 572-9726, Fax: (808) 572-5934.**

**Type:** Cottage & house rental.
**Clientele:** 50% gay & lesbian & 50% straight clientele.
**Transportation:** Rental car is best, $30 for pickup from airport.
**To Gay Bars:** 40 minutes.
**Rooms:** 3 cottages, one 3-bdrm house & one 1-bdrm apartment with queen or king beds.
**Bathrooms:** All private bath/toilets.
**Vegetarian:** Chef & vegetarian food available with prior notice.
**Complimentary:** Fresh fruit, tea, coffee & tropical flowers from estate gardens.
**Dates Open:** All year.
**High Season:** June-Sept & Dec-March.
**Rates:** $60-$200 plus tax.
**Discounts:** For 4 days or longer.
**Rsv'tns:** Required.
**Reserve Through:** Travel agent or call direct.
**Minimum Stay:** 2 nights.
**Parking:** Ample, free off-street parking.
**In-Room:** Color TV, VCR, stereo/compact disc player, kitchen, telephone, ceiling fans.
**On-Premises:** Two outside BBQs, covered lanai for house & covered lanai at common area for cottages.
**Exercise/Health:** Private spa for house & garden spa for cottages.
**Swimming:** Pool with house, 8 miles to beach, 1/4 mile to waterfall, natural pools.
**Sunbathing:** At poolside or on private patios.
**Nudity:** Permitted in pool area & around spas.
**Smoking:** Permitted outdoors.
**Pets:** Not permitted.
**Handicap Access:** Main house is accessible.
**Children:** Over 12 years permitted.
**Languages:** English.

## Keiki Ananda

Gay-Friendly 50/50 ♀♂

### *Upcountry Maui – Where Humans and Gods Mingle*

Nestled on the side of breathtaking Haleakala Crater, ***Keiki Ananda*** has spectacular vistas of the West Mountains, Iao Valley and the Pacific Ocean. Within walking distance to the shops and cafes of Makawao, we are only a 15-minute drive to beautiful Baldwin Beach. Facilities include a spacious yoga and meditation room, clothing-optional swimming pool, outdoor hot tub, and access to tennis courts. Maui's treasures lie open to you: waterfalls cascading into sacred pools, hiking through a redwood forest on majestic Haleakala, snorkeling at La Perouse Bay, and swimming in cobalt-blue and clear-aqua ocean waters, maybe even with dolphins.

**Address: Makawao, HI**
**Tel: (808) 573-2225 or (808) 572-8496.**

**Type:** Bed & breakfast retreat center.
**Clientele:** 50% gay & lesbian & 50% straight clientele
**Transportation:** Car is best.
**To Gay Bars:** 8 mi to Hamburger Mary's in Wailuku, a 20 min drive.
**Rooms:** 4 rooms with double beds.
**Bathrooms:** 2 shared bath/shower/toilets.
**Vegetarian:** Vegetarian communal kitchen available. Vegetarian food available in nearby restaurants & cafes.
**Dates Open:** All year.
**High Season:** January-March.
**Rates:** $50-$75.
**Discounts:** 7th night free.
**Rsv'tns:** Required.
**Reserve Through:** Call direct.
**Parking:** Adequate free off-street parking.
**On-Premises:** Meeting rooms, laundry faciities, yoga/meditation room.
**Exercise/Health:** Jacuzzi, massage, yoga/meditation instruction. Nearby gym, weights.
**Swimming:** Pool on premises. Nearby Ocean.
**Sunbathing:** Poolside, on common sun decks, at beach.
**Nudity:** Permitted in pool area.
**Smoking:** Not permitted on premises. All sleeping rooms are non-smoking.
**Pets:** Not permitted.
**Handicap Access:** No.
**Children:** Welcome, can share room with parents.
**Languages:** English, French, Spanish.
**Your Host:** Mick.

## Koa Kai Rentals

**Gay/Lesbian ♀♂**

We offer a wide variety of accommodations throughout Maui, from B&Bs to condos or houses. We feature a very nicely furnished private studio apartment for those wanting to vacation on a budget and still have a nice place in which to stay. Included in the apartment are light cooking facilities, TV/VCR, a shower/bath, linens, beach equipment, etc. ***Koa Kai*** is within walking distance of the beach, parks, shopping and restaurants, a ten-minute drive to Little Beach at Makena, or 30 minutes to Lahaina. Non-smoking only, please.

**Address: Island Surf #401, Kihei, HI 96753**
**Tel: (800) 399-6058 ex. 33, (808) 879-6058, Fax: (808) 875-4274.**
**E-mails: cloy@aloha.net or Maui4Fun@aol.com.**

**Type:** Rentals.
**Clientele:** Mostly gay & lesbian w/ some straight clientele
**Transportation:** Car from airport.
**To Gay Bars:** 15 miles, a 20 minute drive.
**Rooms:** Rms with dbl beds.
**Bathrooms:** Private bath/toilet/shower.
**Dates Open:** All year.
**High Season:** Nov-Mar & Jun-Aug.
**Rates:** $42 per night, $250 per week.
**Discounts:** Monthly discount.
**Rsv'tns:** Required.
**Reserve Through:** Travel agent or call direct.
**Minimum Stay:** 4-night minimum.
**Parking:** Ample free off-street parking.
**In-Room:** AC, ceiling fans, color cable TV, VCR, kitchen, coffee & tea-making facilities, refrigerator.
**Exercise/Health:** Nearby gym.
**Swimming:** Pool on premises, ocean nearby.
**Sunbathing:** Poolside, at beach.
**Nudity:** Inquire.
**Smoking:** Non-smoking room only.
**Pets:** Not permitted.
**Handicap Access:** No.
**Languages:** English, some French, Spanish, Japanese.
**Your Host:** Cloy & John.

# OAHU - HONOLULU

## Hotel Honolulu

**Gay/Lesbian ♀♂**

Although it is in the heart of Waikiki, ***Hotel Honolulu*** has been carefully designed to be different from any other in modern day Hawaii. We are trying to create an oasis in time to take our guests back to the quieter, more gentle and relaxed way of life in these beautiful islands. Large and small studios and suites each have a different theme. All have kitchens, baths and outside lanai. Enjoy the rooftop garden sun deck for relaxation and comfort. We are two blocks from the beach and next door to our best gay clubs and the nicest restaurants and shops in the famed Kuhio district.

**Address: 376 Kaiolu St, Honolulu, HI 96815**
**Tel: (808) 926-2766, (800) 426-2766 (US/CAN), Fax: (808) 922-3326.**

**Type:** Hotel.
**Clientele:** Good mix of gay men & women.
**Transportation:** Pre-arranged airport/Waikiki shuttle, or taxi. 1st class airport shuttle R/T is $25 with lei greeting.
**To Gay Bars:** The main gay bars are on our block.
**Rooms:** 15 rms & 10 suites with king or queen beds.
**Bathrooms:** All private.
**Comp.:** Coffee & tea.
**Dates Open:** All year.
**High Season:** Nov-March.
**Rates:** $69-$119.
**Credit Cards:** MC, VISA, Amex, Diners, Discover & JCB.
**Rsv'tns:** Preferred.
**Reserve Through:** Call direct or reserve through your travel agent.
**Minimum Stay:** 4 days from Dec 20 to Jan 6.
**Parking:** Adequate off-street, covered, pay parking. Least expensive on the island.
**In-Room:** Color TV, AC, ceiling fans, telephone, kitchen & refrigerator.
**On-Premises:** Laundry room & garden sun deck.
**Exercise/Health:** Massage on premises. Nearby gym & sauna.
**Swimming:** Ocean beach 2 blocks away.
**Sunbathing:** On beach & common sun deck (lanai).
**Smoking:** Permitted without restrictions.
**Pets:** Small pets permitted.
**Handicap Access:** No. Only on the 1st floor.
**Children:** Permitted.
**Languages:** English, Spanish, French, German & Hawaiian.
**Your Host:** John, Rob, Elliott, Karen, Guy, Todd.

IGTA

## Pacific Ocean Holidays

Gay/Lesbian ♀♂

### *Hawaii Vacations for Gay Men & Women*

***Pacific Ocean Holidays*** specializes in Hawaii vacation packages for gay travelers. Choose when to travel, the length of stay, the island or islands to visit, and the price range and type of lodgings desired. We package a selection of gay and gay-friendly bed and breakfast homes, resort hotels, and condominiums. On Oahu, our Waikiki packages include lodging, flower lei greeting, airport transfers and a gay-hosted welcome and orientation meeting. Kauai, Maui, and Hawaii (Big Island) packages include lodging and rental car. All packages also include a personalized itinerary, applicable taxes, and our gay "Pocket Guide to Hawaii." Flights to and between the islands can also be included.

***Pacific Ocean Holidays*** provides a convenient, hassle-free way to arrange the basic components of your Hawaii vacation through one reliable and knowledgable source. In business since 1982, we've earned a reputation for personal, individualized, and friendly service, with attention to detail. ***Pacific Ocean Holidays*** is licensed by the State of Hawaii and is a charter member of the International Gay Travel Association. Call or write for our free gay Hawaii vacation brochure.

**Address: PO Box 88245, Dept IP, Honolulu, HI 96830-8245**
**Tel: (808) 923-2400, (800) 735-6600, Fax: (808) 923-2499,**
**E-mail: poh@hi.net. http://gayhawaii.com.**

**Type:** Bed & breakfasts, hotels & condos.
**Clientele:** Gay & lesbian
**Credit Cards:** MC, VISA, Amex, Discover, Novus.
**Rsv'tns:** Required.
**Reserve Through:** Travel agent or call direct.
**Minimum Stay:** 3 nights.
**Languages:** English.

## The Mango House

Q-NET Women ♀

### *Oahu's Only Gay & Lesbian B&B*

***The Mango House,*** a delightful alternative to Waikiki hotels, has views of the ocean, Honolulu, Punchbowl Crater, and the harbor. From your breezy corner room, you'll see mango trees in the backyard. Wake to the aroma of baking bread, served with island juice, fresh fruit and Kona coffee. Explore Hanauma Bay, a snorkeler's paradise; Japanese temples, bamboo forests; waterfalls and hidden pools. Sun and swim at the island's best beaches. Six years of serving you. As one guest said, "Great food, great views, great advice, great location!"

**Address: 2087 Iholena St, Honolulu, HI 96817**
**Tel: Tel/Fax: (808) 595-6682 or (800) 77-MANGO.**
**E-mail: mango@pixi.com.**

**Type:** Bed & breakfast.
**Clientele:** Mostly women with men welcome
**Transportation:** Taxi from airport, $13, rental car is best.
**To Gay Bars:** 15 minutes to gay & lesbian bars.

*continued next page*

**Rooms:** 2 rooms with queen or king beds, plus 1-bdrm cottage (sleeps 4).
**Bathrooms:** 1 private, 1 shared.
**Meals:** Aloha continental breakfast with homemade bread & mango jam.
**Vegetarian:** We accommodate special diets.
**Complimentary:** Passion-orange fruit juice on arrival.
**Dates Open:** All year.
**Rates:** $63-$99, plus tax.
**Discounts:** 10% for 7 days.
**Credit Cards:** Amex, Discover.
**Rsv'tns:** We accept short-notice reservations, but call first.
**Reserve Through:** Travel agent or call direct.
**Minimum Stay:** 3 days. For shorter stays call 5 days ahead.
**Parking:** Ample, on-street parking.
**On-Premises:** TV/VCR, laundry facilities, beach chairs, snorkeling, cooler & ice, beach towels, maps.
**Exercise/Health:** Ocean snorkeling, basketball court across the street.
**Swimming:** Waikiki & Queen's Surf area 15-min. drive, Kailua (windsurfing) is 20 min.
**Sunbathing:** At ocean beach or on patio.
**Nudity:** OK, if guests don't mind the neighbors!
**Smoking:** Permitted outdoors.
**Pets:** No, we have a pet parakeet in the household.
**Handicap Access:** No, stairs.
**Children:** Permitted, if over 10 years.
**Languages:** English & limited Spanish.

IGTA

## Waikiki AA Studios (Bed & Breakfast Honolulu & Statewide)

**Gay-Friendly** ♀♂

### *One Call Does it All!*

***Waikiki AA Studios,*** Hawaii's largest B&B agency has over 350 studios and bed & breakfasts on all of the islands. We also offer good rates on cars and inter-island flights. Our volume means lower rates! Fax, E-mail or snail mail us for a free brochure. Then contact us by phone (toll-free USA/Canada), E-mail or fax for a give-and-take which will provide us with a better awareness of your desires. We offer places which are actually open on the dates you want, and more information (dates, places, etc) means better help!

**Address: 3242 Kaohinani, Honolulu, HI 96817**
**Tel: (808) 595-7533, (800) 288-4666, Fax: (808) 595-2030,**
**E-mail: BnBsHI@Aloha.net. URL: travelsource.com/bnb/allhi.html.**

**Type:** Studios, hosted rentals & statewide bed & breakfast reservation service.
**Clientele:** Mostly straight clientele with a gay & lesbian following.
**To Gay Bars:** Some are near men's/women's bars.
**Rooms:** 9 studio apartments in Waikiki, 390 homestays & studios in other locations.
**Bathrooms:** All private in Waikiki, private & shared elsewhere.
**Meals:** Breakfast in homestays varies with host.
**Dates Open:** All year.
**High Season:** December 15th-Easter.
**Rates:** $45-$150.
**Discounts:** On weekly & monthly stays.
**Credit Cards:** MC, VISA.
**Rsv'tns:** Recommended.
**Reserve Through:** Travel agent or call direct.
**Minimum Stay:** 3 days.
**Parking:** Both free and pay parking
**In-Room:** Studios have color TV, telephone, AC, kitchen.
**On-Premises:** Studios have laundry facilities.
**Swimming:** Studios have pool, ocean is 1-1/2 blocks away.
**Sunbathing:** At poolside, on beach.
**Smoking:** No restrictions in studios. 25% of homestays permit smoking.
**Pets:** Not permitted.
**Handicap Access:** Some locations are accessible.
**Languages:** English.

## Waikiki Vacation Rentals

**Gay-Friendly** ♀♂

***Waikiki Vacation Rentals*** offers you a range, from budget to deluxe, of fully-furnished condos with full kitchens, washer, dryer, phone and TV. You can reserve weekly, monthly and sometimes daily. Each has a view of city, ocean or mountains. All condos are within walking distance of "Old Waikiki" (gay bars, discos, baths and shops), and the ocean beach. Enjoy the privacy of your own condo apartment (just bring a toothbrush) while catching the nightlife of Waikiki. This is our 19th year in business!

**Address: 1860 Ala Moana Blvd #108, Honolulu, HI 96815**
**Tel: (808) 946-9371 or (800) 543-5663, Fax: (808) 922-9418,**
**E-mail: compuserve72324,2620.**

**Type:** Condominium rentals.
**Clientele:** Both straight & gay men & women.
**Transportation:** Airport shuttle, cab or rental car.
**To Gay Bars:** 1-3 blocks to men's & women's bars.
**Rooms:** 20 apartments with single, double, queen or king beds.
**Bathrooms:** All private.
**Dates Open:** All year.
**High Season:** Thanksgiving to Easter.
**Rates:** Low season \$55-\$135, high season \$75-\$185.
**Discounts:** For monthly stays, 10%-20%.
**Credit Cards:** MC, VISA, Amex, Diners, JCB, Discover.
**Rsv'tns:** 1-4 months in advance for high season.
**Reserve Through:** Travel agent or call direct.
**Minimum Stay:** 7 days (some exceptions).
**Parking:** Free parking at condos. Fee at hotel/condo.
**In-Room:** Color TV, VCR, telephone, full kitchen, refrigerator, AC, washer, dryer.
**On-Premises:** Laundry facilities.
**Exercise/Health:** Jacuzzi, sauna, paddle tennis.
**Swimming:** Pool & ocean beach.
**Sunbathing:** On beach & sun decks, at poolside or on roof.
**Smoking:** Non-smoking units available.
**Pets:** Not permitted.
**Handicap Access:** No. Bathrooms are regular design.
**Children:** Permitted.
**Languages:** English.
**Your Host:** Walt.

# ILLINOIS

## CENTRAL ILLINOIS

### The Little House On The Prairie

Gay-Friendly ♀♂

### *Home of the Stars*

***The Little House On The Prairie*** is a Queen Anne Victorian homestead surrounded by acres of woodlands, gardens, swimming pool and pond. "It is a showpiece of a home, full of turn-of-the-century Victorian antiques, wooden parquet floors and theater memorabilia...and it is anything but little." (Mike Monson, *Champaign-Urbana News-Gazette*) Guests at ***The Little House On The Prairie*** have included many stars who performed at the The Little Theatre On The Square in Sullivan druing the 60s, 70s and 80s. It is in the heart of Amish country, yet only 3 hours from Chicago and 2 hours from St. Louis.

**Address: PO Box 525, Sullivan, IL 61951. Tel: (217) 728-4727.**

**Type:** Bed & breakfast.
**Clientele:** Mostly straight clientele with a gay & lesbian following.
**Transportation:** Car is best.
**To Gay Bars:** 60 miles to Champaign, IL.
**Rooms:** 4 rooms with single, double & queen beds.
**Bathrooms:** 2 private shower/toilets, 2 private bath/shower/toilets.
**Meals:** Full breakfast.
**Vegetarian:** Available if asked for in advance.
**Complimentary:** Wine, tea, cheese, crackers & fruit. Mints in room.
**Dates Open:** April 1 thru January 1.
**High Season:** June thru August. Usually sold out in advance.
**Rates:** \$55-\$75.
**Rsv'tns:** Required.
**Reserve Through:** Call direct.
**Parking:** Ample free parking.
**In-Room:** AC, maid service & video tape library. 1 room with color TV & VCR. Coffee/tea-making facilities available.
**On-Premises:** Meeting rooms & TV lounge.
**Exercise/Health:** Jacuzzi on premises. Nearby gym, weights, sauna & massage.
**Swimming:** Pool on premises. Nearby lake.
**Sunbathing:** At poolside.
**Nudity:** Permitted in the wooded area.
**Smoking:** Permitted in sun room & outdoor areas.
**Pets:** Not permitted.
**Handicap Access:** No.
**Children:** Not especially welcome.
**Languages:** English, French & Italian.
**Your Host:** Guy & Kirk.

# CHICAGO

## Best Western Inn of Chicago

Gay-Friendly ♀♂

### *"Chicago's Best Value," 1995/1996 Zagat Survey rating*

The ***Best Western Inn of Chicago*** is on Ohio Street, just one block east of North Michigan Avenue and is in the heart of The Magnificent Mile, home of Bloomingdales, Nieman Marcus, Marshall Field's, art museums and galleries. The hotel is close to the nightlife district and Chicago's business and financial centers. Located only 30 minutes from O'Hare Airport, 25 minutes from Midway Airport and five minutes from McCormick Place, the ***Inn of Chicago*** is easily accessible.

Originally, the St. Clair Hotel, the Inn of Chicago is a 22-storey highrise downtown hotel offering 357 tastefully-decorated rooms. We offer 26 suites/luxury penthouse suites which feature wet bars, mini refrigerators and large sunken tubs. All of our guest rooms feature remote control color TV with in-room movies. The hotel also features valet and room service. The area's most popular health club is adjacent to the hotel.

The Newsmakers Restaurant and All Stars Sports Lounge, decorated with historical news displays and broadcast journalism memorabilia, offers American cuisine to patrons of the hotel. Our elegant conference facilities have full amenities and a professional staff to cater meetings and banquets on the Mezzanine level for up to 250 attendees. Additionally, the Rooftop Terrace offers a breathtaking view of downtown Chicago and Lake Michigan.

The ***Best Western Inn of Chicago*** welcomes you and your guests to a wonderful lodging experience you'll never forget. For reservations, please call Tim Heim or Pete Zudyk at the numbers below.

**Address: 162 E Ohio, Chicago, IL**
**Tel: (312) 573-3105, Fax: (312) 573-3140.**

**Type:** Hotel with restaurant & gift shop.
**Clientele:** Mostly straight with a gay/lesbian following
**Transportation:** Car is best. Fee for Airport Express shuttle service from airport.
**To Gay Bars:** 2-5 minute walk or 10-minute drive.
**Rooms:** 358 rooms, 26 suites/luxury penthouse suites.
**Bathrooms:** All private.
**Vegetarian:** Available in full-service restaurant on premises.
**Dates Open:** All year.
**Rates:** $89-$129.
**Discounts:** AAA, AARP, inquire about other groups/ organizations.
**Credit Cards:** MC, Visa, Amex, Diners, Discover.
**Rsv'tns:** Required. Ask for Tim.
**Reserve Through:** Travel agent or call direct.
**Parking:** Ample pay parking.
**In-Room:** AC, color cable TV, phone, maid, room & laundry service,
**On-Premises:** Meeting rooms, laundry facilities.
**Exercise/Health:** Nearby gym with weights, Jacuzzi, sauna, steam & massage.
**Swimming:** Nearby lake.
**Sunbathing:** On roof.
**Pets:** No.
**Handicap Access:** Yes.
**Children:** Welcome.
**Languages:** English, Spanish.
**Your Host:** Ask for Tim Heim or Pete Zudyk.

IGTA

## City Suites Hotel

Gay-Friendly ♀♂

***The City Suites Hotel*** offers a touch of European style with comfortable and convenient accommodations at affordable rates. Located on Chicago's dynamic near north side, close to famous Halsted St., Wrigley Field and the eclectic Sheffield/ Belmont area, we're in the heart of Chicago's gay community. Only steps from our door, you'll find the city's finest dining, shopping, theatres and exciting nightlife. The ***City Suites*** is truly Chicago's best value!

**Address: 933 West Belmont, Chicago, IL 60657**
**Tel: (312) 404-3400, Fax: (312) 404-3405. Reservations: (800) CITY-108.**

**Type:** Hotel.
**Clientele:** Mostly straight, with a gay & lesbian following.
**Transportation:** Taxi.
**To Gay Bars:** 1 block to gay/lesbian bar.
**Rooms:** 16 guest rooms & 29 suites.
**Bathrooms:** All private.
**Meals:** Continental breakfast.
**Dates Open:** All year.
**Rates:** $85-$99.
**Discounts:** Group.
**Credit Cards:** MC, VISA, Amex & Discover.
**Rsv'tns:** Recommended.
**Reserve Through:** Travel agent or call direct.
**Parking:** Ample, off-street, pay parking.
**In-Room:** Maid & room service, telephone, AC, color cable TV.
**On-Premises:** Laundry facilities.
**Exercise/Health:** Discounted daily rates at nearby health club with gym & weights.
**Swimming:** Lake Michigan nearby.
**Sunbathing:** At the lake.
**Smoking:** No restrictions.
**Pets:** Small pets with pre-approval.
**Handicap Access:** No.
**Children:** Permitted.
**Languages:** English.

IGTA

## The House of Two Urns

Gay-Friendly ♀♂

***The House of Two Urns*** earned its name from the pair of concrete urns at the top of its roof and the repeated motif in the stained-glass windows. This charming two-flat, eclectically furnished with antiques and local art, is near downtown, the gallery district, art bars and alternative theater venues. It is very convenient to public transportation from O'Hare airport and to downtown, is close to the expressway, and has off-street parking. A side garden produces fruits and berries which seasonally grace the breakfast table and patio chairs offer a place to lounge and watch the raspberries ripen in the garden.

**Address: 1239 N Greenview Ave, Chicago, IL 60622-3318**
**Tel: (312) 235-1408.**

**Type:** Bed & breakfast.
**Clientele:** Mainly straight with gay/lesbian following.
**Transportation:** Blue Line subway from O'Hare airport to Division is best or 2 blocks from expressway by car.
**To Gay Bars:** 28 blocks to Newtown, a 10-minute drive.
**Rooms:** 3 rooms with double beds.
**Bathrooms:** 2 shared.
**Meals:** Expanded continental breakfast.
**Vegetarian:** Always.
**Comp:** Coffee & soda.
**Dates Open:** All year.
**High Season:** Mar-Nov.
**Rates:** $50-$85.
**Discounts:** For stays of 1 week or longer & during off-season.
**Credit Cards:** MC, VISA, Amex.
**Rsv'tns:** Required. 1-week cancellation fee.
**Reserve Thru:** Call direct.
**Minimum Stay:** 2 nights.
**Parking:** Limited free off-street parking.
**In-Room:** AC, 2 rooms with ceiling fans.
**On-Premises:** TV lounge, telephone, refrigerator, 2 sitting rooms.
**Swimming:** 1 block to outdoor pool, 8 blocks to enclosed pool.
**Sunbathing:** In the garden.
**Smoking:** Not permitted indoors.
**Pets:** Not permitted.
**Handicap Access:** No.
**Children:** Permitted.
**Languages:** English, German, French & Spanish.
**Your Host:** Kapra & Kalina.

## Old Town Bed & Breakfast

Q-NET Gay/Lesbian ♀♂

***Old Town Bed & Breakfast*** is a modern townhouse splendidly furnished and decorated with pictures and art objects from three centuries. A walled garden, library with easy chairs, marble bath with oversized tub, and cherrywood sleighbeds invite rest, reflection and renewal. Lake Michigan, Lincoln Park and an urban village surround. Parking is ample. Public transportation is best. North Michigan Avenue shopping, Gold Coast mansions and fine restaurants are a five- to 12-minute walk. If you prefer complete privacy, you can have the run of the entire second floor. Just ask us when you make your reservation.

**Address: 1451 N North Park Ave, Chicago, IL 60610-1226**
**Tel: (312) 440-9268.**

**Type:** Bed & breakfast.
**Clientele:** Mostly gay & lesbian/some straight clientele
**Transportation:** All transportation is best.
**To Gay Bars:** 2 blocks.
**Rms:** 2 rms w/ queen beds.
**Bathrooms:** 1-1/2 shared or ask for the private bath option.
**Meals:** Cont. breakfast.
**Vegetarian:** Always avail.
**Complimentary:** Tea, coffee & juice.
**Dates Open:** All year.
**Rates:** $90 for all rooms.
**Discounts:** Extended stays.
**Credit Cards:** MC, Visa, Amex.
**Reserve Through:** Travel agent or call direct.
**Parking:** Ample off-street parking.
**In-Room:** Color cable TV, video tape library, AC, telephone & laundry service.
**On-Premises:** TV lounge with fireplace, meeting rms.
**Exercise/Health:** Nearby gym.
**Swimming:** Nearby pool/lake
**Sunbathing:** In enclosed private garden.
**Nudity:** Permitted upstairs.
**Smoking:** Not permitted.
**Pets:** Not permitted.
**Languages:** English, German, French, Italian & Spanish.
**Your Host:** Michael.

## Park Brompton Inn

Gay-Friendly ♀♂

### *English Elegance with the Flair of Chicago Style*

In the tradition of fine, old English inns, the ***Park Brompton Inn*** offers a romantic 19th-century atmosphere on Chicago's bustling North Side. Poster beds and tapestry furnishings lend a hint of Dickensian spirit to finely appointed rooms. Steps away from the park and Lake Michigan, ***Park Brompton Inn*** is located in Chicago's largest gay district, where fine dining, shopping and

theatres abound. Wrigley Field, Halsted Street, Lincoln Park Zoo and a beautiful lakefront are nearby, and it's a ten-minute ride to downtown.

**Address: 528 W Brompton, Chicago, IL 60657**
**Tel: (312) 404-3499, Fax: (312) 404-3495. Reservations: (800) PARK-108.**

**Type:** Hotel.
**Clientele:** Mostly straight clientele with a gay/lesbian following.
**Transportation:** Taxi.
**To Gay Bars:** 1 block to gay/lesbian bars.
**Rooms:** 7 suites with kitchenettes, 25 single rooms.
**Bathrooms:** All private.
**Meals:** Continental breakfast.
**Dates Open:** All year.
**Rates:** $85-$99.
**Discounts:** Group.
**Credit Cards:** MC, VISA, Amex & Discover.
**Rsv'tns:** Recommended.
**Reserve Through:** Travel agent or call direct.
**Parking:** Ample off-street pay parking.
**In-Room:** Maid service, telephone, AC & color cable TV.
**On-Premises:** Laundry facilities.
**Swimming:** Lake Michigan nearby.
**Sunbathing:** At the lake.
**Smoking:** No restrictions.
**Pets:** Not permitted.
**Handicap Access:** No.
**Children:** Permitted.
**Languages:** English.

## Surf Hotel

**Gay-Friendly ♀♂**

On a quiet, tree-lined street in Lincoln Park, yet just 10 minutes from downtown Chicago, the ***Surf Hotel*** combines atmosphere with accessibility. We're steps away from Chicago's beautiful lakefront, the park, the zoo, the city's finest restaurants and Chicago's version of the Off-Broadway theatre district. Built in 1920, the ***Surf*** offers tastefully appointed rooms and is a truly affordable alternative for discriminating guests who prefer personality and ambiance when choosing lodgings.

**Address: 555 W Surf, Chicago, IL 60657**
**Tel: (312) 528-8400, Fax: (312) 528-8483.**
**Reservations: (800) SURF-108.**

**Type:** Hotel.
**Clientele:** Mainly straight clientele with a gay/lesbian following.
**Transportation:** Taxi is best.
**To Gay Bars:** One block.
**Rooms:** 20 singles, 31 doubles & 4 suites.
**Bathrooms:** All private.
**Meals:** Continental breakfast.
**Vegetarian:** Available nearby.
**Dates Open:** All year.
**Rates:** $85-$99.
**Discounts:** Group.
**Credit Cards:** MC, VISA, Amex, Discover.
**Rsv'tns:** Recommended.
**Reserve Through:** Travel agent or call direct.
**Parking:** Ample, off-street pay parking.
**In-Room:** Color cable TV, AC, maid service. Limited room service.
**On-Premises:** Laundry facilities.
**Exercise/Health:** Discounted daily rates at nearby health club with gym & weights.
**Swimming:** At nearby Lake Michigan.
**Sunbathing:** At the lake.
**Smoking:** Permitted without restrictions.
**Pets:** Not permitted.
**Handicap Access:** No.
**Children:** Permitted.
**Languages:** English.

## Villa Toscana Guest House

Gay/Lesbian ♀♂

### *A European-Style Guest House*

Located in the beautiful East Lakeview neighborhood, ***Villa Toscana*** is in the heart of Chicago's most vibrant gay neighborhood. Literally steps from our front door is the nightclub and theater district and the beautiful Lake Michigan shoreline. Our 1890s coach house offers wonderful gardens which are perfect for relaxation, entertainment or private receptions. Make yourself comfortable near the wood-burning fire in the living room and enjoy an expanded continental breakfast each morning in our dining room, or if you prefer, have breakfast in bed.

**Address: 3447 N Halsted, Chicago, IL 60657-2414**
**Tel: (800) 684-5755, (312) 404-2643.**

**Type:** Guesthouse.
**Clientele:** Mostly gay with some straight clientele
**Transportation:** Subway.
**To Gay Bars:** Next door.
**Rooms:** 6 dbls & 1 triple.
**Bathrooms:** 2 priv., 5 shared.
**Meals:** Expanded continental breakfast.
**Dates Open:** All year.
**High Season:** May-Nov.
**Rates:** $79 weekdays, $89 weekends. Room with private bath $99.
**Credit Cards:** MC, Visa, Amex, Discover.
**Rsv'tns:** Required.
**Reserve Through:** Travel agent or call direct.
**Minimum Stay:** Required.
**Parking:** Off-street parking available upon request.
**In-Room:** Color TV, AC & room service.
**On-Premises:** Meeting rms.
**Exercise/Health:** Hot tub.
**Swimming:** 2 blks to lake.
**Sunbathing:** On common sun decks.
**Languages:** English, Italian & Spanish.

# IOWA

## NEWTON

## La Corsette Maison Inn & The Sister Inn

Gay-Friendly ♀♂

### *Two Historical Properties*

***La Corsette Maison Inn***, a Mission-style mansion built in 1909, is acclaimed by historians as one of the finest examples of Arts and Crafts architecture in the Midwest. The original mission oak woodwork, art nouveau windows, and brass light fixtures highlight the decor. Guest rooms are furnished in French country decor, with goose down comforters and pillows. Enjoy a gourmet dinner in the 4-1/2 star restaurant preceded by a history and tour of the inn. ***The Sister Inn,*** a 140-year-old Federal-style building, features two luxurious bed chambers, both lavishly furnished and designed with privacy in mind. We're a 25-minute drive from Des Moines.

**Address: 629 1st Ave E, Newton, IA 50208**
**Tel: (515) 792-6833, Fax: (515) 792-6597.**

**Type:** Two inns, one with restaurant.
**Clientele:** Mainly straight clientele with a gay & lesbian following.
**Transportation:** Car is best, free pick up from airport.
**To Gay Bars:** 25 minutes to Des Moines.
**Rooms:** 5 doubles, 2 suites with double, queen & king beds.
**Bathrooms:** All private.
**Meals:** Full breakfast.
**Vegetarian:** By prior arrangement.
**Complimentary:** Tea, coffee, pop & snacks.
**Dates Open:** All year.
**High Season:** May through August, December.
**Rates:** $65-$185.
**Discounts:** Corporate discount with corporate number.
**Credit Cards:** MC, VISA, Amex.
**Reserve Through:** Call direct or travel agent.
**Minimum Stay:** Required at certain peak times.
**Parking:** Ample off-street parking.
**In-Room:** Ceiling fans, AC, double whirlpools, fireplaces. Phones & color TV upon request.
**On-Premises:** Meeting rooms & laundry facilities.
**Swimming:** At nearby pool.

**Smoking:** Permitted outside only, all rooms non-smoking.
**Pets:** Permitted by prior arrangement, but not in rooms.
**Handicap Access:** No.
**Children:** Permitted by pre-arrangement.
**Languages:** English.
**Your Host:** Kay.

# LOUISIANA

## NEW ORLEANS

### A Private Garden

Gay/Lesbian ♀♂

#### *Romantic Hideaway Near New Orleans' Garden District*

There is ***A Private Garden*** in the historic Faubourg Lafayette. Here, your romantic hideaway can be a studio or a two-room apartment set in a secluded patio garden with a spa. Eighteenth-century decor is complemented by a private bath, cable TV, telephone and videos. Just a block away, catch the St. Charles streetcar line for an easy 10-minute ride to the French Quarter, or walk to some of the city's best restaurants.

**Address:** 1718 Philip St, New Orleans, LA 70113
**Tel:** (504) 523-1776 (Tel/Fax).

**Type:** Bed & breakfast.
**Clientele:** Good mix of gay men & women
**To Gay Bars:** 1 mile or 10 minutes by car.
**Rooms:** 2 self-contained apartments with single, double & queen beds.
**Bathrooms:** 2 private.
**Meals:** Expanded continental buffet breakfast.
**Dates Open:** All year.
**High Season:** Mardi Gras & Jazzfest.
**Rates:** $50-$75, excluding Mardi Gras & Jazzfest. Please inquire.
**Rsv'tns:** Required.
**Reserve Thru:** Call direct.
**Parking:** Ample on-street parking.
**In-Room:** Color cable TV, VCR, video tape library, AC, ceiling fans, kitchen, ref., coffee/tea maker, tele., maid & laundry serv.
**On-Premises:** Laundry fac.
**Exercise/Health:** Jacuzzi.
**Swimming:** Local pools avail.
**Sunbathing:** On the patio.
**Nudity:** Permitted. Entire compound is private.
**Smoking:** Permitted.
**Children:** Not especially welcomed.
**Languages:** English.

### Bourgoyne Guest House

Gay/Lesbian ♀♂

#### *A Courtyard Retreat on Bourbon Street*

The excitement of Bourbon Street, coupled with a courtyard retreat from the hullabaloo, is what ***Bourgoyne Guest House*** offers visitors to the fabled French Quarter. Fine restaurants, museums, bars, discos...everything you'd want to see in the old section of the city is an easy walk from our central location. Guest accommodations range from cozy studios to spacious one- and two-bedroom suites of unusual style and elegance. All are furnished with antiques and all have private baths, kitchens, air conditioning and telephones.

*continued next page*

**Address: 839 rue Bourbon, New Orleans, LA 70116**
**Tel: (504) 524-3621 or (504) 525-3983.**

**Type:** Guesthouse.
**Clientele:** Mostly gay & lesbian with some straight clientele.
**Transportation:** Taxi or airport shuttle.
**To Gay Bars:** 1 blk to men's bar, 7 blks to women's bars.
**Rooms:** 3 rms & 2 suites.
**Bathrooms:** All private.
**Dates Open:** All year.
**Rates:** $70-$160.
**Credit Cards:** MC & VISA.
**Rsv'tns:** Recommended.
**Reserve Through:** Travel agent or call direct.
**Parking:** Off-street pay parking nearby.
**In-Room:** AC, color TV, telephones, complete kitchens, maid & laundry service.
**On-Premises:** Meeting rooms, laundry facilities, kitchen.
**Sunbathing:** On the patio.
**Smoking:** Permitted without restrictions.
**Children:** Permitted.
**Languages:** English & French.

## Boys On Burgundy

Gay/Lesbian ♂

***Boys on Burgundy*** is located in the heart of the French Quarter, only steps from the bars and famous New Orleans sights and restaurants. This spacious, quiet B&B with friendly, courteous hosts, offers reasonable rates, cable TV, unlimited local calls and large, comfortable rooms that make you feel at home. Everyone is invited to enjoy our large, well-landscaped patio. No standard institutional hotel stay here! Members of Gala Choruses and NOGMC.

**Address: 1030 Burgundy St, New Orleans, LA 70116**
**Tel: (504) 524-2987, (800) 487-8731.**

**Type:** Bed & breakfast.
**Clientele:** Men.
**Transportation:** Airport shuttle service.
**To Gay Bars:** 3 blocks.
**Rooms:** 3 rooms with king beds.
**Bathrooms:** 1 private bath/shower/toilet, 1 shared bath/shower/toilet.
**Meals:** Cont. breakfast.
**Vegetarian:** Avail. nearby.
**Dates Open:** All year.
**High Season:** Sept- May.
**Rates:** Call for rates.
**Credit Cards:** MC & VISA.
**Rsv'tns:** Required.
**Reserve Thru:** Call direct.
**Minimum Stay:** 2 nights, except for certain holidays.
**Parking:** On-street parking.
**In-Room:** Color cable TV, AC, telephone.
**On-Premises:** Kitchen, refrigerator, coffee/ tea-making facilities, large, well-landscaped patio.
**Exercise/Health:** Nearby gym, weights, spa, sauna, steam & massage.
**Swimming:** Nearby pool.
**Sunbathing:** On the patio & at private clubs.
**Smoking:** Permitted on patio only.
**Pets:** Not permitted.
**Handicap Access:** No.
**Children:** Not especially welcome.
**Languages:** English.

## Bywater B&B

Q-NET Women ♀

***Bywater B&B*** is a late Victorian "double shot-gun" cottage in the Bywater neighborhood, a short distance from Faubourg Marigny and the French Quarter and close to tourist attractions. Decorated with contemporary Southern folk art, guest space includes living room, library, dining room, kitchen and enclosed backyard patio. Groups can be accommodated with special prior arrangement. This is a women-owned B&B.

**Address: 1026 Clouet St, New Orleans, LA 70117. Tel: (504) 944-8438.**

**Type:** Bed & breakfast.
**Clientele:** Mostly women with men welcome.
**Transportation:** Car or taxi.
**To Gay Bars:** 1 mile or a 5-minute drive.
**Rooms:** 3 rooms with king or double beds.
**Bathrooms:** 1 private bath/shower/toilet, 2 private sinks, 2 shared bath/ shower/toilets.
**Meals:** Expanded continental breakfast.
**Vegetarian:** Request in advance. Vegetarian restaurants nearby.
**Comp.:** Coffee & tea.
**Dates Open:** All year.
**Rates:** $60-$75.
**Discounts:** Negotiable on stays of two weeks or more.
**Rsv'tns:** Required.
**Reserve Through:** Travel agent or call direct.
**Minimum Stay:** 2 nights on weekends, longer during Jazz Fest & Mardi Gras.
**Parking:** Ample on-street parking.
**In-Room:** AC, ceiling fans.
**On-Premises:** TV lounge, laundry facilities, video tape library.
**Sunbathing:** On the patio.
**Smoking:** Permitted only outdoors & on rear patio.
**Pets:** Permitted with advance arrangements.
**Handicap Access:** No.
**Children:** Welcome with advance arrangements.
**Languages:** English.
**Your Host:** Betty-Carol & Ken.

## Chateau Negara

Gay-Friendly ♀♂

### *A Restoration Wonder on Esplanade Avenue*

Experience antebellum New Orleans in this small, private and quaint guesthouse. ***Chateau Negara*** has many of the original features which made it an elegant mansion when it was built in 1865. These include ornate plasterwork, 11 functioning fireplaces, hardwood floors and 14-foot ceilings. There is cypress millwork throughout the home, as well as wrought iron railings and fences, a hand-carved mahogany banister, pocket doors, marble mantles, period furnishings, and much more. Our large tropical gardens are home to many native Louisiana trees and flowers. And, most importantly, we offer plenty of Southern Hospitality.

**Address: 1923 Esplanade Ave, New Orleans, LA 70116-1706**
**Tel: (504) 947-1343, Fax: (504) 947-4754,**
**E-mail: chateauneg@aol.com.**

**Type:** Bed & breakfast.
**Clientele:** Mostly straight clientele with a gay/lesbian following
**Transportation:** Airport, bus or train. Complimentary airport limo service.
**To Gay Bars:** 15 blocks to gay bars.
**Rooms:** 1 room, 2 suites with queen beds.
**Bathrooms:** Private: 2 bath/toilets, shared: 1 bath/shower/toilet.
**Meals:** Full breakfast.
**Vegetarian:** Available by request.
**Complimentary:** Complimentary bar in parlors. Complimentary beer, soft drinks & snacks in suites.
**Dates Open:** All year.
**High Season:** Sept-April.
**Rates:** High season (Sept-May): $75-$200, low season (June-August): $50-$125.
**Discounts:** On stays of 4 plus nights.
**Credit Cards:** MC, Visa, Amex.
**Rsv'tns:** Required.
**Reserve Through:** Travel agent or call direct.
**Minimum Stay:** 2 nights.
**Parking:** Ample free off-street parking.
**In-Room:** Color cable TV, VCR, telephone, ceiling fans, AC, kitchen, maid service.
**On-Premises:** Video tape library.
**Exercise/Health:** Jacuzzi, massage.
**Sunbathing:** On patio.
**Pets:** Not permitted.
**Languages:** English.

IGTA

## Fourteen Twelve Thalia, A Bed and Breakfast

Gay/Lesbian ♀♂

Brant-lee and Terry wish to welcome you into their home, ***Fourteen Twelve Thalia, A Bed & Breakfast.*** Your spacious, bright and comfortable one-bedroom apartment in this renovated Victorian house has a king-sized bed, private bath, kitchen with microwave, a large living room with queen-sized sofa sleeper, access to laundry facilities, color cable TV and a private entrance. The patio is available for sunbathing and relaxing among the flowers. Our location in the lower Garden District is convenient to the French Quarter, downtown and the art and warehouse districts, the convention center and Super Dome.

**Address: 1412 Thalia, New Orleans, LA 70130**
**Tel: (504) 522-0453, E-mail: grisgris@ix.netcom.com.**

*continued next page*

**Type:** Bed & breakfast.
**Clientele:** Mostly gay & lesbian with some straight clientele.
**Transportation:** Car, streetcar or taxi.
**To Gay Bars:** 14 blocks to French Quarter bars. From 5-20 minutes by car, taxi or streetcar.
**Rooms:** Self-contained apartment with king bed, queen sleeper sofa & private entrance. For 2-4 people.
**Bathrooms:** Private.
**Meals:** Breakfast furnishings supplied for self-catering kitchen.
**Vegetarian:** Available with advance notice.
**Complimentary:** Tea, coffee, juices & fresh fruit.
**Dates Open:** All year.
**High Season:** Mardi Gras, Jazz Fest, Sugar Bowl/New Years.
**Rates:** $75-$95 or $125-$175 during special events.
**Discounts:** For stays of more than 3 nights.
**Rsv'tns:** Required.
**Reserve Through:** Call direct.
**Minimum Stay:** 2 nights. Mardi Gras 4 nights, other special events 3 nights.
**Parking:** Ample on-street parking.
**In-Room:** Color cable TV, AC, stereo, telephone, ceiling fans, kitchen & refrigerator. Washer/dryer available.
**On-Premises:** Laundry facilities.
**Sunbathing:** On the patio.
**Smoking:** Not permitted in the apartment. Permitted on deck or patio.
**Pets:** Small pets that are crate trained.
**Handicap Access:** Yes. Low steps, wide doors, accessible bath.
**Children:** Welcomed but limited to 2.
**Languages:** English.

## The Greenhouse

### *A New Orleans Tropical Guesthouse*

***The Greenhouse, A Tropical New Orleans Guest House*** is a beautiful 1840's New Orleans grand home which has been converted into a guesthouse. Surrounded by tropical plants, and conveniently located in the Lower Garden District, it is near to all New Orleans has to offer. Its 6 rooms feature king-sized beds, private baths and mini-refrigerators.

***The Greenhouse*** is only 12 blocks from the French Quarter, three blocks from the St. Charles Avenue streetcar and five blocks from the Convention Center. Also nearby are antique shops, art galleries and many fine New Orleans restaurants. In addition, free secured parking, limited free shuttle service to the Quarter, complimentary continental breakfast, daily maid service and an on-site, full service travel agency are all reasons for staying at ***The Greenhouse.*** Lifelong residents of the area, your hosts Jesse and Keith will help you enjoy New Orleans to its fullest.

**Address: 1212 Magazine St, New Orleans, LA 70130**
**Tel: (504) 561-8400, (800) 966-1303, Fax: (504) 525-1306,**
**E-mail: SFCF11A@Prodigy.com.**

**Type:** Bed & breakfast guesthouse.
**Clientele:** Mostly gay & lesbian with some straight clientele
**Transportation:** Airport shuttle van or taxi.
**To Gay Bars:** 12 blks, 1 mi., a 20-min. walk, a 10-min. drive.
**Rooms:** 6 rms with king beds.
**Bathrooms:** Private: 5 shower/toilets, 1 bath/shower/toilet.
**Meals:** Cont. breakfast.
**Vegetarian:** 14 blocks to vegetarian restaurant.
**Complimentary:** Mints on pillow, morning coffee.
**Dates Open:** All year.
**High Season:** Fall & spring.
**Rates:** Low season (summer) $55, high season (fall, winter, spring) $85, special events $125.
**Discounts:** Weekly rate 10% off, monthly rate 25% off.
**Credit Cards:** Amex, Visa, MC, Discover.
**Rsv'tns:** Required.
**Reserve Through:** Travel agent or call direct.
**Minimum Stay:** Required only on special events (Mardi Gras, Jazz Fest, etc.)
**Parking:** Ample free off-street parking.
**In-Room:** AC, color TV, ceiling fans, refrigerator, maid service.
**On-Premises:** TV lounge,

laundry facilities, copier, fax, travel agency.
**Exercise/Health:** Weights. Nearby gym, weights, Jacuzzi, sauna, steam, massage.
**Swimming:** Pool.
**Sunbathing:** On patio.
**Nudity:** OK by pool.
**Smoking:** Permitted only in rooms or outside. No non-smoking rooms available.
**Pets:** Not permitted.
**Handicap Access:** No.
**Children:** No one under 16.
**Languages:** English, Spanish.
**Your Host:** Jesse & Keith.

## Lafitte Guest House

**Gay-Friendly 50/50 ♀♂**

### *The French Quarter's Premier Guest House For Over 40 Years*

This elegant French manor house, meticulously restored to its original splendor and furnished in fine antiques and reproductions, has all the comforts of home, including air conditioning. Located in the quiet, residential section of famous Bourbon St., ***Lafitte Guest House*** is just steps from the French Quarter's attractions. Continental breakfast is served in your room, in our tropical courtyard or in our Victorian parlour. Wine and hors d'oeuvres are served each evening at cocktail hour. Parking is available on the premises.

**Address: 1003 Bourbon St, New Orleans, LA 70116**
**Tel: (504) 581-2678 (Tel/Fax) or (800) 331-7971.**

**Type:** Bed & breakfast guesthouse.
**Clientele:** 50% gay & lesbian & 50% straight clientele.
**Transportation:** Limo from airport. Pick up from airport or train, $21 taxi, $65 limo (for 2).
**To Gay Bars:** 1 block.
**Rooms:** 12 rooms, 2 suites & 2 apartments with double, queen or king beds.
**Bathrooms:** 7 private bath/toilets & 7 private shower/toilets.
**Meals:** Continental breakfast.
**Vegetarian:** Vegetarian food nearby.
**Complimentary:** Wine & hors d'oeuvres.
**Dates Open:** All year.
**High Season:** Sept 1st-Dec 1st, Jan 1st-May 31st.
**Rates:** 1-bdrm $79-$165, 2-bdrm suite $210-$270.
**Discounts:** AAA 10%.
**Credit Cards:** MC, VISA, Amex & Discover.
**Rsv'tns:** Required with deposit.
**Reserve Through:** Travel agent or call direct.
**Minimum Stay:** 2 days on weekends. Inquire for special events.
**Parking:** Ample off-street parking.
**In-Room:** Color TV, AC, telephone & maid service. Some rooms have refrigerators & ceiling fans.
**On-Premises:** Victorian parlor & courtyard.
**Exercise/Health:** Nearby gym, weights, Jacuzzi/spa, sauna, steam & massage.
**Swimming:** Available at two of our off-premises townhouses.
**Smoking:** Not permitted in house.
**Pets:** Not permitted.
**Handicap Access:** No.
**Children:** Permitted.
**Languages:** English.
**Your Host:** Bill & Robert.

## The Lions Inn

**Men ♂**

***The Lions Inn*** is a handsome, 1840's private home with guest rooms and is located in the historic Faubourg-Marigny area, 5 blocks from the French Quarter. Amenities include central air, private baths, cable TV, VCR & CD, garden, swimming pool and continental breakfast.

**Address: 2517 Chartres St, New Orleans, LA 70117**
**Tel: (504) 945-2339, (504) 949-7321.**

**Type:** Bed & breakfast.
**Clientele:** Men only
**Transportation:** Taxi from airport or RR station.
**To Gay Bars:** 2 blocks or 5 minutes by foot.
**Rooms:** 2 rooms & 1 suite with queen beds.
**Bathrooms:** Private & shared.
**Meals:** Continental breakfast.
**Dates Open:** All year.
**Rates:** $50-$100 except special events & holidays.
**Discounts:** 10% on stays of 4 nights or more.
**Credit Cards:** MC, VISA.
**Rsv'tns:** Required.
**Reserve Thru:** Call direct.
**Minimum Stay:** 2 days.
**Parking:** Ample on-street parking.
**In-Room:** AC, color cable TV, ceiling fans & telephone.
**Exercise/Health:** Jacuzzi. Nearby gym.
**Swimming:** Pool on premises.
**Sunbathing:** At poolside.
**Smoking:** Not permitted in rooms.
**Pets:** Not permitted.
**Handicap Access:** No.
**Children:** Not especially welcome.
**Languages:** English.
**Your Host:** Jon & Earl.

# Macarty Park Guest House

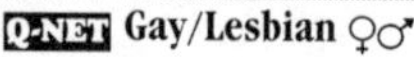


## *A Tropical Paradise in the City*

Enjoy beautiful, small, private poolside cottages, spacious suites and rooms in this Eastlake Victorian home. Step out of your room into lush, tropical gardens and jump into the sparkling pool. Enjoy the tranquility of the cool water on moonlit nights. Rooms are tastefully decorated in antique and reproduction furnishings, and are impeccably clean, each with a private bath. Located in a national historical district, ***Macarty Park*** is just five minutes from the French Quarter. All this for a fraction of what you would pay elsewhere!

**Address: 3820 Burgundy St, New Orleans, LA 70117-5708**
**Tel: (504) 943-4994, (800) 521-2790, Fax: (504) 943-4999.**

**Type:** Bed & breakfast guesthouse with cottages.
**Clientele:** Mostly gay & lesbian with some straight clientele
**Transportation:** Cab from airport. Pickup from Amtrak available.
**To Gay Bars:** A 2-minute drive, 10 blocks.
**Rooms:** 6 rooms & 2 cottages with king, queen, full or twin beds.
**Bathrooms:** All private.
**Meals:** Continental breakfast.
**Complimentary:** Brewed coffee & tea.
**Dates Open:** All year.
**Rates:** Off season $39-$115, In season $59-$115 (except special events).
**Credit Cards:** MC, VISA , Amex.
**Rsv'tns:** Required with deposit.
**Reserve Through:** Travel agent or call direct.
**Minimum Stay:** 2 days on weekends.
**Parking:** Ample free off-street parking.
**In-Room:** Color TV, AC, telephone & maid service. Some accommodations have kitchen, refrigerator, ceiling fans, coffee & tea-making facilities.
**Exercise/Health:** Complete universal gym with rowing machine, free weights, ab machine.
**Swimming:** In-ground heated pool on premises.
**Sunbathing:** At poolside, on common sun decks & on patio.
**Nudity:** Permitted around pool.
**Smoking:** Permitted without restrictions.
**Pets:** Not permitted.
**Handicap Access:** No.
**Children:** Not especially welcomed.
**Languages:** English & French.
**Your Host:** John.

IGTA

## Maison Burgundy B&B

Gay/Lesbian ♀♂

### *Minutes from the Heart of the French Quarter*

***Maison Burgundy,*** newly renovated and located in the historic Marigny Triangle area of New Orleans, stands out as one of the area's premier Greek Revival landmark buildings. The bed & breakfast offers two luxurious suites, each with antique furnishings and accessories, private baths, wet bars, cable color televisions, individually controlled air conditioners and heat, private entrances and off-street parking. Each suite accommodates four adults comfortably. Continental breakfast is served every morning in the Grand Dining Room of the house and, if you prefer, in-room service is also available. ***Maison Burgundy*** is minutes away from the heart of the French Quarter which is easily accessible by riverfront streetcar, French Quarter Trolley or, for a small fare, take a taxi.

**Address: 1860 Burgundy, New Orleans, LA 70116-1923**
**Tel: (504) 948-2355, (800) 863-8813, Fax: (504) 944-8578.**

**Type:** Bed & breakfast guest home.
**Clientele:** Mostly gay & lesbian with some straight clientele
**Transportation:** Taxi or airport shuttle.
**To Gay Bars:** 2 blocks to French Quarter, 10 blocks to main gay bars.
**Rooms:** 2 suites.
**Bathrooms:** All private.
**Meals:** Cont. breakfast.
**Dates Open:** All year.
**High Season:** October-May, Jazz Fest, Mardi Gras & Sugar Bowl.
**Rates:** $125-$175.
**Discounts:** On stays of 2 weeks or more.
**Credit Cards:** MC, Visa, Amex, Discover.
**Rsv'tns:** Req'd with deposit.
**Reserve Through:** Travel agent or call direct.
**Minimum Stay:** 1 night.
**Parking:** Off-street parking.
**In-Room:** Cable color TV, private phone, wet bar, central AC/heat, maid service, refrigerator, microwave, ceiling fans.
**On-Premises:** Patios.
**Smoking:** Permitted.
**Pets:** Not permitted.
**Handicap Access:** No.
**Children:** Not permitted.
**Languages:** English, Spanish.
**Your Host:** Carlos & Greg.

## Mentone Bed & Breakfast

Gay/Lesbian ♀♂

***Mentone Bed & Breakfast*** offers a suite in a Victorian home in the Faubourg Marigny district next to the historic French Quarter. The suite is furnished with antiques and Oriental rugs, has thirteen-foot ceilings, a sitting room, and a private entrance. The sound of the paddle wheels on the river and of the horse-drawn carriages in the street below lull guests to sleep in the evenings. Enjoy the solitude of our home and tropical garden, or venture five blocks into the heart of the Quarter for entertainment and nightlife.

**Address: 1437 Pauger St, New Orleans, LA 70116. Tel: (504) 943-3019.**

**Type:** Bed & breakfast.
**Clientele:** Mostly gay & lesbian with some straight clientele.
**Transportation:** Shuttle, taxi or limo from airport at expense.
**To Gay Bars:** 3-4 blocks.
**Rooms:** 1 suite with double bed.
**Bathrooms:** All private

*continued next page*

shower/toilets.
**Meals:** Expanded continental breakfast of pastries or bread, fruit bowl.
**Complimentary:** Champagne, coffee, & tea.
**Dates Open:** All year except Christmas.
**High Season:** Sep1-June1.
**Rates:** $75-$100 except for special events.
**Discounts:** Reduction after 7-night stay.
**Rsv'tns:** Preferred.
**Reserve Thru:** Call direct.
**Minimum Stay:** On weekends and for special events.
**Parking:** Adequate free on-street parking or limited off-street free parking.
**In-Room:** Color TV, AC, ceiling fans, telephone, kitchenette, refrigerator & coffee & tea-making facilities.
**Smoking:** On the balcony off the suite. Non-smoking room.
**Pets:** Not permitted.
**Handicap Access:** No.
**Children:** Permitted on approval.
**Languages:** English & limited French.

## Nine Twelve Pauline Street

Gay/Lesbian ♀♂

### *New Orleans – A City Spiced with Unusual Charm*

Located in the residential neighborhood of Bywater, a National Historic District, ***912 Pauline Street*** is a raised and renovated Mediterranean-style home with a distinctive Spanish tile roof. About one mile from the French Quarter and four blocks from the Mississippi River, this spacious and bright first-floor, 2-bedroom apartment has a private, lighted entrance, cable TV, stereo and electronic security. The kitchen is stocked with self-catering breakfast foods and beverages. The charm, warmth and affordability of ***912 Pauline Street*** is ideal for visitors wanting to do business in "The Big Easy," or those wanting to reinforce its reputation as "The Big Sleazy."

**Address: 912 Pauline St, New Orleans, LA**
**Tel: (504) 948-6827, E-mail: bareskin@ix.netcom.com**

**Type:** Bed & breakfast.
**Clientele:** Mostly gay & lesbian with some straight clientele
**Transportation:** Cab from airport, or car.
**To Gay Bars:** 12 blocks, a 10 minute walk, a 2 minute drive.
**Rooms:** 1 apartment with double or queen beds.
**Bathrooms:** Private bath & toilet.
**Meals:** Cont. breakfast.
**Vegetarian:** No meat served. 1 vegetarian restaurant 2 miles away.
**Complimentary:** Coffee & tea provided (self-catering) in kitchen.
**Dates Open:** All year.
**Rates:** $65-$175.
**Rsv'tns:** Suggested for Mardi Gras, Southern Decadence, national events.
**Reserve Through:** Call direct.
**Minimum Stay:** Required.
**Parking:** Ample on-street parking.
**In-Room:** Color cable TV, AC, telephone, kitchen, refrigerator, coffee & tea-making facilities.
**On-Premises:** Large, plant-filled raised veranda, backyard patio & fish pond.
**Exercise/Health:** Nearby gym, weights, sauna, steam, massage.
**Swimming:** 8 blocks to G/L/B pool club, swimsuit optional.
**Sunbathing:** On patio.
**Smoking:** Permitted outside only, on porches or pond-side.
**Pets:** Not permitted.
**Handicap Access:** Yes.
**Children:** No.
**Languages:** English.
**Your Host:** Larry & Steve.

## Parkview Marigny Bed & Breakfast

**Gay-Friendly 50/50 ♀♂**

***Parkview Marigny*** offers comfortable accommodations and cozy atmosphere in a quaint Creole townhouse. Centrally-located, across from Washington Square and adjacent to the French Quarter, the bed & breakfast is surrounded by restaurants, bars, jazz clubs, theatres, and curio shops. ***Parkview Marigny*** has been newly renovated and expanded into five well-appointed guest rooms, each with private bath. A continental breakfast is served in the dining room. Guests can enjoy visiting in the living room with a view of the park, or in the private courtyard.

**Address: 726 Frenchmen St, New Orleans, LA 70116**
**Tel: (504) 945-7875. Reservations: (800) 729-4640.**

**Type:** Bed & breakfast.
**Clientele:** 50% gay & lesbian & 50% straight clientele.
**Transportation:** Taxi.
**To Gay Bars:** 5-minute walk.
**Rooms:** 5 rooms with double, queen or king beds.
**Bathrooms:** All private.
**Meals:** Continental breakfast.
**Complimentary:** Coffee, orange juice.
**Dates Open:** All year.
**High Season:** New Year, Jazz Fest, Mardi Gras.
**Rates:** Summer $70-$80. Fall, winter, spring $80-$110. Special events $125-$160.
**Rsv'tns:** Required.
**Reserve Through:** Call direct.
**Minimum Stay:** 2 days.
**Parking:** Limited on-street parking.
**In-Room:** Color cable TV, AC, ceiling fans.
**Sunbathing:** On the patio.
**Smoking:** Permitted in courtyard only.
**Pets:** Not permitted.
**Handicap Access:** No.
**Children:** Not permitted.
**Languages:** English.

IGTA

## Rober House

**Gay/Lesbian ♀♂**

Welcome to America's most fascinating city, whose unique personality was blended from many cultures. New Orleans offers you fun, music, excitement and delicious foods. Come, experience and capture the charm of the French Quarter at ***Rober House.*** Here, in a quiet, residential location, our one-bedroom, living, kitchen and full-bath condos are fully furnished and have all the amenities, plus courtyard and swimming pool. Three of the apartments can sleep up to 4 people. Great savings only minutes from fabulous restaurants and tourist attractions.

**Address: 822 Ursulines St, New Orleans, LA 70116-2422**
**Tel: (504) 529-4663 or 523-1246.**

**Type:** Guesthouse.
**Clientele:** Mostly gay & lesbian with some straight clientele
**Transportation:** Taxi from airport $21. Shuttle bus, $10 per person, stops across the street.
**To Gay Bars:** Two blocks to 1 bar & three blocks to 4 other bars, all in the same direction.
**Rooms:** 5 apartments (3 apts. sleep up to 4 people each) with queen beds & queen sofa beds.
**Bathrooms:** All private.
**Vegetarian:** Health restaurant nearby.
**Complimentary:** Coffee.
**Dates Open:** All year.
**High Season:** Special events weeks & weekends.
**Rates:** July 1-Aug 27, $69-$89. Rest of year, $90-$125, except special events periods (call for rates).
**Discounts:** Weekly rates.
**Credit Cards:** All accepted.
**Rsv'tns:** Required.
**Reserve Through:** Travel agent or call direct.
**Minimum Stay:** 3 days in summer & 2 days rest of year.
**Parking:** On-street parking & plenty of parking garages near Canal St.
**In-Room:** Color TV, AC, ceiling fans, telephone & kitchen with refrigerator.
**Swimming:** Pool.
**Sunbathing:** At poolside.
**Nudity:** Permitted poolside if no one else objects.
**Smoking:** Preferably outside the apartments.
**Pets:** Permitted except for snakes & other reptiles.
**Handicap Access:** 1 unit is accessible with help.
**Children:** Welcomed.
**Languages:** English, German & Danish.

## Royal Barracks Guest House

**Gay/Lesbian ♀♂**

In a newly-renovated Victorian home located in a quiet, residential neighborhood, a charming French lady will offer you the hospitality of the historical French Quarter. Within a few blocks are 24-hour restaurants, bars and delicatessens. Rooms at ***Royal Barracks*** are individually decorated, have private entrances and have all modern conveniences. All open onto our high-walled, private patio with wet bar, refrigerator and ice maker. Our avid return customers, many of whom often book a year in advance, consider their accommodations here their own secluded, private hideaway.

**Address: 717 Barracks St, New Orleans, LA 70116**
**Tel: (504) 529-7269, Fax: (504) 529-7298.**

**Type:** Guesthouse.
**Clientele:** Mostly gay & lesbian with some straight clientele
**Transportation:** $10 per person airport shuttle, taxi $20 flat fee.
**To Gay Bars:** 1/2 block to men's & 7 blocks to women's bars.
**Rooms:** 4 rooms & 1 suite with double & queen beds.
**Bathrooms:** All private.
**Meals:** Expanded continental breakfast.
**Complimentary:** Kenwood water, fruits, cookies, coffee & tea.
**Dates Open:** All year.
**High Season:** April (Jazz Fest) & February (Mardi Gras).
**Rates:** Jun 15-Sep 15, $65-$95. Winter, $75-$130.
**Credit Cards:** MC, Visa.
**Rsv'tns:** Required.
**Reserve Through:** Travel agent or call direct.
**Parking:** On-street parking.
**In-Room:** Color TV, telephone, ceiling fans, AC & maid service.
**On-Premises:** Ice machine & refrigerator in the courtyard.
**Exercise/Health:** Jacuzzi.
**Smoking:** Permitted without restrictions.
**Pets:** Not permitted.
**Handicap Access:** No.
**Children:** Permitted.
**Languages:** French, English & Spanish.
**Your Host:** Christine & John.

## Ursuline Guesthouse

**Gay/Lesbian ♀♂**

Our guesthouse is located in the midst of the French Quarter, near restaurants, shops, museums and all that makes New Orleans famous. Constructed in the 18th century, ***Ursuline Guest House*** is today an historical structure enhanced with all the modern amenities desirable to the out-of-town guest. All rooms have modern bathrooms, air conditioning, color cable TV, carpeting or hardwood floors, are furnished with an eclectic blend of furniture, and some open onto a serene, old French Quarter courtyard with wrought iron furniture and a hot tub. We are confident you will be pleased.

**Address: 708 rue des Ursulines, New Orleans, LA 70116**
**Tel: (504) 525-8509, (800) 654-2351, Fax: (504) 525-8408.**

**Type:** Guesthouse.
**Clientele:** Mostly gay & lesbian with some straight clientele
**Transportation:** Airport shuttle $10. Taxi $21 for 1 or 2 people.
**To Gay Bars:** 3 blocks.
**Rooms:** 13 rooms with single, double & queen beds.
**Bathrooms:** All private.
**Meals:** Continental breakfast.
**Vegetarian:** Vegetarian restaurant within walking distance.
**Complimentary:** Coffee. Wine in courtyard each evening.
**Dates Open:** All year.
**High Season:** Sept-May.
**Rates:** $75-$120. Higher on holidays & for special events.
**Credit Cards:** MC, Visa, Amex.
**Rsv'tns:** Recommended.
**Reserve Thru:** Call direct.
**Minimum Stay:** Two nights weekends & 3-5 days during special events & holidays.
**Parking:** Limited off-street parking $7/day.
**In-Room:** Color TV, AC, direct dial telephone & maid service.
**On-Premises:** Reading room, meeting room.
**Exercise/Health:** Whirlpool in courtyard.
**Smoking:** Permitted without restrictions.
**Pets:** Permitted with restrictions.
**Handicap Access:** Yes, limited.
**Children:** Not especially welcomed.
**Languages:** English.

# MAINE

## AUGUSTA

### Maple Hill Farm B&B Inn

Gay-Friendly ♀♂

*Get Away From It All, Yet Be Near It All...*

On 62-acres just minutes from Augusta, ***Maple Hill Farm*** is the only B&B Inn in the Capitol area. Breakfast is hearty country fare, cooked to order from our menu. Guest rooms provide a variety of amenities, including private bath and a whirlpool for two! ***Maple Hill Farm*** provides an excellent "base camp" from which to explore Maine. Hike through fields and woods, enjoy the private swimming hole, or relax in front of the fireplace. The coast, lakes, mountains and Freeport shopping are all within an hour's drive. Hallowell, just 3 miles away, is the gay community for this area.

**Address: Outlet Rd, RR1 Box 1145, Hallowell, ME 04347**
**Tel: (207) 622-2708, (800) 622-2708, Fax: (207) 622-0655,**
**E-mail: maple@mint.net.**

**Type:** Bed & breakfast with gallery.
**Clientele:** Mostly straight clientele with a gay & lesbian following.
**Transportation:** Car is best. Rentals available at Portland or Augusta airports.
**To Gay Bars:** 5 miles to P.J.'s in Augusta. 1 hour to Portland bars.
**Rooms:** 6 rooms & 1 suite with double or queen beds.
**Bathrooms:** Private: 3 shower/toilets, 1 full bath. 1 shared full bath.
**Campsites:** Rustic camping adjacent to small spring-fed pond in woods. Very private.
**Meals:** Full breakfast cooked to order from menu. Lunch & dinner with liquor service.
**Vegetarian:** Cooked to order breakfast. Excellent vegetarian-oriented restaurant nearby.
**Complimentary:** Evening tea or coffee. Mints in room. Bathroom amenities.
**Dates Open:** All year.
**High Season:** July-October (summer & fall foliage).
**Rates:** Summer $55-$105 winter $45-$95.
**Discounts:** Government rates available.
**Credit Cards:** MC, VISA, Amex, Diners & Discover.
**Rsv'tns:** Recommended.
**Reserve Through:** Travel agent or call direct.
**Minimum Stay:** Required some peak summer & fall weekends.
**Parking:** Ample free off-street parking.
**In-Room:** AC, telephone, color TV, clock radio & maid service. 1 room with Jacuzzi bath.
**On-Premises:** TV lounge, meeting rooms, fax machine.
**Exercise/Health:** Jacuzzi in 1 guest room. Nearby gym & massage.
**Swimming:** Swimming hole in the woods. 1 mile to lake.
**Sunbathing:** On common sun decks & at the swimming hole.
**Nudity:** Permitted at swimming hole.
**Smoking:** Permitted outside or on covered porch only, not inside building or rooms.
**Pets:** Not permitted.
**Handicap Access:** Yes. Ramp to 1st floor guest room & fully accessible bathroom.
**Children:** Well-behaved children over 8 are welcome. Younger children by permission only.
**Languages:** English, some French.
**Your Host:** Scott & Vince.

# BAR HARBOR

## Devilstone Oceanfront Inn

**Gay/Lesbian ♀♂**

### *On the Famous Bar Harbor Shorepath, Yet Only a Block from Town*

Early neighbors of the Rockefellers and Pulitzers, ***Devilstone*** was one of the original estates built on the shorepath in 1885, with unusual romantic gardens flowing to the ocean's edge on nearly two acres. Located on Mt. Desert Island, Bar Harbor and Acadia National Park (ANP is five minutes from us) offer biking, golfing, kayaking, sailing, hiking, climbing, whalewatching cruises, etc. Movies and nearly 75 restaurants are all a short walk from the inn. Very quiet, peaceful and beautifully designed, ***Devilstone*** is the perfect place to relax.

**Address: PO Box 801, Bar Harbor, ME. Tel: (207) 288-2933.**

**Type:** Inn.
**Clientele:** Mostly gay & lesbian with some straight clientele.
**Transport.:** Car is best.
**Rooms:** 6 rooms with queen or king beds.
**Bathrooms:** 6 private bath/tub/shower/toilets.
**Meals:** Expanded continental breakfast.
**Vegetarian:** Many restaurants nearby.
**Complimentary:** Afternoon tea, coffee, cocktail set ups, munchies, mints on pillows.
**Dates Open:** May 15-October 15.
**High Season:** Summer.
**Rates:** $95-$295/night.
**Discounts:** On stays of 1 week or more.
**Credit Cards:** MC, VISA.
**Rsv'tns:** Required.
**Reserve Thru:** Call direct.
**Minimum Stay:** Inquire.
**Parking:** Ample free off-street parking.
**In-Room:** Beautiful sitting areas, maid service. AC in some rooms.
**On-Premises:** The beautiful shorepath & ponds.
**Exercise/Health:** Horseshoes, weights, Jacuzzi. Nearby gym, weights.
**Swimming:** Ocean on premises. Nearby lake.
**Sunbathing:** On common sun decks, beach, patio.
**Smoking:** No smoking.
**Pets:** Not permitted.
**Languages:** English.
IGTA

## Lindenwood Inn

**Gay-Friendly ♀♂**

### *A Quiet Place by the Harbor*

Built at the turn of the century, ***Lindenwood Inn*** derives its name from the stately linden trees that still line the front lawn now, as they did then. Recently remodeled, each room is individually decorated and has a private bath. The inn is filled with an eclectic mix of art and furnishings gathered by the host in his travels. Many rooms feature harbor views from sun-drenched balconies. Relax and unwind in one of the inn's elegant sitting rooms, or on the large, shaded porch, while listening to the sounds of the harbor just a few steps away.

**Address: Box 1328, Clark Point Rd, Southwest Harbor, ME 04679 Tel: (207) 244-5335.**

**Type:** Inn.
**Clientele:** Mostly straight clientele with a gay & lesbian following
**Transportation:** Car is best. Pick up from airport.
**To Gay Bars:** 40 miles or 1 hour by car.
**Rooms:** 15 rooms, 5 suites & 3 cottages with dbl or queen beds.
**Bathrooms:** All private & 3 housekeeping cottages.
**Meals:** Full breakfast.
**Vegetarian:** Available upon request.
**Complimentary:** Tea, coffee & setup service.
**Dates Open:** All year.
**High Season:** Jul-Oct.
**Rates:** Jul-Sept: $85-$195; Sept-Oct 15: $75-$185; Oct 16-June 30: $65-$[illegible]5.
**Cred. Crds.:** MC, Visa, Amex.
**Rsv'tns:** Sugg. in sum.
**Reserve Thru:** Call direct.
**Min. Stay:** Summer only.
**Parking:** Ample free off-street parking.
**In-Room:** Ceiling fans & maid service.
**On-Premises:** Meeting rms, sitting rooms with fireplaces, balconies, guest kitchen & priv. access to water.
**Exercise/Health:** Nearby gym, weights, Jacuzzi/spa, sauna, steam & massage.
**Swimming:** Nearby ocean, river & lake.
**Sunbathing:** On private sun decks & nearby beach.
**Nudity:** Nude beach near.
**Smoking:** Permitted on porches only.
**Children:** Not welcomed.
**Languages:** English.

## Manor House Inn

Gay-Friendly ♀♂

### *Bar Harbor's Historic Victorian Inn*

The moment you step into the front entry, a romantic Victorian past becomes the present. Our elegant common rooms are decorated with antiques, Victorian wallcoverings, original maple floors and several working fireplaces. Our in-town location on tree-lined West St. lets you enjoy privacy, while staying within easy walking distance of Bar Harbor's fine shops, restaurants, whale watching, schooner rides, bike rentals, and even Bar Island. The spacious suites at ***Manor House Inn*** are graciously furnished, have working fireplaces, private baths, garden views and king-sized beds.

**Address: 106 West St, Bar Harbor, ME 04609**
**Tel: (207) 288-3759, (800) 437-0088.**

**Type:** Bed & breakfast.
**Clientele:** Mostly straight clientele with a gay/lesbian following.
**Transportation:** Car is best.
**Rooms:** 9 rooms & 5 suites with queen or king beds.
**Bathrooms:** All private baths.
**Meals:** Full breakfast.
**Complimentary:** Tea, coffee, lemonade, iced tea & apple cider in season.
**Dates Open:** May through October.
**High Season:** July through October.
**Rates:** Seasonal $85-165, off season $50-$125.
**Credit Cards:** MC & VISA.
**Rsv'tns:** Highly recommended as early as possible.
**Reserve Through:** Call direct.
**Minimum Stay:** 2 nights July & August & holiday weekends.
**Parking:** Adequate on-street & off-street parking.
**In-Room:** Maid service. Some rooms have fireplaces, cottages have color cable TV.
**On-Premises:** TV lounge, veranda & gardens.
**Swimming:** Beaches at the ocean or nearby lakes.
**Sunbathing:** On the beach.
**Smoking:** Not permitted.
**Pets:** Not permitted.
**Children:** Permitted (12 years and up).
**Languages:** English.

# BELFAST

## Alden House Bed & Breakfast

Q-NET Gay-Owned 50/50 ♀♂

### *Seventh Heaven in One of the Top Five Culturally Cool Towns in the U.S.*

Come to the coast and enjoy an authentic, affordable New England community. ***The Alden House*** (c. 1840), located in the heart of the historic district, is graced with a hand-carved cherry staircase and mantel, several marble fireplaces, German silver hardware, a curved pocket door and ornate woodwork. The town has lovely shops, art galleries and restaurants and was named by *USA Today* as one of the top five "culturally cool" towns in the U.S. Activities abound, including antiquing, skiing, biking & hiking, the theatre, cruises and train excursions. Commitment ceremonies are welcomed.

**Address: 63 Church St, Belfast, ME 04915. Tel: (207) 338-2151.**

**Type:** Gay-owned & -operated bed & breakfast.
**Clientele:** 50% gay & lesbian & 50% straight clientele
**Transportation:** Car, or air to Bangor or Portland, ME.
**To Gay Bars:** 37 miles, a 40 min drive.
**Rooms:** 7 rooms with single, double or queen beds.
**Bathrooms:** 5 private shower/toilets, 2 shared bath/shower/toilets.
**Meals:** Full breakfast.
**Vegetarian:** Available upon request, with notice.
**Complimentary:** Coffee, tea, lemonade.
**Dates Open:** All year.
**High Season:** July-beginning of October.
**Rates:** $65-$95.
**Discounts:** Extended stay discounts.
**Credit Cards:** MC, Visa, Amex.
**Reserve Thru:** Call direct.
**Parking:** Ample off-street parking.

*continued next page*

**In-Room:** VCR, maid service.
**On-Premises:** Video tape library.
**Exercise/Health:** Massage. Nearby gym, weights, Jacuzzi, sauna.
**Swimming:** Nearby pool & ocean.
**Smoking:** Permitted on outside porches only.
**Pets:** Not permitted.
**Handicap Access:** No. First-floor room has some accessibility.
**Children:** No.
**Languages:** English.
**Your Host:** Jessica & Marla.

# COREA - ACADIA AREA

## The Black Duck Inn on Corea Harbor

Gay-Friendly ♀♂

### *Explore the Real Downeast!*

Retreat from the hassles of daily city life on 12 acres in a tranquil, Downeast fishing village. The land is full of rock outcrops (to sit, read, paint, or birdwatch), wild berries, hidden tidal bays, and salt marshes. From ***The Black Duck Inn,*** enjoy the sight of one of the most picturesque harbors in Maine. The inn is only a few miles from the Schoodic section of Acadia National Park and is close to other wildlife sanctuaries, a fresh water pond, sand beaches, public golf courses, antique shops, and restaurants.

**Address: PO Box 39, Crowley Island Rd, Corea, ME 04624**
**Tel: (207) 963-2689, Fax: (207) 963-7495,**
**E-mail: bduck@acadia.net.**

**Type:** Bed & breakfast.
**Clientele:** Mostly straight clientele with a gay/lesbian following.
**Transportation:** Car is best. Free pick up from boat into harbor.
**To Gay Bars:** 50 miles.
**Rooms:** 3 rooms, 1 suite, 2 cottages with single, double or queen beds.
**Bathrooms:** Private: 3 shower/toilets, 1 bath/shower/toilet. 1 shared bath/shower/toilet.
**Meals:** Full breakfast.
**Vegetarian:** Vegan by advance request, otherwise fully available. Restaurants nearby in season.
**Complimentary:** Early coffee (6:30 am).
**Dates Open:** All year.
**High Season:** July-September.
**Rates:** Winter $60-$90, summer $70-$130.
**Discounts:** On weekly & monthly cottage rentals, without breakfast.
**Credit Cards:** MC, VISA.
**Reserve Through:** Travel agent or call direct.
**Minimum Stay:** 3 nights in cottages.
**Parking:** Ample free off-street parking.
**In-Room:** Maid service.
**On-Premises:** Meeting rooms, TV lounge, VCR, library, fireplaces, fax.
**Exercise/Health:** Trails on premises.
**Swimming:** Ocean, nearby lake.
**Sunbathing:** On patio, at beach.
**Smoking:** No smoking in house or cottages.
**Pets:** Not permitted.
**Handicap Access:** No.
**Children:** Please inquire.
**Languages:** English, Danish.
**Your Host:** Barry & Bob.

# KENNEBUNK

## Arundel Meadows Inn

Gay-Friendly ♀♂

### *A Relaxing Getaway With a Four-Star Breakfast!*

Small and personal, this nineteenth-century farmhouse has rooms and suites decorated in art and antiques, with private bathrooms and summer air conditioning. Three rooms have working fireplaces and all have comfortable sitting areas for reading and relaxing. Nearby Kennebunkport has antiques, artists' studios and excellent restaurants. Golf, tennis, fishing and cross-country skiing are readily accessible. At ***Arundel Meadows Inn,*** guests enjoy spring picnic meadows, summer flower gardens, fall foliage and winter fires in the living room.

**Address: PO Box 1129, Kennebunk, ME 04043-1129**
**Tel: (207) 985-3770.**

**Type:** Bed & breakfast.
**Clientele:** Mostly straight clientele, with gays & lesbians welcome.
**Transportation:** Car is best.
**To Gay Bars:** 10 miles to Ogunquit, ME, 25 miles to Portland, ME gay bars.
**Rooms:** Five rooms and two suites with single, double, queen and king beds.
**Bathrooms:** All private.
**Meals:** Full breakfast.
**Vegetarian:** Available upon request.
**Complimentary:** Afternoon tea.
**Dates Open:** All year (subject to change).
**High Season:** Memorial Day through Columbus Day.
**Rates:** Summer $75-$125, winter $55-$85.
**Discounts:** 10% on 5 nights or more.
**Credit Cards:** MC & VISA.
**Rsv'tns:** Required.
**Reserve Through:** Call direct.
**Minimum Stay:** 2 days on weekends Memorial Day through Columbus Day.
**Parking:** Adequate free off-street parking.
**In-Room:** AC & maid service. 3 rooms have color TV.
**Swimming:** Ocean beach is nearby.
**Sunbathing:** At the beach, on the patio, 2 rooms with private sun decks.
**Smoking:** Not permitted.
**Pets:** Not permitted.
**Handicap Access:** Yes.
**Children:** Not permitted under 12 years of age.
**Languages:** English.

# NAPLES

## Lamb's Mill Inn

Q-NET Gay-Friendly ♀♂

### *Ewe Hike, Ewe Bike, Ewe Ski, Ewe ZZzzz...*

***Lamb's Mill Inn*** is a small country inn nestled among the foothills of the White Mountains in the picturesque village of Naples. Surrounded by two of Maine's largest lakes, Sebago and Long Lake, Naples is the hub of summertime water activities in this area. Winter brings cross-country and alpine skiers, snowmobilers and ice fishermen. The spectacular fall foliage invites hikers and bikers to hit the trails. In spring, canoeing the Saco River and nearby ponds is a popular pastime. The inn is a 19th-century farmhouse, newly renovated and abounding with country charm. Our six rooms offer a romantic atmosphere and feature private baths. You will awaken to the aroma of a full country breakfast served in our two gracious dining rooms. Enjoy the privacy and scenic beauty of twenty acres of field and woods, or a leisurely stroll to the charming village. Browse along the causeway and discover parasailing, aerial sightseeing, watercycling, windsurfing and tours on the Songo River Queen. Play golf and tennis, or visit the many country fairs and flea markets. Dine in gourmet restaurants, or sample local Yankee recipes in small cafes and diners. To end an exciting day, unwind in our hot tub. All this and more is yours at ***Lamb's Mill Inn,*** an inn for all seasons.

**Address: Box 676, Lamb's Mill Rd, Naples, ME 04055**
**Tel: (207) 693-6253.**

**Type:** Bed & breakfast inn.
**Clientele:** Large gay & lesbian clientele
**Transportation:** Car from Portland airport 25 miles away.
**To Gay Bars:** 25 miles to Portland gay/lesbian bars.
**Rooms:** 6 rooms with 1 king, 4 queens, 1 full bed.
**Bathrooms:** All private.
**Meals:** Full gourmet breakfast.
**Vegetarian:** Yes.
**Complimentary:** Ice & munchies available in afternoon as well as tea & coffee.
**Dates Open:** All year.
**High Season:** Summer & for fall foliage.
**Rates:** High peak (May 16-Labor Day) $85-$105; Peak (Sept-Dec 31) $75-$95; Low (Jan-May 15) $65-$85.
**Discounts:** Sixth consecutive night free. 15% midweek (Mon-Thurs) for 3 night stay.
**Credit Cards:** MC & VISA.
**Rsv'tns:** Recommended.
**Reserve Through:** Travel agent or call direct.

*continued next page*

**Minimum Stay:** Two nights on weekends in high season.
**Parking:** Ample free off-street parking.
**In-Room:** Color cable TV, maid service, refrigerators.
**On-Premises:** 2 private dining rooms, 2 TV lounges, stereo, BBQ's, 1 reading & game lounge.
**Exercise/Health:** Hot tub, treadmill, canoeing, windsurfing, parasailing, boat rides, water cycling, trails, downhill skiing, bicycling.
**Swimming:** Town beach is at the bottom of our hill on Long Lake.
**Sunbathing:** On patio, private sun decks or anywhere on 20 acres.
**Smoking:** Permitted outside.
**Pets:** Not permitted.
**Handicap Access:** No.
**Children:** Not permitted.
**Languages:** English.

IGTA

# NORTHPORT

## Sign of the Owl B&B

**Gay/Lesbian ♀♂**

Visit with us in our 1794 Maine farmhouse nine miles north of Camden's beautiful harbor. ***Sign of the Owl*** is convenient for day trips to Acadia Nat'l Park, Vinalhaven, Bar Harbor and Islesboro. A sandy public beach is but 2 miles from the house and a small private beach is a 10-minute walk through the woods. Many fine restaurants, gift and antique shops are nearby. The bathroom is shared, so please be considerate of other guests.

**Address: 243 Atlantic Highway, Northport, ME 04849**
**Tel: (207) 338-4669.**

**Type:** Bed & breakfast with an antique shop.
**Clientele:** Mostly gay & lesbian with some straight clientele
**Transportation:** Rent a car at Bangor airport.
**To Gay Bars:** Nearest gay bars are in Portland, a 2-hour drive.
**Rooms:** 3 rooms with single or double beds.
**Bathrooms:** 1 shared bath/shower/toilet & 1 shared shower/toilet.
**Meals:** Full gourmet break.
**Vegetarian:** Available upon request.
**Dates Open:** All year.
**High Season:** July-Sep.
**Rates:** $35-$65.
**Discounts:** Stay one week, 7th day free.
**Credit Cards:** MC, VISA, Amex.
**Rsv'tns:** Recommended.
**Reserve Thru:** Call direct.
**Parking:** Ample free off-street parking.
**In-Room:** Maid service, color or B&W TV.
**On-Premises:** Meeting rms, cent. heat, TV lounge.
**Exercise/Health:** Hiking, swimming, bike trails.
**Swimming:** 4-min. walk to ocean beach, 6 mi. to lake.
**Sunbathing:** On ocean beach, at lakeside, in backyard.
**Smoking:** Permitted outside only.
**Pets:** Permitted with prior arrangement.
**Children:** Not permitted.
**Languages:** English.
**Your Host:** John & Duncan.

# OGUNQUIT

## Admiral's Inn & Guesthouse

**Gay-Owned ♀♂**

### *Unique in Ogunquit...*

***The Admiral's Inn*** is located 65 miles north of Boston in Ogunquit, Maine. Our spacious grounds are within walking distance of the beach and all other village pleasures, and the privacy of our backyard pool is perfect for enjoying a morning or late-night swim, or a quiet afternoon retreat. We are unique in that we offer not only

traditional guesthouse accommodations, but also efficiency and motel rooms with refrigerators and private baths. All rooms are air-conditioned and have electic heat and television. ***Admiral's Inn*** is gay-owned and -operated.

**Address: #70 US Rt. 1, PO Box 2241, Ogunquit, ME 03907**
**Tel: (207) 646-7093.**

**Type:** Bed & breakfast guesthouse & motel.
**Clientele:** Mostly gay & lesbian clientele. Straight-friendly
**Transportation:** Car is best.
**To Gay Bars:** 1/4 mile (a 5 min walk) to men's/women's bars.
**Rooms:** 3 doubles, 5 efficiencies, 1 apartment, 5 quads.
**Bathrooms:** 9 private, 8 shared.
**Campsites:** 6 RV parking (electric & water hookups only), 6 tent spaces.
**Meals:** Continental breakfast for rooms in guesthouse.
**Vegetarian:** 1/2 mile to vegetarian restaurant.
**Complimentary:** Morning coffee.
**Dates Open:** All year.
**High Season:** Mid-June thru mid-Sept.
**Rates:** Summer $45-$108, winter $35-$65.
**Credit Cards:** MC, Visa, Amex, Discover.
**Rsv'tns:** Strongly recommended during high season.
**Reserve Through:** Call direct.
**Minimum Stay:** 2 nights during summer, 3 nights on holidays.
**Parking:** Ample, free parking, 2 lots on property.
**In-Room:** Color TV, AC, maid service, some with kitchen, refrigerator.
**On-Premises:** TV lounge, laundry facilities.
**Exercise/Health:** Nearby gym, weights, Jacuzzi, sauna, massage.
**Swimming:** Outdoor pool on premises. 10 min walk to beach.
**Sunbathing:** At poolside or on the beach.
**Nudity:** At guest discretion.
**Smoking:** Permitted outside.
**Pets:** Not permitted.
**Handicap Access:** Yes, 2 rooms.
**Children:** Not encouraged.
**Languages:** English.

## Beauport Inn and Cafe

**Gay-Friendly 50/50 ♀♂**

### *Comfortable Elegance*

The ***Beauport Inn*** is a cozy, expanded cape-style home with an attached gourmet cafe. Located on Shore Road on the trolley line, approximately halfway between town center and Perkins Cove, our inn provides a quiet location within easy walking distance to shops, restaurants, the beach, the Playhouse and the Marginal Way walking path. Relax in our pine-panelled living room with piano and fireplace, our comfortable TV area or on our deck overlooking the gardens. Breakfast is served in the dining room or may be enjoyed on the deck.

**Address: PO Box 1793, 102 Shore Rd, Ogunquit, ME 03907**
**Tel: (800) 646-8681, (207) 646-8680.**

**Type:** Bed & breakfast with gourmet cafe.
**Clientele:** 50% gay & lesbian & 50% straight clientele.
**Transportation:** Car is best.
**To Gay Bars:** 1/2 mile. A 10-minute walk or 3-minute drive.
**Rooms:** 6 rooms with twin or queen beds.
**Bathrooms:** All private.
**Meals:** Expanded continental breakfast.
**Vegetarian:** At nearby restaurants.
**Dates Open:** March 1st to December 15th.
**High Season:** July & August.
**Rates:** Summer $95. Fall & spring $65.
**Discounts:** 10% for weekly stays.
**Credit Cards:** MC, VISA.
**Rsv'tns:** Required.
**Reserve Through:** Call direct.
**Minimum Stay:** Required.
**Parking:** Adequate free off-street parking.
**In-Room:** AC & maid service. 2 rooms have private balconies.
**On-Premises:** TV lounge.
**Exercise/Health:** Nearby gym, massage & golf.
**Swimming:** Nearby ocean.
**Sunbathing:** On common sun decks & at the beach.
**Smoking:** Permitted outside only. Entire house is non-smoking.
**Pets:** Not permitted.
**Handicap Access:** Cafe is accessible.
**Children:** Welcome over 10 years of age.
**Languages:** English, Spanish.

## Heritage of Ogunquit

Q-NET Women ♀

### *"Beautiful Place by the Sea"*

***Heritage of Ogunquit*** is a new Victorian reproduction in a quiet area which is just an eight-minute walk to the beach, cove and the fabulous Marginal Way floral footpath along the ocean's edge. ***The Heritage*** features a hot tub, giant cedar deck, sitting room with TV and VCR, refrigerator and microwave. Expanded continental breakfast is served overlooking perennial gardens and five acres of woods. Check out the new "kd Lang Loft," with private entry, deck and more! Lesbian-owned and -operated.

**Address: PO Box 1295, Ogunquit, ME 03907**
**Tel: (207) 646-7787,**
**E-mail: heritageo@cybertours.com.**

**Type:** Bed & breakfast.
**Clientele:** 99% women with men welcome
**Transportation:** Car. Pick up from airport in Portland, ME, $30 roundtrip, from bus in Portsmouth, NH, $25 roundtrip.
**To Gay Bars:** 5-minute walk.
**Rooms:** 5 rooms with queen beds. 1 room has additional single bed & 2 have double futons.
**Bathrooms:** 3 private bath/toilets & 2 shared bath/shower/toilets.
**Meals:** Expanded continental breakfast.
**Vegetarian:** Nearby restaurant.
**Dates Open:** All year.
**High Season:** July & August.
**Rates:** $50-$95.
**Discounts:** Weekly & weekdays off season.
**Credit Cards:** MC & Visa.
**Rsv'tns:** Recommended.
**Reserve Through:** Call direct.
**Minimum Stay:** 2 nights on weekends & 3 nights on holiday weekends.
**Parking:** Ample free off-street parking.
**In-Room:** Ceiling fans. Loft has AC, microwave, refrigerator, TV, VCR, toaster oven, sitting area.
**On-Premises:** Common room with TV, VCR, refrigerator & microwave.
**Exercise/Health:** Hot tub & mini exercise area with treadmill & free weights.
**Swimming:** Ocean nearby.
**Sunbathing:** On common sun decks & at the beach.
**Smoking:** Not permitted indoors.
**Pets:** Permitted on occasion. Call for details.
**Handicap Access:** No.
**Children:** Welcome.
**Languages:** English, limited German & Spanish.
**Your Host:** Rica.

## THE INN at Two Village Square

Gay/Lesbian ♀♂

### *Ogunquit, Maine–The Quiet Alternative*

***THE INN at Two Village Square***, a spacious Victorian summer home, perches on a wooded hillside overlooking Ogunquit, yet is secluded amidst the trees of our five acres. Our heated pool and hot tub are surrounded by greenery on three sides, with a wall of glass doors providing ocean views. Public rooms are furnished in a light, summery style. Guest rooms are on three levels, some with ocean views, others looking into the treetops. We are gratified by the number of lesbian and gay guests who return to enjoy vacations, celebrate special occasions, renew friendships or make new acquaintances.

**Address: 135 US Rte 1, PO Box 864, Ogunquit, ME 03907**
**Tel: (207) 646-5779,**
**E-mail: theinntvs@aol.com.**

**Type:** Bed & breakfast inn.
**Clientele:** Good mix of gays & lesbians
**Transportation:** Car. Free pick up from airport or bus in Portsmouth NH.
**To Gay Bars:** 2-minute walk to gay & lesbian dance bar & piano bar.
**Rooms:** 18 rooms with double, queen or king beds.
**Bathrooms:** Private: 14 full baths, 3 sinks. Shared: 1 full bath, 2 toilets.
**Meals:** Expanded continental breakfast.
**Complimentary:** Tea/coffee in guest kitchen. In season: Tues pm BBQ; Sat nite get-acquainted party (also holidays).
**Dates Open:** May-Columbus Day.
**High Season:** Late June-Labor Day.
**Rates:** In season $60-$125. Spring & fall $40-$70.
**Discounts:** Ask about spring & fall specials.
**Credit Cards:** MC, Visa, Amex & Discover. Debit cards.
**Rsv'tns:** Strongly recommended in season.
**Reserve Thru:** Call direct.
**Minimum Stay:** On holidays and in season. Short stays as space permits.
**Parking:** Ample free off-street parking.
**In-Room:** Color TV, AC, ceiling fans & maid service.
**On-Premises:** Common sitting rooms, TV lounge, public telephone, & piano. Shared guest kitchen with refrigerator for cold food preparation & serving.
**Exercise/Health:** Gym, hot tub & bicycles. Massage nearby.
**Swimming:** Heated pool on premises. Gay section of beach a short walk away.
**Sunbathing:** On poolside deck, sun deck, or nearby public beach.
**Smoking:** Not permitted in common rooms.
**Pets:** Not permitted (facilities for cats & dogs nearby).
**Handicap Access:** Minimal accessibility.
**Languages:** English.

## Leisure Inn

Gay-Friendly 50/50 ♀♂

### *The Warm Feelings of Grandmother's House*

Capture the feel of coastal village life in Ogunquit, a picturesque resort town by the sea. ***Leisure Inn*** is traditionally Maine, with uniquely-decorated guest rooms reflecting all the charm of old New England. In summer, there's plenty of fun in the sun, but have you ever known the sensation of walking the beach after the first snow of autumn? Everything in Ogunquit is within walking distance, from fine restaurants, to quaint and interesting shops. We're only a five-minute walk from the beach.

**Address: 6 School St, PO Box 2113, Ogunquit, ME 03907**
**Tel: (207) 646-2737, Fax: (207) 646-2471.**

**Type:** Bed & breakfast guesthouse, cottages, apts.
**Clientele:** 50% gay & lesbian & 50% straight clientele.
**Transportation:** Car is best.
**Rooms:** 12 rooms, 3 apartments & 3 cottages with double & queen beds.
**Bathrooms:** 12 private, others share.
**Meals:** Cont. breakfast.
**Dates Open:** May-Oct.
**Rates:** $58-$82.
**Credit Cards:** MC, VISA.
**Rsv'tns:** Preferred (and advised for July & August).
**Reserve Thru:** Call direct.
**Minimum Stay:** Two days on weekends, 3 on summer holiday weekends.
**Parking:** Ample, free off-street parking.
**In-Room:** Room service, most have color TV, AC, some kitchens.
**On-Prem:** Meeting rooms.
**Swimming:** Short walk to ocean beach.
**Sunbathing:** At beach, on patio.
**Pets:** Not permitted.
**Languages:** English, French.

## Moon Over Maine

Q-NET Gay/Lesbian ♀♂

### *Tranquility and Romance Await You*

***Moon Over Maine,*** built in 1839, has been beautifully restored. Many rooms feature original New England pine floors and gabled ceilings and most have direct access to the multilevel deck, overlooking a wooded yard. It will take you two minutes to walk to Ogunquit's gay nightlife and five minutes to walk to the beach. Spend a relaxing day at the beach and a quiet evening with us. Gaze at the moon as you sit in the hot tub or simply relax with someone you love.

**Address: PO Box 1478, 6 Berwick Rd, Ogunquit, ME 03907**
**Tel: (207) 646-MOON (6666), (800) 851-6837,**
**E-mail: MoonMaine@aol.com.**

*continued next page*

**Type:** Bed & breakfast.
**Clientele:** Mostly gay & lesbian with some straight clientele.
**Transport.:** Car is best.
**To Gay Bars:** 1 blk to The Club or The Front Porch.
**Rooms:** 9 rooms with queen beds.
**Bathrooms:** All private shower/toilets.
**Meals:** Expanded continental breakfast.
**Vegetarian:** Breakfast is vegetarian. Most local restaurants have vegetarian entrees.
**Complimentary:** Soft drinks, candy.
**Dates Open:** April-Nov.
**High Season:** June-Aug.
**Rates:** Summer $65-$120, winter $35-$65.
**Discounts:** 5th night is free, discs. on weekly stays.
**Credit Cards:** MC, Visa, Discover.
**Reserve Through:** Travel agent or call direct.
**Minimum Stay:** July-Aug: 2 nights on weekends.
**Parking:** Adequate free off-street parking.
**In-Room:** Color cable TV, AC, maid service.
**Exercise/Health:** Jacuzzi. Nearby gym, weights, massage.
**Swimming:** Ocean nearby.
**Sunbathing:** On common sun decks & at beach.
**Smoking:** Permitted outside only.
**Pets:** Not permitted.
**Handicap Access:** No.
**Children:** No.
**Languages:** English.
**Your Host:** John.

## Ogunquit House

**Gay-Friendly 50/50 ♀♂**

Originally a schoolhouse in 1880, ***Ogunquit House*** is now a tastefully-restored bed and breakfast in a country setting at the edge of town. We offer a clean, comfortable, reasonably-priced vacation spot. Guest rooms are spacious, with both private and shared baths. Beach, restaurants, shops, movies and art galleries are all within walking distance. Ogunquit's trolley stops almost at your door to bring you to the Marginal Way, Perkins Cove and The Playhouse.

**Address: 3 Glen Ave, Box 1883, Ogunquit, ME 03907**
**Tel: (207) 646-2967.**

**Type:** Bed & breakfast & cottages.
**Clientele:** 50% gay & lesbian & 50% straight clientele.
**Transportation:** Car is best.
**To Gay Bars:** 2 blocks to men's/women's bars.
**Rooms:** 6 rooms & 4 cottages with single, queen or king beds.
**Bathrooms:** 8 private, others share.
**Meals:** Continental breakfast.
**Vegetarian:** Three nearby restaurants offer vegetarian food.
**Dates Open:** March 15-January 2.
**High Season:** July through August.
**Rates:** $59-$135 summer, $45-$70 winter.
**Credit Cards:** MC, VISA, Discover.
**Rsv'tns:** Recommended.
**Reserve Through:** Call direct.
**Minimum Stay:** Summer 2 nights, holidays 3 nights.
**Parking:** Ample free off-street parking.
**In-Room:** Maid service, AC, some have kitchen or refrigerator and color cable TV.
**On-Premises:** TV lounge.
**Swimming:** 5-minute walk to ocean beach.
**Sunbathing:** On beach, patio, or private sun decks.
**Smoking:** Permitted with restrictions.
**Pets:** Permitted with restrictions in the cottages.
**Handicap Access:** No.
**Children:** Permitted in cottages, over 12 only in the inn.
**Languages:** English.

# PEMBROKE

## Yellow Birch Farm

**Gay/Lesbian ♀**

### *An Organic Farm in Downeast Maine*

***Yellow Birch Farm*** is a working farm near wild, unspoiled Cobscook Bay, 20 minutes from historic Eastport and half an hour from New Brunswick, Canada. The area is a nature lover's paradise of particular interest to birdwatchers. In this scenic, serene setting, we raise livestock and organic vegetables, and do farmwork with a team of oxen. Our seasonal, two-room guest cottage has a full kitchen, woodstove, outdoor hot shower, and outhouse. The spacious, year-round studio features a woodstove, skylights, private entrance, and a full bath.

**Address: RR 1, Box 248-A, Pembroke, ME 04666. Tel: (207) 726-5807.**

**Type:** B&B or weekly rental in a cottage or large studio.
**Clientele:** Mostly gay women
**Transport:** Car is best.
**To Gay Bars:** 2-1/2 hours to Bangor.
**Rooms:** One cottage with bunk beds & queen futon & 1 lg studio with queen bed.
**Bathrooms:** 1 private bath/ toilet & 1 private outhouse & outdoor hot shower.
**Meals:** Expanded continental breakfast.
**Vegetarian:** Organically raised vegetables available from the farm.
**Dates Open:** Studio, all year. Cottage, May-Oct.
**Rates:** $45 double, $15 each additional person.
**Discounts:** Housekeeping basis. $250 wk double occupancy, $50 per additional guest.
**Rsv'tns:** Required.
**Reserve Through:** Travel agent or call direct.
**Parking:** Ample parking.
**In-Room:** Kitchen, refrigerator, color TV & ceiling fan.
**Swimming:** Nearby lakes & ocean.
**Nudity:** Permitted anywhere.
**Smoking:** Permitted outside.
**Pets:** Not permitted.
**Children:** Please inquire.
**Languages:** English & French.
**Your Host:** Bunny.

# SEBAGO LAKE REGION

## Maine-ly For You

Gay/Lesbian ♀♂

### *Home of Maine's Women's Music Festivals*

***Maine-ly For You*** is a complete resort on 33 acres, with cottages and campsites along an 1800-foot waterfront beach equipped with dock and swimming float. The accent is on outdoor activities, such as water sports, hiking on trails, mountain climbing, exploring ice caves, canoeing, etc. We also have a softball field. Usually, the clientele is mixed, but twice a year, the entire place is reserved for 4-day women's music festivals with crafts, entertainment and workshops. Please check with us for details about these womens' festivals.

**Address: RR2 Box 745, Waterford, ME 04088**
**Tel: (207) 583-6980.**

**Type:** Lakeside cottages and campground.
**Clientele:** Mainly gay & lesbian. Women's festivals June & August or Sept
**Transportation:** Car is best.
**To Gay Bars:** 45 min by car to Portland, 30 min to Lewiston.
**Rooms:** 20 rustic cottages.
**Bathrooms:** All private.
**Campsites:** 45 wooded sites, 20 waterfront sites, all with electric & water. Modern, clean restrooms with flush toilets & free showers, recreation room.
**Dates Open:** May 15-Oct 15th.
**High Season:** Late June to Labor Day.
**Rates:** Campsites: wooded $18, waterfront $25. Call for rates on cottages.
**Rsv'tns:** Recommended. Required during 1 week, please inquire.
**Reserve Through:** Call direct.
**Minimum Stay:** 1 week for cottages.
**Parking:** Ample parking.
**In-Room:** Kitchen, refrigerator, some heat.
**On-Premises:** Meeting rooms, TV lounge, laundry facilities, recreation room, country store, boat rentals.
**Exercise/Health:** Swimming, boating, hiking, fishing, softball, basketball.
**Swimming:** In lake on premises.
**Sunbathing:** On the beach by the lake.
**Smoking:** No smoking in bath house, lodge, or recreation room.
**Pets:** Permitted, on leash with deposit.
**Handicap Access:** Partially, inquire.
**Children:** Permitted.
**Languages:** English, some French.
**Your Host:** Rita.

# MARYLAND

## ANNAPOLIS

### William Page Inn

Gay-Friendly ♀♂

#### *B&B Inn Close to Annapolis Naval Academy*

Planning to visit the U.S. Naval Academy? Then why not stay at ***The William Page Inn*** in the historical district, just 50 yards from the visitor's gate of the academy. Built in 1908, this dark brown, cedar-shingle, wood-frame structure was the local Democratic party clubhouse for more than 50 years. The B&B inn is a handsomely renovated turn-of-the-century home, furnished with genuine antiques and period reproductions, with a feeling of quiet, hushed, elegance, and Victorian splendor. We are a Mobil & AAA-rated approved establishment.

**Address: 8 Martin St, Annapolis, MD 21401**
**Tel: (410) 626-1506, (800) 364-4160, Fax: (410) 263-4841,**
**E-mail: wmpageinn@aol.com.**

**Type:** Bed & breakfast.
**Clientele:** Mainly straight with gay & lesbian following
**Transportation:** Car is best. Add'l. charge for pick up from airport, train or bus.
**To Gay Bars:** 40 minutes to DC bars/Baltimore bars.
**Rooms:** 4 rooms & 1 suite with queen beds.
**Bathrooms:** 3 private bath/toilet/showers, 2 shared bath/shower/toilets.
**Meals:** Full breakfast.
**Vegetarian:** Available upon request.
**Complimentary:** Wet bar set up, complimentary sodas.
**Dates Open:** All year.
**High Season:** Mar-Nov.
**Rates:** $85-$175.
**Discounts:** Mid week, stays of 5 or more days, winter rates.
**Credit Cards:** MC, Visa.
**Rsv'tns:** Required, but walk-ins welcome.
**Reserve Through:** Travel agent or call direct.
**Minimum Stay:** For special events & high season weekends.
**Parking:** Limited free off-street parking.
**In-Room:** AC, maid service. Color cable TV in suite.
**Exercise/Health:** Jacuzzi en suite.
**Swimming:** Nearby state park beach, 2 hrs to ocean beach.
**Sunbathing:** At nearby state park beach.
**Smoking:** Permitted outdoors.
**Pets:** Not permitted.
**Handicap Access:** No.
**Children:** Permitted if 12 yrs, or older.
**Languages:** English.
**Your Host:** Robert & Greg.

## BALTIMORE

### Abacrombie Badger Bed & Breakfast

Gay-Friendly 50/50 ♀♂

#### *Elegant Lodgings in Baltimore's Cultural Center*

Across the street from the Meyerhoff Symphony Hall and two blocks from the Lyric Opera House, the Theater Project, and the beginning of Baltimore's Antique Row sits ***Abacrombie Badger***. Music lovers, business people, visitors, and Baltimoreans will find the 12 individually-decorated rooms in this renovated

1880's townhouse a delight. Guests are welcome to relax in the parlor or enjoy a meal at the restaurant. The B&B subscribes to the highest standards of service, comfort, and cleanliness.

**Address: 58 W Biddle St, Baltimore, MD 21201**
**Tel: (410) 244-7227, Fax: (410) 244-8415.**

**Type:** Bed & breakfast with restaurant & bar.
**Clientele:** 50% gay & lesbian & 50% straight clientele
**Transportation:** Car or taxi. Light rail from airport to Cultural Center stop.
**To Gay Bars:** 1 block, a 1 minute walk.
**Rooms:** 12 rooms with single & queen beds.
**Bathrooms:** All private.
**Meals:** Expanded continental breakfast.
**Vegetarian:** Fresh fruit & homemade bread with breakfast. Six blocks to vegetarian restaurants.
**Complimentary:** Chocolates.
**Dates Open:** All year.
**High Season:** March-November.
**Rates:** $79-$159.
**Credit Cards:** MC, Visa, Amex, Diners, Discover.
**Rsv'tns:** Required.
**Reserve Through:** Travel agent or call direct.
**Minimum Stay:** 2 nights on weekends during high season.
**Parking:** Ample free off-street parking. Parking lot adjoins B&B.
**In-Room:** Color cable TV, AC, telephone, maid service.
**Smoking:** Permitted outdoors only.
**Pets:** Not permitted.
**Handicap Access:** No.
**Children:** Well-mannered children over 10 years of age welcome.
**Languages:** English, French, German, Dutch.
**Your Host:** Paul & Collin.

## Mr. Mole Bed & Breakfast

Gay-Friendly ♀♂

### *Maryland's Only Four-Star Award B&B (1995 & 1996 Mobil Travel Guides)*

***Mr. Mole*** has renovated his grand 1870 Baltimore row house on historic Bolton Hill, close to downtown, Inner Harbor, the Symphony and Antique Row, to provide gracious accommodations for discriminating guests. The comfortable, English-style decor, with 18th- and 19th-century antiques, adorns five spacious suites with private phones and full baths. Two suites offer a private sitting room and two bedrooms. Garage parking, with automatic door opener, is included, as is a hearty Dutch-style breakfast of homemade bread, cake, meat, cheese and fruit.

**Address: 1601 Bolton St, Baltimore, MD 21217**
**Tel: (410) 728-1179 or Fax: (410) 728-3379.**

**Type:** Bed & breakfast.
**Clientele:** Mostly straight clientele with a gay & lesbian following.
**Transportation:** Car or taxi.
**To Gay Bars:** Five minutes by car to gay/lesbian bars.
**Rooms:** 3 rooms & 2 suites with queen beds.
**Bathrooms:** All private bath/toilets.
**Meals:** Expanded continental breakfast.
**Complimentary:** Chocolates.
**Dates Open:** All year.
**High Season:** Mar-Nov.
**Rates:** $97-$155.
**Credit Cards:** MC, Visa, Discover, Amex, Diners Club.
**Rsv'tns:** Required.
**Reserve Through:** Travel agent or call direct.
**Minimum Stay:** 2 nights on weekends in high season.
**Parking:** Free parking in garage with automatic opener.
**In-Room:** Maid service, AC, telephone & clock radio.
**Smoking:** Permitted outdoors only.
**Pets:** Not permitted.
**Children:** Well-mannered children over 10 years welcome.
**Languages:** English.

# CUMBERLAND

## Red Lamp Post

**Gay/Lesbian ♀♂**

We would like to welcome you to ***Red Lamp Post,*** our living home. Become part of the environment and enjoy the company of your hosts Kery and Gary. Located just 3 miles from historic downtown Cumberland, we are near antique shops, the C&O Canal, the new Allegheny Central Railroad, Early American historic sites, scenic beauty, Rocky Gap State Park, Deep Creek Lake, winter sports, hiking and biking trails. Enjoy homemade breakfast and snacks and refreshments in the evening.

**Address: 849 Braddock Rd, Cumberland, MD 21502. Tel: (301) 777-3262.**

**Type:** Bed & breakfast.
**Clientele:** Mostly gay & lesbian with some straight clientele.
**Transportation:** Car or free pick-up at train or airport from DC or Pittsburgh (commuter from Pittsburgh).
**To Gay Bars:** New bar in Cumberland, 1-1/2 hours to Hagerstown, Altoona, Morgantown bars.
**Rooms:** 3 rooms with full or queen beds.
**Bathrooms:** 1-1/2 shared.
**Campsites:** Nearby.
**Meals:** Full breakfast included, dinner available at additional cost.
**Veget.:** Avail. on request.
**Complimentary:** Cocktails, refreshments upon arrival.
**Dates Open:** All year.
**High Season:** Sum.& fall.
**Rates:** $55 sgl, $65 dbl. Inquire about specials.
**Disc:** For 3 days or more.
**Credit Cards:** MC & VISA.
**Rsv'tns:** Required.
**Reserve Thru:** Call direct.
**Minimum Stay:** Req'd during special events in the area.
**Parking:** Adequate free off-street parking.
**In-Room:** AC, cable TV, elec. blanket & ceiling fans.
**On-Premises:** Living room & TV lounge with fireplaces, sunroom or deck for breakfast.
**Exercise/Health:** Weights, rowing machine, stationary cycle, spa.
**Swimming:** 10 minutes by car to lake.
**Sunbathing:** On patio.
**Smoking:** Permitted in designated areas.
**Children:** Not permitted.
**Languages:** English.
**Your Host:** Kery.

# MASSACHUSETTS

# AMHERST

## Ivy House B&B

**Gay-Friendly 50/50 ♀♂**

### *In a College Town Four Miles from Northampton*

Our colonial cape home, portions circa 1740, has been handsomely restored with distinctive interiors, exposed beams, fireplace, country kitchen, and new baths. The patio and landscaped grounds add to the atmosphere of this romantic setting. ***Ivy House*** is close to the Northampton scene, Cummington gay beach, and Vermont, just a block from the U. Mass. Fine Arts Center, and near the homes of Robert Frost and Emily Dickinson. The Five Colleges, Old Deerfield, Brimfield, and the Berkshires, are also convenient. Host John welcomes both men and women.

**Address: 1 Sunset Court, Amherst, MA 01002**
**Tel: (413) 549-7554, Fax: (413) 549-1238.**

**Type:** Bed & breakfast.
**Clientele:** 50% gay & lesbian & 50% straight clientele.
**Transportation:** Car is best. Pick up from Hartford-Springfield airport $25 per person, $5 from Amherst bus or train station.
**To Gay Bars:** 5 miles.
**Rooms:** 1 rm with queen bed & 1 rm with twin beds.
**Bathrooms:** 2 baths.
**Meals:** Full breakfast.
**Dates Open:** All year.
**High Season:** Mid-May college graduations and fall foliage.
**Rates:** $50-$80
**Discounts:** For midweek or more than 6 nights.
**Rsv'tns:** Required.
**Reserve Through:** Travel agent or call direct.
**Minimum Stay:** 2 nights at peak periods & most Fri-Sat.
**Parking:** Adequate free off-street parking.

**On-Premises:** Laundry facilities for guests.
**Swimming:** Nearby pool, river & lake.
**Sunbathing:** On the patio.
**Smoking:** Outside on porch only.
**Pets:** Not permitted.
**Children:** Welcome over 12 years of age only.
**Languages:** English, French & Spanish.
**Your Host:** John.

# BARRE

## The Jenkins Inn and Restaurant

Gay-Friendly ♀♂

### *We Are in the Center of Massachusetts*

Located in a quaint New England town, unspoiled by commercialism, ***The Jenkins Inn*** offers peace and comfort to the weary traveler. An antique shop, herb farm and restaurants are in town, with brochures displayed at our guesthouse. A homemade full breakfast is served in our breakfast room with views from ten windows. Wraparound porch, balconies and an English garden are on site. There is a full-service restaurant & bar on premises.

**Address: 7 West Street, Route 122, Barre, MA 01005**
**Tel: (508) 355-6444, (800) 378-7373.**

**Type:** Bed & breakfast inn.
**Clientele:** Mostly straight clientele with a 30% gay & lesbian following
**Transportation:** Car is best.
**To Gay Bars:** 35 minutes to Worcester, 1 hr to Springfield & Northampton gay/lesbian bars.
**Rooms:** 5 doubles.
**Baths:** 3 private, 1 shared.
**Meals:** Full breakfast.
**Complimentary:** Ice and glasses available.
**Dates Open:** All year.
**High Season:** October foliage season, Brimfield antique shows.
**Rates:** $80-$125.
**Credit Cards:** MC, Visa, Discover, Amex.
**Rsv'tns:** Preferred.
**Reserve Through:** Travel agent or call direct.
**Minimum Stay:** 2 nights on weekends & holidays.
**Parking:** Adequate, free off-street parking.
**In-Room:** Maid service, AC, ceiling fans.
**On-Premises:** Two common rooms, fireplaces, wrap-around porch, English garden.
**Swimming:** 7 miles to lake in state park.
**Smoking:** No smoking indoors.
**Pets:** Permitted with prior arrangement.
**Children:** Permitted if over 12 years.
**Languages:** English.
**Your Host:** David & Joseph.

# BOSTON

## Amsterdammertje

Gay/Lesbian ♀♂

### *A Little of Holland in Boston*

***Amsterdammertje*** Euro-American B&B is for the discriminating, sophisticated, down-to-earth, value-conscious traveler. This home-away-from-home in a beautiful and quiet setting at the ocean is barely 20 minutes by car from downtown Boston (45 minutes by public transportation). Boston and its surroundings definitely warrant a visit of seven to ten days, depending on your own pace and on how far you wish to travel. Your host, the Flying Dutchman, will provide one personally guided tour, other obligations permitting. Call, write, or fax for a brochure, reservation form, and inn policy.

*continued next page*

**Address: PO Box 865, Boston, MA 02103. Tel: (617) 471-8454 (Tel/Fax).**

**Type:** Bed & breakfast.
**Clientele:** Mostly gay & lesbian with some straight clientele
**Transportation:** Car or public transportation (subway & bus). Charge for pick up, please inquire.
**To Gay Bars:** 10 miles, a 12-minute drive.
**Rooms:** 3 rooms with twin or queen beds.
**Bathrooms:** 1 private shower/toilet, 2 shared bath/shower/toilets.
**Meals:** Full breakfast.
**Vegetarian:** Available.
**Dates Open:** All year.
**High Season:** April-October.
**Rates:** $55-$100, weekly: $340-$640.
**Rsv'tns:** Required.
**Reserve Through:** Call direct.
**Minimum Stay:** 3 days. Exceptions possible if/when space is available.
**Parking:** Ample free off-street parking.
**On-Premises:** In living room & kitchen: color cable TV, VCR, telephone, refrigerator. Charge for fax & laundry service.
**Exercise/Health:** Skiing 20-minutes to 2 hours away. Gym in downtown Boston with weights, sauna, steam, massage.
**Swimming:** Nearby pool, ocean, lake.
**Sunbathing:** On patio, at beach.
**Smoking:** No smoking permitted.
**Pets:** Generally not permitted. Arrangements could be made.
**Handicap Access:** No.
**Children:** Preferably 10 years and older.
**Languages:** English, Dutch, German, French, Italian, Spanish, Polish.

## Chandler Inn

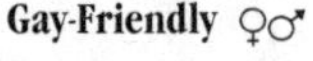

Gay-Friendly ♀♂

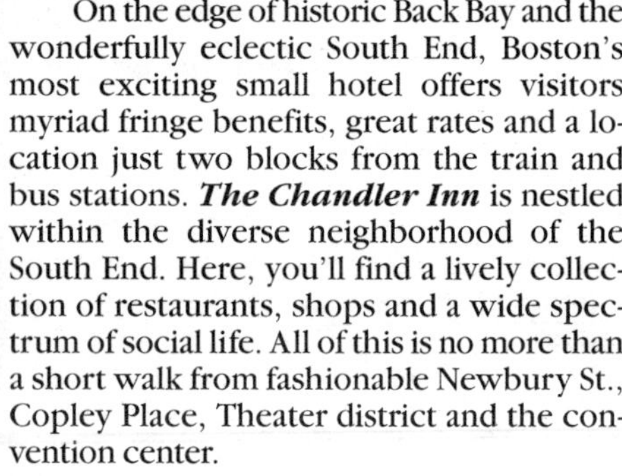

### *Location, Location, Location!*

On the edge of historic Back Bay and the wonderfully eclectic South End, Boston's most exciting small hotel offers visitors myriad fringe benefits, great rates and a location just two blocks from the train and bus stations. ***The Chandler Inn*** is nestled within the diverse neighborhood of the South End. Here, you'll find a lively collection of restaurants, shops and a wide spectrum of social life. All of this is no more than a short walk from fashionable Newbury St., Copley Place, Theater district and the convention center.

**Address: 26 Chandler St, Boston, MA 02116**
**Tel: (617) 482-3450, (800) 842-3450.**
**E-mail: inn3450@ix.netcom.com.**

**Type:** Bed & breakfast hotel with gay bar on premises.
**Clientele:** Mostly straight clientele with a gay & lesbian following
**Transportation:** Taxi from airport $15. 2 block walk from Back Bay Amtrak/subway station.
**To Gay Bars:** Gay/lesbian bar inside building.
**Rooms:** 56 doubles.
**Bathrooms:** All private.
**Meals:** Continental breakfast.
**Dates Open:** All year.
**High Season:** April-November.
**Rates:** Singles $74-$99. Doubles $84-$109.
**Discounts:** AARP, off-season.
**Credit Cards:** All credit cards.
**Rsv'tns:** Required.
**Reserve Through:** Travel agent or call direct.
**Minimum Stay:** 2 nights on weekends in season.
**Parking:** Limited on-street parking. Municipal lots 2 blocks away.
**In-Room:** Private direct-dial telephone, color TV & AC.
**Exercise/Health:** Discount at Metropolitan Health Club 1 block away.
**Sunbathing:** On Boston's Esplanade, a ten minute walk from the hotel.
**Smoking:** Permitted. 16 non-smoking rooms, no smoking in common areas.
**Pets:** Permitted.
**Handicap Access:** No.
**Children:** Permitted.
**Languages:** English, Spanish, & French.

IGTA

# Four-Sixty-Three Beacon Street Guest House

Gay-Friendly 50/50 ♀♂

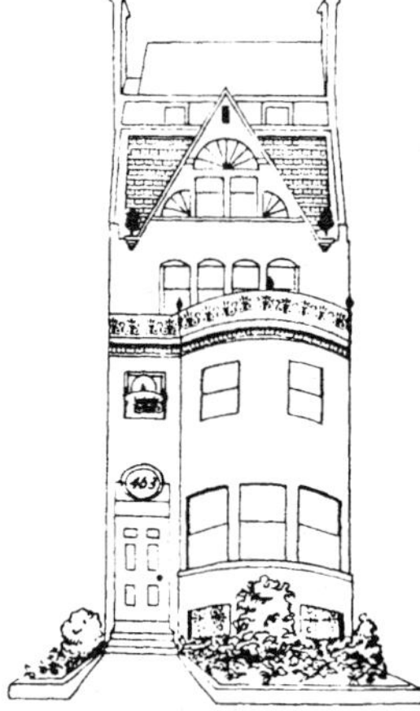

## *Boston's Best Slept Secret*

Located in Boston's historic Back Bay, the ***463 Beacon Street Guest House*** offers a comfortable and affordable hotel alternative. Our turn-of-the-century brownstone-style building includes private baths, kitchenettes, cable TV, air conditioning and complimentary local phone service, Our warm, quiet, residential setting is near public transportation, the Prudential-Hynes Convention Center, colleges, restaurants, and is minutes away from downtown Boston and Cambridge. Discounted weekly & monthly rates and parking available.

**Address: 463 Beacon St, Boston, MA 02115**
**Tel: (617) 536-1302, Fax: (617) 247-8876.**

**Type:** Guesthouse.
**Clientele:** 50% gay & lesbian & 50% straight clientele.
**Transportation:** Taxi, public transportation, airport shuttle bus.
**To Gay Bars:** Five minutes by car to gay bars.
**Rooms:** 20 rooms with double & king beds.
**Bathrooms:** 16 private bath/toilets, 4 sink/washbasins only.
**Meals:** Meals not included.
**Complimentary:** Coffee, tea.
**Dates Open:** All year.
**High Season:** May-October.
**Rates:** $55-$90 per night.
**Discounts:** Discounts for weekly & monthly stays.
**Credit Cards:** MC, Visa, Amex.
**Rsv'tns:** Required.
**Reserve Through:** Travel agent or call direct.
**Parking:** Limited off-street parking.
**In-Room:** Color cable TV, telephone, AC, kitchenette with refrigerator.
**On-Premises:** Laundry facilities.
**Sunbathing:** 1 unit with private deck.
**Smoking:** Permitted with some restrictions.
**Pets:** Not permitted.
**Handicap Access:** No.
**Children:** Permitted.
**Languages:** English, French & Spanish.

# Greater Boston Hospitality

Gay-Friendly ♀♂

## *An Uncommonly Civilized Way to Travel*

***Greater Boston Hospitality*** offers superb accommodations in the Boston area in hundreds of friendly, private homes and inns, all of which are carefully screened for comfort, cleanliness and congeniality of hosts. Bed and breakfasts range from Federal to Colonial to Georgian, from cozy to luxury, from city to suburb to country. Neighborhoods throughout Boston are included. Many of our accommodations include parking. All include breakfast and knowledgeable, friendly hosts. Be it for business or pleasure, we'll help you to have a welcoming and wonderful time.

**Address: PO Box 1142, Brookline, MA 02146. Tel: (617) 277-5430.**

**Type:** Reservation service for bed & breakfasts, guesthouses & inns.
**Clientele:** Good selection of very gay-friendly accommodations
**To Gay Bars:** 10 blocks or 1/2 mile from most accommodations.
**Rooms:** 180 rooms & 10 suites with single, double, queen or king beds.
**Bathrooms:** 160 private. Shared 10 bath/shower/toilets & 18 showers only. Most have private baths.
**Meals:** Expanded continental, continental, or full breakfast.
**Vegetarian:** Several vegetarian restaurants in the greater Boston area.
**Complimentary:** Many hosts offer cold &/or hot drinks, candy & flowers.
**Dates Open:** All year.
**High Season:** Apr 1-Dec 1.
**Rates:** $50-$130.
**Discounts:** Inquire, discounts vary.
**Credit Cards:** MC, Visa, Amex (depending on location).
**Rsv'tns:** Required.

*continued next page*

**Reserve Through:** Travel agent or call direct.
**Parking:** Adequate parking: free, pay, off- & on-street.
**In-Room:** Color cable TV, AC, phone & maid service, depending on location.
**On-Premises:** Libraries, pianos & decks in various locations.
**Exercise/Health:** Gym, weights, sauna, steam, massage in various locations.
**Swimming:** Pools on premises & nearby pool, ocean & lake.
**Sunbathing:** On patios.
**Smoking:** Generally permitted outside only.
**Pets:** Not permitted.
**Handicap Access:** Some.
**Children:** Inquire.
**Languages:** English, French, Italian, Spanish, German.
**Your Host:** Kelly, Lauren & Jack.

## Victorian Bed & Breakfast

**Women ♀**

### *TLC in Massive Doses*

Our guests say: "Thanks for such friendly hospitality, helpful Boston hints and great food. You two are a delight!" "We feel like we've found a home in the big city." "The best place, the best hosts!" ***Victorian Bed & Breakfast*** offers elegant and comfortable accommodations just 5 minutes from Boston's Copley Place. All the tourist attractions of the city, plus gay and lesbian bars are nearby. We're sure you'll find your accommodations feel just like home...only better!

**Address: Boston, MA. Tel: (617) 536-3285.**

**Type:** Bed & breakfast.
**Clientele:** Women only.
**Transportation:** Car or taxi from airport, easy subway trip from airport.
**To Gay Bars:** Close to all gay/lesbian bars.
**Rooms:** 1 room accommodates up to 4 women with king-sized bed & double couch.
**Bathrooms:** Private bath/toilet.
**Meals:** Full breakfast.
**Vegetarian:** Food to please all tastes and needs.
**Complimentary:** Soft drinks.
**Dates Open:** All year.
**High Season:** All year.
**Rates:** $50 for 1, $65 for 2, $75 for 3 & $85 for 4.
**Rsv'tns:** Required.
**Reserve Through:** Call direct.
**Minimum Stay:** 2 nights on weekends.
**Parking:** Free off-street parking.
**In-Room:** Large living room, easy chairs, black & white TV, AC, laundry done by hostess, if stay longer than 4 nights, maid service.
**Smoking:** Not permitted.
**Pets:** Not permitted. We have 3 cats in residence.
**Handicap Access:** No.
**Children:** Not permitted.
**Languages:** English.
**Your Host:** Claire & Lois.

# GREENFIELD

## The Brandt House

**Gay-Friendly ♀♂**

### *The Luxury of a Real Feather Bed Awaits You in Western Massachusetts*

Enjoy the pleasures of cozy fireplaces, breezy porches, patios, a full-sized pool table, and whirlpool baths. ***The Brandt House,*** an elegant turn-of-the-century Colonial Revival mansion, has original beautiful woodwork and personally selected furnishings and decor. Relax in the comfort of our spacious, light-filled guest bedrooms that include featherbeds, a private bath, remote cable TV, telephone (upon request),

and AC. Guestrooms with fireplaces, skylights and suites of rooms are available. The B&B is a short drive from craft fairs, auctions, a championship golf course, ice skating, cross-country skiing and is five minutes from historic Deerfield. We're ideally situated to the north of Northampton and south of Brattleboro, Vermont.

**Address: 29 Highland Ave, Greenfield, MA**
**Tel: (800) 235-3329, (413) 774-3329, Fax: (413) 772-2908,**
**E-mail: brandt@crocker.com. http://www.brandt-house.com.**

**Type:** Country inn.
**Clientele:** Mostly straight clientele with a gay & lesbian following
**Transportation:** 1 hour drive from Bradly Int'l Airport in Hartford, CT; 2 hr drive from Logan Airport in Boston; 3 hr drive from New York City.
**To Gay Bars:** 20-minute drive to Northampton, MA or 30-minute drive to Brattleboro, VT.
**Rooms:** 7 rooms & 1 suite with single, queen or king beds.
**Bathrooms:** 5 private bath/toilet/showers. In suite: 2 shared bath/toilet/showers.
**Meals:** Expanded home-cooked continental breakfast or full breakfast on weekends.
**Vegetarian:** Breakfast menu cards ask for any dietary restrictions. 2 vegetarian restaurants nearby.
**Complimentary:** Champagne for special occasions.
**Dates Open:** All year.
**High Season:** May-October.
**Rates:** $90-$165.
**Discounts:** Ad & coupon specials. Special weekly & corporate rates.
**Credit Cards:** MC, Visa, Amex, Discover, Novus.
**Rsv'tns:** Required. Walk-ins accepted.
**Reserve Through:** Travel agent or call direct.
**Parking:** Ample off-street parking.
**In-Room:** Color cable TV, AC, ceiling fans, phones.
**On-Premises:** Meeting rooms, sun porch with TV, wraparound decks, large covered porch, fireplaces, billiard room.
**Exercise/Health:** Nearby gym, weights, Jacuzzi, sauna, steam & massage.
**Swimming:** River & lake nearby.
**Sunbathing:** On the patio & common sun decks.
**Smoking:** House is non-smoking. Smoking permitted on outside covered porch.
**Pets:** Dogs permitted. Restrictions determined at time of reservation.
**Handicap Access:** No.
**Children:** Permitted.
**Your Host:** Phoebe (innkeeper) & large staff.

# LENOX

## Summer Hill Farm

Gay-Friendly ♀♂

### *Berkshire Arts and a Country Setting*

Enjoy the beauty and culture of the Berkshires at ***Summer Hill Farm,*** a 200-year-old colonial farmhouse on a 20-acre horse farm. Rooms are pleasantly furnished with English family antiques. Delicious country breakfasts are served family-style in the dining room or on the sunporch. A haybarn has been newly converted to a delightful, spacious, 2-room, all-season guest cottage. We're in the country, yet minutes from Tanglewood, Jacob's Pillow Dance, theatres, fine art galleries, restaurants and shops. Choose from a wide variety of outdoor activities. The countryside is beautiful in all seasons. Come for the fall colors or our winter wonderland.

**Address: 950 East St, Lenox, MA 01240**
**Tel: (413) 442-2057, (800) 442-2059.**

**Type:** Bed & breakfast.
**Clientele:** Mostly straight clientele with a gay & lesbian following.
**Transportation:** Car is best. No charge for pick up from local bus.
**Rooms:** 6 rooms with single, double, queen or king beds.
**Bathrooms:** All private.
**Meals:** Full home-cooked breakfast. Continental breakfast in cottage.
**Vegetarian:** Available with special request.
**Dates Open:** All year.
**High Season:** Mid June-Labor Day & October.
**Rates:** Summer & October $85-$185. Winter & spring $60-$130.
**Discounts:** For groups & stays of a week or more, up to 20% discount; mid-week reductions.
**Credit Cards:** Visa, MC, Amex.
**Rsv'tns:** Required.
**Reserve Through:** Call direct.
**Minimum Stay:** On July, August, October & holiday weekends.
**Parking:** Ample free off-street parking.

*continued next page*

**In-Room:** Color cable TV, AC, maid service. 2 rooms with fireplaces, 1 with ref. Cottage: coffee/tea-making facilities, refrigerator, TV, AC, microwave, toaster.
**Exercise/Health:** Riding by arrangement. Nearby gym, sauna, massage, hiking, biking, canoeing, skiing, tennis, horseback riding.
**Swimming:** 5 miles to lake.
**Sunbathing:** On private or common sun decks & on the lawns.
**Smoking:** No smoking indoors.
**Pets:** Not permitted.
**Handicap Access:** Yes. Cottage only.
**Children:** Infants, & children 5 & over. Must be well-behaved & closely supervised.
**Languages:** English.
**Your Host:** Michael & Sonya.

## Walker House

Gay-Friendly ♀♂

### *A Most Harmonious Place to Visit*

***Walker House,*** is an 1804-era federal manor, furnished in antiques, on 3 acres of gardens and woods near the center of the picturesque village of Lenox. Rooms, decorated with a musical theme honoring composers, such as Beethoven and Mozart, have private baths, some with claw-foot tubs and fireplaces. Our library theatre features a large-screen video projection system. Walk to galleries, shops and good restaurants. Tanglewood, Jacob's Pillow and summer theatres are only a short drive.

**Address: 64 Walker St, Lenox, MA 01240**
**Tel: (413) 637-1271, (800) 235-3098, Fax: (413) 637-2387,**
**E-mail: phoudekevgernet.net.**

**Type:** Bed & breakfast inn.
**Clientele:** Mainly straight with a gay & lesbian following
**Transportation:** Car is best. 1 block from New York & Boston buses.
**To Gay Bars:** 35 miles to Albany & Northampton.
**Rooms:** 8 rooms with single, double, queen or king beds.
**Bathrooms:** All private.
**Meals:** Expanded continental breakfast.
**Vegetarian:** Breakfasts have no meat; other vegetarian meals available at restaurants within walking distance.
**Complimentary:** Bottle of wine in room, afternoon tea each day.
**Dates Open:** All year.
**High Season:** July, August, October.
**Rates:** Summer $70-$180, Oct $70-$150, Sept & Nov-Jun $60-$120.
**Discounts:** 10% off for single persons in rooms depending on availability.
**Rsv'tns:** Advisable during busy periods.
**Reserve Through:** Call direct.
**Minimum Stay:** On holidays & summer weekends.
**Parking:** Ample free on- & off-street parking.
**In-Room:** AC, maid service.
**On-Premises:** Meeting rooms, TV lounge, library theatre with large-screen video projection system.
**Exercise/Health:** Nearby gym, massage.
**Swimming:** Nearby river & lake.
**Sunbathing:** On the patio, lawns & garden, at the beach.
**Smoking:** Non-smoking property.
**Pets:** Permitted by prior approval at reservation time.
**Handicap Access:** Yes. 3 1st-floor rooms accessible.
**Children:** 12 years of age & older welcome.
**Languages:** English, Spanish, French.

# MARTHA'S VINEYARD

## Captain Dexter House of Edgartown

Gay-Friendly ♀♂

Romantic guest rooms, each uniquely different, are distinctively decorated with fine furnishings to create the warmth and ambiance of an elegant private home. Each has its own bathroom. Several have working fireplaces and four-poster beds with white lace canopies. At ***Captain Dexter House of Edgartown,*** rooms are richly appointed with many amenities, to let you know how special you are to us. Fresh, home-baked breakfast breads are served in our elegant dining room or enchanting flower-filled garden. It's only a short stroll to the town, harbor, shopping and dining.

**Address: 35 Pease Point Way, PO Box 2798, Edgartown, MA 02539**
**Tel: (508) 627-7289, Fax: (508) 627-3328.**

**Type:** Bed & breakfast.
**Clientele:** Mostly straight clientele with a gay & lesbian following.
**Transportation:** Car to ferry or airport.
**To Gay Bars:** Gay organization & 1 gay-friendly bar on island.
**Rooms:** 11 rooms with double or queen beds.
**Bathrooms:** All private baths.
**Meals:** Expanded continental breakfast.
**Complimentary:** Lemonade, sherry.
**Dates Open:** April through November.
**High Season:** Mid June through Labor Day.
**Rates:** Summer $110-$200, winter $65-$175.
**Credit Cards:** MC, VISA, Amex & Diners.
**Reserve Through:** Travel agent or call direct.
**Minimum Stay:** Required on high season weekends.
**Parking:** Ample off-street parking.
**In-Room:** Maid service, most rooms with AC & ceiling fans.
**On-Premises:** Meeting rooms, laundry facilities, refrigerator.
**Exercise/Health:** Nearby aerobics classes & gym.
**Swimming:** At nearby ocean beach.
**Sunbathing:** In yards & at nearby ocean beach.
**Nudity:** Permitted on beach at Gay Head.
**Smoking:** Permitted in all rooms.
**Pets:** Not permitted.
**Handicap Access:** No.
**Children:** Permitted. Prefer 12 years or older.
**Languages:** English.

## Martha's Place

Q-NET Gay-Friendly 50/50 ♀♂

### *Come Pamper Yourself in Style*

***Martha's Place*** is a stately Greek Revival overlooking Vineyard Haven Harbor, two blocks from the ferry, village shops, restaurants and the beach. Rooms boast harbor views and are beautifully decorated with fine antiques, oriental carpets and crystal chandeliers. Other amenities include private baths, bathrobes, fireplaces and Jacuzzi. Breakfast in bed is available and the pampering continues at night with turndown service in wonderful beds dressed in fine Egyptian cotton linens. Afternoon tea and cocktails are served. To enhance your enjoyment of Martha's Vineyard, we have tennis, beach chairs and coolers, bicycles and more! Your host's previous experience as an employee of Ritz Carlton hotels is evident in the style of hospitality at ***Martha's Place.*** As a guest at our island escape, your stay will be an especially memorable one.

**Address: 114 Main St, PO Box 1182, Vineyard Haven, MA 02658**
**Tel: (508) 693-0253.**

**Type:** Inn.
**Clientele:** 50% gay & lesbian & 50% straight clientele
**Transportation:** Ferry. Taxi is a maximum $10 rate about anywhere on island.
**To Gay Bars:** 1-1/2 hours to Boston or Provincetown gay bars.
**Rooms:** 6 rooms with double or queen beds.
**Bathrooms:** 2 rooms with shower/toilet/sink, 4 rooms with tub/shower/toilet/sink.
**Meals:** Expanded continental breakfast. Breakfast in bed available.
**Vegetarian:** Available nearby.
**Complimentary:** Open bar at tea time in afternoon, liqueur after dinner in room, turndown chocolates & bottled water.
**Dates Open:** All year.
**High Season:** June-September.
**Rates:** Summer $175-$275, fall $150-$250, winter $125-$225.
**Credit Cards:** MC, Visa.
**Rsv'tns:** Required.
**Reserve Through:** Travel agent or call direct.
**Minimum Stay:** 3 nights on holiday weekends.
**Parking:** Ample free off-street parking.
**In-Room:** AC, color cable TV, VCR, room, laundry & maid service.
**On-Premises:** Meeting rooms, TV lounge, fax, copier.
**Exercise/Health:** Jacuzzi. Nearby gym, weights, sauna, Jacuzzi, steam, massage.

*continued next page*

**Swimming:** Nearby pool, ocean, lake.
**Sunbathing:** At beach & in side yard.
**Nudity:** Permitted at beach.
**Smoking:** Permitted outside. All rooms are non-smoking.
**Pets:** Not permitted.
**Handicap Access:** Yes.
**Children:** No.
**Languages:** English.
**Your Host:** Richard & Martin.

IGTA

# NORTHAMPTON

## Innamorata

**Women ♀**

### *For Romance and Relaxation*

Northampton, the lesbian mecca, abounds with great food, cultural events and shopping. Nearby are many athletic, historical and cultural activities. With so much to do here, ***Innamorata*** is your perfect getaway. Our seven-acre, secluded country estate has open lawns surrounded by spectacular woods. Our three spacious pine guest rooms are decorated with flowers and homemade country touches. We have an extensive women's library, a living room with fireplace and a huge sunporch for our guests' relaxation. Bountiful, delicious breakfasts are served in a warm familial atmosphere. Yvonne and Kristen welcome you!

**Address: 47 Main St, PO Box 113, Goshen, MA 01032-0113**
**Tel: (413) 268-0300.**

**Type:** Bed & breakfast guesthouse.
**Clientele:** Mostly women with men welcome.
**Transportation:** Car is necessary.
**To Gay Bars:** 12 miles or 20 minutes by car.
**Rooms:** 3 rooms with queen beds.
**Bathrooms:** 1 shared bath/shower/toilet.
**Meals:** Expanded continental breakfast.
**Vegetarian:** Always available upon request. Many vegetarian choices in Northampton.
**Complimentary:** Beverage upon arrival.
**Dates Open:** All year.
**High Season:** May-Oct.
**Rates:** $60-$95 per room, double occupancy.
**Discounts:** 10% on stays of 4 or more days.
**Rsv'tns:** Required.
**Reserve Thru:** Call direct.
**Minimum Stay:** 2 nights on weekends & holidays.
**Parking:** Ample free off-street parking, covered if necessary.
**On-Premises:** Meeting rooms, TV lounge, living room with fireplace, library & sunporch.
**Exercise/Health:** Massage by appointment. Tennis, hiking, cross-country/downhill skiing, biking & canoeing.
**Swimming:** Lake & river nearby.
**Sunbathing:** On the lawns.
**Nudity:** Permitted with discretion on secluded lawns.
**Smoking:** Permitted outside only.
**Pets:** Not permitted.
**Handicap Access:** No, all bedrooms are upstairs.
**Children:** No. Kids' weekends available. Please inquire.
**Languages:** English.

## Tin Roof Bed & Breakfast

**Women ♀**

### *Visit Lesbianville, USA*

***Tin Roof*** is a turn-of-the-century farmhouse in the scenic Connecticut River Valley, five minutes from Northampton.

Our peaceful backyard has panoramic views of the Berkshire Hills and gardens galore. Breakfast features home-baked muffins, fruit, yogurt, granola, juice and hot beverage of choice. There's color TV, a lesbian video library and a front porch with porch swing. Whether you're considering moving to the area or just visiting, your long-time resident hosts will give you lots of local information and acclimate you to the area. Friendly felines in residence.

**Address: PO Box 296, Hadley, MA 01035. Tel: (413) 586-8665.**

**Type:** Bed & breakfast.
**Clientele:** A women's space where lesbian-friendly men are welcome.
**Transportation:** From Hartford airport, rent a car or take a bus to Northampton.
**To Gay Bars:** 10 minutes to gay/lesbian bars.
**Rooms:** 3 rooms with double beds.

**Bathrooms:** 1 shared bath/shower/toilet, 1 shared toilet.
**Meals:** Expanded continental breakfast.
**Vegetarian:** Upon request.
**Dates Open:** All year.
**Rates:** Sgl $55, $60 dbl.
**Discounts:** 7th night free.
**Rsv'tns:** Required.
**Reserve Thru:** Call direct.
**Minimum Stay:** 2 nights on weekends & holidays.
**Parking:** Ample off-street parking.
**On-Premises:** Laundry facilities, TV in living room.
**Exercise/Health:** Nearby health club.
**Swimming:** In nearby river.
**Sunbathing:** In the garden.
**Smoking:** Permitted outside.
**Pets:** Not permitted.
**Languages:** English.
**Your Host:** Jane & Diane.

# PROVINCETOWN

## Admiral's Landing Guest House

Gay/Lesbian ♀♂

### *You've Been Waiting a Long Time to Get Away*

***Admiral's Landing Guest House...*** One block from the bay beach, shops and restaurants, offering spacious rooms with private baths, parking and a friendly, social atmosphere. Provincetown has miles of sandy beaches and dunes, wonderful shops and restaurants. Dance the night away or sit and gaze at the moon over Cape Cod Bay. Call or write for photo brochure, or visit our web site.

**Address: 158 Bradford St, Provincetown, MA 02657**
**Tel: (508) 487-9665,**
**Fax: (508) 487-4437,**
**E-mail: adm158@capecod.net.**
**http://www.ptown.com/ptown/admiralslanding/**

**Type:** Guesthouse & efficiency studios.
**Clientele:** Gay men & women
**Transportation:** Courtesy transportation from airport with prior arrangement.
**To Gay Bars:** 3 blocks to men's bar. 5-minutes' walk to women's bar.
**Rooms:** 6 doubles & 2 efficiencies.
**Bathrooms:** 4 private & 2 shared. Studio efficiencies have private baths.
**Meals:** Continental breakfast, afternoon snacks.
**Dates Open:** All year. Studios Apr 15-Nov 15 only.
**High Season:** May-September.
**Rates:** Summer & holidays: $74-$109; winter: $34-$64; spring/fall $44-$79.
**Discounts:** Group rates.
**Credit Cards:** MC, VISA.
**Rsv'tns:** Strongly recommended.
**Reserve Through:** Travel agent or call direct.
**Minimum Stay:** Holiday weekends & July-August.
**Parking:** Free off-street parking.
**In-Room:** Maid service, ceiling fans.
**On-Premises:** Patio, guest phone, TV lounge with video library.
**Exercise/Health:** Gym nearby.
**Swimming:** Ocean beach nearby.
**Sunbathing:** On ocean beach or patio.
**Smoking:** Permitted in studios.
**Pets:** Permitted in studios.
**Handicap Access:** Studios have limited accessibility.
**Children:** Not permitted.
**Languages:** English.
**Your Host:** Chuck & Peter

## Ampersand Guesthouse

**Gay/Lesbian ♂**

***Ampersand Guesthouse*** is a fine example of mid-nineteenth century Greek Revival architecture located in the neighborly west end of Provincetown, just a short walk from town center. Each of the bedrooms is unique in its layout, creating a range of accommodations from suites of two to three rooms, to shared baths, to private baths. All are furnished in a careful blend of contemporary appointments and restored antiques, many original to the house. There is also a studio apartment that looks out on both the water and the yard.

Continental breakfast is served daily in the large, gracious living room, a gathering place for guests throughout the day & evening. It has a fireplace seating arrangement, a gaming table and a dining area for relaxing and socializing. And guests have use of the yard as well as a second-story sun deck which commands a view of the harbor and Commercial Street. You may be looking for a quiet, restful time for meeting new friends, walking or sunbathing on the nearby beaches, and enjoying the singular views of nature around Provincetown. Or you may be seeking the bustle of a resort town famous for its shops, restaurants, and active social life. In either case, ***Ampersand Guesthouse*** provides a delightful home base both in season and off.

**Address: 6 Cottage St, PO Box 832, Provincetown, MA 02657**
**Tel: (508) 487-0959.**

**Type:** Guesthouse.
**Clientele:** Mostly men with women welcome.
**Transportation:** Take taxi from the airport or walk from town center.
**To Gay Bars:** 6 blocks to men's bars.
**Rooms:** 11 rooms & 1 apartment with double or queen beds.
**Bathrooms:** 9 private bath/toilets & 2 shared bath/shower/toilets.
**Meals:** Cont. breakfast.
**Dates Open:** All year.
**High Season:** Memorial Day-Labor Day week.
**Rates:** $51-$71 off season, $71-$126 high season.
**Credit Cards:** MC, VISA & Amex.
**Rsv'tns:** Required.
**Reserve Thru:** Call direct.
**Minimum Stay:** 5 nights in July & Aug, 2 nights on May, June & Sept. weekends & off-season holidays.
**Parking:** Limited free off-street parking.
**In-Room:** Maid service.
**On-Premises:** TV lounge.
**Swimming:** Ocean beach nearby.
**Sunbathing:** Sun decks.
**Smoking:** Permitted in rooms. Living room smoke-free.
**Pets:** Not permitted.
**Children:** Not permitted.
**Languages:** English.
**Your Host:** Bob & Ken.

## Bayview Wharf Apartments

**Women ♀**

Overlooking the Cape's most picturesque harbor, ***Bayview Wharf Apartments*** is a perfect place to relax and enjoy your holiday in the gayest town in the Northeast. We are located in the center of Provincetown, near all local shops, restaurants, and bars. The beaches are nearby, ideal for swimming and sunbathing. We extend a warm welcome to our guests and hope to see you soon in Provincetown.

**Address: 421 Commercial St, Provincetown, MA 02657**
**Tel: (508) 487-1600.**

**Type:** Apartments.
**Clientele:** Mostly women with men welcome
**Transportation:** Car, train or bus.
**To Gay Bars:** 1/2 block.
**Rooms:** 10 apartments (condos) with double or queen beds.
**Bathrooms:** All private.
**Dates Open:** All year.
**High Season:** May 15-Sept 15.
**Rates:** In season $700-$1400 per week, off season $600-$900 per week.
**Rsv'tns:** Required.
**Reserve Through:** Call direct.
**Minimum Stay:** 1 week in season, 3 nights off season.
**Parking:** Adequate free & pay parking within 1/2 block.
**In-Room:** Color cable TV, ceiling fans, refrigerator, kitchen, coffee/tea-making facilities. Some have AC, telephone.
**Exercise/Health:** Nearby gym, weights, Jacuzzi, sauna, steam, massage.
**Swimming:** Bay on premises, ocean nearby.
**Sunbathing:** On common sun decks, beach.
**Smoking:** Permitted. Some non-smoking units available.
**Pets:** Permitted with pet deposit.
**Handicap Access:** Some units accessible.
**Children:** Welcome.
**Languages:** English, German.

## Beaconlite Guest House

Gay/Lesbian ♀♂

### *A Provincetown Tradition Like No Other*

Awaken to the aroma of freshly-brewed coffee and home-baked cakes and breads. Relax in the English country house charm of our elegant bedrooms and spacious drawing rooms, complete with open fire, grand piano, and antique furnishings. Multi-level sun decks provide panoramic views of Provincetown. ***Beaconlite's*** exceptional reputation for pampered comfort and caring service has grown by the word of mouth of our many returning guests. We truly become your home away from home! Editor's Choice Award 1996 & 1997 – Out and About.

**Address: 12 & 16 Winthrop St, Provincetown, MA 02657**
**Tel: (508) 487-9603 (Tel/Fax), (800) 696-9603. Call #16 Winthrop St. at (508) 487-4605 (Tel/Fax), (800) 422-4605.**

**Type:** Guesthouse.
**Clientele:** Mostly men in high season. Good mix of men & women at other times
**Transportation:** Car, ferry or air from Boston. Free airport/ferry pick up provided if arranged.
**To Gay Bars:** 2 minutes' walk to gay bars, 1/2 block to tea dance.
**Rooms:** 12 rooms, 3 suites & 1 apartment with double, queen or king beds.
**Bathrooms:** 5 private bath/toilets & 11 private shower/toilets.
**Meals:** Gourmet continental breakfast.
**Vegetarian:** local rest.
**Compliment.:** Coffee & tea.
**Dates Open:** All year.
**High Season:** Mid June to mid September.
**Rates:** High season $80-$180, off-season $45-$120.
**Discounts:** Off season: 5+ days, 15% (Nov 1-May 15), 10% for returning guests.
**Credit Cards:** MC, Visa, Amex, Discover.
**Rsv'tns:** Required.
**Reserve Through:** Call direct or travel agent.
**Minimum Stay:** 5 to 7 days during high season.
**Parking:** Free off-street parking, 1 car per room.
**In-Room:** Color cable TV, VCR, AC, ceiling fan, telephone, refrigerator, daily laundry & maid serice.
**On-Premises:** TV lounge, grand piano, fireplace, laundry services, fax & internet services, cycle storage.
**Exercise/Health:** Nearby gym, bike hire, massage. In-house massage on season.
**Swim:** Nearby pool & ocean.
**Sunbathing:** On private sun decks.
**Smoking:** A non-smoking guesthouse, except on outside decks.
**Your Host:** Trevor, Stephen & Patrick.

IGTA

## Benchmark Inn & Annex

Gay/Lesbian ♀♂

### *The Best is For You*

Debuting in April, 1997, ***Benchmark Inn*** promises top-notch comfort and style. On a quiet side street near the center of Provincetown, six brand-new individually climate-controlled bedrooms and a penthouse suite offer a variety of luxuries. The long list of deluxe amenities includes fireplaces, whirlpool baths, wet bars with refrigerator, private balconied entrances and stunning harbor views. Next door is ***Benchmark Annex,*** a cozy, quiet gem with a beautiful flowering garden, dip pool and large sun deck. Moderate tariffs make this an attractive choice for your Provincetown getaway.

**Address: 6-8 Dyer Street, Provincetown, MA 02657**
**Tel: (508) 487-7440, (888) 487-7440, Fax: (508) 487-7442.**

**Type:** Bed & breakfast.
**Clientele:** Mostly gay & lesbian with some straight clientele
**Transportation:** Free parking or airport pick up. Ferry from Boston in summer or 5 blocks to bus.
**To Gay Bars:** 3 blocks, a 3 minute walk.
**Rooms:** 14 rooms, 1 suite with single, double or queen beds.
**Bathrooms:** Private: 4 bath/toilet/showers, 4 bath/toilets, 5 shower/toilets. Shared: 2 bath/shower/toilets.
**Meals:** Expanded continental breakfast. Room delivery for inn guests.
**Vegetarian:** Very good options at virtually every restaurant.
**Complimentary:** Snack basket for inn guests, hard candy.
**Dates Open:** All year.
**High Season:** Memorial Day wknd & mid-June-mid-Sept.
**Rates:** Summer $65-$275, mid $49-$225, winter (inn only) $75-$175.
**Discounts:** 10% off for stays of 1 week or longer during off season.
**Credit Cards:** MC, Visa, Discover, Amex.
**Rsv'tns:** Strongly recommended for summer & special events.
**Reserve Through:** Travel agent or call direct.
**Minimum Stay:** 7 nights during 4th of July, 4-5 nights summer wknds, 2-3 nights mid-season wknds.
**Parking:** Limited free parking, 1 space per room.
**In-Room:** Color cable TV, telephone, AC, ceiling fans, safe, hair dryer, refrigerator, maid service.
**On-Premises:** Fax service.
**Exercise/Health:** Nearby gym, weights, sauna, massage.
**Swimming:** Pool on premises.
**Sunbathing:** Poolside, at beach, on private sun decks.
**Nudity:** Permitted at the beach.
**Smoking:** Permitted in some bedrooms. Non-smoking rooms available.
**Pets:** Permitted in some rooms, off-season only. Please call ahead for details.
**Children:** Welcome over 6 years of age.
**Languages:** English.

## Boatslip Beach Club

Gay/Lesbian ♀♂

### *Simply the Best for Over 25 Years!*

The ***Boatslip Beach Club***, beginning its 30th season, is a 45-room contemporary resort on Provincetown Harbor. Thirty-three rooms have glass doors opening onto private balconies overlooking our fabulous deck, pool, private beach and the bay.

All rooms have either one queen or two double beds, private baths, direct-dial phones and color cable TV. Off-street parking, morning coffee, admission to Tea Dance and sun cots are all complimentary. We offer a full-service restaurant, poolside grille and raw bar and evening entertainment. Call or write your hosts: ***Peter Simpson and Jim Carlino*** for further information....***YOU OWE IT TO YOURSELF!!!***.

Address: 161 Commercial St Box 393, Provincetown, MA 02657
Tel: (800) 451-SLIP (7547), (508) 487-1669, Fax: (508) 487-6021.

**Type:** Hotel with restaurant, bar, disco, card & gift shop, & sportswear boutique.
**Clientele:** Gay & lesbian. Good mix of men & women
**Transportation:** Car is best. Walk from ferry.
**To Gay Bars:** Bar on premises, good mix of men & women. Women's bar 2 blocks away.
**Rooms:** 30 rooms with double beds & 15 rooms with queen beds.
**Bathrooms:** All private bath/toilets.
**Vegetarian:** Available.
**Complimentary:** Morning coffee, sun cots, admission to Tea Dance.
**Dates Open:** April thru October.
**High Season:** June 18th-September 7th.
**Rates:** Off season $65-$95. In season $120-$160.
**Discounts:** Group rates available. Call for information.
**Credit Cards:** MC & VISA.
**Rsv'tns:** Strongly recommended in season.
**Reserve Thru:** Call direct.
**Minimum Stay:** Three nights by reservation, less if available.
**Parking:** Ample free covered off-street parking.
**In-Room:** Color cable TV, direct-dial phones, maid service, limited room service. Ceiling fans in some rooms.
**On-Premises:** Meeting rooms, public telephone, central heat, restaurant & bar.
**Exercise/Health:** Nearby gym, weights & massage.
**Swimming:** Pool or ocean beach.
**Sunbathing:** On beach, private/common sun decks or poolside.
**Smoking:** Permitted without restrictions.
**Pets:** Not permitted.
**Handicap Access:** No.
**Children:** Permitted, but not recommended.
**Languages:** English.
**Your Host:** Peter & Jim

IGTA

# The Bradford Carver House

**Gay/Lesbian ♂**

## *Your Home away from Home – Where There Are No Strangers, Only Friends You Haven't Met!*

***The Bradford Carver House*** was built in the mid-nineteenth century and is conveniently located in the heart of Provincetown. Experience our warm hospitality and cozy accommodations in a friendly and relaxed atmosphere. Our rooms, most with private baths, are perfect for those who seek the charm of a guesthouse. A complimentary continental breakfast is served each morning on our patio. Come join us at ***The Bradford Carver House*** and we will make your stay a memorable one.

**Address:** 70 Bradford St, Provincetown, MA 02657
**Tel:** (508) 487-4966 (Tel/Fax), (800) 826-9083.

**Type:** Guesthouse.
**Clientele:** Mostly men with women welcome
**Transportation:** Bus, car, ferry or plane.
**To Gay Bars:** Across street, others 1 or 2 blocks.
**Rooms:** 5 rooms with single or double beds.
**Bathrooms:** Private: 1 shower/toilet, 2 bath/shower/toilets. Shared: 2 bath/shower/toilets.
**Meals:** Expanded continental breakfast.
**Vegetarian:** In nearby restaurants.
**Dates Open:** All year.
**High Season:** Mid-June thru mid-September, Memorial Day weekend.
**Rates:** Summer $60-$99, fall & spring $50-$79, winter $40-$69.
**Discounts:** Nov 15-May 15. Stay 4 nights pay for 3 and at off season rates, too. Excludes holidays & special events.
**Credit Cards:** MC, Visa, Amex, Discover.
**Rsv'tns:** Highly recommended in season.
**Reserve Through:** Call direct or travel agent.
**Minimum Stay:** Required July thru Labor Day & Women's Week, 5-night minimum.
**Parking:** Free off street parking.
**In-Room:** AC, color cable TV, VCR, refrigerator, ceiling fans, maid service.
**On-Premises:** Guest telephone, TV lounge, common patio.
**Exercise/Health:** Local gym nearby.
**Swimming:** Nearby pool, bay & ocean.
**Sunbathing:** On patio.
**Smoking:** Permitted in common room.
**Pets:** Permitted with prior arrangements, must be quiet.
**Handicap Access:** No.
**Children:** No.
**Languages:** English, Tagalog (Pilipino).
**Your Host:** Bill & José.

# The Brass Key Guesthouse

Gay/Lesbian ♂

## *Unique in Provincetown*

***The Brass Key Guesthouse*** is renowned for providing gay and lesbian travelers with the finest in luxury accommodations, attentive service and meticulous housekeeping. In concert with numerous accolades from its guests and from travel writers of the gay media, ***The Brass Key*** is one of five gay-designated lodgings throughout the United States to receive *Out & About's* coveted Editor's Choice award (1994-1996).

Located on a quiet side street in the heart of town, ten guest rooms in a restored 1828 sea captain's home and two charming private cottages overlook the heated dip pool and landscaped courtyard. All accommodations offer traditional New England architecture enhanced by English and American Country antiques. Yet no two rooms are alike: each presents its own special warmth and personality with details such as a vaulted skylit ceiling, a teddy bear loft, a working fireplace, framed antique quilts or courtyard and harbor views.

Throughout the four seasons, ***The Brass Key*** presents a private and exclusive retreat. In the early Spring, flowering tulips, forsythia, azalea and rhododendron greet guests. From Memorial Day through September, the action shifts to the sun: while many guests enjoy the seashore beaches, others relax and socialize in the enclosed courtyard. In the Fall, as crisp nights complement the warm days of Indian summer, and later, throughout the quiet of Winter, a blazing fire in the hearth accords the perfect backdrop to savor a bottle of wine and ward off the outside chill.

Guests of ***The Brass Key*** are offered every amenity to ensure their year-round comfort: individually-controlled heating and air-conditioning, telephone, color cable televisions with VCR and videocassette library, refrigerator, hair dryer, Caswell-Massey bath toiletries; some deluxe rooms further feature fireplaces, king beds and oversized whirlpool baths.

The staff of ***The Brass Key*** looks forward to the pleasure of your company.

**Address: 9 Court St, Provincetown, MA 02657**
**Tel: (508) 487-9005, (800) 842-9858, Fax: (508) 487-9020.**

**Type:** Bed & breakfast guesthouse.
**Clientele:** Mostly men with women very welcome.
**Transportation:** Ferry, auto, or plane from Boston. Provincetown airport taxi $5.
**To Gay Bars:** 2 blocks to gay & lesbian bars.
**Rooms:** 10 rooms & 2 cottages with queen or king beds.
**Bathrooms:** All private.
**Meals:** Expanded continental breakfast.
**Complimentary:** Afternoon cocktails.
**Dates Open:** All year.
**High Season:** Mid-June to mid-September, also holidays, special weekends.
**Rates:** In season $165-$230 & off season $65-$145.
**Credit Cards:** Amex, Discover, MC, VISA.
**Rsv'tns:** Highly recommended.
**Reserve Through:** Travel agent or call direct.
**Minimum Stay:** Required in season, during holidays & special events.
**Parking:** Ample free off-street parking.
**In-Room:** Color cable TV, VCR, video tape library, AC, telephone, ceiling fan,

*continued next page*

refrigerator, fireplace, whirlpool bath, hair dryer, bathrobes. Laundry, maid & turndown service.
**On-Premises:** Spacious living room w/ breakfast area, wood-burning fireplace.
**Exercise/Health:** Whirlpool spa & nearby gym.
**Swimming:** Heated pool on the premises; also nearby ocean beaches.
**Sunbathing:** Poolside courtyard & sun decks.
**Smoking:** Non-smoking rooms available.
**Pets:** Not permitted.
**Handicap Access:** Yes. Wheelchair parking & ramp. 1 guestroom/bath for the physically challenged.
**Children:** Not permitted.
**Languages:** English.

IGTA

## The Buoy

**Gay/Lesbian ♀♂**

***The Buoy*** is located conveniently in the center of Provincetown, close to everything that this gay & lesbian resort town has to offer. Near shops and restaurants, the inn is also just a short distance from the beach. Of the nine guestrooms, two have king beds, private baths and cable television. There is also cable TV in the common room for your enjoyment. In the summer, the backyard is perfect for sunning and relaxing your cares away. We offer morning coffee, off-season rates, and parking is also available.

**Address: 97 Bradford St, Provincetown, MA 02657**
**Tel: (508) 487-3082, (800) 648-0364, Fax: (508) 487-4887.**

**Type:** Guesthouse.
**Clientele:** Good mix of gay men & women
**To Gay Bars:** 1/2 block to major discos.
**Rooms:** 1 single, 7 doubles, 1 triple.
**Bathrooms:** 2 private, 3 shared.
**Meals:** Cont. breakfast.
**Dates Open:** All year.
**High Season:** June-Aug.
**Rates:** In-season $50-$90, off-season $35-$75.
**Credit Cards:** MC, Visa.
**Rsv'tns:** Required with 1/2 deposit within 5 days of booking.
**Reserve Thru:** Call direct.
**Minimum Stay:** 3 nights; 5 nights on holidays.
**Parking:** 6 spaces off premises.
**In-Room:** Maid service, rooms with private bath have color cable TV.
**On-Premises:** Cable TV in common room.
**Swimming:** Ocean beach nearby.
**Sunbathing:** On the beach or deck.
**Smoking:** Permitted without restrictions.
**Pets:** Not permitted.
**Handicap Access:** No.
**Children:** Not permitted.
**Languages:** English.

## Cape View Motel

**Gay-Friendly 50/50 ♀♂**

### *The Motel with the Picturesque View of the Harbor*

***Cape View Motel,*** sitting on the hightest bluff in North Truro, is very much in the Provincetown area, but is away from the bustle of downtown. Its position means that every unit has a panoramic view of the harbor and bay. Nearby white sand beaches and rolling dunes are postcard perfect. Enjoy a day of swimming and sunning along the shore, or simply relax by the pool.

Picturesque Provincetown is only eight minutes from the motel where galleries, nightclubs, theaters, shops, boutiques, and restaurants abound. Quaint Wellfleet village – home of the famous Wellfleet oysters – is less than 10 minutes to the south and also has many charming restaurants, shops, and boutiques. Fine craftsmen are plentiful in the area and a leisurely day of exploring can be well rewarded by the discovery of unique artisans and unsurpassed scenery.

For athletes, golf and tennis are available nearby or you can bike or ride horses along the scenic trails of the National Seashore Park. Dune rides, whale watching, fishing excursions and sightseeing helicopter and plane rides can be arranged.

When you are ready to relax after sightseeing, the motel's spacious, comfortable rooms have color cable TVs, while deluxe efficiencies have private balconies and telephones with free local calls. Air conditioning, king-sized beds, and free morning coffee are also among the amenities offered for your comfort and enjoyment.

**Address: Rte 6, PO Box 114, North Truro, MA 02652**
**Tel: (508) 487-0363, (800) 224-3232.**

**Type:** Motel.
**Clientele:** 50% gay & lesbian & 50% straight clientele.
**Transportation:** Car is best. Provincetown Airport or Ferry, then taxi. Pick up from airport.
**To Gay Bars:** 8-minute drive.
**Rooms:** 32 rooms with 2 doubles or 1 king bed. 20 units have completely equipped kitchens.
**Bathrooms:** All private.
**Meals:** Morning coffee.
**Complimentary:** Free ice 24 hours.
**Dates Open:** Apr 15-Nov 1.
**High Season:** June 28-Sept 7 (Labor Day).
**Rates:** Off season $45-$59.90, in season $65-$89.90.
**Discounts:** 5% for weekly stays.
**Credit Cards:** MC, VISA, Discover.
**Rsv'tns:** Highly suggested.
**Reserve Thru:** Call direct.
**Minimum Stay:** 2 nights on weekends, more on certain holidays.
**Parking:** Ample free off-street parking.
**In-Room:** Color cable TV, AC, telephone, kitchen, refrigerator & maid service.
**Swimming:** Pool on premises, beaches nearby.
**Sunbathing:** At poolside, on the beach & on private sun decks.
**Nudity:** Permitted on private sun decks.
**Smoking:** Permitted everywhere.
**Pets:** Not permitted.
**Handicap Access:** No.
**Children:** Permitted.
**Languages:** English & French.

## Captain's House

**Gay/Lesbian ♂**

***The Captain's House*** is one of the oldest guesthouses of Provincetown. Built more than a century ago, it represents the typical architecture and simple elegance of a bygone era. Though on busy Commercial St., we're located up a secluded little alley where there is an absence of noise and a lot of unexpected privacy. Our charming little patio is great for morning coffee, cook-outs or sun tanning, and you will find the common room to be most comfortable. Our rooms are charming, immaculate and comfortable, with reasonable rates.

**Address: 350-A Commercial St, Provincetown, MA 02657**
**Tel: Guest phone: (508) 487-9794, Reservations: (800) 457-8885.**

**Type:** Guesthouse.
**Clientele:** Mostly men with women welcome.
**Transportation:** Taxi from airport 5 min. 2-min. walk from bus, ferry.
**To Gay Bars:** 5-10 minutes' walk to everything.
**Rooms:** 1 small single, 8 doubles & 2 rooms with 2 beds.
**Bathrooms:** 3 private & 2 shared. All rooms have sinks.
**Meals:** Continental breakfast.
**Dates Open:** All year.
**High Season:** Memorial Day-Labor Day.
**Rates:** $45-$85.
**Discounts:** By request on stays of 7 days or more.
**Credit Cards:** MC, VISA, Amex, Discover.
**Rsv'tns:** Necessary, as soon as possible.
**Reserve Through:** Call direct.
**Parking:** Free parking.
**In-Room:** Color TV, maid service, refrigerator, & ceiling or window fans.
**On-Premises:** TV lounge, public telephone, & central heat.
**Swimming:** Ocean beach nearby.
**Sunbathing:** On beach or private patio.
**Smoking:** Permitted with restrictions.
**Pets:** Not permitted.
**Handicap Access:** No.
**Children:** Not permitted.
**Languages:** English.
**Your Host:** David & Bob.

## Carl's Guest House

Q-NET Men ♂

### *Where Strangers Become Friends*

Our house is decorated in the clean, simple manner most suited to a beach vacation. Friendly, decent guys come from around the world to enjoy sea, sun and sand. At ***Carl's Guest House,*** all guest rooms are private, clean, comfortable and fairly priced. You can kick off your shoes and relax in an inviting living room with stereo, cable TV and a selection of video tapes of all ratings. We have been catering to gay ***gentlemen*** since 1975.

**Address: 68 Bradford St, Provincetown, MA 02657**
**Tel: (508) 487-1650, (800) 348-CARL,**
**E-mail: carlptwn@tiac.net. http://www.tiac.net/users/carlptwn.**

**Type:** Guesthouse.
**Clientele:** Men
**Transportation:** $1 bus, $5 taxi from airport; short walk from bus stn & boat dock.
**Rooms:** 14 rms with sgl, double or queen beds.
**Bathrooms:** Private & semi-private.
**Meals:** Complimentary coffee, tea, soups and ice in lounge service area.
**Complimentary:** Coffee, tea, etc.
**Dates Open:** All year.
**High Season:** Mid-June to mid-September.
**Rates:** Summer $55-$100, other times $30-$60.
**Discounts:** For groups, gay business organizations during off season.
**Credit Cards:** MC & VISA.
**Reserve Thru:** Call direct.
**Parking:** Limited off-street & adequate on-street parking.
**In-Room:** Color TV, private sun decks, patios, AC, fridge, ceiling fans.
**On-Premises:** TV lounge with color cable TV & VCR.
**Exercise/Health:** Nearby gym.
**Swimming:** One block to ocean beach.
**Sunbathing:** On beach, private or common sun deck.
**Nudity:** Permitted on sun decks, in shower rooms.
**Smoking:** Smoking areas are limited.
**Children:** Not permitted.
**Languages:** English.

## The Chicago House

Gay/Lesbian ♀♂

### *When in P-Town, Think of Chicago... (House, That Is!)*

***Chicago House,*** surrounded by charming gardens, canopied porches, inviting decks and patios, offers guests ten attractive rooms, nearly all with private bath, and three apartments with kitchenettes. Guests return each year, to the two historical Cape Cod homes that make up ***Chicago House,*** for the delicious homemade muffins and cakes baked daily for continental breakfast. One of the oldest established P-Town guesthouses, we stay open all year, offering a roaring fire in the common room in winter. We're centrally located, but on a quiet side street.

**Address: 6 Winslow St, Provincetown, MA 02657**
**Tel: (508) 487-0537, (800) SEE-PTOWN (733-7869), Fax: (508) 487-6212.**
**E-mail: mongooseiv@aol.com.**

**Type:** Bed & breakfast guesthouse.
**Clientele:** Good mix of gay men & women.
**Transportation:** Car or boat from Boston. Free pick up from airport & ferry dock.
**To Gay Bars:** 1 block or 1 min walk.
**Rooms:** 10 rooms, 1 apartment & 2 studio apartments with single, double, queen or king beds.
**Bathrooms:** Private: 1 bath/toilet, 8 shower/toilets. Others share.
**Meals:** Cont. breakfast.
**Vegetarian:** Available in restaurants.
**Complimentary:** Tea, coffee, mints on pillow.
**Dates Open:** All year.
**High Season:** July & Aug.
**Rates:** Summer $49-175 & winter $25-135.
**Credit Cards:** MC, Visa, Amex.
**Rsv'tns:** Suggested.
**Reserve Thru:** Call direct.
**Minimum Stay:** During July & August.
**Parking:** Adequate, free off-street parking.
**In-Room:** Color TV, maid service, kitchen & ref.
**On-Premises:** TV lounge, meeting rooms, courtesy phone & guest refrigerator.
**Exercise/Health:** Gym & weights nearby.
**Swimming:** Nearby pool & ocean beach.
**Sunbathing:** On patio or nearby poolside & ocean beach.
**Smoking:** Permitted.
**Pets:** Permitted with advance notice & some restrictions.
**Children:** Permitted off season.
**Languages:** English.

## Coat of Arms

Gay/Lesbian ♂

***Coat of Arms*** is a vintage 1810 New England Colonial home which was converted to Victorian in 1886. It's located in central Provincetown at the tip of Cape Cod. Rooms are comfortable and cozy and, like many guest houses in Provincetown, have shared baths. Entertain your personal guests in the lounge, which has a large private bar where you can keep your own bottles. ***Coat of Arms*** is within strolling distance of fine restaurants, gift shops, theaters, artists' studios and gay bars and clubs.

**Address: 7 Johnson St, Provincetown, MA 02657**
**Tel: (508) 487-0816, (800) 224-8230.**

**Type:** Guesthouse.
**Clientele:** Mostly men with women welcome
**Transportation:** Taxi from airport 10 min or less, 5 min walk from ferry & bus.
**To Gay Bars:** 1-2 minutes to bar.
**Rooms:** 10 rms w/single/twin, dbl/queen beds.
**Bathrooms:** 4 shared showers.
**Meals:** Coffee & pastries in the morning only.
**Complimentary:** Ice, set-ups at bar.
**Dates Open:** March 15 to November 1.
**High Season:** June thru September.
**Rates:** $50-$75 summer, $35-$55 off season.
**Rsv'tns:** Recommended.
**Reserve Through:** Call direct.
**Minimum Stay:** 4 days in summer, 7 for Carnival week, 4th of July, Labor Day.
**Parking:** Limited free off-street parking.
**In-Room:** Maid service, ceiling fans.
**On-Premises:** TV lounge.
**Swimming:** Ocean beach 100 yards.
**Sunbathing:** On the beach, patio or common sun decks.
**Smoking:** Not permitted in home.
**Pets:** Not permitted.
**Handicap Access:** No.
**Children:** Not permitted.
**Languages:** English.
**Your Host:** Skip & Arpina.

## The Commons

Q-NET Gay/Lesbian ♀♂

### *Provincetown Historical Commission's 1995 Best Restoration Award*

Awake to the call of seagulls gliding over Cape Cod Bay at ***The Commons***, a charming seaside resort nestled in a garden just off lively Commercial Street and across from Cape Cod Bay. Mornings in Provincetown are famous for the pristine clarity of "Cape light," and you can see it for yourself from the private balconies, 19th-century bay windows, and popular streetside Upper Deck at ***The Commons.***

This mid-19th-century house has been an inn for decades and, in 1995, underwent extensive restoration. All rooms now have new private baths and are furnished with oversized comfortable beds and a blend of modern and antique furnishings. The inn received the 1995 Preservation Award for Best Restoration from the Provincetown Historical Commission.

Among the attractions of ***The Commons*** is the bistro-style res-

*continued next page*

taurant, located on Commercial Street. The Bistro serves fresh seafood, wood-oven pizzas, and innovative cuisine with a French accent. Outdoor dining at the streetside cafe and the Upper Deck with harbor views makes The Bistro one of Provincetown's liveliest eateries. You can also enjoy cappuccino and fresh-baked muffins in

the morning, a nightcap in the intimate bar, or champagne in your own room.

If you choose to venture out, Cape Cod Bay Beach is only steps away, right across Commercial Street. Provincetown's Gallery District begins just down the block; terrific shopping and the outrageous downtown scene are a 10-minute walk at the center of town. We also have historic lighthouses, scenic trails for hiking or biking, and incredible whale watching. Of course, being at Land's End, Provincetown is surrounded by the Atlantic Ocean, with miles of unspoiled beaches and soaring sand dunes.

**Address: 386 Commercial St, PO Box 1037, Provincetown, MA 02657**
**Tel: (508) 487-7800, (800) 487-0784.**

**Type:** Guesthouse with restaurant & bar.
**Clientele:** Mostly gay & lesbian with some straight clientele
**Transportation:** Taxi from Provincetown airport.
**To Gay Bars:** Bar on premises. Other bars & disco 8 blocks, a 10-minute walk.
**Rooms:** 12 rooms & 2 suites with single, queen or king beds.
**Bathrooms:** Private: 11 shower/toilets, 3 bath/shower/toilets.
**Meals:** Expanded continental breakfast.
**Vegetarian:** Several vegetarian items available at bistro on premises.
**Dates Open:** All year.
**High Season:** June-Sept.
**Rates:** Summer $85-$135, winter $50-$90.
**Discounts:** Off-season only for extended stays & multiple room bookings.
**Credit Cards:** MC, Visa, Amex.
**Rsv'tns:** Required.
**Reserve Through:** Travel agent or call direct.
**Minimum Stay:** Required.
**Parking:** Adequate free off-street parking.
**In-Room:** Color cable TV, AC, ceiling fans, maid & room service.
**On-Premises:** Restaurant available to host private functions.
**Exercise/Health:** Nearby gym, weights, massage.
**Swimming:** Nearby pool & ocean.
**Sunbathing:** On private sun decks, in garden & at beach.
**Smoking:** Permitted in rooms, bar, outside deck.
**Pets:** Permitted, $10 pet charge.
**Handicap Access:** No.
**Children:** No.
**Languages:** English, Spanish.
**Your Host:** Carl & Chuck.

## Dexter's Inn

**Gay/Lesbian ♀♂**

### *Come Out to Provincetown & Feel at Home With Us*

The experience of a lifetime awaits you in Provincetown. The sea, the sunsets, the people and ***Dexter's Inn*** are here for your pleasure. Enjoy homemade muffins or breads, juice, and coffee each morning on the flower garden patio or in the cozy hospitality room. The sun deck and patio are perfect places to meet new friends or share quiet moments with your special someone. A brief stroll will lead you to Cape Cod Bay, shops, galleries, and restaurants. UNDER NEW OWNERSHIP.

**Address: 6 Conwell St, Provincetown, MA 02657.**
**Tel: (508) 487-1911, (888) 521-1999.**

**Type:** Bed & breakfast guesthouse.
**Clientele:** Gay & lesbian. Good mix men & women.
**Transportation:** Car, plane, bus or ferry. Free airport pick up available.
**To Gay Bars:** 5-min walk.
**Rooms:** 15 rooms with double beds.
**Bathrooms:** 12 private shower/toilets & 1 shared bath/shower/toilet.
**Meals:** Expanded continental breakfast.
**Dates Open:** All year.
**High Season:** July & Aug.
**Rates:** $75-$95 summer, $50-$60 off season.
**Discounts:** Special off-season rates for long stays.
**Credit Cards:** MC & VISA.
**Rsv'tns:** Recommended.
**Reserve Thru:** Call direct.
**Minimum Stay:** In high season, for summer weekends (May, June, September) and holidays.
**Parking:** Free ample park.
**In-Room:** Maid service, color cable TV.
**On-Premises:** Sun deck, patio, TV lounge, fridge.
**Swimming:** Ocean beach.
**Sunbathing:** On ocean beach or sun deck.
**Smoking:** Permitted on sun deck & in outdoor areas.
**Pets:** Not permitted.
**Handicap Access:** Lmtd.
**Children:** Not permitted.
**Languages:** English.

## Dusty Miller Inn

Women ♀

### *Guests Thrive on the Friendly, Easy Atmosphere!*

Making guests feel at home is our specialty at ***Dusty Miller Inn.*** The pleasant comfort of our porch rocking chairs seems to promote interesting conversations, and friendships are struck there. Our porch rockers also give you a great vantage point for peoplewatching. Expect to feel at ease and in the perfect mood to enjoy the fun of Provincetown. Our rooms are well-appointed and comfortable.

**Address: 82 Bradford St, Provincetown, MA 02657. Tel: (508) 487-2213.**

**Type:** Guesthouse.
**Clientele:** Mostly women with men welcome
**Transportation:** Taxi. Free pick up from airport with at least one week prior arrangement.
**To Gay Bars:** Across street.
**Rooms:** 12 rooms & 1 apartment, all doubles.
**Bathrooms:** 10 private, others share.
**Meals:** Morning coffee/tea.
**Dates Open:** All year.
**High Season:** Memorial Day to Labor Day.
**Rates:** In season: $68-$78 double, $115 apt. Off season: $45-$55 double, $80 apartment.
**Credit Cards:** MC, Visa.
**Rsv'tns:** Required.
**Reserve Thru:** Call direct.
**Minimum Stay:** Rooms: 2 nights in season (holidays 3 nights). Apts: 2 nights (in season 7 nights).
**Parking:** 1 space per room on premises or in private lot approximately 1 blk away.
**In-Room:** Maid service. Ceiling fans, fans, or AC in all rooms. Color TV, ref. in 7 rooms & apt. Other rms have B&W TV & access to ref. & color TV.
**On-Premises:** BBQ grills, common room, phone .
**Swimming:** Ocean beach nearby.
**Sunbathing:** On the beach or in the front yard.
**Smoking:** Permitted without restrictions.
**Pets:** Permitted in designated rooms.
**Children:** Permitted.
**Languages:** English.

## 1807 House

Gay/Lesbian ♀♂

### *Comfort and Privacy 50 Yards from the Beach*

This sought-after spot for discerning gay travelers since 1977 stands just 50 yards from the beach. ***1807 House,*** located in Provincetown's famous West End, is an origianl 1807 cedar-shingled main house facing the beach and bay. The addition joining it to the remodeled carriage house and the separate secluded garden cottage each contain additional studios and apartments with kitchens. Miles of unspoiled sand dunes, beaches, hiking, bicycling, and horse trails are close by. From ***1807 House,*** it's an easy walk to Provincetown's galleries, restaurants, gay bars, and discos.

**Addr: 54 Commercial St, Provincetown, MA 02657**
**Tel: (508) 487-2173, E-mail: ptown1807@aol.com.**

**Type:** Bed & breakfast & guesthouse.
**Clientele:** Mostly gay & lesbian with some straight clientele
**Transportation:** Car, plane, ferry, bus. Free pick up from airport or ferry dock.
**To Gay Bars:** 1/2 mile or a 10-minute walk.
**Rooms:** 3 rooms & 5 apartments with single, double or king beds.
**Bathrooms:** 5 private & 3 shared bath/toilet/showers.

*continued next page*

**Meals:** Continental breakfast (for rooms).
**Vegetarian:** Excellent restaurants nearby.
**Complimentary:** Setup service.
**Dates Open:** All year.
**High Season:** Memorial Day thru mid-Sept.
**Rates:** Summer $58-$125, winter $48-$85.
**Credit Cards:** MC, Visa, Amex.
**Reserve Through:** Travel agent or call direct.
**Minimum Stay:** Please inquire.
**Parking:** Ample free off-street parking.
**In-Room:** Color cable TV, coffee/tea-making facilities, refrigerator. Some rooms with AC, ceiling fans. Apartments have kitchen.
**On-Premises:** Meeting room.
**Exercise/Health:** Nearby gym, weights & massage.
**Swimming:** Nearby ocean & bay.
**Sunbathing:** On patio, private sun decks, in private garden.
**Smoking:** Permitted in some units.
**Pets:** Not permitted.
**Handicap Access:** No.
**Children:** No.
**Languages:** English.
**Your Host:** Court & Dean.

## Elephant Walk Inn

**Gay/Lesbian ♀♂**

### *Elephant Walk "Unforgettable"*

***Elephant Walk Inn*** was built as a private country home in 1917. The large mission-style house was converted to an inn some years later. Its proximity to the center of town and the then existing railroad made it a favorite stop for early Provincetown visitors.

ELEPHANT WALK INN

The decor of the inn recalls the romantic feeling of an Edwardian house of the past. Many of the rooms are decorated with original paintings, prints and antiques. One room has a canopy bed, another a four-poster, while brass and enamel beds grace two others. Old captain's bureaus, antique tables and Oriental carpets are scattered about.

However, to this echo of the past have been added the modern conveniences of the present. Each guest room has its own private bath as well as a remote cable color TV, a small refrigerator, and a ceiling fan. Air-conditioning is also available as an option.

Continental breakfast is served each morning on the glass-enclosed front porch where guests can also find a varied supply of reading material. Some guests enjoy their coffee on the large second floor sun deck which is at the rear of the inn overlooking the landscaped garden. The deck, with its scattering of summer furniture, is a favorite gathering spot for guests to meet and to enjoy a drink after a day at the beach.

Free parking is provided on the premises. Although a car is not necessary for seeing Provincetown with its myriad shops, restaurants and clubs, it is convenient to have one for exploring and finding a secluded beach with windswept dunes. June and September are the perfect times to do that. The days are warm and bright and although everything is open, there are no crowds.

Please call or write for a free brochure.

**Address: 156 Bradford St, Provincetown, MA 02657**
**Tel: (508) 487-2543 or (800) 889-WALK (9255). Guest ph: (508) 487-2195.**

**Type:** Bed & breakfast.
**Clientele:** Good mix of gay men & women.
**Transportation:** Pick up from airport, ferry or bus available.
**To Gay Bars:** 5-minute walk to men's, women's bars.
**Rooms:** 8 rooms with double, queen or king beds.
**Bathrooms:** All private shower/toilets.
**Meals:** Continental breakfast.
**Dates Open:** April 15-November 10.
**High Season:** June 20-September 7.
**Rates:** In season $89-$95, off season $46-$79.
**Discounts:** One night free on weekly stays Apr 15-

Jun 7, Sep 14-Oct 9.
**Credit Cards:** MC, Visa, Amex, Diners, Discover.
**Rsv'tns:** Required 4-8 wks in advance in high season.
**Reserve Through:** Call direct.
**Minimum Stay:** 3 nights in season, more on weekends, holidays.
**Parking:** Ample free off-street parking.
**In-Room:** Maid service, color TV, refrigerator, ceiling fans, some with air-conditioning.
**On-Premises:** Lounge, sun deck. Guest phone in lounge.
**Swimming:** Ocean beach 1-1/2 blocks.
**Sunbathing:** On beach or common sun deck.
**Smoking:** Permitted in rooms, not in lounge.
**Pets:** Not permitted.
**Handicap Access:** No.
**Children:** Usually not permitted. Please inquire.
**Languages:** English.
**Your Host:** Len.

## The Fairbanks Inn

Q-NET Gay/Lesbian ♀♂

### *There is magic here...*

This 18th-century sea captain's house, rich in history, with its elegant architecture, roaring fireplaces, sensuous beds, wide plank floors from the ship of the captain who built it, brass candlesticks & cast-iron latches, infinite treasures from the past, and a philosophy of decadence, will enchant you. Mornings, smell the aroma of fresh-ground coffee, crumb cakes baking, and cinnamon and butter melting. Breakfast in the gorgeous courtyard garden, on the sun porch, or take it back to your room for a lingering breakfast in bed... Our guest rooms range from original antique-filled rooms to luxurious country-style suites. If a sun-drenched bed is where you'd like to spend your afternoon, indulge your pleasure by reserving our penthouse.

**Address:** 90 Bradford St, Provincetown, MA 02657
**Tel:** (508) 487-0386, (800) FAIRBNK, **Fax:** (508) 487-3540,
**E-mail:** fairbank@capecod.net. www.capecod.net.

**Type:** Bed & breakfast.
**Clientele:** Good mix of gays & lesbians
**To Gay Bars:** 1/2 block, a 2-minute walk.
**Rooms:** 13 rooms, 1 suite, 1 apartment with double or king beds.
**Bathrooms:** All private.
**Meals:** Expanded continental breakfast.
**Vegetarian:** Available nearby.
**Complimentary:** Tea & coffee, mints on pillow, cookies.
**Dates Open:** All year.
**High Season:** End of June-Labor Day
**Rates:** In-season $95-$175, off-season $50-$120.
**Discounts:** For groups renting several rooms in house.
**Credit Cards:** MC, Visa, Amex.
**Rsv'tns:** Suggested for high season.
**Reserve Through:** Travel agent or call direct.
**Minimum Stay:** Varies with season.
**Parking:** Adequate free off-street parking.
**In-Room:** Color cable TV, AC, maid service. Some rooms with VCR, kitchen, refrigerator, ceiling fans.
**On-Premises:** Public phone, living room, sun deck, sun porch, fax, E-mail, video tape library.
**Exercise/Health:** Nearby gym, weights, massage.
**Swimming:** In nearby ocean.
**Sunbathing:** On ocean beach, common sundecks, patio.
**Smoking:** All guest rooms are non-smoking. Permitted outside only.
**Pets:** Not permitted.
**Handicap Access:** No.
**Children:** Age restrictions may apply.
**Languages:** English, German.

## Gabriel's

**Women ♀**

### *Perhaps There Really are Small Corners of This Earth That Come Close to Heaven*

*Come close to heaven.*

In the Heart of Provincetown • Conference Center • Workshops • Breakfast • Gym • Jacuzzis • Steam Room • Sauna In-room Phones • Sun Decks • Barbecue • Fireplaces • Bicycles • Parking • Cable TV • Air Conditioning • Business Services • Group Rates Available

Since 1979, ***Gabriel's*** has welcomed women and their friends to two beautiful old homes graced by antique furnishings, patios and gardens. Each guest room and suite, decorated differently, is distinguished by its own personality. We also offer modern conveniences such as fax, e-mail and copy services; cable TV, VCRs, in-room phones and fully-equipped kitchens.

Whether you take a soothing soak in one of our two hot tubs, unwind in our steam room or sauna, lounge on the sun decks, work out in our exercise area, relax in the common room around a fire, or set out at twilight towards the bright lights of Commercial Street, or the last, purple light of day fading over Herring Cove, you're certain to experience the unique character of Provincetown and the cozy hospitality of ***Gabriel's.***

We are also home to *Siren's Workshop Center* offering a variety of classes for body, mind and spirit. Our lovely sky-lit meeting space is available year-round to both individuals and groups for conferences, ceremonies or other special events. Please accept our invitation to join us anytime in the comfortable, safe and heavenly setting of ***Gabriel's.*** Warmly, *Gabriel Brooke, Innkeeper*

**Address: 104 Bradford St, Provincetown, MA 02657**
**Tel: (800) 9MY-ANGEL, (508) 487-3232, Fax: (508) 487-1605,**
**E-mail: gabriels@provincetown.com.**
**http://www.provincetown.com/gabriels.**

**Type:** Guesthouse & workshop center.
**Clientele:** Mostly women with men welcome
**Transportation:** Free pick up from airport, bus or ferry dock.
**To Gay Bars:** 1 block.
**Rooms:** 10 room & 10 apartments with double or queen beds.
**Bathrooms:** 16 private baths. 4 shared baths.
**Meals:** Homemade breakfast.
**Complimentary:** Coffee, tea, juice, fruit, muffins, cereal, chocolates on pillow.
**Dates Open:** All year.
**High Season:** Memorial Day to Labor Day week.
**Rates:** Winter $50-$100, Border season $65-$120, high season $75-$150.
**Discounts:** Nov 1st-Apr 1st, 3rd night free with coupon, coupons for repeat guests.
**Credit Cards:** MC, VISA, Amex, Discover.
**Rsv'tns:** Recommended.
**Reserve Through:** Travel agent or call direct.
**Minimum Stay:** 2 nights in season & on weekends off season.
**Parking:** Reserved parking in a nearby lot for $3 per night.
**In-Room:** Cable TV, telephones, housekeeping service, fully equipped kitchens (in apartments). Some rooms with refrigerators, AC, ceiling fans & fireplaces.
**On-Premises:** TV lounge, conference room, library, games, common kitchen for light meals, two gardens.
**Exercise/Health:** Yoga classes, 2 outdoor hot tubs, sauna, steam room, exercise room, discounts on massage.
**Swimming:** Nearby ocean beach.
**Sunbathing:** On beach and common sun decks.
**Nudity:** Permitted on patio in our enclosed yard.
**Smoking:** Permitted with restrictions, smoke-free rooms available.
**Pets:** Usually not permitted, but sometimes we bend.
**Handicap Access:** No.
**Children:** Permitted.
**Languages:** English, French.

## The GrandView Inn

**Gay/Lesbian ♂**

***The GrandView Inn,*** an 1870's renovated captain's home, is perfectly located in Provincetown's West End only one block from the beach. Savor the spectacular views of the bay from either of our sun decks or venture into the excitement of Commercial Street, only steps away. Charming and convenient, ***The GrandView Inn*** enjoys numerous repeat guests who consider it home when in Provincetown.

**Address: No. 4 Conant St, Provincetown, MA 02657**
**Tel: (508) 487-9193. E-mail: gndview@capecod.net.**

**Type:** Guesthouse.
**Clientele:** Mostly men with women welcome
**Transportation:** Plane from Boston to P'town airport, taxi to inn. Boat 9:30am from Boston, walk to inn.
**To Gay Bars:** 1 block to nearest bar, 1 min walk to afternoon tea dance.
**Rooms:** 12 rooms with single or double beds.
**Bathrooms:** Private, semi-private & shared.
**Meals:** Continental breakfast in season.
**Vegetarian:** Health food restaurants nearby.
**Complimentary:** Coffee & juices available in common room daily in season.
**Dates Open:** All year.
**High Season:** June 20-September 5.
**Rates:** High season $45-$100, low season $40-$70.
**Credit Cards:** MC, Visa, Amex.
**Rsv'tns:** Recommended.
**Reserve Through:** Call direct.
**Minimum Stay:** Major holidays during high season.
**Parking:** Adequate parking.
**In-Room:** Maid service.
**On-Premises:** TV lounge, common room, kitchen.
**Exercise/Health:** High-tech gym a 2-minute walk.
**Swimming:** Within walking distance.
**Sunbathing:** On common sun decks & nearby beaches.
**Smoking:** Permitted in designated areas.
**Pets:** Not permitted.
**Handicap Access:** No.
**Children:** No.
**Languages:** English.
**Your Host:** Ed & Brian.

## Gull Walk Inn

**Q-NET Women ♀**

### *The Oldest Women's Guesthouse in Provincetown*

Established in 1978, ***The Gull Walk Inn*** is the oldest women's guesthouse in Provincetown. The inn is located in the center of town, a block from Town Hall and MacMillan Wharf. This ensures that you'll be near everything and yet be sheltered from the hustle and bustle of town life. ***The Gull Walk*** is a small inn with five simple and clean guest rooms and two large shared baths. With its two porches (one with a distant water view), common room and large private garden, you are welcomed to relax and feel at home.

**Address: 300A Commercial St, Provincetown, MA 02657**
**Tel: (508) 487-9027 (Tel/Fax), (800) 309-4725.**

**Type:** Guesthouse.
**Clientele:** Women only
**To Gay Bars:** 2 minutes to women's bar.
**Rooms:** 3 dbl and 2 quads.
**Bathrooms:** 2 shared.
**Meals:** Cont. breakfast.
**Vegetarian:** Restaurant 3 houses away, also health food store 4 houses away.
**Complimentary:** Coffee, tea.
**Dates Open:** All year.
**High Season:** May-Sep.
**Rates:** Oct-Apr $45, May-Sept $65.

*continued next page*

**Rsv'tns:** Required.
**Reserve Through:** Call direct.
**Minimum Stay:** During holidays only.
**Parking:** Ample free on- & off-street & reserved pay parking.
**On-Premises:** Meeting room, TV lounge, refrigerator in hall, microwave, VCR.
**Exercise/Health:** Gym & weights 1 block away.
**Swimming:** Ocean beach.
**Sunbathing:** On ocean beach, common sundecks or on lawn.
**Smoking:** Permitted outdoors.
**Pets:** Not permitted.
**Handicap Access:** No.
**Children:** Not permitted.
**Languages:** English.
**Your Host:** Kathy & Polly.

## The Haven House

Q-NET Gay/Lesbian ♂

### *Extraordinary Value, Poolside Fun*

The atmosphere of ***The Haven House*** reflects the call for the simple pleasures of a Provincetown vacation: comfortable accommodations, poolside fun, and a heart-of-town location ideal for shopping and evening entertainment. Unique in Provincetown, this charming compound of two 19th-century homes and an adjoining carriage house surrounds a sparkling heated pool and expansive sun decks.

Guests enjoy morning coffee and homemade muffins poolside, then roam the miles of seashore beaches, or simply relax in sun chaises on the property. Later, exploration of Provincetown's shops, restaurants and nightlife is easy from this convenient location, just one block from the harborfront. Guest accommodations vary from very comfortable, larger poolside rooms featuring private bath and air conditioning to simpler, shared-bath rooms; every guestroom offers color television, mini-refrigerator and a choice of double, queen or twin beds.

Friendly service, careful housekeeping, comfortable charm and poolside fun. an extraordinary value in the heart of Provincetown. Join us this season! "★★★ - Recommended," Out & About.

**Address: 12 Carver St, Provincetown, MA 02657**
**Tel: (508) 487-3031, (800) 261-2450, Fax: (508) 487-4177.**

**Type:** Bed & breakfast guesthouse.
**Clientele:** Mostly men with women welcome
**Transportation:** Car, plane or ferry from Boston. Provincetown airport taxi $5.
**To Gay Bars:** Men's bar across the street, others within 1-3 blocks.
**Rooms:** 19 rooms & 1 3-bedroom suite.
**Bathrooms:** 14 private. Other rooms share baths.
**Meals:** Continental breakfast.
**Dates Open:** All year.
**High Season:** Mid-June thru mid-September, also some holidays, special weekends.
**Rates:** In season $65-$130. Off season $30-$80.
**Credit Cards:** Amex, Discover, MC, Visa.
**Rsv'tns:** Highly recommended.
**Reserve Through:** Travel agent or call direct.
**Minimum Stay:** Required in season, during holidays & special events.
**Parking:** Ample, free off-street parking.
**In-Room:** Color cable TV, refrigerator. Some rooms with AC. Maid service.
**On-Premises:** Coin laundry.
**Exercise/Health:** Nearby full-service gym.
**Swimming:** Heated pool on premises. Nearby ocean beaches.
**Sunbathing:** In poolside courtyard.
**Pets:** Not permitted.
**Handicap Access:** No.
**Children:** No.
**Languages:** English.

## Heritage House

Gay/Lesbian ♀♂

### *Having a Wonderful Time...Wish You Were Here!*

Our house, with thirteen rooms on three floors, a large common room, two verandas and views of Cape Cod Bay and the harbor, is next door to the Heritage Museum between Commercial Street and Bradford Street. Some of the best people watching in Provincetown is to be had from the upper and lower verandas of ***Heritage House.*** Shops, the bay beach and many fine restaurants are just a short walk from our door. Our fluffy towels, fresh and crisp linens, sparkling-clean bathrooms, delicious coffee, homemade muffins and a friendly, comfortable atmosphere will help make your stay a pleasant one. We are committed to providing our guests with all these things and more. As your hosts, we'd like to help you enjoy the magic of Provincetown.

**Address: 7 Center St, Provincetown, MA 02657**
**Tel: (508) 487-3692,**
**E-mail: HeritageH@aol.com.**

**Type:** Guesthouse.
**Clientele:** Mostly gay & lesbian with some straight clientele
**Transportation:** Car or fly into Provincetown Airport from Boston's Logan Airport. Free pick up from airport & ferry wharf.
**To Gay Bars:** 5-minute walk to women's & men's bars.
**Rooms:** 13 rooms & 1 2-bedroom condo with single, double or king beds.
**Bathrooms:** 4 shared bath/shower/toilets. Condo with private bath.
**Meals:** Buffet breakfast.
**Vegetarian:** Breakfast is mostly vegetarian & restaurants featuring vegetarian selections are only a 5-minute walk.
**Complimentary:** Ice available. Ref. on each floor.
**Dates Open:** All year.
**High Season:** Jun-Sep & holiday weekends.
**Rates:** In season \$50-\$120, off season \$40-\$100.
**Discounts:** Off-season group rates available.
**Credit Cards:** MC, VISA & Amex.
**Rsv'tns:** Preferred.
**Reserve Thru:** Call direct.
**Minimum Stay:** 2 nights for in-season weekends & 3 nights on holiday weekends.
**Parking:** Free off-street parking.
**In-Room:** Maid service.
**On-Premises:** TV lounge with color cable TV & VCR.
**Exercise/Health:** Gym, weights & massage nearby.
**Swimming:** In nearby ocean.
**Sunbathing:** At the beach.
**Smoking:** Permitted without restrictions.
**Pets:** Not permitted.
**Children:** Not especially welcomed.
**Languages:** English.

## Hotel Piaf

Q-NET Gay/Lesbian ♀♂

### *A Very Small, Very French Guesthouse in Provincetown*

In the heart of Provincetown, the ***Hotel Piaf*** is a completely restored 1820 Cape, offering the finest service, luxurious informality, and the greatest attention to detail. The house has three rooms and one suite each with its own private full bath, telephone, and cable TV.

The house, just a minute's walk from Town Hall and the Meeting House, sits in the middle of a large garden with hammocks strung between tall locust trees and Adirondack chairs here and there for an afternoon's lazy read. The inn is furnished

*continued next page*

with a mix of the owner's family antiques and comfy, overstuffed chairs. Down comforters, terry cloth robes, European bath products, and fresh flowers are just a few of the comforts we've included.

Continental breakfast (included in your room rate) consists of a croissant or brioche, depending on the baker's whim, coffee, tea, espresso or cappucino, and juice. A booklet in each room gives recommendations for local dining and sightseeing. We are happy to make dinner reservations for you, reconfirm your travel plans with the airlines, and take you to the airport or meet your flight if you let us know in advance.

Relax on the deck, take a short walk to the ferry wharf and the Boston boat, or borrow our second-hand bicycles to explore Provincetown. We want your stay with us to be as comfortable, special, pampered, and relaxing as we like when we're on vacation. We are small and our facilities are historic and charming not lavish and grand, but we believe our attention to detail and our commitment to your comfort is unparalleled in town.

**Address: 3 Prince St, Provincetown, MA 02657.**
**Tel: (508) 487-7458, (800) 340-PIAF, Fax: (508) 487-8646,**
**http://www.tiac.net/users/ptown/piaf.html,**
**E-mail: otelpiaf@capecod.net.**

**Type:** Bed & breakfast.
**Clientele:** Mostly gay & lesbian with some straight clientele
**Transportation:** Car, plane, ferry. Free pick up from airport, bus, ferry dock.
**To Gay Bars:** 1 block, a 4-minute walk.
**Rooms:** 3 rooms, 1 suite with double or king beds.
**Bathrooms:** All private bath/toilets.
**Meals:** Cont. breakfast.
**Vegetarian:** Available nearby.
**Complimentary:** Cocktails, set-up service, tea & coffee, mints on pillow.
**Dates Open:** May-Dec.
**Rates:** $55-$155.
**Credit Cards:** MC, VISA, Amex.
**Rsv'tns:** Required.
**Reserve Through:** Travel agent or call direct.
**Minimum Stay:** Required on holiday weekends.
**Parking:** Adequate free parking.
**In-Room:** Color cable TV, VCR, telephone, maid, room & laundry service.
**On-Premises:** Video tape library, living & dining rooms, garden.
**Exercise/Health:** Nearby gym, weights, massage.
**Swimming:** Ocean nearby.
**Sunbathing:** On common sun decks, in garden.
**Smoking:** Permitted outside. No non-smoking rooms available.
**Pets:** Not permitted.
**Children:** Welcome.
**Languages:** English, French.

## Lamplighter Inn & Cottage

Q-NET **Gay/Lesbian** ♂

### *Gentle Sea Breezes and the Grace and Charm of Yesteryear*

***Lamplighter Inn*** is just a stroll to most beaches and the center of town. Our antique sea captain's home is on one of Provincetown's highest hills, overlooking Cape Cod Bay, and is within walking distance of all restaurants, shops and bars. Our inn is immaculate, and we strive to assure that your stay will always be remembered. Our must-see gardens include a water garden, cacti, rare shrubs and perennials. Come relax and enjoy Provincetown at the ***Lamplighter Inn.*** Please visit our website at http://www.CapeCodAccess.com/Lamplighter.

**Address: 26 Bradford St, Provincetown, MA 02657**
**Tel: (508) 487-2529, (800) 263-6574, Fax: (508) 487-0079,**
**E-mail: lamplite@lamplite.com. http://www.CapeCodAccess.com/Lamplighter.**

**Type:** Bed & breakfast guesthouse & cottage.
**Clientele:** Mostly men with women very welcome
**Transportation:** Car, bus. Ferry or Cape Air from Boston. Free pick up from airport, bus, ferry dock.
**To Gay Bars:** 3 blocks or 1/8 mile, a 5 minute walk.
**Rooms:** 7 rooms, 2 suites & 1 cottage with double, queen or king beds.
**Bathrooms:** 8 private baths, 2 semi-private baths.
**Meals:** Expanded continental breakfast.
**Vegetarian:** Available at local restaurants, delis & grocery stores. 5-minute walk to A&P.
**Complimentary:** Turn-down service, ice.
**Dates Open:** All year.
**High Season:** Mid-June through mid-September.
**Rates:** Winter $45-$75, spring & fall $55-$129, summer $89-$179.
**Discounts:** Off-season specials & discounts on longer stays.
**Credit Cards:** MC, Visa, Amex.
**Rsv'tns:** Required during peak season, holidays & special events.
**Reserve Through:** Call direct or travel agent.
**Minimum Stay:** Highly recommended during peak season, holidays & special events.
**Parking:** Free off-street parking, 1 car per room.
**In-Room:** Color cable TV, VCR, AC, telephones, ceiling fans, maid service, robes, kitchen, refrigerators.
**On-Premises:** Roof-top sun deck, bicycle rack, patios, BBQ grill, video library, fax machine, laundry service.
**Exercise/Health:** Local gym nearby. Weights, massage.
**Swimming:** At nearby pool, ocean, lake or bay.
**Sunbathing:** On private roof-top sun deck.
**Nudity:** Permitted on roof-top deck.
**Smoking:** Non-smoking rooms. Smoking permitted on sun deck and in outdoor areas.
**Pets:** Not permitted.
**Handicap Access:** No.
**Children:** Not especially welcomed.
**Languages:** English.
**Your Host:** Steve & Brent.

IGTA

## Land's End Inn

**Gay/Friendly 50/50 ♀♂**

### *Relax in Victorian Comfort*

***Land's End Inn*** commands a splendid windswept location with breathtaking views of Provincetown and the whole of Cape Cod from on high. Built in the late Victorian period, the inn still houses part of the original owner's collection of oriental wood carvings and stained glass. Spacious rooms furnished with antiques provide a lived-in atmosphere where the modern world has not entered. Here in the quiet west end, we're close to ocean beaches, restaurants and nightlife.

BLAKE GARDENER, PHOTOGRAPHER

**Address: 22 Commercial St, Provincetown, MA 02657. Tel: (508) 487-0706, (800) 276-7088.**

**Type:** Bed & breakfast guesthouse.
**Clientele:** 50% gay & lesbian & 50% straight clientele
**Transportation:** Car is best or fly via Provincetown Airport. Bus & ferry runs from Boston Memorial Day-Labor Day.
**To Gay Bars:** 15-min walk to men's/women's bars.
**Rooms:** 13 rooms, 1 suite & 2 apartments with double or queen beds.
**Bathrooms:** 16 private bath/toilets.
**Meals:** Continental breakfast.
**Dates Open:** All year.
**High Season:** Memorial Day Weekend-September 30.
**Rates:** $90-$295.

*continued next page*

**Credit Cards:** MC, Visa.
**Rsv'tns:** Recommended.
**Reserve Through:** Call direct.
**Minimum Stay:** Summer 5-7 days, off-season weekends and some holidays have minimums.
**Parking:** Ample free off- & on-street parking.
**In-Room:** Maid service. Some units with kitchens & ceiling fans.
**On-Premises:** Public telephone, refrigerator, living rooms.
**Swimming:** Nearby ocean.
**Sunbathing:** On private sun decks, lawn or nearby beach.
**Smoking:** Not permitted inside. Permitted on decks, porches & in garden.
**Pets:** Not permitted.
**Handicap Access:** No.
**Children:** Permitted if under 1 year or over 12.
**Languages:** English.
**Your Host:** Anthony.

## Lotus Guest House

**Gay/Lesbian ♀♂**

***Lotus Guest House*** is situated in a beautiful Victorian building in the heart of town near beaches, bus, and ferry. The guesthouse has large, spacious rooms with private or shared bath, and a beautiful 2-bedroom suite with a private balcony overlooking Commercial Street. There is a charming common deck where you can enjoy a morning coffee or just relax and socialize. The centralized location of this guesthouse enables you to walk to every restaurant, nightclub, shop, and gallery in town.

**Address: 296 Commercial St, Provincetown, MA 02657**
**Tel: (508) 487-4644.**

**Type:** Guesthouse with boutique.
**Clientele:** Mostly gay/lesbian
**Transportation:** Taxi from airport, Boston Ferry & bus lines 1/2 block.
**To Gay Bars:** 1 block.
**Rooms:** 12 rooms & 1 suite with double beds.
**Bathrooms:** 3 private bath/toilets & 2 shared bath/shower/toilets.
**Complimentary:** Morning coffee.
**Dates Open:** May through October.
**High Season:** July & Aug.
**Rates:** In season $55-$110, off season $35-$80.
**Discounts:** Call about weekly specials.
**Credit Cards:** MC, VISA & Amex.
**Rsv'tns:** Recommended.
**Reserve Through:** Travel agent or call direct.
**Minimum Stay:** 3 nights weekends, 3-7 nights holidays, call.
**Parking:** Limited on-street parking, Municipal & private lots 1/2 block away.
**In-Room:** Maid service & ceiling fans.
**On-Premises:** Large common deck, tables & chairs in garden.
**Swimming:** Ocean beach.
**Sunbathing:** On beach & patio.
**Smoking:** Permitted.
**Pets:** Not permitted.
**Handicap Access:** No.
**Languages:** English.

## Normandy House

**Gay-Friendly 50/50 ♀♂**

### *A Room With More Than Just A View*

Awaken each morning to a gentle sea breeze and sweeping ocean views of Provincetown harbor and Cape Cod Bay. Then, join us in our sun-drenched common room for continental breakfast. Rooms have TV, VCR and refrigerator, and all have air conditioning. Furnishings range from contemporary to antiques. Shed the accumulated tensions of urban living by relaxing on the sun deck with panoramic views of the lower cape, or melt those frazzled nerves away in the hot tub! ***Normandy House*** is your haven by the sea.

**Address: 184 Bradford St, Provincetown, MA 02657**
**Tel: (508) 487-1197 or (800) 487-1197.**

**Type:** Guesthouse.
**Clientele:** 50% gay & lesbian & 50% straight clientele
**To Gay Bars:** 10-min. walk to men's/women's bars.
**Rooms:** 7 rooms & 1 apt. with dbl. or queen beds.
**Bathrooms:** 5 priv./2 shared.
**Meals:** Cont. breakfast.
**Compliment.:** Ice & mixes.
**Dates Open:** All year.
**High Season:** Mid-June to mid-September.
**Rates:** High season $80-$145, low season $55-$98.
**Credit Cards:** MC, VISA, Amex.
**Rsv'tns:** Required.
**Reserve Thru:** Call direct.
**Minimum Stay:** 4 nights on Memorial Day weekend, 7 nights on big holidays & Carnival.
**Parking:** Limited free off-street parking.
**In-Room:** Cable color TV, VCR, video tape library, AC, ceiling fans, tele., kitchen, refrigerator & maid service.
**On-Premises:** Lovely common rooms w/sun porch, sun deck, Jacuzzi.
**Exercise/Health:** Jacuzzi.
**Swimming:** Nearby town beach & National Seashore beaches.
**Sunbathing:** On common sun deck, patio & at nearby beaches.
**Nudity:** On sun deck with discretion.
**Smoking:** Permitted. Non-smoking room available.
**Languages:** English.
**Your Host:** Dennis.

# Ravenwood Guestrooms & Apartments

**Women ♀**

## *Quiet Accommodation in the Gallery District*

Originally a sea captain's residence, ***Ravenwood*** now offers comfortable and inviting guestrooms and apartments to Provincetown visitors. Some rooms have ocean views. Other features are decks, beamed ceilings and Casa Blanca fans. Guests relax in an enclosed backyard with flower gardens, statues and fountain. Each accommodation has its own outside sitting deck or picnic area. We are centrally located, directly across the street from the harbor, near the beach and only a 10-minute stroll to the center of town. A Cape Cod cottage is also available for long weekends or by the week.

**Address: 462 Commercial St, Provincetown, MA 02657**
**Tel: (508) 487-3203.**

**Type:** Guest room & year-round apartments, condo & year-round cottage.
**Clientele:** Women. Men permitted only if accompanied by their women friends.
**Transportation:** Plane, bus, ferry, car from Boston.
**To Gay Bars:** 5 blocks to men's/women's bars.
**Rooms:** 1 room, 3 apartments, 1 cottage & 1 oceanfront condo.
**Bathrooms:** All have private shower & toilet.
**Vegetarian:** Available at many nearby restaurants.
**Complimentary:** Mints on pillows, private catering of flowers, champagne, balloons, etc can be arranged.
**Dates Open:** All year.
**High Season:** Spring whale watching, fall foliage, winter holidays & July & August.
**Rates:** Summer $75-$125, winter $50-$110.
**Discounts:** Off season third consecutive night free.
**Credit Cards:** All major cards accepted for deposit only.
**Rsv'tns:** Recommended.
**Reserve Through:** Travel agent or call direct.
**Minimum Stay:** 3 nights holiday wknds, 7 nights July-Aug & Oct Women's Week. Inquire about shorter stays.
**Parking:** Ample off-street parking. 1 private spot per room. Other parking available
**In-Room:** Color cable TV, ceiling fans & refrigerators. Apts have kitchens.
**On-Premises:** Patio, BBQ, private fenced-in yards or private decks. Special arrangements available for commitment ceremonies or domestic partner registration.
**Exercise/Health:** Gym & Jacuzzi 4 blks, massage available.
**Swimming:** At ocean beach.
**Sunbathing:** On ocean beach, private sun decks & in private garden.
**Nudity:** Permitted on private decks of apts.
**Smoking:** Permitted without restrictions. Non-smoking rooms available.
**Pets:** Not permitted.
**Handicap Access:** Studios are accessible.
**Children:** Permitted (age restrictions).
**Languages:** English, French.
**Your Host:** Valerie.

## Roomers

Q-NET Gay/Lesbian ♂

Provincetown...the name alone evokes thoughts of a quaint fishing village surrounded by beautiful beaches and untamed sand dunes, fine restaurants and a shopper's paradise. ***Roomers*** guesthouse maintains the charms of the past, but has the crisp, clean, contemporary feel of today. Each room is decorated with quality antiques and has private bath, queen-sized bed, ceiling fan, TV and refrigerator. Cozy and intimate...that's ***Roomers'*** style.

**Address: 8 Carver St, Provincetown, MA 02657. Tel: (508) 487-3532.**

**Type:** Guesthouse.
**Clientele:** Mostly men with women welcome
**Transportation:** Free pickup from airport or ferry.
**To Gay Bars:** Gay bar across street, more 1-3 blks.
**Rooms:** 9 rooms with twin or queen beds.
**Bathrooms:** All private.
**Meals:** Cont. breakfast.
**Dates Open:** April-Dec.
**High Season:** Memorial Day weekend, July, August & Labor Day weekend.
**Rates:** In-season $105-$140, off-season $65-$105.
**Cred Crds:** Visa, Amex, MC.
**Rsv'tns:** Required.
**Reserve Thru:** Call direct.
**Min. Stay:** 5 days in-season.
**Parking:** Free off-street parking, 1 space per room.
**In-Room:** Refrigerator, maid service, color cable TV.
**On-Premises:** 2 com rms.
**Sunbathing:** In side yard.
**Smoking:** Permitted.
**Children:** Not permitted.
**Languages:** English.
**Your Host:** Andrew.

## Rose & Crown Guest House

Gay/Lesbian ♀♂

### *Where if It's Worth Doing, It's Worth Over-Doing*

***The Rose & Crown*** is a classic Georgian square rigger, built in the 1780's. A ship's figurehead greets visitors from her post above the paneled front door. During restoration, wide floorboards were uncovered and pegged posts and beams exposed. An appealing clutter of Victorian antiques and art fills every nook. The Barbie- & Ken-decorated water garden, fast becoming THE Provincetown attraction, is a must for any photographer.

**Address: 158 Commercial St, Provincetown, MA 02657**
**Tel: (508) 487-3332, E-mail: campbarbie@wn.net.**
**http://www.ptown.com/ptown/rosecrown/.**

**Type:** Guesthouse.
**Clientele:** Good mix of gay men & women
**Trans.:** P/U from airport.
**To Gay Bars:** Men's across street, wom's. 3 blks.
**Rooms:** 6 rooms, 1 apartment & 1 cottage with sgl, queen or king beds.
**Baths:** 5 private, 3 shared.
**Meals:** Cont. breakfast.
**Dates Open:** All year.
**High Season:** Memorial Day thru September.
**Rates:** Rooms $25-$95, cottages & apts. $65-$150.
**Discounts:** Varies.
**Cre. Crds:** MC, VISA, Diners.
**Rsv'tns:** Req'd. in season.
**Reserve Through:** Travel agent or call direct.
**Minimum Stay:** On particular holidays.
**Parking:** Lmt'd pay parking.
**In-Room:** Color TV, ceiling fans & maid service. Kitchen in apts & cottage.
**Exerc/Health:** Nearby gym.
**Swimming:** Nearby ocean beach & pool.
**Smoking:** Permitted in room & outside. Not permitted in common rooms.
**Pets:** Perm. only in cottage.
**Children:** Not welcome.
**Your Host:** Sam.

## Rose Acre

Women ♀

### *A Provincetown Classic*

and women's house offering rooms, apartments and a cottage called "Rosebud." Enjoy the unhurried atmosphere of a rambling old-fashioned 1840 Cape house. Tucked down a private drive, ***Rose Acre*** offers decks, gardens and parking. Visit us where the light is bright, streets are narrow, and the minds are broad. Always open, brochure available.

**Address: 5 Center St, Provincetown, MA 02657. Tel: (508) 487-2347.**

**Type:** Apartments, cottage & guest rooms.
**Clientele:** Women only.
**Transportation:** From Boston: car, plane (Cape Air) or ferry boat, pick up from airport, bus, ferry dock.
**To Gay Bars:** 1 blk to bars.
**Rooms:** 2 rms, 4 apts & 1 cottage with double beds.
**Bathrooms:** All private.
**Comp:** Coffee, tea.
**Dates Open:** All year.
**High Season:** Jun-Aug.
**Rates:** Apts. & cottage $70-$140, rms $65-$70.
**Discounts:** Off-season on request.
**Rsv'tns:** Preferred.
**Reserve Thru:** Call direct.
**Minimum Stay:** 5 nights in high season.
**Parking:** Adequate off-street parking.
**In-Room:** Color cable TV, coffee/tea-making facilities. All apartments have full kitchens, rooms have use of kitchen & refrigerator.
**Exercise/Health:** Nearby gym.
**Swimming:** Ocean beach nearby.
**Sunbathing:** On the beach, common sun deck & in private yard.
**Smoking:** Permitted except in sleeping rooms in house.
**Children:** Not permitted.
**Languages:** English.

## Sandpiper Beach House

Gay/Lesbian ♀♂

The *Sandpiper* is a beautiful thirteen-room turreted Victorian guesthouse on the beach next to the world-famous Boatslip. All rooms have private baths and color cable television, and several boast glass doors and private balconies overlooking the harbor. Most have lovely bay views. Complimentary off-street parking and morning coffee are available. Meet other house guests or play the piano in the lovely living room. Use of our private beach and the Boatslip's pool, sun cots, and free admission to Tea Dance at the Boatslip are also included. We are open year-round and off-season rates are available. Please call or write for further information.

**Address: 165 Commercial St, PO Box 646, Provincetown, MA 02657 Tel: (508) 487-1928 or (800) 354-8628.**

**Type:** Guesthouse.
**Clientele:** Gay & lesbian. Good mix of men & women
**Transportation:** Car is best, or taxi from airport.
**To Gay Bars:** Next door to men's & 2 blocks to women's bar.
**Rooms:** 10 rooms with double beds & 3 with queen beds.
**Bathrooms:** All private shower/toilets.
**Meals:** Cont. breakfast.
**Complimentary:** Mints on pillows.
**Dates Open:** All year.
**High Season:** Jun 18-Sep 9.
**Rates:** $55-$130.
**Discounts:** Off-season rates available.
**Credit Cards:** MC, VISA & Discover.
**Rsv'tns:** Required in season. Strongly recommended off season
**Reserve Thru:** Call direct.
**Minimum Stay:** 6 nights in season. Varies off season.
**Parking:** Adequate free off-street parking.
**In-Room:** Cable color TV, ceiling fans & maid service. Most have AC, some with refrigerators, all with direct-dial phones.
**On-Premises:** Common room with piano, large veranda & patio.
**Exercise/Health:** Nearby gym, weights & massage.
**Swimming:** Pool next door in season. Ocean beach.
**Sunbathing:** At poolside, on beach, private sun decks or patio.
**Smoking:** Permitted.
**Handicap Access:** Limited.
**Children:** Permitted, but not recommended.
**Your Host:** Fred.

IGTA

## Sea Drift Inn

**Men ♂**

***Sea Drift*** is a complex of two guesthouses catering to gay men. We're within walking distance of all restaurants, shops and bars. We provide such amenities as extra beach towels, parking passes, aspirin and items you might forget to pack. Eighteen double rooms with European-style shared baths have daily maid service. A private bar has ice, mixers and limes, stereo, TV/VCR with movies. BBQ facilities for guests are outside, as are a sundeck and expanded garden and patio. We serve continental breakfast and occasionally host cocktail parties.

**Address: 80 Bradford St, Provincetown, MA 02657. Tel: (508) 487-3686.**

**Type:** Guesthouse.
**Clientele:** Men only
**Transportation:** Free p/u from Provincetown Airport.
**To Gay Bars:** 1 block to men's bars.
**Rooms:** 18 rooms with single or double beds.
**Bathrooms:** 5 shared bath/shower/toilets.
**Meals:** Cont. breakfast.
**Complimentary:** Set-up service, ice.
**Dates Open:** All year.
**High Season:** July & Aug.
**Rates:** $45-$80.
**Discounts:** 10% on each night after 7 days.
**Credit Cards:** MC, VISA & Discover.
**Rsv'tns:** Highly recommended.
**Reserve Thru:** Call direct.
**Minimum Stay:** 2 nights on weekends & 5 on holidays.
**Parking:** Limited, free, off-street parking.
**In-Room:** Maid, room & laundry service.
**On-Premises:** Outside deck.
**Swimming:** 2 blocks to ocean beach.
**Sunbathing:** On deck or beach.
**Smoking:** Permitted without restrictions.
**Children:** Not permitted.
**Languages:** English.
**Your Host:** Dick.

## ShireMax Inn

**Gay/Lesbian ♂**

The ***ShireMax Inn,*** named for our two Samoyed-Husky dogs, is in its 12th season and is known as your home away from home with that extra added comfortableness and charm. The innkeeper is happy to tend to your needs and to provide extra amenities not offered by other establishments. In fact, many people arrive as new guests and leave as friends. Choose from two apartments and seven rooms in the main house. The common room is a great place for socializing, sipping a cocktail, or watching a movie from the selection of more than 600. We offer a cool front porch, sun deck and a shaded, gardened yard with gas grill.

**Address: 5 Tremont St, Provincetown, MA 02657**
**Tel: (508) 487-1233, Toll-free: (888) SHIREMAX (744-7362).**

**Type:** Guesthouse inn.
**Clientele:** Mostly men with women welcome
**Transportation:** Free pick up from ferry, bus or airport.
**To Gay Bars:** 4 blocks to men's & 5 blocks to women's bars.
**Rooms:** 7 rooms & 2 apartments with double, queen or king beds.
**Bathrooms:** 4 private shower/toilets & 1 shared shower/toilet.
**Meals:** Expanded continental breakfast & snack.
**Dates Open:** April 15-New Years.
**High Season:** June 15-Sept 10th, Memorial Day weekend & New Years Eve.
**Rates:** Rooms $35-$90, apartments $500-$750 weekly. (3rd & 4th person $10 extra per night.)
**Credit Cards:** MC, Visa.
**Rsv'tns:** Recommended 2 mths in advance, in season.
**Reserve Thru:** Call direct.
**Minimum Stay:** 3 days in June, 5-7 in July & Aug.
**Parking:** Ample free off-street parking.
**In-Room:** Color TV & VCR in apts. Rooms with private baths have maid service.

**On-Premises:** Kitchen, TV lounge, guest phone, in-house movies, iron, ironing board, beach chairs, umbrellas & blankets.
**Swimming:** Ocean beach 1/2 block.
**Sunbathing:** On the beach, private or common sun deck.
**Nudity:** Permitted on private apartment decks only.
**Smoking:** Permitted without restrictions.
**Pets:** Pets permitted with prior arrangement, must be quiet pets.
**Handi. Access:** Limited.
**Languages:** English.
**Your Host:** Jack & Bob.

## Six Webster Place

Gay/Lesbian ♀♂

### *A 1750's Bed & Breakfast*

***Six Webster Place*** is a newly restored 1750's bed and breakfast located on a quiet lane in the heart of historic Provincetown. This historic home is an ideal year-round retreat for guests who seek a small and intimate colonial atmosphere in the spirit and style of Ye Old New England. The architecture, layout and amenities are of a grace and character of a bygone era, recently improved for modern convenience and comfort (yes, indoor plumbing was installed in 1986). In addition to our traditional guest rooms with working fireplaces and private baths, we now offer luxury apartments as well. http://ptown.com/ptown/lodging/sixwebster

**Address: 6 Webster Place, Provincetown, MA 02657**
**Tel: (508) 487-2266, (800) 6 WEBSTER.**

**Type:** Bed & breakfast.
**Clientele:** Mostly gay & lesbian with some straight clientele
**Transportation:** Free pickup from airport, bus, ferry.
**To Gay Bars:** 1 block to men's/women's bars.
**Rooms:** 7 rooms, 2 suites & 3 apts with double, queen or king beds.
**Bathrooms:** Private: 6 shower/toilets, 2 full baths. 2 shared full baths.
**Meals:** Expanded continental breakfast.
**Vegetarian:** All vegetarian.
**Dates Open:** All year.
**High Season:** June-Oct.
**Rates:** Summer $50-$95, winter $35-$75.
**Credit Cards:** MC, Visa, Amex & Discover.
**Rsv'tns:** Recommended.
**Reserve Through:** Travel agent or call direct.
**Minimum Stay:** 5 days in July & August.
**Parking:** Free off-street parking (1 space per rental).
**In-Room:** Maid service, color TV/VCR, ceiling fans. Most rooms have fireplaces.
**On-Premises:** TV lounge.
**Exercise/Health:** Jacuzzi.
**Swimming:** Ocean beach, bay beach.
**Sunbathing:** On beach, common sun decks & patio.
**Smoking:** Permitted without restrictions.
**Pets:** Permitted.
**Handicap Access:** Studio apartment is accessible.
**Children:** Permitted in off-season.

IGTA

## Sunset Inn

Gay/Lesbian ♀♂

### *You'll Love the Sunsets from The Sunset*

The ***Sunset Inn*** is one of Provincetown's oldest guesthouses. Built in the mid-nineteenth century as a private home, it has been a guesthouse welcoming visitors for more than half a century. If the ***Sunset Inn*** looks familiar, it may be that you've seen one of the many paintings or photographs depicting the building. Scores of artists have been attracted by the stately elegance and beauty of the inn. Among them renowned local artist Robert Kennedy, whose paintings of the inn can be found in art galleries throughout the country, and American artist Edward Hopper, whose famous painting of the inn entitled *Rooms for Tourist* hangs in the permanent collection at the Yale University Art Gallery in New Haven.

At the ***Sunset Inn*** you're in the heart of Provincetown, just one block from the center of town and the beach. Stroll down Commercial Street and browse the unique shops and galleries that have made Provincetown famous. Enjoy dinner at one of the many fine restaurants the town has to offer; from hot dogs to haute cuisine, you're sure to find what you crave. And, of course, there is the legendary excitement of the Provincetown nightlife with cabarets, comedy shows, dance clubs and nightclubs – all within walking distance of the inn. For the outdoor types, we are close to the National Seashore bike trails, whale watching, fishing boats, dune rides and airplane sightseeing.

We offer spacious, comfortable guest rooms, each distinct in its decor. You'll find all the modern conveniences, yet we've retained the cozy warmth of a Cape Cod inn. Our sun decks and porches afford spectacular views of Provincetown Harbor and are a perfect vantage point from which to view Provincetown's sunsets. We've carefully created a cordial and informal setting to ensure that your stay with us is comfortable and relaxed.

**Address: 142 Bradford St, Provincetown, MA 02657**
**Tel: (508) 487-9810, (800) 965-1801.**

**Type:** Guesthouse.
**Clientele:** Mostly gay & lesbian with some straight clientele
**Transportation:** Car, airplane, ferry from Boston. Free pick up from Provincetown airport.
**To Gay Bars:** 3 blocks to gay bars.
**Rooms:** 20 rms with sgl, double or queen beds.
**Bathrooms:** 8 private shower/toilets, 6 shared bath/shower/toilets.
**Meals:** Cont. breakfast.
**Vegetarian:** Available nearby.
**Complimentary:** Ice.
**Dates Open:** Apr 15-Nov 1.
**High Season:** June 28-Labor Day Week.
**Rates:** Off season (spring & fall): $40-$59; high season (summer): $59-$99.
**Discounts:** 8% discount on weekly stay.
**Credit Cards:** MC, Visa, Discover.
**Rsv'tns:** Highly suggested.
**Reserve Through:** Travel agent or call direct.
**Minimum Stay:** 2 nights weekends, 4 nights Memorial Day, 5 nights 4th of July & Labor Day.
**Parking:** Ample free off-street parking.
**In-Room:** Maid service. Color TV in rms. with priv. baths.
**On-Premises:** TV lounge.
**Exercise/Health:** Nearby gym, weights, massage.
**Swimming:** In nearby ocean & bay.
**Sunbathing:** On common sun decks, at beach.
**Nudity:** Permitted on top deck.
**Smoking:** Permitted in room.
**Pets:** Not permitted.
**Handicap Access:** No.
**Children:** No.
**Languages:** English.

## Three Peaks

Gay/Lesbian ♀♂

### ... A Victorian Bed and Breakfast

Comfort is what is emphasized at ***Three Peaks,*** an 1870's Victorian house originally built as a summer home for a prominent Midwestern family. Today it is a perfect B&B for guests visiting Provincetown. It is located in the East End where art galleries, shops, restaurants, and entertainment are within a few minutes' walk. Town beaches are a block away, while the National Seashore beaches of Herring Cove and Race Point are within bike or driving distance. In season, the town "Loop" bus provides transportation to all areas. After sightseeing, relax on the patio/deck or on the rockers on the wraparound front porch.

**Address: 210 Bradford St, Provincetown, MA 02657**
**Tel: (800) 286-1715 or (508) 487-1717.**

**Type:** Bed & breakfast.
**Clientele:** Good mix of gays & lesbians
**Transportation:** Free airport, bus or ferry dock "shuttle" service.
**To Gay Bars:** 10-15 minute walk.
**Rooms:** 5 rooms with queen or double beds, 2 apartments with double beds.
**Bathrooms:** All private bath/toilets.
**Meals:** Continental breakfast.
**Complimentary:** Juice bar.
**Dates Open:** All year.
**High Season:** Memorial Day weekend through Labor Day weekend.
**Rates:** In-season $85-$115, mid-season $65-$95, off-season $55-$85.
**Discounts:** 10% on stays of 7 or more nights, mid- & off-season specials.
**Credit Cards:** MC, Visa, Discover.
**Rsv'tns:** Recommended for high season.
**Reserve Through:** Call direct.
**Minimum Stay:** 2-3 nights. 4-5 nights for holidays & special events.
**Parking:** Ample free off-street parking.
**In-Room:** Color cable TV & refrigerator. In-season AC or ceiling fans, VCR in apartments.
**On-Premises:** Common room/reading room, outdoor patio/sun deck, garden areas, bike rack.
**Exercise/Health:** Nearby gym, tennis, bicycle rental & bicycle trails.
**Swimming:** One block to bay beach.
**Sunbathing:** On patio/deck & nearby beach.
**Smoking:** Smoke-free atmosphere.
**Pets:** Not permitted.
**Handicap Access:** No.
**Children:** Not especially welcome.
**Languages:** English.
**Your Host:** Walt & John.

## The Tucker Inn at Twelve Center

Gay/Lesbian ♀♂

### *A Romantic Country Inn by the Sea*

*circa 1870*

***The Tucker Inn at Twelve Center,*** originally a sea captain's home, pays tribute to Provincetown's history and Captain Miles B. Tucker's tradition of gracious hospitality. There are eight spacious, antique-filled rooms and two fully equipped cottages, available for weekly rentals. The inn is located on a quiet side street in the heart of Provincetown. A complimentary continental breakfast is served daily in the comfortable living room or on a private tree-shaded patio. There is ample on-site parking.

**Address: 12 Center St, Provincetown, MA 02657**
**Tel: (508) 487-0381, Fax: (508) 487-6236.**

**Type:** Bed & breakfast inn.
**Clientele:** Mostly gay & lesbian
**To Gay Bars:** A 2-minute walk to gay & lesbian bars.
**Rooms:** 6 queens & 2 doubles, 2 fully equipped cottage apartments.
**Bathrooms:** Private baths in queen rooms, semi-private in doubles.
**Meals:** Expanded continental breakfast (all homemade specialties).
**Complimentary:** Beach chairs & towels, daily room fresh.
**Dates Open:** May 1-Nov 1.
**Rates:** $90-$125 high season, $70-$100 low season.
**Credit Cards:** Visa, MC.
**Rsv'tns:** Suggested.
**Reserve Through:** Call direct.
**Minimum Stay:** 3 nights July-August, 5 nights holidays & Women's Week.
**Parking:** Ample parking on premises.
**In-Room:** Cable TV, ceiling fans, spacious antique-filled rooms.
**On-Premises:** Patio & yard for quiet relaxation, bike rack.
**Swimming:** In nearby bay, 1 block.
**Sunbathing:** In yard or back patio.
**Smoking:** Permitted outside.
**Pets:** Not permitted.

## Watership Inn

Gay/Lesbian ♂

A home to ship captains in the seafaring days of the 1820's, ***Watership Inn*** is now a comfortable inn. Enjoy the fresh, salt air, clean skies and bright, Cape Cod sunshine. Walk the beaches or cycle the miles of trails through the dunes. ***Watership Inn*** is half a block from the harbor, right in the center of town, close to everything, yet on a quiet sidestreet.

**Address: 7 Winthrop St, Provincetown, MA 02657. Tel: (508) 487-0094, (800) 330-9413, Fax: (508) 487-2797, E-mail: watership@cyberq.com.**

**Type:** Bed & breakfast.
**Clientele:** Mostly men with women welcome.
**To Gay Bars:** 2 blocks to all gay bars.
**Rooms:** 14 rooms & 1 apartment with double beds.
**Bathrooms:** 14 private shower/toilet, others share.
**Meals:** Expanded continental breakfast.
**Complimentary:** Ice & mixers.
**Dates Open:** All year.
**Rates:** Rooms $31-$112, apartment $73-$159 per night.
**Credit Cards:** MC, VISA, Amex & Discover.
**Rsv'tns:** Required.
**Reserve Through:** Call direct. May call through travel agent in winter.
**Minimum Stay:** Required on some holiday weekends.
**Parking:** Ample free parking.
**In-Room:** Maid service, color TVs, 1 ceiling fan.
**Swimming:** At nearby pool & ocean beach.
**Sunbathing:** On private & common sun decks.
**Smoking:** Permitted without restrictions.
**Pets:** Not permitted.
**Handicap Access:** No.
**Children:** Not permitted.
**Languages:** English.

## Windamar House

**Women ♀**

***Windamar House*** is one of Provincetown's most beautiful, historical, seaside properties. It stands on half an acre with colorful English flower gardens and manicured lawns. This mini-estate is directly across from Cape Cod Bay in the quiet east end. From the moment you step into ***Windamar's*** elegant, two-story entrance hall and take the winding staircase to one of her fine guest rooms, you know that you are in a very special place. Every detail in this stately home, circa 1840, has been lovingly attended to. Each room has its own unique decor, tastefully wallpapered and filled with antiques and original artwork. The front rooms have water views and the others have views of the gardens. No matter the location of your room, you have a pleasant view of a natural setting. One of the most popular accommodations is the dramatic studio room that features a cathedral ceiling, an entire wall of glass overlooking the gardens and an antique carved bed. The penthouse apartment has expansive water views, skylights, exposed beams and cathedral ceiling...a wonderful mix of old and new. The centrally located common room offers guests a pleasant mingling space and use of refrigerator, microwave and cable TV with VCR. Continental breakfast features fresh-baked muffins and breads. It's only a 15-minute walk through the east end gallery district to the downtown area, just far enough away from the hustle-bustle, but close enough to enjoy the nightlife, restaurants, shops and galleries that Provincetown offers. Provincetown Tennis Club is a 3-minute walk. At low tide, guests can take a romantic stroll on the tidal flats directly across the street and view the town from a totally different vantage point. The clientele is mostly women, with men most welcome. In the off-season, the entire house can be booked for reunions, special events, small conferences or seminars.

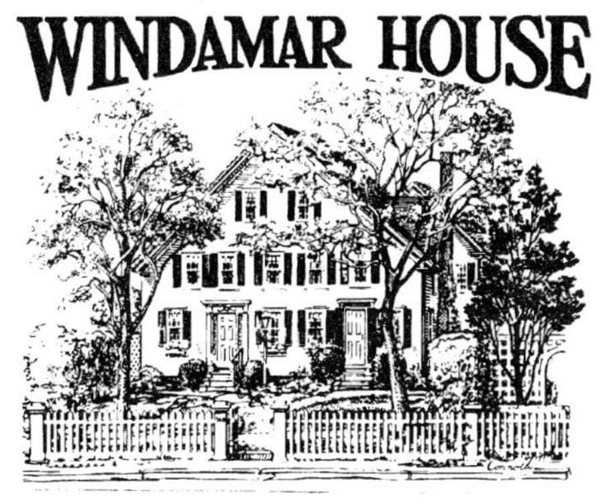


**Address: 568 Commercial St, Provincetown, MA 02657**
**Tel: (508) 487-0599, Fax: (508) 487-7505.**

**Type:** Bed & breakfast guesthouse.
**Clientele:** Mostly women with men welcome. Some straight clientele off season
**Transportation:** Car or plane. Free pick up from airport, bus or ferry dock.
**To Gay Bars:** 20-minute leisurely walk.
**Rooms:** 6 rooms & 2 fully equipped apartments with double or queen beds.
**Bathrooms:** 4 private shower/toilets. 4 rooms share 3 baths.
**Meals:** Continental breakfast.
**Vegetarian:** Provincetown has a lot available for vegetarians.
**Dates Open:** All year.
**High Season:** June 15-September 15.
**Rates:** Summer: rooms $60-$125; apts $775-$885/wk. Off season: $45-$85; apts $85-$95/day. Mid season: $55-$95; apts $650-$750/wk
**Discounts:** Off season, long stays, or booking the whole house.
**Rsv'tns:** Required.
**Reserve Through:** Call direct.
**Minimum Stay:** 5 nights on July 4th & Labor Day, 4 nights Memorial Day.
**Parking:** Ample free off-street parking. Full private lot at rear of the property.
**In-Room:** Maid service.
**On-Premises:** TV/VCR lounge, common room with refrigerator & microwave.
**Exercise/Health:** 3-minute walk to tennis club. Massage can be arranged.
**Swimming:** Cape Cod Bay 300 feet directly across the street. Nearby ocean beach.
**Sunbathing:** On Windamar's exceptional estate-like grounds or at the beach.
**Smoking:** No.
**Pets:** Not permitted.
**Handicap Access:** No.
**Children:** Not permitted.
**Languages:** English & French.
**Your Host:** Bette.
IGTA

# STURBRIDGE - WARE

## Wildwood Inn

Gay-Friendly ♀

### *We Specialize in Friendliness*

***Wildwood***, cozy, old-fashioned, inexpensive, specializes in friendliness. While privacy's respected, staying here is more like visiting old friends. We're 1-1/2 hours from Boston, 3 from NYC. We're near Old Sturbridge Village, historic Deerfield, Amherst and Northampton's women's community. This 1880's Victorian has well cared-for wood floors and American primitive furnishings. Guests enjoy the cozy parlor with its books, games, jigsaw puzzles and signed original fireplace, plus rooms with heirloom quilts and early cradles. Fredi's yummy breakfasts will energize you for any activity. Relax on the wraparound front porch, play croquet, or wander the grounds, woods and river behind.

**Address: 121 Church St, Ware, MA 01082**
**Tel: (413) 967-7798, (800) 860-8098.**

**Type:** Bed & breakfast.
**Clientele:** Mostly straight clientele with a lesbian following, gay men welcome
**Transportation:** Car is best, bus available from major cities to Palmer, MA, taxi to Ware.
**To Gay Bars:** 30-40 minutes to Worcester or Northampton gay & lesbian bars.
**Rooms:** 7 doubles, 2 twins.
**Bathrooms:** 7 private, 1 shared.
**Meals:** Full breakfast with homemade muffins, peach butter, juice, tea, coffee, Wildwood's famous "Country Yummies."
**Vegetarian:** Breakfast meats served separately, if at all.
**Complimentary:** Mulled cider or herb tea in winter, BYOB, cold lemonade in summer.
**Dates Open:** All year.
**High Season:** May through October.
**Rates:** Summer $55-$80, winter $50-$75.
**Discounts:** 10% off for stays of 7 days or more, for longer stays.
**Credit Cards:** Amex, MC, Visa.
**Rsv'tns:** Highly recommended.
**Reserve Through:** Travel agent or call direct.
**Parking:** Ample, safe, outdoor, off-street parking.
**In-Room:** AC, ceiling & table fans.
**Exercise/Health:** At nearby Nautilus Works.
**Swimming:** At nearby pool or pond.
**Sunbathing:** At pond or the inn grounds.
**Smoking:** Permitted outdoors.
**Pets:** Not permitted, kennels in town.
**Handicap Access:** Yes.
**Children:** Permitted if over 6 years.
**Languages:** English.
**Your Host:** Fraidell & Richard.

# MICHIGAN

## SAUGATUCK - DOUGLAS

### Campit

Gay/Lesbian ♂

*Where Friendly People Camp*

When visiting Saugatuck, gay & lesbian campers can stay in an all gay-operated, all gay and lesbian campground located just 7 miles from Saugatuck's gay beach and 6 miles from the gay bars. ***Campit*** features all the usual amenities, such as mini-store with ice and soft drinks, modern bath and shower facilities and a game room. We're also near a supermarket, so it's easy to make a run for that one item you forgot to pack.

**Address: 6635 118th Ave, Fennville, MI 49408. Tel: (616) 543-4335.**

**Type:** Campground.
**Clientele:** Mostly men with women welcome.
**Transportation:** Car is best.
**To Gay Bars:** 10 minutes to men's/women's bars in Saugatuck.
**Rooms:** 60 campsites.
**Campsites:** 37 hookups (electric only), 30 tent sites & 30 RV parking spaces with modern toilets & showers, also "Portajohns" throughout the park.
**Dates Open:** May 1st-Nov 1st.
**Rates:** $10 per person, $3 per night for electric. Rates slightly higher on holidays.
**Discounts:** Group rates.
**Rsv'tns:** Required on holiday weekends.
**Reserve Through:** Call direct.
**Minimum Stay:** 3 nights on holidays.
**Parking:** Plenty of off-street parking.
**On-Premises:** TV lounge & laundry facilities.
**Exercise/Health:** Free weights.
**Swimming:** At the lake in Saugatuck.
**Pets:** Permitted, if on leashes.
**Handicap Access:** No, steps up to restrooms.
**Children:** Not permitted.
**Languages:** English.

### Douglas Dunes Resort

Gay/Lesbian ♀♂

***Douglas Dunes Resort*** is located in the Saugatuck/Douglas area, along the Lake Michigan shoreline. Accommodations range from deluxe motel rooms and cottage suites to steam bath-style rooms. Guests can lounge at our large heated pool with bar service, dine at our award-winning *Le Cabaret Cafe,* dance the evening away in our disco, enjoy entertainment in the cabaret, or just relax in our bistro bar or garden deck. In winter, enjoy cross-country skiing or snowmobiling.

**Address: 333 Blue Star Highway, Douglas, MI 49406**
**Tel: (616) 857-1401, Fax: (616) 857-4052.**

**Type:** Motel with restaurant, bar & disco.
**Clientele:** Good mix of gay men & women
**Transportation:** Car is best. Bus, Amtrak, airport in Grand Rapids.
**To Gay Bars:** On premises.
**Rooms:** 23 rooms, 23 steam bath-style rooms, 3 suites & 10 cottages with double or king beds.
**Bathrooms:** 36 private bath/toilets. Steam bath-style have showers, share baths.
**Vegetarian:** Available upon request.
**Dates Open:** All year.
**High Season:** Summer.
**Rates:** Winter $48, summer $25-$125.
**Credit Cards:** MC, Visa, Amex, Diners & Discover.
**Rsv'tns:** Required.
**Reserve Through:** Travel agent or call direct.
**Minimum Stay:** Weekend packages.
**Parking:** Ample off-street parking.
**In-Room:** Color TV, AC, telephone, ceiling fans, maid & room service.
**On-Premises:** Meeting rooms, TV lounge.
**Exercise/Health:** Nearby gym.
**Swimming:** Pool on premises, 1/2 mi to lake.
**Sunbathing:** At poolside.
**Smoking:** Permitted.
**Pets:** Permitted with deposit & not left alone.
**Handicap Access:** Yes.
**Children:** Permitted.
**Languages:** English.

IGTA

## The Kirby House

Gay/Lesbian ♀♂

A beautifully-restored 105-year-old Victorian manor on the state historical registry, ***The Kirby House*** is known for its comfortable elegance, warm hospitality and sumptuous breakfast/brunch buffets. Entirely furnished with turn-of-the-century antiques, the house becomes an adventure into days gone by. The establishment offers a beautiful, secluded pool, hot tub and sunning decks overlooking acres of woodland. ***The Kirby House*** is more than a place to stay, it's a place to linger.

**Address: PO Box 1174, Saugatuck, MI 49453**
**Tel: (616) 857-2904 (Tel/Fax), (800) 521-6473.**

**Type:** Bed & breakfast.
**Clientele:** Mostly gay & lesbian/some straight clientele
**Transportation:** Car is best. Free pick up from Amtrak, bus and airport.
**To Gay Bars:** 4 blks to bars.
**Rooms:** 8 rms with single, double or queen beds.
**Bathrooms:** 6 priv./2 share.
**Meals:** Full breakfast buffet.
**Vegetarian:** Available upon request.
**Dates Open:** All year.
**High Season:** June-Oct.
**Rates:** $85-$125.
**Discounts:** 10% on extended stays and vacation packages. Sun-Thurs package-5 nights for price of 4.
**Credit Cards:** MC, Visa, Amex & Discover.
**Rsv'tns:** Required.
**Reserve Through:** Travel agent or call direct.
**Minimum Stay:** 3 nights July & August wknds. 2 nights other wknds.
**Parking:** Ample off-street parking.
**In-Room:** Maid service & ceiling fans.
**On-Premises:** Courtesy telephone, kitchen privileges, ice & gas BBQ.
**Exercise/Health:** Bicycles, Jacuzzi & X-country skis.
**Swimming:** Pool or lake.
**Sunbathing:** At poolside, lakeside or on common sun decks.
**Nudity:** 2 mi. to nude beach.
**Smoking:** Permitted in common areas.
**Pets:** Permitted with restrictions.
**Children:** Permitted weekdays with prior arrangement.
**Your Host:** Loren & Marsha.

## Moore's Creek Inn

Gay/Lesbian ♀♂

### *Where Friendships Are Formed*

Saugatuck is a quaint, little village 3 hours from Detroit and 2 1/2 from Chicago. It's known as a popular beach resort for gays and lesbians and as an artistic haven, and it has a large selection of specialty shops. ***Moore's Creek Inn*** is an old-fashioned farmhouse, over 100 years old. Rooms are decorated in different themes: The Erte Elegance room is filled with Erte prints. Walt's Woom has Disney paraphernalia. The Teddy Bear Den features small and large stuffed bears. Two gathering rooms have grand piano, movie library and a 50-inch TV.

**Address: 820 Holland St, Saugatuck, MI 49453**
**Tel: (616) 857-2411, (800) 838-5864.**

**Type:** Bed & breakfast.
**Clientele:** Mainly gay & lesbian with some straight clientele
**Transportation:** Car is best. Free pick up from airport.
**To Gay Bars:** 3 miles or ten-minute drive.
**Rooms:** 4 rooms with single or double beds.
**Bathrooms:** 4 private shower/toilets.
**Meals:** Full breakfast.
**Vegetarian:** Cold or hot cereals, fruit & cheese.
**Complimentary:** Tea, coffee, mixes for cocktails (no alcohol). Evening wine & cheese tasting.
**Dates Open:** All year.
**High Season:** May-Sep.
**Rates:** Summer $75-$95, winter $65-$85.
**Discounts:** Four or more days, 10% off, full occupancy party 10% off.
**Credit Cards:** MC, Visa.
**Rsv'tns:** Required.
**Reserve Through:** Travel agent or call direct.
**Min. Stay:** 2 days in season.
**Parking:** Ample off-street parking.
**In-Room:** Ceiling fans.
**On-Premises:** Meeting rooms, TV lounge.
**Exercise/Health:** Massage at nearby salon.
**Swimming:** At nearby lake.
**Sunbathing:** On the beach.
**Smoking:** Permitted in 1st floor gathering rooms only, not in bedrooms.
**Pets:** Not permitted.
**Children:** Not encouraged.
**Languages:** English.
**Your Host:** Clif & Fred.

## Newnham SunCatcher Inn

**Gay/Lesbian ♀♂**

***Newnham SunCatcher Inn*** is on a secluded lot in the heart of Saugatuck's business district, close to shops, restaurants, recreation and the lake beaches. The turn-of-the-century home with wraparound porch, complete with gingerbread carvings, has been carefully restored to the grandeur of its day. Period furniture once again graces its 5 bedrooms. Behind the main house, a two-cottage suite provides more private accommodations. Features are a large sun deck, hot tub and swimming pool.

**Address: 131 Griffith, Box 1106, Saugatuck, MI 49453**
**Tel: (616) 857-4249,**
**http://wwwbbonline.com/mi/suncatcher/index.html.**

**Type:** Bed & breakfast.
**Clientele:** Mostly gay & lesbian/some straight clientele.
**Transportation:** Free pick up from airport, train.
**To Gay Bars:** 3-minute drive to gay/lesbian bars.
**Rooms:** 5 doubles, 2-cottage suite (cottage is a guest house with complete facilities).
**Bathrooms:** 3 private, others share.
**Meals:** Full breakfast.
**Complimentary:** Tea, coffee, juices, mints on pillow.
**Dates Open:** All year.
**High Season:** May-Oct.
**Rates:** Rooms $65-$85 weekdays & off-season weekends, $75-$100 summer weekends; call for cottage rates.
**Discounts:** During off-season.
**Credit Cards:** MC, VISA.
**Rsv'tns:** Required.
**Reserve Thru:** Call direct.
**Minimum Stay:** 2 nights on weekends.
**Parking:** Ample free off-street parking.
**In-Room:** AC.
**On-Premises:** Common room, meeting room, fireplace, TV lounge, telephone, kitchen available.
**Exercise/Health:** Jacuzzi.
**Swimming:** In-ground heated swimming pool.
**Sunbathing:** At poolside or on private sun decks.
**Nudity:** 3 mi to nude beach.
**Smoking:** Permitted on outside deck only.
**Pets:** Not permitted.
**Children:** Permitted weekdays only.
**Languages:** English.

# SOUTHWEST MICHIGAN

## Cozy Cottages

**Gay/Lesbian ♀♂**

### *Cozy Up in Cozy Cottages*

Cozy up for a weekend getaway or crosscountry stopover in our ***Cozy Cottages,*** in New Buffalo, Michigan, just 1-1/2 hours from Chicago and five blocks from Lake Michigan. Walk on the beach or explore a pretty little town with fine restaurants, art galleries and jewelry shops...or cross-country ski...or visit the National & State Dunes Parks nearby. Men, women, children, small dogs – everyone is welcome. One cottage is a two-bedroom with electric fireplace, the other is a three-bedroom with gas fireplace. Both have full kitchens, microwaves, color TV and VCR, telephones and AC. Towels and linens are provided.

*continued next page*

**Address: Envoy Resort Properties, 740 N Rush St #609, Chicago, IL 60611**
**Tel: (312) 787-2400, Fax: (312) 787-7109, (800) 44-ENVOY (36869).**

**Type:** Cottages.
**Clientele:** Mostly gay & lesbian with some straight clientele
**Transportation:** Car is best, but train is available once a day.
**To Gay Bars:** 50 miles, a 1 hour drive.
**Rooms:** 1 2-bedroom cottage & 1 3-bedroom cottage with single, double or queen beds.
**Vegetarian:** Most nearby restaurants offer excellent vegetarian fare.
**Dates Open:** All year.
**High Season:** July & August.
**Rates:** $200-$350 3-night weekend; $400-$800 per week.
**Discounts:** Discounts for both cottages rented together & for early bookings for high season.
**Rsv'tns:** Required.
**Reserve Through:** Travel agent or call direct.
**Minimum Stay:** Required.
**Parking:** Ample off-street parking.
**In-Room:** AC, color TV, VCR, telephone, ceiling fans, kitchen, coffee & tea-making facilities, dishwasher, refrigerator.
**On-Premises:** Laundry facilities.
**Exercise/Health:** Nearby gym, weights, Jacuzzi, sauna, steam, massage.
**Swimming:** Nearby pool & lake.
**Sunbathing:** On private sun decks.
**Smoking:** Up to discretion of cottage renter.
**Pets:** Small pets permitted.
**Handicap Access:** No.
**Children:** Welcomed.
**Languages:** English.

# MINNESOTA

## DULUTH

### Stanford Inn

Q-NET **Gay/Lesbian** ♀♂

The ***Stanford Inn,*** Minnesota's first gay-owned bed & breakfast, is an elegant Victorian home built in 1886. There is natural woodwork and hardwood floors throughout and the entrance is graced by a hand-carved oak staircase and an eight-foot stained glass window. The 4 bedrooms are all charmingly decorated with period antiques, the suite has a private bath, and all accommodations include complete gourmet breakfast and room service coffee. We are located two blocks from Leif Erickson Park, the Rose Garden, Lake Superior, and within walking distance of shops and restaurants.

**Address: 1415 E Superior St, Duluth, MN 55805**
**Tel: (218) 724-3044.**
**http://www.visitduluth.com/stanford.**

**Type:** Bed & breakfast.
**Clientele:** Mostly gay & lesbian with a following of straight clientele
**Transportation:** Car is best.
**Rooms:** 3 rooms & 1 suite.
**Bathrooms:** 1 private & 2 shared.
**Meals:** Full gourmet breakfast & room service coffee.
**Vegetarian:** Available upon request.
**Complimentary:** Coffee, tea, & juices.
**Dates Open:** All year.
**High Season:** May through Oct.
**Rates:** $75-$115.
**Discounts:** For weekdays (Sun-Thur), groups, also corporate & single rates.
**Credit Cards:** MC, Visa, Amex, Discover.
**Rsv'tns:** Required.
**Reserve Through:** Call direct.
**Parking:** Adequate off-street & on-street parking.
**In-Room:** Room service.
**On-Premises:** TV lounge.
**Exercise/Health:** Sauna.
**Swimming:** Lake 2 blocks. Creek 1 mile.
**Sunbathing:** On the beach.
**Nudity:** Permitted at creek, 1 mile away. Directions on request.
**Smoking:** Permitted on the porch.
**Pets:** Permitted with restrictions.
**Handicap Access:** No.
**Children:** OK with prior arrangement.
**Languages:** English.

# KENYON

## Dancing Winds Farm

Gay/Lesbian ♀♂

### *Where the Relaxed & Unexpected are a "Whey" of Life!*

Imagine a relaxed, country setting with goats frolicking in the pastures and women working in the cheese plant and on the farm. We are proud to be Minnesota's first Farmstead Goat Cheese Plant and purveyors of quality-tasting, award-winning, low-fat/low-sodium fresh cheeses. You can watch us milking the goats, making the cheeses, or just kick back and enjoy the peaceful surroundings. Long walks, star-gazing, birdwatching, bicycling, canoeing, swimming, x-country skiing, snowshoeing or reading by the stone fireplace are what ***Dancing Winds Farm*** is all about!

**Address: 6863 Co. #12 Blvd, Kenyon, MN. Tel: (507) 789-6606.**

**Type:** Bed & breakfast, campground with licensed cheesery on farmstead.
**Clientele:** Men & women
**Transportation:** Car is best.
**To Gay Bars:** 60 miles to Minneapolis & 40 miles to Rochester gay/lesbian bars.
**Rooms:** 1 private unit separate from main house, sleeps up to 6 people.
**Bathrooms:** Private bath/ shower/toilet & shared shower/toilet.
**Campsites:** 3 tent sites with shower & toilet available. Evening bonfires upon request, weather permitting.
**Meals:** Full breakfast, fresh goat's milk & cheeses. Specialty is goat cheese omelets & fresh biscuits!
**Vegetarian:** Available upon request.
**Complimentary:** Tea, coffee, juices.
**Dates Open:** All year.
**High Season:** Feb-Mar, summer months & early spring for kidding season, Fall Colors season.
**Rates:** Private unit, pp: $42.50 (breakfast inc.), Economy Rate, pp/per night $35. Camping (2 persons/site) $10, b'fast extra.
**Discounts:** Work exchange available. Weekend & traveler's specials.
**Rsv'tns:** Required at most times.
**Reserve Thru:** Call direct.
**Parking:** Ample, free off-street parking.
**In-Room:** Heat, ceiling fans. Private unit: kitchen, living room with patio & deck.
**On-Premises:** Stone fireplace, TV/VCR. Laundry facilities at extra charge.
**Exercise/Health:** Plenty of work to do: throwing hay bales, fencing, milking goats & goat wrangling in general!
**Swimming:** River & pool nearby.
**Sunbathing:** In yard.
**Smoking:** Permitted outdoors ONLY.
**Pets:** Permitted by previous permission ONLY.
**Handicap Access:** 1st floor with help. Otherwise, no. Old farmhouse.
**Children:** Permitted by previous permission only.
**Languages:** English, limited French.
**Your Host:** Mary.

# MINNEAPOLIS - ST PAUL

## Abbotts Como Villa

Gay/Lesbian ♀♂

***Abbotts Como Villa*** is an 1875 restored Victorian home, offering guests the choice of three antique-filled rooms. Each room is furnished with Victorian antiques and comes with a breakfast served on china and crystal in the dining room. Hometown innkeeper, Ron, is a native Minnesotan who will see to it that guests know about all of the hidden-away sights there are to see. Close to bars and restaurants, the B&B is 10 minutes from downtown Minneapolis/St. Paul, and is one block from 450-acre Como Park with its free zoo, conservatory, lake and golf course.

**Address: St Paul, MN 55108. Tel: (612) 647-0471.**

**Type:** Bed & breakfast.
**Clientele:** Mostly gay & lesbian with some straight clientele
**Transportation:** Car is easier, but busline is nearby.
**To Gay Bars:** 1-1/2 miles.

*continued next page*

**Rooms:** 4 rooms.
**Bathrooms:** 1 room with private shower. 2 rooms share shower.
**Meals:** Continental breakfast Monday-Thursday, full breakfast on weekends.
**Vegetarian:** Available upon request.
**Complimentary:** Coffee, juice, tea, soda & cookies.
**Dates Open:** All year.
**Rates:** $65 weekdays, $70-$78 weekends.
**Discounts:** On longer stays.
**Credit Cards:** VISA, MC & Discover.
**Rsv'tns:** Required.
**Reserve Through:** Travel agent or call direct.
**Parking:** Ample free off-street parking in horseshoe driveway.
**In-Room:** AC, maid & room service. Color TV & VCR available upon request.
**On-Premises:** TV lounge, baby grand piano & covered porches.
**Exercise/Health:** Gym nearby.
**Swimming:** 6 blocks to pool.
**Smoking:** Permitted outside only.
**Pets:** Not permitted.
**Handicap Access:** No.
**Children:** Not permitted.
**Languages:** English.
**Your Host:** Ron.

## Be Yourself Inn — Twin Cities

**Gay/Lesbian ♂**

Jon and Phillip invite you to relax and be yourself in their, 4-level, 4,200 sq. ft. executive home. We're 10-20 minutes from the airport, the Mall of America, gay bars and downtown. The fully-enclosed grounds have an expansive deck that's great for natural sunning. In winter, enjoy the living room's fire place, vaulted beamed ceilings and views of snow-covered evergreens. A delicious breakfast, Happy Hour, and a large, mirrored, queen sized bedroom are just some of the extra touches that will make ***Be Yourself Inn – Twin Cities*** your home away from home.

**Address: 1093 Snelling Ave South, St. Paul, MN 55116**
**Tel: (612) 698-3571 or Fax: (612) 699-3840.**

**Type:** Bed & breakfast.
**Clientele:** Men.
**To Gay Bars:** 8 min drive.
**Rooms:** 2 rms/queen beds.
**Bathrooms:** All private.
**Meals:** Full breakfast.
**Vegetarian:** Available daily.
**Complimentary:** Coffee, tea, soft drinks, mineral water & beer at all times. Happy Hour drinks 5-6:30pm daily.
**Dates Open:** All year.
**Rates:** $60-$85 per night.
**Discounts:** One coupon per stay for 10% off next total bill for one stay. Good for one year.
**Credit Cards:** MC, VISA.
**Rsv'tns:** Required.
**Reserve Through:** Travel agent or call direct.
**Parking:** Ample free off-street parking.
**In-Room:** Color TV/VCR.
**On-Premises:** Meeting rms, TV lounge, AC, laundry fac. for guests, use of complete lower level kitchen.
**Swimming:** Walk to pool, 10 min drive to Mississippi River & Twin City Lakes.
**Sunbathing:** On private sun deck.
**Nudity:** Permitted on private deck.
**Smoking:** Not permitted.
**Pets:** Not permitted.
**Languages:** English, Spanish.
**Your Host:** Jon & Phillip

# MISSOURI

## KANSAS CITY

### Doanleigh Wallagh Inn

**Gay-Friendly ♀♂**

***Casual Elegance Where All Your Needs are Attended to***

European and American antiques enhance the Georgian architecture of the ***Doanleigh Wallagh Inn,*** centrally located between the famed Country Club Plaza and Hallmark Crown Center. A delicious, full, gourmet breakfast awaits both leisure and business travelers each morning; the butler's pantry is always stocked with sodas, juices, and snack foods. Enjoy a room with fireplace, deck or whirlpool tub, and pamper yourself by curling up in luxurious robes. And if you must work during your stay, the guest office center provides free local phone and faxes, as well as computer modem access.

**Address: 217 East 37th St, Kansas City, MO 64111**
**Tel: (816) 753-2667, Fax: (816) 531-5185.**

**Type:** Bed & breakfast.
**Clientele:** Mostly straight clientele with a gay & lesbian following.
**Transportation:** Car is best, airport shuttle.
**To Gay Bars:** 2 blocks to nearest gay/lesbian bar. 5 minutes by foot or car to others.
**Rooms:** 5 rooms with queen or king beds.
**Bathrooms:** All private. Some with Jacuzzi.
**Meals:** Full gourmet breakfast, evening wine & hors d'oeuvres.
**Vegetarian:** Always available.
**Complimentary:** Homemade cookies, fruit juices, soda, snacks, coffee, tea, weekend wine & cheese, local newspaper.
**Dates Open:** All year.
**Rates:** $90-$135.
**Discounts:** Corporate rates available Sun-Thurs.
**Credit Cards:** MC, VISA, Amex, Discover.
**Rsv'tns:** Required.
**Reserve Through:** Travel agent or call direct.
**Minimum Stay:** 2 nights some holiday weekends.
**Parking:** Ample free off-street parking.
**In-Room:** Maid service, color cable TV, speaker phone, AC, computer hookup. Some rooms with fireplace, deck or whirlpool tub.
**On-Premises:** Grand piano, meeting rooms, TV lounge, laundry facilities, fax.
**Exercise/Health:** 5-minute drive to Golds gym, tennis courts, walking paths.
**Smoking:** Permitted on outdoor porches.
**Pets:** Not permitted.
**Handicap Access:** No.
**Children:** Permitted, please inquire.
**Languages:** English.
**Your Host:** Terry & Cynthia.

# ST LOUIS

## A St. Louis Guesthouse in Historic Soulard

**Gay/Lesbian ♂**

### *Come Home to St. Louis*

***A St. Louis Guesthouse,*** in historical Soulard, is tucked between downtown, Busch Stadium, the Anheuser Busch Brewery and the Farmers Market. A gay bar and restaurant are next door. Of the eight apartments in the building, three are available as guest suites. Each has two large rooms, phone, a private bath, AC, wet bar with refrigerator and a private entrance opening onto a pleasant courtyard with hot tub. If your visit to St. Louis is for business or pleasure, please consider ***A St. Louis Guesthouse*** your home away from home.

ST. LOUIS
GUESTHOUSE
In Historic Soulard

St. Louis Mo.

**Address: 1032-38 Allen Ave, St Louis, MO 63104**
**Tel: (314) 773-1016.**

**Type:** Guesthouse.
**Clientele:** Mostly men with women welcome.
**Transportation:** Car is best. Free pick up from airport, bus or train.
**To Gay Bars:** Next door.
**Rooms:** 3 suites with double or queen beds.
**Bathrooms:** All private shower/toilets.
**Complimentary:** Coffee, tea & hot chocolate always available.
**Dates Open:** All year.
**Rates:** $50.
**Discounts:** Weekly rate.
**Credit Cards:** Amex, Discover, VISA, MC.
**Rsv'tns:** Required.
**Reserve Thru:** Call direct.
**Parking:** Ample free off-street & on-street parking.
**In-Room:** Color cable TV, ceiling fans, refrigerator, coffee/tea-maker, telephone (free local calls), maid service & laundry service, AC.
**On-Premises:** Laundry facilities, BBQ, hot tub in courtyard.
**Exercise/Health:** Non-sexual massage is $40.
**Sunbathing:** In courtyard.
**Nudity:** In hot tub after sunset.
**Smoking:** Permitted.
**Pets:** Not permitted.
**Handicap Access:** No.
**Children:** Not permitted.
**Languages:** English.
**Your Host:** Garry & Billy.

## Brewers House Bed & Breakfast

Gay/Lesbian ♀♂

***Brewers House*** is a Civil War-vintage home, whose location amidst several breweries, is minutes from downtown and only blocks from bars, restaurants and shops. Some rooms feature fireplaces and unusual items. The hot tub in the intimate garden area offers total privacy. Enjoy a view of downtown from the deck. Visit the Soulard Market, a colorful open-air market established in 1790, or Anheuser-Busch, home of the world's largest brewery (free tours include the Clydesdales and beer tasting), or take a ride to the top of the Gateway Arch.

**Address: 1829 Lami Street, St. Louis, MO 63104. Tel: (314) 771-1542.**

**Type:** Bed & breakfast.
**Clientele:** Good mix of gays & lesbians.
**Transportation:** Car is best or cab from Transit Station. Free pick up from train.
**To Gay Bars:** 7 blocks or 1/2 mile. 15 minutes by foot, 5 minutes by car.
**Rooms:** 3 with double or king beds.
**Bathrooms:** 1 private bath/toilet, 1 private sink & 1 shared bath/shower/toilet.
**Meals:** Expanded continental breakfast.
**Vegetarian:** Available upon request. Restaurant nearby.
**Complimentary:** Coffee always available.
**Dates Open:** All year.
**Rates:** $55-$60.
**Discounts:** 7th day free.
**Credit Cards:** MC & VISA.
**Rsv'tns:** Recommended.
**Reserve Through:** Travel agent or call direct.
**Parking:** Ample parking.
**In-Room:** Color cable TV, AC, ceiling fans, maid service & laundry service.
**On-Premises:** TV lounge.
**Exercise/Health:** Jacuzzi.
**Sunbathing:** On common sun decks.
**Nudity:** Permitted in Jacuzzi in secluded garden.
**Smoking:** Permitted.
**Pets:** Permitted, but call ahead.
**Handicap Access:** No.
**Children:** Permitted.
**Languages:** English.

## Napoleon's Retreat Bed & Breakfast

Gay-Friendly 50/50 ♀♂

### *Follow Napoleon...Retreat in Style!*

***Napoleon's Retreat,*** an elegantly-appointed French second-empire townhouse dating to the 1880s, is in St. Louis' Lafayette Square, one of the nation's oldest historical districts. In our four spacious bedrooms, guests enjoy the elegant ambiance of antiques along with conveniences such as color TVs and telephones. Conveniently close to St. Louis' Union Station shopping and entertainment complex, Busch Stadium and Brewery, Gateway Arch and riverfront park, Cherokee St. Antique Row and world-renowned Missouri Botanical Gardens, as well as excellent dining and shopping. The perfect retreat for business or pleasure.

**Address: 1815 Lafayette Ave, St Louis, MO 63104. Tel: (314) 772-6979.**

**Type:** Bed & breakfast guesthouse.
**Clientele:** 50% gay & lesbian & 50% straight clientele.
**Transportation:** Car. From airport 20 minutes on Hwy 70. 1 mile to MetroLink station.
**To Gay Bars:** 5 blocks or 1 mile. 20-minute walk or 5-minute drive.
**Rooms:** 4 rooms with queen beds.
**Bathrooms:** All private.
**Meals:** Full breakfast.
**Vegetarian:** Can easily accommodate special diets.
**Complimentary:** Tea, coffee, juices, sodas, sherry, homemade chocolate chip cookies.
**Dates Open:** All year.
**Rates:** $65-$85.
**Credit Cards:** MC, Visa, Amex.
**Rsv'tns:** Required.
**Reserve Through:** Travel agent or call direct.
**Parking:** Ample on-street parking.
**In-Room:** Color cable TV, AC, ceiling fans, telephone, clock radio & maid service.
**On-Premises:** Meeting rooms.
**Exercise/Health:** 2 miles to YMCA with gym, weights, Jacuzzi, sauna, steam & massage.
**Swimming:** Pool at YMCA.
**Sunbathing:** In patio area.
**Smoking:** Permitted outside only.
**Pets:** Not permitted.
**Handicap Access:** No.
**Children:** Permitted.
**Languages:** English.
**Your Host:** Michael & Jeff.

# NEVADA

## LAS VEGAS

### Desert Rainbow Inn

Men ♂

## *Announcing Las Vegas' First Adults-Only, Clothing-Optional ALL GAY MALE Motel*

OPENING SUMMER, 1997: Can you imagine an all-gay motel located in the heart of it all, just minutes from all the excitement you can only find in Las Vegas, Nevada and just minutes from McCarren Airport? Can you imagine a motel that features the ultimate in relaxation with approximately 30 king-sized rooms (and two suites). Each will have king-sized beds and color cable television (with one channel carrying adult male entertainment), showers with dual shower heads, refrigerators in every room and elegance at every turn.

The ***Desert Rainbow Inn*** will be fully air conditioned and have total motel water purification (purified drinking water from every faucet), juice bar and continental breakfast served daily in the morning, and coin-operated laundry facilities. Its large private courtyard will be landscaped like a tropical paradise with a swimming pool designed as a lagoon and waterfall. There will also be an exotic steam room, sauna, limited video poker gaming, easy access to the Strip on Las Vegas Boulevard, limousine service to and from the airport, shuttle service to the exciting Strip, ample parking, a completely ALL-MALE staff, 24-hour security guard service on the premises, handicap-accessibility, plus a whole lot more!

Now you have a place where you can completely unwind, make new friends and enjoy the lush surroundings after visiting all the casinos and other attractions. The ***Desert Rainbow Inn*** is being designed with you in mind and with amenities not found in many gay resorts throughout the US. So, take your clothes off and pretend you're on a tropical island away from it all! Our friendly, customer service-oriented, all-male staff and ***Desert Rainbow*** owners Eldon Garrett and Rick Rodrigues will make your stay a very memorable one. OPENING SUMMER, 1997.

**Tel: (702) 221-4301 (recorded message) or (702) 362-0484 (voice), Fax: (702) 362-7113.**

**Type:** Motel inn with juice bar.
**Clientele:** Men only
**Transportation:** Car is best. Shuttle service to & from airport.
**To Gay Bars:** 2 miles, a 15 min drive.
**Rooms:** 28 rooms & 2 suites with king beds (pillow-top mattresses, the ultimate).
**Bathrooms:** 30 private shower/toilets.
**Meals:** Continental breakfast.
**Vegetarian:** Available nearby.
**Complimentary:** Coffee, fruit juices.
**Dates Open:** All year.
**High Season:** All seasons, especially during conventions.
**Rates:** $100-$150.
**Credit Cards:** MC, Visa, Amex, Discover.

*continued next page*

**Reserve Through:** Travel agent or call direct.
**Parking:** Ample free parking.
**In-Room:** Color cable TV, telephone, AC, coffee & tea-making facilities, refrigerator, maid service.
**On-Premises:** Meeting rooms, coin-operated laundry facilities.
**Exercise/Health:** Jacuzzi, sauna, steam.
**Swimming:** Pool on premises. Lake nearby.
**Sunbathing:** Poolside.
**Nudity:** Permitted in courtyard.
**Smoking:** Permitted in courtyard. Non-smoking rooms available.
**Pets:** Not permitted.
**Handicap Access:** Yes.
**Children:** No.

## Las Vegas Private Bed & Breakfast

Gay/Lesbian ♂

### *Lucky You!*

My home, ***Las Vegas Private Bed & Breakfast,*** features a unique, European decor with lots of amenities. Outside are tropical plants and trees around the pool area. Further back are the aviaries, with tropical birds and parrots. Las Vegas has 24-hour entertainment. Other activities: desert sightseeing, water sports on Lake Mead, private sailboats with catered dining, Grand Canyon tours in a private plane, Laughlin excursions, alpine mountain tours, winter skiing, and hiking to hot springs along the Colorado River.

**Address: Las Vegas, NV. Tel: (702) 384-1129 (Tel/Fax).**

**Type:** Bed & breakfast.
**Clientele:** Mostly men with women welcome
**Transportation:** Pick up from airport at minimal charge.
**To Gay Bars:** 5-block walk to gay bars.
**Rooms:** 2 rooms & 1 suite with queen or king beds.
**Bathrooms:** 2 shared full bathrooms, one with whirlpool. Outside hot/cold shower.
**Meals:** Full breakfast & evening snack, other meals by request.
**Vegetarian:** Available upon request.
**Complimentary:** Cocktail, etc.
**Dates Open:** All year.
**High Season:** Spring & late summer, holidays.
**Rates:** One person $59, double $79, triple $12 add'l.
**Discounts:** 25% after 7-day stay.
**Rsv'tns:** Required.
**Reserve Through:** Travel agent or call direct.
**Minimum Stay:** Weekend 2 nights, Saturday arrival OK.
**Parking:** On-street parking.
**In-Room:** Color cable TV, VCR, AC, ceiling fans, room service & laundry service.
**On-Premises:** Meeting rooms, laundry facilities.
**Exercise/Health:** Jacuzzi, sauna & hot tub.
**Swimming:** Pool on premises.
**Sunbathing:** At poolside or on the patio.
**Nudity:** Permitted without restrictions.
**Smoking:** Permitted outdoors in most areas.
**Pets:** Permitted with prearrangement.
**Handicap Access:** No, not wheelchair accessible.
**Children:** Not permitted.
**Languages:** English, German, French, Danish, Swedish & Norwegian.
**Your Host:** Ole.

# NEW HAMPSHIRE

## ASHLAND

## Country Options

Gay-Friendly 50/50 ♀♂

Our location in the foothills of the White Mountains makes ***Country Options*** an easily accessible getaway destination. We're just two hours from Boston and visitors are assured abundant natural beauty and diverse outdoor activities year-round. We are on the main street of a busy little village with shops, restaurants and a bike rental/repair shop nearby. The area offers a challenging golf course and unspoiled Squam Lake, where *On Golden Pond* was filmed. The inn offers a comfortable, relaxed atmosphere, antique decorations and newly-decorated common areas and bathrooms.

**Address: 27-29 N Main St, Ashland, NH 03217. Tel: (603) 968-7958.**

**Type:** Bed & breakfast.
**Clientele:** 50% gay & lesbian & 50% straight clientele
**Transportation:** Car is best. We will pick up from bus station in Plymouth.
**To Gay Bars:** 1 hour to Manchester gay/lesbian bars.
**Rooms:** 4 rooms with double beds.
**Bathrooms:** 2 shared bath/shower/toilets.
**Meals:** Full breakfast.
**Vegetarian:** Upon request.
**Dates Open:** All year.
**High Season:** Fall foliage.
**Rates:** Singles $35, doubles $45-$50.
**Rsv'tns:** Recommended.
**Reserve Through:** Call direct.
**Minimum Stay:** 2 nights on holiday weekends.
**Parking:** Adequate free off-street parking.
**In-Room:** Self-controlled heat.
**On-Premises:** TV lounge.
**Swimming:** River, lake or nearby indoor pool.
**Sunbathing:** On nearby beach or in small backyard area at the inn.
**Smoking:** No smoking.
**Pets:** Not permitted.
**Handicap Access:** No.
**Children:** Permitted, but infants not encouraged.
**Languages:** English.

# BETHLEHEM

## The Highlands Inn

Q-NET Women ♀

### *A Lesbian Paradise!*

Surrounded by 100 scenic mountain acres, ***The Highlands Inn*** is a 200-year-old lovingly restored farmhouse that has operated as a country inn for more than 100 years. Fifteen miles of trails, for walking hand-in-hand or cross-country skiing in winter, grace the property. An enormous heated pool with sun deck is a gathering place for swimmers and sunworshippers alike.

Spacious, comfortable common areas include: an enormous fireplaced living room, a library, a tremendous, sunny breakfast room, TV/VCRs with an excellent gay & lesbian video collection, an enclosed wicker-filled sunporch, and a private whirlpool spa.

Commitment ceremonies, honeymoon packages and special events are available. Join us for spectacular fall colors, super winter skiing, lush mountain springtime and all summer sports. We're here for you year round – a lesbian paradise! The inn is conveniently located just 2-1/2 hours from Boston and the Maine coast, 4-1/2 hours from Provincetown, and three hours from Montreal. 1995 Out & About Editor's Choice Award.

**Address: Box 118 (IP), Bethlehem, NH 03574. Tel: (603) 869-3978.**

**Type:** Bed & breakfast inn.
**Clientele:** A women-only lesbian paradise
**Transportation:** Car is best. Closest major airport: Manchester, NH 1-1/2 hrs. Free pick up from bus.
**To Gay Bars:** 1-1/2 hours to gay/lesbian bars.
**Rooms:** 19 rooms & 1 cottage with double or queen beds.
**Bathrooms:** 14 private bath/toilets. Shared: 2 bath/shower/toilets, 1 toilet only.
**Meals:** Deluxe continental breakfast.
**Vegetarian:** Breakfasts don't include meat. Vegetarian options at most local restaurants.
**Complimentary:** Lemonade, cider, popcorn, pretzels, coffee & tea.
**Dates Open:** All year.
**High Season:** Summer, fall & winter weekends.
**Rates:** Rooms $55-$110.
**Discounts:** For longer stays varying seasonally (ex. 15-20% off 7-night stay year-round, except holidays).
**Credit Cards:** MC & VISA.
**Rsv'tns:** Recommended. (Sign always says No Vacancy. Ignore it if driving by without reservations).

*continued next page*

**Reserve Through:** Call direct or travel agent.
**Minimum Stay:** On in-season weekends 2 nights. Longer on holidays.
**Parking:** Ample free parking.
**In-Room:** Self-controlled heat & maid service. Some rooms have kitchens available & some have TVs/ VCRs. Video tape library, refrigerator, coffee & tea-making facilties.
**On-Premises:** TV lounge, VCRs, use of the farmhouse's full kitchen, library, piano, BBQ grills, stereo & boardgames.
**Exercise/Health:** Hot tub, Jacuzzi & lawn games. Massage can be arranged.
**Swimming:** Heated pool, nearby rivers & lakes.
**Sunbathing:** On common sun deck or at poolside.
**Nudity:** Topless sunbathing fine.
**Smoking:** Permitted in smoking area. Most areas & rooms are smoke-free.
**Pets:** Permitted in certain rooms, with prior arrangement.
**Handicap Access:** Yes.
**Children:** Permitted with a gay parent.
**Languages:** English.
**Your Host:** Grace.

IGTA

# CENTRE HARBOR

## Red Hill Inn

Gay-Friendly ♀♂

### *Quiet, Peaceful and Secluded, Yet Close to Everything...*

The ***Red Hill Inn*** is a restored estate on sixty acres overlooking the White Mountains and Squam Lake. In the heart of the Lakes Region, two hours north of Boston, our guest rooms offer beautiful views of fields, woods or mountains. All rooms have private baths and telephones and are decorated with beautiful antiques. Many rooms have fireplaces, some have Jacuzzis and some suites also feature sitting rooms. The inn boasts a wonderful restaurant, where everything is made from scratch, and a small lounge where we have a fireplace and weekend entertainment. Come see the beautiful New Hampshire countryside and experience an authentic country inn!

**Address: RFD #1, Box 99M, Centre Harbor, NH 03226**
**Tel: (603) 279-7001.**

**Type:** Inn with bar and restaurant, cross-country ski trails.
**Clientele:** Mostly straight clientele with a gay/lesbian following
**Transportation:** Car is best. Free pick up from airport or bus.
**To Gay Bars:** 90-minute drive to Manchester gay/ lesbian bars.
**Rooms:** 17 rooms, 3 suites & 1 cottage with single, double, queen or king beds.
**Bathrooms:** All private.
**Meals:** Full breakfast.
**Vegetarian:** On our menu nightly.
**Dates Open:** All year.
**High Season:** Mid-June through November 1st.
**Rates:** $42-$165.
**Discounts:** For longer stays.
**Credit Cards:** MC, VISA, Amex, Diners, Carte Blanche & Discover.
**Rsv'tns:** Helpful.
**Reserve Through:** Travel agent or call direct.
**Minimum Stay:** 2 nights on weekends in season.
**Parking:** Ample free parking.
**In-Room:** Telephone & maid service. 5 rooms have Jacuzzis & 13 have fireplaces.
**On-Premises:** Private dining rooms, meeting rooms, TV lounge, public telephone & central heat.
**Exercise/Health:** 5 rooms have Jacuzzis.
**Swimming:** At nearby lake.
**Sunbathing:** On beach.
**Smoking:** Permitted without restrictions.
**Pets:** Not permitted.
**Handicap Access:** No.
**Children:** Well-behaved only!
**Languages:** English.

IGTA

# FRANCONIA

## Bungay Jar

Gay-Friendly ♀

### *Conducive to Romance & Quiet Pleasures*

Stroll through an enchanted wood, discover a hidden river, reflect on a mountain, star gaze on a private balcony, sip afternoon tea by a water-lily pond, enjoy a fireside chat, have a relaxing sauna and massage, soak in a six-foot tub, nap in a king-sized canopy bed, and awaken to a medley of morning aromas – wood smoke, mountain air, and wild blueberry pancakes. Built from an 18th-century barn, the ***Bungay Jar*** and its exuberant gardens have been featured on the cover of national magazines such as *Country Accents, American Homestyle and Gardens* and *Yankee.*

The seven large guest rooms and suites with mountain or woodland views include such welcoming touches as lavish linens, handmade quilts, ornate beds, and comfortable chairs or a desk for reading and writing. The Stargazer Room on the third floor has stenciled stars on the ceiling. There are four skylights, one directly over the king-sized bed and another over the bathtub that is in the main part of the room. The brightly lit room has thick wall-to-wall carpeting, stained glass windows, bent-branch furniture, and an antique gas fireplace. The Cinnamon Room on the second floor has a queen-sized bed, a six-foot long soaking tub (originally owned by Benny Goodman), and a balcony. The Garden Suite has king bed, fireplace, VCR, private bath, and French doors to the garden. The Rose Suite has a king-sized pencil post bed and a private balcony overlooking the two-story, fireplaced common rooms. There is also a sauna on the second floor for guests' enjoyment. Breakfast specialties include oatmeal pancakes with pure maple syrup, popovers, and fresh fruit salads. By the way, ***Bungay Jar*** is an unusual wind that comes from the southern part of Easton Valley, especially in the spring, roaring along the ridge, shaking, and jarring in a strange rhythmic fashion.

**Address: PO Box 15, Easton Valley Rd, Franconia, NH 03580**
**Tel: (603) 823-7775, Fax: (603) 444-0100.**

**Type:** Bed & breakfast.
**Clientele:** Mostly straight. Strong lesbian following, especially in winter, men always welcome
**Transportation:** Car is best.
**To Gay Bars:** 15 min from Highland Inn.
**Rooms:** 7 rooms, single, double, queen or king beds.
**Bathrooms:** Private: 3 bath/toilets, 2 shower/toilets. 1 shared shower/ toilet/sink.
**Meals:** Full breakfast & afternoon tea & snacks.
**Vegetarian:** All breakfasts (meat served separately). Please inform us of dairy product intolerance.
**Complimentary:** Afternoon snack with tea.
**Dates Open:** All year.
**High Season:** July-October.
**Rates:** Fall foliage $75-$130, all other seasons: $70-$105.
**Discounts:** Inquire.
**Credit Cards:** MC, Visa, Discover, Amex.
**Rsv'tns:** Advised.
**Reserve Through:** Call direct.
**Minimum Stay:** 2 nights some weekends & foliage season.
**Parking:** Ample, off-street parking (15 acres).
**In-Room:** Maid service.
**On-Premises:** Fireplaces,

*continued next page*

common area, telephone. **Exercise/Health:** Sauna, hiking trails. Massage by appointment. **Swimming:** At nearby pool, river, lake, swimming hole. **Sunbathing:** On many porches & hammock. **Nudity:** Permitted in private, 2-person sauna. **Smoking:** Not permitted. **Pets:** Not permitted. **Handicap Access:** No. **Children:** Permitted over age 6. **Languages:** English.

## The Horse & Hound Inn

Gay-Friendly ♂

Off the beaten path at the base of Franconia's Cannon Mountain and adjacent to White Mountains National Forest and the Franconia Notch State Park is one of New England's finest traditional inns. Visitors to ***The Horse & Hound Inn*** are treated to a quiet, relaxed atmosphere of pine paneling, three cozy fireplaces and comfortable guest rooms. The area supports plenty of activities such as hiking, boating, cross-country skiing, antiquing, and sightseeing. There are also bluegrass festivals, chamber music concerts, craft demonstrations, and museums.

**Address: 205 Wells Rd, Franconia, NH 03580**
**Tel: (603) 823-5501, (800) 450-5501.**

**Type:** Bed & breakfast inn with restaurant & lounge. **Clientele:** Mostly straight clientele with a gay male following **Transportation:** Car is best. **To Gay Bars:** 1-1/2 hrs to Manchester, NH, 2-1/2 hrs to Boston, MA. **Rooms:** 8 rooms & 2 suites with double, queen or king beds. **Bathrooms:** Private: 7 bath/toilets, 1 shower/toilet. 2 shared bath/shower/toilets. **Meals:** Full breakfast & dinner with map. **Vegetarian:** Always available. **Dates Open:** Closed April-early May & November till Thanksgiving. **High Season:** Fall foliage Sep 15-Oct 15 & old time Dec 26-Mar 31. **Rates:** $79.95 double, $67.65 single. **Discounts:** Mention ^Inn Places!^ for 20% discount Sun-Thur, 10% Fri-Sat. **Credit Cards:** MC, Visa, Amex, Diners & Discover. **Rsv'tns:** Preferred. **Reserve Through:** Travel agent or call direct. **Parking:** Ample free off-street parking. **In-Room:** Window fans & maid service. **On-Premises:** TV lounge, VCR in lobby & laundry facilities. **Exercise/Health:** Gym with nautilus 12 miles. **Swimming:** 1-1/2 mi to lake, $2.50 fee. **Sunbathing:** On grassy backyard. **Smoking:** Permitted except in dining room & lobby. **Pets:** Permitted, $10 charge. **Handicap Access:** No. **Children:** Permitted, additional charge. **Languages:** English. **Your Host:** Bill & Jim.

# HART'S LOCATION

## The Notchland Inn

Gay-Friendly ♀♂

### *A Magical Location...Naturally Secluded*

Get away from it all, relax and rejuvenate at our comfortable 1862 granite mansion located on 400 acres in the midst of beautiful mountain vistas. ***The Notchland Inn*** rests atop a knoll at the base of Mount Bemis and looks out upon Mounts Hope and Crawford.

Within ***The Notchland Inn,*** experience the comforts and pleasures of attentive and friendly hospitality! Settle in to one of our seven guest rooms or four spacious suites, each individually appointed and all with woodburning fireplaces and private baths. The front parlor is a perfect place to sit by the fire and read or to visit with other guests. The music room draws guests to the piano, or to the stereo to listen to music they personally select. The sun room offers a great place to sip your coffee and read a novel or just enjoy the great views.

In the evening, ***Notchland's*** wonderful 5-course dinner is served in a romantic, fireplaced dining room looking out to the gazebo by our pond. Our Chef creates a new menu each day, her elegant flair respecting the traditional while exploring the excitement of international cuisines. Morning brings a bountiful country breakfast to fuel you for the adventures of the day.

Nature's wonders abound at ***Notchland*** and include 8,000 feet of Saco River frontage and two of the area's best swimming holes. The Davis Path hiking trail starts just across the road from the Inn. Other activities to enjoy are mountain biking, cross-country skiing, snowshoeing, fishing, or soaking in the wood-fired hot tub which sits in a gazebo by the pond. For animal lovers there's a Burnese Mountain dog, a Belgian draft horse, miniature horses and two llamas.

Nearby attractions include: Crawford Notch, ski areas, shopping at North Conway's antiques, arts & crafts, and factory outlet stores, and the Mount Washington Auto Road & Cog Railway.

**Address: Hart's Location, NH 03812-9999**
**Tel: Reservations: (800) 866-6131 or (603) 374-6131, Fax: (603) 374-6168, E-mail: notchland@aol.com.**

**Type:** Inn with restaurant with full liquor license.
**Clientele:** Mostly straight clientele with a gay & lesbian following.
**Transportation:** Car is best. Free pick up from bus.
**To Gay Bars:** 2 hours to Manchester, NH. 2+ hours to Portland, ME.
**Rooms:** 7 rooms & 4 suites with single, queen or king beds.
**Bathrooms:** 6 private shower/toilets & 5 private bath/shower/toilets.
**Meals:** Full breakfast & dinner.
**Vegetarian:** Available with advance notice (dinners by reservation, prepared to order). All dietary restrictions considered.
**Complimentary:** Various treats at various times.
**Dates Open:** All year.
**High Season:** Foliage (Sep 15-Oct 20) & Christmas to New Year (Dec 23-Jan 1).
**Rates:** Per person per night MAP double occupancy: $85-$95, Holiday & foliage $100-$115.

*continued next page*

**Discounts:** 2, 3, 4 & 5 night mid-week packages (per person per package, MAP, double occupancy) $155-$375.
**Credit Cards:** MC, Visa, Amex, Discover.
**Rsv'tns:** Subject to prior booking.
**Reserve Through:** Travel agent or call direct.
**Minimum Stay:** Required at times.
**Parking:** Ample free off-street parking.
**In-Room:** Maid service, some ceiling fans.
**On-Premises:** Meeting rooms.
**Exercise/Health:** Spa, massage by appointment. Nearby gym, weights, Jacuzzi, sauna, steam, massage, skiing, sleigh & carriage rides.
**Swimming:** River on premises. Nearby pool, river & lake.
**Sunbathing:** On patio, lawns or at the beach.
**Smoking:** Non-smoking environment.
**Pets:** Not permitted.
**Handicap Access:** No.
**Children:** Mature children only. No TV. Many animals & outdoor activities.
**Languages:** English.
**Your Host:** Les & Ed.

# KEENE

## Post and Beam Bed & Breakfast

**Gay-Friendly ♀♂**

### *"There Are No Strangers – Only Friends We Haven't Met"*

The Monadnock Region, known for its New England charm and "Currier & Ives" appeal, is home to ***The Post and Beam Bed & Breakfast,*** a 1797 restored Colonial farmstead. Guests love the quiet, cozy romantic atmosphere, and marvel at the posts and beams, wide pine floors and fireplaces. Nearby are hiking trails, biking, golfing, fishing, cross-country skiing, swimming and gorgeous fall foliage. The region is also rich in art galleries, music, theater, covered bridges and great shopping. Your friendly innkeepers will make your stay comfortable and relaxing, and serve you bountiful homemade breakfasts. Groups are welcome.

**Address: HCR 33, Box 380, Centre St, Sullivan, NH 03445**
**Tel: (603) 847-3330, Fax: (603) 847-3306.**
**E-mail: postandbeam@top.monad.net.**
**http://www.nhweb.com/postandbeam/.**

**Type:** Bed & breakfast.
**Clientele:** Mostly straight clientele with a gay & lesbian following
**Transportation:** Car is best. Closest major airport: Manchester, NH (1 hr). Free pick up from bus in Keene.
**To Gay Bars:** A 1-hour drive to Manchester gay bars. 2 hours to Boston, MA bars.
**Rooms:** 6 rooms with single, queen or king beds.
**Bathrooms:** Private: 2 shower/toilets, 1 WC only. 4 shared bath/shower/toilets.
**Meals:** Full or continental breakfast.
**Vegetarian:** All breakfasts. Please inform us of dairy product intolerance.
**Complimentary:** Afternoon tea, cookies, snacks, apples.
**Dates Open:** All year.
**High Season:** Mid-June thru Nov 1.
**Rates:** High season $60-$90, low season $49-$79.
**Discounts:** Mention Inn Places for 10% discount. Seniors 10% discount.
**Credit Cards:** MC, Visa.
**Rsv'tns:** Preferred.
**Reserve Through:** Call direct.
**Minimum Stay:** 2 nights during fall foliage & holiday weekends.
**Parking:** Ample free off-street parking.
**In-Room:** Window fans, maid service. Some rooms have AC.
**On-Premises:** TV lounge, video tape & book libraries, telephone.
**Exercise/Health:** Nearby gym, massage.
**Swimming:** Nearby river, lake.
**Sunbathing:** On grounds.
**Smoking:** Permitted only in designated areas. No smoking in bedrooms.
**Pets:** Not permitted.
**Handicap Access:** Yes.
**Children:** Must be at least 8 years old.
**Languages:** English, French.
**Your Host:** Darcy & Priscilla.

# NORTH CONWAY - CHOCORUA

## Mt. Chocorua View House Bed & Breakfast

Gay-Friendly ♀♂

Welcome to ***The Mt. Chocorua View House.*** Built in 1845 and beautifully restored, it is furnished with a warm and cozy old-fashioned charm. This beautiful colonial home features a woodburning Franklin fireplace, paddle fans, porches and many unique antiques which take you back in time to a bygone era. Conveniently located in the upper lakes region, you are minutes from lakes, mountains, shopping outlets, and the many antique and gift shops that dot the area. Close by is the "Barnstormers Playhouse," the oldest summer playhouse in New Hampshire, and also one of the first in the nation. Mornings, enjoy a delicious and bountiful country breakfast served in a lovely antique-furnished dining room. Private bathrooms available, with some shared. Non-smoking, no pets.

**Address: Rte 16, PO Box 348, Chocorua, NH 03817-0348**
**Tel: (603) 323-8350.**

**Type:** Bed & breakfast.
**Clientele:** Mainly straight with some gay & lesbian clientele.
**Transportation:** Car is best. Bus stop about 2000 ft. Pick up from bus.
**To Gay Bars:** 1 hour to Manchester or Portsmouth, NH, or Portland & Ogunquit, ME.
**Rooms:** 6 rooms & 1 suite with single or double beds.
**Bathrooms:** 4 private full baths. 1 shared full bath with shower, 1 half bath.
**Meals:** Full breakfast.
**Vegetarian:** Available.
**Complimentary:** Coffee, tea, hot chocolate, & lemonade. Setups always available.
**Dates Open:** All year.
**High Season:** July to September. October for autumn foliage.
**Rates:** Shared baths from $55; Private baths from $75; Suite from $85. Mid-week rates $45, $55, $75. For Autumn Foliage add $10.
**Credit Cards:** MC, VISA, Amex, Discover.
**Rsv'tns:** Requested for priority confirmation.
**Reserve Through:** Call direct.
**Parking:** Ample free parking.
**In-Room:** Ceiling fans.
**On-Premises:** TV lounge, guest living room, dining room, kitchen, & enclosed porch. Cable TV in living room.
**Exercise/Health:** Boating.
**Swimming:** Lake Chocorua & White Mt. State Park lake 2 miles, Silver Lake 3 miles.
**Sunbathing:** On common sun decks & lawn in back of inn.
**Smoking:** Smoke-free B&B.
**Pets:** No pets.
**Handicap Access:** No.
**Children:** Permitted.
**Languages:** English & German.
**Your Host:** Eric.

# NEW JERSEY

# PLAINFIELD

## The Pillars of Plainfield Bed & Breakfast

Q-NET Gay-Friendly 50/50 ♀♂

### *Sylvan Seclusion With Easy Access to Manhattan*

***The Pillars*** is a lovingly-restored Victorian/Georgian mansion. Relax by the Music Room fire, read a book from the living room library, play the organ, listen to the stereo, watch a video. Swedish breakfast at ***The Pillars*** is expanded continental, served at your convenience, but you may wish to cook your own in the huge kitchen. We have over 20 years' experience in the hospitality industry and are eager to offer a quality experience to our guests. Plainfield is a beautiful town with easy access to Manhattan by commuter train. It's a town where rainbow flags and windsocks can be seen on local houses and is fast becoming the "Gay Capital of New Jersey."

*continued next page*

Address: 922 Central Ave, Plainfield, NJ 07060-2311
Tel: (908) 753-0922 (Tel/Fax), (888) PILLARS (745-5277).
E-mail: Pillars2@juno.com. http://cimarron.net/usa/nj/pillars.html.

**Type:** Bed & breakfast.
**Clientele:** 50% gay & lesbian & 50% straight clientele
**Transportation:** Train or bus to Plainfield, car or taxi to house.
**To Gay Bars:** 1/2 mile. 8 miles to the famous "Den" at Rutgers University.
**Rooms:** 3 suites with twin or queen beds.
**Bathrooms:** All private bath/shower/toilets.
**Campsites:** Parking for self-contained RV with electric & water hookup.
**Meals:** Expanded continental breakfast.
**Vegetarian:** Facilities to prepare your own vegetarian meals.
**Complimentary:** Coffee, tea. Beverages afternoon & evening.
**Dates Open:** All year.
**Rates:** $50-$105.
**Discounts:** Call for discounts.
**Credit Cards:** Visa, MC, Discover.
**Rsv'tns:** Required.
**Reserve Through:** Travel agent or call direct.
**Parking:** Ample off-street parking.
**In-Room:** AC, coffee/tea-making facilities, maid & room service.
**On-Premises:** Meeting rooms, TV lounge, VCR, stereo, organ, laundry & kitchen facilities, library & fireplace.
**Exercise/Health:** Health clubs in the area.
**Swimming:** Outstanding gay nude beach at nearby Sandy Hook.
**Sunbathing:** In secluded backyard.
**Smoking:** Permitted only on the sun porch in inclement weather.
**Pets:** Well-behaved dogs permitted with prior arrangement. We have a Cairn Terrier.
**Handicap Access:** No.
**Children:** Welcome under 2 years old & over 12 years old. Crib, playpen & cots available.
**Languages:** English.
**Your Host:** Chuck & Tom.

IGTA

# NEW MEXICO

## ALBUQUERQUE

### The Casitas at Old Town

Gay/Lesbian ♀♂

## *A Glimpse of the Past Beneath a Sea of Sky*

Enjoy the hospitable warmth and comfort of New Mexico's classic adobe dwellings on the secluded edge of Albuquerque's oldest historical area. ***Casitas at Old Town*** are early dwellings restored to modern comfort with fireplace, kitchen area, bedroom, bath and patio, all furnished with authentic New Mexico pieces. Stroll into the plaza of nearby Old Town with its adjacent museums, drive an hour to Santa Fe, or just relax in absolute privacy...with one foot in the past.

Address: 1604 Old Town Rd NW, Albuquerque, NM. Tel: (505) 843-7479.

**Type:** Suites with private entrances.
**Clientele:** Mostly gay & lesbian with some straight clientele
**Transportation:** Car is best.
**To Gay Bars:** A 15-minute drive to men's & women's bars.
**Rooms:** 2 suites with double or queen bed.
**Bathrooms:** 2 private shower/toilets.
**Vegetarian:** 1 block to vegetarian food.
**Complimentary:** Tea & coffee makings in each suite.
**Dates Open:** All year.
**Rates:** $85 all year.
**Discounts:** On extended stays.
**Rsv'tns:** Preferred.
**Reserve Through:** Travel agent or call direct.
**Parking:** Ample off-street parking.
**In-Room:** AC, kitchen, refrigerator, coffee & tea-making facilities.
**Exercise/Health:** Nearby gym.
**Sunbathing:** On the patio.
**Nudity:** Permitted on patios.
**Smoking:** Not permitted.
**Pets:** Not permitted.
**Handicap Access:** No.
**Children:** Not especially welcome.
**Languages:** English, minimal Spanish.

## Dave's B&B on the Rio Grande

Gay/Lesbian ♂

### *Casual and Private for Gays and Leatherfolk*

In a quiet residential area, convenient to Old Town and downtown, 1 mile north of I-40, ***Dave's B&B*** is decorated with original art, including Indian kachinas, pottery and rugs. All advertising is directed solely to gays, lesbians and leatherfolk. The emphasis is on privacy and a casual, make-yourself-at-home style. My southwest adobe-style home is surrounded by seven-foot privacy walls and patios with trees, fountain, hot tub and sunning areas. Both rooms open directly onto patios. The master suite has a fireplace, unique four-poster bed and a large adjoining bath/dressing area.

Address: PO Box 27214, Albuquerque, NM 87125-7214
Tel: (505) 247-8312, Fax: (505) 842-0733,
E-mail: DavesBB@Rt66.com. http://www.rt66.com/~davesbb.

**Type:** Bed & Breakfast.
**Clientele:** Mostly gay men with women welcome.
**Transportation:** Car is best.
**To Gay Bars:** Convenient to gay bars.
**Rooms:** 1 room & 1 suite with queen beds.
**Bathrooms:** All private.
**Meals:** Expanded continental breakfast. Low-fat/special diets catered to.
**Vegetarian:** Always avail.
**Complimentary:** Regular & decaf coffee, herbal tea, soda, juices, beer, wine.
**Dates Open:** All year.
**High Seas.:** May 15-Oct 15.
**Rates:** High season $75-$95. Off season $65-$85.
**Discounts:** Available on stays over 4 days.
**Credit Cards:** MC & VISA.
**Rsv'tns:** Required, but check if passing through.
**Reserve Thru:** Call direct.
**Minimum Stay:** 2 nights on weekends.
**Parking:** Ample garage parking plus RV space.
**In-Room:** Color TV, VCR, ceiling fan, tele. & maid serv. One rm with fireplace.
**On-Premises:** Living room with fireplace & piano, laundry facilities, kitchen privileges, computer, fax.
**Exercise/Health:** Outdoor hot tub, weights, rowing machine. Motorcycle/mountain bike rentals & tours available. Nearby gym.
**Sunbathing:** On walled patio.
**Nudity:** Permitted on the rear patio & in the hot tub.
**Smoking:** Permitted.
**Pets:** Not permitted.
**Handicap Access:** Yes, ground floor.
**Children:** Not permitted.
**Languages:** English.
**Your Host:** Dave.

## Golden Guesthouse

Gay/Lesbian ♀♂

### *Peace, Privacy and Southwestern Flair*

Peace, quiet and privacy surround ***Golden Guesthouse,*** our charming, spacious one-bedroom casita, designed and completed in 1996. The front porch is perfect for the morning light and the living room features a kiva fireplace for cozy, romantic winter evenings. Brimming with Southwestern style, the bathroom features a shower created for two. The guesthouse is a quick block from the Rio Grande Nature Center and only minutes from Albuquerque's museums and Old Town Plaza. We are happy to offer directions, make suggestions, or leave you absolutely alone with the hope of making your stay a memorable and soul-soothing experience.

Address: 2645 Decker NW, Albuquerque, NM 87107
Tel: (505) 344-5995, (888) DEBBIE G (332-2434), Fax: (505) 344-3434,
E-mail: GoldenGH@aol.com.

*continued next page*

**Type:** Guesthouse.
**Clientele:** Mostly gay & lesbian with some straight clientele
**Transportation:** Car is best.
**To Gay Bars:** 3 miles to gay bars.
**Rooms:** 1 cottage with queen bed.
**Bathrooms:** Private shower/toilet.
**Meals:** Continental breakfast.
**Vegetarian:** Available upon request.
**Complimentary:** Beer, wine, champagne upon request, sodas, juice, bottled water, bagels, snacks.
**Dates Open:** All year.
**Rates:** $85 daily, $420 weekly.
**Discounts:** Ask for Inn Places discount price of $69 daily.
**Rsv'tns:** Recommended or take a chance.
**Parking:** Ample free off-street parking.
**In-Room:** AC, ceiling fans, coffee & tea-making facilities, refrigerator, kitchen area.
**Exercise/Health:** Nearby gym, massage, mountain bicycle rental (will deliver).
**Sunbathing:** On patio.
**Nudity:** Permitted on private patio.
**Smoking:** No cigarette smoking.
**Pets:** Not permitted.
**Handicap Access:** No.
**Children:** Call to inquire.
**Languages:** English.

## Hacienda Antigua Bed and Breakfast

Q-NET Gay-Friendly ♀♂

### *Secluded, Serene and Romantic – Featured on TLC's "Great Country Inns"*

Walk through the massive carved gates of ***Hacienda Antigua*** and step back in time. The gentle courtyard with its big cottonwood tree and abundance of flowers is the heart of this 200-year-old adobe hacienda. In summer, relax on the peaceful portal or bask in the sun by the large swimming pool. In winter enjoy a crackling piñon fire in your own kiva fireplace. Enjoy the outdoor Jacuzzi year-round. Visitors linger, not wanting to leave the warm Southwestern hospitality, full breakfasts, and splendid rooms comfortably furnished with antiques. Member New Mexico & Albuquerque B&B Associations.

**Address: 6708 Tierra Dr NW, Albuquerque, NM 87107**
**Tel: (505) 345-5399, (800) 484-2385, code no. 9954.**

**Type:** Bed & breakfast.
**Clientele:** Mostly straight clientele with gays & lesbians welcome
**Transportation:** Car is best.
**To Gay Bars:** 1-5 miles.
**Rooms:** 4 rooms & 1 suite with single, double, queen or king beds.
**Bathrooms:** All private.
**Meals:** Full breakfast.
**Vegetarian:** Served upon request. Our breakfasts are ample & we will accommodate any dietary request.
**Complimentary:** Glass of wine. Chocolates in the room.
**Dates Open:** All year.
**High Season:** Aug, Sept, Oct.
**Rates:** $85-$150.
**Credit Cards:** MC & VISA.
**Rsv'tns:** Required.
**Reserve Through:** Travel agent or call direct.
**Parking:** Ample free off-street parking.
**In-Room:** AC, ceiling fans & fireplaces.
**On-Premises:** TV lounge.
**Exercise/Health:** Jacuzzi on premises. Gym & weights nearby.
**Swimming:** Pool on premises.
**Sunbathing:** At poolside or on the patio.
**Smoking:** Permitted outside.
**Pets:** Not permitted.
**Handicap Access:** No.
**Children:** Limited acceptance.
**Languages:** English.

## Hateful Missy & Granny Butch's Boudoir & Manure Emporium

Gay/Lesbian ♀

### *A Rather Queer Bed & Breakfast – The Gravy May be Lumpy, But the Beds Ain't*

Yippy-Ki-Yay! ***Hateful Missy & Granny Butch*** have relocated to a twelve-acre ranch south of Albuquerque in the Rio Grande Valley and we are definitely "for the birds." Located close to two major bird and wildlife sanctuaries, our stunning two-story adobe home boasts beamed ceilings, brick floors, wood-burning stoves, a luxurious Jacuzzi tub, huge picture windows for all sorts of bird watching (ho-ho!), cable TV, VCRs and selected videos.

Relax, hike, mountain bike to the river for a romantic picnic, punch a dogie, slap a hog, get bitten by a red ant, shoot pool, or go to Albu-*queer*qe for even more excitement. Then, come home to terrific food, prepared, whenever possible, with Missy's home-grown organic veggies. Granny Butch's mean cuisine "a la New Mexico" will leave you breathless. Be tortured by our canine coordinator, Rotten Long-Young. Remember! The gravy may be lumpy, but the beds ain't. Call soon. Operators must be standing by somewhere.

**Address: PO Box 556, Veguita, NM 87062**
**Tel: (800) 397-2482, (505) 861-3328.**

**Type:** Bed & breakfast with Granny Butch's Genital Store & Art Gallery
**Clientele:** Mostly women with men very welcome
**Transportation:** Car is necessary, poor public transportation. 1 free round-trip pick up, if absolutely necessary, from airport, bus, train. $25 round-trip charge thereafter.
**To Gay Bars:** 45 miles. 45 minutes by car.
**Rooms:** 3 rooms, 1 suite with 1 king & 3 queen beds.
**Bathrooms:** 3 bath/shower/toilet rooms, suite has Jacuzzi. Only at full capacity does anyone share.
**Campsites:** 2 RV parking spaces only.
**Meals:** Full breakfast. Other meals, picnic or box lunches available at nominal price.
**Vegetarian:** Simply indicate your need.
**Complimentary:** Wine or sparkling cider, cheese, cracker basket, fruit juices, fruit, snacks, X-rated candy on pillows.
**Dates Open:** All year.
**High Season:** September-March.
**Rates:** $85-$125. During holidays & special events (balloon fiesta, etc) $100-$150.
**Discounts:** Weekly rates except during holidays & special events.
**Rsv'tns:** Preferred.
**Reserve Through:** Travel agent or call direct.
**Minimum Stay:** Required during holidays & special events.
**Parking:** Ample free parking. Some covered parking.
**In-Room:** Color cable TV, VCR, ceiling fans, refrigerator, coffee & tea-making facilities, room, maid & laundry service. Telephone in 2 rooms.
**On-Premises:** TV lounge, video tape library, video & parlour games, jigsaw puzzles, pool table, etc. Computer, fax, laundry facilities.
**Exercise/Health:** Massage by appointment, Jacuzzi, mountain bikes, hiking, bird watching at 2 huge bird & wildlife sanctuaries. Waterskiing, boating & fishing at nearby lake.
**Swimming:** At huge nearby man-made lake.
**Sunbathing:** Everywhere on premises & on patio.
**Nudity:** Permitted everywhere on premises.
**Smoking:** We are a non-smoking facility. Outdoor smoking is fine.
**Pets:** Permitted, must be well-mannered, sociable & housebroken.
**Handicap Access:** No.
**Children:** We accept no children.
**Languages:** English, some French, Spanish, Japanese.
**Your Host:** Butch & Rita.

## The Rainbow Lodge Bed & Breakfast

Q-NET Gay-Friendly 50/50 ♀♂

### *Sweeping Vistas, Southwest Elegance, and a Hot Tub with Mountain Views*

Escape to the Land of Enchantment and to the ***Rainbow Lodge.*** We are conveniently located on the historic Turquoise Trail in the Sandia Mountains, between Albuquerque and Santa Fe, just 25 minutes from the Albuquerque airport. The ***Rainbow Lodge*** provides panoramic views, sweeping vistas and Southwest-style elegance. Occupying over 6,000 square feet, the lodge has beamed ceilings, flagstone and wooden floors, seven fireplaces, a hot tub overlooking the mountains, an expansive brick-covered terrace, an adobe-walled courtyard, a water fountain, and even miniature donkeys to entertain you.

Colorful and unique suites await you at the ***Rainbow Lodge,*** including private bathrooms, queen-sized beds, sitting areas, color TVs and beautiful mountain views. Some of our suites offer a kitchen, fireplace, VCR and CD player. Guests are treated to a delicious breakfast, including New Mexico specialties, homemade muffins, freshly baked breads, seasonal fruit, gourmet coffees, teas and juices. A plate of homemade cookies awaits all guests upon arrival.

The entertainment in New Mexico is limited only by your imagination. Enjoy striking contrasts in seasons with golden autumns, dazzling white winters, clear blue springs and sun-drenched summers. Day trips include hiking, skiing, mountain biking, horseback riding, hot air ballooning, horse racing and river rafting. There are also Native American pueblo tours, ancient ruins, spectacular restaurants, as well as endless art galleries and gift shops which capture the spirit of the Southwest. At the end of the day, pamper yourself in our steaming hot tub and relax while gazing at the Sandia skies and the star-filled nights.

If you need the ultimate ESCAPE, New Mexico and the ***Rainbow Lodge*** can be your place to renew worn spirits, rekindle a romance, or be your home base for all of the enchanting excitement that New Mexico has to offer.

**Address: 115 Frost Rd, Sandia Park, NM 87047**
**Tel: (505) 281-7100. E-mail: rainbowbed@aol.com.**

**Type:** Bed & breakfast.
**Clientele:** 50% gay & lesbian & 50% straight clientele
**Transportation:** Car is best, 25 miles from airport.
**To Gay Bars:** 16 miles.
**Rooms:** 4 suites with queen beds.
**Bathrooms:** Private.
**Meals:** Full breakfast.
**Vegetarian:** Available upon request.
**Complimentary:** Gourmet cookies, coffee, herbal tea, soda, fully stocked non-alcoholic wet bar with snacks.
**Dates Open:** All year.
**High Season:** Summer & fall.
**Rates:** $70-$100.
**Discounts:** Discounts for week-long stays.
**Credit Cards:** MC, Visa, Amex, Discover.
**Rsv'tns:** Highly recommended.
**Reserve Through:** Travel agent or call direct.
**Minimum Stay:** 2 nights on weekends.
**Parking:** Ample free parking on site.
**In-Room:** Color TV, VCR, CD stereo, ceiling fan, fireplace, kitchen, coffee/tea-making facilities, refrigerator, laundry & room service.

**On-Premises:** Meeting rooms, laundry facilities.
**Exercise/Health:** Hiking, biking, skiing. Outdoor hot tub.
**Sunbathing:** On common sun decks.
**Nudity:** Permitted in hot tub, with discretion.
**Smoking:** Permitted on terrace. All rooms non-smoking.
**Pets:** Permitted in available on-site kennels.
**Handicap Access:** No.
**Children:** Not especially welcomed.
**Languages:** English.
**Your Host:** Rusty, Jody & Sue.

## Rio Grande House

**Gay-Friendly ♀♂**

This landmark adobe residence, ***Rio Grande House,*** is located near historic Old Town, major museums and the Rio Grande nature center. Southwestern charm is reflected throughout with beamed ceilings, brick floors, Kiva fireplaces and museum-quality antiques. Collectibles from East Africa, Nepal, Pakistan and Yemen are used to decorate each room.

**Address: 3100 Rio Grande Blvd NW, Albuquerque, NM 87107**
**Tel: (505) 345-0120.**

**Type:** Bed & breakfast.
**Clientele:** Mostly straight clientele with a gay & lesbian following.
**Transportation:** Car is best.
**To Gay Bars:** 15-minute drive.
**Rooms:** 5 rooms with double, queen or king beds.
**Bathrooms:** All private shower/toilets.
**Meals:** Full breakfast.
**Vegetarian:** Available upon request.
**Dates Open:** All year.
**High Season:** June to October.
**Rates:** $50-$95.
**Rsv'tns:** Required.
**Reserve Through:** Call direct.
**Parking:** Ample off-street parking.
**In-Room:** Color TV, AC & telephone.
**On-Premises:** Laundry facilities.
**Sunbathing:** On patio.
**Smoking:** Permitted. Non-smoking rooms available.
**Pets:** Not permitted.
**Handicap Access:** No.
**Children:** Not permitted.
**Languages:** English.

## W.E. Mauger Estate

**Gay-Friendly 50/50 ♀♂**

### *Linda Ronstadt Slept Here!*

From the ***W.E. Mauger Estate*** in the heart of Albuquerque you can walk to old town, museums, the aquarium, the convention center, shops, and restaurants. This 1897 restored Victorian B&B on the national registry has three floors with eight elegant suites, all private baths, and a hot tub. Guests can enjoy a full gourmet breakfast, hors d'oeuvres, the peace and quiet of the area, and ample private parking. The B&B has a three-star rating by Mobile and a three-diamond rating by AAA.

**Address: 701 Roma Ave NW, Albuquerque, NM 87102**
**Tel: (505) 242-8755, Fax: (505) 842-8835.**
**http://www.thuntek.net/tc_arts/mauger.**

**Type:** Bed & breakfast.
**Clientele:** 50% gay & lesbian & 50% straight clientele
**Transportation:** Car is best or taxi.
**To Gay Bars:** 3 miles by car.
**Rooms:** 7 rooms & 1 suite with single, double, queen or king beds.
**Bathrooms:** All private baths with showers.
**Meals:** Full breakfast.
**Vegetarian:** Available if pre ordered.
**Complimentary:** Wine, cheese, juice, cookies, brownies, chips, fruit, candy & coffee.
**Dates Open:** All year.
**High Season:** Mar thru Oct.
**Rates:** $69-$125.
**Discounts:** Long stays, booking whole house.
**Credit Cards:** MC, Visa, Amex & Diners.
**Rsv'tns:** Required.
**Reserve Through:** Call direct.
**Minimum Stay:** 2 nights for special events.
**Parking:** Ample, free, off-street parking, private lot, will accept RV.
**In-Room:** Color TV, maid & room service, AC, ceiling fans, coffee/tea-making facilities & refrigerator.
**On-Premises:** TV lounge, meeting rooms, catering for special occasions.
**Swimming:** In nearby river.
**Sunbathing:** On patio.
**Smoking:** Permitted in designated outside areas.
**Pets:** Call to inquire.
**Handicap Access:** No.
**Children:** Call to inquire.
**Languages:** English.
**Your Host:** Alan & Valerie.

## W.J. Marsh House Victorian B&B

Gay-Friendly 50/50 ♀♂

### *We Even Have A Ghost!*

The ***W.J. Marsh House Victorian Bed & Breakfast,*** built in 1892, is on the National Register of Historical Places and is located in Albuquerque's old *Railroad Town* historic district. The six unique guest rooms are brimming with antiques. Two female ghosts, dressed in turn-of-the-century gowns, are often seen in the Rose Room. We're five minutes from the airport, walking distance from UNM and the convention center downtown, and a few minutes drive from Old Town, the zoo and nature center, museums, the Indian Pueblo Cultural Center, and the world's longest, highest tramway.

**Address: 301 Edith SE, Albuquerque, NM 87102**
**Tel: (505) 247-1001, Toll-free: (888) WJ MARSH (956-2774).**

**Type:** Bed & breakfast inn with separate Victorian cottage.
**Clientele:** 50% gay & lesbian & 50% straight clientele.
**Transportation:** Car is best. Cab from airport less than $10 one way.
**To Gay Bars:** 2-3 miles to gay & lesbian bars.
**Rooms:** 6 rooms, 1 cottage with single, double or queen beds.
**Bathrooms:** 2 private toilets with shared shower & 2 shared bath/shower/toilets.
**Meals:** Full gourmet breakfast in house. Full kitchen in cottage (breakfast not provided).
**Vegetarian:** Available with prior notice. Many vegetarian restaurants nearby.
**Complimentary:** Depends on time of year & mood of the Innkeeper. Alcohol is not provided.
**Dates Open:** All year.
**High Season:** First week of October (International Balloon Fiesta). Make reservations by July.
**Rates:** Single $50-$105, double $80-$115. Cottage $400 per week for 2, $500 per week for 3 or 4.
**Discounts:** Stays of one week or more.
**Credit Cards:** VISA, MC.
**Rsv'tns:** Preferred. Same-day calls accepted IF space is available.
**Reserve Thru:** Call direct.
**Minimum Stay:** During Balloon Fiesta: 3 nights weekends, 2 nights during the week.
**Parking:** Ample free off-street & on-street parking. Well-lit walkways to entrances.
**In-Room:** AC & maid service. Color cable TV, ceiling fans & kitchen in cottage. Laundry service on request.
**On-Premises:** Meeting rooms, laun. fac. & phone.
**Exercise/Health:** Self-guided walking tours. Nearby gym, Jacuzzi, sauna, steam & massage.
**Swimming:** Nearby pools, river & lakes.
**Smoking:** Not permitted anywhere, not even on the grounds!
**Pets:** Not permitted.
**Handicap Access:** No, sorry.
**Children:** Permitted in cottage only. Permitted in main house if 12 or older.
**Languages:** English, Spanish, French.

# ESPAÑOLA

## The Inn of La Mesilla

Gay-Friendly 50/50 ♀♂

### *The Essence of Northern New Mexico*

***The Inn of La Mesilla*** is a private residence bordering the Santa Clara Indian Reservation. The Hoemann's invite you to enjoy two private bedrooms, each with private bath. Our pueblo-style home has Mexican tile throughout. The Inn has a new hot tub with large, festive deck for sunning or enjoying views. The Inn is minutes from Chimayo, Puye Cliffs, Santa Fe, Taos and eight northern Indian pueblos. A full breakfast is served, and afternoon snacks are available from 5:00-6:00 pm. Two Springer Spaniels, Pork Chop and Te-Bone, reside in home.

**Address: Rt 1, Box 368A, Española, NM 87532. Tel: (505) 753-5368.**

**Type:** Bed & breakfast.
**Clientele:** 50% gay & lesbian & 50% straight clientele
**Transportation:** Car is best.
**To Gay Bars:** 30 minutes to Santa Fe.
**Rooms:** 2 rooms with queen or king bed.
**Bathrooms:** All private bath/showers.
**Meals:** Full breakfast & afternoon refreshments.
**Vegetarian:** Special veggie dishes for breakfast

if requested in advance.
**Complimentary:** Afternoon snacks between 5pm-6pm.
**Dates Open:** All year.
**Rates:** $90.
**Discounts:** 10% to senior citizens.
**Rsv'tns:** Required.
**Reserve Through:** Travel agent or call direct.
**Parking:** Ample free parking.
**In-Room:** Color cable TV & ceiling fans.
**On-Premises:** TV lounge, baby grand piano & use of refrigerator for sodas & such.
**Exercise/Health:** Hot tub on premises. Nearby gym, hot springs & massage.
**Sunbathing:** On hot tub deck.
**Smoking:** Permitted outside only.
**Pets:** Not permitted. Kennel 5 minutes away.
**Handicap Access:** No.
**Children:** Not permitted.
**Languages:** English, some Spanish.

## Ranchito San Pedro de Cócono

Q-NET **Gay-Friendly 50/50** ♀♂

### *A Special Place to Stay While Exploring Northern New Mexico*

Española, New Mexico, known as the "low-rider capital of the world," is fast becoming the sightseeing center of Northern New Mexico. Española, established for its central trade route location, is shaped and surrounded by Native American and Hispanic art and cultural history, a contemporary and traditional art market, spectacular landscapes, all kinds of outdoor recreation, hot springs, Santa Fe nightlife, the eight Northern Pueblos (special places that will renew one's spirit), and the best red chili in the state!

***Ranchito San Pedro de Cócono*** (Little San Pedro Turkey Ranch) is home and studio for watercolor artist/teacher Jan Hart, and is located in one of the oldest neighborhoods at the southern edge of Española. No longer an operational turkey ranch, the ranch buildings include a charming pueblo-style ranch house B&B, three artist studios, and open gallery and a racing-pigeon loft. The rural past of the San Pedro neighborhood is still visible in the adobe houses, apple orchards and *acequias* (irrigation ditches), the one-lane access road lined with ancient cottonwood trees, and the Santa Clara Pueblo land just across the road. During your stay at ***Ranchito San Pedro*** you will enjoy the solar-oriented private room and bath, access to the kitchen, an outdoor patio with kiva fireplace and all the sunshine, starlight and coyote serenades you desire.

Trained as an architect, Jan has an abiding appreciation for the charm and authenticity of this part of Northern New Mexico, as well as plenty of ideas for the ranchito's future. She will be happy to offer suggested outings to the nearby spectacular vistas and other little-known New Mexico "off-the -beaten-track" treasures such as Abiquiu, where Georgia O'Keeffe lived and painted, Ghost Ranch, El Rito, Dixon, Ojo Caliente, Chimayo, the High Road, Puye Cliffs, the Turquoise Trail, Black Mesa... And if you'd like to try a class in watercolor or drawing, just ask! Jan probably has just what you want!

**Address: PO Box 1849, Española, NM 87532. Tel: (505) 753-0583.**

*continued next page*

**Type:** Bed & breakfast.
**Clientele:** Half 'n half straight/gay-lesbian
**Transportation:** Car is best. Shuttle available from Albuquerque to Santa Fe (will pickup there).
**To Gay Bars:** 18 miles to Santa Fe gay bars.
**Rooms:** 2 rooms with king, queen or single beds.
**Bathrooms:** Shared bath/shower/toilet.
**Meals:** Continental breakfast, casual, on your schedule.
**Vegetarian:** Available in Española.
**Complimentary:** Tea & coffee.
**Dates Open:** All year.
**High Season:** May-October.
**Rates:** $45-$65.
**Discounts:** For stays longer than 3 days.
**Credit Cards:** MC, Visa.
**Rsv'tns:** Required.
**Reserve Through:** Call direct.
**Parking:** Ample, free off-street parking.
**In-Room:** Telephone, ceiling fans, evap cooling maid service.
**On-Premises:** Laundry facilities ($3 per load), color TV, VCR. Art classes (your schedule).
**Exercise/Health:** Country walks. Nearby gym, weights, massage.
**Swimming:** Nearby river. Ojo Caliente, 20 miles.
**Sunbathing:** On patio.
**Smoking:** Permitted outside. Both rooms are non-smoking.
**Pets:** Please inquire.
**Handicap Access:** Yes, but help needed to negotiate dirt driveway & gravel path to front door.
**Children:** Please inquire.
**Languages:** English, Spanish (un poco).
**Your Host:** Jan.

# SANTA FE

## Arius Compound

Q-NET Gay-Friendly ♀♂

### *Experience Adobe Living...*

...in your own authentic Santa Fe *Casita*, ideally located on Canyon Road, the heart of Santa Fe's historic East Side with charming shops, galleries and fine restaurants. Up a quiet lane, surrounded by high adobe walls filled with gardens, patios, fruit trees and our ever-hot redwood tub, each *Casita* has 1 or 2 bedrooms, fully-equipped kitchen, living room with corner Kiva fireplace (wood provided), private bath or shower, private patio and loads of Southwest style. Don't be a visitor. Live here, at ***Arius Compound,*** if only for a few days.

**Address: PO Box 1111, 1018-1/2 Canyon Rd, Santa Fe, NM 87504-1111**
**Tel: Out of Town: (800) 735-8453,**
**Local: (505) 982-2621, Fax: (505) 989-8280.**
**E-mail: len@ariuscompound.com.**

**Type:** Cottages.
**Clientele:** 60% straight & 40% gay & lesbian clientele
**Transportation:** Car is best.
**Rooms:** 3 cottages (two 1-br & one 2-br) with single, double or queen beds. Futon sleepers in living rooms.
**Bathrooms:** 2 private shower/toilets & 1 private bath/shower/toilet.
**Dates Open:** All year.
**High Season:** July-August.
**Rates:** 1-bedrm: low $80, high $115. 2-bedrm: low $135, high $175.
**Credit Cards:** MC, Visa, Amex, Discover.
**Rsv'tns:** Not required, but usually sold out without reservations.
**Reserve Thru:** Call direct.
**Parking:** Adequate off-street parking.
**In-Room:** Color cable TV, telephone, ceiling fans, kitchen, refrigerator, coffee & tea-making facilities.
**Exercise/Health:** Jacuzzi.
**Swimming:** Nearby pool.
**Sunbathing:** On private & common sun decks & patio.
**Smoking:** Permitted outside. Non-smoking rooms available.
**Pets:** Permitted. Check first.
**Handicap Access:** No.
**Children:** Welcome.
**Languages:** English.
**Your Host:** Len & Robbie.

## Four Kachinas Inn Bed & Breakfast

Gay-Friendly ♀♂

### *Our Breakfasts Will Win Your Acclaim*

On a quiet street, built around a private courtyard, ***Four Kachinas Inn*** is a short walk from the historic Santa Fe Plaza via the Old Santa Fe Trail. Rooms have private baths & entrances and southwestern furnishings which include antique Navajo rugs, Hopi kachina dolls, handcrafted wooden furniture and saltillo tile floors. A continental-plus breakfast, prepared by our award-winning baker, is served in your room. Rated 3 diamonds by AAA. **Guest Comments:** *"I was born in New Mexico, and this B&B felt like home....Great breakfasts here, too." -Felix, Berkeley, CA*

**Address: 512 Webber St, Santa Fe, NM 87501**
**Tel: (505) 982-2550, (800) 397-2564.**

**Type:** Bed & breakfast.
**Clientele:** Mostly straight clientele with gays & lesbians welcome.
**Transportation:** Car is best.
**To Gay Bars:** 3 blocks. A 10-minute walk or 5-minute drive.
**Rooms:** 5 rooms with single, queen or king beds.
**Bathrooms:** All private.
**Meals:** Expanded continental breakfast.
**Vegetarian:** Available.
**Complimentary:** Tea, soft drinks & cookies every afternoon in guest lounge.
**Dates Open:** Feb 1-Jan 4.
**High Season:** May 1-Oct 31 & major holidays.
**Rates:** High seas. $98-$125. Low seas. $88-$110.
**Credit Cards:** MC, VISA, Discover.
**Rsv'tns:** Required.
**Reserve Through:** Travel agent or call direct.
**Minimum Stay:** 3 nights high season weekends, 2 nights low season wknds. 3-5 nights certain holidays & special events.
**Parking:** Adequate free off-street parking.
**In-Room:** Color cable TV, ceiling fans, tele. & maid serv.
**On-Premises:** Guest lounge (no TV).
**Exercise/Health:** Nearby gym, weights, Jacuzzi, sauna, steam & massage.
**Swimming:** Nearby pool.
**Sunbathing:** On the patio.
**Smoking:** Permitted outside only. All rooms are non-smoking.
**Handicap Access:** Yes. 1 room & guest lounge are wheelchair accessible.
**Children:** Not especially welcome.
**Languages:** English, Spanish, some French.
**Your Host:** Andrew & John.

## Inn of the Turquoise Bear

Q-NET Gay/Lesbian ♀♂

### *Where the Action Is... Stay Gay in Santa Fe!*

The ***Inn of the Turquoise Bear*** occupies the home of Witter Bynner (1881-1968), a prominent gay citizen of Santa Fe, active in cultural and political affairs. A noted poet, essayist and translator, Bynner was a staunch advocate of human rights (supporting the suffrage movement and the rights of Native Americans and other minorities) and a vocal opponent of censorship.

Bynner's rambling adobe villa, built in Spanish-Pueblo Revival style from a core of rooms dating to the mid 1800's, is one of Santa Fe's most important historic estates. With its signature portico, tall pines, magnificent rock terraces, meandering paths, and flower gardens, the inn offers guests a

*continued next page*

romantic retreat close to the center of Santa Fe. As the largest gay-oriented bed & breakfast in Santa Fe, the ***Turquoise Bear*** is the perfect choice for both couples and individuals traveling alone.

Bynner and Robert Hunt, his lover of more than 30 years, were famous for the riotous parties they hosted in this house, referred to by Ansel Adams, a frequent visitor, as "Bynner's Bashes." Their home was the gathering place for the creative and fun-loving elite of Santa Fe and guests from around the world. Their celebrity guests included D.H. & Frieda Lawrence, Igor Stravinsky, Willa Cather, Errol Flynn, Martha Graham, Christopher Isherwood, Georgia O'Keeffe, Rita Hayworth, Thornton Wilder, Robert Frost – and many others.

Ralph and Robert, the new owners of the Witter Bynner Estate, reside on the property. Their goals are to rekindle the spirit of excitement, creativity, freedom and hospitality for which this remarkable home was renowned; to protect, restore and extend the legacy of its famous gay creator; and to provide their guests with the experience of a unique setting that captures the essence of traditional Santa Fe. Whether you are coming to New Mexico for the opera, the art scene, the museums, skiing, hiking, exploring Native American and Hispanic cultures, or just to relax away from it all, the ***Inn of the Turquoise Bear*** is the place to stay in Santa Fe. Robert and Ralph look forward to the privilege of serving as your hosts during your visit.

**Address: 342 E Buena Vista Street, Santa Fe, NM 87501**
**Tel: (505) 983-0798, (800) 396-4104, Fax: (505) 988-4225,**
**E-mail: bluebear@roadrunner.com.**

**Type:** Bed & breakfast inn.
**Clientele:** 70% gay & lesbian and 30% straight clientele
**Transportation:** Car is best, shuttle bus from Albuquerque airport.
**To Gay Bars:** 8 blks, 1 mi, 20 min walk, a 2 min drive.
**Rooms:** 9 rms, 2 suites with dbl, queen or king beds.
**Bathrooms:** Private: 1 bath/toilet, 4 shower/toilets, 4 bath/shower/toilets. Shared: 1 shower only.
**Meals:** Expanded continental breakfast.
**Vegetarian:** Available nearby.
**Complimentary:** Tea, coffee & fruit all day. Wine & cheese in afternoon. Sherry & brandy in common room. Chocolates on pillows.
**Dates Open:** All year.
**High Seas.:** Apr-Oct & Dec.
**Rates:** Per room, dbl occ.: high season $90-$210, low season $80-$180.
**Discounts:** 10% for AAA, AARP & Weekly rate.
**Credit Cards:** MC, Visa, Amex.
**Rsv'tns:** Required, but we accept late inquiries.
**Reserve Through:** Travel agent or call direct.
**Minimum Stay:** Required during certain holidays.
**Parking:** Ample free, walled/ gated off-street parking.
**In-Room:** Color cable TV, VCR, fans, telephone, maid service. Some rooms have refrigerators.
**On-Premises:** Meeting rooms, video tape, book libraries, fax (send/ rec.).
**Exercise/Health:** Jacuzzi. Nearby gym, weights, Jacuzzi, sauna, steam, massage.
**Swimming:** Pool nearby.
**Sunbathing:** On patios.
**Nudity:** Permitted in various patio areas.
**Smoking:** Permitted on patios, not in rms or public rms.
**Pets:** Small pets OK in some rooms.
**Handicap Access:** One guest rm accessible, no access to rest of the building.
**Children:** Over 12 years OK, but children discouraged.
**Languages:** English, Spanish, French, Norwegian, German.
**Your Host:** Ralph & Robert.

IGTA

## Open Sky B&B

**Gay-Friendly 50/50 ♀♂**

### *An Endless Open Vista*

Want to get away from it all? ***Open Sky B&B*** is a spacious and serene adobe with spectacular open views of Jamez, the Sangre de Cristo and Ortiz Mountains, and Santa Fe. Located off the historical Turquoise Trail in the countryside of Santa Fe, this B&B offers privacy and peace to enjoy the natural beauty that has made this area popular. Three rooms furnished in southwest decor have king- or queen-sized beds and private baths. A breakfast of fresh breads and fruit is served at individual tables outside the rooms.

**Address: 134 Turquoise Trail, Santa Fe, NM 87505**
**Tel: (505) 471-3475, (800) 244-3475, E-mail: skymiller@aol.com.**

**Type:** Bed & breakfast.
**Clientele:** 50% gay & lesbian & 50% straight clientele
**Transportation:** Car is best, shuttlejack from airport.
**To Gay Bars:** 16 miles.
**Rooms:** 3 rooms with queen or king beds.
**Bathrooms:** All private
**Meals:** Expanded continental breakfast.
**Vegetarian:** Available upon request.
**Complimentary:** Gour. coffee, herb teas, fresh flowers!
**Dates Open:** All year.
**High Season:** Sum. & holi.
**Rates:** $70-$120.
**Disc:** 10% for 7 + nights.
**Credit Cards:** Visa, MC, Discover, Amex.
**Rsv'tns:** Preferred for guaranteed availability.
**Reserve Through:** Call direct or travel agent.
**Parking:** Ample off-street SAFE parking.
**In-Room:** Color TV, telephone, refrigerator.
**On-Premises:** Large 600 sq. ft. living room with fireplace.
**Exercise/Health:** Jacuzzi, cross-country skiing, hiking, bicycling & massage.
**Swimming:** At nearby river & lake.
**Sunbathing:** On the patio.
**Smoking:** Permitted outside only. Entire B&B is smoke-free.
**Pets:** Please inquire.
**Handicap Access:** Yes.
**Children:** Permitted with restrictions.
**Languages:** English & German.

## The Triangle Inn-Santa Fe

**Gay/Lesbian ♀♂**

### *Internationally Acclaimed... Exclusively Lesbian & Gay*

Santa Fe is one of the world's most desirable destinations, offering the visitor an extraordinary range of vacationing opportunities. ***The Triangle Inn*** is Santa Fe's sole exclusively lesbian and gay property and is the perfect retreat from which to explore all that Northern New Mexico offers.

The Inn is a rustic adobe compound, dating from the turn of the century, located on an acre of pinon- and juniper-studded land. It offers nine very distinct private casitas, ranging from studios to a two-bedroom house. Each is furnished in Southwestern style with Mexican and handmade furniture and has living and sleeping areas, kitchenettes and private baths. Most have kiva fireplaces and private patios. Special attention has been paid to details – the rooms are appointed with TV/VCRs, stereo/ CD players, air conditioning, telephones, and down comforters. Further amenities include gourmet teas, coffees and cocoas, bath robes and spa towels. A scrumptious continental breakfast is provided to you, in your casita, each day.

***The Triangle Inn*** has two large courtyards. The Hacienda Courtyard boasts a stunning free-standing portal with an outdoor fireplace and guest gathering areas. Afternoon refreshments are provided in this delightful setting, which is also frequently used for commitment ceremonies and other functions. The Main Courtyard, around which most of the casitas are situated, has extensive plantings, a large hot tub, deck and sunbathing areas.

Although Santa Fe is not a gay resort, our visitors always find themselves comfortable in this small but sophisticated artist colony. The region offers more opportunities than most – world-class opera, a famed art market, 260 restaurants, miles of hiking and skiing trails, native American pueblos and ruins, Spanish and Mexican culture, and, of course, our world-renowned views. Come to ***The Triangle Inn – Santa Fe*** and discover the real Southwest!

**Address:** PO Box 3235, Santa Fe, NM 87501
**Tel:** (505) 455-3375 (Tel/Fax), **E-mail:** TriangleSF@aol.com.

*continued next page*

**Type:** Inn.
**Clientele:** Good mix of gays & lesbians.
**Transportation:** Car is best.
**To Gay Bars:** 10 miles to gay/lesbian bars.
**Rooms:** 9 cottages with queen & king beds & kitchenettes.
**Bathrooms:** All private.
**Meals:** Expanded continental breakfast & fully equipped kitchen.
**Vegetarian:** All breakfasts are vegetarian.
**Complimentary:** Gourmet coffee, herbal teas, juices, snacks & afternoon cocktail gatherings.
**Dates Open:** All year.
**High Season:** April-October, Thanksgiving & Christmas.
**Rates:** Low season $70-$125. High season $80-$135.
**Discounts:** On weekly stays.
**Credit Cards:** MC, VISA & Eurocard.
**Rsv'tns:** Recommended.
**Reserve Through:** Travel agent or call direct.
**Minimum Stay:** 3 days during holidays.
**Parking:** Ample, free, off-street parking.
**In-Room:** TV/VCR, stereo/CD player, AC, telephone, ceiling fans, robes, spa towels, kitchenettes, refrigerator, coffee/tea-making facilities & maid service. Some rooms have fireplaces.
**On-Premises:** 2 common courtyards (1 with covered portal & outdoor fireplace, 1 with hot tub & sun deck), VCR tape library, games.
**Exercise/Health:** Jacuzzi on premises. Nearby gym, weights, sauna, steam & massage.
**Swimming:** Nearby pool.
**Sunbathing:** On private & common sun decks.
**Smoking:** Non-smoking rooms available.
**Pets:** Permitted with advance notice ($5 per day).
**Handicap Access:** Yes.
**Children:** Children of all ages welcome.
**Languages:** English & Spanish.
**Your Host:** Sarah & Karan.

# TAOS

## The Ruby Slipper

SEE SPECIAL PAGE 25 COLOR SECTION

Q-NET Gay/Lesbian ♀♂

### *A Perfect Balance of Privacy & Personal Attention*

At ***The Ruby Slipper,*** our guest rooms, individually decorated with handmade furniture, have private baths and fireplace or woodstove. Breakfast specialties include scrumptious breakfast burritos, omelettes and banana pancakes. Our lovely grounds are complete with an outdoor hot tub. A vacation in Taos might include hiking, horseback riding, world-class skiing, gallery viewing, shopping or visiting Taos Pueblo. ***The Ruby Slipper*** is Northern New Mexico's most popular and relaxing gay-friendly bed and breakfast. Come see what everybody's talking about!

**Address: PO Box 2069, Taos, NM 87571. Tel: (505) 758-0613.**

**Type:** Bed & breakfast.
**Clientele:** Mostly gay/lesbian with some straight clientele.
**Transportation:** Car is best. 2-1/2 hours from Albuquerque by car. Taxi from bus stop to Ruby Slipper, $5.
**To Gay Bars:** 1-1/4 hours to Santa Fe gay & lesbian bars.
**Rooms:** 7 rooms with dbl, queen or king beds.
**Bathrooms:** All private.
**Meals:** Full breakfast.
**Vegetarian:** Available.
**Complimentary:** In-room coffee-maker/fresh ground coffee & assorted teas.
**Dates Open:** All year.
**High Season:** Summer, holidays and ski season.
**Rates:** $79-$104 per night for two, $94-$119 for Xmas holidays.
**Discounts:** On weekly stays, if booked directly.
**Credit Cards:** MC, Visa, Amex, Discover.
**Rsv'tns:** Recommended.
**Reserve Through:** Travel agent or call direct.
**Minimum Stay:** 2-3 days on holidays.
**Parking:** Adequate free off-street parking.
**In-Room:** Maid service, some fireplaces, ceil. fans, coffee/tea-making facilities.
**On-Premises:** Telephone, common room for guests, refrigerator stocked with items for purchase.
**Exercise/Health:** Hot tub on the premises, health club in town.
**Swimming:** 10 minutes to pool, 20 to Rio Grande.
**Sunbathing:** On hot tub deck or patio.
**Nudity:** Permitted in the hot tub.
**Smoking:** Permitted outdoors.
**Handicap Access:** Yes, call for details.
**Children:** Permitted.

IGTA

# NEW YORK

## ANGELICA

### Jones Pond Campground

Men ♂

*Jones Pond Campground* is an all-male, adult retreat on 119 rustic acres with two large natural trails and 135 sites. All trailer and RV sites have electric & water hookups, picnic tables and fireplaces. Many tent sites have picnic tables and fireplaces, and some have water and electric. The camp store has basic supplies and grocery items. There is a two-story recreation hall, a large pond, a 65-foot swimming pool, volleyball and basketball courts, and a baseball diamond. Events include variety, car & craft shows, Leather weekends, Christmas in July, pool/pizza parties, and Fantasy weekends.

**Address: 9835 Old State Rd, Angelica, NY 14709-9729**
**Tel: (716) 567-8100, Fax: (716) 567-4518,**
**E-mail: jonespond-dorin@worldnet.att.net.**

**Type:** Campground.
**Clientele:** Men only
**Transportation:** Car is best.
**To Gay Bars:** 1-1/2 hr to Buffalo or Rochester.
**Rooms:** Trailers for rent (you supply bedding & utensils).
**Bathrooms:** 2 shower/toilet facilities/4 showers each.
**Campsites:** Tent & trailer sites, 135 with elec. & water.
**Dates Open:** May 2-Oct 5.
**High Season:** July-Sep.
**Rates:** Rates vary, call for brochure.
**Discounts:** For weekly & monthly stays.
**Credit Cards:** Visa, MC, Discover, Novus.
**Rsv'tns:** Required, with a $20 deposit.
**Reserve Thru:** Call direct.
**Parking:** Ample free parking.
**On-Premises:** TV lounge, exercise area, gathering room, dance room with DJ.
**Exercise/Health:** Weights.
**Swim.:** Pool on premises.
**Sunbathing:** At poolside.
**Nudity:** Permitted at the pool & in nonrestricted areas.
**Smoking:** Permitted.
**Pets:** Permitted on leash.
**Handicap Access:** Yes.
**Children:** Not permitted.
**Your Host:** Wayne & Roger.

## CATSKILL MOUNTAINS

### Bradstan Country Hotel

Gay-Friendly ♀♂

## *That Uptown Feeling in Upstate N.Y.*

After a 21 month, painstaking renovation, ***Bradstan Country Hotel*** was awarded The First Sullivan County Board of Realtors Award for Architectural Excellence. In addition to our large comfortable rooms, the ***Bradstan*** also features a 70-foot private deck and a 60-foot front porch overlooking beautiful White Lake, where your favorite water activities are at your beck and call. At the end of the day, order up your favorite cocktail and enjoy the live cabaret entertainment in ***Bradstan's*** own piano bar lounge. All this just 2 hours from NYC. Ask us about hosting your special affair or meeting at our inn.

**Address: Route 17B, PO Box 312, White Lake, NY 12786**
**Tel: (914) 583-4114 (Tel/Fax).**

**Type:** Bed & breakfast inn with cottages & bar.
**Clientele:** Mainly straight clientele with a gay & lesbian following.
**Transportation:** Car is best, no charge for pick up, prior arrangement required.
**To Gay Bars:** Piano bar on premises w/ mixed crowd.
**Rooms:** 2 rooms, 3 suites & 2 cottages with queen beds.
**Bathrooms:** All private.
**Meals:** Expanded continental breakfast.
**Vegetarian:** Our breakfast is acceptable for vegetarians.
**Dates Open:** Open weekends all year & 7 days a week from 4/1 to 8/31.
**High Season:** Memorial Day to Labor Day.

*continued next page*

**Rates:** $105-$115 summer, $75-$85 winter.
**Discounts:** Discounts available to groups & stays of 5 nights or more.
**Credit Cards:** MC, VISA, Discover, Amex.
**Rsv'tns:** Recommended.
**Reserve Thru:** Call direct.
**Minimum Stay:** 2 night min. stay on weekends from Memorial Day to 10/31.
**Parking:** Free adequate on-street & off-street parking.
**In-Room:** B&B: AC, maid service, ceiling fans. Year-round cottages have color cable TV, full kitchens.
**On-Premises:** Piano lounge, meeting rooms.
**Swimming:** At private lake.
**Sunbathing:** On sun deck or private lake front.
**Smoking:** Permitted.
**Pets:** Not permitted.
**Children:** Permitted with prior arrangement, over the age of 8.
**Languages:** English.
**Your Host:** Scott & Edward.

# COOPERSTOWN

## Toad Hall

Gay-Friendly ♀♂

***Toad Hall,*** circa 1824, is a large stone farmhouse restored to highlight its early American ambiance, featuring the original beehive bread oven. Large bedrooms have private baths tiled in slate. Downstairs are eclectic furnishings and a wall mural depicting local history. In 1992, *Country Living Magazine* featured us in March, and *Country Inns Magazine* in December. ***Toad Hall*** is minutes from both the baseball and soccer halls of fame, the Glimmerglass Opera, the Fenimore House Folk Art Museum, the Farmer's Museum, the Corvette Museum and Lake Otsego.

**Address: RD 1 Box 120, Fly Creek, NY 13337. Tel: (607) 547-5774.**

**Type:** Bed & breakfast with custom furniture, folk art & gift shop.
**Clientele:** Mostly straight clientele with a gay & lesbian following
**Transportation:** Car.
**To Gay Bars:** 30 minutes to Utica gay/lesbian bars.
**Rooms:** 3 rooms with queen beds.
**Bathrooms:** All private bath/toilets.
**Meals:** Full breakfast.
**Vegetarian:** Upon advance request.
**Complimentary:** Coffee, tea, upon request.
**Dates Open:** All year.
**High Season:** June -Oct.
**Rates:** $85.
**Credit Cards:** MC, Visa, Amex & Discover.
**Rsv'tns:** Required in sum.
**Reserve Through:** Travel agent or call direct.
**Minimum Stay:** Holiday weekends.
**Parking:** Ample off-street parking.
**In-Room:** Color cable TV, AC & ceiling fans.
**Exercise/Health:** Nearby gym, weights, Jacuzzi, sauna, steam, massage, bowling, handball & nautilus.
**Swimming:** Six mi to lake.
**Sunbathing:** At lakeside or on sun deck.
**Smoking:** Not permitted.
**Children:** Permitted 12 years & over.
**Languages:** English, limited Spanish.

# EAST HAMPTON

## Centennial House

Gay Friendly ♀♂

### *Welcome to Another, Less Hurried Era*

Sumptuous describes the impression ***Centennial House*** makes as you leave the hectic world behind. Crystal chandeliers, a breasted fireplace, and a concert grand grace the parlor filled with antiques and collectibles in the English eclectic style. The formal dining room is lush with Scalamandre silk draperies and Chippendale chairs around a commodious table groaning each morning with the house specialties: banana buttermilk pancakes, blueberry and strawberry French toast, eggs, and slabs of ham. Each guest room, with a variety of antique furnishings, has a private bath, robes, fresh flowers, and chocolate truffles.

**Address: 13 Woods Lane, East Hampton, NY 11937**
**Tel: (516) 324-9414, Fax: (516) 324-2681.**

**Type:** Bed & breakfast.
**Clientele:** Mostly straight clientele with a gay/lesbian following
**Transportation:** Car is essential.
**To Gay Bars:** 1 mile, a 10-minute drive to The Swamp.
**Rooms:** 5 rooms with double, queen or king beds.
**Bathrooms:** Private: 2 shower/toilets, 3 bath/shower/toilets.
**Meals:** Full breakfast.
**Vegetarian:** On request. Available nearby.
**Complimentary:** Sherry, port, sparkling water, snack bags, chocolate truffles.
**Dates Open:** All year.
**High Season:** June-August.
**Rates:** High season $225-$375, quiet season $150-$300.
**Discounts:** Midweek discounts.
**Credit Cards:** MC, Visa.
**Rsv'tns:** Required.
**Reserve Through:** Call direct.
**Minimum Stay:** Required.
**Parking:** Ample free off-street parking.
**In-Room:** Color cable TV, VCR, telephone, AC, maid service.
**On-Premises:** Meeting rooms, fax & secreterial services, video tape library.
**Exercise/Health:** Gym, weights, massage. Nearby gym, weights, Jacuzzi, sauna, steam, massage.
**Swimming:** Pool on premises. Nearby ocean.
**Sunbathing:** At poolside & at beach.
**Smoking:** No smoking indoors.
**Pets:** Not permitted.
**Handicap Access:** No.
**Children:** Welcome over 12 years of age only.
**Languages:** English, French.
**Your Host:** Harry & David.

# ELMIRA - CORNING

## Rufus Tanner House

**Gay-Friendly 50/50 ♀♂**

"Peaceful," "A great time," and "Can we live here?" are some of the comments we've had from guests at our 1864 Greek Revival farmhouse. Wonderful antiques help retain the charm of the tastefully and comfortably updated interior. Find a spot on our 2-1/2 acres of lawn and garden to relax or hold your commitment ceremony, and a romantic dinner for 2 is always a possibility, followed by a dip in the outdoor hot tub. Stay with us at ***Rufus Tanner House*** just 1 or 2 nights or enjoy one of our packages. See you soon!

**Address: 60 Sagetown Rd, Pine City, NY 14871. Tel: (607) 732-0213.**

**Type:** Bed & breakfast.
**Clientele:** 50% gay & lesbian & 50% straight clientele.
**Transportation:** Car is best. Free pick up from airport or bus.
**To Gay Bars:** 15 minutes to David & The Body Shop in Elmira, 45 minutes to Common Ground in Ithaca.
**Rooms:** 3 rooms with doubles & 1 queen bed.
**Bathrooms:** All private & 1 with Jacuzzi.
**Meals:** Choice of breakfast.
**Vegetarian:** Available upon request.
**Complimentary:** Tea, juice, soda.
**Dates Open:** All year.
**High Season:** May 1-November 1.
**Rates:** $40-$95 per night for two, $5 each extra guest.
**Discounts:** Special honeymoon & weekend packages & long-term stays of 4 or more nights.
**Credit Cards:** MC & VISA.
**Rsv'tns:** Preferred.
**Reserve Through:** Travel agent or call direct.
**Parking:** Ample free off-street parking.
**In-Room:** Maid & room service.
**On-Premises:** Baby grand piano, CDs, color cable TV, VCR, small video tape library, telephone, refrigerator, laundry facilities for long-term guests.
**Exercise/Health:** Weight machine, treadmill, running areas, outdoor hot tub. Jacuzzi in one room & nearby full service fitness center.
**Swimming:** Nearby creek. 45 min to Cayuga & Seneca Lakes.
**Sunbathing:** On common sun decks.
**Nudity:** Permitted in hot tub.
**Smoking:** Not permitted.
**Pets:** Not permitted.
**Handicap Access:** No.
**Children:** Permitted if well-behaved.
**Languages:** English.
**Your Host:** Bill & John.

# FIRE ISLAND

## Belvedere

Men ♂

For magnificent terrace views over 100 miles of water, with superb sunsets, stay at ***Belvedere.*** Many of our rooms have terraces because this old mansion was built in the tradition of a Venetian palace, complete with towers, domes, statuary and fountains. There are also sun decks, a hot tub, a Roman swimming pool and an extensive gym. Though our rooms are not large, they have frescoed ceilings, antiques, Oriental rugs and crystal chandeliers. Most have private baths.

**Address: Box 4026, Cherry Grove, Fire Island, NY 11782**
**Tel: (516) 597-6448.**

**Type:** Guesthouse and cottages.
**Clientele:** Men only
**Transportation:** Car, Long Island RR or air.
**To Gay Bars:** 2 blocks or a 5-minute walk.
**Rooms:** 30 rooms, 5 suites & 30 cottages with single, double & king beds.
**Bathrooms:** 20 private bath/toilets & 10 private sink/washbasins. Others share.
**Meals:** Continental breakfast weekends & holidays.
**Complimentary:** Coffee always available & cocktail parties on holiday weekends.
**Dates Open:** May 1st-Oct 15th.
**Rates:** Rooms $80-$100 weekdays, $300-$450 weekends.
**Credit Cards:** MC, Visa & Amex.
**Rsv'tns:** Required.
**Reserve Through:** Call direct.
**Parking:** Ample pay parking at ferry terminal on mainland.
**In-Room:** Refrigerator & ceiling fans. Some color TVs & VCRs.
**On-Premises:** TV lounge & coffee/tea-making facilities.
**Exercise/Health:** Gym, weights & Jacuzzi.
**Swimming:** Pool & 5 minutes to ocean beach.
**Sunbathing:** At poolside, beach, patio, roof, private and common sun decks.
**Nudity:** Permitted in all sunbathing areas.
**Pets:** Not permitted.
**Handicap Access:** Yes.
**Children:** Not permitted.
**Languages:** English & French.

IGTA

## Carousel Guest House

Men ♂

### *Sun, Surf & Solace Far From the Manhattan Crowd*

Fire Island is an island of contrasts. Here is the absence of autos, the presence of deer, the lull of the surf and the beat of the disco. Set in a garden among holly, cherry, pine, calendula, rose and zinnia, the ***Carousel Guest House*** offers a charming retreat near both the beach and Fire Island's gay night life.

**Address: PO Box 4001, Cherry Grove, Fire Island, NY 11782-0998**
**Tel: (516) 597-6612.**

**Type:** Guesthouse.
**Clientele:** Mostly men.
**Transportation:** Sayville ferry to island, then 2-minute walk.
**To Gay Bars:** 1 minute to bars.
**Rooms:** 2 rooms with twin beds & 9 with double beds.
**Bathrooms:** 3 shared & an outdoor shower.
**Meals:** Continental breakfast.
**Dates Open:** Spring (May)-fall (Oct).
**Rates:** $62-$175.
**Credit Cards:** MC, VISA & Amex.
**Rsv'tns:** Highly recommended.
**Reserve Through:** Call direct.
**Minimum Stay:** 2 nights on weekends.
**Swimming:** Ocean beach 300 ft away.
**Sunbathing:** On beach or common sun decks.
**Smoking:** Permitted.
**Pets:** Not permitted.
**Handicap Access:** No.
**Children:** Not permitted.
**Languages:** English.

## Cherry Grove Beach Hotel

Gay/Lesbian ♀♂

***Cherry Grove Beach Hotel,*** Fire Island's largest hotel, is located in the heart of town, only steps from the beach, restaurants, shops and bars. Choose between our economy and deluxe room with refrigerator, microwave, air conditioning, television/VCRs and telephones. Ask about reserving a room and receiving additional nights for only $19.97! It is home to the Ice Palace, offering New York's top DJs, drag shows, guest entertainers and theme parties. Lounge by our 30' by 60' pool or roam freely with deer on the finest natural beach in the world!

**Address: PO Box 537, Sayville, NY 11782-0537. Tel: (516) 597-6600.**

**Type:** Hotel with bar & disco.
**Clientele:** Good mix of gay men & women.
**Transportation:** Ferry.
**To Gay Bars:** Within 200 feet of 5 gay bars.
**Rooms:** 64 studio apartments with high rise sleep sofas for 2.
**Bathrooms:** All private.
**Vegetarian:** 3 restaurants have vegetarian alternatives.
**Dates Open:** May 1-October 1.
**High Season:** Memorial Day-Labor Day.
**Rates:** Off season $39-$299 & in season $69-$399.
**Discounts:** Group & mid-week. Ask about additional nights at $19.97.
**Credit Cards:** MC, VISA, Amex & Discover.
**Rsv'tns:** Required.
**Reserve Through:** Call direct.
**Minimum Stay:** Two nights on weekends.
**Parking:** At ferry terminal on the other side.
**In-Room:** Color TV, AC, maid service, telephone, ceiling fans, kitchen & refrigerator.
**Swimming:** In the 30' x 60' pool or at nearby ocean beach.
**Sunbathing:** At poolside or on the beach.
**Nudity:** Permitted on the beach.
**Smoking:** Permitted. Non-smoking rooms are available.
**Pets:** Not permitted.
**Handicap Access:** Yes. Rooms available.
**Children:** Not permitted.
**Languages:** English.
**Your Host:** Isaac.

# ITHACA

## Pleasant Grove B&B

Gay-Friendly 60/40 ♀♂

### *Ithaca and the Finger Lakes Wine Country*

***Pleasant Grove*** is a comfortable country home from the 1930s above the west shore of Cayuga Lake in the Finger Lakes wine country. Panoramic views from the deck make afternoon tea and morning breakfast special times. Hike, birdwatch and cross-country ski in our fields and woods. Taughannock Falls State Park provides swimming and boating on Cayuga Lake. Four golf courses are minutes away. Wineries, antique shops and fine restaurants make a visit memorable. Both Cornell University and Ithaca College are fifteen minutes away.

**Address: 1779 Trumansburg Rd (Rte 96), Jacksonville, NY 14854-0009**
**Tel: (607) 387-5420, (800) 398-3963, E-mail: jlg4@cornell.edu.**

**Type:** Bed & breakfast.
**Clientele:** 60% gay & lesbian & 40% straight clientele.
**Transportation:** Car.
**To Gay Bars:** 10 miles from gay/lesbian bar.
**Rooms:** 3 rooms with queen beds.
**Bathrooms:** 1 private, others share.
**Meals:** Full breakfast.
**Vegetarian:** Always available.
**Complimentary:** Afternoon tea, coffee.
**Dates Open:** All year.
**High Season:** May-Oct.
**Rates:** $60-$75.
**Rsv'tns:** Preferred.
**Reserve Through:** Call direct.

*continued next page*

**Minimum Stay:** During major university & college weekends.
**Parking:** Ample, free off-street parking.
**Exercise/Health:** Cross-country skiing, hiking & birdwatching. Golf courses nearby.
**Swimming:** Cayuga Lake & streams nearby.
**Sunbathing:** Common sun decks.
**Smoking:** Not permitted in the house.
**Pets:** Not permitted.
**Handicap Access:** No.
**Children:** Permitted over 12 years old by prior arrangement.
**Languages:** English & German.
**Your Host:** James & Robert.

# LAKE GEORGE

## King Hendrick Motel

Gay-Friendly ♀♂

### *Escape to the Adirondacks!*

***King Hendrick Motel*** consists of cabins and deluxe efficiencies in a quiet, secluded location three miles south of the village. All guest quarters have air conditioning, telephone and color cable TV. There is a private back deck with a panoramic view of the hills, a picnic area in the woods, a pool, walking/bike trails to the lake and spectacular fall foliage. We are only 20 minutes from Saratoga Springs with its antiquing and factory outlet shopping. Other area attractions are whitewater rafting, horseback riding, hiking, the Saratoga Performing Arts Center, the mineral baths and wonderful amusement parks.

**Address: 1602 State Route 9, Lake George, NY 12845**
**Tel: (518) 792-0418.**

**Type:** Motel, cabins & efficiencies.
**Clientele:** Mostly straight clientele with a gay/lesbian following
**Transportation:** Car is best.
**To Gay Bars:** 3 miles to gay/lesbian bar.
**Rooms:** 3 rooms, 8 apartments & 16 cottages with double beds.
**Bathrooms:** All private.
**Meals:** Continental breakfast.
**Dates Open:** All year.
**High Season:** Memorial Day through Labor Day, fall foliage.
**Rates:** $45-$120.
**Credit Cards:** MC, Visa, Amex & Discover.
**Rsv'tns:** Required.
**Reserve Through:** Call direct.
**Parking:** Ample free off-street parking.
**In-Room:** Color cable TV, AC, telephone, maid service & refrigerator.
**On-Premises:** Screened porch.
**Exercise/Health:** Nearby gym, sauna, steam, massage.
**Swimming:** Pool on premises, 3 miles to lake.
**Sunbathing:** At poolside & on private & common sun decks.
**Smoking:** Permitted.
**Pets:** Permitted.
**Children:** Welcome.
**Languages:** English & French.
**Your Host:** Nicole.

# LONG ISLAND

## One Thirty-Two North Main

Gay/Lesbian ♂

### *The Hot Place to be COOL This Summer*

To make each guest feel like a personal friend visiting has been the primary objective at ***One Thirty-Two North Main*** for 25 summers. On two tranquil acres, just steps from quaint village shops and trendy restaurants, we offer fifteen accommodations in various locations, including the main house, the annex, the cottage and the cabana, and an unusually inviting large and secluded swimming pool surrounded by a "jungle" of trees. From ***One Thirty-Two,*** it's a 5-minute drive or bike ride to one of the world's most beautiful beaches.

**Address: 132 N Main St, East Hampton, NY 11937**
**Tel: (516) 324-2246 or (516) 324-9771.**

**Type:** Mini-resort.
**Clientele:** Mostly men with women welcome.
**Transportation:** Car, train or bus. Short walk from Long Island RR station, Hampton Jitney & Hamptons on My Mind bus stops.
**To Gay Bars:** 4 miles to bar, disco & restaurant.
**Rooms:** 13 rooms, 1 apartment & 1 cottage with single, double or queen beds.
**Bathrooms:** 5 private shower/toilets & 8 shared bath/shower/toilets.
**Meals:** Continental breakfast.
**Dates Open:** May-Sept.
**High Season:** All weekends from July 4th to Labor Day.
**Rates:** $70-$225.
**Discounts:** On stays including 5 weekdays.
**Credit Cards:** MC, VISA, Amex.
**Rsv'tns:** Required.
**Reserve Through:** Travel agent or call direct.
**Minimum Stay:** 2 nights on weekends in July & August.
**Parking:** Ample free off-street parking.
**In-Room:** Maid service, refrigerator, ceiling fans. Some accommodations have AC.
**On-Premises:** TV lounge.
**Exercise/Health:** Nearby gym, weights, steam & massage.
**Swimming:** 20 ft by 50 ft pool on premises, 1 mile to ocean beach.
**Sunbathing:** At poolside, on patio or ocean beach.
**Nudity:** Permitted at poolside.
**Smoking:** Permitted without restrictions.
**Pets:** Permitted in cabana.
**Handicap Access:** Yes, very small step at back entrance.
**Children:** Permitted in annex or cabana.
**Languages:** English, Italian.
**Your Host:** Tony

IGTA

# NEW PALTZ

## The Golden Bear Farm

Q-NET Gay/Lesbian ♀♂

### *A 1784 Country Inn Less Than Two Hours from New York City*

Nestled in a 12-acre country setting, less than two hours from New York City is our historic 1784 stone house, ***Golden Bear Farm.*** The romantic guest rooms are appointed with feather beds and antique furnishings. Weather permitting, breakfasts are served on the outdoor patio overlooking the pool and meadows. The many wonderfully delicious and tempting breakfast offerings include savory Belgian waffles with fresh fruit and strawberry cream, a variety of omelettes, homemade popovers and quiche of the day. There is always a tasty array of fresh juices and a supply of tasty muffins such as maple-pecan, Swiss cheese and zucchini, and German apple.

Each evening, an elegant dinner is served on Wedgewood china and crystal in the candlelit dining room. The meals are prepared by the owner/chefs of the inn who were trained at the renowned Culinary Institute of America. Featured among the choices of entrees are chateaubriand for two, rack of lamb, poached salmon with lemon beurre blanc, and a seafood medly of scallops, shrimp and lobster in a creamy white sauce. Each dish is accompanied with locally grown vegetables. Vegetarian meals and low-fat dishes are always available upon request.

***Golden Bear Farm*** is in close proximity to the Mohonk Mt. House and Minnewaska State Park. Other historic and cultural attractions include FDR's home, the Vanderbilt mansion, old stone houses in New Paltz and Hurley, local college theater and concerts, local wineries, ski areas, Woodstock and West Point. **TO OPEN SPRING, 1997.**

*continued next page*

**Address: 1 Forest Glen Rd, New Paltz, NY 12561. Tel: (914) 255-1515.**

**Type:** Country inn.
**Clientele:** Mostly gay & lesbian with some straight clientele
**Transportation:** Car is best. Non-stop bus from NYC. Shuttle to Stewart Airport in Newburg, NY. Free pick up from train in Poughkeepsie or bus in New Paltz.
**To Gay Bars:** 12 mile, a 20 min drive to gay bars.
**Rooms:** 5-7 rooms, 1 suite with double or queen beds.
**Bathrooms:** 5 private bath/toilets, 2 shared bath/shower/toilets.
**Meals:** Continental breakfast Mon-Thurs. Expanded continental breakfast Fri-Sun. Dinner nightly.
**Vegetarian:** Always available with notice at time of reservation.
**Complimentary:** Set-up service, tea & coffee, mints on pillow.
**Dates Open:** All year.
**High Season:** April-Oct.
**Rates:** Inquire.
**Discounts:** Inquire.
**Credit Cards:** MC, Visa, Amex.
**Rsv'tns:** Required.
**Reserve Through:** Travel agent or call direct.
**Minimum Stay:** Required on certain holiday weekends.
**Parking:** Ample free off-street parking.
**In-Room:** Ceiling fans, coffee & tea-making facilities, VCR, maid & laundry service. Color TV in some rooms.
**On-Premises:** TV lounge, video tape library, fax, computer.
**Exercise/Health:** Massage. Spa to be completed in 1998.
**Swimming:** Pool on premises. Minnewaska State Park lake nearby.
**Sunbathing:** Poolside & on patio.
**Nudity:** Permitted poolside.
**Smoking:** Permitted in common rooms.
**Pets:** Ask when reservations are made.
**Your Host:** Robert & Jim.

# NEW YORK

## A Bed & Breakfast Abode, Ltd

Gay-Friendly ♀♂

### *Privacy & Luxury in a NYC Brownstone or Apartment*

Have your heart set on staying in one of those delightful, restored brownstones? Or how about a contemporary luxury apartment in the heart of Manhattan? ***Abode*** selects hosts with great care, and all homes are personally inspected to ensure the highest standards of cleanliness, attractiveness and hospitality. All the attractions of New York City–theatres, museums, galleries, restaurants, parks and shopping–are within easy reach. Select an unhosted contemporary luxury apartment or a private apartment, with country inn ambiance, in an owner-occupied brownstone.

**Address: PO Box 20022, New York, NY 10021**
**Tel: (212) 472-2000, (800) 835-8880.**

**Type:** Reservation service organization.
**Clientele:** Mostly straight clientele with a gay/lesbian following
**Transportation:** Taxi.
**To Gay Bars:** Within a few blocks in most Manhattan neighborhoods.
**Rooms:** 200 apartments. Most have queen beds, some double, some king.
**Bathrooms:** All private.
**Meals:** Fixings for continental breakfast provided in most apartments.
**Vegetarian:** Nearby supermarkets.
**Dates Open:** All year.
**Rates:** $100-$325 per night.
**Discounts:** Special rates for extended stays of 1 month or longer.
**Credit Cards:** Amex.
**Rsv'tns:** Required.
**Reserve Through:** Call direct.
**Minimum Stay:** Required.
**Parking:** Ample pay parking.
**In-Room:** Color/color cable TV, VCR, AC, telephone, answering machine, kitchen, refrigerator, coffee & tea-making facilities. Daily maid service can be arranged at guests' expense.
**On-Premises:** Laundry facilities at several apartments.
**Smoking:** We have smoking & non-smoking accommodations.
**Pets:** Not permitted.
**Handicap Access:** No.
**Children:** Over 12 years permitted in some apartments. Please inquire.
**Languages:** English.

# A Greenwich Village Habitué

Gay-Friendly 50/50 ♀♂

## *Your Perfect Home Away From Home*

***A Greenwich Village Habitué*** has fully-appointed apartments available in an owner-occupied 1830's Federal brownstone in the historic West Village. Antique filled apartments come complete with living room, sleeping alcove, dining alcove, fully-equipped kitchen and full bath. The apartments overlook a formal English garden. They are perfect for both business or tourism and are only a short distance from the Convention Center.

***As Quoted by Mimi Reed of*** **Food and Wine Magazine:** *"It was to our delight, an immaculate, graciously stocked and elegantly furnished apartment (with a mahogany sleigh bed) in a brownstone. It seemed a great bargain."*

**Address: New York's West Village. Tel: (212) 243-6495.**

**Type:** Private, fully-equipped apartments.
**Clientele:** Sophisticated, well-traveled persons, some of whom are gay & lesbian.
**Transportation:** Taxi or Cary bus.
**To Gay Bars:** Walking distance to most gay & lesbian bars.
**Rooms:** 2 fully-appointed private apartments with queen beds.
**Bathrooms:** Private.
**Vegetarian:** Complete vegetarian/health food center nearby.
**Dates Open:** All year.
**Rates:** $125 plus taxes (single or double occupancy).
**Rsv'tns:** Advance reservation required.
**Reserve Thru:** Call direct.
**Minimum Stay:** 3 nights.
**Parking:** Limited on-street pay parking.
**In-Room:** AC, color TV, telephone, answering machine, full kitchen, refrigerator, coffee & tea-making facilities. Daily maid service available for additional charge.
**Exercise/Health:** Nearby gym.
**Smoking:** Not permitted.
**Languages:** English, Spanish.
**Your Host:** Matthew & Lewis.

# Chelsea Mews Guesthouse

Gay ♂

## *Friendly, Private & Affordable*

Ours is an old fashioned atmosphere, with Victorian garden. Guestrooms are furnished with antiques, and there is even an antique shop on the ground floor. You'll find the location of ***Chelsea Mews*** very convenient to all attractions, transportation and shopping. Advance reservations are advised.

**Address: 344 W 15th St, New York, NY 10011**
**Tel: (212) 255-9174.**

**Type:** Guesthouse.
**Clientele:** All male
**Transportation:** Any city transportation.
**To Gay Bars:** 1-1/2 blocks.
**Rooms:** 8 rooms with single or double beds.
**Bathrooms:** 1 private bath/toilet, others share bath/shower/toilet.
**Meals:** Continental breakfast of coffee.
**Dates Open:** All year.
**Rates:** $75-$150.
**Rsv'tns:** Required.
**Reserve Through:** Call direct.
**Parking:** Ample on-street pay parking.
**In-Room:** Color TV, AC, telephone, refrigerator, coffee-making facilities & maid service.
**On-Premises:** Garden.
**Smoking:** All rooms non-smoking.
**Pets:** Not permitted.
**Handicap Access:** No.
**Children:** Not especially welcomed.
**Languages:** English.

## Chelsea Pines Inn

Q-NET Gay/Lesbian ♂

### *Your Passport to Gay New York*

*Fodor's Gay Guide USA* calls us "The best-known gay accommodation in the city... equidistant from the Village and Chelsea attractions... this 1850 town house is run by a helpful staff and has small but pleasantly furnished rooms... it's a great deal!" Bordering Greenwich Village and Chelsea, two of the most colorful and interesting gay areas of New York City, the ***Chelsea Pines Inn*** is the ideal place from which tourists can explore the city. A short walk away are restaurants, shops, clubs, and bars. The famous Christopher Street area is just 10 minutes away by foot. Both subway and bus stops at the corner make the entire city easily accessible.

The inn has newly decorated rooms, guest areas, and hallways; new carpeting; new lighting; and new colors. Charmingly decorated with vintage movie posters, the rooms have full- or queen-sized beds, direct-dial phones, air conditioning and central heating, color cable TVs with free HBO, refrigerators, and washing facilities. Daily maid service and a fax service is also available. And, despite its recent renovation, the inn still has modest rates.

A complimentary, expanded continental breakfast includes fresh fruit and homemade bread and is available in the outdoor garden when the weather permits. The inn is centrally located for airline travelers – JFK Airport is 45-60 minutes away, La Guardia Airport is 25-30 minutes away, and Newark Airport is 30-45 minutes from the inn.

**Address: 317 W 14th St, New York, NY 10014**
**Tel: (212) 929-1023, Fax: (212) 620-5646, E-mail: cpiny@aol.com.**

**Type:** Bed & breakfast inn.
**Clientele:** Mostly men with women welcome
**Transportation:** Car service to inn or bus to Manhattan, then taxi or subway.
**To Gay Bars:** 1/2 block to men's, 5-minute walk to women's bars.
**Rooms:** 25 rooms with double or queen beds.
**Bathrooms:** 5 private & 7 semi-private, others share. Sink in every room.
**Meals:** Expanded continental breakfast with homemade bread.
**Vegetarian:** Vegetarian restaurant nearby.
**Complimentary:** Coffee & cookies all day.
**Dates Open:** All year.
**High Season:** Spring, summer & fall.
**Rates:** \$75-\$99 plus taxes.
**Credit Cards:** All major cards.
**Rsv'tns:** Recommended.
**Reserve Through:** Call/fax direct, or travel agent.
**Minimum Stay:** 3 nights on weekends, 4 nights on holidays.
**Parking:** Paid parking in lot or garage (1 block).
**In-Room:** Maid service, color cable TV with free HBO, AC, phone & refrigerator.
**On-Premises:** Garden.
**Exercise/Health:** 1 block to gym.
**Smoking:** Permitted.
**Pets:** Not permitted.
**Handicap Access:** No.
**Children:** Not permitted.
**Languages:** English.
**Your Host:** Al, Jay & Tom.

IGTA

## Colonial House Inn

Q-NET Gay/Lesbian ♀♂

### *Being Gay Is Only Part of Our Charm*

***Colonial House*** is like a European hotel. The inn, on a quiet street in Chelsea, has 20 modern and impeccably clean rooms. All have color cable TV, radio and air conditioning, sinks and direct-dial phone. Some rooms have private baths and fireplaces. Most have refrigerators. The roof sun deck and homemade muffins at breakfast round out the amenities, but the real attraction here is service, including a 24-hour concierge. If you have any trepidation about the Big Apple, this is the place to stay. Winner of Out & About 1994-'96 Editor's Choice Award.

**Address: 318 W 22nd St, New York, NY 10011**
**Tel: (212) 243-9669, (800) 689-3779, Fax: (212) 633-1612.**

**Type:** Bed & breakfast inn.
**Clientele:** Good mix of gays & lesbians
**Transportation:** Airport bus to city, then taxi. Self-pay car service. Will arrange pick up from airport.
**To Gay Bars:** 1/2 block to several men's, 10-minute walk to women's bars.
**Rooms:** 20 rooms.
**Bathrooms:** 12 shared baths & 8 private. All rooms have washing facilities.
**Meals:** Continental breakfast. Fresh-baked homemade muffins, bagels, special house-blend coffee, assorted juices daily, fresh fruit & cereal.
**Complimentary:** Tea, coffee & mints.
**Dates Open:** All year.
**Rates:** $65-$99 daily, $420-$665 weekly, + tax.
**Discounts:** Weekly rates available.
**Credit Cards:** Not accepted.
**Rsv'tns:** Recommended.
**Reserve Through:** Travel agent or call direct.
**Parking:** On-street parking or 1/2 block to off-street pay parking.
**In-Room:** Maid service, color cable TV, AC, direct dial phones, radios, alarm clocks, some with refrigerators or fireplaces.
**On-Premises:** TV lounge.
**Exercise/Health:** Weights on premises. Gym & massage nearby.
**Sunbathing:** On common sun deck or rooftop.
**Nudity:** Permitted on sun deck.
**Smoking:** Permitted in rms.
**Pets:** Not permitted.
**Children:** Mature children permitted.
**Languages:** English, Spanish, Italian, French, German.

IGTA

## East Village Bed & Breakfast

Q-NET Women ♀

***East Village Bed & Breakfast*** is situated in a tasteful second-floor apartment located in an urban, multi-cultural, multi-ethnic neighborhood close to shops, galleries and affordable restaurants. Greenwich Village, SoHo, Chinatown and other areas of interest are within easy reach. The kitchen comes complete with items for preparing your own continental breakfast. You are usually on your own in your own apartment.

**Address: 244 E 7th St #6, New York, NY 10009. Tel: (212) 260-1865.**

**Type:** Bed & breakfast.
**Clientele:** Women only
**Transportation:** Airport bus to Grand Central Station or Port Authority in Manhattan. Then taxi or bus.
**To Gay Bars:** Twenty minute bus ride or a little longer walk.
**Rooms:** 2 rooms with single or double bed.
**Bathrooms:** 1 shared bath/shower/toilet.
**Meals:** Self-service continental breakfast.
**Complimentary:** Coffee, tea, juices & snacks.
**Dates Open:** All year.
**Rates:** $50-$75 per day for 1 or 2 people.
**Rsv'tns:** Required.
**Reserve Thru:** Call direct.
**Minimum Stay:** 2 nights on weekends.
**Parking:** Adequate free on-street parking.
**In-Room:** AC & telephone.
**On-Premises:** Guests may use kitchen, refrigerator & watch TV.
**Smoking:** Not permitted.
**Pets:** Usually permitted but call in advance.
**Handicap Access:** No. There are stairs.
**Children:** Permitted.
**Languages:** English.

# The New York Bed & Breakfast Reservation Center

Q-NET Gay ♂

## *Perfect Accommodations in New York, San Francisco, South Beach and Paris*

Having started out as the host of a Manhattan bed and breakfast, I know that potential guests appreciate getting a clear and honest description of the accommodations and of the surrounding neighborhood before they book. I know they appreciate dealing with a person who is not only interested in booking once, but looking down the road for repeat business.

***The New York Bed & Breakfast Reservation Center*** offers a wide variety of bed and breakfast accommodations in New York City at prices ranging from $60 to $90 per night. Several are within a few blocks of major Midtown hotels and theatres. We also have private studios and apartments for people who wish to be on their own. Unhosted facilities start at $100 per night, some less. Apartments are also available by the month. Our clients are not only tourists, but corporations who are trying to cut down on their corporate travel expenses. Our hosts are New Yorkers who make their guest rooms or apartments available for paying guests. Our hosted accommodations include continental breakfast.

All accommodations are personally inspected. I turn down an average of seven out of ten inquiries to join our center, although many have been doing bed and breakfast for years. I prefer to turn down a property, rather than to place someone in an accommodation that is not satisfactory. We can suggest reasonably-priced airport pick up to facilitate getting into New York. Aside from finding the most appropriate accommodations for our guests, we try to enhance their stay in New York by assisting in every way possible. And now, you can also call us for accommodations in San Francisco, CA, South Beach/Miami, FL and Paris, France.

**Address: Suite 221, 331 West 57th St, New York, NY 10019**
**Tel: (212) 977-3512, (800) 747-0868.**

**Type:** Bed & breakfast & apartments.
**Clientele:** Gay
**Transportation:** Taxi is best. Charge for pick up from public transportation stations.
**To Gay Bars:** Walking distance to most, depending on the accommodation.
**Rooms:** 25 rooms, 10 suites & 15 apartments.
**Bathrooms:** Most are private, but some are shared.
**Meals:** Continental breakfast at hosted accommodations.
**Complimentary:** Tea & coffee.
**Dates Open:** All year.
**Rates:** $60-$90 hosted or $100-$150 unhosted private apartments.
**Credit Cards:** Amex.
**Rsv'tns:** Required.
**Reserve Through:** Travel agent or call direct.
**Minimum Stay:** 2 days.
**Parking:** Variety of adequate parking conditions. On-street pay parking.
**In-Room:** Color TV, AC, ceiling fans, telephone, kitchen, & refrigerator.
**On-Premises:** Doorman & concierge service with secured buildings.
**Sunbathing:** On private sun decks when available.
**Smoking:** Permitted sometimes.
**Pets:** Permitted sometimes.
**Handicap Access:** Some are accessible.
**Children:** Permitted.
**Languages:** English, Spanish & French.

IGTA

## Three Thirty-Three West 88th Associates

Gay/Lesbian ♀♂

### *Beautifully-Furnished Apartments in Manhattan*

For visits to New York, consider these exceptional one-bedroom apartments, just restored, in an 1890's brownstone on the west side of Manhattan, directly across the park from the Metropolitan Museum of Art. From ***333 West 88th's*** safe and advantageous location, it's an easy trip, via subway or bus, to the theater district, the World Trade Center and the ferry to the Statue of Liberty. You can walk to Lincoln Center. Riverside Park, whose handsome promenade overlooks the Hudson, is 200 feet from the door. Apartments are unhosted, giving guests maximum independence. Coffee and tea are provided, and nearby groceries are open 24 hours a day.

**Address: 333 West 88th St, New York, NY 10024**
**Tel: (212) 724-9818, (800) 724-9888.**

**Type:** Bed & breakfast.
**Clientele:** Mostly gay & lesbian w/ some straight clientele
**Transportation:** Taxi from airports. #1 subway line to 86th St Station.
**To Gay Bars:** 8 blocks.
**Rooms:** Unhosted B&B apts & hosted B&B rooms.
**Bathrooms:** All private.
**Complimentary:** Coffee & tea set-up.
**Dates Open:** All year.
**Rates:** $420-$709 weekly.
**Discounts:** Jan/Feb -20%.
**Rsv'tns:** None with deposit.
**Reserve Thru:** Call direct.
**Minimum Stay:** 2-4 days.
**Parking:** Limited free on-street parking. Nearby garages suggested.
**In-Room:** Color TV, AC, telephone, kitchen & HiFi.
**Smoking:** Permitted.
**Pets:** Well-behaved animals permitted.
**Children:** Welcome.
**Your Host:** Albert.

# SENECA FALLS

## Guion House

Gay-Friendly ♀♂

The ***Guion House Bed & breakfast*** is a beautiful 1876 Second Empire home located in the historic district, one block from downtown, shops, museums and Women's Rights National Park.

**Address: 32 Cayuga St, Seneca Falls, NY 13148**
**Tel: (315) 568-8129, (800) 631-8919.**

**Type:** Bed & breakfast.
**Clientele:** Mostly straight clientele with a gay/lesbian following.
**Transportation:** Car is best.
**To Gay Bars:** 1 hour to Syracuse or Rochester gay & lesbian bars.
**Rooms:** 2 queens, 1 full, 1 room with 2 twin beds, rollaways available.
**Bathrooms:** 2 private, 1 shared.
**Meals:** Full candlelight breakfast.
**Vegetarian:** Available upon request.
**Dates Open:** Year round.
**High Season:** July, August, September, October.
**Rates:** $55-$85.
**Discounts:** For 4 + days.
**Credit Cards:** MC & VISA.
**Rsv'tns:** Suggested.
**Reserve Through:** Call direct.
**Parking:** Free off-street parking on premises.
**In-Room:** AC, maid service.
**On-Premises:** Library, double parlor.
**Exercise/Health:** Hiking at state parks, 5 minutes.
**Swimming:** 5 minutes to state park & lake.
**Smoking:** Permitted outdoors.
**Pets:** Not permitted.
**Handicap Access:** No.
**Children:** Children over 12 welcome.
**Languages:** English.

# WOODSTOCK AREA

## River Run Bed & Breakfast Inn

Q-NET Gay-Friendly ♀♂

### *A Century of Welcome*

Our exquisite 1887 Queen Anne "cottage" is surrounded by the Catskill Forest Preserve, with its magnificent hiking trails, splendid foliage and superb skiing. Our eclectic Victorian village features tennis, swimming, theatre, museum, antiques, a weekly country auction, horseback riding, and a variety of restaurants. Rejuvenate on our delightful wraparound porch or in our book-filled parlor, complete with piano and fireplace. Step into the oak-floored dining room, bathed in the colors of the inn's signature stained-glass windows, and enjoy homemade breakfasts and refreshments. At ***River Run,*** all are welcome, and all are made comfortable.

**Address: Main St, Fleischmanns, NY 12430**
**Tel: (914) 254-4884.**

**Type:** Bed & breakfast, 35 minutes from Woodstock, NY.
**Clientele:** Mostly straight clientele with a significant gay & lesbian following
**Transportation:** Car is best. Trailways bus stops at our front door, direct from NYC.
**To Gay Bars:** 35 miles or a 50-minute drive to Kingston.
**Rooms:** 8 rooms & 1 apartment with single, double, queen or king beds.
**Bathrooms:** Private: 3 shower/toilets, 3 bath/shower/toilets. 2 shared full baths.
**Meals:** Deluxe continental breakfast.
**Vegetarian:** Available upon request. Most diets accommodated.
**Complimentary:** Afternoon refreshments.
**Dates Open:** All year.
**High Season:** Memorial Day-Labor Day, Sep-Oct (foliage), Dec-Mar (skiing).
**Rates:** $50-$95.
**Discounts:** 10% for single & 4 or more night stays.
**Credit Cards:** MC, VISA.
**Rsv'tns:** Strongly recommended. Walk-ins accommodated if space is available.
**Reserve Through:** Travel agent or call direct.
**Minimum Stay:** 2 nights weekends, 3 nights holiday weekends.
**Parking:** Ample free on-street parking.
**In-Room:** Color & B/W TV, maid service. Kitchen in apartment.
**On-Premises:** TV lounge, VCR, tea-making facilities, fireplace & piano.
**Exercise/Health:** Massage. Nearby gym.
**Swimming:** Stream on premises. Nearby pool, river & lake.
**Sunbathing:** On private grounds & at nearby pool.
**Smoking:** Inn is non-smoking except for apartment accommodation.
**Pets:** Well-behaved, fully-trained, well-socialized pets permitted.
**Handicap Access:** Yes. Apartment is on ground level.
**Children:** Welcome. Rollaway, crib available.
**Languages:** English, French, German.
**Your Host:** Larry.

# NORTH CAROLINA

## ASHEVILLE

### Another Point of View

Gay/Lesbian ♀♂

#### *A View to Remember*

Covered decks on three sides of ***Another Point of View,*** a beautiful, nicely appointed guest apartment, provide spectacular, panoramic long-range views of Little Pisgah Mountain and Bearwallow Mountain. The apartment, with woodstove, is completely private with easy access to the Blue Ridge Parkway, Bat Cave, Chimney Rock, and Lake Lure. It's only minutes to downtown Asheville's dining, dancing, bars, and entertainment, and only 11 miles from the Biltmore House.

**Address: 108 Weeping Cherry Forest Rd, Fairview, NC**
**Tel: (704) 628-0005.**

**Type:** Guest apartment.
**Clientele:** Mostly gay & lesbian with some straight clientele.
**Transportation:** Car is best.
**To Gay Bars:** 10-15 minutes by car.
**Rooms:** 1 apt with queen bed & queen sleeper.
**Bathrooms:** Private bath/shower/toilet.
**Vegetarian:** Many vegetarian restaurants in town.
**Complimentary:** Welcome fruit & wine basket.
**Dates Open:** All year.
**High Season:** April-Oct.
**Rates:** 2 people $80/night; 3-4 people $100/night; $500 per week.
**Rsv'tns:** Required.
**Reserve Thru:** Call direct.
**Minimum Stay:** 2 nights.
**Parking:** Ample free off-street parking.
**In-Room:** Color TV, VCR, phone, kitchen, ref., microwave, ceiling fans, AC.
**On-Premises:** Stove, washer/dryer. Cooking & dining supplies provided.
**Sunbathing:** On sun decks.
**Smoking:** Permitted on outside deck only.
**Pets:** Not permitted.
**Children:** No.

### The Bird's Nest Bed & Kitchen

Women ♀

#### *Country Living in the City*

Seclusion and quiet are yours just a short walk from downtown Asheville, when you stay with us at ***The Bird's Nest Bed & Kitchen.*** Our inn sits on top of a hill overlooking both the city and the beautiful Blue Ridge Mountains. The views are magnificent. Your accommodations have a private entrance, private bath, master bedroom with sunporch, fully-equipped kitchen, and guests also have their own private living room and dining room on the second floor of our home. Boating, hiking, skiing and horseback riding are all available in the area.

**Address: 41 Oak Park Rd, Asheville, NC 28801. Tel: (704) 252-2381.**

**Type:** Guesthouse.
**Clientele:** Mostly women with men welcome
**Transportation:** Car is best.
**To Gay Bars:** 1 mile.
**Rooms:** 1 apartment with double & queen bed.
**Bathrooms:** Private.
**Vegetarian:** There are 2 excellent vegetarian restaurants within 1 mile.
**Complimentary:** Coffee, tea, cereal & staples.
**Dates Open:** All year.
**High Season:** May-Nov.

**Rates:** $75-$85 per night for 1-2 people. $400/week.
**Credit Cards:** MC, Visa, Discover, Amex.
**Rsv'tns:** Required.
**Reserve Thru:** Call direct.
**Minimum Stay:** 2 nights on weekends.
**Parking:** Ample off-street parking.
**In-Room:** AC, color TV, VCR, stereo, ceiling fans, telephone, kitchen, & ref.
**Exercise/Health:** Gym, weights, Jacuzzi, sauna, steam, & massage all 1/2 mile away.
**Swimming:** Pool 1/2 mile away.
**Sunbathing:** On private sun decks.
**Smoking:** Permitted outside.
**Pets:** Not permitted.
**Children:** Permitted on approval.
**Languages:** English & Spanish.
**Your Host:** Elizabeth Ann.

## Camp Pleiades

Q-NET Women ♀

### *A Mountain Retreat for Women*

Slow your pace and enjoy a new appreciation of nature at private, heavily wooded ***Camp Pleiades,*** a 67-acre mountain resort with stream-fed swimming pond and hiking trails leading into the Appalachian Trail. Activities include swimming, hiking, mountain biking, sports, arts and crafts, nature studies, bird watching, gardening, and general relaxation. Tennis, horseback riding and whitwater rafting are nearby. Theme weeks and weekends, such as Artist Residency Week and Family Camp, are scheduled throughout the season. Private and group cabins are available, some with bath. The central shower house has hot showers and flush toilets. Three family-style meals are served daily.

**Address: Route 2, Box 250, Hughes Gap Rd, Bakersville, NC 28705**
**Tel: summer (704) 688-9201, Fax: (704) 688-3449.**
**Winter call (904) 241-3050, Fax: (904) 241-3628.**
**E-mail: starcamp@aol.com.**

**Type:** Mountain resort with clothing shop.
**Clientele:** Women, with men welcome for Family Camp, group bookings, Labor Day-Halloween
**Transportation:** All major highway access or by air to Asheville or Tri-cities airport, TN. Fee for airport pickup.
**To Gay Bars:** 35 miles to Johnson City, TN.
**Rooms:** 11 cabins with single, double or queen beds.
**Bathrooms:** Private: 2 shower/toilets, 1 WC only. Shower house: 6 private showers, flush toilets & sinks, 1 tub, hot/cold H2O.
**Meals:** American Plan, picnic lunches for hikers & day trippers.
**Vegetarian:** Available.
**Complimentary:** Coffee, tea, cocoa, lemonade, snacks.
**Dates Open:** Memorial Day-Halloween.
**Rates:** Daily $45-$85, weekly $285-$535. Special rates for theme weeks & special events.
**Discounts:** 10% for groups of 6 or more in 1 cabin.
**Credit Cards:** MC, Visa, Amex.
**Rsv'tns:** Required.
**Reserve Through:** Call direct.
**Minimum Stay:** 2-day minimum.
**Parking:** Ample free off-street parking.
**On-Premises:** Meeting space, TV lounge with VCR & videos, library, board games, hammocks.
**Exercise/Health:** Hiking, sports.
**Swimming:** Pond on premises. Nearby pool, river & lakes.
**Sunbathing:** At pond & in open glens around property.
**Smoking:** Permitted in designated areas only. All buidings are non-smoking.
**Pets:** No pets.
**Handicap Access:** No. Sign language interpreters available with advance notice.
**Children:** Welcome with adult supervision & during annual Family Camp.
**Languages:** English.
**Your Host:** Barbara & Jacque.

## Carolina Bed & Breakfast

**Gay-Friendly ♀♂**

***Carolina Bed & Breakfast,*** a very comfortable 1900 Colonial Revival home, is located near downtown Asheville in the Montford Historic District. Five second-floor guest rooms are decorated in antiques and collectibles. All have private baths and air-conditioning and four have working fireplaces. There are two parlors and two porches for our guests to use and lovely gardens to stroll through. We are close to Biltmore House, the Blue Ridge Parkway, Great Smokey Mountains, regional crafts, excellent restaurants and shopping.

**Address: 177 Cumberland Ave, Asheville, NC. Tel: (704) 254-3608.**

**Type:** Bed & breakfast.
**Clientele:** Mostly straight clientele with a gay & lesbian following.
**Transportation:** Auto is best.
**To Gay Bars:** 1/2 mile. A 10-minute walk or 2-minute drive.
**Rooms:** 5 rooms with queen beds.
**Bathrooms:** 2 private bath/toilets & 3 private shower/toilets.
**Meals:** Full breakfast.
**Vegetarian:** Available upon request. There is an excellent vegetarian restaurant downtown.
**Complimentary:** Afternoon refreshments. Candy in guest rooms & public areas.
**Dates Open:** All year.
**High Season:** Apr-Dec.
**Rates:** $85-$100.
**Credit Cards:** MC, Visa, Discover, Amex.
**Rsv'tns:** Required.
**Reserve Through:** Travel agent or call direct.
**Minimum Stay:** 2 nights weekends & 3 nights on holiday weekends.
**Parking:** Ample off-street parking.
**In-Room:** AC & ceiling fans. Some rooms with fireplaces.
**Exercise/Health:** Massage. Nearby gym, weights, Jacuzzi & massage.
**Smoking:** Limited to porches only.
**Pets:** Not permitted.
**Handicap Access:** No.
**Children:** 12 years of age & older.
**Languages:** English.
**Your Host:** Sam & Karin.

## Emy's Nook

**Women ♀**

### *Quiet and Cozy Accommodations with a Homegrown Touch*

***Emy's Nook*** is situated in in-town Asheville, the premiere city of the western North Carolina mountains. Our guest space is for women who want the convenience of being in an attractive and tranquil place in the city combined with easy access to mountain fun. ***Emy's Nook*** is an Arts & Crafts-style home in a quiet tree-lined neighborhood, an area ideal for walking and cycling. We are only five minutes from the wide variety of shops, restaurants and nightlife that Asheville has to offer. Our accommodations are quiet and cozy with a homegrown touch.

**Address: 248 Forest Hill Dr, Asheville, NC 28803**
**Tel: (704) 281-4122 (Tel/Fax).**

**Type:** Guesthouse.
**Clientele:** Women only
**Transportation:** Car is best, airport, bus or train. We're on downtown bus line. Free pick up from bus, train. Pick up from airport $10 (pre-arranged, if possible).
**To Gay Bars:** A 25 minute walk, a 10 minute drive.
**Rooms:** 2 rooms with queen bed.
**Bathrooms:** One shared bath/shower/toilet.
**Meals:** Light continental breakfast.
**Vegetarian:** Many vegetarian possibilities nearby.
**Complimentary:** Tea & coffee.
**Dates Open:** All year.
**High Season:** April-Christmas.
**Rates:** $40 & $45 per night.
**Discounts:** 5% on stays of 4 or more nights.
**Rsv'tns:** Required.
**Reserve Through:** Travel agent or call direct.
**Parking:** Ample free on- or off-street parking. Street parking is very quiet with little traffic.
**In-Room:** B&W or color TV, ceiling fans, coffee & tea-making facilities.
**On-Premises:** Laundry facilities.
**Exercise/Health:** Nearby gym, weights, massage.
**Swimming:** Nearby river & lake.
**Sunbathing:** In private yard.
**Smoking:** Permitted on patio. All rooms are non-smoking.
**Pets:** Not permitted.
**Handicap Access:** No.
**Children:** No.
**Languages:** English.

## Mountain Laurel B&B

Women ♀

### *Distinctive, Classy Comfort in a Secluded, Mountain Setting*

***Mountain Laurel*** is in a new, contemporary home nestled into a ridge surrounded by mountain views, a secluded, private cove and 13 wooded acres. Gourmet breakfasts are a specialty, featuring such items as Eggs Benedict, blueberry pancakes, pecan waffles, french omelettes accompanied by orange juice, fresh fruit, homemade jams and plenty of coffee. Though there are many fine restaurants in nearby Asheville, you may choose to dine at the B&B. There's plenty to do, from whitewater rafting or hiking to the many diversions Asheville has to offer. Give ***Mountain Laurel*** a try. You won't be disappointed.

**Address: 139 Lee Dotson Rd, Fairview, NC 28730. Tel: (704) 628-9903.**

**Type:** Bed & breakfast.
**Clientele:** Mostly women with men welcome. Women-only space arranged upon request.
**Transportation:** Air to Asheville, then rent car or drive your own car.
**To Gay Bars:** 30 minutes to Asheville & 3 gay bars.
**Rooms:** 3 rooms with queen or king beds.
**Bathrooms:** All private full baths.
**Meals:** Full gourmet breakfast from a menu. Dinner with advance notice at additional charge. Gourmet menu.
**Vegetarian:** Available upon request. Vegetarian entrees on dinner menu.
**Complimentary:** Mints on pillows & cocktail set-ups.
**Dates Open:** All year.
**Rates:** $80-$100 double occupancy.
**Discounts:** Coupon specials in off season. Will trade accommodations with other B&B proprietors.
**Rsv'tns:** Required 2 weeks in advance.
**Reserve Through:** Call direct.
**Minimum Stay:** 2 nights July 1-Nov 1.
**Parking:** Ample free off-street parking.
**In-Room:** Ceiling fans, color TV & VCR. Phone & CD player in one room.
**On-Premises:** TV lounge, pool table, game room, piano, laundry facilities & refrigerator space.
**Exercise/Health:** 6-person hot tub, excercise equipment. Jacuzzi in 1 room. Hiking trails. Tubing & rafting 1 hour away in mountains.
**Swimming:** In Lake Lure 20 minutes away.
**Sunbathing:** On private & common sun decks.
**Nudity:** Permitted in 6-person hot tub under the stars or for sunbathing on decks.
**Smoking:** No smoking in house. Smokers are respected.
**Pets:** Not permitted.
**Handicap Access:** No. Could make some arrangements. Inquire.
**Children:** Not permitted.
**Languages:** English.

## Sophie's Comfort

Women ♀

### *Escape from Your Busy World to Sophie's Mountain Bliss*

At ***Sophie's Comfort*** enjoy a private upstairs area consisting of bedroom, bath and a morning room. Cuddle up and enjoy the view of the spectacular Blue Ridge Mountains from your windows. We are located ten minutes from the village of Black Mountain where you will find unique shops, delicious casual dining, crafts and antiques. Asheville restaurants, bars and dancing, the Biltmore Estate, arts and entertainment are just 20 minutes away. Front door hiking trails, outdoor activities and the Blue Ridge Parkway are special features of ***Sophie's Comfort.***

**Tel: (803) 787-5777 (Reservations).**

**Type:** Bed & breakfast.
**Clientele:** Women only
**Transportation:** Car is best.
**To Gay Bars:** A 30 minute drive.
**Rooms:** 1 suite with single or double beds.
**Bathrooms:** Private bath/toilet/shower.
**Campsites:** Parking is by side of house on a private road. Special arrangements must be made for van & RV parking.
**Meals:** Vegetarian continental breakfast. No meat served.
**Vegetarian:** 1 vegetarian restaurant in Black Mountain, several in Asheville.
**Complimentary:** Tea & coffee.
**Dates Open:** March 1-November 31.
**High Season:** May-October.

*continued next page*

**Rates:** $45-$55.
**Rsv'tns:** Required.
**Reserve Through:** Call direct.
**Minimum Stay:** 2 days & nights.
**Parking:** Limited on-street parking. Van & RV parking by special arrangement.
**In-Room:** Ceiling fans, coffee & tea-making facilities, CD/tape player radio.
**Smoking:** Permitted outside only.
**Pets:** Not permitted.
**Handicap Access:** No.
**Children:** No.

## Twenty-Seven Blake Street

Women. ♀

### *Charmingly Romantic, Private Gardens, Warm Hospitality*

If ***27 Blake Street*** were a character she would be a real lady – impeccably dressed, charmingly graceful and very personable. Come share 100 years of romantic charm (c. 1897) in this beautiful, turreted Victorian home, surrounded by gardens in a historic neighborhood. Your romantic room has a comfortable side porch, private entrance, private bath and fine antique furnishings. We are convenient to downtown, the Blue Ridge Parkway, gorgeous trails and waterfalls and the Biltmore Estate and village. We also cheerfully assist in directing guests to outstanding local restaurants.

Tel: (704) 252-7390.

**Type:** Bed (no breakfast).
**Clientele:** Women
**Transportation:** Easy walk to downtown. Car is best for exploring countryside.
**To Gay Bars:** Three minutes to 4 bars.
**Rooms:** 1 rm with dbl bed.
**Bathrooms:** 1 private.
**Meals:** Fine coffees in rm.
**Dates Open:** Usually all year.
**High Season:** October.
**Rates:** $65.
**Rsv'tns:** Appreciated.
**Reserve Thru:** Call direct.
**Minimum Stay:** 2 nights on weekends.
**Parking:** Off-street parking in lower garden area.
**In-Room:** Color cable TV, AC.
**Exercise/Health:** Hiking trails, rafting, gyms, tennis courts all nearby.
**Swimming:** Nearby pool, river, waterfalls & mountain streams with sliding rock.
**Smoking:** Outside, please. Smoke-free room.
**Pets:** Not permitted.
**Children:** Not permitted.

# BAT CAVE

## Old Mill B&B

Gay/Lesbian ♀♂

Come, be lulled to sleep on the banks of a rushing mountain stream in spectacular Hickory Nut Gorge. ***Old Mill B&B*** provides rustic comfort in rooms overlooking the river and hearty breakfasts of eggs benedict or soda-water pancakes with sausage and homemade apple sauce to fortify you for days of hiking, tubing, rafting, canoeing, tennis or golf. Shopping and dining are all close by, as is Asheville, Biltmore House, the Blue Ridge Parkway, Chimney Rock Park, Lake Lure, Flat Rock Playhouse, and the Carl Sandburg Home.

**Address: Hwy 64/74-A/9, Lake Lure Hwy, Box 252, Bat Cave, NC 28710**
**Tel: (704) 625-4256.**

**Type:** Bed & breakfast with gift shop.
**Clientele:** Mostly gay & lesbian with some straight clientele
**Transportation:** Car is best.
**To Gay Bars:** 20 miles to Asheville gay/lesbian bars.
**Rooms:** 4 rooms.
**Bathrooms:** All private.
**Meals:** Full breakfast.
**Complimentary:** Drinks on arrival.
**Dates Open:** All year.
**Rates:** $35-$85.
**Discounts:** 10% for INN Places readers.
**Credit Cards:** MC, Visa, Amex, Discover.
**Rsv'tns:** Recommended.
**Reserve Through:** Travel agent or call direct.
**Minimum Stay:** 2 nights on weekends.
**Parking:** Ample free on-street parking.
**In-Room:** Maid service, ceiling fans, & sitting areas. 3 rooms have color TV.
**On-Premises:** TV lounge with VCR.
**Exercise/Health:** Soloflex & hot tub.
**Swimming:** River out back with tubing.
**Sunbathing:** Sun decks.
**Smoking:** Permitted without restrictions.
**Pets:** Permitted with restrictions.
**Handicap Access:** Limited accessibility.
**Children:** Please call.
**Languages:** English & limited Spanish.
**Your Host:** Walt.

# BLOWING ROCK

## Stone Pillar B&B

Q-NET Gay-Friendly ♀♂

### *A Mountain Getaway for You & a Special Friend*

Visit ***Stone Pillar B&B*** for a homey atmosphere in a friendly, scenic mountain community on the Blue Ridge Parkway. ***Stone Pillar*** provides easy access to a quaint village and antique, craft, and specialty shops, fine restaurants, summer theatre, hiking, cross-country ski trails, seven ski slopes and some of the most beautiful scenery in the Blue Ridge Mtns. Relax in the rock garden or in front of a warm fire. Your hosts, George and Ron, can help you plan a variety of activities and events to make your visit to Blowing Rock a memorable one.

**Address: PO Box 1881, 144 Pine St, Blowing Rock, NC 28605**
**Tel: (704) 295-4141, (800) 962-9955.**
**E-mail: stonepillar@blowingrock.com.**
**http:www.blowingrock.com/northcarolina/stonepillar.**

**Type:** Bed & breakfast.
**Clientele:** Mostly straight clientele with a gay & lesbian following.
**Transportation:** Private auto is best.
**To Gay Bars:** 30 miles to Hickory, NC, gay bars.
**Rooms:** 6 rooms with single, double or queen beds.
**Bathrooms:** All private.
**Meals:** Full breakfast.
**Vegetarian:** Available with 24 hrs notice.
**Dates Open:** All year.
**High Season:** Summer & fall foliage.
**Rates:** $60-$95 summer, $55-$85 winter.
**Discounts:** 10% on stays of 4 nights, 10% for group taking the entire house.
**Credit Cards:** MC & VISA.
**Rsv'tns:** Advisable 4 weeks ahead in peak season.
**Reserve Through:** Call direct.
**Minimum Stay:** 2 nights on weekends, high season, & holidays.
**Parking:** Ample, off-street parking.
**In-Room:** Alarms, radios, ceiling fans.
**On-Premises:** Living & dining areas with fireplace.
**Exercise/Health:** All degrees of hiking trails nearby, whitewater rafting.
**Swimming:** 2 blocks to town pool.
**Smoking:** Permitted outdoors.
**Pets:** Not permitted.
**Handicap Access:** 1 room is handicap accessible.
**Children:** Not encouraged.
**Languages:** English.
**Your Host:** George & Ron.

# CHAPEL HILL

## Joan's Place

Women ♀

***Joan's Place*** is a B & B for women in my home, offering a rustic setting, secluded among trees, with a serene and picturesque environment. I have 2 bedrooms, one large with double bed, one smaller with double bed. There is a shared, full bath across the hall. Guests have access to my living room, with TV and stereo, ping-pong room downstairs, and large deck overlooking the trees. I am 2 miles south of Chapel Hill and UNC Campus, with easy access to Raleigh, Durham and Research Triangle Park.

**Address: c/o M. Joan Stiven, 1443 Poinsett Dr, Chapel Hill, NC 27514**
**Tel: (919) 942-5621.**

**Type:** Bed & breakfast.
**Clientele:** Women only
**Transportation:** Personal car only.
**To Gay Bars:** About 8 miles to Durham gay bar.
**Rooms:** 2 rooms with double beds.
**Bathrooms:** 1 shared bath/shower/toilet.
**Meals:** Continental breakfast.
**Vegetarian:** Available upon request. 2 vegetarian stores & vegetarian restaurants nearby.
**Complimentary:** Tea, coffee & juices.
**Dates Open:** All year.
**High Season:** Spring, summer and fall.
**Rates:** $45-$48 per night.
**Discounts:** Weekly rates.
**Rsv'tns:** Preferred.
**Reserve Through:** Call direct.
**Parking:** Ample, free off-street parking.
**In-Room:** AC & telephone.
**On-Premises:** TV lounge.
**Smoking:** Permitted outdoors.
**Pets:** Not permitted.
**Handicap Access:** No.
**Children:** Not permitted.
**Languages:** English.
**Your Host:** Joan.

# CRYSTAL COAST

## William & Garland Motel

Gay-Friendly ♀♂

### *Simple Accommodations in an Oceanside Setting*

***William & Garland Motel,*** a small family business, is oceanside with a lovely nature trail walkway to the beach. There are no phones and no pool. The rooms are clean and comfortable and guests who are quiet and who come to relax and enjoy a peaceful atmosphere are appreciated. The beach is located on a 20-acre plot called the Salter Path Dunes Natural Area. It is not crowded and is great for sunning, swimming, and fishing. Very good seafood restaurants – some with lounges – are within walking distance.

**Address: PO Box 204, Hwy #58, Salter Path, NC 28575**
**Tel: (919) 247-3733.**

**Type:** Motel with beach access & kitchen facilities.
**Clientele:** Mostly straight clientele with a gay/lesbian following.
**Transportation:** Car is best.
**Rooms:** 8 rms & 3 mobile homes with double beds.
**Bathrooms:** Private: 8 shower/toilets, 3 bath/shower/toilets.
**Meals:** Restaurants nearby.
**Vegetarian:** Possibly available at nearby restaurant.
**Dates Open:** Apr 1-Nov 30.
**High Season:** Memorial Day weekend-Labor Day.
**Rates:** $45-$60.
**Discounts:** 10% discount for paid stay of 7 nights.
**Credit Cards:** MC, VISA, Discover.
**Rsv'tns:** It's a good idea.
**Reserve Thru:** Call direct.
**Minimum Stay:** Required.
**Parking:** Adequate free parking.
**In-Room:** Color cable TV, AC, coffee/tea-making facilities, kitchen, ref.
**Exercise/Health:** Nearby fishing, amusement park.
**Swimming:** At nearby ocean.
**Sunbathing:** At beach.
**Smoking:** Permitted. No non-smoking rooms.
**Pets:** Permitted, 25 lbs & smaller.
**Children:** Permitted if quiet & well-behaved.

# WILMINGTON

## Rosehill Inn Bed & Breakfast

Q-NET Gay-Friendly ♀♂

### *Experience the Romance of a Bygone Era*

Welcome to ***Rosehill Inn,*** located in the heart of Wilmington's historic district, a wonderful place to relax and unwind. Built in 1848, the inn has been lovingly restored as an elegant yet comfortable bed and breakfast with an eclectic mix of antiques, sumptuous fabrics, fine linens, and beautiful gardens. Each of the large, luxurious guest rooms has been individually designed and decorated. They include a private bath, downy soft comforter, large fluffy towels, and a plush robe for your enjoyment. The 7,000-square-foot house is climate controlled for year-round comfort.

The inn is located just three blocks from the Cape Fear River. Wilmington's renovated riverfront and downtown district provide abundant opportunities for fine dining, outstanding entertainment, and unique shopping. The sparkling blue waters of the Atlantic Ocean, wide beaches, and world-class golf courses are within a 20-minute drive from the inn.

Included in your stay are afternoon refreshments served in our two parlors, nightly turn-down service with sweets, and a generous and healthy breakfast of homemade delights. Use of our bicycles, early morning coffee service, and many "little extras" make your stay memorable. The inn is suitable for children ages 12 and older. Smoking is permitted only on the verandas where you will find cozy seating. The inn has no televisions, ensuring a quiet atmosphere.

**Address: 114 South 3rd St, Wilmington, NC**
**Tel: (910) 815-0250, (800) 815-0250, Fax: (910) 815-0350.**

**Type:** Bed & breakfast.
**Clientele:** Mostly straight clientele with some gays & lesbians
**Transportation:** Car is best, 10 minutes from airport, boat via Intracoastal Waterway to Cape Fear River to Wilmington waterfront. Airport pick up by prior arrangement $10.
**To Gay Bars:** 1 block, a 4-5 minute walk.
**Rooms:** 6 rooms with queen or king beds.
**Bathrooms:** Private: 4 shower/toilets, 2 bath/shower/toilets.
**Meals:** Full breakfast.
**Vegetarian:** Available by request. Several restaurants nearby.
**Complimentary:** Sweets with turndown, soda, spring water, afternoon cookies & refreshments.
**Dates Open:** All year.
**High Season:** April 1-Jan 4.
**Rates:** High $125-$165, low $99-$135.
**Discounts:** Corporate Sun-Thurs $89-$110.
**Credit Cards:** MC, Visa, Amex, Discover.
**Rsv'tns:** Required. Walk-ins based on availability.
**Reserve Through:** Call direct.
**Minimum Stay:** 2-night minimum on weekends during high season, festivals & holidays.
**Parking:** Ample on-street & some off-street parking.
**In-Room:** AC, maid & laundry service. Some rooms have ceiling fans.
**On-Premises:** Meeting room, fax.
**Exercise/Health:** Massage by prior arrangement. Nearby gym & massage.
**Swimming:** Ocean 20 minutes away.
**Sunbathing:** At ocean beach.
**Smoking:** Permitted outside on verandas. All rooms non-smoking.
**Pets:** Not permitted.
**Handicap Access:** No.
**Children:** Only 12 years & older.
**Languages:** English.
**Your Host:** Dennis & Laurel.

## Taylor House Inn

Gay-Friendly ♀♂

### *Join Us for Candlelit Breakfast*

In historical downtown Wilmington, minutes from some of North Carolina's finest beaches, ***Taylor House Inn*** provides gracious, European-style accommodations and personalized service in a massive, turn-of-the-century residence. Spacious, individually-decorated guest rooms have ceiling fans, fireplaces, private baths with claw-footed tubs, oriental rugs, queen-sized beds, comfortable sitting areas and antiques. Breakfast is served by candlelight, using china, silver, linen and sparkling crystal.

**Address: 14 North Seventh St, Wilmington, NC 28401**
**Tel: (910) 763-7581 or (800) 382-9982.**

**Type:** Inn.
**Clientele:** Mostly straight clientele with a gay & lesbian following.
**Transportation:** Car is best. Free pick up from airport & bus.
**To Gay Bars:** 8 blocks.
**Rooms:** 5 rooms with king or queen beds.
**Bathrooms:** All private.
**Meals:** Full breakfast.
**Vegetarian:** Available upon request at time of arrival.
**Complimentary:** Wine, beer, set-up service & sherry in room.
**Dates Open:** All year.
**High Season:** April-Oct.
**Rates:** $90-$180.
**Discounts:** 10% discount for 3 or more nights.
**Credit Cards:** MC, VISA & Amex.
**Rsv'tns:** Required.
**Reserve Through:** Travel agent or call direct.
**Minimum Stay:** 2 days on weekends Apr-Nov.
**Parking:** Ample on-street parking.
**In-Room:** AC, ceiling fans, telephone, coffee & tea-making facilities, room service, laundry service & maid service.
**On-Premises:** Laundry facilities.
**Exercise/Health:** Nearby gym, weights & tennis. Fee for all.
**Swimming:** 15-minute drive to ocean beach.
**Sunbathing:** On the patio & at the beach.
**Smoking:** Permitted outside only.
**Pets:** Not permitted.
**Handicap Access:** No.
**Children:** Children 12 & older accepted.
**Languages:** English.
**Your Host:** Glenda.

# OHIO

# CINCINNATI

## Prospect Hill B&B

Gay-Friendly 50/50 ♀♂

### *The Perfect Country Retreat in the City*

We invite you to join us at the ***Prospect Hill Bed & Breakfast,*** an elegantly-restored 1867 Italianate townhouse with spectacular views of downtown Cincinnati. We're nestled into a wooded hillside in the Prospect Hill National Historical District, within a mile of most gay bars and restaurants, and only 15 blocks from the convention center. Your comfort is assured in our spacious rooms. A large six-person hot tub, antiques and wood-burning fireplaces compliment your romantic getaway. *"Thanks for making me feel like I was on vacation even though I was not."*

**Address: 408 Boal St, Cincinnati, OH 45210. Tel: (513) 421-4408.**

**Type:** Bed & breakfast.
**Clientele:** 50% straight & 50% gay & lesbian clientele.
**Transportation:** Car is best.
**To Gay Bars:** 8 blocks to gay/lesbian bar & restaurant.
**Rooms:** 4 rooms with double or queen beds.
**Bathrooms:** 2 private & 1 shared bath/shower/toilet.
**Meals:** Breakfast buffet.
**Vegetarian:** Available upon request.
**Complimentary:** Mints on pillows, tea, coffee, soft drinks, cookies, fruit basket.
**Dates Open:** All year.
**Rates:** $89-$129.
**Discounts:** 10% for 1 week or more.

**Credit Cards:** MC, VISA, Amex, Discover.
**Rsv'tns:** Recommended.
**Reserve Through:** Call direct.
**Minimum Stay:** 2 nights certain weekends. Not required otherwise.
**Parking:** Ample, free off-street parking.
**In-Room:** Color TV, central AC.
**On-Premises:** Woodburning fireplace, telephone, refrigerator, coffee/tea-maker, large side deck, shade trees.
**Exercise/Health:** Jacuzzi on premises. Gym, weights, Jacuzzi, sauna, steam nearby.
**Swimming:** Nearby pool.
**Sunbathing:** On common sun decks.
**Smoking:** Permitted outside.
**Pets:** Not permitted.
**Handicap Access:** No.
**Children:** Permitted if 12 years or older.
**Languages:** English.
**Your Host:** Gary & Tony.

# OKLAHOMA

## OKLAHOMA CITY

### America's Crossroads

Men ♂

#### *Private Homestays in Oklahoma City*

***America's Crossroads*** is the reservation service for a network of homes in the metropolitan Oklahoma City area. Since 1994, Les and Michael have offered the traditional European-style bed & breakast they love. All homestays include a full breakfast on request, and most homes in our network can accommodate up to four people at one time. We are geared to the gay traveler and provide a selection of gay-owned and -operated homes. With I-35, I-40 and I-44 all passing through the metro area, this is an ideal stopover for the cross-country traveler, putting you at ***America's Crossroads.***

Address: PO Box 270642, Oklahoma City, OK 73137
Tel: (405) 495-1111, E-mail: LesMike91@aol.com.
http://members.aol.com/LesMike91/lesmike9.htm.

**Type:** Private homestays.
**Clientele:** Men only
**Transportation:** Private car best.
**To Gay Bars:** 5-15 min.
**Rooms:** 3 homes, each w/ 2 rms with queen beds.
**Bathrooms:** Priv. & shared.
**Meals:** Full breakfast upon request.
**Vegetarian:** Available with advance notice.
**Dates Open:** All year.
**Rates:** Per night rates from $25 (single) & $30 (double).
**Rsv'tns:** Min. 1 week advance.
**Reserve Thru:** Call direct.
**Minimum Stay:** None.
**Parking:** On- & off-street parking.
**In-Room:** Tele., radio, AC.
**Exercise/Health:** Free weights & exercise bicycle. Jacuzzi, hot tub available.
**Sunbathing:** On patios.
**Nudity:** Permitted in hot tubs only.
**Smoking:** Permitted in some locations, please inquire.
**Pets:** Not permitted.
**Children:** No.
**Languages:** English.
**Your Host:** Les & Michael.

### Habana Inn

Gay/Lesbian ♂

#### *The Heart of Gay Nightlife in One Complex*

The ***Habana Inn*** complex is the hub of gay nightlife in Oklahoma City, within walking distance of a unique gay area with many gay businesses. This 200-room hotel, with two large heated swimming pools, has everything: Gusher's Restaurant is open daily with reasonably priced, excellent food; The Copa Club and the Finishline, a country western bar; and Jungle Red, a large pride store. Plan your next convention or vacation at the ***Habana Inn.***

Address: 2200 NW 39th Expwy, Oklahoma City, OK 73112
Tel: (405) 528-2221, (800) 988-2221.

*continued next page*

**Type:** Motel, bar, restaurant & gift shop.
**Clientele:** Mostly men with women welcome
**Transportation:** Airport shuttle or car.
**To Gay Bars:** On premises.
**Rooms:** 175 singles, doubles & some suites.
**Bathrooms:** All private.
**Meals:** Restaurant on premises.
**Dates Open:** All year.
**High Season:** June-Aug.
**Rates:** $34.95-$130.
**Discounts:** Weekly rates available.
**Credit Cards:** MC, Visa, Amex, Discover.
**Rsv'tns:** Recommended for holidays & weekends.
**Reserve Thru:** Call direct.
**Minimum Stay:** 3 nights on holidays.
**Parking:** Ample free on-site parking.
**In-Room:** Maid service, color cable TV, tele., AC.
**Swimming:** 2 heated pools.
**Sunbathing:** At poolside.
**Smoking:** Permitted without restrictions.
**Pets:** Permitted with prior arrangement.
**Handicap Access:** Yes.
**Children:** Permitted but not encouraged.
**Languages:** English.

# OREGON

## ASHLAND - MEDFORD

### Will's Reste

**Gay/Lesbian ♀♂**

## *Shakespeare's Neighbor*

***Will's Reste,*** our small, intimate, friendly and well-located cottage, offers comfortable accommodations a few blocks from the Oregon Shakespeare Festival Theatres, Lithia Park and some of Oregon's finest restaurants. Set between the Siskiyou and Cascade Mountains, at 2000 feet, Ashland offers unsurpassed views, cross-country and downhill skiing, many internationally-known cultural events and almost every type of outdoor recreation. Enjoy the peace and serenity of Ashland, a welcome respite from today's frantic lifestyle. So park your car, forget it, and enjoy one of the West's favorite destinations.

**Address: 298 Hargadine St, Ashland, OR 97520**
**Tel: (541) 482-4394.**

**Type:** Traveller's accommodations.
**Clientele:** Mainly gay & lesbian with some straight clientele.
**Transportation:** Car is best, pick up from airport $10.
**To Gay Bars:** 3 blks.
**Rooms:** Self-contained guest house with queen bed.
**Bathrooms:** Private.
**Dates Open:** All year.
**High Season:** July, August, September & ski season.
**Rates:** $75 plus 7% tax.
**Discounts:** Weekly rates ($400 per week).
**Rsv'tns:** Recommended.
**Reserve Through:** Travel agent or call direct.
**Parking:** Adequate free on-street parking.
**In-Room:** Coffee/tea-making facilities, kitchen, ref.
**Exercise/Health:** Hot tub and outdoor shower, nearby mineral baths & gym.
**Swimming:** Nearby pool and lake, river 30 miles.
**Sunbathing:** On patio or private sun decks.
**Nudity:** Permitted in hot tub at discretion of other guests.
**Smoking:** Permitted outdoors only.
**Pets:** No, resident dog & cat.
**Handicap Access:** Please inquire.
**Children:** Please inquire.
**Languages:** English, limited French, Spanish.

# BROOKINGS

## South Coast Inn Bed & Breakfast

Q-NET Gay-Friendly 50/50 ♀♂

### *Charm & Comfort on Oregon's Rugged, Unspoiled Southern Coast*

Surrender yourself to turn-of-the-century hospitality. Enjoy coffee in front of the stone fireplace. Relax in the spa or sauna, or bask in the warmth of beautiful antiques. Wake up to a gourmet breakfast and a beautiful ocean view. ***South Coast Inn*** is centrally located in Brookings, on the southern Oregon coast. Built in 1917, and designed by Bernard Maybeck, the inn exhibits the grace and charm of a spacious craftsman-style home. AAA-approved member of PAII.

**Address: 516 Redwood St, Brookings, OR 97415**
**Tel: (800) 525-9273, (541) 469-5557, Fax: 469-6615,**
**E-mail: scoastin@wave.net.**

**Type:** Bed & breakfast.
**Clientele:** 50% gay & lesbian & 50% straight clientele.
**Transportation:** Car is best.
**Rooms:** 3 rooms with queen beds. 1 cottage.
**Bathrooms:** 1 private bath/toilet & 3 private shower/toilets.
**Meals:** Full breakfast.
**Dates Open:** All year.
**High Season:** Memorial Day through September.
**Rates:** $79-$89.
**Discounts:** 10% senior.
**Credit Cards:** MC, VISA, Amex & Discover.
**Rsv'tns:** Suggested.
**Reserve Through:** Travel agent or call direct.
**Parking:** Ample free off-street parking.
**In-Room:** Color cable TV, VCRs & ceiling fans. Cottage has kitchenette.
**Exer./Health:** Indoor Jacuzzi & sauna, Universal gym.
**Swimming:** Nearby pool, river & ocean.
**Sunbathing:** On the patio, common sun decks & at the beach.
**Smoking:** Permitted outside only.
**Children:** Welcomed if 12 or over.
**Languages:** English.
**Your Host:** Ken & Keith.

# PORTLAND

## Holladay House

Gay-Friendly ♀

The hospitality of two grandmothers makes you feel welcome at ***Holladay House.*** We're close to a large shopping mall, congenial markets and coffee bars, and only fifteen minutes from downtown Portland, via light-rail. Mary Rose will help you locate places of women's musical interest. When visiting Portland, enjoy our breakfast and clean, comfortable rooms. We hope you find our neighborhood as special as we do.

**Address: 1735 NE Wasco, Portland, OR 97232. Tel: (503) 282-3172.**

**Type:** Bed & breakfast.
**Clientele:** A gay female following with some straight clientele
**Transportation:** Bus & light-rail from airport, bus from train & Greyhound. Free pick up from airport, bus, train if timely.
**Rooms:** 2 rooms with single or double beds.
**Bathrooms:** 1 shared bath/shower/toilet.
**Meals:** Guests' choice breakfast.

*continued next page*

**Vegetarian:** Just ask. **Dates Open:** All year. **High Season:** Summer. **Rates:** $40-$55. **Rsv'tns:** Required, with 1 night's rate as deposit. **Reserve Thru:** Call direct. **Parking:** Adequate on-street parking. **Exercise/Health:** 20 min to pool, 40 min to river & lake, 2 hrs to ocean beach. **Smoking:** Permitted. Rooms well-aired, non-smokers encouraged. **Pets:** 1 dog on premises, 1 guest dog permitted. **Handicap Access:** Stairs to front door, bedrooms. Not WC accessible. **Children:** Permitted, considered as guests. **Languages:** English, minimal German, French & Spanish. **Your Host:** Rose & Mary.

## MacMaster House circa 1895

Gay-Friendly ♀♂

### *Location–FABULOUS!*

Adjacent to Portland's scenic Washington Park and the beautiful Japanese and Rose Test Gardens, this historic Colonial mansion is perfect for those who want to be near downtown nestled in a quiet neighborhood. Popular hiking trails are nearby, as well as the fashionable 23rd Avenue cafe/boutique district. Spacious bedrooms are furnished with European antiques and have their own small library, desk, dressing table and reading chair. Seven fireplaces cozy things up, and a full breakfast is served in the elegant dining room. Seven guest rooms are available, some with private bath and fireplace.

**Address: 1041 SW Vista Ave, Portland, OR 97205**
**Tel: (503) 223-7362, (800) 774-9523, Fax: (503) 224-8808.**
**http://www.site-works.com/machouse.htm.**

**Type:** Bed & breakfast with antique shop. **Clientele:** Mostly straight clientele with a gay & lesbian following **Transportation:** Super Shuttle door-to-door (800) RIDE-PDX. Car is ok. **To Gay Bars:** 15-20 min. by foot. **Rooms:** 7 rooms & 2 suites with double or queen beds. **Bathrooms:** 2 private, others share. **Meals:** Full breakfast. **Complimentary:** Red & white wine, local ale, sodas & fruit juices in guest's refrigerator. **Dates Open:** All year. **High Season:** May-Oct. **Rates:** $75-$115 plus lodging tax. **Credit Cards:** MC, Visa, Amex & Discover. **Rsv'tns:** Advisable. **Reserve Thru:** Call direct. **Parking:** Limited on-street parking. **In-Room:** Color TV & AC. **Exercise/Health:** Facilities nearby. **Swimming:** At nearby pool. **Sunbathing:** 15 min to Sauvie Island. **Smoking:** Permitted on veranda only. **Pets:** Dog in residence. **Handicap Access:** No, stairs. **Children:** Not especially welcomed. Permitted over 14 years old. **Languages:** English, French.

## Sullivan's Gulch Bed & Breakfast

Gay/Lesbian ♀♂

### *Western Hospitality Celebrating Diversity*

***Sullivan's Gulch Bed & Breakfast,*** a lovely 1904 home, decorated with Western art and Native American art & artifacts, is in the charming, quiet area of NE Portland known as Sullivan's Gulch. Near the famed Lloyd Center shopping mall and cinemas, the Convention Center and the Coliseum, we're also two blocks from NE Broadway's shops, microbreweries and restaurants, and minutes from downtown. We serve an expanded continental breakfast that celebrates our local bakeries and the natural abundance of the Pacific Northwest.

**Address: 1744 NE Clackamas Street, Portland, OR 97232**
**Tel: (503) 331-1104, Fax: (503) 331-1575,**
**E-mail: BBSKIP@TELEPORT.COM.**

**Type:** Bed & breakfast.
**Clientele:** Mostly gay & lesbian with gay-friendly straight folk welcome.
**Transportation:** Car is best. Public transportation nearby. We offer free pick up service from all terminals.
**To Gay Bars:** 5 blocks.
**Rooms:** 3 rooms with queen beds.
**Bathrooms:** 2 private, 1 shared.
**Meals:** Expanded continental breakfast, special requests honored.
**Vegetarian:** Special requests honored.
**Complimentary:** Coffee & tea available all day.
**Dates Open:** All year.
**High Season:** Summer.
**Rates:** $65-$75 plus tax, double occupancy.
**Discounts:** Available for extended stays.
**Credit Cards:** VISA, MC & Amex.
**Rsv'tns:** Required.
**Reserve Through:** Travel agent or call direct.
**Parking:** Adequate free off-street & on-street parking.
**In-Room:** Cable TV, ceiling fans. Breakfast served in room upon request.
**Exercise/Health:** Gyms nearby.
**Sunbathing:** On common sun deck.
**Nudity:** 20 minutes to nude beach.
**Smoking:** Not permitted.
**Pets:** Resident dog. Well-behaved dogs permitted.
**Handicap Access:** No. Many steps.
**Children:** Lesbian & gay families welcome.
**Languages:** English.
**Your Host:** Skip & Jack.

IGTA

# ROGUE RIVER

## Whispering Pines Bed & Breakfast/Retreat

Gay/Lesbian ♀♂

### *Peace & Quiet & Country Comfort*

Cradled in the Cascade foothills of Southern Oregon, just 15 minutes off Interstate 5, peace and solitude abound on the 32 acres of pine and pasture that make up ***Whispering Pines Bed & Breakfast/Retreat.*** In summer, swim in our pool, or enjoy river rafting, fishing, hiking, biking and nearby cultural activities such as the Oregon Shakespeare Festival and the Britt Music Festival. In winter, ski your cares away, then return to our steamy hot tub. Or just sit back, relax, and enjoy the quiet of our rural setting.

**Address: 9188 W. Evans Creek Rd, Rogue River, OR 97537**
**Tel: (541) 582-1757, (800) 788-1757.**

**Type:** Bed & breakfast.
**Clientele:** Mainly gay/lesbian with some straight clientele.
**Transportation:** Car is best. Pick up from bus or Medford airport, fee or free depends on length of stay. Small charge for other trips.
**To Gay Bars:** One hour to Ashland gay/mixed bar.
**Rooms:** 2 rooms with queen beds, 1 bunkhouse with 3 doubles (sleeps 6).
**Bathrooms:** Rooms share 1 bath. Bunkhouse has shower & composting toilet.
**Campsites:** RV's & camping available.
**Meals:** Full country breakfast.
**Vegetarian:** Available upon request.
**Dates Open:** All year.
**High Season:** May-Oct.
**Rates:** Rooms $55-$65 double occupancy.
**Discounts:** 10% for 3 or more nights (loft excluded).
**Rsv'tns:** Preferred.
**Reserve Through:** Call direct.
**Parking:** Ample, free off-street parking.
**In-Room:** AC.
**On-Premises:** TV lounge.
**Exercise/Health:** Hot tub.
**Swimming:** Pool on premises, river nearby.
**Sunbathing:** At poolside or on private & common sun decks.
**Nudity:** Permitted.
**Smoking:** Permitted in a very limited outside location only.
**Pets:** Not permitted.
**Handicap Access:** No.
**Children:** Permitted by special arrangement.
**Languages:** English.
**Your Host:** Lorna & Karen.

# WALDPORT

## Cliff House Bed & Breakfast

Gay-Friendly ♀♂

### *Pampered Elegance By the Sea*

***Cliff House,*** a luxuriously restored older home with lots of history and a spectacular ocean view, allows you to escape to a peaceful atmosphere and refresh the spirit in a romantic setting amid shore pines. Eight miles of uninterrupted beach run in front of the house. Each room has plush bedding and is uniquely decorated with antiques, and has its own ocean or bay view, cedar bath, and balcony. Three rooms have antique parlor stoves. Lounge on a chaise, play croquet, walk, explore the beach, sail, deep-sea fish or go whalewatching. Northwest Best Places gives us 3 stars!

**Address: Box 436, Yaquina John Pt, 1450 Adahi St, Waldport, OR 97394**
**Tel: (541) 563-2506, Fax: (541) 563-4393.**

**Type:** Bed & breakfast.
**Clientele:** Mostly straight clientele with a gay/lesbian following.
**Transportation:** Car is best. Will arrange for rental car or pick up from local airport or pick up from Waldport bus station.
**To Gay Bars:** 1-3/4 hrs. to Eugene gay/lesbian bars.
**Rooms:** 4 rooms & 1 suite with queen or king beds.
**Bathrooms:** All private.
**Campsites:** Available nearby.
**Meals:** Full breakfast.
**Vegetarian:** Always available upon request.
**Complimentary:** Afternoon tea & occasional aperitifs, goodies in room.
**Dates Open:** March-October or by special reservation.
**High Season:** July-Sept.
**Rates:** $120-$150. Bridal Suite $245.
**Credit Cards:** Accept MC, Visa or Discover to hold room. Prefer cash or check for payment.
**Rsv'tns:** 14-day cancellation notice ($20 fee regardless).
**Reserve Thru:** Call direct.
**Minimum Stay:** 2 days on weekends, holidays, longer in season.
**Parking:** Ample free parking.
**In-Room:** Color cable TV & VCR. 2 rooms have refrigerator.
**On-Premises:** Meeting room, VCR & TV, grand piano, game table, dining room, telephone, fireplace.
**Exercise/Health:** Massage, golf, horseback riding, croquet, 10-jet hot tub. Massage by appointment.
**Swimming:** Ocean beach, river.
**Sunbathing:** On the beach, balconies or common sun decks.
**Nudity:** Permitted in hot tub or sauna steam room.
**Smoking:** Permitted outdoors.
**Pets:** Not permitted, but kennel nearby.
**Handicap Access:** Yes.
**Children:** Not permitted.
**Languages:** English, Spanish.
**Your Host:** Gabrielle & George.

# YACHATS

## The Oregon House

Q-NET Gay-Friendly ♀♂

### *See the Coast From Our Point of View*

High on a cliff above the Pacific Ocean, ***Oregon House*** is like no other property on the Oregon coast. Surrounding the complex are 3 1/2 acres of forest, lawn and wooded trails, a creek crossed by arched wooden bridges, a lighted trail down the cliff to the beach. The beach is ideal for bonfires and picnics, tidepooling, mussel gathering, kite flying and collecting sand dollars. Lodgings, decorated in country inn style, are sited across the property. Five have fireplaces, three have Jacuzzi tubs, one has a private hot tub and fireplace, nine have kitchens and all have private baths.

**Address: 94288 Hwy 101, Yachats, OR 97498**
**Tel: (541) 547-3329.**

**Type:** Inn with small gift shop.
**Clientele:** Mostly straight with a gay & lesbian following
**Transportation:** Car is best.
**To Gay Bars:** 1-1/2 hrs or 80 miles to Eugene.
**Rooms:** 2 rooms, 7 suites & 1 cottage with single, queen or king beds.
**Bathrooms:** All private bath/toilets.
**Dates Open:** All year.
**High Season:** May 15-October 15, every weekend, holiday & school break.
**Rates:** High season $45-$105 plus tax, low season $35-$95 plus tax.
**Credit Cards:** MC, VISA, Diners & Discover.
**Rsv'tns:** Recommended.
**Reserve Through:** Call direct.
**Minimum Stay:** 3 nights July, August & some holidays & 2 night weekends some holidays & high season.
**Parking:** Adequate free off-street parking.
**In-Room:** Ceiling fans, kitchen, refrigerator & coffee/tea-making facilities.
**On-Premises:** Telephone.
**Exercise/Health:** Jacuzzi in 3 rooms, hot tub in 1 room.
**Swimming:** Ocean beach for the hardy.
**Sunbathing:** On the beach, patio & private sun decks.
**Smoking:** Permitted outside only.
**Pets:** Not permitted.
**Handicap Access:** One room.
**Children:** Permitted if well-behaved.
**Languages:** English.
**Your Host:** Bob & Joyce.

## See Vue

**Gay-Friendly 50/50 ♀♂**

### *Lodging Where the Mountains Meet the Sea*

A coastal landmark since 1945, the ***See Vue,*** with its spectacular ocean view, is nestled between the breathtaking Coast Mountains and the everchanging Pacific Ocean. Room motifs range from the quaint Granny's Rooms to the northwest American Indian Salish Room. Fireplaces, antiques and flourishing indoor plants contribute to the homey and restful serenity. There is easy access to miles of hiking trails, tidepools, Heceta Head Lighthouse, Sea Lion Caves, restaurants and coastal shopping.

**Address: 95590 Hwy 101, Yachats, OR 97498**
**Tel: (541) 547-3227, Fax: (541) 547-4726.**

**Type:** Motel.
**Clientele:** 50% gay & lesbian & 50% straight clientele
**Transportation:** Car is best.
**To Gay Bars:** 1-1/2 hours to gay bars in Eugene, OR.
**Rooms:** 6 rooms, 4 suites & 1 cottage with single or double beds.
**Bathrooms:** All private.
**Dates Open:** All year.
**High Season:** May 16-October 15.
**Rates:** Summer $42-$65, winter $35-$58.
**Credit Cards:** MC, Visa.
**Rsv'tns:** Recommended at least 3 weeks in advance.
**Reserve Through:** Call direct.
**Minimum Stay:** On rooms with kitchen or fireplace, 2 nights on weekends or in high season.
**Parking:** Ample off-street parking.
**In-Room:** Color TV, some kitchens & fireplaces.
**On-Premises:** Massage.
**Swimming:** In the ocean, if you are brave (cold water!).
**Sunbathing:** On ocean beach.
**Smoking:** Permitted with restrictions; some non-smoking rooms.
**Pets:** Permitted if not left unattended. $5 per pet, per night charge.
**Handicap Access:** No.
**Children:** Permitted.
**Languages:** English.

# PENNSYLVANIA

## KUTZTOWN

### Grim's Manor

Gay/Lesbian ♀♂

The 200-year-old ***Grim's Manor*** site, at the edge of Pennsylvania Dutch country, includes a historic stone farmhouse on five secluded acres of land. Step back in time, experiencing the history of this home and its laid-back, noncommercial atmosphere, while enjoying all modern comforts. The property includes a huge restored barn, complete with hex signs. The manor is near the city of Reading, antique shops, Doe Mountain skiing, Hawk Mountain birdwatching, the Clove Hill Winery, Crystal Cave, Dorney Park and Wildwater Kingdom.

**Address: 10 Kern Road, Kutztown, PA 19530. Tel: (610) 683-7089.**

**Type:** Bed & breakfast.
**Clientele:** Mostly gay & lesbian with some straight clientele.
**Transportation:** Car is best, free pick up from Allentown or Reading Airport or Bieber Bus Tours in Kutztown from NYC.
**To Gay Bars:** 1/2 hr to Reading/Allentown, PA, 1 1/4 hrs to Philadelphia, 2 hrs to NYC.
**Rooms:** 4 rooms with queen beds (3 with fireplaces).
**Bathrooms:** All private shower/toilets.
**Meals:** Full breakfast, served all-you-can-eat homestyle.
**Vegetarian:** Available upon request.
**Complimentary:** Light refreshments upon arrival, bedside snack, soft drinks, morning coffee tray.
**Dates Open:** All year.
**High Season:** Kutztown, PA German Festival—July 4th week.
**Rates:** $60-$65.
**Rsv'tns:** Required.
**Reserve Thru:** Call direct.
**Parking:** Ample free off-street parking.
**In Room:** Color TV, AC, ceiling fans & maid service. Some rooms with fireplaces.
**On-Premises:** TV lounge, VCR, laundry facilities, kitchen & indoor spa.
**Swimming:** At nearby pool or Dorney Park & Wildwater Kingdom.
**Sunbathing:** On the lawn.
**Smoking:** Permitted with consideration for others.
**Pets:** Not permitted.
**Children:** Permitted with consideration for others.
**Languages:** English.

## NEW HOPE

### Fox & Hound B&B of New Hope

Gay-Friendly 50/50 ♀♂

On two beautiful acres of park-like, formal grounds stands ***Fox & Hound B&B,*** a fully-restored historic 1850's stone manor. Full gourmet breakfasts are served on our outside patio or in our spacious dining room. Our ample guest rooms, all with private baths and four-poster canopy beds, are furnished with a fine blend of period antiques and are air-conditioned for your comfort. Guest rooms with 2 beds are available. Within walking distance of the center of New Hope, guests can also enjoy tennis, the swimming pool and carriage rides, upon request. AAA/Mobil Guide-approved.

Address: 246 W Bridge St, New Hope, PA 18938
Tel: (215) 862-5082 or (800) 862-5082 (outside of PA).

**Type:** Bed & breakfast.
**Clientele:** 50% gay & lesbian & 50% straight clientele.
**Transportation:** Car is best. Trans Bridge Bus lines from New Jersey & Port Authority NYC. Pick up from bus.
**To Gay Bars:** One block walking distance (4 minutes).
**Rooms:** 5 rooms with twin, double & queen beds.
**Bathrooms:** All private.
**Meals:** Continental breakfast Mon-Fri, full breakfast Sun.
**Vegetarian:** Available upon request.
**Dates Open:** All year.
**High Season:** October.
**Rates:** Summer, spring, fall, Sun-Thurs $60-$80, Fri, Sat, $110-$120, winter specials.
**Discounts:** Corporate & long term.
**Credit Cards:** MC, VISA & Amex.
**Rsv'tns:** Required, especially on weekends. In high season required 2-3 weeks in advance.
**Reserve Through:** Call direct.
**Minimum Stay:** Call for details.
**Parking:** Ample, free off-street parking.
**In-Room:** Maid service, AC, ceiling fans, fireplaces, TV upon request.
**On-Premises:** Use of kitchen on limited basis.
**Exercise/Health:** Tubing & canoeing at nearby river.
**Swimming:** Pool within walking distance, Delaware river 1/4 mile.
**Sunbathing:** At poolside.
**Smoking:** Permitted throughout house.
**Pets:** Not permitted.
**Handicap Access:** No.
**Children:** Permitted if 14 or older.
**Languages:** English.

# NEW MILFORD

## Oneida Campground and Lodge

Gay/Lesbian ♂

*Oneida Camp* offers 100 wooded and meadowed acres with well-spaced campsites. Cottages and campsites use the bath house, which has hot showers and modern facilities. We are also a spiritual retreat where you can experience comradeship as you commune with new friends. There is a show on Saturday night, volleyball and a nature trail. Our disco features a DJ. Beverages are sometimes supplied on weekends at the disco. There is occasional leadership at the meditation center. Nudity is permitted. Call for directions to the campground.

Address: PO Box 537, New Milford, PA 18834
Tel: (717) 465-7011 or (717) 853-3503.

**Type:** Campground and lodge with clubhouse, sauna, disco & rental cottages.
**Clientele:** Mostly men with women present frequently
**Transportation:** Small charge for pick up ($10 one way) from Binghamton bus or airport.
**To Gay Bars:** 20 miles to Binghamton, NY gay bars.
**Rooms:** 12 rooms & 2 cottages with single & double beds.
**Bathrooms:** Shared: 4 tubs, 5 showers & 9 bath/shower/toilets.
**Campsites:** 35 tent sites & 20 sites with dump station, electric & water.
**Meals:** Coffee hour on Sunday morning, restaurants are 3 miles away.
**Complimentary:** Saturday night at disco.
**Dates Open:** Closed Nov 25-Mar 15. Call ahead for off season camping or lodge.
**High Season:** May-Oct.
**Rates:** Reasonable & vary according to days & number accommodated.
**Discounts:** 10% for pre-registered groups of 10 or more. 25% camping discount Oct 16-Apr 30.
**Rsv'tns:** Necessary during holiday weekends.
**Reserve Thru:** Call direct.
**Minimum Stay:** No min. even day camping ok.
**Parking:** Ample free parking.
**In-Room:** Color TV, refrigerator, stove, light housekeeping in general area outside room.
**On-Premises:** TV lounge, library, meditation center, fitness center, use of kit.
**Exercise/Health:** Sauna.
**Swimming:** Spring-fed lake or swim pond. Planning above-ground pool for 1997.
**Sunbathing:** On the patio & at poolside.
**Nudity:** Permitted on the grounds.
**Smoking:** Permitted in most areas unless posted.
**Pets:** Permitted, but must be controlled.
**Handicap Access:** Not recommended for wheelchairs.
**Children:** Permitted, parent or guardian required & at discretion of owner.
**Languages:** English, A.S.L.

# PHILADELPHIA

## Antique Row Bed & Breakfast

Gay-Friendly 50/50 ♀♂

### *Perfectly Positioned for the Gay/Lesbian Communities*

***Antique Row B&B*** is centrally located for business and tourism, only a few blocks from the convention center. We're a small European-style B&B with mixed clientele. Rooms in this 180-year-old townhouse are attractively furnished with comfortable beds, down comforters, designer linens and sufficient pillows for watching TV and reading in bed. The color cable TV has Bravo, CineMax and Showtime. A more spacious fully furnished flat for added privacy is available, as well as an additional accommodation across the street.

**Address: 341 South 12th St, Philadelphia, PA 19107**
**Tel: (215) 592-7802, Fax: (215) 592-9692.**

**Type:** Bed & breakfast & fully furnished flat.
**Clientele:** 50% gay & lesbian & 50% straight clientele
**Transportation:** Easy access for all forms of transportation.
**To Gay Bars:** Within a few blocks of most gay & lesbian bars.
**Rooms:** 5 rooms & 1 apartment with double or queen beds.
**Bathrooms:** 2 private shower/toilets & 2 shared bath/shower/toilets.
**Meals:** Full breakfast.
**Vegetarian:** Within walking distance to several vegetarian restaurants.
**Dates Open:** All year.
**High Season:** April-October.
**Rates:** $40-$85.
**Discounts:** Extended stays.
**Rsv'tns:** Recommended.
**Reserve Through:** Call direct.
**Parking:** Off-street pay parking ($5.75 for 24 hours). Recommended for safety.
**In-Room:** Color cable TV & AC. Apartment has telephone, kitchen, refrigerator & coffee & tea-making facilities.
**Smoking:** Permitted.
**Pets:** Not permitted.
**Handicap Access:** No.
**Children:** Case-by-case depending on child's age, season & available accommodations.
**Languages:** English, a little Spanish & a little German.

## The Best Nest

Women ♀

Homey, friendly and personal service awaits you when you visit ***The Best Nest.*** Our city/country town house is located in a quiet residential community, near the edge of Philadelphia, with lots of parks and hiking trails only one-half mile from us. We are five miles from the Philadelphia Art Museum, City Hall, Liberty Bell and other historical places of interest. Public transportation is right at the corner for your convenience in accessing the city and its many sights.

**Address: PO Box 23236, Philadelphia, PA 19124. Tel: (215) 482-2677.**

**Type:** Guesthouse.
**Clientele:** Women only
**Transportation:** Taxi from airport. Pick up from airport, bus or train $15.
**To Gay Bars:** 5 miles from Philadelphia gay bars.
**Rooms:** 1 single, 1 dbl.
**Bathrooms:** 1-1/2 shared baths.
**Meals:** Continental breakfast.
**Complimentary:** Tea, coffee, juice.
**Dates Open:** All year.
**High Season:** May-November.
**Rates:** Single $50, double $60.
**Discounts:** 10% for weekly stays.
**Rsv'tns:** Required.
**Reserve Through:** Call direct.
**Parking:** Limited free off-street parking.
**In-Room:** Telephone, color TV, self-controlled AC.
**On-Premises:** Laundry facilities.
**Exercise/Health:** Massage available nearby, for fee, with appointment.
**Swimming:** Public pool in summer, 1 block.
**Sunbathing:** On patio.
**Smoking:** No smoking in bedrooms. Other areas available for smoking.
**Pets:** Not permitted.
**Handicap Access:** No.
**Children:** Welcome, ages 8 & up preferred.
**Languages:** English.
**Your Host:** Carol & Chris.

## Glen Isle Farm Country Inn

**Gay-Friendly 50/50 ♀♂**

Come and experience, as did George Washington on June 3, 1773, the "historic hospitality" of ***Glen Isle Farm.*** At that time, the farm was known as the Ship Inn. Other guests have included James Buchanan, before he became the fifteenth president of the United States, as well as the United States Continental Congress, while on its way to York. During The Civil War, ***Glen Isle Farm*** was a stop on the underground railroad, thus it has an important place in civil rights history. Today, the farm is a secluded 8-acre gentleman's estate. The approach is down a long, heavily-wooded drive and across a small stone bridge. The drive circles up to the imposing front entrance, leading you up granite steps and across a broad checkerboard porch of black slate, white marble and red brick, through a glass vestibule and to the wide front door. Once inside, you can feel the wonderful sense of history present in this 266-year-old home.

On your visit, you might enjoy a cool autumn afternoon in the upstairs sunroom, sipping a cappuccino or glass of sherry. Watch the fall colors and the shadows, as they gently cross the walled garden. Play a tune on the grand piano in the music room or just curl up with a good book from the selection in the library. If you are the more active type, you may want to take one of the many day trips available. Visit historic Valley Forge. Take the train to Philadelphia, the nation's first capital. Go antiquing, or visit beautiful Longwood Gardens and the Brandywine River Museum, the home of the Wyeth school and collection. You may want to take a bike ride or go hiking on the many nearby roads and trails. Maybe you've come in May to attend the Devon Horse Show, or to see some of the nearby Amish country, and enjoy a slice of Shoofly Pie. Come and experience the "historic hospitality" that is ***Glen Isle Farm.***

**Address: Downingtown, PA 19335-2239**
**Tel: (610) 269-9100, Reservations/Info: (800) 269-1730,**
**Fax: (610) 269-9191.**

**Type:** Bed & breakfast inn.
**Clientele:** 50% gay & lesbian & 50% straight clientele.
**Transportation:** Car or train. Free pick up from train or airport shuttle.
**To Gay Bars:** 30 miles, or 40 minutes by car, to Norristown or Philadelphia.
**Rooms:** 3 rooms with queen or king beds.
**Bathrooms:** 1 private, 2 shared.
**Meals:** Full breakfast, other meals by arrangement. Our restaurant is licensed by the county.
**Vegetarian:** Available with prior arrangement.
**Dates Open:** All year.
**High Season:** April through October.
**Rates:** $49-$89 + tax.
**Discounts:** 10% on stays of 7 or more nights. Seniors 10%.
**Credit Cards:** MC, Visa, Discover.
**Rsv'tns:** Required.
**Reserve Through:** Travel agent or call direct.
**Parking:** Ample off-street parking.
**On-Premises:** TV lounge. Weddings, reunions & business meeting space available.
**Swimming:** Nearby river & lake.
**Sunbathing:** On the patio or in the yard.
**Smoking:** Permitted outdoors only.
**Pets:** Not permitted. Dogs in residence.
**Handicap Access:** Limited.
**Children:** By arrangement.
**Languages:** English.
**Your Host:** Glenn & Tim.

## Uncles Upstairs Inn

Gay/Lesbian ♂

### *We're More Than Friends – We're Family!*

Service is at the heart of ***Uncles Upstairs Inn*** on Locust Street, the hub of the gay district and cultural and business areas. Under the direction of the innkeeper, the meticulously restored interior rooms featuring traditional furnishings, original art, and personal touches, make guests feel at home. The totally renovated, turn-of-the-century historical building has seven rooms each with queen beds and private baths. Continental breakfasts are served with a friendly smile and afternoon and evening cocktails are served in the cocktail lounge.

**Address: 1220 Locust St, Philadelphia, PA 19107**
**Tel: (215) 546-6660, Fax: (215) 546-1653.**

**Type:** Bed & breakfast with gay/lesbian bar.
**Clientele:** Mostly men with women welcome
**Transportation:** Car is best, taxi from airport.
**To Gay Bars:** Gay bar on prem., others within 3 blks.
**Rooms:** 7 rooms with queen beds.
**Bathrooms:** Al private bath/toilets.
**Meals:** Cont. breakfast.
**Vegetarian:** Avail. nearby.
**Dates Open:** All year.
**Rates:** $85-$110.
**Discounts:** 10% discount for stays of 7 days.
**Credit Cards:** MC, Visa.
**Rsv'tns:** Requested.
**Reserve Through:** Travel agent or call direct.
**Parking:** Ample off-street pay parking.
**In-Room:** Color TV, AC, telephone, ceiling fans, refrigerator, maid service.
**Exercise/Health:** Nearby gym, weights, sauna, steam.
**Pets:** Permitted with deposit.
**Languages:** English, Span.
**Your Host:** Mort.

# PITTSBURGH

## The Inn on the Mexican War Streets

Gay/Lesbian ♂

### *In the Historic Old Allegheny District...*

Come experience the adventure and convenience of inner-city living in a gentrified way, just minutes from downtown shopping, nightlife and other attractions. Staying at the ***Inn on the Mexican War Streets,*** in an historic district of Victorian-era row houses in Pittsburgh's Northside, puts you in the heart of what used to be the city of Allegheny. While at the inn, relax and experience the tranquillity of the rear courtyard, listen to the fountain or sit by the fireplace and enjoy some refreshments. Whichever room you choose, each will radiate a character and charm of its own...and the hospitality that is truly Pittsburgh.

**Address: 1606 Buena Vista St, Pittsburgh, PA 15212. Tel: (412) 231-6544.**

**Type:** Inn.
**Clientele:** Mostly men with women welcome
**Transportation:** Airport taxi or airport bus to town, then taxi. $10 pick up from airport, train or bus.
**To Gay Bars:** 8 blocks, a 15-minute walk, a 5-minute drive.
**Rooms:** 3 rooms, 12 apartments, bunkhouse with single, queen, king or bunk beds.
**Bathrooms:** Private: 1 shower/toilet, 12 bath/shower/toilets. Shared: 1 bath/shower/toilet.
**Meals:** Expanded continental breakfast.
**Complimentary:** Fresh fruit on arrival, homemade cookies at night, mints.
**Dates Open:** All year.
**Rates:** $65-$85.
**Discounts:** On stays of 5 days or longer.
**Credit Cards:** VISA.
**Rsv'tns:** Required.
**Reserve Through:** Call direct.
**Parking:** Ample, on- & off-street parking.
**In-Room:** AC, color cable TV, VCR, video tape library, phone, kitchen, refrigerator, ceiling fans, coffee/tea-making facilities, maid & laundry service.
**On-Premises:** TV lounge, laundry facilities, landscaped courtyard.
**Exercise/Health:** Nearby gym, sauna, weights, steam, sauna.
**Swimming:** Nearby pool.
**Sunbathing:** On private sun decks, in courtyard.
**Smoking:** Permitted in rooms or outside. Not permitted in common areas.
**Pets:** Not permitted.
**Handicap Access:** No.
**Children:** No.
**Your Host:** Jeffery & Karl.

# POCONOS MTN AREA

## Blueberry Ridge

Women ♀

### *For That Romantic Country Feeling*

Pat and Greta, of ***Blueberry Ridge,*** offer you friendship and warmth in the company of women. In a beautiful, secluded cedar house, you'll relax in the hot tub or by the wood-burning stove while enjoying a panoramic view of the Delaware Water Gap. Stroll the woods or go out for a romantic dinner. Winter brings skiing, ice skating, sleigh riding. Summer offers canoeing, whitewater rafting, riding, hiking, golf, tennis. Year-round interests include auctions, antique & candle shopping.

**Address: Mail to: McCarrick/Moran, RR 1 Box 67, Scotrun, PA 18355 Tel: (717) 629-5036 or (516) 473-6701.**

**Type:** Bed & breakfast guesthouse.
**Clientele:** Women only.
**Transportation:** Car is best.
**To Gay Bars:** 10 miles or 20 minutes by car to Rainbow Mountain Disco.
**Rooms:** 4 rooms with double & king beds.
**Bathrooms:** 1 private, others shared
**Meals:** Full country breakfast. Holiday weekend specials include all meals.
**Complimentary:** Baked goods, tea & coffee.
**Dates Open:** All year.
**Rates:** Rooms $55-$70.
**Rsv'tns:** Required.
**Reserve Through:** Call direct.
**Parking:** Ample off-street parking.
**In-Room:** TV, ceiling fan & some rooms have VCRs.
**On-Premises:** TV lounge, videos, kitchen.
**Exercise/Health:** Outdoor hot tub.
**Swimming:** River is 5 miles away.
**Sunbathing:** On common sun decks.
**Nudity:** Permitted in the hot tub.
**Smoking:** Permitted outdoors.
**Pets:** Not permitted.
**Handicap Access:** No.
**Children:** Permitted.
**Languages:** English, Spanish.

## Rainbow Mountain Resort

Gay/Lesbian ♀♂

### *Our Finest Amenity: "Enjoying The Freedom To Be Yourself"*

***Rainbow Mountain Resort*** has a style and setting like no other resort of its kind. You will find us nestled high atop a Pocono mountainside on 85 private, wooded acres with a spectacular view of the surrounding mountains. Welcoming both men and women, we are open year-round, and have a friendly, courteous staff to serve you. Dine on fabulous four-course gourmet meals and full American breakfasts, join the crowd in the Dance Club or relax in the Lizard Lounge. Our Olympic-sized outdoor pool is just what the doctor ordered for the summer. Take in a day of antique shopping, or hike the many beautiful trails in the fall. Ski some of the best mountains in Pennsylvania during the winter. Take a romantic horseback ride or canoe down the Delaware River in the spring. Come to ***Rainbow Mountain Resort*** to play, to celebrate, to get a good night's sleep. Choose from one of our 46 lovely, antique-filled rooms or cabins. There is always something to do in this four-season resort area. But remember, our finest amenity will always be ***"Enjoying The Freedom To Be Yourself."***

**Address: RD #8, Box 8174, East Stroudsburg, PA 18301**
**Tel: (717) 223-8484, E-mail: Mountain@prolog.ptd.net.**
**http://www.rainbowmountain.com.**

**Type:** Resort with dance club, piano bar, patio dining, pool bar & restaurant.
**Clientele:** Good mix of gay men & women.
**Transportation:** Car is best or bus to Stroudsburg, then taxi.
**To Gay Bars:** Gay & lesbian bar on premises.
**Rooms:** 30 rooms & 16 cottages with double & queen beds. Cottages are seasonal, May-October.
**Bathrooms:** 36 private & 2 shared in lodge.
**Meals:** Full breakfast & dinner.
**Vegetarian:** Limited availability on menu.
**Dates Open:** All year.
**High Season:** 4-season resort area.
**Rates:** $55-$95, includes breakfast & dinner.
**Discounts:** For groups over 25 people, except some holidays.
**Credit Cards:** MC, VISA, Amex & Discover.
**Rsv'tns:** Recommended two weeks in advance.
**Reserve Through:** Travel agent or call direct.
**Minimum Stay:** 2 nights on weekends. 3 nights on holidays.
**Parking:** Ample free off-street parking.
**In-Room:** Maid service, color TV, ceiling fans & AC.
**On-Premises:** Meeting room.
**Exercise/Health:** Tennis, volleyball, badminton, horseshoes, hiking, basketball, paddle & row boats, & skiing.
**Swimming:** Outdoor Olympic-sized pool with pool bar.
**Sunbathing:** At poolside.
**Smoking:** Permitted. Smoking & non-smoking dining area.
**Pets:** Not permitted.
**Handicap Access:** No.
**Children:** Adult-oriented resort.
**Languages:** English.
**Your Host:** Georgeann & Laura.

IGTA

## Stoney Ridge

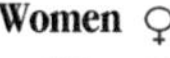
Women ♀

For a respite from the city, stay at ***Stoney Ridge,*** our charming new cedar log home in the secluded Pocono Mountains of Pennsylvania. The house is beautifully furnished with antiques to give it that warm country feeling, while providing all the modern conveniences. Within 10 miles of here, you can enjoy restaurants, skiing, canoeing, hiking, trout fishing, dancing, antiquing, etc.

**Address: mail to: P. McCarrick, RR 1 Box 67, Scotrun, PA 18355**
**Tel: (717) 629-5036 or (516) 473-6701.**

**Type:** Cedar log home with 2 bedrooms, stone fireplace.
**Clientele:** Women only
**Transportation:** Car is best.
**To Gay Bars:** 10-minute drive to Rainbow Mountain disco/restaurant.
**Rooms:** Cabin with 2 double bedrooms.
**Bathrooms:** 1-1/2 baths.
**Dates Open:** All year.
**Rates:** $250/$450/$1250, by weekend, week, month.
**Rsv'tns:** Required.
**Reserve Through:** Call direct.
**Parking:** Ample off-street parking.
**In-Room:** Telephone.
**On-Premises:** TV lounge with VCR.
**Swimming:** River & lake nearby.
**Smoking:** Permitted without restrictions.
**Pets:** Permitted.
**Children:** Permitted.
**Languages:** English & Spanish.

# SCRANTON

## Hillside Campgrounds

Men ♂

***Hillside*** is a men-only campground, in the mountains of NE Pennsylvania on over 176 acres of private woodlands (45 of which are a very private play area) with nudity permitted throughout. We have RV hookups, parking and tent sites, 2 sites for groups of 50 or more, rental cabins, two large, clean bathhouses, flush toilets, and showers. There's a pool, volleyball and a rec hall with occasional impromptu amateur entertainment and get-togethers. There are nature trails, small streams, Friday and Saturday disco and a Saturday evening bonfire. We're halfway between Binghamton, NY and Scranton, PA, just off I-81. Call for directions.

**Address: Mail to: PO Box 726, Binghamton, NY 13902**
**Tel: (717) 756-2007.**

**Type:** Campground with disco, snack bar, & camping supplies.
**Clientele:** Men only
**Transportation:** Private automobile is best.
**To Gay Bars:** 30 miles.
**Campsites:** 200+ sites. Most have electric & water. 2 bath houses.
**Dates Open:** May 1st-Oct 15th.
**Rates:** From $30 to $56 for 2 nights weekends. Weeknights $15.
**Discounts:** For longer stays.
**Rsv'tns:** Required.
**Reserve Through:** Call direct.
**Minimum Stay:** On weekends & holidays.
**Parking:** Ample off-street parking.
**On-Premises:** Rec room with DJ and disco on weekends. Different theme weekends all summer.
**Exercise/Health:** Volleyball court & free weights.
**Swimming:** Pool on premises.
**Sunbathing:** At poolside.
**Nudity:** Permitted anywhere on our 176-plus acres.
**Smoking:** Permitted without restrictions.
**Pets:** Permitted. No dogs at pool. Pick up excrement. Dogs must not disturb guests.
**Handicap Access:** Yes.
**Children:** Not permitted.
**Languages:** English.
**Your Host:** Dave & Dan

# RHODE ISLAND

## NEWPORT

### Brinley Victorian Inn

**Gay-Friendly ♀♂**

Romantically decorated with fine antiques, Trompe l'Oeil period wallpapers and satin-and-lace window treatments, ***Brinley Victorian Inn*** is a haven of peace in this city by the sea. In the heart of Newport's historic district, the ***Brinley*** is within walking distance of historic sites, including the oldest Episcopal church and America's first synagogue. Close by are the *gilded era* mansions of the 19th century, hundreds of 17th-century colonials, the famed America's Cup waterfront, unique shops and restaurants, magnificent beaches and two gay bars.

**Address: 23 Brinley St, Newport, RI 02840**
**Tel: (401) 849-7645, (800) 999-8523, Fax: (401) 845-9634.**

**Type:** Bed & breakfast inn.
**Clientele:** Mostly straight clientele with a gay/lesbian following
**Transportation:** By car.
**To Gay Bars:** Within walking dist. to gay/lesbian bars.
**Rooms:** 17 doubles, including 1 suite.
**Bathrooms:** 13 private, others share 2 bathrooms.
**Meals:** Cont. breakfast.
**Complimentary:** Bottle of champagne for special occasions.
**Dates Open:** All year.
**High Seas:** May 23-Oct 1.
**Rates:** Please call for rates.
**Discounts:** Mid-week & longer stays, multiple reservations (5 rooms).
**Credit Cards:** MC, Visa.
**Rsv'tns:** Recommended.
**Reserve Through:** Travel agent or call direct.
**Minimum Stay:** 2 nights on in-season weekends, 3 on holiday weekends.
**Parking:** Adequate, free on- and off-street parking.
**In-Room:** Maid service, AC, ceiling fans, refrigerators (some rooms).
**On-Premises:** 2 porches, 2 parlors, library & patio courtyard.
**Swimming:** Ocean beach or bay.
**Sunbathing:** On beach and in private courtyard.
**Smoking:** Permitted in rooms only.
**Children:** 8 years & older, at owner's discretion.

### Captain James Preston House

**Q-NET Gay-Friendly ♀♂**

#### *A Charming Victorian Inn in the Heart of Historic Newport*

This delightful B&B, located in a large Victorian home, includes two cozy sitting rooms, a dining room and a sunny breakfast porch. It's an easy walk to all of Newport's unique attractions – the harbor, mansions, Cliff Walk, beaches and shopping. There's even ample off-street parking. Comfortably furnished accommodations at the ***Captain James Preston House*** include two doubles, one single and two queens. The inn's namesake, Captain Preston, served in the English Navy during the 18th century. His descendent, Paul Preston, also a captain, enjoys hosting guests year round and has excellent contacts for local sporting, entertainment and outdoor activities.

**Address: 378 Spring St, Newport, RI 02840**
**Tel: (401) 847-4386, Fax: (401) 847-1093.**
**E-mail: EEXK82A@prodigy.com.**

**Type:** Bed & breakfast.
**Clientele:** Mostly straight with a gay/lesbian following
**Transportation:** From airport by shuttle. From train by bus (local bus line) or taxi. Bus station a 10 min walk to inn. Ask about pick up.
**To Gay Bars:** 5 min walk.
**Rooms:** 5 rooms with single, dbl. or queen beds.
**Bathrooms:** 1 private shower/toilet. 2 shared bath/shower/toilets.
**Meals:** Expanded continental breakfast.
**Vegetarian:** Available with prior notice.
**Complimentary:** Tea in afternoon, if requested.

**Dates Open:** All year.
**High Season:** Summer.
**Rates:** Summer $100-$150, winter $60-$100.
**Discounts:** Inquire about extended stays.
**Rsv'tns:** Recommended.
**Reserve Through:** Travel agent or call direct.
**Parking:** Adequate free off-street parking.
**In-Room:** Ceiling fans, maid service.
**On-Premises:** TV lounge, meeting rooms, business services, laundry facilities.
**Exercise/Health:** Nearby gym, tennis, kayaking, sailing.
**Swimming:** Nearby pool & ocean.
**Sunbath:** At beach & patio.
**Smoking:** Permitted on porches. Non-smoking rooms available.
**Handicap Access:** Yes.
**Languages:** English, French.
**Your Host:** Paul.

## Hydrangea House Inn

Q-NET Gay-Friendly 50/50 ♀♂

### *Quiet Sophistication in the "City by the Sea"*

During the "gilded" period of Newport, when America's wealthy families were building lavish summer homes and bringing with them every luxury, a little luxury found its way to the natives of Newport, themselves. Gardeners who worked on the mansion grounds, it is said, took home cuttings of the exotic plants they cared for, among them the hydrangea, and grew them in their own gardens. We have taken our name from the hydrangea, which blooms all over Newport, because we, like the gardeners, have brought a little luxury home, and we would love to share that feeling of old, luxurious Newport with you.

Built in 1876, this Victorian townhouse has been carefully transformed, and its 6 guest rooms, each with its own sumptuous personality, is elegantly decorated with antiques. Plush carpeting, thick cozy towels, crystal water glasses, long-stemmed goblets for your wine setups, and afternoon refreshments all help make your stay a real luxury. Your day will start with our gratifying hot buffet breakfast served in the contemporary fine art gallery. For your enjoyment we will serve our special blend of ***Hydrangea House*** coffee, fresh squeezed juice, home-baked bread and granola, and perhaps raspberry pancakes or seasoned scrambled eggs. The gallery may also serve as a unique setting for small conferences and business meetings. Our location is right on Bellevue Avenue just 1/4 mile from the mansions and in the center of Newport's "Walking District," within steps of antique shops, clothing stores, galleries, ocean beaches and historical points of interest. Your hosts will be happy to recommend restaurants and popular night spots. Buses and the airport shuttle stop outside our door. We know you'll love it here: In 1989, the **Boston Globe** said of the inn, *"In a city renowned for its lodging, the **Hydrangea House** is not to be missed!"* We're not a mansion, just a special place that's home away from home, with our welcome mat out for new friends.

**Address:** 16 Bellevue Ave, Newport, RI 02840
**Tel:** (401) 846-4435, (800) 945-4667, **Fax:** (401) 846-6602,
**E-mail:** bandbinn@ids.net.

**Type:** Bed & breakfast with contemporary art gallery.
**Clientele:** 50% gay & lesbian & 50% straight clientele
**Transportation:** Car is best. Pick up from airport by shuttle $13 per person. Bus station 5-min walk to inn. Local bus line, taxi.
**To Gay Bars:** 5-minute walk to gay/lesbian bars.
**Rooms:** 6 rooms with double, queen, king beds.
**Bathrooms:** All private bath/toilets.
**Meals:** Full breakfast.
**Vegetarian:** Available upon request.

*continued next page*

**Complimentary:** Homemade chocolate chip cookies, afternoon tea & lemonade.
**Dates Open:** All year.
**High Season:** May-Oct.
**Rates:** Summer $115-$139, Suite $250. Off season $75-$105, Suite $195.
**Discounts:** Inquire for extended stays.
**Credit Cards:** MC & VISA.
**Rsv'tns:** Required, walk-ins based on availability.
**Reserve Through:** Travel agent or call direct.
**Minimum Stay:** 2 days June-Sept & weekends all year. 3 days on holidays.
**Parking:** Ample free off-street parking on site.
**In-Room:** AC, refrigerator & maid service.
**On-Premises:** Meeting rms.
**Exercise/Health:** Massage by appt. Gym with weights, exercise room, aerobic class, $8-$12 day 5 min away.
**Swimming:** 5-minute walk to ocean beach.
**Sunbathing:** On beach or common sun decks.
**Smoking:** Permitted outdoors ONLY.
**Pets:** Not permitted.
**Children:** Permitted.

# Melville House Inn

Q-NET **Gay-Friendly** ♀♂

## *Where the Past Is Present*

Staying at the ***Melville House Inn*** is like a step back into the past. Built c. 1750, the house is located in the heart of the historical Hill section of Newport, where the streets are still lit by gas. The French General, Rochambeau, quartered some of his troops here when they fought in the Revolutionary War under George Washington. The house where Washington and his envoy, Major General Marquis de Lafayette, met Rochambeau is across the street.

Although the ***Melville House Inn*** is on one of Newport's quietest streets, it is only one block from Thames Street and the harborfront, and many of the city's finest restaurants, antique shops and galleries. We're within walking distance of many places of worship, such as Touro Synagogue (the oldest in the U.S.), Trinity Church (c. 1726) and St. Mary's (where President Kennedy married Jacqueline). The Tennis Hall of Fame; the famous and lavish mansions of the Vanderbilts, Astors and Belmonts; The Naval War College; and Newport's finest ocean beaches are just a very short drive.

The seven rooms, furnished in traditional Colonial style, are available with both private and shared baths. A romantic fireplace suite is available during the cold months. Guests in the suite are greeted with champagne upon arrival, treated to after-dinner drinks and served breakfast in bed the next day. The full breakfast features homemade granola, muffins and various other baked breads, such as buttermilk biscuits, bagels, scones, Yankee cornbread and Rhode Island Johnnycakes. Afternoon tea is served daily. Guests enjoy a cup of tea or our special Melville House Blend coffee, a glass of sherry and biscotti, as we discuss the day's activities and our favorite places for dinner. Your hosts, Vince and David, will share with you their Newport experiences and will do their best to make your visit as pleasant as possible. Stay at the ***Melville House Inn,*** "Where the Past is Present."

**Address: 39 Clarke St, Newport, RI 02840**
**Tel: (401) 847-0640, (800) 711-7184, Fax: (404) 847-0956,**
**E-mail: innkeepri@aol.com.**

**Type:** Bed & breakfast.
**Clientele:** Mostly straight clientele with a gay & lesbian following
**Transportation:** Car is best. Short walk from bus station. Limo from Providence Airport.
**To Gay Bars:** 2 blocks.
**Rooms:** 7 rooms with single, double or king beds. 1 fireplace suite available in winter.
**Bathrooms:** 5 private shower/toilets & 2 shared bath/shower/toilets.
**Meals:** Full breakfast.
**Veget.:** Served daily.
**Complimentary:** Tea & sherry at 4pm with refresh-

ments & homemade biscotti. Hot soup in winter.
**Dates Open:** All year.
**High Season:** Memorial Day-Columbus Day.
**Rates:** Summer $115-$135 & winter $85-$110. Fireplace suite $165.
**Discounts:** On stays of 3 or more nights.
**Credit Cards:** MC, Visa, Amex, Discover.
**Rsv'tns:** Suggested for weekends & holidays.
**Reserve Through:** Travel agent or call direct.
**Minimum Stay:** 2 nights on weekends & 3 nights on holidays & special events.
**Parking:** Ample free off-street parking.
**In-Room:** AC & maid serv.
**Exercise/Health:** Health club nearby.
**Swimming:** In nearby ocean.
**Sunbathing:** At the beach.
**Smoking:** Not permitted.
**Pets:** Dewey and Spike, the feline innkeepers, do not want to share their affections.

# SOUTH CAROLINA

## CHARLESTON

### Charleston Columns Guesthouse

**Gay/Lesbian ♀♂**

## *The Charleston Experience: Ultimate Charm and Warm Hospitality*

To the residents of Charleston, life in the Historic District is like stepping back into history and sharing timeless charm and majestic beauty on a daily basis. Charleston offers a serene reflection of a lifestyle that has all but vanished. When you come to visit, you will want to stay in accommodations befitting the "Charleston Experience." From the moment you arrive at ***Charleston Columns,*** you feel the charm and hospitality for which Charleston is renown. Every effort is made to make your stay memorable.

Begin your day with a healthy continental breakfast, and experience the warm, friendly hospitality that you naturally expect of "The Old South." Information on tours and entertainment, restaurant recommendations, and complimentary maps are cheerfully provided upon request. When you are ready to "do Charleston," staff members will gladly arrange a tour of antebellum homes, a horse-drawn carriage ride around the city, a harbor tour, a guided walking tour or even bicycle rentals.

Like the beautiful city of Charleston, the guesthouse is an elegant survivor of a tempestuous past. Built as a private residence in 1855 for Edward Simonton, a prominent Charleston lawyer, state legislator, Confederate officer and federal judge, it has been the home of a number of notable Charlestonian and South Carolinian public figures. In keeping with its history, the suites, guest rooms and public rooms are graced with 19th-century period-style furnishings and antiques, designer linens, Oriental rugs and ceiling fans (although the entire house is air conditioned). The stately living room, dining room and porches provide a comfortable setting for relaxation and congenial entertainment.

***Charleston Columns Guesthouse*** is located in the Historic District of downtown Charleston, an easy walk to historic sites, great shopping and exciting

*continued next page*

nightlife. The people of Charleston have been welcoming guests for over 300 years, and they know how to make you feel welcome and right at home. Come see for yourself!

**Address: 8 Vanderhorst St, Charleston, SC 29403-6121**
**Tel: (803) 722-7341, E-mail: CHS65@AOL.COM.**

**Type:** Guesthouse.
**Clientele:** Good mix of gays & lesbians
**Transportation:** Car is best.
**To Gay Bars:** 2 blocks or a 5-minute walk, 2 minute drive.
**Rooms:** 4 rooms & 2 suites with queen or king beds.
**Bathrooms:** 4 private bath/shower/toilets, 1 shared bath/shower/toilet.
**Meals:** Continental breakfast. Gourmet coffee, tea, juices, fresh fruit, yogurt, cereals, pastries.
**Dates Open:** All year.
**High Season:** Mar-Nov.
**Rates:** For 2 guests: suites $110-$125, doubles $75-$90. $10 less for singles. Tax included.
**Discounts:** One night free for 7-night stay.
**Rsv'tns:** Recommended.
**Reserve Through:** Travel agent or call direct.
**Parking:** Adequate free off-street parking.
**In-Room:** Color cable TV, AC, ceiling fans, maid & laundry service.
**On-Premises:** TV lounge, laundry facilities for guests.
**Swimming:** 7 miles to gay beach.
**Smoking:** Permitted in kitchen & on porches.
**Pets:** Not permitted.
**Handicap Access:** No.
**Languages:** English.
**Your Host:** Frank & Jim.

## Crabapple Cottage

Q-NET **Gay/Lesbian** ♀♂

### *Nothing Could Be Finer...*

***Crabapple Cottage*** is situated in the center of a 7000-acre wildlife preserve and is adjacent to one of the most historic and beautiful plantation properties in the South. Surrounded by huge live oaks and tall pine trees, this wonderfully quaint cottage has the feel of a rustic country cabin, combined with the charm and comfort of an English country cottage. While ceiling beams of rich cypress wood, floors of beautiful heart pine, and a floor-to-ceiling brick fireplace add to the rustic flavor, the comfortable living room decorated with chintz-covered sofa and chairs add to the charm and coziness of ***Crabapple Cottage.***

There is a completely stocked kitchenette, equipped for a stay of any length, which can be stocked as you request for an additional fee. At the very least, we will provide for you a complimentary bottle of wine and a wide selection of breakfast consumables. Walk through the French doors to the great outdoors and you will find a private heated swimming pool, lounge chairs, and a beautifully landscaped garden. You will also find yourself surrounded by nature at it's finest. Walk or bicycle to your heart's content along marked trails. Want a glimpse of an alligator? We'll take you on a boat cruise down the river for a nominal fee. The beautiful city of Charleston is but 30 minutes away and has plenty to offer. Or, like us, you may be so completely ensconced in your cottage and in the surrounding pine forest that you'll forget about Charleston altogether.

**Address: Pine Grove Plantation, 300 Medway Rd, Goose Creek, SC 29445. Tel: (803) 797-6855, Fax: (803) 824-0435, E-mail: sccottage@aol.com.**

**Type:** Cottage.
**Clientele:** Mostly gay & lesbian with some straight clientele
**Transportation:** Car is best. Complimentary pick up from airport, train.
**To Gay Bars:** 30-min drive.
**Rooms:** 1 cottage with queen bed.
**Bathrooms:** Private bath/toilet/shower.
**Meals:** Full breakfast.
**Vegetarian:** Hosts are vegetarian. We will prepare lunches &/or dinners for an additional charge.
**Complimentary:** Bottle of wine, tea & coffee.
**Dates Open:** All year.
**High Season:** Feb-May & Oct-Dec.
**Rates:** Summer $75-$95, winter $95-$135.
**Discounts:** On extended weekly/monthly stays.
**Credit Cards:** MC, Visa.
**Rsv'tns:** Required.
**Reserve Through:** Travel agent or call direct.
**Minimum Stay:** 2 nights.
**Parking:** Ample free parking. Property inside electric gates, vehicles & contents completely safe.
**In-Room:** Color TV, VCR, phone, ceiling fans, AC, coffee/tea-making facilities, kitchen, ref., maid service.
**On-Premises:** Computer, fax, laundry facilities.
**Exercise/Health:** Massage.
**Swimming:** Pool on premises. Ocean nearby.
**Sunbathing:** Poolside.
**Nudity:** Permitted poolside.
**Smoking:** Permitted outside cottage only.
**Pets:** Permitted, complimentary facilities on property provided for pets. No pets in pool.
**Handicap Access:** Yes.
**Children:** Welcome. Please call for restrictions.
**Languages:** English, moderate French.
**Your Host:** Wendy & Brenda.

## Eighteen Fifty-Four Bed & Breakfast

Gay/Lesbian ♀♂

### *A Tropical Retreat in the Heart of Charleston*

Centrally located in Harleston Village, one of the premier restored areas of Charleston's renowned National Register historical district, ***1854*** is sited in an unusual antebellum edifice of distinctive Italianate design. Both suites are charmingly decorated with an eclectic mix of antique and modern furnishings, original art and sculpture. They have private entrance and access to a rear garden nestled in a lush grove of banana trees and other tropical plantings. The city's best restaurants, gay bars and shopping are a short walk away.

**Address:** 34 Montagu Street, Charleston, SC 29401. **Tel:** (803) 723-4789.

**Type:** Bed & breakfast.
**Clientele:** Mostly gay & lesbian with some straight clientele
**Transportation:** Car is best.
**To Gay Bars:** Four blocks or ten minutes to all local gay bars.
**Rooms:** 2 full suites with double beds.
**Bathrooms:** All private bath/toilets.
**Meals:** Cont. breakfast.
**Vegetarian:** Available with advance notice.
**Dates Open:** All year.
**Rates:** $95-$115. Rates may vary seasonally.
**Discounts:** 10% discount for stays of 3 + nights.
**Rsv'tns:** Required, but will accept late call-ins.
**Reserve Through:** Travel agent or call direct.
**Parking:** Ample free on-street parking.
**In-Room:** Kitchen, refrigerator, AC, color TV, maid service & private outdoor garden area.
**On-Premises:** Lush tropical garden.
**Swimming:** 10-15 miles from all Charleston beaches, including Folly Beach gay area.
**Smoking:** Permitted.
**Children:** Permitted with advance notice only. No infants.
**Languages:** English.

# SOUTH DAKOTA

## RAPID CITY - BLACK HILLS

## Camp Michael B&B

Gay/Lesbian ♀♂

### *Out and About in the Black Hills*

Situated about 12 miles from Rapid City, ***Camp Michael*** is surrounded by the beautiful and serene atmosphere of the Black Hills of South Dakota. Our guests always comment on the absolute quiet of our place. Tourist attractions such as Mt. Rushmore, Devils Tower, the Badlands, Custer State Park and Deadwood are all

*continued next page*

within easy access. We give you a farm-style breakfast that you'll think Grandma made. You'll also have your own living room, private entrance and verandah. A great place to stay for a great price.

**Address: 13051 Bogus Jim Rd, Rapid City, SD 57702**
**Tel: (605) 342-5590, E-mail: campmike 1@aol.com.**

**Type:** Bed & breakfast 12 miles outside Rapid City, 15 minutes from Mt. Rushmore.
**Clientele:** Gay & lesbian. Good mix of men & women
**Transportation:** Car is best.
**Rooms:** 3 rooms with dbl, queen or king beds.
**Bathrooms:** 2 shared bath/shower/toilets.
**Meals:** Full farm-style breakfast. Supper, if you arrive in time.
**Vegetarian:** Upon request.
**Complimentary:** Tea & coffee.
**Dates Open:** All year.
**High Season:** May-Sep.
**Rates:** $50-$75 per room.
**Discounts:** Weekly rates.
**Rsv'tns:** Preferred.
**Reserve Thru:** Call direct.
**Parking:** Ample free off-street parking.
**In-Room:** Ceiling fans, color TV, VCR, coffee & tea-making facilities, kitchen, refrigerator, maid & laundry service.
**On-Premises:** TV lounge, video tape & reading libraries, laundry facilities, wet bar, refrigerator, microwave.
**Exercise/Health:** Power Rider, walking, hiking.
**Sunbathing:** On grounds.
**Nudity:** Open for discussion & depends on clientele.
**Smoking:** Permitted on verandah & in smoking room.
**Pets:** Permitted (dogs, cats, horses).
**Children:** Welcome.
**Languages:** English, sign language.
**Your Host:** Michael & Mike.

# TENNESSEE

## GREENEVILLE

### Timberfell Lodge

Men ♂

## *Impeccable Accommodations, Inspired Cuisine & Courteous Staff*

***Timberfell*** is a fully self-contained gay men's resort, including two lodging facilities, *The Lodge* and *The Poolhouse Annex Building. The Lodge* is a beautiful three-story stone and log guesthouse nestled in a lush, wooded hollow, with 250 acres of mountain trails and springs and an oak barn, surrounded by grassy meadowland. *The Lodge,* decorated with a lovely, eclectic collection of antiques and Oriental rugs, overlooks a pond and a picturesque willow tree. Guests enjoy a charming living room with a ceiling fan, a large stone fireplace, wide screen TV, VCR, a full video library and a stereo. *The Poolhouse Annex building,* the newest lodging facility at ***Timberfell,*** is highlighted by the *Corral Room.* This beautiful room is the largest guest room. It comes complete with a large sitting area, a king-sized bed, TV, VCR, stocked bar refrigerator, private sink, private bath and a veranda with a great view. Also, there are the new *Roommate Rooms,* with two double beds in each room. A full gourmet breakfast, hors d'oeuvres, and dinner are included for all guests, for example, French omelets or buckwheat waffles served with blueberries, pure maple syrup and whipped cream. All gourmet dinners are prepared with the highest-quality ingredients, right down to our homemade desserts and fresh-ground café Angelica. Our chef studied under French President Mitterrand's former personal chef. The chef and his accomplished sous-chef are on duty daily to create the finest of gourmet dining experiences. All of the deluxe rooms are furnished with king- or queen-sized beds, TV, VCR, down pillows and handmade quilts. Nearby attractions include Dollywood, Biltmore Estates, the Appalachian Trail, whitewater rafting and historical Jonesborough, Tennessee.

**Address: 2240 Van Hill Rd, Greeneville, TN 37745**
**Tel: (423) 234-0833 or (800) 437-0118.**

**Type:** Resort.
**Clientele:** Men only, levi/leather & naturists welcome.
**Transportation:** Pick up from airport & bus.
**To Gay Bars:** 30 miles or a half-hour drive.
**Rooms:** 15 rooms w/ bunk, dbl, queen or king beds.
**Bathrooms:** 4 private shower/toilets, 2 private sinks. Others share.
**Campsites:** 4 RV parking spaces & 50 tent sites. Campers have full bath house clean-up facilities. Electric, sewer & water.
**Meals:** Modified American Plan: full breakfast, appetizer trays, full dinner with wine.
**Vegetarian:** Available upon request.
**Complimentary:** Toiletry baskets & terry cloth robes.
**Dates Open:** All year.
**High Season:** Apr-Oct.
**Rates:** $94-$169 single occupancy ($60 for additional person). $94 bunkroom. Campsites $35 with lodge privileges extra.
**Discounts:** 7th night free on stay of 7 days or more.
**Credit Cards:** MC, VISA, Amex & Discover.
**Rsv'tns:** Required.
**Reserve Through:** Travel agent or call direct.
**Minimum Stay:** 2 nights on holidays.
**Parking:** Free off-street secured parking.
**In-Room:** Color TV, housekeeping & laundry service. Deluxe rooms have VCR, bar ref. & coffee pots.
**On-Premises:** Central AC, living room with entertainment center & 24-person dining room.
**Exercise/Health:** 20-person sauna, 8-person Jacuzzi, massages, bikes, bench press, gravity inversion, fishing & hiking trails & canoe.
**Swimming:** 20 x 40 foot heated pool on premises.
**Sunbathing:** At poolside, pond, on common sun deck or in backyard.
**Nudity:** Permitted inside lodge and on all 250 acres.
**Smoking:** A smoking area is set aside for winter.
**Pets:** Call ahead.
**Children:** Not permitted.

IGTA

# NEWPORT

## Christopher Place

Q-NET Gay-Owned 50/50 ♀♂

SEE SPECIAL COLOR SECTION PAGE 28

### *We're Easy to Find, but Hard to Forget*

Surrounded by expansive mountain views, this premiere bed & breakfast includes over 200 acres to explore, a pool, tennis court and sauna. Relax by the marble fireplace in the library, retreat to the game room, or enjoy a hearty mountain meal in our restaurant. Romantic rooms are available with a hot tub or fireplace. Off I-40 at exit 435, ***Christopher Place*** is just 32 scenic miles from Gatlinburg and Pigeon Forge. Perfect for special occasions and gatherings. Rated 4 diamonds by AAA. Gay-owned & -operated.

**Address: 1500 Pinnacles Way, Newport, TN 37821**
**Tel: (423) 623-6555 (Tel/Fax), (800) 595-9441 (for brochure).**

**Type:** Gay-owned & -operated inn with restaurant.
**Clientele:** 50% gay & lesbian clientele
**Transportation:** Car is best. $25 for pick up from airport.
**To Gay Bars:** 40 miles or an hour drive.
**Rooms:** 9 rooms & 1 suite with double, queen or king beds.

*continued next page*

**Bathrooms:** Private: 2 bath/toilets, 4 shower/toilets & 4 bath/shower/toilets. **Meals:** Full breakfast. **Vegetarian:** Available with 24-hour notice. **Complimentary:** Afternoon tea & lemonade. **Dates Open:** All year. **High Season:** Jul-Oct. **Rates:** $99-$199. **Discounts:** Special gift to Inn Places readers. **Credit Cards:** MC & Visa. **Rsv'tns:** Recommended. **Reserve Through:** Travel agent or call direct. **Minimum Stay:** Some holidays or special weekends. **Parking:** Ample free off-street parking. **In-Room:** AC, ceiling fans & maid service. Some rooms with hot tubs & fireplaces. **On-Premises:** TV lounge, VCR, video tape library, meeting rooms, game room, tanning bed, fax, copy, word processing equipment. **Exercise/Health:** Sauna & weights. **Swimming:** Pool on premises. **Sunbathing:** At poolside. **Nudity:** Permitted in sauna. **Smoking:** Permitted in game room & on porches. **Pets:** Not permitted. **Handicap Access:** Yes. **Children:** Ages 12 & over welcomed. **Languages:** English. **Your Host:** Drew.

IGTA

# TEXAS

## AUSTIN

### Park Lane Guesthouse

Gay/Lesbian ♀♂

*Discover the Live Music Capital of the World*

Entertainment and natural beauty abound year-round in Austin. ***Park Lane Guesthouse,*** a restored traditional Texas home, is five minutes from shops and restaurants and only one mile to the lively downtown entertainment district, gay bars, the river, parks, and hike and bike trails. Located in historic Travis Heights neighborhood, the spacious private cottage surrounded by gardens and ancient live oaks has a full kitchen. There is a cozy guest room with private bath in the main house. Come discover friendly Austin with us.

**Address: 221 Park Lane, Austin, TX 78704**
**Tel: (512) 447-7460, (800) 492-8827.**

**Type:** Cottage & guesthouse. **Clientele:** Mostly gay & lesbian with some straight clientele. **Transportation:** Car or taxi from airport, or call for pick up from airport, train, bus ($10 each way). **To Gay Bars:** 10 blocks, a 20-minute walk, a 5-minute drive. **Rooms:** 1 room in house, 3 rooms in cottage with double or queen beds. **Bathrooms:** Private shower/toilet. 2-person tiled shower in cottage. **Meals:** Expanded continental breakfast. **Vegetarian:** Breakfast is vegetarian, 3-5 block to 5 restaurants. **Complimentary:** Tea, coffee always available. **Dates Open:** All year. **High Season:** October-May. **Rates:** Guestroom in main house: single $65, double $75. Cottage (accommodates 4): $100 double ($15 each addt'l person). **Discounts:** 1 night free with full week's stay. **Rsv'tns:** Required. **Reserve Through:** Call direct. **Parking:** Ample off-street. **In-Room:** AC, maid service, coffee/tea-making facilities, ceiling fans. Cottage: color TV, VCR, kitchen, refrigerator, ceiling fans. **Exercise/Health:** Massage on premises & nearby. Jacuzzi in summer, 1997. **Swimming:** Pool in summer, 1997. Nearby pool, river, lake. **Sunbathing:** At poolside, on common sun decks. **Smoking:** Permitted outside only. All rooms are non-smoking. **Pets:** Permitted with prior notice & pet deposit. **Handicap Access:** Cottage is accessible. **Children:** Welcome, but there are no special facilities. **Languages:** English.

## Summit House

Gay/Lesbian ♀♂

### *Best Breakfast in Texas!*

Located on an old Indian campground above the Colorado River, the house and herb gardens nestled under 100-year-old oak trees give the feeling of a secluded hideaway. The guesthouse is close to the hearbeat of Austin, just minutes from downtown, quaint shopping and dining. We have a very down-home atmosphere at the ***Summit House.*** Your host, David, will be helpful in letting you know what is going on in the Live Music Capital of the World. He also conducts shopping and gourmet tours of Austin, as well as a variety of sightseeing tours of the city, including the gay nightlife. Come experience the true feeling ot Texas!

**Address: 1204 Summit St, Austin, TX 78741-1158. Tel: (512) 445-5304.**

**Type:** Guesthouse.
**Clientele:** Gay & lesbian, straight-friendly
**Transport.:** Car, taxi, bus.
**To Gay Bars:** 15 minute walk, a 5 minute drive.
**Rooms:** 2 suites w/ queen beds, 1 single with a 3/4 bed.
**Bathrooms:** 1 shared & 1 outdoor shower garden.
**Meals:** Full down-home breakfast.
**Vegetarian:** Available. Vegetarian markets & restaurants nearby.
**Complimentary:** Wine, beer, iced tea, coffee, juice, home-baked goodies & fresh fruit.
**Dates Open:** All year.
**High Season:** Oct-May.
**Rates:** Sgl or double $69.
**Discounts:** Stay 5 nights, 6th night is free.
**Rsv'tns:** Recommended
**Reserve Thru:** Call direct.
**Parking:** Off-street parking.
**In-Room:** Central AC & heat, ceiling fans, sitting area, color TV, phone service, large windows, natural fabrics, flowers.
**On-Premises:** Great trees, natural garden setting, lots of birds and wildlife.
**Exercise/Health:** Massage, weights, hike & bike trail.
**Swimming:** Nearby public pools. 2 miles to Barton Springs, one of the world's best swimming holes.
**Sunbathing:** On patio.
**Nudity:** Permitted in private sunning area.
**Smoking:** Outside only.
**Children:** Not welcomed.
**Languages:** English.
**Your Host:** David.

# CORPUS CHRISTI - ROCKPORT

## Anthony's by the Sea

Gay/Lesbian ♀♂

A few minutes from Padre Island National Seashore, ***Anthony's by the Sea*** is hidden by live oaks on two thirds of an acre with pool and therapy spa and spacious lawn. Choose from four bedrooms (some with private baths and seating areas) or two guest cottages, which have private baths, living rooms, dining areas, and fully-equipped kitchens with dishwasher and microwave. The lanai is covered and carpeted, with chandeliers, BBQ, and fountains. Gourmet breakfasts are served in an open dining area or on the patio where guests can watch hummingbirds, butterflies, squirrels, and geckos.

**Address: 732 S Pearl, Rockport, TX 78382**
**Tel: (512) 729-6100, (800) 460-2557.**

**Type:** Bed & breakfast.
**Clientele:** Mostly gay & lesbian with some straight clientele.
**Transportation:** Car is best.
**To Gay Bars:** 30 miles to Corpus Christi bars. 10 miles to gay-friendly bar.
**Rooms:** 4 rooms & 1 cottage. 550 sq ft Spanish Suite w/wet bar, 17' x 17' living area & king bed.
**Bathrooms:** 3 private & 1 shared.
**Meals:** Full gourmet breakfast.
**Vegetarian:** Available upon request.
**Complimentary:** Juices, iced tea, coffee, lemonade, & an afternoon snack.
**Dates Open:** All year.
**Rates:** $50-$95.
**Discounts:** 7th day free.
**Rsv'tns:** Requested.
**Reserve Through:** Travel agent or call direct.
**Parking:** Carports.
**In-Room:** Color TV, VCR, AC, ceiling fans, refrigerator & maid service.
**On-Premises:** TV lounge, laundry facilities, telephone & full, covered lanai with fans & chandeliers.
**Exercise/Health:** Weights & Jacuzzi.
**Swimming:** Pool on premises. 5 blocks to beach.
**Sunbathing:** On common sun decks & at the beach 5 blocks away.
**Nudity:** Permitted by the pool.
**Smoking:** Permitted with restrictions.
**Pets:** On approval.
**Children:** Permitted in the cottage.
**Languages:** English & Span.
**Your Host:** Tony & Denis

# DALLAS

## Courtyard on the Trail

Gay/Lesbian ♀♂

### *Maximum Comfort, Privacy and Convenience*

Enter through arched gates into a relaxing and memorable experience at ***Courtyard on the Trail.*** While close to downtown and North Dallas, we are far enough removed to afford guests a country setting in which to kick back and relax. The B&B is decorated with elegant antique and modern furnishings, fine linens and art. Your bedroom has direct access to the pool and courtyard through French doors, affording you maximum comfort, privacy and convenience. Luxuriate in your marble bathroom's extra-large bathtub while contemplating the beautiful clouds painted on a blue sky overhead. Whether you are in town for business or celebrating a special occasion, your host will ensure a personalized, first-class stay.

**Address: 8045 Forest Trail, Dallas, TX 75238**
**Tel: (214) 553-9700 (Tel/Fax), (800) 484-6260 pin #0465.**
**E-mail: akrubs4u@aol.com.**

**Type:** Bed & breakfast.
**Clientele:** Mostly gay & lesbian with some straight clientele
**Transportation:** Car. Pick up service if prearranged.
**To Gay Bars:** 6 miles, a 15 minute drive.
**Rooms:** 3 rooms with king or queen beds.
**Bathrooms:** 3 private bath/toilet/showers.
**Meals:** Full breakfast. Dinner if prearranged.
**Vegetarian:** Available if prearranged. Vegetarian cuisine within 1 mile.
**Complimentary:** Wine, fruit & delectables upon arrival & each day thereafter. Mints on pillows each night. Champagne for special occasions.
**Dates Open:** All year.
**High Season:** June-Nov.
**Rates:** $85-$140.
**Discounts:** Mon-Thurs 10%. Extended stays over 3 days 10%. All repeat customers 10%.
**Credit Cards:** MC, Visa.
**Rsv'tns:** Required.
**Reserve Through:** Travel agent or call direct.
**Parking:** Ample off-street parking.
**In-Room:** AC, color cable TV, VCR, telephone, ceiling fans, maid & laundry service.
**On-Premises:** Meeting rooms, fax & computer, video tape library, private garden.
**Exercise/Health:** Massage.
**Swimming:** Pool on premises.
**Sunbathing:** Poolside, in hammock in private garden.
**Nudity:** Permitted poolside with discretion.
**Smoking:** Permitted outside only.
**Pets:** Not permitted.
**Handicap Access:** No.
**Children:** No.
**Languages:** English.
**Your Host:** Alan.

## Inn on Fairmount

Gay/Lesbian ♀♂

### *The Ambiance of an Inn, the Luxury of a Fine Hotel*

The ***Inn on Fairmount*** is located in the heart of the Oak Lawn/Turtle Creek area, minutes from restaurants, clubs and the Dallas Market Center.

There are seven finely-furnished bedrooms and suites with private baths, a beautifully decorated lounge and a Jacuzzi. Coffee is placed outside your door each morning. Continental breakfast is served in the lounge as is evening wine and cheese. For the ambiance of an inn and the luxury of a fine hotel, spend a night or two with us and experience the style and good taste which is the ***Inn on Fairmount!***

**Address: 3701 Fairmount, Dallas, TX 75219**
**Tel: (214) 522-2800 or Fax: (214) 522-2898.**

**Type:** Bed & breakfast inn.
**Clientele:** Mostly gay & lesbian with some straight clientele
**Transportation:** Car or airport shuttle.
**To Gay Bars:** 2-1/2 blocks.
**Rooms:** 7 rooms with twin, queen & king beds.
**Bathrooms:** All private.
**Meals:** Cont. breakfast.
**Complimentary:** Evening wine & cheese hour.
**Dates Open:** All year.
**Rates:** Per night: rooms $85, mini-suites $100, 2-room suite $125.
**Discs:** On longer stays.
**Credit Cards:** MC, Visa.
**Rsv'tns:** Recommended, especially on weekends.
**Reserve Through:** Travel agent or call direct.
**Parking:** Ample free off-street parking.
**In-Room:** Color TV, AC, telephone, video tape library, maid service. Some rooms with ceiling fans. VCR in 2-room suite.
**On-Premises:** Fax machine.
**Exercise/Health:** Jacuzzi.
**Sunbathing:** On common sun decks.
**Smoking:** Not in lobby.
**Pets:** Not permitted.
**Handicap Access:** 1 room with widened doors.
**Children:** Not especially welcome.
**Languages:** English, Spanish.
**Your Host:** Michael.

# HOUSTON

## The Lovett Inn

Gay/Lesbian ♀♂

### *You'll Love It at the Lovett!*

Originally the home of a former mayor, ***The Lovett Inn*** now offers unique client lodging and distinctive catering accommodations for corporate meetings, seminars, retreats and receptions. Guest rooms and suites, each restored with antiques, have queen-sized beds, adjoining bathrooms, color TV and telephone. Surrounding the inn are landscaped grounds with box hedges and brick paths, a swimming pool and a spa in a magnificent setting.

**Address: 501 Lovett Blvd, Houston, TX 77006**
**Tel: (713) 522-5224, Fax: 528-6708, (800) 779-5224.**

**Type:** Inn.
**Clientele:** 75% gay & 25% straight clientele.
**Transportation:** Airport shuttle to downtown Hyatt, then taxi.
**To Gay Bars:** 1/2 block to gay/lesbian bars.
**Rooms:** 3 rooms, 3 suites, 1 apartment & 1 cottage with double, queen or king beds.
**Bathrooms:** All private. 3 with whirlpool baths.
**Meals:** Continental breakfast.

*continued next page*

**Vegetarian:** Available.
**Complimentary:** Tea, coffee, candy in rooms.
**Dates Open:** All year.
**Rates:** $65-$150.
**Discounts:** Group and long-term rates.
**Credit Cards:** MC, Visa, Amex, Discover.
**Rsv'tns:** Suggested.
**Reserve Through:** Call direct.
**Minimum Stay:** Required at peak times.
**Parking:** Ample, free parking.
**In-Room:** Color cable TV, VCR, kitchen, coffee & tea-making facilities & laundry service.
**On-Premises:** Meeting rooms & TV lounge. Laundry available.
**Exercise/Health:** Jacuzzi. Nearby gym, weights, Jacuzzi, sauna, steam & massage.
**Swimming:** Pool on premises, 30-60 minutes to ocean beach, lake.
**Sunbathing:** At poolside or on private sun decks.
**Smoking:** Permitted in public areas & in some smoke-friendly rooms.
**Pets:** Permitted on approval.
**Handicap Access:** No.
**Children:** Permitted on approval.
**Languages:** English.
IGTA

# PORT ARANSAS

## Seahorse Inn

Q-NET Gay/Lesbian ♀♂

### *Gay-Owned & -Operated Since 1956*

Experience the warmth of Port Aransas at the ***Seahorse Inn.*** We are secluded high atop a sand dune, a short sandy stroll to the beach. In-room antiques and classical decor complete the uncluttered ambience of the inn's ocean view units. In addition to eighteen miles of unobstructed white sandy beaches, we have a very private, clothing optional, heated pool surrounded by tropical gardens. ***The Seahorse Inn*** provides a charming European style tastefully set on the wild dunes of Mustang Island and sun-drenched Port Aransas.

**Address: PO Box 426, Port Aransas, TX 78373. Tel: (512) 749-5221.**

**Type:** Self-catering guesthouse with separate entrances. Completely private.
**Clientele:** Good mix of gay men & lesbians with very few straight clientele
**Transportation:** Car is best. Free pick up from local airport (for private planes). Can arrange pick up at Corpus Christi Int'l airport.
**To Gay Bars:** 28 miles to gay bars in Corpus Christi.
**Rooms:** 1 room, 1 suite, 1 cottage & 12 efficiencies All units have cooking facilities.
**Bathrooms:** All private.
**Meals:** Self-catering.
**Complimentary:** Coffee & tea.
**Dates Open:** All year.
**High Season:** March-October.
**Rates:** From $55 for one or two people.
**Discounts:** Seventh night is free.
**Credit Cards:** MC, Visa, Amex, Discover.
**Rsv'tns:** Recommended.
**Reserve Through:** Call direct.
**Minimum Stay:** During certain periods. Please inquire.
**Parking:** Adequate, free off-street parking.
**In-Room:** Color cable TV, AC, ceiling fans, kitchen, refrigerator. Optional maid service at extra charge for 2-day stays.
**On-Premises:** Meeting rooms.
**Swimming:** In heated pool or nearby ocean. 20 miles to gay beach.
**Sunbathing:** At poolside, beach, patio, common sun decks.
**Nudity:** Permitted poolside.
**Smoking:** Permitted.
**Pets:** Trained pets welcome.
**Handicap Access:** No.
**Children:** No.
**Languages:** English.
**Your Host:** Hunter & Rod.

# SAN ANTONIO

## Adelynne's Summit Haus & Summit Haus II

Gay/Lesbian ♀♂

### *Welcome, Wilkommen, Bienvenidos, Bienvenue, Benvenuto, C'mon Over, Stay Awhile...*

***Adelynne's Summit Haus & Summit Haus II*** are two elegant 1920's bed and breakfast accommodations. Just minutes north of San Antonio's downtown historical, multicultural attractions, they offer luxury, comfort and privacy for less than most hotels. Furnishings include rare Biedermeier antiques, crystal, porcelain, Persian and Oriental rugs and French and English antiques. The adjacent 2000-square-foot cottage is beautifully-furnished with all the comforts of elegant accommodations in our tradition of Texas hospitality.

**Address: 427 W Summit, San Antonio, TX 78212**
**Tel: (800) 972-7266, (210) 736-6272, (210) 828-3045, Fax: (210) 737-8244.**

**Type:** Bed & breakfast.
**Clientele:** Gay & lesbian. Good mix of men & women.
**Transportation:** Car.
**To Gay Bars:** 1 mile or 5 minutes by car.
**Rooms:** 2 rooms, 1 suite & 1 cottage with double, queen or king beds.
**Bathrooms:** 3 private bath/toilets & 1 private shower/toilet.
**Meals:** Full breakfast.
**Complimentary:** Brandy, cognac, soft drinks & beer.
**Dates Open:** All year.
**Rates:** $67.50-$150.
**Credit Cards:** MC, VISA, Amex.
**Rsv'tns:** Required.
**Reserve Thru:** Call direct.
**Minimum Stay:** 2 nights on weekends.
**Parking:** Ample free off-street parking.
**In-Room:** Color TV, AC, tele., ceiling fans, ref., coffee/tea-making facilities.
**On-Premises:** Meeting rooms & laundry facilities.
**Sunbathing:** In the backyard & on common sun decks.
**Smoking:** Outside on decks. Other areas non-smoking.
**Pets:** Not permitted.
**Children:** Will accept children over 10 years of age.
**Languages:** English & German.

## Arbor House Hotel

Q-NET Gay-Owned ♀♂

### *The Best-Kept Secret in Downtown San Antonio*

The ***Arbor House Hotel*** invites you to the most unique all-suites hotel in San Antonio. Although it looks like a B&B, the four buildings, built in 1903, have central AC/heat, state-of-the-art phone and messaging systems, private baths and furnishings unlike any hotel you have ever visited. The location is convenient to the Riverwalk and downtown, but you won't have to fight the crowds to "get away from it all" – just relax in our formal gardens under the grape arbor. Come see for yourself – you will be forever grateful that you found us.

*continued next page*

**Address: 339 S. Presa St, San Antonio, TX 78205**
**Tel: (210) 472-2005, Toll-free: (888) 272-6700, Fax: (210) 472-2007.**

**Type:** Hotel.
**Clientele:** Mostly straight clientele. Looking to increase gay & lesbian clientele
**Transportation:** Airport limo or taxi.
**To Gay Bars:** 2 blocks, a 5 minute walk, a 2 minute drive.
**Rooms:** 11 suites with king or double beds.
**Bathrooms:** Private: 3 shower/toilets, 8 bath/shower/toilets.
**Meals:** Continental breakfast.
**Vegetarian:** Inquire. Available nearby.
**Complimentary:** Coffeemaker in all suites.
**Dates Open:** All year.
**Rates:** $140-$250.
**Credit Cards:** MC, Visa, Amex, Discover.
**Rsv'tns:** Required.
**Reserve Through:** Travel agent or call direct.
**Minimum Stay:** Required on holiday weekends.
**Parking:** Adequate free off-street parking.
**In-Room:** AC, color cable TV, telephone, coffee & tea-making facilities, maid service. Some rooms have refrigerators & ceiling fans.
**Exercise/Health:** 1 block to Riverwalk, nearby weights, Jacuzzi, sauna, massage.
**Swimming:** Pool nearby.
**Sunbathing:** Poolside & on patio.
**Smoking:** Permitted outside, on porch & on balcony. All suites are non-smoking.
**Pets:** Small-medium dogs permitted (under 25 lbs), $15 charge per night.
**Handicap Access:** No.
**Children:** Welcome.
**Languages:** English.
**Your Host:** Reg & Dale.

IGTA

## The Garden Cottage

**Gay/Lesbian ♀♂**

Come to ***The Garden Cottage*** in San Antonio. There's no place like it! We offer privacy and a country-style atmosphere, yet we're minutes from downtown, shopping, restaurants, museums, and public gardens. Our cozy cottage, shaded by Texas pecan trees in a quiet residential neighborhood, is conveniently located near San Antonio's historic and cultural attractions. San Antonio is home to the Alamo, River Walk, and its five Spanish missions are part of the National Park System.

**Address: San Antonio, TX. Tel: (210) 828-4539 (tel/fax), (800) 235-7215.**

**Type:** Cottage adjacent to the San Antonio Botanical Gardens.
**Clientele:** Mainly gay/lesbian with some straight clientele.
**Transportation:** Taxi, rental car, or bus.
**To Gay Bars:** 6 blocks to gay bar, 15-20 min to lesbian bars.
**Rooms:** 1 cottage with double beds.
**Bathrooms:** 1 private shower/toilet.
**Complimentary:** Drinks, snacks, fruit, popcorn.
**Dates Open:** All year.
**High Season:** March-May & Sept-Nov.
**Rates:** $50-$80.
**Discounts:** Weekly rate $250-$350.
**Rsv'tns:** Required.
**Reserve Through:** Call direct.
**Minimum Stay:** 2 nights.
**Parking:** Ample, free off-street parking.
**In-Room:** Color cable TV, VCR, AC, telephone, ceiling fans, kitchen, refrigerator, coffee & tea-making facilities.
**On-Premises:** Laundry facilities upon request.
**Exercise/Health:** Massage $30-$40.
**Swimming:** 15 min to public pool, 1 hr to river, lake, 2 hrs to ocean beach.
**Sunbathing:** On patio.
**Smoking:** Permitted on porch.
**Pets:** Not permitted.
**Handicap Access:** Not wheelchair accessible.
**Children:** No.
**Languages:** English, German.

## San Antonio Bed & Breakfast

**Gay/Lesbian ♀♂**

### *A Chili Bowl of Culture*

Eclectic and stately, with its 32-foot octagonal tower, this 1891 homestead, ***San Antonio B&B,*** is situated in the King William Historical Neighborhood two blocks from the Riverwalk. Uniquely decorated rooms have private or semi-private entrances. Relax outdoors under the grape arbor, the three arched porticos or on the second-story veranda. We serve breakfast in the formal dining room adjacent to the music room. A touch of the Old West, a trace of the South, a taste of Mexico. That's totally San Antonio! Currently under renovation.

**Address: 510 E Guenther, San Antonio, TX 78210-1133**
**Tel: (210) 222-1828.**

**Type:** Bed & breakfast.
**Clientele:** Gay & lesbian
**Transportation:** Car is best. Shuttle bus to downtown.
**To Gay Bars:** 12 blocks or 1/2 mile. 15 minutes by foot or 3 minutes by car.
**Rooms:** 3 rms w/ full beds.
**Bathrooms:** 2 private bath/toilets & 1 shared bath/shower/toilet.
**Meals:** Full breakfast weekends. Continental breakfast weekdays.
**Vegetarian:** Available upon request.
**Comp.:** Fruit & wine.
**Dates Open:** All year.
**High Season:** Fiesta, 3rd week in April.
**Rates:** From $85.
**Rsv'tns:** Required.
**Reserve Thru:** Call direct.
**Parking:** Off-street shaded parking.
**In-Room:** Color TV, AC, housekeeping & room serv.
**On-Premises:** Laund. fac.
**Exercise/Health:** Jacuzzi & nearby YMCA.
**Sunbathing:** On common sun decks.
**Smoking:** Perm. outdoors.
**Pets:** Not permitted.
**Handicap Access:** Handicapped welcome. Tell us your needs.
**Children:** Any age welcomed.

# SOUTH PADRE ISLAND

## Upper Deck, A Guesthouse

Q-NET Gay/Lesbian ♀♂

### *An Island of Pure Fun and Relaxation*

***Upper Deck*** is the only openly gay establishment in the vicinity. There is a strong representation of Hispanics in the area, because of our close proximity to Mexico, Matamoros being only 30 minutes away. Convenient air connections are available to Harlingen via Continental, American and Southwest Airlines. Mexican airlines serve other area cities. South Padre Island is world-famous for deep-sea fishing. Bay fishing, pier fishing and surf fishing are also extremely popular. This area is the home of the area's largest shrimping fleet. Bring your surfboard or wind surfer for some exciting action. Shop or party in Matamoros, Mexico. Enjoy one of the nation's top beaches. Visit the Gladys Porter Zoo in Brownsville, TX, the home of endangered species. Nearby Laguna at Atascosa National Wildlife Preserve is a delight for birders and wildlife enthusiasts. A nude beach, some 15 miles to the north, is a quiet refuge for fun and relaxation.

Our hotel is designed for the gay or lesbian traveler who is interested in meeting new friends, or for lovers who want to enjoy a getaway where they can unwind and be themselves. Now under new ownership, the building is being updated and renewed to provide guests with the most comfortable environment possible. The Crews Quarters Bar is an addition to the hotel and is becoming one of the hot spots in the Rio Grande Valley. The entire inn can be booked by gay and lesbian groups for conferences, meetings, parties, etc. The area abounds in excellent and moderately priced restaurants.

**Address: 120 E Atol, Box 2309, South Padre Island, TX 78597**
**Tel: (210) 761-5953, Fax: (210) 761-4288.**

**Type:** Hotel.
**Clientele:** Good mix of gay men & women
**Transportation:** Hotel limo service (24 hr notice, addt'l fee). Airport shuttle service available (small charge).
**To Gay Bars:** Crews Quarters Bar in hotel, 1 hr to Harlingen gay bars. Gays discreetly frequent straight bars nearby.
**Rooms:** 19 recently renovated rooms with double, king, queen, Craftmatic, waterbeds, bunk beds & daily locker rental.
**Bathrooms:** All private.
**Meals:** Complimentary coffee & Danish pastry 9am-12 noon.
**Dates Open:** All year.
**High Season:** February 12-Labor Day.
**Rates:** $36-$160.
**Discounts:** Call for special rates.
**Credit Cards:** MC, Visa.
**Rsv'tns:** Recommended.
**Reserve Through:** Call direct.
**Minimum Stay:** 2 nights weekends, 3 on holidays.
**Parking:** Parking lot on premises for hotel & bar.
**In-Room:** Color remote TV, ceiling fans, AC & maid service.
**On-Premises:** TV lounge, laundry facilities, game room, kitchen, soda machine.
**Exercise/Health:** Jacuzzi on premises. Horseback riding, jet ski, bike rental nearby.
**Swimming:** Heated pool & ocean.
**Sunbathing:** On beach, common sun deck or at poolside.
**Nudity:** Permitted in pool & Jacuzzi. Nude beach nearby.
**Smoking:** Non-smoking rooms available.
**Pets:** Not permitted.
**Handicap Access:** Hotel, no. Bar, yes.
**Children:** Not permitted.
**Languages:** English, Spanish.

# UTAH

## ESCALANTE

### Rainbow Country Tours and Bed & Breakfast

Q-NET Gay-Friendly 50/50 ♀♂

***Experience A Truly Unique Indoor/Outdoor Adventure...***

The spectacular wilderness of the Grand Staircase Escalante National Monument surrounds you at ***Rainbow Country B&B,*** a hilltop B&B with views of nearby mountains and slick rock. Conveniently located near a charming rustic town and four national parks, our modern home offers spa, pool table, cable TV, full breakfast and optional jeep & hiking tours. We specialize in taking guests "off the beaten path" to enjoy outdoor activities like hiking, jeep tours, horseback riding, bicycling and camp-outs in a vast private locale. We are open all year. Call for a free, detailed brochure.

**Address: 586 E 300 S, Escalante, UT 84726**
**Tel: (801) 826-4567, (800) 252-UTAH (8824).**

**Type:** Bed & breakfast guesthouse with jeep tours.
**Clientele:** 50% gay & lesbian & 50% hetero clientele
**Transportation:** Car or commuter flight from Las Vegas or Salt Lake City. Free pick up from Bryce Canyon airport.
**To Gay Bars:** 200 miles.
**Rooms:** 4 rooms with single, double, queen or king beds.
**Bathrooms:** 2 shared bath/shower/toilets & 1 shared toilet.
**Campsites:** 2 RV parking only.
**Meals:** Full breakfast.
**Vegetarian:** Almost always available.
**Complimentary:** Coffee, tea, soft drinks & munchies.
**Dates Open:** All year.
**Rates:** $45-$55.
**Discounts:** Group rates, travel agents 10%.
**Credit Cards:** MC & VISA.
**Reserve Through:** Travel agent or call direct.
**Parking:** Ample free off-street parking.
**In-Room:** AC.
**On-Premises:** TV lounge.
**Swimming:** River & lake nearby.
**Sunbathing:** On common sun decks.
**Smoking:** Permitted outside.
**Pets:** Well-trained pets permitted.
**Handicap Access:** No.
**Languages:** English.
**Your Host:** Gene.

## MOAB

### Mt. Peale Bed & Breakfast Country Inn

Gay-Friendly 50/50 ♀♂

***A Mountain Paradise in Southeastern Utah***

A short 35 miles southeast of Moab, ***Mt. Peale Bed & Breakfast*** rests at the base of Southeastern Utah's greatest peaks, the La Sal Mountains. Each guestroom is individually decorated, representing the natural diversity of the area. The Garden Nook represents the wildflowers & birds of Mt. Peale; The Timber Trek illuminates the unforgettable terrain and wildlife of the La Sal Mountains; and The Sea Cove reflects the innkeepers' love of the sea. A nutritious breakfast is served daily inside or outdoors on the deck. The area's summer and winter activities include hiking, four-wheeling, biking, fishing, skiing, snowmobiling and snow shoeing.

**Address: PO Box 366, LaSal, UT 84530**
**Tel: (801) 686-2284 (Tel/Fax), mobile: (801) 260-1305.**

**Type:** Bed & breakfast & cottages.
**Clientele:** 50% gay & lesbian & 50% straight clientele
**Transportation:** Car, 4-wheel drive helpful, airport in Moab. Free pickup from Moab airport or Monticello airstrip with Inn Places ad.
**To Gay Bars:** 150 miles to gay bars.
**Rooms:** 3 rooms, 1 cottage with double (extended) or queen beds. Single beds in 1997.
**Bathrooms:** Private shower/toilets, 1 shared bath/shower/toilet.
**Meals:** Buffet breakfast, family-style dinner, picnic available.
**Vegetarian:** Available, specify when making reservation.
**Complimentary:** Fruit drinks, wine set-ups, cocktails, tea & coffee.
**Dates Open:** All year.
**High Season:** Apr-Jul & Sept-Nov.
**Rates:** $65-$120.
**Discounts:** 10%-15% weekdays during low season.
**Credit Cards:** MC, Visa, Discover.
**Rsv'tns:** Required, walk-ins accepted.
**Reserve Through:** Travel agent or call direct.
**Minimum Stay:** Required Dec 25-Jan 1 & any festival wknd. 2 nights holiday wknds.
**Parking:** Adequate free parking.
**In-Room:** Maid, room & laundry service, portable phone.
**On-Premises:** Meeting rooms, TV lounge, fax, phone, modem, laundry service ($3 per load).
**Exercise/Health:** Volleyball, basketball, horseshoes, Jacuzzi, massage by appointment when making reservation.
**Swimming:** Nearby river, lakes.
**Sunbathing:** On common sun decks, on hot tub deck.
**Smoking:** Permitted outside.
**Pets:** Please inquire.
**Handicap Access:** No.
**Children:** Welcome.

# SALT LAKE CITY

## Anton Boxrud B&B

Gay-Friendly ♀♂

### *Salt Lake's Closest B&B to Downtown*

When looking for a warm homebase from which to explore Salt Lake City and the Wasatch mountains, we invite you to relax in the casual elegance of our historic home, ***Anton Boxrud B&B.*** Half a block from the Governor's Mansion, we are the closest B&B to downtown, just a 15-minute walk. In the evenings, enjoy complimentary beverages and snacks. The hot tub can provide liquid refreshment of a different kind. We serve full breakfasts featuring Grandma Glady's freshly baked cinnamon buns.

**Address: 57 South 600 East, Salt Lake City, UT 84102**
**Tel: (801) 363-8035, (800) 524-5511, Fax: (801) 596-1316.**

**Type:** Bed & breakfast.
**Clientele:** Mostly straight clientele with a gay & lesbian following.
**Transportation:** Car or taxi.
**To Gay Bars:** 8 blocks.
**Rooms:** 6 rooms & 1 suite with single, queen or king beds.
**Bathrooms:** Private: 2 shower/toilets, 3 full baths. Shared: 1 full bath, 1 shower.
**Meals:** Full breakfast.
**Complimentary:** Evening snacks, beverages, coffee & tea.
**Dates Open:** All year.
**High Season:** Jun-Oct (summer) & Jan-Mar (ski season).
**Rates:** $59-$129.
**Credit Cards:** MC, Visa, Amex, Diners, Discover.
**Rsv'tns:** Recommended.
**Reserve Through:** Call direct.
**Minimum Stay:** 2 nights on weekends.
**Parking:** Ample on-street & off-street covered parking.
**In-Room:** AC, mints, terrycloth robes, flowers, shampoo & soap, maid service.
**On-Premises:** TV lounge, meeting rooms.
**Exercise/Health:** Jacuzzi on premises. Nearby gym, weights, Jacuzzi, sauna, steam & massage.
**Swimming:** Nearby pool & lake.
**Sunbathing:** At the beach.
**Smoking:** Permitted outside only.
**Pets:** Not permitted.
**Handicap Access:** No.
**Children:** Welcome.
**Languages:** English, French.
**Your Host:** Jane & Jerome.

# SOUTH CENTRAL UTAH

## SkyRidge, A Bed & Breakfast Inn

Gay-Friendly ♀♂

### *Karen & Sally Will Treat You to Red Cliffs, Sandstone Domes, and Forested Mountains*

***SkyRidge B&B*** sits on 75 beautiful acres, surrounded by some of the most magnificent scenery Southern Utah has to offer. **AAA has awarded the inn 4 Diamonds and guests have rated SkyRidge as one of the top inns in Utah's State B&B Association.** The inn features an eclectic decor, including art furnishings such as a painted fireplace decorated with 30 pounds of roofing nails, created by the nationally exhibited artist-owner Karen Kesler. Each of the five rooms has a private bath, queen-sized bed, TV/ VCR and phone. Rooms with patio, deck, Jacuzzi or hot tub are available. Sally Elliot, co-owner and chef, indicates "Guest favorites include croissant French toast and a made-to-order fresh vegetable or smoked trout omelet." Experience this spectacular park - cooler than Arches/Zion in the summer and less crowded than both!

**Address: near Capitol Reef National Park, Torrey, UT**
**Tel: (801) 425-3222 (Tel/Fax).**

**Type:** Bed & breakfast.
**Clientele:** Mostly straight clientele with a gay/lesbian following
**Transportation:** Car is best (we recommend a 4-wheel drive if staying 3-4 days), 3-1/2 hrs to Salt Lake City airport.
**Rooms:** 5 rooms with queen beds.
**Bathrooms:** Private: 1 Jacuzzi tub/toilet, 1 shower & hot tub/toilet, 3 bath/ shower/toilets.
**Meals:** Full breakfast.
**Vegetarian:** All breakfasts are vegetarian, 2 restaurants in town w/ vegetarian dinners.
**Complimentary:** Sherry, fruit, soft drinks, tea & candy dish 24hrs in dining room. Chocolates in room, hors d'oeuvres in afternoon.
**Dates Open:** All year.
**High Season:** May-early June & September-October.
**Rates:** $82-$120.
**Discounts:** Sun-Thurs, Jan-Mar, 10%, except holidays.
**Credit Cards:** MC, Visa.
**Rsv'tns:** Highly recommended.
**Reserve Through:** Travel agent or call direct.
**Minimum Stay:** Required Sept 15-Oct 15 only on weekends.
**Parking:** Ample free off-street parking.
**In-Room:** Color TV, VCR, ceiling fans, maid service.
**On-Premises:** Living room with fireplace, gallery, library, video tape library, games, guest telephone in entry, large front porch for watching sunsets.
**Exercise/Health:** 75 acres for hiking or biking.
**Swimming:** Nearby streams & waterfalls.
**Sunbathing:** On patio & private sun decks.
**Smoking:** Permitted on front porch only.
**Pets:** Not permitted.
**Handicap Access:** No.
**Children:** 10+ yrs welcome in main house. Younger accommodated in room w/ outside entrance.
**Languages:** English.
**Your Host:** Karen & Sally.

# ZION NATIONAL PARK

## Red Rock Inn

Gay-Friendly ♀♂

Experience the spectacular red rock cliffs of Zion National Park in relaxed comfort at ***Red Rock Inn.*** Each of our five rooms is individually decorated to offer a unique flavor and ambiance. They all have patios with a view and private baths (4 rooms feature jetted tubs, suite has outdoor hot tub). Enjoy your complimentary breakfast (delivered in a basket to your door each morning) in the shade of an old pecan tree as you plan your day in one of the world's most beautiful and inspiring natural wonders.

**Address: 998 Zion Park Blvd, PO Box 273, Springdale, UT 84767 Tel: (801) 772-3139.**

**Type:** Intimate bed & breakfast cottages.
**Clientele:** Mostly straight clientele with a gay & lesbian following.
**Transportation:** Car is the only way.
**To Gay Bars:** 150 miles to Las Vegas.
**Rooms:** 3 rooms with queen beds, 1 with king bed, 1 2-room suite.
**Bathrooms:** Private: 4 whirlpool bath/shower/toilet, 1 full bath.
**Meals:** Full breakfast.
**Vegetarian:** Available with prior arrangements.
**Dates Open:** All year.
**High Season:** May to Sep.
**Rates:** $69-$140.
**Credit Cards:** MC, Visa, Amex & Discover.
**Rsv'tns:** Required in high season.
**Reserve Thru:** Call direct.
**Minimum Stay:** 2 nights on holidays.
**Parking:** Adequate free off-street parking.
**In-Room:** Color cable TV, AC, ceiling fans & maid service. Suite has VCR.
**Exercise/Health:** Massage available by appointment.
**Swimming:** Nearby pool & river.
**Sunbathing:** On private sun decks & patios, common patio & lawn.
**Smoking:** Not permitted.
**Pets:** Not permitted.
**Handicap Access:** Yes. One unit & garden area.
**Children:** Allowed with special arrangements.
**Languages:** English.

# VERMONT

## ANDOVER

### The Inn at HighView

Q-NET Gay-Friendly ♀♂

***Vermont the Way You Always Dreamed It Would Be...***

...but the way you've never found it, until now. Everyone who arrives at ***The Inn at HighView*** has the same breathless reaction to the serenity of the surrounding hills. The inn's hilltop location offers incredible peace, tranquility and seclusion, yet is convenient to all the activities that bring you to Vermont, such as skiing, golf, tennis and antiquing. Ski cross-country or hike our 72 acres. Swim in our unique rock garden pool. Enjoy our gourmet dinner, relax by a blazing fire, snuggle under a down comforter in a canopy bed, or gaze 50 miles over pristine mountains.

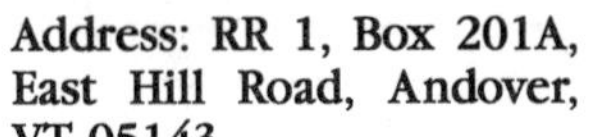

**Address: RR 1, Box 201A, East Hill Road, Andover, VT 05143**
**Tel: (802) 875-2724, Fax: (802) 875-4021.**

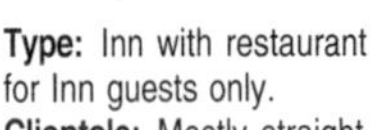

**Type:** Inn with restaurant for Inn guests only.
**Clientele:** Mostly straight with a gay & lesbian following
**Transportation:** Car is best. Amtrak to Bellows Falls, VT (19 mi), Albany, NY (83 mi). Taxi from Bellows Falls $20. Limo from Albany $90.
**To Gay Bars:** 1.5 hours by car. Proximity to a bar is NOT the reason to come here!
**Rooms:** 6 rooms & 2 suites with single, double, queen or king beds.
**Bathrooms:** 6 private bath/toilet/showers & 3 private shower/toilets.
**Meals:** Full breakfast with dinner available on most weekend nights at a prix fixe rate.
**Vegetarian:** We specialize in Italian cuisine and have many pasta dishes without meat.
**Complimentary:** Sherry in room & turn-down service. Tea & coffee always. Conferences receive coffee service, snacks.
**Dates Open:** All year except for 2 weeks in November & 2 weeks in April.
**High Season:** Sep 15 through Oct 25, Christmas holiday week, & all of February.
**Rates:** Fall/Winter: $95-$135 double occupancy. $20 per extra person in suite. Summer: $89 midweek double occupancy.
**Discounts:** For mid-week stays in winter & for longer than 2 days on weekends when no 3-night minimum is in effect.
**Credit Cards:** MC & Visa.
**Rsv'tns:** Required.
**Reserve Through:** Travel agent or call direct.
**Minimum Stay:** 3 nights on holiday weekends & week between Christmas & New Year.
**Parking:** Ample free off-street parking.
**In-Room:** Maid & laundry service. 1 room with fireplace, 3 with canopy beds, 7 with private balconies & entrances, 2 with AC.
**On-Premises:** Meeting rooms, TV lounge, laundry facilities, gazebo with view, BBQ picnic area, game room, huge fireplace with comfortable couches in living room, library & CD player.
**Exercise/Health:** Sauna.
**Swimming:** Pool on premises.
**Sunbathing:** At poolside.
**Smoking:** Permitted outside only.
**Pets:** Small pets sometimes permitted depending on how full we are. Please inquire.
**Handicap Access:** 1 room accessible, but doorway is narrow.
**Children:** Permitted in suites only except during peak season. Please inquire.
**Languages:** English, Italian & Spanish.
**Your Host:** Greg & Sal.

# ARLINGTON

## Candlelight Motel

Gay-Friendly ♀♂

### *Four Spectacular Seasons to Explore Vermont*

In the charming village of Arlington, Vermont, once the home of Norman Rockwell, ***Candlelight Motel*** is nestled in a valley with magnificent mountain views. Your room has a comfortable bed, private bath, air conditioning and color cable TV. Join us for continental breakfast by the fireplace. Good restaurants are nearby. Vermont has brilliant red and gold foliage in autumn, nearby skiing in winter, and crystal clear days and cool nights in the spring. Four seasons of activities include fishing, hiking, biking, canoeing and skiing. AAA & Mobil rated.

**Address: Rt 7A, PO Box 97, Arlington, VT 05250**
**Tel: (802) 375-6647, (800) 348-5294.**

**Type:** Motel with fireside lounge.
**Clientele:** Mostly straight clientele with a gay & lesbian following.
**Transportation:** Car.
**To Gay Bars:** 1-hr drive to bar in Brattleboro area. 1-1/4 hr drive to gay & lesbian bars in Albany, NY.
**Rooms:** 17 rooms with double or queen beds.
**Bathrooms:** All private bath/toilets.
**Meals:** Cont. breakfast.
**Complimentary:** Coffee, tea & juices.
**Dates Open:** All year.
**High Season:** Fall foliage.
**Rates:** $45-$75.
**Discounts:** Group bookings & ski packages.
**Credit Cards:** MC, VISA & Amex.
**Rsv'tns:** Recommended.
**Reserve Thru:** Call direct.
**Minimum Stay:** On holiday weekends.
**Parking:** Ample free off-street parking.
**In-Room:** Color cable TV, AC, telephone & maid service. Refs. in 14 rooms.
**On-Premises:** Fireside lounge.
**Swimming:** Pool on premises.
**Sunbathing:** At poolside.
**Smoking:** Permitted. Non-smoking rooms available.
**Pets:** Not permitted.
**Children:** Permitted with restrictions.

IGTA

# BURLINGTON

## Howden Cottage

Gay-Friendly ♀♂

***Howden Cottage*** offers cozy lodging and warm hospitality in the atmosphere of an artist's home. We're located in downtown Burlington, convenient to The Marketplace Shopping Mall, Lake Champlain, cinemas, night spots, churches, great restaurants, theatre, concerts, the U. of Vermont and the Medical Center Hospital of Vermont. The Shelburne Museum is a short drive away, as are several major ski areas and Vermont's spectacular fall foliage. Breakfast is served in our solarium. Owner-occupied & -run.

**Address: 32 N Champlain St, Burlington, VT 05401-4320**
**Tel: (802) 864-7198.**

**Type:** Bed & breakfast.
**Clientele:** Mostly straight clientele with a gay/lesbian following.
**Transportation:** Bus stop is one block away.
**To Gay Bars:** 2-1/2 blocks to gay/lesbian bar.
**Rooms:** 2 rooms & 1 suite with single, double or queen beds.
**Bathrooms:** 1 private shower/toilet, 2 sinks & 1 shared bath/shower/toilet.
**Meals:** Continental breakfast.
**Dates Open:** All year.
**High Season:** July-October.
**Rates:** $39-$89.
**Credit Cards:** MC & VISA.
**Rsv'tns:** Suggested.
**Reserve Through:** Call direct.
**Parking:** Adequate off-street & on-street parking.
**In-Room:** Sinks in room, AC/heat.
**Exercise/Health:** Nearby gym, weights, Jacuzzi, sauna, steam, massage.
**Swimming:** In the lake or at the YMCA or nearby river.
**Sunbathing:** Lakeside.
**Nudity:** Permitted at nearby river & quarry.
**Smoking:** Not permitted.
**Pets:** Not permitted.
**Handicap Access:** No.
**Children:** Permitted with prior arrangement.
**Languages:** English.
**Your Host:** Bruce.

# CENTRAL VERMONT

## Autumn Crest Inn

Gay-Friendly ♀♂

### *Vermont Magazine Loves Our Romantic Inn!*

"Perched on a knoll overlooking the panoramic Williamstown valley and surrounded by the barns and pastures of a 46-acre work-horse farm, the comfortable, unpretentious inn conveys a refreshing sense of rural authenticity." *—Vermont Magazine* ***Autumn Crest Inn*** is a 180-year-old restored farmstead nestled among verdant fields and forest. Enjoy the cozy fireplace in the living room and cross-country skiing in winter, the wraparound porch, trail rides, horseback riding lessons, hiking, biking in summer and world-class dinners and robust breakfasts year-round.

**Address: Box 1540 Clark Rd, Williamstown, VT**
**Tel: (802) 433-6627, (800) 339-6627.**

**Type:** Inn w/ gourmet rest.
**Clientele:** Mostly straight clientele with a gay & lesbian following
**Transportation:** Auto, air to Burlington VT, Amtrak to Montpelier VT. Pick up from airport, train, bus in Burlington, $20 one way.
**To Gay Bars:** 1 hr to Burlington.
**Rooms:** 16 rms & 2 suites with sgl, dbl or queen beds.
**Bathrooms:** All private.
**Meals:** Full breakfast, map with dinner on request only.
**Vegetarian:** Available upon request, other special diets accommodated.
**Comp.:** Coffee, tea.
**Dates Open:** All year.
**High Season:** Winter, Dec thru Mar, summer, June-Aug, fall, Sept, Oct.
**Rates:** Summer & winter, $88-$138 per room, fall, $98-$148 per room.
**Discounts:** Group disc.
**Credit Cards:** MC, VISA, Amex, Diners & Carte Blanche.
**Rsv'tns:** Required.
**Reserve Through:** Travel agent or call direct.
**Minimum Stay:** Required during fall foliage season & major holidays.
**Parking:** Ample free off-street parking.
**In-Room:** Color TV, maid service.
**On-Premises:** Private dining rooms, full liquor license.
**Swimming:** Pond on prem.
**Sunbathing:** On grass near pond/lawn near inn.
**Smoking:** Non-smoking rooms available, smoking permitted in living room.
**Pets:** Permitted with advance notice/$25 deposit. Dogs on leash at all times.
**Handicap Access:** Yes. One room meets handicapped requirements.
**Children:** Not especially welcome, under 10 years old discouraged.

# FAIR HAVEN

## Maplewood Inn

Q-NET Gay-Friendly ♀♂

### *Where Great Expectations Are Surpassed*

Rediscover romance in this exquisite 1843 Greek Revival inn listed on Vermont's historical register, with national register status pending. Once part of a prosperous dairy, ***Maplewood Inn*** was transformed into a warm and inviting inn in 1986 after remaining in one family for more than 100 years. Experience panoramic country views, spectacular sunsets, and a romantic and intimate atmosphere amid many fine antiques.

The inn is conveniently located in Central Vermont's Lake Region near lakes, skiing, historical sites, museums, shopping, and great restaurants. It's also close to many New York State destinations like Lake George and Fort Ticonderoga.

The first-class accommodations are expertly decorated in outstanding period decor. Doubles feature four-poster and brass beds, all private baths, and seating areas, and most have working fireplaces. Suites feature a full living room, large bedroom, bath, and fireplace. All accommodations have AC, fans, radios, color TVs with HBO, and in-room phones (on request). Fax and copier service is available for business travelers. Small meetings and retreats are also accommodated. Fine touches such as evening turn-down service with custom-made chocolates, custom toiletries, and excellent appointments are our standard. Bicycles and a canoe are available. Relax in the common rooms: the Breakfast Room with complimentary hot beverages, snacks, and set ups; Gathering Room with library; and the Parlor with complimentary cordial bar and games. Begin your day with a bountiful breakfast buffet.

The inn has been featured in *Country Magazine, New England Getaways, Americana, Innsider Magazine,* and more than 30 guidebooks. We are Vermont's only AAA 3-diamond, Mobile 3-star and AB+BA 3-crown-rated B&B. We are a member of the Professional Association of Innkeepers International, the American B&B Association, National B&B Association, and many chambers of commerce. Come today for a memorable stay – where great expectations are surpassed.

**Address: Route 22A South, Fair Haven, VT 05743**
**Tel: (802) 265-8039, (800) 253-7729, Fax: (802) 265-8210,**
**E-mail: maplewd@sover.net. http://www.sover.net/~maplewd.**

**Type:** Bed & breakfast.
**Clientele:** Mostly straight clientele with a growing gay & lesbian following
**Transportation:** Car. Rentals at Albany, NY & Burlington, VT airports & at Amtrak in Ft. Edward, NY (Glen Falls Hertz delivers to stn.).
**Rooms:** 3 rooms & 2 suites with double or queen beds, rollaway bed available.
**Bathrooms:** All private.
**Meals:** Expanded continental breakfast.
**Vegetarian:** Breakfast is basically vegetarian. Vegetarian food in town & in nearby Rutland.
**Complimentary:** Cordials in parlor, hot beverages & snacks in breakfast room, turndown service with chocolates.
**Dates Open:** All year.
**High Season:** Jul-Oct.
**Rates:** $75-$120. $5 higher during Fall Foliage & some holidays.
**Discounts:** 10% on stays of over 5 nights, off-season specials, group discounts for rental of entire inn.
**Credit Cards:** MC, Visa, Amex, Diners, Discover, Carte Blanche, Novus, Bravo.
**Rsv'tns:** Recommended.
**Reserve Through:** Yes.
**Minimum Stay:** 2 nights for foliage weekends, Christmas week, & some special events & holidays.
**Parking:** Ample free private on-premises parking. Night lighting, very safe.
**In-Room:** Color cable TV, AC, fireplaces, fans, radios & maid service. VCR & refrigerator in 1 suite. Telephone by request.
**On-Premises:** Meeting rooms, copier service, fax.
**Exercise/Health:** Nearby gym, weights & massage.
**Swimming:** Nearby lake.
**Sunbathing:** On the patio.
**Smoking:** Permitted in 2 guest rooms or on outside porch. Most rooms are non-smoking rooms.
**Pets:** Not permitted. Kennels nearby.
**Handicap Access:** No.
**Children:** Permitted by prior approval if 8 years or older or under 1 year old.
**Languages:** English.
**Your Host:** Cindy & Doug.

# SHAFTSBURY

## Country Cousin

Gay/Lesbian ♀♂

### *Experience Vermont's Gay Bed & Breakfast*

Located on 15 beautifully landscaped acres, ***Country Cousin*** is a truly traditional bed and breakfast housed in an 1824 Greek Revival farmhouse. It is nestled in a valley between the West Mountains and the Green Mountains of Southwestern Vermont, just north of Bennington. ***Country Cousin*** is surrounded by Vermont's year-round activities. Three major downhill ski areas are within 30 minutes and you can cross-country ski right from the front door. Enjoy biking, canoeing or horseback riding through the Green Mountains. Antiquing and sightseeing along historic Route 7A, exploring Vermont's quaint hamlets, or enjoying the outlet stores and gourmet dining of nearby Manchester are other popular activities. You may, however, just prefer to curl up next to the fireplace with a good book or relax in the sun and enjoy the company of our friendly guests and staff.

The spacious farmhouse offers two common areas for guests: a quiet antique-filled living room with views of Mt. Equinox and a magnificent post and beam music room with cathedral ceilings, stained-glass, grand piano and a 25-foot natural stone fireplace. The music room leads to a large sunning deck complete with wooden tub. The rolling lawns beyond take you to two large spring-fed ponds, perfect for nude swimming and sunbathing, with clothing being optional. Our inn offers four uniquely decorated guest rooms, some with feather beds, down comforters, or patchwork quilts. Warm robes are provided and guests are encouraged to enjoy the public areas in comfort. A full country breakfast is served daily after morning coffee in front of the fireplace. Afternoon tea, snacks and conversation are also a part of our hospitality. We are sure you will enjoy our country retreat and return again and again, as so many of our guests have!

**Address: RR 1, Box 212 Old Depot Rd, Shaftsbury, VT 05262**
**Tel: (802) 375-6985 or (800) 479-6985.**

**Type:** Bed & breakfast.
**Clientele:** Gay & lesbian
**Transportation:** Pick up from bus $5.
**To Gay Bars:** 1 hr to Brattleboro, VT & 1-1/4 hours by car to Albany, NY.
**Rooms:** 5 rooms with double or queen beds.
**Bathrooms:** All private.
**Meals:** Full breakfast.
**Vegetarian:** Available on request.
**Complimentary:** Tea, coffee, juices, snacks.
**Dates Open:** All year.
**High Season:** Fall.
**Rates:** $60-$75 (surcharge: $10/night for holidays, $20/night for fall foliage).
**Discounts:** Weekday & weekly rates.
**Credit Cards:** MC, VISA.
**Rsv'tns:** Recommended.
**Reserve Through:** Travel agent or call direct.
**Minimum Stay:** 2 days on weekends preferred, but not essential.
**Parking:** Adequate off-street parking.
**On-Premises:** Music room with stone fireplace & great room, partial AC.
**Exercise/Health:** Wooden hot tub.

**Swimming:** 2 ponds on premises.
**Sunbathing:** On sun deck.
**Nudity:** Permitted on deck, in spa & pond areas.
**Smoking:** Permitted outdoors.
**Pets:** Permitted with prearrangement.
**Handicap Access:** Yes, with some restrictions.
**Children:** With prearrangement.
**Languages:** English, Spanish.

# STOWE

## Arcadia House

Gay/Lesbian ♀♂

### *Simple Elegance*

Surrounded by mountain and valley views, the ***Arcadia House*** offers woodland paths, country meadows, river frontage and several ponds. Wildflower meadows and gardens surround the house creating a peaceful atmosphere, and Stowe, Smugglers' Notch and Jay Peak, three of Vermont's premiere ski areas, are a 30-minute drive. Your hosts offer first-class amenities and bountiful, healthful breakfasts. To ensure peace and privacy, the ***Arcadia House*** has only one guest room in a separate wing of the house, with a private entrance, large sleeping quarters, self-controlled heat and private bath.

**Address: PO Box 520, Hyde Park, VT**
**Tel: (802) 888-9147.**

**Type:** Bed & breakfast.
**Clientele:** Mostly gay & lesbian with some straight clientele.
**Transportation:** Car is best.
**Rooms:** 1 room with queen bed.
**Bathrooms:** Private.
**Meals:** Expanded continental breakfast. Dinners & picnic lunches by special request, at extra charge.
**Vegetarian:** Vegetarian restaurants in town.
**Complimentary:** Tea, coffee & juices.
**Dates Open:** All year.
**High Season:** Summer, September-October.
**Rates:** $85/night ($95 on holiday weekends).
**Discounts:** 10% on stay of 3 or more nights.
**Credit Cards:** MC, VISA.
**Rsv'tns:** Required.
**Reserve Through:** Call direct.
**Minimum Stay:** 2 nights on holiday weekends & in September.
**Parking:** Ample free off-street parking.
**In-Room:** AC, color TV, phone, ceiling fans, maid service.
**On-Premises:** Perennial, herb & organic veggie gardens, orchard, ponds, river, private patio.
**Exercise/Health:** Hiking trails.
**Swimming:** In river & pond on premises and in nearby river & lake.
**Sunbathing:** On patio & pond dock.
**Nudity:** Permitted at pond & sunning areas.
**Smoking:** Not permitted.
**Pets:** Not permitted.
**Handicap Access:** No.
**Children:** No.
**Languages:** English, limited French & German.
**Your Host:** Ed & John.

## Buccaneer Country Lodge

Gay/Lesbian ♀♂

### *A Treasure Chest of Vermont Hospitality*

Experience Vermont hospitality and discover why our guests return year after year. Stowe is the ski capital of the East and ***Buccaneer Country Lodge*** is minutes from village, mountain, nightlife, recreational activities and special events. Suites have full kitchens, one queen bed and two twin beds. One suite has its own fireplace. Motel rooms have two double beds or a queen-size bed, and refrigerator. All have private bath, cable TV, phone and air conditioning. **READER COMMENT:** *"Building in immaculate condition, grounds well landscaped, pool well maintained, pleasant dining room, owners pleasant and helpful."* Peter, Seattle, WA.

**Address: 3214 Mountain Rd, Stowe, VT 05672**
**Tel: (802) 253-4772, (800) 543-1293.**

**Type:** Bed & breakfast motel.
**Clientele:** Good mix of gay men & women with some straight clientele
**Transportation:** Car.
**To Gay Bars:** 30-minute drive to Burlington, VT gay/lesbian bars.
**Rooms:** 8 rooms & 4 suites with single, double or queen beds.
**Bathrooms:** All private.
**Meals:** Full breakfast, except in spring.
**Complimentary:** Hot soup & hot mulled cider during ski season.
**Dates Open:** All year.
**High Season:** Dec 19th-Jan 3rd, fall foliage season.
**Rates:** Rooms $49-$225, depending on season.
**Discounts:** 10% on a non-holiday midweek stay (Sun-Thurs).
**Credit Cards:** MC, Visa.
**Rsv'tns:** Recommended.
**Reserve Through:** Travel agent or call direct.
**Minimum Stay:** 2 nights (3 nights during holidays).
**Parking:** Free parking.
**In-Room:** Cable color TV, telephone, AC, maid service, refrigerator, some kitchens.
**On-Premises:** TV lounge, hot tub.
**Exercise/Health:** Hot tub.
**Swimming:** Pool on premises, lake.
**Sunbathing:** At poolside.
**Smoking:** Not permitted in dining room & public areas. Non-smoking rooms available.
**Pets:** Not permitted.
**Handicap Access:** No.
**Children:** Permitted.
**Languages:** English, Spanish, French.

## Fitch Hill Inn

Gay-Friendly ♀♂

### *Elegant, But Not Stuffy*

Historic ***Fitch Hill Inn,*** c. 1794, occupies a hill overlooking the magnificent Green Mountains. Its location, central to Vermont's all-season vacation country, offers a special opportunity to enjoy the true Vermont experience. This is the town in which Charles Kuralt said he would like to settle. Antique-decorated guest rooms all have spectacular views. Breakfasts and, by arrangement, gourmet dinners, are prepared by the innkeeper. The library has video tapes, books, and an atmosphere of comfort and ease. The newly-renovated 18th century living room is wonderful for music, reading, and sitting by the fireside.

**Address: RFD 1 Box 1879, Fitch Hill Rd, Hyde Park, VT 05655**
**Tel: (802) 888-3834, (800) 639-2903, Fax: (802) 888-7789.**

**Type:** Bed & breakfast inn with restaurant for guests only.
**Clientele:** Mostly straight with a gay & lesbian following.
**Transportation:** Car is best. We do not pick up from Burlington International Airport except for those on extended stays.
**To Gay Bars:** 40 miles to Burlington.
**Rooms:** 4 rooms with 2 queen & 2 doubles, 1 suite with 2 single beds & 1 double bed. 1 efficiency apt with queen bed.
**Bathrooms:** All private.
**Meals:** Full breakfast.
**Vegetarian:** Available with reservation & prior arrangement.
**Complimentary:** Tea, sherry, snacks, bathrobes, bottled water. Maple syrup & candy in rooms.
**Dates Open:** All year.
**High Season:** Dec 25-Jan 3 & Sept 15-Oct 15.
**Rates:** $69-$145.
**Discounts:** On stays over 2 days (except during high season), 10% for AAA.
**Credit Cards:** MC, VISA, Amex.
**Rsv'tns:** Suggested.
**Reserve Through:** Travel agent or call direct.
**Minimum Stay:** 2 nights

during high seasons.
**Parking:** Ample off-street parking.
**In-Room:** Maid & laundry service, color TV, telephone, ceiling fans, 300+ video library. Apartment has fireplace. Suite: AC, color cable TV, living room.
**On-Premises:** Meeting rooms, TV lounge, VCR library. Kitchen & refrigerator privileges available.
**Exercise/Health:** Hot tub, skiing, hiking, biking, horseback riding, golf & canoeing.
**Swimming:** Lake & river nearby.
**Sunbathing:** On the beach.
**Smoking:** Not permitted inside. Permitted on 3 outdoor porches.
**Pets:** Not permitted.
**Handicap Access:** No.
**Children:** Permitted over 3.
**Languages:** English, Spanish & some French.
**Your Host:** Richard & Stanley.

## Honeywood Country Lodge

Gay-Friendly ♀♂

### *Experience Vermont Hospitality at Its Best*

Experience the ambiance and luxury of a country inn with the privacy of a motel. At ***Honeywood Country Lodge*** we're famous for early-morning baking and continental-plus breakfasts. Our large tastefully decorated rooms have cathedral ceilings and patio doors leading to a common balcony and our four acres of land. The rooms feature double and queen brass or canopy beds with handmade quilts. Enjoy mountain views or dabble your feet in the brook which runs behind our property. In winter, cross-country ski from your door. We are the closest AAA Three-Diamond lodging to the slopes at Stowe Mountain Resort.

**Address: 4527 Mountain Rd, Stowe, VT 05672**
**Tel: (802) 253-4124, (800) 659-6289.**

**Type:** Bed & breakfast motel.
**Clientele:** Mostly straight clientele with a gay & lesbian following
**Transportation:** Pick up from airport, train, bus & ferry dock. We use a local taxi service which usually charges $20-$50.
**To Gay Bars:** 30 miles to Burlington gay bars.
**Rooms:** 12 rooms, 1 suite with single, double or queen beds.
**Bathrooms:** Private: 1 shower/toilet, 12 bath/toilet/showers.
**Meals:** Expanded continental breakfast.
**Vegetarian:** Available nearby.
**Complimentary:** Afternoon wine & cheese.
**Dates Open:** All year.
**High Season:** Sept 15-Oct 20, Dec 24-Jan 2.
**Rates:** Summer $62-$99, winter $66-$129, high season $89-$159.
**Discounts:** Seniors and multi-day discounts 3 days or more. Not available during peak periods.
**Credit Cards:** MC, Visa, Amex, Discover.
**Rsv'tns:** Recommended in regular & high season.
**Reserve Through:** Travel agent or call direct.
**Minimum Stay:** 2 nights on weekends, 3-4 nights high season.
**Parking:** Ample free off-street parking.
**In-Room:** AC, color cable TV, telephone, ceiling fans, refrigerator, kitchen, maid service. Some rooms have fireplaces & efficiencies.
**Exercise/Health:** Jacuzzi. Nearby gym, weights, Jacuzzi, sauna, steam, massage.
**Swimming:** Pool, river on premises. Nearby river & lake.
**Sunbathing:** Poolside & on grass near rooms or pool.
**Smoking:** Permitted outside or in smoking rooms. Non-smoking rooms available.
**Pets:** Not permitted.
**Handicap Access:** Yes, 1 room handicap-equipped with some restrictions.
**Children:** We accommodate families with 1 or 2 well-behaved children.
**Languages:** English.
**Your Host:** Carolyn & Bill.

# WATERBURY-STOWE AREA

## Grünberg Haus Bed & Breakfast

Gay-Friendly ♀♂

### *Spontaneous Personal Attention in a Handbuilt Austrian Chalet*

Our romantic Austrian inn, ***Grünberg Haus,*** rests on a quiet hillside in Vermont's Green Mountains, perfect for trips to Stowe, Montpelier, Waterbury and Burlington. Choose guest rooms with wonderful views from carved wood balconies, secluded cabins hidden along wooded trails or a spectacular carriage house with skywindows, balconies and modern kitchen. Relax by the fire or warm-weather Jacuzzi, ski expertly-groomed cross-country trails, gather fresh eggs or listen to innkeeper Chris playing the grand piano as you savor your imaginative, memorable breakfast. Explore Vermont.

**Address:** RR2, Box 1595 IP, Route 100 South, Waterbury-Stowe, VT 05676-9621
**Tel:** (802) 244-7726, (800) 800-7760,
**E-mail:** grunhaus@aol.com.

**Type:** Bed & breakfast guesthouse & cabins.
**Clientele:** Mostly straight clientele with a gay & lesbian following.
**Transportation:** Car is best, pick up from airport $25, bus $5, ferry dock $25, train $5.
**To Gay Bars:** 25 miles to Pearl's in Burlington, VT.
**Rooms:** 10 rooms, 1 suite & 3 cottages with single, double or queen beds.
**Bathrooms:** 9 private shower/toilets & others share shower/toilets.
**Meals:** Full, musical breakfast.
**Vegetarian:** Breakfast always vegetarian.
**Complimentary:** Set-ups, soft drinks, coffee & tea, cordials & snacks. BYOB OK.
**Dates Open:** All year.
**High Season:** Feb & March, July-October & Christmas.
**Rates:** $55-$140.
**Discounts:** 10% for seniors & stays of 4 or more days.
**Credit Cards:** MC, VISA, Amex, En Route & Discover.
**Rsv'tns:** Suggested.
**Reserve Through:** Travel agent or call direct.
**Parking:** Ample free off-street parking.
**In-Room:** Maid service, fans & balcony. One kitchen unit.
**On-Premises:** Tennis court, Steinway grand piano, library, fireplace, chickens, BYOB pub. Groomed cross-country ski center.
**Exercise/Health:** Jacuzzi, sauna, 40 acres for hiking.
**Swimming:** Pool, river or lake nearby.
**Sunbathing:** At poolside, by river or lake or on common sun decks.
**Nudity:** Clothing-optional swimming areas nearby.
**Smoking:** Permitted outside.
**Pets:** Not permitted. Pick up & delivery of pets at registered kennel is available.
**Handicap Access:** No.
**Children:** Permitted.
**Languages:** English.
**Your Host:** Chris & Mark.

# WOODSTOCK AREA

## Maitland Swan House

Q-NET Gay-Friendly ♀♂

### *Vermont Scenery & Refreshing Green Mountain Air – Newly Redecorated in Country French*

On a quiet road in the village of Taftsville, ***Maitland Swan House*** offers gracious accommodation in an early 19th-century Greek Revival home. Each bedroom has its own character and a private bath. Awaken to fresh-brewed coffee and fresh juice. There's plenty to do within minutes of the inn, such as golf, hiking, biking, swimming and horseback riding. Autumn brings glorious color to the hills and fields. Winter brings glistening snow and skiing minutes from the inn. Guests are welcome to join our family feast on holidays.

**Address: Happy Valley Rd, PO Box 105, Taftsville, VT 05073**
**Tel: (802) 457-4435 (Tel/Fax), (800) 959-1404.**

**Type:** Bed & breakfast.
**Clientele:** Mostly straight clientele with a gay & lesbian following
**Transportation:** Car is best.
**To Gay Bars:** One hour to Brattleboro.
**Rooms:** 3 rms & a cottage.
**Bathrooms:** All private.
**Meals:** Coupons good for up to $8 per person at your choice of 3 local rest.
**Complimentary:** Port or wine.
**Dates Open:** All year.
**High Season:** Late Sept to Oct.
**Rates:** Summer $95-$175, winter $85-$235. Fall foliage $150/room.
**Discounts:** If you take the whole house for 3 or more nights, 15%.
**Rsv'tns:** Required.
**Reserve Through:** Travel agent or call direct.
**Minimum Stay:** 2 nights during high season.
**Parking:** Ample free off-street parking.
**In-Room:** Kitchen in cottage. Color cable TV in all bedrooms.
**On-Premises:** Living room, den/library.
**Exercise/Health:** Arrangements for use of local health club, golf course & ski areas can be arranged.
**Swimming:** Wading stream on the premises.
**Sunbathing:** On the patio.
**Smoking:** Not indoors.
**Children:** Permitted over 12 years old in main house. Smaller children in cottage.
**Lang.:** English, French, German, Spanish, Hebrew.
**Your Host:** Nelson & Jerusha.

# VIRGINIA

# CAPE CHARLES

## Wilson-Lee House Bed & Breakfast

Gay-Friendly ♀♂

### *Relaxation as it Should Be in the Land That Time Forgot*

On Virginia's Eastern Shore in historic Cape Charles, life moves at a deliciously slower pace. The ***Wilson-Lee House Bed & Breakfast***, furnished with heirloom antiques and modern classics, offers six luxurious rooms, each with private bath. The James W. Lee Room features a splendid whirlpool. Mornings, full Southern breakfasts are served and, after dark, the nightlife in Norfolk awaits just 45 minutes across the Chesapeake Bay Bridge Tunnel. With the beach only steps away, sunset sails can be arranged at your request. Pamper yourself – you deserve it.

**Address: 403 Tazewell Ave, Cape Charles, VA 23310-3217**
**Tel: (757) 331-1954, Fax: (757) 331-8133, E-mail: WLHBnB@aol.com.**

*continued next page*

**Type:** Bed & breakfast.
**Clientele:** Mostly straight clientele
**Transportation:** Car is best, Norfolk Int'l airport.
**To Gay Bars:** 40 miles, a 50 minute drive.
**Rooms:** 6 rooms with queen beds.
**Bathrooms:** All private. One with whirlpool & 1 private bath across hall.
**Meals:** Full breakfast.
**Vegetarian:** Can be arranged with adv. notice.
**Complimentary:** Welcome mint on pillow. Afternoon tea, setups provided, BYOB.
**Dates Open:** All year.
**High Season:** Late April to mid-November.
**Rates:** High season $85-$120, low season $50-$75.
**Credit Cards:** MC, Visa.
**Rsv'tns:** Required.
**Reserve Through:** Travel agent or call direct.
**Parking:** Ample free off-street parking.
**In-Room:** AC, AM/FM clock radio & stereo CD player. Color cable TV available.
**On-Premises:** Meeting rms, video tape & CD libraries.
**Swimming:** 5-10 minute walk to Chesapeake Bay beach, drive to ocean.
**Sunbathing:** At beach.
**Smoking:** Permitted on NON-enclosed porch.
**Children:** Only children over 12 years of age.
**Languages:** English.
**Your Host:** David, Leon.

IGTA

# NELLYSFORD

## The Mark Addy

**Gay-Friendly ♀♂**

### *Lodging in an Elegant Tradition*

***The Mark Addy*** is conveniently located between the beautiful Blue Ridge Mountains and Thomas Jefferson's Charlottesville. This beautifully restored and lovingly appointed country inn dates back to 1884, offering all who stay here the richness of a bygone era. The charming rooms and luxurious suites have private bathrooms with either a double whirlpool bath, double shower, or an antique claw-foot tub with shower. Much of what we know about gracious living and warm welcomes we learned from our family. It is with considerable pride and affection that this historic home bears their names.

**Address: 56 Rodes Farm Dr, Nellysford, VA 22958**
**Tel: (804) 361-1101, (800) 278-2154.**

**Type:** Country inn.
**Clientele:** Mostly straight with a gay & lesbian following
**Transportation:** Airport or Amtrak pick up available at extra charge.
**To Gay Bars:** 30 min.
**Rooms:** Rooms & suites.
**Bathrooms:** All priv. Dbl. whirlpool bath, double shower or tub with shower.
**Meals:** Bountiful breakfast. Dinner. Catering available.
**Vegetarian:** Upon request.
**Complimentary:** In guest kitchen: beer, soda, juice, iced tea, VA peanuts, homemade cookies.
**Dates Open:** All year.
**Rates:** $90-$135.
**Discounts:** Some avail. Sun-Thurs or for ext. stays.
**Credit Cards:** MC, Visa.
**Rsv'tns:** Required.
**Reserve Through:** Travel agent or call direct.
**Minimum Stay:** 2 nights in Oct, Feb, May & holidays.
**In-Room:** Down comforters, liqueur decanters, local goat's milk skin products, central AC.
**On-Premises:** 5 porches.
**Exercise/Health:** Excercise facilities nearby.
**Swimming:** Swim. nearby.
**Smoking:** On porches only.
**Handicap Access:** 1 rm totally wheelchair accessible.
**Children:** Permitted age 12 & over.
**Languages:** English, German.
**Your Host:** John & Saverio.

# NEW MARKET

## A Touch of Country

**Gay-Friendly 50/50 ♀♂**

### *Daydream on the Porch Swings...*

...or stroll through town, stopping at antique and gift shops, sampling savory fare at local restaurants. There's no need for detailed itineraries, for you've come to relax at ***A Touch of Country,*** our restored 1870's Shenandoah Valley home in historic New Market. We've gone to great lengths to create a warm, friendly atmosphere for your stay, setting the tone with antiques and country collectibles. Come morning, a down-home country breakfast fortifies you for visiting the Blue Ridge Mtns., New Market Battlefield, caverns and other points of interest.

**Address: 9329 Congress St, New Market, VA. Tel: (540) 740-8030.**

**Type:** Bed & breakfast.
**Clientele:** 50% gay & lesbian & 50% straight clientele.
**Transportation:** Car.
**To Gay Bars:** 1-1/2 hrs to gay bar in Charlottesville or 2 hours to DC.
**Rooms:** 6 rooms with double or queen beds.
**Bathrooms:** All private shower/sink/toilets.
**Meals:** Full breakfast.
**Vegetarian:** Available with advance request.
**Complimentary:** Soda available upon arrival.
**Dates Open:** All year.
**High Season:** September-November.
**Rates:** $60-$75, plus tax.
**Discounts:** For longer stays.
**Credit Cards:** MC, VISA, Discover, Amex.
**Rsv'tns:** Recommended.
**Reserve Through:** Travel agent or call direct.
**Minimum Stay:** 2 days on holiday weekends & October weekends.
**Parking:** Adequate free off-street parking.
**In-Room:** Self-controlled AC.
**On-Premises:** TV lounge.
**Swimming:** At nearby pool.
**Smoking:** Not permitted.
**Pets:** Not permitted.
**Handicap Access:** No.
**Children:** Permitted if well-behaved and over 12 years old.
**Languages:** English.
**Your Host:** Jean & Dawn.

# RICHMOND

## Bellmont Manor Bed & Breakfast and Silver Rooster Antiques

Gay-Friendly 50/50 ♀♂

### *Thrill Your Taste Buds and Your Appetite for History*

Having a country gourmet breakfast arrive at your door with silver service is indeed special, and it is yours for the asking at ***Bellmont Manor,*** where gracious Southern hospitality is accented by great food. The house and its four bedrooms have been filled with an eclectic array of furniture, pictures, glass, brass, and china, including antiques and Virginia heirlooms. Only 20 minutes from downtown Richmond, VA, ***Bellmont Manor*** is surrounded by a treasure-trove of historic sites and museums for guests to visit.

**Address: 6600 Belmont Rd, Chesterfield, VA 23832. Tel: (804) 745-0106.**

**Type:** Bed & breakfast with antique shop.
**Clientele:** 50% gay & lesbian & 50% straight clientele
**Transportation:** Car is best. Pick up from airport & train station, $20 charge.
**To Gay Bars:** 5 miles or a 15-min drive.
**Rooms:** 4 rooms with single, double or queen beds.
**Bathrooms:** Private & shared.
**Meals:** Full breakfast.
**Vegetarian:** Available by prior arrangement.
**Complimentary:** Wine, tea, coffee, hors d'oeuvres.
**Dates Open:** All year.
**Rates:** $55-$125, plus tax.
**Discounts:** 10% on stays of 3 nights or more.
**Credit Cards:** MC, VISA, Discover.
**Rsv'tns:** Required.
**Reserve Through:** Travel agent or call direct.
**Minimum Stay:** 2 nights on weekends.
**Parking:** Ample free off-street parking.
**In-Room:** AC, black & white TV, ceiling fans, phone, maid & room service.
**On-Premises:** TV lounge.
**Exercise/Health:** Gym nearby.
**Swimming:** Pool & river nearby.
**Sunbathing:** On patio.
**Smoking:** Permitted outside only.
**Pets:** Not permitted. Dogs on premises.
**Handicap Access:** Yes. 1 room with accessible bath.
**Children:** No.
**Languages:** English.
**Your Host:** Uly & Worth.

# WASHINGTON

## BELLINGHAM

### Marc-James Manor

Q-NET Gay/Lesbian ♀♂

***Marc-James Manor*** B&B is a contemporary interpretation of an English manor house, situated on nearly two acres in the Highland Heights district of Bellingham. The guest suite has a private entrance off a semi-secluded courtyard, queen-sized bed, private bath, wet bar, wood-burning fireplace, and private bath. Guests can choose between a continental breakfast served in their room or on the patio, or, if preferred, a late morning brunch served in the main hall. The B&B is located one hour south of Vancouver and 90 minutes north of Seattle, close to museums, shopping, and the general arts community.

**Address: 2925 Vining St, Bellingham, WA 98226. Tel: (360) 738-4919.**

**Type:** Bed & breakfast.
**Clientele:** Mostly gay & lesbian with some straight clientele
**Transportation:** Car is best. $5 pick up charge from airport, train, ferry dock.
**To Gay Bars:** 15-min drive.
**Rooms:** 1 suite with queen bed.
**Bathrooms:** Private bath/toilet.
**Meals:** Full breakfast.
**Vegetarian:** Always available.
**Complimentary:** Tea on day of arrival, chocolate on pillow, sherry & port in room. High tea from 4:30pm-5:30pm.
**Dates Open:** All year.
**High Season:** April-Oct.
**Rates:** $95-$125.
**Discounts:** Special rate for relocaters $75.
**Rsv'tns:** Required.
**Reserve Thru:** Call direct.
**Minimum Stay:** 2 days on weekends during high season.
**Parking:** Adequate free off-street parking.
**In-Room:** Coffee/tea-making facilities, refrigerator.
**On-Premises:** Meeting rooms, TV lounge, solarium, laundry facilities.
**Exercise/Health:** Jacuzzi, sauna.
**Swimming:** Nearby lake.
**Sunbathing:** On patio.
**Nudity:** Permitted in solarium hot tub, not protected from hosts' view.
**Smoking:** Not permitted.
**Pets:** Not permitted. 3 dogs & 2 cats in residence.
**Handicap Access:** No.
**Children:** Facility not designed for children.
**Languages:** English.
**Your Host:** Marc & Jim.

## CHELAN

### Mary Kay's Romantic Whaley Mansion Inn

Q-NET Gay-Friendly ♀♂

#### *Take Someone You Love to Mary Kay's*

Slip off your shoes, sink into our soft carpets, snuggle into our satin sheets, sip your own champagne and enjoy our superb coffee and our own hand-dipped truffles. ***Mary Kay's Romantic Whaley Mansion Inn*** is listed by AAA as a 4-diamond B&B. We specialize in romantic rendezvous, birthdays, anniversaries, honeymoons, retreats and marriage encounters. We have six elegant bedrooms with private baths in a historical Victorian mansion. The candlelit breakfast is presented on crystal and sterling silver in the formal dining room. All rooms have VCR, color TV, refrigerators, and free movies.

Address: 415 Third St, Chelan, WA 98816
Tel: (509) 682-5735, (800) 729-2408 (USA & Canada), Fax: (509) 682-5385.
E-mail: whaley@televar.com.
http://www.lakechelan.com/whaley.htm.

**Type:** Bed & breakfast.
**Clientele:** Mostly straight clientele with a gay/lesbian following
**Transportation:** Car is best. Free pick up from bus or airport in Chelan.
**To Gay Bars:** 175 mi from Seattle gay/lesbian bars.
**Rooms:** 6 rooms with dbl, queen or king beds.
**Bathrooms:** All private.
**Meals:** 5-course candlelight breakfast.
**Vegetarian:** Always available.
**Complimentary:** Chocolates & truffles.
**Dates Open:** All year.
**High Season:** Memorial Day-Labor Day & Christmas-Valentines' Day.
**Rates:** $115-$135 summer.
**Discounts:** Off-season specials. 1st night regular price, 2nd night 1/2 price.
**Credit Cards:** MC, Visa.
**Rsv'tns:** Required. 72-hour cancellation policy.
**Reserve Through:** Call direct.
**Minimum Stay:** 2 days on weekends, 3 days on holidays.
**Parking:** Ample off-street parking.
**In-Room:** Color TV, VCR, AC, ceiling fans, refrigerators, maid service & free movies.
**On-Premises:** Meeting rooms, TV lounge, laundry facilities, & player piano.
**Exercise/Health:** Cross-country skiing, boating, tennis courts, hiking & walking trails. Nearby fitness center.
**Swimming:** At Lake Chelan.
**Sunbathing:** On common sun decks.
**Smoking:** Permitted outdoors.
**Pets:** Not permitted.
**Handicap Access:** No.
**Children:** Not permitted, unless renting whole house.
**Languages:** English.
**Your Host:** Mary Kay & Carol.

# INDEX

## Wild Lily Ranch

Gay/Lesbian ♀♂

### *A Rustic Forest Retreat under Towering Cedars & Firs*

In the Cascade Mountains one hour from Seattle, near the gay-friendly town of Index, are several cozy cabins made of cedar logs and cobblestones known as ***Wild Lily Ranch.*** Each cabin has a woodstove or fireplace and loft with skylights. They also have large picture windows with mini-blinds, dutch doors, small rustic porches looking out over the Skykomish River, nicely-finished hardwood floors, and spectacular views from every window. Among the many local activities available to guests are whitewater rafting, horseback riding and cross-country and downhill skiing. Luxury camping is available in two tents, each with double beds on wooden platforms with linens provided. A buffet breakfast is served in the picnic area each morning.

Address: PO Box 313, Index, WA 98256. Tel: (360) 793-2103.

**Type:** Bed & breakfast with luxury camping available in 2 tents.
**Clientele:** Mainly gay & lesbian with some straight clientele
**To Gay Bars:** Gay-friendly bars in Index.
**Rooms:** Small log cabins.
**Bathrooms:** Modern, shared, centrally located bath house with bath/shower/toilets.
**Campsites:** 2-room tents already set up on the beach also with double beds & linens provided.
**Meals:** Continental breakfast.
**Dates Open:** All year.
**High Season:** June, July, August, September.
**Rates:** $65 all year, $10 for each additional person.
**Discounts:** 5 days or more 10% off.
**Rsv'tns:** Required.
**Reserve Through:** Call direct.
**Minimum Stay:** 2-days on weekends.
**Parking:** Ample free parking.
**In-Room:** Refrigerator, fireplaces, cable color TV in cabins.
**Exercise/Health:** Recreational building has Jacuzzi, sauna, tropical plants.
**Swimming:** In river on premises.
**Sunbathing:** On the beach.
**Nudity:** Permitted on the beach with discretion.
**Smoking:** Permitted outside only.
**Pets:** Permitted with $10 daily pet fee.
**Handicap Access:** No.
**Children:** Not permitted.
**Languages:** English.
**Your Host:** Mike.

# LA CONNER

## The Heron in La Conner

Gay-Friendly ♀♂

### *Fine Lodging in La Conner*

***The Heron in La Conner,*** with views of flowers and farm fields, Mount Baker and the Cascade Range, offers fine lodging to guests visiting this lovely community. We serve a continental breakfast in our parlor, the privacy of your room, or out on any of our three back decks. Our backyard hot tub provides soothing relaxation in a peaceful garden environment. La Conner has many shops and restaurants appealing to all tastes and there are local parks and scenic areas to hike, bike or stroll through. We're at the entrance of La Conner. Mt. Baker and the Cascades are an hour's drive, and Whidbey Island and Anacortes are less than 30 minutes away.

**Address: 117 Maple Street, PO Box 716, La Conner, WA 98257**
**Tel: (360) 466-4626.**

**Type:** Inn.
**Clientele:** Mostly straight clientele with a gay/lesbian following
**Transportation:** Car.
**Rooms:** 9 rooms & 3 suites with dbl or queen beds.
**Bathrooms:** All private bath/toilets.
**Meals:** Expanded continental breakfast.
**Vegetarian:** Available upon request.
**Complimentary:** Candy, popcorn, cookies.
**Dates Open:** All year.
**High Season:** April & June-September.
**Rates:** Summer $70-$160, winter $60-$160.
**Credit Cards:** MC, Visa, Amex.
**Reserve Through:** Travel agent or call direct.
**Parking:** Adequate free parking.
**In-Room:** Color TV, telephone. Some rooms have color cable TV.
**On-Premises:** Meeting rooms, video tape library, laundry facilities.
**Exercise/Health:** Hot tub in back yard.
**Sunbathing:** On common sun decks.
**Smoking:** Permitted outside.
**Pets:** Permitted at manager's discretion.
**Handicap Access:** Yes. 1 room on 1st floor.
**Children:** Well-mannered children always welcome.
**Languages:** English.
**Your Host:** Glenda.

## White Swan Guest House

Gay-Friendly ♀♂

### *The Best-Kept Secret in La Conner*

Welcome to the ***White Swan Guest House,*** an 1890's farmhouse with wicker chairs on the porch, piles of books and a platter of homemade chocolate chip cookies on the sideboard, English-style gardens, fruit trees and acres of farmland. Country breakfast is served in our sunny yellow dining room. The Garden Cottage is a perfect romantic hideaway, with private bath, kitchen and sun deck. Visit nearby La Conner, a charming waterfront village. ***White Swan*** is ninety miles from Vancouver, BC, one hour north of Seattle and close to the San Juan Islands' and Victoria ferries.

**Address: 1388 Moore Rd, Mt Vernon, WA 98273. Tel: (360) 445-6805.**

**Type:** Bed & breakfast guesthouse.
**Clientele:** Mostly straight clientele with a gay/lesbian following.
**Rooms:** 3 rooms & one large cottage for up to 4 persons. Queen & king beds.

**Bathrooms:** 2 shared in older home, 1 private in cottage.
**Meals:** Expanded country continental breakfast, with muffins, fruit, coffee.
**Vegetarian:** Only vegetarian food is served.
**Complimentary:** Fresh chocolate chip cookies always available.
**Dates Open:** All year.
**High Season:** Months of July & August & Tulip time (April 1st-30th).
**Rates:** Single $65, double $75, cottage $125-$185.
**Credit Cards:** MC, VISA.
**Rsv'tns:** Preferred.
**Reserve Thru:** Call direct.
**Parking:** Ample off-street parking.
**In-Room:** Maid & laundry service, kitchen available in cottage.
**On-Premises:** Kitchen, lounge, gorgeous flower garden, sun deck.
**Sunbathing:** On lawn or on cottage's private sun deck.
**Smoking:** Permitted outdoors only.
**Pets:** Not permitted.
**Handicap Access:** No.
**Children:** Welcome in garden cottage.
**Languages:** English.
**Your Host:** Peter.

# LOPEZ ISLAND

## Inn At Swifts Bay

Gay-Friendly ♀♂

### *A Small Inn with a National Reputation*

Since 1988, ***The Inn At Swifts Bay*** has gained national recognition as one of the finest accommodations in the beautiful San Juan Islands of Washington State. This elegant country home sits on three wooded acres with a private beach nearby. The inn has five quiet and romantic guest rooms, three with private baths and fireplaces. Two common areas also have fireplaces. The hot tub is at the edge of the woods – we provide robes and slippers. Here's what others say about the inn.

"The most memorable part of the trip...a stay at Inn At Swifts Bay...the setting is beautiful and serene, the accommodations excellent, and the food of gourmet quality!" – *San Francisco Sunday Chronicle-Examiner*

"Stateroom elegant." – *Vogue*

"Entrust yourself to the warm hospitality of the Inn At Swifts Bay. In the morning, one of the greatest pleasures of your stay awaits, a breakfast that is famous island-wide!" – *Brides Magazine*

"Those who appreciate luxury and superb cuisine will find the Inn At Swifts Bay to their liking. The Tudor-style inn is classy, stylish and oh, so comfortable...a breakfast that is nothing short of sensational!" – *West Coast Bed & Breakfast Guide*

**Inn Places Reader Commment:** "The inn is impeccably and tastefully decorated. Everything is done with warmth and quality. All of your needs and desires are met before you know what you want. The inn has a sense of class I have dreamed about, but have never found."

**Address: Lopez Island, WA 98261**
**Tel: (360) 468-3636, Fax: (360) 468-3637,**
**E-mail: SWIFTINN@aol.com. http://www.pgsi.com/swiftsbay.**

*continued next page*

**Type:** Bed & breakfast inn & cottage.
**Clientele:** Mostly straight clientele with a gay/lesbian following
**Transportation:** By car ferry from Anacortes or daily plane from Seattle, Anacortes. Pick up from airport, ferry dock, or marina.
**To Gay Bars:** Drive 1 hr to Bellingham or Everett. 1-1/2 hrs to Seattle bars.
**Rooms:** 2 rooms, 3 suites & 1 cottage with queen beds.
**Bathrooms:** 4 private shower/toilets & 1 shared bath/shower/toilet.
**Meals:** Full breakfast.
**Vegetarian:** Dietary restrictions considered with advance notice at time of reservation.
**Complimentary:** Sherry in living room. Fridge with mineral waters, microwave popcorn & tea.
**Dates Open:** All year.
**High Season:** May-Oct.
**Rates:** $85-$225.
**Discounts:** For extended stays in off season.
**Credit Cards:** MC, Visa, Discover & Amex.
**Rsv'tns:** Required.
**Reserve Through:** Call direct.
**Minimum Stay:** Only on holiday weekends.
**Parking:** Ample free off-street parking.
**In-Room:** Maid service.
**On-Premises:** Telephone in library, VCR with film library, refrigerator with ice & mineral water.
**Exercise/Health:** Hot tub & massage (by appointment only), exercise studio & sauna
**Swimming:** Ocean or lake (very cold!).
**Sunbathing:** On beach, patio or lawn.
**Nudity:** Permitted in the hot tub.
**Smoking:** Not permitted inside.
**Pets:** Not permitted.
**Handicap Access:** No.
**Children:** Not permitted.
**Languages:** English, limited German & Portuguese.
**Your Host:** Robert & Christopher.

IGTA

# LUMMI ISLAND

## Retreat on Lummi Island

Gay/Lesbian ♀♂

### *Take a 10-Minute Ride to Tranquility and Beautiful Views*

The entire downstairs of our home provides guests with kitchen and bath, two bedrooms, large living and dining spaces and spectacular views. From the house, surrounded by pastures, an orchard and an active wetland, you can see the sun rise over the North Cascades and observe ships sailing through Rosario Strait. Walk to beaches, the folksy general store, bike rentals and Lummi's rural artistic community or hike and bike the 5-mile island.

**Address: Tel: (360) 671-6371, ask for Mary Ellen or Marie.**
**E-mail: okeefe@pacificrim.net.**

**Type:** House.
**Clientele:** Gay & lesbian
**Transportation:** Car is best.
**To Gay Bars:** 30 miles, a 40-50 min drive.
**Rooms:** 2 bedrooms with double beds & 1 double futon in living room.
**Bathrooms:** 1 bathroom with full shower & bathtub.
**Dates Open:** All year.
**High Season:** June-Sept.
**Rates:** $80 per night for 1-2 people. $10 per night each additional person.
**Rsv'tns:** Required.
**Reserve Through:** Call direct.
**Minimum Stay:** 2 nights.
**Parking:** Ample free off-street parking.
**In-Room:** House: ceiling fans, CD player, kitchen, refrigerator, coffee & tea-making facilities.
**On-Premises:** Meeting rooms, laundry facilities.
**Exercise/Health:** Walking.
**Sunbathing:** In big yard.
**Smoking:** Permitted outside only.
**Pets:** No pets.
**Handicap Access:** No, 2 steps to enter house.
**Children:** Welcome.
**Languages:** English.

# MARYSVILLE

## Equinox Inn

Gay/Lesbian ♀♂

***Equinox Inn*** is situated on 2-1/2 acres in a serene natural wooded setting on the Tulilap Indian reservation. This two-bedroom Northwest-style inn features contemporary furnishings mixed with antiques. Sleep in The Wizard's Nook under the eves or in The Beltane, a sunny spacious room with luxury bath, aromatherapy and candlelight. The local area is great for canoeing in sheltered waters or try your hand at pier fishing or, in season, crabbing and clamming. Nearby attractions include the Tulilap tribal center, while shopping, dining and the Tulilap Casino are a 15-30 minute's drive from the inn.

**Address: 13522 12th Ave NW, Marysville, WA. Tel: (360) 652-1198.**

**Type:** Bed & breakfast.
**Clientele:** Mostly gay & lesbian with some straight clientele
**Transportation:** Car is best. Pick up available, please inquire.
**To Gay Bars:** A 30 min drive.
**Rooms:** 2 rooms with double or king beds.
**Bathrooms:** Private bath/toilets.
**Meals:** Full breakfast. Picnic lunch or Medieval supper at extra cost.
**Vegetarian:** Available upon request.
**Complimentary:** Before-dinner wine.
**Dates Open:** All year.
**High Season:** June-Aug.
**Rates:** $75-$85.
**Rsv'tns:** Required.
**Reserve Through:** Call direct.
**Parking:** Ample on-street parking.
**In-Room:** Black & white TV.
**On-Premises:** TV lounge, meeting rooms.
**Exercise/Health:** Massage (can be booked at time of reservation).
**Swimming:** Puget Sound & lake on premises, lake nearby.
**Sunbathing:** On common sun decks.
**Smoking:** Permitted on deck.

# OCEAN PARK

## Shakti Cove Cottages

Gay/Lesbian ♀♂

### *Experience the Peacefulness of Shakti Cove*

Though much of the Long Beach peninsula is heavily touristed, you'll find Ocean Park much quieter. ***Shakti Cove Cottages*** is a group of secluded cottages on three wooded acres. They're rustic, but have all the amenities you'll require. Don't expect chic, but DO expect quiet, privacy and the smell of the ocean. It's a five-minute walk to the world's longest (28 miles) beach. Stroll in search of driftwood or sand dollars and go clam digging in season, or try some of the great restaurants nearby. Midway between Seattle and Portland, it's a good place to kick back and relax.

**Address: PO Box 385, Ocean Park, WA 98640. Tel: (360) 665-4000.**

**Type:** Cottages.
**Clientele:** Mainly gay & lesbian with some straight clientele
**Transportation:** Car is best.
**To Gay Bars:** 2-1/2 hours to Portland, Oregon.
**Rooms:** 10 cottages with queen beds.
**Bathrooms:** All private.
**Dates Open:** All year.
**High Season:** June, July, August.
**Rates:** $60-$70.
**Discounts:** October-March 3 nights for 2.
**Credit Cards:** MC, Visa.
**Rsv'tns:** Suggested.
**Reserve Through:** Call direct.
**Parking:** Ample free covered parking.
**In-Room:** Color TV, kitchen, refrigerator.
**Swimming:** 5 min walk to ocean beach.
**Sunbathing:** On the beach.
**Smoking:** Permitted.
**Pets:** Permitted.
**Handicap Access:** No.
**Children:** Permitted.
**Languages:** English.
**Your Host:** Liz & Celia.

# ORCAS ISLAND

## Rose Cottage

Women ♀

### *Orcas Island, Gem of the San Juans*

***Rose Cottage*** is a cozy, private waterfront sanctuary for two on Orcas Island. It has a spectacular sunrise view of Mount Baker, a sunny deck and a long, private pebble beach. Situated above an artist's studio, it nestles among old firs and looks over fragrant vegetable and flower gardens and meandering lawns that end down at the beach. Orcas has excellent kayaking, biking, fishing, hiking and fresh-

*continued next page*

water swimming. Moran State Park is within five miles. The local village, Eastsound, handy for groceries, restaurants and theater, is just under two miles away.

**Address: Rt 2, Box 951, Eastsound, WA 98245. Tel: (360) 376-2076.**

**Type:** Guesthouse.
**Clientele:** Mostly women with men welcome.
**Transportation:** Car is best. Free pick up from airport.
**To Gay Bars:** 80 miles north to Vancouver, BC or 80 miles south to Seattle, WA.
**Rooms:** 1 cottage with double bed.
**Bathrooms:** Private shower/toilet.
**Vegetarian:** Organic food store & several restaurants with vegetarian meals 2 miles away.
**Complimentary:** Tea, coffee, cookies & flowers. (Fresh eggs when the hens are laying!)
**Dates Open:** All year.
**High Season:** Jun through Sept.
**Rates:** Summer $80 per night. Winter $70 per night.
**Discounts:** Weekly rates 10% discount.
**Rsv'tns:** Required.
**Reserve Through:** Travel agent or call direct.
**Minimum Stay:** 2 nights weekends & 3 nights holiday weekends.
**Parking:** Off-street parking for one car.
**In-Room:** Kitchen, refrigerator & coffee/tea-making facilities.
**On-Premises:** Deck.
**Exercise/Health:** Gym, weights, sauna, steam & massage nearby.
**Swimming:** Ocean beach on premises. Pool & lake nearby.
**Sunbathing:** At the beach & on private sun deck.
**Nudity:** Permitted on private deck with discretion.
**Smoking:** Not permitted.
**Pets:** Not permitted.
**Handicap Access:** No.
**Children:** Not permitted.
**Languages:** English, French & Italian.

# PORT TOWNSEND

## Ravenscroft Inn

Gay-Friendly ♀♂

### *Take a Short Trip to Far Away...*

One of the most romantic hideaways in the Pacific Northwest is located high on a bluff overlooking historic Port Townsend, the Olympic Peninsula's Victorian seaport. The ***Ravenscroft Inn*** is noted for its colonial style, a replication of a historic Charleston single house.

The Inn offers a unique combination of colonial hospitality, mixed with a casual air that spells comfort to its guests. The hosts take great pleasure in looking after their guests' special requests, whether it's dinner, theatre, concert reservations, or arranging for flowers or champagne, all are carried out with ease and alacrity.

While staying at the ***Ravenscroft Inn,*** you can explore the Olympic National Park, walk the seven mile sand spit at Dungeness or hike through North America's only rainforest. Port Townsend and its environs meets all your vacation requirements offering scenic beauty, theatre, unparalleled dining, boating, biking, fishing, kayaking and hiking. Top this off with a delectable breakfast and fresh roasted gourmet coffee, served each morning. **Guest Comment**: "There was never a detail left unattended."

**Address: 533 Quincy St, Port Townsend, WA 98368**
**Tel: (360) 385-2784, (800) 782-2691, Fax: (360) 385-6724.**

**Type:** Bed & breakfast.
**Clientele:** Mainly straight with a gay & lesbian following
**Transportation:** Car is best. Free pick up from Port Townsend Airport (from Seattle via Port Townsend Airways).
**To Gay Bars:** 2 hrs by car.
**Rooms:** 8 rooms & 2 suites with single, queen or king beds.
**Bathrooms:** 4 private bath/shower/toilets & 5 private shower/toilets.
**Meals:** Full breakfast.
**Vegetarian:** Available on request. When making reservation, all dietary restrictions addressed.
**Complimentary:** Sherry, coffee, tea, set-up service, juices.
**Dates Open:** All year.
**High Season:** May 15-Oct 15.
**Rates:** $68-$165 May 15-Oct 15, $65-$140 Oct 16-May 14.
**Discounts:** Single discount.
**Credit Cards:** MC, VISA, Amex & Discover.
**Rsv'tns:** Required.
**Reserve Thru:** Call direct.
**Minimum Stay:** Some weekends, special holidays & special events.
**Parking:** Ample free off-street parking.
**In-Room:** Color TV on request, maid service.
**On-Premises:** Meeting room, library, great room.
**Exercise/Health:** Soaking tub in suite, gym available, weights, Jacuzzi, sauna, steam & massage at nearby Athletic Club.
**Swimming:** At local school pool.
**Sunbathing:** On common sun decks & at beach.
**Smoking:** Permitted on outdoor balconies only.
**Pets:** Not permitted.
**Children:** Permitted over 12 years of age.
**Languages:** English.

# SEATTLE

## Bacon Mansion

Gay-Friendly ♀♂

### *Seattle's Finest B&B for Sun (and Rain!) Lovers!*

***The Bacon Mansion*** is an elegant English Tudor house in the Harvard-Belmont Historical District. Here in Capitol Hill, one of Seattle's most exciting neighborhoods, dining, sightseeing, nightlife and boutiques are just a few blocks away. A variety of well-appointed accommodations, from moderate rooms to suites and even a carriage house, warmly welcome every guest. Eight rooms have private baths. We have immense, beautifully decorated day rooms and a large, private, partially-covered patio for sun (and rain!) lovers. Don't miss it!

**Address: 959 Broadway East, Seattle, WA 98102**
**Tel: (206) 329-1864, (800) 240-1864, Fax: (206) 860-9025.**

**Type:** Bed & breakfast guesthouse.
**Clientele:** 40% gay & lesbian & 60% straight clientele.
**Transportation:** Shuttle Express from airport, taxi from train.
**To Gay Bars:** Two blocks to famous Elite Tavern on Broadway.
**Rooms:** 7 rooms & 3 suites with double or queen beds.
**Bathrooms:** Private: 4 shower/toilet, 4 full baths. 2 shared full baths.
**Meals:** Buffet breakfast.
**Vegetarian:** Always available.
**Complimentary:** Tea, coffee, mints on pillow.
**Dates Open:** All year.
**High Season:** May through October.
**Rates:** Summer $69-$130, winter $62-$120.
**Discounts:** 10% on stays of over 6 nights, winter only.
**Credit Cards:** MC, VISA, Amex, Discover.
**Rsv'tns:** Required.
**Reserve Through:** Call direct.
**Minimum Stay:** Required.
**Parking:** Ample, off-street parking.
**In-Room:** Color TV, telephone & maid service.
**On-Premises:** Meeting rooms, refrigerator & fax.
**Exercise/Health:** Nearby gym, weights & massage.
**Swimming:** At nearby pool & lake.
**Sunbathing:** On patio & common sun deck.
**Smoking:** Permitted outside only.
**Pets:** Not permitted.
**Handicap Access:** One suite accessible.
**Children:** Permitted in some rooms only.
**Languages:** English.
**Your Host:** Daryl.

## Bed & Breakfast on Broadway

Gay-Friendly 50/50 ♀♂

Welcome to ***Bed & Breakfast on Broadway,*** situated in a tree-lined, residential neighborhood one block from the popular and lively Broadway shopping, restaurant and theater district. This distinctive 1901 Pacific Northwest-style house has been faithfully restored to its original splendour and is filled with antiques and art objects. Original paintings and contemporary works of art by Northwest artists, as well as our own resident artist, Russ Lyons, are on display throughout the house. There are four charming guest rooms with private bath, and a scrumptious continental breakfast is served in the dining room.

**Address: 722 Broadway E., Seattle, WA 98102**
**Tel: (206) 329-8933, Toll-free: (888) 329-8933, Fax: (206) 726-0918.**

**Type:** Bed & breakfast.
**Clientele:** 50% gay & lesbian & 50% straight clientele
**Transportation:** Car, taxi or Super Shuttle.
**To Gay Bars:** 1 block.
**Rooms:** 4 rooms with queen beds.
**Bathrooms:** 4 private bath/toilets.
**Meals:** Expanded continental breakfast.
**Vegetarian:** Always available upon request.
**Dates Open:** All year.
**High Season:** May-Sept.
**Rates:** Summer $85-$95, winter $75-$85.
**Credit Cards:** MC, Visa, Amex.
**Rsv'tns:** Recommended 2-3 weeks in advance.
**Reserve Through:** Call direct.
**Minimum Stay:** 2 nights on weekends, 3 nights on holidays.
**Parking:** Limited off-street parking.
**In-Room:** Color cable TV, maid service.
**Exercise/Health:** Nearby gym, weights.
**Swimming:** Nearby pool, ocean, lake.
**Smoking:** Inquire.
**Pets:** Not permitted.
**Handicap Access:** No.
**Children:** No.
**Languages:** English, Tagalog, a little Japanese.
**Your Host:** Don & Russ.

## Bellevue Place Bed & Breakfast

Q-NET Gay-Friendly 50/50 ♀♂

### *A 1905 Storybook House on Seattle's Capitol Hill*

***Bellevue Place,*** located in the Landmark District of Seattle's Capitol Hill, is a 1905 "storybook" house with leaded glass and Victorian charm. As your innkeepers, we wish is to ensure that guests will find two things as perfect as possible during their stay with us: the beds and the breakfasts. Our queen beds have cotton bedding and down comforters, as well as very comfortable high-quality mattresses and springs. In addition, fresh towels are provided daily. Breakfasts at ***Bellevue Place*** feature fresh seasonal fruits, juices, croissants, muffins and jam. We also serve either pancakes and meats, casseroles, or various other egg dishes.

Our all-white house with columned porch, swing, manicured lawns, arabesque windows, tapestry rugs and three comfortably furnished sitting areas provides a great sense of *home away from home.* Retire with a book to the swing on the columned porch, or enjoy strolling the manicured lawns. Parking is available and public transportation is just two blocks away. ***Bellevue Place*** is close to Broadway restaurants and stores and Volunteer park, and is a 20-minute walk to downtown Seattle shops and the public market. The two innkeepers are happy to guide your tourist or business plans on a daily basis.

**Address: 1111 Bellevue Place East, Seattle, WA**
**Tel: (206) 325-9253, (800) 325-9253, Fax: (206) 455-0785.**

**Type:** Bed & breakfast.
**Clientele:** 50% gay & lesbian & 50% straight clientele
**Transportation:** Shuttle express, rental car, airporter & city bus.
**To Gay Bars:** 5 blocks to gay bars.
**Rooms:** 3 rooms with queen beds.
**Bathrooms:** 2 shared bath/shower/toilets.
**Meals:** Full breakfast.
**Vegetarian:** Request when making reservation.
**Complimentary:** Cocktails, set-up service, tea & coffee, mints on pillow.
**Dates Open:** All year.
**High Season:** May 15-October 15.
**Rates:** Single or double $95, plus tax.
**Discounts:** 7 days for the price of 6.
**Credit Cards:** MC, Visa, Amex, Bancard, Discover.
**Rsv'tns:** Required.
**Reserve Through:** Travel agent or call direct.
**Minimum Stay:** Required.
**Parking:** Adequate on-street parking.
**In-Room:** Color TV, telephone, maid service.
**Exercise/Health:** Nearby gym, weights, steam, massage.
**Sunbathing:** On patio.
**Smoking:** Permitted on porches & patios. B&B is non-smoking.
**Pets:** Not permitted.
**Handicap Access:** No.
**Children:** No.
**Languages:** English.
**Your Host:** Gunner.

## Capitol Hill Inn

Q-NET Gay-Friendly 50/50 ♀♂

### *You Can't Be Any Closer*

***Capitol Hill Inn,*** an elegantly restored 1903 Queen Anne, delights guests with treasures from a bygone era. Elaborate restoration details include custom-designed wall coverings, period chandeliers, and original, intricately carved wood mouldings. Rooms are lavishly furnished with European antiques, brass beds and down comforters, which are especially cozy on crisp, Seattle nights. A sumptuous breakfast includes such items as blintzes, lox and bagels, quiche and fresh fruit. There are issues of *NY Times,* books, and magazines in the parlor and AAA has given us a 3 diamond rating. We're six blocks from the Convention Center. Recommended: AAA 3 diamonds, Best Places Pacific Northwest, Best Places to Kiss. Member: Seattle Visitors & Convention Bureau, Seattle B&B Assn.

**Address: 1713 Belmont Ave, Seattle, WA 98122**
**Tel: (206) 323-1955, Fax: (206) 322-3809.**

**Type:** Bed & breakfast.
**Clientele:** 50% gay & lesbian & 50% straight clientele
**Transportation:** Airport shuttle $14 per person or taxi approx. $30.
**To Gay Bars:** 1 block.
**Rooms:** 6 rooms with single, double, queen or king beds.
**Bathrooms:** All private bathrooms, 2 rooms have private 1/2 baths & shared hall shower.
**Meals:** Full breakfast.
**Vegetarian:** Available upon request.
**Dates Open:** All year.
**Rates:** $85-$165.
**Discounts:** 10% in off-season, winter only.
**Credit Cards:** MC, Visa & Amex.
**Rsv'tns:** Recommended.
**Reserve Through:** Call direct.
**Parking:** Free parking.
**In-Room:** Maid service. Americana & Sherlock Holmes suites have fireplace, Jacuzzi & queen beds.
**On-Premises:** Parlors, living room, public telephone.
**Exercise/Health:** Jacuzzis in two suites.
**Swimming:** At downtown health club.
**Smoking:** Permitted on the porch or outdoors.
**Pets:** Not permitted.
**Handicap Access:** No, stairs.
**Children:** Not permitted.
**Languages:** English.
**Your Host:** Katie & Joanne.

# Chambered Nautilus Bed & Breakfast Inn

Gay-Friendly ♀♂

## *A Classic Seattle-style Inn*

Welcome to ***Chambered Nautilus,*** a classic Seattle-style B&B inn combining the warmth of a country inn with excellent access to the city's theaters, bars, restaurants and shopping. An elegant 1915 Georgian mansion, it has fine views of the Cascade Mountains and is perched on a peaceful hill in Seattle's University district. Guest rooms are large, airy and comfortably furnished with American and English antiques. A full breakfast completes your stay with fresh fruit, juice, granola, a wide array of entrees and plenty of fresh-roasted Seattle coffee! We welcome guests to share the comfortable, gracious ambiance of this classic inn.

**Address: 5005 22nd Ave NE, Seattle, WA 98105**
**Tel: (206) 522-2536, Fax: (206) 528-0898.**

**Type:** Bed & breakfast inn.
**Clientele:** 80%/20%, mainly straight with a gay & lesbian following
**Transportation:** Your own car or airport shuttle or taxi to our front door.
**To Gay Bars:** Less than 10 minutes' drive or 20 minutes' by bus to gay/lesbian bars.
**Rooms:** 6 rooms.
**Bathrooms:** 4 private, 1 shared.
**Meals:** Full breakfast.
**Vegetarian:** On request.
**Complimentary:** Afternoon & evening tea and home-made cookies.
**Dates Open:** All year.
**High Season:** May-Oct.
**Rates:** $79-$105.
**Discounts:** 10% discount in winter only. Discounts available to U. of Washington visiting faculty, off-season only.
**Credit Cards:** MC, Visa, Amex.
**Rsv'tns:** Strongly recommended (6-8 weeks in season), 1 week cancellation policy.
**Reserve Through:** Call direct.
**Minimum Stay:** 3 days on holiday weekends, 2 on summer weekends.
**Parking:** Adequate free on-street parking.
**In-Room:** Maid service, clock radio. 4 rooms have porches.
**On-Premises:** Meeting rooms, living room w/ fireplace, sun porch, large yard & garden, library, guest refrigerator, phone & fax available.
**Exercise/Health:** Spa & gym nearby.
**Swimming:** Lake swimming nearby.
**Sunbathing:** On room porches with discretion.
**Smoking:** No smoking in the inn. Permitted outside in garden only.
**Pets:** Not permitted.
**Handicap Access:** No.
**Children:** Under 12 by prior arrangement only.
**Languages:** English & French.
**Your Host:** Joyce & Steve.

## Gaslight Inn

Q-NET Gay/Lesbian ♀♂

Welcome to ***Gaslight Inn,*** a Seattle four-square house built in 1906. In restoring the inn, we have brought out the home's original turn-of-the-century ambiance and warmth, while keeping in mind the additional conveniences and contemporary style needed by travelers in the nineties. The interior is appointed in exacting detail, with strikingly rich, dark colors, oak paneling, and an enormous entryway and staircase.

***Gaslight Inn's*** comfortable and unique rooms and suites are furnished with quality double or queen-sized beds, refrigerator and television. Additional features for your special needs, such as private bath and phone service, are available in some rooms. Some rooms also have decks with fabulous views or fireplaces. The living room, with its large oak fireplace, is always an inviting room, as is the library. Through the late spring and summer, we encourage you to relax and unwind at poolside with a glass of wine after a long, busy day. This private, inground, heated pool with several decks and interesting plant arrangements, is found at the back of the inn.

***Gaslight Inn*** is convenient to central Seattle's every attraction: Volunteer Park, City Center, and to a plethora of gay and lesbian bars, restaurants and retail stores in the Broadway district. All of us at ***Gaslight Inn*** send you a warm advance welcome to Seattle.

**Address: 1727 15th Ave, Seattle, WA 98122**
**Tel: (206) 325-3654, Fax: (206) 328-4803.**

**Type:** Guesthouse.
**Clientele:** Mostly gay/lesbian with some straight clientele
**Transportation:** Shuttle Express from airport $15. (206) 286-4800 to reserve ride.
**To Gay Bars:** 2 blocks to men's bars, 3 blocks to women's bars.
**Rooms:** 9 doubles, 5 suites.
**Bathrooms:** 11 private, others share.
**Meals:** Expanded continental breakfast.
**Complimentary:** Coffee, tea & juices, fresh fruit, pastries.
**Dates Open:** All year.
**High Season:** Summer.
**Rates:** $68-$148.
**Discounts:** 5% for cash payment.
**Credit Cards:** MC, Visa & Amex.
**Rsv'tns:** Recommended at least 2 weeks in advance.
**Reserve Through:** Call direct.
**Minimum Stay:** 2 days on weekends, 3 days on holidays.
**Parking:** Ample on-street & off-street parking.
**In-Room:** Color TV, maid service & refrigerator.
**On-Premises:** Meeting rooms, living room, library, public telephone.
**Swimming:** Seasonal heated pool.
**Sunbathing:** On private or common sun decks or at poolside.
**Smoking:** Permitted on decks & porches only.
**Pets:** Not permitted.
**Handicap Access:** No.
**Children:** Not permitted.
**Languages:** English.
**Your Host:** Trevor, Stephen & John.

IGTA

## Hill House Bed & Breakfast

Q-NET Gay-Owned 50/50 ♀♂

### *Experience the Romance*

Wake up to the fragrant smell of fresh brewed coffee, the sweet sound of Baroque music, and the voluptuous pleasure of down comforters. Experience the romance of the ***Hill House Bed & Breakfast***, a recently restored 1903 Victorian home located on historic Capitol Hill, just minutes from downtown attractions and the convention center and a short walk to many restaurants, nightclubs and shops. Choose from five differently-appointed, elegant rooms. Also enjoy a scrumptious full breakfast and plenty of personal attention from your hosts. AAA has rated us with three diamonds, and we have ample free parking on premises.

**Address: 1113 E John St, Seattle, WA 98102**
**Tel: (206) 720-7161, (800) 720-7161, Fax: (206) 323-0772,**
**E-mail: hillhouse@uspan.com. http://uspan.com/hillhouse.**

**Type:** Bed & breakfast.
**Clientele:** 50% gay & lesbian & 50% straight clientele
**Transportation:** Public transportation from the airport: cabs, shuttles, rental cars.
**To Gay Bars:** 6 blocks.
**Rooms:** 3 rooms & 2 suites with queen beds.
**Bathrooms:** 1 shared & 3 private.
**Meals:** Full gourmet breakfast.
**Vegetarian:** Available upon request.
**Complimentary:** Mints, coffee, tea & cocoa.
**Dates Open:** All year.
**High Season:** May 15-November 14.
**Rates:** Winter $65-$95 & summer $70-$105.
**Discounts:** Weekly rates in low season.
**Credit Cards:** MC, Visa, Amex, Discover.
**Rsv'tns:** Required with 1 week cancellation policy.
**Reserve Thru:** Call direct.
**Minimum Stay:** 3 nights on holiday weekends & 2 nights on weekends.
**Parking:** Ample free off-street & on-street parking.
**In-Room:** Variety of facilities, some rooms have phones.
**On-Premises:** Guest refrigerator, CD library, sun deck, sitting & reading room.
**Exercise/Health:** Gym, weights, Jacuzzi, sauna & steam at nearby health clubs.
**Swimming:** At nearby gay beach on Lake Washington.
**Sunbathing:** On common sun decks.
**Smoking:** Smoking allowed outside on porches.
**Pets:** Not permitted.
**Handicap Access:** No special access.
**Children:** Not permitted.
**Languages:** English, Filipino.
**Your Host:** Ken & Eric.

## Inn the Woods

Women ♀

### *Immerse Yourself in the Tranquility*

***Inn the Woods*** is a peaceful, private bed and breakfast for women only. A warm, spacious log home on five acres, ***Inn the Woods*** offers two large guest rooms furnished with wicker, antiques, down comforters and original artwork. A hot tub, decks for sunbathing, picnic areas and walking trails complete the setting. A full gourmet breakfast in bed awaits you each morning. One hour from Seattle or Olympia and ten minutes from picture-postcard Gig Harbor, guests will find exquisite dining, antiques, galleries and shops to suit all tastes. One to two hours from the Olympic Peninsula, Cascade Mountains, San Juan Islands or Victoria, Canada. Guests may enjoy sailing aboard the owners' private sailboat.

**Address: 4416 150th St Ct NW, Gig Harbor, WA. Tel: (206) 857-4954.**

**Type:** Bed & breakfast inn 1 hour outside Seattle.
**Clientele:** Women only
**Transportation:** Car is best.
**To Gay Bars:** 20 minutes to Tacoma, 1 hour to Seattle.
**Rooms:** 2 rooms with queen or double bed.
**Bathrooms:** 1 private sink, 1 shared bath/toilet.
**Meals:** Full breakfast in bed.
**Vegetarian:** Will accommodate any dietary desires or restrictions.
**Complimentary:** Home baked treats, mints at bedside.
**Dates Open:** Sept 1-May 1 open weekends only.
**High Season:** Summer, May-September.
**Rates:** $95 per night all year.
**Discounts:** 10% for weekly stay.
**Rsv'tns:** Required.
**Reserve Through:** Call direct.
**Minimum Stay:** 2 nights on

holiday weekends.
**Parking:** Ample free off-street parking.
**On-Premises:** Large stone fireplace in living area, piano, music, parlor games, laundry facilities.
**Exercise/Health:** Hot tub/spa & private sailing excursions.
**Swimming:** At nearby ocean, river & lake.
**Sunbathing:** On common sun decks.
**Nudity:** Permitted in hot tub at guests' discretion.
**Smoking:** Permitted on deck area only.
**Pets:** Not permitted.
**Handicap Access:** Wheelchair ramp. Inquire about bath facilities.
**Children:** Not permitted.
**Languages:** English.

## Landes House

Gay/Lesbian ♀♂

***Landes House*** is an historic turn-of-the-century home a short walk from the shops and restaurants of the popular Broadway district. It is named for Bertha Landes, Seattle's only woman mayor, who was elected in 1926. The house has a warm and inviting ambiance, large gracious day rooms, elaborate woodwork and a private garden courtyard with hot tub. Most rooms have private baths, and several have private decks with views of Seattle's skyline, Puget Sound and the Olympic Mtns.

**Address: 712 11th Ave E, Seattle, WA 98102**
**Tel: (206) 329-8781, (888) 329-8781,**
**Fax: (206) 324-0934.**

**Type:** Bed & breakfast.
**Clientele:** Mostly gay/lesbian with some straight clientele
**Transportation:** For airport shuttle, call 622-1424 or (800) 942-0711.
**To Gay Bars:** 2-10 blocks to most men's & women's bars.
**Rooms:** 10 rms & 1 apt with queen or king beds.
**Bathrooms:** 9 private, others share.
**Meals:** Expanded continental breakfast.
**Vegetarian:** Always available, 3 blocks to The Gravity Bar.
**Complimentary:** Coffee, tea, summer beverages.
**Dates Open:** All year.
**High Season:** April-Oct.
**Rates:** Winter $64-$170, summer $68-$180.
**Discounts:** 7th night free.
**Credit Cards:** MC, Visa.
**Rsv'tns:** Strongly suggested (6-8 weeks in season).
**Reserve Thru:** Call direct.
**Minimum Stay:** 2 nights on weekends, 3 on holidays.
**Parking:** Adequate free off-street parking.
**In-Room:** Color TV, tele, maid service, ceiling fans.
**On-Premises:** Laundry facilities.
**Exercise/Health:** Hot tub.
**Swimming:** Lake & beach nearby.
**Sunbathing:** On private & common sun decks.
**Nudity:** Permitted in hot tub.
**Smoking:** Permitted (Non-smoking rooms available).
**Pets:** Not permitted.
**Handicap Access:** No.
**Children:** Not permitted.
**Languages:** English.
**Your Host:** Tom, Dave & Jim.

## Roberta's Bed & Breakfast

Gay-Friendly ♀♂

### *A Capital Welcome on Capitol Hill*

The leafy historic neighborhood circling Volunteer Park is a tranquil and beautiful oasis in the heart of "happening" Seattle. Volunteer Park, which is just around the corner from our bed & breakfast, includes the Seattle Art Museum's Asian Art collection, the Observation Tower and the Conservatory. A short walk along tree-lined avenues of lovingly-maintained turn-of-the-century homes and en-

*continued next page*

viable gardens will deposit you in Capitol Hill's lively area of shops, cafes and restaurants. Broadway, Seattle's heartbeat, is only a few blocks away. Beyond that is the rest of the city with its many famous sights, including The Seattle Center, Pike Place Market, the waterfront, Space Needle and the International District. The surrounding mountains, lakes and beaches are also all within easy access.

If this convenient location and Doris Day setting were not enough, Roberta's welcome alone would secure the success of your stay. ***Roberta's Bed & Breakfast*** is exactly that, with all the warmth and comfort of a real home. You may choose from five sunny bedrooms furnished with many books and a variety of antiques. All bedrooms have queen-sized beds, and four of the rooms have private baths.

Roberta boasts the wealth of knowledge that only a native can, and she is hell-bent on ensuring that you enjoy the best of this wonderful city. She is well-equipped with newspapers, maps and ideas, and the rooms are bursting with information and enjoyable books. But don't look for the word "overeat" in Roberta's dictionary – it's not there. Roberta serves a wild-west-sized breakfast of home cooking, accompanied by spirited conversation and laughter, that will see you through to dinner. If you remind her (and if she likes you) she'll bake cookies for you. We hope you enjoy your visit at ***Roberta's,*** whether you are a first-time guest or an old friend.

**Address: 1147-16 Avenue East, Seattle, WA 98112**
**Tel: (206) 329-3326, Fax: (206) 324-2149, E-mail: robertasbb@aol.com.**

**Type:** Bed & breakfast.
**Clientele:** Mostly straight clientele with a gay/lesbian following
**Transportation:** Super Shuttle $18. Please inquire about pick up service.
**To Gay Bars:** 8 blocks, 3/4 mile, a 15 minute walk, a 5 minute drive.
**Rooms:** 4 rooms, 1 suite with queen beds.
**Bathrooms:** Private: 1 bath/toilet, 4 shower/toilets.
**Meals:** Full breakfast.
**Vegetarian:** All vegetarian served here, no meat at all.
**Complimentary:** Wake-up coffee & tea in room. Coffee & tea anytime, cookies sometimes.
**Dates Open:** All year.
**High Season:** June-Sep.
**Rates:** High $90-$125, Low $85-$115.
**Credit Cards:** MC, Visa.
**Rsv'tns:** Required.
**Reserve Through:** Call direct.
**Parking:** Ample on-street parking on a quiet, sleepy street.
**In-Room:** Maid service.
**On-Premises:** Meeting rms, coffee & tea-makings.
**Exercise/Health:** Nearby gym.
**Swimming:** Nearby pool & lake.
**Smoking:** No smoking.
**Pets:** Not permitted.
**Handicap Access:** No.
**Languages:** English.
**Your Host:** Roberta.

# WHIDBEY ISLAND - LANGLEY

## Galittoire

**Gay-Owned ♀♂**

### *European Graciousness, American Spaciousness*

***Galittoire*** exudes the notion of being more than just a guesthouse. It provides an ideal setting for physical, mental and spiritual refreshment and revitalization. It "...is a sleek, contemporary B&B that's almost sensual in its attention to detail." – *1994-95 Northwest Best Places* In addition, ***Galittoire*** is one of the highest-rated bed and breakfasts on Whidbey Island according to *The Best Places to Kiss in the Northwest.*

Located on Whidbey Island in Puget Sound, ***Galittoire*** encompasses over ten acres of woodlands and offers luxurious accommodations in a serene setting.

The guesthouse, sited in a glade ringed with trees and surrounded by lawn sloping to forest, seems an extension of the natural world with its many windows, glass doors and skylights. The name *Galittoire* is a hybrid derived from the French "galetoire," meaning "first step towards freedom" and the Mayan "galeto," which translates as "a place of feasting and celebration."

A perfect place from which to explore the unique character of the island, its beaches, farms and small towns, ***Galittoire*** is a short distance from the seaside village of Langley. Langley strikes a pleasant balance between slow-paced existence and intriguing discovery. The notion of timelessness contributes in giving Langley a way of life that locals fight to preserve and that bustle-weary escapees from the city long to experience.

At ***Galittoire,*** equal emphasis is placed on "bed" and "breakfast" to realize the best of both. Each of the guest suites is built to enhance maximum privacy. The finest king-sized beds and down bedding assure a good night's sleep. In an elegant sunlit dining room, a gourmet breakfast is served complemented by spiced fruits and homemade freezer jams, honey sweetened mousse, whipped butters or fruit compotes. ***Galittoire*** combines European graciousness with American spaciousness.

***Galittoire*** pleases and pampers its guests with a variety of diversions. For indoor pleasures, a sauna, hot tub and Jacuzzi are provided, in addition to an exercise room, entertainment room and library. Complimentary transportation to and from the ferry landing, bicycles and island tour information are also available.

**Address: 5444 S Coles Rd, Langley, Whidbey Island, WA 98260-9508**
**Tel: (360) 221-0548,**
**E-mail: galittoire@whidby.com. http://www.whidbey.com/galittoire.**

**Type:** Bed & breakfast.
**Clientele:** 35% gay & lesbian clientele
**Transportation:** Car is best. Shuttle Express from Seattle airport to Mukilteo, then ferry to Clinton. Call for free pick up from ferry.
**To Gay Bars:** 45-min drive to Everett, 1 hr to Seattle.
**Rooms:** 2 suites with king beds.
**Bathrooms:** Private bath/toilets.
**Meals:** Full gourmet breakfast. 4-course dinner service at $75 per person by prior arrangement.
**Vegetarian:** Dietary restrictions considered with advance notice. Vegetarian food also available at local restaurants.
**Complimentary:** Juices, seltzer, tea & coffee always available. Fresh fruits in suites at turndown time.
**Dates Open:** All year.
**High Season:** May-Sep.
**Rates:** $175-$245.
**Discounts:** For extended stay in off season.
**Credit Cards:** MC, Visa, Discover, Amex.
**Rsv'tns:** Required.
**Reserve Thru:** Call direct.
**Minimum Stay:** 2-night minimum on weekends.
**Parking:** Ample free parking.
**In-Room:** Room & maid service.
**On-Premises:** TV lounge, video tape library, telephone, business services & laundry facilities. Ideal setting for executive retreats, weddings & union ceremonies.
**Exercise/Health:** Gym, weights, Jacuzzi, sauna, hot tub & massage on premises.
**Swimming:** Nearby ocean & lake.
**Sunbathing:** On common sun decks, on the lawn or in the woods. At nearby beach.
**Smoking:** On exterior decks only. Main house & suites are strictly non-smoking.
**Pets:** Not permitted.
**Handicap Access:** No. 2 steps into main house & into single-level suite.
**Children:** Third parties $50 additional per night.
**Languages:** English, Hindi.
**Your Host:** Mahésh.

## The Gallery Suite

**Gay-Friendly 50/50 ♀♂**

### *Art by the Sea*

Escape to Langley for a quiet, romantic weekend. Enjoy our regional contemporary art collection and the island's beautiful sunsets. This quaint Victorian town has three fine restaurants, art galleries, shopping, antique shops and many nearby beaches. Come to ***The Gallery Suite*** for a stay in an artfully-appointed waterfront suite with an unobstructed view of Saratoga Passage and Camano Head. Breathe sea air from the spacious deck. Picturesque, seaside Langley is just outside your door.

*continued next page*

**Address: PO Box 458, Langley, WA 98260. Tel: (360) 221-2978.**

**Type:** Bed & breakfast with art gallery.
**Clientele:** 50% gay & lesbian & 50% straight clientele.
**Transportation:** Car, airport shuttle, ferry boat. Pick up from ferry dock.
**To Gay Bars:** 1 hour to gay/lesbian bars.
**Rooms:** 1 suite with queen bed.
**Bathrooms:** 1 private.
**Meals:** Continental breakfast.
**Complimentary:** Swiss chocolates, beverages, fruit & cheese.
**Dates Open:** All year.
**High Season:** Memorial Day-Labor Day.
**Rates:** $110 1st night, $100 2nd night & $90 for 3rd & subsequent nights.
**Credit Cards:** MC, VISA, Amex & Discover.
**Rsv'tns:** Required, 1 week cancellation policy.
**Reserve Through:** Travel agent or call direct.
**Minimum Stay:** 2 nights on holidays, weekends.
**Parking:** Ample free off-street parking.
**In-Room:** Maid service, refrigerator, coffee pot, toaster oven.
**Exercise/Health:** Local gym nearby, massage available.
**Swimming:** Lake & saltwater passage 1/2 hour drive.
**Sunbathing:** On private sun decks or patio.
**Smoking:** Not permitted.
**Pets:** Permitted with special permission.
**Handicap Access:** No.
**Children:** Not permitted.
**Languages:** English.

# WEST VIRGINIA

## HUTTONSVILLE

### Richard's Country Inn

**Gay-Friendly ♀♂**

***Richard's Country Inn*** is a pre-Civil-War mansion restored as a bed and breakfast inn with full-service bar and restaurant. We are close to state parks and national forest, and outdoor activities abound, such as mountain bike tours (rentals available), cave exploring, hiking, trout fly-fishing, whitewater rafting, downhill and cross-country skiing, as well as more civilized sports, like golfing. Our guests say they like the clean, cool air. A favorite of tourists is the Cass restored railroad which regularly toils up and down the mountains. Skiing in these mountains, by the way, is the best east of the Rockies.

**Address: US 219 Route 1 Box 11-A-1, Huttonsville, WV 26273**
**Tel: (304) 335-6659, (800) 636-7434.**

**Type:** Bed & breakfast inn & cottage with restaurant/bar.
**Clientele:** Mostly straight clientele with a gay & lesbian following
**Transportation:** Car is best.
**To Gay Bars:** 1-3/4 hours to Morgantown, WV.
**Rooms:** 15 rms & 1 cottage.
**Bathrooms:** 10 private, others share.
**Meals:** Full breakfast.
**Vegetarian:** Always available.
**Dates Open:** All year.
**Rates:** Rooms $60-$80 for 2 including full breakfast. Cottage $85-$150.
**Credit Cards:** MC, Visa, Amex.
**Rsv'tns:** Advisable.
**Reserve Through:** Travel agent or call direct.
**Parking:** Ample free off-street parking.
**In-Room:** Maid service. Some rooms have AC, some have ceiling fans.
**On-Premises:** TV lounge & meeting rooms.
**Exercise/Health:** Excellent downhill & cross-country skiing.
**Swimming:** Nearby public pool & river.
**Sunbathing:** On common sun decks.
**Smoking:** Non-smoking rooms available.
**Pets:** Permitted in some rooms.
**Children:** Welcome.
**Languages:** English.
**Your Host:** Richard.

# LOST RIVER

## The Guest House

Gay/Lesbian ♀♂

### *Come to the Mountains 2 Hours from the Washington, DC Beltway*

Our ***Guest House*** sits high above the Lost River Valley at the edge of a national forest. Extensive views and absolute privacy provide our guests the peace and quiet they deserve. In our main lodge, guests tend to gather around the immense native stone fireplace. Another living room is surrounded by windows with views of the mountains and valley. There are wraparound porches at treetop level. Ladderback rockers are everywhere. After arrival, soak away your city tensions in our indoor hot tub. By morning, you'll be in a mountain frame of mind. Breakfasts are served family-style, with fresh fruit, yogurt and traditional country fare.

The house holds thirteen spacious rooms with private baths, central air conditioning and a heated pool. Such outdoor activities as white water rafting, rock climbing, hiking, horseback riding, canoeing and fishing are all available in the area. The one-million-acre George Washington National Forest is adjacent to the property. Rockcliff Lake and Lost River State park are nearby.

**Address: H.C. 83 Box 18, Settlers Valley, Lost River, WV 26810**
**Tel: (304) 897-5707, Fax: (304) 897-5707, E-mail: guesthse@cfw.com.**

**Type:** Bed & breakfast guesthouse & mini-resort.
**Clientele:** Gay & lesbian
**Transportation:** Car is best.
**To Gay Bars:** 2-1/2 hours to Washington, DC, or Richmond, VA, gay bars.
**Rooms:** 13 rooms & 1 cottage with single, double or queen beds.
**Bathrooms:** All private shower/toilets.
**Meals:** Full breakfast. Extra charge: Saturday pm candlelight dinner. All 3 meals prepared for groups with prior notice.
**Vegetarian:** Available.
**Complimentary:** Tea, coffee, juices, wine & beer.
**Dates Open:** All year.
**High Season:** Apr - Nov.
**Rates:** $75-$95.
**Discounts:** For senior citizens, AARP.
**Credit Cards:** MC, Visa, Amex, Diners, Carte Blanche, Discover.
**Rsv'tns:** Suggested.
**Reserve Through:** Call direct.
**Parking:** Ample free parking.
**In-Room:** AC, ceiling fans, maid service.
**On-Premises:** Private dining rooms, TV lounge, conference meeting rooms. Main house has kitchen, 2 large living rooms with fireplaces. 4000 sq ft main lodge open to guests.
**Exercise/Health:** Spa complex with indoor, in-ground, 10-person spa, outdoor Jacuzzi, 8-person steam room. Separate massage therapy room, licensed massage therapist on staff.
**Swimming:** Outdoor heated in-ground pool w/ Jacuzzi on premises. River & lake nearby.
**Sunbathing:** At poolside.
**Smoking:** Smoking areas available.
**Pets:** Not permitted.
**Handicap Access:** No.
**Children:** Not permitted.
**Languages:** English & French.
**Your Host:** Bob, David & Tammy.

# WISCONSIN

## DELAVAN

### The Allyn Mansion Inn

Gay-Friendly ♀♂

***"Inside...the Year is Always 1885" – Country Living Magazine***

Grand Prize winner of the Great American Home Awards presented by the National Trust for Historic Preservation and recipient of the Wisconsin Historical Society's Certificate of Commendation for Historic Preservation because of its "exceptionally thorough and meticulous restoration," the ***Allyn Mansion*** ranks as one of the finest restoration efforts in the nation. Along with walnut woodwork, frescoed ceilings, ten marble fireplaces and other original features, the mansion is completely furnished in authentic Victorian antiques. Guests enjoy the use of three formal parlors and two grand pianos.

**Address: 511 E Walworth Ave, Delavan, WI 53115**
**Tel: (414) 728-9090, Fax: (414) 728-0201.**

**Type:** Bed & breakfast with gift & antique shop.
**Clientele:** Mostly straight clientele with a gay & lesbian following.
**Transportation:** Car is best. Airport bus from Chicago or Milwaukee. Pick up from bus.
**To Gay Bars:** 35 miles.
**Rooms:** 8 rooms with single, dbl or queen beds.
**Bathrooms:** Shared: 7 full baths, 3 bathtubs only & 4 showers only.
**Meals:** Full breakfast.
**Vegetarian:** Available upon request.
**Complimentary:** Wine & cheese at 6 pm.
**Dates Open:** All year.
**High Season:** May-Feb.
**Rates:** $60 (single, corporate rate). $100 (2nd floor, queen beds, working fireplace).
**Credit Cards:** MC & VISA.
**Rsv'tns:** Required.
**Reserve Through:** Call direct. (Travel agents weekdays only.)
**Minimum Stay:** No Sat-night-only stays (Fri-Sat or Sat-Sun minimum).
**Parking:** Ample free off-street parking.
**In-Room:** AC. Some rooms with working fireplace.
**On-Premises:** Fax & meeting space.
**Exercise/Health:** Nearby gym, weights, Jacuzzi, sauna, steam & massage.
**Swimming:** Nearby pool & lake.
**Smoking:** Strictly forbidden anywhere in the house.
**Pets:** Not permitted.
**Handicap Access:** No.
**Children:** Not especially welcome.
**Languages:** English & French.
**Your Host:** Ron & Joe.

## MADISON

### Chase On The Hill Bed & Breakfast

Gay-Friendly 50/50 ♀♂

***Escape to the Country!***

You are invited to kick off your shoes and enjoy the charm and hospitality of ***Chase On The Hill,*** a cozy farmhouse built in 1846. Guestrooms are filled with fresh air and sunshine, providing an ideal atmosphere for peace and relaxation.

The master bedroom features skylights, queen bed and private bath. Antique furnishings, a woodburning stove and a miniature grand piano will add to your enjoyment, along with farm animals on premises and cats in residence. We welcome you to our comfortable retreat in the rolling hills of Wisconsin, easily accessible from Madison, Milwaukee and Chicago.

**Address: 11624 State Road 26, Milton, WI 53563. Tel: (608) 868-6646.**

**Type:** Bed & breakfast.
**Clientele:** 50% gay & lesbian & 50% straight clientele.
**Transportation:** Car is best. Free pick up from bus.
**To Gay Bars:** 9 miles to Janesville, 35 miles to Madison.
**Rooms:** 3 rms with queen, dbl or trundle beds.
**Bathrooms:** 1 private bath/toilet, 1 shared bath/shower/toilet.
**Meals:** Full breakfast.
**Vegetarian:** Vegetarian breakfast served with advance notice.
**Complimentary:** Afternoon beverages, chocolates on nightstand.
**Dates Open:** All year.
**High Season:** Summer.
**Rates:** $45-$70 all year.
**Discounts:** For single occupancy.
**Credit Cards:** MC, VISA & Discover.
**Rsv'tns:** Required.
**Reserve Through:** Call direct.
**Parking:** Ample free off-street parking.
**On-Premises:** AC, meeting rooms, TV lounge, Fax.
**Swimming:** Lakes nearby.
**Sunbathing:** On the patio.
**Smoking:** Permitted outdoors only.
**Pets:** Not permitted.
**Handicap Access:** No.
**Children:** Welcome if over 12 years old.
**Languages:** English, Spanish, elementary German.
**Your Host:** Michael.

# STURGEON BAY - DOOR COUNTY

## Chanticleer Guesthouse

**Gay-Friendly 50/50 ♀♂**

### *A Romantic Country Inn*

Welcome to the ***Chanticleer,*** situated on 30 private acres in picturesque Door County, WI. With over 250 miles of shoreline, 12 lighthouses, 7 state parks and countless antique and gift shops, you're not far from unlimited fun and adventure. The ***Chanticleer's*** majestic maples and delicate fields of wild flowers are a grand sight as you stroll on our nature trail. After your walk, tour our beautiful gardens, lounge poolside or relax on your private terrace overlooking the ***Chanticleer's*** serene countryside. All deluxe suites include double whirlpools, fireplaces and breakfast delivered to your room.

**Address: 4072 Cherry Rd, Sturgeon Bay, WI 54235. Tel: (414) 746-0334.**

**Type:** Bed & breakfast.
**Clientele:** 50% gay & lesbian & 50% straight clientele.
**Transportation:** Car.
**To Gay Bars:** 45 miles or a 50-minute drive to 5 bars in Green Bay.
**Rooms:** 8 suites (6 with queen & 2 with king beds).
**Bathrooms:** All private bath/toilet/showers.
**Meals:** Expanded continental breakfast.
**Vegetarian:** Our breakfast is vegetarian. Vegetarian restaurants nearby.
**Complimentary:** Tea, coffee, juice, cookies & fresh fruit.
**Dates Open:** All year.
**High Season:** Jun-Oct for summer festivals, fall & pumpkin festivals. Feb-Mar for ski season.
**Rates:** $115-$175.
**Discounts:** 10% summer 5 or more days. 10% winter 3 or more days (Sun-Thurs). Weekday specials.
**Credit Cards:** MC, Visa, Discover.
**Rsv'tns:** Required. Walk-ins welcome if rooms available.
**Reserve Through:** Call direct.
**Minimum Stay:** 2 nights on weekends.
**Parking:** Ample free off-street parking in paved lot.
**In-Room:** Color TV, VCR, CD & cassette stereo, AC, coffee/tea-making facilities, ceiling fans, refrigerator,

*continued next page*

fireplace, double whirlpool tub, room & maid service.
**On-Premises:** Meeting rooms.
**Exercise/Health:** Sauna on premises. Nearby gym & weights.
**Swimming:** Heated pool on premises, nearby lake.
**Sunbathing:** At poolside, on patio & private & common sun decks.
**Smoking:** Permitted with restrictions. Non-smoking sleeping rooms available.
**Pets:** Not permitted.
**Handicap Access:** No.
**Children:** Not especially welcome.
**Languages:** English.
**Your Host:** Bryon & Darrin.

# WASCOTT

## Wilderness Way Resort & Campground

Women ♀

***Wilderness Way*** is a women-owned resort and campground on 10 wooded acres with a lake. It's secluded, yet accessible to restaurants and points of interest. Two-bedroom units have kitchens, and linens and towels are furnished. Tent sites and full RV hookups offer maximum privacy and quiet. All sites have tables and fireplaces or grills. Bathrooms include sinks, flush toilets and hot showers. The commons building has a large stone fireplace, offering warmth and cheer on cool, rainy days and nights, and a bug-free refuge from mid-summer's buzzings.

**Address: PO Box 176, Wascott, WI 54890. Tel: (715) 466-2635.**

**Type:** Resort campground.
**Clientele:** Women only
**Transportation:** Car is best.
**To Gay Bars:** 45 minutes to women's bars.
**Rooms:** Five 2-bedroom cabins.
**Bathrooms:** All private.
**Campsites:** 6 sites with electric hookup & 20 tent sites with showers & rest rooms.
**Complimentary:** Boat & canoe use with cabin.
**Dates Open:** All year.
**High Season:** Memorial Day-Labor Day.
**Rates:** Cabins (for 2) $48-$68 daily, $270-$390 weekly. Add'l person $8-$10. Camping $20 for two. Electric hookup $4.
**Discounts:** Visa, MC, Discover.
**Rsv'tns:** Required.
**Reserve Through:** Call direct.
**Minimum Stay:** 2 nights for cabins on weekends.
**Parking:** Free parking.
**In-Room:** Kitchen, cooking utensils, fans, linens, & towels.
**Exercise/Health:** Boats, canoes, hiking, biking, volleyball.
**Swimming:** In the lake.
**Sunbathing:** On the beach by the lake or anywhere on the property.
**Smoking:** Permitted, with restrictions.
**Pets:** $5 add'l charge in cabins, $2 if camping. Owner must keep pet leashed & in view.
**Handicap Access:** Bathrooms in camping area.
**Children:** Permitted and welcomed.
**Languages:** English.

# WYOMING

# JACKSON

## Bar H Ranch

Women ♀

### *The Undiscovered Side of the Grand Tetons*

In addition to regularly planned trail riding and horsepacking trips, ***Bar H Ranch*** offers loft accommodation to guests scheduling their own activities. The newly-remodeled barn loft is quite luxurious with lodgepole pine walls and ceilings, wall-to-wall carpet, and oak floors in kitchen and bath. The modern kitchen is fully-equipped with Jenn Aire range and breakfast bar. The bathroom sports a bathtub with claw feet. Sun yourself on the large deck, use the picnic table and chairs, BBQ, or relax and enjoy the fabulous views. Yellowstone and Grand Teton Nat'l Parks and Jackson Hole are all easy drives from the ranch.

**Address: Box 297, Driggs, WY 83422. Tel: (208) 354-2906.**

**Type:** Self-contained, private ranch accommodation on a working cattle ranch.
**Clientele:** Mostly women with men welcome.
**Transportation:** Car is best. Rental cars available from Jackson Hole Airport.
**Rooms:** Loft, tipi or B&B in main house.
**Bathrooms:** Private bath.
**Meals:** Full breakfast for B&B only.
**Vegetarian:** Vegetarian food nearby.
**Dates Open:** Spring-fall. Closed in winter.
**Rates:** Loft $90/night, $580/wk. Tipi $50/night, $300/wk. B&B $90/night.
**Rsv'tns:** Highly recommended.
**Reserve Through:** Call direct.
**Minimum Stay:** 2 nights in loft.
**Parking:** Ample off-street parking on ranch.
**In-Room:** Color TV, VCR, telephone, fully-equipped kitchen, dishwasher, Jenn Aire range with oven, refrigerator.
**On-Premises:** Deck & BBQ.
**Exercise/Health:** Horseback riding, hiking, fly fishing, cycling.
**Swimming:** Nearby river, lake and public natural hot water pool.
**Sunbathing:** On private sun deck.
**Smoking:** Permitted on deck.
**Pets:** Cat with prior permission, dog may be acceptable.
**Handicap Access:** No.
**Children:** Inquire.
**Languages:** English.
**Your Host:** Edie & Gloria.

## Fish Creek Lodging

Gay/Lesbian ♀♂

### *Bed & Kitchen – Fix Your Own Damn Breakfast*

Nestled in the foothills of the Grand Teton Mountain Range, a secluded log cabin offers solitude and natural beauty for a truly peaceful getaway. Enjoy hiking, fishing, skiing, viewing wildlife or just relax. Visit nearby Yellowstone National Park, Grand Teton National Park and Jackson Hole, Wyoming. Fish the Henry's Fork of the Snake River and Warm River, or ski from your doorstep across the rolling meadows and surrounding forests. ***Fish Creek Lodging,*** a newly remodeled cabin, is fully furnished with everything you need for a perfect vacation.

**Address: Warm River, PO Box 833, Ashton, ID 83420-0833**
**Tel: (208) 652-7566.**

**Type:** Log cabin.
**Clientele:** Gay & lesbian. Good mix of men & women.
**Transportation:** Rental cars available from Jackson Hole & Idaho Falls, ID airports.
**Rooms:** Cabin with queen beds.
**Bathrooms:** All private.
**Dates Open:** All year.
**High Season:** Summer & fall.
**Rates:** Summer $75-$90 per night. Winter $90-$115 per night for 2 people.
**Discounts:** Weekly & monthly rates.
**Rsv'tns:** Highly recommended.
**Reserve Thru:** Call direct.
**Minimum Stay:** 2 nights.
**Parking:** Acres of off-street parking, some covered.
**In-Room:** All conveniences, full kitchen, TV/VCR, woodstove.
**Swimming:** Nearby rivers & lakes.
**Sunbathing:** On patio, private sun decks & 20 acres.
**Smoking:** Smoking outside only.
**Pets:** With prior permission.
**Handicap Access:** No.
**Children:** Permitted, but not especially welcome.
**Languages:** English.

## Redmond Guest House

Gay-Friendly 50/50 ♀♂

The ***Redmond Guest House*** is situated on a quiet, residential street, five blocks from Jackson's town square. Guests enjoy privacy in the back garden with barbecue and outdoor furniture. The guest house features lodgepole-pine furniture, a large brick fireplace, color TV and private bath with a queen-sized bed. Guests prepare their own breakfasts. The beautiful Jackson valley has long been a premier vacation destination. Even the Northern Plains Indians journeyed here in summer to gather healing herbs and hunt.

**Address: Box 616, Jackson, WY 83001. Tel: (307) 733-4003.**

**Type:** Guesthouse.
**Clientele:** 50% gay & lesbian & 50% straight clientele.
**Transportation:** Car is best. Free pick up from airport.
**Rooms:** 1 apartment with single & queen bed.
**Bathrooms:** Private.
**Dates Open:** May 1st-September 15th.
**High Season:** June - Sep.
**Rates:** Per night: $110.
**Discounts:** 10% discount if you mention Inn Places, 10% senior citizen discount.
**Rsv'tns:** Preferred.
**Reserve Thru:** Call direct.
**Minimum Stay:** 2 nights on weekends, 3 nights on holidays.
**Parking:** Ample off-street parking.

*continued next page*

**In-Room:** Color cable TV, kitchen, refrigerator, coffee & tea-making facilities.
**On-Premises:** BBQ & outdoor furniture.
**Sunbathing:** On the patio.
**Smoking:** Permitted outside only.
**Pets:** May be permitted, please inquire.
**Handicap Access:** No.
**Children:** Permitted.
**Languages:** English.
**Your Host:** Sue Ann

# THERMOPOLIS

## Out West Bed & Breakfast

Gay-Friendly 50/50 ♀♂

### *Thermopolis – Home of the World's Largest Mineral Hot Spring*

Overlooking the Owl Creek Mountains, ***Out West B&B,*** a unique Queen Anne home, was built in 1908 from hand-cast Ashlar stone. Among the B&B's many unique features are a bellcast roof, ornate staircase, beaded ceilings and original leaded stained-glass windows. Thermopolis is home to Hot Springs State Park's World's Largest Mineral Hot Spring, where you can relax while soaking in the Jacuzzi, or swim or slide in the pools. Other activities in the area include whitewater rafting, visiting the Indian petroglyphs and the Wyoming Dinosaur Center. We are just 136 miles from Yellowstone National Park and 84 miles from Cody, Wyoming.

**Address: 1344 Broadway, Thermopolis, WY 82443**
**Tel: (307) 864-2700.**

**Type:** Bed & breakfast with antique & gift shop.
**Clientele:** 50% gay & lesbian & 50% straight clientele
**Transportation:** Car is best.
**Rooms:** 4 rooms (1double bed, 3 queen beds).
**Bathrooms:** Shared: 1 upstairs bath/shower/toilet, 1 toilet/sink on main floor.
**Meals:** Full breakfast.
**Vegetarian:** Available if requested when making reservation.
**Complimentary:** Tea & coffee, mints & candy in room.
**Dates Open:** All year.
**High Season:** June-Aug.
**Rates:** $40-$50.
**Credit Cards:** Discover, Amex. MC & Visa accepted Apr 1-Sept 30 ONLY.
**Rsv'tns:** Strongly recommended.
**Reserve Through:** Call direct.
**Parking:** Ample free on-street.
**On-Premises:** TV lounge.
**Exercise/Health:** Nearby Jacuzzi, steam, massage.
**Swimming:** Nearby pool & river.
**Sunbathing:** At commercial pools in state park.
**Smoking:** House is non-smoking.
**Pets:** Not permitted.
**Handicap Access:** No.
**Children:** Not encouraged.
**Languages:** English.

# RV & CAMPING INDEX

## EUROPE


**FRANCE**
DOMME — La Dordogne Camping de Femmes ... 47
SOUTHWEST FRANCE - RURAL
Roussa ... 53
Saouis ... 53
**IRELAND**
CORK — Amazonia ... 64
**NETHERLANDS**
DONKERBROEK
`t Zijpad ... 86


## PACIFIC (Australia)


**NEW SOUTH WALES**
BERRY — Tara Country Retreat ... 133
**QUEENSLAND**
CAIRNS — Witchencroft ... 149


## PACIFIC (New Zealand)


**SOUTH ISLAND**
CHRISTCHURCH
Frauenreisehaus (The Homestead) ... 163


## CARIBBEAN


**BRITISH WEST INDIES**
JAMAICA — Tingalaya's B&B ... 198
**PUERTO RICO**
VIEQUES ISLAND
New Dawn Caribbean Retreat & Guest House ... 204


## CANADA


**ONTARIO**
HAMILTON — Cedars Tent & Trailer Park ... 182


## UNITED STATES


**ALASKA**
FAIRBANKS — Alta's Bed and Breakfast ... 226
**ARIZONA**
SEDONA — Huff 'n Puff Straw Bale Inn ... 232
Paradise by the Creek B&B ... 233
TUCSON — Montecito House ... 238
**ARKANSAS**
EUREKA SPRINGS
Greenwood Hollow Ridge ... 242
**CALIFORNIA**
CLEARLAKE AREA
Sea Breeze Resort ... 247
GOLD COUNTRY - SIERRA FOOTHILLS
Rancho Cicada ... 248
RUSSIAN RIVER
Highlands Resort ... 278
Willows, The ... 282
**FLORIDA**
ORLANDO — Things Worth Remembering ... 353
**HAWAII**
HAWAII - BIG ISLAND
Kalani Oceanside Eco-Resort ... 367
Volcano Ranch ... 372
Wood Valley B&B Inn ... 373
**MAINE**
AUGUSTA — Maple Hill Farm B&B Inn ... 403
OGUNQUIT — Admiral's Inn & Guesthouse .. 408
SEBAGO LAKE REGION
Maine-ly For You ... 413
**MICHIGAN**
SAUGATUCK — Campit ... 457
**MINNESOTA**
KENYON — Dancing Winds Farm ... 461
**NEW JERSEY**
PLAINFIELD — Pillars of Plainfield B&B ... 473
**NEW MEXICO**
ALBUQUERQUE
Hateful Missy & Granny Butch's ... 477
**NEW YORK**
ANGELICA — Jones Pond Campground ... 487
**OREGON**
ROGUE RIVER — Whispering Pines B&B /Retreat ... 515
**PENNSYLVANIA**
NEW MILFORD
Oneida Campground ... 519
SCRANTON — Hillside Campgrounds ... 525
**TENNESSEE**
GREENEVILLE — Timberfell Lodge ... 532
**UTAH**
ESCALANTE — Rainbow Country Tours B&B ... 542
**WASHINGTON**
INDEX — Wild Lily Ranch ... 559
**WISCONSIN**
WASCOTT — Wilderness Way Resort & Campground ... 578

# WOMEN'S INDEX

## EUROPE


**FRANCE**

BRITTANY — Chez Jacqueline ........ 46

DOMME — La Dordogne Camping de Femmes ........ 47

SOUTHWEST FRANCE - RURAL
- Hilltop Cantegrive Farmhouses ........ 51
- Mondès ........ 52
- Roussa ........ 53
- Saouis ........ 53

**GERMANY**

BERLIN — Artemisia, Women Only Hotel ........ 55

BRUNKEN WESTERWALD — Lichtquelle, Frauenbildungsstätte ........ 58

CHARLOTTENBERG — Frauenlandhaus ........ 58

OSTFRIESLAND — Frauenferienhof Ostfriesland ........ 60

TIEFENBACH — Frauenferienhaus Tiefenbach/Silbersee ........ 62

ZULPICH LOVENICH — Frauenbildungshaus Zülpich-Lövenich ........ 62

**IRELAND**

CORK — Amazonia ........ 64

**ITALY**

ACQUI TERME — La Filanda Guesthouse ........ 69

ISOLA D'ELBA — Casa Scala ........ 70

**NETHERLANDS**

AMSTERDAM — Liliane's Home; Guesthouse for Women Only ........ 81

DONKERBROEK — 't Zijpad ........ 86

**SPAIN**

TARRAGONA — MontyMar ........ 93

**UK - WALES**

AMMANFORD - DYFED — Apple Cottage ........ 129

SNOWDONIA NATIONAL PARK — Dewis Cyfarfod ........ 131


## PACIFIC (Australia)


**NEW SOUTH WALES**

NORTHERN NEW SOUTH WALES — A Slice of Heaven Rural Retreat for Women ........ 135

**QUEENSLAND**

CAIRNS
- Fifty-Four Cinderella Street ........ 10,147
- Witchencroft ........ 149


## PACIFIC (New Zealand)


**NORTH ISLAND**

WELLINGTON — Mermaid, The ........ 163

**SOUTH ISLAND**

CHRISTCHURCH — Frauenreisehaus (The Homestead) ........ 163


## CARIBBEAN


**DOMINICAN REPUBLIC**

CABARETE — Purple Paradise ........ 198

**PUERTO RICO**

VIEQUES ISLAND — New Dawn Caribbean Retreat & Guest House ........ 204


## CANADA


**BRITISH COLUMBIA**

TOFINO — Wind Rider, A Guest House for Women ........ 172

VANCOUVER — Hawks Avenue B&B ........ 175

**ONTARIO**

OTTAWA — Le jardin des Trembles ........ 182

**QUEBEC**

MONTREAL
- La Douillette ........ 191
- Pension Vallières ........ 193


## UNITED STATES


**ARIZONA**

SEDONA
- Paradise by the Creek B&B ........ 233
- Paradise Ranch ........ 234

TUCSON — Montecito House ........ 238

**CALIFORNIA**

BIG BEAR LAKE — Beary Merry Mansion ........ 246

LAKE TAHOE AREA
Holly's ... 252
MENDOCINO COUNTY
Sallie & Eileen's Place ... 262
PALM SPRINGS
Bee Charmer Inn ... 265
SAN FRANCISCO
Carl Street Unicorn House ... 293
SONOMA COUNTY
Asti Ranch ... 306

**DELAWARE**
MILTON Honeysuckle ... 313

**FLORIDA**
KEY WEST Island Key Courts of Key West, The ... 337
Rainbow House ... 21, 343
SEBASTIAN Pink Lady Inn, The ... 355
TAMPA Birdsong B&B ... 356

**GEORGIA**
SENOIA Culpepper House B&B ... 363

**HAWAII**
HAWAII - BIG ISLAND
Paauhau Plantation House ... 369
Wood Valley B&B Inn ... 373
MAUI Hale Makaleka ... 380
OAHU - HONOLULU
The Mango House ... 385

**LOUISIANA**
NEW ORLEANS
Bywater B&B ... 394

**MAINE**
OGUNQUIT Heritage of Ogunquit ... 410
PEMBROKE Yellow Birch Farm ... 412
SEBAGO LAKE REGION
Maine-ly For You ... 413

**MASSACHUSETTS**
BOSTON Victorian Bed & Breakfast ... 420
NORTHAMPTON
Innamorata ... 424
Tin Roof Bed & Breakfast ... 424
PROVINCETOWN
Bayview Wharf Apartments ... 426
Dusty Miller Inn ... 437
Gabriel's ... 440
Gull Walk Inn ... 441
Ravenwood Guestrooms & Apts ... 447
Rose Acre ... 448
Windamar House ... 455
STURBRIDGE - WARE
Wildwood Inn ... 456

**NEW HAMPSHIRE**
BETHLEHEM Highlands Inn, The ... 467
FRANCONIA Bungay Jar ... 469

**NEW MEXICO**
ALBUQUERQUE
Hateful Missy & Granny Butch's ... 477

**NEW YORK**
NEW YORK East Village Bed & Breakfast ... 498

**NORTH CAROLINA**
ASHEVILLE Bird's Nest Bed & Kitchen ... 502
Camp Pleiades ... 503
Emy's Nook ... 504
Mountain Laurel B&B ... 505
Sophie's Comfort ... 505
Twenty-Seven Blake Street ... 506
CHAPEL HILL Joan's Place ... 508

**OREGON**
PORTLAND Holladay House ... 513

**PENNSYLVANIA**
PHILADELPHIA
Best Nest, The ... 520
POCONOS Blueberry Ridge ... 523
Stoney Ridge ... 525

**WASHINGTON**
ORCAS ISLAND
Rose Cottage ... 563
SEATTLE Inn the Woods ... 570

**WISCONSIN**
WASCOTT Wilderness Way Resort & Campground ... 578

**WYOMING**
JACKSON Bar H Ranch ... 578

# PLEASE COMMENT...

Name of the inn: ______________________________

Location of inn: city ____________ country ______________

When did you stay there? month ____________ year ____________

Did you find that the accommodations were as described in the listing?

❑ Yes ❑ No

Explain: ______________________________

______________________________

______________________________

______________________________

______________________________

______________________________

______________________________

Sometimes, readers' comments are included in inns' descriptions. If you wish, your name can be included after your comments. If you DO want your name used, print your name as you would like it to appear and the city you come from.

Name ______________________________

City ______________________________

If you do NOT wish your name printed, please give it to us below for our private use in verifying your stay at the location.

Name (NOT to be published): ______________________________

If you run out of space, use another sheet of paper.

Mail to:
**Ferrari International Publishing, Inc.**
P.O. Box 37887, Phoenix, AZ 85069 USA
Tel: (602) 863-2408 Fax: (602) 439-3952
E-mail: ferrari@q-net.com

# THE FERRARI GUIDES™

## ORDER FORM

Please Send The Following Ferrari Guides To:

NAME

ADDRESS

CITY/STATE (PROVINCE)

ZIP/POSTAL CODE COUNTRY

| ITEM | PRICE/BK | QUANTITY | TOTAL |
|---|---|---|---|
| **SUBSCRIPTION TO FERRARI GUIDES** | | | |
| 3-BOOK SET FOR MEN (Includes Shipping in US/CANADA) | $41.95 | | |
| 3-BOOK SET FOR WOMEN (Includes Shipping in US/CANADA) | $41.95 | | |
| **SINGLE COPIES** | | | |
| Ferrari Guides' Gay Travel A to Z™ | $16.00 | | |
| Ferrari Guides' Men's Travel in Your Pocket™ | $16.00 | | |
| Ferrari Guides' Women's Travel in Your Pocket™ | $14.00 | | |
| Ferrari Guides' Inn Places® | $16.00 | | |

| SHIPPING: | USA | CANADA |
|---|---|---|
| ONE BOOK | $4.50 | $6.50 |
| TWO BOOKS | $5.50 | $7.50 |
| THREE BOOKS | $6.00 | $8.50 |
| FOUR BOOKS | $6.50 | $9.50 |

**PLEASE ENCLOSE THIS AMOUNT**

All prices are in US dollars. Prices good for US & Canada only.
All other countries: Please fax/phone/e-mail for additional shipping cost.

**SEND TO:**

**Ferrari International Publishing, Inc.**

P.O. Box 37887, Phoenix, AZ 85069 USA
Tel: (602) 863-2408 Fax: (602) 439-3952
E-mail: ferrari@q-net.com
Internet Orders: http://www.q-net.com

# INDEX TO ACCOMMODATIONS

## ABC


A Bed & Breakfast Abode, Ltd ... 494
A Greenwich Village Habitué ... 495
A Private Garden ... 393
A Slice of Heaven Rural Retreat for Women ... 135
A St. Louis Guesthouse in Historic Soulard ... 463
A Touch of Country ... 556
Abaca Palms ... 157
Abacrombie Badger Bed & Breakfast ... 414
Abbotts Como Villa ... 461
Acapulco Las Palmas ... 214
Adams House, The ... 312
Adelynne's Summit Haus & Summit Haus II ... 539
Admiral's Court ... 324
Admiral's Inn & Guesthouse ... 408
Admiral's Landing Guest House ... 23, 425
Adobe Rose Inn Bed & Breakfast ... 234
Alacoque Bed & Breakfast ... 187
Alamo Square Bed & Breakfast Inn ... 288
Albion Guest House, The, ... 173
Alden House Bed & Breakfast ... 405
Alexander Resort ... 263
Alexander's Guesthouse ... 328
Allender Apartments ... 145
Allyn Mansion Inn, The ... 576
Aloha Kauai Bed & Breakfast ... 373
Alpha Lodge Private Hotel ... 100
Alta's Bed and Breakfast ... 226
Amaryllis Guest House, The ... 126
Amazonia ... 64
Amelia Island Williams House ... 322
America's Crossroads ... 511
Ampersand Guesthouse ... 426
Amsterdam House BV ... 73
Amsterdam Toff's ... 74
Amsterdammertje ... 417
Anco Hotel-Bar ... 75
Andora Inn ... 289
Andrea & Janet's Maui Condos ... 378
Anfora's Dreams ... 378
Anna's Three Bears ... 290
Annie's Jughandle Beach B&B Inn ... 262
Another Point of View ... 502
Ansley Inn ... 358
Anthony's by the Sea ... 535
Antique Row Bed & Breakfast ... 520
Anton Boxrud B&B ... 543
Apple Cottage ... 129
Applewood Inn and Restaurant ... 15, 274
Arbor House Hotel ... 539
Arbour Glen B&B Victorian Inn & Guesthouse ... 240
Arcadia House ... 551
ARCO Hotel — Norddeutscher Hof ... 55
Arctic Feather B&B ... 224
Ardmory House Hotel ... 128
Aries Guest House ... 127
Arius Compound ... 482
Arizona Royal Villa ... 229
Arizona Sunburst Inn ... 230
Armadillo Guest House, The ... 127
Artemisia, Women Only Hotel ... 55
Arundel Meadows Inn ... 406
Ashbeian Hotel ... 98
Aspen Lodge ... 161
Asti Ranch ... 306
Atherton Hotel ... 291
Atlantic Shores Resort ... 329
Atrium/Vista Grande/Mirage ... 264
Au Bon Vivant Guest House ... 188
Auchendean Lodge Hotel ... 125
Aurora Winds, An Exceptional B&B Resort ... 225
Autumn Crest Inn ... 548
Aux Berges ... 189
Bacon Mansion ... 565
Bahama Hotel, The ... 324
Balboa Park Inn ... 284
Balconies, The ... 153
Bales Mead ... 120
Bar H Ranch ... 578
Barracks, The ... 136
Barrington's Private Hotel ... 101
Bathley Guest House ... 118
Bavarian House, The ... 251
Bayview Wharf Apartments ... 426
Be Yourself Inn — Twin Cities ... 462
Beach Place, The ... 285
Beaconlite Guest House ... 23, 427
Beary Merry Mansion ... 246
Beauport Inn and Cafe ... 409
Beck's Motor Lodge ... 292
Bed & Breakfast on Broadway ... 566
Bee Charmer Inn ... 265
Bellevue Place Bed & Breakfast ... 566
Bellmont Manor Bed & Breakfast and Silver Rooster ... 557
Belvedere ... 490
Benchmark Inn & Annex ... 428
Best Nest, The ... 520
Best Western Inn of Chicago ... 388
Big Ruby's Guesthouse (Ft Lauderdale) ... 325
Big Ruby's Guesthouse (Key West) ... 329
Bird's Nest Bed & Kitchen, The ... 502
Birdsong Bed and Breakfast ... 356
Black Duck Inn on Corea Harbor, The ... 406
Black Stallion Inn ... 292
Blackbeard's Castle ... 208
Blue Ewe ... 170
Blue Parrot Inn ... 330
Blueberry Ridge ... 523
Boatslip Beach Club ... 24, 429
Bock's Bed & Breakfast ... 293
Bonaventure, The ... 359
Bourgoyne Guest House ... 393
Boys On Burgundy ... 394
Bradford Carver House, The ... 430
Bradstan Country Hotel ... 487
Brandt House, The ... 420
Brass Key Guesthouse, The (Key West) ... 331
Brass Key Guesthouse, The (Provincetown) ... 431
Brenton, The ... 317
Brewers House Bed & Breakfast ... 464

Brickfield Hill Bed & Breakfast Inn ... 137
Brickfields Terrace ... 152
Brighton Court Craven Hotel ... 102
Brinley Victorian Inn ... 526
Bromptons Guesthouse ... 112
Buccaneer Country Lodge ... 552
Bull Lodge ... 122
Bungalow 't Staaksken ... 41
Bungay Jar ... 469
Buoy, The ... 432
Burnside ... 183
Bygone Beautys Cottages ... 134
Bywater B&B ... 394
C&G Bed & Breakfast House ... 76
California Motor Inn ... 154
Camp Michael B&B ... 531
Camp Pleiades ... 503
Campit ... 457
Candlelight Motel ... 547
Candler Park Patio Apartment ... 360
Canyon Club Hotel ... 265
Cape View Motel ... 432
Capitol Hill Guest House ... 318
Capitol Hill Inn ... 567
Captain Dexter House of Edgartown ... 422
Captain James Preston House ... 526
Captain's House ... 433
Captain's Quarters ... 11, 199
Carl Street Unicorn House ... 293
Carl's Guest House ... 434
Carolina Bed & Breakfast ... 504
Carousel Guest House ... 490
Cartwright Hotel, The ... 294
Casa Alegre Bed & Breakfast Inn ... 235
Casa Alexio ... 90
Casa Amigos ... 87
Casa Aurora ... 216
Casa Fantasía ... 217
Casa Laguna Bed & Breakfast Inn ... 12, 250
Casa Le Mar ... 215
Casa Lorenzo ... 89
Casa Marhaba ... 88
Casa Panoramica ... 218
Casa Pequena ... 88
Casa Scala ... 70
Casa Tierra Adobe Bed & Breakfast Inn ... 236
Casitas at Old Town, The ... 474
Castillo Inn ... 294
Catalina Park Inn ... 236
Catnaps 1892 Downtown Guesthouse ... 184
Catnaps Private Guest House ... 102
Cedars Tent & Trailer Park ... 182
Centennial House ... 488
Centre Apartments Amsterdam ... 77
Chalet in the Pines ... 228
Chambered Nautilus Bed & Breakfast Inn ... 568
Chandler Inn ... 418
Chanticleer Guesthouse ... 577
Charleston Columns Guesthouse ... 529
Chase On The Hill Bed & Breakfast ... 576
Château Cherrier B&B ... 190
Chateau Negara ... 395
Chateau Tivoli ... 295
Chelsea House ... 332
Chelsea Mews Guesthouse ... 496
Chelsea Pines Inn ... 497
Cheney Lake Bed & Breakfast ... 226
Cherry Grove Beach Hotel ... 491
Cheviot View Guest House ... 117
Chez Jacqueline ... 46
Chicago House, The ... 434
Christopher Place ... 28, 533
City Suites Hotel ... 389
Claddagh House Bed & Breakfast ... 178
Cliff House Bed & Breakfast ... 516
Cliff House Hotel at the Beach ... 120
Clone Zone Luxury Apartments ... 113
Clone Zone Manchester Holiday Apartment ... 116
Coast Inn ... 250
Coat of Arms ... 435
Cockford Hall ... 119
Coconut Grove ... 333
Coffee Boy Cottages ... 37
Colibri Bed & Breakfast ... 174
Colonial House Inn ... 498
Colours, The Guest Mansion Key West ... 333
Colours, The Mantell Guest Inn ... 347
Columbia Cottage Guest House ... 174
Columns Resort ... 266
Commons, The ... 24, 435
Cooper Island Beach Club ... 205
Coral Tree Inn ... 334
Corinda's Cottages ... 152
Cottages, The ... 34
Country Comfort Bed & Breakfast ... 244
Country Cousin ... 550
Country Options ... 466
Courtfield Hotel ... 130
Courtyard on the Trail ... 28, 536
Coward's Guest House ... 102
Cozy Cactus ... 232
Cozy Cottages ... 459
Crabapple Cottage ... 530
Creffield, The ... 99
Crestow House ... 108
Culpepper House B&B ... 363
Curry House ... 334

## DEF

Dairy Hollow House ... 241
Dancing Winds Farm ... 461
Dave's B&B on the Rio Grande ... 475
Desert Paradise Hotel ... 267
Desert Rainbow Inn ... 465
Devilstone Oceanfront Inn ... 404
Dewis Cyfarfod ... 131
Dexter's Inn ... 436
Dillinger House Bed & Breakfast ... 237
Divine Lake Nature's Sport & Spa Resort ... 185
Dmitri's Guesthouse ... 285
Doanleigh Wallagh Inn ... 462
Doin' It Right — in Puerto Vallarta ... 219
Douglas Dunes Resort ... 457
Dragon's Den, The ... 354
Dundonald House, The ... 185
Dunsany Bed & Breakfast ... 65
Dusty Miller Inn ... 437
Duval House ... 335
East Village Bed & Breakfast ... 498
Edgecliffe Hotel, The ... 111
Edward Lodge ... 145
Eighteen Fifty-Four Bed & Breakfast ... 531
Eighteen Thirty-Six California St ... 318

Eighteen-O-Seven (1807) House ..... 25, 437
El Mirasol Villas ..... 268
Elephant Walk Inn ..... 438
Ellesmere House ..... 122
Elmwood House B&B ..... 245
Embassy Guest House - Condado ..... 201
Embassy Inn ..... 319
Emy's Nook ..... 504
Equator ..... 336
Equinox Inn ..... 562
Essex Hotel, The ..... 296
European Guest House ..... 348
Fairbanks Inn, The ..... 439
Fairfield Lodge ..... 66
Fern Falls ..... 14, 275
Fern Grove Inn ..... 276
Field of Dreams ..... 146
Fifty-Four Cinderella Street ..... 10, 147
Finns Pension ..... 45
Fish Creek Lodging ..... 579
Fitch Hill Inn ..... 552
Fountain Inn, The ..... 97
Four Kachinas Inn Bed & Breakfast ..... 483
Four-Sixty-Three Beacon Street Guest House ..... 419
Fourteen Twelve Thalia, A Bed and Breakfast ..... 395
Fox & Hound B&B of New Hope ..... 518
Foxwood Bed & Breakfast, The ..... 168
Frankies Guesthouse ..... 67
Frauenbildungshaus Zülpich-Lövenich ..... 62
Frauenferienhaus Tiefenbach/Silbersee ..... 62
Frauenferienhof Ostfriesland ..... 60
Frauenlandhaus ..... 58
Frauenreisehaus (The Homestead) ..... 163
Frog Pond Guesthouse, The ..... 353
Furama Hotel Central ..... 138
Furama Hotel Darling Harbour ..... 138

## GHI

Gabriel's ..... 440
Gaige House Inn ..... 16, 304
Galittoire ..... 572
Gallery Suite, The ..... 573
Garden Cottage, The ..... 540
Gaslight Inn ..... 31, 569
Gaslight Inn Bed & Breakfast ..... 361
Gatehouse, The ..... 154
George IV Hotel ..... 103
Glen Isle Farm Country Inn ..... 521
Glenborough Inn ..... 303
Golden Apple Ranch ..... 277
Golden Bamboo Ranch ..... 379
Golden Bear Farm, The ..... 27, 493
Golden Guesthouse ..... 475
Governors on Fitzroy B&B ..... 139
Gram's Place B&B Guesthouse ..... 356
GrandView Inn, The ..... 441
Greater Boston Hospitality ..... 419
Green Rose ..... 170
Greenhouse, The ..... 396
Greenways Apartments ..... 150
Greenwood Hollow Ridge ..... 242
Grim's Manor ..... 518
Grove Guest House, The ..... 256
Grünberg Haus Bed & Breakfast ..... 554
Guest House, The ..... 575
Guion House ..... 500
Gull Walk Inn ..... 441
Guys Bed & Breakfast Noosa Heads ..... 149
Habana Inn ..... 511
Hacienda Antigua Bed and Breakfast ..... 476
Hale Aloha Guest Ranch ..... 364
Hale Kipa 'O Pele ..... 365
Hale Makaleka ..... 380
Hale Ohia Cottages ..... 366
Halfway to Hana House ..... 380
Hartley House Inn ..... 283
Hateful Missy & Granny Butch's Boudoir & Manure Em ..... 477
Haven House, The ..... 442
Hawks Avenue Bed & Breakfast ..... 175
Heritage House ..... 443
Heritage of Ogunquit ..... 410
Heron House ..... 336
Heron in La Conner, The ..... 560
Hibiscus House B&B ..... 357
Highland Dell Inn Bed & Breakfast ..... 16, 278
Highlands Inn, The ..... 467
Highlands Resort ..... 278
Hill House Bed & Breakfast ..... 570
Hillside Campgrounds ..... 525
Hilltop Cantegrive Farmhouses ..... 51
Hodgkinson's Hotel & Restaurant ..... 109
Holladay House ..... 513
Holloway Motel ..... 256
Holly's ..... 252
Honeysuckle ..... 313
Honeywood Country Lodge ..... 553
Horse & Hound Inn, The ..... 470
Hostal Hispano ..... 91
Hostellerie des Trois Forces ..... 200
Hostellerie Ten Lande ..... 40
Hotel Aero ..... 78
Hotel Alt Graz ..... 59
Hotel Aspen ..... 307
Hotel Casa Blanca de Manuel Antonio S.A. ..... 210
Hotel Central Marais ..... 48
Hotel Colours, The Guest Residence San Jose ..... 211
Hotel des Nations ..... 49
Hotel Elysium ..... 63
Hotel Goldenes Schwert ..... 95
Hotel Honolulu ..... 384
Hotel Kekoldi ..... 212
Hotel Kerlinga ..... 40
Hotel Louxor ..... 49
Hotel Mocking Bird Hill ..... 196
Hotel Piaf ..... 443
Hotel Romàntic i La Renaixença ..... 92
Hotel Rosamar ..... 90
Hotel Sander ..... 79
Hotel Scalinata di Spagna ..... 71
Hotel Seven Bridges ..... 80
Hotel Sonnenhof ..... 61
Hotel "The Village" ..... 78
Hotel Villa Schuler ..... 72
Hotel Wilhelmina ..... 80
Hotel Windsor ..... 44
House of a Thousand Flowers ..... 279
House of Two Urns, The ..... 389
Howden Cottage ..... 547
Huckleberry Springs ..... 279
Hudsons Guest House ..... 104
Huelo Point Flower Farm B&B ..... 381
Huff 'n Puff Straw Bale Inn, The ..... 232
Hydrangea House Inn ..... 527

Inn at 410 Bed & Breakfast, The ... 229
Inn at HighView, The ... 29, 546
Inn At Swifts Bay ... 30, 561
INN at Two Village Square, THE ... 410
Inn Essence ... 253
Inn Exile ... 13, 269
Inn of La Mesilla, The ... 480
Inn of the Turquoise Bear ... 26, 483
Inn On Castro ... 17, 297
Inn on Fairmount ... 537
Inn on the Mexican War Streets, The ... 522
Inn San Francisco, The ... 297
Inn the Woods ... 570
Innamorata ... 424
INNdulge Palm Springs ... 268
Inntimate ... 270
InnTrigue ... 270
Interludes ... 123
Island Key Courts of Key West, The ... 337
Island Watch B&B ... 227
Ivanhoe Inn ... 304
Ivy House B&B ... 416

## JKL

Jack & Tom's Maui Condos ... 382
Jacques' Cottage ... 280
Jefferson House, The ... 348
Jenkins Inn and Restaurant, The ... 417
Joan's Place ... 508
Joel House ... 34
Joluva Guesthouse & Villa La Roca Beach House ... 213
Jones Pond Campground ... 487
Kailua Maui Gardens ... 382
Kalani Oceanside Eco-Resort ... 367
Kalihiwai Jungle Home ... 374
Kalorama Guest House at Kalorama Park, The ... 319
Kasa Korbett ... 286
Kealakekua Bay B&B ... 368
Keating House ... 286
Keiki Ananda ... 383
Kennard Hotel, The ... 97
King Hendrick Motel ... 492
King Henry Arms ... 325
King's Head ... 157
Kirby House, The ... 458
Koa Kai Rentals ... 384
Künstler-Pension Sarah Petersen ... 59
La Concha Beach Resort ... 216
La Conciergerie Guest House ... 10, 190
La Corsette Maison Inn & The Sister Inn ... 392
La Dordogne Camping de Femmes ... 47
La Douillette ... 191
La Filanda Guesthouse ... 69
La Salamandre ... 46
La-Te-Da Hotel ... 338
Lafitte Guest House ... 397
Laird O'Cockpen Hotel ... 155
Lakeside B 'n B Tahoe ... 13, 254
Lamb's Mill Inn ... 407
Lamplighter Inn & Cottage ... 444
Landes House ... 571
Land's End Inn ... 445
Larry's B & B ... 230
Las Vegas Private Bed & Breakfast ... 466
Lawley on Guildford, The ... 158
Le Coureur des Bois ... 193
Le jardin des Trembles ... 182
Le Montrose Suite Hotel De Gran Luxe ... 257
Le Parc Hotel ... 258
Le Rêve Hotel ... 259
Le St. Christophe Bed & Breakfast ... 192
Leelin Wikiup B&B ... 249
Leisure Inn ... 411
Lichtquelle, Frauenbildungsstätte ... 58
Lightbourn Inn ... 339
Lighthouse Court ... 339
Liliane's Home; Guesthouse for Women Only ... 81
Lindenwood Inn ... 404
Lions Inn, The ... 397
Little House On The Prairie, The ... 387
Lodge, The ... 96
Lombard Central, A Super 8 Hotel, The ... 17, 298
Lotus Guest House ... 446
Lotus Hotel ... 38
Lovett Inn, The ... 537

## MNO

Macarty Park Guest House ... 398
MacMaster House circa 1895 ... 514
Maes B&B ... 82
Mahina Kai ... 22, 375
Maine-ly For You ... 413
Maison Burgundy B&B ... 399
Maitland-Swan House ... 555
Mala Lani (Heavenly Garden) Guest House ... 375
Mallard Guest Houses, The ... 314
Mangrove House ... 340
Manor House Boutique Hotel ... 140
Manor House Inn ... 405
Mansfield House ... 128
Mansion Inn, The ... 261
Maple Hill Farm B&B Inn ... 403
Maplewood Inn ... 548
Marc-James Manor ... 558
Mark Addy, The ... 556
Martha's Place ... 423
Marti's Guest Ranch ... 233
Mary Kay's Romantic Whaley Mansion Inn ... 558
Melbourne Guesthouse, The ... 155
Melville House Inn ... 528
Mentone Bed & Breakfast ... 200
Mermaid, The ... 163
Metro Hotel, The ... 299
Miami River Inn ... 349
Michael and Sebastian's ... 201
Mile Hi Bed/Breakfast ... 310
Mission San Francisco ... 220
Mohala Ke Ola B&B Retreat ... 376
Mondès ... 52
Montecito House ... 238
MontyMar ... 93
Moon Over Maine ... 411
Moore's Creek Inn ... 458
Morandi alla Crocetta ... 70
Mountain Laurel B&B ... 505
Mountain Lodge Resort ... 280
Mr. Mole Bed & Breakfast ... 415
Mt. Chocorua View House Bed & Breakfast ... 473
Mt. Peale Bed & Breakfast Country Inn ... 542
Muscle & Art B&B ... 197
Napoleon's Retreat Bed & Breakfast ... 464
Nelson House ... 176

New Dawn Caribbean Retreat & Guest House ................. 204
New York Bed & Breakfast Reservation Center, The ............ 499
Newnham SunCatcher Inn ........................................ 459
Newton Street Station ........................................ 341
Nine Twelve Barnard Bed & Breakfast ........................ 363
Nine Twelve Pauline Street ................................ 22, 400
Noosa Cove ........................................................ 150
Normandy House .................................................. 446
Normandy South .................................................. 350
Notchland Inn, The ............................................. 471
Noupoort Guest Farm ............................................ 35
Number Seven Guesthouse ..................................... 114
Numero Uno Guest House ...................................... 202
"O Canada" House ................................................ 177
Oak Bay Guest House .......................................... 179
Oasis, A Guest House .......................................... 341
Observatory Hotel, The ........................................ 140
Ocean Walk Guest House ...................................... 203
Ocean Wilderness ................................................ 180
Ogunquit House .................................................. 412
Old Mill B&B ...................................................... 506
Old Town Bed & Breakfast ..................................... 390
On The Beach Resort ........................................... 207
One Sixty-Three Drummond Street ............................ 156
One Thirty-Two North Main .................................... 492
One-Sixty (160) Regents Park Road .......................... 115
Oneida Campground and Lodge ................................ 519
Open Sky B&B ..................................................... 484
Oregon House, The .............................................. 516
Orongo Bay Homestead ......................................... 161
Orton Terrace ..................................................... 326
Our Place Papaikou's B&B ..................................... 369
Out West Bed & Breakfast ..................................... 580

## PQ

P.T. Barnum Estate ............................................. 310
Paauhau Plantation House .................................... 369
Pacific Ocean Holidays ........................................ 385
Palapas in Yelapa ............................................... 221
Pali Kai ............................................................ 377
Palms on Las Olas, The ........................................ 326
Pamalu ............................................................. 370
Paradise by the Creek B&B .................................... 233
Paradise Cove .................................................... 281
Paradise Ranch ................................................... 234
Park Brompton Inn ............................................... 390
Park Lane Guesthouse .......................................... 534
Park Lodge Hotel ................................................ 141
Park Manor Suites Hotel ....................................... 287
Parkview Marigny Bed & Breakfast ........................... 401
Pauleda House Hotel ........................................... 124
Pennant Hall ...................................................... 131
Penryn House ..................................................... 106
Pension Niebuhr ................................................. 56
Pension Vallières ................................................ 193
Penzion David Hotel ............................................ 43
Pikes Peak Paradise B&B ...................................... 309
Pillars of Plainfield B&B ....................................... 473
Pilot House Guest House & Duval Suites .................... 342
Pine Cove Inn, The ............................................. 248
Pines of Key West .............................................. 343
Pink Lady Inn, The ............................................. 355
Pleasant Grove B&B ............................................ 491
Pond Mountain Lodge & Resort ............................... 242
Post and Beam Bed & Breakfast .............................. 472
Prague Home Stay ............................................... 44
Prieuré des Granges ............................................ 54
Private Paris Accommodations ................................. 50
Prospect Hill B&B ............................................... 510
Purple Paradise ................................................. 198

## RST

R.B.R. Farms ...................................................... 370
Rainbow Country Tours and Bed & Breakfast ................. 542
Rainbow House (NZ) ............................................ 164
Rainbow House (FL) ......................................... 21, 343
Rainbow Lodge Bed & Breakfast, The ......................... 478
Rainbow Mountain Resort ...................................... 524
Ramada Hotel West Hollywood ................................. 260
Rams Head, The ................................................. 314
Ranchito San Pedro de Cócono ............................... 481
Rancho Cicada .................................................. 248
Ravensbourne Hotel ............................................ 100
Ravenscroft Inn ............................................. 29, 564
Ravenswood Hotel .............................................. 121
Ravenwood Guestrooms & Apts ................................ 447
Red Hill Inn ...................................................... 468
Red Lamp Post .................................................. 416
Red Rock Inn ..................................................... 545
Red Squirrel Lodge ............................................. 121
Redmond Guest House .......................................... 579
Regis House ...................................................... 128
Rehoboth Guest House ......................................... 315
Renoir Hotel ................................................. 18, 299
Residence Linareva ............................................. 166
Retreat on Lummi Island ....................................... 562
Richard's Country Inn .......................................... 574
Richmond Hotel .................................................. 351
Rideau View Inn ................................................. 183
Rio Grande House ............................................... 479
Rio Villa Beach Resort ......................................... 282
Rising Star Ranch ............................................... 308
River Run Bed & Breakfast Inn ................................ 501
Riverside Apartments ........................................... 83
Rober House ...................................................... 401
Roberta's Bed & Breakfast ..................................... 571
Rochdale .......................................................... 151
Rock Cottage Gardens ......................................... 243
Room With a View ............................................... 64
Roomers ........................................................... 448
Rose & Crown Guest House ................................... 448
Rose Acre ......................................................... 448
Rose Cottage ..................................................... 563
Rosehill in the Fern ............................................. 106
Rosehill Inn Bed & Breakfast ................................... 509
Roseland Guest House ......................................... 125
Roussa ............................................................. 53
Royal Barracks Guest House .................................. 402
Royal Drive Cottages ........................................... 377
Royal Palms, The ............................................... 327
Ruby Slipper, The ........................................... 25, 486
Rufus Tanner House ............................................ 489
Rural Roots Bed and Breakfast ................................ 178
Ryn Anneth ....................................................... 107
Saharan Motor Hotel ............................................ 260
Sallie & Eileen's Place ......................................... 262
Samurai, The ..................................................... 371
San Antonio Bed & Breakfast .................................. 540
San Francisco Cottage ...................................... 18, 300
San Vicente Inn & Resort ...................................... 261
Sandpiper Beach House ........................................ 449
Santa Fe Luxury Bed & Breakfast ............................. 135

Santiago Resort ... 14, 271
Saouis ... 53
Sea Breeze Resort ... 247
Sea Drift Inn ... 450
Sea Isle Resort ... 344
Sea Oats by the Gulf ... 354
Seahorse Inn ... 538
See Vue ... 517
Shakti Cove Cottages ... 563
Shalimar Hotel ... 104
Sheraton Key West All-Suite Resort ... 345
ShireMax Inn ... 450
SierraWood Guest House ... 255
Sign of the Owl B&B ... 408
Silver Lake ... 20, 316
Simonton Court Historic Inn & Cottages ... 346
Simpsons of Potts Point ... 142
Sinclairs Guest House ... 105
Singel Suite — The Bed & Breakfast Suites ... 84
Six Webster Place ... 451
SkyRidge, A Bed & Breakfast Inn ... 544
Smoketree Resort ... 246
Sonoma Chalet B&B ... 305
Sophie's Comfort ... 505
South Coast Inn Bed & Breakfast ... 513
Spring Valley Guest Ranch ... 194
Stanford Inn ... 460
Stewart's B&B ... 231
Stone Pillar B&B ... 507
Stoney Ridge ... 525
Stoneybroke House ... 68
Stratford Lodge ... 117
Sullivan's Gulch Bed & Breakfast ... 514
Summer Hill Farm ... 421
Summer Place, The ... 317
Summerhill Guest House ... 171
Summit House ... 535
Sunhead of 1617 ... 85
Sunset Inn ... 452
Surf Hotel ... 391
Swanbourne Guest House ... 159
Sydney Star Accommodation ... 143
`t Zijpad ... 86
Tara Country Retreat ... 133
Taylor House Inn ... 510
Ten Cawthra Square B&B & Guesthouse ... 186
The Mango House ... 385
Things Worth Remembering ... 353
Three Peaks ... 453
Three Thirty-Three West 88th Associates ... 500
Timberfell Lodge ... 532
Tin Roof Bed & Breakfast ... 424
Tingalaya's Bed & Breakfast ... 198
Toad Hall ... 488
Tom's House Berlin ... 57
Tortuga Roja Bed & Breakfast ... 12, 239
Tremadoc Guest House ... 99
Triangle Inn ... 272
Triangle Inn-Santa Fe, The ... 485
Triangle Pointe ... 362
Troutbeck ... 162
Tucker Inn at Twelve Center, The ... 454
Turtle Cove Resort Cairns ... 148
Twenty-Four Henry Guesthouse ... 301
Twenty-Seven Blake Street ... 506
Tybesta Tolfrue ... 130

## UVW

Uncles Upstairs Inn ... 522
Upper Deck, A Guesthouse ... 541
Upper Echelons ... 362
Ursuline Guesthouse ... 402
Vallarta Cora ... 222
Victoria Court Sydney ... 144
Victoria Oaks Inn ... 311
Victorian Bed & Breakfast ... 420
Villa, The (Palm Springs) ... 273
Villa, The (SF) ... 19, 301
Villa, The (FL) ... 323
Villa Toscana Guest House ... 392
Villas of Fort Recovery Estate ... 206
Volcano Ranch: Inn & Bunkhouse ... 372
W.E. Mauger Estate ... 479
W.J. Marsh House Victorian B&B ... 480
Waikiki AA Studios (Bed & Breakfast Honolulu & Sta ... 386
Waikiki Vacation Rentals ... 386
Walker House ... 422
Warham Old Post Office Cottage ... 118
Watership Inn ... 454
Weekender Bed & Breakfast, The ... 180
West Wind Guest House, The ... 171
Westend Hotel & Cosmo Bar ... 86
Westways Guest House ... 169
Whispering Pines B&B ... 306
Whispering Pines Bed & Breakfast/Retreat ... 515
Whistler Retreat, The ... 181
White Horse Hotel ... 94
White House Hotel ... 110
White Swan Guest House ... 560
Wild Lily Ranch ... 559
Wilderness Way Resort & Campground ... 578
Wildwood Inn ... 456
William & Garland Motel ... 508
William Lewis House, The ... 320
William Page Inn ... 414
Willow Retreat ... 263
Willows, The (Russian River) ... 282
Willows, The (SF) ... 302
Will's Reste ... 512
Wilson-Lee House Bed & Breakfast ... 555
Wind Rider, A Guest House for Women ... 172
Windamar House ... 455
Windsor Cottage ... 231
Windsor Inn ... 321
Witchencroft ... 149
Wood Valley B&B Inn ... 373

## XYZ

Yellow Birch Farm ... 412
Your Private Art Deco Apartment in South Beach ... 352